D1029353

THE ORIGINS OF ENGLISH WORDS

The Origins of English Words

A Discursive Dictionary of Indo-European Roots

Joseph T. Shipley

THE JOHNS HOPKINS UNIVERSITY PRESS
Baltimore and London

Published 1984

Printed in the United States of America
89 88 7 6 5

The Johns Hopkins University Press
701 West 40th Street
Baltimore, Maryland 21211
The Johns Hopkins Press Ltd., London

The paper in this book is acid-free and meets the guidelines for permanence and durability of the Committee on Production Guidelines for Book Longevity of the Council on Library Resources.

Library of Congress Cataloging in Publication Data

Shipley, Joseph Twadell, 1893-
The origins of English words.

Bibliography: pp. xxxi–xxxii.
Includes index.
1. English language–Etymology. 2. English language–Word formation. 3. English language–Roots.
4. Indo-European languages–Etymology. I. Title.
PE1571.S46 1984 422 83-8415
ISBN 0-8018-3004-4

Language is the garden of man's mind;
its fertility, and its beauty, rise from its roots.

Il faut cultiver notre jardin.
—Candide

Contents

Acknowledgments

Any dictionary, especially a discursive one such as this, bears a heavy debt to forebears in many times and languages. Some nearer ones are mentioned in the bibliography. Many others, named in the book, by their wit, wisdom, and quest of beauty, have helped brighten the text, have helped to form this book and me.

More specifically, I wish to extend thanks to Ruth Busch for her painstaking and patient preparation of the index of English words. Thanks go most closely to my wife, Shirley, for not only enduring but encouraging the many hours of concentration that after six years have culminated in this volume. I wish also to express my appreciation of the interest and assistance of William P. Sisler, Humanities Editor of the Johns Hopkins University Press, and of the concern and meticulous care of copy editor Penny Moudrianakis, in helping bring *The Origins of English Words* to its finished form. Beyond all these, the responsibility for the book, with its inevitable flaws and revealed foibles, but also, I trust, some measure of illumination, rests with me. So be it. Benedicite.

Joseph T. Shipley
New York and London

Introduction

The most widespread of all language families is the Indo-European, of which English began as a minor branch, but now is the largest, in vocabulary, in number of native speakers, and in the extent of its use around the world. From tongues in Western Asia some four thousand years ago the Indo-European forms moved south in Sanskrit and other Indian languages, and in other branches across Europe and ultimately to the far ends of the Americas. Along the Mediterranean Sea they grew into Greek and Latin, and from the latter, the speech of Rome, came the Romance languages, Italian, Spanish, Portuguese, Romanian, French. Westward through Europe came the Celtic and Germanic branches, northward turned the Scandinavian, and eastward spread the Baltic and Slavic, including the Russian. English, which in its earliest form was Germanic (Anglo-Saxon), developed as a mingling of branches, as first the Celts, then after the Saxons the Danes and the Normans, took hold upon the island. The Normans were originally from Scandinavia, but during long residence in Normandy had absorbed a dialect of French, itself an outgrowth of "vulgar" Latin, the speech of the soldiers and traders (and, later, Christian missionaries), who carried the Roman words with their goods, their weapons, and their faith.

Readers familiar with the Bible will remember the three sons of Noah, whose descendants spread through the known world. From Shem came the Semites, Arabs and Jews. The children of Ham went into Egypt and down the African continent. The children of Japheth went into Asia Minor, where Noah's great-grandson Nimrod built the Tower of Babel. They then spread westward, Japheth's son Iavan, for example, being linked with Ionia, Greece. With the Norman conquest of England under William, called "the Conqueror," but owing much to Halley's Comet, the appearance of which was interpreted as an omen of disaster and broke King Harold's morale (shown on the famous Bayeux tapestry, the comet has been traced since 12 B.C., was last seen in 1910, and is scheduled to appear again in 1986)—after William won the Battle of Hastings in 1066, the Norman French dialect became the official language of the country, in church (with Latin), in royal court, and in law court. For some three hundred fifty years Anglo-Saxon and Norman French competed, and gradually merged, until Chaucer's poems and Caxton's printing press set the crown upon their fusion into English.

In the shuffle and friction of these tongues, English lost many of the inflections that had burdened the earlier words. In the Romance languages all nouns are still either masculine or feminine (in German, or neuter); the adjectives vary in form (French *le, la;* German *der, die, das*) to fit the gender of the noun. English nouns have but three forms—nominative, possessive, and plural—although the pronouns retain the genders (*he, she, it*) as well as the objective case (*me, him, her,* and fadingly *whom*). Other languages may have five cases, or more, indicating various aspects of relationship. What English expresses with prepositions—*to, for, by, from,* and the like—other languages may indicate by various endings of the root word. But by their roots ye shall know them.

Sir William Jones (1745–1794), while a judge in Calcutta, declared: "No philologer can examine the Sanskrit, Greek, and Latin, without believing them to have sprung from some common source, which, perhaps, no longer exists." He was right: the original speech, the primal Indo-European from which a hundred languages have flowered, was unwritten, and therefore left no records. It was almost a century and a half later that philologists, by a backward coursing—by comparing the different developments in Sanskrit, Greek, and the Slavic, Celtic, Germanic, and Romance branches, and by identifying family likenesses and regular shiftings of sounds—became able to postulate with considerable confidence a large number of the Indo-European roots from which current words proliferated. In some instances, the primal root is but slightly changed in the modern variations. *Mama,* perhaps formed from the *m.m.m.* of the suckling babe, is *meter* in Greek, *mater* in Latin, *mère* in French, *Mutter* in German (which still capitalizes all its nouns), *moder* in Danish, *mat* in Russian, *mother* in English; it embraces all the nursing *mammals.* We return to this every time we call something *yum-yum. Papa* exemplifies one of the regular sound changes, as tribes, which grew to nations, branched off on their separate ways. Surviving in Latin as *pater* (Jupiter is Zeus-pater), in Italian as *papa* and the papal seat of the pope, and in French as *père,* it makes the Germanic shift from a *p* sound to an *f* sound in the German *Vater,* Danish *fader,* and English *father.* By noting such resemblances and changes, it is possible to construct a single origin of seemingly diverse words. Thus, one Indo-European root may have burgeoned not only into a word in many languages but into a number of words in one language, as in English.

On the other hand, different roots, journeying by diverse routes down the ages, may in our day appear in a single form, and one current word form may even have come to mean its own opposite (for example, *cleave*). A view of the complexity of language growth may be had by considering the English form *c.o.n.* As a word, *con* has several meanings, from different pathways. It means against, as in arguments pro and con. In navigation, to con is to direct steering, as from the conning tower. It means to examine carefully, to commit to memory, from the Early English *cunnan,* to know, to be able, whence also our word *I can.* This meaning is traced to the prolific root *gen,* to know. Then there is to con, to swindle: they conned him out of his sweepstakes winnings. This is a shortening of *confidence game,* in which the confidence man, con man, seeks to win your trust so as to cheat you. Finally—as a separate word—we use *con* from the Italian, to mean with, especially in musical terms, *con brio, con amore,* and more.

Note that the first *con* means against, the last means with. Yet these two opposites spring from the one Indo-European root *kom,* meaning beside. If two things are next to each other, they may be friends or opponents. Thus from *kom* came *con, contra, against;* and *com, together, with.* A *companion* is one with whom you break bread (Latin *panem*). *Country* is the land lying against (next to) the town.

We have far from ended the *c.o.n.* story. As an abbreviation, *con* may represent a dozen words: *connection, consolidate, consols, conclusion.* In law, after a woman's name, *con.* means wife (Latin *conjunx,* joined); and *crim. con.* is the legal euphemism for unlawful sexual intercourse. Nor is this all. As a prefix, *con-* may mean against, as in *contradict, control.* But in the great majority of its occurrences the prefix *con-* is a shift, for easier sounding, of *com-*, together. *Com-* remains before *b, m,* and *p;* it changes before *c, d, f, g, j, n, q, s, t,* or *v; combination, compassion;* but *congress, constant, convention.* And sometimes the prefix has no meaning save that it adds force to the root idea, as an intensive: *conceal, condemn, conflagration.*

There are, of course, some words beginning with *c.o.n.* that are not involved in this pattern. On New York's Coney Island men once went shooting *coneys,* rabbits. In Elizabethan tales, however, *coney-catching* does not refer to rabbits: *coney* (as later gull and pigeon) was slang for an easy mark, a dupe. Another such word (of which the origin is unknown) may be hunted in a guessing game by syllables: My first is company; my second shuns company; my third summons company; and my whole puzzles company. The word is *co/nun/drum.* Word ways are multiplex.

English, perhaps because of its early blending, has continued to welcome into its vocabulary, sometimes with no change, words not only from other branches of Indo-European but also from many other language families around the world. American Indian, Chinese, Arabic, Hebrew (the last two are of the Hamitic-Semitic family, named for Noah's sons Ham and Shem, but this is not merely biblical; the Egyptians' first name for their land was Ham), various African families, Eskimo, and more, have all given us good English words. English has borrowed more freely than any other tongue. The French have long objected to the assimilation of foreign terms; they speak scornfully of *Franglais,* the acceptance of English expressions. And recently the Soviet Union has protested against the "corruption" of Russian by English absorptions. English, on the contrary, welcomes new words that identify new items or ideas from any land: Greek *euphoria,* French *garage* (automobile barn), Swedish *ombudsman,* Afrikaans *apartheid,* Japanese *karate* (empty hand) and *judo* (gentle way). It embraces concise or colorful expressions from any source: Spanish *pronto,* French *détente,* Russian *sputnik,* Latin *condominium,* Latin *etc.* (*et cetera:* and others). This ingathering is a continuing process. New words may also be invented, or formed by combining already existing words or roots. *Gas,* said its creator, Jan Baptist van Helmont, in 1640, was formed by analogy with the word *chaos.* Gelett Burgess in this century invented the word *blurb* because it "sounds like a publisher." *Kodak* was coined by cameraman George Eastman, who thought that *k* has a commanding sound. *Radar* (*ra*dio *d*etecting *a*nd *r*anging) and *scuba* (*s*elf-*c*ontained *u*nderwater *b*reathing *a*pparatus) are acrostics, words fashioned from the first letters of the words they represent. *Chortle* (by Lewis Carroll) is a fusion of *chuckle* and *snort.* Word ways are weird.

Combinations are very frequent, and continually fashioned: *railroad, paperback, skyscraper,* then *highriser.* English is likely, especially in the sciences, to combine its words from Greek or Latin roots. Thus *anthropology* means the study of man. Greek *logos* (word, talk, reason, logic) provides many English words ending in *(o)logy,* meaning the study of. *Gynecology* is the (medical) study of women. An *androgyne* is a man with marked characteristics of a woman; a *gynander* is a woman with marked characteristics of a man. We may call either of these a *hermaphrodite,* from a Greek myth: the son of Hermes and Aphrodite, Hermaphroditos, was granted his plea to be forever joined with his beloved Salmacis. Aphrodite gives us such English words as *aphrodisiac.* Greek Hermes (Roman Mercury) was the patron god of both merchants and thieves; hence such words as *mercurial* and the slippery metal *mercury; hermetic* is from Hermes Trismegistus (thrice greatest), a name applied to the Egyptian god of astrology and magic, supposed inventor of a way of sealing vessels airtight.

Also from classical myth comes the term *psychology.* Psyche (breath, soul) was briefly the mate of the child-god (not of love, as is commonly said, but of desire) Greek Eros (Roman Cupid): these names give us material *cupidity,* the many *erogenous* zones, and *erotica. Erotetic,* however, means pertaining to questioning, Socrates' method of seeking truth. George Bernard Shaw was a member of the English Erotetic Society before he, with Beatrice and Sidney Webb, left it in 1884 to form the Fabian Society. This was named after a historical figure, Quintus *Fabius* Maximus Verrucosus, called Cunctator (the Delayer) from his hit-and-run tactics, which harassed the flanks of Hannibal's army while avoiding pitched battle, and gradually wore down his strength to the destruction of Carthage. The Fabians advocate a gradualist socialism, to be attained by winning majority approval, as opposed to the Communist "instant" imposition from above.

The Greek root *anth,* meaning man, is also found in the name *Alexander,* meaning protector of men. *Philander* should mean lover of men; as a verb, it has a livelier sense, from stories and plays that have so named a *philanderer.* Mr. Antrobus, referring to the first man, Adam, is with Eve and Cain a character in Thornton Wilder's *The Skin of Our Teeth.*

The forms from *anthr* have become intertwined with those from another root, *andr, anther,* referring to the bloom of the plant world. The form *anther* has come unchanged into English, meaning the organ of a flower that secretes its pollen. *Anth* or *anthem* occurs at the beginning, middle, or end of numerous flower names. *Polyanthus* names the primrose family–but *polyandrous* means having more than one husband at a time. A *chrysanthemum* is a golden flower (Greek *khrusos,* gold). The word *anthem* by itself, however, means a hymn of praise or loyalty, such as the national anthem; from Greek *antiphonos* (a voice against), it was originally a song chanted alternately by two choirs. In this sense, we have taken *antiphon* into English. *Anthology* reverses the usual sense of the ending; it means not the study of flowers, but a bouquet, a garland, of words. Word ways, while usually explicable, are always unpredictable.

The endings of words must be watched carefully for the changes they make in the root significance. To distinguish between a *gourmand* and a *gourmet,* one must take the second portion. Love turns to hate when *Francophile* turns to *Francophobe.* Greek *phobos* means dread, but fear gives birth to hatred. There are too many *phobias,* but the *phil* words also abound. *Philanthropy,* love of man. *Philadelphia,* (city of) brotherly love. *Philip,* lover of horses (hippopotamus, river horse; hippodrome, course for racing horses). *Philosophy,* love of wisdom. The first American college fraternity, the honor society ΦBK, Phi Beta Kappa, founded in 1776, takes its name from the initials of its motto, *Philosophia biou kubernetes:* Philosophy the pilot of life. *Cybernetics* is the technique of "piloting," of control processes; the new word *cybernate* means to control by computer. Word ways are wander-ful, and wonderful.

Wonderful is a genuine word, a valid counter in the exchange of ideas; *wanderful* is a false coinage, a counterfeit (French *feit* from Latin *factum,* made) made against but in imitation of a coveted or currently accepted form. The first counter, a token, springs from Latin *computare:* to clear, to compute; the second is from the widespread *con,* against. Again we are reminded that as one root may send forth several words, so one current form may have grown from several roots. Ideas and experiences are infinite; to express them, we have 26 letters and some 45 sounds.

Some words, though long, are easy to trace. An *electroencephalogram* is the writing (gram, graph) of the electric movements of the brain (Greek *en,* in; *kephale,* head). Some words, though short, have traced a longer trail. *Taxi* is a shortening of *taxicab,* itself a cutting of *taximeter cabriolet;* in other words, a little (originally two-wheeled) vehicle that bounds like a goat (Capri, island of capering goats), equipped with a device that measures and sets a price. But the word ways are not trivial (Latin *tri via:* gossip, where three roads meet). Words are flashlights turned upon our thoughts.

It should be noted that the original Indo-European words were fashioned to denote material objects or specific events that impinged directly upon the senses, or immediate emotions. It may have been centuries before these terms were extended from physical to mental activity, from the concrete to the abstract; and finally, perhaps, were given figurative uses and applications. Thus the language grew with the growth of its makers and users, from nomads to farmers, to the citizen and his civilization; from immediate concerns to general principles, from observation to speculation; across the centuries from myth and magic to religion, philosophy, and science. The process, of course, continues along with us.

A number of words came into our language group after the great migrations that separated the various branches of the Indo-European family, so that, while we may trace an English word to Germanic, Latin, or Greek, it may lack analogues in Celtic, say, and Sanskrit, and thus not permit the extraction of a common root. The various additions to our Indo-European heritage from later or alien sources, however, have not basically altered its nature; these have, when necessary, been transformed to fit the pattern of our speech. A bird named in Arabic *al qadus* (*al* is Arabic for *the:* the famous caliph Harun al Rashid, of the Arabian Nights, is Aaron the Upright) became Portuguese *alcatraz,* which we retain as the name of an island prison; but the color of the bird (Latin *alba,* white) led the way to English *albatross.* The greater number of our English words, however, can be traced through various branches of the family to an inferred Indo-European root. This volume lists the most productive of these roots, and notes the various and frequently diverse English words into which they have been fashioned. It is the compiler's hope that such a listing and description will illuminate our living language and give impetus to its further growth, and that it will also advance the recognition that we share a vivid and boundless treasury of speech which has spread widely among our brother nations, as the second language in virtually every land where it is not the first—a language that increasingly embraces, in its trends and tendrils, all mankind.

Frequent Word Forms and Transformations

Most of the words we use in our everyday speech have come into English by way of the Germanic Anglo-Saxon line. In the great body of our vocabulary, however, especially if we count the scientific terms, by far the majority of our words have traveled through Greek or Latin, often reaching English via French. During these journeyings, certain patterns of form or transformation have recurred so frequently that, instead of repeating them time after time in the discussion of individual roots, it seems wise to set them down in advance. Recognition of these patterns will make clear many of the word associations and current forms that have evolved from the faraway Indo-European roots.

The most frequent silent letter is *e* at the end of a word. This, however, often has the effect of lengthening the preceding vowel, as in *human, humane; dam, dame; them, theme; kit, kite; not, note; cut, cute.*

We are told that more than half of all English words end in *e, s, t,* or *d.* For *d,* add the past tense of verbs; and for *s,* the third person singular present tense of verbs; the plural and the possessive of nouns—and the total is magnified.

The editors of the *American Heritage Word Frequency Book* (1971) counted over a million words, and found that the word *the* occurs almost three times as often as the second most frequent word, *of.* The first twelve most frequently used words are; (1) *the,* (2) *of,* (3) *and,* (4) *a,* (5) *to,* (6) *in,* (7) *is,* (8) *you,* (9) *that,* (10) *it,* (11) *he,* (12) *for.* The first word of more than one syllable is (48) *about,* followed by (55) *many,* (60) *other,* (61) *into.* The first noun is (60) *time,* followed by (79) *people,* (90) *water,* (95) *words,* (116) *day.* Note that *you* is eighth; *he,* eleventh; *they,* nineteenth; while *I* comes trailing at twenty-fourth. Apparently we are not especially egotistical.

Consonant Shiftings

Many of the consonantal variations have been set into a pattern known as Grimm's Law, established in 1822 by the fairy tale man, Jakob Grimm. Here it is, as applied to English.

Words that in early times began with one of the sounds listed below, may later have changed to the next sound to the right.

Gutturals: g, k, kh (h), g
Examples: *g*enus, *k*in; *ch*oler, *g*all; *h*ost, *g*uest
Dentals: d, t, th (f), d
Examples: *d*ual, *t*wo; *t*riple, *th*ree; *f*ume, *d*ust
Labials: (v) b, p, ph (f), b (v)
Examples: *b*ucket, *p*ocket; *p*aternal, *f*atherly; *f*ragile, *b*reak

The original sound may have come to us in words along the Mediterranean route; the change, via the Germanic movement. Thus the root *pleu* (meaning flow) through Greek and Latin gave English *pluvial* and *plutocracy;* from Germanic *flug* came *flow, flee, flight.* The *k* to *kh* sound shift appears in Spanish *c*aballo, French *ch*eval, English *c*avalry and *ch*ivalry. (The two foreign words also show the *b.v* shift: ca*b*allo, che*v*al.) Also, in Germanic, the *k* or *kh* sound may become *h:* the root *kam*-er (meaning vault, vaulted room) gives us *camera–camera obscura:* dark room–and *comrade,* who shared a room; but also, via Low German *heben,* gives us the vaulted heaven.

The sounds *d, t, th,* have always been confused by careless speakers; their interchange abides in the language. German *Theater* and French *théâtre* begin with the same two letters as English *theater,* but their sound is *t,* as opposed to our *th*. In earlier English, such words as *author* and *Catholic* were spoken with a *t* sound, as we still say *Thomas.* Shakespeare punned in his title *Much Ado About Nothing* (pronounced *Noting*): to carry along the plot, many things must be noted, as by eavesdropping, or discerned through the blundering of Dogberry. Like other good playwrights, Shakespeare makes the title clear within the play. Don Pedro, urging Balthasar to sing (act 2, scene 3), says:

Don Pedro: . . . if thou wilt hold longer argument,
Do it in notes.
Balthasar: Note this before my notes;
There's not a note of mine that's worth the noting.
Don Pedro: Why, these are very crotchets that he speaks–
Note, notes, forsooth, and nothing.

For fear that the word *crotchets* will not alert the modern reader, a footnote in the 1952 G. B. Harrison edition notes: "Nothing: a pun on noting." (We need not make much ado about noting that Shakespeare anticipated the claimants of

Bacon as the author of the plays, their arguments based on anagrams deciphered in the dramas. For the title *Much Adoe About Nothing,* so spelled in the earliest printing, the 1600 Quarto, and in the First Folio of 1623, is an anagram of "Bacon? O, naught due to him!")

Vowel Actions

Indo-European words were never written; they were spoken by heedless illiterates who (as speakers of dialects around the world today) tended to slur sounds, drop any sound that got in the way of rapid expression, or add any that made for smoother flow. Looking along such changes, one can sympathize with Voltaire's remark that in etymology vowels do not count, and consonants count very little. Even our more "enlightened" age has trouble accounting for all the changes.

A few vowel changes may be noted. Between two consonants that go well together the vowel may be dropped. Thus the root *bhel,* which gives English *bellows,* drops the vowel to form the English *bladder.*

Where Greek has *o,* Latin may have *e;* as cosmo*gony*, in*gen*uity. Here, too, the vowel may be dropped; hence *gn,* a*gn*ostic; Germanic *kn, kn*ow. And the changes continue; that first consonant, becoming silent, may also be dropped, as early Latin *gnotus* turned into English *note.* Within a word, the two letters may be sounded: *agnostic, recognize;* one is silent at the end, as in *benign,* but note *malignant.* German *Knabe:* boy, with the *k* sounded, became English *knave,* with silent *k.*

Greek *u* is usually turned into English *y*, as *gune,* woman, gives us *gynecology.* The *Oxford English Dictionary* lists *hubristic* as "irregular for hybristic." Words beginning with *i* in Greek or Latin may begin with *j* or *y* in English, as *ius, iuris,* justice, jury; *iuvenis, iuventus,* young, youth; *iuvenilis,* juvenile.

It may offer validity to Voltaire to consider the vagaries of a few vowel sounds. Thus *head, hear, heard, hearken.* The farmer may *sow* the seed, then use the *sow* for meat.

R. B. Sheridan (in parliament):	Where shall I find a more foolish knave or a more knavish fool than this?
Eager Honorable Gentleman:	Hear! Hear!

There are seven sounds of the combination o.u.g.h.: (1) *au: plough, slough* (: morass); Edward FitzGerald uses spelling as well as rhyme in "bough . . . thou . . . Paradise enow."* (2) *uff: slough* (as a snake its skin), *enough, rough, tough.* (3) *up: hiccough.* (4) *ock: hough.* (5) *off: cough, trough.* (6) *oo: through.* (7) *oh:*

*"A book of verses underneath the bough, / A Jug of Wine, a Loaf of Bread—and Thou / Beside me singing in the Wilderness— / Ah, Wilderness were Paradise enow."—*Rubáiyát of Omar Khayyám.* (Eugene O'Neill's one happy play is entitled *Ah, Wilderness.*)

dough, although; losing the accent in *furlough;* becoming little more than a breath in *thoroughly.*

Contrariwise, the one sound *mean,* according to its meaning, has grown from three roots: *medhyo* (the golden mean, median); *mei* (low, nasty); and *meino* (denote).

Confounded Sounds

Some consonantal sounds are not part of the speech equipment of certain peoples; for example, many languages lack the clickings of the Hottentots. Words are then altered to fit the phonetic habit. The Bible (Judges 12) tells of an early instance of this: 42,000 Ephraimites were slain at a River Jordan ford by the Gileadites under Jephthah, betrayed by their inability to pronounce *shibboleth,* which they sounded with an initial *s.* We now use *shibboleth* to mean a password. Arabic *Salaam,* peace, is Hebrew *Shalom;* Israeli Begin used both forms when signing the treaty of peace with Egypt. The Semites are the descendants of Shem.

Most widespread of such shiftings is that of *l* and *r.* The Chinese have no sound *r;* the Japanese, no *l.* A fabulous monster came into being at the moment of the birth of Confucius; its reproduction on Chinese pottery we know as *kylin;* on Japanese, it is *kirin.* In a hotel in Tokyo, I was talking with a newly elected member of the Olympic Games Committee, meeting there, when a Japanese member came over and asked whether they might hold a cocktail party the next afternoon, "to cerebrate your erection." With a glance at me, and well-controlled countenance, the new member graciously acquiesced.

Even when a mouth can form both sounds, the two often shift. Amsterdam is on the Amstel River. English (Shakespeare's) Harry le Roi was Prince Hal. From the "gramarye" of medieval witchcraft and alchemy, *grammar* and *glamour* (originally a spell, still the spell of beauty) are variants of a single word. From *amphora* came *ampulla* and *ampoule.* A *peregrine* is a *pilgrim.* The medieval name for *Majorca* was *Majolica,* which still names a style of pottery from that island. *Angola* and *angora* are both from Turkish *Ankara. Scandal* and *slander* are both from a single Greek word. Latin *prunum* became Anglo-Saxon *plum* before it came again into the language as *prune.* Agatha Christie, in *Elephants Can Remember,* speaks of twin sisters Dorothy and Margaret, "known colloquially as Dolly and Molly." The Spanish officer *coronel* is French *colonel,* each sounded as spelled; English spells it the French way, but returns to the *r* and sounds it like the inside of a nut. Greek *aster* and Latin *stella* have both come into English, in *star* and *stellar, constellation* and *astrology*—which may prophesy *disaster,* the friendly stars turned away.

These *l.r* alternations are found "from China to Peru"; they not only occur on every continent but recur in every time. Ancient Greek *polis,* city, gives us *Constantinople,* the *metropolis* (mother city) and the *politics* in which we are, willy-nilly, involved; in Sanskrit, *city* is *pur,* whence *Singapore.* The map of India is dotted with names ending in *puram* or *pur,* such as *Mahabalipuram, Rampur,* and the one that has come into English as the riding breeches and boots, the *jodhpurs.* In America, *Minneapolis* combines the Greek word for city with the Sioux word for water. In Egyptian hieroglyphics one symbol, a lion couchant, represents both sounds, *l* and *r.* In the Minoan Linear A script, used on the island of Crete from 3000 to 1500 B.C., Cyrus H. Gordon, who deciphered it, asks us to "note that *l* and *r* are not differentiated." The Latin suffix *alis:* pertaining to, Englished in *spiritual, punctual,* etc., changed to *aris* when there was an *l* in the preceding syllable, giving us such words as *consular, lunar, regular, similar, solar, stellar.* By the natives of India the two sounds might be confusedly combined, as Rudyard Kipling noted: the woman of Shamlegh tells Kim that, although she is now an unbeliever, she once was a *Ker-listian* (Christian). Even the sometimes humorous pun slips into the sound story: *pun* is shortened from the earlier *pundigrion,* from the Italian *punctiglio,* meaning a fine point, as in the English *punctilio.* W. S. Gilbert, for the plot of *The Pirates of Penzance,* takes advantage of the confusion: nursemaid Ruth apprentices her ward Frederic to a *pirate* instead of a *pilot.* Roll the sounds *l* and *r* along your tongue, and you may sense the reason.

Metathesis

Metathesis, the transposition of a sound, may occur in bumbling speech. It has created blunders (some devised for humor), which, after the Reverend W. A. Spooner (1844–1930), Warden of New College, Oxford, we call *spoonerisms:* "It is kisstomary to cuss the bride." But metathesis may also influence the form of a word. Old English *bridd* became our *bird. Thrill* was earlier *thyrl.* In current use are the cardinal number *three* and the ordinal *third* (not *thrid,* although Gower in 1393 said that air "is eke the thridde element": earth, water, air, fire).

Cardinal is a good example of how meanings multiply. It has no Indo-European root, for the object it names did not exist in those roving days. When the Romans built houses, and devised swinging doors, they coined the word *cardo, cardinis,* adjective *cardinalis* (perhaps fashioned by metathesis from Greek *krado,* a quivering spray on a branch, then a swing—and note the English *cradle,* the infant's swinging bed) to name the hinge. Hence, anything on which another thing hinges: the cardinal veins that start circulation in the human embryo; the four cardinal points of the compass, of the year, of a horoscope; the cardinal numbers, which, giving quantity without kind or order, enable us to calculate; the cardinal sins (the "seven deadly" ones: pride, lust, envy, anger, covetousness, gluttony, sloth), on which our stay in hellfire hinges, contrasted with the seven cardinal virtues (natural: justice, prudence, temperance, fortitude; theological: faith, hope, charity), which swing open the doors of paradise. And the members of the Catholic College of Cardinals, who choose one of their number as representative of God on earth, the pope. From the cassock of the cardinal the color is named; from the color, (1) an 18th-century lady's cloak, (2) a bird, (3) a flower, (4) a fish—which seems oceans away from a door hinge.

Germanic *flug* became *fugl,* whence our *fowl. Vogel* is German for *bird.* Latin *scintilla* came directly into English, giving us *scintillate* as well; by metathesis it is also the source of *tinsel* and *stencil.*

Reduplication

A sound may, in early speech, be reduplicated, as we say *chat* and *chitchat; hurry-scurry.* From the root *sta,* Greek *histani* led to English *system;* Latin *si-st*, to English *assist, exist,* and more.

Verbal Forms

Words may come into English from various parts of a verb. Latin *sto, stare,* to stand, present participle *stans, stantem,* past participle *status* (taken directly into English), gives us such differing words as *stow, store, circumstance, extant, instant, prostitute, state, stationary.* Many English words with *ant*—*infant* (Latin *infans, infantem,* not speaking), *substantial, triumphant, contestant*—have come from a Latin present participle. As a prefix, however, *ant* may come from either *ante,* before (*anticipate, antediluvian*) or *anti,* against (*antagonist, antimacassar:* protection on chair against hair oil, which in Victorian days was imported from Macassar, a port on Sulawesi, Indonesia). When a Latin verb is reduplicated or affixed, the vowel may change: thus *stare* became *constituere,* to stand together, whence your and your country's *constitution.*

Lost Sounds

Roots beginning with *s* before a consonant may lose the *s*. The root *stern:* stiff, comes directly into English. But the Germanic form, without the *s,* applied to prickly plants, became English *thorn* (originally sounded *torn,* as a skirt may be). Modified again, via Swedish, it gave English *turbot,* a spiny flatfish. Similarly, the root *stene,* whence *stentorian,* also gave us *thunder* and the Norse god of thunder, Thor, after whom we name Thursday.

Other initial letters also may be sloughed, as we noticed with *gn.* And some letters retained in today's spelling may no longer be sounded, though their retention helps us to trace their story. Note the loss of the *w* sound in such names as Warwick and Greenwich. Indeed, every letter of the alphabet is silent in some word: *a*, inst*e*a*d*; *b*, de*b*t; *c*, a*c*quaintance . . . *z*, jazz. A full alphabetical list of silent letters is in my book *In Praise of English.*

N Changes

The sound *n* varies perhaps most frequently. It is sometimes added, the root sound being "nasalized." Thus the root *tag:* touch, gives us *tangible* and *tangent* as well as *tact* and *tactile.* Similarly *sac:* to make holy, whence *sacred, sacerdotal,* also provides *sanctify;* via French, *saint;* and via Dutch, *Santa Claus.*

Or the *n* may be dropped. In this way the pronominal root *nes* gave English *us, our, ours.* Latin retained the *n* of *nes;* hence *paternoster,* the prayer to our Father (in heaven), and the medieval *nostrum,* literally "our own": a secret recipe, concocted by the man, usually a quack, that sold it.

In Greek the letter gamma, before kappa, chi, khi, or another gamma, was pronounced *n:* Greek *agkura:* bent, English *angle, anchor;* Greek *aggelus:* messenger, English *angel,* messenger of the Lord.

In 15th-century English, smooth flow of sound occasionally added an *n,* as *message* led to *messenger, passage* to *passenger* (instead of *passager,* which is the French form); *n* was inserted also in *celandine, nightingale, popinjay, porringer, scavenger.* A curious double action came in *agnail:* this had lost an *n,* from *angnail, ang* meaning pain, as in *anguish;* then, from the tiny loose flesh at the edge, it came to be called *hangnail.* At about the same time (as discussed below, under "Folk Etymology," the *n* sound sometimes shifted between two words: the Fool in *King Lear* calls the King *Nuncle,* for Mine Uncle; a*n* *u*mpire was *a* *n*on-pair (not even), the odd man out, asked to referee.

"Full" Words

Words ending in the Latin suffix *osus:* full of, may come into English as *bellicose, grandiose, verbose;* or as *courageous, ostentatious, pious* (full of piety). Usually the *ose* form is more learned, taken directly from the Latin, whereas the *ous* form came via French. In scientific words, more recently formed, there is another contrast; the *ous,* as in *ferrous* (of iron) indicates less of the substance than the *ic* ending, as in *ferric.* Greek *osis* is discussed later.

Learned Creations

In the 16th and 17th centuries, in the fervor of the English Renaissance, writers took pride in the invention of words from Greek and Latin sources. They proudly put forth their own creations, and disdainfully put down those of their fellows.

Thus Puttenham in 1589 boasted of having formed *scientific, idiom, methodical, savage, audacious, numerosity, implete, politien;* the last three have not survived. In 1592 Thomas Nashe heaped scorn upon Gabriel Harvey for having coined *jovial, rascality, notoriety, extensively.* In his play *The Poetaster* Ben Jonson makes John Marston spew out the words *retrograde, damp, strenuous, spurious, defunct, clumsy, prorump, obstupefact, ventositous;* the last three died aborning, although *obstupefact* sounds worth a resurrection.

Shakespeare, as might be expected, was the greatest wordfacturologist of them all. Well known is his one-time *honorificabilitudinitatibus,* with its long alternation of consonants and vowels. Less well known is the fact that of the 17,677 words Shakespeare used in his works, well over 1700 are recorded there for the first time, one new word in every ten. Here is a tiny sampling: *aerial, assassination, auspicious, barefaced, castigate, clangor, critic, critical, compunctious, countless, what the dickens, eventful, laughable, leapfrog, misplaced, monumental, seamy, lapse, hurry, perusal, sportive, impartial.* Some of his inventions, naturally, were less successful; he complicated *clog* as *enclog;* he tried *ensky, barky, barry, brisky.* And in *Love's Labor's Lost** he has the schoolmaster Holofernes mock the fantastical Spaniard Armado—well named for ridicule, after the recent defeat of the "invincible" Spanish Armada—for saying *dout* instead of *doubt, det* instead of *debt, abominable* instead of *abhominable.* All three of these are due to the new interest in the classics. Until the late 16th century, *det* was the regular spelling; then direct from Latin came English *debit,* and in its train *debt.* Similarly *dout,* after *dubious,* was supplanted by *doubt*—oddly, in this trail, for almost three centuries *doughty* was spelled *doubty.* With Shakespeare's third word, he made the wrong choice, as though from Latin *homo, hominem,* man, meaning away from man, unnatural, hateful, instead of *omen, ominem,* away from the omen. In the First Folio the word occurs 18 times, always spelled *abhominable.* While the etymological (Greek *etumos,* true) spelling has been restored, the misunderstanding has permanently altered the meaning. Among other spelling changes due to classical influence are the shift from *rime* to *rhyme,* and the transposition of the *h* from the earlier English *rethorick.*

Sometimes the word borrowed directly from the classics gives more intensity to the meaning: thus, Germanic *fire,* French *flame,* Latin *conflagration,* Greek *holocaust* (total burning).

Since the Renaissance, most new words have been coined by physicians, inventors, and scientists to label new diseases, devices, discoveries, and ideas. Medical men—especially, recently, psychiatrists and Freudians—have reveled in word formation. A patient may feel reassured on the assumption that if a doctor can name the ailment, he can in all likelihood cure it. A dreaded exception, still,

*Spelled *labor* on the title page of the First Quarto (1598), "as it was presented before her Highnes this last Christmas"—the first time Shakespeare's name appeared on any play.

is cancer, for which he therefore seeks less ominous names such as *carcinoma;* a *carcinogen* is a cancer-producing substance.

Frequent among medical terms are certain suffixes. Greek *osis,* full of, coming via Latin in such general terms as *voluptuous* and *grandiose,* appears direct in *tuberculosis,* full of little tubers; *arteriosclerosis,* arteries clogging, the channels filling up. *Metamorphosis* is a full change of shape. The *itis* suffix is used to mean enlarged or inflamed: *tonsilitis, appendicitis.* An atom (Greek *a,* not; *temnein, tom,* to cut) is the tiniest item, which cannot be divided–though now we know better. The suffix *(o)tomy* means to incise, cut into, as in *anatomy.* The suffix *ectomy* means to cut out, to remove. Hence *hysterectomy,* removal of the uterus; *hysterotomy,* incision, as in the Caesarian operation–from Latin *caedere, caesum,* to cut, but in legend the manner of the delivery of Julius Caesar. (The first Caesarian operation, we are told, was ordered by Numa, first king of Rome, about 700 B.C., some 650 years before Julius Caesar. Caesar's mother was alive when he wrote his account of the Gallic Wars; in ancient times, the operation was performed only on an already dead woman, to try to save her unborn child.) *Mastectomy* is the removal of a breast; *orchidectomy,* of a testicle (*orchis, orchidem;* the flower named from the shape of the root-bulb). *Phlebotomy* is bloodletting, cutting a vein.

Physicians and scientists today are seldom expert in the classical languages, and may blunder in their creation of words. In their *Dictionary of Psychological and Psychoanalytical Terms,* H. B. and A. C. English set a prefatory jingle, mocking such misuse of the classical roots. There are many words ending in *mania;* even more–some 275–in *phobia;* yet these authors state that in no case is the compound with *phobia* "clearer, more convenient, more euphonious, or less ambiguous, than if the morbid fear had been characterized in English." Yet the eager wordsmiths continue. A new term might mean an increase in salary or prestige. A mountain on Mars or a disease might even be named for its describer. A chemical company, marketing some 80 new products a year, has had a computer spell out 37,000 possible names. Now there are international committees to fashion and establish names in scientific fields.

Echoic Words

A number of words are imitative (also called echoic or onomatopoetic). Some present the sound that they name: *crash, smack, crack, smash; buzz, hiss, click, whippoorwill* (from the bird's call). Others have been modified along the way from Indo-European to bring them nearer the speaker's idea of the sound. The root *pneu:* breath, gives us, via Greek, *pneumatic, pneumonia,* etc.; but the Germanic form, *fneasan,* has been echoically altered and reaches English as *sneeze.* Peoples of different tongues, however, also hear differently: it is enlightening as well as amusing to note, say, Japanese or even French, Danish, German, and English echoic words for the crowing of a cock, the growl of a dog, the purr of a cat. Imitation has played an incalculable part in word formation.

Folk Etymology

Another activity that has helped shape language is what is called folk etymology, the turning of an unfamiliar word toward one that is more common. Thus, *crevisse* became *crayfish. Pentis,* a lean-to, was transfigured to *penthouse.* When laymen began to write (an activity that for centuries was the almost exclusive function of the clergy; reading, too: a man could escape hanging by reading a "neck-verse," winning transfer from king's to ecclesiastical court), they sometimes shifted *n* from *an* to the following word, or vice versa–*a* becoming *an*–because they did not know, when they wrote it down, to which word to attach the sound. Thus *a napron* became *an apron;* the less common *napkin* and *napery* were not confused. The venomous snake, *a nadder,* became *an adder;* contrariwise, the little salamander, *an ewt,* became *a newt.*

Folk change may also result from tribal taboo, or fear of the wrath of a god. In Hebrew, the name Englished as *JHVH* (Jehovah) was never sounded. In Greek, the Furies were called *Eumenides,* "daughters of kindness." This process, known as euphemism, has changed many an unpleasant word, and it still functions in many forms. Behind a woman's back, one might remark that her face would stop a clock; to her, it would be more diplomatic to declare: "Whenever I look at you, time stands still." The voice with the smile wins.

Juncture

Juncture and pause–the transitions between sounds in speech–are important and, as we have seen under "Folk Etymology," may play a part in word creation. Talking, said the Autocrat of the Breakfast Table, "is like playing on the harp: there is as much in laying the hands on the strings to stop their vibrations as in twanging on them to bring out their music." Every actor knows that pauses are as precious as sound. Indeed, without proper pause, speech would be a confusing continuum of noises.

"Fairy Ann! Fairy Ann!" cried Kipling in *Thy Servant Dog* (1930). The expression, listed in *OED*'s third supplement under *san fairy ann,* was a transferred juncture brought back by the soldiers of World War I from the French *Ça ne fait rien:* It doesn't matter. Without language hopping, too often *It's mother love* turns out to be *smother-love.* Under *juncture* in *OED*'s second supplement, a quotation calls for distinction of *nitrate, night rate,* and *Nye trait.*

Improper juncture may lead to misunderstanding. Simultaneous translators at the UN once made "The Secretariat's sphere of competence" become in four languages "the Secretariat's fear of competence." And who can blame the rural adolescent who heard on the radio: "Eugene O'Neill won the Pullet Surprise"? A briefly extended pause may add emphasis to what follows it. Juncture remains a basic aspect of speech.

Letter Sounds

Finally, it should be noted that even in closely related languages of the Indo-European family, letters may represent different sounds. Latin *v* is English *w*. German *w* is English *v*. German *v* is English *f*. In both the United States and England, *school* and *orchestra* have a *k* sound; but *schedule* is pronounced *skedule* in the one country and *shedule* in the other. Scandinavian *fisk* and German *Fisch* are both pronounced as English *fish*. An American in Scandinavia may be permitted a smile if a native friend telephones that it is a clear, crisp day, and suggests that they go "she-ing"; he'll provide the "shees"—which they would both spell *s.k.i.s.*

In William the Conqueror's census roll (1086), Shipley is spelled Sciplea (pronounced sheep-lea). Schacosper is among the 83 spellings of the family name of our greatest playwright; also Sashpierre and Chacsper; his grandfather was named Shakeschafte. (We are told that a family is not truly Old American unless there is a horsethief on the tree; Shakespeare is truly Old English, for the earliest recorded fellow of that ilk, William Sakspere of Clopton, who died in 1248, was hanged for robbery. The family prestige had been given luster by the only Englishman to become pope, Adrian IV [d. 1159]; he was of the peaceful [spears-into-pruning-forks] branch: Nicholas Breakspear.)

While such differences may confuse a person trying to speak a foreign tongue, they have contributed to word formation: from French *gentil*, pronounced *zhontee*, has come English *jaunty*. Other odd shiftings play from tongue to tongue. English *Alps* is French *Alpes*. Little change of sound. But with one spelling what we call *Paris* the French call *Paree*. English *pine* (the tree) is French *pin* (sounded *pa*-nasalized); reverse the languages, and sound and sense also change: English *pin*, French *pine* (sounded *peen*) meaning *penis*.

These are some of the ways in which an Indo-European root may have been transformed during the journey across continents and centuries into English. The body of this book lists the most important and fertile Indo-European roots with the English words they have become and with relevant quotations and expansions.

Notes on Usage

Some Indo-European roots may seem quite different from the English words associated with them. It should be remembered that they have grown over a period of some four thousand years, and have spread into more than a hundred languages. The differences between, say, Hittite, Phrygian, Minoan, Sumerian, Tocharian, Persian, Pashto, Annamese, Oscan, Latvian, Wendish, or Ukrainian, and English—all members of one family—make them mutually unintelligible; yet by tracing vowel and consonantal changes, by separating prefixes, suffixes, and midfixes from the basic stems, scholars have been able to follow seemingly quite different words back to a single root. The most frequent of these forms and transformations are presented here with their current English derivatives. It should also be remembered that English began as a minor branch of the Germanic limb of the Indo-European tree.

In the long growth of English, the language has taken many words from tongues outside the Indo-European spread. There have been perhaps ten thousand languages since humankind advanced from grunts to words. Most of these have been set into a hundred or so families, every family apparently unrelated to the others, with different psychological organization, different structural patterns, different sound elements and emphases, different roots.

The number of sounds, and letters to represent them, being limited, we may expect repetition, so that a single root form may have more than one meaning. Few have more than two separate senses; but the root *weik* and the root *wel* are listed with five meanings, and the exceptional *wer* has thirteen different meanings from which words have sprung. Indeed, this spread is duplicated in the growth of words in any one language. Few have more than two separate senses; but the various meanings of *make* occupy 59 columns in the *Oxford English Dictionary*, and the definition of *cell* depends upon whether you are thinking of biology, electricity, politics, or prison.

A figurative use of a word, quite different from its literal meaning, may continue in a language along with the original, or survive after the original, literal sense has lapsed from use. Thus the noun *pluck,* first used of feathers, for three hundred years meant the heart, liver, and lights of an animal, which the huntsman plucked out and tossed to the dogs, or the farmer plucked for food. About 1850, sports writers, seeking variety of terminology–the viscera being considered the seat of courage–applied the literal term to "the quality of courageous (heartful) persistence despite difficulty," and the noun *pluck* took on its present meaning. The persistence of folk physiology and human imagery is illustrated by the fact that today persons seeking colorful variety may go right back to the viscera and exclaim, "That guy's got guts!" or may more learnedly speak of intestinal fortitude; conversely, one's bowels are loosed with fear.

Names of living things begin with the species, which, for the animal kingdom, is defined as "a group of populations capable of interbreeding, a group that is reproductively isolated from other such groups." Beyond these specific congenital creatures, scientists have arranged larger taxonomic groupings, from species upward through genus (plural genera), family, order, class, phylum, to kingdom. Macaulay's schoolboy knew the story of the little goose-girl who was questioned by the passing king: "How many kingdoms are there?" "Three, animal, vegetable, and mineral." "And to which do I belong?" Starry-eyed, she looked at the magnificently garbed stranger and replied: "You belong to the kingdom of God."

Tracing mankind through this arrangement, we have: kingdom: *animal;* phylum: *chordata;* class: *mammalia;* order: *primate;* family: *hominidae;* genus: *homo;* species: *sapiens.* The last three groups are enough for recognition. In zoology, all family names end *idae;* in botany, all end *aceae.*

Because of figurative application or meaning shifts, some of the Indo-European roots have produced English words that seem to be in surprising juxtaposition. From the most fertile root, *gn,* for example, have come many English words, including *know, enormous, genius, ignoble, uncouth, quaint, puny, reconnaissance, physiognomy, pregnant,* and *jaunty.*

Choice of letters to represent sounds may vary among contemporary scholars. Some use *q,* with no following *u,* where others prefer *k.* Since the sound, not the symbol, is significant, I have used *k* as the initial letter of such roots. For similar reasons, *w* is here the single *u,* and *j* is–as it was for centuries–*i.*

Some words, coming into English by different journeys from one root, have given us what are called doublets: *regal, royal; captive, caitiff.* Occasionally there are more than two variants: for example, *dais, desk, disc, discus, dish, disk.*

Bibliography

The greatest work of general English lexicography is the *New English Dictionary on Historical Principles,* issued in fascicule from 1884 to 1928 under the general editorship of James A. H. Murray and reissued in 1933 in twelve volumes and a supplement as the *Oxford English Dictionary.* It is frequently referred to in the body of this book as *OED.* Under the editorship of R. W. Burchfield, four more supplements are now appearing: A–G, 1972; H–N, 1976; O–Scz, 1982 . . .

The *Rhyming Dictionary* of J. Walker, first published in 1775, used and referred to by Byron, one of the oldest reference works still in active use, lists some fifty-five thousand words alphabetized by their last letters. It begins *a, baa;* and ends *humbuzz, fuzz.* Thus, if the reader wishes to know how many English words end, say, with *ly* or *acy,* Walker gives a not exhaustive yet approximate count. I have used him for this purpose, and may say "JWalker lists . . ."

Methods of word development are discussed in the author's *In Praise of English* (1977). Those that wish to pursue the subject further might consult the following:

Beechin, C. L. *A Dictionary of Eponyms* (1979).

Brown, Roland W. *Composition of Scientific Words* (1954).

Brugman, K. *Grundriss der vergleichenden Grammatik der indogermanische Sprache* (1896–1916).

Buck, Carl D. *Dictionary of Selected Synonyms in the Principal Indo-European Languages* (1949, 1965). Arranged somewhat like Roget's *Thesaurus,* with English words translated into 22 languages.

Carnoy, A. J. *Dictionnaire étymologique du proto-indo-européen,* vol. 39. Louvain: Bibliothèque du Muséon (1955).

Cuny, A. *Invitation à l'étude comparative des langues indo-européenes et des langues chamito-sémitiques* (1946).

Dowson, John. *A Classical Dictionary of Hindu Mythology, Religion, Geography, History, and Literature,* 3d ed. (1914).

Elcock, W. D. *The Romance Languages* (1960, 1975).
Ernout, A., and Meillet, A. *Dictionnaire étymologique de la langue latine,* 4th ed. (1959).
Fennell, C. A. N. *The Stanford Dictionary of Anglicized Words and Phrases* (1964).
Flood, W. E. *The Origin of Chemical Names* (1903).
Frisk, Hjalmar. *Griechisches Etymologisches Wörterbuch* (1955).
Grandsaignes d'Hauterive, Robert. *Dictionnaire des racines des langues indo-européenes* (1949).
Great Languages Series. Faber & Faber (1931-1949).
Klein, Ernest. *A Comprehensive Etymological Dictionary of the English Language,* 2 vols. (1966, 1967).
Lehman, W. P. *Historical Linguistics* (1962).
Levi, Sylvain, et al. *Pre-Aryan and Pre-Dravidian in India* (1929).
Lockwood, W. B. *Panorama of Indo-European Languages* (1972).
——. *Languages of the British Isles, Past and Present* (1975).
Mayrhofer, Manfred. *A Concise Etymological Sanskrit Dictionary* (1956).
Meillet, Antoine. *Introduction à l'étude comparative des langues indo-européenes* (1964).
——. *The Indo-European Dialects,* trans. S. N. Rosenberg (1967).
Menninger, Karl. *Number Words and Number Symbols* (1969).
Oxford Classical Dictionary, 2d ed. (1970), s.v., "comparative philology."
Pikkusaari, Lauri T. *New Light on the Indo-European Language* (1961).
Pisani, Vittore. *Introduzione alla linguista indoeuropea* (1939, 1948).
——. *Crestomazia indoeuropea* (1947).
——. *Glottologia indoeuropea* (1949).
Plowden, C. C. *A Manual of Place Names,* 2d ed. (1970).
Pokorny, Julius. *Indogermanisches Etymologisches Wörterbuch* (1948, 1969).
——. *Vergleichendes Wörterbuch der indogermanischen Sprachen* (1973).
Saussure, Ferdinand du. *Course in General Linguistics,* ed. E. Ball, C. Sechellay, and A. Reidlinger (1959).
Shipley, Joseph T. *Dictionary of Word Origins* (1945, 1982).
——. *Dictionary of Early English* (1955).
Skinner, Henry Alan. *The Origin of Medical Terms* (1970).
Walde, Alois, and Hofmann, J. B. *Lateinisches Etymologisches Wörterbuch* (1938-55).
Walde, Alois, and Pokorny, J. *Vergleichendes Wörterbuch der indogermanischen Sprachen.* Walde died in 1924; the work was completed by Pokorny (1926-30).
Zahradnik, Jiří. *Insects* (1977).

List of Abbreviations

Arab	Arabic
Aram	Aramaic
Av	Avestan
Bulg	Bulgarian
Celt	Celtic
Dan	Danish
Du	Dutch
E	English
EE	Early English
Etr	Etruscan
Fr	French
Gael	Gaelic
Gall	Gallic
Gc	Germanic
Gk	Greek
Gm	German
Hebr	Hebrew
Hung	Hungarian
Icel	Icelandic
IE	Indo-European
Ir	Irish
Iran	Iranian
It	Italian
L	Latin
LGk	Late Greek
LL	Late (Vulgar) Latin
Malay	Malaysian
MDu	Middle Dutch
ME	Middle English
Norw	Norwegian
ODu	Old Dutch
OE	Old English
OED	*Oxford English Dictionary*
OFr	Old French
OGm	Old German
OHG	Old High German
OInd	Old Indian
OIr	Old Irish
OIran	Old Iranian
OIt	Old Italian
OL	Old Latin
ONorse	Old Norse
OPers	Old Persian
OProv	Old Provençal
OSlav	Old Slavic
OSw	Old Swedish
Pers	Persian
Phoen	Phoenician
Pkr	Prakrit
Port	Portuguese
Prov	Provençal
Rom	Romanic
Rum	Rumanian
Russ	Russian
Scand	Scandinavian
Scot	Scots
SCr	Serbo-Croatian
Sem	Semitic
Skr	Sanskrit
Slav	Slavic
Sp	Spanish
Sw	Swedish
Turk	Turkish
W	Welsh

abel: originally, fruit of a tree. Gc, *apple. dapple,* from the varied color of the early fruit skin. A colorful poem by Gerard Manley Hopkins begins: "Glory be to God for dappled things."

For *apple-pie order,* see *caput. apple cider; apple dumpling.* "Coleridge holds that a man cannot have a pure mind who refuses apple dumpling. I am not certain but he is right"—Charles Lamb, *Essays of Elia.* Although not originating there, the U.S. has taken this fruit into its folklore: "as American as apple pie."

An apple pie without some cheese
Is like a kiss without a squeeze.
—Folk rhyme

An *apple-pie bed,* as a practical joke, with a sheet so folded that one cannot get one's legs in, may be a corruption of Fr *nappe pliée:* folded sheet.

Remember Johnny Appleseed,
All ye who love the apple;
He served his kind by word and deed
In God's grand greenwood chapel.
—William H. Venable

John *"Appleseed"* Chapman (1774–1847) traveled through the new land starting orchards; helped the new land to blossom. Vachel Lindsay wrote a poem *In Praise of Johnny Appleseed.*

love apple: the tomato, Gm *Liebesapfel,* Fr *pomme d'amour,* has had a curious history. A member of the nightshade family, all of which contain poisonous alkaloids, it was taken from its native America and grown as an attractive plant, but not eaten by the English and the Americans until after 1830. Chambers's *Encyclopaedia* of 1753 wonderingly records: "Tomato, the Portuguese name for the lycopersicon (Persian wolf) or love-apple, a fruit eaten either stewed or raw by the Spaniards and Italians and by the Jew families of England." In 1856 Emerson remarked: "I find the sea life an acquired taste, like that for tomatoes." As late as 1867 it was dismissed as something "the Feejeans eat at their feasts of human flesh, and is therefore called the cannibals' tomato." Once it grew familiar as food, the tomato was considered an aphrodisiac, hence love apple; perhaps the belief grew from the name, which is a mistranslation of It *pomodoro,* not from *adorare:* to adore, but from *d'or:* of gold, from the yellow fruit, or *de Moro:* of the Moors. See *teue.*

L *pomum,* Fr *pomme,* also at first meant any tree fruit. Hence there remains question as to the exact nature of the apple Eve ate in the Garden of Eden, a bit of which stuck in the throat of her man, still a sign of the first sin, the Adam's apple—actually, the projecting cartilage of the larynx. "In Adam's fall We sinned all" ran the Colonial ABC hornbooks. See *do; per VI c.*

applejack is brandy from cider. To *apple-polish* or *apple-shine* is to curry favor, as the schoolboy hopefully sets a shiny red apple on his teacher's desk.

The *apple of discord* started the Trojan War; when not invited to the wedding feast of Peleus and Thetis (parents of Achilles), the goddess of discord, Eris, tossed in a golden apple, "for the fairest." Three goddesses claimed it. Paris of Troy, son of Priam, was their choice as judge. Hera (Roman Juno) promised Paris greatness; Athene (Roman Minerva), success in war; Aphrodite (Roman Venus), the loveliest woman. The most beautiful woman, Helen—daughter of Leda by Zeus in the guise of a swan—was wife of the Greek Menelaus; her departure with Paris started the ten-year Trojan War. Dr. Faustus, in Marlowe's play (1588), exclaims when Mephistophilis materializes Helen:

Was this the face that launched a thousand ships,
And burnt the topless towers of Ilium?
Sweet Helen, make me immortal with a kiss.

Events in the last year of the Trojan War are told in Homer's epic the *Iliad;* the Trojan state, Ilium, was founded by King Ilus. (Homer does not mention the story of the apple.) See *neuos.* And of course there is the apple that struck Newton with the force of gravity.

From L *pomum* came E *pomade; pomegranate:* seedy apple. *pomelo:* grapefruit, Fr *pampelmousse. pommel,* from the shape, as on the poles of a bed, hilt of a sword, front of a saddle, and, in the 15th c., a woman's breast. *pomology.* The Roman goddess of fruits was *Pomona.* There are over 50 more words from this source in *OED.* Beyond these, "a word fitly spoken is like apples of gold in pictures of silver" (Bible, Proverbs 25); and, of course, the one that is "the apple of my eye."

Besides *abel* and *pomum,* Gk *melon,* Doric *malon,* and L *malum* were also used of tree fruit with fleshy skin, as opposed to L *nux:* nut with hard shell. Thus Gk *melopepon:* ripe apple; see *peku.* Gk *melimelon:* honeyapple, in Portuguese became (*l.r* shift) *marmelo:* quince, which was used before orange to make *marmalade.* Hence also *malic* acid; *melanite. c(h)amomile* (Gk *khamaimelon;* see *ghdhem*) was earthapple. *Ab ovo usque ad mala:* from egg to apples, was the Roman equivalent of our "from soup to nuts."

During the Middle Ages L *malum,* for the apple the Tempter gave to Eve and she to Adam, was linked with *mal,* as the root of all evil. Thus *malfeasance,* and all the *maladies* that have plagued mankind, were seen as springing from the apple that led to the fall of man in the primordial garden. Fortunately, the fruit has so lost the sense of its *malfunctioning* as to give rise to the orchardmen's slogan: "An apple a day keeps the doctor away." Temptation: wholesomeness; it is with mixed feelings that one calls New York City "the Big Apple." See *deu; melo.*

The apple is the favorite fruit of Americans. *A Dictionary of Americanisms* (1951) gives 40 combinations beginning with *apple,* as *apple dowdy, applejack, appleparing:* a preserving bee; and lists 41 ending with *apple,* as *bake-apple, swamp apple.*

Warmth and peace within,
And savory sniff from cellar door of spicy apple bin.

applesauce; also as slang: "That's all applesauce!"—explained in *Century Magazine* (Autumn 1929) as "a camouflage of flattery, derived from the boarding-house trick of serving plenty of this cheap comestible when richer fare is scanty." A goodly portion has been called "applesauce of purest ray serene."

Leigh Hunt, after two years' imprisonment for his articles about the prince regent, showed his criminal tendencies in the *Song of the Fairies* (1818):

Stolen sweets are always sweeter;
Stolen kisses much completer;
Stolen looks are nice in chapels;
Stolen, stolen, be your apples.

Though now rarely experienced, it is still fun to glean windfalls in a roadside orchard.

ag: lead, drive, push; do; weigh. Gk, *demagogue,* leader of the people. *hypnagogic. pedagogue:* child-leader. *synagogue:* a leading together of at least ten males over the age of thirteen, the Jewish quorum, called a *minyon* (*Quorum* is L "of whom . . ." with a specified number). See *pou; men I.*

protagonist; antagonist. antagonize. anagoge. agony. choragus. Gk *axioma:* weighty. *axiom, axiology; chronaxy.*

L *agere, agendum, actum.* agenda. *act, redactor; reaction, agent. agile, agitate.* L *cogo, coactum:* press together. *coaction. coagulate. cogency. cogitate:* weigh in the mind. *exact, exaction, exiguous, exigent; intransigent. stratagem. strategy. assay; essay. epact; transact; retroactive.* With L *ambi:* around (see *ambhi*) came *ambage, ambiguous; embassy, ambassador.* Sir Henry Wotton in 1604 neatly declared that "an ambassador is an honest man sent to lie abroad for the good of his country." *fumigate; fustigate; levigate; litigation.* L *ex-ags-men; examine, examination; exact.*

From driving cattle in the open fields came *agrarian, agrestial; agriculture; agro-,* as *agriology, agronomy. acre:* originally, pasture land; *acreage.* God's *acre:* the cemetery. *acorn;* first, fruit of the field (*agran,* changed by association with corn). *peregrination:* a driving through, as for new pastures; *peregrine,* whence (*l.r* shift) *pilgrim;* also used as proper names, as in Tobias Smollett's picaresque novel, *Peregrine Pickle* (1751) (see *per*); and *Pilgrim's Progress,* written in prison in 1678 by John Bunyan, which the Pilgrim Fathers brought with them to the New World and with which the Bible formed the complete library of many a New England home. The Pilgrims landed at Plymouth Rock in 1620 and, we are told, fell first upon their knees and then upon the aborigines. There followed our first Thanksgiving.

From this root probably *air:* of cattle of good stock, as also in "an air of distinction." Fr, *debonair.* Possibly *area; eyrie.* Also via Fr, *cache, cachet; cachepot:* decorative cover for a flower pot.

agh: to be afraid. *awe.*

agher: daytime. Gc, *day, today. daisy* (day's eye). *dawn.* See *dei.*

agu(e)si: *ax; adz.*

aguhno: lamb. *yean; yeanling.*

ai I: allot. *etiology.* Gk *diaiton:* arrange one's life. *diet.*

ai II: utter. Gk *ainigma. enigma.* Several critics have described several books or plays—e.g., *Waiting for Godot* (1952), by Samuel Beckett—as "a mystery wrapped in an enigma," following Winston Churchill's reference on 1 Oct. 1939 to the action of Russia as "a riddle wrapped in a mystery inside an enigma."

aidh: surge; burn. Gk, *ether.* L, *(a)estival, (a)estivate. estuary. oast.* L *aedes:* hearth, whence *edifice; edify. OED* defines 12 relevant words beginning *edif.* From OE *an aelan:* to burn, associated with L *nigellum,* diminutive of *niger: black,* as when burned, came *anneal.*

aier: Gc, *early, ere, or. erst* (superlative); *erstwhile.*

aig: goat. From the goatskin shield of Athene, *aegis.* Gk *tragos: tragedy:* goat song; *tragic,* etc. In their dramatic contests the ancient Greeks presented three plays (a trilogy) on a tragic theme, followed by a burlesque satyr play. A satyr is a goatlike demigod; hence goat song; also, a goat (to be sacrificed) was a prize in the early sung-and-danced dramas. Pan, god of nature, had a man's head and torso; a goat's ears, horns, and (two) legs.

"The world is a comedy to those that think, a tragedy to those that feel."—Horace Walpole, letter of 16 Aug. 1776. (In 1775 he had written: "By the waters of Babylon we sit down and weep, when we think of thee, O America!")

aios: metal. ore. L *aes, aeris:* copper, bronze. From cutting the ore (*tem:* cut) came bits that were cut and used to calculate; hence *era; esteem, estimate, inestimable. aeneous, aeruginous, aerugo.* Via Fr, *aim, aimless.*

"Illi robur et aes triplex/Circa pectus erat, qui fragilem truci/Commisit pelago ratem/Primus" [His heart was mailed in oak and triple brass,/who first committed a frail bark/to the rough sea]. So wrote Horace. He also boasted of his poetry, *Exegi monumentum aere perennius:* I have erected a memorial more enduring than brass.

aiu: vital force; long life, eternity. Gk, *eon.* L *aetatis; aevum:* age. *coeval; coetaneous; simultaneous. longevity. medieval, primeval. eternal, sempiternal; eternity.* Gc, *aught, ay; ever, aye; every, everything. age, ageless; nonage. no, naught, never;* see *ne* and the more active negative root *nek.* Also probably related is the dangerous *nighttime,* L *nox, noctis;* see *nekut.*

La Rochefoucauld, in *Maxims* (1665), observed: "Age loves to give good precepts, to console itself for being no longer able to give bad examples."

King Solomon and King David led very merry lives,
With very many concubines and very many wives,
Until old age came creeping, with very many qualms,
Then Solomon wrote the Proverbs, and David wrote the Psalms.
—James A. Naylor

ak: sharp, sour, pointed; hence top, tip. Gk, *acme. acne,* from an error, Gk *m* written as *n. acmite. acrobat:* first, performing atiptoe. *oxygen* (see *el 8*). *oxalic. paroxysm. paragon; mediocre. acropolis:* city on the hill. *acrophobia. OED* has five columns of relevant words beginning *acro,* as *acronym; acrostic* (see *steigh*). *acid, acidity; acrid. acrimony. acantha, acanthion; acanthus,* from the shape of the leaves. *pyracantha. acumen; acute,* also shortened to *cute.* Gc, *egg* (*on*); *edge; eager, vinegar; ear* (of corn). Via OE, *hammer.*

aks: axis. This is a strengthened form of *ag:* to move, drive. Gk, *axon.* L, *axis. axil:* point where branch extends to twig; *axilla:* point where shoulder extends to arm: *armpit. axillary.* By extension (L *agsla?, ala:* wing), *alar, alate; aliped; aileron. aisle. axial, coaxial.* Gc, *axle.*

akua: water. The importance of water was early recognized; it took several roots; see *aue; nebh; ug.* L, *aqueous, aquarium, aquatic; aqueduct; aquamarine. aqua fortis, aqua regia, aqua vitae.* Fr, *eau de vie;* Gaelic *usquebaugh:* whiskey. More recently, *aquacade, aquabatics, aqualung, aquanaut.* Fr, *aquarelle, gouache, aquatint. Aquarius,* the Water Carrier, is the eleventh sign of the zodiac; see *guei.* The eagle, genus *Aquila,* is the water-colored bird. *aquiline.* Fr *eau:* water; hence *eager:* literally, water-spear: a tidal flood.

Island is "land on water," the first syllable changed from Gc *ey* to *is* (silent *s*) by association with *isle,* which was L *insula,* probably from *in salo:* in the salt (sea). Thus also *islet,* as the islets of Langerhans (P. Langerhans, d. 1888) in the pancreas, source of insulin. Reil's island (Johann C. Reil, d. 1813) is a tiny lobe of the cerebrum, in the deep lateral fissure of Sylvius. The Sylvian fissure in the human brain is named for Franz de la Boë Sylvius (d. 1672), as is sylvite. See *sal I.*

insular; peninsula (L *paena:* next to, almost, as in *penultimate;* see *al II*); *insulation, isolate.* OFr *aiguiere: ewer. sewer* (*ex-aqua*).

An interesting suggestion connects *island,* early *yland,* with the eye. Parts of the body are used figuratively in geography: the mouth of a river, the brow and foot of a hill, an arm of the sea. A headland; thus, too, an eye-land: dark "earth" of the iris surrounded by water. Frisian, the tongue nearest to English, still has *ey:* island. A small island, as in the Thames, is called an *eyot.* The island of Jersey (pronounced *Jarzee*) may have been Caesar's (Czar's) eye; similarly, such forms in other place names, as *Battersea, Molesey, Bermondsey,* and the initial *e* of *Eton:* town on river. The first part of *Chelsea* is from OE *chesil:* gravel, "small pebbles, as on a beach." "It is with passions as it is with fire and water; they are good servants, but bad masters"—Sir Roger L'Estrange, *Æsop's Fables* (trans. 1692), 38.

al I: nourish, hence grow (tall, old). Gk, *althea* (marshmallow family, thought to heal). L, *aliment, alimentary* (canal). *alimony. alma mater; alumna, alumnus* (plurals *alumnae, alumni*). *altitude, altimeter. exalt. adolescent, adult. coalesce. obsolescent* and *obsolete,* from this root, have altered form and meaning from association with L *solere, solitum:* to grow used to, be accustomed, from which came *insolent:* attitude to which one is unaccustomed. (*insult* first meant to leap upon; see *sel IV.*) *-esce* is the inceptive form; *adolescent:* on the way to being adult. *abolish* (*ab:* from).

L *pro-al, prole. proles, prolific, proliferate. proletariat:* first, grown for menial or military use (see *seni*). Fr, *enhance. hawser. haughty, hauteur, hautboy; oboe* (see *bhurs*). It, *alto, altissimo; contralto. rialto.* Gc, *alderman; eld, elder; old. old-fashioned. old-timer. old wives' tale. Old-worldly.*

Dickens, *Dombey and Son* (1848): "Her eyes would play the devil with the youngsters before long—'and the oldsters too, if you come to that,' added the Major." *auld lang syne.*

"The old man has already done what the young man hopes to do: live long."

al II: beyond, other. Gk *allos:* other. *allegory. allelomorph; allogen; diallage, hypallage. agio. catallactic. allactite. allagite. synallagmatic; trophallaxis. parallel, parallelogram, parallelopiped* (see *ped*). *unparalleled; parallective. parallax.*

Distances across space are measured by light-years, or by parallax. A light-year is the distance that light (at 186,000 miles a second) travels in a year, about 5.88×10^{12} miles. The parallax is the difference in the angle made by the line of vision to an object distant in space, measured from two points of observation, as at the opposite extremes of the earth's annual rotation; the farther the celestial object, the smaller the parallax. A *par*allax of one *sec*ond of arc is called a *parsec* (from the first syllable of each of the words); it equals 3.258 light-years, or about 1.92×10^{13} miles.

When quacks with pills political would dope us,
When politics absorbs the livelong day,
I like to think upon that star Canopus,
So far, so far away.

Greatest of visioned suns, they say who list 'em;
To weigh it science almost must despair,
Its shell would hold our whole dinged solar system,
Nor ever know 'twas there . . .

For after one has had about a week of
The arguments of friends as well as foes,

A star that has no parallax to speak of
Conduces to repose.
—Bert Leston Taylor, *Canopus*

allopathy: medical treatment opposed to *homeopathy,* which acts on the principle that like cures like. *allogamy; allogeneous* (vs. *homogeneous*). *allomorph; allonymous. allograph:* written by another, opposed to *autograph; holograph* is entirely handwritten. *allophilian:* outsider (neither Indo-European nor Semitic). *allotropy:* chemical unity with physical difference, as carbon, coal, graphite, diamond; first used by J. J. Berzelius (1841). Fr, *aubain* (of another *ban:* tribe). *allotrio-,* as *allotriophagy. Allobroges; Alsatia. A(l)lemanni. allemande:* German dance. *ataunt.*

L *alias:* otherwise. *alias, alien. alter, alternate. altercation. altruism. subaltern. alibi* is a blend of *alius:* other, and *ibi:* there: elsewhere. L *ultra:* beyond. *ne plus ultra:* the uttermost. *ultrasonic; ultraviolet.* In the sense of excessive, transcending the limits of, *OED* says *ultra* "has become very prolific in English use," as *ultramicroscopic. ulterior* (motive); *ultimate, ultimatum.*

adulterer, adultery. adulterate: to change to something other. Johnson's *Dictionary* quotes *The Spectator:* "The present war has so adulterated our tongue with strange words, that it would be impossible for one of our greatgrandfathers to know what posterity has been doing."

penult, antepenult (L *paene:* almost, thus also *penumbra, peninsula* [see *akua*].) L *ille:* that one; Fr *le, la;* Sp *el; alligator* (*el ligarto des Indias:* the lizard of the Indies). Fr, *outrage.* Gc, *else.*

al III: wander; go. L, *ambulate, circumambulate, perambulator; funambulist;* see *dhun. amble, preamble* (see *ambhi*). After the Wife of Bath delivers a prologue of 828 lines, in Chaucer's *Canterbury Tales,* the Friar says to her:

Now dame—quod he—so have I joye or bliss,
This is a long preamble of a tale!

Thereupon the Summoner rebukes him:

Lo!—quod the Summoner—Goddes armes two!
A frere will entremette him ever-mo.
Lo, gode man, a fly and eke a frere
Wol falle in every dish and eek matere.
What spekestow of preambulacion?
What! amble, or trot, or pees, or go sit down;
Thou lettest our disport in this manere.

entremette: meddle. *lettest:* hinderest. *disport:* later shortened to *sport;* see *per II.* Chaucer's frank urinary suggestion was too strong for later ears. Shakespeare's Autolycus, in *The Winter's Tale,* puts it in what is glossed as "a notable euphemism": "I shall but look upon the hedge, and follow thee"—although I do not put it past the Elizabethan actor to have sounded the *look* like *leak.* For women, there was a sweeter expression: Beaumont, in *The Knight of the Burning Pestle,* ii, 4, has Humphry say to the fair Lucia, almost echoing Chaucer:

Up and ride,
Or if it please you, walk for your repose,
Or sit, or if you will, go pluck a rose.

Again a note: "euphemism for relieving nature." In Swift's *Directions to Servants* (1745), a maid complains about the need for a dank dark cupboard because milady disdains going into the garden "to pluck a rose." Yesterday's facetious euphemism was "I have to see a man about a dog."

hallucinate (mental wandering). OFr *alley; purlieu. aleatory* (the dice go haphazardly). *Alea jacta est:* The die is cast. See *bher I.*

albh: whiteness. Gk, *alphos; alphitomancy.* L, *alb, albino; albite. album,* from the white sheets. *alburnum; albumen.* Fr *aubade:* dawn song. *auburn,* meaning influenced by brown. L *dealbare,* Fr *dauber; daub.* "Perfidious Albion": England, so called by the French, who approached by the white cliffs of Dover.

ambhi: around, both. Some of its uses fuse with *al III.* Gk, *amphitheatre, amphodelite. amphoteric:* either acid or base. *amphora:* two-handed jar, diminutive *ampulla* (*l.r* shift); *ampule; ampulliform.* L, *ambageous; ambiguous; ambient; ambidextrous. amputate. ambition:* first, the going around of candidates, still practiced (see *kand*). *amble,* etc. *ambulance* (OFr *hôpital ambulant*). *ambivalence,* coined by Sigmund Freud. *ancile; ancipitous.* It, *andante, andantino.*

Gc, *bivouac:* by, but. Gc *bi,* E *be,* is a most prolific prefix. First meaning around, then all around, it came to be used as an intensive, for emphasis. Editor James Murray spoke of 1500 such words from which to select for *OED; OED* lists 262, then details others in 39 columns. They seem to fall into five groups: (1) Many have become obsolete, as *bebass:* to kiss all over; *becack.* (2) Of some, the simple form, without the prefix, has lapsed, as *bewildered, behavior, beware.* (3) Some have now a different meaning from the simple form, as *bequest, becoming* (*Mourning Becomes Electra,* play by Eugene O'Neill). (4) Some differ from the simple form in use, part of speech, as *beguile,* verb; *guile,* noun. *befoul, befriend, benighted.* (5) In some, emphasis is merely added to the simple form, as *bedaubed, befuddled, bewail, bespatter, beloved.*

ambsace: both aces; lowest throw, hence bad luck.

amer: a day. Gk *hemera. hemeralopia.* With *epi:* within, upon, came *ephemerid, ephemeris; ephemeron* (plural *ephemera*). As the Roman emperor Marcus Aurelius Antoninus (d. 130) remarked in his *Meditations:* "All is ephemeral–even fame and the famous."

amma. Baby talk, reduplicated form of *ma,* sound of suckling; *mamma.* See *ma II,* with which this root is intertwined. *amah:* wet-nurse, in India. Gk *meter:* mother. *metropolis:* mother city; first, see of a chief bishop of the Mother Church. *metropolitan. metronymic. metrorrhagia* (Gk *metron:* womb). L and E *mater; alma mater; matriculate. maternal, maternity, matron. matroclinous. matrix:* first, the uterus. *material, matter,* etc.

What is mind? No matter.
What is matter? Never mind.
–*Punch* 30 (1855): 19

L *amare, amatum:* love. *amateur, amatory, amorous; amour, enamored.* It, *inamorata. paramour. amity, enmity; enemy, inimical.* Sp, *amigo.* Fr *commère:* godmother; Scot *cummer.* L *amita:* father's sister; OFr *ante,* aunt. *mama, mamma; mammary, mammilla, mammal. Mammalia,* coined by Carolus Linnaeus, whose *Systema Naturae* (1737) began the modern classification of plants and animals. Gc, *mother, motherly, motherless, mother-in-law. mother,* in the sense of slimy material, such as the bacterial mass that converts wine to vinegar, may take that meaning from thought of the afterbirth, or possibly from Du *modder:* mud.

Sayings about amour are numberless. *Amare et sapere vix deo conceditur:* To love and be wise is rarely granted even to a god. Through association of the verb *amare* and the noun *amor* with the passions–sex constantly rearing!–the 4th c.

translation of the Bible into Latin tended to avoid the words. The verb is used 51 times; the noun, 20. Instead *caritas:* dearness, occurs 101 times–resulting in our familiarity with "faith hope and charity" instead of love–*dilectio,* implying esteem as well as affection, 43 times; and its verb, *diligo, dilectum,* 422 times. Nevertheless, *amor omnia vincit:* love conquers all.

Giving of alms is not from *amma,* but from Gk *eleos,* pity, expanded to *eleemon:* pitiful, expanded to *eleemosune,* L *eleemosyna:* pity. Thence *eleemosynary,* which sensibly reversed the lengthening process; this seven-syllable adjective was folkchanged with the Lord High Almoner, who distributes the royal (now monosyllabic) alms. Hawthorne, in *The Marble Faun* (1860), speaks of "food for the flock of eleemosynary doves."

Students, not to mention alumni, like to write burlesques and parodies, often little more than extended graffiti. Alfred Jarry's *Ubu Roi* (1896), translated as *King Turd,* the prototype of the theatre of the absurd, was a schoolboy's burlesque of a disliked teacher. John O'Keeffe, called by Hazlitt "the English Molière," was victim of a student parody, of a song from *The Agreeable Surprise* (1793). Here are two stanzas with the chorus after the laughingly lubricated perversion:

Amo, amas, I love a lass
As a cedar tall and slender.
Sweet cowslips' grace her nom'nitive
  case,
And she's of the feminine gender . . .
Oh how bella my puella!
I'll kiss secula seculorum;
If I've luck sir, she's my uxor,
O dies benedictorum!

Amo, amas, I loved a lass,
And she was tall and slender.
Amatus amantis, I took down her
  panties
And tickled her feminine gender.
Rorum corum, sunt divorum,
Harum scarum divo!
Tag rag, merry derry, periwig and
  hatband,
Hic hoc horum, genetivo!

For other instances, see quotations under *ken III, ker III.*

an: on. Gk, *ana:* same of each, in prescriptions (see *sem*). *ana:* collection relating to a person or place, usually as a suffix: *Lincolniana, Americana.* Gc, *on, onslaught. aloft. anlage.* As a prefix, *ana:* up, again, anew; back, over again. *OED* has 35 columns of relevant words, from *anabaptist* to *anatropous:* "heels over head"; of an inverted plant nucleus, opposite of *orthotropous*–with 43 more words in its 1972 supplement. Thus, via It, *analfabeti;* though illiteracy does not necessarily mean ignorance; we are told that there have been Italian *analfabeti* who knew cantos of Dante by heart. *anacamptic:* relating to reflection; *anaclastic:* relating to refraction. In *anarchy* and *anodyne,* the *a* is negative. *analysis* (Gk *luein:* loosen), opposite of *synthesis,* but see *dhe.*

anathema means things devoted, at first to God, but since usually sacrificed, they shifted to the devil; *anathema maranatha* is generally deemed the deepest damnation–so regarded in the Tyndale, Wyclif, and King James bibles–but recent scholarship separates the expressions. Paul ends his First Epistle to the Corinthians: "If anyone has no love for the Lord, let him be accursed" (*anathema*). The next word, *maranatha,* is now translated "Our Lord, come!"

andh: bloom. Gk, *anther. crysanthemum* (Gk *khrusos:* gold, probably from Semitic). *dianthus.* Prefix *anth,* as *anthesis:* a flower's span of life, from bud to fall of seed. *OED* gives 40 relevant words beginnning *anth. anthos;* see *urod.* For *anthro:* man, as prefix, see *nert.*

Suffix *anthous,* as *monanthous, ananthous. antholysis, anthomania. syn-*

anthous: flowers and leaves together. There are over 200,000 named species of plants.

andho: dark; shade. See *dhue I.* L, *umbel, umbra, umbrage. umbrella. adumbrate. penumbra.* Fr, *somber.* Sp, *sombrero,* shades the face. The umbrella was in ancient days borne over a potentate, to mark his high authority and protect him from the rays of the sun. Its use in northern lands came much later, against the rain (see *ombhr*). For Fr *parapluie,* see *per V.* Gay, in *Trivia* (1712), declares:

Let Persian maids the umbrella's ribs display
To guard their beauties from the sunny ray,
Or sweating slaves support the shady load
When eastern monarchs show their state abroad;
Britain in winter only knows its aid,
To guard from chilly showers the walking maid.

In 18th c. coffeehouses, umbrellas were kept to lend to patrons. Hence an ironic advertisement in *The Tatler:* "The young gentleman belonging to the Custom House who in fear of rain borrowed the umbrella from Wilk's Coffee House shall the next time be welcome to the maid's pattens." In December 1758, a Doctor Shebbaird "stood in the pillory, having a footman with an umbrella to keep off the rain." C. C. Colron, in *Lacon* (1822), bk. ii, mentions a man "as completely at a loss as a Dutchman without his pipe, a Frenchman without his mistress, an Italian without his fiddle or an Englishman without his umbrella."

an(e): breathe, breath; that which animates. Via Av, *prana:* breath of life. *ahura:* a good spirit. *asura:* first a good, then an evil, spirit; *Vitrasura. Ahuramazda:* chief spirit; shortened to *Ormazd:* Zoroastrian god of good. *Mazdaism:* the religion, sometimes spelled *Mazdeism* by association with *deism.* The Parsi (name derived from *Persia*), the surviving Zoroastrians, in their morning prayer ask for three admirable things: good thoughts, good words, good deeds.

L, *animal, animalcule,* and the whole animal kingdom. *animation; OED* has 43 related words. *animadvert. animosity. unanimous, magnanimous. pusillanimous:* like a little boy (see *pou*). *equanimity;* the first element in this word, from L *aequus:* equal, also gives us *equality, equation, equable.* The partly imitative *anslare* gave English *anhelation; inhale, exhale, exhalation,* etc. *asthma. halitus. halitosis* came into common use from its euphemistic thrust in advertisements, instead of "foul breath."

Many names of familiar animals have come surprisingly late. The only animal truly domesticated is the cat; the word may be African, but is first seen as LL *catta. kitten* may be imitative: "Here kt, kt, kt, kitty." These terms are closely intertwined with *tickle* (a change by metathesis of *kittle*), with sexual application. *OED* says "tickly-kittly." Langland, in *Piers Plowman* (1362), describes a woman "tikel of her tayl . . . common to knaves and all." To *tickle* was early used for what was later called petting and necking; to *kittle* meant to rouse, also to give birth. *OED* defines *tickle-tail* as a wanton woman, "now dialectal." And *pussy,* perhaps also imitative, is still a slang term for the vagina, as *cat-house* is vulgar for a brothel. The same entanglement occurs in French: *chat:* cat; *chaton:* kitten, both also slang for *con:* cunt; and *chatouiller:* tickle. *purr, mew, mewl, miau(l),* are all imitative.

A caterpillar is a hairy cat; see *pilo. catcall* is from the hideous noise a tomcat on the prowl can make at night; the end of *caterwaul* is imitative. *cat's eye* is a semiprecious stone that gives a shifting reflection. *cat's cradle* is a seeming tangle of string woven on the hands in a game; it comes off disentangled. *catamountain.*

A *cat-burglar,* also called a second-story man, climbs up the outside of a building, agile as a cat. A Cheshire cat vanishes, all but the grin; first mentioned in 1770, it can be seen disappearing in the illustrations to *Alice in Wonderland* (1866). A *cattail* is a plant familiar near marshes. The *cat-o'-nine-tails* is so called because its nine knotted thongs make marks like a cat's scratches; W. S. Gilbert makes play with "the cat" in *H.M.S. Pinafore.* A cat, of course, has "nine lives"; but the nine tails are supposed to represent the holy number *three* taken in itself (squared): a divine instrument of chastisement. See *pilo.*

Using someone as a *cat's paw* arose from the fable of the monkey that persuaded a cat to pull his roasted chestnuts out of the fire. Other combinations of cat include *cat nap:* a short sleep while sitting; *catnip;* "raining cats and dogs."

The dog, trained to guard sheep in the field, and for various purposes in hunting, was OE *docga.* For hound, see *kuon.* Into the 19th c. a dog-whipper was a church official whose function was to keep dogs from running about during services; a new one was appointed at Exeter Cathedral in 1856. The *Oxford Companion to English Literature* describes 46 dogs "famous in history, myth, or fiction." Dogs are put through their paces for prizes at many shows, and are the principal occupants, often with elaborate tombstones, of pet cemeteries.

In the Bible, the dog is mentioned 18 times, the cat, not once.

Other "domestic" animals are farmyard creatures (for *farm,* see *dher III;* for *yard,* see *gher IV*) raised for food, or trained as beasts of burden. Chief of these is the horse, trained also for riding, for racing, for the hunt. OE *hors;* see also *eku.* For *mare,* see *marko;* for *pony, filly,* and *foal,* see *pou;* for *steed* and *stallion,* see *sta.* L *caballus:* horse, gave English *cavalcade, cavalry, cavalier;* via Fr, *chevalier:* first, man on a horse, knight; thence *chivalry,* etc.

It *cavaliere servente* was a knight in devoted service of a married woman, as prescribed in the medieval circles of "courtly love." Courtly love, sung by Provençal troubadours of the 11th c. spread through Italy in the "sweet new style" of Dante and Petrarch; into France, into England, even into Germany with the *Minnesingers:* songsters of love. The early great poet of the Minnelied was Walther von der Vogelweide (d. 1230), who is in Wagner's opera *Tannhäuser.* Courtly love was favored by Eleanor of Aquitaine (1122–1204), queen of Louis VII of France, then of Henry II of England, mother of two English kings, Richard I and John. (England's claim to her province, Aquitaine [about half of southern France] led to 400 years of French-English wars.) Courtly love animated *The Courtier* (1518), by Baldassare Castiglione, translated into English in 1561 by Sir Thomas Hoby, influencing among others Sidney and Spenser. It was the basic attitude of chivalry for 500 years, flowing over into deep devotion to the Virgin Mary and in England to the Virgin Queen.

A *cheval glass* is a large mirror on a "wooden horse" with swivels and on wheels, permitting various views, especially of a woman preparing her display for a formal function. Hence also *clotheshorse. hobby-horse,* in Shakespeare's day, was also used of a prostitute, whom any man might ride; Armado, in *Love's Labor's Lost,* iii, 1, takes offense when the term is used by Moth, who thereupon substitutes *hackney,* which was a horse anyone might hire. (Note the similar sound, for wordplay: *horse, whores.*) There was, much earlier, the Trojan horse, within the belly of which hid the Greeks that captured the city.

As man's most useful neighbor, the horse found frequent reference. The word and listed compounds take up 12 *OED* columns; others are detailed in 18 columns more, from *horseback . . . horse chestnut:* a large inedible variety–unlike the French marron, delicious when glazed or creamed–used in the East, said Gerarde in his *Herbal* (1597), to cure horses of the cough . . . *horse laugh* (*haw*

haw) . . . *horsemanship* . . . *horseplay* . . . *horsetail* (see *eku*) . . . *horsewhip* . . . to *horsy*. Among the many sayings are: "a horse of another color"; "work like a horse"; "don't look a gift horse in the mouth"; "you're flogging a dead horse." A *wooden horse,* "foaled of an acorn," is the English gallows.

The horse has close relatives. A mule is the sterile offspring of a jackass and a mare. For *ass,* see *asinus*—though *asinine* refers to humans. The donkey, a domesticated ass, is named for its dun color (see *dheu I*); the ending is probably influenced by *monkey*. For *ass,* the buttocks, see *ors.*

The cow family provides the most nourishment: milk, butter, cheese, meat. See *guou.* For bull, see *beu. bovine, beef. bullock,* a castrated bull, is a diminutive of *bull;* its plural may have influenced the word *ox,* also a castrated bull; see *ugu.* An oxpecker is a bird that feeds on ticks from the animal's back. An Oxonian marks a person or thing connected with Oxford University, from OE *Oxenaford,* in the river there. Oxtail makes a good soup.

A *bull's-eye* is the dark circle in the center of a target, marking an excellent shot. *calf,* OE *cealf,* is a yearling; and from the root *uet:* year, via L *vitulus,* comes *veal.* To "kill the fatted calf" is for a special feast on someone's returning, as in the biblical reception of the prodigal son (Luke 15:11–32). Allusions to the prodigal son are innumerable, as in *The Merchant of Venice* (ii, 6); Jonson's *Every Man in His Humour* (v, 1); *Robinson Crusoe;* and Scott's *Fair Maid of Perth.*

Partridge's *Dictionary of the Underworld* (1950) devotes almost six columns to *bull, bully,* and their compounds. During the days when flogging was a common punishment, a dose of 25 lashes was called a *tester;* 50, a *bob;* 75, a *bull;* and 100, a *canary;* these names were borrowed from slang terms for money, a *tester* being sixpence; a *bob,* a shilling; a *bull,* a crown; and a *canary,* a (gold) guinea. "A bull out of harness" is a plain-clothes policeman. "A bull in a china shop" implies wanton, indiscriminate destruction. See *beu.*

To throw the bull—"That's a lot (load) of bull!"—may now imply *bullshit;* earlier, it may have brought to mind the story of the proud Persian prince who, to display his skill to his bride, shot a deer in full leap, so that the arrow pierced at once its heel and its heart. When she said, "One takes that for granted," he in his fury ordered her executed. She explained to the officer that the prince loved her, and would one day handsomely reward the officer were she still alive; a generous gift of jewels persuaded him she was right. Living in a far corner of the princedom, she took a newborn calf in her arms and bore it to the roof of her home, repeating this daily for two years, by which time she was carrying a full-grown bull. She had word sent to the prince. When he came, saw, and marvelled, she lifted her veil and said: "One takes that for granted." Surprised and delighted, he restored her to his heart and his throne. That's indeed a load of bull! See *bhel I.*

The word *lamb* is from the root *el:* brown. *sheep,* with *shepherd,* came from OE *sceap.* For *mutton* (also for Saxon vs. Norman animal terms), see *mel I.* The Lord, we are told, will separate the sheep from the goats—saved souls from lost souls—on Judgment Day (see *ghaido, kapr*).

Apparently content to be in the farmyard are the poultry family; see *pou.* hen is from the root *kan:* sing; not melodious, but as Fr *chantecler* indicates, loud and clear. *chick* is from *kue. cock* is imitative; *cock-a-doodle-doo,* Fr *cocorico;* whence also *cackle.* There is an old saw: "If you would have a hen lay, you must bear with her cackling." *coquette:* flirt, and *cocotte:* prostitute, were first baby-words for *chicken.* Here, too, *cockerel,* and the fabulous *cockatrice.*

a tale of cock and bull has been given two origins. Some trace it to a nonsensical story of a cock that turned into a bull; this has the corroboration of Fr *coc-à-l'ane:* cock to jackass. Others state that it arose in antipapist Reformation days, mocking an official proclamation (bull) of the pope, the seal of which (*bulla*) bore a picture of St. Peter with the humbling reminder of a cock, from Jesus' prophecy (Matthew 26:30–75) that Peter would deny the Lord three times before the cock crowed. "'L––d!,' said my mother, 'what is all this story about?' 'A cock and a bull,' said Yorick.–'And one of the best of its kind I ever heard.'" So ends Laurence Sterne's *Tristram Shandy* (1760–67).

high cockalorum, with its mock-Latin ending, a cry of triumph in some 19th c. games, now is applied to a little fellow with a big opinion of himself. There are only guesses as to the origin of the now frequent *cocktail. cocaleekie,* a creamed chicken soup with leek, is delicious. The *cock of the walk* is supreme on his dunghill. A *cock's comb,* part of the court jester's headgear, became *coxcomb:* a conceited dandy. From its resemblance to a cock's head, the early tap or faucet was called a *cock;* from the tap came the use of *cock* to mean penis. *cocksure:* secure as a tap; not a drop of doubt can drip through. Such overconfidence reminds one of Ambrose Bierce's *Devil's Dictionary* definition of *positive:* mistaken at the top of one's voice. See *auei.*

Other words are more or less accidentally "cocked" (as a gun might literally be–the gun *cock* is from the animal, via the tap). A *coxswain* was in charge of a *cockboat:* a tender on a large ship; the word is from L *caudex:* tree trunk, block of wood. (Split the woodblock into writing tablets and there come the words *codex* and *code.*) *cockatoo* is imitative, but first in Malay *kakatu.* And *cockroach* is from Sp *cucaracha,* both ends folkchanged.

The first recorded use of *rooster* was in 1822; this euphemism, *rooster* for *cock,* occurred in the U.S., where prudery preceded, and some say exceeded, that of Victorian England. The rooster, of course, rules the *roost* (OE *hrost:* framework). Hens, however, have their own "pecking order" and know which in the yard have priority when the farmer's wife scatters the grain. The turkey cock got its name from a misunderstanding; the North American bird was at first identified with the guinea fowl, called *turkey* because it came via Turkey, first into Portugal. For *fowl,* see *pleu.* The turkey was introduced into England about 1550. Tusser, in *500 Points of Husbandry* (1585), pictures a hearty Christmas dinner:

> Beef, mutton, and porke, shred pies of the best,
> Pig, veals, goose and capon, and turkie well drest,
> Cheese, apples, and nuts, jolie carols to heare,
> As then, in the countrie, is counted good cheare.

duck is an Old English word, related to *dive,* as is the other sense of the word, *to duck,* and the *ducking stool,* onto which a scold was tied, and dipped into the village pond to cool her temper and temper her tongue; it was last used to duck one Jenny Piper at Leominster, in 1809. *duckling* and *gosling* are diminutives (see *sap;* for *goose, gander,* see *ghans*). A few terms in other fields call upon the goose. *gooseflesh,* as on a cold human, resembles that of the plucked bird. The *goosestep* of Hitler's army resembled a bird's walk. A tailor's *goose* is a smoothing iron, from the neck shape of the handle. *gossamer* is folkchanged from goosesummer (U.S. Indian summer), when goose is traditionally served for dinner, and fine "gossamer" cobwebs sparkle with dew in the grass. A *goose-egg:* zero, in scoring games, comes from the shape; matched in tennis by the score of *love,* from Fr *l'oeuf:* the egg. The name *tennis* itself came via Fr *Tenez!:* Hold! Make ready!, originally cried when the server was ready. (Robert Frost, in a lecture of 17 May 1935, scornfully remarked: "Writing free verse is like playing tennis with the net down.") *To give someone the goose* used to mean to hiss a performer off the stage; recently, from the bird's intrusive beak, it has come to mean to poke someone in the buttocks.

The bird's often seemingly aimless behavior makes it a symbol of foolishness; hence the cry, "You silly goose!" Thus, when the Athenians in 554 B.C. submitted docilely to the dictatorship of Peisistratus, Solon observed: "Each man of you, individually, walketh like a fox, but collectively ye are geese!" But the Romans carried a golden goose in annual procession to the Capitol, in memory of the geese in the Temple of Juno, who in the 4th century B.C. alerted the citizens by their cackling when scouts of the hostile Goths penetrated the city by night.

The goose fits midway between the duck and the swan. For *swan* (genus *Cygnus;* hence *cygnet:* young swan) see *suen:* sound—though its best-known sound is the swan song, at the moment of its dying. All the swans of England belong to the Crown.

Note that the Saxon words here are all monosyllabic.

pigge is ME; *hog,* perhaps Celt; for *swine,* see *sus.* The term *guinea pig* has had an odd development. *Guinea* is the European name of a country and bay of West Africa; from gold mined there the first English guinea (worth a pound and a shilling) was coined in 1663. In the 19th c., noblemen "with more rank than money" lent their names as directors of companies (which thus hoped to attract investors) for the guinea and meal provided at each board meeting; they were called *guinea pigs.* The actual guinea pig came not from Africa but from Guiana, in South America. But the term *guinea* was applied loosely, usually in scorn, to various persons, as to Italians; and to the midshipmen of the British navy—explained by saying "The guinea pig is neither a pig nor a native of Guinea; a midshipman is neither a sailor nor an officer" (see *medhi*). In this century, the South American rodent was found useful in experimentation, whence the use of *guinea pig* for a human so used.

Not a household pet but a frequent household pest is the mouse; see *mus.* Its cousin vermin, the rat, has been an even greater pest, as shown in the lamentable tale of *The Pied Piper of Hamelin,* which Browning brings to a bathetic close with his rhyme:

So, Willy, let you and me be wipers
Of scores out with all men, especially pipers,
And whether they free us from rats or from mice,
If we promise them aught, let us keep our promise.

About a million species of animals have been distinguished and described, of which some 300,000 species are beetles; see *bheid.* "Man is a tool-making animal"—Benjamin Franklin. It has also been remarked that man is the cooking animal. Mark Twain found another distinction: "Man is the only animal that blushes. Or needs to."

Ten animals, in Muslim legend, have been admitted into paradise: (1) Abraham's ram, sacrificed instead of his son Isaac. The Mohammedans trace their descent from Abraham, who is mentioned in their daily prayers. (2) Noah's dove. (3) Jonah's whale. (4) Moses' ox. Mount Sinai, where Moses talked with God and received the Ten Commandments, has come in English to symbolize human contact with supernal values. Thus, writes James Russell Lowell in *The Vision of Sir Launfal* (1848):

Not only around our infancy
Doth heaven with all its splendors lie;
Daily, with souls that cringe and plot,
We Sinais climb and know it not.

(5) Solomon's ant: "Go to the ant, thou sluggard." (6) The lapwing of Bilqis, which bade Solomon to send for her; hence the *Song of Songs.* (7) Balaam's ass. (8) Mohammed's ass, Al Borak. (9) The camel of the prophet Salih, a forerunner of Mohammed. (10) The dog, Kratim, of the Seven Sleepers, who fled from the Decian persecution, A.D. 250. They slept for 309 years, their cave guarded by the dog; when they awoke, Kratim barked in joy and died. The legend apparently grew from a literal interpretation of the Bible, 1 Corinthians 15: those that "fall asleep in Christ" will reawaken.

"The last enemy to be destroyed is death."

angh: squeeze: painful. (Many words first meaning acts were shifted to feelings.) Gk, *angina; quinsy.* L, *anxiety, anxious; anguish.* Gc, *(agnail) hangnail. anger. angst.*

anghui: snake. Vedic, *ahi:* mythological serpent, identified with Vitrasura, demon of drought, foe of Indra; see *ane.* Gk, by taboo transformation, *ophis. ophidian, ophiclide, ophiology. ophite:* serpentine stone. Gk *ekhinos:* hedgehog, snake-eater. *echino-,* as *echinodorus, echinops; echidna; echinus.* L, *anguine, anguiliform. ask:* a newt.

ank: bend; something bent or curved. Skr, *palanquin,* from its bent bearers, or its reeds and cloth bottom sagging. Gk, *anchor. ankylosis; ankle.* L, *unciform; uncinal, uncinus; uncus.* Gc, *angle, angler; angular. Anglo-*(Saxon), from the shape of their native land, *Angul,* in Schleswig. A young priest, Gregory, seeing some blond slaves in Rome, inquired, then exclaimed: "Not Angles but Angels!" In 597, as Pope Gregory I, he sent Augustine with 40 monks to Kent, and Christianized England (*Angle-land*). Thence *Anglican, Anglophile,* etc., and all the English. Gregory, "the Great," also established the primacy of the bishop of Rome, as pope (*papa:* father) of all Catholics everywhere. *catholic,* Gk *cataholos,* means universal, as in the phrase "of catholic taste."

ano: ring. L, *anal, anus.* Diminutive *annular, annulet; annelida.* For *annul,* see *ne.*

ant: in front of, before; thus also opposite, opposed, against; the end. Skr *Vedanta:* "the end of knowledge" in Hindu philosophy. L prefix *ant:* before, begins many words, as *antecedent, antediluvian, anteroom, anterior; antemeridian,* A.M. *advance, advantage, vanguard.* Also *ancient, antiquity, antique, antic.* Robert Bridges wrote *An Ancient to Ancients:*

Sophocles, Plato, Socrates,
Gentlemen,
Pythagoras, Thucydides,
Herodotus and Homer—yea,
Clement, Augustin, Origen,
Burnt brightlier toward their setting day,
Gentlemen.

L prefix *ant:* against, is even more frequent, as *antagonist, antipathy, antipodes, antibiotic; antichrist. answer* was first a swearing against. Both forms are still live; thus we may say *anti-Nixon* as well as *ante-Nixon.*

Gc, *along; and; unto, until.* A variant of *until* is *till,* a form that has three other distinct meanings: (1) to prepare soil for planting; (2) glacial debris; (3) a compartment for ready money.

Here also the Germanic prefix *un,* indicating reversal (not the negative *un,* for which see *ne*), as *unearth, unlock, unloose, undo. end* first meant opposite the beginning, as in a polarity; positive vs. negative; black vs. white; blessed vs. damned; top vs. bottom of the pole. *ancestor* is short for *antecestre,* which also appears in English, but rarely. *antecedent.*

The Greek and Latin prefix has taken several forms: (1) *a,* as *agnostic;* (2) *an,* as *anomaly.* Thus we have both *antarctic* and *anarchic, anarchy.* (3) *ana,* as *anachronism, anachorism;* see *kann.* (4) *ant,* as well as *ante* and *anti. antaphrodisiac.* And sometimes *anti* means not against but before, as *anticipate, antipasto. antiae:* forelocks, by which one must grasp Opportunity, he being a rapidly passing old gentleman, all bald behind. James Murray had to decide which of over 500 *anti* words to include in the *OED;* associated *ant* words take 60 columns. See *ne.*

Dryden translated Ovid's *Art of Love,* I:

To see and to be seen, in heaps they run,
Some to undo, and some to be undone.

Oliver Wendell Holmes, in *A Modest Request,* speaks of "lean, hungry anti-everythings."

ap, apo: reach, extend; put; hence, away. Gk prefix *apo* (*koluptein:* cover), *apocalypse:* revelation, as to St. John on Patmos. (*khruptein:* hide), *apocrypha.* (Gk *deiknunai:* show; L *dicere:* tell), *apod(e)ictic.* (Gk *ge:* earth), *apogee.* (*plessein:* strike), *apoplexy. OED* has 26 columns of *apo* words, as *apologue, apologize, apotheosis. apostate; apostasy:* "standing away," defection, was first used by Wyclif, who died in 1384, but whose body was disinterred in 1415, burned, and thrown into the River Swift.

L *apt, aptitude, attitude; adapt, adept, inept; apex.* L prefix *ab:* from, away, lacking. *abiogenesis:* production of life from nonliving matter, coined by Thomas Huxley in 1870; still not attained save in science fiction. *abdomen* (L *abdo:* hide; *do, dare:* do, put): the "hidden" part of the body. *abortion* (*oriri:* to rise); *abduct; abolition, aborigine. OED* has over 100 columns of relevant words, from *abacinate:* an old form of punishment, blinding by holding a red-hot iron near the eyes, . . . to *abusive,* and the unused word *abvolate:* fly away.

The prolific verb L *pono, ponere, postum, positum:* put, place, was shortened from *pozno,* which is *(a)po-s(i)no;* see *sei. apposite, apposition, component, compose, composite, composition, compost. compound; contrapose. deponent, depose, deposit; dispose. expound, expose, exposition. impound; impose; impost, impostor. interposition, juxtaposition. opponent, oppose, opposition; ovipost. pose, position, positive; posture, post* (see *sta*). *postillion; postiche. prepositor, preposition. preposterous:* "full of before and after." *proponent, propose, proposition, propound, provost; purpose. repose, repository; superpose, suppose, supposition; transpose.* L *co-ap, copula; copulation; couple,* verb and noun.

"That's a poser!" *pose* in the sense of baffle is the shortening of *oppose;* and from *opposal* may have come *a puzzle;* whence also *puzzlement.*

post: behind, after; afterward, is a frequent and live prefix, as in *post-Dadaist; post-Watergate. OED* lists 99 such words, from *postapostolic* to *postuterine.* It then details 118 relevant words, from *postabdomen . . . postgraduate . . . postnuptial . . . postprandial . . .* to *postzygapophysis.* A few Latin *post* expressions are still familiar: *(ex) post facto:* after the fact. *post-mortem:* after the death; often used figuratively of a discussion when a game, or the like, is over. *post meridiem:* after noon, P.M. *post scriptum:* written after, P.S. *post hoc, ergo propter hoc:* after this hence on account of this; the logical fallacy of accepting sequence for consequence.

Omnes animal post coitum triste est: Every animal, after coition, is sad. In *Memories* (1966), E. M. Bowra was reminded, by this, of the London firm of solicitors Mann, Rogers and Greaves. (The Germanic name *Hrodgar:* Roger, meant famed for the spear.) *Roger,* meaning "got ya," O.K., is drawn from the radio practice of using names to identify letters; *Roger* (for the letter *R*) an abbreviation of "message *received,* understood, and accepted." *Roger:* "I'll take care of it."

Gc, *aft, after; ebb. of, off, offal* (what falls off). *evening, eftsoons.* Via Norse *öfugr:* turned backward, E *awkward. April,* when the days are clearly extending.

> "Hold off! Unhand me, grey-beard loon!"
> Eftsoons his hand dropt he.
> —Coleridge, *The Ancient Mariner*

> Whanne that Aprille with his shoures sote
> The droghte of March hath perced to the rote . . .
> [So Chaucer starts his pilgrimage to Canterbury.]

Freud, in *The Psychotherapy of Everyday Life,* 8, makes one of his characteristic leaps in the dark: "Occasionally I have had to admit to myself that the annoying, awkward stepping aside in the street, whereby for some seconds one steps . . . always in the same direction as the other person . . . conceals erotic purposes under the mask of awkwardness." As Sir Thomas Browne noted, in *Hydriotaphia* (1658), "The long habit of living indisposeth us from dying."

apsa. Gc, *aspen.*

> Willows whiten, aspens quiver,
> Little breezes dusk and shiver.
> —Tennyson, *The Lady of Shalott*

ar I: reckon, arrange, fit; join, joint. Gk *arthron:* joint. *arthritis. arthr(o)-,* as *arthropod, arthrospore; OED* lists eight such. *anarthrous, diarthrous; enarthrosis, synarthrosis.* Gk superlative *aristos:* fittest, best. *Arista:* N.Y. high school honor society. *aristocracy. arete:* virtue. *Aristides:* son of the best. Gk *Aristoteles:* by far the best (*tele,* as in telephone: far-speaking), E *Aristotle. Aristocles:* famed as the best; family name of the philosopher known to posterity as Plato; see *pela.* Thus also *Sophocles:* famed for wisdom.

Note Gk *ariston:* breakfast, whence *aristology,* study or art of dining; see *past.* On the basis of a few satires, the Romans have been grossly misunderstood, as when M. Collins, in *Pen Sketches* (1871), declares: "The Romans . . . defied all rules of aristology by their abominable excesses." The Roman vomitorium was not what the word first brings to mind; always in the plural, the vomitoria were the exits of the great amphitheatres. The word has been used figuratively, as when *Blackwell's Magazine* in 1830 spoke of "our three great theatres, which Mr. Prynne proved long ago to be vomitories of vice." J. Wilson, in *Noctes Ambrosiana* (1826), wrote of a man with "his tongue stuck dumb in his cheek, and the vomitory of vociferation hermetically sealed." See *uem.*

Gk *armos:* harmony. Gk *arithmos:* arrangement; applied to numbers by Archimedes (d. 212 B.C.). *arithmetic.* Arithmetic is divided into four branches, misnamed by the Mock Turtle, who in *Alice's Adventures in Wonderland* explains: "I took only the regular course: Reeling and Writhing . . . Ambition, Distraction, Uglification, and Derision." Alice's creator, Charles Lutwidge Dogdson (Lewis Carroll) was a deacon, and lecturer in mathematics at Oxford. (Mock turtle soup, popular since 1783, is made with a calf's head, and the Tenniel drawing of the

Mock Turtle in *Alice* has a calf's head, feet, and tail, with an erect turtle-shell body. It was the Mock Turtle who, angry at Alice's stupidity, explained: "We called him Tortoise because he taught us.")

logarithm. In numerology, *arithmogram* is the sum of the numerical values in a word or passage, to be applied in practical counsel. L *ars, artem:* arrangement. *art, artisan, artist; artifice; artful, artless.* As Quintilian knew, *ars est celare artem:* art consists in concealing the art. *articulate. inert; inertia.* From the diminutive *articula* came *article* and *artillery.* L *ordo, ordinem. order, ordinal; ordinary. co-ordinate, inordinate, subordinate. exordium. primordial. ornament, ornate; adorn. suborn.*

L *arma. arms. alarm* (It *all'arme:* To arms!). Sp *armada* (destroyed by the English in 1588); *armadillo; armor, armament; armature. armory; army. disarm; rearm. armoire. armillary. armistice;* see *sta.*

From dropping the initial *a* came *rate, ratify; rite, ritual; ratio, irrational.* Via Fr, *reason, reasonable.* "One ought, every day at least, to hear a little song, read a good poem, see a fine picture and, if it be possible, speak a few reasonable words"—Goethe, *Wilhelm Meister's Apprenticeship* (1796).

Via OFr, *arraign, deraign.* Gc, *arm,* which first included the shoulder (the "join"); hence *armomancy. read; rede. hatred; kindred;* see *gn. riddle* has been used for a thousand years to mean a dark saying, the sense of which must be guessed; and almost as long to mean a coarse sieve, for arranging: separating chaff from corn, ashes from cinders, etc. Hence also verb uses: *to riddle* may mean to puzzle; but *Riddle me this* means Solve this riddle—and *to riddle,* as with bullets, is to make holes, as in a sieve.

Three books by popular writers present unsolved riddles. The Jester in Gilbert's *Yeomen of the Guard* inquires: "Can you tell me, Sir, why a cook's brain-pan is like an overwound clock?" When the Lieutenant brushes him off, he laments: "Just my luck; my best conundrum wasted!" Lewis Carroll's Mad Hatter asks: "Why is a raven like a writing desk?" Alice gives up: "What's the answer?" The Mad Hatter: "I haven't the slightest idea." Archie Goodwin, detective Nero Wolfe's legman, in Rex Stout's *Some Buried Caesar,* asks Lily Rowan: "Do you know the difference between a Catholic and a river that runs uphill?"—and comments: "She didn't, and I told her, and we babbled on."

Suggestions have been made for all three. The last, being by a nonliterary man, is the simplest. In the 1896 preface to the sixth edition, Carroll answered his riddle: "Because it can produce a few notes, though they are *very* flat, and it is never put with the wrong end in front. This, however, is merely an afterthought; the Riddle as originally invented, had no answer at all." English children had given it one: "Because neither can climb a tree." And an ingenious suggestion appeared in the American *Cyclopaedia of Puzzles* (1914): "Because Poe wrote on both."

"Three things there are . . . aye, four," says the Bible; and lovers of Carroll's Alice might chide me if I were to omit the White Queen's "lovely riddle" about a fish. Her jingle ends with her vainly trying to lift the dish-cover off the fish:

> For it holds it like glue—
> Holds the lid to the dish, while it lies in the middle:
> Which is easiest to do,
> Un-dish-cover the dish, or dishcover the riddle?

Before Alice responds, there is tumult in the Looking Glass world; she awakes; and the reader can go fish for the riddle.

When Shakespeare, a canny playwright, gives a riddle, he gives the answer—thrice. As Dull, in *Love's Labor's Lost,* puts it:

Dull: You two are bookmen: can you tell me by your wit
What was a month old at Cain's birth that's not five weeks old as yet?

Holofernes: Dictynna, goodman Dull . . . a title to Phoebe, to Luna, to the moon. [*Then he explains:*]
The moon was a month old when Adam was no more,
And raught not to five weeks when he came to five score.
—Th'allusion holds in the exchange. [*Then goodman Dull presses the point home:*]
The prolusion holds in the exchange, for the moon is never but a month old.

Gilbert, in *The Gondoliers,* thoughtfully added:

Life's perhaps the only riddle
That we shrink from giving up.

ar II: burn, dry. Gk, *azalea;* grows best in dry soil. L, *ardent, ardor. arson, arid.* Gc, *ash, ashen.*

are: work. *arable.*

arek: hold, guard. Gk *ekh-horkos:* oath. *exorcise, exorcism;* usually with bell, book, and candle; book being the Bible. L, *exercise. coercion. ark. arcane.*

arg: shine; clear; white. Gk, *argil, argyrol.* Possibly *argonaut,* sailor from Argos, oldest Greek city, bright on the Peloponnesian gulf. L, *argent,* in heraldry abbreviated *arg;* the symbol of the chemical element silver is *Ag;* see *el 47. argentiferous. argentine. Argentina.*

ari: ruler. *Aryan,* self-given name. It was claimed by the Nazis, whose name is short for *Na*tionalso*zi*alist, the party (founded in 1912, before World War I) that came to power with Hitler in 1933.

?arkh: begin, take the lead; hence, ruler. This root produced two sets of words. (1) Related to the beginning of things, early times. With prefixes *arch, arch(a)eo, OED* lists 25 and details 58 such words, as *archaic, archetype, archegonium, archaeology.* (2) As chief or leader. *OED* lists 125 words and details 120 more. *OED*'s 1972 supplement adds 16 words of the first sense, and 14 of the second.

Shakespeare, in *Richard III,* exclaims at "the most arch [*k* sound] deed of pitious massacre." Spenser, in *The Faerie Queene,* uses Archimage (chief magician) to personify Hypocrisy. Several of these words, as *archliar, archfiend,* are used of Satan, the *archdevil.* You have to guess (or remember) which, like *archangel,* take the *k* sound, and which, like *archbishop,* take the *ch.*

An *architect* is a master builder. *archeus* was used by Paracelsus (d. 1541) to name the vital force that produces all animal and vegetable growth and behavior. He located the main *archeus* in the stomach, with other *archei* regulating other human actions. *archives* were, first, records of the rulers of a state. *OED* lists *architemple,* from LL, but adds: "it could hardly be an English compound"—apparently feeling about hybrids as did the man who brushed aside television: "No good can come of it; it's half-Latin and half-Greek."

Archimedes (literally, chief guardian), Greek mathematician (d. 212 B.C.), declared that if he had a long enough lever he could lift the world. He did invent the Archimedean screw for raising water, which is still used in Egypt.

An *archipelago* (Gk *pelagos:* sea) was first the chief Greek sea, the Aegean, which has many islands; by transfer, a cluster of many islands; see *pela.* The root also appears at the end of words, as *monarch; anarchy, oligarchy.* JWalker lists 22 words ending *archy:* ruler, chief.

"I am monarch of all I survey"—Alexander Selkirk, marooned on Juan Fernandez Island, 1704–8, model for Defoe's Robinson Crusoe.

arq: bow and arrow. L, *arc, arcade; archiform, arch, arcuate.* Gc, *arrow.*

?asinus: ass. See *ane; ors.* Gk *onos,* L *asinus.* Gk *agros:* field; hence *onager;* wild ass; also used to name a catapult. M. F. Sheldon, in 1886, translating Flaubert's *Salammbo:* "Catapults were frequently called onagers, because they were like wild asses, which threw stones by kicking." L, *ass, jackass; asinine.* Sp, *asinego.* More than the jackass is intended in the old saw, "Every ass likes to hear himself bray."

at: go; especially, the going round of the year. L *annus* (*at-nus*): year. *annual, anniversary; annuity. annals. superannuated;* Lamb has an amusing yet touching essay on *The Superannuated Man. biennial,* etc., on to the *millennium.*

atos (baby talk): elder relative. *atavism.* See *pa.*

atr: fire; fire-blackened. L, *atrabilious,* translation of Gk, *melancholy:* black bile (see *akua; ug*). *atrocious:* with black looks; *atrocity.* Perhaps *atrium:* Roman room with central fireplace and hole in ceiling; some call this folk etymology, and link the word to the Etruscan town Atria, where this type of room was supposedly first constructed. The American Indian approximated this in his tepee.

au I: down. Skr *au ter:* cross over. *avatar.* The god Vishnu had many avatars, especially: 6th, Parashurana; 7th, Ramachandra, chief figure in the *Ramayama;* 8th, Balarama, elder brother of the most important reincarnation of Vishnu, the 9th, Krishna. In Sanskrit, both *Rama* and *Krishna* mean black. *Chem,* the native word for Egypt, which the Greeks also used, likewise means black, from the rich soil after the receding of the annual flood of the Nile; hence, *alchemy,* superseded by *chemistry, chemotherapy,* and the host of modern *chemicals.* For large portions of our earth, black is beautiful.

Russ, *ukase.* See *kers II.*

au II: draw water; suck. L *haurire, haustum. haustellum, haustorium. exhaust.*

au III: elder relative. L *avunculus. avuncular. uncle.* Ir *O'.*

au IV: desire, hence dare. *avaricious. avid. audacious.* "Ambition is but avarice on stilts"—Walter Savage Landor, *Lord Brooke and Sir Philip Sidney.*

aud: speak, sing; an extension of *aus:* ear. Gk *aoidos:* singer. *ode, epode.* Gk *epi:* upon; *episodos:* coming in, originally the entrance of the Greek tragic chorus, which came in singing; E *episode. hymnody, melody, monody, parody; prosody:* not prose, but rules of verse. *psalmody; rhapsody; threnody. palinode. comedy:* first, song at a village festival (Gk *khome:* village); whence Milton's Comus, spirit of rural merrymaking. *encomium. afikoman* (Hebr from Gk: at a festival). *tragedy* is goat song; see *aig;* played especially at the festival of Dionysus in early Spring, called by the *Oxford Companion to Classical Literature* "a period of anxiety in a primitive community, of longing that the spirit of vegetation may duly be reborn, and of consequent intercession."

Gk *tragos:* he-goat, literally gnawer, gave English also *trout* (with sharp teeth); *trogon, troglodyte;* and the monster *tragelaph:* half-goat, half-stag.

au(e): water; wave. Skr *vari:* water; *vati:* he blows; *varsha:* the rainy season. Gk *Ouranos,* god of the heavens and the rain; Roman Jupiter Pluvius; husband of Gea (see *ge*), goddess of earth. *Venus Urania* represented the "heavenly," the spiritual, aspect of love; by transfer, *uranism* was applied to Platonic love; by degeneration, to Socratic love. Thus E *uranism* came to mean homosexual love; *urning,* male homosexual (feminine, *urninde*). The first two of these three words are in the *Oxford Dictionary of English Etymology;* but none of them was granted entry into the somewhat prudish *OED.* J. A. H. Murray was a self-educated, learned lexicographer, but a Victorian of rigid standards (as other entries show); the current editor, R. W. Burchfield, promises rectification. *OED* does, however, define 43 words beginning *ur,* relating to our heavenly roof, the roof of the mouth, or the element uranium; see *el 92.*

Gk *hudra:* water snake. *hydra:* many headed monster of the Lerna marshes in the Peloponnesus; for every head cut off, two at once appeared; Hercules killed it with a heated sword, thus cauterizing the neck as he cut off the head. The giant crab helping the hydra was crushed beneath Hercules' foot; it became the constellation Cancer (*cancer* means crab; see *kar*), fourth sign of the zodiac; see *guei.* Hydra is an equatorial constellation, near the constellation Centaurus, which is named for another monster, half horse, half man. The centaur Chiron was a healer; hence *centaury,* the healing plant he used. And Hydrus is a southern constellation near Mensa; see *men I.*

hydra and *hydra-headed* are still used, figuratively, of difficulties that increase as one fights them. Also *hydrant; hydraulic:* first, of a water-organ. *hydrogen* (see *el 1*). *hydro-,* as *hydroelectric, hydrokinetics, hydrolysis. OED* lists 112 words beginning *hydro,* as *hydrocycle:* velocipede propelled in water; often, on park lakes, shaped like a swan. *hydroextractor:* centrifugal machine for drying clothes, now commonly called *drier. OED* details other relevant words in 31 columns, from *hydantoic, hydatic,* through *hydrophobia* (see *ugu*); *hydrophore:* instrument to draw water samples from depths; *hydroxide;* to *hydruria. hydurilic acid. hydroxyl:* the molecule OH, which forms bases, phenols, alcohols. *hydrocephalic:* with enlarged skull, compressed brain. *dehydrate; anhydrous.*

clepsydra: water-clock; the water trickles, "steals" away; Gk *kleptein:* steal, whence also *kleptomaniac. dropsy* is short for *hydropsy.* Gk *ouron:* urine. *urinal, urinalysis, urinate, uroscopy; urogenital; urotoxic, ureter, urethra, uretic; diuretic; enuresis; pyuria. OED* lists eight words beginning *urino;* it details 17, from *uric* to *urinous.* Note that the first sense of L *urina* was water; some doctors still speak of passing (making) water. This sense held in England through the 17th c. *urination:* the act of diving. Cockeram's 1623 *Dictionary* defines *urinate:* "to dive or swimme under water." A letter of 1682 states: "His Majesty's urinator, Mr. Curtis, published in the *Gazette* how he had practised." Then the bodily urine, micturition, drowned out the other meaning. See *meigh.*

L *unda:* wave. *undate* (but not *undated*); *inundated. undulant. abound, abundant; superabundance. redound; redundant. surround,* first *surund,* originally meant to overflow; form and meaning changed by association with *around. sound the depths,* as with plumb line or radar. Samuel Clemens took his pen name, Mark Twain, from the measure on a Mississippi River plumb line.

Fr *ondine, undine;* coined by Paracelsus (d. 1541) to name a still-water spirit; see *nymph* under *gn;* about her, many yarns have been spun: one is dramatized in *Ondine,* by Jean Giraudoux (1939). If a man and an undine fall truly in love, she becomes human, and mortal. In *Vashti,* by Augusta Wilson (1867), we are told that "foaming cataracts braided glittering spray into spectral similitude of undine tresses and undine faces." But take heed; Carlyle, in *Frederick the Great* (1837), mentions "the gallop home of the undined generals," who wanted spirits stronger than water could supply. See *seu I.*

L *lutra* (*udra* and *utrum:* mud): otter. *nutria.* Fr *onde:* wave. *ondograph; ondometer; ondoyant.* Gc, *water; wash.* Gm *Wasser; vaseline.* See *akua; nebh; uer VII; ugu.*

And Noah he often said to his wife, when he sat down to dine,
I don't care where the water goes if it doesn't get into the wine.
—G. K. Chesterton, *Wine and Water*

auei: bird; egg. Gk *oon* (two syllables), *oocyte, oogamy, oogonism,* etc. L *avis. aviary, aviculture, aviation.* LL *struthio:* ostrich. From the bird's supposed trick of hiding its head in the sand when in danger, *ostrichism* is used to mean refusal to face unpleasant facts. The ostrich, largest extant bird, runs rapidly; *bustard, au contraire,* is from L *avis tarda:* slow bird. The *ocarina* (L diminutive *avicula* with *l.r* shift) is named for its shape.

L *auspex:* observer of birds' entrails, for divination; *auspices, auspicious.* L *ovum:* egg. *oval; ovule, ovum, ovary, ovi-,* as *oviduct. oviparous:* born from the egg, as the chicken and the cobra; opposed to *viviparous:* delivered alive, as man and the viper. Gc *ei:* egg. *kidney* is OE *kidenei,* plural *kideneiren,* confused with *eiren,* plural of *ei.*

cockney, originally a "cock's egg," a bad or unfertilized egg; then applied in mockery to a city-dweller, a greenhorn, pictured as asking how to cook a haycock; strictly, one born within sound of Bow bells, London. Two other origins are suggested. Some trace *cockney* to Fr *coquin;* rascal; this is itself from Fr *coq:* cock, imitative of the rooster's call; Skr *kakila;* L *coco coco* or *cucucuru;* E *cock-a-doodle-do;* see *ane; kokila.* The other suggestion is emphasized by the Rev. Alexander Dyce, in *A Glossary to the Works of Shakespeare* (1902): "There is hardly a doubt that it originates in a Utopian region of indolence and luxury, formerly denominated the country of Cockaigne"—the word applied satirically to London. Its use, however, seems to contradict this; thus Shakespeare, in *Twelfth Night,* iv, 1: "I am afraid this great lubber, the world, will prove a cockney." More mockingly, the Fool in *Lear* as the King wept; "Cry to it, Nuncle, as the cockney did to the eels when she put 'em i' the paste alive. . . . 'Twas her brother that, in pure kindess to his horse, buttered his hay."

Johnson's *Dictionary* calls *cocksure* "a word of contempt." Lord Melbourne is quoted, in *Spectator,* 30 Nov. 1889, as saying: "I wish I were as cocksure of anything as Tom Macaulay is of everything." At first the word meant simply safe, secure, as though stopped by a cock, a closed faucet; as when in *1 Henry IV,* ii, 1, the Gadshill robbery is being planned with Prince Hal: "We steal as in a castle, cocksure." See *ane.*

> The wiles and guiles that women work,
> Dissembled with an outward show,
> The tricks and toys that in them lurk,
> The cock that treads them shall not know.
> —Shakespeare, *The Passionate Pilgrim*

aues: dawn, therefore bright, east; also, dawn of the world. Gk, *eoan, eoanthropus, eolithic, eocene, eosin, eohippus,* etc. Gk *Eos,* Roman *Aurora,* goddess of the dawn. L, *aurora* (*borealis:* of the north). From the gold of the dawn, L *aurum;* hence the symbol of the chemical element gold, *Au;* see *el 79. aureate, aureole; oriflamme:* golden flame, the banner of St. Denis. *orient;* see *ergh. oriole.* Sp *El Dorado:* the golden land. *Aureomycin* (Gk *mukhes:* fungus, mucus; whence also *mycology, myxoma,* etc.).

> "Over the mountains of the moon,
> Down the valley of the shadow,
> Ride, boldly ride,"
> The shade replied,
> "If you seek for Eldorado."
> —Poe, *Eldorado*

aug: increase. Gk, *auxesis.* L, *augment, auction; auxiliary. author, authority, authorize. augur,* from whom the celebrant hoped divine increase; *augury. inaugurate. august:* favorable; the month was named for Augustus Caesar; see *sek.* Gc, *eke. a n*ickname was folkchanged from a*n e*kename. *wax:* to grow, opposed to *wane;* see *eu. waist*—too often seen to expand.

The young Nathaniel Hawthorne (b. 1804) wrote to his mother: "I don't want to be a doctor, and live by men's diseases; nor a minister, to live by their sins; nor a lawyer, to live by their quarrels. So I don't think there's anything left for me but to be an author."

auku: cooking pot. Sp, *olla-podrida;* rotten pot; hence, mixture, medley. *olio.* Gc, *oven.*

au(s): ear; hear, perceive. See also *aud.* Skr, *vada:* speech; *theravada:* speech of the elders. Gk *ous, ot-. otacoustic, otalgia. otary:* the seal, with external ears. *oto-*, as *otocranial, otorrhea. myosotis:* a plant, the "mouse ear." *parotid.* Gk *aesthenesthai:* perceive, feel. *aesthetics; an(a)esthetic,* etc.

L *audire, auditum:* hear. *audit, audition, auditorium, audible, audience. OED* details 28 relevant words beginning *audio.* Its 1972 supplement adds 15, as *audiometer, audiofrequency; audio-visual* (teaching aids). *audiophile:* devotee of high-fidelity (hi-fi) recordings. Note the concerned counsel of St. Auguste (d. 430) in *De Duabus Animabus: Audi partem alteram:* Hear the other party (lest a person "hear one and judge two"). *aural, auricle, ausculation.* OFr *escoute, scout.* Via Fr, *obey* (hear and heed); *obedience; obeisance.* Gc, *oyer, oyez.*

"Everybody has his own theatre, in which he is manager, actor, prompter, playwright, sceneshifter, boxkeeper, doorkeeper, all in one, and audience into the bargain"—J. C. and A. W. Hare, *Guesses at Truth* (1827).

B

baba. Baby talk. *babe, baby; booby. bauble. balbuties:* stammering. *babble:* incomprehensible sounds. *baboon;* OFr *babine:* hanging lip. *barbarian, barbaric, barbarism, barbarous.* (IE *barbarah, balbarah:* non-Aryan: Gk *barbaros:* non-Greek; hence, making unintelligible sounds.) Hindi, *babu:* old man, as in Kipling's *Kim.* It, *bambino. bravo. brigand.* Also as an exclamation of praise, *Bravo!* (feminine, *Brava!*). E *brave:* at first, savage, wild. *bravado: bravura.* Slav, *balalaika.*

Similarly imitative are *gabble, gobble* (as of monkeys); slang *gabfest, gobbledegook,* etc. Also *rabble,* which first meant the noise of confused shouted words, then the ragtag and bobtail that made it.

?baca: berry. For various berries, see *bhel I.* Associated with Bacchus, Roman god of wine, whence *bacchante, bacchanalia. bacciferous, bacciform, baccivorous.* LL *baccalaureatus:* wearing the laurel berry, a sign of victory. *baccalaureate:* the college degree, as won by a bachelor of arts or science—of either sex. Apollo pursued the nymph Daphne, daughter of the river god Peneus, who at her prayer transformed her into a bay tree, the *laurus nobilis*—whereafter Apollo wore a wreath of bay leaves; and the bays, or the laurel wreath, became a symbol of victory or excellence. (A statue by Bernini shows Apollo holding Daphne as she changes into a laurel tree.) The intoxicating powers of the laurel were linked with poetic inspiration, as Apollo was the patron god of medicine and the arts.

A bachelor, in Roman times, was a youth of either sex that worked for a farmer; in medieval times, a *bas chevalier:* young (low) knight, not yet with his own banner, but attendant on a knight who had won his colors; later, also a junior member of a trade guild. (Among the seals, a bachelor is barred from the breeding grounds by the adult males.) Chaucer, in *The Merchant's Tale* (1386), seems to have been the first to write of a bachelor as an unmarried man. *OED* defines 3 words related to *baccalaureate;* 17, to *bacchanals;* 6, to *bacca* (berry); and 8, to *bachelor.*

King Henry VIII is supposed to have exclaimed, on the beheading of Anne Boleyn, mother of the great Queen Elizabeth:

> Cock's bones! Now again I stand
> The jolliest bachelor in the land!

Her own remarks, on the way to the scaffold, were more sober: "Commend me to the King, and tell him he is constant in his course of advancing me; from a private gentlewoman he made me a marquise, and from a marquise a queen; and now, as he hath left no higher degree of earthly honor, he hath made me a martyr."

Swift, in *Polite Conversation* (1738), defined Bachelor's fare: bread, cheese, and kisses. After a 19 Nov. 1891 cartoon in *Life,* there soon was a stock joke in American minstrel shows:

> *Interlocutor to End Man:* Sambo, can you tell me why married men live longer than bachelors?
> *Sambo:* They don't live longer—it only seems so.

bak: rod, staff. Gk, *bacterium,* plural *bacteria,* from the shape. *bacteriology, bactericidal,* etc. *OED* has 9 relevant words beginning *bacteri-;* its 1972 supplement adds 22, as *bacteriolysin, bacteriophage.* L *baculum,* used in English as the technical name for the penis bone, found in all primates except man. *baculine, baculite, baculometry. bacillus.* Via Fr, *baguette. debacle. imbecile* (needing support). Gc, *peg.*

bamb. Imitative. Gk, *bomb. bound* (leap). *bounce:* first, a resounding thump or explosion; Shakespeare, in *King John:* "He speaks plain cannon fire, and smoke, and bounce."

bat: to beat (imitative). L *battuere. bat, batter, battery, battle, battlement. abate. combat. debate. rebate.*

The ending of battledore is disputed. Sp *batador* was a beetle used to beat clothes in washing, as still in many parts of the world. But "battledore and shuttlecock" was an aristocrats' game; possibly the ending is *d'or:* of gold, as a bat with a gilded handle. the shuttlecock was made with feathers; for *shuttle,* see *skeud.*

From this root also ONorse *beytill:* penis, which reminds one that a bull's pizzle was used for flogging; Scott, in a 17 June 1814 letter to Southey, spoke of the "wholesome discipline of a bull's pizzle and straitjacket." *beetle* also came—no one knows how—to mean projecting, overhanging, as in *Hamlet,* i, 4; *beetle-browed;* also figuratively, as when Sidney spoke of "high hills that lifted up their beetil-browes." For the insect *beetle,* see *bheid.*

"Heaven's gift takes earth's abatement"—Browning, *One Word More.*

bel: strong. (L *de:* from, without, *debilitate, debility*). Russ, *bolshevik.*

bend: point. Gael, *ben:* mountain peak. Gc, *pen. pound,* for confining animals; first, an enclosure of stakes. *impound. compound* may be from Malay *kampong:* an enclosed place. OE, *pintle.*

beu; bhel, bhleu: swelling, flowing, flowering. Gk *phallos; phallus. ithyphallic* (*ithy:* erect; carried at festivals of Bacchus). *phallus impudicus:* the stinkhorn fungus, from its shape. Gk *phullon:* leaf. *efflorescence. flower, flour* (the "flower" of the meal). *Flora,* Roman goddess of flowers, vs. *Faunus,* god of nature; *flora* and *fauna* came to be used of the plant and the animal world. (The *faun,* like Pan, like the satyr, was pictured as half man, half goat.) *florid. Florida. florist, flourish. deflower. cauliflower,* folkchanged from *colyflory,* L *caulis:* stem. *Phyllis,* flowering maiden; sometimes spelled *Phillis* and associated with Gk *philos:* love (see *bhili*). From Milton's use in *L'Allegro,*

Herbs and other country messes
Which the neat-handed Phillis dresses,

Phillis has come to be used as a name for a pretty waitress.

Via OFr *girofle* from Gk *karyophullon:* the clove tree, *karyon:* nut, and *phullon:* leaf, came E *gillyflower.* And *anthophyllite* is from LL *anthophyllum:* flower leaf; see *andh. xanthophyll* (*xanthos:* yellow), as in autumnal leaves. *foil:* first, a leaflike design, as on a Gothic window. *trefoil,* etc. *folio; portfolio. exfoliate, defoliation. foliage.* The suffix *phyl(l),* as in *lithophyl, chlorophyll* (Gk *chloros:* green). JWalker has 15 words ending *phyllous,* as *aphyllous:* without leaves; *microphyllous, polyphyllous. Phylloxera* (Gk *xeros:* dry, whence the recent *Xerox*): genus of insects that feed on plants.

L *bulla. bill, billet; billow. bilge. bowl. bull* and its diminutive *bullock,* from the prominent penis. See *ane. ballocks. bulla, bullet, bulletin. ebullient; boil, parboil.* Perhaps *bully. bullion. bouilli, bouillon. bouillabaisse* is the imperative of two Provençal words meaning boil and lower (*abase;* jestingly, from the speed at which the fish is cooked).

This bouillabaisse a noble dish is—
A sort of soup, or broth, or brew,
Or hotchpotch of all sorts of fishes
That Greenwich never could outdo;
Green herbs, red peppers, mussels, saffron,
Soles, onions, garlic, roach and dace:
All these you eat at Terre's tavern
In that one dish of bouillabaisse.
—Thackeray, *Ballad of Bouillabaisse*

Bill(y) is a common hypocoristic term for *William.* It has other uses; as a highwayman's club, or a piece of lead tied in one end of a handkerchief; as the name of various plants and animals; *billy-button:* various flowers; *billy-biter:* a titmouse; *billy-wix:* an owl; and the *billy-goat* (female, *nanny-goat*). *OED* says of *billy,* meaning fellow: "of unknown derivation. It has been compared with bully, but to little purpose." Of *billy,* meaning brother, and its feminine, *tittie, OED* comments: "Both are now considered rude." *billycock:* a kind of hat, was earlier *bully-cocked:* as worn by bullies. It was in vogue at Oxford around 1720; the suggestion that it was named after Billy Coke of the noble Leicester family, "for whom the first billycock was made" around 1775, is folk etymology.

buccal: puffed out cheeks. *buckle. debouch* (Fr *bouche:* mouth); *disembogue.*

ball; boll, rocambole; bole. bubo. bulk; bulwark. blob; bloat. blain; blister. blot. blubber. blast. isinglass (Dutch *huus:* sturgeon, *blass:* bladder; folkchanged from its transparency, like glass). *ballot*—"Bullets or ballots govern the world." *balloon; bale:* large bundle.

L *follis:* bellows. *follicle. folly; fool:* windbag. *foolhardy. foolproof. foolscap,* from the early watermark design on the paper. Beaumont, in the prologue to *The Knight of the Burning Pestle* (1613), speaks words relevant today: "knowing it to the wise to be as great pleasure to hear counsel mixed with wit as to the foolish to have sport mixed with rudeness." The fights between rival spectators at ancient chariot races are matched by the mobs at rock concerts, international football games, and other so-called sports of our times.

L *fluere, fluctum:* flow. *fluid, fluent; fluctuate. fluorine* (see *el 9*). *fluoride. flux; flush, affluent, confluence.* L and E *flatus.* (divine) *afflatus. flatulent. deflate;* and too frequent *inflation.* (The five-cent ice-cream soda of my childhood now sells for $2.50.) *flavor. flageolet; flautist; flute. effluvium; mellifluous; superfluous. flout. influence,* etc. *influenza.* Sp, *bolero.* Fr, *bouillon, bouillabaisse; soufflé.*

Gc, *poach, pouch; poke,* its diminutive *pocket* (if you buy a pig in a poke, you may have to let the cat out of the bag). *pucker; pout. bud, blade, blossom, bloom, blow.* From analogy with a red flower, but flowing, *blood; bleeding. big; bosom; boast.* The same word in Old English was used for both the bellows and the belly. Shakespeare, in *As You Like It* (The Seven Ages of Man, ii, 7), speaks of "the Justice, In fair round belly with good capon lined." The word *belly* largely lapsed from use in prudish Victorian days; see *stoman. bellow, blister. bolster. boulder.* Fr, *boulevard. bold, embolden,* etc. *bawd;* first, a bold, lively person. *bawdry,* the noun, has been largely replaced by the adjective *bawdy,* as in the essay and glossary *Shakespeare's Bawdy,* by Eric Partridge.

When Mercutio, in *Romeo and Juliet,* says smilingly: "The bawdy hand of the dial is now upon the prick of noon," two definitions of prick are literal: *OED,* 3, "a measuring mark on a dial or scale"; *OED,* 9, "the precise instant." The word *bawdy* slips in a third meaning: *OED,* 17, "the penis." Shylock uses the word in its basic sense: "If you prick us, do we not bleed?"

bawdry was not a concept of the early tribe. The word *bawd* first appeared in English as *bawdstrot* (bold strutter), applied to a procurer of either sex; but since 1700 *bawd* has been purely feminine.

O, for a draft of vintage! that hath been
Cooled a long age in the deep-delved earth,
Tasting of Flora and the country green,
Dance, and Provençal song, and sunburnt mirth.
—Keats, *Ode to a Nightingale*

bha I: speak. Gk *pheme:* voice, *phasis:* speech. *apophasis. ephemia, aphasia.*

Polyphemus: much spoken of; the one-eyed Cyclops whom captive Odysseus blinded, escaping by clinging beneath a ram as Polyphemus let his flock out to graze. *Polyphemus* is also a silkworm moth with an eye-spot on its hind wings. Phemius, the minstrel with Penelope and her suitors while Odysseus was away.

blaspheme, blame. euphemistic, euphemis. Gk *phonè:* sound. *gramophone, telephone. phoneme, phonetics,* etc. *antiphon,* shortened to *anthem. symphony. euphony.* For *phony, fake,* see *esu.*

L *fari:* speak; *fans, fantem:* speaking; *fatum:* spoken. *infant:* not speaking. *infantry:* "Theirs but to do and die." Sp, *Infante. prefatory. affable:* easy to speak to. *ineffable:* that which cannot be put into words, vs. unspeakable: that which should not be put into words. *fable, fabulous, confabulation. fame, famous, infamous; defamatory. fate:* it is spoken. L *fate:* the Fates: Clotho holds the distaff; Lachesis weaves the thread of life; implacable Atropos cuts it. Beside them smiling stands their sister Tyche: success. *fatal. fairy; fay;* Fr, *fée. Fata Morgana*, sister of the legendary King Arthur, now used of a mirage; *Morgana* is roundabout from Gk *margarites:* pearl. *faerie:* enchantment.

Also *preface; prophet. profess, professor,* etc. *confession. confiteor:* first word of the Latin church confessional. *nefarious, bifarious, multifarious,* etc. It, *fantaccini, fantassin.* Gc, *ban:* summons; first, feudal call to arms, going to all; hence E *banal;* then excommunication, forbidding. *banns; banish, abandon. contraband; bandit. boon* (a *boon companion,* however, is from L *bonus:* good, jovial).

The Loves of the Triangles, by Frere, Canning, and Ellis, a parody of Erasmus Darwin's *Loves of the Plants* (1789), in its passage on *Three:*

> So, the three Fates, beneath grim Pluto's roof,
> Strain the dun warp, and weave the murky woof;
> Till deadly Atropos with fatal shears
> Slits the thin promise of th'expected years,
> While midst the dungeon's gloom or battle's din
> Ambition's victims perish, as They spin.

bha II: shine; light; bright; hence, appearing. Gk *phainein:* show; *phantasia:* appearance. *diaphanous:* showing through. *phase, phantom, phantasmagoria: phanerogram. phenomenon. fantasia, fantastic, fantasy, fancy, fanciful. cellophane. sycophant:* fig-shower, to curry favor with the ancient excise officer; it has, however, been suggested that this may be from the perennial obscene gesture of "showing the fig" (It *fico*), as in the sycophant's mind behind his subservient manner. *hierophant.*

epiphany: religious term that James Joyce secularized, meaning a sudden enlightenment. *theophany:* the manifestation of a god; Jehovah showed only his back side to Moses, lest the full vision blind him (Bible, Exodus 33:20). (Semele, when at Juno's jealous instigation she persuaded her lover Jupiter to appear in all his majesty, was by his brilliance instantly consumed to ashes.) *theophany* had earlier been secularized and shortened to *tiffany,* applied to sheer silks which, as Philomel Holland said in 1601, "instead of apparell to cover and hide, show women naked through them"—manifestation of a goddess, belike! For a time such women were called Evites, after Eve, who walked naked and unashamed in the Garden. Addison, in *The Guardian,* no. 134 (1713), commented on "the many in all public places who show so great an inclination to be Evites," anticipating our nudist beaches and the "flashing" of sprites on a college campus. In 1977 I saw a young woman, completely naked save for sandals, turning the corner at Piccadilly Circus, London, to stroll down the avenue; when a shocked elderly woman complained to an officer, he replied: "My beat ends here, Madam," and walked the other way. The "see-through" material, gauze, is from Gaza, where Samson enjoyed a harlot; we still speak of the Gaza Strip. (Note that *evite, evitate,* are early verbs meaning to avoid; *The Merry Wives of Windsor* says: "She doth evitate and shun a thousand irreligious cursed hours." These forms are from L *vitare:* whence also *inevitable* and, via Fr, *avoid* and *unavoidable.*)

Gk *phos, phot-:* light. *phot, photic, photograph, photostat. OED* lists 79 words beginning *photo,* and details 98. A *photographee* is a person that poses for a *photographer. photogenic* is defined as "produced by light on a sensitized surface"; the present application to a person that looks well on a photograph might be expressed more accurately by *euphotic;* see *esu. phosphorous; phosphorescent; phosphorus;* see *el 15.*

L, *banner, bandoleer. band:* first, troops under a displayed banner. Via It, *bandits,* who usually appear suddenly. Gc, *beacon, beckon. berry:* the bright fruit of the bush; see *bhel I. buoy,* to be seen and heeded.

"You who listen with credulity to the whispers of fancy, and pursue with eagerness the phantoms of hope . . . attend to the history of Rasselas, Prince of Abyssinia"—Samuel Johnson, *Rasselas* (1759), written in a week to pay his mother's debts and funeral costs.

bhad: good. See *gledh.* Gc (OE *bet*), *better, best. batten. to boot:* for further advantage; hence, a *bootless quest,* which means not barefoot but bare of favorable result.

booties, and the *boots* one may wear, come via OE *bote.* Hence also *bootblack, bootlick,* and the onerous task of lifting oneself by one's own *bootstraps.* A *bootlegger* was orignially a smuggler who hid hides of liquor in the loose tops of his high boots. The two senses of the word *boot* are combined in the Victorian utterance regarding "a scoundrel, and a good one to boot."

bhag: share (especially food). Skr, *Bhaga:* god of wealth; literally, Distributor. *pagoda:* first, house of the lord. *bahadur:* English officer in India. The *Bhagavad-Gita* is the noted "song of the lord" Krishna (: Black) to his friend Arjuna (: White) in the *Mahabharata.* Pers *baksheesh.*

Gk *phagein:* eat. *esophagus. phagedena. sarcophagus:* stone that "consumes" flesh. *phago-,* as *phagocyte,* coined in 1884 by Elie Metchnikoff: the white blood corpuscle "stuffing a bacterium in its jaws, engulfer of the invaders"; see *past. bacteriophage,* often shortened to *phage. dysphagia; polyphagia. oophage* and other words ending in *phage;* thus L *-vore,* as *insectivore.* Both the Greek and the Latin ending are frequent in English. For a taste: *coprophagous,* as the dung beetle; *galactophagous,* as mammalian infants; *ichthyophagous:* of fish-eating; *rhizophagous:* of roots; *androphagous,* as cannibals; *ophiophagous,* of snakes, as the mongoose (canned rattlesnake is available for the human *ophiophage*); *poephagous:* of grass, as the cow and the kangaroo; *mysophagous:* of fungus, mushroom; *ostreophagous:* of oysters, as humans in the "R" months; *lithophagous:* eating one's way through stone, as some molluscs; *dendrophagous:* of bark; *entomophagous:* of insects; *zoophagous,* of animals; *hippophagous:* of the horse (in France many butchers specialize in horsemeat); *xylophagous:* of wood. *polyophagous* is Greek; the more inclusive *omnivorous* is Latin. Also *apivorous:* of bees; *baccivorous:* of berries, even as you and I; *succivorous:* of sap; *lignivorous:* of wood; *fucivorous:* of seaweed, as the Japanese; *mucivorous:* of plant juices; *mellivorous:* of honey ("he on honey-dew hath fed, and drunk the milk of Paradise"—Coleridge, *Kubla Khan*); *vermivorous:* of grubs, as small fish; *granivorous:* of grain; *graminivorous:* of grasses; *ranivorous:* of frogs, their legs a French delicacy; *carnivorous; ossivorous:* of bones, the joy of dogs; *sanguinivorous,* as mosquitoes, leeches, and vampire bats. *rhypophagous:* eating of filth. *allotriophagy:* unnatural appetite, excessive or bizarre. See *dheigh N 2 f.*

bhaghu: elbow; shoulder. Gc, *elbow. bough.* "The boughs that bear most hang lowest." Human application: those that achieve most are most unassuming. *bow* of a ship.

bhago: tree. *beech. buckwheat,* its seeds resembling *beechnuts. bark,* used for Runic writing; boys may still write on the white birch; hence *book.* There has been questioning of the value both of literacy and of books. In the Bible, Ecclesiastes, we find the complaint: "Of making many books there is no end." Callimachus in 250 B.C. stated *Mega biblion mega kakon:* The greater the book, the greater the harm, as when an antisocial idea is cogently, luringly, presented. Samuel Johnson declared that, as an evil society has many laws, so an ignorant society has many books. Emerson advised: "Never read any book that is not a year old," which would ban most bestsellers. For literacy (which Plato felt was bad for the memory) see that word in my *Dictionary of World Literary Terms.* Milton, in *Areopagitica,* nobly affirmed: "A good book is the precious life-blood of a master spirit, embalmed and treasured up on purpose to a life beyond life."

bhar: bristle. L *fastus. fastidious, fastigate, fastuous.* Gc, *barse. bass,* spiny-finned. *beard.* Gods, Adam, and other early men and monarchs are usually represented with a beard. The early Egyptians wore a chin beard, frizzled, dyed, hennaed, or plaited with gold thread; from 3000 to 1580 B.C. a false golden beard was worn by kings, and some queens, as a sign of sovereignty. The Grecian beard was curly; the Roman, trimmed; but in the Roman Empire shaving became general about 450 B.C. partly for greater safety in close combat, not to be grasped by the beard. When Pope Leo III shaved, in 795, the Roman Catholic clergy followed his practice, and still generally do.

Fashions in beards have varied. Among the most frequent have been: (1) vandyke: from the chin, short and pointed, as in the painting of Sir Anthony Van Dyke (Dyck) (d. 1641), court painter to Charles I of England; it is sometimes called a charlie, from portraits of the King. (2) imperial: lower lip and chin, after Napoleon III. (3) goatee: from the chin, perhaps scraggly, but coming to a point, as on the billygoat. (4) barbula; also, from Fr, *pic-à-devant:* a tuft under the lower lip; diminutive of *barb,* which first meant beard; hence *barber.* (5) sideburns: from the ears, on both sides of the face, chin shaved, as worn by General Ambrose E. Burnside, Union commander (twice relieved of his command) in the Civil War. (6) muttonchops: a fuller variety of the preceding, narrow on top, then widening: named for its shape. (7) dundrearies: long side whiskers, chin and lips clear; named after E. A. Sothern as Lord Dundreary in *Our American Cousin* (1858), by Tom Taylor, a hit on both sides of the ocean; worn again when the son, E. H. Sothern (b. 1859), repeated the role. (*Our American Cousin* is the play Lincoln was watching at Ford's Theatre in Washington on 14 Apr. 1865, when he was assassinated.) (8) galways: ear to ear, right around the chin; probably from Galway County, Ireland. Other varieties are worn at will. A general term for hair allowed to grow on the face in addition to the mustache is *whiskers.*

Whiskers were probably so named because they suggest a brush, *whisk* being imitative of the swish of a brush on clothes. Similarly echoic is *whist,* as in shuffling cards; though the interjection *Whist!*—from which came the name of the card game—was used for what is now the *Sh!* of silence. The game of bridge, developed from whist, is also echoic, probably from Russ *birich:* official caller, what in England used to be the town crier. *Gee whizz!* and *whistle* are similarly echoic.

From the shape of a beard, and the fact that most bearded monarchs are represented with a weapon, came E *barb; barbel.* Also *rebarbative.* LL, *barbicel, barbule. Lombard* (*Longobardus*). From the Lombardy pawnbrokers, *lombard* came to be used (as on Lombard Street, London) for a banker or moneylender (in early days, the two were one); from the miscellaneous material a pawnbroker took, *lumber* was used to mean odds and ends; as early as 1662 it was used in the U.S. for roughly sawed timber. *OED* gives 32 combinations of *lumber,* as *lumberjack. lumberpie:* minced fish or flesh with eggs, baked in a pie. Pope, in his *Essay on Criticism* (1711), speaks of

The bookful blockhead ignorantly read,
With loads of learned lumber in his head.

"You will hang like an icicle on a Dutchman's beard"—*Twelfth Night,* iii,1.

bhareku: crowd, stuff, cover. Gk, *diaphragm. cataphract.* L, *farcy, infarct. frequent. forcemeat:* mincemeat; a variant of *farce,* which first meant stuffing; thence, jokes "stuffed in" to a quack's palaver, etc. See *sa.* The last 33 words of Steven Weinberg's *The First Three Minutes* (1976): "The effort to understand the universe is one of the very few things that lift human life a little above the level of farce, and give it some of the grace of tragedy."

bhares: barley. L, *farina, farinaceous. farrago:* originally, mixed meal. Gc. *barley; barn. bastard:* conceived in a barn; but note L *bastum,* E *bat:* packsaddle (a *batman* is the servant of a British cavalry officer; a *bat-horse,* one that carries army supplies); some consider this the source of *bastard,* as though conceived on a packsaddle by the roadside or, indeed, in a barn. Royal bastards were frequently acknowledged and ennobled by their fathers; such sons of Charles II of England were named *Fitzroy,* which means son of the king. Swinburne had other thoughts in *A Song in Time of Order* (1852):

When the devil's riddle is mastered,
And the galley-bench creaks with a Pope,
We shall see Buonaparte the bastard
Kick heels with his neck in a rope.

bhasko: gathering; bundle. Gk, *bast; baste* first meant to sew with bast, as a binding. L *fasces,* plural of *fascis:* bundle of tied rods with a projecting axe, borne before the ancient Roman magistrate as a sign of his authority; recalled by Mussolini, it gave English *fascist* and *fascism.* The Italian Fascists were organized in Mar. 1919 to oppose Bolshevism; Mussolini took control in Oct. 1922.

L *fascinum:* a phallus-shaped charm. *fascinate. fascinator:* a soft head-shawl; not in *OED* but in its 1933 supplement, which says "now disused"; the 1972 supplement gives later examples, as R. Harvey, *Curtain Time* (1949): the ladies "with snowflakes caught in their lacy fascinators." Prov, *bastille.* The Paris prison The Bastille was destroyed by the revolutionists on 14 July 1789. Bastille Day is celebrated by the French with fireworks, as is 4 July, Independence Day in the U.S.

bhau(t): knock, strike off; hence an end, stumpy. From figurative use in Latin came *confute, refutation.* From the sexual application of violent action (as still in English slang) came L *futuere:* to copulate, E *footle, footy.*

The Germanic forms were more fertile, and remained physical; *beat, beetle:* a mallet; *bushel:* to tap often, to mend; *baste, lambaste.* Hence also *butt,* as a goat; *butt,* the end, then an end left, as of a cigar. *buttock;* probably *butt,* a target. Also *buttress; abut, debut, rebut. sackbut.* Via Fr *bouter:* strike against, push, came E *button.*

Via Swedish *bott:* thick, came the *turbot,* a stumpy fish; *botling:* "little stumpy," the chub; also *halibut:* a similar fish eaten on holy days. (Men used to swear "By my halidom"; sometimes, as by Horace Walpole in *The Castle of Otranto* (1765), "By my halidame," as though "By my Holy Lady." See *kailo.*)

bhe: warm. Gc, *bath, bathe; bake.* Possibly OIr *Brigit,* goddess of fire; hence *Bridget; biddy:* talkative old woman, also applied—partly imitative—to a chicken; *chickabiddy.* Note also *Jenny wren* and *Molly sparrow.* Possibly *bacon,* though this may mean sliced from the back (of the hog). Gc, *zwieback:* twice baked, which is also the meaning of *biscuit* (Fr). Fr, *bain:* bath. *bain-Marie:* double boiler.

Marie, Fr for *Miriam,* sister of Moses, of repute in alchemy. She watched as Moses lay hidden in the reeds; when Pharoah's daughter picked up the baby, Miriam volunteered to find a wet-nurse, and brought her own and Moses' mother. The name *Moses* is probably from an Egyptian word meaning to beget (with divine implications, as in the god Thutmose); but Pharaoh's daughter (Bible, Exodus 2:10) says she named the baby *Moses* (Hebr *M'sh'h*) because she drew him out (Hebr *m'sh'h*) of the water. From the frequent nickname *Mose* among Southern slaves came the phrase *mosey along.*

baignoire was a 19th c. word for a theatre box; Browning, in *Red Cotton Nightcap Country* (1873), wonders:

Should one display
One's robe a trifle over the baignoire edge . . .

bagnio was originally a bathhouse for sweating and cupping, a treatment for syphilis; but soon came to mean brothel; the play *The Suspicious Husband* (1747) suggests: "Carry her to a bagnio, and there you may lodge with her." The Turkish bath, hummum, met the same fate; the Hummums, opened in Covent Garden in 1631, were soon suppressed for reasons of immorality.

The only two licensed theatres in London from 1662 to 1843, Covent Garden and Drury Lane, have constrasted names. *Covent* is a form of *convent,* a retreat for pious virgins; *Drury* is from OE *druery:* sexual love. At Covent Garden in 1728 the license-holder, illiterate John Rich, produced John Gay's *The Beggar's Opera,* which "made Gay rich and Rich gay." From Bath in Somersetshire, England (still supplied by a Roman reservoir dating from the 1st c. A.D.), comes the *bath chair;* and at Bath for twenty years until 1813 (his patron the Prince Regent, later George IV) George Bryan ("Beau") Brummel reigned as *arbiter elegantiarum.* Brummel, "the grandson of a gentleman's gentleman," strutted and gambled excessively, but fell from royal favor and in 1840 died in a pauper's lunatic asylum.

bathetic is defined as "sinking" in literary style; Gk, *bathos,* depth, but used in contrast with, or unsuccessfully aiming at, *pathos,* the *pathetic. OED* calls *bathetic* "a favourite word of reviewers." Hence also *bathometer, bathokolpian, bathybius; bathymetry. OED* defines *bathing* as "the exposing of oneself or others to the free action of water etc. by immersion or suffusion." The "etc." allows for grand dames who bathe in milk, and starlets who bathe (before intimate spectators) in champagne. Also *shower bath,* frequent where Americans fare.

bhedh: dig. L *fodere, fossum. fossa, fosse, fossette. fossil. fossorial. bothrium; cyclobothra.* Gc, *bed,* first, in a garden.

The frolic Wind that breathes the Spring,
Zephyr, with Aurora playing
As he met her once, aMaying,
There on beds of violets blue
And fresh-blown roses washed in dew,
Filled her with thee, a daughter fair,
So buxom, blithe, and debonair. . . .
—Milton, *L'Allegro,* which ends:
That Orpheus self may heave his head
From golden slumber on a bed
Of heaped Elysian flowers, and hear

Such strains as would have won the ear
Of Pluto to have quite set free
His half-regained Eurydice.
These delights if thou canst give,
Mirth, with thee I mean to live.

Henry King, bishop of Chichester (d. 1669), reflects quite a different mood:

Sleep on, my Love, in thy cold bed,
Never to be disquieted.
The wind blows out; the bubble dies;
The Spring entombed in Autumn lies;
The dew dries up; the star is shot;
The flight is past; and man forgot.

bheg: break. Nasalized, *bank:* first, river bank, where the stream's smooth line is broken; by extension, *bench* of a moneylender, as on the square before a church, whence Jesus drove the moneychangers (needed at a synagogue, as Roman and other coins had a graven image). *banco. bankrupt:* broken bench. *charabanc. mountebank;* stood on a bench in the public square. *saltimbanco. bunco.* Fr, *banquet.* Gc, *bench, disbench. bang* is echoic.

bhegu: run. Gk *phebesthai:* run in terror. *Phobos,* Greek god of terror, son of Mars, Greek god of war; hence, appropriately, Phobos is one of the satellites of the planet Mars. Hence *hydrophobia* and some 275 other *phobias* listed in the *Oxford Psychiatric Dictionary,* as *astrophobia, automysophobia, parthenophobia.*

bhei: bee—source of sweetness and light. Caught in Samson's riddle, after seeing bees hived in the carcass of a lion he had slain:

Out of the eater came something to eat;
Out of the strong came something sweet.

When, through his wife's treachery, the wedding guests gave him the answer, Samson (Bible, Judges 14) slew 30 Philistines to get the garments for his forfeit; the Philistines then burned the bride's father's home, with her and her father inside. Samson ruled Israel for 20 years before Delilah smiled his life away: a double warning against confiding in women. For more *bees*, see *hum.*

bheid: strike, split; bite. L *findere, fissum. fission,* as recently of the atom. *fissure. vent;* spelling changed by association with Fr *vent:* wind, which goes through it; see *ue.* Gc, the weapons *bill* and *beak. bit, bite; bait,* for fish to bite. *bitter; bite the tongue; embitter. boat;* split tree; *boatswain. abet, giblet. bezzle;* first, of cattle bitten by gadflies; *embezzle* (bitten, stung).

The *beetle:* biting insect, is of the family of *Coleoptera:* sheath-winged, its front wings covering the back ones. Some 300,000 species of beetle have been named, more than all the varieties of plants, some one-quarter of all living kinds. The largest beetle, the goliath of equatorial Africa, is the size of a mouse, with an almost one-foot wing-span; the smallest, the *Ptiilidae,* living in the spore tubes of fungus, are smaller than the dot on this *i.* The next most numerous family is of butterflies and moths; see *ane,* toward the end; *lep I; kel VI, spend II.* For another use of *beetle,* see *bat.*

"Loud and bitter words indicate a weak cause"—Victor Hugo.

bheidh: trust. Gk *pistis:* faith. *pistology.* L *fidere,* variant *fidare, fidavi:* trust. *Fidius,* Roman god of faith, surname of Jupiter, often used in oaths. *fiduciary. confide, confident, confidant. diffident.* To defy first meant to renounce faith or allegiance; *defiance. affiance, fiancée. federal, confederation. fidelity;* via Fr, *fealty. affidavit,* sometimes corrupted to "on my davy." *Fidei Defensor:* Defender of the Faith, a title of the British monarch bestowed by Pope Leo X upon King Henry VIII in 1521, and kept ever since, despite the fact that in fifteen years Henry broke with Rome and was declared by Parliament the "sole supreme head of the church and the clergy of England." *fideism, fidelious. fideicide:* breacher of trust. *bonafide; bona fides; mala fides; perfidy. faith, faithful. By my fay!* And the trusty dog *Fido.*

"If anyone doubts my veracity, I can only say that I pity his want of faith"—Baron Münchhausen, *Narrative* (1785).

Gc, *bead:* first, prayer; then, tiny ball or chip to tell (keep count of) the prayers. *bide, abode, bode, foreboding.* The word *bad* has been attributed to this root, but seems more closely related to OE *baedling:* sodomite; *OED* remarks: "There have been other, more dubious suggestions." Sallust (d. 34 B.C.) used *Punica fide:* with Carthaginian faith, to mean treachery; the phrase became proverbial in English as *Punic faith.*

Bunyan in *Pilgrim's Progress* tells us: "Now Giant Despair had a wife, and her name was Diffidence."

bheigu: shining. Gk *Phoebe:* Artemis, goddess of the moon. *Phoebus:* Apollo, god of the sun. The bird name *phoebe,* partly shaped after the goddess, is imitative of the bird's call. Phoebe is the ninth moon of Saturn.

O Proserpina!
For the flowers now that frighted thou let'st fall
From Dis's waggon! daffodills,
That come before the swallow dares, and take
The winds of March with beauty; violets dim,
But sweeter than the lids of Juno's eyes
Or Cytherea's breath; pale primeroses,
That die unmarried, ere they can behold
Bright Phoebus in his strength—a malady
Most incident to maids; bold oxlips and
The crown imperial; lilies of all kinds . . .
—*The Winter's Tale,* iv, 3

bhel I (by *l.r* shift, also *bher, bhrek*): shine; blaze, burn; shimmer like a flame; hence, move to and fro; hence, bright colors and objects. Gk, *phlox. phlogiston:* supposed flammable essence, named by Raphael Elgin in 1600; when Joseph Priestley discovered oxygen in 1774, he called it *dephlogisticated air.* Hence also *phlegmon. phlegopite* (Gk *ops, opos:* eye; fiery-looking); *antiphlogistic. Phlegethon:* river of fire in Hades; see *kau II.* The coastal region below Mount Vesuvius was known as *Campi Phlegraei:* the flaming fields. This is the title of a two-volume description (1775) by Sir William Hamilton, who as ambassador of England to the court of Naples promoted the excavation of Herculaneum and Pompeii.

L, *fulgent, effulgent, fulgurant. flagrant, conflagration. in flagrante (delicto):* in the blaze of the transgression, caught in the act. *delicto* is a noun from the past participle of L *delinquo, delictum:* to fall short, fail, be at fault; see *leiku.*

Via Fr, *flame, flambeau; inflammable; inflame.* Because many took the *in* of *inflammable* to be a negative, trucks bearing such material are now labeled "Flammable." *flamboyant. flamingo. fulminate. flavescent; flavoprotein.*

Gc, *bald:* shiny-pated. *bright; bleak, blaze.* To blaze a trail is to cut off bark, leaving a white spot as a guide. *blink:* dazzled. *blind* (Don't gaze at the sun!).

blend; bleach; blench; blemish. blanch. blank; blanket. blancmange. blonde, blizzard. blood, blue, blush, black: burned. See colors, under *kel VI.*

With *l.r* shift came *bear; berserk,* as the Norse warrior in *bearskin. beaver. brown, brunette. burnish. bream* (shimmering in the water). *braid, embroider. bridle* (verb; the noun *bridle* took its name from the movement of the horse's head when the bit is tugged). First in Scotland, in the 15th c., *bridle* was used of a headpiece with bit, for a termagant. Lydgate in 1430 said: "Sensuality holdeth the bridle of lecherous insolence"; more literally the court at Macclesfield ordered "a brydle for a curste quean," wearing which she was carted and displayed through the town; and still in England in 1753 they used a "bridle for correcting scolding women." In the fashionable world of the 18th c., however, *to bridle* was one of a young woman's weapons; Cowper, in *Hope* (1781), speaks of "the flirted fan, the bridle, and the toss." In the countryside, a *bridlebridge* was one a rider could cross on horseback, too narrow for a vehicle. In riding days, the *bridle hand* was the left hand, which holds it. No relation to *bridal,* of course, no matter which holds the reins.

birch (see *bhago*). *-bert:* bright, as in *Albert, Herbert, Robert; Bertha. filbert,* the hazel nut, which is picked on St. Philibert's Day, Aug. 22. *Gilbert;* hence, for William Gilbert (d. 1603), *gilbert,* unit of magnetomotive force; for Davies Gilbert (d. 1839), the mineral *gilbertite;* and for William Schwenck Gilbert (d. 1911 saving a woman from drowning), *Gilbertian:* relating to, or in the style of, his comic poems and plays.

berry: the bright fruit of the bush. Thus both parts of *blackberry* and *blueberry* are from the same root. *cranberry* was *craneberry,* the stamens resembling the bird's beak; from where it grows, also called *bogberry* and *fenberry*—best known in cranberry sauce. *strawberry* may be named for its imbedded strawlike flecks, or for its strawlike runners; indeed, from the runners, some link the word with *stray.* It is memorialized in *The Compleat Angler,* by Izaak Walton, who quotes Dr. William Boteler: "Doubtless God could have made a better berry, but doubtless God never did." D. G. Cooley, however, in *Eat and Get Slim* (1945), warns, "One man's strawberries are another man's hives." See *ster I.* If you taste a chokeberry, you will agree that it deserves the name. For *mulberry,* genus *Morus,* see *moro.* For *naseberry,* see *melit.*

Spiced ale with sops of bread is called *aleberry,* by folkchange from *alebrey:* ale and *briw:* pottage, whence *brew* and *brewery.* A similar dish with water instead of ale is *breadberry,* which was common on the tables of the poor for four centuries. The *hackberry* is the *hagberry, hedgeberry,* favorite of the *hag, hedge-demon;* see *kagh.* The *coral berry* is a type of *snowberry,* both named for their color. There are also the *cloudberry,* the *crowberry,* and the *batberry.* The *bramberry* is a short form of *brambleberry,* which is, from the bush's prickles, another name for *blackberry;* see the nursery rhyme under *magh. Quinsyberry,* the black currant, bitter in the throat, is named for *quinsy, cynanche,* from Gk *kunos:* dog (see *kuon*) and *anchein:* throttle. The *baneberry,* as its name implies, is poisonous; it grows on the herb christopher.

The *sheepberry,* also called *nannyberry* (*nanny goat,* paired with *billy goat; Nanny,* pet name for Anne; *nannyhouse* in the 18th and 19th c. meant brothel, the goat being proverbially lecherous), is named for its shape, like the animal's droppings. Of the *soapberry* there are 15 species, mainly tropical; the fruit contains saponin, which lathers in water. The *bearberry,* astringent, with pink blossoms, is the favorite food of the grouse; there is also a *blackbearberry.* There are two suggestions as to the origin of *gooseberry.* It may be from Gc *kraus:* curly, folkchanged to E *goose.* Or, since it ripens about the feast day of St. John, it may have been Gc *Johannesbeeren,* shortened to *Janbeeren,* folkchanged to *Gansbeeren,* then literally translated as gooseberry. The *wild gooseberry* is also called *dogberry,* and Dogberry is the foolish constable in Shakespeare's *Much Ado About Nothing.* The delicious dessert *gooseberry fool* gets its gooseberry by God's grace and its folly by analogy with the equally ambrosial meal-ender, the trifle; see *tene 9.* Some suggest that the *fool* is folkchanged from Fr *foulé:* crushed, as the berries are. Many good dishes came with Charles II from France, the French cuisine being virtually unrivaled in the West until Chinese food came in.

The English also enjoy the *bilberry,* which they call the *whortleberry* (for the *w,* see *kailo:* whole) or *hurtleberry,* shortened to *hurt.* As the *Pall Mall Gazette* of 29 July 1887 pointed out: "*Hurting* is a process that involves nothing worse than the picking of the hurt, otherwise known as the hurtleberry" (in Sweden, the *lingonberry,* cousin to the American *huckleberry,* not to be confused with the smoother *blueberry*). The *red whortleberry* is also called the *cowberry.* (*hurt:* to harm, was originally a term in jousting: L *juxta:* together; see *ieug.*)

The *raspberry,* still a favorite, is linked, by Cockney rhyming slang, to the "Bronx cheer," the razz; the full rhyming term being *raspberry tart:* to give someone the razz is to direct toward him a sound like the noisy noisome expulsion of anal wind. The *black raspberry,* on the other hand, is a delicious fruit almost gone from the market. Four berries are recent hybrids. Crossing a raspberry and a dewberry, Helge Ness in 1921 produced the *nessberry;* earlier, in 1881, Judge James H. Logan had grown the *loganberry,* "with the shape of a blackberry, the color of a raspberry, and a combination of their flavors." Combining this hybrid with the two berries it came from, Rudolf Boysen about 1940 created the *boysenberry.* These three are from the U.S. Announced from Britain in 1980, from the same berries, is the *tayberry,* cultivated beside the River Tay near Dundee.

The *bayberry,* fruit of the American wax-myrtle, is not eaten, but a spray of it makes a long-lasting and a pleasing decoration. The *barberry,* strongly acid, is sugared as a conserve; its bark yields a yellow dye. Longfellow, in *Hiawatha* (1855), admires the way "the tangled barberry bushes hang their tufts of crimson berries."

Although *OED* lists 14 *queen-* combinations, there does not seem to be a berry called queensberry; but Sir John Sholto Douglas, eighth marquis of Queensberry, is remembered for having established the rules of modern boxing, including the use of padded gloves and the count of ten for the knockout; and his ancestor the fourth duke of Queensberry (d. 1810) is credited with having developed horse racing in England. The duke was satirized by Burns, and pictured by Wordsworth and, in *The Virginians,* by Thackeray.

The *farkleberry,* also called the *fartleberry* and the *sparkleberry,* is the "tree huckleberry." Among animal berries is the *wolfberry.* The *squawberry* is also called *osoberry* (Sp *oso:* bear) and *deerberry.* The varieties are not exhausted, although the reader may be.

Blackberries, as every farmer's son knows, are red when they are green. Else you're a greenhorn.

bhel II: cry. L *flere:* weep. *feeble; foible.* Fr *bave:* drivel. *bavadage.* Gc, *bawl, bellow, blear, blare.* (The *Germanii* were a noisy lot!) *belch. bell.* By sound association, *belfry* came to be used of a bell tower; it is not of this root; see *bhergh.*

bheld: strike; one quick movement. *bolt:* a heavy arrow. *bolt the door:* one push into the slot. *bolt food.* A horse may bolt. From lightning, the *thunderbolt.*

bhelk: beam. Gk, *phalanx; phalangeal.* L, *fulcrum.* It, *balcony.* Fr, *debauch;* first, to rough out timber; then to turn someone (*de:* away) from his work. *ébauchoir:* a roughing chisel. Gc, *balk, block; bole; bulk; blockhead; bulkhead.*

bhendh: bind. Skr, *band, bandage; bandanna.* Pers, *cummerbund* (*kamar:* waist). Gc, *bin,* first made of tied reeds. *bind, bend, bond, bondage. bund, bundle; riband, ribbon.* Browning, lamenting Wordsworth's political shift, with consequent honors, begins *The Lost Leader* (the first line alluding to Judas Iscariot):

> Just for a handful of silver he left us,
> Just for a riband to stick in his coat.

"Next to the wound, what woman makes best is the bandage"—Barbey d'Aurevilly.

bhengh: thick, dense. Gk *pakhus. OED* lists 39 zoological, botanical, and pathological terms beginning *pach(y),* as *pachycardian:* thick-hearted, *pachycephalic:* thick-skulled, either of which might be used figuratively; it details six such words, as *pachyderm, pachyntic.* Not in *OED* are the genera *Pachysandra:* of the box family; *Pachystina:* of the staff-tree family. For a "thick-skinned," insensitive person, *pachydermatic* has not come into general use. (The *ch* is pronounced *k,* as in *orchestra, chasm, strychnine,* and other words from Greek sources.)

bher I: carry, bear, bring. Gk, *amphora, ampoule, anaphora; euphoria. metaphor. perimeter,* measured by pi, its first letter in Gk, Π. *paraphernalia.* Suffixes *phore,* as in *semaphore,* and *phorus,* as in *gonophorous. phosphorus:* light-bearer, being *phosphorescent;* see *el 15. Phosphor* is a poetic name for the morning star. *phosphene:* seeing stars, the impression of light from pressure on the eye. *OED* lists 21 and details 46 relevant words beginning *phos,* as *phosphate; phosphoprotein:* protein, such as casein, that is bound with phosphoric acid.

L *ferre, tuli, latum:* to bear. *fertile:* able to bear. *feretory.* The *ferret* was used to hunt and bring out rabbits and rats; hence *to ferret out*—though some suggest it may be a diminutive of L *fur;* thief; see *fur. afferent. circumference; conference; defer, different; efferent. opprobrium:* brought forward against one. *infer; offer, offertory; proffer; prefer; refer, referee. suffer; transfer. collation. dilate; dilatory. translate. vociferate. ablative.* The suffix *ferous;* JWalker lists 160 such, as *herbiferous, odoriferous, proliferous, vociferous.* (*fermium* is from Enrico Fermi; see *el 100.*)

fortune; bearer of good or evil. *fortuitous.* From the tossing of dice (L *alea*) came E *aleatory.* Caesar, crossing the forbidden river Rubicon, toward Rome, exclaimed *Alea jacta est:* The die is cast. *Rubicon* is sometimes used for a moment of critical decision. It was by a similar "tossing" (Bible, 1 Samuel 10:20) that Samuel made Saul king of the Jews.

The word *serendipity:* happy chance, was formed from Horace Walpole's tale of *The Three Princes of Serendip* (1754), to whom such good fortune fell. *Serendib* (There is no *p* sound in Arabic) was the Arab name of the island of Ceylon, recently changed again, to Sri Lanka. *Serendip* itself is a folkchange from Skr *Simhaladvipa:* Dwelling-Place-of-Lions Island. An intended instance of serendipity occurred when in 521 B.C. seven noble Persians had killed the pretender Smerdis, who sought to usurp the throne on the death of Cambyses. They agreed to ride the next morning to the hill outside Babylon, where the one whose horse neighed first would be acclaimed king. This was Darius, a Zoroastrian, who became a good ruler; he built many roads, with post stages for rapid communication; he dug a canal from the Nile to the Red Sea; but he was defeated by the Greeks at Marathon, 490 B.C. Tradition has it, however, that Darius's groom, on the night before the choice, led Darius's horse to the hilltop and there mated him with a mare; the next morning the horse, remembering, neighed, and Darius was king. Thus was set a precedent followed for 2500 years in many games of "chance."

Fr, *berceuse:* cradle song. Gc, *bear, forebear(s); bairn, birth, born, borne. forbear. bore. bier. (wheel)barrow. burly. burden. bring. berth* (earlier *birth*).

The insouciance of Sir Thomas Vanbrugh is neatly portrayed in the dialogue of his play *The Provok'd Wife* (1697), i, 1:

Belinda: Ay, but you know we must return good for evil.
Lady Brute: That may be a mistake in the translation.

bher II: cut, pierce; break. Gk *pharuggos:* cleft, chasm; hence, throat. *pharynx; pharyngeal.* L, *foralite; foramen; forficate; perforate; interfere.* It, *bordello:* first a hut of planks, a hovel; thence Fr, *brothel.* Gc, *bole, bore. board; garboard; starboard:* "steerboard." *cupboard. border. barrow:* castrated pig. *brittle.* Scand, *smorgasbord:* smear-goose-table.

bher(e)gh: high; fort or town on a height; hence strong; protect; secure. L, *fort, fortress, fortitude; fortify. enforce, reinforce; effort.* There's an old Chinese saying, among many attributed to Confucius: "It takes little effort to watch a man carry a load."

It, *forte, fortissimo; pianoforte,* shortened to *piano.* Perhaps *ghetto,* from *borghetto:* small town. Fr, *forte:* strong point. *bourgeois.* Gc, *iceberg. borough, burgher, burgomaster. burglar:* town thief, opposed to highwayman. *belfry, l.r* shift; first, a movable tower set against the wall of a besieged city; now a usually separate bell tower; see *bhel II. bury; burial. bargain. borrow:* first, to give as a pledge, to go bail for. *scabbard:* sword guard. *harbor, harbinger:* both first meant an army shelter.

Many city names end in *berg, burgh,* or *bury;* thus *Canterbury, Bloomsbury; Pittsburg* in California, Kansas, and Texas; *Pittsburgh* in Pennsylvania. *Edinburgh.* From *Hamburg* comes the ground meat *hamburger;* mistaking the first syllable led to such compounds as *beefburger, cheeseburger.* (*Frankfurt* gave us the popular *frankfurter,* familiarly known, from its dachshund shape, as the *hot dog.*)

In the marketplace of Bruges stands the belfry, old and brown;
Thrice consumed and thrice rebuilded, still it watches o'er the town.
As the summer morn was breaking, on that lofty tower I stood,
And the world threw off the darkness, like the weeds of widowhood.
—Longfellow, *The Belfry of Bruges*

bherem: to project; a rough edge (extension of *bher II*). *brim. bream:* clean a ship's bottom. *underbrush. broom:* first, the plant, then a cleaning instrument of its twigs. The same shift occurred with *brush* and *scrub, scrub* being actually a variant form of *shrub.* We still use *scrub* for "brushwood or stunted forest growth"; it was thence applied to "a stunted or insignificant person"; and now, to a secondary, unofficial group, as a *scrub team.*

bhereu: stir; warm, boiling. Gk, *phreatic.* L, *effervescent. ferment. fervent; fervid. fervor. fry.* Gc, *breath:* warm exhaled air; *breathing. breeze. barm; bread; broth. brew; brewis; imbrue. broil, embroil, brood, breed. braise; brazier. brawn. brand, brandish, brandy; burn. brimstone. bourne. burn:* a flowing stream; also in names, as *Bannockburn, Burnside.* The *burbot* is a freshwater fish that stirs up muddy bottoms. (Fr *bourboter:* to wallow in mud.) A *Bourbon*—used figuratively of an "unteachably aristocratic" person—was a member of the family that once ruled Naples, Spain, and France (France, 1589–1792 and 1815–1848); now applied to a whiskey first made in Bourbon County, Kentucky; the name is from a town in central France, changed from *Borvo,* a primitive god of warmth. *brewster,* first, a female brewer, survives as a name—used by Susan Glaspell in her one-act satire on psychoanalysis, *Suppressed Desires* (1914), in which the name Stephen Brewster contains the "unconscious" wish: "Step hen, be rooster."

bhes I: scrape, rub off, smooth; crumble; hence pebble, sand. Compounded as *bhesamatho* in Gk *psammos, amados;* L *sabulum:* sand. *sabulous; saburra. psammite. psephite. psephism:* ancient Greek voting with pebbles; later, with pellets—white for Aye, black for No; hence, *blackball. psora; psoriasis. palimpsest* (*palin:* again; smoothed and used over). *ammodyte:* sand burrower, a venomous snake. *ammocate.*

Gk *psilos:* simple, bare, smooth; see *bhili. epsilon, upsilon.* The Greek alphabet has *o* twice: omicron, little *o;* omega, big *o.* The Bible, Revelation 1:8, uses the first and last Greek letters: "I am alpha and omega, the beginning and the ending, saith the Lord."

Jupiter appeared as a man with ram's horns to rescue Hercules, parched in the sandy Libyan desert; from the sand, he was worshiped there as Jupiter *Ammon* (also *Amen;* hence Egyptian rulers, supposed descendants of the god, often had names including his, as *Amenhotep*). The god's wife was then hailed as Juno *Ammonia.* The *Amonii:* dwellers of the sands, were a nation of Egypto-Ethiopian origin. The great temple of Jupiter Ammon—its oracle having been founded, we are told, 18 centuries before Augustus, almost as long before Christ as we are after—was widely famed. From the sands where the camels waited while their masters prayed for good omens, there was first extracted *sal ammoniac.* Thence *ammonia;* though in the Middle Ages this was sometimes spelled *armonia* (Gk: fastening, gum ammonia was used as cement); some scholars thence trace the word to *Armenia*—which has Mount Ararat, but not much sand.

Thus the prefix *ammo,* as *ammophilous. ammotherapy:* sand baths. *ammo* is also used colloquially as short for *ammunition;* see *mei III. ammonal, amine. amino,* as *amino acid, aminophenal, aminopterin.* The Swiss Jacob Amen, or Ammon, in the late 17th c. led the strict Amish sect of the Mennonites, who had been founded by the Frieslander Menno Simons (b. 1492).

Gc, *sand, sandy. Sandy,* a Scottish shortening of Alexander, is also a nickname of boys with appropriately colored hair. *sandpaper, sandpiper, sandworm. sandwort* (*wort:* plant used for food or medicine). *sandblind* is a folkchange from *sam:* half; but note also *gravelblind* and *stoneblind;* see *caput.* The name *Sandwich* comes from *sandy village* (*wich* from L *vicus;* see *ueik I*). John Montague, fourth earl of Sandwich (d. 1792), was too ardent a gambler to stop to eat; he had slices of bread brought to him with meat between, and gave his name to the ubiquitous *sandwich.* The *sandwichman,* himself sandwiched between two advertising boards, may still be seen on crowded streets.

Mock on, mock on, Voltaire, Rousseau;
Mock on, mock on, 'tis all in vain!
You throw the sand against the wind,
And the wind blows it back again.
—William Blake, *Mock On*

bhes II: breathe. Imitative of inhalation and exhalation, which are from L *halare,* also imitative, whence *halitosis.* Gk *psukhe:* soul, spirit. The story of Cupid and Psyche is told in *The Golden Ass* of Apuleius (b. A.D. 125) and translated by Walter Pater in *Marius the Epicurean.* Hence *psyche, psychedelic, psychic, psychiatric,* etc. *psychology, psychopath, psychotic. psychoanalysis* (a better translation from the German would have omitted the *o*). *psychosomatic. metempsychosis. panpsychism.*

Here once, through an alley Titanic
Of cypress, I roamed with my soul—
Of cypress, with Psyche, my soul.
—Edgar Allan Poe, *Ulalume* (1847)

bheu: be; dwell; grow. Gk *phusis:* nature. *physics,* and *physical* things. *OED* has 130 related words and compounds. A *physician* was first a student of natural science; *doctor* means learned; see *dek. physiology. physiognomy. physique.* Human physique is divided into three main types: (1) asthenic: lean, flat-chested, with narrow shoulders; (2) athletic: with large bones and muscles; (3) pyknic: with rounded contours of face and body. *neophyte.* JWalker has 15 words ending *phyte:* relating to plant life, as *epiphyte, saprophyte.* A *zoophyte* is an animal that resembles a plant, as coral and sponge. Gk *phulon:* tribe, that dwells together. *phyletic, phylogeny, phylum; symphysis.*

Euphuism is named after the style of Lyly's *Euphues* (1579); literally, well-being; see *esu. imp,* via L from Gk *emphutos:* implant, first meant to graft; hence, a young shoot; this was applied to a mischievous child; then, in partly amused annoyance, to a "child of the Devil."

L *fieri:* to become. *fiat:* literally, Let it be done! *Fiat lux:* Let there be light—and there was light. *Fiat iustitia et ruant coeli:* Let justice be done though the heavens fall!, said William Watson in 1602. "Let justice be done and be seen to be done," says the British House of Lords when it agrees to try a case. Here, too, is the word *future:* what is to be.

dubious: to be of two minds; *dubitation, indubitably.* Fr *doubt. superb:* to be above, superior. *tribe:* a division, third part, of the Roman people. *tribunal, tribune; tribute;* see *tre. probe; probable; probity:* righteous living. *reprobate. proof, prove, approve; disprove; reprove.*

Gc, *be, been. beam; boom* (of a sail). *big. booth. build, bound, bondage, husband* comes via ONorse *hus:* house, and *buandi:* dwelling; hence *husbandry; husband* your resources. Matthew Prior, in 1709, gave husbands three lines of good advice—and a forlorn fourth:

Be to her virtues very kind,
Be to her faults a little blind;
Let all her ways be unconfined,
And clap a padlock on her mind.

Boer: farmer; *boor. neighbor:* nearby farmer. *bower; bowery. byre; by(e)law.* The last element of Gaelic *eisteddfod* (*eistedd:* sit), annual assembly and contest of Welsh poets. The Bowery, New York, was for years a symbol of a dangerous city slum; it had many "flop houses," where homeless drifters and hopeless drunkards might sleep for a pittance; it used to house the diamond center of the city, where an incautious rustic might be sold a "goldbrick" or a share of the Brooklyn Bridge; and it gave entrance to the underground opium dens for the gory gangsters of the Tong wars of Chinatown. Hence the popular song "The Bowery, the Bowery, I'll never go there anymore."

Then to the bower they came,
Naked they came to the smooth-swarded bower,
And at their feet the crocus brake like fire,

Violet, amaracus, and asphodel,
Lotos and lilies.
—Tennyson, *Œnone*

bheudh: aware, enlightened. Skr, *bo tree, bodhi tree* (Skr *bodhi:* awakening). *Bodhisatta. Buddhism.* Prince Siddhartha, Gautama Buddha ("the enlightened"), found the Way under a pipal (*bo*) tree at Buddh Gaya in 530 B.C. Gc, *bid, forbid; verboten. bode, foreboding.* Norse *ombudsman:* aware of both sides; see *ambhi. beadle,* who carried a rod to prod aware those that snored in church. See *es.*

Berowne, in *Love's Labor's Lost,* iii, 1, protests:

I, forsooth, in love! I that have been love's whip,
A very beadle to a humorous sigh,
A critic, nay, a night-watch constable,
A domineering pedant o'er the boy . . .
This senior-junior, giant-dwarf, Dan Cupid,
Regent of love rhymes, lord of folded arms . . .
Dread prince of plackets, king of codpieces . . .
—Oh, my little heart!—
What! I love! I sue! I seek a wife!
Go to, it is a plague
That Cupid will impose for my neglect
Of his almighty dreadful little might.
[*Go read the rest.*]

Cupid, "prince of plackets," follows a crooked trail. Fr *plaquer:* to press, lie flat, was used of a breastplate, then of a dress. E *placket* (a diminutive of *placard*), from a dress, was used of a slit at the top of a dress for easier putting on and off; then, in Tudor slang, for the slit in the flesh beneath. Edgar, "Poor Tom" the pretended madman in *King Lear,* iii, 4, says: "Keep thy hand out of plackets"; see *burd; per VI f; tel.*

bheug I: flee. L, *fugitive. centrifugal* (opposed to *centripetal;* see *pet I*). *refuge, refugee. subterfuge. fugacious.* Suffix *fuge,* in *febrifuge, insectifuge, vermifuge. basifuge:* that which discourages kissing. *fugue.*

bheug II: bend, fold; curve; swell. Gk *ptukh. diptych, triptych, polyptych* (*ch* pronounced *k*). Gc, *bow:* bend in respect; also *bow,* bent to drive an arrow. *crossbow,* for which the yew tree was preferred; see *ei II.* Also *bow window; bowlegs,* and the beautiful *rainbow. akimbo. bagel,* from the shape. *buxom:* first, flexible, amenable. *bight. bog. bout:* first, a turn, as in ploughing; then a round, as in boxing. Thus also *boustrephedon:* writing one line right to left, alternately left to right, as on early Greek statues—turns like those of an ox (Gk *bous*) in ploughing.

You may grind their souls in the self-same mill,
You may bind them, heart and brow;
But the poet will follow the rainbow still,
And his brother will follow the plow.
—John Boyle O'Reilly, *The Rainbow's Treasure* (1873)

bheug III: enjoy, perform. Nasalized, L, *function, perfunctory; defunct.*

bhili: loving. Gk *philos: philosophy:* love of wisdom. Pythagoras, 6th c. B.C., was the first to call himself philosopher; the earlier term, *sophos:* wise man, seemed to him immodest. A pretender to wisdom is a *psilosopher* (Gk *psilos:* mere, bare).

Psilanthropy is pretended philanthropy; but also, in theology, the doctrine that Jesus is a mere man. *Psilogy* is empty talk. see *bhes I.* "Philosophy begins in wonder"—Socrates.

philharmonic. Francophile, bibliophile, etc. *Philadelphia:* (city of) brotherly love; Gk *delphos:* womb; *adelphos:* from one womb. (The dolphin is named for the female's womb; see *guelbh.*) *oxyphil(e), acidophil(e), acidophilus. anemophilous:* breeze-loving; also used of plants fertilized by wind-borne pollen. *heliophilous:* sun-loving, as many flowers and beach bathers.

philter: love potion. *philtrum:* dimple in the upper lip, which invites kissing. *philomel:* "lover of song," the nightingale. *OED* lists 81 words beginning *phil(o),* plus a few humorous nonce words, as *philofinancitive, philofoxhuntingness;* it details 19 columns of relevant words, *philadelphian . . . philoprogenitive . . . philtrous.* The philosopher's stone, which can turn base metals into gold, was the supreme quest of the alchemists.

Philip: lover of horses; Gk *hippos:* horse; see *eku.* A philippic, invective speech, however, takes its name from the orations of Demosthenes against Philip of Macedon, 4th c. B.C. The Philippines, a cluster of some 7100 islands in the Malay Archipelago, were named after Philip II of Spain. From the Philippines—some say, rather, by folkchange from Gm *Vielliebchen:* much beloved darling—comes a playful game, philippine or philopena. If a nut, such as an almond, is found to have two kernels, the finder offers one to a person of the other sex; at their next meeting, the first to cry Fillipeena! wins a gift. Mark Twain, in *Pudd'nhead Wilson,* uses the term *human philopena* to mean a twin.

The graduate degree Ph.D., *Philosophiae Doctor:* "learned in the love of wisdom," came from German practice to England and America; first conferred in the U.S. at Yale in 1861 (though an honorary Doctor of Laws degree was conferred at Harvard in 1773). William James, in *Memories and Studies* (1903), noted that "a Ph.D. in philosophy would prove little . . . as to one's ability to teach literature."

pamphelet: all-loving, was a 16th c. term for a prostitute. *pamphlet* was the diminutive of *Pamphilus,* title and hero of a short Latin amatory poem of the 12th c., which was so popular throughout the 13th c.—students at the University of Paris were chided for reading it instead of serious works—that *pamphlet* became the general term for a booklet.

Syphilis (: loving together; but some trace the first syllable to the root *sus:* swine, which see) was the title of a Latin poem of 1530, by the Veronese physician Girolamo Fracastoro, about a shepherd named Syphilis, supposedly the first sufferer from the disease, of which Fracastoro himself is said to have died. The book, *Syphilis, sive Morbus Gallicus,* was translated in 1686 by Nahum Tate as *Syphilis, or a Poetical History of the French Disease.* The French called syphilis "the Italian sickness."

The French are generally considered to be rather xenophobic than xenophilic. Gk *xenos:* stranger, might mean either guest or enemy. like L *hostis,* which gave English both *mine host* of the hospitable inn and the *hosts* of the *hostile* army. The *host:* bread consecrated in the Eucharist, is from L *hostia:* a victim for sacrifice, from *hostis:* stranger. Strange are the turns of human expression.

"I am ruminating," said Dickens' Mr. Pickwick, "on the strange mutability of human affairs." "Ah, I see—in at the palace door one day, out at the window the next. Philosopher, Sir?" "An observer of human nature, Sir," said Mr. Pickwick.

When all philosophies shall fail
This word alone shall fit:
That a sage feels too small for life,
And a fool too large for it.
—G. K. Chesterton, *Ballad of the White Horse*

bhlag: strike. L, *flagellation, flagitious. flail, flog.* In compounds, *afflict, conflict, inflict.* "Affliction, like the iron-smith, shapes as it smites." Via ONorse *ledr-blaka:* leatherflapper; Dan *afen-bakke:* evening bat, came the flying mammal, E *bat.*

Come into the garden, Maud,
For the black bat, night, has flown.
—Tennyson, *Maud*

bhoso: naked. Gc, *bare.* OSw, *ballast:* a "bare" load, not cargo, just for the balance and weight.

Back and side go bare, go bare,
Both foot and hand go cold;
But belly God send thee good ale enough,
Whether it be new or old.
—Song in *Gammer Gurton's Needle* (1566), ii

bhrag: emit a smell, pleasant or not. L, *fragrare, fragrantum. fragrant,* (*l.r* shift) *flair.* Gc *brach,* which hunts by the scent.

Anthony Trollope, in *Miss Mackenzie* (1865), presses an analogy: "With many women I doubt whether there be any more effectual way of touching their hearts than ill-using them and then confessing it. If you wish to get the sweetest fragrance from the herb at your feet, tread on it and bruise it."

bhrater: brother. Skr, *pal.* Gk, *phratry.* L, *fra, friar, fraternal, fraternity. fratricide* began early, with Cain and Abel. Fr, *confrère.* Gc, *brother, brotherhood,* etc. R. L. Stevenson ends his story *The Black Arrow* with a fighting man's conversion: "So Lawless had his will, and died a friar."

bhreg, bhrei: rub; prick as with a spit; break. L *frangere, fractum. fracas. fraction:* first, the breaking of bread in the Eucharist. In arithmetic, a vulgar fraction is one expressed by a line with a numerator above and a denominator below, as 3/4; a decimal fraction, by a dot between the units and the tenths, as 17.7425. In a speech on 10 Oct. 1953 Winston Churchill confessed: "Personally, I like short words and vulgar fractions." One early meaning of *fraction* was brawling; hence, *fractious,* the ending as on *captious;* see *kap. fracture. fragment; fragile* and its doublet via Fr, *frail. frailty* (thy name is woman: *Hamlet,* i, 2).

franion, the end as on *companion,* is probably via OFr *fraignant:* breaking, *fraigneis:* uproar; hence a gay, reckless fellow, as used by Lamb in 1810; see *kad II,* though by Spenser, in *The Faerie Queene,* v, 3, applied to a loose woman. Also *anfractuous:* of a broken, irregular shore (*ambi:* around). *diffraction; refractory. refrain:* breaking back the sequence of a song; for the verb *refrain,* see *ghren. frangible, infrangible, infringe. irrefragable. saxifrage:* "stone-breaker" plant. *suffrage:* first, voting with shards. *suffragette.*

L *fricare, fricatum:* rub. *fray; friable, fricative, friction. fritter. dentifrice. fricandeau, fricandel, fricasee.* Newton, in a letter of 15 Dec. 1716, describes the production of static electricity: "a piece of amber or resin fricated on silk cloth."

frig: first, to move about restlessly, to agitate the body or limbs; then–one meaning of L *fricere, frictum* is to become erect–it was used for sexual intercourse, also for masturbation. Thomas D'Urfey, in *Pills to Purge Melancholy* (1719), sets a jingle:

O! how they do frig it,
Jump it and jigg it.

Hence, *fricatrix,* a whore, or a self-enjoying female; Jonson, in *Volpone* (1605), iv, 2, speaks of "a lewd harlot, a base fricatrice." Hence also *firk,* a very frequent word with a variety of meanings, driven out in the early 17th c., when it came to the form and meaning of *fuck;* see *gay,* under *es.*

Also *defray. osprey,* earlier *ossifrage:* "bone-breaker," a fish-eating hawk, the ending folkchanged to match *bird of prey.* Gc, *brash, breach, break, broke, broken; brick. burst; bruise;* in heraldry, *debruise. brake* is (1) the old past tense of *break;* (2) a device for breaking off movement. A *broker* was first a *broacher* of wine casks; hence a dealer in wine, then a more general agent. A *broach* was first a tool for broaching casks; then, an opening; also used figuratively, as by Addison in 1712: "I broached my project of a news-paper." Hence also *brooch; brochure; brocade, brocatel.* OFr, *brisance; debris.* It, *broccoli,* diminutive of *brocco:* spit, stalk.

Samuel Johnson in 1780 (Boswell's *Life of Samuel Johnson* [1791]): "Among the anfractuosities of the human mind, I know not if it may not be true, that there is a superstitious reluctance to sit for a picture." In Johnson's time, a painting took time; today there seems a ready response to pose for a quick photograph.

bhreus: swell. *breast. brisket. browse:* first of cattle browsing on budding twigs.

bhru: edge. *brow.* From a beam used as a side, *bridge.*

bhrud: enjoy. *fructify. usufruct. frugal. frumentaceous. frumenty.* It, *tutti-frutti.* Fr, *fruit, fruition.* Gc, *brook:* to put up with; now often with a negative. Shakespeare, in *Love's Labor's Lost,* iv, 2, notes that "many can brook the weather that like not the wind." Byron, in *Don Juan,* x, is more materialistic:

Alas, how deeply painful is all payment! . . .
They hate a murderer much less than a claimant . . .
Kill a man's family, and he may brook it–
But keep your hands out of his breeches' pocket.

bhudh: bottom: L *fundus:* bottom. *to found:* "lay the bottom" of; start. *foundation. profound; founder. to fund:* supply means for the start. *fundament, fundamental.* Gc, *bottom.* Among the 19 definitions of *bottom* is one, common in Shakespeare's time: "a clew or nucleus on which to wind thread," that makes appropriate the name *Bottom* in *A Midsummer Night's Dream,* for the man is a weaver. And when Bottom is transmogrified into an ass, it seems likely that Shakespeare is still playing on the name, although the first recorded (i.e. written) use of *bottom* for what *OED* calls "the sitting part of a man" is by Erasmus Darwin in 1794. It was on 20 Apr. 1761 that Samuel Johnson, in mixed company, remarked: "The woman had a bottom of good sense." To the immediate tittering he responded: "Where's the merriment? I say the woman was fundamentally sensible." His almost farcical attempt to rectify the situation may still amuse us.

bhugo: male animal. Fr. *butcher.* Gc, *buck; springbok.*

bhuko: water weeds, possibly of Hebrew origin. Gk, *phukos:* seaweed. *OED* lists 15 biological words beginning *phyco,* as *phycocyanin, phycology, phycoxanthin.*

L *fucus:* seaweed; algae; red dye. Hence *fucoid, fucivorous; fucaceous. Zygophyceae:* class of algae (*zygo:* yoked). *Fucus:* genus, brown algae. From the use of the dye as a cosmetic, also *fuco'd:* painted; *fucal:* specious, fair-seeming; *fucatious:* deceitful. Kingsley, in *Westward Ho!* (1855), warns of a "painted, patched, fucussed, periwigged, bolstered Charybdis." Earlier the word had been turned in sexual wordplay: Middleton, in *A Fair Quarrel* (1617), iv, 1, presents two tyro "Roarers" who try out their taunting on a Captain and his two trollops, Priss and Meg: "I say she is a bronstrops; and this is a fucus"–Priss interrupts: "No indeed, Sir: we are both fucusses." (*bronstrops* is Middleton's word for a *bawdstrot:* literally, "bold or lively strutter," first used of a pander or pimp; after 1700, only feminine: a procuress.)

?bhurig: (Skr) shears. See *gib; leg II.* L *furca:* fork. *furcate, bifurcate, trifurcate.* Fr, *fourchée, fourchette. carfax,* via Fr *carrefour* from L *quadrifurcum:* point where four roads meet.

Neither the pitchfork, two-pronged, nor the table fork is a nomadic instrument. The word *furca* first appeared in connection with hay. In the Late Roman Empire and the Middle Ages, two-pronged forks were used for serving meat, which was eaten (as still by Henry VIII) with the fingers. The table fork, soon with jeweled handle, came into use in the Italian Renaissance, but was not a common piece for dining, even among the upper classes, until the mid-17th c. Gentlemen used to carry a personal fork on their journeys. Ben Jonson, in *Volpone* (1605), pointed out the novelty: "You must learn the use and handling of the silver fork at meals."

Beyond the widened use of the fork, one may note its figurative application, as in the historical Morton's fork. John Morton (?1420–1500) was an opportunist, a turncoat. He chose correctly when Henry Earl of Richmond killed King Richard III at Bosworth Field in 1485, becoming Henry VII, first king of the House of Tudor. Henry made Morton a cardinal, and for Henry he impaled the gentry on one of the prongs of Morton's fork: "You can't be spending much, so how about something for the King?" "You're spending so much you must be rich, so how about something for the King?"

The *Oxford Dictionary of National Biography* states that Morton "probably wrote 'The History of Richard III', usually ascribed to Sir Thomas More" (who'd been a page in Morton's household). This book is the source of Shakespeare's play, and of the picture of Richard, the hunchback villain, that has lasted to our day, despite recent historians' attempts to rehabilitate the much-maligned monarch. J. D. Mackie, in *The Earlier Tudors* (1952), of the Oxford History of England series, still accepting "More's picture of the restless, suspicious tyrant," adds: "Yet, if we judged by the records of his parliaments he would rank as an enlightened ruler; he was popular as a good soldier. . . . even after the murder of the [two] princes the bishop of St. David's could write of him: "God hath sent hym to us for the wele of us all.'" Josephine Tey, in her book *The Daughter of Time* (Truth is the daughter of time), uses the detective-story technique to expose the falsity of the usual notion of Richard, the most prominent English instance of tonypandy. See *gib.*

Tonypandy has been suggested as the name for a false story accepted as historical. "The Boston Massacre," 5 Mar. 1770: the mob threw stones at a sentry before the Customs House. "Washington could not tell a lie": into the 20th c. full credence was given to Parson Weems's tale of the cherry tree. Tonypandy is a town in Wales where "the Government used troops in 1910 to shoot down Welsh miners striking for their rights": actually, the chief constable requested the troops to stop the riots and the looting; Churchill sent not soldiers but metropolitan police "armed" with rolled-up mackintoshes, creating a few bloody noses. Several countries in 1982 were protesting Japan's rewriting of history for its schoolbooks. Russia, in books and encyclopedias, has made this practice routine. Tonypandy is international and perennial. Or do I write with a national, sociopolitical bias? A lexicographer should not argue but should report.

Incidentally, England has never had a fourth King Richard–nor, after the extraction of the Magna Carta from an unwilling king, a second ruler with the most frequent of Christian names, *John.* There are 84 *St. Johns.*

?bibli. Our Indo-European ancestors, doing no writing, had no use for its instruments. Early writing was mainly carved or scratched on marble. The Egyptians discovered they could write on the inner bark of the papyrus, which came into Greece by way of the Phoenician port the Greeks called Bublos. From *papyrus* came E *paper,* etc., and from *Bublos* the various words beginning *biblio. OED* lists 40, and details 48, including *bibliography, bibliophile.* A *bibliopole* is a bookseller, a pleasant occupation before paperbacks and mass semiliteracy. *bibliomancy:* divination by opening the Bible at random and building upon the first words seen or touched. By less pious scholars the works of Virgil were often used; this was called *sortes Virgilianae.*

The Bible has been described as lacking in humor, but from the very beginning it is rich in wordplay. Genesis 2:7: "Then the Lord God formed man [*adham*] of dust [*adhama*]." Genesis 2:23: "She shall be called woman [*ishshah*] because she was taken out of man [*ish*]." In Genesis 4:1 Eve says: "I have gotten [*qanah*] a man [Cain] with the help of the Lord." And so on, past the Psalms, a number of which are alphabetic acrostics. See *es;* for an example from the New Testament, see *caput.*

?bomb. Imitative of the humming of insects. Gk, L, E *bombus:* a humming in the ears; *bombous.* Gk *bombux,* E *bombyx:* genus of moths, family *Bombycidae,* which includes the silkworm moth. *bombic. bombycinous. bombilation; bombinate. bombylious:* of the bumblebee fly. From the 16th c. into the 19th, *bombycine* was a silk fabric, now *bombasine.* Transferred to "tree silk" (i.e., cotton) fabrics, as *bombazine, bombace, bombasie,* etc., which were used for padding, it came to English as *bombast,* used figuratively of inflated language. *OED* defines 8 words beginning *bombast.* Coleridge speaks of "mental bombast, as distinguished from verbal."

Entomologists have recently noted the scent *bombykol,* "a single molecule of which will tremble the hairs of any male [moth] within miles and send him driving upwind in a confusion of ardor."–Lewis Thomas, *The Lives of a Cell* (1974).

?borbor. Partly imitative. Gk *borboros:* filth. *borborite:* a person of filthy thought or ideas; applied first to a sect of the Gnostics; in the 16th and 17th c., to a sect of Mennonites. *borborology:* filthy talk. *borborygmus:* rumbling of the bowels; *borborygmous.* See *perd.*

braghu, mreghu: short. Gk *brakhion:* shorter; hence the upper arm, shorter than the forearm. *amphibrach:* short at both ends, as the metrical foot: a short syllable, then a long, then a short. *tribrach. brace, bracelet; embrace.*

OED details 7 words relating to the arm, beginning *brach.* It lists 11 and details 4 beginning *brach(y),* (Gk *brakhus:* short), as *brachiate, brachycephalic, brachylogy.* It also lists 3 beginning *brachisto,* from the superlative; shortest, as *brachistochrone* (*khronos:* time): the curve of quickest gravitational descent of an object moving through the air.

L, *breve, brevet; abbreviate, breviary. OED* lists 4 and details 18 relevant words, as *brevity, breviped,* and let us hope "pithy" *breviloquence.* Via Fr, *brief, abridge. brassiere,* shortened to *bra;* Fr *bras:* arm. Gc, *pretzel,* like linked arms.

merry (short and sweet; note the Gm *Kurtzweil:* pastime, merriment; literally, short time). *mirth.*

Macaulay, with his usual overstatement, declared that Calandrino, in Boccaccio's *Decameron* (8th day, 9th tale) "made all Europe merry for more than four centuries."

buff: swelling cheeks; to puff out. Imitative. L, *buff, buffer; rebuff. bluff:* first, to swell up; also imitative. It, *buffo.* Fr, *opéra bouffe.* Gc, *puff, puffin, puffy.*

The word *buff,* from two sources, provides a good example of the way meanings may spread. (1) From the sense of a sudden puff came the use for a blow, a *buffet,* as in boxing; hence, the sound of flesh being struck; also, *to stand buff,* firm against a blow. (2) Via Fr *buffle* from Gk *bous:* cow, ox, came *buffalo* (first, water buffalo). Hence (3) the hide, stout leather. Then (4) the human "hide," the skin, as in *stripped to the buff.* Police and military jackets were made of leather; hence (5) the *Buffs,* as the third regiment of the line; and more generally, (6) a fellow, also called a *buffer.* Then, the fellow that's "it" (blindfolded) in the game of Blind Man's Buff. Also (7) *buff,* to clean or polish, rubbing first with soft leather. Hence *buff* came to be used (8) for the color of the leather, usually a dull, light yellow. Shakespeare, in *The Comedy of Errors,* iv, 2, speaks of a "suit of buff." In New York, the uniform of the volunteer firemen was this color; thence (9) the vogue use, a *buff,* an enthusiast, as Mayor La Guardia, who had a fire alarm installed in his office and used to speed to the scene of a conflagration. Thus a skating buff, a word buff.

At the same time, sense (1) was spreading. Thus It, *buffo,* a slapstick comic actor, puffing out jests with bursts of laughter; whence also *buffoon.* And Fr *bouffer:* to give a burst of laughter; this meaning is in Cotgrave's English wordbook of 1611. In Victorian days, the game of "Knock, knock" was based on this meaning. At a party, someone knocks on the door with a cane. "Who's there?" "Buff." "Buff who?" "Buff you"—the person then comes in and makes faces and funny or clever remarks until someone laughs. The laugher is handed the cane and goes out to be the next Buff. In recent revival, the game is purely verbal and involves making up clever or comic names, as one that draws in Shakespeare: "Who's there?" "Mandy." "Mandy who?" "Man delights me not; no, nor woman neither"—Hamlet's words to Rosenkrantz and Guildenstern. A much earlier variant of the game was played in 1283, as in the "first comic opera," *Le Jeu de Robert et Marion,* by Adam de la Halle (lines 427–470 in the Axton-Stevens translation: *Medieval French Plays* [Oxford, 1971]), "the game of St. Coisne." A gift is brought by a petitioner to someone as the saint; if the saint's words and ways make the donor laugh, the donor "loses" and must in turn play the saint. The perennial element is the endeavor to make the listeners laugh. Saint Coisne, or Cosme, was the patron saint of physicians, also of the famous Florentine family the Medici, several men of which—as Cosimo the Elder (d. 1464), "the father of his country," and Cosimo II, "the Great" (d. 1574)—were named after the saint. *Medici,* of course, means doctor, and the laughter is legended:

For human ills, three cures are Heaven-sent:
Dr. Diet, Dr. Quiet, and Dr. Merriment.

?burd. Imitative of the drone of a bee; then of the drone of a bagpipe. The bagpipe, known to us from Scotland, was in early use in North Africa, and spread through Europe. There are references to it in Greek and Latin as early as A.D. 100. The primitive bag was a whole sheepskin or goatskin; the base drone accompaniment was two octaves below the melody pipe. It was early used in festivals; military use, with drums, grew in the 18th c. It had various names, as It *zampogna,* Fr *cornemuse;* the musette was popular for the pastoral dances of the court of Louis XI.

From the sound, used as accompaniment to a song, *burdon* came to mean a chorus, a refrain; then the word was, as *OED* puts it, "completely merged" with *burden.* Thus, in *As You Like It,* iii, 2: "I would sing my song without a burthen; thou bringst me out of tune"; and in *The Tempest,* i, 2: "Foote it featly heere and there, and sweet Sprights beare the burthen."

This becomes more complicated in the description of the peddler Autolycus in *The Winter's Tale* (iv, 4): "He has the prettiest love songs for maids, so without bawdry, which is strange, with such delicate burdens of dildos and fadings, 'jump her and thump her'." Strange indeed! And Shakespeare knew the audience would be amused, for these "burdens" were directly sexual. *dildo* was used as a nonsense word in many refrains, as "Sing trang dildo lee"; S. Holland in *Don Zara del Fogo* (1656):

> That gods may view, with a dildo-doo,
> What we bake and what we brew—

but it had common currency as (1) an artificial phallus: (2) a term of contempt for a man, like vulgar E *prick* and Fr *con;* and from their shape (3) a curl on a courtier's wig; (4) a dildo-glass, a testtube; (5) a dildo-bush: a prickly green shrub without leaves or blossoms. Meanings (1) and (5) persist. In *Live and Let Die,* 16, Ian Fleming in 1954 mentions a dildo cactus alongside the road from Jamaica airport. *fade* came via OFr from a blend of L *fatuus:* silly, and *vapidus:* spiritless; but "with a fading," says *OED,* "was the refrain of a popular song of an indecent character"—so popular that a number of later songs were written "to the tune of *With a fading.*" Autolycus's own phrases match his lewd inclination; he tells of a crowd so intently absorbed in a ballad singer that "you might have pinched a placket, it was senseless; 'twas nothing to geld a codpiece of a purse." See *bheudh; per VI; tel.*

?burs: bag. Gk and L *bursa:* hide; leather bag. *bursa; bursitis; bursiform. burse; disburse; imburse, reimburse.* Via OE, *purse.* Sp, *bolson:* bag-shaped depression, as in southern U.S. and Mexico. Scot, *sporran.*

Also the *Bourse,* financial center of Paris; called "the Street" in London, "Wall Street" in New York; "the Rialto" in Venice. The last is via It *rivo alto:* deep river, old name of the island now Venice; it is also applied to the famous bridge there, with many shops of goldsmiths; and there Shylock shook his head at the hard-hearted Christians.

> Who steals my purse steals trash; 'tis something, nothing;
> 'Twas mine, 'tis his, and has been slave to thousands . . .
> —*Othello,* iii, 3

Note: The letter *c* does not appear in early alphabets, and is unnecessary, as its sounds are expressed either by *k* or by *s*. The combination *ch* is still sounded *k* in words from Greek, as *scholar, orchestra* (*skedule* in the U.S., although *shedule* in England); in most other cases *ch* is a comparatively recent change from *ci,* as in *charlatan, chicken, child, chin.*

ca. Imitative. *cackle. quack.* Fr *cane:* duck; male, *canard:* drake; *caneton:* male duckling; female *canette.* E *canard* was first used of a quacking sound; Fraser's *Magazine* in 1841 pictured "a ragged starveling canarding on a clarionet." About 1850 came the use of *canard* as a hoax, a joke at somebody's expense—borrowed from the Fr *vendre des canards à moitié:* to half-sell ducks.

Also imitative are *caw, cawk.* Jeffries, in *Wild Life* (1879), reports that rooks "before diving utter a gurgling sound like the usual caw prolonged—caw-wouk." In *A Midsummer Night's Dream,* Puck tells Oberon, king of the fairies, that on seeing Bottom transmogrified into an ass, the rude mechanicals scattered like "choughs rising and cawing at the gun's report."

caca: defecate; feces. Baby talk, *cacca,* used in baby training. Gk *Kakos,* son of Vulcan, who terrorized the country around Mt. Aventinus, until killed by Hercules. Used in compounds to mean bad, as *cachexy;* see *segh. kakistocracy. cacodyl. cacoepy. cacophonous. cacogenics;* see *gn.* With *a* negative, *Acacetus:* not bad, was a name of Mercury, as the shrewd persuader, often to mischief or to thievery.

cacoethes (Gk *ethos:* custom): bad habit, as in *cacoethes scribendi:* itch to be writing, also dubbed *graphomania.* See *ker III.* The scribbler's itch, pandemic since print, is no new affliction. The biblical book Ecclesiastes, of the third c. B.C., laments (12:12) that "of making many books there is no end." And the Roman Juvenal, who died in our second century, remarks, as Dryden translated:

> But since the world with writing is possest,
> I'll versify in spite, and do my best
> To make as much waste-paper as the rest.

caconym; cacography. Akin are *rhyparography,* Gk *rhupos:* filth; and the *rhyparographer,* flooding the flourishing "sex shops" in many Western lands. *cacodyl,* from its foul odor. *mazocacothesis:* malposition of the placenta.

A nonrepetitive form of *caca* appears in Gk *kopros:* dung, whence *coprolite, coprology, coprophilous, coprophagy,* etc. L *cacare:* poppycock (*pap:* soft; literally, soft shit). Via Norse, *cucking stool.* Note that *cacomistle* is unrelated to *caca* or to *mistletoe;* it is a Nahwatl (American Indian) word, meaning half-lion.

Classes in eugenics used to be proffered, as horrible examples, the sordid generations of the Jukes family of New York, and the Kallikaks of New Jersey, one branch of which passed on good genes; the other, faulty. *Kallikak* is a coined pseudonym, from *cal:* good, and *caca.* See next root.

cal: good; good-looking, beautiful. Gk *kallos:* beauty. *kaleidophone:* instrument to make sound waves visible in patterns of light. *kaleidoscope. callisthenics:* beautiful strength; *OED* says "chiefly a term of young ladies' boarding schools." *calligraphy,* a not wholly lost art.

calomel: beautiful black; calomel is white, but was first made from a black powder; see *mel II.* W. S. Gilbert, in *Patience,* seized upon this purgative in his mockery of poetic affectation:

> Is it, and can it be,
> Nature hath this decree,
> Nothing poetic in the world shall dwell?
> Or that, in all her works,
> Something poetic lurks,
> Even in colocynth and calomel?
> I cannot tell.

"Nonsense!" cries Patience. "Nonsense, yes, perhaps," admits one of the infatuated ladies; "but oh, what precious nonsense!"

Calliope: beautiful-voiced (four syllables, long *i*); Muse of epic poetry; debased into the steam *calliope* (pronounced kaliōpe) of the circus parade and the showboat. *callicebus:* South American monkey.

Callisto: most beautiful, was a nymph; Zeus, who loved all lovely females, made her the mother of Arcas, from whom the Arcadians claimed descent. *Et in Arcadia ego:* I too have been in Arcady, pictured as a land of pastoral delights; see *es.* Zeus's jealous wife, Hera, changed Callisto into a bear, whereupon Zeus set her in the sky as the constellation Ursa Major, the Great Bear; see *ger V.*

Callirrhoe: beautifully flowing, was a sea nymph; is also a genus of the mallow family. Another Callirrhoe was wife of Alcmaeon, who killed his mother when she had his father murdered; after which Alcmaeon lived a more wretched life than Orestes, who had done the same thing; see *kuei 1.*

Several plants have won the name of beauty, as the *calla lily,* and the genera *Callicarpa* (: fruit; L *carpere:* pluck); *Callitriche* (hair: a water-weed); *Calluna* (heath); *Hemerocallis* (beauty of a day: kind of lily); *Hymenocallis* (membrane: the amaryllis).

Aphrodite Callipyge: of the beautiful buttocks (Gk *puge:* rump, whence *pygal, pygidium*), was a frequent subject of paintings, of *callipygian* bloom. *steatopygian* is from Gk *stear, steat-:* solid fat, whence also *stearic acid, steatolysis;* see *stei.* Among some African tribes, *steatopygia* is considered *callipygian.* Sir Thomas Browne—enlightened in many respects, although his testimony caused the burning of two women as witches—in 1646 spoke of women "largely composed behind"; and in our tense and troubled times, it is pleasant to see a woman composed.

calophantic: putting on a show of beauty, as with cosmetics: "the art of beautifying the body." Modern cosmetics is a special application (Gk *cosmeticos,* contrasted with *chaotic*) of *cosmos,* which first meant world order rising out of primordial chaos: empty space; see *ghe.* From *cosmos,* English has recently formed *cosmonaut:* a sailor through space. There are 77 related words in *OED* beginning *cosm,* as *cosmopolitan. cosmorama:* peep show of "all the world in a box," originally applied to a show on Regent Street, London, then especially to the Great Exhibition of 1851, the first "World's Fair."

L *mundus* traveled in the opposite direction from cosmos; it first meant feminine adornment; but as early as 1290 E *mound* was used to mean the world; by 1550 it had become limited to the golden orb used as a symbol of royal power, representing the terrestrial world; *mound* is still so used in heraldry. In Ben Jonson's *Cynthia's Revels* (1599), a mound is presented to the monarch, signifying Queen Elizabeth. The more worldly concern of the self-adorning woman, as opposed to other-worldly emphasis, is preserved in the words *mundane, mundanity;* via Fr, *la monde:* society; *demimonde* and the *demimondaines.* The *orb*—which has replaced this sense of mound in common use—is from L *orbus,* whence also *orbicular,* and the planets (stars, galaxies) in their *orbit. Securus iudicat orbis terrarum:* "Final is the judgment of the earthly orb," said St. Augustine (d. 430), who had earlier prayed: "Grant me chastity and continence, but not quite yet." There is also W. S. Gilbert's mighty plaint to the terrestrial orb, which ends:

It's true I've got no shirts to wear;
It's true my butcher's bill is due;
It's true my prospects all look blue—
But don't let that unsettle you!
Never you mind!
Roll on! (It rolls on.)

caput: head. There is much under this head. A root *ghebhel:* head, has also been suggested; but save for Gc *gable* and perhaps the Gk *cephalic* group, our English words seem to spring from L *caput, capitis:* head. Gk *kephale:* cephalic index; *hydrocephalus; microcephalous, brachycephalous, macrocephalous, megacephalous, mesocephalous.* The recently isolated *enkephaline. biceps, triceps;* for *forceps,* see *kap. Cephalonia* is an Ionian island west of Greece, with headlands.

Bucephalus (: ox-head) was the steed of Alexander the Great, son of Philip II of Macedon. *Alexander* means protector of men; the king is praised in the history books for his patience, "as at the siege of Tyre" (Gk *Tyros*); but it was there that his conquests almost ended. He was about to abandon the protracted siege and return to Greece when he dreamed he had captured a satyr (Gk *satyros*); in the morning the oneirocritics exclaimed *Sa Tyros!* Tyre is his! He led an assault that took the city, and marched on until he "wept" that there were no more worlds to conquer. He died in 323 B.C., after having founded Alexandria in Egypt and the Greek Pharaonic dynasty, of which the best known is Caesar's and Antony's Cleopatra, celebrated by Shakespeare and Shaw.

L, *capital, chattel, cattle* (used for exchange; still counted by the head). *captain, cadet; chief, chieftain; corporal,* Fr *caporal.* Fr, *capitain;* Gm *Hauptmann:* head man; Cossack ataman; Polish hetman. *capital punishment* (Off with his head!). Gc *beheading;* L *decapitation;* Gk *kephalotomy. capital letter; capital city. capitalism. capsize* (head first); *precipitate* (headlong). *precipice* (headland). *cape. cap;* hence, *to cap the climax. capstan.*

cape: a cloak with hood; especially the cape of St. Martin, a holy relic, guarded by the chaplain in the chapel (It *cappella;* there's no organ there; hence *a cappella:* from the chapel: singing without accompaniment). From the hoods worn by the Knights of the Garter, an attendant on the Queen became *chaperon.* OE *chapiter:* heading, then division of a book, *chapter;* then a meeting to read a chapter of the Bible; thence the *chapter of a fraternity.*

L *caput mortuum:* death's head, skull at the feast; *memento mori:* reminder of our common fate. It, *capo, capuche; capuchin.* Fr, *capote, caparison; caprice, capricious.* It *capriccio,* combining *head* and *riccio:* hedgehog, first meant hair standing on end, like porcupine bristles; then, influenced by *capra:* goat (see *kapr*), was used of a lively leaping step, or a sudden turn of mind, as with the unpredictably random randy goat.

occiput, occipital (L *ob:* back, opposed to the front part of the head, *sinciput, sin* being a variant of *semi:* half). *capillary:* first, of hair on the head; then, a hair-thin blood vessel. Fr *bechevet:* two-headed. *tête-à-tête;* Fr *tête* is from L *testa:* pot; first, slang for *head,* now the established French term. *cap-à-pie:* head to foot in fine fettle, was folkchanged to *apple-pie order. kerchief,* Fr *couvrechef; handkerchief:* a cloth held in the hand to cover the head, as when a woman enters a Catholic church; also put to other use. The first handkerchiefs in England were probably used by King Richard II, who reigned from 1377 (aged ten) to 1399: "little pieces of cloth given to the lord King for carrying in his hand to wipe and clean his nose." The poor boy must have been susceptible to colds—or unhappy.

The hood, a *cowl* (OE *cugele,* L *cucullus,* whence also *cucullated,* and the muscle *cucullaris:* cap-shaped) may be of Gaulish origin; it led Robert Browning into an odd blunder. At the end of *Pippa Passes,* he rhymes "owls and bats" with "cowls and twats." Browning had evidently read, in *Vanity of Vanities* (1660), the lines:

> They talkt of his having a Cardinall's hat;
> They'd send him as soon an old maid's twat.

and he assumed, as *cowl* was a man's hood, *twat* was a woman's. He had evidently not consulted Bailey's 1727 *Dictionary*, which defines *twat* as *pudendum mulieri. twat-scourer* was a scornful 17th c. term for a gynecologist. (We pronounce the mistaken word to rhyme with *what.*)

L *ad caput venire:* to come to a head, to end, became Fr *venir à chef,* the end of which made E *achieve.* Shakespeare in *Henry V* says, "Let them atchieve me, and then sell my bones." But the happy ending prevailed: again Shakespeare, *Twelfth Night:* "Some are born great, some achieve greatness . . ." Old English used *bonchief;* we retain the *mischief;* Shakespeare coined *mischievous.* Edward Gibbon, in *The Decline and Fall of the Roman Empire* (1776), said of Comnenus Andronicus: "In every deed of mischief he had a heart to resolve, a head to contrive, and a hand to execute." (The Comnenus family ruled the Eastern Roman Empire from 1057 to 1204, and were kings of Trebizond from 1204 to 1461. See Anna Comnena, under *porpur.*)

Fr, *camouflage,* via It *capo muffare:* muffle the head. Gc, OE *heafod:* head; *headlong, headstrong; heading, headline. heady.* Prefix *head,* as *headmaster. gable;* Goethe's *Über allen Gipfeln ist Ruh:* Over every mountaintop is peace.

In desperation, a man grasped by the cape might slip out of it and—as a follower of Jesus exemplified (Bible, Mark 14:51)—L *ex cappa,* Fr *échapper:* escape!

While we may speak of a person as "out of his mind," it is hard to escape from one's head. There may be more than accidental relation between Aram *kephas:* rock, and Gk *kephas:* head. When Jesus (Matthew 16) says to Simon Bar Jonah: "Thou art Peter, and on this rock I will build my church," he is establishing the Catholic Church with wordplay. The name and the rock are the same in Greek; Peter is petrified into St. Peter's at the Vatican. And the pun was in the original Aramaic: *Kephas* the man, *kephas* the rock. It holds also in French: *Pierre* the person, *pierre* the rock. *Bonehead* and *blockhead* are slang terms that carry on the association. *petrosal* is an anatomical term referring to the temporal bone around the inner ear.

From Gk *petros* came other English words: *petroglyph, petrology; saltpeter; parsley,* of the family *Petroselinum:* rock celery; and especially *petroleum:* oil from rock, with its offshoots *petrol* (Step on the gas!), *petrolatum, petrochemistry, petrodollar,* etc. Nor should we overlook that sentimental mime *Pierrot:* little Peter, prominent in commedia dell'arte, with Harlequin, Columbine (little dove) and Pantaleone; see Pan under *keu II.*

As Shakespeare observes in *Romeo and Juliet:* "Stony limits cannot keep love out." *rockabye baby. rock-and-roll.* "A noble man disdains to hide his head"—

Robert Greene, *Alphonsus* (1588). "Fine art is that in which the hand, the head, and the heart of man go together"—Ruskin, *The Two Paths.*

?char: idle chat; patter. Imitative. *charade. charlatan.* Ben Jonson, in *Volpone,* ii, 2, uses the Italian plural, *ciarlatani.*

coc: rooster's call. Imitative; see *kokila.* Fr *cocorico;* E *cock-a-doodle-doo,* etc. *cackle. clap, flap, plop, swat,* are also imitative; *flyflapper* has been superseded by *flyswatter.*

In the 19th c. *flapdoodle* (perhaps combining flapping wings and rooster crow) was coined to mean nonsense. Captain (Frederick) Marryat, in his *Peter Simple* (1833), records: "The gentleman has eaten no small quantity of flapdoodle in his lifetime." "What's that, O'Brien?" "Why, Peter, it's the stuff they feed fools on." In their *Dictionary of Slang* Barrère and Leland define *flapdoodlers* as "charlatan namby-pamby political speakers"—especially rife before election. Also the *doodler.*

?cruc: cross; move back and forth, as when making the sign of the cross. L, *cross, crucial, crucifix, crucify. excruciating.* Fr, *crusade. cruise:* sail to and fro; *cruiser.* See *ger III.*

cub, qeb: to be lying down. See also *gue.* L *incumbere, incumbentis, incubitum:* lie upon; apply oneself to. *cubicle; incubator. cubit, cubitus. incubus:* first, the male demon, lying on top; *succuba* (incorrectly but more frequently *succubus*): the female demon, lying beneath; the existence of these demonic lovers was recognized in medieval law, both ecclesiastical and civil. Fr, *covey, couvade. accumbent, decumbent; incumbency, incumbent; procumbent, recumbent, succumb.*

The *Encyclopaedia Britannica* of 1979 clarified: "The truth is the succubus is only a species of the nightmare"; yet in 1818 C. K. Sharpe in *The Law's Memorialls* said of Benedict of Berne: "For forty years, he had kept up an amatory commerce with a succubus, called Hermeline." *Incubus* is now used figuratively of any burden hard to remove; though recently a heroin addict is said to have "a monkey on his back."

cucu. Imitative of the bird's call. *cuckoo.* A song of 1250:

> Sumer is icumen in,
> Lhude sing cuccu! . . .
> Sing cuccu, nu, sing cuccu,
> Sing cuccu, sing cuccu, nu!

Thomas Nashe has a refrain: "Cuckoo, jug-jug, pu-we, to-witta-woo." A couplet by Wordsworth has suffered a cruel addition, as for a test:

> O cuckoo! Shall I call thee bird,
> Or but a wandering voice?
> State the alternative preferred,
> With reasons for your choice.

cuculiform. cuckoopint; from *cuckoo pintle:* penis, from the shape of the spadix. *OED* lists 28 and details 10 combinations, as *cuckoo-buds, cuckoo clock.* The repetitive cuckoo call was annoying (*Merchant of Venice:* "He knows me as the blind man knows the cuckoo, by the bad voice"), then was deemed foolish, whence the slang *cuckoo:* foolish, "off one's trolley."

The cuckoo lays her eggs in the nests of other birds, who hatch and feed the nestling; the Fool found a figure in this to picture Lear's fate (i, 4, 235): "The hedge-sparrow fed the cuckoo so long that it had it head bit off by it young." Hence, the *cuckold:* a husband unaware of his wife's digression. In Old French, *coucou, cucu,* meant both the bird and the husband; today the bird is *coucou;* the unfortunate but frequent man, *cocu.* Hence *cuckoldize,* etc. The spring song at the end of *Love's Labor's Lost* has the refrain:

Cuckoo, cuckoo! Oh, word of fear,
Unpleasing to a married ear.

The cuckold appears in Chaucer, *The Miller's Prologue;* in Spenser's *The Faerie Queene,* iii; 40 times in Shakespeare, 8 of them in *The Merry Wives;* in Burns, *Oh Willie;* and in Emerson's essay *The Over-Soul.* Fielding's *Tom Jones* refers to "gentlemen who profess the art of cuckold-making." Cuckolds' Point was a lovers' rendezvous along the Thames near Greenwich. See *ueid.*

?cura, coir: care. L, *cure, curative; curator,* short for *procurator:* overseer, caretaker. Hence also *procure, procuress, procuration, procuratory,* and the shorter forms *proctor* and *proxy.*

curious: first, taking care, "of curious workmanship"; *curiosity. curette, curettage. curate; sinecure:* first, benefice without cure (care) of souls, as of a priest not assigned to a parish. *incurable:* no care can help. *procure; secure. accurate. manicure, pedicure.* L *excurare;* E *scour.* It *pococurante:* devil-may-care. Gm *Kursaal:* main room at a health resort. Thus also Fr *salle,* as in *salle à manger:* dining room. Fr, *sure, surety, ensure, insurance.* Gc, *care, careful, carelessness,* etc.

To the Trojan proposal to give Helen back to the Greeks (*Troilus and Cressida,* ii, 2), Hector, warning his fellow Trojans against overconfidence, exclaims:

The wound of peace is surety,
Surety secure.

da I. Baby talk; imitative. The first two sounds an infant makes seem to be *ma* and *pa,* intake and output. Shortly thereafter come *da, dad, daddy,* the first inkling that thought's being added to feeling. Hence *da-da,* the artistic movement in the second half of the 19th c.

While *da I* may suffice for English terms, the more inclusive root is *tara,* which see. See also *amma; ma II; pa.*

da II: divide. Gk *daimon:* divider of destiny. *daimon, demon;* see *esu. demoniacal; demiurge; eudemonic; pandemonium. geodesy. demos:* first, district, then its inhabitants; *deme, democracy,* and all the *democrats. demagogue:* (mis)leader of the people.

The Federal(ist) Party with Madison led the fight for the adoption of the U.S. Constitution, then was powerful with Washington and Hamilton. The Democratic-Republican Party was organized in 1792 by Jefferson; in 1828, under

Andrew Jackson, it split. The Republican Party was reorganized in 1854, to oppose slavery. *republican* is from L *res publica:* public concern; L *populus,* which may be from Etruscan; hence, *populace, population, depopulate, repopulate; public, publicity; people;* Sp, *pueblo.* The ending of *democracy* is from Gk *khratos:* rule. Hence also *aristocracy, autocracy, ochlocracy;* JWalker lists 32 relevant words, as *bureaucracy, gerontocracy.* It appears also in names, as *Socrates:* ?ruler by wisdom; *Hippocrates:* ?controller of horses–from whom *hippocras:* mixed wine and spices, once used as a medicine, filtered through Hippocrates' bag or sleeve: a coneshaped sieve; and the *Hippocratic oath,* still taken by persons beginning the practice of medicine.

L *damnare, damnatum. damn, damnation.*

There's a great text in Galatians
Once you trip on it, entails
Twenty-nine distinct damnations,
One sure, if another fails.
—Browning, *Soliloquy in a Spanish Cloister* [The text is Galatians 5:19–21.]

damage; indemnify. condemn. Gc, *time,* also *tide,* which wait for no man, and divide our days. *tidings. eventide, summertide, Yuletide* (wherein *tide* means time). *deal,* as in cards. *dole. fardel:* a fourth part. *ordeal.*

Sir Thomas Browne, in *Religio Medici* (1643), wondered: "Who can speak of eternity without a solecism, or think thereof without an ecstasy? Time we may comprehend; 'tis but five days elder than ourselves." (*solecism:* a substandard use, is from *Soloi,* an Athenian colony in Cilicia, which spoke a scorned dialect. For *ecstasy,* see *sta.*)

Browning, in *A Grammarian's Funeral,* is emphatic:

What's time? Leave Now for dogs and apes!
Man has forever.

dakru: weeping. Skr *acru.* Gk *dakru(on), dakruma. dakruotimon:* honored with tears. OL *dacruma;* L *lacrima.* Gc *tagr;* E *tear.* "The soul would have no rainbow had the eye no tears."

There are 15 entries in *OED,* from *lachrymable* to *lachrymous,* including *Lachrymae Christi* (tears of Christ): a strong sweet red Italian wine. *lachrymatory:* a small vase for holding tears; that of the emperor Nero has been preserved. *OED*'s Supplement II adds *lachrymator:* tear gas; and *lachrymogenic:* inducing tears, as onions and sob-sister movies. The supplement notes that the "etymologically correct form" *lacrimal* is now frequent in scientific use. The *y* crept in from the cognate Greek *dakru,* Greek upsilon being regularly rendered as English *y.* The *ch* was introduced in medieval L before an *r,* as in *anchor, sepulchre, pulchritude, Christ.*

sunt lacrimae rerum
[the sense of tears in mortal things]
—Virgil, *The Aeneid,* i

dam: tame, overcome. Gk, *adamant:* untamed, *a* negative; hence *diamond,* the significant *a* dropped, as also *adown:* off the hill (*down:* hill) became *down.* The *i* in *diamond* was influenced by Gk *diaphanes:* showing through, transparent.

L *dominate, predominate, indomitable* (see *dem*). Fr, *daunt.* Gc, *tame.*

When Eve upon the first of men
The apple pressed with specious cant,
Oh! what a thousand pities then
That Adam was not adamant.
—Thomas Hood, *A Reflection* (1827)

dau: burn, torment. L *duellum, bellum. bellicose. belligerent. duel. rebel. revel:* first, to rebel, raise a tumult; then softened to having a high old time.

There was a sound of revelry by night,
And Belgium's capital had gathered then
Her beauty and her chivalry, and bright
The lamps shone o'er fair women and brave men . . .
And all went merry as a marriage-bell—
But hush! hark! a deep sound strikes like a rising knell!
—Byron, *Childe Harold*

de, do: Prepositional root, meaning to or from. L, *de, dem:* down. *defer:* first, to lower. *deteriorate. idem. tandem:* first, right to the moment; then, at length; then applied, at first jocosely, to mean lengthwise, one behind the other, as horses thus harnessed. For more than two in this order, Americans speak of "Indian file," as the autochthonous Americans moved one after the other on forest trails.

Gc, *to, too, onto. toward; untoward.* Du *tattoo* (partly imitative): drumbeat; first, at closing time; earlier *taptoe:* putting the taps "to" (shutting them) when it was time to close the taverns.

dei: clear; the bright sun; the clear sky; hence, the abode of the gods; god. Skr *Dyaus:* god of the sky and weather. *Dyauspitar:* heavenly father; with mother earth. Hence Gk, *Zeus* (genitive *Dios*), his consort *Dione* (also a name of their daughter *Aphrodite*). Probably *Dionysus:* god first of fertility, then of wine and revelry, as in the festivals the Dionysia. *Dionysiac;* the names *Dionysius, Dion, Denis.* Hence, too, *Diana:* goddess of the moon. *Janus Dianus:* two-headed god of gates; see *ei. Dioscuri:* sons of Zeus; see *ker VI.* Also (via *Zeus-peter*) L *Jupiter; Jovis, Jove;* whence *jovial. Julius;* from Julius Caesar, *July. Julian, julienne; Jules. Juno,* earlier *Divona,* queen of the Roman gods. OHG *Zio,* ONorse *Tyr,* OE *Tiu;* Teutonic god of war, as Roman Mars; hence E *Tuesday,* Fr *Mardi. Mardi gras:* literally, Fat Tuesday: a day of festivity before Ash Wednesday and the restrained mood of Lent, celebrated especially in France and in New Orleans, Louisiana. *Lent* is via Gc *langan-tin,* OE *lengten:* long days. The sprinkling of ashes, or daubing them on the forehead, was initiated by Gregory the Great, pope from 590 to 604.

Other terms from Skr: *devangari:* divine script; the Sanskrit alphabet. *Devi:* goddess; especially Sati, wife of Shiva, who, when she felt humiliated by the god Shiva—who had killed her father—cremated herself and was reborn as Parvati, wife of Shiva, thus giving hope to all believing women, who followed her practice of *sati* or *suttee:* immolation on the late husband's funeral pyre, a persisting practice. *devadasi:* maidservant of the god: temple dancer, formerly used for religious prostitution. *Dewali:* Hindu holy fall festival.

Various names of persons and things: *Dorothea, Dorothy, Theodore:* gift of God (see *do*). *deodar:* divine tree, the sacred cedar. *Diosma:* "divine odor," the rue. *Dionaea:* genus, the sundew family. *Diomedes:* advised by Zeus.

From the meaning "the sky," was coined the word *eudiometer:* first, to measure the "good weather"; then, any gas (see *esu*). From the sense of "clear," "bright," came the recent *psychedelic:* relating to things seen by the "psyche." And a number of scientific terms with *a* negative, hence unseen: *Adelia,* genus of the olive family with tiny flowers. *adelite:* an opaque mineral. *adelocodonic; adelomorphous; adelopod.*

The names *Adelaide; Adeline,* shortened to *Aline, Lina; Adella, Della; Adolph; Alice* (Gc *Adalhald*); *Athelstan,* are from Gc *adal:* noble.

Related to *Dionysus* is *dionise:* a precious stone, black veined with red, a medieval "preservative" against drunkenness.

The Romans had two forms for god: *deus,* and *divus,* adjective *divinus.* From the former came Fr *dieu,* E *adieu,* the pious *prie-dieu* and the irreverent *Pardie!* Also *deicide, deify, deism. deity* was coined by St. Augustine after LL *deitas,* Gk *deotes.* (Note *deicer:* that which removes, or prevents, formation of ice, as on windows of automobiles and airplanes.) A *deodand* was a thing that had caused the death of a person, therefore was forfeited, "to be given to God," used for a pious purpose. A *joss:* an idol, in Far Eastern Pidgin English, from Port *deos.* From the latter, *divine, divinity* ("that shapes our ends"); *divination,* and *the divining rod.*

The sunshine brings the day, L *dies. Dies irae:* first words of a 13th c. hymn, "Day of Wrath." *dies non:* legal holiday, no business. *diurnal. diuturnal, diuturnity:* partway to eternity. *journal, journalism, journey:* first, a day's trip, a day's work; *journeyman:* one that works by the day. *dial, diary; diet:* assembly. *sojourn; adjourn* (*sine die:* without specifying a day for the next meeting). *circadian:* in a rhythm of about 24 hours. *quotidian, meridian. antemeridian, postmeridian:* A.M. and P.M., which make up the day. *pridian. dismal:* "bad day"—two a month.

O Henry, in *Options* (1909), remarks: "The reception they were going to put up would make the Mardi Gras in New Orleans look like an afternoon tea in Bury St. Edmunds with a curate's aunt." See *ker III; prai.*

deik: show, utter, and consequences thereof. Gk, *deictic, apodeictic:* clearly shown. *paradigm.* Perhaps *policy,* but see *pele.* Gk *dike:* justice ("shown to be done"). *syndic:* a judge in ancient Greece; then (*syn:* together, with) a council; a group with a common purpose; hence *syndicate, syndication. theodicy:* justifying an all-good all-powerful god in a world of evil.

The world had a pleasant beginning
Until Adam spoiled it by sinning;
  We hope that the story
  Will end in God's glory,
But so far the other side's winning.

Gk *dikein:* show forth; throw. *disc, disk, discus, dish, desk, dais.* L, *benediction, malediction. Maledicta:* Society for the Study of Aggressive Language. *edict; judicate, judicial, judge; jurisdiction;* see *ieuos. prejudice. diction, interdiction; dictionary. dictum.* Via It, *ditto, ditty. condition. dictate, dictator; abdicate, dedication, indicate; index. valedictory. vindicate; vindictive. verdict, veridical, indict.* Fr, *indite; avenge, revenge.* L, *digit* (a finger's a pointer); *dital, hallux. digitalis,* after Gm *Fingerhut:* thimble, shape of the foxglove, from which the medicine is extracted. *prestidigitator.* L *praedicare:* proclaim. *predict, predicate;* via Fr, *preach.* Gc, *teach, toe, take; token, betoken.*

"Dictionaries are like watches, the worst is better than none; and the best cannot be expected to go quite true," said the compiler of the first outstanding English dictionary, Samuel Johnson; his remark remains true of dictionaries, if not of watches. In Thackeray's *Vanity Fair,* Miss Pinkerton gives a copy of

Johnson's *Dictionary* to every scholar leaving her academy; Becky Sharp tossed hers into the garden as her coach drove away. Lewis Carroll, in *Four Riddles,* protests and proposes:

Yet what are all such qualities to me
Whose thoughts are full of indices and surds?

$$x^2 + 7x + 53$$
$$= 11/3$$

dek I: take, accept; hence, seemly; take in, hence learn. Hindi, *diksha:* initiation before being accepted. Gk *doxa:* opinion, *dogma, dogmatic; docoglossus; diplodocus; adiadochokinesis. diadoche. pandect. synecdoche. doxaster, doxographer; doxology. paradox.* Bishop William Warburton in 1750 stated: "Orthodoxy is my doxy; heterodoxy is another man's doxy." Carlyle called these *mydoxy* and *thydoxy.* Perhaps because women are capable of taking in men, came the Elizabethan use—with which the bishop was in all likelihood familiar: "Doxies, i.e. she-beggars, trulls, wenches, whores, being neither maids, wives, nor widows, will for good victuals, or a very small piece of money, prostitute their bodies, protesting that they never did so before, and that sheer necessity drove them to it—though they are common hackneys." They bargain, often with lewd proposals and provocations, "till at length few words are best, the bargain's made, and the pox is cheaply purchased at the price of a guinea." (Swift, by the way, advised greeting one's enemies not with the words *Pax Vobiscum:* Peace be with you, but, with the same pronunciation, *Pox Vobiscum.*) *hackney* and *hack* may be named for Hackney, a town in Middlesex, England, that trained horses anyone might ride; if so, it was borrowed in OFr as *haquenée,* Sp *haca:* nag, an ambling horse for ladies; if these be the source, then the town is folk etymology.

L *decent; docile; decorate. decorous; indecorous. Dulce et decorum est pro patria mori:* Sweet and fitting it is to die for one's country—Horace (d. 8 B.C.), *Odes.*

Wilfred Owen protested:

My friend, you would not tell with such high zest
To children ardent for some desperate glory,
That old lie: dulce et decorum est
Pro patria mori.

Owen should ponder the last words of Nathan Hale. And look around: world brotherhood remains a beautiful dream.

L, *doctrinaire, indoctrinate. deign; disdain; dignify, dignity, indignity; indignant; condign. Infra dig. didactic. disciple, discipline. docent; doctor, doctorate. doctrine, document,* etc. Fr, *dainty;* first, fastidious in taking.

Sun worshipers, at morning prayer in thanks for rebirth of light, had south on the *dexter,* right-hand side; hence, *dext(e)rous.* Opposed is the *sinister,* left-hand side. *sinistrorse:* turning to the left, anticlockwise. The French word for *left, gauche,* also means clumsy in both French and English. L, *dexterity; ambidexterous:* as though with two right hands. *dextral; dextrine:* turns the plane of polarization of light to the right, as also *dextrose, dextrorse; dextrorotation:* clockwise. *OED* lists 11 and details 20 words beginning *dextr.* Its 1972 supplement adds six relevant words, including *dex(tro)amphetamine,* also called *Dexedrine* and "pep pill." *dextrocardiac:* one whose heart is—literally—on the right side; not yet applied figuratively.

Opposed to orthodox dogma is, of course, the heretic, whose heresy consists in exercising individual choice (Gk *hairein:* choose) instead of conforming to the officially accepted creed. It was on this ground that Joan of Arc was burned. Gk *orthos:* straight, right, is a frequent English prefix, as in *orthodontics, orthography. orthopterans* (May they avoid your house!); *orthognathous; orthoptic.* Gk *heteros* (IE *sm-tero;* see *sem*): one of two, other, different, forms a frequent opposing prefix, as *heterochromatic, heterochromosome, heterodyne. heterogeneous* (vs. *homogeneous*), *heterogenesis.* "In no country perhaps in the world is the law so general a study. . . . This study renders men acute, inquisitive, dexterous, prompt in attack, ready in defence, full of resources. . . . They augur misgovernment at a distance, and snuff the approach of tyranny in every tainted breeze"—Edmund Burke, speech on Conciliation with America, 22 Mar. 1775, long used as a model of argumentation in writing classes.

dek II: hair, fringe; plug. Sp, *taco,* from the shape. Via Fr, *shako; tache, tack.* The source of *hardtack* is unknown; possibly at first figurative: "hard as tacks to chew." Gc *taegl; tail; tag;* first, differently shaped or colored tip of a tail, then an attached label; then used more generally and figuratively. The *tag* that names a game is a variant of *tig* and *tick,* imitative of a light touch. Similarly *tick-tack-toe* begins with the sound of the stylus striking the slate; the *toe* is perhaps short for *total.* The *tick-tock* of a clock is of course also imitative.

dekm: ten. L *decem. decade, decagon, decagram, dodecahedron. decimal. decimate. decennial, decenary. doyen, dean, decemvir. December:* tenth month when the year began with March. *dime. Septuagint* (L *ginta:* ten times); earliest translation of the Old Testament into Greek, arranged by Ptolemy II Philadelphus of Egypt (d. 246 B.C.), who according to legend had Eleazar, High Priest of Jerusalem, send 70 Jews (more correctly, 72, six from each of the twelve tribes of Israel) to the island of Pharos, where in separate cells for 70 days they produced identical translations! In the above names, by the way, *El* is Hebrew for *god;* it also appears in *Elijah, Elisha, Gabriel, Raphael,* etc., and Arab *Allah* (*al-ilah:* the high god). *Beelzebub:* "god of flies," in Milton's *Paradise Lost* is made a fallen angel, hence a devil. Thus also *Baal,* chief Phoenician male deity; his consort in the Septuagint is *Astarte,* Hebr *Astoreth,* assimilated to Gk *Aphrodite. Jerusalem,* Hebr *Yerushalaim,* was translated into Greek as *Hierosoluma:* (city of) Holy Peace. Hebr *Shalom* and Arab *salaam,* both meaning peace, are from Sem *aslama:* submit (to God); whence also *Islam, Moslem, Muslim; Islamabad:* capital of Pakistan, etc. See *eis.* "Jerusalem letters" were tattooed on pilgrims as a token of their visit to the holy city. See *nebh.*

Gc, *ten, tenth. thirteen:* three and ten, and so through the teens. *twenty:* two tens; *thirty;* three, etc. For *center,* see *kent.* The word for ten tens took various forms. Skr *satam,* E *satem.* Some philologists distinguish such Indo-European satem languages as Iranian, Armenian, Balto-Slavic, in which the *k* sound becomes *s* or *sh,* from the centum group, which kept the guttural *k.* Gk *hekaton; hecatomb* (*hekaton, bous*): sacrifice of a hundred oxen. *hectare, hectograph, hectometer,* etc. L and E *centum. cent, percent; centenary, centennial. centime, centavo; centesimal. centigrade. centillion.*

A *cento,* a poem made from lines of other poems, is from the root *kenth:* rag; the Jester's song in Gilbert's *The Yeomen of the Guard*—"A wand'ring minstrel I, a thing of rags and patches"—refers to both attire and repertoire. The monster *centaur* is from the name of a savage tribe in Thessaly; the creature has the head, arms, and trunk of a man, the body and legs of a horse. (When the South American Indians first saw a mounted European, they thought the figure was all one white god.)

The *cornflower,* used as medicine by the centaur Chiron, a healer, is also called *centaury.* Two genera of plants are *Centaurea* and *Centaurium.* There is a constellation *Centaurus.* The *bucentaur,* so called from the boat's figurehead, was the State Barge of Venice, from which on Ascension Day the doge dropped a ring into the Adriatic to marry the city and the sea. *Bucephalus* (ox-headed) was the warhorse of Alexander the Great; when Alexander expressed dissatisfaction with his portrait by Apelles, Bucephalus whinnied at the horse in the picture; Apelles said, "Your horse knows better."

Gc, *hundred, hundredfold, hundredth.* For the ten animals Muslim legend says were admitted to paradise, see *ane.*

del I: trick; recount. Gk *dole* (guile). *dolerite;* its components puzzled the scientists. *sedulous* (*se:* apart, without: no trickery). *subdolous.* Gc, *tale, talk, tell, told; till, until.*

They went and told the sexton and
The sexton tolled the bell.
—Thomas Hood, *Faithless Nelly Brown* (1839)

del II: cut; carve; harm. Gk *daidalos:* cut with art; *Daedalus,* the inventor who built the labyrinth for Minos, king of Crete, to confine the Minotaur. This monster—half man, half bull—was conceived by Minos's wife Pasiphae with Poseidon's sacred bull, which Minos had refused to return to Poseidon. Imprisoned, Daedalus made wings for himself and his son Icarus; they flew away; but the son flew too near the sun, the wax fastening his wings melted, and he fell and drowned in what was thereafter called the Icarian Sea. Hence *daedalian:* skilful; *Icarian:* rash and ruinous. "Expectations are oft exalted on Icarian wings, and fall"—Shelley. The French communist Etienne Cabet wrote of an ideal republic, Icaria (*Voyage en Icarie* [1840]), and established communistic settlements with that name at Mauvoo, Illinois, and elsewhere in the U.S.; they all failed.

L *dolere:* suffer. *dolorous; doleful; dole; condolence, indolent.* Gc *tilt, tiller.*

del III, dlong: long. *longevity. longitude. along; belong; oblong; prolong. purloin:* first, delay. *Longobardus:* Lombard, lumber (see *bhar*). Gc, *long, length; Lent* (as days grow longer). *linger.*

dem: house, household. Gk *dems-pot; despot* (ruler of the house; see *pot*). L *dominus:* master, hence the Lord. *dominie. dominical. domicile; domain. dominate, domineer, dominion;* see *dam. condominium. major-domo. domestic, domesticated. dome. predominant.* It, *domino:* first, a cleric's hooded cape; then a cape worn at a masquerade; hence, a mask; finally, a counter in a game, the first to use all his pieces being the master. The irrepressible Rabelais, when ill, asked to be wrapped in his *domino* (cape) because *Beati qui in Domino moriuntur:* Blessed are they that die in the Lord.

It, *don, donna, madonna; belladonna.* Fr, *dame, madam(e); demoiselle, mademoiselle; damsel. donjon* (keep); *dungeon; danger* (in the master's power). Sp, *duenna.* Gc, *dam, beldam, grandam. tame; timber; toft. Dan,* an honorary, sometimes humorous, title: *Dan Cupid.* "Dan Chaucer, well of English undefiled"—Spenser, *The Faerie Queene,* iv.

none would be heard
Or writ so oft in all the world as those,—
Dan Chaucer, mighty Shakespeare, then for third
The classic Milton, and to us arose
Shelley, with liquid music in the word.
—Robert Bridges, *The Growth of Love*

St. Dominic in 1215 founded the Dominican Order (L *Dominicanes*): most noted member, Thomas Aquinas; most notorious, Torquemada. As directors of the Inquisition the *Dominicanes* were nicknamed *Domini canes:* hounds of the Lord. (For *canine,* see *kuon.*) Perhaps from this, Francis Thompson drew the figure for his best-known poem, *The Hound of Heaven* (1893), which pictures Jesus pursuing the man tempted to sin. From their appropriate attire, the Dominicans are also known as the Black Friars; the Carmelites are the White Friars; the Franciscans, the Gray Friars.

den(k): bite. Gk *odon, odontis:* tooth. *odontology; OED* lists 19 and details 17 relevant words beginning *odont. acrodont; periodontal; prosthodontics. mastodon.* L *dens, dentis. dental, dentist, dentifrice, dentine; edentate. Edentata:* order of mammals with no front teeth, as the ant-eater, armadillo, sloth. *dentil; denture. indent. indenture:* first a deed between two parties, as for apprenticeship or service in the colonies: two copies written on one sheet, then torn or cut in a serrated line, for future matching and identification—as early as 1300. Hence, a zigzag line, as in *Purchas' Pilgrimage* (1614): "Their crisses or daggers are two foot long, waved indenture fashion, and poysoned." *indenture language:* early officialese, bureaucrap; Ascham, in *The Scholemaster* (1568), advised: "Take Halles *Cronicle,* where much good matter is quite harmed with indenture English, and first change strange and inkhorn terms into proper and commonly used English." *indentwise;* an early use of this recently vogue suffix; see *ueid.*

Fr *dandelion:* lion's tooth; see *leo.* Gc, *tooth, tusk. tongs. tang. zinc,* which becomes jagged when heated.

"You cannot forget if you would those golden kisses all over the cheeks of the meadow, queerly called dandelions"—Henry Ward Beecher (d. 1887), *Star Papers.*

dens: thick; flat. L, *dense, density. condense.* Gk, *dasy,* as in *dasymeter. dasyure:* thick-tailed. Plant genera, *Dasylirion,* of the lily family; *Dasystephana:* of the gentians. *dasypus:* the armadillo.

deph: stamp; thing stamped or prepared. Gk *diphthera:* hide prepared for writing. *diphtheria,* from the false membrane.

L, probably via Etr, *littera. literal, literary, literature, littérateur. illiteracy,* and the too many *illiterate. alliteration, transliteration; obliterate.* Fr, *belles-lettres.* Few know the first line of the couplet from Charles Churchill's *The Prophecy of Famine* (1763), of writers

Who often, without success, have prayed
For apt alliteration's artful aid.

literocrat, literocracy, coined in 1946 (in *China,* ed. H. F. MacNair, United Nations series) by Chi Chen Wang to describe person and system in China, beginning at least as far back as 500 B.C., of selecting government officials by examinations in the classics. In the early days only priests and aristocrats read and wrote, but by the time of Confucius (d. 479 B.C.), commoners had caught the literacy fever, and competition for government posts became increasingly keen, lasting, through dynastic changes, until 1905. In an 1842 letter to Auguste Comte, J. S. Mill, for the same system, used the less attractive term *pedantocracy;* see *pou.*

litter might at times seem an appropriate term for what is called *literature,* but was first a bed; see *legh;* then, and still, a carried couch; its use for odds and ends, rubbish, is an extension from the straw once used for bedding, as pictured by Swift (1730) when Strephon ventures into Chloe's dressing room:

Strephon took a swift survey
Of all the litter as it lay . . .

View them litter'd on the floor,
Or strung on pegs behind the door.
[*The rest grows odoriferous.*]

For arguments for and against literacy, see my *Dictionary of World Literary Terms* (1970).

der: peel, rip off, flay. Gk and E *derma:* skin. *dermatitis. Dermaptera:* order of insects, the earwigs. *OED* lists 31 words beginning *dermat(o),* as *dermatology,* and 29 beginning *dermo.* JWalker lists ten words ending *derm,* as *malacoderm:* soft skinned; *echinoderm:* prickly; *pachyderm:* thick. *epidermis. xerodermy* (Gk *xeros:* dry). *taxidermy* (Gk *taxis:* arrangement).

L, *drab:* harlot; *drabbing:* whoring, as in *Hamlet,* ii, 1. Gc, *drape:* first, piece torn off. *drab:* cloth. *traps, trappings:* clothes. *tear; darn. tetter, tart. turd* (dropped off).

derbh: roll; compress. L, *turbary.* Gc, *topsy-turvy. turf.*

d(e)re: do. Gk *drama, dramatize; dramaturgy* (first in Lessing's *Hamburgische Dramaturgie* [1767]). *drastic.*

derk: look at. Hindi, *darshana:* school of Hindu philosophy. Gk *drakon:* with the evil eye. *dragon; tarragon; estragon.* The Athenian Draco in 621 B.C. drew up a severe civil code; hence, *Draconian.* L, *Draconic, dragonet, dragoon.* Draco is a constellation between Ursa Major and Ursa Minor. There are three plant genera: *Dracaena,* lily family; *Dracocephalum:* dragonhead, from the form of the corolla; *Dracontium:* dragonwort. L *dracunculus:* writhing—like the twenty-foot dragon (paper, with persons under) of Chinese festivals. *rankle.*

deru: solid; hence wood and associated ideas, as lasting, holding firm. Skr, *deodar. germander;* see *ghdhem.* Gk *dendron:* tree. *dendrite, dendroid; dendrochronology:* calculating dates by tree rings. *philodendron. rhododendron. OED* lists 13 *dendr(o)* words, as *dendroheliophallic,* and details 13, from *dendral* to *dendrology. druid. drupe. dryad, hamadryad.*

L, *durable, durance* (vile); *duration; during. duress. dour. dura mater. duramen. endure, perdurable; indurate; obdurate.* Gc, *tree. tar:* first, from the tree. *trough:* wooden, holds securely; *tray. trig, trim.*

true: it holds fast. "The truth shall make you free."—Bible, John 8. *trust, trusty; truce; trow, tryst.* Mark Twain, in *Puddinhead Wilson's Calendar,* warned: "Truth is the most valuable thing in the world. Let us economize it." Oliver Wendell Holmes, in his "logical story" of the one-hoss shay, pauses to press a point:

In fact, there's nothing that keeps its youth,
So far as I know, but a tree and truth.
(This is a moral that runs at large;
Take it—You're welcome. No extra charge.)

Schopenhauer contrariwise observed: "Truth is allowed only a brief interval of victory between the two long periods when it is condemned as paradox or belittled as trivial."

deu: perform, be able, work well; hence, win respect; revere. Gk, *dynamo, dynamometer; dynamic, thermodynamics. dynasty. dynamite,* named in 1876 by Alfred B. Nobel; with the money it earned him he established the Nobel Prizes, in 1896. *dyne; aerodyne; neutrodyne.* For *anodyne,* see *ed.*

L *beare, beatum:* bless. *beatific, beatify, beatitude. beatification* is the Catholic stage prior to canonization, sainthood. *Beatrice,* who inspired Dante. L *bellus:* fine. *belvedere, clarabella.* Via It, *bella-donna:* fair lady; also a poisonous plant, *Atropa bella,* the juice of which was used to dilate the pupil of the eye. (*pupil* because of the tiny image—L *pupillus,* feminine *pupilla,* diminutive of *pupus:* boy, *pupa:* girl—reflected therein.) Via Fr, *embellish. belle;* masculine, *beau. beauty. beau geste:* an act without profit, purely for the graciousness of the gesture. Hence the use of *beau* in Fr to mean in vain: *Vous l'avez beau dit*—well said, but of no use.

L (*duonus*) *bonus:* good. *bonus, magnum bonum. bounty; Lady Bountiful,* a "comic" cartoon figure become a general term. *bonafide:* in good faith. Fr, *bonbon, bonne bouche; debon(n)aire. embonpoint. bonne, bonhomie.* Celt, *bonny, boon.* Sp, *bonito. bonanza* rose from a misunderstanding; L *malacia:* calm at sea, from Gk *malakhia:* softness, was taken to be from L *malus:* bad, and hence was countered by the use of *bonus:* good, *bene:* well.

The prefixes *mal* and *bene* form contrasting pairs, as *benediction, malediction;* also thus paired are *benefactor, benevolent, benign.* Johnson's *Dictionary* (1755) said of *benison:* "not now used unless ludicrously"; *OED* calls it "poetic or quaint" for *benediction;* it survives in church usage; but *malison* dropped out by the end of the 19th c. *beneficence* remains; *maleficence,* along with *malefic* and 9 other forms in *OED* (*maleficiate:* to bewitch, especially, to deprive of potency; occasional male impotence "was generally ascribed to maleficiation"; Urquhart, translating Rabelais [1692], spoke of "drugs which make the taker cold, maleficiated"), is no longer used. Burke in *Reflections on the French Revolution* (1790), remarked that the "law itself is only beneficence acting by a rule."

In such words unpaired, nonetheless, the evil exceeds the good: *benefice, beneficial, beneficiary, benefit;* but *malefic, malentendu, malfeasance, malicious, malinger, malism, malodorous, malpractice, maltreat,* and *malaise, maladjusted, malady.* Some have said that the world is a Lewis Carroll nightmare, with Malice in Blunderland.

It is possible that the first element in *benzoin,* from Arab *luban jawi:* frankincense of Java (the *lu* dropped as though an article, Fr *le:* the), was folkchanged by the influence of *bene:* good. *OED* lists 24 and details 7 related words, as *benzene, benzoline;* its 1972 supplement lists 3 more, as *benzocaine,* and details 4 more, as *benzedrine.*

The liqueur *benedictine* was made by monks of the Benedictine Order, founded about 529; in 1980 the British Museum gave an exhibition celebrating the 1500th anniversary of the birth of St. Benedict and the influence of his Order on English life and art.

From *bene* also *benison; beneficence. benedict:* literally, well-spoken; the sense, a bachelor married in spite of himself, is from the character Benedick in Shakespeare's *Much Ado About Nothing. Boniface,* used of a pleasant innkeeper, is from the character Will Boniface in Farquhar's play *The Beaux' Stratagem* (1707). The Beaufort scale of wind velocity, devised by Sir Francis Beaufort in 1805, is an accidental aptronymic: the scale ranges from calm to hurricane, and *beau* means fair, *fort* means powerful.

'Tis not a lip or eye, we beauty call,
But the joint force and full result of all.
—Pope, *Essay in Criticism*

deuk: lead. L *ducere, ductum. ducal, duke, duchess, duchy, ducat, dock, duct, ductile; aqueduct, viaduct. conducive, conduct; nonconductor; conduit. abduct. adduce; deduct, deduce; educe, education; subdue, traduce, traduction. redoubt:* outwork, place of retreat; the *b* was inserted by association with *redoubt:* to dread, from L *dubitare;* see *duo.*

It, *condottiere*. Fr, *douche*. Gc, *tug*. *wanton* (lacking leadership; see *eu*). *taut; team, teem; tie; tow.*

The East Indian R. Manikin was quoted in *The Observer* of 30 Mar. 1947: "If you educate a man you educate a person, but if you educate a woman you educate a family." Note that *education* means "leading out" not "pouring in"; aiding toward self-expression, toward realization of potentiality.

dhabh: fit together. L *faber*. *fabricate; fabric. fable* (? see *bha I*). Fr, *forge, forgery*. Gc, *daft:* first, suited, gentle; then meek, then stupid. *deft*. The Chorus, in *Henry V*, v, speaks of "the quick forge and working-house of thought."

dhal: to bloom. Gk *thallos:* green shoot. *Thallophyte; thallus, prothallus. Thalia*, the blooming lass, one of the three Graces; see *esu; gel I*. Ir, *dulse*.

thallium (see *el 81*), named for the green line in its spectrum; hence *thallous* for compounds of valence 1; *thallic* for those of valence 3.

dhar: hold. Skr, *dharma:* justice; see *ker I. dharmas(h)astra:* book of laws. *dharmasala:* resting place, as at a shrine. *dharma:* fasting at a debtor's door, one way of inducing payment. Darius (OPers *Darayavahush*): he that holds to the good. A number of words for native "holders" in British India end with *dar*, as *aumildar* (holder of records), *tahsildar* (district collector), *defterdar* (chief revenue man), *bahadar* (tax-free landholder), *jagheedar* (person on annuity), *zemindar* (landholder), *talukdar* (estate owner), *dizdar* (castle warden), *subahdar* (province governor), *silladar* (weapon-holder, cavalry man), *ressaldar* (cavalry commander) and its doublet *sirdar* (commander), *jhavildar* (squad-holder, sergeant), *jemadar* (troop-holder, lieutenant), *killadar* (fort commander); also *thanadar* (chief of police), *foujdar* (judge in criminal court). *chobdar* ("stick-holder," servant), *chokdar* (porter).

Gk, *thorax; mesothorax. therapeutic. hydrotherapy*, etc. *throne*. L *firmus. firm, firmament. affirm, affirmative; confirm; infirm, infirmary. frenum. refrain*. Gc, *farm, farmer:* landholder.

> From his brimstone bed at break of day
> Awalking the Devil is gone,
> To visit his snug little farm the earth
> And see how his stock goes on.
> —Coleridge, *The Devil's Thoughts*

dhe I, dho: set down; make, shape. Gk (reduplicated) *tithenai:* put. *theme. Themos:* god of justice and law (that which is set down). *thesis, antithesis* and (higher) *synthesis*, Hegel's three dialectical steps. *anathema;* see *an. diathesis; epenthesis; metathesis; parenthesis. prothesis. prosthesis; prosthetics. hypothesis. synthetic. apophthegm*, shortened to *apothem. thesaurus:* set down carefully.

L *facere, factum:* make, made. *fact, factotum:* jack-of-all-trades. *factitious, fictitious. facient, facinorous, factual; fiction. facile, difficult; facility, faculty. faction* was first used for a doing, a making, as was *fashion*, as still is the verb *to fashion*. But in Latin, *factionem* was applied to the "makings" of a scorned minor political group, such as "an oligarchical clique"; whence in English the obsolete *factional, factionary, factionate, factioner*, and the still used *factious*. See *sa*.

Also *fetish. Scire facies* (a legal term): Make it known. *factor, factory. face:* originally, shaped, as caught in the saying: "For beauty at twenty, thank God; for beauty at forty, thank your character." "It is the common wonder of all men, how among the many billions of faces there should be none alike"—save, perhaps, those of identical twins, hatched of one ovum. One wonders whether the same is true of creatures other than man, and of, say, leaves of the maple trees. Some of

Picasso's paintings suggest that he was familiar with Humpty Dumpty's words to Alice: "Your face is the same as everybody has. Now, if you had the two eyes on the same side of the nose, for instance."

façade, facet; facial, surface, superficies. affair. It, *affetuoso. deface, efface. prima facie. chafe* (L *calefacere:* to make warm). It, *dolce far niente:* sweet do-nothingness. *facetious.* "One had as good be out of the world as out of fashion," observed Colley Cibber in *Love's Last Shift* (1696)–naively translated into French as *La dernière chemise de l'amour.*

de facto: in reality, as opposed to *de jure:* according to the law. *defeat; defect; deface; defector, deficient, deficit. office, officer, official, officious. affair; affect, affection; affected, affectation. effect, effective, efficient, efficacious. efface. infection. profit. feckless* is shortened from *effectless. feces,* however, is from L *faex, faeces:* sediment, dregs. The basic sense of *defecate* is to clear out the dregs, cleanse, purify. Thus Robert Burton, in *The Anatomy of Melancholy* (1621), states that Luther "began upon a sudden to defecate, and as another sun to drive away, those foggy mists of superstition." And fallible man is comforted by H. Macmillan in *The True Vine* (1870): "By the death of the body, sin is defecated."

perfect: made through, nothing more to be done. *imperfect; pluperfect; perfection.* A perfect number is one equaled by the sum of its factors. The first five perfect numbers are 6; 28; 496; 8,128; and 33,550,336. Thus 1+2+3=6; 1+2+4+7+14=28; figure out the others yourself.

prefect. proficient. refectory. artifact, artifice; edifice; benefice, beneficial, benefit, benefactor; see *deu. beneficence. confection. counterfeit. feasance, malfeasance, misfeasance; malefic, malefactor. magnificence. sacrifice. satisfaction. savoir-faire. suffice, sufficient; superficial; surface; surfeit. facsimile. feasible; feat, feature. manufacture:* first, by hand. *munificent. office. orifice. pontiff; to pontificate:* to speak like a pompous pontiff. *rifacimento.* Suffixes *fic,* as *beatific, pacific, scientific, terrific; fy,* as *edify, justify, petrify, satisfy;* see *dheigh N 15.* Note *verify, simplify, clarify,* the trinity that forms the basis of proper presentation; see *dhe II.*

Gc, *do. halidom* (see *bhaut*). *kingdom, martyrdom;* JWalker lists 33 relevant words, as *boredom, freedom, topsy-turvydom. comfit. discomfiture.* L *abscondere:* set away; hide. *abscond.* An *absconce,* in medieval monasteries, was a dark lantern. *sconce, ensconce. scoundrel.* It, *confetti.* Sp, *bodega. hacienda:* first, things to be done. Fr, *boutique.* Gc, *deed.* Shakespeare, in *Love's Labor's Lost,* turns this to sexual reference when Berowne says of Rosaline:

Ay, and by heaven, one that will do the deed,
Though Argus were her eunuch and her guard.

(A *eunuch* was a harem guard; Argus was the hundred-eyed; only two of his eyes slept at a time; jealous Juno set him to watch Io; when on Zeus's orders Hermes killed Argus, Juno set his eyes into her sacred peacock's tail.)

dhe II: befuddle; vanish. Scand, *dastard.* Gc, *daze* and its frequentative, *dazzle.* Poignant power may rise from simplicity of expression, as in the words of Ferdinand in John Webster's *The Duchess of Malfi* (1612): "Cover her face, mine eyes dazzle; she died young." W. Somerset Maugham, in *The Summing Up* (1938), recognized the writing values: "It seemed to me that I must aim at lucidity, simplicity, euphony. I have put these three qualities in the order of the importance I assigned to them." Had he been speaking of nonfiction, Maugham might have replaced *euphony* with *verity* (see *dhe I*).

dheie: look, consider. Skr, *dhyana:* meditation. Gk *sema:* sign. *semaphor. semantics,* coined in French by Michel Bréal in 1897; *semasiology, sematic, sem(e)iotics, sememe. diseme, triseme.*

dheigh: touch; knead, mix dough, shape clay; put together; fasten. OPers, *paradise* (Gk *peri:* around): first, a garden with a clay wall. The enclosed grounds of St. Peter's in Rome were first called *Paradise. paradisiac.* Fr, *parvis:* enclosed garden. Hindi: *deha, dizdar.* Gk *digma:* touch. *thigmotaxis:* move; *thigmotropism:* turn (to or from), at a touch.

L *fingere, fictum:* form. *figure, disfigure, configuration. feign, feint.* Fr *fainéant:* a do-nothing, folkchanged from OFr *faignant. faint:* weak, is a doublet of *feint,* with shifted meaning. *fictile; fiction:* story put together; *fictitious;* see *dhe I. figment, effigy.* Fr, *fiche, fichu; microfiche.*

Also via L, *fibula:* a clasp or fastener on a garment. *fibulate, infibulate, infibulation.* Richard Browne wrote in 1640, "Your fingers fibulating on your breast," as though fussing with a clasp. *fibulate* was also used of putting a button on a fencing foil (removed by Laertes in his duel with Hamlet; see paragraph below). DeQuincey wrote in 1847: "Hooks and eyes . . . fitted to infibulate him. . . . Infibulate cannot be a plagiarism, because I never saw the word before; and, in fact, I have this moment invented it." (It is listed in Cockeram's wordbook of 1623 and in Bailey's of 1721.) Borrowed from French, *infibulation* was used of occluding the sexual organs, of boys in ancient Rome, of females, still, in Muslim lands. A full-page report on the practice in Sudan, in the London *Observer* of 6 July 1980 says, "The tradition is deeply imbedded," then details the forms. *Clitoridectomy* consists in the removal of the tip of the clitoris. Excision means removal of the entire clitoris and "the paring of the labia minora"; this is known as *Sunna:* tradition. The general procedure, infibulation, "involves excision of all the external genitalia, clitoris and labia minora. The fleshy parts of the labia majora are pared down, leaving enough skin for them to be sewed together. In this way the vulva is closed, except for a small posterior meatus to allow the passage of urine and menstrual flow." This closure remains throughout life, being opened for child-delivery, then immediately reclosed. The report ends: "Although a futile expedient to ensure virginity–in fact, it can hide the lack of it–infibulation is accepted as a sign of chastity."

In *Hamlet* (iv, 7; v, 2), Laertes' infibulated blade is spoken of as "unbated and envenomed." *bate:* to hold back, as "bated breath," is shortened from *abate, a* negative, from L *battuere:* to strike, beat. This has also given us *bat, batter, battery, battle, battledore* (with the shuttlecock), *battue; combat; debate; rebate.*

Gc, *dig, dike, ditch; duff; dough. lady:* loaf-kneader; see *gn.* There are some 40 combinations with *lady,* as *ladyfinger:* a plant, also a cake. Shakespeare (*Antony and Cleopatra,* v, 2) coined *lady-trifles. dairy* was first a place for kneading dough. *fix, affix, fixation. fixity, fixture. antefix, infix, prefix; transfixed. transfigure.*

Then thou wilt not be loth
To leave this Paradise, but shalt possess
A paradise within thee, happier far . . .
They looking back, all th' eastern side beheld
Of Paradise, so late their happy seat . . .
The world was all before them, where to choose
Their place of rest, and Providence their guide:
They hand in hand with wandering steps and slow
Through Eden took their solitary way.
–blind Milton, *Paradise Lost,* xii

dheigh N. Suffixes play so large a part in the formation of English words that it seems appropriate to present some major ones, with the number of relevant words listed in JWalker. Some of the suffixes are live, still used to form new words.

(1) Most frequent is the adverbial ending *ly:* in the manner of, OE *lik,* root *leig.* JWalker lists 4100, as *freshly, smoothly.* Almost 800 end *ally,* as *algebraically, enthusiastically, gradually, tragically.* See *al,* below.

(2) *ous,* adjective ending, L *osus:* full of, as *courageous, pious.* 1400 words from *gibbous* to *polyrhizous.* These may be subdivided:

(a) *aceous,* 100, as *crustaceous, orchidaceous, papaveraceous.* Also *eous,* 175, as *aqueous, courteous, nauseous, righteous.*

(b) *acious,* with nouns ending *acity,* 30, as *audacious, pugnacious, tenacious, vivacious.*

(c) *icious,* 18, as *delicious, judicious, suspicious,* with 52 nouns ending *icity,* as *duplicity, electricity, felicity.*

(d) *ocious, atrocious, ferocious, precocious,* their nouns ending *ocity,* as also *reciprocity* and *velocity;* but 65 nouns ending *osity,* as *animosity, luminosity, pomposity, verbosity.* Over 200 adjectives end *ious,* as *notorious, subconscious;* many drop the suffix to end the noun with *y,* as *acrimonious, ceremonious, harmonious, obsequious.*

(e) *dous,* 17, as *hazardous, nefandous, steganopodous, stupendous, tremendous.*

(f) *gous,* 17, as *analogous, azygous, homologous;* from L *vagus:* wandering, *noctivagous, solivagous.* Also 26 *phagous* (Gk *phagein:* eat, root *bhag*), as *anthropophagous;* some with nouns ending *phage.* These are matched with 23 from L *vorare:* eat, as *herbivorous, piscivorous,* with nouns ending *vore.* See *bhag; garg.*

(g) Some 60 learned words keep closer to L *osus:* full of, as *adipose, bellicose, cellulose, comatose, jocose, otiose, varicose.*

(h) The L *ous* forms are matched with Gc *ful,* 180, as *baleful, bellyful, cupful* (plural *cupfuls,* a measure, as opposed to a number of cups full; similarly *spoonfuls,* etc.; see *pel V*), *disdainful, forceful, sorrowful.* In a few cases, both forms have taken hold, as *piteous, pitiful; beauteous, beautiful.*

(3) *able,* adjective ending, L *abilis,* 1050, as *charitable, lovable, insupportable, untranslatable, viable.* Also 300 ending *ible,* as *incredible, invincible, irascible.* (The *a* is usually from a first-conjugation Latin verb, the *i* from the third conjugation.)

(4) *age,* LL *aticum,* noun, usually indicating relationship, 400, as *breakage, disadvantage, leakage, parentage, salvage, selvage, voltage.*

(5) *al,* L *alia:* undergoing a process, 1400, as *abnormal, conjugal, ephemeral, triumphal.* Some 375 of these end *ial,* as *adverbial, commercial, presidential.* And 400 end *ical,* as *chronological, farcical, lexical, seraphical.* See *ic,* below.

(6) *algia,* Gk *algos:* pain, 23, as *cardialgia, neuralgia, nostalgia.*

(7) *an,* L *anum:* relating to, 400, as *anti-American, arachnidan, diocesan, gargantuan.* See *man,* below. Also 100 *ean,* as *hyperborean, marmorean, protean.* And 325 *ian,* as *antediluvian, custodian, nonagenarian, ruffian, tragedian.*

(8) *ance, ant.* Nouns and adjectives from the present participle of first-conjugation Latin verbs: *ance,* 250, as *circumstance, countenance, disturbance, preponderance, remonstrance; ant,* 450, as *flamboyant, piquant, truant.* From third-conjugation verbs: *ence,* 450, as *coexistence, impenitence, insistence, sequence; ent,* 1000, as *inconsistent, nascent, omnipotent, recurrent.*

(9) *ar,* adjective ending, 150, as *interlinear, peculiar, plantar.* Plus 200 *ular,* as *avuncular, cellular, circular, funicular, octangular* etc., *particular.* See also *er,* below.

(10) *ate,* L *atum,* ending of past participle, first conjugation, 1350, mainly verbs, as *adjudicate, appreciate, checkmate, decimate, emanate, manipulate.* Also adjectives, as *legitimate, obdurate, proximate, ultimate.* Some nouns, as *magnate, potentate, primate. intimate* may be any of these three parts of speech. Some of the verbs and adjectives form nouns ending *ation.*

(11) *crat* (person), *cracy* (state), Gk *kratos:* power, 32, as *aristocracy, democracy, ochlocracy, timocracy.* Associated is

(12) *arch* (person), *archy,* (state), Gk *arkhein:* to rule, 21, as *monarch(y), oligarch(y).*

(13) *er,* L *arius:* one who, 3300, as *gambler, jobber, preacher, teacher, overreacher, usurer.* Also 600 *or,* as *possessor, professor, supervisor, tormentor. soldier, sailor, tinker, tailor* (Fr, *tailler:* to fit, "outfitter to the king"). Also several *ar,* as *avatar, bursar, hospodar, hussar, registrar, vicar.*

The comparative degree of adjectives, indicating more, as *bolder, colder, faster, richer*—with the superlative *est.* Hawthorne, in *American Notebooks* (1863), says, "It had been the beautifullest of weather all day"; but *OED* says "occasionally compared with -er, -est; usually with more, most." Disyllables, as *candid, hardy,* take forms according to harmony and taste; all verbals, as *hurt, biting, refreshed, sequestered,* use *more, most.*

er also has a feminine form, which survives, as in *abbess, hostess,* but is declining. No one would refer to a competent versifier as a poetess, nor dream of sending a diplomatess abroad. The latest *OED* quotation of *diplomatess* is from the *Athenaeum* of 1890. *Mistress,* once a term of high respect, grew into disreputable application; even that is moribund; and its abbreviation, Mrs. (together with Miss) is widely replaced by Ms, to indicate sex without subordination. See *rad I.*

(14) *form,* L *forma:* shape (root *merbh*), 180, as *bulliform, chloroform, inform, oviform.*

(15) *fy,* L *facere, ficare:* make (root *dhe I*), 150, as *beatify, codify, identify, ratify.*

(16) *graph(y),* Gk *graphein:* write (root *gerbh*), 150, as *cinematography, hymenography, lipography, phonography.* The thing written ends *gram,* as *telegram, electroencephalogram.*

(17) *ic:* relating to, L *icus,* adjective ending, 1450, as *demagogic, goliardic, hieroglyphic, pacific, somnific.* Many of these can add *al,* as *enthusiastic(al), fantastic(al), sporadic(al);* usually the *al* form indicates a weaker force. In some cases the simpler form may (also) be used as a noun: *epic(al), lyric(al), magic(al).*

(18) *ice,* L *itia,* ending of feminine nouns (*Fiat justitia et ruant coeli:* Let justice be done though the heavens fall), 37, as *armistice, cockatrice, disservice, jaundice, novice, precipice. delice,* used by Spenser, *Faerie Queene,* ii and v, probably in the sense of Fr *fleur de lys:* lily; *delicious:* full of delight.

(19) *ion,* noun ending, L *ionem, ationem,* 150, as *communion, million* etc., *reunion.* Also 250 *sion,* as *admission, commission, delusion, omission.* And 1700 *tion* (often meaning the act of), as *condemnation, recreation, reformation, sedition.*

(20) *ish,* Gc, but Gk *iskos* (a diminutive ending): somewhat, 375, as *feverish, lavish, lumpish, slavish.* Some verbs, as *abolish, admonish,* whose nouns end *ition.*

(21) *ism,* abstract nouns, Gk *ismos,* L *ismus,* 900, as *atheism, methodism, racialism, vandalism, syllogism.* Many, as *capitalism, individualism, pauperism, terrorism,* have verbs ending *ize* (see *(25)* below). *ism* is also used as a separate word, referring to abstract ideas. Thus James Russell Lowell, in *A Fable for Critics* (1848; published anonymously until others claimed authorship), pictures himself:

There's Lowell, who's striving Parnassus to climb
With a whole bale of isms tied together with rhyme;...
The top of the hill he will ne'er come nigh reaching
Till he learns the distinction twixt singing and preaching.

Many, like Robert Nisbet in *The American Scholar,* Spring 1982, feel that ours is especially an age of isms. Thus *Marxism* has spawned *Stalinism, Leninism, Trotskyism,* moving from "*eponism* into *anonism,*" as *communism, Sovietism, dialectical materialism.* Nisbet mentions 16 more, from *agrarianism* to *vitalism,* "efforts to encapsulate the zeitgeist through exercises in ismatics."

(22) *ite:* belonging to (also used to indicate a mineral), 300, as *tripartite, opposite; anthracite, hyalite, malachite, stalactite.*

(23) *itis,* Gk: swelling, 80, as *appendicitis, bronchitis, peritonitis, poliomyelitis, tonsillitis.*

(24) *ive,* L, adjective ending, 750, as *evasive, exclusive, executive, expensive, explicative, incommunicative, provocative, restive.*

(25) *ize:* make, Gk *izein,* 425, as *fertilize, memorize, scandalize.* Sometimes spelled *ise,* as *advertise.*

(26) *less:* lacking (root *leu I),* 350, as *careless, faithless, hopeless, reckless, meaningless.*

(27) *man,* 200, as *alderman, craftsman, sportsman, statesman, superman.*

(28) *ment,* nouns, mainly of condition or result, 375, as *amazement, bereavement, commitment, pavement.*

(29) *ness,* Gc, indicating quality, or state of being, 2650, as *business, callowness, dreaminess, hollowness, keylessness, restlessness, strictness.*

Let justice roll down like waters,
And righteousness like an ever-flowing stream.
—Bible, Amos 5

(30) *(o)logy:* relating to words, or to the study of . . . (root *leg I*), 370, as *antilogy, brachylogy, genealogy; gynecology, parapsychology.* Lady Lytton, in *Cheveley; or The Man of Honour* (1839), remarked: "a condensation of all the *logics* and all the *ologies,* but, unfortunately, the only ones thoroughly exemplified were tautology and acrology." Tautology results from untaught *ology.*

(31) *plasm:* substance, 130, as *ectoplasm, idioplasm, protoplasm.*

(32) *scope:* relating to vision (root *spek*), 57, as *horoscope, koniscope, sideroscope, telescope. hagioscope:* opening in a church wall, for lepers to see altar and service.

(33) *ship:* quality, rank, skill, 130, as *courtship, friendship, guardianship, hardship, kinship, marksmanship.*

(34) *spasm,* Gk *spasmos:* pull, jerk, 32, as *bronchospasm, enterospasm.*

(35) *tory,* mainly adjectives relating to action, 325, as *aleatory, contradictory, damnatory, ejaculatory, refractory. monetary* and *monitory* are from the same root; see *Juno* in *men I. factory* is short for L *factorium:* first, place where oil was pressed. The Latin ending is preserved in some 15 words, as *emporium, aquarium, solarium, planetarium. sudatorium,* for sweating, as at the sauna or the Turkish bath. *sudarium,* however, means a wiping-cloth, especially the one "miraculously preserving the countenance of Christ." There are over 200 words ending *ium,* as *delirium, millennium, pandemonium, pseudopodium, scholium.*

(36) *ty,* noun and adjective ending, L *-ticum:* state of being, 1250, as *audacity, charity, chastity, clarity, crudity, frailty. spirituality, venality; flighty, fruity, hoity-toity, nutty, witty. finality.*

The ending *try,* though unrelated to *tri:* three, has had a triple development. There are 25 words ending *olatry:* worship, as *autolatry, bibliolatry, idolatry.* There are 45 ending *metry:* measurement, as *trigonometry:* of 3-sided figures; *bathymetry, craniometry.* And there are 59 miscellaneous, as *forestry, gallantry, harlotry, infantry, knight-errantry, pedantry, poetry, psychiatry.*

The Latin ending *ticum* remains in English in *viaticum.* From L *via:* way, *viaticum* means provisions (money and other necessaries) for a journey; but as early as the 16th c. it was used of the Eucharist administered to a dying person as preparation for the journey to the next world. Hence it was turned to figurative use, as in the saying that biography can "nourish you with the viaticum of good examples," or that "education is the best viaticum for old age."

(37) A twofold suffix is *some.* Pronounced with a long *o,* it comes from Gk *soma:* body, and forms half a dozen words, as *chromosome, urosome, microsome;* see *teue.* Sounded like E *sum,* it denotes likeness or tendency; JWalker gives 54 such words, as *cumbersome, frolicsome, handsome, toothsome, troublesome, venturesome.*

For the suffix *wise,* recently a vogue affix, see *ueid.*

H. Bradley, in *The Making of English* (1904), commented on "the freedom with which we can still form derivations [new words] by means of suffixes." Language grows with mankind.

dhe(l) I: suck, suckle; nourishing; hence fruitful, hence happy. Gk *thele:* nipple. *thelium, endothelium, esothelium, epithelium. thelitis.* Prefix *thely,* as *thelyblast; thelyotokous:* producing females only. *theelin:* female hormone.

L, *female:* that which gives suck; *feminine; effeminate. fetal, fetus; feticide:* abortion(ist). *effete* is from *ex-fetus:* worn out from bearing; hence, lacking vigor. *superfetate. fecund, fecundity.* L *felius, filius:* son, sucker (feminine, *filia*). *filial, affiliate. fellatio.* Via OFr, *Fitz,* a prefix meaning son; for the illegitimate sons of Charles II of Great Britain, see *bhares.* L *felix. felicity, felicitations; infelicity.*

L *fenum:* hay, sustenance for cattle. *Foeniculum:* genus, plants of the carrot family. *fennel,* which smells like new-mown hay; *fenugreek:* Greek hay. It, *finochio;* Fr, *sainfoin. fennel* (Gk *marathon*) was taken as a tea, to lose weight; see *bher I.* It was also a symbol of flattery; Ophelia, distributing herbs in *Hamlet,* has yet a method in her madness; she gives a sprig of fennel to Claudius, who had flattered his way to the heart of Queen Gertrude and the throne of Denmark. For *Marathon,* the fennel field, see *niger.* Scand, *dug:* teat.

dhel II, dheub: a hollow; thence a valley, often with a lake. Gc, *dale, dell. deep, depth. dimple. dip, dive, delve. dope:* first, a dipping; a thick liquid. The *dopper,* in South Africa, baptized by dipping. *dump,* partly imitative.

dhem: breathe, smoke. Gc, *damp, damper. dank.*

dhembh: bury. Gk, *epitaph; cenotaph. tritaph. taphrina:* parasitic fungus.

dh(e)r: muddied; obscure. Gk, *ataractic, ataraxia. trachea, trachoma.* Gc, *dark, drab, draff, dregs. drivel. dross. Dublin,* once a muddy stretch along the River Liffey; for *lin,* see *pleu.* Joyce's *Ulysses* tells the story of a Dublin day; his *Finnegans Wake* widens the Liffey across the world; in the West it is the *mississliffey.*

The imaginary Dark Lady of Shakespeare's sonnets has impelled the most misguided search ever made by literal-minded scholars. The "lady," a stereotype of Renaissance love poetry, also in Italy and France, seems real because a genius has drawn her. Incidentally, she is not "dark," but "black"; all such references to her use the second word, save in one instance where *dark* is used to avoid repetition:

For I have sworn thee fair and thought thee bright
Who art as black as hell, and dark as night.

That the characterization refers to spiritual, not physical, attributes, is reiterated in Sonnet 131: "In nothing art thou black save in thy deeds." In *Love's Labor's Lost,* written at about the same time as the sonnets, the King, comparing her to his beloved Princess, calls Rosaline *black,* whereupon Berowne retorts, "No face is fair that is not full so black." Wordsworth smiled acquiescence on the quest of the autobiographical school:

Scorn not the Sonnet, Critic, you have frowned
Mindless of its just honors; with this key
Shakespeare unlocked his heart—

which moved the more analytical Browning to a burst of scorn:

With this same key
"Shakespeare unlocked his heart" once more!
Did Shakespeare? If so, the less Shakespeare he!

The mind that created King Lear's daughters, Lady Macbeth, Cressida, Rosalind, Viola, Portia, Rosaline, needed no personal ache to limn the black-browed, black-hearted "Dark Lady."

Night makes no difference 'twixt the Priest and Clerk;
Joan as my Lady is as good i' th' dark.
—Robert Herrick, *Hesperides*

dh(e)ragh: draw, slide. Slav, *droshky.* Gc, *draft, drag, draught, draw, dray. draughts:* the game in the U.S. called checkers; in Scotland, dambrod. *dredge.* Nasalized, *drink* (draw in); *drunk, drunken; drown.*

Who layeth the beams of his chambers in the waters . . .
All beasts of the field drink thereof: and the wild asses quench their thirst.
Beside them shall the fowls of the air have their habitation;
They sing among the branches.
—*The Book of Common Prayer,* Psalm 104

dhers: of the gods. Gk, *theism, monotheism, polytheism; atheist. theocentric, theocratic. pantheon. theobromine:* "food for the gods." Thus also the food *ambrosia* (Gk *a:* not; *mbrotos:* mortal [see *mer II*]) and the drink *nectar* (*nekros:* corpse [see *nek*]; *tar:* overcome. *Thespis:* divine founder of the drama [see *seku II*]). *theology; theophany* (see *bha II*). *apotheosis. enthusiasm:* spirit of the god within; Mme de Staël said that its etymology is "its noblest definition." *theodicy* (see *deik*). *OED* lists 33 and details 108 relevant words beginning *theo. theory, theorem,* etc., however, are from Gk *theorein:* to view, *theorema:* spectacle, speculation.

L *festus:* holy day, then holiday. *fest, festival, festive, festoon. feria, ferial. gabfest. fair,* as World's Fair. *feast.* It, *fiesta;* Fr, *fête. fane; fanatic,* shortened to *fan. profane:* literally, outside the temple; *profanity. nefarious. feral:* of the dead, used in astrology to indicate doom; not to be confused with *feral:* of a wild beast, especially of a tame animal backsliding, as in Jack London's *Call of the Wild* (1903); see *ghuer.*

"Terms like grace, new birth, justification . . . terms, in short, which with St. Paul are literary terms, theologians have employed as if they were scientific"—Matthew Arnold, *Literature and Dogma* (1873).

dheu I: to smoke; dust; hence rise, fly about, like dust; Fr, *jeter de la poudre aux yeux:* throw dust in one's eyes; hence bewilder, deceive; a demon (see *kagh*); strong smell, confusion; also—"Dust thou art, to dust returnest"—scatter, vanish, die. Bishop Berkeley, in *Principles of Human Knowledge* (1710), cutely and acutely observed: "We have first raised a dust, and then complain we cannot see."

Gk *thuos:* incense. *thyme:* to cause to smoke; used in sacrifices. *thurible, thurifer. thymus* (resembles the thyme bud). *thionic;* the prefix *thio,* as *thio acid, Thiobacillus, thiocyanic, thiophenal. athymia, barythymia. thumos:* spirit. *enthymeme:* one premise kept in the mind. *typhoid, typhus.*

thanatos: death. *thanatoid; thanatotic. athanasy* (*a* negative); with initial *a* sloughed, via OFr *tanesie,* came E *tansy,* its aromatic juice used as a medicine. John Donne wrote a poem (published posthumously, 1644) *Biathanatos,* arguing that suicide is not necessarily a sin. *Thanatopsis:* a look at death, poem written in 1811, at the age of seventeen, by William Cullen Bryant. In the same year Byron wrote a poem entitled *Euthanasia.* The word *euthanasia* has been used since 1640, sometimes figuratively, as by Hume, in *Essays* (1742): "Absolute monarchy . . . is the true euthanasia of the British constitution." As "an act of mercy," euthanasia has often been a vehemently disputed end, as when *The Spectator,* 22 Feb. 1873, ironically observed: "I saw a crab euthanatising a sickly fish, doubtless from the highest motives." The antitheological notion that the soul dies with the body is *thanatism. thanatognomic:* indicating death. *thanatosis:* gangrene.

L, *fume, fumigate; perfume. fuliginous, obfuscate. fury,* from the excesses after inhaling incense at sacrificial festivals, as of the Bacchantes; the maddened women tore to pieces Pentheus, king of Thebes, whose head was borne in triumph by his own unwitting, ecstatic mother, Agave. *furor; the Furies.* See *fur; nebh.*

Gc, *dock,* the plant. *burdock;* its burrs fly away. *dull, dullard; dole, doldrums. deaf-and-dumb; deafen; dizzy. dun; donkey* and *dove,* from the color; *dusk, dusky. down;* the feathers fly; *eiderdown* (*eider:* duck).

dune; down, still used in the plural to mean a mound or hill; the sense of *downward* is from OE *adown:* off the hill, which dropped the *a.* From *town on the hill* came the ending *ton,* as in *Charleston, Binghamton, Newton.* "There never was a good town but had a mire at one end."

Via Fr from Gk *tuphos* came *stew,* which developed several meanings: a stove; a caldron for boiling; hence, the food boiled therein; a room or tub with a steam bath, an early treatment for syphilis; hence, a brothel. Thomas Nashe in 1598(?) exclaimed: "London, what are thy suburbs but licensed stews!" Also, literally, *stewed:* bathed in perspiration, and figuratively, as Hamlet says, "in the rank sweat of an enseamed bed, stew'd in corruption." Hence the slang *stewed,* soaked in alcohol. Note that a *steward* was the keeper not of a stew but of a *stiy:* dwelling place, but also as in *pigsty.*

From *smoke, breath,* as noticeably on cold days—in the same way as L *anima:* air, spirit, led to the word *animal* (see *ane*)—came *deer,* which first meant any animal, as in *King Lear* iii, 4:

But mice and rats and such small deer
Have been Tom's food for seven long year.

reindeer: horned deer.

Liberty's a glorious feast!
—Burns, *The Jolly Beggars*

The World's a bubble, and the Life of man
  Less than a span;
In his conception wretched, from the womb
  So to the tomb;
Cursed from his cradle, and brought up to years
  With cares and fears.
Who then to frail mortality shall trust
But limns the water, or but writes in dust.
  —Bacon, *The World*

dheu II: to be worn out, die (an extension of *dheu I*). Gc, *dearth, die, dead, death; dwine, dwindle.* Despite the legend told in Euripides' play, 438 B.C., of Alcestis, who gives her life in place of her husband Admetus, and is brought back from Hades by Hercules, the old saw is fortunately true: There's no dying by proxy.

dheubh: to tap; a plug, peg. Gc, *dowel. dub,* which has taken various meanings: (1) to tap lightly on the shoulder, as on conferring knighthood; (2) to name humorously; (3) to do something awkwardly or poorly, as to dub a stroke at golf; hence (4) the noun, an awkward person or player; (5) to rub smooth. *To dub a film:* make a second copy, as by adding a translated soundtrack, etc., is shortened from *double,* root *duo.*

dheugh: achieve; hence also tools, etc. Gk, *Pentateuch* (*penta:* five): first, a case for five scrolls; then applied to the contents, the first five books of the Bible. Gc, *doughty.*

dhregh: run; wheel, turn. Gk, *trachelotomy* (a neck is a "turner"). *trechometer. trochal. troche, trochanter, trochlea*—all wheel-shaped. *trochaic, trochee:* "running foot" in verse, long syllable followed by a short one (reversing the more common iambic). *trochilus:* running bird. *trochoid. trochilus. truck; truckle.* A *truckle-bed* was originally a guard's bed, which at dawn was wheeled under the master's; hence, *to truckle under.*

"It did so happen that persons had a single office between them, that had never spoken to each other in their lives; until they found themselves, they knew not how, pigging together, heads and points, in the same truckle-bed."—Edmund Burke, speech on American taxation (1774).

dhreibh: drive. Gc, *drift. snowdrift; drive, drove.* "What is your drift, Sir?"—Samuel Johnson.

dhren: murmur, partly imitative. Gk, *threnetic, threnody.* Gc, *drone. dor:* buzzing insect, as the bumblebee. The sound *drone* is made by the *drone* bee, the non-worker (hence, other senses of the word as applied to humans) waiting to impregnate the queen bee, who thereupon takes over all control of the hive.

dhreu: fall, flow. Gc, *drip, drizzle; droop, drop, dreary, drowse. dripstone.* The *drippings,* for good gravy.

drip was earlier *drib,* whence *dribble, driblet, dribs* and *drabs. drabs* is an echoic variation, as frequently with such paired words as *helter-skelter.* There are only guesses as to the origin of *drab:* a cloth, then a dull color; or of *drab:* a slattern. From the latter came *drab:* to go whoring, as in *Hamlet* ii, 1: "Drinking, fencing, swearing, quarreling, drabbing."

Thomas Walkington, in *The Optick Glass of Humors* (1607), contrasted "a drop of words, a flood of cogitation"—much rarer and more commendable than what has been referred to as diarrhea of words and constipation of ideas.

dhrigh: hairy. Gk *thrikh, trikh. trichiasis:* inturning eyelashes. *trichina:* hairy worm, cause of *trichinosis. trichechine:* of the walrus. Several genera: *Trichodesmium:* algae, hairy-banded; *Tricholoma:* agarics, hairy-bordered; *Trichomanes:* raving hair, a filmy fern; *trichophyton:* hairy plant, a fungus; *Trichosporum:* blushwort, hairy spore; *Trichostema:* blue curl, with hairy stamen. Also *Trichiuridae:* family of "hairy-tailed" fish. *OED* lists 61 *trich(o)* words, botanical, zoological, pathological, and details 15. For mankind classified by hair, see *lei I.*

Note *trichi,* short for *trichinopoli:* a cigar, from a city so named in the state of Madras; its ash serves as a clue for Sherlock Holmes in *A Study in Scarlet.*

dhugeter: daughter.

> O daughter of Death and Priapus,
> Our Lady of Pain.
> —Swinburne, *Dolores*

dhun: cord, rope. L *funis,* diminutive *funiculus.* E *funis:* the umbilical cord. *Funambulist. funipendulous:* hanging by rope or cord, as the sword of Damocles (see *kleu I*) and a parachutist. *funicle. funipotent:* of clever handling of a rope, as by a cowboy. *OED* gives 10 words from *funis. Funaria:* genus of mosses. A funicular railway draws its cars by rope or cable. The song *A Merry Life,* written for the inauguration of the funicular railway up Mount Vesuvius in 1830, begins:

> Some think the world is made for fun and frolic,
> And so do I . . . [*with the chorus, each line repeated*]:
> Listen, listen, music sounds afar . . .
> Funiculi, funicula . . . [*ending*]
> Music sounds afar, funiculi, funicula.

dhur: at, or outside, the door. Pers, *durbar, durgah, durwan.* Gk, *thyroid,* from the shape; its cartilage forms the Adam's apple, as though Eve's offering had stuck in the man's throat (see *abel*). *thyrotropin; thyroxin:* hormone from the thyroid gland. *thyrotoxicosis. OED* lists 26 *thyro-* words, plus 11 *thyroi-.*

L *foris:* outside. (For the English prefix *fore,* meaning before, see *per.*) *forest, afforest, deforestation, reforestation. forfeit. foreclose. foreign;* the *g* is intrusive, as in *sovereign;* see *reg I. foreign* first meant outside; in the 13th c. "a chamber forene" meant an outside privy. In the 15th c. *foreigner* replaced *stranger,* as someone from another country (see *eghs*). By the time of Charlemagne (ruled 768–814), *forum* had come to mean court of justice, and *forest,* unfenced land controlled by the king.

Fr, *dehors; farouche. hors de combat. hors d'oeuvre* (: not part of the main job). *fauburg:* outside the burg; thus also *suburb* (L *urbem:* city; whence also *urban, urbane, urbanity*).

dinghu: tongue. L, *lingua:* tongue; mother tongue. The change from *d* to *l* may be due to the Romans' Sabine wives, or to the link with L *lingere:* lick, the tongue being the licking organ (see *leigh*). *linguist. lingua franca. bilingual,* etc., to *polylingual. lingo* is usually contemptuous, of another's tongue. In 1820 Coleridge coined *linguipotence,* rarely used since. *OED* has 26 *lingu* words, all relating to the tongue or to speech. Fr *langue:* tongue; Old English used *langage,* etc., but by ca. 1300 the *u* had crept into such words from the French.

"Tongue: well that's a wery good thing wen it an't a woman's."—Mr. Weller in Dickens's *Pickwick Papers.* In *The Tempest,* ii, 2, the tipsy Stephano sings, "She had a tongue with a tang." In *Troilus and Cressida,* iv, 5, Ulysses scornfully says of Cressida:

> Fie, fie upon her!
> There's language in her eye, her cheek, her lip,
> Nay, her foot speaks, her wanton spirits look out
> At every joint and motive of her body.

dlku: sweet. Gk, *glycerine; glucose. licorice,* varied to *liquorice; liquorish. lecherous* and *lecher* are from Fr *lécheur;* see *leigh.* L, *dulcet, dulcify. dulcimer* (L *melos:* song). *dulciana:* an organ-stop. *Dulcinea,* the sweet fantasy lady of Cervantes' fancied knight, Don Quixote, whose name gave us *quixotic.*

do: give. Gk *didonai. dose; antidote, anecdote, apodosis. doron:* gift. *Dorothea, Theodore;* via Russ, *Fedor, Fedora;* all mean gift of God. The *fedora hat* is from the play *Fédora* (1882), by Victorien Sardou, from whom *Sardoodledum. Eudora:* good gift; *Isidore:* gift of Isis. By *l.r* shift *Dorothy* becomes *Dolly,* whence the toy *doll.* Probably Gk *duein:* enter (as a temple, to give sacrifice); *ependyma:* membrane covering the ventricles of the brain; *endysis:* the process of growing a new coat of hair. *adytum* (*a* negative): a temple sanctum, which laymen may not enter. *ecdysis:* sloughing of the skin (*do off; doff*). H. L. Mencken coined *ecdysiast* as a euphemistic term for a stripteaser, whose performance has since been outmoded by direct onstage nudity.

L *do, dare, datum; donare, donatum:* give, given, *dado. datum;* plural, *data. date, postdate; dative. die:* that which gives an impression; plural in printing, *dies;* in gambling, *dice. add. addendum* is the gerundive: what should be added; plural, *addenda. addition; edition; perdition;* Fr, *perdu; rendition, render, rent.* "Service is the rent we pay for the space we occupy."

surrender. donation, donor, donative. condone; pardon. dot, dowry; endow; dower, dowager. L *vendere:* vend (give for sale); *vendor; venal.*

L *tradere, traditum:* give over. *tradition; traitor;* via Fr, *treason, betray.* There is an Italian saying, *Traduttore, traditore:* Translator, traitor; but translation, however necessarily imperfect, is nonetheless necessary both in commerce and in literature.

date: a given point in time. The *date* of the palm tree is from Gk *dakhtulus:* finger, from the shape of the fruit; some claim this is folk etymology, and suggest a Semitic source. Into the 17th c. the English *dactyl* was used to name the fruit. A *dactyl* was also one of the ten ("fingers") priests of Cybele, mother of the Greek gods.

dactyl, a measure, a foot in poetry: one long syllable followed by two short, from the sections of a finger; thus *dactyloid. dactylography:* the making or study of fingerprints. *leptodactyl:* slender-toed, as birds. *dactylio-,* of the finger-ring, as *dactylioglyph, dactyliomancy. monodactylous,* as the one-toed horse, whose small ancestor was a *tridactyl. pentadactyl:* humankind. Sir Charles Lyell, in *Principles of Geology* (1830) imagined that the extinct *pterodactyl* (wing-fingered reptile, ? ancestor of the bat) might "flit again through umbrageous groves of tree-ferns."

The rare word *dactylodeiktous:* pointed at, might be worth restoring for learned humor. The (London) *Times* of 27 May 1852 declared: "Oxford must be represented in politics by an universally dactylodeiktous personage." More often, perhaps, pointed at with the finger of scorn.

The *dactylic hexameter* was by far the most popular meter in Latin poetry. An amusing double-dactyl form had a vogue in English in the 1970s. Two examples will show the pattern. I devised the second herewith, and sent it to my friend the poet Melville Cane, then ninety-seven years old, as a challenge. He replied that his muse was still sportive, but averse to formulae.

Higgledy piggledy
Tom Tom the Piper's son
Purloined a porker and
Forthwith he fled.

Passersby said this was
Incomprehensible
Due to the yarmulke
Worn on his head.

Hokery jokery
Sigmund the Freudian
Sought the first thing that a
Man recollects.
Labeled his fantasies
Psychoanalysis,
First and forever con-
Cocted of sex.

Finger-talk, as for the deaf and dumb, is *dactylology.* The alphabet of raised dots, by which the blind can read, was devised in 1834 by Louis Braille. The early Indo-Europeans did not develop the written word. The word *alphabet* is from the first two letters of the Greek writing system, alpha, beta, via Phoen from Hebr *aleph, beth*—the *a* being added because Greek words do not end with *ph* or *t*. But in Hebrew *aleph* means ox; *beth* means house, which the form of the letters resembled; these meanings were lost in Greek, where the symbols had no meaning but their sound; hence the Greek is the first purely literal alphabet. From our letters, for neoliterates, came the *ABC* books, also *abcee, absey.* Shakespeare has, in *King John,* i, 1:

That is Question now,
And then comes Answer like an absey book.

The Roman emperor Geta—killed by his brother and co-emperor Caracalla in A.D. 212—was so impressed with letters that he had his meats served in alphabetical order. Seneca (see *tolku*) understood: "Many that lack even a child's knowledge of letters use books, not as the tools of learning, but as decorations for the dining room."

For the hornbook, see *ker II.* Later came the primer (short *i*), a book for the primary grades. The *New England Primer* had an illustrated and rhymed alphabet, beginning:

In Adam's fall, / We sinnèd all.
Thy life to mend, / This book attend [*picture of the Bible*].
The cat doth play / And after, slay.
A dog will bite / A thief at night . . .
The idle fool / Is whipt at school . . .

The alphabet on a hornbook was usually preceded by a cross; hence it became known as a *crisscross-row,* a *crosse-row,* etc. This term then came to be used of the first step, the basis; Francis Quarles, in *Emblems* (1635), states: "Christ's cross is the crisscross of all our happiness." A youngster learning the alphabet, and asked to recite it, might say: "Christ's cross me speed!" Kingsley, in *Water Babies* (1862)—how many read it now?—tells of "twelve or fourteen neat, rosy, chubby little children, learning their Christ-cross-row."

In *Don Quixote,* part II, chapter 42, Sancho Panza remarks: "I don't even know my ABC's; but to be a good governor, it's enough for me to remember the Christus." "With so good a memory," observed the Duke, "Sancho cannot go wrong." Sancho Panza went, briefly, to govern Barataria. (Barataria came into literature again as the island governed jointly by the two gondoliers in the Gilbert and Sullivan musical; and into history as Barataria Bay of the Gulf of Mexico in Louisiana, where from 1810 to 1814 Jean Lafitte headed a colony of pirates and smugglers.) Bartlett in 1860 defined *crisscross* as a game played on slates by children at school. In England, four straight lines were crossed so as to make nine spaces, in which the numbers *1* to *9* were written; each player in turn closed his eyes and tapped, the number he struck being his score. In the U.S. two players in turn put into the empty spaces, one a cross, one a circle; one wins if he gets three in a row; we call it *tic-tac-toe.* Either way, it's easier than learning the alphabet.

OED has 19 columns of relevant words beginning *chris,* including *Christianomastix:* scourge of Christians. In 1933 *OED* defined *abecedarian* as "one occupied in learning the alphabet. In U.S. the regular school term" The U.S. has now abandoned the term, and almost despaired of the endeavor. Montaigne, in his *Essays* (translated by John Florio in 1603, by Charles Cotton in 1685), looked beyond: "There is an abecedarian ignorance that precedes knowledge, and a doctoral ignorance that comes after it." The Middle Ages used an abecedarian circle, a ring of the letters with a needle to spin, for divination according to the letter at which it stopped. A variation of this became a gambling game, roulette. Thence Russian roulette, in which one aims at oneself a revolver with one or two bullets in the six or eight chambers, and pulls the trigger.

In the early days of the Christian Era, from the Gnostics, who called God *Abrasax,* came the cabalistic charm the *abracadabra,* used to ward off disease and disaster. It was usually worn as an inverted pyramid, the top line spelling *abracadabra* in full, each line below leaving off the last letter of the line above, down to a lone *A.* Its first known use was in a poem of Quintus Serenus Sammonicus, of the 2d c. It has been suggested that *abracadabra* was fashioned after the Jewish words for the Christian trinity: *al:* father; *ben:* son; *ruach acadash:* holy spirit. Note, too, that Abra was a favorite concubine of Solomon's. He jokingly protests—in a 1718 poem by Matthew Prior:

> Abra was ready ere I called her name,
> And though I called another, Abra came.

Solomon, through the Dark Ages, was noted as a magician, a dealer in abracadabra. Robert Burns, in his *First Epistle to John Lapraik,* scoffed at the many who would learn their ABCs:

> If honest nature made you fools,
> What sairs your grammar?

duei: fear. This seems to be a form of the next root, meaning, first, to be of two minds: to trust or mistrust; to run or to fight. Gk *Deimos:* the god Fear, son of Ares (Roman Mars; see *mavors*). Gc, *dire. dinosaur:* fearful lizard; *dinothere:* fearful beast.

duo: two. Gk *di-,* as *dichromatic, dichlorodiphenyltrichloromethane. diphthong* (Gk *phthongos:* sound, whence also *apophthegm*). The *diptich* is less common, as a screen, than the *triptich;* similarly, a *duumvir* was less frequent than a *triumvir;* see *trei. diploma,* says Johnson's *Dictionary:* "written on tables, and folded together . . . plural diplomata"; now cherished as a sign of academic achievement. Presented as an official seal of government assignment, a *diploma* marked a *diplomat,* who employs *diplomacy,* and seeks not to be *undiplomatic. diplomatic(k)* first meant "the art of deciphering old writing."

dipsomania comes from *dipsas,* a fabulous serpent whose bite caused an unquenchable thirst; hence *dipsosis; adipsia,* etc. Contrariwise, the bite causing rabies brings on *hydrophobia:* dread of water; *hydrophic* means not dissolving in water; see *aue.* For *rabies,* see *labh.*

Also the prefix *di* as in *didymium; didynamous. epididymus:* covering of the testicles (Gk *epi:* around; *didymos:* twins). *diptera:* two-winged, as the housefly and the gnat. *OED* lists 14 words beginning *dipter. dicho,* as *dichotomy; dichogamy.*

The Latin prefix *bi,* as *biped; combine. binary. bit,* as applied to computers, is a fusion of *bi*nary dig*it,* as electric calculators use only two figures, *0* and *1,* manifest as alternating current. For *digit,* see *deik. OED* lists 112 words beginning *bi,* and details over 200 relevant words, as *biceps* (two-headed), *bicycle, bigamy, biped, biplane, bivalve.* Its 1972 supplement adds 58, as *bipod* (after *tripod*), *biracial, biquinary:* a computer language.

L *duo. duodecimal, dual; duet.* Via Fr, *deuce; deuce* is also used as a euphemism for the devil—*What the deuce!*—possibly because it is the lowest throw with (two) dice. *double, doublet.* To *dub* a film. Sp, *d(o)ubloon:* gold coin worth two pistoles. *duplicate, reduplicate; duplex, duplicity. dubious:* of two minds. L *dubitare:* doubt. *duodenum* (*duo* and *deni:* ten each), coined by the Greek physician Herophilus (d. 285 B.C.) for the first section of the small intestine, figured as the breadth of 12 fingers. *balance* (*bi* plus LL *lancia:* dish), from the two plates of the old scales; the change of *i* to *a* influenced by Fr *baller:* to dance, as the scales sway up and down. *barouche,* with two wheels.

Gc, *two, twain.* Samuel Langhorne Clemens took his pen name, Mark Twain, from the two-fathom mark on the plumb line of the pilots checking the shifting sands of the Mississippi River. *twayblade:* two-leaved orchid. *twelve:* two left after ten; so also *dozen.* To be sure they met the legal requirements for weight of bread, bakers used to add a loaf when twelve were purchased; hence, *a baker's dozen:* thirteen. *twice; twin. twenty:* two tens. *twig,* dividing in two, to bifurcate, *twill, twine:* of two threads. *twist.*

The ancient Greeks swore solemnly "By the Twelve!", the dozen gods of the Greek (and the Roman) pantheon. Eudoxis, a pupil of Plato, assigned each god one of the twelve signs of the zodiac. Alexander the Great, on his farthest march eastward into Asia, raised an altar to "the Twelve." From the altar in the agora at Athens distances from the city were measured, as now from Charing Cross, London, and Grand Central Station, New York.

Twelve is found in other references, prominently in the twelve months, originally counted by the moon. The Passover song of twelve items may be of Sanskrit origin. There are twelve tribes of Israel, from the twelve sons of Jacob. Jesus had twelve apostles; his believers celebrate "the twelve days of Christmas," which also have a song. Twelve—compact of the three divine aspects, multiplied in the four fourfold earthly components (four corners, four dimensions, four elements, four human humors)—embrace the universe. In quantities, twelve twelves (dozens) make a gross; twelve gross make a great gross. (The Company of Grocers, established in 1344, first dealt "by the gross," wholesale.) And there are of course the cousins of Sir Joseph Porter, first lord of the admiralty, in Gilbert's *Pinafore,* "whom he counted by the dozens." The ancient immortal dozen seldom dozed.

Gm *zwei:* two. *Zwieback:* translation of It *biscotto,* Fr *biscuit:* twice baked. *zwitterion:* a doubly charged ion, positive and negative, which thus forms an electrically neutral molecule.

Chesterton pointed out that there are two ways of looking at twilight; just as a glass may be said to be half-empty or half-full, so twilight may be herald of the bright day, or harbinger of the long darkness: dawn or dusk. The Romans distinguished between the dilucid morning and the crepuscular eve.

When we speak of single combat, we mean one on each side, two opposed, as Goliath's challenge was answered with David's sling, as Rustum unwittingly killed his own son Sohrab; hence *duel.* The early form OL *duellum* widened to *bellum* (two opposed sides); hence *Bellona,* Roman goddess of war; *antebellum, postbellum. rebellion,* softened to, and often beginning with, *revelry.*

"Rebellion is as the sin of witchcraft"—Bible, 1 Samuel 15. "A little rebellion now and then is a good thing"—Thomas Jefferson, letter to James Madison, 30 Jan. 1787.

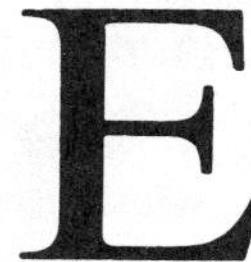

?ebri: drunken. L, *ebriate, ebriety; inebriate;* the *in* is intensive (as *flammable, inflammable*). *sober, sobriety* (*se:* away from, as in *separate*). Both Bishop George Barkeley in *Siris* (1774) and William Cowper in *The Task* (1785) spoke of cups "that cheer but not inebriate"; the bishop was recommending tar water.

> Inebriate of Air—am I—
> And Debauchee of Dew—
> Reeling—through endless summer days—
> From inns of molten blue.
> —Emily Dickinson, No. 214

ed: be hungry: eat. Gk, *anodyne* (*a* negative, away from "gnawing" pain); *acrodynia:* pain in the extremities; *crymodynia:* frostbite; etc. L *edere, esum:* eat; *edax, edacem:* hunger. *edible.* The *New Monthly Magazine* in 1823 characterized a man: "He has vivacity, edacity, and bibacity." An *edacious* person is a little more restrained than a *voracious* one; both words may be used figuratively. Lowell, in *The Biglow Papers* (1862), stated that "Concord Bridge had long since yielded to the edacious tooth of time." He probably knew the Roman saw, *Tempus edax rerum:* Time the devourer of all things.

esculent. comestible. escarole. obedere, obesum: devour. *obese. prandial:* eaten early, as to break fast; *postprandial;* both words now used mainly in pedantic humor.

Gc *eat, etch:* eat away, literally: *fret:* eat away, figuratively. *fressen:* gobble. *frass:* consequence of devouring.

eg I: I. L, *ego, egoism, egotism.* Gc *Ich.* For *me,* see *me I.* George Meredith remarks, in *The Egoist* (1879), "In the book of Egoism it is written, Possession without obligation to the object possessed approaches felicity."

eg II: lack. L *egere, egens. indigent* (OL *indo, endo:* into). So also *indigence. indigene,* however, and *indigenous* are from the same prefix, but from L *gignere, genui:* beget; see *gn.*

eg III: speak. L (*agyo*) *aio:* say. *adage.* With L *pro(d):* before, early, came *prodigy, prodigious.* However, *prodigal:* wasteful, lavish, is from LL *prodigalis,* from L *prodigere* (*prod-agere*): to drive ahead, be wasteful. The prodigal son appears first in Luke 15:11–32, and often since.

Sir Thomas Browne, in *Religio Medici* (1643), i, 15, observed: "We carry within us the wonders we seek without us: there is all Africa and her prodigies within us."

eghs: out. Gk, *exoteric; exotic. exotica* used to be a bookseller's euphemism for *erotica. eschatology. synecdoche.* The prefix *ex:* out, is both Greek and Latin; in Greek it has the *k* sound before a consonant; hence, e.g., *eclipse* (*leipo:* leave). The *ecliptic:* the sun's apparent orbit, was by 450 B.C. divided into the twelve equal periods, or signs, of the zodiac; see *guei. ecdysis* (*ekhduo:* put off, as the slough of serpents; see *do*).

OED lists 17 *ecto* words, as *ectoblast, ectogenous, ectoplasm;* and details 18 columns of relevant words beginning *ec.* The *ecclesia* was a convoked (called out) assembly; a man that addressed it was an *ecclesiast;* with the advent of Christianity, these words were attached to the congregation and the church; *ecclesiastical.*

The Latin prefixes *e, ef, ex,* are very frequent. *ecaudate:* without tail. *OED* has 26 columns of relevant words beginning *ef,* as *effable, efface . . efflorescent . . . effusive. effutiation:* twaddle; an English drama critic, J. Lacy, in 1823, spoke, in words applicable to much onstage today, of "the plotlessness, still-life, puling effutiation of modern plays."

OED remarks that *ex* may be "applied indiscriminately" and has (not counting *extra;* see just below) 363 columns of words beginning *ex,* as *exacerbate . . . excise, existentialism, expand, expose, exterminate, external, extreme, exultation, ex voto. exzodiacal:* of comets, satellites, and the farther planets, with an orbit that passes out of the zodiac. *expresident, exconfidant;* one may even speak of one's divorced spouse as "my ex." *exhaustless.*

extra. extraordinary. extraneous; OFr *estrange:* strange, stranger (see *dhur; en*). J. B. Rhine in 1934 expressed his idea of *extrasensory perception,* known by the initials *ESP;* more technically, *tel(a)esthesis:* feeling from afar. *OED* lists 98 words beginning *extra,* then details 19 columns more, as *extraction, extradition, extragalactic, extramatrimonial, extrapolate, extravaganza.*

"Ethelberta breathed a sort of exclamation, not right out, but stealthily, like a parson's damn."—Thomas Hardy, *The Hand of Ethelberta.*

egni: fire. Skr, *Agni,* god of fire. L *ignis. igneous, ignescent, ignite, ignition; ignis fatuus. ignivomous. OED* defines 20 *ign(i)* words.

ei I, i: go. Skr *jadoo:* a going against, sorcery. *jaun. yana:* on the Righteous Way. *Rathayatra:* procession at a festival. *Ramayana, Hinayana, Mahayana:* lesser and greater Ways of Buddhism.

Gk *ienai:* go; *ion:* going. *ion, anion, cation. disprosium* (see *el 66*) means "hard to approach" (*dys-pro-ienai*). Gk *ichno-:* footprint; sign of one's going. *ichnography; ichnolite, ichnology.* Perhaps *isthmus:* to go across.

L *eo, ire, itum:* go, gone; *iens, ientem:* going; *it:* he goes; *i:* Go! *ambient, ambit, ambition;* L *ambulare:* go about, whence also *amble, preamble, somnambulist;* etc. And via Fr *aller:* go, *alley* and *purlieu,* the ending from Fr *lieu:* place. *cenobite:* going together. *coitus:* a coming together; *coition;* L *coitionem* was used of a coalition, a conspiracy. *exit, exeunt. introit; circuit; issue. initial, initiation, initiative. sedition. iterate, reiteration. itinerate, itinerary.* The *knight errant* went about in search of adventure; frequently one going about may go astray; hence *err.* The roving robber, the highwayman, was called an *errant thief;* pronounced *arrant,* he was obviously an *arrant* (: unmitigated) rogue. (The word *errand,* OE *arende:* message, seems unrelated.) *obituary,* sometimes shortened to *obit:* L *obire mortem:* to go against death.

It, *subito*. E *sudden* came roundabout, via LL *subitanus*, from *subire:* to go under(handedly), unexpectedly. Also *transient, transit, transitive, transition.* A *trance* is, literally, a going across; as *perish* is, literally, a going through. *preterit. commence* is a compound of L *com* and *initiare:* to go in, begin; hence, prepare a ceremony of *initiation* (: take the *initiative*); thus *commencement,* at the end of a college education, is the beginning of adult life in the world outside the classroom. *constable; count* (L *comitem:* one going along), *county, viscount, concomitant.* Gc, *wide.*

Janus was the two-headed Roman god of gates, facing both ways, thus also the god of goings in and out and of beginnings; *January, janitor.* When Rome was at peace, with no need of the rites and the sacrificial ram, the ceremonial gate of Janus in the Forum was closed. Before Shakespearolatry, Dryden, in the *Essay on Dramatic Poesy* (1668), said of the Bard of Avon: "He is the very Janus of poets; he wears almost everywhere two faces; and you have scarce begun to admire the one, ere you despise the other." Quite a different application of the god's name occurs when René, the page of Lady Blanche in Balzac's *Venial Sin* in his *Droll Stories,* utters the fervid exclamation "*Janua coeli,* gate of Heaven!" as he kisses her foot, opening the way to higher favors.

ei II: yew. A tree of many uses; best for the bow and crossbow; frequent in graveyards, a symbol of grief; beautiful in gardens in topiary forms and as polished wood in furniture. See *bheug II; iso.*

Of all the trees in England,
Oak, elder, elm and thorn,
The yew alone brings lamps of peace
For them that lie forlorn.
—Walter de la Mare, *Trees*

What of the bow?
The bow was made in England:
Of true wood, of yew wood,
The wood of English bows.
—Arthur Conan Doyle, *Song of the Bow*

eik: possess. Skr, *ishwara:* owner, ruler; title of the god Shiva. *ixora:* tropical plant. Gc, *ought; owe, own.*

"An ill-favored thing, but mine own"—*As You Like It,* v, 4. "A man possesses nothing certainly save a brief loan of his own body; and yet the body of man is capable of much curious pleasure"—James Branch Cabell, *Jurgen.*

eir, ir: that which goes. An extension of *ei I.* Gk *hora:* a time gone by. *horal, horary, horograph, horologe, horoscope.* The *Horae:* goddesses of the seasons, in the Mediterranean region; originally three. L *hanc ad horum:* this time again; via Fr, *encore.* Gc, *hour, year, yore.* Gm *Yahrzeit:* anniversary.

And so, from hour to hour, we ripe and ripe,
And then, from hour to hour, we rot and rot,
And thereby hangs a tale . . .
My lungs began to crow like chanticleer
That fools should be so deep-contemplative,
And I did laugh sans intermission
An hour by the dial. O noble fool!
Motley's the only wear.
—*As You Like It,* ii, 7

eis: set in quick motion; wrath; divine power. *Asmodeus:* Avestan god of wrath. Gk *hieros:* holy. *hieratic. OED* defines 56 relevant words beginning *hier(o),* as *hieroglyphics.* From the divine power of healing, Gk *iatros:* healer, *iatric, pediatrics, geriatrics,* etc. *podiatry, iatrology. iatrogenic:* of a condition in the patient induced by the doctor, a not infrequent ailment. *OED* has 12 associated words, with 11 in its 1972 supplement, some of these being modifications of or additions to the earlier words. An *iatromathematician* was a doctor (especially in 17th c. Italy) who practiced medicine using astrological calculations of the time to gather herbs, to apply remedies, etc.

Also *Jason,* leader of the Argonauts; and the plant genera *Jasione:* healing; and *Jatropha.* The Greek name *Hierosoluma,* for the holy city of Jerusalem, Hebr *Yerushalayim:* foundation of peace; earlier *Shalem,* whence *Salem,* name of 29 places in the U.S. See *dekm.*

Gk *oistros:* gadfly. *estrogen, estrone. (o)estrus.* Only woman is exempt from regularly recurring *estrus;* alone of all female mammals, woman may be ready for intercourse at any season and hour. And—as Sir Thomas Browne pointed out in 1646—each animal has its particular and single method of copulation; man alone runs the gamut of coital patterns, and adds variations involving other than the usual organs of sexual congress.

L *ira:* anger. *irascible, irate, ire. Dies irae, dies illa . . . ,* opening words of a solemn hymn by Thomas of Celano (ca. 1250); see *tol.* Despite the admonition "Don't get your Irish up!" and the old Irish saying "If there's a government, I'm agin it!" *ire* is not related to *Ireland,* which was earlier *Eire,* from OE *Erin. Erse* is a Gaelic variant of *Irish. Hibernia:* "the wintry land," from L *hibernus:* winter; see *ghei.*

Gc *Eisen:* iron, "the holy metal"; strong, as opposed to the softer bronze. The Iron Age succeeded the Bronze Age in prehistory; it began, in our chronology, about 900 B.C. In classical mythology, it was the last and worst age of the world, following the Golden, Silver, and Bronze ages; hence a period of cruelty and oppression, with the rule of the iron hand.

Mrs. Slipslop, in Fielding's *Joseph Andrews* (1742), uses "ironing" for "irony," for which see *sue II.*

eku: horse. Skr, *Asvins,* twin gods of Vedic mythology; literally, horsemen. Gk *hippos. hippodrome:* race course; *hippopotamus:* river horse. *eohippus. Philip:* lover of horses; for *philippic,* see *bhili. hippalectryon:* horse and cock, a mythical creature. *Xanthippe* (literally, yellow horse; Gk *xanthos,* yellow, whence *xanthic acid, xanthous; xanthophyll,* occurring with chlorophyll) was the scolding wife of Socrates; her name is now used to identify a shrew.

The horse was important to the ancient Greeks. Their second division of citizens consisted of *hippeis:* knight with armored horses. Their cavalry commander was the *hipparch.* The winged horse Pegasus (son of Poseidon, sprung from the blood of the Gorgon Medusa when Perseus beheaded her), with a stamp of his foot, released the fountain *Hippocrene* (: horse fountain) on Mt. Helicon, sacred to the Muses and a source of inspiration. (There were three Gorgons, monsters with serpents for hair; they shared one eye among them: *Euryale:* Far Springer; *Medusa:* Queen; *Stheno:* Mighty. Medusa was the only mortal one; she turned whoever looked on her into stone; Perseus [son of Zeus and Danaë] looked in a mirror to behead her while she slept; he used her head to rescue Andromeda from a sea monster; also to petrify Atlas [see *fur; nebh*]. Perseus is also, in the Milky Way galaxy, the name of the spiral arm that holds our sun.)

O for a beaker full of the warm South,
Full of the true, the blushful Hippocrene,

With beaded bubbles winking at the brim,
And purple-stainèd mouth.
[*Read it all.*]
—Keats, *Ode to a Nightingale*

Oenomaus, king of Pisa in the west of the Peloponnesus, offered his daughter to the man that could beat him in a chariot race; her name was *Hippodamia:* tamer of horses (Gk *daman;* E *tame;* see *dam.* The fallow deer is of the genus *Dama,* whence *doe.*) Pelops, son of Tantalus, won Hippodamia by bribing the king's groom to give his master a chariot with a bad axle, which broke, killing the king. Hippodamia's marriage, and her evil influence on her son Atreus, led to the misfortunes of "the house of Atreus"—which included Agamemnon and Menelaus—a favorite theme of the Greek tragic dramatists.

Hippolyta (: looser of horses" [see *leu*]; a genus of sea horses is called *Hippolyte*) was queen of the Amazons; her marriage to Theseus is celebrated in *A Midsummer Night's Dream,* wherein the bridegroom tells the bride:

The lunatic, the lover, and the poet
Are of imagination all compact.

Cynisca, sister of King Agesilaus of Sparta (d. 360 B.C.), was the only woman that ever won the chariot race in the *hippodrome* of the Olympic Games.

Xenophon, a disciple of Socrates, wrote *Peri Hippikes* [On horsemanship], giving details for buying, breaking, breeding, riding, arming, etc. When Cyrus of Lydia in 401 B.C. fought his brother Artaxerxes II of Persia, 13,000 Greeks joined his forces; one of the Greek generals, Proxenus, invited his friend Xenophon to be a civilian observer. In battle at Cunaxa, near Babylon, Cyrus was killed; the Greek generals, invited to discuss peace, were treacherously seized and slain. Xenophon, as he relates in the *Anabasis,* organized the retreat of the surviving 10,000 Greeks; after two years, on the crest of Mt. Thecker, they saw the sea and joyously exclaimed, "Thalassa! Thalassa!" (Gk *thalassa:* sea, whence E *thalassian, thalassic, thalassophilous. OED* lists 10 and details 8 words beginning *thalass;* it lists 4 beginning *thalatto,* the Attic form, as *thalattocracy.*)

L *equus* (title of play by Peter Shaffer, 1973); *equine, equitation; equestrian,* opposed to *pedestrian* (see *ped*). *equisetum:* the horsetail, which grows near ponds. Darwin in 1847 complained, "His oolitic upright equisetums are dreadful for my submarine flora."

el: L *elementum:* first principle; earlier, letter of the alphabet; hence probably from Gk *elepanta:* ivory letter (Gk *elephantos:* the animal and its tusk; the change from *p* to *m* being Etruscan. L *-mentum:* suffix to form a noun, as in E *supplement, monument, implement, condiment;* see *dheigh N 28*).

Elements: the simple substances of which all material bodies are compounded. Early thought accepted four elements: earth, water, air, fire. These were taken for granted through two thousand years; they entered every phase of life, from medicine and forecasting to entertainment—as at the climax of three months of festivities when Leopold I of Austria (1640–1705) linked his land with Spain by marrying the Infanta. In a pageant presenting an equestrian contest of the four elements (described by Barbara W. Tuchman in "Mankind's Better Moments," in *The American Scholar,* Autumn 1980), a thousand riders for each element preceded a great globe from which emerged horsemen impersonating the fifteen previous Hapsburg emperors, with Leopold in "a silver seashell drawn by eight white horses and carrying seven singers in jeweled robes, who serenaded the Infanta." In a final blaze of a thousand rockets, the sky shone with the five vowels *A E I O U,* acrostic for *Austria est imperare omne Universo:* Austria, ruler of the world.

The classification of the four elements is neither so simple nor so erroneous as it seems. To the alchemist these four "elements" represented not only land, sea, and sky, but the three forms of human excretion—which are as well the three aspects of all matter: solid, liquid, gas—and force. (The word *energy,* first used in this sense in the 17th c., was applied to heat from fire; *power,* as in *horsepower,* was first used in the 19th c.)

Aristotle added a fifth element, the quintessence (L *quintus:* fifth; *essens, essentis:* being, whence *essential; esse:* to be; see *es*), of which the heavenly bodies were composed, latent as the soul in earthly beings. Among the quests of the alchemists was the search for the quintessence of things.

The chemical elements, which we now see as making up all matter, consist basically of atoms, which are formed mainly of positively charged protons, an equal number of negatively charged electrons, and neutrons. The protons are in the nucleus of the atom. The neutrons are stable if within the nucleus, but may exist outside, with a halflife of about 16.6 minutes. The electrons are in orbits around the nucleus. These orbits (shells) can contain $2n^2$ electrons; i.e., the first shell can hold 2; the second, $2 \times 2^2 = 8$; the third $2 \times 3^2 = 18$ . . . ; the last, $2 \times 7^2 = 98$. If the outer shell of an atom is full, it does not enter readily into compounds. In nature, oxygen appears over 99.75% as isotope 0 16; it combines with almost any other element, and forms alcohols, acids, and salts.

The number of neutrons in a nucleus may vary, producing isotopes of the same element. *isotope:* "having the same place," named by Frederick Soddy in 1913: forms of the same element, with the same atomic number but slightly different weights. There are about 300 naturally occurring isotopes; several hundred more have so far been created artificially. Hydrogen may have one neutron in the nucleus, and is then called deuterium (found in 1931); or two, in which case it is called tritium (found in 1935), which is radioactive. Deuterium, also called heavy hydrogen, occurs naturally about once in 6,000 atoms. Tritium is the form used in hydrogen bombs. See *iso.* Isotopes of other elements are not separately named; we speak, e.g., of uranium 235 and uranium 238. Uranium (element 92) has 92 protons and 92 electrons; the isotope number shows the total of protons, electrons, and neutrons.

Uranium is the highest element found in nature; those beyond it in the periodic table, produced artificially, and unstable, are labeled *transuranian.*

Modern chemistry has so far discovered some 106 elements, listed here in the order of their atomic number and followed by their symbol. All but 20 of the elements have known isotopes. The halflife of an isotope is the time it takes for half of the nuclei to disintegrate, a process known as radioactive decay.

The *atom* (Gk: not divisible; see *tem*) is now known to be complex. In addition to the proton, electron, and neutron, 14 other particles within the atom have been identified; each has an opposite antiparticle. Estimates indicate that such particles may total 100. The field has recently been more widely opened by such discoveries as the mu and the pi meson, the "strange" and the "naked charm" quark. The *proton* (Gk *protos:* first (see *per VI*), named by Ernest Rutherford in 1920) is the basis of the atomic nucleus; the number of protons gives the element its atomic number in the periodic table. An equal number of electrons, negatively charged, with a mass of about 9.1006×10^{-28} gram, whirl in concentric shells about the nucleus. *Neutrons* (L *ne:* not, *uter:* either; see *ne*) were postulated by Rutherford in 1920 and discovered in 1932 by James Chadwig;

their mass is 1,839 times that of the electron. The atom measures perhaps 10^{-8} centimeter.

elekhtron is Greek for *amber:* rubbing that produced man's earliest acquaintance with electrical phenomena—except for the heaven-sent lightning, not identified until Benjamin Franklin flew his kite. The word *electric* was coined in 1600 by the English physicist William Gilbert to denote substances that, like amber, attract other substances when rubbed. The 1933 *OED* has 188 words beginning *electr.* The 1972 supplement has 109 more, plus 115 *electro-* compounds. Gk *elekhtron* is related to *elekhtor:* the beaming sun, source of the power.

(1) *hydrogen* (H), "begetter of water," H_2O (see *aue; gn*). Separated by Henry Cavendish in 1776; named in 1787 by A.-L. de Lavoisier. The known universe consists almost entirely of hydrogen.

pH (Gm *Potenz:* power; *H:* hydrogen ion): measure of the acidity or basicity of a solution, developed in 1909 by S. P. L. Sørenson. pH 7 is neutral; below 7, acidic; above 7, alkaline. *pH-stat:* a device for maintaining a stable solution. Some volcanic lakes are extremely acidic, with pH values below 4; a few bodies of water, as Lake Nakuru in Kenya, have very high pH values. pH is of value in agronomy, and in viniculture, to check the acidity of the more than 5,000 varieties of grape.

(2) *helium* (He), Gk *helios:* sun (see *nebh*). Helium is, after hydrogen, the most common element in the universe. It is continuously formed in the stars, from hydrogen, by nuclear fusion. It forms no known compounds. It was noted by P. J. C. Jannsen in the spectrum of the sun during the 1868 eclipse; suggested as an element by Sir Joseph N. Lockyer and Sir Edward Frankland, and isolated by Sir William Ramsay, in 1895. It is the first member of the group of inert gases.

(3) *lithium* (Li), Gk *lithos:* stone, as in *lithography.* (*lite* is a general suffix indicating a mineral.) Baron Jöns J. Berzelius suggested the name *lithia* for the oxide, in 1817, in the belief that it occurred only in minerals. The element was isolated the same year by J. A. Arfvedson.

(4) *beryllium* (Be), Gk *beryllion,* diminutive of *beryllos:* beryl, a mineral and gem found near and named for the city of *Velur,* now *Belur,* in India. It is of the same composition as the emerald. The element was found in the mineral in 1797 by N.-L. Vauquelin and was isolated by A. A. Bussy in 1828.

(5) *boron* (B), Pers *burah:* borax. Extracted from boric acid in 1807 by Sir Humphry Davy, who first called it *boracicum,* then changed the ending by analogy with *carbon.*

(6) *carbon* (C), L *carbonum:* coal. Known from early times, both as coal and as diamond. Davy demonstrated that the diamond is carbon. Carbon occurs in all organic compounds. A soft form of carbon is graphite, used for writing, from Gk *graphein* (see *gerbh*). Carbon 14 (isotope, mass 14, halflife 5,700 years, is used for dating ancient objects containing carbon. The word comes from the root *ker:* burn.

(7) *nitrogen* (N). Described by Rutherford in 1772, but found by Priestley in England and by Scheele in Sweden at about the same time. First recognized as an element by Lavoisier, who called it *azote* (Gk *a:* not; *zoe:* animal life), as it is part of the air animals exhale. J. A. Chaptal coined the name in 1790: *nitrogen,* begetter of *niter* (Gk *nitron:* soda [KNO_3]) or *natron:* sodium carbonate (Na_2CO_3) with ten parts of water. The symbol for sodium, element 11, formerly called *natrium,* remains Na. The *natron lakes* of Egypt were used by the ancients. The best-known compound of nitrogen is *ammonia* (NH_3), named for the Egyptian god *Ammon,* because extracted from the deposits of the camels in the sand as

they awaited their masters worshiping at Ammon's great temple at Thebes. Urine has been used for washing in many lands, as in ancient Rome; Emperor Vespasian (A.D. 9–79) sold it from the public urinals to the launderers (see *piss*). Ammonia has a pungent, irritating odor, but 700 volumes will dissolve in one volume of water, which makes it widely useful for cleansing. From the emperor, *vespasian* is a polite term for what the usual Parisian calls a *pissoir,* a public urinal; Christopher Morley described his tour of the vespasians left in London after the blitzkrieg bombings of World War II. In early England, ammonia was called *spirits of hartshorn,* as it was also extracted from the hoof and horns of hunted hart, deer. Nitrogen is the most common gas in the atmosphere, being 75% of the volume of air; it is a constituent of all living matter.

(8) *oxygen* (O). Discovered by Priestley in 1774, but called *dephlogisticated air.* Gk *oxos:* sharp, acid; *gn:* begetter. Coined by Lavoisier in 1777, from the earlier Fr *principe oxygine:* the acidifying principle. Oxygen is the most abundant element on earth, being 62% of all living matter; plant cells are 75% water (H_2O); animal cells, 65%. *Ozone* (Gk *ozon:* smelling; see *od*) is a molecule consisting of three oxygen atoms instead of the usual two.

(9) *fluorine* (F). From L *fluor:* flux, *fluo:* flow (because it melts). Found by Sir Humphry Davy in *fluorspar,* a nonmetallic mineral. Sir Humphry gives A. M. Ampere credit for suggesting the name; he himself, however, in addition to inventing the *davy:* an early safety lamp for miners, discovered twelve elements—and was the subject of the first *clerihew,* a humorous verse form named after Edmund *Clerihew* Bentley, who, in a boring period of a chemistry class, set down:

Sir Humphry Davy
Abominated gravy.
He lived under the odium
Of having discovered sodium.

More such were published in *Biography for Beginners* (1905), but Bentley is more widely known for his detective story, *Trent's Last Case* (1913). The element was isolated in 1886, by H. Moissan.

(10) *neon* (Ne), Gk *neos:* new; root *neuos.* Coined in 1898 by its discoverers, Ramsay and Morris W. Travers. The gas is used, with an electric current, for the familiar *neon lights.* (At the same time, Ramsay and Travers found krypton [element 36] and xenon [element 54].)

(11) *sodium* (Na), LL *sodanum:* headache remedy, from Arab *suda:* headache. Coined in 1879 by Davy, who extracted it from caustic soda (see *el 7*). Sodium occurs most frequently in its chloride, NaCl, which we use as common salt.

(12) *magnesium* (Mg). From *Magnesia,* a district in Thessaly, which also gives us *magnet* (lodestone), *milk of magnesia,* and element 25, *manganese.* Discovered in 1807 by Davy; found widely but only in compounds. Isolated by Bussy in 1830; if ignited, it burns with a blinding light.

(13) *aluminium* (Al), Gk *aludoimos:* bitter; L *alumen:* bitter salt. Davy named it in 1809: first *alumium;* then *aluminum* (still used in the U.S.); finally *aluminium,* in line with *sodium, potassium,* etc. It is the most abundant metal in the earth's crust.

(14) *silicon* (Si), L *silicis:* flint. Named in 1817 by T. Thompson, as resembling boron and carbon, replacing Davy's 1808 term *silicium.* In the form of its dioxide (SiO_2), *silica,* quartz, it is, next to oxygen, the most abundant element on earth. There are 14 related words in *OED,* including *silicide.*

(15) *phosphorus* (P), Gk *phosphoros:* light-bearer. *Phosphor* is the morning star; root *bha II:* to shine. It was accidentally obtained from urine in 1669 by

Hennig Brandt of Hamburg, who was seeking the philosopher's stone; the name became general ca. 1750. In the 17th c. it was called *noctiluca,* as it glowed at night, being (of course) *phosphorescent,* luminous without sensible heat. A nonmetallic element, it is widespread in compounds; *OED* has over two pages of related words, including *phossy.* One form of Gk *phos:* light, is *phot,* from which five more *OED* pages of *photographical* words. *photuris* is the common glowworm, firefly, lightning bug. *Phosphorus* is the first element the discoverer of which is known.

(16) *sulphur, sulfur* (S), L *sulfur:* brimstone. *OED* allows only the *ph* spelling, but notes "(now U.S.) sulfur"; it gives some six pages of related words. Thus *sulfatara,* a variant of *solfatara:* a volcanic vent emitting sulphurous exhalations, from a volcano near Naples so named.

Sulphur is highly inflammable, and abundant in volcanic regions; hence it is popularly associated with the devil and hellfire. Iago in *Othello* knows that a planted hint, at first hardly noticed, may soon "burn like the mines of sulphur." Gower in 1390 said that sulphur is "thridde" of the "fowre" fundamental spirits of the alchemists, the others, as Chaucer lists them, being quicksilver (mercury, element 80), sal ammoniac (ammonium chloride [NH_4Cl]), and orpiment (L *aurum:* gold, and *pigmentum:* coloring-matter): arsenic trisulphide (As_2S_3). Arsenic is element 33; gold, element 79.

(17) *chlorine* (Cl), Gk *khloros:* green; root *gel I.* Found widely in compounds, especially as common salt, NaCl; see *el 11.* First isolated in 1744, but not recognized as an element until 1810, by Davy, who named it.

(18) *argon* (Ar), Gk *argos:* inactive (*a:* not; *ergon:* work [see *uerg*]). Coined in 1894 by its discoverers, Ramsay, J. W. Strutt, Baron Rayleigh, because it does not unite readily with other elements.

(19) *potassium* (K), Du *potasch:* pot ash; originally obtained from vegetable matter burned in a pot; named by Davy in 1807. Next to lithium, the lightest solid element. Decomposes water when tossed on it, the hydrogen rising in a violet flame. Ure, in *Dictionary of the Arts* (1839), stated that the discovery of potassium led Sir Humphry Davy "through many of the formerly mysterious and untrodden labyrinths of Chemistry." The symbol *K* is from LL *kalium,* from Arab *qali,* whence also *alkali* (Arab *al:* the), *kali* being a name of the glasswort, or saltwort, from which, by calcination, potash is obtained. Rousseau said that Egyptian kali makes the best potash.

(20) *calcium* (Ca), L *calx, calcis:* lime. Coined by Davy, who isolated the metal in 1808. *to calcine* is to reduce to lime: to burn to ashes, as by roasting. Calcium is found only in compounds; when isolated, it is a light yellow metal, about as hard as gold; it oxidizes quickly in moist air, forming quicklime (CaO).

(21) *scandium* (Sc), LL *Scandia:* Scandinavia. L. F. Nilson discovered and named *scandia* (Sc_2O_3) in 1879; later the same year he isolated and named the element. *Scandia* is an island of northern Europe. *Scandinavia* is named after *Skaney,* a district of southern Sweden; *ey,* as in *Jersey,* etc. means island; see *akua.* Mendeléev, when he made the periodic table of elements in 1869, predicted *scandium,* calling it *eka-boron.* (Skr *eka:* one; used of a predicted element one below the name one, in the same group). Mendeléev predicted other elements to fill gaps in the periodic table; these were later found. Thus *eka-aluminium* appeared as *gallium; ekasilicum,* as *germanium; ekaiodine,* as *astatine.*

eka: one, and *dvandva:* pair, a grammatical term for a compound noun, such as prince-consort, dowager-duchess (where *and* can be understood), are the two instances I know of, of the use of Sanskrit in the formation of a current scientific term.

(22) *titanium* (Ti). See *nebh.*

(23) *vanadium* (V). From Norse *Vanadia,* a name of Freya, goddess of love and beauty; perhaps from the beautiful color of its compounds. Named in 1830 by its discoverers, Baron J. J. Berzelius and N. G. Sefström. The metal was actually observed in 1801 by the Mexican A. M. del Rio; but, other analysts disagreeing, he withdrew his claim. With niobium (element 41) and tantalum (element 73), it is in atomic sequence 5b.

(24) *chromium* (Cr), Gk *khromos:* color. See *gher I.*

(25) *manganese* (Mn), from *Magnesia* (see *el 12*). The name was applied, from the 17th c. into the 20th, to a black mineral, *manganese dioxide,* the chief ingredient in glassmaking. The element was announced in 1770 by Kaim; in its separate metallic form it has no practical use (*OED*), but as an alloy with copper and zinc it makes an attractive bronze.

(26) *iron* (Fe), the symbol from L *ferrum:* iron; the word from Gk *ieros:* strong—as contrasted with the other metal most widely used in ancient times, bronze. Gm *Eisen* as in *Eisenhauer* (: *hewer,* horse-shoer); OE *isern, iren;* the word took many forms, the spelling *iron* becoming dominant ca. 1630. The most useful of the metallic elements, though soft (and silver-white) when pure; it is always used in admixtures, usually with carbon, or in alloys and compounds. It most commonly appears in three varieties: *wrought iron,* malleable; *cast iron,* hard but brittle; and *steel,* an alloy with any of eight metals according to the qualities desired. Pure iron in nature is found mainly in meteorites.

(27) *cobalt* (Co), Gc and E *kobold:* a gnome, evil spirit of the mines; Gk *khobolos:* rogue, evil spirit. The metal was known to Paracelsus (d. 1541), but was recognized as an element by Brandt in 1735. It exists in nature only in compounds, especially with arsenic and sulphur; such ores in the mines of Harz and Erzgebirge seemed not only worthless but noxious; hence, the miners gave it its name. *Cobalt blue* is a vivid color, often used to stain glass; *cobalt bloom* is of peach blossom color; *cobalt bronze* is violet.

(28) *nickel* (Ni). Coined by Baron Axel F. von Cronstedt in 1754, from Gm *Kupfernickel:* copper devil, so called in contempt because the copper-colored ore, *nicolite,* yielded no copper. *Nickel* (Old Nick), as the devil, is from Gk *Nikholaos,* the name that gave us also *St. Nicholas, Santa Claus.* The name is from Gk *nikke:* victory, and *laos:* people (whence the statue *Nike Apteros:* Wingless Victory; see *laos*). Nickel forms alloys with most of the other metals; it was 12% of the "copper" penny authorized by Congress in 1857; the old nickel (five-cent piece) has one part nickel to three of copper. In A. C. Gunter's *Miss Nobody of Nowhere* (1890) we read the complaint: "I can't go through Yale on nothing but a fifty-dollar note and two nickels."

(29) *copper* (Cu), Gk *Kupros:* Cyprus, from which much copper came; L *cuprum.* Originally *aes Cyprium:* Cyprian brass; *aes,* Gc *aer,* gave us E *ore.* The "island of cypress trees" is possibly from Hebr *gopher,* the wood of Noah's Ark. This red metal has been known since the fourth millennium B.C. Despite the old call "Brass button, blue coat, couldn't catch a nannygoat," the *copper* or *cop,* the policeman, does not derive the name from this word, but from (originally slang) *cop,* to catch, to nab; *nab* is a variant of *nap,* too common in *kidnap.*

(30) *zinc* (Zn), Gm *Zink, Zinke:* fork prong, jagged projection, from the shape of the metal in a furnace. Best known of its alloys is that with copper, called *brass,* used by the ancient Romans. Iron may be coated with zinc to prevent rust.

(31) *gallium* (Ga), L *Gallia:* France: "All Gaul is divided into three parts"—the opening words of Caesar's *Gallic Wars.* Discovered by spectroscope in zinc

ore in 1875 by Paul Emile Lecoq de Boisbaudran. Note *Lecoq:* the cock, L *gallus;* his name puns with his country's. Gallium was predicted by Mendeléev in 1869 as *eka-aluminium.*

(32) *germanium* (Ge) (see *gal*). predicted by Mendeléev as *eka-silicon.*

(33) *arsenic* (As), Gk *arsenikhon:* yellow orpiment; Pers *zar:* gold, influenced by Gk *arsenikhos:* strong. Many of its compounds are violent poisons. *Yellow arsenic,* orpiment, is trisulphide of arsenic (As_2S_3); as a pigment it is called *king's yellow.* The Greeks knew *red arsenic,* calling it *sandarake.* Arsenic is a link between metallic and nonmetallic substances. *Orpiment* comes via L *aurum pigmentum:* gold coloring. See *el 16.*

(34) *selenium* (Se), Gk *selene:* moon. So named in 1818 by its discoverer, Berzelius, because it resembles tellurium (the "earth element"), element 52, next after selenium in the 6a atomic sequence. Both elements were at first called metallic, but are now regarded as nonmetallic. Selenium has important uses because its electrical resistance is greatly increased by exposure to light, as in the radiophone of A. Graham Bell. Several words with *seleno,* as *selenotropic,* refer not to the element but to the moon.

(35) *bromine* (Br), Gk *bromos:* stench, from the noisome odor of its fumes. Named (Fr *brome*) by its discoverer, A. J. Balard, in 1826. Berzelius gave the name *halogens:* salt begetters, to the atomic sequence 7a: fluorine (element 9); chlorine (element 17); bromine (element 35); iodine (element 53); astatine (element 85). Note that Gk *broma:* food, has come directly into English, meaning food that is masticated, not drunk; *bromatology* is the study of food.

(36) *krypton* (Kr), Gk *kruptos:* hidden. Coined by its discoverers, Sir William Ramsay and M. W. Travers, in 1898, because it had long gone unnoticed. An inert gas, present in very minute quantities in the atmosphere. It was found along with neon (element 10), and xenon (element 54), also inert gases.

(37) *rubidium* (Rb), L *rubidus:* reddish. Named for the two red lines in its spectrum, by Robert W. Bunsen, who discovered this rare silvery metal in 1861, isolating it in 1863. Fifty tons of water were evaporated to obtain 200 grains of two metals: cesium (element 55) and rubidium. It ignites spontaneously in air, reacts violently with water. Bunsen also invented the burner that bears his name.

(38) *strontium* (Sr). Coined by Sir Humphry Davy from *Strontian,* in Scotland, where Cruikshank found it in 1787. Davy isolated it in 1808, and "ventured to denominate" the metals from the alkaline earths: barium (element 56); strontium (element 38); calcium (element 20); and magnium, later magnesium (element 12).

(39) *yttrium* (Y). Coined from the short form of *Ytterby,* Sweden, where it was discovered, three earths (yttria, erbia, and terbia) being separated by A. G. Ekeberg. See also *ytterbium* (element 70). *-ium* is a regular suffix for a metallic element. Yttrium was extracted in 1794 from the earth *yttria,* a white powder, Y_2O_3, obtained from gadolinite (after Johann Gadolin, who called it *ytterbite*). See also *gadolinium* (element 64).

(40) *zirconium* (Zr). Coined in 1789 by the German chemist Martin H. Klaproth from the mineral *zircon,* in which it was found. Fr *zircon* (also *jargon*) is via Port from Pers *zar:* gold; *zargun:* gold-colored; also in arsenic (element 33). Zirconium was not fully isolated until 1914.

(41) *niobium* (Nb), Gk *Niobe,* daughter of Tantalus (tantalum [element 73] is below it in atomic sequence 5b). Charles Hatchett in 1801 examined an ore, found an element, and noted: "having consulted with several of the chemists of the country, I have been induced to give it the name of columbium," after *Columbia,* the gem of the ocean. But as its rediscovery in 1844, in Bavarian

tantalite (from *Tantalus*), "is certainly due to Heinrich Rose, chemists are, for the most part [by 1950], agreed to accept his designation," *niobium.*

Niobe, with six sons and six daughters, boasted of her progenitive superiority over the Titaness Ledo, who had but one child of each sex. Unfortunately for Niobe, the two were deities. Nemesis fell upon hubris (excessive pride) as son Apollo killed Niobe's six sons, and daughter Artemis killed the six daughters. Niobe is pictured as all turned to tears in many literary references, as in *Troilus and Cressida* v, 10:

There is a word will Priam turn to stone,
Make wells, and Niobes of the maids and wives.

Zeus turned Niobe to stone, a rock on Mt. Siphylus, now Yamanla Daği, northeast of Izmir, Turkey, which still weeps (with melting snow). In the 5th c. B.C. an artist known only as *Niobid* Painter represented the story on a large mixing bowl, now in the Louvre; his work was an early attempt to capture depth on a plane surface.

Niobe is also the name of an asteroid discovered by R. Luther in 1861; and of three genera: of trilobites, molluscs, and weaver-birds. *Niobean:* a person "like Niobe, all tears" (*Hamlet*, i, 2); *niobic* and *niobous* refer to compounds of the element.

(42) *molybdenum* (Mo). Coined from Gk *molubdos:* lead. *molybdomancy* is divination by the movements of molten lead. In the 17th c., *molybdena* (also called *molybdenite*) was confused with various ores of lead; the name of the element is an alteration of these. It exists only in compounds.

(43) *technetium* (Tc). Coined by Emilio Segré (b. 1905) from Gk *technicos:* artificial; *techne:* skill, craft. A radioactive metal, the first element synthetically produced, it has 14 isotopes. The most common, Tc 99, emits negative beta rays; it has a halflife of 212,000 years. Isotope Tc 97, found by Carlo Perrier and Segré in 1937 at Berkeley, by bombarding molybdenum (element 42) with deuterons, has a halflife of 2,600,000 years. (How did they figure that out?) In 1952 Paul W. Merrill found Tc in S-type stars. See *el 103.* Technetium was predicted by Mendeléev, as *eka-manganese.*

(44) *ruthenium* (Ru). This rare metal was obtained by Karl K. Klauss in 1844; he gave it the name Wilhelm Osann had suggested for an element he found in 1828, not then confirmed (LL *Rutheni:* Little Russians). Its natural state is a mixture of seven stable isotopes. It is found in platinum ores; first, in the Ural Mountains.

(45) *rhodium* (Rh), Gk *rhodon:* rose. Coined in 1804 by its discoverer, W. H. Wollaston, from the rose-red color of its salts. A very hard white metal.

(46) *palladium* (Pd) (see *gn*). Discovered in 1803 by Wollaston. Often used for the balance-spring in watches. Found a year after the discovery of the minor planet *Pallas;* thence named.

(47) *silver* (Ag), L *argentum.* OE *seolfor:* ultimately from an Akkadian word meaning to refine, smelt. In general use since ancient times; of the precious metals, next to gold. In heraldry, still called *argent.*

(48) *cadmium* (Cd), L *cadmia:* calamine: zinc ore, with which it is found; from Gk *Kadmeia:* Cadmean (earth), from *Cadmus,* the Phoenician founder of Greek Thebes. Named by its discoverer, Friedrich Strohmeyer, in 1817.

(49) *indium* (In), Gk *indikhon:* indigo, short for Indian dye. Named for the color in its spectrum by its discoverers, the color-blind F. Reich and his assistant T. Richter, in 1863. *OED* lists *indicum* (used by the Roman scientist Pliny, who

died trying to observe the eruption of Vesuvius, in A.D. 79) as obsolete for *indigo,* with a curious recipe of 1558: "Steep the indicum in thicke redde wyne."

(50) *tin* (Sn). Symbol from L *stannum:* the word *tin* appears only in Germanic tongues, in Old English as early as 897. Rome imported tin from early Britain. In Britain today, what in America is called a can is called a tin.

(51) *antimony* (Sb). The *an* is perhaps a variant of Arab *al:* the; Gk *stimmi, stibi,* whence the symbol—the word was used in the late 11th c. by the alchemist Constantinus Africanus of Salerno, whom Chaucer, in *The Monk's Tale* (1386), called the "cursed monk, don Constantyn." The French term, *antimoine,* was broken by folk etymology into *anti-moine:* against the monks, who were widely hated in the Middle Ages. The brittle metal is in atomic sequence 5a, which is comprised of elements 7, 15, 33, 51, and 83. The word should not be confused with *antinomy:* a contradiction between seemingly equally logical conclusions; Gk *anti:* against, *nomos:* rule, law.

(52) *tellurium* (Te). Named in 1798 by Klaproth, from L *Tellus, Telluris,* goddess of earth, opposed to element 92, which nine years before he had named *uranium,* from *Uranus,* god of heaven. Tellus is the oldest classical divinity after Chaos. *Hamlet* mentions "neptune's salt wash and Tellus' orbèd ground." *The Gentlemen's Companion* (1738) observes:

> Reason, like Sol to Tellus kind,
> Ripens the products of the mind.

At first deemed a metal, tellurium belongs in atomic sequence 6a with sulphur and selenium. See *tel.*

(53) *iodine* (I), Gk *ion:* violet, *oides:* like (whence the English suffix *oid*). Coined in 1811 by its discoverer, Bernard Courtois, who came upon it accidentally as a manufacturer of saltpeter (so called because it appears as a salty crust on rock; for *peter* as rock, see *caput*). Courtois called it *iode;* Davy added the ending in 1814, to match the other elements in sequence 7a (9, 17, 35, and 85). The name is from the color of its vapor. It is a nonmetallic element found in seaweed.

(54) *xenon* (Xe). Coined in 1898 by its discoverers, Ramsay and Travers, from Gk *xenos:* stranger, because it forms no compounds. It was found with krypton and neon, also inert gases; is present in minute quantities in the air.

(55) *c(a)esium* (Cs). Coined in 1860 when discovered by spectrum analysis by Bunsen and Kirchoff; isolated in 1882. L *caesius:* bluish gray, from two such lines in its spectrum. A rare alkaline metal. In 1859 Bunsen had determined that each element emits a line of characteristic wave length (specific color), and thus had paved the way for spectrum analysis. Cesium 133 is used in atomic clocks for observations of remote space because it emits microwaves of the unvarying frequency of 9,192,131,770 cycles a second, and therefore can maintain accuracy with a deviation of no more than a billionth of a second a day.

(56) *barium* (Ba), Gk *baros:* heavy (see *guer*). Found in 1808 in heavy spar, *barytes,* by Davy, the element itself is comparatively light. It is found only in compounds.

(57) *lanthanum* (La), Gk *lanthanein:* escape notice (whence also *Lethe; lethargy;* via L, *latent.* The study of truth is *alethiology,* from Gk *alethes:* not forgotten). IE root *ladh.* A rare earth metal found by C. G. Mosander in 1839 "concealed" in cerite, oxide of cerium, element 58.

Elements 58 to 71 are called *lanthanides:* children of lanthanum.

(58) *cerium* (Ce). Named by its discoverer, Berzelius, in 1803, after the just-

discovered asteroid *Ceres* (Roman goddess of growth and agriculture); IE root *ker.* A very rare metal, it was found in an abandoned copper mine in Bastunäs, Sweden, in the mineral *cerite.* Klaproth tried to change the name, deeming it too close to Gk *keros:* wax. (From *keros* come *cerecloth, ceromancy, cerography, ceroplasty,* etc. *cerotic acid* is the major component of beeswax.)

(59) *praseodymium* (Pr). See *el 60.*

(60) *neodymium* (Nd). Mosander found a rare metal he thought was an element; he named it *didymium,* from Gk *didumos:* two of two, twin, because it always occurred with lanthanum (element 57). In 1885 A. von Weisbach proved that didymium was two elements, which he named *praseodymium,* from Gk *prasios:* leek green, the color of its salts; and *neodymium,* from Gk *neos:* new.

(61) *promethium* (Pm). A short-lived metallic element named by its discoverers, G. A. Marinsky and L. E. Glendenin, in 1948, after the Titan *Prometheus,* who made mankind out of clay, then stole fire from heaven and taught man the arts—for which Zeus chained him to a rock, where an eagle eternally devours his eternally renewed liver. Robert Bridges wrote a poem on Prometheus; Shelley's *Prometheus Unbound* makes him defeat Zeus. Aeschylus's *Prometheus Bound* (one of the earliest Greek dramas, dated, by a reference to an eruption of Mt. Etna, 478 B.C.) examines the problem of the existence of evil in the world, picturing heroic resistance to tyranny.

(62) *samarium* (Sm). Named by its discoverer, Boisbaudran, in 1879, after the mineral *samarskite,* in which its spectral bands were first seen. This rare mineral, which contains uranium as well, was named in 1847 by H. Rose, after Col. von *Samarski,* a Russian mine officer.

(63) *europium* (Eu). Named by its discoverer, Eugene Demarçay, in 1896, after the continent *Europe.* A rare earth, used in research to absorb neutrons. *Europe* is probably a Semitic word meaning region of the setting sun (west of Asia Minor).

(64) *gadolinium* (Gd). Named by J. C. Marignac in 1880 for the Finn Johann *Gadolin,* who in 1797 had found the silicate *gadolinite.* A rare earth element, it has the highest neutron absorption rate.

(65) *terbium* (Tb). Coined by its discoverer, Mosander, in 1843, from the Swedish town *Ytterby.* Mosander found three elements in gadolinite, and he named the strongest *yttrium;* the next, *terbium;* and the weakest, *erbium.* See *el 39, el 68,* and *el 70.* Denied by other researchers, terbium was confirmed by Delafontaine in 1878.

(66) *dysprosium* (Dy), Gk *dusprositos:* hard to get at; IE root *ei I.* Found by Boisbaudran in 1886, among the heavy rare earths; it was not isolated as a metal until 1906, by Georges Urbain. Used in nuclear research.

(67) *holmium* (Ho). In 1879 Per T. Cleve named holmia after his native city, *Stockholm,* L *Holmia.* In 1886 Boisbaudran found and named the rare earth holmium, of which holmia is the oxide.

(68) *erbium* (Er). See *el 65.* Four elements are named for the one town.

(69) *thulium* (Tm). Found by Boisbaudran in 1886, and named for the mineral thulite (thulium oxide), which was found and named in 1879 by Cleve, from Gk *thule:* farthest north. Thule was called by Polybius, in 145 B.C., a "six days' sail north of Britain." James Thomson, in *Autumn* (1730), speaks of

where the Northern Ocean
Boils round the naked melancholy isles
Of farthest Thule.

Also used in English is Virgil's Latin phrase *ultima Thule:* the uttermost limit.

(70) *ytterbium* (Yb). Found by Mosander in 1843; isolated by Urbain in 1905. See *el 39, el 65,* and *el 68;* all four are rare earth minerals.

(71) *lutetium* (Lu). Coined (first *lutetia,* the oxide) in 1907 by Urbain, from *Lutetia,* a fortified town of the Gaulish tribe Parisii, a town now known as Paris. A rare earth. From *lutetia:* swampland; IE root *leu II.*

(72) *hafnium* (Hf). A rare metal, with elements 22 and 40 in atomic sequence 4b. Found in zirconium ores and named in 1923 by Dirk Coster and George de Hevesy, for *Hafnia,* L for *Copenhagen.*

(73) *tantalum* (Ta). Coined in 1802 by Anders G. Ekeberg, who said it was "in allusion to its incapacity, when immersed in acid, to absorb any." *Tantalus,* rebellious son of Zeus, was immersed to his neck in water, which receded when he tried to drink. From Gk *tantalos:* sufferer, reduplicated *tal-talos,* IE root *tol.*

(74) *tungsten* (W). Coined in 1781 by its discoverer, Karl W. Scheele, from Swedish *tung:* heavy; *sten:* stone. A rare metal, formerly called *tungstenus.* Contained in the mineral *calcium tungstate,* also called *Scheelite.* Also found in wolfram, whence its symbol. Has the highest melting point of any metal. Is used to harden steel; and as a filament in electric lights, since it can be drawn into wire as thin as one-thousandth of an inch.

(75) *rhenium* (Re). Coined in 1925 by its discoverers, Walter K. F. Noddack and his wife, Ida Tacke, with O. C. Berg, from L *Rhenus:* River Rhine (whence also *Rhenish* wine). Predicted by Mendeléev in 1869. A rare metal.

(76) *osmium* (Os). Coined in 1803 by its discoverer, Smithson Tennant, from Gk *osme:* smell, from the strong odor of its poisonous oxide. IE root *od.* A metal of the platinum group. See *el 77* and *el 78.*

(77) *iridium* (Ir). Found, also by Tennant, in the alloy *osmiridium* (also *iridosmine*). Gk *iris, iridos:* rainbow, from "the striking variety of colors, while dissolving in marine acid." Tyndall remarked in 1871 that, when electrified, "this refractory metal emits a light of extraordinary splendor."

(78) *platinum* (Pt). Earlier *platina,* diminutive of Sp *plata,* silver; from its color and source, *platina del Pinto:* little silver of the River Pinto. It occurs worldwide, usually with osmium and iridium. First described as an element by Dr. Lewis in 1754; fusible only at very high temperature. Can be drawn into wire far finer than human hair. Osmium (element 76), iridium (element 77), palladium (element 46), rhodium (element 45), and ruthenium (element 44) are *platinoid* elements. IE root *plat.*

(79) *gold* (Au). Symbol from L *aurum:* gold. IE *gel I:* to shine. Known since ancient times. "A man may buy gold too dear."

(80) *mercury* (Hg). Symbol from L *hydrargyrus:* liquid silver. Also called *quicksilver; quick:* live, as in "the quick and the dead." The name from the sly and slippery *Mercury,* who, besides being Jupiter's messenger, was the god of both merchants and thieves. The only metal that is liquid at ordinary temperatures, it has been found in an Egyptian tomb dating from ca. 1500 B.C., and was known to the ancient Hindus and Chinese. Usually it is a mixture of seven stable isotopes. It is 100 times rarer than copper or zinc, occurring in the earth's crust at the rate of ½ gram per ton of rock. Pure mercury, isotope 198, is obtained by neutron bombardment of Au 197, a reverse of the process vainly sought by the medieval alchemists. Abd-ar-Rahman III, the greatest Moorish king of Spain (fl. A.D. 950) had a fountain of mercury continuously flowing in his courtyard.

(81) *thallium* (Tl). Coined by Sir William Crookes, who found it in 1861 by spectrum analysis. A rare metal. Gk *thallos:* green shoot, from the vivid green line in its spectrum, 0.0005348 millimeter long.

(82) *lead* (Pb), Gc *lod:* lead (see *mlub*). The symbol from L *plumbum:* lead.

Via L from Gk *polubdaina* is *plumbago:* the plant leadwort; also the mineral black lead or graphite (Gk *graphein:* write), which is actually carbon, used in the common "lead pencil." A *plumbate* is an ancient scourge, a lash tipped with leaden balls. Hence, too, the *plumb line,* its weight the *plumbob.* The *plumbator* is the guardian of the leaden seal of the pope. *Plumbum* is from the same root as *molybdenum,* element 42; also the expensive *plumber.* Soft and malleable, lead has long been one of the most useful metals; it is also the heaviest. Early coffins were made of lead; hence, *to be wrapped in lead:* buried.

(83) *bismuth* (Bi), Gm *Bismuth* (now *Wismut,* possibly from *wis mat:* white mass). LL *bismetum,* used by Georgius Agricola in 1529; first described in English in 1668, as metal used in making pewter; a report of 1674 states that the metal was found "some years ago" in the mountains of Bohemia. It was also called *tinglass,* but differs from tin and lead (which are in atomic sequence 4a), its properties being akin to those of antimony (element 51), which is above it in the 5a sequence.

(84) *polonium* (Po), LL *Polonia:* Poland. Named by Pierre Curie and his wife, Marja (Marie) Skłodowska, after her native land. It is a highly radioactive element with 27 isotopes, between mass numbers 192 and 218. Mme Curie discovered radium (element 88) in the residue after uranium and polonium had been extracted from pitchblende, an oxide of uranium. (*polony,* as in Little Buttercup's song in *Pinafore:* "I've chickens and conies, and pretty polonies," is a variant of *baloney,* from *Bologna,* Italy.)

(85) *astatine* (At), Gk *astatos:* not stable, IE root *sta;* whence also E *astasia,* frequent in hysteria. Very unstable; among its isotopes, At 210 has the longest halflife, 8.3 hours. Astatine is the rarest element in nature; perhaps .01 ounce is found in the earth's crust. Radioactive, it resembles iodine, which falls before it in atomic sequence 7a. It was found in 1940 at the U. of California, Berkeley, by Dale R. Corson, K. R. MacKenzie, and Emile Segré, who bombarded bismuth with alpha particles. Like iodine, it concentrates in the thyroid gland of the higher animals. It is the heaviest of the halogens: salt-producers (elements 9, 17, 35, 53, and 85, which form a salt by direct union with a metal). The term *halogen* was coined by Berzelius in 1828.

(86) *radon* (Rn). Coined from *radium* (element 88), but having the *on* ending used for inert gases; in France and Germany, called *niton* (Ramsay's suggestion, LL *nitens:* shining). Formed by disintegration of radium, it is the heaviest gaseous element and has a halflife of 3.823 days. One of its isotopes is called *actinon,* from element 89; its halflife is 3.92 seconds. Colorless, odorless, and tasteless, radon is seven times heavier than air. See *el 90.*

(87) *francium* (Fr). Named after the country *France* by Marguerite Perey, who found it in 1939 while studying actinium 227 (see element 89), which by negative beta decay becomes thorium 227 (see *el 90*); but by alpha emission about 1% becomes francium 223, the most stable of its 19 isotopes, with a halflife of 21 minutes. There is scarcely one ounce of francium in the earth's crust; but since it concentrates in the tumors (not the normal cells) of cancerous rats, it may have therapeutic value.

(88) *radium* (Ra), L *radius:* ray; because it emits rays of energy, glows in the dark. Has 13 isotopes; most common is Ra 226, with a halflife of 1,622 years. See *el 84.* In 1898 Marie Curie observed that pitchblende was some five times more radioactive than its constituent uranium (and polonium, which she had just discovered in the residue) could account for; thus she and Pierre Curie discovered radium; but it was not until 1910 that she and A.-L. Debierne isolated the metal.

(89) *actinium* (Ac), Gk *akhtis, akhtinos:* ray; IE root *nekut.* Coined in 1899 by its discoverer, André-Louis Debierne. Found in uranium ores; produces alpha rays. Its longest isotope, Ac 227, has a halflife of 21.7 years. Elements 90 through 103, mainly synthetic, are called *actinides:* children of actinium. *actinology* is the study of light rays.

(90) *thorium* (Th). A radioactive element; earlier called *thorinum.* Coined in 1828 by Berzelius, from *Thor,* Norse god of thunder, whence also *Thursday.* Only one of its 13 isotopes, Th 232, occurs naturally. Disintegrates into *thoron,* a radioactive isotope of radon (element 86). See *el 91.*

(91) *protactinum* (Pa). Earlier, *protoactinium.* Gk *protos:* first. By losing an alpha particle, disintegrates into actinium (element 89). A metal, it was discovered in 1917, isolated in 1934, by Aristid V. Grosse; occurs in all uranium ores, about 0.34 part of protactinium per million parts of uranium. Its most common isotope, Pa 231, with a halflife of 34,300 years, is found in marine sediment and (with thorium 230, halflife 80,000 years) is used to date sediments as old as 175,000 years.

(92) *uranium* (U). A silvery white metal, basic for nuclear activity. See *nebh.* Isotope U 235, with a halflife of 7.13×10^8 years, is fissionable for nuclear power. The most common isotope, U 238, with a halflife of 4.51×10^9 years, is nonfissionable, but can be irradiated with neutrons to form fissionable plutonium 239 (element 94). Named by Klaproth in 1789 for the planet *Uranus,* discovered by Herschel in 1781 (Gk *Ouranos,* god of the heavens); its radioactive properties were discovered by A. H. Becquerel in 1896.

(93) *neptunium* (Np). See *nebh.* A silvery metal; the first transuranian element artificially produced—in 1940, by Edwin MacMillan and Philip H. Abelson, who bombarded uranium with neutrons from the Berkeley cyclotron. Has 13 isotopes, with halflives from 7.3 minutes to 2.2 million years. Found in slight amounts in uranium ores. Named by McMillan after the planet *Neptune,* the first planet beyond Uranus, just as this is the first element after uranium.

(94) *plutonium* (Pu). Named by Glenn T. Seaborg and Arthur C. Wahl in 1942, after *Pluto,* second planet beyond Uranus; see *el 92* and *el 93.* IE root *pleu.* Pluto was the Greek god of wealth, *Ploutodores:* bestower of riches, as well as god of the underworld (where are also the rich mines). The most poisonous element, plutonium occurs in uranium ores and as the result of neutron bombardment of uranium. It has 15 isotopes, with halflives from 20 minutes to 7.6 million years.

(95) *americum* (Am). Named after the two Americas by G. T. Seaborg in 1944, as corresponding to the rare earth element europium (element 63). Its isotopes have halflives from 25 minutes to 7,950 years; the longest, Am 241 and Am 243, emit alpha rays.

(96) *curium* (Cm). Also named in 1944 by Seaborg, after Pierre and Marie Curie, pioneer workers in radioactivity (just as its corresponding rare earth element, gadolinium [element 64], was named after a pioneer in rare-earth research). It has 13 isotopes, with halflives from 64 minutes to 16.4 million years.

(97) *berkelium* (Bk). Synthesized at and named after *Berkeley* (U. of California), home of a cyclotron and much research, by Stanley G. Thompson, A. Ghiorso, Seaborg, and Kenneth Street, Jr., in 1949. It has 9 isotopes, with halflives from 3 hours to 1,380 years, and is synthesized in helion-ion bombardment of americum (element 95).

(98) *californium* (Cf). Named after the U. of *California* (at Berkeley), where it was found by helium bombardment of curium (element 96) in 1950 by

Thompson and team. Radioactive isotopes, with halflives from 25 minutes to (Cf 251) 800 years. Important for research—e.g., in its 3% decay by spontaneous fission—one microgram releases 170,000,000 neutrons per minute.

(99) *einsteinium* (Es). Named after physicist Albert *Einstein* (1879–1955), whose mathematics led to the discovery of atomic fission. Produced mainly by neutron bombardment of plutonium (element 94). Found in 1952 at Berkeley by Ghiorso and team, and in debris from the first hydrogen bomb explosion, at Eniwetok Atoll, in the South Pacific, in November 1952. It has 12 isotopes, with halflives from 1.2 minutes to 270 days.

(100) *fermium* (Fm). Named after physicist Enrico *Fermi* (1901–1954), who directed the first controlled nuclear chain reaction. Fermium was found in debris from Eniwetok Atoll (see *el 99*), on filter paper from airplanes that flew through the clouds of the explosion, and in the coral of the atoll.

(101) *mendelevium* (Md). Named after chemist Dmitri Ivanovich *Mendeléev* (1834–1907), who in 1871 arranged the periodic table of the elements, leaving gaps and predicting elements to fit them, three of which were discovered in the next 20 years. Mendelevium was the first element synthesized one atom at a time, from helium-ion bombardment of a minute quantity (one billion atoms) of Es 253 (element 99), by a team with Ghiorso, Seaborg, and Thompson at Berkeley.

(102) *nobelium* (No). Named after chemist Alfred Bernhard *Nobel* (1833–96), who concocted dynamite and over 100 other patented items, thereby amassing the wealth that established the Nobel Prizes, which have been awarded annually since 1901. Its discovery was claimed in 1957 by the Nobel Institute in Stockholm, which named it; but experiments in the U.S.S.R. and the U.S. (Berkeley) failed to confirm it; then it was found at Berkeley in 1958 by Ghiorso and team, who bombarded curium (element 96) with carbon ions.

(103) *lawrencium* (Lw). Named after Ernest Orlando *Lawrence,* who in 1939 won the Nobel Prize for his invention of the cyclotron (subatomic particle accelerator), which speeds protons to 1,200,000 electron volts and facilitates nuclear disintegration. Thence the discovery of techneticum (element 43), the first element made artificially. Lawrencium was found in 1961 by Ghiorso and team, who bombarded californium (element 98) with boron (element 5) ions.

The remaining elements are still disputed.

(104) *rutherfordium* (Rf). Synthesized at Berkeley in 1969; named after Ernest *Rutherford,* who discovered alpha particles and established the bases of nuclear physics. Russians claimed its discovery in 1964, naming it *kurchatovium* (Ku), after the nuclear physicist Igor *Kurchatov* (1903–1960); but the halflives of their isotopes were so brief that their findings were judged inconclusive.

(105) *hahnium* (Ha). The Soviets claimed that in 1967 they had synthesized a few atoms of element 105 at Dubna; this has not been confirmed. At Berkeley in 1970 the isotope Ha 260 was obtained and was named after Otto *Hahn* (1879–1968), the discoverer of nuclear fission. The Russians called it *nielsbohrium* (Bo), after the Danish physicist Niels H. D. Bohr (1885–1962).

(106) ___? In July 1974 the Russian Georgii N. Flerov and team claimed discovery of two isotopes of a new element. By bombarding Pb 207 and Pb 208 with a beam of chromium (element 54), they had produced one isotope with a halflife of 0.007 second; the other with a halflife of 0.026 second.

___? In September 1974 at Berkeley, Ghiorso and team bombarded Cf 249 (californium) with O 18 and claimed a new element with a halflife of 0.9 second.

Elements up to 109 have been claimed, but not confirmed or named. There is little doubt, however, that further experiments will lead to further findings.

From the elements, over a million chemical compounds have already been named and described, with more pouring from the laboratories daily.

I am a little world, made cunningly
Of elements, and an angelic sprite.
—John Donne, *Holy Sonnets* (1618)

?elaia: olive. Gk, *olive; oleo, oleaginous. oleograph. oleophilic. oil, oily; petroleum* (Gk *petros:* stone; first extracted from fissures in rock).

oleomargarine, usually shortened to *margarine.* The Society of Butterine Manufacturers voted that the *g* should be sounded *j.* It was named after *margaric acid,* assumed—falsely—to be present in all vegetable oils; this is from Gk *margaron, margarites:* pearl. Hence also *Margaret; magpie* (*Meg* is short for *Margaret; pie:* woodpecker; see *speik*). Also *fata morgana* (*fata:* fairy, roundabout from the more sober *Fates; morgana* via Arab from Gk): a mirage, supposedly due to the sorcery of *Morgan le Fay,* sister but foe of King Arthur. *Margarita* is an island of Venezuela; also, a cocktail with salt encrusted on the glass. For *Oliver,* see *koro.*

OED devotes almost six columns to *olive* and its compounds. An *olive branch* has long been a symbol of peace. Perhaps because children may be thought a source of peace between parents, or from Psalm 128: "Your children will be as olive shoots around your table," the term was used to mean children, as by Jane Austen in *Pride and Prejudice* and by Dickens, who in *Nicholas Nickelby,* 14, mentions "the wife and olive-branches of one Mr. Kenwigs."

An *olive stick* was a pencillike piece of *olive wood,* pointed at one end, with a sharp edge at the other, used to push back the cuticle at the base of the fingernails, to further expose the arc of the "moon" of white, supposedly a sign of aristocratic stock—in the days before revival of the pagan practice of painting the nails.

(e)lei: bend, forearm: limit. L *limes, limitum. limit, delimit; limitation, unlimited, limitless,* etc. *limulus:* king crab. *limb, limber. oblique.* Gc, *elbow. lay figure:* jointed model of a human. *ell:* roughly, distance from elbow to tip of middle finger; later stabilized at 45 inches; surviving mainly in the saying, "Give him an inch and he'll take an ell."

L *limen, liminen:* threshold. *limen. subliminal, sublimation. preliminary; postliminy; eliminate. lintel. sublime* first meant lofty, "up to under the lintel." The five-line nonsense verse, the *limerick,* was popularized in Edward Lear's *Book of Nonsense* (1846); the lines were first called *learicks,* then folkchanged from the supposed game of composing one, with everybody joining in the chorus: "Will you come up to Limerick?" The form is still very popular, many of the jingles being what used to be "unprintable." The form appears in an early nursery rhyme:

Hickory dickory dock,
The mouse ran up the clock;
The clock struck one
And down he run;
Hickory dickory dock.

em: first, take; later, buy. *example, sample. exemplary; exemplify. preempt; premium. prompt, prompter; impromptu.* L *sumere:* take. *sumptuous. assume; consume, consumption; presume, presumption; resume,* Fr *resumé. sumptuary; subsume. diriment:* literally, taking away. The Polish Assembly is *sejm:* literally, taking together; see *ksun.*

When the Indo-European nomadic tribes settled in towns, and commerce began, the root *em* took on the meaning "take by purchase, buy." Even in early times the Roman warning was necessary: *Caveat emptor:* Let the buyer beware; see *keu I.* Thus *emption, exemption; preempt; redeem, redemption;* via Fr, *ransom.*

Nowadays floor-waxing machines and vacuum cleaners have largely eliminated housemaid's knees; but housewife's need has not lessened, has indeed often expanded to a yearning, aptly caught in an unfortunately obsolescent word, *emacity:* itch to be buying. (Note that the ending *-city* forms a noun of which the adjective may be *-cious,* as *capacity, voracity;* see *dheigh N 2.*)

Possibly L *vindemia:* a taking off of the vine. Hence *vintage; wine,* and the widespread wine family, its first taste lost in the *winy* mists of prehistory. *Funk & Wagnalls Standard Dictionary* mentions a few classical wines, known now only from literary references, e.g., the Falernian; then it lists, with tabulated description, some 150 varieties, from Adelantadillo to Zinfandel. As the list seems almost a century old, many new ones have of course been added, and many of these are of non-European cultivation. The wines are grouped in some 20 genera, of which the most important are Asti, Bordeaux, Burgundy, Champagne, Hock, Madeira, Malaga, Port, and Sherry. A rough classification may characterize wines as red or white (with the more recent rosé), dry or sweet, still or sparkling. Poe makes grisly use of *A Cask of Amontillado.* For *Liebfraumilch,* see *glact.* There are also innumerable "family" and "local" wines, *le vin de pays.* "Good wine needs no bush"—now applied more generally—arose from the old practice of announcing a new vintage by putting a bush or ivy spray outside the wineshop. Burton, in *The Anatomy of Melancholy,* speaks of "those two main plagues and dotages of mankind, wine and women." More popular is the feeling expressed in FitzGerald's translation of Omar Khayyám:

A book of verses underneath the bough,
A jug of wine, a loaf of bread—and thou
Beside me singing in the wilderness—
Ah, wilderness were paradise enow!

The word *vinegar* ends with L *acer,* Fr *aigre:* sharp, sour. *viniculture. vintner; vinometer:* how much alcohol? *vineyard.* Fr, *vignette:* first, a vine-branch-shaped ornament. *vinegarroon:* scorpion with sour odor. Gk *oinos:* oenology. *oenomel:* wine and honey. *oenophilist:* lover of wine; a connoisseur, not an alcoholic. The evening primrose is of the genus *Oenothera:* the root smells of wine. The Trojan Paris had a wife, a nymph of Mt. Ida (where he gave Aphrodite, his choice as the most beautiful goddess, the apple). This nymph was *Oenone:* the intoxicating one. Paris deserted her for Helen, but sought her help (too late) when in the Trojan War he was stricken by Philoctetes' poisoned arrow. Draw what moral ye can.

en: in, within, into. This has been a fertile source of English prefixes, and is still used to fashion new words. Only a few examples are given here, however. *en-: enamored, engaged; enable, engender, entrails. OED* lists 212 such words, many obsolete; it details more in 182 columns. Also *endocrine, endoblast, endogamy, endomorph,* etc. *enter-,* as *enterprise, entertain. OED* lists 35 and details 34 words. *entero-:* relating to the intestines; *OED* lists 13 and details 3 words, as *enteritis, enterokinase. en-* also appears as *el-. em-: ellipsis; emphatic.* Also *parenthesis, dysentery; episode. esoteric,* opposed to *exoteric;* see *eghs.* Gk, *entomology,* L, *insect,* both indicate "cut in."

The prefix *in,* from this root, meaning inside, should not be confused with *in,* from root *ne,* meaning not. Between them, fairly evenly, these two prefixes—the same in spelling, but quite different in sense—occupy 771 columns (257 pages) in *OED,* with such words as (inside) *initiation, intricate, invention, investigate;* (not) *incest:* not chaste; *iniquity:* not equity; *invisible.* The world is *incomplete;* the proponents of General Semantics state that at the end of every sentence there is an implied *etc.* These two prefixes also vary before certain consonants, giving us, e.g., *illegible, illegitimate; immaterial, imperfect; irrepressible.* When an *irresistible* force meets an *immovable* body . . .

From the root *en* come four extensions of *in-.* (1) *infra:* below. *OED* lists 68 such words and details 10, as *infraspinatus.* See *ndher.* Also *infra dig,* short for *infra dignitatem:* beneath one's dignity, unbecoming. *infrared* refers to invisible rays below the lowest range of the spectrum, at the pole opposite ultraviolet. (2) *inter-:* between. *OED* lists 276 words, and details 135 columns more, as *intercollegiate, intercrural, interloper, interrupt.* The word *interpersonal* has had considerable recent use. In the 1933 *OED* there is one listing of it, from 1882, linked with *mesmerism.* The 1976 supplement gives nine quotations—e.g., H. S. Sullivan in 1938 stating that psychiatry's "peculiar field is the study of interpersonal phenomena," and Margaret Mead's 1949 mention of "the specific interpersonality of the sexual act." The word *interpersonal* crops up in discussions of aggression, immaturity, conflict. (3) *intra-:* within. *OED* lists 92, then details more in seven columns, as *intragalactic, intramural.* (4) *intro-:* into. *OED* lists 23, then details more in ten columns, as *introduce, intromission, introspection; introvert,* opposed by Carl Jung to *extrovert* (see *re*). In many cases, English has both the basic word and one with the prefix, as *change, interchange; flammable, inflammable* (able to burst into flame). In others, the word came from Latin in the compound form, and the basic term is lacking in English, as *infatuation, infection.* From Gc, *in, inn; inner, into. inside. within.*

Good thoughts his only friends,
His wealth a well-spent age;
The earth his sober inn
And quiet pilgrimage.
—Thomas Campion, *A Book of Airs* (1610)

endher: beneath. L, *inferior; inferiority complex. infernal, inferno. infra dig;* see *en,* of which this root is an extension. Gc, *under, underground, underwater, underwear.*

enek: sufficient; size. Gk *oncos:* mass (as a tumor). *oncology, oncometer, oncotomy,* etc. Gc, *enough.*

"There are three things that are never satisfied, yea, four things that say not, It is enough: The grave, and the barren womb; the earth that is not filled with water; and the fire that sayeth not, It is enough"—Bible, Proverbs. "Love is enough, though the world be a-waning"—William Morris.

engu: internal organ. Gk *aden:* gland. *adenoid; adenoma.* L and E *inguen. inguinal; inguino-,* as *inguinocrural, inguinoscrotal.* Compound root *neughron,* Gk *nephros:* kidney. *nephralgia, nephridium, nephritis.* The jade *nephrite* was supposed to cure kidney ailments. *mesonephron, metanephron; perinephral; pronephron.*

enguo: anoint. L, *unguent. unctious, unctuous; anoint, ointment. preen* meant to anoint, adorn, in anticipation (*pre:* before), folkchanged by association with OE *preen:* to pick, as a bird does when smoothing its feathers. For the religious range, see *gher I.*

enos: burden. L *onus, onerem. onus, onerous; exonerate.* Robert Burton's *Anatomy* *of Melancholy* (1621) has roused more praise than many a better-known book. Samuel Johnson in 1771 called it the only book that "ever took him out of his bed" two hours early. Byron in 1807 said that its reader "will be more improved for literary conversation than by the perusal of any twenty other works with which I am acquainted." In Part II of that volume, seeking remedies for melancholy, Burton states: "Divers have been relieved by exonerating themselves to a faithful friend."

er: separation; hence a network (see *sta,* Samuel Johnson on); apart, infrequent, hence precious. Gk, *eremite, hermit, hermitage.* L, *rare, rarefied, rarity.*

> What is so rare as a day in June?
> Then, if ever, come perfect days.
> —Lowell, *The Vision of Sir Launfal*

More physically, *retiary, reticle, reticule, reticulum; retina.*

> Stone walls do not a prison make,
> Nor iron bars a cage;
> Minds innocent and quiet take
> That for an hermitage.
> —Richard Lovelace, *To Althea, from Prison*

ere: to row. L, *trireme. Remus:* oarsman; as a name, best known through the Brer Rabbit and Tar Baby stories of Uncle Remus, begun in 1880 by Joel Chandler Harris. Russia was early settled by Norsemen; its name comes from the Norse term meaning to journey by water, to row. Gc, *oar, row, rudder.* Note the slang *put in one's oar:* interfere.

> Surely, surely, slumber is more sweet than toil, the shore
> Than labour in the deep mid-ocean, wind and wave and oar;
> Oh rest ye, brother mariners, we will not wander more.
> —Tennyson, *The Lotos-Eaters*

ergh, rei, res: flow; hence rise; exist. See *rei I.* Gk, *orchestra:* first, a place to dance. *orchestration.* L, *orient; origin, original, originate. abortion* (*ab:* away). *river, rivulet;* Fr *rivière,* Riviera. It, *Rialto* (see *burs*).

arrive. derive: first, to turn a stream, as for irrigation. Some tribes buried a leader (as the Goths did Alaric [d. 410]) by diverting a stream, then letting it flow back to hide the body from desecration. A *rival* was a person sharing a stream, at first a colleague, as in *Hamlet:* "If you do meet Horatio and Marcellus, the rivals of my watch . . ." Human nature being what it is, sharers soon vied with, then opposed, one another. *rivalry; unrivaled.*

L *errare;* wander. *err. knight errant; erratic; erratum, erroneous, error, aberration;* see *ei I.* L *ripa:* shore, along which a stream flows; hence rugged, as New England's stern and rock-bound coast. *riparian; rift; rive.*

Gc, *are. earnest:* risen for battle. *race, rear (up); raise, rise; rill; roam.* OE *rinnen, rann, gerunnan; ran, run; runnel. Rhine, Rhenish; rhenium;* see *el 75.* Shakespeare's Sonnet 116 confidently closes:

> If this be error, and upon me proved,
> I never writ, and no man ever loved.

And as Sir William G. Benham (b. 1859) wisely observed, "What is the use of running when you are on the wrong road?"

ert: ground. Gc, *earth. earthenware. OED* gives 15 columns to earth and its compounds, as *earthworm. earthling* was used around the year 1000 for a cultivator of the soil; scientifiction has coined two terms for an inhabitant of our planet, juxtaposed to dwellers on other spheres: *Earthian,* and *Earthman.* Via Dutch come *aardvark* (*vark:* pig) and *aardwolf.*

"I am earth, overtaking all things except words. They alone escape me. Therefore I lie heavy on their makers"—Kipling, *A Book of Words* (1914).

es: be. Skr *asti:* is; *su:* good (see *esu*); *swastika.* This was a symbol of good fortune in the Orient and among American Indians—often with the arms leftward, sinistrorse—long before Hitler made the rightward, dextrorse, clockwise swastika infamous. (The Indians had a simple cross with the gods of the four directions on its arms.) In Northern references, the swastika has been called the cross of Thor; also *fylfot,* being used as a design to "fill the foot" of a stained glass window.

It is also called *gammadion,* as shaped like the Greek letter gamma, Γ, whirled four times. *gamma,* like most Greek letters, is from Semitic: *giml:* camel. There is neat wordplay in the biblical description in Matthew 23: "Blind guides, which strain at a gnat, and swallow a camel" (Aram, *gilm:* gnat; *giml:* camel).

Skr *sat:* existing. *Bodhisattva:* enlightened being; see *bheudh. sattva:* what is, truth. *sati, suttee,* from the goddess *Sati,* bride of Vishnu; see *dei.*

Gk *ontos:* being. *biontic. onto-,* as *ontology, ontologism; ontogeny,* contrasted with *phylogeny* (see *gn*). Gk *etumos:* truth, what is. *etymon, etymology. Homoousian:* of the same essence, as in the Catholic trinity; *Homoiousian:* of like essence. *Heteroousian:* of different essence, as for a non-Christian. See *dheugh; sem.*

No quarrel over one syllable has been more long-lasting or more bitter—Athenius, defending the finally accepted view, was exiled and recalled five times—than that of the Arian heresy, led by Arius of Alexandria (A.D. 256–326), who declared that Jesus was of like essence (*Homoiousian*) but not "one with" God the Father. This belief was condemned as heretical by Emperor Constantine's Council of Nicaea in Asia Minor, A.D. 325, and the doctrine of sameness (*Homoousian*) was set as orthodox. Semi-Arianism, as the Church called the heresy, was favored by Constantine's sons, faded with the death of Constantius II in A.D. 361, but flared up again with Emperor Valens in A.D. 362; it was finally condemned when a second ecumenical council, at Constantinople in A.D. 381, reaffirmed the Nicene Creed. (For *ecumenical,* see *ueik I.*)

Gk *homoi:* like, has come into English as the suffix *oid,* in *celluloid, mastoid, spheroid;* JWalker lists 200 such. Gk *homo:* same, is kept in its entirety, as a prefix. Thus *homogenized* milk is "made the same," the cream completely mingled with the rest. And *homosexual,* often abbreviated *homo,* is not from L *homo, hominem:* man (see *ghdhem*), but is from the Greek root *homo,* and thus may refer to either sex. A homosexual woman may also be called a *lesbian,* from *Lesbos,* the Greek island where in the 6th c. B.C. the greatest poetess, Sappho, sang the delights of such a union; whence also *sapphic.* (Incidentally, the homosexuals' public avowals illustrate one way in which the language continues to change. Once they adopted the word *gay* as their label, its earlier meaning became obsolescent; if their use persists, *gay* in the sense of lively will become obsolete. Thus, too, was driven out of the language the word *firk,* a once-frequent verb with a wide range of meanings, of which only the sexual sense and form, *fuck,* survives).

Words beginning *homi* or *homini* refer to man, as *homicide, hominid;* there are six of each in *OED;* see *manu.* (*hominy,* first recorded by Capt. John Smith in 1629—fed to him by Pocahontas?—is from American Indian.) The much more frequent first elements *homo* and *hom(o)eo* are from Greek, meaning, respectively, same and similar. *OED* lists 55 and details 49 words with *homo,* as *homogamous, homogeneous;* it lists 12 and details 21 with *hom(o)eo,* as *homeopathy, homoeoteleuton.*

homographs are two or more words spelled (written) the same, but with different sound and meaning, as the farmer may *sow* his seed, then feed his *sow. homophones* are two or more words with the same sound, but different spelling and meaning, as *to, too, two; rain, rein, reign. homonyms* is used loosely for these and a third variation, but specifically refers to two or more words of the same spelling and sound but with different meanings; something that is *mine* is not a coal *mine.* (*nym* means name, as also in *antonym, pseudonym;* see *onomen.*)

L *esse:* to be. *essential, essence; entity. quintessence:* a fifth element (L *quintus:* five; see *el*). *pot-esse, posse, possible* (see *poti*). *exist, existentialism* (see *eghs*). *inter-esse:* to be between. *interest, interested, interesting.* Note the difference between *disinterested* (*dis:* apart from, hence impartial) and *uninterested* (not concerned); one may be interested and disinterested in the same matter.

An interesting split occurred with the prefix *pro* (in behalf of) and *esse.* Fairly directly came E *prowess;* but for smooth sounding a *d* was inserted, *prodesse,* from which OE *prud,* E *proud,* whence *pride.* Caustic Alexander Pope exulted in his power:

> Yes, I am proud, and must be proud, to see
> Men not afraid of God afraid of me.

Lord Herney put him in his place:

> The mighty honour of that boast is such
> That hornets and mad dogs may boast as much.

Pride is the first of the seven deadly sins (see below). Dekker, in his discussion of these, says, "Because Pride is the Queene of Sinnes, thou hast chosen her to be thy Concubine." This pride "goeth before destruction," says Proverbs 16:18, and with the Semitic pattern of repetition, "and a haughty spirit before a fall." But there is also a legitimate pride, as when one calls a wholesome child "my pride and joy." Six different flowers have *pride* in their name, as *pride-of-Ohio,* the cowslip. In heraldry, a peacock is "in his pride" when his tail is spread. Among terms for a group (see *ger III*) is *a pride of lions;* but *pride* is also used of animals in sexual heat; thus *Othello,* iii, 3, has "as salt as wolves in pride." And from the notion of "swollen with pride" comes the physical *proud flesh,* swollenness around the edge of a healing wound.

L *id est:* that is; in English usage, usually abbreviated *i.e.* Byron, in *Don Juan,* iv, uses it for an ironic twist: "Arcades ambo, id est, blackguards both." "Arcadians both" usually implies pastoral, innocent pleasures. After Byron's verse, *The Reader's Encyclopedia* (1965) declares: "When used ironically, the term implies that both are simpletons or scoundrels"; probably no one else has thus maligned Arcadians. Several have written of Arcadia, after Virgil's mention of Corydon and Thyrsis, shepherds and poets, *Arcades ambo,* in his *Seventh Eclogue.* Sannazaro wrote a series of most popular Italian verse eclogues, *Arcadia* (1504); Sir Philip Sidney wrote a prose romance, *Arcadia,* for his sister, the Countess of Pembroke, in 1580; the story *Menaphon* (1589) was reprinted ten years later as *Greene's Arcadia;* and Milton wrote *Arcades* for the Dowager Countess of Derby, to be acted and sung by her family, in 1633. The usual happiness suggested by the word is altered in a 17th c. painting by Guercini (Giovanni Fr. Barbieri), whereon shepherds are examining a skull, words below reading *Et in Arcadia ego:* Even in Arcady am I: death. See *cal.*

Gc, *am, are, is.* For *be, been,* see *bheu. sin:* that which is; in the religious concept, the condition of us all. "In Adam's fall, we sinnèd all." The root of *sin* is in the middle of the word. The first words in prayer: "O Lord, be merciful to me, a sinner." The last words of St. Francis of Assisi: "I have sinned against my brother the ass." See *ped.* A 14th c. illuminated manuscript pictures the Seven Deadly Sins: Pride, a knight on a lion; Envy, a monk on a dog; Sloth, a peasant on a donkey; Avarice, a merchant on a badger; Gluttony, a youth on a wolf; Ire, a woman on a boar; Luxury (Lechery), a woman on a goat.

sooth: truth, that which is. *soothsayer. soothe;* first, to show the truth, which is not always soothing.

> If, of all sad words of tongue or pen
> The saddest are "It might have been,"
> More sad are these we daily see:
> "It is, but hadn't ought to be."
> —Bret Harte, parody of Whittier

esu: to be well. An emphatic form of root *es.* Its most fertile form, the Greek prefix *eu,* fills over 24 columns of *OED* with such words as *eucalpytus, eucharist, eulogy . . . euphoria . . . euzeolite. Euphrosyne:* Good Cheer; one of the three Graces; see *dhal: gel I.*

Ascham, in *The Schoolmaster* (1570), wrote: "Euphues is he that is apt by goodness of wit, and appliable by readiness of will, to learning."And in 1578 and 1580 John Lyly made Euphues the chief figure (and title) of two books, the style of which created a vogue—copied and mocked in Shakespeare's *Love's Labor's Lost* (1598)—that lasted for half a century. The title page of Shakespeare's play (which spells *labor* without the current British *u*), the first to bear his name, calls the play "a pleasant conceited comedy," i.e., full of conceits. Among these is the clown Costard's mockery of learned speech in his words to the page Moth as the schoolmaster and the curate come from a meal:

> *Moth:* They have been at a great feast of language, and stolen the scraps.
> *Costard:* O, they have lived long on the almsbasket of words. I marvel thy master hath not eaten thee for a word, for thou art not so long by the head as honorificabilitudinitatibus; thou art easier swallowed than a flap-dragon.

(Note the neat alternation of consonants and vowels in the long mock-Latin word. A flap-dragon is not, like "Moth," a tiny creature, but is a raisin in flaming brandy, which an Elizabethan gentleman might pluck from the flames and extinguish by swallowing.) The scene ends with schoolmaster Holofernes turning to the Constable:

> *Holofernes:* Via, Goodman Dull! Thou hast spoken no word all this while.
> *Dull:* Nor understood none, neither.

Beaumont and Fletcher, in *An Honest Man's Fortune* (1613), poked fun at a courtier with "nothing in him but a piece of Euphues, and twenty dozen of twelvepenny ribband." The affected style of the euphuists is called euphuism. A clerihew by Edmund Clerihew Bentley found a neat rhyme, foisted upon an innocent poet:

> How vigilant was Spenser
> As a literary censor!
> He pointed out that there were too few e's
> In Lyly's Euphues.

euphotic: attractive in light; by extension, in photographs; also applied to the depth of water—up to 30 feet—that is light enough for *photosynthesis,* the greening of plants, to take place.

Gk and E *daimon* (not from this root) named a divinity. According to *OED,* "one's genius or demon," originally a guiding spirit that is with one all the days of one's life. But as men tended to blame their daimon for their faults and misfortunes, he soon came to be regarded as rather a misguiding spirit, the current sense of *demon.* Socrates claimed to be guided by a *daimonium* (diminutive), a sort of (*OED*) "divine principle or agency"; his accusers transformed this into a demon of evil, a term the Christian Fathers applied widely. It was not always thus; in *Antony and Cleopatra,* ii, 3, we hear the soothsayer warning Antony to be on guard against Octavius Caesar:

O Antony. . . .
Thy daemon, that thy spirit which keeps thee, is
Noble, courageous, high, unmatchable,
Where Caesar's is not, but near him thy angel
Becomes a fear, as being overpowered. . . .
If thou dost play with him at any game
Thou art sure to lose. . . . I say again, thy spirit
Is all afraid to govern thee near him.

As late as 1937, in *Something of Myself,* Kipling advised: "When your Daemon is in charge, do not try to think consciously. Drift, wait, and obey." The surrealists, seeking spontaneity, made this their practice. Because of the evil turn of *demon,* new words were needed; thus *eudemon:* a friendly spirit; *agathodemon* (Gk *agathos:* good, whence also *agathism:* a deferred optimism; *agathokakological:* compounded of good and evil, as on this earth—and *Agatha Christie*). The Eleventh House in astrology, source of good, is also called *eudemon;* see *guei.* The system of ethics that deems happiness the proper and basic quest of man, and the justification for his actions—"life, liberty, and the pursuit of happiness" —is *eudemonism.*

Gk *phonè:* sound, gives us *euphony;* see *dhe II. phony:* fake, may have originated as learned slang: *mere sound—et praeterea nihil:* sound and nothing more. It was first spoken in Greek by a man who tried to make a meal of a nightingale, then exclaimed, "You are a sound, and nothing more!" (A less enticing suggestion is that *phony* is folkchanged from *fawney:* a gilt finger-ring used in the "fawney rig": pretending to find what seems to be a gold ring, and with it cheating a gull who "happens to be" nearby.)

We say *'phone;* the Greeks said *phonè.* The use of the silent final *e* in English has been questioned. James Howell as far back as 1645 pointed out that foreigners sounded *done, some, come,* etc., as disyllables. This would have been correct English in Chaucer's time; even after Shakespeare, words like *discovered* were spelled *discover'd* if the *e* was to be silent. In French poetry, a final silent *e* is counted as an unstressed syllable. In English words such as *some* and *come,* the *e* may seem superfluous, but it lengthens the preceding vowel in such cases as *Dan, Dane; den, dene; din, dine; do, doe; dun, dune;* and it changes the preceding sound in *sooth, soothe.*

Euphorbiaceae: good-bearers, perhaps after a 1st c. Greek physician. *Euphorbus:* a very large plant family which includes the poinsettia and is a source of latex, rubber, and castor oil. The euphorbiaceous *stillingia* is named after "bluestocking" Stillingfleet; see *blue,* under *kel VI.* Other *eu* plant names are *eucalyptus:* well covered (the bud has a cap); *eucharis:* goodly grace, genus, amaryllis family (*OED:* "much in request for bouquets"; from the same elements is the Catholic Eucharist); *euclea:* good fame, genus, ebony family; *euphrasia:* pleasing to the mind (*euphrainein:* to cheer; *phren:* mind, as in *phrenology*): genus, figwort family; and the euphemistic *euonymus:* pleasantly named, a poisonous genus, the spindle tree. Calling the Furies *Eumenides:* pleasant-minded, expresses a fervent hope. There are also personal names, as *Eudora:* of good gifts, generous; *Euclid:* well-known, Greek mathematician of 300 B.C., exponent of (*Euclidian*) geometry; *Eunice:* pleasant success (*Nike:* Victory; see *laos*); *Eugene:* well born, whence also *eugenics; Eulalia:* pleasant-speaking. Also *euthanasia:* pleasant death; see *dheu I. eupepsia,* opposite of *dyspepsia. eudiometer:* having a good sky, coined by Priestley from *dios:* Zeus; see *dei.*

A word with strong influence on the English language has been *euphemy* (Gk *eu* and *pheme:* prophetic saying, speech; L *fama:* report, talk). A *euphemism* is a substitution of a bland or pleasant term for one that is considered blasphemous or obscene, or otherwise offensive to current taste or sense of decency. The most notorious spoiler of classics was Thomas Bowdler, who, egged on by his sister, in 1818 cut from Shakespeare (later from Gibbon too) whatever he deemed should not be read aloud to a family gathering; to describe this we have coined the verb *to bowdlerize.*

The practice of avoiding terms that might embarrass the ladies was at its height in Queen Victoria's moldy days. It is mocked in Gilbert's *H.M.S. Pinafore,* whose Captain protests:

Though "Bother it!" I may
Occasionally say,
I never use a big, big D.

But the practice has been continuous and, despite contemporary license, persists. I trace the changing attitudes in a chapter of my *In Praise of English;* here it must suffice to glance at the ways men have made words by mincing an oath, using *euphemy* as a bow to the First Commandment: "Thou shalt not take the name of the Lord thy God in vain." Men have sounded the first letter of the deity, *Gee!,* which is also a stopping short of *Jesus;* they have altered the last sound, *Gosh!* Of the more complicated discombobulations, *Odsbodkins* recalls the infant Jesus; it means "God's little body." *OED* states that *od,* as a minced form of *God,* was "very frequent in the 17th and early 18th c.," and lists 31 terms, including *odzooks:* God's hooks (more commonly *Gadzooks*); *odsoons:* God's wounds. *Ods fish!:* God's flesh, as in the Eucharist, was a favorite ejaculation of King Charles II. Fielding, in *Tom Jones,* has *od rabbit it* (*God drat it, odrat it*): all for *God damn it.*

Bob Acres, in Sheridan's *The Rivals* (1775), proposes the "oath referential," explaining (ii,1) that it should fit the person speaking, spoken of, or spoken to. His words, "The oath should be an echo to the sense," echo Pope's *Essay in Criticism,* 1, 364–65:

'Tis not enough no harshness gives offence,
The sound must seem an echo of the sense.

Among Acres' oaths are "Odds whips and wheels!" . . . "Odds triggers and flint!" . . . "Odds blushes and blooms!" Thus, one might cry to a lawyer, "By jury and torts!"; to a chef, "By garlic and thyme!" Acres ends by roundly declaring, "Damns have had their day." (For *od* as the force that animates all nature, see *hule.*)

Other languages, of course, have other euphemisms. Fr *Parbleu!* shies away from *Par dieu!;* a dictionary translates it "By Jove," which was a round oath for a proper Victorian. Hotspur, in frank Elizabethan times (in Shakespeare's *1 Henry IV*), bids his wife:

Swear me, Kate, like a lady, as thou art,
A good mouth-filling oath, and leave "in sooth"
And such protests of pepper-gingerbread
To velvet-guards and Sunday citizens.

The Great Queen Elizabeth set her courtiers a vivid example. *Gadzooks, Gorblimey,* and *Bejabbers!* It has been suggested that *Dear me!* is a softening of It *Dio mio:* My God! *Misery me!* is not directly from *misery,* but folkchanged from *Miserere me, Deus:* Have mercy on me, O God (the first words of the Fifty-first Psalm, in the Vulgate). See *kerd.*

eti: beyond. L *et cetera:* and the others; abbreviated *etc.* An "ornamental substitute" for *et cetera*–used by Chesterfield in a letter of 9 March 1748, by Rossetti in one of 23 Oct. 1876, and by Shaw in a review of 1889–is *et hoc genus omne:* and all of that sort. Gc, *eddy.*

etman: breath. Skr, *atman:* the principle of life. *mahatma:* great of soul.

eu: be lacking; empty. L *vacare:* to be empty; *vacans, vacantem:* lying empty; *vacuus:* empty. *vacant, vacate, vacation; vacuity, vacuous. vacuum. evacuate. vain, vanity.* "Vanity of vanities, all is vanity"–Ecclesiastes 1:2. "It beareth the name of Vanity Fair"–John Bunyan in *Pilgrim's Progress* (1678)–whence the title of Thackeray's novel *Vanity Fair* (1847). *vanish; evanescent. vaunt:* empty boast. *void; avoid, devoid; devastate. vast:* first, empty space–"In the dead wast and middle of the night"–*Hamlet. avoidable, unavoidable,* with their probable doublets *evitable, inevitable;* though the latter two may come from *e, ex:* out of, *via:* way, (un)able to get out of the way.

"There is no good in arguing with the inevitable. The only argument available with an east wind is to put on your overcoat"–Lowell, *Democracy* (1884).

Yon rising moon that looks for us again,
How oft hereafter will she wax and wane;
How oft hereafter rising look for us
Through this same garden–and for *one* in vain!
–FitzGerald, *Rubáiyát of Omar Khayyám*

Abraham Tucker, in *The Light of Nature Pursued* (1768), V, iii, pictured the vanity of man: "The best of us are in the same situation with the ass carrying the image of the goddess Cybele: the opening crowd fall prostrate on each side as he passes; but he would sell for no more at a fair than his brother long-ears, carrying two bundles of rags with a gypsy brat in each."

The Davenant family kept the Crown Tavern in Oxford, where Shakespeare may have stopped on his way between Stratford-upon-Avon and London; and the poet and playwright Sir William Davenant allowed himself to be thought the playwright's son, "in which way," commented John Aubrey (1626–1697), "his mother had a very light report, whereby she was called a whore." Thomas Hearne (1695–1735) in his diary corroborates: "The boy was sent for from school; a head of the college (who was pretty well acquainted with the affairs of the family) asked him whither he was going in such haste. The boy replies 'To my godfather Shakespeare.' 'Fie, child,' says the old gentleman, 'have you not learned that you must not take the name of the Lord in vain?'"

Gc, *want:* first meaning lack, but now giving greater emphasis to the consequent emotion, desire. *unwanted.* OE *wan:* dark, dull, hence gloomy, came to have a negative sense, linked with *wane:* to lessen (opposed to *wax;* see *aug*). Thus *wanton* (OE *towen:* trained): first, poorly trained, undisciplined. *OED* gives 15 obsolete words using the prefix *wan,* as *wanease, wanhap.* Almost forgotten is *wanhope,* gentler than *despair,* softer than *hope against hope.* Morris, in *Earthly Paradise* (1870), says, "But creeping wanhope he did still withstand."

Gc *hoffen,* E *hope; hopeful, hopeless, unhoping; hope chest.* Hannah More, in *David* (1782), v, neatly pictured "Fair hope, with smiling face but ling'ring feet."

eudh: udder. L *uber. uberous:* fruitful. *exuberant.* Gc, *udder.*

euoi: cry of joy, as at Bacchanalian orgies. "Maenads who cry loud Evoe!"—Shelley, *Prometheus Unbound.* L, *ovation.*

eus: burn; itch. Gk, *eurus:* scorching wind. L *urere, ustum. ustion; ustulation. combustible, combustion. bust:* first, over a cremated body. *Ustilago:* genus of fungi, "the itching plant." *uredo. urtica:* the nettle. *urticaria; urtication.* Gc, *embers.* See *ker V.*

?fin: end. Possibly a compression of *fig-snis:* firmly set; L *figere,* also *fingere:* fasten. *final, finality; finish. finial* (a variant of *final*): an adornment at the end. Sp *Cape Finisterre* is the same as E *Land's End:* the farthest point jutting into the westward ocean. *finite, infinite; ad infinitum* (like the fleas). *infinitesimal,* coined by Leibnitz (d. 1716) after L *centesimus:* hundredth, etc.; hence, mathematically, one divided by infinity.

finance: originally, paying (thus ending) a debt; *financial, financier. trephine;* L *tres fines:* three ends; described in 1628 by its inventor, Dr. John Woodall, as an instrument for cutting out bone, especially of the skull; the form of the word was influenced by *trepan,* on which it was an improvement.

The 1933 *OED* presents *His Finalityship,* but not *finalize;* this vogue word blooms in *OED*'s 1972 supplement with 15 quotations, the earliest dating from 1922. *affinity; confine, confinement; define, definition, definitive; refined, refinement, superfine, finical, finicking, finicky.*

The form *fine* has developed various senses (1) a penalty payment, the final agreement. (2) finished, hence consummate in quality, as *finery.* The remaining senses are outgrowths of this: (3) delicately wrought, opposed to *coarse:* "He draweth out the thread of his verbosity finer than the staple of his argument"—*Love's Labor's Lost.* (4) sharp-pointed, keen-edged: "What fine chisel Could ever yet cut breath?"—*The Winter's Tale.* (5) subtle; sensitive to delicate distinction: "For here the Trojans taste our dearest repute with their finest palate"—*Troilus and Cressida.* (6) admirably conceived or expressed; often used ironically: "A fine way to paint soul, by painting body so ill"—Browning, *Fra Lippo Lippi.* (7) exquisite, beautiful: "A shepherdess so fine perdie, So lively young and passing fair"—Bartholomew Young, *Diana Enamorata* (1598). (8) delightful.

"Cuckoo! Cuckoo! Was ever a May so fine!"—Tennyson, *The Window.* Fine-weather friends, who turn away when things turn foul. (9) marking an end, as in the mnemonic jingle of the months:

Except February, which, in fine,
Has 28, in Leap Year 29.

finale. finalist; finesse. Fr, *fines herbes:* chopped small. It, *finè.* In ancient Rome it became a proverb that *finis coronat opus:* the end crowns the work. *Finis.*

?frons: front. This may be an extended form of the root *bhrem:* to project. L *frons:* forehead. *front, frontage, frontier.* (A *frown* appears on the forehead, but the word seems to stem from a Celtic term for *nose.*) *affront, confront, effrontery. frontispiece* is folkchanged from *frontispice;* see *spek.*

fur: wrathful. L, fury. The *Furies,* because they wracked the mind, were also called *Maniai:* that made men mad; see *men I;* also *Erinyes* (root *erei:* to move, stir up, rouse). In an appeasing mood they were called *Eumenides:* daughters of kindness; see *esu.* These demons of vengeance were born of Gea, the goddess Earth, from the dripping seed of her emasculated son and husband, Uranus. Just, but merciless, they were *Alecto:* unrelenting wrath; *Tisiphone:* avenger of murder; and *Megara:* ever-jealous, scourge of the unchaste. They were winged, and serpent-haired; and they led a host of attendant furies. They first appear in literature in *Eumenides,* third play of Aeschylus's tragic trilogy, which won first prize in 458 B.C. and is the only extant ancient trilogy. More recently they swarm in Sartre's *The Flies;* see *huei I.*

The ending *ides:* daughters, also marks the sea nymphs, the *Atlantides,* daughters of Atlas (see *nebh*); and also the *Nereids,* the 50 daughters of Nereus, son of Pontus, early god of the sea—whence *Hellespont:* sea of the Hellenes, the Greeks. Hellen was the mythical ancestor of the Greeks; the judges at the Olympic Games were *Hellenodikai:* spokesmen of the Greeks. The Olympic Games were founded by Heracles (Hercules); for their duration, all but athletic rivalry held truce. As they were religious in intent, they took their name from Mt. Olympus, in the clouds whereof was the abode of the gods. The ancient Greek calendar began—Year 1—with the first Olympic Games, our 776 B.C.; the games were abolished with the fall of Greece in A.D. 393, by the Roman emperor Theodosius I. They were reestablished at Athens in 1896, with, unfortunately, less regard for amateur status or freedom from political pressure.

Helen "of Troy," taken from Greece by the Trojan Paris, was the essence of Hellenic beauty. The name *Helen* may be "the bright one," from *Helios,* the sun; or possibly from Gk *hellein:* to turn or twist, from her behavior, submissively from Menelaus to Paris and back. The Irish form of the name is *Aileen, Eileen, Mavourneen:* my darling.

Nereids were attendant upon the later sea god Neptune; it is thus appropriate that the satellite of the planet Neptune, discovered in 1846, should be named *Nereid*—a contrary nymph, however, for she revolves around the planet in the direction opposite to that of most members of the solar system. *Nerita* is a genus of sea-snail; *nereis,* a marine worm.

Nereus was the tutor of Aphrodite *Anadyomene:* born of the sea, who as goddess of universal desire was worshiped as *Pandemos:* of all the people, anticipating Sigmund Freud's ubiquitous *libido;* see *leubh.* When Aphrodite was wounded by Diomedes and in revenge teased his wife into infidelity, Zeus (as told in the *Iliad*) reminded the goddess that her sphere was love, not war—a phrase recently recaptured as a slogan. Her son was Eros, the child-god of desire, who drove his victims with axe and whip; his Roman counterpart, young Cupid, used bow with arrow to the heart. Hence E *sweetheart; erotic* and its trail of words, and *cupidity*. See *nebh.* Cupid's mother, Venus, while she provides English with *venerable* and *veneration,* is also responsible for *venery* and *venereal;* to avoid association with these, the scientifiction inhabitants of her planet are called not *Venerians* but *Venusians* (though perhaps the pulpish coiner did not know Latin). *Venus* has lingered pleasantly in plant names, as *Venus's flowerbasket, Venus's girdle, Venus's-hair, Venus's looking-glass.* See *uen*.

Furtive is from L *fur:* thief, whence, via OFr and *l.r* shift, came *felon, felonious, felony;* see *bher I. FUR* was branded on the brow of a convicted thief, who then was commonly called a "three-letter man," which phrase has prouder significance in college circles today, as one who has earned the varsity letter in three sports.

ga: rejoice. Gk *Ganymede:* rejoicing in men, cupbearer and beloved of Zeus (Roman Jupiter), from which dual role he ousted Hebe, goddess of youth (from whom the ephebic oath, on entering manhood). From one of Ganymede's functions, folkchange brought English *catamite.* Hence also *Ganymede,* the largest satellite of the planet Jupiter. *OED* lists 7 relevant words begnning *hebe,* as *hebecarpous, hebephrenia*—not to be confused with the 9 words from L *hebes, hebetum:* dull, as *hebetate, hebetude. Hebe* is also sixth of the counted asteroids. Milton, in *L'Allegro,* summons

Quips and cranks, and wanton wiles,
Nods, and becks and wreathèd smiles
Such as hang on Hebe's cheeks,
Sport, that wrinkled care derides,
And Laughter holding both his sides.

Shakespeare, in *Antony and Cleopatra,* 3, 13, says "Come, let's have one other *gawdy* night"; and *gaudy night* has come to be an annual commemorative festival at many British colleges. Dorothy L. Sayers, in her detective novel *Gaudy Night* (1936), indulges in a rare poetic flight, giving a sonnet the octet of which is written by the heroine Harriet Vane, the sestet being added by the amateur detective Lord Peter Wimsey:

Here then at home, by no more storms distrest,
    Folding laborious hands we sit, wings furled;
    Here in close perfume lies the rose-leaf curled,
Here the sun stands and knows not east nor west,
Here no tide runs; we have come, last and best,
    From the wide zone in dizzying circles hurled

To the still centre where the spinning world
Sleeps on its axis, to the heart of rest.
Lay on thy whips, O Love, that we upright
Poised on the perilous point, in no lax bed
May sleep, as tension at the verberant core
Of music sleeps; for, if thou spare to smite
Staggering, we stoop, stooping, fall dumb and dead,
And, dying so, sleep our sweet sleep no more.

At the story's end, the noble detective and the lady share the oddest–and the neatest–proposal in all fiction:

"Placetne, magistra?"

"Placet."

The Proctor, stumping grimly past with averted eyes, reflected that Oxford was losing all sense of dignity. But what could he do? If Senior Members of the University chose to stand–in their gowns too!–closely and passionately embracing in New College Lane right under the Warden's window, he was powerless to prevent it. He primly settled his white bands and went upon his walk unheeded, and no hand plucked his velvet sleeve.

gal, gar. Imitative of cry or shout. L *gallus:* cock, the calling bird. *gallinaceous. galeeny.* Sp, *gallinazo;* Fr, *gallinule. gallium* (see *el 31*). *galimatias,* from noisily disputing students, but possibly a folkchange from LL *ballimathia:* bawdy songs. *garrulous, garrulity.* Gc, *charm* (cast a spell). *care,* as *Take care!* In the 18th c., *Gardyloo!,* from Fr *Gardez l'eau:* Watch out for the water, as the slops were poured out of the window; see *leuk.*

By metathesis, *slogan. slughorn,* now *slogan,* was misunderstood by Chatterton (d. 1770) in his re-creations of early English verse, and followed by Browning in *Childe Roland* (1855): "Dauntless the slughorn to my lips I set, and blew."

German (with a hard *g*) was the Celtic name for the shouting Germanii, who came roaring into battle. In 1886 Klemes A. Winkler discovered a chemical element, which he named after his native land, *germanium;* see *el 32.* Also *germanite; Germanophobe,* etc. A *Germantown* is a small covered wagon, used by the westering pioneers, first made at Germantown, Pennsylvania.

Gc, *call.* John Masefield, in *Sea Fever,* rejoices, repeating the first seven words to start each stanza:

I must down to the seas again, for the call of the running tide
Is a wild call and a clear call that will not be denied . . .
And all I ask is a merry yarn from a laughing fellow-rover,
And quiet sleep and a sweet dream when the long trick's over.

Poet Laureate John Betjeman's 1978 preface to Masefield's *Selected Poems* begins: "John Masefield wrote two lyrics which will be remembered as long as the language lasts–I must go down to the seas again . . ." *eight* words–showing how long the laureate's memory–debasing the power and drive of poetry to wistful, hackneyed prose. "The difference between the right word and the almost right word," said Mark Twain, "is the difference between lightning and the lightning bug." Pope captured the converse:

True wit is nature to advantage dressed,
What oft was thought, but ne'er so well expressed.

clap, clatter, clack, crack, crackle. And in the theatre, via Fr, those hired to applaud, the *claqueurs* of the *claque*. Via *karo:* lament, OE *cearig:* sorrowful, came *chary*. Laertes, in *Hamlet*, warns his sister Ophelia against the prince's suit:

And keep you in the rear of your affection,
Out of the shot and danger of desire.
The chariest maid is prodigal enough
If she unmask her beauty to the moon . . .

As the barber wrapped his towel about Archelaus, king of Macedonia, he inquired: "How shall I cut your hair, Sire?" The king answered: "In silence"—Plutarch, *On Garrulity* (ca. A.D. 95).

gar: praise. A special use of the root *ga*. L *Gratia Dei:* Praise be to the Lord. *grace*. "It is the grace of lambs to suckle kneeling."—Chinese proverb. *gracile; gracious; grateful, gratify. gratis, gratuity. graceless, disgrace,* etc. *agree; disagreeable. congratulations. ingrate* (*in:* not); *ingratiate* (*in:* into). The three *Graces* were *Aglaia:* Brightness, *Euphrosyne:* Good Cheer, and *Thalia:* Bloom. See the Muses, under *men I*.

Sp, *gracioso*. Fr, *maugré*. Celt, *bard*, singer of praises. Charles Lamb, pondering grace before meals, wondered why there is none before books, those spiritual meals: "a grace before Milton, a grace before Shakespeare, a devotional exercise proper to be said before reading *The Faerie Queene.*"

Such stains there are, as when a Grace
Sprinkles another's laughing face
With nectar, and runs on.
—Walter Savage Landor, *On Catullus*

garg. Imitative of throat sounds. Gk *bronkhus:* windpipe. *bronchia, bronchus; bronchitis,* coined in 1808 by Charles Bedham. Also *branchia, branchiform,* etc. *hellebore* (Gk *hellos:* fawn, and *bro:* eaten by fawns). *theobromine,* a bitter compound, but from *Theobroma:* food of the gods, a genus of chocolate plants; coined by Carolus Linnaeus (d. 1778). From the form *guer,* L *vorare,* came *devour; voracious, omnivorous,* etc. See *bhag; dheigh N 2 f.*

gorge. gargle, gurgle; gurges, gurgitation, ingurgitation, regurgitate. gargoyle, the grotesque figure on churches, is in function a spout to pour off rain. It was Fr *gargouille:* gullet; and *Gargouille* was a fabulous dragon that lived in the River Seine in the 7th c. and devoured the inhabitants of Rouen until killed by the virtuous Romanus, bishop of Rome.

The *l.r* shift led to *glut, deglution, deglutition; gullet; glutton.* (*glutton:* the wolverine, is a translation of Gm *Vielgrass:* great gobbler, which is a mistranslation of Norw *fjeldfrass:* wolverine; literally, mountain cat.) *gargantuan,* from Rabelais' *Gargantua,* the gluttonous giant. The father looked at the babe in the cradle and exclaimed: *Que grand tu as!* How large you are! Hence its name, although Rabelais drew upon a friendly giant of French folklore. (Kenneth Tynan may have had a Rabelaisian memory when he called his nudist show *O! Calcutta! O! quel cul t'as!* What a backside you have!) As Gargantua grew, he unwittingly swallowed five pilgrims, staffs and all, in a salad. Cf. *guretso.*

jargon: literally, noise with the throat. *beagle:* open throat, from its barking. Probably *gormandize* and *gourmand;* these influenced the form and meaning of *gourmet,* from Fr *gromet:* wine merchant's assistant. Also *goliard,* the medieval wandering and guzzling student, who wrote ribald and drinking songs, supposedly named after *Golias,* god of the thirsty.

?ge: earth. Gk, *G(a)ea,* the goddess earth. *apogee, perigee. epigeous. geode, geodesy, geoid. George:* first, farmer. *georgic;* Virgil's *Georgics,* on peasant life and farming.

geo-, as *geocentric, geography, geology. geometry* was developed by the Egyptians to replot the rich earth when the annual flooding of the Nile had receded. *OED* lists 23 words beginning *geo,* and details others in 15 columns.

gel I, ghel: bright, smooth; bright colors; shiny objects; hence ice, freezing. Pers, *zircon,* one variety of which is called *jargon. zirconium;* see *el 17.*

Various chemical compounds are listed in *OED,* beginning as follows: *chol-,* 6 words; *chole-,* 15; *cholester-,* 9; *cholo-,* 16. In addition, *OED* 1933 details 23 words. The 1972 supplement adds 6, including *cholesterol,* "formerly cholesterin"; the *Science News Letter* of 1 Oct. 1955 warned that cholesterol "plays a large part in hardening of the arteries, leads to the formation of gallstones in experimental animals." *OED* also lists the following variants: *chlor-,* 15; *chloral-,* 6; *chlorophyll-,* 5; *chloro-* (green), 17, as *chlorotile; chloro-* (relating to *chlorine*), 21, as *chlorohydric.* Its 1972 supplement details 25 more, including *chlorosis:* green sickness; *chloroma, Chloromycetin; chloretone. chloroacetophenone,* more familiarly known as teargas.

cholic; chole; cholera. melancholy. choleric (from yellow bile), *melancholic* (from black bile); these are two of the four body humors, which are supposed to influence one's character; see *ugu.*

Gk, *Aglaia:* one of the three Graces, "the shining one"; see *dhal; esu; gar.*

L, *glabella; glabrous. glaucous; glaucoma; gall, gallstones.*

Gc, *clean, cleanse. glance, gleam, glimmer, glimpse, glint, glisten, glister.* Gm *Gelt. gold.* "All that glisters is not gold." *gilt. gill:* first, a cooling vessel. *gull:* bright-colored bird.

gull: to deceive, is from the figurative use of the bird to mean an easy mark. Similarly used have been *coney* (rabbit) and *pigeon.* Robert Greene, who died in 1592 from "an excess of pickled herring and Rhenish wine"—who wrote the first allusion to Shakespeare, the country lout presuming to be a playwright: "upstart crow . . . an absolute Johannes-fac-totum . . . the only Shake-scene in a country" —also wrote four books on cony-catching. John Galsworthy wrote a play, *The Pigeon* (1912), about a man of whom everyone took advantage.

Gc, *glare, glass, glaze, gloss.* (*gloss:* to explain, and *gloss over* are from Gk and L *glossa:* tongue; see *glokh*). *gleaming; glow, glower. glad* (bright spirits); *glee,* also *glee club. gleed* (glowing coal). *gloat. yellow.* By *l.r* shift, *green.* (For *yellow, green,* and *gold,* see also *kel VI.*) From this root come both *yolk* and *glair:* the yellow and the white of an egg. The yolk is also called *vitellus;* see *uet.*

Ice being shiny, we have *gelid, glacier, glacial, glacis. glide, glissade. chill, cool, cold. keel:* to cool, as by stirring. *glib:* first, literally, slippery. *gelatine.* Via Fr, *jelly; Jello.*

When icicles hang by the wall,
And Dick, the shepherd, blows his nail,
And Tom bears logs into the hall,
And milk comes frozen home in pail;
When blood is nipp'd and ways be foul
Then nightly sings the staring owl—
Tu-whit,
Tu-who, a merry note,
While greasy Joan doth keel the pot.
—*Love's Labor's Lost.*

gel II: form a ball, lump; hence, cohere. Gk, *ganglion. glioma:* a sticky tumor; *gliomatosis. gluteus. neuroglia* (Gk *glia:* glue).

L, *glue:* first used of birdlime, to hold the bird on a branch, for capture.

gluten, glutinous. agglutinate; agglomeration; conglobate, conglomeration. glebe, gleet: sticky discharge. *globe, globule.*

Gc, *clamp, claw, cleat, clench, clinch, cling, clunch, clutch. cleave:* to cling; for *cleave:* to cut apart, see *gleubh.* "Therefore shall a man leave his father and his mother, and shall cleave unto his wife, and they shall be one flesh"—Genesis 2:24 ("one flesh," of course, in the next generation). *cleavers. catchweed.*

clam; hence slang, *to clam up. clammy. clay. clasp, clip; cliff; clamber, climb. cleat. clue* or *clew:* first, a ball of thread, such as Ariadne gave Theseus, to enable him to kill the Minotaur in the labyrinth, then find his way out. *clod, clot; cloud* (a mass); *clout, club; clump; clutter. clever* first meant quick at holding, thus "catching on." Perhaps *cloth,* first meaning the material that clings; a TV commercial today announces a spray to take the "cling" from cloth garments. *gall(nut),* ellagic acid, from *oak gall,* coined by Henri Braconnot, who reversed Fr *galle:* gallnut, and added a suffix. Perhaps *clown:* lumpkin.

From its sticky sap, *clover.* The usual three-leaf kind is to the farmer a sign of good soil; the less frequent four-leaf clover is widely deemed a sign of good luck. The Irish prefer a special three-leaf form called *shamrock,* folkchanged from Ir *seamrog,* diminutive of *seamar:* clover. The shamrock preserves the memory of St. Patrick, whom Pope Celestine I sent in 432 to convert the Irish; at Wicklow, when he declared that the Trinity was contained in the Unity, the scornful Druids were ready to stone him; then he picked a shamrock and said, "Father and Son and Holy Ghost, as these three leaves, grow on a single stalk." Ireland was converted; Patrick is its saint; the shamrock is its emblem. *Patrick,* like *patrician:* noble, is from L *pater, patrem:* father.

> Only a man harrowing clods,
> In a slow silent walk
> With an old horse that stumbles and nods
> Half asleep as they stalk.
> Only thin smoke without flame
> From the heaps of couch grass;
> Yet this will go onward the same
> Though Dynasties pass.
> —Hardy, *In Time of 'the Breaking of Nations'*

gembh: bud, tooth. Gk, *gomphosis, agomphious.* L, *gem, gemmate.* Gc, *cam, comb;* Scot, *kame.* OE *acumbe:* combing off. *oakum.* The obsolete verb *kemb,* which gave way to *comb,* survives, usually for humor, in the otherwise archaic past participle, *kempt.* Wyclif, whose translation of the Bible was finished by 1388, declared, "If a man have a kempt head, then he is a lecherous man." So much for cleanliness beside godliness! Condemned at the Council of Constance in 1415, Wyclif was disinterred, burned, and thrown into the River Swift. Youthful disregard has kept alive the term *unkempt.*

gem(e): marry. *gamic, gamete,* first used in science by Gregor Mendel, who in 1865 announced the Mendelian law of heredity. *gamogenesis. gametophore. gamophyllous. cryptogamous. monogamy,* etc., *polygamy. endogamy:* only within the tribe; *exogamy:* only outside the tribe; *heterogamy. Gamelion,* seventh month of the Attic calendar, from mid-January to mid-February, was the month of marriages; children might be born in pleasant weather. *bigamy* (L *bi-:* two) and *digamy* (Gk *di-:* two) have grown apart; the former means two at a time; the latter, two in succession. Thus *bigamous; digamous:* in, or making, a second marriage. In Gilbert's *Trial By Jury* we find the following colloquy:

Defendant: You cannot eat breakfast all day,
Nor is it the act of a sinner,
When breakfast is taken away
To turn your attention to dinner . . .
But this I am willing to say,
If it will appease her sorrow,
I'll marry this lady today
And I'll marry that lady tomorrow.
Judge: That seems a reasonable proposition,
To which, I think, your client may agree.
Counsel: But I submit, my Lord, with all submission,
To marry two at once is Burglaree!

gen: pinch, squeeze; hit hard; result of compressing, etc. Gc, *knap, knapsack. knag. gnar. knell. knead; knit. nag. knob, knock. knot:* wood pressed tight. *knoll. knuckle.*

Gm *Knecht:* vassal; *knave:* first, a servant, hence a rascal. A *knight* (the word is given over eight columns in *OED*) was first a servant to an overlord or king; then, one that had "earned his spurs": could ride a horse and fight under his own banner; for a time, one devoted to the service of a lady. Also *knight errant;* see *ei.* A *carpet knight* was one whose powers were exerted rather in ladies' boudoirs than on battlefields; first, one not knighted on the field or for his feats there. Charles Major's *When Knighthood was in Flower* (1898) was a very popular romantic historical novel of 16th c. England. The first line of Spenser's *The Faerie Queene* is "A gentle knight was pricking on the plain."

geph: jaw. *chafer:* beetle; *cockchafer, chaff, chaffer. chaffinch;* see *spingo. jole,* more commonly *jowl:* "cheek by jowl" is used of persons sitting or working in close association. From *chattering teeth* probably comes *shiver.*

Oh, to be in England
Now that April's there . . .
While the chaffinch sings on the orchard bough
In England—now!
—Browning, *Home Thoughts from Abroad*

ger I: assemble. Gk and E, *agora:* place of assembly, marketplace. *agoraphobia. category; categorize:* first, public accusation; *panegyric:* public praise. *allegory. paregoric:* literally, soothing the crowd.

L *grex, gregem:* herd. *gregarious. aggregate; congregation; segregation. egregious:* out of the herd. Gc, *cram.*

"A man's life of any worth is a continual allegory . . . Shakespeare led a life of allegory; his works are the comments on it"—Keats, letter of 3 May 1819.

ger II: make noise. Imitative. Gk, *crane.* The *geranium,* from its shape, is also called *crane's-bill.* L, *grackle.* Gc, *cranberry,* earlier *craneberry* (see *bhel I*). *crake, croak, crow.* Fr, *pedigree:* foot of crane, the shape of the "family tree."

cur was used of the cooing pigeon and of the braying ass, before it clung to the snarling, unpedigreed, and often unwanted dog. *curmur* has been used of cats pleasantly together, but also, as in Scott's *Old Mortality* (1816): "A glass of brandy to three glasses of wine prevents the curmurring in the stomach." *curmudgeon* belongs here, but has won a place in the mockery of etymological divagations: Johnson, in his *Dictionary* (1755), notes under *curmudgeon,* "unknown correspondent: *coeur méchant,* 'evil or malicious heart'"—which a later, less harmless drudge (John Ash, 1775) passed on as "from the French *coeur,* unknown, and *méchant,* a correspondent." Actually, the *cur* of curmudgeon is an application of dog to human; for the second part, take your choice among dialectical *mudge:* bruise; *midge:* the insect; and OE *midgern:* fatty guts.

ger III: twist, crooked; hooked; squeezed together, etc. It, *group.* Fr, *crèche.* Gc, *carp:* pick at minor things. *cart:* small wagon, as a *pushcart.* We are cautioned not to put the cart before the horse, and it is usually easier to pull than to push. *cradle, crib; cramp, crimp; crank; creek* (winding); *creep; cringe; crinkle. cripple, crutch. crochet, crotchet. accroach. encroach.* (By hook or by) *crook. crooked. crock; croft. crouch. croup. croupier, crupper. crumb, crumble, crumple, crumpet.*

kernel. grape: first, the hook used to harvest the product of the vine. *grapple. grovel:* bending low; coined by Shakespeare. *agraffe. crozier. lacrosse:* game named for the shape of the stick. *Cross* is via L *crux, crucis,* whence also *crux, crucial. crucifixion* seems a method of dispatch of Phoenician origin. *crucifer, cruciform;* a *crucible* was first a light-holder before the cross behind the altar. (*altar* was folkchanged from L *adolere:* to burn, by association with *altus:* high, comparative *altior;* an altar was originally a place, usually on high ground, for burning a sacrifice.) See *cruc.*

There are many words naming groups of creatures. Some of these were farmers' terms, as a *flock* of sheep, a *herd* of cattle—although English has *shepherd* as well as *herdsman.* A *pot* of apples was 5 pecks; a *pot* of butter, 14 pounds. In venery, a gentleman could not qualify as a sportsman unless he knew the proper group terms: as a *school* (folkchanged from *shoal*) of fish; a *covey* of partridge (*cove, cover,* from the nest); a *rafter* of *turkeys* (*raft:* a large collection; whence also *riffraff* and *raffish*); a *gang* of elk; a *skulk* of foxes; a *nest* of rabbits; farther off, a *pride* of lions.

The earliest list of such terms is *The Book of St. Albans* (1486), by Dame Juliana Berners. More recent are *An Exaltation of Larks* (1970), by James Lipton, and the Ivan Sparkes *Dictionary of . . . Group Terms* (1975). Some of the terms are derogatory, as an *abomination* of monks, a *riot* of Romans. A few have been folkchanged, as a *chirm* (: chatter) became a *charm* (of goldfinches). Many have been created by word-fanciers seeking clever or humorous pairing, as a *guzzle* of aldermen, an *entrance* of actresses, a *column* of accountants, a *frown* of critics, a *gaggle* of gossips (earlier, of geese on water; a *skein* of geese in flight), a *zeal* of zebras. Noticing a *haunting* of whores near the London Dorchester Hotel, I was reminded of the three Oxford professors who tried to cap one another's climax: a *flourish* of strumpets, a *jam* of tarts, an *anthology* of pros. In his *English Grammar* (1817), William Cobbett spoke, somewhat sardonically, of "nouns of number, such as Mob, Parliament, Rabble, House of Commons, Regiment, Court of King's Bench, Den of Thieves, and the like."

"He that would eat the kernel must crack the shell'—Latin proverb.

ger IV: grow old. Pers, *Zoroaster; Zarathustra:* literally, owner of old camels. His words, of about 100 B.C., are recorded in the *Zend-Avesta:* "Thus spake Zarathustra." Confucius had his say some 500 years later. The *Zoroastrian* god of light was *Ormuzd;* whence also *Mazdaism.* The morning prayer of the current followers of Zoroaster (called *Parsi,* from *Persia*) is for "good thoughts, good words, good deeds," a worthy trinity. Gk *ageratum* (*a* negative): a perennial flower.

The 1933 *OED* defines *gerocomical:* pertaining to the treatment of the aged; also *gerocomy; gerontarchical, gerontic; gerontocracy. gerontogeous:* "of plants, etc., belonging to the Old World, to the eastern hemisphere." *OED*'s 1972 supplement adds *gerontocratic, gerontology, gerontomorphic, gerontophil,* etc., and the "new" branch of medicine, *geriatrics,* suggested by I. L. Nascher in the

N.Y. Medical Journal of 21 Aug. 1909 "to cover the same field in old age as is covered by pediatrics in childhood." The *New Scientist* of 19 Jan. 1967 complained that "there is in Britain only one university chair in geriatrics, and none in gerontology." The fields have flourished since then. The London *Times* of 16 Feb. 1963 reported "a new and deceptive form of restraint that has appeared in certain mental hospitals to fill the vacuum left by the straitjacket—the geriatric chair."

ger V, gren: to ripen, grow old; an extension of *ger IV.* L *granum:* grain, seed. *grain, granary; grange. granule, granulated, granulose. garner; garnet* (Fr *grenate*); *pomegranate:* seedy fruit. *granite:* a granular rock; *OED* defines 14 related words. gravy is a misreading of OFr *grane:* seed-sprinkled. *grenade. engrained. filigree* is folkchanged from *filigrane.* Gc, *corn* (on the cob); *corny* in English slang means drunk, especially red and pimply from drink; in the U.S. it is applied to an action or remark such as might come from a country bumpkin. For *corn* on the foot, see *ker II. kernel.*

churl: old fellow. Hence also *Carl, Caroline; Charles;* Fr *Charlemagne:* Charles the Great and the Carolingian concerns. *carline* is still Scots for an old woman. *Charles's Wain,* the Big Dipper, the Great Bear, was named after Charlemagne because the neighboring *Arcturus:* the Bear watcher, was (erroneously) associated with the other medieval hero, King Arthur. The ancients had observed that the polar stars never "set"; never sink below the horizon. Homer's *Odyssey,* v, pictures Odysseus

Gazing with fixed eye on the Pleiades,
Boötes setting late, and the Great Bear,
By others called the Wain, which, wheeling round,
Looks ever toward Orion, and alone
Dips not into the waters of the deep.

?ger VI: act, do, carry; pile up (not traced before L *gerere, gestum*). *gerent, gerund; gest, gesticulate. gesture; jest. gestation. armiger. belligerent. congeries. register. congested. digest; ingest, egest. suggest.* In the 14th c. OE *weorpan:* throw, was superseded by *cast,* possibly from this root. *OED* gives over 20 columns to *cast,* with two dozen meanings and with combinations such as *cast about, cast aside, castaway, castoff.* Also *broadcast; downcast; forecast; outcast; overcast; roughcast.*

When in disgrace with fortune and men's eyes
I all alone beweep my outcast state . . .
For thy sweet love remembered such wealth brings
That then I scorn to change my state with kings.
—Shakespeare, Sonnet 29

gerbh: scratch, carve. Gk *graphein:* incise; *gramma:* letter. *gram, grammar; diagram; ungrammatical. gramophone, phonograph. graph, graphology. graphite:* used for the "lead" in pencils; actually, a form of carbon (see *el 6*). *graft:* from the resemblance of the pointed shoot to a stylus. From *graft* (in botany and surgery): something added on, came the use in—shall I say?—economics and politics. *epigraph. autograph, holograph, monograph.* JWalker has 84 words ending *graph. biographer. stenography* (Gk *stenos:* narrow, short). *epigram; program.* JWalker has 33 words ending *gram,* as *aerogram, parallelogram; telegram:* message sent by *telegraph.*

In an early instance of "fem lib," G. K. Chesterton reported, "Twenty million young women rose to their feet with the cry 'We will not be dictated to!' and promptly became stenographers." J. M. Barrie pictures a frustrated yet determined wife in *The Twelve-Pound Look* (1908), £12 being the sum she needed to buy a typewriter and independence.

It, *graffito* (plural, *graffiti*). Many games, including the crossword puzzle and "Scrabble," use varieties of the *anagram,* which is basically a rearrangement of the letters of a word or phrase so as to form another: e.g., *time, item, mite, emit.* A special form of this is the *palindrome* (Gk *palindromos:* running back): a word or sentence that reads the same forward and back. Thus *noon.* And "A man, a plan, a canal, Panama."

The anagram has played a minor role in word formation. *aconitic acid* is tribasic; its dibasic fellow is *itaconic acid.* The *ohm,* named after the German physicist Georg Simon Ohm, is the unit of electrical resistance; its reciprocal, the unit of conductance, is the *mho.* See *gher III.* Anagrams grow in plant names: *tellima* from *mitella; Amopuria* from *Mapouria.* They work with cities: *Tokyo,* the royal head; *Kyoto,* the religious heart, of Japan. Ellery Queen sets the clue to one of his mysteries, *The Fourth Side of the Triangle,* in a series of anagrams.

What do these four words—*thorn, sate, shout, stew*—have in common? Each is an anagram of a cardinal point of the compass.

Tetragrammaton: four-letter word, especially J H V H, standing for the not-to-be-spoken-or-written name of the Lord. Fourteen letters for four.

Gc, *carve. scratch, scrawl, scribble;* but see *sek. crab, crawl. crawfish* and *crayfish* are folkchanged from OE *crevise,* Fr *écrevisse.*

glamour is by *l.r* shift from *gramarye:* enchantment, Fr *grimoire.* Until about 1600 there was a *Magister Glomeriae:* Master of Glomery, at Cambridge University. He is now usually explained as head of the (Latin) Grammar School; but a Cambridge University statute of 1591 states: "The Master of Grammar shall be brought by the beadle to the place where the Master of Glomerye dwelleth at iii of the clock, and the Master of Glomery shall go before." The word *glamour* is generally supposed to have been introduced into literary language by Scott in *The Lay of the Last Minstrel* (1805), but Burns wrote in 1789:

> Ye gipsy gang that deal in glamor,
> And you deep-read in hell's black grammar,
> Warlocks and witches . . .

No longer magic, *glamour* still means alluring charm. It should keep the *u* spelling, for association with *amour.*

?ges: carry on, perform. L *gerere, gestum. gest, gestation. gesticulate, gesture;* see *ger VI. gerent; gerundive. jest. jester. OED*'s 1972 supplement defines *beau geste* as "a display of magnanimity"; it is an act performed for the sake of grace rather than need. *congestion. ingest, digest, egest, register. suggest. congeries. armiger; belligerent.* The usurper Antonio, plotting his brother Prospero's death in *The Tempest,* ii, 1, says of the people, "They'll take suggestion as a cat laps milk."

geu: hollow place, or what it might hold; lump, round object, etc. Gk, probably *kobold:* a sprite inhabiting hollows and mines, from whom *cobalt;* via Fr, *goblin.* Gc *cubbyhole. cot, cottage, pigeon cote; coterie. haycock,* to which the Victorians preferred *haystack. cudgel,* lumped at one end; Gk *rhopalos:* cudgel, has given English *rhopalic;* see *uer II. chubby,* and the fish the *chub. chitterlings,* from the protrusive abdomen. OE *coppe:* spider; *cobweb. cower. coop. cogwheel. keel:* first, of round-bottomed ships. *cod:* bag, hence *codpiece* (see *ghel II*); thus, from its shape, the *codfish.*

Nasalized, Gm *Kunt, cunt.* Among Shakespeare's words for the female intercrural foramen are *ring, eye, circle, O, nothing;* as in Mercutio's words in *Romeo and Juliet,* ii, 1, or when Hamlet is saucy throughout his words with Ophelia as they prepare to watch the play:

Hamlet: Lady, shall I lie in your lap?
Ophelia: No, my lord.
Hamlet: I mean, my head upon your lap.
Ophelia: Aye, my lord.
Hamlet: Do you think I meant country matters?
Ophelia: I think nothing, my lord.
Hamlet: That's a fair thought to lie between maids' legs.
Ophelia: What is, my lord?
Hamlet: Nothing.
Ophelia: You are merry, my lord.
Hamlet: Who, I?

Even the simple-seeming word *lap* was double-dipped for Ophelia; one meaning it had in Shakespeare's time is "the female pudendum"; *The Body of Man* (1615) says: "The clitoris is a small body . . . placed in the height of the lap."

ghaido. Gc, *goat.* See *ane.*

ghais: stick to. L *haerere. adhere, adhesion; cohere, coherent; inhere, inherent. hesitate:* be stuck. For *inherit* and *heir,* see *ghe.*

ghaiso: spear. Gc, *garfish. garlic:* spear leek. Probably *gerfalcon.* Several names: *Edgar:* happy with spear; *Oscar:* godlike with spear; *Roger:* famed with spear; *Gerald:* spear-wielder; *Gerard:* spear power; *Gervais:* spear vassal. *Gertrude:* true to the spear.

ghans: goose family. Gk *khen. chenopod:* goosefoot, a plant also (perhaps by folk-change from the Greek) called *Good Henry;* and its equivalent in L, Fr, and Gm. "In Cambridgeshire it is called good King Henry"—Gerarde's *Herbal* (1597).

L *(h)anser. anserine; merganser.* Gc, *goose, gander; gosling; goshawk.* Norse, *smorgasbord:* goose-fat table. *goosestep* occurs in 1806, as to balance on each leg alternately, swinging the other back and forth; D. L. Richardson says, in a sonnet of 1825:

Oft with aching bones
I marched the goose-step, cursing Serjeant Jones.

The word's use in reference to the brisk march without bending the knees seems to have appeared first in English in *Mr. Britling Sees It Through* (1916), by H. G. Wells; notorious in Hitler's troops, this goosestep has been adopted by some other nations, especially for ceremonial parades.

Fiddlepins end! Get out, you blazing ass!
Gabble o' the goose. Don't bugaboo-baby me!
—C. S. Calverley, *The Cock and the Bull* (1866)

ghau: call upon, invoke; hence, the one invoked, the deity. Gc *guth,* Gm *Gott. god, godhead, godsend. godchild, godparent, godmother, godfather. gossip:* first, the one that bore the infant (*sib*) to baptism, thus undertaking responsibility for its religious upbringing; see *spel. Godfrey* (Gc *fridu:* peace). *giddy* (OE *gudig:* possessed by God). *good-by(e),* compressed from *God be by ye. God* is not related to *good;* see *ghedh.*

ghdhem: of the earth. Pers, *zamindar. germander:* ground-oak. Gk, *chthonic. chthonian, chthonograph. autochthonous. Erysichthon:* tearer-up of earth: a monster who destroyed trees in the sacred grove of Demeter, Greek goddess of agriculture; she cursed him with an insatiable appetite, and he finally devoured himself. (Among intemperate eaters was *Cambis,* king of Lydia, who [as described by F. W. Hackwood in *Good Cheer*] "had an appetite so fiercely compelling that one night the glutton unfortunately devoured his wife.")

chameleon: ground-lion. *Chamomila:* genus, the earth-apple; *camomile.* Four other plant genera: *Chamaecyparis:* ground-cypress; *Chamasdaphne:* ground-heath; *Chamaelirium:* devil's bit; *Camelina:* "ground-flax," mustard. The flower *camellia* was named for the Jesuit traveler George J. Kamel (d. 1706).

In Latin, the initial sound was sloughed. *humus:* earth; *homo, hominis:* earthling, man. "Dust thou art." *humanus:* human. *humus; inhume, exhume.* L *postumus:* last, hence last-born, was blended with *posthumus:* born when the father was in the ground; hence E *posthumous. homage. homicide. hominid, hominoid. homunculus. human, humane, humanitarian, humanity, inhuman; humanism,* etc. *humble, humiliate; humility.* Hence the expression *to eat humble pie:* to submit to humiliation; this is a folkchange from the literal pie made of the "umbles" of a deer; Thomas Love Peacock, in *Maid Marian* (1822), an evocation of earlier days, says: "Robin helped him largely to humble pie . . . and the other dainties of his table." The later use was made by Charles Reade, in *Hard Cash* (1863): "The 'scornful dog' had to eat wormwood pudding and humble pie." See *lendh I.*

Sp, *hombre,* whence the card game *ombre.* Fr *bonhomie.* Scot, *duniwassal.* Russ, *zemstvo.* Gc, second element in *bridegroom,* folkchanged from OE *gume:* man, by association with *groom:* servant.

Homo sum; humanum nil a me alienum puto: "I am a man; I deem nothing human alien to me"—Terence, *Heautontimoroumenos*—The self-tormentor (163 B.C.).

ghdhies: yester. Fr *hier;* Gm *Gestern:* yesterday. *yestreen.* And Dante Gabriel Rossetti's inspired translation of François Villon's refrain:

Mais ou sont les neiges d'antan?
But where are the snows of yesteryear?

ghdhu: fish. Gk *ichthus. ichthyology. ichthyoid.* Two extinct creatures: *ichthyornis:* fish-bird, and *ichthyosaurus:* fish-lizard. *ichthyosis:* scaly skin. *OED* lists 26 words beginning *ichthy,* as *ichthyolatry:* fish worship, as of Dagon, fish-man deity of the ancient Philistines; and it details 26 more. *ichthyophthalmite* is the fish-eye stone.

The fish was a symbol of the early Christians, a secret recognition sign in times of persecution, because the letters of the Greek word *i.ch.th.u.s* are the initial letters of *Iesous Christus, Theou, Uios, Soter:* Jesus, Anointed, God's Son, Savior.

The most remarkable such symbol, used as an amulet, etc., laid on a pregnant woman's abdomen for a healthy child, was the holy square

S A T O R
A R E P O
T E N E T
O P E R A
R O T A S

Seeming to say "Arepo the sower holds the wheels in the work," this square, reading the same up and down, left or right, has a cross in the middle reading *tenet* (L): he holds; E *tenet:* a held belief. The letters of the square can be rearranged in a single large cross, reading *Paternoster* from top and from left, with four letters omitted: *a, o, a, o* (which surround the inner cross, *tenet*). Set these at the four tips; they are alpha and omega: "I am Alpha and Omega, the beginning and the ending, saith the Lord"—Bible, Revelation of St. John. And all of the letters can be arranged to spell *Oro Te, Pater; oro Te, Pater, sanas:* "I pray to thee, Father, Thou healest." Thus the fivefold square is a fourfold Christian symbol; 5 + 4 = 9, 3 X 3, which is the Holy Trinity enfolded in itself, sealing the sign of the faithful.

ghe: lack; go without (in both senses: not having; and not belonging, outside); give up; be empty—hence, empty place, country as opposed to town. Gk *choris:* apart; *chorein:* yield place, withdraw; *chora:* place, country; *chorisis:* separation. Hence *chorion, chorizontes; anchoret,* later *anchorite. enchorial; epichorial, choristate; chorisis,* in botany; *choristophyllous. parachor:* literally, holds its place; a chemical constant. For *chorus,* etc., see *gher IV.* L *haerere. heir* (to what's left), *heritage, heredity; inherit, disinherit; exheredate.*

ghebh: give, receive. "O Lady! We receive but what we give"—Coleridge, *Dejection.* L *habere, habitum:* have, hold. *habit, habitude; habitat, inhabitant; cohabit.* L *habilis:* able to hold; expert. JWalker lists some 1050 adjectives (first conjugation, Latin) ending *able;* also about 300 (third conjugation) ending *ible,* and as many nouns ending *bility;* see *dheigh N 3. have. behavior. adhibit, exhibition, inhibition, prohibition.*

"The nature of men is always the same; it is their habits that separate them"—Confucius, *Analects* (ca. 500 B.C.). "Habits are first cobwebs, then cables"—Spanish proverb.

L *debere, debitum:* away from having. *debit, debt, debtor; indebted. debenture.* LL *debutus:* due; *dutiful, duty; endeavor.* Sinai: duty; Calvary: love.

inhabit. malady (LL *male habitum*). *habitation; habilitate. binnacle,* short for *habitaculum:* little building. *prebend* (from *pre* and the gerundive *habendum:* what ought to be given); thus also *provender. habiliment:* stump, was folkchanged in sound and sense by association with *habit,* which means both the custom and the costume; thence, via Fr, *déshabillé.*

habeas corpus: You may have the body. Fr, *avoirdupois; devoir.* Gc, *gavel:* tribute; the collector of the hated salt tax, in Dickens' *Tale of Two Cities,* is *Gabelle.* Probably *gavel,* hammer at auctions and formal meetings.

Edward Gibbon, in his *Memoirs* (1896), noted a too frequent attitude: "Dr. —— well remembered that he had a salary to receive, and only forgot that he had a duty to perform."

Samuel Johnson, in his *Shakespeare* (1765), makes the charge, "A quibble is to Shakespeare what vapours are to the traveller: he follows it at all adventures; it is sure to lead him out of his way, and sure to engulf him in the mire." William was far from unaware of this willfulness in his spirit: he rings all the changes on his name *Will* in Sonnets 135 and 136; and he may well have had a feeling of smiling self-mockery when he made Holofernes, after a bad pun in *Love's Labor's Lost,* add complacently: "This is a gift that I have, simple, simple, a foolish extravagant spirit, full of forms, figures, shapes, ideas, apprehension, notions, revolutions. These are begot in the ventricle of memory, nourished in the womb of pia mater, and delivered upon the mellowing of occasion. . . . *Vir sap qui pauca loquitur* [He's a wise man that says little]." See *sap.*

ghedh: join, fit; hence, going well together. See *bhad.* Gc, *gather, forgather. together. gad* (OE *gadeling:* companion). *garboard:* plank that fits on a ship's keel. *good. Thank goodness!* is a euphemism for *Thank God!* See *ghau; spel.* The suffix *ness,* usually added to an adjective to name its quality, is very frequent; JWalker lists 2656 words ending *ness,* as *blindness, fondness, gladness, kindness.* See *dheigh N 29.*

The evil that men do lives after them,
The good is oft interrèd with their bones.
—Mark Antony in *Julius Caesar*

ghel I: call. Imitative. Gk *kelidon:* the swallow. *celandine.* Gc, *gale; nightingale;* the *n* is intrusive, for easier flow. *yell, yelp.*

And such a yell was there,
Of sudden and portentous birth,
As if men fought upon the earth,
And fiends in upper air.
—Scott, *Marmion*

ghel II: cut. *geld, gelding. gilt:* young sow.

g(h)enu: angle, bend; hence (in Latin), knee. Thus *genuflect,* as a knight to his lord or his lady; formerly, as a man proposing marriage. From the Roman practice of the father's accepting a newborn son as legitimate by setting the infant on his knee, comes our word *genuine.* (Some claim it means "born in the family"; see *gn.*) In Greek, the change to *o* provided *goniometer,* which measures angles; *diagonal, polygon,* and the *Pentagon* (five-sided). The Germanic change to *kn* gave us *knee* and *kneel.*

The *gonyaulax* (knee-furrow) is a tiny protozoon that sometimes fills warm ocean waters, over 50 million per quart; off the Florida coast in 1947 thousands of fish died from the gonyaulax infestation, commonly known as *red tide.*

Given by some as a separate root, but probably from *g(h)enu* because of the sharp angle to the face, *genu* also means the jawbone, the chin. Hence *genial:* relating to the chin; for the other *genial,* see *gn.* Via Greek came *gonys:* the underpart of a bird's beak. *Prognathous:* with protrusive jaw, of a gnathic index over 103; contrasted with *orthognathous:* normal; and *opisthognathous:* of receding jaw. The *Syngnathidae:* jaws together, are the family of pipefish. *Chaetognatha:* phylum, the arrowworms, with bristly jaws; *Cynognathus:* dog-jawed, genus of large carnivorous reptiles of the Triassic period.

Here also Skr *hanu:* jaw; whence the "jawful" chattering monkey, E *hanuman;* and *Hanuman* the monkey leader in the Indian epic, the *Ramayama.*

gnathonic: sycophantic, which is derived from this root, comes directly from the parasite *Gnatho* in Terence's Latin comedy, *The Eunuch;* there are six words derived from *Gnatho* in *OED.* Also in Terence's play is *Thraso,* the *miles gloriosus:* braggart soldier; see *dhers.* Shakespeare, in *As You Like It,* v, 2, speaks of "Caesar's thrasonical brag of 'I came, saw, and overcame.'" See *ker III.* In *2 Henry IV,* iv, 3, he had remarked: "I may justly say, with the hooknosed fellow of Rome, 'I came, saw, and overcame.'" His first use of the expression gives the Latin as well, in the fantastical Armado's love letter in *Love's Labor's Lost,* iv, 1: "Me it was that might rightly say *Veni, vidi, vici,* which to annothonize in the vulgar—O base and obscure vulgar!—videlicet, He came, saw, and overcame." In 1683, when Jan Sobieski sent Pope Innocent XI the Mussulman standards he had captured at Vienna, he also sent the pious message: "I came, I saw, God conquered." Caesar's boast produced a less pious piece of learned graffito, sanctified for years—now in large print and framed behind glass—in the New York Harvard Club Men's Room, spelled in the hope (though the last word shows, hardly in the expectation) that a Harvard man would remember that the Romans pronounced *v* as *w: Veni, vidi, wiwi.* It was a Columbia professor, Brander Matthews, who in the first decades of our century used to declare: "A gentleman need not know Latin, but he should at least have forgotten it." See *dhers.*

In the at-first unpublished preface to *Don Juan* (1818), Byron applied both the Terentian names to Wordsworth, who had shifted from Liberal to Tory and been rewarded with a government post: "This Thraso of poetry has long been a Gnatho in politics."

On parent knees, a naked new-born child,
Weeping thou sat'st, when all around thee smiled;
So live that, sinking in thy last long sleep,
Calm thou may'st smile, while all around thee weep.
—Sir William Jones, *Persian Miscellany* (1780)

gher I: scratch, scrape away; hence, rough surface; rub, smear, tinge. Skr *ghat:* where sins are rubbed away, shrine; then, the stepways down to the sacred River Ganges at Benares, especially the "burning ghats," where pious Hindus are cremated, their ashes being thrown into the river. The Ganges is especially holy there, as for six miles it makes a U-turn back toward its godly source.

Kalighat: shrine of Kali; the black, terrific tongue of Agni, god of fire; then separately, goddess of destruction. *Kalighat* was also the early name of Calcutta; site of the "Black Hole," a garrison strong-room about 18 feet square, wherein 146 British prisoners were confined the night of 20 June 1756, during the Sepoy rebellion; in the morning, only 23 were alive. *Kali* means black. *Kali Nag:* black snake, is the elephant in Kipling's *The Jungle Book.*

Gk *khriein:* anoint; *chrisma:* unguent. *chrism. christen,* which identifies a Christian. *Christ:* the anointed, translation of Hebr *Messiah. Christopher:* bearer of Christ. *Christmas:* the Christ mass.

'Twas a thief said the last kind word to Christ.
Christ took the kindness and forgave the theft.
—Browning, *The Ring and the Book,* vi

The Turks borrowed *chrisma* as *khorozma,* for a depilatory; it came back via It and Fr as (cosmetic) *cream;* the word *cream* was long used for *chrism; creambox,* for *chrismatory.* In 1563 Thomas Becon explained: "The byshop must annoynt them with chrisme, commonly called creame." Goldsmith, in 1765:

In vain she tries her paste and creams
To smooth her face and hide its seams.

"You can't beat our milk, but you can whip our cream." *cream of the jest, cream of the crop:* the best. *cream of the wilderness:* gin, in the 19th c. Wild West. From *chrism* to *Christmas, OED* has 20 columns of relevant words. Also *Eucharist.*

Gk, *character:* originally a mark scratched on stone (or branded on a felon); hence, distinguishing features. *characterization, charactery,* etc.

From rough surface to skin, to color of skin, to color in general, came Gk *chroma, chromatos,* and English words such as *chrome, chromatic, achromatic; monochrome, dichromatic, heliochrome, homochromous, parachroma. OED* lists 9 and details 12 words beginning *chromato,* as *chromatophore, chromatoscope.* It lists 9 and details 12 beginning *chromo,* as *chromosome, chromophyll. chromolithograph,* which may be abbreviated *chromo.* Hence also *erythrochroic* (Gk *eruthro:* red); *cacochroid. chromium,* the chemical element (24) isolated by Nicolas-Louis Vauquelin in 1797, was first called *chrome* for its brilliantly colored compounds, the gem *emerald* from the oxide, *ruby* from the acid. Note that *chromatic* has also been transferred to music.

Also *gash;* via Celt, *gravel.* Gc, *grits, groats, gruel. grain, granule;* but see *ger V,* which overlaps. *grind, grist, gristle;* see *ghren. gruesome:* rubbing one the wrong way. *great,* which first meant gross-grained.

Probably also *gross,* which today as an adjective commonly implies coarseness or excessiveness; as "gross misbehavior." As a noun, it has had several senses: various thick coins, as Gm *Groschen;* It *grosso.* E *groat* was a great or "thick" penny; when coined in 1351, it equaled four pence. In finance, *gross* applies to an all-inclusive sum, opposed to *net.* As a measure, a *gross* is a dozen dozen; a *great gross* is a dozen gross. A *grocer* was first a wholesale merchant, dealing by the gross, as in the English Company of Grocers, established in 1344 to deal in spices and other produce from abroad; *grocery* was for a time spelled *grossery. grocer's itch* was a type of eczema, among those handling coarse produce, such as raw sugar. See *guertso.*

Here, too, *grosbeak. engross, engrossing. grogram* was folkchanged from Fr *grosgrain.* And when Admiral Vernon of the British Navy, in August 1740, ordered that the sailors' daily allowance of rum be diluted with water, his nickname, "Old Grog," from his grogram cloak, was shortened to *grog* as the name of the drink. If you drank too much, you became *groggy.* See *ker I.*

gher II: desire, delight. Gk *Eucharist. charism. charisma* is not in the 1933 *OED,* but it is in *OED*'s 1972 supplement, its first current use being dated 1947. Applied especially to President John F. Kennedy, it led the English *Listener* of 7 Feb. 1963 to wonder about a change of "the institutions of Western democracy into a kind of tribal form with a charismatic tribal leader."

The aromatic *chervil* and the plant genera *Eleocharis:* delight of the marsh; *hydrocharis; Eucharis:* delightful delight, the amaryllus family. *Amaryllus* is a shepherdess in the idyls of Theocritus. Virgil's *First Eclogue* sounds her praise: "Thou teachest the responsive woods to call Amaryllus fair." and Milton queries, in *Lycidas,*

Were it not better done, as others use,
To sport with Amaryllus in the shade . . .

L, *exhortatory; hortative, hortatory.* Gc, *greedy. yearn.*

Charon, who ferried the dead across the River Styx, may have been given his name, "the pleasant one," with the hope of receiving a warm welcome—not the fires of Tartarus!—when it was one's turn to take the voyage to "the undiscovered country from whose bourn No traveler returns." See *kau II.*

The *Eucharist:* giving of thanks and sharing of joy, is a memory of the Last Supper, a Passover feast, of Jesus and his disciples before his betrayal. At this service, the consecrated bread and wine, in which, says the *Maryknoll Catholic Dictionary,* "the body and blood of Christ is really, truly, and substantially contained, for the purpose of giving spiritual nourishment to the soul," are absorbed by the recipients. This service, first by St. Ambrose in A.D. 385, is now commonly known as *mass,* from the closing sentence: *Ite, missa est:* Go, this is the sending. The word has been used as the ending of several festive services, as *Candlemas, Michaelmas,* and, most popularly, *Christmas.*

The sentence used in consecrating the mass bread (now a wafer)—*Hoc est corpus meum:* This is my body—has been deemed the origin of a magician's words before he performs a transformation trick; but these can be traced to the medieval goliards, students that sang and drank their way from university to university, making obeisance to the Lord of Misrule, Golias ("Glutton," from L *gula:* gullet), and imposing magical tricks on the country and town folk, with mock-Latin incantations such as *Max pax max Deus adimax,* which turned into *hocus-pocus,* and ultimately into what properly named the trick, a *hoax.*

gher III: gray. *gray, grey; graybeard, greyhound; graylag, grayling. grilse. Griselda:* gray battle-maid. Fr *grisaille. grisette:* working girl, clad in gray. *grizzled; grizzly bear.*

ambergris. The word *amber* is from Arabic. *amber,* fossil resin, is found mainly on the southern shore of the Baltic Sea; it was first called *amber jaune* (yellow) to distinguish it from *ambergris* (gray), which is a morbid secretion of the sperm whale found floating in warm seas or washed ashore. The word *ambergris* has been folkchanged to *ambergrease* and, especially in the classical revival of the 17th c., *ambergreece. Amber,* especially with embedded insects, twigs, and other fossil substances, has long been prized for amulets and jewelry; thus in 1691, of Cleopatra: "The fair queen of Egypt she wore a commode, and on top there was a laced amber."

Since amber, when rubbed, becomes, as *OED* puts it, "notably electric," and thus was man's first close contact with such phenomena, the Greek name for amber, *elektron,* came to be used for the entire field of *electromagnetic* charges, *electricity,* the *electron,* and hundreds of other terms. Many mature persons have had an *electrocardiogram,* though they may have been lucky to avoid an *electroencephalogram;* fewer have had to suffer *electrocution.* The telephone, telegraph, television, electric lights, radio, transistors, and the new world and words of the computer and micromechanics, are the most manifest of the spreading activities due to man's use of electricity. It reaches out in all the sciences, in medicine, in architecture, in the arts, and in many ways is still developing, with more to come. With electric and electronic devices helping us to probe the vast outer ranges of the expanding universe, the infinitesimal whirls within the atom, and that most complex of all our concerns, the interfiliations of the human brain, there will be many further findings, and their fit new words.

It is interesting to note that all the units of electricity take their name from workers in the field:

Unit of electric —		
capacity	*farad*	E, Michael Faraday, 1881
quantity	*coulomb*	Fr, C. A. de Coulomb, 1881
current	*ampere*	Fr, André M. Ampère, 1881
energy	*joule*	E, James P. Joule, 1882
frequency	*hertz*	Gm, Heinrich Hertz, 1928
motive force	*volt*	It, Count Alessandro Volta, 1873
resistance	*ohm*	Gm, Georg S. Ohm, 1861, 1881
conductivity	*mho*	(reciprocal of ohm), 1883
power	*watt*	Scot, James Watt, 1882

Sources: 1861, British Association Meeting, Manchester. 1881, Paris Electric Congress. 1882, British Association President's Address: "A watt, then, expresses the rate of an ampere multiplied by a volt, while a horsepower is 746 watts. . . . The watt is the rate of doing work when a current of one ampere passes through a resistance of one ohm."

In the field of electromagnetic forces are further units from names: *faraday* (*faradic, faradization*); *henry; maxwell; newton; weber.* From *gauss,* electromagnetic density, came in World War II the word *degauss:* make a ship immune to magnetic mines. Perhaps the only recently described unit not named for a scientist is the *dyne;* see *deu.*

Let beam upon my inward view
Those eyes of deep, soft, lucent hue—
Eyes too expressive to be blue,
Too lovely to be gray.
—M. Arnold, *Faded Leaves*

gher IV: seize; embrace, enclose, enclosure. Gk *khoros:* enclosed place for dancing. Hence *choric, chorus, choir, chorister, chorale. Terpsichore. choragus. choriamb. chorea:* St. Vitus's dance.

Gk *cheir:* hand, with opposed thumb, the grasping organ. *cheiranthus,* etc. *chirotonize:* vote by show of hands. *chirocracy:* government by the strong hand, "the mailed fist." *chirurgeon:* hand-worker, shortened to *surgeon. chiromachy,* hand-to-hand fighting; boxing. *chironomy; chiromancy; chiromantic* (Keep his hands away!), *chirosopher,* etc. The centaur *Chiron* was famed as a doctor—the "laying on" of hands. *enchiridion:* a handbook. *chiropractor; chiropodist:* hand-to-foot man.

Gk *khronos:* time, embracing all things. *chronaxy. chronic, isochronous. anachronism, metachronism, parachronism. chronometer; chronoscope. chronograph.* There is also a *chronanagram.*

gird, girdle, girt, girth. Via Fr *jardin, jardiniere; garden.* "God Almighty first planted a garden"—Francis Bacon, *Essays.* Gm, *Kindergarten.* The *gardenia* is named after the American botanist Alexander Garden (d. 1791). Gc, OE *geard, yard;* Scot, *kailyard. orchard. hortus siccus:* dry garden: herbarium, or collection of dried plants. *hortal, hortensial; Hortense. horticolous, hortulan. horticulture* is care of growth in an orchard or garden, as opposed to *agriculture,* in a field; see *ag.*

The River Jordan has had an odd influence on a set of English words. At first a *jordan* was a bottle—a flat-bottomed globe with a long neck—in which pilgrims brought back water from the holy Jordan ("There's one wide river to cross"); you can still buy Jordan water at Mideastern stores in New York City. From its shape, the jordan was used to hold urine for analysis; then it became a urinal, a chamber pot; Shakespeare, in *1 Henry IV,* ii, 1, has a porter protest: "Why they will allow us ne'er a jordan, and then we leak in your chimney." For two centuries around Shakespeare, the term *a jordan* was also used in scorn of a silly person, a noodle, in recent vogue slang from Russian-Yiddish, *a nudnik.* Then, from a curious reading of Jacob's words in Genesis 32:10: "with only my staff I crossed this Jordan," the word was slang—so recorded in the *Dictionary of the Canting Crew* (1700)—for a blow with a staff. These meanings have passed; all that is left is the *jordan almond*—which has no relation to the river, but is a folk-change from Fr *jardin:* garden: a cultivated variety of the pleasant nut, first grown in Malaga. *The Pall Mall Gazette* of 24 Jan. 1888 said: "With the Malaga raisins go the Jordan almonds, with which they are always eaten." A century later, they remain a popular admixture.

Also *courtyard.* A court was first an enclosed yard around a palace. *court holy water* was from the 16th through the 18th c. a phrase for fair promises not meant to be kept (as today in political campaigns); in *King Lear* the King is reproached by the Fool, who on the stormy heath regrets that they had left the inhospitable daughter's castle: "O Nuncle, court holy water in a dry house is better than this rain water out o' door."

From the manners of a court came *courteous, courtesy.* "The grace of God is in courtesy"—Hilaire Belloc. *curts(e)y; courtier.* A *courtesan* was originally a man attached to the court of a prince; then especially (It *cortigiano*) a member of the papal curia. Being forbidden to marry, many of these men acquired a feminine *courtesan* (It *cortigiana*); there were in Rome in 1565 "many thousand Cortigians well regarded." The distinction was made clear in 1607: "Your whore is for every rascall, but your curtizan is for your courtier"—far from what Cotgrove in 1608 called "a hedge-whore, lazie queane, lowsie trull, filthie curtall, doxie, mort." Francis Bacon in 1608 set her in a figure, admonishing that "knowledge may not be as a courtesan, for pleasure, but as a spouse, for generation."

Lord Herbert of Cherbury (d. 1648) wrote a pleasant ditty to his fair:

Now that the April of your youth adorns
The garden of your face . . .

The kiss of the sun for pardon,
The song of the birds for mirth,
One is nearer God's heart in a garden
Than anywhere else on earth.
—Dorothy Gurney (d. 1932)

gher V: gut. Gk *khorion:* afterbirth. *chorion.* Gk *khorde,* L *chorda:* gut, string. *cord, cordon; chordal, chordate. harpisichord; tetrachord.* L, *hernia. haruspex:* entrail examiner, diviner; see *spek.*

As unto the bow the cord is,
So unto the man is woman;
Though she binds him, she obeys him,
Though she draws him, yet she follows;
Useless each without the other!
—Longfellow, *Hiawatha*

ghers: to bristle. Gk, *chersonese:* literally, rough, barren island. Applied to the peninsula of Thrace; then, any peninsula. *choiros:* pig, the bristly beast. *chiros:* hedgehog. hence the suffix *choerus,* as *hydrochoerus. chride:* barleycorn; E *crith:* unit of weight. L, *Hordeum,* genus of barley. *orgeat. (h)ericius:* hedgehog. *horrere:* hair stands on end. *horrendous, horrible, horrid, horrific, horripilation, horrisonant; horror,* first roughness, then mingled terror and repugnance.

It *capo:* head, as *capo* of the Mafia (see *caput*), plus *riccio:* hedgehog, E *capriccio; caprice:* first a shiver, then a whim. An *urchin* was first a hedgehog, then a "pricking" boy. Gc, *gorse,* a prickly shrub.

gheslo: probable origin of Greek and Latin terms for *thousand.* Gk *chilioi, chiliad,* and all the *kilo-* terms, as *kilogram* and *kilometer* (in French, abbreviated *kilo*). L *mille. mil, mile* (*milia passum:* a thousand paces). *mill, millionaire; milliped:* thousand-legger. *millennium. milfoil;* It, *millefiori. milliard,* etc.

gheu: pour. Gk *khein:* pour; *khulos, khumos:* juice. *chyle, chyluria; chylify; chyme, chymify. OED* defines 9 words beginning *chyli;* 8, *chylo;* it lists 6 and details 8 beginning *chyme.* An earlier spelling of *chemistry* was *chymistry,* as though the art of pouring (mixtures). *ecchymosis; enchymatous, mesenchyma, prosenchyma. choana, chonolith; chytra, synchytrium.*

urachus: passes the urine; see *nebh.* OL *hundere,* L *fundere, fusum:* pour. *foundry; funnel; fuse, fusion; confound, confuse; diffuse, effusive; profusion; refund; refuse* (noun accented on first syllable; verb, on last). *transfusion,* etc. *futile* (poured too easily; leaky, useless). *refutation, refute,* may be from this root, or from *bhat:* to strike down; also *confute.* Gc, *gut, gush, gust. ingot; lingot* (misheard from Fr *l'ingot*); thus also E *nugget,* earlier *a n*igget, from *an in*got. Norse, *geyser.* Jonson's Epigram 118 runs: "Gut eats all day, and lechers all the night . . . / Lust it comes out, that Gluttony took in."

ghi: open wide. Gk, *chasm. chaos.* Jan Baptista von Helmont (d. 1644), who is credited with coining the word *gas,* said he based it on the word *chaos;* but Paracelsus (d. 1541) used the word *gas* to mean air. *OED* lists 85 combinations of *gas,* as *gas-gauge, gas-ring;* and details 17 more, as *gasify, gaslight; gasoline,* often abbreviated, as in "Step on the gas!" *coal-gas,* about 1800, was the first gas used for illumination.

L *hiare, hiatum. hiatus. dehiscence.* Gc, *yawn; gap, gape. gill:* a ravine. *lammergeier:* voracious vulture, "lamb-eater."

Guns aren't lawful,
Nooses give;
Gas smells awful;
You might as well live.
—Dorothy Parker, *Résumé*

P. Hood, in 1883, mentions "the lass with the lantern, the constant attendant of every lady who might happen in those gasless days to be out after nightfall."

ghostis: stranger; hence to be welcomed or feared; break bread, or break his head. L *hospes, hospitis (hosti-potis:* lord of strangers; see *poti). Hospes,* Roman god of strangers. L *hostis:* stranger. Thus "mine host" of the *hospitable* hotel. *hospice, hostel, hostler, ostler. hospital, hospitality.* But also the *hosts* of *hostile* armies, and *hostage.*

The *host:* bread consecrated at the Eucharist, is from L *hostia:* a victim for sacrifice, from *hostis:* stranger. Strange are the turns of human thought.

Slav *hospodar:* lord of strangers; Russ *gospodin.* Gc, *guest.*

Perhaps cognate with this root is Gk *xenos:* stranger, also enemy or guest; see *xenos.*

In this house with starry dome,
Floored with gemlike plains and seas,
Shall I never feel at home,
Never wholly be at ease? . . .

On from room to room I stray,
Yet mine host can ne'er espy,
And I know not to this day
Whether guest or captive I.
—William Watson, *World-Strangeness*

ghou(e): to honor. L *favere. favor, favorite.* Gc, *gawk:* stare at.

"He that goeth about to persuade a multitude that they are not so well governed as they ought to be, shall never want attentive and favourable hearers"—Richard Hooker, *Of the Lawes of Ecclesiasticall Politie* (1594).

ghre: become green. Gc, *green,* but see *gel I. grow. grass, grasshopper.* "Many persons have a grasshopper mind, apop from stem to stalk." *OED* devotes four columns to the word *grass;* then lists 112 combinations, as *grass-guard, grass-work;* then details 15 relevant words, as *grassman, grass widow,* plus 6 *grasshopper* combinations.

"You may eat . . . the grasshopper according to its kind"—Bible, Leviticus 11:22 (ca. 700 B.C.). You may also drink a *grasshopper:* a cocktail mixing crème de menthe, crème de cacao, and cream, dating from ca. A.D. 1969.

ghrebh I: hollow; dig, scratch. Gc, *grave, greave, groove; grub. engrave.*

We'll sit contentedly
And eat our pot of honey on the grave.
—George Meredith, *Modern Love*

ghrebh II: seize, gather, select. Gc, *grab, grabble. grape* was first a hook—with which the bunches of grapes were plucked; hence, the fruit. grapple. *graps* became *grasp*. Probably *grip, gripe, grope;* see *ghreib.* Hence *garb:* a sheaf of wheat; obsolete save in heraldry. The form persists in *garbage,* which originally meant offal, or wheat, hay, and corn (stalks) taken as food for cattle. Hence probably also *garble,* which originally meant to sift, select, (*OED*) "take the pick of"; then came to mean select (*OED*) "with a view to misrepresentation." Thus *garbling* seems usually intentional.

ghredh: step, go. L *gradus, gressum:* walk. *gradual, gradation; gradatim; graduation.* Suffix *grade:* way of walking, as *saltigrade; plantigrade,* walking as bears and humans do. *grade, degrade, retrograde. degree. aggression. congress, progress, regress, retrogress, transgression. gressorial. gradient; ingredient. egress;* when his circus side show was crowded, Barnum used to put up a sign: "This way to the egress," and persons expecting to find a female egret or the like found themselves on the street. This is not a *digression.* Laurence Sterne, in *Tristram Shandy* (1760–67), specialized in digressions from a digression. As he declares in Book I, "Digressions, incontestably, are the sunshine;—they are the life, the soul of reading;—take them out of this book for instance—you might as well take the book along with them." *Et ego in Arcadia.*

ghreib: take hold of, a variant of *ghrebh II.* Gk *gruph,* perhaps borrowed from the Hittites: *griffin.* The *hippogriff* is the fabulous half-horse, half-griffin. *(la)grippe* may be imitative of the cough that seizes you. *griff(e):* claw-like ornament; *griffonage. gripe* first meant to grasp. Also *gripsack.*

ghrem: wrathful. Partly imitative. *grim, grimace.* Softened to *grumble.* Russ, *pogrom.*

ghren: rub, grind. Extended form of *gher I.* Probably Gk *chondros:* granule, gristle; hence E *chondroma; chondrodite; enchondrona, perichondrium, synchondrosis, mitochondrion* (see *mei IV*). *hypochondria:* literally, below the (breastbone) cartilage; the morbid sense of illness was supposed to rise from the abdomen. *hypochondriac.* L *frendere:* gnash the teeth; *frenum:* horse's bit. *frenum, frenulum; refrain,* but see *dhar. furfur, furfuraceous; OED* defines 6 more.

Gc, *grind, ground, grist.* "All is not grist that comes to the mill."

ghuer: wild beast. Gk *ther,* diminutive *therion. panther. theroid. paleothere; theropod; dinotherium; megathere. Therevidae, Thereva:* family and genus of stiletto flies. *Therediidae:* family of spiders. *therianthropic:* of a monster, man and beast, especially of a god worshiped in the form of a beast, as in ancient Egypt. "Cleopatra's grandmother was a black cat." *OED* lists 11 and details 2 words beginning *therio.*

The Cretan Andromachus, ca. A.D. 50, concocted a cure for poison from 61 ingredients, mainly the dried flesh of vipers, which he called *theriache antidotos;* whence E *theriac,* then *treacle.*

L *ferus:* wild, *ferox, ferocis:* wild-looking, *feral, fierce; ferocious, ferocity.* See *dhes.* William Cowper, in *The Task* (1784), vi, speaks of "anger insignificantly fierce."

If I were fierce and bald and short of breath,
I'd live with scarlet Majors at the Base,
And speed glum heroes up the line to death.
—Siegfried Sassoon, *Base Details*

gib: humped. L, *gibbous, gibbosity.* Gc, *?hunch, hump; humpback, hunchback.* To "have a hunch" may be related to the notion that rubbing a hunchback's hunch brings good luck.

The nursery rhyme Humpty Dumpty was first recorded in 1803; it was used by Lewis Carroll in *Through the Looking Glass* (1871), the reduplication suggesting round-bellied, egg-shaped.

hump was first used in the 18th c.; *humpback* was a change from *crump-backed, crump-shouldered.* The Second Quarto of Shakespeare's *Richard III* has *hunch-backed;* the First Folio has *bunch-backed.*

The story of Richard III is still questioned. The villain pictured by Shakespeare was drawn from the *History of Richard III,* supposedly by Sir Thomas More, who was eight when Richard died, in 1485. In 1491, More was a page in the household of Bishop John Morton; see *bhurig.* For instance, instead of the hump and withered arm Shakespeare gives him, Richard in reality had merely one shoulder slightly higher than the other. In addition to historians' efforts to rehabilitate King Richard, Josephine Tey (pseudonym of Elizabeth Mackintosh), in *The Daughter of Time,* uses the detective-story technique to clear him of various charges, such as the London Tower murder of young Edward V and his brother. And Archie, in Rex Stout's *A Family Affair,* says that his boss, detective Nero Wolf, "was down on More because he had smeared Richard III." There is a saying that truth will out; but so far, the literary version in Shakespeare's play remains the general picture of "crouchback Richard."

> The camel's hump is an ugly lump
> Which well you may see at the Zoo;
> But uglier yet is the hump we get
> From having too little to do.
> —Kipling, *Just-So Stories*

gieu: chew. ?L *gingiva:* gum. *gingivitis.* Gc, *chew.* "Some books are to be tasted, others to be swallowed, and some few to be chewed and digested"—Francis Bacon, *Essays,* "Of Studies."

?gigas: Gk *gigas, gigantos. giant, gigantic. giantism, gigantomachy:* battle of the Titans and the gods. the name *Gigas* was applied to any son of Tartarus, lord of the underworld, and Ge, goddess of Earth. See also *nebh.*

?glact: milk. (It is surprising, considering that milk is as ancient as mammals, that no Indo-European root seems to exist for it. See also *melg.*) Gk *galaktos.* The sugars are a closely related family. Let us begin with milk sugar, *lactose* ($C_{12}H_{22}O_{11}$). Upon hydrolysis (combination with water, H_2O), this forms *galactose* ($C_6H_{12}O_6$) and *glucose* ($C_6H_{12}O_6$). Glucose is also called *dextrose,* because it is dextrorotatory, turning polarized light to the right, clockwise; it is found in fruits and human blood, and is the chief source of protoplasmic energy. *fructose,* also called *levulose,* as it is levorotatory, turning light to the left, is found in honey and many fruits, and is used as an intravenous nutrient; it is also an isomer of glucose. (Isomers are substances of the same chemical formula, but their molecules are arranged differently.) Galactose occurs in both dextro- and levo-rotatory forms, and it produces (both the substances and the names) the rare sugar *talose* and a crystalline sugar, *tagatose*—both of which are also isomers of glucose ($C_6H_{12}O_6$). Most generally known of the family is *sucrose* ($C_{12}H_{22}O_{11}$, an isomer of lactose), which occurs in sugar cane, beet sugar, and maple sap, and which by hydrolysis yields dextrose and levulose.

galactogogue; galactometer (how much water in the milk?); *galactopoietic; galactorrhea. galaxy,* the Milky Way, or island universe; by extension, any star universe; figuratively, any cluster of human "stars."

The average galaxy contains some 100 billion stars. Instead of spreading randomly through space, galaxies tend to gather in clusters. The Virgo "constellation," for example, is actually a cluster of 2500 galaxies. Our own Milky Way galaxy is a member of a smaller group of some 20 galaxies; our sun is far out on an arm of the spiral, which makes a complete revolution once in 250 million years.

Of the galaxies in our cluster, the two nearest to us form the "Magellanic Clouds" in the southern sky (named for Ferdinand Magellan, who in 1520 sailed south and through the Strait of Magellan from the Atlantic to the Pacific Ocean). These "clouds" are some 180,000 light-years away, but are surrounded by a hydrogen cloud that may extend to our Milky Way. They are irregular in shape, and smaller than our galaxy, having a mere 10 billion or so stars apiece.

Strangely, external galaxies (outside the Milky Way) were identified only in 1924, by Edwin P. Hubble. Once known, they were swiftly surveyed; it is now estimated that there are some 10^{11} galaxies in observable space. The "expansion of the universe" is marked by a widening of the distance between clusters, within each of which the member galaxies maintain their fellowship. The diameter of a galaxy may be some 2,000,000 light-years.

galax: a white-flowered plant. *Polygalacea, Polygala:* family and genus, the milkwort. *Galactia:* genus, the milk pea. The *galaxia* was an ancient Greek festival at which a boiled mixture of barley, pulse, and milk was enjoyed by the participants.

Galatea was a sea nymph whose story is told in Ovid's *Metamorphoses:* she loved the Sicilian shepherd Acis, but the jealous Cyclops Polyphemus (later blinded by Odysseus) crushed Acis as he lay in her arms. *Galatea* is also a milkmaid in the *Third Eclogue* of Virgil.

L, *lactic, lactate, lactation, lacteal, lactescent. lacti-,* as *lactiferous; lacto-,* as *lactometer. OED* defines 40 relevant words. OFr *laitues,* E *lettuce,* with milky juice.

From the 15th c. through the 17th, *lac virginis* (literally, milk of the virgin) named a cosmetic; since the mid-19th c. it has named a wine; also translated into Gm, *Liebfraumilch.* See *per VI c.*

gleubh: carve, split. Gk, *glyph, glyptic. anaglyph; dactylioglyph; triglyph. hieroglyphics:* holy carvings.

L *glubere:* peel. *glume,* peels off.

Gc, *cleave,* as with the butcher's cleaver; for *cleave:* to cling to, see *gel II.* Thus, from different roots may rise one form, even to mean its own opposite. Such a form is an *autantonym:* a fast runner runs rapidly; a fast color doesn't run at all.

clove, a divided bulb; the plural, *cloves,* names a spice. *cleft,* perhaps *cliff.* South African Du, *kloof:* ravine. *cloven-footed,* the *cloven hoof,* as of the ostrich, swine, and the devil.

Nose, nose, jolly red nose,
And who gave thee this jolly red nose?
Nutmegs and ginger, cinnamon and cloves,
And they gave me this jolly red nose.

This song comes from a compilation of rounds and catches, *Deuteromelia* (1609), by Thomas Ravenscroft. The *deuter* means two; the first such collection printed in English was also by Ravenscroft, earlier the same year, *Pammelia* (*Pan Melia:* all song). The quoted song is remembered because it was sung in Beaumont and Fletcher's *Knight of the Burning Pestle* (1613).

glokh: point. Gk *glossa, glotta:* tongue; thence, one's native tongue; explain. *gloss; glossary. glossolalia* may lead to *glossalgia.* (Gk *algos:* pain. JWalker lists 23 relevant words ending *algia,* as *neuralgia.*) One type of glossolalia is *battology:* empty repetition, named by Herodotus after one *Battos,* a stammerer; but *battos* may be imitative; *battosos:* full of buh-buh-buh.

glottis, epiglottis. monoglot, polyglot, etc. *Pangloss:* explains everything: main character in Voltaire's *Candide* (1758), who shows how every misfortune helps make ours "the best of all possible worlds." *Voltaire* is a pseudonym, an anagram of the author's real name: Arouet l.j. (*le jeune:* Junior), with *j* equivalent to *i,* and *u* to *v,* as they were in his day.

Hence also various terms in botany and zoology, as *bugloss:* ox-tongued, from the leaf shape; *triglochin:* with three-pointed fruit; *cynoglossum:* hound's tongue; *tachyglossus:* quick-tongued, as the ant-eater; *hippoglossus; docoglossa; proglottid.*

?glor. L and E *gloria:* music and/or song (doxology) in praise of the Lord, as *Gloria in excelsis Deo:* "Glory to God in the highest, and on earth peace to men of good will."

glorify; gloriole; glorious, glory. Sic transit gloria mundi: So passes the glory of the world—Thomas à Kempis, *De Imitatione Christi* (1486).

gn, gen. This root is so prolific that some scholars divide it in two. It defies partition. For its two meanings, to know and to beget, continue to entwine through the linguistic changes. Thus the Gc *k* shift turns it to E *know,* and *know* may refer to mental or carnal familiarity; in the 1611 King James Bible (Genesis 4:1 and elsewhere): "Adam knew his wife, Eve, and she conceived"—followed by the inevitable "begat." Thus also Gm *Kind* and the obsolete E *kindle:* the young of an animal, which persist in the verb *kindle:* to beget. Shakespeare, in *As You Like It,* iii, 2, has Rosalind say, "As the coney [rabbit] that you see dwell where it is kindled." To *kindle* a fire is to beget the flame; from the Latin form of this root we have *ignite.* We retain the word *kin,* and have adopted Gm *kindergarten* and *Kriss Kringle,* little Christ Child.

A punning rhyme is made in the Massinger-Dekker play *The Virgin Martyr* (1622): "A pox on your Christian cocatrices! They cry, like poulterers' wives, No money, no coney." In fact, the rabbit may have gotten its earlier name, *coney,* from its prolific nature. Since the word *coney* appears in the Bible, a pious euphemistic note advises: "It is familiarly pronounced cunny, but cōney is proper for solemn reading." Perhaps a similar primness gave the long vowel to *Coney Island,* New York, named for the rabbits the early Americans hunted there. From the "knowing" sense came the word *cunning;* but from the "begat" sense came *cunny* (alpha and omega, the beginning and the end of the begetting), *cunt, cunnilingus.*

In Sanskrit the root became *yoni,* the intercrural cleft; this stands as a base for the erect *lingam* (Skr: sign of the male), from cigar-butt size to nine feet, on the some 3,000 shrines in the holy city of Benares, most of them wet with water from the sacred River Ganges, sprinkled by pious women praying for a male child. The navel of Vishnu, object of Hindu contemplation (often symbolized by one's own) is linked in worship with the yoni.

With the root *gen* via Latin come *generate, generator* and *generatrix, progeny* down the *generations* with the *genitals,* rarely by *parthenogenesis,* which is, however, common among the lower plants and invertebrate animals, including the drone bee. Pallas Athene was worshiped in the *Parthenon* on the acropolis of Athens—from which Lord Elgin took the marbles now in the British Museum. Both Gk *parthenos* and Gk *pallas, pallados,* mean virgin. Hence E *parthenic.* Also *Palladium:* a statue in Troy on which hung the fate of the city; used as the name of various "motion picture palaces." *Pallas* is the name given the asteroid discovered by Heinrich W. M. Olbers in 1802, after which element 46, *palladium,* was named by its discoverer W. H. Wollaston in 1803. *Palladian*, however, refers to the style of the Italian architect Andrea *Palladio* (1518–1580).

Gk *pallas:* maiden, is related to Gk *pallaxis:* concubine of a married man, and to IE *pairika* (*l.r* shift): beautiful women seducing pious men; it is linked with *Bilqis*, Queen of Sheba, who visited Solomon, taking his child back within her; she is celebrated in *The Song of Songs.*

Hence also *peri:* first a seductive, then a helpful, fairy, caught in the title of the Gilbert and Sullivan musical *Iolanthe; or, the Peer and the Peri.* (Three of their musicals with titles beginning with *P–Pinafore, Pirates of Penzance,* and *Patience*–had been so successful that when they chose a title without a *P,* they doubled the lucky letter in the subtitle.

The *genitive* case is the case of origin, hence of belonging; but its use in grammar is a mistranslation of the Greek word meaning *generic. gender, engender, genesis* and its compounds, as *palingenesis.* JWalker lists 36 words ending *genesis,* as *psychogenesis, abiogenesis, xenogenesis.* Also *genus, congener, congenital; epigene; epigenous:* growing outside, as a fungus on a leaf. *primogeniture, genitor, progenitor.* More compounds with *-geny,* as in the observation that *ontogeny* encapsulates *phylogeny* (individual growth recapitulates the evolution of the species; hence our embryonic gills, the appendix, and other vestigia, such as the male foreskin, a safeguard when men hunted and when they trained naked, as in the gymnasium, Gk *gumnos:* naked).

Polygeny and *polygenism* (L *poly:* many) refer to the belief that Adam and Eve were not humanity's sole parents, that mankind (*homo, hominem*) sprang from independent pairs of *hominoids* (*-oid:* like) in various times and climes.

On *pregnancy: pregnant* means before (L *pre*) giving birth. The unrelated *impregnable* (L *in:* not, and OFr *prenable:* able to be taken) absorbed the *g* from the neighboring potency of *impregnate* and swallowed the earlier *impregnable* (*in:* into), which meant fertile, able to be made pregnant.

Here also are *miscegenation, degenerate,* and *regeneration; genocide; gentile; indigene, indigenous* (for *indigent,* see *eg II*); *androgenous; homogenized, homogeneous; heterogeneous,* and numerous words with the suffix *gen,* as *hydrogen:* water-begetter; *halogen:* salt-producer; *oxygen:* acid-begetter. *hallucinogen:* a drug, such as LSD (acrostic of lysurgic acid diethylamide, named in 1952), that produces delusions and changes in perception; used sometimes in psychotherapy, more frequently to "take a trip" to euphoria. *orogeny:* formation of mountains.

The head of the *gens* is the *general, generalissimo. gendarme.* The spirit assigned to one at birth is one's *genius* (the mythical *genie* is adapted from Arab *jinee,* active in the *Thousand and One Nights*). *eugenics* is the study or practice of good breeding; see *esu;* its neglect may lead to *cacogenesis* (see *caca*) according to one's *genes.*

Friendly ties account for *gentle,* which first meant born in the family, the *gentry;* hence well-born, a *gentleman. lady* (OE *hlaef-diger:* loaf-kneader) is now paired with *gentleman,* but more precisely, as still in England, is the mate of the lord (*hlaefweard:* loaf-warden). From such an association came also *genteel.*

A *genteelism,* however, is an incorrect expression achieved in an effort to indicate one's superior breeding, superior taste, or superior knowledge, especially of grammar, and thereby revealing its absence; saying, for instance, "We smiled at those whom we felt were trying to keep up with the Joneses"; wherein the subject of "were trying" should be the more common and therefore avoided "who." Thus the popular mystery writer John Creasey, in *Danger for the Baron:* "He was a tall, lean man whom even the cynics agreed was handsome."

From L *lectum genialis:* nuptial bed, hence sociable, came *genial; congenial;*

generous. Fr *gentil,* pronounced *ghontee,* became E *jaunty.* Here, too, are *ingenious, ingenuity, ingenuous* and *disingenuous.* Via L *ingenium:* inborn talent, came *engine* (product of talent) and *engineer,* earlier *enginer* ("hoist with his own petar"–*Hamlet* iii, 4), etc.

By way of a reduplicated form, L *gignere:* to bring forth, came *gingerly,* which first meant in well-bred fashion, as to the manor born. *gingerly* has no relation of source or sense with *ginger,* which was OE *gingifer* (Skr *srngam:* horn, *vera:* body, from its antler-shaped root).

Within a word, Latin usually kept the letter *g* and the sound; hence *agnate, cognate, cognition, cognizant, recognizant, recognize.* At the end of a word, the *g* sound was often lost: *benignant,* but *benign* (both originally meaning well-born: *noblesse oblige!*); *malign, malignant.* Often the initial *g* was dropped; hence *natal, native, nativity, nation, nature; nascent;* in compounds, *innate, neonate, connate; extraneous.* Through French came *genre, née, naive; Noël* (L *natalis dies:* birthday of Jesus). Also *connoisseur, reconnaissance; Renaissance,* generalized as *renascence. nascent.* OFr *puisné:* born later (silent *s*), gave English *puny.* Also from this *generous* root, via L *germen* (a smoothing of *genmen:* bud, embryo), came *germ, germinate, germinal, germane,* and your *cousin-german.*

From Greek are *gonad, epigone:* of a later, "inferior" generation; compounds with *gono,* as *gonosphere. OED* lists 15 words beginning *gono-,* from *gonoblast* to *gonozooid;* its 1972 supplement adds 14, from *gonochorism* to *gonotocont, gonotome.*

gonorrhea was in the 16th c. spelled *gomoria,* in the belief, stressed by Andrew Boorde in *The Breviary of Health* (1547), that the disease was an infliction upon the inhabitants of Sodom and Gomorrah. Thus the sin, *sodomy,* took the name of one city; and the punishment, that of the other. In fact, the form we use is also based on a misconception; to Gk *rhoia:* flux, was added *gon* because the discharge was supposed to be a flow of semen.

Here also are suffixes: *gonium,* as in *epigonium; gony,* as in *cosmogony.* Thomas Browne, in his discussion of popular fallacies, *Pseudodoxia Epidemica* (1646), scoffed at believers in *telegony* (Gk *tele-:* far, as in *telephone*); he refused to accept a jury's verdict that a woman had become pregnant while bathing in a stream down-current from a man who had ejaculated in the water. Artificial insemination is a modern form of telegony. But *telegony* is also used to mean the supposed influence of a previous sire on the offspring of the same mother by a subsequent sire.

By way of Greek, *gn* led to *gnosis: cognition,* knowledge; especially, a higher knowledge of spiritual things. Thus, Thomas Stanley, in *The History of Philosophy* (1656), said: "The Souls of the Gods have a dijudicative Faculty, called Gnosis." In the early Christian centuries there were several sects of *Gnostics,* some of whom declared that all matter is evil, that *gnosis* "frees the spirit from the slavery of material things"; they were all denounced as heretic. Milton, in *Tetrachordon* (1645), described *gnosticism* as "of little reading, which holds ever with hardest obstinacy what it took up with easiest credulity."

Hence also *prognosis, diagnosis.* With *a* negative, *agnostic;* suggested by Thomas H. Huxley in 1869, "from St. Paul's mention of the altar to *the unknown God.*" The agnostic holds that the existence of anything beyond material phenomena is unknown and in all likelihood unknowable. As Bishop Fraser said in *The Manchester Guardian* of 25 Nov. 1880, "The agnostic neither denied nor affirmed God, he simply put him on one side."

physiognomy (Gk *gnomos:* interpreter). The *gnomon* of a sundial shadows forth the hour if the sun is shining. *Non numero horas nisi serenas:* I count only the hours that are serene. A *gnome* is a knowing remark; there are 18 words compounded of *gnome* in *OED.* The little *gnome* that guards underground treasure was named in 1530 by Paracelsus (Aureolus Philippus Theophrastus Bombastus von Hohenheim), who had studied the mechanics of mining. He named four spirits inhabiting the four elements: *sylphs,* air; *gnomes,* earth; *nymphs,* water; *salamanders,* fire. *gnomes* travel in earth as fish do in water, birds in air. Perhaps the name was formed from *geo:* earth, and *nomos:* rule, order. In 1978 a *Gnome Society* was organized in England. The United States has been equally receptive; by Christmas 1978 the illustrated volume *Gnomes* had been on the *New York Times* best-seller list for 50 weeks. You can buy a gnome calendar, or material to build a gnome house to place in a hollow of the garden (I suppose, thinking of bird houses hung on suburban front-lawn trees) to lure the lively creatures.

Words from Latin in the "know" range are even more numerous: *ignore, ignoramus* (literally, we do not know); for *ignorance,* see *ne; sek II.* With the silent *g* dropped came *note, notice, notion, notify, notable, notorious.* From L *nobilis:* knowable, worthy of being known, came *noble, nobility; ignoble.* Also *annotate, connotation, denotation; notary; prothonotary* (Gk *protos:* first): chief clerk. The *prothonotary warbler,* significant in the Hiss-Chambers treason case, has the golden color of the old formal clerical robe. See *onomen.*

L *norma:* carpenter's square, to know by, to give order to, gave English *norm, normal, abnormal; enormous* (out of the norm). L *(g)narus:* known, hence told, gave English *narrate, narrative.* With two intensive prefixes, *ad* and *com,* L *adcognoscere:* to know thoroughly, via Fr *acointer,* produced *acquaint* and *acquaintance,* in which down the ages the thoroughness lapsed.

L *cognitus,* contracted to OFr *cointe,* led to E *quaint,* which first meant knowing, then turned to putting on an air of knowing, affected, then softened to pleasantly odd. Chaucer in 1386 used *quaint* and *queynte* as spellings for *cunt,* which Richard Burton in his 1888 translation of *The Arabian Nights* spelled *coynte.* Andrew Marvell's lines *To His Coy Mistress* (1650) seem to play on this sense of *quaint:*

But at my back I always hear
Time's wingèd chariot hurrying near:
And yonder all before us lie
Deserts of vast eternity.
Thy beauty shall no more be found:
Nor, in thy marble vault, shall sound
My echoing song; then worms shall try
That long-preserved virginity,
And your quaint honor turn to dust,
And into ashes all my lust.
The grave's a fine and private place,
But none, I think, do there embrace.

Along the Germanic route, the head of the *kith,* of little *kinchin,* the *kin* and *kindred,* is the *king* (OE *cynning*), chief of the *kind* (noun), who is expected to be *kind* (adjective). *Kind* was early pronounced with a short *i,* and still is in German. There is a bitter pun in Hamlet's first words in Shakespeare's play: "A little less than kin, and more than kind." In *The Merchant of Venice,* copulation is called "the deed of kind," as when a couple has *kindled.*

Also along the Germanic line came *ken, kenning; know, knowledge, acknowledge; can:* know how; *con; couth:* knowing how, and the now more frequent *uncouth.*

By no means completing the list are *nevus* (*gnaevus:* inborn: birthmark); *genetics, montigenous; antigen; archigonium, oogonium, perigonium. oogenesis. gonococcus,* isolated in 1882 by Dr. A. L. S. Neisser. *primogenital; ultimogeniture:* inheritance by the youngest—and, by the Indic pathway, *mirza* (*emir* and *zadan:* high-born) and *shahzadah:* son of the *Shah,* heir apparent.

The association of these two sets of meanings in the one root shows the early sense of their essential unity: knowledge is power; to know how, to produce; to ken, to kindle. *Savoir pour prévoir pour pouvoir* is the neat French wording: to know, to figure ahead, to function. One may speculate that the notion of "knowing," the self-examination it involves, and the need of a word to name it, arose in human consciousness at about the time men grew aware of the tie between copulation and conception. (*conception* and *conceive,* in Later Latin, took the same dual application, genital and mental.) I think, therefore I am. I know, therefore I can. Again the French (Paul Claudel): *Naître, pour tout, c'est connaître. Tout naissance est un connaissance:* To be born is to come to know. All birth is awakening to knowledge.

> When Adam delved and Eve span,
> Who was then the gentleman?
>
> —John Ball's sermon (for which he was executed) at the start of Wat Tyler's Rebellion, 1381. Tyler led his men to London, where he was killed by the Lord Mayor.

?grand. L *grandem. grand, grandeur; grandiloquent. aggrandize.* It, *grandiose.* Sp, *grandee.* Fr, *grandpère. grandmother,* etc., of the third generation. *grandam. greatgrandchild,* etc.

gras: devour. A variant of *garg.* Gk *grastis:* fodder. *cress:* edible plant; *watercress. gaster:* stomach, belly. *gastrocnemius:* belly of the calf of the leg. *gastrology. gastronomy.* "Civilized man cannot live without cooks"—Owen Meredith; as George Meredith puts it in *The Ordeal of Richard Feverel:* "Kissing don't last; cookery do!" *OED* lists 20 and details 44 words beginning *gaster* or *gastr(o),* including the three types of *gastromancy. gastriloquy.* Its 1972 supplement lists 14 more, and details 4, including the hormone *gastrin.*

L (*grasmen*) *gramen:* fodder. *gram* was first a chickpea. *grama, gramacidine; gramineous. graminivorous,* as cattle and vegetarians.

gru: grunt. Imitative. *grouch. grouse:* complain. *grudge. disgruntled;* the basic form, *gruntled,* is sometimes revived for humor. *gurnard:* fish that grunts when taken out of the water. *Like a fish out of water* has become a cliché for a person in an incongruous situation. For *fish,* see *peisk.*

gua, gue(n): come; go. Skr, *jagat:* moving creatures, the human world. *Juggernaut, Jagannath:* names of Krishna, god of destruction, who goes about the world demanding sacrifice. *jaconet,* fabric first made at *Jagannath,* a town in Bengal.

Gk *bainein:* go; *basis:* stepping, place for foothold. *base, basic, basis. bema:* step, platform. *acrobat:* first, one on the tips of the toes, as in classical ballet. *amphisbaena:* monster going both ways, as a serpent with a head at each end; called by Pliny (d. A.D. 79) "a symbol of treachery." Aeschylus, in *Agamemnon* (458 B.C.): "What odious monster shall I call her? An amphisbaena?" Tennyson, in *Queen Mary,* iii, calls a heretic and traitor "an amphisbaena, each end a sting."

anabasis, catabasis, metabasis, parabasis. diabetes: going through (of excessive urine), named by the 2d c. physician Aretaeus of Cappadocia. *hyperbaton.*

presby-: coming before; hence old; thus *presbyter:* church elder. *presbyopia:*

impaired hearing and/or sight, due to old age; see *per VI d*. The *base* in chemistry, as opposed to acid and salt, was named in 1754 by G.-F. Rouelle; hence *monobasic,* etc. *baseball* is named for its four bases.

L *venire, ventum:* come. *Venire facies:* "You shall make come" persons from whom to select a jury; a person thus called is a *venireman.*

"Prevent us, O Lord, in all our doings!"—*The Book of Common Prayer* (1548); i.e., Come before us and prepare the way. Alas, human action on coming before led to the current meaning of *prevent:* "First come, first served, and the Devil take the hindmost."

advent, adventitious; adventure, venture, misadventure. avenue; venue. circumvent. convene. convenient; convention; contravene. coven: a coming together, now restricted to witches and the like. *covenant. convent. Covent Garden,* London, was in 1633 the site of the *Convent of St. Peter. event, eventuate; intervene. invent:* come upon. *subvention. supervene.* For *venter, ventricle,* see *udero;* for *vent, ventilation,* see *ue.* Fr, *revenant; revenue; parvenu; souvenir.* Gc *come, become, welcome.*

As the Earl of Chesterfield said in 1748: "Advice is seldom welcome."

guadh: sink. Gk, *abyss. bathos:* first used for the tumble from the sublime to the ridiculous in Pope's essay *Peri Bathos; or, The Art of Sinking in Poetry* (1727), which was a parody of Longinus's *On the Sublime,* of perhaps the 1st c. A.D. And Pope illustrated *bathos* in his *Dunciad* (1728). Dr. McLaren remarked in 1875: "It is as absurd bathos as to say the essentials of a judge are learning, integrity, and an ermine robe." Dickens employed the tumble of *bathos* for humor, as in *The Pickwick Papers:* "Miss Bolo rose from the table considerably agitated, and went straight home, in a flood of tears and a sedan chair."

Hence *bathetic, bathotic. bathybius,* coined by Huxley in 1868. *OED* gives 9 relevant words beginning *bath,* including *bathukolpian:* deep-bosomed; and *bathetic,* which it noted is "a favorite word with reviewers." Its 1972 supplement lists 12 words beginning *bathy:* deep, and details 4, including *bathysphere,* coined by William Beebe in 1930; and *bathyscaphe,* coined by Auguste Piccard in 1947 for his deep-sea diving vessel. *bathorse,* however, is a packhorse; so *batman:* officer's servant.

Ernst Haeckel in 1891 coined *benthos:* the deep sea bottom; also, organisms living there, by analogy with Gk *penthos:* grief; Gk and E *pathos.* From *pathos* to *bathos* is a treacherously easy slip, but a Humpty Dumpty fall:

And all the King's horses and all the King's men
Couldn't put pathos together again.

From this root (but see *kuenth*) came also *pathetic, pathogen, pathology,* etc. *neuropathy; protopathic. allopathy* vs. *homeopathy. antipathy; empathy; sympathetic,* etc. JWalker has 20 words ending *pathy,* including *apathy,* and *dipsopathy:* treatment of dipsomania by enforced abstinence, instead of AA (Alcoholics Anonymous). *telepathy,* breeder of ESP (Extra-Sensory Perception).

nepenthe: ne-penthe: grief-remover; Poe found the word in *The Odyssey,* iv; he used it in internal rhyme in *The Raven:*

"Wretch," I cried, "thy God hath lent thee—by these angels
he hath sent thee
Respite—respite and nepenthe from thy memories of Lenore!
Quaff, oh quaff this kind nepenthe, and forget this lost Lenore!"
Quoth the raven: "Nevermore."

gue: bend, curve; thus a rise or a hollow. This root came into English via compounds.

(1) *gueb:* bend, rise; arch. L, *cubicle, cubit. incubus, succuba* (see *cub*). *cacuminal.* Via Celtic, *combe, coomb.* (2) *gued:* pouch. *cud; quid. cod,* the fish. *cod:* a pouch, such as holds the testicles; *codpiece. peasecod. coddle. cuttlefish:* pouch-fish. (3) *guel.* L *columna. column. colliculus; colline. colonnade. culminate. excel:* rise beyond. *Excelsior. colonel:* first, leader of a column of soldiers. Via Norse, *how:* mound. *hill, hillock. holm:* rising from the water; hence *Stockholm,* etc. Gc, *high. hawker, huckster, hunker:* all bent over, pack on back. (4) *guep. cup, cupel. cupola. cupule. cove. Gyps:* genus of vultures, cave-dwelling bird. (5) *guer. gyre:*

> 'Twas brillig, and the slithy toves
> Did gyre and gimble in the wabe.
> —Lewis Carroll, *The Jabberwocky* (?wacky
> jabber), in *Through the Looking Glass* (1872)

Also *autogyro; gyroplane; gyroscope. gyromancy:* spin until dizzy; foretell by direction or spot of the fall. *circumgyrate. girandole. girasole:* bends toward the sun. (6) *guet:* throat (hollow). *guttural. goiter.* L *botellus,* diminutive of *botulus:* sausage. *bowel. botulism. guetumen; bitumen.* Fr, *béton:* mixture of mud and pitch. *Betula:* genus of birch trees, from which the Gauls extracted tar. *boyau.* OE, *chitterlings.*

> The shades of night were falling fast
> As through an Alpine village passed
> A youth, who bore, 'mid snow and ice,
> A banner with the strange device,
> Excelsior!
> —Longfellow, *Excelsior*

guebh: dip, slip, sink. Gk *baptisma. baptism, Baptist, Anabaptist; baptize. baphia. baptisia;* the sap is dipped into, for dyeing; also *phlobaphene:* the bark. Perhaps Gc *quacksalver, quagmire, quaver,* though the first syllable of these may be imitative: "quack quack quack" goes the *quack-doctor,* shortened to *quack. quagmire* was earlier *quake-mire,* as it does. Gm *quabbeln,* E *quiver:* tremble. Hence *quake* and probably the *Quakers:* common term—though they use it not; coined in 1650 by Justice Gervase Bennet of Derby—for members of the Society of Friends, whose founder, George Fox (d. 1691), bade them "tremble at the word of the Lord." (Fox is involved in the brilliant conversation of Bernard Shaw's play *In Good King Charles's Golden Days* [1939].) *Quaker gun:* a wooden, dummy weapon, named for the Quakers' opposition to war.

guei: live, alive. Skr, *jiva:* vital energy. Gk *hugies* (*su-gueiyes:* living well). *Hygeia:* goddess of health. Gk *bios:* life. *aerobic; amphibious. bathybius. cenobite. microbe* (see *sme*). *necrobiosis* (see *ken*). *symbiosis. limnobium, lithobium.*

bio-, as *biomedical, biography; autobiography. OED* lists 18 words beginning *bio,* and details 27 relevant words. The field has grown; *OED*'s 1972 supplement lists 41 more, as *biodegradable, biozone,* and details a further 38 new terms, as *biochore, biosphere; biotin:* vitamin H. *biopsy;* its opposite, *necropsy,* has been replaced by *autopsy,* which first meant seeing with one's own eyes. Seeing is believing.

Gk *zoe:* life. *zoetic. zoon; zooblast; zoogamy; zooid; zoolite,* etc.; *zoology* and the *zoo*—in all but *zoo,* the first three letters make two syllables. *zoolatry,* as with the golden calf when Moses brought down the Ten Commandments. *azote* (*a* negative): nitrogen, in which life does not survive; *azoic.* The *Paleozoic,*

Mesozoic, Neozoic, and *Cenozoic* ages of the earth. For *zoo OED* lists 60 and details 41 relevant words, as *zoophyte; zoomorphism. zoon:* a unit of organic life, coined in 1864 by Herbert Spencer.

Maid of Athens, ere we part,
Give, oh give me back my heart!
Or, since that has left my breast,
Keep it now, and take the rest!
Hear my vow before I go:
Zoe nou, sas agapo.

To these words, addressed by Byron to Theresa Macri, daughter of his hostess in Athens, Byron appended a note in the printed edition of 1812, about the Greek refrain: "Romaic expression of tenderness. If I translate it, I may offend the gentlemen, as it may seem that I supposed they could not; and if I do not, I may affront the ladies. For fear of any misconstruction on the part of the latter I shall do so, begging the pardon of the learned. It means 'My life, I love you', which sounds very prettily in all languages, and is as much in fashion in Greece at this day as, Juvenal tells us, the first two words were among the Roman ladies, whose erotic expressions were all Hellenised." Those first two words, euphemistically described by Lord Byron, were the usual come-on greeting of the prostitute in antiquity.

L *vivus:* living. *viable. vivisection. viviparous,* whence *viper:* bearing its young alive, not in eggs like some snakes, e.g. the cobra; read Kipling's *Rikki-Tikki-Tavi.* See *auei. vivacity; vivid; vivify; revive. vital, vitality; the vitals. victuals. vitamin(e),* first *i* short in England, long in the U.S.; coined in 1913 by the biochemist Casimir Funk, from *vita* and *amine,* from ammonia (see *bhes I; el 7*). *convivial. vivarium. Vitaphone:* early talking motion picture.

aqua vitae: water of life, also the meaning of Ir *usquebaugh,* which became E *whiskey;* see *akua.* It, *Viva! viva voce.* Fr, on the *qui vive. Vive ___:* Long live ___! *savoir vivre. vivandière:* woman who sold wine, provisions, and often herself to the soldiers. Gc, *quitch:* a kind of grass, also folkchanged to *couch grass.* L *argentum vivum,* translated as quicksilver. The quick (and the dead).

The zodiac (Gk *zoidion:* small carved animal figure): circle in the sky, *zoidiakos kuklos,* with twelve signs encompassing the year, is basic in astrological calculations. Newspapers in many parts of the world present daily zodiacal forecasts; in India the many marriage advertisements request zodiacal details, for the happy union of horoscopic mates. The signs are:

Name		*Root*	*Dates*
1. Aries	The Ram	*er*	Mar. 21–Apr. 20
2. Taurus	The Bull	*teu*	Apr. 21–May 20
3. Gemini	The Twins	*iem*	May 21–June 20
4. Cancer	The Crab	*kar*	June 21–July 21
5. Leo	The Lion	*leo*	July 22–Aug. 21
6. Virgo	The Virgin	*maghos*	Aug. 22–Sept. 21
7. Libra	The Scales (Balance)	*lithra*	Sept. 22–Oct. 22
8. Scorpio	The Scorpion	Gk *scorpion*	Oct. 23–Nov. 21
9. Sagittarius	The Archer	L *sagitta*	Nov. 22–Dec. 20
10. Capricorn(us)	The Goat's Horn	*kapr*	Dec. 21–Jan. 19
11. Aquarius	The Water Carrier	*akua*	Jan. 20–Feb. 18
12. Pisces	The Fish(es)	*peisk*	Feb. 19–Mar. 20

Each of the twelve signs occupies a house (30° of the heavenly circle), dominated by one of the seven heavenly bodies supposedly revolving around Earth, in this order: Aries (Mars), First House; then Venus, Mercury, Moon, Sun, Mercury, Venus, Mars, Jupiter, Saturn, Saturn, Jupiter. The first ten houses "control" various dispositions and likelihoods. The Eleventh House "confers" benefits and friends, hence is called *eudemon;* see *esu.* The Twelfth House "brings on" losses and enemies.

The twelve signs of the zodiac are also grouped in four sets of three, associated, in repeated order, with the four elements: fire (Aries, Leo, Sagittarius), earth, air, water.

Keats pictures Shakespeare and his comrades of the Mermaid Tavern as

Souls of poets dead and gone . . .
Pledging with contented smack
The Mermaid in the Zodiac.

guel I: pierce, destroy. Gc, *qualm; quell. kill.*

guel II: move about, throw—possibly by slang, as our *throw the bull,* applied to various aspects of speech. Gk and L, *diabolic:* to throw aslant, attack, slander; and its doublet, *devilish.* Hence *the devil,* on whose tempting many blame their lapses. As Rabelais declared,

When the devil was sick, the devil a monk would be;
When the devil was well, the devil a monk was he!

deviled eggs, like temptations, are well spiced. Thus *devil's food cake:* a dark chocolate cake, contrasted with the snow-white angel food cake. *devilish; devil-may-care. devil's bit:* a plant, the blazing star, with a foul taste. *devil's advocate:* originally in theological use, as at heresy trials of the Inquisition, one that takes the opposing view, to test validity or truth. *Eblis,* prince of the fallen angels. Note that *Lucifer* means light-bearer, comparable to Gk *Prometheus* (who was punished by the gods for bringing fire to man). Fr, *diablerie.* Baudelaire, poet of the French "diabolic" school, said: "The cleverest ruse of the devil is to persuade us he does not exist."

Gk, *disc, discus, disk, dish; dais, desk. discobolus:* discus thrower; especially, statue by Myron, 5th c. B.C. Replicas are in the Vatican and the British Museum. *amphibole, amphibology. hyperbola, hyperbole. parable; parabola, paraboloid. metabolic, metabolism, catabolism; embolism. ecbolic:* throwing out, causing abortion. *ballista; ballistics. bolometer. symbol:* two ideas or images thrown together. *problem. emblem:* literally, thrown on; see *porpur.*

Samuel Butler was given a pension of £100 by Charles II, but died (1680) in penury; his monument in Westminster Abbey reads:

The poet's fate is here in emblem shown:
He asked for bread and he received a stone.

It, *parlando.* Fr, *pourparler, parlance; parliament,* where one cannot be sued for one's words. *parley. parole:* first, a captured knight's pledge that he'd accept the conditions set for his release. *parlor:* first, a room in a convent where the nuns were allowed to speak with visitors through a grating. From *Parlez-vous français?:* Do you speak French? in the 18th and 19th c., for humor or mockery, came *parleyvoo:* a Frenchman. The London *Sporting Times* in 1815 bunched "Jockeys, Jews, and Parleyvoos, Courtezans and Quakers." Gilbert, in the Bab ballad "The Darned Mounseer," has an English sailor tell how a French merchantman his ship tried to capture turned out to be a frigate that fired on them, so they sailed hastily away:

And I wager in their joy
They kissed each others cheek
(Which is what them furriners do)
And they blessed their lucky stars
We were hardy British tars
Who had pity on a poor Parleyvoo,
D'ye see?
Who had pity on a poor Parleyvoo.

ballad: first, a song to be danced to; *ball:* a dancing party. *ballet, ballerina. bayadere.*

The farmer's daughter hath soft brown hair
(Butter and eggs, and a pound of cheese)
And I met with a ballad, I can't say where,
Which wholly consisted of lines like these.
—C. S. Calverley, *Ballad*

guel III: to fly. Hindi, *garuda:* mythical bird. L, *volage, volant, volitant, volatile, volitation. volley. volplane. volucrine.* Fr, *vol-au-vent* (literally, flight with the wind): a light pastry shell. *mouche volant:* speck that seems to move in front of the eye.

guelbh: womb. Gk *delphis, delphinos;* L *delphinus:* E *dolphin,* named for the womb of the female, being not fish but mammal. *Delphinidae:* family of whales that includes the dolphin. *delphinium:* the flower, from its shape.

When the god Apollo came to Pytho, he slew Python, the female dragon that dominated the region; he assumed the shape of a dolphin to establish his oracle, the place being thence called *Delphi.* He uttered his prophecies through the mouth of a local priestess (always over fifty years of age); they were delivered in hexameters, sometimes with faulty meter and diction, which puzzled the hearers: did the god blunder? The prophecies were often two-tongued, fitting whatever might transpire; as when a king, asking what would happen if he went to war, was assured: "You will be happy." He was killed. But there was an old Greek saying, which Sophocles used more than once; with it he ended the masterpiece of classical drama, *Oedipus the King:* Count no man happy until he is dead.

OED has 15 related words, as *delphinestrian:* rider on a dolphin, as often in fountain statuary, after *equestrian* and *pedestrian.* Oberon, in *A Midsummer Night's Dream,* ii, 1, reminds Puck of such a rider:

once I sat upon a promontory
And heard a mermaid, on a dolphin's back,
Uttering such dulcet and harmonious breath
That the rude sea grew civil at her song,
And certain stars shot madly from their spheres
To hear the sea maid's music.

The *dauphin,* from the three dolphins on the coat-of-arms of the lords of the province therefore called *Dauphiné* (L *Delphinatus*), first worn by Guido IV, count of Vienna (d. 1142). When Humbert III ceded Dauphiné to Philip of Valois in 1349, he stipulated that *Dauphin* be perpetuated as the title of the eldest son of the French king. The three dolphins were formalized as three fleurs-de-lis; but the name continued until 1830, longer than the kings.

Gk *adelphos:* of one womb, brother. *adelpholite. adelphous, monodelphia,* etc. *polydelphia:* several stamens bound together. *Philadelphia:* (city of) brotherly love; see *bhili.* In early Christian art, the dolphin was a symbol of love (occasionally, of diligence or speed). Spenser, in *Colin Clouts* (1595), sweetly observes: "The Lyon chose his mate, the Turtle Dove her deare, the Dolphin his owne Dolphinet."

guen: woman, the bearing human; related to *g(e)n:* to beget. Pers *zan:* woman. *zenana.* From Greek, several English prefixes: *gyn,* as *gynarchy; gyne,* as *gynephobia; gyn(a)eco,* as *gyn(a)ecologist;* and *gyno,* as *gynocracy. epigynous. gynecomastia:* enlarged breasts on the male. Perhaps also the feminine ending of *regina,* official title of the British queen; see *reg I.*

A *gynander* is a woman with marked characteristics of the male; the converse is *androgyne. Polygyny* is having more than one wife at a time; its converse is *polyandry;* both are included in *polygamy.* See *geme; gn; nert.*

From the Germanic shift to the *k* sound (Gothic *qino:* woman) came E *queen* and *quean. quean,* revived by Scott in *Rob Roy* (1818) to mean a young woman, was widely used in the 16th and 17th c. to mean a hussy. The drinking song in Sheridan's *The School for Scandal* (1777) sets the toasts:

Here's to the maiden of bashful fifteen,
Here's to the widow of fifty;
Here's to the flaunting, extravagant quean,
And here's to the housewife that's thrifty.

Probably *wench,* which at first was not derogatory, from OE *quen* and Du *je,* a term of affection, as *kinje:* dear child. (Similarly, *ji* in India is added as a sign of affection and esteem, as *Gandhiji; guruji:* revered teacher.)

In Gaelic the form became *bean:* woman, as, in Irish, *bean sidhe:* fairy; then, in English, *banshee,* a creature of sad omen, from the belief that the banshee wails before someone is to die.

guer: swollen, heavy, powerful. Skr, *guru:* weighted with wisdom. Gk *bruein:* swell. *embryo,* swelling within. *embryology. baros:* weight. *ventrobaric,* as in a treatise by Archimedes (208 B.C.) on the center of gravity. *barometer,* designed by Robert Boyle in 1665. *isobar. barium,* element 56, found by Sir Humphry Davy in *barytes:* heavy spar. *baritone. barythymia:* heaviness of spirit. *baruria. Briareus:* 100-handed giant.

L *brutus:* heavy, dull. *brute. gravis; grave, gravitate, gravity. grief, grieve, grievance; aggrieved. aggravate. gravid.* It, *brigade; brigand.* Gc, *blitzkrieg:* lightning power. *quern:* millstone.

For thence—a paradox
Which comforts as it mocks—
Life will succeed in that it seems to fail:
What I aspired to be
And was not, comforts me:
A brute I might have been, but would not sink i' the scale.
[*Read it all.*]
—Browning, *Rabbi Ben Ezra*

guet: speak. *bequeathe; bequest. quoth,* from this root, took the *o* by association with *quote* (L *quota pars:* so large a part), first used to mark off chapters of a book. Hence also *quota:* see *kuo.*

guhdhei: be consumed; die away. Gk *phthisic, phthisis, phthisicky; phthisiology. phthinode; phthinoplasm.* Southey in 1843 mentioned "a science which Jeremy the thrice-illustrious Bentham calls phthisozoics": the art of destroying noxious creatures.

Gk *phtora:* destruction. *phthorine,* old name for *fluorine,* element 9, from the corrosive force of hydrofluoric acid.

guhdher: spoil. Gk *phtheir:* louse (hence slang, to louse things up). *phthiriatic:* a polite way of calling a person or thing lousy—and the hearer will have trouble looking it up, because the *ph* is not sounded. The *British Medical Journal* of 4 Nov. 1899 commented that lice "caused little inconvenience and afforded employment to the *phthirophagous* natives": scratch, catch, despatch. Monkeys seem to enjoy them too. OE, *ick,* shortened from LL *ichthyophthirius:* fish-louse. See *ghdhu; lus.*

The shorter *OED* (1933, 1973) gives just four words with the first four letters *phth.* Note their pronunciations:

1. *phthaline:* pertaining to naphthaline, sounded *fth*
2. *phthiriasis:* excessive pediculosis, sounded *th*
3. *phthisic:* pulmonary consumption, sounded *t*
4. *phthisis:* same as (3), any of the three sounds above

guhen: strike, wound, destroy. L *defendere, defensum* (*de:* away): ward off. *defend. Heaven forfend!* Aphetic from *defense* came *fence, fend, fender* (on the early American railroads called *cowcatcher*); *fens:* a call in games that exempts the caller from capture. *offend, offensive.* The *phoenix,* "blood-red" bird that after 500 years builds and kindles its own funeral pyre, and rises anew from the ashes. *Bellerophon,* name given to Hipponous, son of Glaucus, king of Ephyre, as "slayer of monsters"; he had killed the Chimera. Bellerophon was sent from the court of Proteus, king of Argos, with a sealed letter requesting the recipient to kill the bearer (somewhat as Hamlet was sent to England); hence a message inimical to its bearer has been called *a letter of Bellerophon.*

Gc, *gonfalon,* earlier *gonfanon:* war banner. *gun:* in 1330 (before gunpowder), used of a catapult, from the feminine name *Gunnhilda;* in Scandinavian both *gunnr* and *hildr* meant war. Thus *Gunther:* bold in war. *Big Bertha* is another weapon named for a woman, who in this case can be identified; she was Frau Bertha Krupp von Bohlen und Halbach, owner of the Krupp steel works from 1903 to 1943. England's *Sphere* of 20 July 1918 said: "Big Bertha spoke for the first time on March 23, and at the sound of her voice Paris was intensely surprised." *OED* lists 76 compounds of *gun,* plus 5 for *gunnery* and 13 for *gunner,* including *Gunner's daughter:* a gun to which a sailor was "spliced" for a whipping; and it details 28 relevant words, as *gun-shy, gunpowder, guncotton, gunman.*

guher: idea of heat. Gk *thermos:* warm. *thermae, thermion; thermometer; thermo-,* as *thermochemistry, thermodynamics, thermophile,* etc. *OED* lists 84 words starting *therm(o),* as *thermocall:* a heat-started fire alarm; it details 58, as *thermaesthesia:* sensitivity to hot and cold. *therm* was suggested as a basic unit of heat, but lost to *calorie.* One calorie is the amount of heat required to raise one kilogram of water 1°C. In ca. 1890 *calorie* was also applied to the energy-producing value of food. See *kel I.*

The *thermos flask* was devised by Sir James Dewar in 1904; it was named in 1907. The *thermostat* is designed to keep a room at the desired temperature. The ancient Gk *thermopaulion,* L *thermopalium,* both used, rarely, in English, was a tavern serving hot drinks; a *thermopote* is one that drinks them—e.g., today, Japanese saki, Christmas eggnogg, and other liquid imbibitions, as coffee, tea, and hot lemonade.

L *fornax:* furnace; *fornix:* arch, vault; *fornicatus:* vaulted; *furnus:* oven, bakery. The vaulted archways under the Roman aqueducts held the ovens for the free bread for the Roman poor, the theory being that "bread and circuses"

*–pan et circenses–*would keep the people pacified (an ancient form of "welfare"). As these vaulted ways were thus kept warm, they became the rendezvous for lovers and the haunts of whores, whence the word *fornication* and a dozen related terms in *OED.* Milton wrote in 1649: "They shall hate the great whore . . . and yet shall lament the fall of Babylon where they fornicated with her." Etheredge was more complaisant in his play *She wou'd if she cou'd* (1668): "We are resolved to fornicate in private." Note that *fornicate* as an adjective means arched; in botany it is used of branches bending over.

Also *furnace.* Fr, *petits fours.* Gc, *warm, warmth. Schabzieger* (*dwi-guher*), *sapsago:* twice-warmed cheese.

guhisl: tendon; thread; trifle. L *filare:* spin; *filum:* thread. *filament, file, ficelle, filigree; filet, fillet. defile* (marching); *enfilade; profile; purfle. Filaria:* genus of worms. *Filago:* genus of thistle. *Gifola* (anagram of *filago*): genus of cotton rose. From the variant *hilum* (tiny thread, fiber) came *nihil* (*ne-hilum:* not so much as a thread); E *nil; nihilism,* coined by F. H. Jacobi in 1819. *annihilate.* In all likelihood *vilipend* (with 7 more forms in *OED*) was an error in a Plautus manuscript for *nilipendere:* value as nothing.

Several wise observations have hung upon *nothing.* Horace, in the *Odes,* says *Nil desperandum:* Never give up. In the *Ars Poetica* he moves from exhortation to wiser counsel: *Tu nihil invita dices faciesve Minerva:* Say nothing, and do nothing, unless Minerva approves (Minerva, of course, being the goddess of wisdom). And Lucretius sets an axiom of science: *Nil posse creavi de nilo:* Nothing can be made out of nothing. On these scores, nothing more need be said.

guhren: midriff; region of the heart; hence, in ancient belief, activity of the mind. Gk *phrenos,* (*phrenetic*) *frenetic* and its doublet *frantic. frenzy. phrenic; phrenitis. phronesis:* intelligence. Aristophanes, in *The Clouds* (421 B.C.), mockingly pictured Socrates hanging in a basket above his fellow-mortals as a *phrontist:* deep-thinker, but actually in the clouds; this picture, said Plato in the *Apology,* hurt Socrates when on trial for his life in 399 B.C. more than the actual charges; and in 1875 Browning wrote a poem, *Aristophanes' Apology,* therefor.

phrenology: seeking the mind through the skull. *OED* has 26 relevant words beginning *phren(o). Phrenocosmia:* the world of the mind, has been the name of various literary societies. *schizophrenia. euphrasy. Euphrasia:* genus, figwort. *Phronima:* genus of crustaceans. *Euphrosyne:* of a merry mind, one of the three Graces; see *gar. Neophron;* see *neuos.*

Sophronia: of keen mind (combined with Gk *sophron*). From a play by James Thomson (1730), titled with the heroine's name, comes a line often quoted to show how absurd iambic pentameter can be: "Oh! Sophonisba! Sophonisba! Oh!" At the opposite pole is Pope's mockery in his *Essay on Criticism* (1711): "And ten low words oft creep in one dull line." See Milton, under *pen.*

Sophia, goddess of wisdom, and the beautiful shrine *Santa Sophia,* still in Istanbul. *sophist, sophism, sophistry.* The *Sophists* in ancient Greece were teachers of rhetoric and logic; they came to be regarded as verbal tricksters, able to "make the worse reason seem the better"; it was such charges that Aristophanes heaped upon Socrates, whose Socratic method is still soundly used. When his class was studying philosophical idealism, and a student queried: "How do I know that I exist?" Professor Morris Raphael Cohen replied: "Who's asking?"

sophomore: wise fool; see *moro.* This is a folkchange from *sophumer.* A college listing of 1688 names the four years: "Fresh men; Sophy Moores; Junior Soph, or Sophister, and lastly, Senior Soph." The suffix *sophy,* as in *pansophy; theosophy.* The meaning of *philosophy:* love of wisdom, has been extended; it has been divided, as into natural and moral philosophy; and in the Middle Ages "the philosopher's stone" was the supreme quest of the alchemists, who hoped to turn baser metals into gold.

A clerk ther was of Oxenford also . . .
But al be that he was a philosophre,
Yet hadde he but litel gold in cofre.
—Chaucer, *The Canterbury Tales*

gultur: vulture, and other creatures. Skr, *gaur:* wild ox. *gayal; goral. nilgai* (*nilgau, nylghau*): literally, blue cow. *Gautama* (The Buddha): literally, son of the best ox. *gopura:* first, cow gate.

Gk *bous:* ox. *boustrophedon:* writing as an ox moves in plowing: one line right to left, next line left to right, as on old carvings. *hecatomb* (*b* from *bous*): sacrifice of 100 bulls. L *bos, bovem,* diminutive *buculus. bovine. bugle:* first, a horn. Shakespeare in *The Winter's Tale,* iv, speaks of a bugle-bracelet.

bulimia (*bous,* plus Gk *limos:* hunger): "hungry as an ox," with variant spellings and figurative use. Thomas Fuller, "chaplain in extraordinary" to Charles II, in his *Commentary on Ruth* (1654), spoke of "the boulimie of all-consuming time"; in 1853 Thomas Hood said: "Novel reading is to some constitutions a sort of literary bullimy."

Also *butyl, butyric, butyraceous. butter,* earlier called *cow-cheese.* (Note that *buttery* [L *buttis:* cask] is a storeroom for liquor, whence *butt, butler; bottle.*) *bucentaur:* front half, man; rear half, bull. *Bucephalus:* literally, ox-head; horse of Alexander the Great. *buceros:* a bird, the hornbill. *Buchloe:* genus, buffalo grass. *bucellas:* a white wine from Bucellas, a town near Lisbon.

Fr, *boeuf, beef.* Gc, *vulture, vulturine. bull; ox; cow,* perhaps imitative. *cowslip. kine.* Possibly—by way of *cow dung,* hence annoying, especially when soft—*bother* (This may be tangled with a variant root, *guou.*)

Oh! the roast beef of old England,
And old England's roast beef!
—Fielding, *Grub Street Opera,* 1731

The heroine of this burlesque is named *Sweetissa.*

guretso: thick, fat; in great quantity. Gc, *gross.* Via Fr, *grosgrain* (*s* silent). See *gher I. groschen:* German coins. *grosz* (plural *groszy*): Polish coins.

Zangwill, in *The Children of the Ghetto* (1892), exhorted: "With our groschen let us rebuild Jerusalem."

?gutta: drop; also, a place where drops flow. L *guttur:* throat. *goiter.* See *gue 6.* L *gutta:* drop; E *gutta:* a droplike ornament in architecture. *gout:* a drop, as in *Macbeth,* ii, 1:

I see thee still,
And on thy blade and dudgeon gouts of blood,
Which was not so before.

gout: the disease, supposedly caused by morbid drops, "a defluxion of humours"; *OED* has 9 associated entries. *guttersnipe:* first, one that gathers up refuse, perhaps from the practice of the bird *snipe. gutter.* What used to pass along a gutter is pictured in Swift's *A City Shower* (1710):

Now from all parts the swelling kennels flow,
And bear their trophies with them as they go:
Filth of all hues and odours seem to tell
What streets they sailed from, by the sight and smell . . .

Sweepings from butchers' stalls, dung, guts, and blood,
Drowned puppies, stinking sprats, all drenched in mud,
Dead cats and turnip-tops come tumbling down the flood.

Swift then uses his last three lines for literary criticism, with the note: "These triplets and alexandrines were brought in by Dryden and other poets in the reign of Charles II. They were the mere effect of haste, idleness, and want of money; and have been wholly avoided by the best poets since."

H

ha. Imitative of surprise or derision. *ha-ha;* also *haw-haw.* French etymologists say that the *ha!* of surprise at seeing it gave its name to the *ha-ha:* a fence in a ditch, to keep animals out of a garden but not to spoil the view. *haw,* however, is Old English for an enclosure bordered by a hedge or ditch.

haw is also the name of the third eyelid in some animals, as dog and horse, which can expand to sweep dust off the eyeball. This may bring a ha! of surprise to a man, who for such an intrusion has only his tears.

?haifst: speed, violence. Gc, *haste.* (*Festina lente,* said Suetonius: Make haste slowly. The more haste, the less speed. *speed* first meant power; then success, as in the pleasant farewell, *God speed you!*) *hasten. hasty pudding:* in England, oatmeal porridge; in New England, cornmeal mush; called *hasty* because it takes no longer to prepare than to eat.

Father and I went down to camp, along with Captain Goodin,
And there we saw the men and boys, as thick as hasty puddin'.
Yankee Doodle, fill your cup,
Yankee Doodle, Dandy;
Yankee Doodle, drink it up,
And with the girls be handy.
Yankee Doodle went to town, riding on a pony,
Stuck a feather in his hat, and called it macaroni.

A *macaroni* (see *men III*): a fop, a dandy, drew his name from the *Macaroni Club* (founded in London ca. 1760), a group of men who had taken the Grand Tour, and affected the manners and cuisine of Italy. See *kred I; ueid.* The *Oxford Magazine* in 1770 declared: "There is indeed a kind of animal, neither male nor female, a thing of the neuter gender, lately started up among us. It is called a Macaroni. It talks without meaning, it smiles without pleasantry, it eats without appetite, it rides without exercise, it wenches without passion." It wears two watches, Mme D'Arblay observed in her *Diary,* 9 Dec. 1783, and a beribbon'd lovelock.

Richard Brinsley Sheridan, playwright and orator-statesman (he opposed the

British war in America, but declined a proffered gift from the Continental Congress), was described as "a macaroni and brilliant lounger in the Carlton House" —home of the Prince of Wales, then regent, then George IV, to whom Sheridan was confidential adviser.

As late as 1831, in *Sartor Resartus,* Carlyle declared that "a Dandy is a clothes-wearing man, a man whose trade, office, and existence consists in the wearing of clothes." (*Sartor Resartus:* The Tailor Repatched, clothes Carlyle's own life with the speculation of *Professor Teufelsdrökh:* Professor Devil's Dung. He goes through a sort of dialectic conversion, from the Everlasting No through the Center of Indifference to the Everlasting Yes, an acceptance of the present which demands rigorous honesty, facing the facts of life, so that "The Emperor is naked" need never be cried.

Heaven shall forgive you [Bridge] at dawn,
The clothes you wear—or do not wear.
—G. K. Chesterton

There is also a *macaroni penguin,* named for its crest, which resembles the macaroni coiffure. The food *macaroni* is a kind of pasta, a wheaten paste dried and rolled into tubes, like the thinner *vermicelli.* A *macaroon,* though mainly of ground almonds, glair (egg whites), and sugar, is also from It *maccherone, maccarone,* the singular of *maccaroni.* Just as macaroni is mixed with butter and cheese, tomato sauce, clam sauce, etc., so *macaronic verse* mixes Latin words with vernacular words or words given Latin endings, for burlesque effect. These words come from Gk *makharia:* happiness, which one feels while eating pasta. *vermicelli* is literally little worm; see *uer II; spaghetti* is the diminutive of It, *spago:* string.

fop is from OE *foppi:* fool; whence also *fob:* to make a fool of, to cheat; and *fub:* cheat. A *dandy* (corruption of *Andrew,* Gk *andreias:* manly) is perhaps from the earlier *jack-a-dandy!* buffoon, assistant to a mountebank, influenced by *jackanapes* (*Jack of Naples:* a clown, or a monkey, from Naples; a court fool, as the jack of playing cards). Such performers came to England from Italy, as Dryden noted in 1673:

The Italian merryandrews took their place,
And quite debauched the stage with lewd grimace.

He also, in 1679, pictured a clown "like Merry Andrew on the low rope, copying lubberly the same tricks which his master is so dexterously performing on the high." The dandy is what the French, a little later, called the *Incroyable* and the *Merveilleux.* We are told of a *merveilleuse* who walked "half-naked in the Champs Élysées." These "Elysian Fields" name the grander "Fifth Avenue" of Paris, from the Arc de Triomphe to the Louvre, former palace of the French kings, now the great art museum. *louvre:* literally, place of the she-wolf; Fr *louve;* see *ulkuos.*

?honos. L *honorem; honor, honorable; honorarium; honorific,* etc. College degrees may be awarded *honoris causa. honest, honesty.* Frank Harris divided his life into three degrees: getting on, getting honor, getting honest.

He that acts on the principle that "honesty is the best policy" is basically not an honest man.

?hule. Gk *hule:* forest; *khule:* wood. *hylozoic; hylotheism.* "The woods were God's first temples." The Druids ate acorns of the holy oak before their prophecies. Many varieties of acorn are edible; they were an early food, as shown in the saying "Acorns were good until wheat was ground." The Druid ritual upon plucking the oak mistletoe was mentioned by Caesar and Pliny; there is a long article on mistletoe in the *Standard Dictionary of Folklore,* which repeats Skeat's account of its origin, via OE *mistel,* from Gc *mist:* dung. The United Ancient Order of Druids calls its lodges "groves." The oak was also a special tree to Jupiter.

Here also *hylobates:* forest walkers, the gibbon. *methylene. hydroxyl. benzoyle. hylophagous,* also *xylophagous,* as certain insects and men that chew toothpicks. *xylophone. OED* lists 26 relevant words beginning *xyl(o),* and details 21; for *hyl(o)* it lists 29 and details 13, from *hyla:* tree toad, to *hylozoist.* Gnostic theology divides humanity according to three principles: the *hylic* (materialistic), the *psychic,* and the *pneumatic,* with Cain, Abel, and Seth, the three sons of Adam and Eve, as respective representatives.

Baron Karl von Reichenbach, in *Dynamics,* published in English in 1850, suggested *odyl* as the basic force in material things; he found the *od* force in mesmerism, hypnosis, and in all nature. "Everyone will admit it to be desirable," he wrote, "that a monosyllabic word beginning with a vowel be selected, for the sake of the convenient conjunction in the manifold compound words." He thereupon compounded such terms as *biod, chymod, crystallod, heliod, magnetod, elod* (electric force); and for them all, *pantod.* See *esu.* Elizabeth Barrett Browning, in *Aurora Leigh* (1858), mentions

> That od force of German Reichenbach
> Which still from female fingertips burns blue.

Those that today know of the *od* terms think them merely odd. Yet the word has lingered; as recently as 1936 Carter Dickson, in *The Magic-Lantern Murders,* has Dr. Keppel dissociate himself from "odyllic quackery." Then there come to mind, perhaps inevitably, the names *Odile* and *Odette,* of the false and the true princess—the essence of evil with a mask of beauty; the soul of innocence in a body of beauty—in the most romantic, sad, and glowing of dance dramas, *Swan Lake,* with music as modern as Tchaikovsky, and story as old as love beyond life.

Recently (dropping the *h*) *ylem:* the primordial matter, called "obsolete" in *Webster's Dictionary, Third Edition* (1966), has been revived by George Gamow and others to name the first stuff—postulated as neutrons—which in the tiny time after the "big bang" may have started our universe, and out of which the chemical elements took form. This pattern is elaborated by Steven Weinberg in *The First Three Minutes* (1976). Note, however, that Fred Hoyle, professor of astronomy at Cambridge, in *The Nature of the Universe* (1950, 1960), and others reject the notion of a primal explosion, the big bang, and put forward in its place the concept of continuous creation, galaxies passing away, new galaxies being endlessly born.

Contrasted with these, Bernard Shaw limited himself to what he called "the Life Force." Much earlier, and more persistingly, the initiating force, the pervasive essence, had been acknowledged as God. No doubt further hypothetical quintessences will be proclaimed.

hum, hmm, ahem. Imitative. *hummingbird.* In 1751 *The Student* (London) spoke of "the superlative advantages arising from the use of the new-invented science, called humbug." Though the "science" is not traced to either *hum* or *bug—OED* says there have been "many guesses" as to its origin—there is the story of the three students who meticulously joined the head of a bee and the body of a beetle to the legs of a praying mantis and took the result to the professor of entomology to identify. "H'm. Was it alive when you found it?" "Yes." "Did it hum?" "Yes, Sir." "H'm. Then it must be a humbug." *Si non e vero, e ben trovato:* If it's not true; it's truly trove. The professor lacked *humbuggability.* See *kem IV.*

Scribner's Magazine in Oct. 1925 hailed Ph[ineas] T. Barnum as Ph.D. in *humbugology;* see *bhili.* More frequent is *humbuggery,* though this form may have been avoided because of *buggery:* sodomy, which is from L *Bulgarus:* Bulgarian; in his *Dictionary of Slang,* Eric Partridge repeats a Catholic slur: "The Albigensian heretics were often perverts." The term *bugger* has lost this scorn, and may mean just "a chap"; Fr *un bon bougre:* a good fellow.

One may *hum* a tune. The *hum* of the bee is gentler than the buzz (also imitative). Both appear in the riddle Longfellow sets in *Kavanagh,* 4: "The square root of half a number of bees, and also nine-tenths of the whole, alighted on the jasmines, and a female bee buzzed response to the hum of the male enclosed at night in a water-lily. O beautiful damsel, tell me the number of bees." Other unsolved riddles appear under the root *ar I.*

I

i. A pointing root used in various compounds. L *id est:* that is (abbreviated *i.e.*). *idem, ibidem. identical, identification, identify, identity. ipseity. Ipse dictum:* he himself has said it; used first in Greek—*autos epha*—of the sayings of Pythagoras, a widely influential thinker of the 6th c. B.C. Cicero (d. 43 B.C.), the Roman with greatest influence on language and literature for 1500 years, declared: *Ipse autem erat Pythagoras:* This "he himself" was Pythagoras. (This lasted longer than the recent decade's "Confucius say.")

ipso facto. if. Touchstone, in *As You Like It,* v, 4, says: "Your If is the only peacemaker; much virtue in If." When Athens sent a message: "If we take Sparta, we'll not leave one stone on stone," the Spartans replied with a single word: "If." They lived in the region of Greece called Lakonia; from their reputation for conciseness came E *laconic.*

ia: to be roused; to seek. Gk *zetetikos* (reduplicated form): inquiring. Sir Thomas Urquhart, who is best known for his translation of Rabelais, explained in *Trissotetras* (1645): "Zetetic is said of loxogonospherical moods which agree in the same quaesitas"—a perfect example of *ignotum per ignotius:* (defining) the unknown by the more unknown. Logic has been called "zetetic, or the art of seeking." Bernard Shaw was a member of the London *Zetetic Society* before he organized the Fabian Society. The latter took its name from Quintus *Fabius* Maximus Verrucosus (d. 203 B.C.), called *Cunctator:* the Delayer, because of the tactics he used against Hannibal, harassing his flanks but avoiding pitched battle until he wore out the Carthaginian army. *Delenda est Carthago:* Carthage must be destroyed. The Fabians advocate a gradual change, when the majority is ready, as opposed to the "instant Utopia" ordained by the Communists. The Aldine device (of the family of Aldus Manutius 1449–1515, early printers), *Festina lente:* Make haste slowly, was translated by Sir Thomas Browne as "celerity contempered with cunctation."

Also *zeal, zealot, zealous; jealous, jealousy.* "I the Lord thy God am a jealous God, and visit the sins of the fathers upon the children unto the third and fourth generation—Bible, Exodus 20:5.

iag I: worship; sacrifice; holy. Skr, *Yajna:* Vedic god of sacrifice. *yasna:* one of the four divisions of the *Avesta,* sacred book of the Parsi, survivors of the Zoroastrians; see *ger IV.*

Gk, *trisagion:* thrice holy, an orthodox hymn. *OED* lists 5 words beginning *hagi(o)* and details 14, as *hagiocracy, hagiographic, hagioscope. hagiosidere:* holy iron, was a plate struck by the Christian Greeks under Turkish rule to summon worshipers; the Turks forbade the clanging of church bells. Turks were summoned to prayer five times a day by the call of the muezzin from the minaret. Also *Agnes:* the chaste; see *nana.*

iag II: hunt, chase. Gc *jaeger. yacht,* shortened from *jachtschiff:* chasing ship; still used for international races. *yaw:* first, hunt; then move to and fro; now applied to a ship's deviating from a straight course. *yager:* hunter; also a proper name. If he had been born nearer Sherwood Forest than the Schwarzwald, Moritz Jagendorf would have been Morris Huntington.

ie: send, throw, throw down. Gk, *paresis, catheter. enema. diesis; aphesis, aphetic. aph(a)eresis; di(a)eresis; synesis; syn(a)eresis. ephetae:* ancient Athenian court of 51 citizens, to which cases of homicide were sent. Possibly *hairein:* choose. *heresy:* making one's own choice instead of accepting orthodox dogma; *heresiarch, heretic.*

L *iacere, iactum:* throw down; hence refute, disprove; its frequentative *iactare, iactatum:* shake, flourish; examine, discuss; boast of. *jactitation; jactation. jest, jet.*

Several terms may be associated here. *jetsam:* goods cast overboard to lighten a ship in difficulty. *flotsam:* the part of the wreckage that does not sink (see *pleu*). *lagan:* goods flung overboard, sinking, but with a buoy to enable recovery (see *legh*). *benthos:* aggregate of organisms living on the bottom of bodies of water (see *guadh*). *nekton:* aggregate of organisms swimming (see *sna*). *plankton:* aggregate of organisms that float or drift with the current or tide (see *plak*).

jetty; joist; jut. gist: first, a lying place; *agist:* lying place for cattle. Combinations include *abject; adjacent, circumjacent.* A doublet of *adjacent* via OFr is *ease:* comfortable lying place. *at ease;* hence *easy; disease.* It, *adagio:* literally, at ease. An *amice* is a garment thrown about one. Also *conjectural; dejection; ejaculate, eject; injection; interject; object, objection, objective; subject, subjection; subjective. adjective; parget; project, projection; reject. subjacent, superjacent; trajectory.* It, *traghetto:* where the gondola sets you down.

My object all sublime
I shall achieve in time,
To let the punishment fit the crime,
The punishment fit the crime.
—G. S. Gilbert, *The Mikado*

ieg. Gc, *ice, iceberg, icicle.* Via Icelandic, *jokiell:* snow mountain. *Isolde* (*Iseult*): literally, ice rule. Her lover was *Tristan* (*Tristram*): literally, troubling sadness; Fr *triste:* sad.

iegua: youthful force; see *ieu.* Gk, *Hebe,* goddess of youth; cupbearer to the gods on Olympus; hence applied to a pretty barmaid. *Hebe* is also the sixth of the asteroids.

The asteroids are improperly named; they are not "starlike"; but, with orbits mainly between Mars and Jupiter, are rather minor planets—possible fragments of a broken planet; they range in diameter from ca. 800 kilometers to ca. 200; and they themselves may break into meteors. Four were discovered between 1801 and 1807: *Ceres, Pallas, Juno,* and *Vesta. Ceres* was named on 1 Jan. 1801 by its discoverer, Giuseppe Piazzi of Palermo, Sicily, of which island Ceres was patron goddess; most of those discovered since have been given feminine names. *Astraea,* the fifth, was identified in 1845; by 1890, 300 were known; by 1940, 7500; and it is estimated that there may be some 50,000 of these minor planets orbiting the sun. Astronomers called them "the vermin of the sky" until 1898, when Eros, coming within 23 million kilometers of Earth, enabled more accurate calculation of heavenly phenomena, and thus brought the asteroids into favor. Incidentally, acrostics have entered their names. The U.S.S.R recognized the American Relief Administration's aid during the 1922–23 famine by giving an asteroid they found the name *Ara;* and Reinuth, identifying eight, gave them names beginning with the letters of a fellow-astronomer's name, G. Strache.

hebephrenia, coined in 1871 by psychiatrist Ewald Hecker. Probably *hebetude,* from the moodiness of youth. Several terms in botany, as *hebeanthous, hebegynous, hebepetalous.*

ephebus: Greek young man, eighteen to twenty years old. The *ephebic oath* he took upon entering man's estate is in modern form taken by graduates of various colleges, as the College of the City of New York.

?ieiun. L *jejunus:* fasting, jejune. *jejunum:* named by Galen in the 2d c. A.D.; upon necroscopy, he always found this part of the small intestine empty. Fr *déjeuner:* to break fast. OFr *desjejeuner,* shortened to *disner;* whence E *dine, dinner.*

I know what wages beauty gives,
How hard a life her servant lives,
Yet praise the winters gone;
There is not a fool can call me friend,
And I may dine at journey's end
With Landor and with Donne.
—Yeats, *To a Young Beauty*

iek: speak (Umbr, pray; Gc, confess; elsewhere, lighter in tone). L *jocare; jocus:* jest; cause of joy. Hence *jewel* (L *jocalis;* Fr *joyau:* jewel; *joie:* joy). *joke, jokelet; jocose, jocular.* OFr *jeu parti:* even play; E *jeopardy.* Via Fr, *jeu.* Baby talk, reduplicated (*jouet; jou-jou*), E *ju-ju:* charm. *jongleur:* "A wand'ring minstrel I." *juggle; juggler,* with patter to introduce tricks and befuddle beholders.

"You could read Kant by yourself, if you wanted; but you must share a joke" —R. L. Stevenson.

ieku-rt: liver. Gk *hepatos. hepar, heparin; hepatic, hepatitis.* L *iecur; iecoris. jecoral.* L *gizeria:* cooked poultry entrails. *gizzard* (perhaps from Pers *jigar;* possibly from Hebrew).

iem: to be full; therefore to split; pair. L *gemellus,* diminutive of *geminus:* twin. *gemination, gemel, gemellus;* Fr, *jumeau:* twin. *Gemini:* the twins, Castor and Pollux; third sign of the zodiac; see *guei. bigeminal; trigeminal,* of *triplets;* etc. *trigeminus:* triple-branched facial muscle.

Also *gemelliparous, geminiflorous. geminate leaves* are a pair from one node. *gimbal. gimmal* was an early word for a finger-ring that could be separated into two; also for a hinge, which "twinned" boards, etc. Thus, in 1623, "the Water Poet," Taylor, spoke of

an hostess with a tongue
As nimble as it had on gimmals hung.

In Shakespeare's *Henry V,* iv, 2, the French are confident of victory, and Grandgré belittles the English, foredooming their steeds:

The gum down-roping from their pale-dead eyes,
And in their pale dull mouths the gimmal'd bit
Lies foul with chaw'd grass, still and motionless;
And their executors, the knavish crows,
Fly o'er them, all impatient for their hour.

Identical twins, always of the same sex, are born of one ovum that divides; other twins are born of two ova that are fertilized at the same time.

ies: boil, seethe. Gk *zeain. eczema. apozem. zeolite:* literally, boiling-stone. Gc, *yeast. guhr; kieselguhr.* See *ieug.*

ieu: young man; see *iegua.* L, *juvenal, juvenile, juvenescent; rejuvenation. Juno,* the youthful one, queen of the Roman gods; hence the month *June;* see also *dei.* Via W, *Evan.* Gc, *young, youngling, youngster; youth. junker, younker.* Du *juffrauw:* young woman. *euphroe;* see *per VI c.*

yeoman (young man); first, a young noble serving as page in a royal family; Sir Gareth spent a year as kitchen-knave at King Arthur's court. *Yeomen of the Guard:* the hundred chosen to serve directly with the English monarch; also called *Beefeaters. beefeater,* however, does not mean that they grow stalwart on "the roast beef of old England"; it is a folkchange from Fr *buffetier:* server of the (royal) buffet. Later research finds that this source was deduced from a spelling error in the French, and insists that *beefeater* means just what it says.

Gaudeamus igitur, iuvenes dum sumus.
[Let us rejoice then, while we are young.]
—Students' song, 1267

And what is so rare as a day in June?
Then, if ever, come perfect days . . .
—Lowell, *The Vision of Sir Launfal*

ieug, ius: join together, unite; shake together, mix; things so shaken, as juice; product of mixture, as ferment and leaven. See *ies.* Skr, *yoga,* the discipline; *yogi,* the disciple. *Yuga:* one of the four ages that unite history.

Gk *zugon:* yoke, pair. Gk and E *zeugma. zeuxite:* a variety of tourmaline, named through a "learned translation" of *unity,* from *Hull Unity,* a place in Cornwall where it was found. *ite* is the usual ending for a mineral or rock. *epizeuxis. zygoma;* the *zygomatic arch* of the skull was described by Galen in the 2d c. A.D. Suffix *zygous,* as in *heterozygous, azygous. syzygy. OED* lists 16 and details 20 words beginning *zyg(o),* as *zygodactyl, zygospore; zygote:* union of two gametes, first cell of a person-to-be.

Compound root *ius-ma,* Gk *zume:* ferment. *enzyme,* coined by Wilhelm Kühne in 1878. *OED* lists 23 and details 13 words beginning *zym(o),* as *zymin(e), zymogen, zymosis, zymurgy.*

L *iugista, iuxta:* together; *iugum:* yoke. *juxtapose, juxtaposition. OED* lists 4 more such words, and its 1972 supplement adds *juxtaglomerula* and *juxtapositive.* Max Muller, in a lecture of 1868, spoke of "the three stages in the history of the Aryan languages: the juxtapositional, the combinatory and the inflectional." *jugular. conjugal* (bliss); *conjugation. subjugate.*

L nasalized, *iungere, unxi, unctum, junctum. join, joinery, joint; adjoin, adjunct; conjoin, conjunction; conjunctivitis. disjoin, disjunctive; enjoin, injunction; rejoin, rejoinder; subjunctive. junction, juncture. joust; jostle.*

Sp, *junta, junto.* Gc, *juice, verjuice* (Fr *vert:* green). "Many a juicy morsel whets the palate." *yoke,* thence perhaps *yokel.*

"Edmund Baehr complained one day to God that he should sit up there in the sky with His pailful of the water of genius beside Him, dip in His finger, splash a drop on this one, on that, on a third, get bored, pick up the pail, pour the whole of it on the zygote of Beethoven"–Gustav Eckstein, in the delightfully written and immensely informative *The Body Has a Head* (1970).

Oh! here
Will I set up my everlasting rest,
And shake the yoke of inauspicious stars
From this world-wearied flesh.
–*Romeo and Juliet,* v, 3

ieuos: sacred, binding; hence, the law. L *ius, iuris:* that which is binding; *iurare:* to take an oath. *juror, jury; juridical, jurisprudence,* etc. *abjure, adjuration; adjure; conjure; injury, perjury. objurgation. just, unjust, justice, injustice; justify; adjust.*

With L *dicere:* show, speak, came *judicatory, judicious, jurisdiction; adjudicate; prejudice. jurat.* Sp, *juramentado:* a Mohammedan who took an oath to die killing Christians. The state of early justice in Spanish America, especially along the U.S. border, may be judged from the fact that Sp *juggado:* courtroom, became folkchanged into E slang *hoosegow:* jail.

?im: copy. L, *image, imago. imagination,* etc. *imitate, emulate, emulous. Emil, Emilia.* L *Aemilius* (name of a Roman gens): literally, rivaling. "In every parting there is an image of death"–George Eliot, "The Sad Fortunes of the Rev. Amos Barton," *Scenes from Clerical Life.*

ios: gird. Gk, *zone, evzone. zonal, zonar; zonule. zoster. Zostera:* genus of eelgrass. *Zonuridae:* literally, belt-tail, family of lizards. For *girdle,* see *gher IV.*

The earth's surface has been divided into five zones: from the South Pole, the frigid zone of the Antarctic Circle; the southern temperate zone, extending to the Tropic of Capricorn; the torrid zone, bisected by the equator and extending to the Tropic of Cancer; the north temperate zone, extending to the Arctic Circle, marking the north frigid zone,which is capped by the North Pole. The equator is an imagined plane passing through the center of the earth perpendicular to the plane of the earth's rotation; the word is short for L *circulus aequator dies et noctis:* circle equalizer of day and night; the sun crosses it at the spring and the fall equinox, when the hours of day and night are equal. The sun is apparently moving toward one of the Tropics, 23 degrees, 27 minutes, north and south of the equator, which it reaches, respectively, at the summer and the winter solstice, before its apparent turn to return. For *solstice,* see *sta.*

?iso: equal. Gk *isos. isochromatic, isochronous, isosceles* (Gk *skele:* leg). *isomeric:* of the same chemical composition but different molecular arrangement. *OED* lists 71 words with the prefix *iso,* plus 13 chemical terms, and details 110 words, from *isobar* to *isotropy.* Its 1976 Supplement adds 46 columns more, the most important new word being *isotope;* isotopes are forms of an element with the same number of protons but a different number of neutrons in the nucleus. There are some 300 naturally occurring isotopes; several hundred more, most of them very short-lived, have been formed artificially. They are usually identified by the mass number (total of electrons, protons, and neutrons) as uranium 235 (fissionable) and uranium 238 (nonfissionable, but when bombarded by neutrons accepts one neutron and becomes fissionable plutonium 239). See *el.*

The ending of *isotope* is from Gk *topos:* place; the various isotopes of an element occupy the same place in the atomic number sequence. Also, from Aristotle's

Ta Topika: "commonplace" themes for discussion, come *topic, topical. topiary* first referred to a garden place, but now is applied to the trimming of trees and shrubs into various shapes, as in a formal garden.

iu I. The plural pronoun: Gc, *you; ye.*

> Abandon hope, all ye who enter here.
> —Dante, *The Inferno*

iu II: shout. Imitative. Gk *iuzein:* call. *jinx;* from *jynx:* the wryneck, the "shouting bird," used in witchcraft.

L *iubilare, iubilatum:* exult. *jubilant, jubilation. Jubilate:* the Hundredth Psalm, from its first word in the Latin Vulgate. Also imitative: *yodel,* first used in English by Scott in 1830; and *yowl.*

J

?jing. *jangle* and *jingle* are among a group of echoic, or imitative, words: *tang, ting, tingle, tink, tinker, tinkle.* Note that there is an early E *tang:* seaweed, whence *tangle:* originally, to form a mass like seaweed. Also imitative, *jog* and *joggle.* One could make long lists of words that are imitative of sounds; here are just a few examples:

(1) of living things: *ah, ai, baa, boo* (*bogy, bugaboo*), *bowwow, buzz, cackle, caw, chatter, coo, gobble, groan, growl, hiss, howl, meow, mew, moo, peep, purr, scream, scratch, sneeze, sniffle, snore, snort, squeal, trump, trumpet, whine, whinney, whisper, whistle, yackety-yak, yelp, yowl.* (The root *iu,* as in *yodel,* meant a shout of joy; *Yo ho ho and a bottle of rum!* Thence E *jubilation;* possibly also *joy,* via L *gaudia;* see *esu.* Thus also *joyous, rejoice, gaud,* and *gaudy night* at English universities. From the same root came *Ganymede:* literally, rejoicing in cunning; and, from a corrupt use Zeus made of Ganymede, the corrupted form *catamite.*)

(2) of other natural sounds: *bing bang boom, clang, clank, clink, crack, crackle, crash, jangle, knock, pitapat, peak, rap, rattle, slam, slap, snap, tap, tattoo, thump, ticktock, whiz, zip, zipper.* For Edgar Allan Poe's 1849 *tintinnabulation,* see *stene. OED* gives 12 such words, from *tintinnabulant* to *tintinnate,* their use going back to 1787. The sound was apparently first associated with cow bells.

Some imitative terms are less frequently used, as the nonce word of Tennyson in *Far-Far-Away:* "The mellow lin-lan-lone of evening bells."

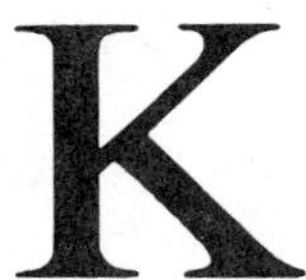

ka: desire. Skr, *Kama,* Hindu god of love. *Kamasutra* (*sutra:* thread, string, string of sayings; thence also *suture;* see *siu*): Hindu cyclopedia of love. L *caritas:* love; in the Bible, First Epistle of Paul, transliterated instead of translated: "And now abideth faith, hope, charity, these three; but the greatest of these is charity."

"Write me as one that loves his fellow men"—Leigh Hunt, *Abu Ben Adhem* ("Abu Ben Adhem, may his tribe increase. . .").

By a downgrading twist, L *cara,* Gc *huore:* sweetheart, turned out as E *whore;* for the *w* see *kailo:* whole. Vicar of Dean Prior, Robert Herrick, in *Hesperides* (1648), found an ironical turn:

Scribble for whoredom whips his wife, and cryes
He'll slit her nose, but blubb'ring she replyes:
Good Sir, make no more cuts i' th' outward skin,
One slit's enough to let Adultry in.

Nose-slitting was then listed as a felony punishable by death.

kad I: fall; befall; fall dead. L *cadere, cadentem, casurus:* fall, falling, fallen. *caducity, caducous. case* (as it falls out). *casual; casualty. occasion. cadaver. cadence. cascade. chute,* as when you shoot the chutes at an amusement park. *parachute:* protection against a fall; (see *per V*). *accident, incident, incidental; coincide, coincidence.* "One is an incident; two is coincident; three, and you nab it; four is a habit."

Occident, the place of the falling sun. *cheat, escheat. decadence, decay. deciduous;* the leaves fall, opposed to the evergreen. *chance;* especially, in LL, fall of the dice. *chancy.*

chancellor is from L *cancelli:* latticework, railings; he sat near the crossbars around the judge's chair. From the crossbars used in "crossing out" came *cancel, cancellated, cancellation.* For *cancer,* see *kar.* Also *chance-medley. recidivist.* It, *cadenza.* See *kat.*

S. E. Morison, in The *Oxford History of the United States* (1965), writes: "America was discovered accidentally by a great seaman who was looking for something else, and most of the exploration for the next fifty years was done in the hope of getting through or around it. America was named after a man who discovered no part of the New World. History is like that, very chancy." (It was a German geographer, Martin Waldseemüller, who in 1507 published the accounts of Amerigo Vespucci and suggested that the new lands be named *America.*)

All nature is but art unknown to thee,
All chance, direction which thou canst not see.
—Pope, *Essay on Man*

kad II: sorrow, hatred, etc. Gk *kedos:* sorrow. *accidie, acedy:* the fourth cardinal sin; see *kerd.* Fr *haine; heinous.* Gc, *hate, hatred. epicedium:* dirge. Lamb wrote a parody of Michael Drayton, an *Epicedium* addressed to his "fine merry franions, Wanton companions":

—Death, that last stinger,
Finis-writer, end-bringer,
Has laid his chill finger
on ye.

The first volume of Drayton's poems, *The Harmony of the Church,* was burned by public order in 1591. For *franion,* see *bhreg.*

kadh: protect, cover. Gc, *hat. hood; hoddie. heed.* L *cassidus,* from *kadh-tis; Cassis:* genus of molluscs–of which there are some 100,000 species. *Cassida:* genus of beetles–of which there are some 200,000 species, the largest number in the animal kingdom.

kagh: seize, hold; enclosure (first, of wickerwork). L *cohum:* strap holding plow-beam to yoke; *inchoare:* to harness, to begin. *inchoate.* Possibly *colum:* sieve; *colare, colatum:* filter, flow. *colander. cullis; percolate. portcullis. cavea:* cage; diminutive *caveola; cage; gaol, jail. cadge* is a back formation from *cadger:* hawker with eggs, poultry, etc., in a wicker basket. Fr, *gabion. gabion, gabionade,* and four more words in *OED.* It, *cabinet.* Du, *decoy* (*de:* the; *kooi:* cage, from *cavea*). *cajole:* first, chatter like a jay in a cage.

> Her beauty was sold for an old man's gold;
> She's a bird in a gilded cage.
> –A. J. Lamb, 1900

Fr, *coulee, couloir, coulisse. machiolate.* Gc, *cay, key, quay, haw:* enclosure; *hawthorn.* (*hem* and *haw* are imitative; see *ha.*) *hay; hedge. hag:* OE *haegtesse:* hedge demon; *tesse* is feminine from *diz:* devil, from *dheu I:* to fly about like dust, invisibly.

Gm *Hexe:* witch; E *hex. hagberry* (see *bhel I*). *hagfish, haggard:* first, hedge-bird, wild hawk; hence, wild looking. For *ha-ha:* hedge, see *ha.*

> Stone walls do not a prison make,
> Nor iron bars a cage;
> Minds innocent and quiet take
> That for an hermitage,
> If I have freedom in my love
> And in my soul am free,
> Angels alone, that soar above,
> Enjoy such liberty.
> –Richard Lovelace, *To Althea, from Prison* (1642)

There is little room for such feelings in the overcrowded prisons of today.

kaghlo: pebble. Gc, *hail, hailstone.*

kai: hot, shining. See *kati; kel I.* Gc, *hot, heat, hoarse:* dried out; earlier *hos,* the *r* from association with *harsh.*

kaiko: lacking vision. Related to Gk *khaikhias:* North Wind, the dark one. *c(a)ecum:* the blind gut. *cecity. Cecil. In regione caecorum, rex est luscus:* In the realm of the blind, the one-eyed man is king–Erasmus, *Adagia* (1523). As Andrew Marvell expressed it in 1665, "Among the blind, the one-eye blinkard reigns." Thomas Fuller in 1732 translated a Greek query: "What has a blind man to do with a mirror?" (Queen Elizabeth I, who had keen eyes, permitted no mirrors in her palaces for her last twenty years.) There have been many sayings of the kind. Homer, in *The Odyssey,* 17: "The blind man calls to the deaf." Ennius, "the father of Roman literature," whose epic *Annales* introduced the hexameter in Latin verse, spoke of "men who see not their own path, yet point the way to others." In the Bible, Matthew 15:14: "And if the blind lead the blind, both shall fall into the ditch." (Demagogues never take heed.) Cervantes, Bunyan, Carlyle, are among others who have developed such thoughts. A frequently repeated proverb from Tudor times throws light on a dark corner of culinary concern: "The blind man eats many a fly." Those that could see brushed them aside, or picked them out of the gravy. George Farquhar, in his play *Love and a Bottle* (1699), reached the finale: "When the blind leads the blind, no wonder they both fall into—matrimony."

kailo: of good omen; unharmed, well. Skr, *kevalin:* a soul freed from matter, in the faith of the Jains—whose priests officiate entirely free from clothing.

Norse, *Helga, Olga.* Fr. *Héloise.* Most noted of that name is the beloved of Abelard; he was emasculated by order of her uncle, Fulbert; he died in 1142, on his way to Rome to answer charges of heresy, and was buried by Héloise in the oratory of the Paraclete, which his students had built for him and where she was prioress; she was buried beside him 22 years later; their tomb is now in Père Lachaise Cemetery, Paris.

celibate: first, a healthy person; then, one living alone. Let well enough alone. *hail, halidom, holy. hollyhock* is *holy hock* (: marrow); *holly,* however, is from the root *kel:* to prick, from its spiny leaves.

whole, wholesome. In the 15th c. *w* was added to many words beginning with *h,* but by 1600 had been dropped from almost all but *who* and *whole* and their compounds, and *whore. heal, healthy. hail,* at first in the greeting: *Be thou hail! Hail and farewell,* L *Ave atque vale;* note the good-by wish: *Fare well! Good-by(e)* is *God be by ye. halse:* first, to greet; then, to keep healthy, to exorcise evil.

kait: bright, spotted. See *kai.* Skr, *svarga:* bright sky. *Sura,* the sun god. *cheeta, chital. chintz. chit:* a note. See *sauel.* Probably L, *celestial.* A *Celestial* may be a Chinese, one from "the heavenly kingdom." *celesta:* "the bells of heaven." *caesius, celeste:* sky-blue. *ceil; ceiling. cerulean.*

Gk *Selene:* goddess of the moon. *paraselena. Selachii,* order of phosphorescent fish. *OED* lists 16 and details 31 relevant words beginning *selen,* as *selenide, selenology, selenyl. selenium;* see *el 34.*

Fr, *Selena, Céline.* Gc, the suffix *heit:* bright; hence applied to a usually pleasant or dignified state. E suffix *hood;* JWalker lists 29, as *hardihood, neighborhood, widowhood. When Knighthood Was in Flower* (1898), is the title of a very popular romantic picture of 16th c. England, by Charles Major, depicting the love of Queen Mary for Charles Brandon.

kaito: woodland. Gc, *heath, heathen. heather. hoyden.*

O ye who tread the Narrow Way
By Tophet-flare to Judgment Day,
Be gentle when the heathen pray
To Buddha in Kamakura!
—Kipling, *Kim*

kak: enable. Skr *siksati:* learns; *saknoti:* is competent. *Shakti* (wife of Shiva), Hindu goddess of generative power, to whom a *shakta* prays for a son. *Sikh:* disciple; member of the Hindu sect founded by the guru Nanak in the early 16th c. (*Singh* is the last name of every Sikh after his initiation into manhood. The *Penny Cyclopedia* [1838] declares: "The Sikhs consider the profession of arms the religious duty of every individual." The Sikhs must possess five things: a dagger, an iron bracelet, short breeches, long hair (never cut; twined under the turban), and a comb. Their creed is "one of those inflammable things a spark might kindle into a flame" (I have found them temperate and keen observers of what is happening in India today.)

kal: strike; break; things broken off. Gk *kholaphos:* blow. *cope, coup, coupé, coupon, recoup. culpable:* worthy of a blow; *culprit; exculpate. khlema:* twig. *clematis. khlados:* branch. *cladocean; phylloclade. khlan, khlastos:* break, broken.

clastic, aclastic, anaclastic, cataclasm. oligoclase, orthoclase, periclase. iconclast. khleros: bit of wood broken off, for casting lots. *clerk, clerical, clergy.*

L, *calamity. colobium, coloboma. gladius:* sword. *gladiate, gladiator. gladius:* swordfish. *gladiolus:* literally, little sword, named by Pliny for the shape of its leaves. *glaive.* See *uag II.*

Celt, *claymore:* two-handed sword. Gc, *holt:* copse (Note *copse, coppice:* grove of small trees used for firewood, etc., from Fr *couper:* cut). *OED* mentions that *holt* appears in many names. *Holtland* became *Holland. halt:* lame. *hilt. Hilda, Matilda:* of the woods.

kam: bend, curve; a vault. Pers *kamar:* girdle; *cummerbund.* Gk, *anacampsis:* the bend of light (reflection, refraction) or sound (echo). L, via Fr, *jamb, jambeau; gamb. gam:* leg; now slang. *gambit. gambol. gammon* has various meanings. Directly from this root: leg of pork, Fr. *jambon:* ham; thus *gammon* (and spinach). *gammon,* as in *backgammon,* may be from OE *gamen:* a game. *To give gammon* was 18th and 19th c. slang for bumping into a person or otherwise attracting his attention while a confederate robs him; the practice, if not the phrase, continues. From this use, *gammon* came more generally to mean chatter; then, ridiculous nonsense; Dickens, in *The Pickwick Papers* (1837): "Some people maintains that an Englishman's house is his castle. That's gammon."

It, *gambado. viola da gamba:* held between the legs.

Gk *kampsai:* bent, curved, turned around. *sconce:* small, curved earthwork, fort. *ensconce:* first, to put earthwork around; Gm *schanz:* stone breastwork. Gk *khampe:* winding of a river; L *campus:* field, camp; the college *campus. campaign; encamp, decamp; scamp, scamper.* Various genera: *Camptosorus:* of ferns, from the flexible fruit; *Camponotus:* of ants, "bending backs." Gk *khampe:* caterpillar; *Campodea:* insects that bend as they move along; *Campephagidae:* family of birds, the shrike; *Campephilus:* the woodpecker; both birds eat the rippling creatures; see *bhag; bhili.*

The *caterpillar* is the "hairy cat"; see *pilo.* L *cattus* (feminine, *catta*) may be of African origin; Cleopatra's grandmother–or was it her greatgrandmother?–was a sacred black cat. The *cat-o'-nine-tails* is called "the cat" in Gilbert's *H.M.S. Pinafore.* See *ane; kat.* Hence also *catamount, caterwaul.* Du *meerkat:* literally, sea cat. Fr, *chatoyant.* Diminutives are *kitten* and *kitty. kittle:* engender, used mainly in the past tense; see *gn.*

L *camera:* arched roof, vault. *camera,* from *camera obscura:* dark chamber. *in camera:* (heard) in the judge's private *chamber. antechamber, chamberlain.* Sp, *camara.* Fr, *camarilla, champerty; champignon:* mushroom of the fields. *champaign; champion. champagne;* hence also the province in France, whence the wine.

Possibly *chimney:* first, a vaulted opening, as over a forge, as in a primitive tent or hut; also in some modern homes with a fireplace in the middle of the living room. See *kau I. camaraderie. comrade:* one that shares a chamber; first, of soldiers in barracks, comrades-in-arms. Du *cambret; cabaret. bicameral.* Gc *kem-en,* OGm *heben:* heaven, the vault of the sky. Good heavens!

"Alas! poor Yorick. . . . Where be your gibes now? Your gambols? Your songs? . . . Now get you to my lady's chamber, and tell her, let her paint an inch thick, to this favour she must come"–Hamlet, contemplating the skull of the Court Jester.

kan: sing. L *canere;* frequentative *cantare, cantatum. canorus. cantor, precentor, succentor. chant.* Fr, *chantage* (a sour note!) *chanson. enchanting, disenchanting.* L and E *carmen:* the song; *Carmen:* the singer. *charm;* first, a chanting to cast a spell. *incantation. recant, descant. cant* was first a beggar's whining tale; hence, hypocritical talk. (the beggar tots of India are taught enough English to plead "No mama, no papa" while from a distance a calculating parent keeps watch.) *concert. incentive,* "setting the tune." *accent. Oscines:* suborder of singing birds; first, singing for augury. *accentor, buccinator,* for blowing music.

It, *cantabile; cantata, canto, canzone.* Fr, *cantatrice.* A *canterbury* is a music stand, named for the cathedral in Canterbury where Thomas à Becket was murdered by four knights of King Henry II in 1170, as in Tennyson's play *Becket* (1884) and T. S. Eliot's *Murder in the Cathedral* (1935). The shrine there was a frequent goal of pilgrims, as in Chaucer's *Canterbury Tales* (1386); hence, *canter:* first, the pace of horses on the London-Canterbury road. In 1538 the shrine was plundered by Henry VIII, and the name of St. Thomas à Becket was expunged from the English church calendar.

Lesser singers are Fr, *chantecler,* and Gc, *hen;* see *ane.*

> Clear your mind of cant.
> —Johnson, in Boswell's
> *Life of Samuel Johnson,*
> 15 May 1783

kand: shine; be white; glow with heat. Skr, *sanders, santal. sandalwood,* burned for incense; *santalaceous. sandarac.* The *sandal* on the foot is the shoe of *Sandal,* a Lydian god.

L, *candent, incandescent; candelabrum; candle.* Fr, *chandelier. incense;* the verb *incense:* to anger, is also from this root, as we may say a person "gets hot" about something; *incendiary.* King Alfred the Great used candles to keep track of the time, having them made so that they burned out in just four hours.

candid. candidate; in ancient Rome, those seeking office went about in a white toga, a symbol of honesty—not worn by campaigning candidates today. *canescent:* to grow white, has been associated with old age; also *canities.*

The glowworm family is called *Cicindelidae,* reduplicated, as is the glow: "Shine little glowworm, glimmer, glimmer." *Candide* is the shining but naive hero of Voltaire's satire *Candide, or Optimism* (1759), which carries him into many misfortunes around this "best of all possible worlds," ending with the wise thought: "Let us cultivate our own garden." There we may bring blossom.

> How far that little candle throws his beams!
> So shines a good deed in a naughty world.
> —Portia, in *The Merchant of Venice,* v, 1

kann: reed, hemp. Skr *sunah; sunn:* East Indian hemp. Gk *kanon:* rod, rule, perhaps from Assyrian. *canon.*

> Oh! that the Everlasting had not fix'd
> His canon 'gainst self-slaughter!
> —Hamlet, in his first soliloquy

L *canna:* reed, tube. *canal, channel, cannel,* and *kennel* (: gutter) are doublets. *cannula:* a small tube; *cannon:* a large one. *cane.* (tin) *can; canister.*

Sp, *canasta;* first played in Argentina with a canister of cards. *canyon, cañada; canions. Canna:* genus of reeds. L, *cannabis:* genus of hemp, also called *marijuana, Maryjane.* It, *cannelloni:* tubes of pasta filled with meat, cheese, or a sweet.

canvas; first, woven of hemp. *canvass:* first, to sift through canvas; hence, to examine carefully; then to discuss, collect opinions; then, especially, to solicit subscriptions or votes.

One of Shakespeare's anachronisms—an anachorism occurs in his reference to the seacoast of Bohemia; see *ksei*—comes in King John's warning the citizens of Angiers that the French are armed against them:

The cannons have their bowels full of wrath
And ready mounted are they to spit forth
Their iron indignation 'gainst your walls.—

King John died in 1216; cannon were first used when Edward III won the battle of Crécy with longbows and four bombards, 26 Aug. 1346, the first important battle of the Hundred Years' War.

In a cavern, in a canyon,
Excavating for a mine,
Dwelt a miner, forty-niner,
And his daughter, Clementine.
Oh, my darling, oh, my darling,
Oh, my darling Clementine!
—Percy Montrose, 19th c.

kanth: corner; edge. L *cantus:* iron ring around a wagonwheel. *cant:* a slope. Possibly *cantankerous:* on edge; the ending by association with *rancorous. canteen. cantle, cantlet. canthus:* corner of the eye. *canton:* corner of land; hence *Kent*, at the edge of England on the Channel. *chamfer. contline. decant:* pour from the edge, gently.

kap: take, grasp, hold. L *capere, captum. capable, capacity, capacious,* etc. *caption, captious* (see *bhreg*). *captor, captivate, captivity. captive* and *caitiff* are doublets, as are *chase* and *catch. cable. capstan. ketch. mercaptan:* substance that "takes" mercury. *cabas, cabbage:* pilfer.

Capias: L imperative: "Arrest him!" *catch. cop, copper:* slang for police officer; not from the metal, despite the scornful jingle from the days when a town had a grazing-common:

Brass button, blue coat,
Couldn't catch a nannygoat!

In the early 1900s, goats roamed on Washington Heights (Goat Hill, Cogan's Bluff, overlooking the Speedway and the Polo Grounds, New York City); see *kapr.*

catchpoll: bumbailiff; tax collectors were wont to confiscate poultry, L *pullus; pullet, poult;* see *ane.* The "poll," however, may refer to the individual to be caught; OE *polle:* head, as at the polls or polling booth on Election Day. We still count cattle by the head. Also *pollard; polled;* and *pollywog:* wiggling little head.

L *capsa:* box. *case; chase, enchase; chassis. chess* (on pontoon); *encase, casement. caisson; capsule. cash:* ready money, kept in a handy box. *casket* (This is not a diminutive of *cask,* which is from LL *quassicare:* break; LL *quassare:* shake violently; L *quatere, quassum:* shake; *see* kuet.) *capsa:* especially, a box for books. It, *cassone.*

Capsella: genus of mustard. *Capsicum:* genus of potato; see *poi.*

copepod: a tiny crustacean. *aucupate:* to catch birds. *cachalot,* from the hilt-like shape of the whale's head. *capistrate, captation. disciple, discipline. anticipate; emancipation; mancipate. participate; reciprocate.*

L *concipere, conceptum,* via OFr *conceivre,* E *conceive,* in mind or body. *deceive, perceive; perception, apperception; imperceptible. conceit, deceit; receive, receptacle, recipe, receipt, reception. inception, incipient:* beginning to take hold.

intercept, intussusception. acceptance; except; excipient. forceps. conception; contraceptive. precept. recuperate, recover. susceptible. nuncupative: taking (designating) one's heirs. *precipice. purchase. prince* is shortened from *princeps, principem* (*primo-capus*): holding the first place. *principal, principality, principle. municipal. usucapion:* holding ownership by uninterrupted use.

occupant, occupation, occupy. OED adds a special note after its definition "8. occupy: to deal with, or have to do with, sexually; to cohabit": "The disuse of this term in the 17th and most of the 18th c. is notable. . . . This avoidance seems to be due to its vulgar employment in sense 8. Cf. Shakespeare *2 Henry IV* ii, 14, 161: 'A Captain! God's light, these villains will make the word as odious as the word occupy, which was an excellent good word before it was ill-used.'" Ben Jonson in 1637 commented on its avoidance "by many, out of their own obscene apprehensions"; and Queen Elizabeth I's godson Sir John Harington indicates the origin of its sexual use in his ironic epigram *To Lesbia, a Great Lady:*

Lesbia doth laugh to hear sellers and buyers
Called by the name Substantial Occupyers;
Lesbia, the word was good while good folks used it,
You marred it that with Chaucer's jest abused it:
But good or bad, how ere the word be made,
Lesbia is loth, perhaps, to leave the trade.

This significance lends poignancy to Othello's despairing cry when he is convinced of Desdemona's unfaithfulness: "Farewell. Othello's occupation's gone!"

Sp, *caja, cajera; recado.* Gc, *haft, have, haven. heave, heavy, heft. behoof, beh(o)ove. hawk.*

kaph. Gc, *hoof. OED* gives more than two columns to *hoof* and its compounds. Most domestic quadrupeds are hoofed, as opposed to clawed.

kapr. L *caper:* goat. *caper. capriole.* From Gk *capparis* came the *caper* (*Capparis spinosa*), the bud of which is used in foods. Shakespeare plays on the two meanings in *Twelfth Night,* i, 2:

Sir Andrew Aguecheek: Faith! I can cut a caper! (*dances awkwardly*).
Sir Toby Belch: And I can cut the mutton to 't.

Capricorn, the cape and the constellation, from the goat-horn shape. The constellation is the tenth sign of the zodiac; see *guei.* The Tropic of Capricorn marks the border between the tropic and the south temperate zone, which the sun reaches on Dec. 21; opposite is the Tropic of Cancer, edge of the north temperate zone, reached by the sun on June 21. See *ios; kar.*

Capella: brightest star, Alpha, in the constellation Auriga. *Capri,* island with many wild goats; on its highest point, in A.D. 26, Emperor Tiberius built his palace. *caprine.* Possibly *caprice, capricious, capriccio;* but see *caput. capric, caproic, caprylic:* fatty acids with a goat smell; their salts are *caprate, caproate, caprylate.*

chevron, cheverel, chevrotain. caprification: pollinizing the goat-fig. *Capreolus:* genus of roe deer. *Caprella:* genus of crustacea. *Caprimulgidae:* family of birds, the *goatsuckers. Caprifoliaceae:* family of honeysuckles. *capercailzie,* however, is possibly a shift from L *caballus* (see *horse,* under root *ane*); Gael *capull coille:* literally, horse of the wood; a large grouse.

Our *cab* is short for *cabriolet:* first, a light, two-wheeled vehicle that bounced on the dirt roads of France like a bounding goat; compounded as *taxicab:* one equipped with a *taximeter:* device for noting distances and computing fares.

kar, krak: hard; strong, powerful. Skr *kankar:* gravel. *kunkur:* coarse limestone. Gk *kratos:* power. *Epicrates:* genus of boa constrictor, the hard-squeezer. *pancratium:* the power struggles at the Olympic Games, wrestling and boxing. *acratia:* loss of power.

aristocracy. JWalker lists 32 words ending *cracy,* as *autocracy, plutocracy;* see *dheigh N 11.* James Bryce, in *The American Commonwealth* (1888), states: "The commonest of the old charges against democracy was that it passes into ochlocracy." *ochlocracy:* mob rule. A danger unknown to Bryce was *unionocracy,* a horrible hybrid word! Kurtz's *Church History* (1849), states: "For the first half of the tenth century, Theodora and her equally infamous daughters filled the see of Peter with their paramours, their sons and grandsons–the so-called pornocracy." Kurtz's book, translated in 1891, was popular in a period when privileged persons, by the "voice of God," were granted a code of conduct for their neighbors.

Gk *kharuon:* nut, kernel. *carina. careen:* first, a ship's keel; then, tipping to expose the keel. *karyo, caryo:* prefix referring to a nucleus, as *karyokinesis, karyolysis, karyostenosis. OED* lists 12, the earliest from 1874; and in its 1976 supplement lists 5 more and details 6. Thus *prokaryocyte, prokaryotic, eukaryotic.*

Gk *kharkhinos:* hard-shelled creature, the crab. From its clutching bite, *carcinogen, carcinoma, carcinomatosis.* There are 5 associated words in *OED,* 4 more in the 1972 supplement. L *cancer:* crab; *cancer. Cancer* is the fourth sign of the zodiac; see *guei;* for *Tropic of Cancer,* see *kapr. canker, chancre.*

It, *arditi:* storm troops in World War II. Fr *écrevisse,* folkchanged to E *crayfish.* W, *crag.* Gc *krabblen:* grope (Gm *Krebs:* crab). *crawl. scrawl* may blend *scribble* and *crawl. crab. crab apple,* from the taste. *crabbed, crabby. hard, harden, hardy, hardihood, hardship, hardtack, hardware. standard* is a blending of OFr *estendre:* spread out, and *-ard:* bold, although some of its meanings grew from association with *stand.* The suffix *ard* appears in various names, meaning powerful, bold: thus *Bernard,* ___ as a bear; *Everard,* ___ as a boar; *Gerard,* ___ with the spear; *Gunther,* ___ in war; *Leonard,* ___ as a lion; *Reynard,* ___ in counsel (Reynard the Fox); *Richard,* ___ as ruler (Richard the Lionheart).

Crabbed age and youth cannot live together;
Youth is full of pleasure, age is full of care.
Youth like summer morn, age like winter weather,
Youth like summer brave, age like winter bare . . .
Age, I do abhor thee; youth, I do adore thee.
    Oh, my love, my love is young!
Age, I do defy thee! Oh, sweet shepherd, hie thee,
    For methinks thou stayst too long.
    –Shakespeare, *The Passionate Pilgrim,* xii

kars: scratch; rub. L *carmen, carminen; carminare:* to card wool. *carduus:* thistle. *carminative:* of carding wool; hence, by the medieval theory of humours, to comb out excess gas from stomach or bowels. *cardonicillo; cardoon. Carduus:* genus of prickly herbs. *Carex:* genus of plants, as the sedge, scratching. *(Swiss) chard. carline:* thistle, linked in legend with *Charlemagne, Carolus Magnus.* Gc, *harsh.*

Somehow, 'tis seldom or never
The two hit it off as they should;
The good are so harsh to the clever,
The clever so rude to the good!
    –Elizabeth Wordsworth, 1900

kas: gray. L (*cas-nos*), *canescent.* Gc, *hare, harrier.* For *harry,* see *koro.*

kas(tr): cut. L *castrare, castratum. castus:* pure; cut free from fault. *caste; castigate* (see *tag I*). *castrate. chaste, chasten, chastize, chastity; incest.* Possibly *catharsis; acatharsia:* filth (*a* negative). *Catherine, Katharine. carere, caritatum:* cut away from; lack. *caret:* it is missing; the sign ∧ . *cassus:* empty. *quash* (but see *kuet*). *castra:* ground cut clear; hence *camp. castramentation. castellated. castellan,* doublet of *chatelain. chateau. alcazar,* roundabout from Latin via Arabic (*al:* the) and Spanish. A castle had a protective moat and ground cut clear, anciently for the "mile walk" before royal residences: dismount and come afoot to prevent surprise; to be prepared for friend or foe; it was thus that Banquo could be slain in *Macbeth.*

Roman camps in Britain left names, spelled in three ways as by the local sounds. *Lancaster, Westchester, Leicester* (*Lester, Leicestershire*). *Worcester* (*Wooster*); *Worcestershire* (Celtic place name, Latin camp, Saxon county) remains as the name of a sauce.

kat: thrown or dropped down; hence animal offspring. *cadelle. catulus:* puppy. *cat.* Gk prefix *cat(a); cath:* completely. *catabolism:* breaking down what metabolism builds up. *catachresis; cataclysm; catastrophe. catarrh; catarrhina:* gorilla, orangutan, etc., with nostrils downward. *cataglottism:* a tongue-kiss. *catamidiate:* to put to shame. *cataract. catalectic, acatalectic. catheter.*

cathedral: seat of a bishop (*ecclesia cathedralis:* church of the seat). *ex cathedra. catholic. catholicon:* cure-all. *catocathartic. catogenic.* The *catacombs* of Rome were accidentally uncovered in 1578. *OED* has 125 related terms beginning *cat(a).*

Other *cata* terms include *catamite:* folkchanged from *Ganymede,* among other things cupbearer to Zeus. *catamaran* is from a Tamil word meaning tied tree; it has recently been extended to the *trimaran:* three hulls "tied" together, with water between. *catamount* is short for *cat-o'-mountain. paramount* is from L *par,* with *a mont:* up the hill; hence, topmost. *catawampus* is a word coined as a humorous exaggeration; thus Bulwer Lytton, in *My Novel* (1852), finds himself "catawampously chewed up by a mercenary cormorant of a capitalist."

kau I: burn. Gk *khauma:* heat of the sun. *calm.* Fr, *chomage:* first, stopping work during heat; now, when workers become hot-headed. *chimney,* but see *kam. khalon:* wood for burning, whence also *khalopodos:* a wooden foot, shoemaker's last; E *caliber. khairein:* burn. *caeoma:* fiery-red rust. *caustic; cauterize. encaustic,* folkshortened to *ink. catacaustic, diacaustic; hypocaust. holocaust:* complete burning. *Caucasian:* the shining people; possibly, those that get sunburned. *Nausicaä:* burner of ships, maiden in the *Odyssey* who welcomes the shipwrecked Odysseus. See *kel I.*

> Like that self-begotten bird
> In the Arabian woods embost,
> That no second knows, nor third,
> And lay erewhile a holocaust.
> —Milton, *Samson Agonistes* (1671)

kau II. Imitative. Skr, *chukar, chikhor, chuckoor:* partridge, said to eat fire; possibly influenced by preceding root. Gk *kokuein:* wail. *Cocytus,* River of Lamentation, is one of the five rivers of Hades; actually, like the Acheron, it was an unwholesome river in Epirus which flowed partly underground. Shakespeare in *A Midsummer Night's Dream,* and Milton in *Comus* ("sooty Acheron") and *Paradise Lost,* ii ("Sad Acheron of sorrow, black and deep"), speak of Acheron. Sometimes the name is used for the infernal regions. The Styx, a supposedly poisonous stream in Arcadia, ended underground, obviously in Hades. Hades (Gk *Aides:* the unseen) was both the god and the land of the dead; then, although Tartarus was an abyss for the damned, Hades became synonymous with the Christian hell. *Acheron* probably meant marshwater, but Greek mythology related it to *achos:* woe. *Acherusia* was a lake near Memphis, Egypt, whereover the dead were ferried by Charon, for judgment. The name *Charon* is euphemistic, meaning the lovely one; see *gher II.* Transferred to Greece by Orpheus, the ferry crossed the River Styx. *Acherusias* was the cave through which Hercules descended to Hades, releasing his friends Theseus and Pirithous and, as the twelfth and last of his "labours," dragging the three-headed guardian dog Cerberus out of Hades. The five rivers there are *Acheron:* woeful; *Cocytus:* wailing; *Lethe:* forgetful (see *ladh*); *Phlegethon:* fiery (see *bhel I*); and *Styx:* hateful. Milton describes them in *Paradise Lost,* ii, 570–86.

kau III: strike; cut. L *cudere, cudus. incus* (anvil, to strike on): the middle bone of the ear, from its shape. *caudex:* first, a cut tree trunk; then, a writing tablet therefrom; hence, *code, codex, codify; codicil.* A foxtail was often cut as a trophy of the hunt; hence *caudal. cue,* as for billiards; via Fr, *queue,* as for a bus. See *kel VIII* and *ker III,* which intertwine.

Perhaps *cause*—"striking off" the action—and its derivatives, *causal, causate, accuse, accusative;* Fr, *causerie, excuse, recusant,* etc. A *cue* for an actor is the first letter of L *quando:* when, stage direction for an appearance.

A cockboat is a small boat, as cut from a tree trunk; hence *coxswain.*

Norse, *hag:* notch, cut; and its frequentative *haggle:* first, cut crudely, mangle. Celt, *haggis,* which is chopped up. Gc, *hew; hoe; hay. hagberry* is *hedgeberry.* See *kagh; bhel I.*

Do you know the difference between hay and straw? Any farmer's boy can show you—even when he can't tell left from right. During the American Civil War the illiterate farm boys tucked a wisp of hay in the left shoe, one of straw in the right, and drilled to the tune of "Hay foot, Straw foot, Forward march away. . . ." Make hay while the sun shines.

Douglas Jerrold (d. 1837) in his *Wit and Opinions* said of Australia: "Earth here is so kind that you just tickle her with a hoe and she laughs with a harvest."

kaul: stalk. Gk *khaulos. cauliflower. cole. coleslaw* (Du *sla:* salad). *kohlrabi. kale;* Scot, *kailyard. cauline, caulescent; caulis; acauline, acaulescent.* OIr, *colcannon:* white-headed cabbage, potato and cabbage. *colza. chou:* ornament on a dress. *amplexicaul, nudicaul. Caulerpa:* genus of marine algae. *Eriocaulon:* genus, the pipewort (Gk *erion:* wool, at the base of the stalk).

ke: sharpen; pointed. Skr, *sikhara:* pyramidal tower (no fewer than three allowed up together, for fear a "suicide pact" may be a murder). Gk *konos:* cone. *conarium:* the pineal gland of the brain, which Descartes believed was the seat of the soul.

Gc, *hone.* Note that *hone* (Fr *hon-hon*) is also a whining sound: "I heard him honing and moaning for Moscow"—Seeley, *The Life and Times of Stein* (1878).

kedr. Gk, *cedar,* perhaps from the Hebrew; wood used in burning sacrifices. Of the long-famous cedars of Lebanon, a few small groves remain. L, *citron, citric acid, citrus. citrul. Citrullus:* genus of the cucumber family.

> And lucent syrops, tinct with cinnamon,
> Manna and dates, in Argosy transferred
> From Fez, and spicèd dainties, every one,
> From silken Samarcand to cedar'd Lebanon.
> —Keats, *The Eve of St. Agnes,* 30

keg: catch, hook. Gc, *hack, hake. hook. hooker:* fishing boat; now slang for a street-walker, who "hooks" men in. *hackle, hatchel. heckle:* first, comb for carding flax. Du *haakbus,* via Fr *arc, (h)arquebus:* hook-gun. *hackbut. nuthatch. hackencreuz:* hooked cross, Nazi swastika. *hockey,* from the shape of the stick; better on ice.

hackney: a horse or carriage for hire (more common now as *hack*), from the town *Hackney,* in Middlesex, noted for its trained and placid horses; it came to mean a sorry jade; hence, *hackneyed:* without freshness or interest.

Roll out your rubber-tired carriage,
Oh, roll out your rubber-tired hack;
There's twelve men goin' to the churchyard
And eleven comin' back.
He was her man, but he done her wrong.
—"Frankie and Johnnie," 19th c. American folksong

hackle, the flax comb, though not the cock's comb (whence the strutting coxcomb) is used to mean the feathers on the cock's neck; hence, to have one's hackles up is to be roused, angry. "A cock of a different hackle" usually means a more dangerous opponent. Also *hackle:* covering, a skin or garment; the conical top over a beehive; the straw case of an Italian wine flask; and the fish the stickleback.

A *hackster:* a swaggering ruffian, especially of the 17th and 18th c., a prostitute's bully; what we call *pimp. hackwork:* writing by a "hired drudge"; Sir Francis Palgrave (who compiled *The Golden Treasury*) said in 1851: "Hackwork is of course out of the question."

kei I: move; rouse. Gk *khinein. cinema,* earlier *kinematograph. kinematics. kin(a)esthesia; hyperkinesis. telekinesis.* L *ciere, citum. cite* first meant to summon, to rouse to motion. *citation; excite; incite; recitation. oscitancy. resuscitate; solicit.* Fr, *(sans) souci:* unroused. Gc, *hight, behight; hest, behest.*

"A wound in the solicitor is a very serious thing"—Samuel "Erewhon" Butler, *The Humor of Homer* (1892).

kei II: lie down, sleep; settle; hence home, friendly, dear. Skr, *Shiva, Siva:* friendly, euphemistic name for the Hindu god of destruction; in earlier times, with the name *Rudra:* weeping, worshiped with human sacrifice. According to Hindu belief, destruction implies reincarnation; the god of destruction is therefore represented by the *lingam:* phallus; he is known by a thousand and eight names.

Gk, *ammocete:* lamprey larva, lying in sand. *kheimai:* lie asleep, whence another euphemism, E *cemetery:* a sleeping-place. *coma. incunabula. cimelia:* things stored away; *cimeliarch. neossin, neossology:* of young birds: newly lying down. *perissad:* literally, lying beyond; in chemistry, having an odd valence. *perissodactyl:* with an odd number of toes.

L *civis:* of the home. *civic, civil, civility; city, citizen,* etc. *civilization, citadel. Civis Romanus sum:* I am a Roman citizen. Cicero remarked that, anywhere in the world, a man need merely state this to win instant respect. From ca. 1850, for some ninety years, the Englishman revived the attitude.

Gk, *eme, oom:* uncle, living with the grandfather. *haunt.* The dying Antony, at the end of Shakespeare's play, bids love and Cleopatra wait:

Eros!—I come, my queen. Eros! Stay for me:
Where souls do couch on flowers, we'll hand in hand,
And with our sprightly sport make the souls gaze;
Dido and her Aeneas shall want troops,
And all the haunt be ours.

Wordsworth, in *The Excursion,* speaks more meditatively of "the mind of man, my haunt, and the main region of my song."

home, homelike, homely, homework. hamlet. Many place names use *ham,* as *Pelham, Southampton.*

In *ford,* in *ham,* in *ley* and *ton*
The most of English surnames run.
—R. Verstegen, *Restitution . . . English Nation* (1608)

From *Birmingham* came *brummagem:* cheap and showy, as Birmingham ware. *homespun. Heinrich, Henry:* ruler of the home. *hind:* servant living with the family. *hamesucken:* assault in one's own home. *Bohemia:* home of the Boii; whence *Bohemian.*

hide: early English measure of land, enough for one free family and dependents, roughly 120 acres. When Dido came to Africa, she bought "enough land to be encompassed by a bull's hide": she then cut the hide into thin strips, enclosing enough land to hold a citadel, which she called *Byrsa* (Gk *bursa:* hide); it grew to be Carthage. There Aeneas gave her one of the garments of Helen of Troy. When the gods commanded him to leave, Dido died—and English schoolboys in Latin grammar class used to say and "thus was di-do-dum[b]."

Abraham Cowley, in *The Mistress* (1647), anticipated Wordsworth's sonnet "The world is too much with us":

Well then, I now do plainly see
This busy world and I shall ne'er agree;
The very honey of all earthly joy
Does of all sweets the soonest cloy,
And they (methinks) deserve my pity,
Who for it can endure the stings,
The crowd, and buzz, and murmurings
Of this great hive, the city.

keiro, koiro: grey; old, hence worthy. *hue, hoar, hoarfrost. horehound;* the *d* added to round out the sound. Gc, *Herr,* translating L *senior:* elder, as of the church. *Junker:* young Herr; Du, *junker,* E *youngster.*

herring: the grey fish. *herringbone,* from the pattern. *herring pond:* facetious name for the Atlantic Ocean. *OED* has 23 columns for the word *red,* including *red herring* (the color when smoked), used in such phrases as "neither fowl, nor flesh, nor good red herring" and, especially, "to draw a red herring across the trail": to destroy the scent dogs have been following; generalized, to seek to divert attention from the main point. See *reudh.*

The man in the wilderness askèd me
How many strawberries grow in the sea?
I answered him, as I thought good,
As many as red herrings grow in the wood.

Sir Toby Belch in *Twelfth Night* exclaims: "A plague o' these pickle herrings!"—which G. B. Harrison, in his edition of Shakespeare, glosses: "very salt and indigestible, and so causing thirst and wind."

keku: excrete. A variant of *caca,* which see. Gk *copros:* dung. *coprolite, coprolith; coprology. coprophagous,* as the dung beetle. *OED* lists 7 and details 8 relevant words beginning *copro.* (*coproperty,* though conjoined, should not be confused.) *Coprosma:* genus of madder, from the smell. Swinburne, in a study of Ben Jonson (1889), remarked: "All English readers, I trust, will agree with me that coprology should be left to Frenchmen." Akin, but more anguished, is the cry—title of a play now (1983) in its twelfth year in London—*No Sex, Please, We're British!*

kel I: warm. L *calor:* heat; *calere:* to be warm; *calidus:* hot. See *dhe I; kai. ca(u)ldron; caudle. calefacient, calenture; calorescence, calorifacient, calorific, calorimeter,* and all your *calories* (singular, *calorie*). *decalescent; recalescence. chafe, chafing dish. chaff* is a doublet of *chafe:* to warm; then, to tease; the meaning *trivia* is influenced by *chaff:* a husk. *nonchalant* (Cool it!). *scald* (*ex-caldus*); *scaldino.*

Fr, *chowder. chauffer, chauffeur. chaudmellé. chaudpisse. chaudron:* color of fire. Note that on French water-taps the letter *C* indicates not cold, but *chaud:* hot. Gc, *lee,* sheltered from the cold. *lukewarm.* Cold hands, but a warm heart.

kel II; kla: shout, resound; thence summon, instruct, make clear. Partly imitative. extended from sound to sight, as today *clear sound, clear view.* Gk *khalein:* summon for worship. *ecclesiastic, ecclesiology. Ecclesiastes. paraclete.*

L *calare:* proclaim; *clamare:* cry out. *calends:* day of the new moon and the new month in ancient Rome; see *neun.* "On the Greek Kalends" is a learned way of saying "never," as "on the 30th of February." Roman accounts being settled on the calends, the records were kept in a *calendar.* Because early writings were on scrolls, *calends* may be related to *cylinder;* see *skel.* Various *calendars*—records of the *days*—have been used. In the Western world:

Greek: beginning with the first Olympic Games; see *fur.*

Roman: beginning A.U.C., *ab urbe condita:* from the founding of the city, 752 B.C. The first day of the month was the calends; then was announced the ides, the day of the full moon; the ninth day before the ides was the nones. It was on the ides of March, 44 B.C., that Julius Caesar was assassinated.

Julian: established by Julius Caesar, 46 B.C., generally used until the

Gregorian: essentially ours, correcting the Julian, established by Pope Gregory XIII in 1582. Caesar's year was eleven minutes ten seconds longer than one revolution of the earth around the sun; when in 1752 the English accepted the Gregorian correction, the day after Wednesday, 2 Sept., became Thursday, 14 Sept.

Ecclesiastical: in Catholic countries, a listing of Saints' days, of feasts and fasts, etc., some of which vary from year to year, mainly depending on the date of Easter.

Revolutionary: year 1 began 22 Sept. 1792 with the founding of the first French Republic; abolished by Napoleon on New Year's Eve, 1805.

Other long-used calendars include:

Jewish: beginning with "the Creation," 3761 B.C.E. (before the Christian Era).

Chinese: a lunar year, starting in 2397 B.C.

Hindu: began ca. A.D. 400; a new month begins when the sun enters a new sign of the zodiac.

Moslem: began 16 July 622, the day after the hegira, Mohammed's journey from Mecca to Medina, the beginning of the spread of Islam, now the religion of the Arab world, its holy book the Koran (Arab *Qur'an:* reading).

Also *intercalary. class:* first, one of the six divisions of the Roman populace, as classified for military service. *classify, classical,* etc. *Calendula:* genus of thistles, supposed to blossom at calends time. *claim; clamant, clamor; acclaim; declaim, exclaim, proclaim, reclaim,* and their nouns, as *acclamation.* L *clarus. clarinet, clarify, clarity, clarion; clear. claret* is a clear drink. Probably *council:* called together, and *counsel; consult:* call for counsel; but see *sel III. conciliate. nomenclature.*

It, *chiaroscuro.* Fr, *chanticleer; clairvoyance; éclair.* Gc *low.* "The lowing herd wind slowly o'er the lea"—Gray's *Elegy. Clara, Clare, Clarice, Clarinda.* The first *Clarence* was Lionel, Duke of Clarence (d. 1368), third son of Edward III; Lionel married the heiress of Clare in Suffolk, founded by Richard de Clare after the Norman Conquest in 1066. The name *Claribel* was coined by Tennyson.

"Who is this that darkeneth counsel by words without knowledge?"—Bible, Job.

kel III: dark color; grey, blue, black. Gk *khelainos. columbarium. Columbella:* genus of gastropods. *culver. caliginous. Calaeno:* the dark, one of the harpies.

Columba: genus of pigeons. The flower *columbine* resembles a cluster of doves. *Columbine,* his "little pigeon," was the sweetheart of Harlequin in the commedia dell'arte and in pantomime. The story of Christopher *Columbus* has echoes of the dove that brought the green sprig to Noah's Ark. *Columbia,* the gem of the ocean. See *mel III.*

kel IV: something elevated; hill. Gk *kholonos:* summit. *colophon; colophony. Kolophon:* a hilltop town in Lydia. L *celsus:* elevated; *columen:* peak; *columna:* pillar. *column, columnar. colonnade; culmination.* L *excellere:* rise out of; *excellens:* rising, surpassing. *excel, excellent, excelsior.* There is a nice but significant distinction between the desire for excellence and the desire to excel.

Gc, *hill, hillock; hillbilly. holm,* an island, rising from a lake or river; also in place names, as *Stockholm,* whence *holmium (el 67).*

The *colon,* whence *colonic,* and *Escherichia coli* (after T. *Escherich* [d. 1911]), of which there are many thousands in your intestines—which run from the pylorus through the small intestine (duodenum, jejunum, and ileum, over 20 coiled feet) to the large intestine (c[a]ecum, with the vermiform appendix dangling, colon, sigmoid, rectum, ending with the anus, over 3 more feet within you). *anus:* L *anus:* ring. *vermiform appendix:* worm-shaped hanger-on. *caecum:* blind (pouch). *colon:* column. *duodenum:* 12 each; calculated by the Greek physician Herophilus (d. 280 B.C.) to be as long as the breadth of 12 fingers. *ileum:* L *ilium:* groin. *jejunum:* fasting; see *ieiun. pylorus:* Gk *puloros:* guardian of the gate; entranceway from stomach to intestines. L *rectum:* straight; Galen, who named it, dissected only animals, which have a straight section there; humans do not. *sigmoid:* shaped like the Greek letter sigma.

The punctuation mark *colon* first indicated a limb, then a section of a talk. Similarly, a *comma* was first a shorter passage. A complete unit of speech, which we call a *sentence,* was earlier called a *period,* marked (as still, usually) by a point. We may still say that a man talks in rounded periods.

The Costa Rican coin *colon* is from Cristóbal *Colón,* known in English as Christopher Columbus; see *kel III.* A *colonel* was first the leader of a column; in America's southern states in the 19th c., any gentleman over forty was ipso facto addressed as *colonel,* pronounced like the inside of a nut.

kel V: to prick. Gc, *holly. holm oak.* See *kailo. holly* was earlier called *hulver;* and in the 18th c. *hulver-head* meant a silly fellow.

kel VI: hollow; to cover; to hide. Gk *khaluptein;* E *conceal. Calypso,* goddess of silence, who held Odysseus for seven of the ten years of his return from Troy. *calybite; calyptra; calyptrogen. eucalyptus:* well covered, with a cap over the bud. *apocalypse* (*apo:* out of, thus revealed, as in the book Revelation). *coleo-,* as *coleopteron:* sheath-winged, as the beetle (see *lep I; bheid*). *coleorhiza; coleus.*

L and E *color:* covers the surface. *cell, cellar, cellular; conceal. occult. cilium:*

eyelid. *cilia. seel,* as of a hawk in training; Macbeth (iii, 2) calls upon "seeling night." *supercilious:* literally, lift of the eyebrow. *clam:* secretly. *clam* and the slang *clam up. clandestine.*

Gc, *Hel,* Norse goddess of the dead; and *hell,* the hidden place that awaits us. *Valhalla. hall; hole, hollow. holster. haugh. heaume; helmet. Anselm:* with a divine helmet. *Kenelm:* bold helmet. *Wilhelm, William, Wilhelmina:* wearing helmet with a will. *will-o'-the-wisp. hull. husk* (*huskin:* little house). Probably *house, housewife; husband* (householder). *housing. hoard* (hidden treasure). *hose, hosiery. caboose* (cabin house). *hut, hutch, hutment.* See *krup.*

She never told her love,
But let concealment, like a worm i' the bud,
Feed on her damask cheek . . .
She sat like patience on a monument,
Smiling at grief.
—*Twelfth Night,* ii, 4

Colors naturally draw attention to themselves; they develop figurative uses and compounds, only a few of which can be mentioned here.

White—presence of all colors—and its compounds occupy 37 columns in *OED.* To *whitewash:* figuratively, to clear of charges of misconduct, often without disproving them. To *show the white feather* (not seen on a game cock) is to manifest cowardice; so also to be *white-livered:* lacking in choler, in the old theory of the four humours as determinants of one's nature. Often, as with *white lie, white magic,* the word means harmless, or good, as opposed to black. *Whitsunday* is *white Sunday,* from the robes of the newly baptized. A *whitecap* is (1) a bird; (2) a mushroom; (3) usually in the plural, white-crested waves.

Black—absence of all color—and its compounds occupy 18 *OED* columns. A *blackguard* was first a kitchen knave who cleaned the pots. *The pot calls the kettle black* may be used when one scoundrel reviles another; they are "tarred with the same brush." *blackmail* was first a sum paid by farmers along the Scotch-English border for protection against marauders; it has taken other meaning, but the "protection racket" is far from outmoded. Here also *black market, blackjack; blacklist. Black Mass* is a supposedly satanic rite, obscenely parodying the Catholic service.

Also *blacksmith. black walnut,* a delicious variety, but hard to crack, and almost off the market. *black sheep:* the undesirables in the human flock. *black widow spider. black tie:* an informal way of indicating men's semiformal wear. *blackleg:* a swindler in gambling. (*OED* comprehensively notes: "As in other slang expressions, the origin of the name is lost; of the various guesses current none seem [*sic*] worth notice.") Joseph Black (d. 1799) discovered carbon dioxide, which with oxygen establishes an important symbiotic link between plant and animal life.

A *black hole*—the name suggested by John A. Wheeler—is the not yet confirmed but theoretically widely accepted phenomenon of a star of such density that one "the size of a thimble" might have a mass from ten million to five billion times the mass of the sun; its gravity would draw inward all radiation, seeming to stop time and space, and of course it would be invisible (hence "black hole"). The theoretical point at which "density becomes infinite and time and space in effect disappear" is called a singularity. Karl Schwarzchild from his deathbed sent Einstein the calculations marking the point at which light would turn back upon itself and thus cut the region off from outside. Let us turn to

Red, with its compounds, occupies 27 *OED* columns. A *red-blooded* person is supposedly hearty, vigorous, as opposed to the more restrained and possibly effete blue-blooded aristocrat. A *red-letter* day, from early church writing, is a holy day, or other important day in one's life. A person taken *red-handed* (first used by Scott, in 1819) is caught in the act, as with the blood of the victim still on his fingers. Scott also said: "redcap is a popular appellation of that class of spirits which haunts old castles"; but in the U.S. a *redcap* was a porter in the heyday of the railroad. Via Fr, *redingote* is a borrowed pronunciation of E *riding coat.*

Yellow and its compounds take 12 *OED* columns, but the usually favored *gold* takes 16. A *yellowbelly* is literally a frog; figuratively, a coward; thus *yellow, yellow streak. yellow fever; yellow jaundice. yellow* was first applied to writing in 1840, to such yellow-paper-covered novels as those of Paul de Kock, selling in the U.S. at 25 cents. Poe spoke in 1846 of "the eternal insignificance of the yellow-backed pamphleteering." In 1895 the *New York World* introduced a cartoon "The Yellow Kid," which gave rise to the term *yellow journalism.* The London *Times* of 9 Nov. 1906 said that President Roosevelt used "the whole weight of his authority and influence against the yellow candidate"—newsman William Randolph Hearst. In the 19th c. *the yellow peril* alluded to the Chinese, although *yaller girl* and *high yaller* were applied to mulatto, quadroon, and octoroon Negroes. In the 17th c., *to wear yellow hose* meant to be jealous.

More popular and pleasant is *gold.* The *Golden Age.* There were also the *golden rule* (Matthew, 7), the *golden calf* (Exodus 32) and the *golden mean;* see *medhi. Goldilocks* has been used of more girls than the folktale lassie; it also names a plant with a cluster of golden flowers. The *goldsmith,* into the 18th c., was also a banker. On the other hand, for 300 years a *goldfinder* was the man that cleaned out the privies (probably a pun on the color of feces and of coins that might have fallen when clothes were loosed). In John Crowne's play *Sir Courtly Nice* (1685) the gentleman is indignant: "A goldfinder, Madam? Look into jakes for bits o' money? I had a spirit above it." See *lap.* In 1889 A. H. Bullen collected an anthology he called *Musa Proterva* [Wanton Muse], but with Victorian reticence left out much material, asking: "Who would care to watch a crew of goldfinders dancing around the shrine of Venus Cloacina?"

Gold bricks used to be sold along with shares in the Brooklyn Bridge. (In 1983, during a vast repair job, parts of the Brooklyn Bridge were sold by the city as souvenirs.) A *gold digger,* although she will not reject diamonds, assumes the permanence of the gold standard.

Green, widespread in nature, and its compounds fill 27 *OED* columns. Thus the *greensward,* the *greenwoods,* and the *greenhouse. To give a girl a green gown* meant to roll and romp with her in the grass, often with the implication of taking her virginity. Herrick, in his 1648 poem urging Corinna to rise to celebrate the May Day, says that already "many a green gown has been given." (Note that *May Day* [Fr *M'aidez:* Help!] is now the international radio call for help, supplementing the *S.O.S.* of the Morse code.)

Armado, in *Love's Labor's Lost,* recognizes that "green, indeed, is the color of love." From the sense of springtide freshness, *green gallant* (Fr, *vert galant*) is applied to a still-lusty old man. From the sense of *green,* unripe, comes *greenhorn;* see the end of *bhel I.* On the other hand, the *green-eyed monster* is jealousy. The 1580 ballad *My Lady Greensleeves* popularized the name as that of an inconstant lover; Shakespeare refers to the tune in *The Merry Wives.*

Blue and its compounds occupy 11 *OED* columns. Often it means despondency; *Blue Monday* (back to work after the weekend) may find one with *the blues.* Byron felt that way, in *Don Juan,* x:

Though six days smoothly run,
The seventh will bring blue devils, or a dun.

A *blue gown* in 17th c. Scotland was the robe of a licensed beggar; in England (Robert Nares's *Glossary* [1822]) it was "the dress of ignominy of a harlot in the house of correction." A *bluestocking*—fading now—grew from the blue worsted stockings of the botanist Benjamin Stillingfleet (see *esu*), who around 1748 was a great conversationalist in Bath and London; the term was applied to women who sought to become learned and literary; they gathered mainly at the homes of Mrs. Montague, Mrs. Vesey, and Mrs. Ord in London, where cardplaying was eschewed for conversation, and the men neglected formal dress with its black silk stockings. The term *bluestockingers* was first used (by Admiral Boscawen) in scorn; later, the *habitués* were called *the Blues.* De Quincey in 1858 called them "totally extinct."

A *blue ribbon,* from the one worn by members of the Order of the Garter (see *ken III*), became a symbol of first prize in all sorts of competition. Nor can we overlook the *blue laws* of the puritanical spirit. *blue mold* is the source of penicillin.

kel VII: to speed, drive; crowd. Gk, *klonus.* In the 1933 *OED, clone* is listed as an obsolete form of *clean.* In the current sense of propagating asexually from a sexually produced ancestor, or the result thereof, *clone* is from Gk *klon:* twig.

L *celer:* rapid. *celerity; accelerate, decelerate. acolyte. anacoluthon. proceleusmatic. celebris:* of a crowded place; hence renowned. *celebration, celebrity.* Gc, *hold:* first, drive cattle, then tend, then keep. Du, *avast!:* behold! *halt. hodden:* coarse cloth held at home, not sent out for sale.

kel VIII; (s)kel: cut, divide. See *kau III; ker III.* Gk *khleros:* a chip cut off for casting lots. *clerk, clerical, clergy.* For *laity,* see *laos. calamity.* L *culter:* knife. *cut, cutlass, cutler, cutlery, cutlet. coutel, co(u)lter; cultrate.*

Possibly *coward,* via L *cauda:* tail, whence also *caudal, caudate.* A coward was a turntail. *Cowardy-custard!,* a children's cry, from the yielding dessert. Adults also often make the accusation; there are four words to label it: *cowardry* (in Spenser, *cowardree*); *cowardship* (Shakespeare); *cowardliness;* and now the most frequent, *cowardice.* A gallimaufry of clever but frothy songs by the English actor-playwright Noel Coward was produced at the London Mermaid Theatre in 1972 under the title *Cowardy Custard.*

L *scalpere, scalptum:* carve. *scalp, scalpel; sculptor, sculpture.* Gc, *scales,* on a fish; *scales,* on a balance; *scale:* to climb. *scall, scald, scallop, skull,* divided from the body. *Skoal!,* as when drinking from a skull. *skulduggery,* the end a humorous coinage. *shell,* with cutting edge. *shelf. shellac. shield. shelter:* first, of a troop with shields (cut wood covered with hide).

skill: divide, distinguish. *slit. half, halve. behalf. hilt. holt:* wood for cutting (see *kal*). *hollandaise.* It, *scaglia, scagliola.* Scot, *claymore* (see *kal*). Fr, *calotte:* skullcap. *caul.* Gc, *skilling; shilling:* coin with a pictured shield.

Still amorous, and fond, and billing,
Like Philip and Mary on a shilling.
—Samuel Butler, *Hudibras* (1678)

Ben Jonson commented on a prophecy of his day involving this ruling pair:

When Hempe is spun
England's done.

He explained that the word *hempe* is made up of the initial letters of the names of five English monarchs, in order: Henry VIII, Edward VI, Mary with Philip, and Elizabeth; and that there was wide expectation that when the great queen died, heirless, confusion would envelop the land. The prophecy was more pleasantly fulfilled: the next ruler, James I, was king not of England but of Great Britain and Ireland.

> Take, take (says Justice) take ye each a shell:
> (We thrive at Westminster on fools like you)
> 'Twas a fat oyster–live in peace–adieu.
> –Pope, translating Boileau

kel IX: dispute; deceive. L, *cavil, calumny. challenge.*

"Be thou as chaste as ice, as pure as snow, thou shalt not escape calumny"–*Hamlet*, iii, 1.

kelb. Gc, *help, helpless,* etc. *helpmate,* folkchanged from *helpmeet.* See *med.*

keleuo: bald. *Calvary;* L *calvaria* translated Gk *khranion* (E *cranium*), translating Aram *gulgutha:* skull. *Golgotha,* named for its shape, the hill where Jesus was crucified.

Calvin, calvities. Calvatia: genus of fungi.

The wounded sergeant, meeting King Duncan at the beginning of *Macbeth,* boasts of the prowess of Macbeth and Banquo:

> If I say sooth, I must report they were
> As cannons overcharged with double cracks,
> So they
> Doubly redoubled strokes upon the foe
> Except they meant to bathe in reeking wounds
> Or memorize another Golgotha
> I cannot tell–
> But I am weak, my gashes call for help.

kelp, (s)kelp: grasp. Gc, *halter. helm, helmsman. halberd. helve.*

kem I: cover. It, *camisado:* night attack, white shirt covering armor to distinguish friend from foe. Fr, *camise, camisole; chemise; shimmy* (Shake the shirt!) Gc, *heaven,* as earth's cover. See *skeu.*

kem II: short; hornless. Via Norse, *scant.* Gc, *hind; gemsbok. chamois.* See *ker I.*

kem III: compress; enclose. *hem* of skirt, doubled over. *hem and haw* is imitative. See *kem IV* and *ken.*

kem IV. Imitative. *hem. hum; humdrum. humblebee, bumblebee. humbuzz:* the cockchafer; also, notched wood on a string, which buzzes when swung.

To eat humble pie: to be humiliated, is folkplay on the word *humble;* see *ghdhem.*

humbug, of unknown origin, came into use about 1750; see *hum.* In Jan. 1751 *The Student, or the Oxford and Cambridge Monthly Miscellany* commented: "There is a word very much in vogue with the people of taste and fashion, which, though it has not even the penumbra of a meaning, yet makes up the sum total of the wit, sense, and judgement of the aforesaid people. . . . I will venture to affirm that this Humbug is neither an English word, nor a derivative from any other language. . . . It is a fine make-weight in conversation, and some great men deceive themselves so egregiously as to think they mean something by it." Lord Churchill exclaimed in 1884 what many have since thought: "The whole legislature of the Government has been a gigantic humbug, a stupendous imposture, and a prodigious fraud." Disraeli had wondered, in *Coningsby,* forty years before, whether they had a government of humdrum or humbug. In the 19th c., *humbug* was the name of a lump of peppermint-flavored toffee; also, a nipper to grasp the nose of a refractory bull.

ken I: blink and associated movements; scrape; hence ashes, dust. Gk *khonia:* dust;

lime. *cinerarium,* for the cremated; *cinerary, incinerator. Cineraria:* genus of asters with down on the leaves. *conidium. conio-,* as *coniology, coniomycetes; coniospermous. Cycloconium:* genus of fungi. *Gymnoconia:* genus of rusts. *pneumoconiosis. aconite:* without dust; in the arena, implying no struggle, quick death; hence used of monkshood, a deadly poison.

anthraconite: black limestone marble (Gk *anthrax:* coal, whence *anthrax, anthracite*). Gc, *nap; neap* (tide); *nip, niggard, niggle, nibble, nod.*

ken II: make an effort, strive. Gk *diakhonos* (*dia:* through, thorough): servant. *deacon, archdeacon, diaconate.* L *conari, conatum:* try. *conation, ratiocination. tirocinium* (L *tiro:* recruit; E *tyro*). *vaticinate* (L and E *vates:* prophet, seer).

larceny came roundabout, via L *latrocinium,* from Gk *latron:* mercenary; *latreia* meant both hired labor (not expected to be faithful or honest) and service to the gods (there still are hired mourners); whence the word *idolatry* and more; see *lei II.*

ken III: new. Gk *khainos:* fresh, new. *kainite. Cenozoic. -cene,* as *Eocene, Pleiocene.* L *recentem,* recent. Fr, *rinse:* make fresh.

enc(a)enia: first, a dedicatory festival; then, an anniversary feast, a "renewal" of the joy, as annually at the Temple of Jerusalem or on Founder's Day (in June) at Oxford. The London *Telegraph* of 2 July 1978 quoted a piece written "on reading that Mr. Peregrine Worsthorne was unable to talk to a beautiful young woman at the luncheon because her thigh was being stroked by a bearded professor":

At the grand encaenia lunch, What a dreary bunch!
Heads of Houses, Former Fellows, Boring wives in pinks and yellows!
But if you bring a girl as guest All may still be for the best;
Let All Souls be bodies too: Soft and female, next to you.
As the dishes pass you by, You may stroke a silken thigh,
Now *allegro,* now *andante,* Lest Perry catch you *in flagrante.*
But if the lady prove not coy, When coffee's served, then attaboy!
If we were young we'd join that dance, *Honi soit qui mal y pense.*

Thus do old functions take the pattern of the times, giving new life to an almost forgotten word. The final French, "Shame to him that thinks ill of this," was spoken by King Edward III of England while dancing with Joan, countess of Salisbury, on 23 Apr. 1349; onlookers had tittered as he retrieved her dropped garter. He then founded the Most Noble Order of the Garter, England's most exclusive honor, which today has, outside the royal family, only 25 members.

Shakespeare quotes the French saying in *The Merry Wives,* v, 5. Herrick knew the incident's effect:

A sweet disorder in the dress
Kindles in clothes a wantonness.

Soame Jenyns, in *The Art of Dancing* (1752), deemed it wise to add a warning:

Let each fair maid, who fears to be disgraced,
Ever be sure to tie her garters fast,
Lest the loose string, amidst the public hall,
A wished-for prize to some proud fop should fall.

garter came to English from the Gaulish *garr:* leg, via Norman French *garet:* bend of the knee; whence also Fr *jarretière:* garter. The most widely distributed reptile in North America is the genus *Thamnophis:* the garter snake; it is harmless, but when disturbed lets loose a foul secretion from its anal gland.

ken IV: empty. Gk *khenos. cenotaph:* tomb monument to a person not buried there. *kenosis; kenotron; kenozooid. kenodoxy:* the desire for, or study of, vainglory; apparently never used, but entered in 17th and 18th c. dictionaries.

keneko: honey. See *melit.* Gk *khankhos:* pale yellow. *honey, honeycomb. honeymoon:* month of marital sweetness. L, *Cnicus:* genus of thistles. Jonathan Swift, in *The Battle of the Books* (1699), pointed out that bees "fill our hives with honey and wax, thus furnishing mankind with the two noblest of things, which are sweetness and light." Coleridge, in *Kubla Khan,* pictured an inspired song so that listeners would cry:

> Weave a circle round him thrice,
> And close your eyes with holy dread,
> For he on honey-dew hath fed,
> And drunk the milk of Paradise.

We have taken *honeydew* to name a melon.

Some scholars trace *beeswax* to the root *uosko,* which in English leads only to this word; others suggest *ueg:* to weave, from the appearance of the honeycomb. More productive (of words) is Gk *kheros:* beeswax; from it come *cere, cerecloth, cerement,* with 16 associated words in *OED.* Some have suggested this as the origin of *sincere;* cracked statues and other objects of marble were mended with wax; hence (*sine-ceros;* without wax, pure) *sincere.* But see *ker VI; ker VII.*

cerumen: earwax. *ceruse:* white lead. *cerusite. kerite,* a 19th c. insulation. *Cereus:* genus of cacti. *Cerinthe:* genus of borage plants. *Cerion:* genus of snails. *adipocere. meliceria:* honeycomb tumor. *ozocerite. tricerion,* in the Eastern Church. Sp, *ciruela.* Fr, *cierge. ceremony,* first used by Wycliffe, in 1380, is from Latin, perhaps first referring to rites at *Caere,* near Rome.

> What infinite heart's ease
> Must kings neglect, that private men enjoy!
> And what have kings that privates have not too,
> Save ceremony, save general ceremony?
> —King Henry V, in Shakespeare's play

kenk I: bind, clasp, enfold. L *cingere, cinctum. cinct, cinch; It's a cinch:* having a firm hold, hence easy. *cincture, cingulum; cinter. precinct. succinct. surcingle. shingles.* Fr, *enceinte:* (1) *in:* not: ungirdled, pregnant; (2) *in:* within: girded around, enclosure.

kenk II: be dry: feel pain. Gc, *hunger, hungry. OED* gives 5 columns to *hunger* and associated words. *starve* first meant to die, and until the 17th c. the term *hunger-starve* was used to make the manner specific. The jejunum is sometimes called the *hungry gut;* see *kel IV.* Into the 18th c. it was believed that a mad dog had a *hungry-worm* under its tongue.

"The best sauce in the world is hunger"—Cervantes, *Don Quixote,* 2, iii, 5.

kenk III: curve, bend. L and E *coxa:* hip. Fr, *cuisses:* thigh armor. *coxalgia; coxitis.* Sp, *quijote:* thigh; thus the name of Cervantes' hero "the famous Don Quixote de la Mancha, otherwise called the Knight of the Woeful Countenance." From him, *quixotic; quixotism, quixotry.* Gc, *heel* (rounded). *round heel* came into several uses, mainly slang: in sports, one who is easily defeated; especially in boxing, one who is easily knocked down. *round heel(s):* in the U.S. a girl "of easy virtue," ready to fall down for intercourse; in England a plain-clothes detective, from his silent rubber heels. And see *tuxedo,* under the root *ulkuo.*

hough, hock, of a horse. Perhaps *hockey,* from the curved stick. *hock* has had other meanings: (1) the last sheaf of a harvest, brought in with festive decorations, as in Herrick's *Hesperides* (1648):

> The harvest swains and wenches bound
> With joy, to see the hock-cart crowned.

(2) a teasing, dancing around, while collecting money for parish use, by the women on *Hock-Monday,* by the men on *Hock-Tuesday,* in the second week after Easter Sunday in Old England. (3) *Hocktide,* the season thus begun, with its warmer days, was marked by festivities, some of which were celebrated into the 19th c.; it was matched by Michaelmas, 29 Sept., the start of the colder season after harvest. (4) a white wine from *Hochheim,* Germany; short for *hockheimer.* (5) a special card in various games; in the U.S. the last card dealt in faro, a popular game among the pioneers. Since the last card paid nothing, *to be in hock* meant (6) to be in trouble; slang, in prison (Du *hok:* hovel, doghouse, jail). Thence (7) having to put possessions in the *hockshop.*

kens: assess; set in order. Probably Gk *cosmos:* the ordered universe, out of chaos. *cosmic.* The 1933 *OED* lists 6 and details 60 relevant *cosm(o)* words, as *cosmogony, cosmology, cosmopolitan; OED*'s 1972 supplement adds new meanings to 7 of these, then adds 11 new words, as *cosmonaut, cosmotron. cosmetics* (for the ordered countenance); *cosmetology. microcosm; macrocosm.*

L *censere:* evaluate, judge. *census:* first, the rating of property for tax purposes. An ancient Roman might post at his doorway a list of his landholdings around the world, partly for admiration, but also as a guide to hospitality for his journeying friends in those hotelless times. *excise. recension. censure; censor, censorious, censorship.* For *bowdlerize,* see *esu; peu II.*

"Unfortunately it has been our experience that there is a distinct affinity between fools and censorship. It seems to be one of those treading grounds where they rush in"—Heywood Broun (d. 1939). "I don't set up for being a cosmopolite, which to my mind signifies being polite to every country except your own"—Thomas Hood, *Up the Rhine* (1840).

Freedom of speech and freedom of publication are still debated concerns.

kent: goad; prick, as a compass point when marking a circle. Gk and E *cestus:* girdle. *cestum.* L *centrum. center, centralization,* etc. *centripetal, centrifugal, concentrate. eccentric; paracentric, paracentesis. centrobaric; centrosome. anthropocentric, egocentric, heliocentric,* etc. *cento:* a poem consisting of lines from other poems, is from L *cento:* patchwork.

> He that hath light within his own clear breast
> May sit i' the centre and enjoy bright day.
> —Milton, *Comus*

ker I, (s)ker(b): bend, turn, move around. A varied root: moving around, then settling in colonies; or turning the land with a plow, turning back and forth as oxen plowing. Skr, *chukker; hackery;* via Port, *jack:* a tree with large yellow fruit. *kakra:* circle, wheel; in combinations, as *cakravatin:* world rule, the wheel symbolizing the sun, the lotus, and the wheel of life; *dharmasakra:* the wheel of law; see *dhar.*

Gk *khukhlos:* circle. *cycle, cyclas; cyclamen; hemicycle, bicycle,* etc. *pericycle. (en)cyclop(a)edia:* circle of knowledge (*paideia:* education, from *pais, paid:* child). An *encyclopedic* mind. *encyclical:* papal letter for general circulation.

In ancient Greece, the *Cyclops,* plural *Cyclopes,* with one, round eye. In the U.S., the "circle" of the Ku Klux Klan. *Cyclades:* a roughly circular cluster of

Greek islands, some 220, around Delos, where Apollo and Artemis were born. *Cyclobothra:* genus of lilies. *Cyclonium:* genus of fungi. *Cycloloma:* genus of the goosefoot family. *Crambe:* genus of the mustard plant.

Gk *khrambe:* cabbage, from the crinkled leaves that turn into a round head. Figuratively, from L *crambe repetita:* twice-served cabbage, came *crambo:* the game of matching rhymes, with a forfeit if one repeats a word. An example from 1630 runs: "Where every jovial Tinker, for his chink, may cry, mine host, to crambe! *give us drinke; and do not clinke, but skinke, or else you stinke.*" Pepys, in his diary entry for 20 May 1660, tells of playing crambo in a carriage on the way to The Hague. *Dumb Crambo* is a variety of acting out a to-be-guessed rhyme word; similar to what Hollywood recently called "the game," which Queen Elizabeth II of England is said to enjoy playing with her houseguests.

The prefix *cycl(o)* is live; *OED*'s 1972 supplement lists 20 such new words, as *cycloid:* of manic-depressive personality, circling high and low; *cyclonite; cyclophosphamide; cyclotron.* Also *range, rank. cornice, corona, crown,* and *crowned monarchs. circa; circle; circular. circum-,* as *circumference, circumnavigate, circumstantial. circumbilivagination,* as in Urquhart's translation of Rabelais. *OED* lists 70 such words, and details 27 columns more, as *circumstance.* Dryden, in his 1681 play *The Spanish Friar,* declares: "I shall fetch him back with a circumbendibus." This word, with its mock-Latin ending, attracted Pope in *Peri Bathos,* Goldsmith in *She Stoops to Conquer,* and Scott in *Waverley.*

In 1526 Tindale preached that "the circumcision of the heart is the true circumcision"; the ancient practice continues among Muslims and Jews. In 1581 the antipapist J. Bell gave the word a new turn, deriding the tonsure of the monks: "that shaveling and cowled rout, with bare scraped scalps, being a new-fangled mark of circumcision." The first of January (the eighth day after his birth) is the festival of Jesus' circumcision, now largely ignored, though in some Catholic countries (e.g., France) it is still favored over Christmas as the day for giving gifts. Finally, we are told that "circuminsession denominates the co-inter-existence within one another of the three aspects of the divine trinity."

The *Circumlocution Office,* in Dickens' *Little Dorrit,* symbolizes the persistent red tape and roundabout dilatory fussiness of government departments.

The familiar *circus*—The Ringling Brothers, Barnum & Bailey ("the greatest show on earth")—spread from a circular meeting place, as where roads spread starlike out, at Piccadilly and other such Circuses in London; or a great circular structure around an arena, as the Circus Maximus of ancient Rome, rimmed with statues of heroes and gods, which Pope tumbles satirically in *The Dunciad* (1729):

> See, the cirque falls, th' unpillar'd temple nods,
> Streets paved with heroes, Tiber choked with gods.

OED defines 57 relevant words beginning *circ,* as *circuitous, circularize. cricoid, curve. search:* go around; *research:* around and around. *crissum:* circle of feathers around a bird's cloaca; *OED* prudishly defines this as from L *crissare: 'clunem movere'* which in English means to move the buttocks in intercourse.

The word *cyclone* was coined in 1848 by H. Paddington as a general term for whirling storms. These had developed different names in different parts of the world. Sp, *tornado:* turned, was influenced by L *tonare:* to thunder; see *stene.* Off Australia such storms are called *willy-willies.* Fitzroy's *Weather Book* of 1863 defines *willie-waw, willie-willie,* as a "whirlwind squall." Kipling, in *Kim,* speaks of a place in the Himalayas where "storm and wandering wullie-wa got up to dance."

The Dutch sailor Willy de Roos in 1973 made a solo circumnavigation of the world; in 1977 made the first solo trip through the Northwest Passage (last traversed by Amundsen with a crew of six in 1906); and has asked the Soviet Union for permission to make a solo trip through the Northeast Passage (last navigated in 1880) in his 42-foot ketch, the *Williwaw.*

The term *whirlwind* is self-explanatory; see *kuerp.* The familiar term in the southwestern U.S. is *twister;* it was a twister that lifted Dorothy to meet the Wizard of Oz. The word *typhoon* seems imitative of the ominous approach, then roar, of the tempest; it comes to us from various sources, and has had 16 recorded English spellings. Chinese *t'ai fung* means big wind. The Portuguese borrowed the word from Hindi *tufan.* In Greek mythology *Typhon* was the god of gales, son of the tempestuous giant *Typhoeus,* whom the gods buried under Etna and whose strugglings bring on the mountain's eruptions. Note that Gk *Tuphon* is related to *tuphein:* to cloud, to smoke; whence also *typhus* and *typhoid. OED* lists 6 and details 5 related words.

A cyclone, with a dreadful calm of minimum barometric pressure at its center, may attain a speed of 300 miles an hour. In the Northern Hemisphere, cyclonic winds revolve counterclockwise; in the Southern, they revolve clockwise; anticyclones, usually without rain, reverse the whirl. In their seasons, the major cyclones have been given, alphabetically as they occur, feminine names, with a perhaps humorous literal application of the last line of Goethe's *Faust: Das Ewig-Weibliche zieht uns hinan:* The eternal feminine uplifts us.

Milton, in *Paradise Lost,* pictures the storm:

> Others with vast Typhoean rage rend up
> Both rocks and hills, and ride the air in whirlwind.

Since 1950 *cyclamates* (abbreviating *cyclohexylsulphamates*) have become important. The *New Scientist* of 1 Jan. 1970 stated: "The cyclamate issue is certainly stimulating research into ways of satisfying man's sweet tooth. . . . Cyclamates are only 30 times sweeter than sucrose, and saccharine 300 times sweeter." As I write, *aspartame* is being tested; a substance 200 times sweeter than sucrose, it seems, nonetheless, actually to reduce weight rather than fatten.

sugar and its doublet, *jaggery* (unrefined sugar), are from Skr *sarkara:* gravel; sugar. Hence *seersucker:* literally, milk and sugar. The word takes two forms in Greek: (1) *khrokhe:* pebble; whence *crocodile:* pebble-worm; (2) *sakhkharon;* whence *saccharin(e); saccharose, sucrate, sucramine, saccharometer,* etc. *sucrose* (see *glact*). *sucre,* an Ecuadoran monetary unit, is named for General Antonio José de Sucre, chief lieutenant of Simon Bolivar in the 1821 campaign against Spain. From sucrose in sugar cane, rum is made—earlier called *rumbullion,* probably imitative of the satisfying stomach rumble as one rubs one's belly after a good swallow of the drink. Diluted rum is grog; see *gher I.* As Byron ironically observes in *Don Juan,* ii:

> There's naught, no doubt, so much the spirit calms
> As rum and true religion.

By *l.r* shift came Gk *polos:* axis, axle; whence the north and south *pole* of an axis, on which planets and wheels turn. Hence also *pulley.* The stretch from end to end makes a *polarity;* many "opposites"—good and evil, hot and cold—are the two ends of a polarity, with an extending range of intermediate degrees. The end of a polarity is Gk *telos,* thus applied to things (1) far off; (2) at the end, finished, fulfilled. Hence *telium, telson. autotelic. entelechy; entelodont. telesterion. telegnosis. telegraph, telephone, telescope. telepathy. teleology. television. philately:*

love of stamps. The stamp indicates that nothing further need be paid for the missive's journey. See *tol; steu.*

Telemachus: far-fighter, son of Odysseus and Penelope, and *Telegonus:* born faraway, son of Odysseus and Circe, are mingled in myth. Telegonus unwittingly slew his father in battle, then married Penelope; their son, Italus, founded Tibur in the land he gave his name to, Italy. Telemachus, after his father died, married Circe; their son, Latinus, gave his name to the language of the Romans, Latin.

OED lists 54 *tele-* words, and details 15 columns more. *telekinesis.*

Gk, *paleo-:* far off in time. *OED* lists 42 *paleo-* words, and details 17, as *Paleolithic:* of the stone age; *paleology.* Gk *palin:* again, turned full circle. *palimpsest; palindrome; palinode.* Edmund Lear declared that when he felt lonely he turned to the Bible and found a *palingenesis.*

L *crispus:* bent; curly. *crepe; crest. crestate. crinite, crinoline. crisp, crispate. curb. curve, curvature; curvet. culere, cultus:* turn the ground. *cult, cultivate, culture,* etc. JWalker lists 19 *-culture* words, as *agriculture,* in the field; *horticulture,* in garden and orchard; *apiculture, pisciculture, viticulture. colon:* the punctuation mark, sign of a "turn" in a sentence. *colon:* the turning intestines; *colitis,* etc. Hence also *colonial:* moved to another land; and the thirteen original *colonies.*

cologne is named for the city, now in Germany, that was *Colonia Agrippina,* the birthplace of Agrippina, niece of the Roman emperor Claudius, whose wife she replaced in the emperor's affections; Agrippina persuaded Claudius to set aside his own son and name her son, Nero, as his heir, then poisoned him, in A.D. 54.

The suffix *colous:* living in, as *pratincolous:* meadow-dwelling; *terricolous, saxicolous. ancillary. bucolic. col; collar.* Fr, *accolade, décolleté. hauberk, hawberk. hausse-col; hawse. inquiline.* Slavic *kolo:* wheel. *calash; kolach:* round cake; *kolo:* round dance.

Gc *hring:* ring. *ranch, range, arrange, derange, disarrange. rank; ring, rung:* round of a ladder. Early officers stood in a ring to hear the commander; hence *harangue,* the first *a* slipping in for smoother sounding. *riband, ribbon* (first, around the neck). Also *ridge, ruck, rucksack. ramp, rimple, rumple. scrimp. shrimp. shrink, shrivel. fallow:* ground turned but unseeded. W, *cromlech.*

> My joy, my grief, my hope, my love,
> Do all within this circle move.
> A narrow compass! And yet there
> Dwell all that's good, and all that's fair:
> Give me but what this riband bound,
> Take all the rest the world goes round.
> —Edmund Waller, *On a Girdle* (1685)

ker II: horn, horned animal; head, face, brain. Skr, *sarangousty; seerband; seerpaw; serang; seraskier, sircar, sirdar. mahseer. ginger,* from the shape of the root; *zingiberene, zingerone; Zingiberaceae* and *Zingiber:* family and genus of the ginger plant.

Gk *khranion:* skull. *cranium. migraine* (*mi* short for *hemi:* half; it usually affects one side of the head). *olecranon:* "head" of the elbow, tip of the "funny bone," the humerus. *keras:* horn. *OED* lists 6 relevant words beginning *kera;* then 12, mainly referring to the cornea of the eye, beginning *kerat(o);* and details 10, as *keratinize, keratose. carat:* grain, like a foot-corn. *cerastes:* horned viper. *ceratoid; keratin.*

Ceratodus: genus of fish. *cladoceran:* water-flea. *cerastium:* chickweed, from the shape of the pod. *rhinoceros. triceratops:* three-horned dinosaur. *cerebrum,* and its diminutive *cerebellum. cerebrate; cerebrose. cernuous. cervical. Corydalis:* genus of the fumewort family. *Coryneum:* genus of fungi.

corymb. coryphaeus: head of Greek chorus. Gk *khara:* head. *cheerful* (to be of good cheer): first, of pleasant countenance. Boswell, in his *Life of Samuel Johnson* (1778), reports Oliver Edwards as lamenting: "I have tried, too, in my time, to be a philosopher; but, I don't know how, cheerfulness was always breaking in."

carrot (horn-shaped). *charivari:* heavy head, from the noise. *crios:* ram, always ready to butt. *criosphinx,* which is *criocephalous,* its body a lion's. Prefix *crio,* as *criocerate, crioceratite. crious,* however, is an old word meaning full of cry, noisy.

L *cornu:* horn. *corn. cornea. cornel:* cherry tree. *cornet. corner. Cornelius,* and from its Dutch diminutive, *keeshond. cornelian; carnelian,* influenced by L *carnem:* flesh, from its color. *corniculate. cornucopia, Capricorn;* see *kapr. cavicorn, clavicorn. lamellicorn. bicorn,* etc.

The *unicorn* was known around the world; its one horn, spiral, up to 36 inches in length, had a white base, black middle, and red tip. Wild, yet at once submissive to a virgin, it was a symbol of both fierceness and chastity. Spenser in *The Faerie Queene* wrote:

Like as a lyon, whose imperiall powre
A proud rebellious Unicorne defies

—and the lion and the unicorn still face each other across the British coat-of arms. Its horn was fashioned into a drinking cup as a charm against poison, and powdered was an antidote. In 1605 Pope Pius III paid 12,000 gold pieces for one, giving substance to Dekker's remark in *The Gull's Hornbook* (1609) that the horn "is worth half a city." The unicorn lingers in legend and heraldry, and has a permanent place in the sky in its Greek translation, *Monoceros:* a constellation near Canis Major.

Fr, *cervine, serval:* ferocious stag-hunter. *cervelat; saveloy:* first, of pig's brains. Gc *hreinn. reindeer. rinderpest. hart;* Du, *hartebeest. hartshorn:* first obtained from harts' antlers. *runt. hurt:* first, from the butting ram. *rother:* horned cattle. *horn, alpenhorn, flugelhorn, krummhorn, waldhorn; hornblende. hornbeam:* a tree; *hornbill:* a bird. *hornet.*

The *hornbook* was first a sheet pasted on a board with a handle and covered for protection with a sheet of transparent horn. On it were usually written the alphabet and the Lord's Prayer, with a "Christ" cross to start; hence, "to learn one's criss-cross row." Also called *abecedarian,* from the first four letters. See *do.* Also *horntail, hornworm, hornwort, horny.*

Milton, in *Paradise Lost,* x, speaks of

Complicated monsters, head and tail,
Scorpion and asp, and Amphisbaena dire,
Cerastes horned, Hydrus, and Ellops drear.

Private Willis, on guard outside Parliament in Gilbert's *Iolanthe,* pictures the English lawmakers:

When in the House M P's divide,
If they've a brain and cerebellum too,
They've got to leave that brain outside
And vote just as their leaders tell 'em to.

ker III, sker: scratch, cut, pluck, gather, dig, separate, sift. See also *kel VIII; sek.* This is another prolific root, for scratching became writing; and sifting led to judging, discriminating; and cutting led to the use of cut things, as bark, hide, food.

Gk *khrinein:* separate, sift; hence dispute, answer, judge. *apocrine. eccrinology; endocrine, exocrine. crisis; epicrisis, epicritic. hypocrisy, hypocritical;* originally from an answering actor; hence, one playing a part. "Hypocrisy is the bow vice makes to virtue."

criterion; critic, criticism. In the 18th c., said the *Parliamentary Gazeteer,* "the critics sat on the stage, and were supplied with pipes and tobacco." And Benjamin Disraeli remarked: "It is easier to be critical than correct."

L *crimen, criminem:* possibly from the sense of judgment, *crime,* etc.; but see *ker IV.* "The atrocious crime of being a young man, I shall attempt neither to palliate nor to deny"—William Pitt, maiden speech in the House of Commons, 27 Jan. 1741.

L *curtus:* cut short. *curt, curtal, curtail. cutty stool:* a stool with the legs cut short; in 18th and early 19th c. Scotland, "offenders against chastity" were seated on one in church for a public rebuke by the minister.

In Burns's *Tam o' Shanter,* tipsy Tam spies on a coven of witches, watching a "winsome wench" in a *cutty sark* (short shift) dancing so spiritedly that he forgets himself and cries out: "Weel done, Cutty Sark!" Thus revealed, pursued, he gallops away, fortunately reaching running water (which, it seems, Scottish witches dare not cross) in time to escape not by a hair but with the loss of only his horse's tail. That's Burns's tale.

Gc, *scar, score; shard; share, plowshare; shear; shred. scabbard. short, shirt, skirt, kirtle. harrow. sharp. scrap, scrape, scratch.* Du, *scrabble. shrub; scrub:* first, a small tree.

> Some for renown on scraps of learning dote,
> And think they grow immortal as they quote.
> —Edward Young, *Love of Fame* (1725),
> satire 1 (and don't quote this quotation
> against this book!)

scurf, scurvy. LL *scorbutus,* Russian *skrobota:* scratch; *scorbutic;* hence (*a* negative) *ascorbic acid* ($C_6H_8O_6$), which is vitamin C. From *scrofa:* sow, "rooter, digger," *scrofulae:* little pigs, was applied to the swollen glands that mark *scrofula. Scrofula* was "the king's evil," supposedly cured by the monarch's laying on of hands. The king's touch began in England with Edward the Confessor in 1042 and ended with the death of Queen Anne in 1714; the ritual was dropped from the *Book of Common Prayer* in 1719. Macaulay records that Charles II touched 92,107 afflicted persons; in 1684 some were trampled to death in the crush. The disease became apparent in infancy; Samuel Johnson, aged three, was touched by Queen Anne in 1712. *OED* has 12 associated words, as *scrofulosis, scrofuloderma.*

L *carpere:* pluck (see *pilo*). *carpet,* first woven of cuttings. Gk *kharpos:* fruit, plucked. *carpel. carpinus:* hornbeam, with notched, "cut-in" leaves. *carp. excerpt. scarce:* first, picked out, choice. *scorpion. acarpous, acrocarpous, amphicarpic. cremocarp* breaks into *mericarp* on the *carpophore:* part of flower to which the ovule-bearing *carpel* is attached. Also *endocarp, epicarp, mesocarp, metacarp; monocarpic; pericarp, schizocarp, syncarp, xylocarp. carpogonium, carpophagous, carpophyll. discerp, discerptible.* Nasalized, *snug.*

It, *sgraffito, graffito* (plural, *graffiti*), which may be found anywhere, as on

N.Y. subway cars; usually written by neoliterates. For learned graffiti, see *ghenu; ken III.* L *cernere, certum, cretum:* sift; *cribrum:* sieve. *cribriform. excrement:* sifted out. *excrete.* Gc, *scrutiny.* A *riddle* was a sieve; hence *riddled,* as with buckshot. For the puzzling *riddle,* see *ar I. garble* also first meant to sift. *ascertain, certain; certificate, certify, certitude, incertitude, uncertain. concern. concert. crayon* is from *terra creta:* sifted earth; hence also *cretaceous. corium.* Fr *cuirasse. currier, excoriate. skirmish* referred first to the hide on a shield. *Scaramouche* (It via Fr; literally, skirmish) is the boastful coward in the commedia dell'arte. *scrimmage, scrummage, scrum.* L and E *cortex. decorticate.* Gk *khoris:* bedbug (cutter). *coreopsis.* L *carnis:* flesh, cut off. *carnal, charnel; carrion; carnivorous, carnage; incarnate, incarnation, caruncle.* Fr, *acharnement; chair:* flesh color. *carnation,* from the color. *charogne,* whence *crone* (mere flesh and bones). Shakespeare, in *Macbeth:*

> Will all great Neptune's ocean wash this blood
> Clean from my hand: No, this my hand will rather
> The multitudinous seas incarnadine . . .

The carnival feast and festival was first on Shrove Tuesday (Fr, *Mardi Gras:* literally, Fat Tuesday; see *dei*), the day before Ash Wednesday, which is the beginning of Lent, during which, until Easter, Catholics eat no meat. *carnival* is from L *carne levare:* to lighten, rise from, flesh; it is said to have come by folk etymology from *carne vale:* Flesh, farewell! On Ash Wednesday, Catholics wear a spot of ash on the brow. In a practice begun by Gregory the Great (pope, A.D. 590–604; enforced celibacy of the clergy; arranged the Gregorian chant), the palms blessed on Palm Sunday are hung in the household throughout the year (a custom still observed in many homes in Spain), then burned to use the ashes on Ash Wednesday.

Gk *khormos:* tree trunk, branches cut off. *corm.* L *cena:* meal, cut food. *cenacle:* dining room; in the Vulgate Bible, the room where Jesus and his disciples ate the Last Supper. L *scribere, scriptum:* cut in; hence write. *scarify. scribe, scrivener*—on whom Chaucer blamed any misprints or censorable matter. *ascribe, ascription, circumscribe, conscript, describe,* etc. Fr, *escritoire. inscribe, interscription, manuscript. postscript,* abbreviated *P.S. prescribe, prescription, proscribe, rescript. scribble, script, scriptorium; scripture;* with capital *S,* the Bible. *scruple. shrift, shrive, Shrovetide. subscribe, superscription, transcribe,* etc.

"The Devil can cite Scripture for his purpose"—Shakespeare, *The Merchant of Venice.*

> *Tenet insanabile multos*
> *Scribendi cacoethes et aegro in corde senescit.*
> [An incurable itch to be writing takes hold of many,
> and grows old in their troubled heart.]
> —Juvenal, *Satires,* A.D. 128. See caca.

ker IV, kr: cry out. Imitative; see *skrei.* Gk *khorax,* L *corvus:* raven. *coracine,* from its black color; as also the *crucian* fish, a kind of carp. *corbeau,* as in La Fontaine's fable of the fox and the raven (1668). *Corvus:* genus of crows. *Corbaccio:* raven, and *Corvino:* crow, are sycophantic characters in Jonson's *Volpone; or, The Fox* (1605). *corbel,* shaped like a raven's beak; *coracoid. corbel's fee:* part of a deer left by the hunters for the ravens. *corbine, corvine. cormorant* (earlier *cormarant*): sea raven.

L *crepare, crepitare, crepitum* (Lewis and Short's *Latin Dictionary*): "rattle, crack, creak, rustle, clatter, tingle, jingle, chink . . . resound, prattle, prate."

crepitate; decrepit. decrepitate; discrepancy. craven. crevasse, crevice. kestrel. L *crimen, criminem:* first, cry of distress, call for help; then transferred to the reason for the call. *incriminate; recrimination. OED* defines 24 relevant words beginning *crim. crime, criminal;* see *ker III. crim. con.,* short for *criminal conversation:* legal term for adultery. Byron plays a "con game" in *Don Juan,* xv, with *crim con* and *nem con* (*nemine contradicente*): no one contradicting, unanimously:

And then he had her good looks–that point was carried
Nem con amongst the women, which I grieve
To say leads to crim con with the married–
A case which to the juries we may leave.

cry may be imitative, but has been traced to L *quiritare,* which first meant addressing the Romans (*Quirites:* Roman citizens), appealing for help. The *Quirinal* was one of the Seven Hills of Rome; *Quirinus* was an early Roman god of war; but *Quirites* may have come from the Sabine town of *Cures.*

Sp, *quebracho:* very hard wood, "breaks the axe"; the first element in the word is from L *crepitare.* Gc, *ring, retch; crack, crackle, creak, crake, croak, crow. crowbar,* with beaklike tip. *cricket,* the insect; how the game got the name is disputed. *grackle, raven, rook, rookery.* The name of the French playwright *Corneille* means rook. *rookie,* from *recruit,* was influenced by the bird.

"Titus Antoninus Pius. . . . His reign is marked by the rare advantage of furnishing very few materials for history, which is, indeed, little more than the register of the crimes, follies, and misfortunes of mankind"–Edward Gibbon, *The Decline and Fall of the Roman Empire* (1776), chap. 2.

"Quoth the raven, Nevermore."

ker V: heat, burn. Gk *kheramos:* potter's clay, pottery. *ceramics.* L *carbonem. carbon, carbonaceous; carbonado, carborundum; carboxyl. carbuncle; escarbuncle.* It, *carbonari:* literally, charcoal burners. L *cremare, crematum:* burn. *cremation, crematory.* Gc, *hearth.* See *eus.*

ker VI: grow. Gk *khoros:* youth; *khora:* maiden. *Cora,* epithet of Persephone, daughter of Demeter, Greek goddess of growth; see *Ceres,* next paragraph. *Corinna. curetes,* gods of youth, worshiped on Crete and perhaps giving the island its name. *Halicore:* literally, sea maiden; genus of aquatic mammals. *hypocoristic:* an added, pet, name. *Dioscuri:* literally, growth of the god; Castor and Pollux, twin sons of Zeus (see *dei*).

L *Ceres,* Roman goddess of growth. *cereal. cerium* (see *el 58*) was named after the asteroid *Ceres,* discovered in 1801; see *iegua. creare, creatum:* to bring forth, hence rear; *crescere, cretum:* to spring forth. *create, creation, creature, recreation, re-creation. creole:* reared in one's house. *crescendo, crescent, concrescence; concrete. accrue, excrescence; increase, increment; decrease, decrement. crew* first meant reinforcements. Fr, *recruit.* Some scholars place *sincere* here, as from *sem:* one, and *ker:* of one growth, but see *keneko* and *ker VII.*

According to Ptolemy (Claudius Ptolemaius, ca. A.D. 135, whose list of the magnitudes of 1,022 stars, grouped in 48 constellations, was authoritative until the Renaissance and the discovery of the telescope) the creation of the world occurred in 4004 B.C., a date accepted by many Christians long after Darwin set evolutionism against creationism. For a time, there was sharp opposition–one was either a Darwinian atheist or a creationist Christian–but the Church survived, through its ability to absorb and adapt generally accepted ideas. Some "fundamentalists," rejecting Darwin, persist; and President Reagan has admitted a measure of dubitancy.

ker VII: harm, destroy. Gk, *Kor:* goddess of death. *keraunos:* thunderbolt. *ceraunite, ceraunograph, ceraunoscope.* L, *caries, carious; sincere* (*sine* without, without decay; but see *keneko* and *ker VI*).

kerd: heart. Gk *khardia. cardia, cardiac, cardialgia, cardiology, carditis. Cardiospermum:* genus of soapberry. *dexocardiac, diplocardiac, endocardium, epicardium. pericardium; megalocardia, myocardia. electrocardiogram,* etc. *OED* lists 7 and details 13 relevant words beginning *cardi(o),* with 14 more related to *cardo, cardinis:* hinge, the "heart" of an arrangement, of which more below.

L *cor, cordem:* heart. *core, cordate, cordial, cordiform.* L *courageous* is Gc *heartful. courage. accord. concord:* hearts beating as one. *accordant. accordion* (modeled on *clarion*). *discord. record* (on the tablet of your heart).

misericord; miserere: have pity, mercy–in your heart. The Fifty-first Psalm begins *Miserere me Deus:* Have mercy on me, O Lord! *misericord(ia)* developed several senses: (1) an indulgence, relaxation of a religious rule; (2) a monastic room where such indulgence, especially of food, was allowed; (3) the underside of a hinged seat in a church stall, for a cleric to lean against during a long service; often decorated with a wood carving, solemn or satirical; still to be seen in old cathedrals; (4) a dagger, 13th to 17th c., for giving the *coup de grace* to a severely wounded knight–an early form of euthanasia (see *dheu I*). From the same root came *miser, miserly, miserable, miserabilism. Misery me!,* an exclamation of wretchedness or plea for pity, as in the refrain of the luckless jester Jack Point in Gilbert's *Yeomen of the Guard:*

Misery me! lackaday dee!
He sipped no sup, and he craved no crumb,
As he sighed for the love of a ladye.

Also *quarry:* hunted game, from the heart's being given to the hounds. Ir *(Mother) machree.* Gc, *heart, sweetheart. To learn by heart; to take to heart,* etc. *OED* devotes over 23 columns to *heart* and its compounds. Tracing L *credere:* believe, to this root is folk etymology, from the protesting oath *Cross my heart and hope to die. . . .* See *kred I. Have a heart.* The *codling apple* (see *sap*) is folk-changed from Fr *coeur-de-leon:* lionheart, as *dandelion* is folkchanged from *dent* (tooth) *de leon,* from the shape of the leaves; explained in French dictionaries as "another name for the *pissenlit*": pissabed. To the meadows of my childhood, Italians used to travel to gather leaves for *pissabed salad,* also called *chicory* (Gk *khikhore*), the root of which may be ground and mixed with coffee.

L *cardo, cardinis:* hinge. E *cardinal* has spread widely. From a doorhinge, it moved figuratively to things upon which something important hinges. Thus the seven *cardinal virtues,* upon which hinge the gates to paradise: four "natural" (prudence, fortitude, temperance, justice); three "theological" (faith, hope, and charity [love]). Opposed to the seven virtues are the seven *cardinal sins,* "from which," says the *Maryknoll Catholic Dictionary,* "other sins arise": pride, envy, covetousness, sloth, anger, lust, gluttony. There are also the four *cardinal motives* –pleasure, use, honor (*noblesse oblige!*), necessity–on which our actions hinge. The *cardinal points of the horizon* (compass) are *N*orth, *E*ast, *W*est, *S*outh, with NEWS from all quarters. The *cardinal numbers* (1,2,3, etc.) are those upon which calculations hinge, as opposed to the *ordinal numbers* (first, second, third, etc.), which describe the order or arrangement of things. The *cardinal points of the ecliptic,* important for the seasons and in astrology, are the two points of the spring and the fall equinox and the two of the summer and the winter solstice (see *sta*), which occur in the zodiacal signs of Aries, Cancer, Libra, and Capricorn, which astrologers call the First, Fourth, Seventh, and Tenth House respectively.

And of course there is the *College of Cardinals* of the Roman Catholic Church, upon which, since 1173, has hinged the succession of the popes, representatives of God on Earth. From the cardinal's cap and cassock comes the name of the color *cardinal;* from the color, an 18th and 19th c. ladies' cloak, a bird, a flower, and a fish—which is oceans away from a door hinge.

When Henry VIII's two cardinals seek to persuade Queen Katharine to accept divorce, she exclaims, in Shakespeare's play:

> Holy men I thought ye,
> Upon my soul, two reverend cardinal virtues;
> But cardinal sins and hollow hearts I fear ye;
> Mend 'em, for shame, my lords.

Henry VIII was first performed on 29 June 1613; wadding from a salvo of cannon in the play set fire to the roof, and the Globe Theatre burned to the ground. And Shakespeare wrote no more.

kerdh. Gc, *herd, herdsman; shepherd, swineherd.*

> She walks—the lady of my delight—
> A shepherdess of sheep.
> —Alice Meynell, 1922, who should have known better

kere: blend, mix; cook. Gk, *khrasis. crater:* first, a mixing bowl. *crateriform. acrasia:* literally, unmixed. *acratia:* not strong, is from Gk *khratos:* power, rule; see *da II. dyscrasia. syncretism. idiosyncrasy* (Gk *idios:* one's own, peculiar to. Hence also *idiom, idiomatic; idiolect; idiomorphic; idioplasm. idiot; idiocy* [first spelled *idiotcy*].)

grail, graal: the platter Jesus used at the Last Supper, as the *Holy Grail,* usually pictured as a cup. Read Lowell's *The Vision of Sir Launfal.* The Holy Grail is also called *sangreal:* holy cup, blent with Fr *sang real:* actual—or royal—blood, with thought of the platter on which Joseph of Arimathea caught the blood of the crucified Jesus.

ker(s) I: run. L *currere, cursum. current, decurrent, excurrent, percurrent, recurrent. course, concourse, discourse, intercourse, recourse. concur, incur, occur, recur,* etc. *cursive, discursive, excursion, excursus. cursory. precursor. curule. curricle, curriculum, curricular. succor, succural. corral. corridor.*

Despite the pun in Julian Sharman's *A Cursory History of Swearing* (1884), there is no direct track between this root and *curse,* unless it developed figuratively from "running down" a person: "May misfortune run upon you!" No other origin has been suggested.

Sigmund Freud's daughter, Anna, reported that he said: "The first human that hurled a curse instead of a rock was the founder of civilization." As was often the case with Freud, he was lured by a gleaming Fata Morgana; the first human that hurled a curse did not do so "instead" of throwing a rock; he hurled the curse with the rock, or because the rock—now rocket—had missed its target. Perhaps the first hundred million, and not yet the last. It was the custom, until guns lent distance to the fight, to rush howling and cursing into combat.

L *carrus:* wagon. *car, cart;* but see *ger III. career, careering. cargo. carry. cark:* literally, to load. *carpenter:* cart-maker. It, *coranto; carroccio.* Fr, *courante, courier. cariole; caroche, caricature:* literally, a loading. *chargé d'affaires. charabanc. corsair.* Gc, *hussar. carriage* first meant something to be carried; thus the King James Bible, Acts 21:15: "After those days we took up our carriages and went up to Jerusalem." Cranmer's Bible (1539) says "burthens"; the Geneva

Bible (1557) says "fardels"; the Oxford Standard Version (1946, 1962) dodges the issue by saying "we made ready."

"I understood Christ was a carpenter"—William Blake. With literary criticism in mind, Samuel Johnson wrote: "You may scold a carpenter who has made you a bad table, though you cannot make a table. It is not your trade to make tables."

kers II: black. Skr, *Krishna:* the black one; ninth avatar of Vishnu. Russ, *chernozem:* black earth. Egyptian *khem:* black earth after the annual Nile flood; hence *alchemy* and *chemistry;* see *au I.* As Dryden described many of us in *Absalom and Achitophel* (1681),

A man so various that he seemed to be
Not one, but all mankind's epitome:
Stiff in opinions, always in the wrong,
Was everything by starts, and nothing long;
But in the course of one revolving moon
Was chemist, fiddler, statesman, and buffoon.

kert: twist together. Gk *khurtos,* L *cratis:* wickerwork. L *crassus:* thick, solid. *cartilage, cartilaginous. crate; crass; creel.* Gc, *hurdle:* first a fence, then as in a hurdle race. *hurst:* thicket of brushwood; frequent in names, as *Amherst, Elmhurst. grate:* framework. *grid, griddle, gridiron; grill, grille.*

keu I: watch, notice; hence see, hear. Skr, *kavi:* ancient language of Java. Gk *akhouein. acoustics. kudos:* renown. *Laocoon* (four syllables; from Gk *laos:* people, and *khoeo:* watch over): priest of Apollo at Troy who warned against taking the Greeks' wooden horse into the city; he and his two sons were squeezed to death by serpents sent by the gods, who were tired of the ten-year war. The Latin words, from Virgil's *Aeneid,* ii, are: *Equo ne credite. Timeo Danaos et dona ferentes:* Trust not the horse. I fear the Greeks, even bearing gifts. The expression—often just *Timeo Danaos*—came into learned use as a more general cautionary term. See *kuei I.*

L *cavere, cautum:* be on guard. *cautel, cautelous; caution, precaution. caveat.* A principle in trading: *Caveat emptor:* Let the buyer beware; the Latin verb has become an English noun. *Cave canem:* Beware of the dog; sign seen in the ruins of Pompeii.

There comes irresistibly to mind a serendipitous find of Newman Levy, the lawyer-poet: a poem by the wealthy Roman Maecenas, sent with a gift to a cute contortionist whom he liked to watch "in a little road-house by the Tarpeian Rock, the Cave Canem it was called" (as Parisian basement bistros today might be called *Cave Maroque, Cave Pig Alley*). What makes it precious is that in all probability the poem was composed by the poet Horace for his patron. The original Latin is not available, but here is the Newman Levy rendering:

Lady, when you coily twist your
Leg behind your dexter ear,
This here bard can scarce resist your
Girlish charms, Pholoë dear.

You're so modest, coy, and winsome;
Such a supple grace you've got,
When you tie your body in some
Sort of bow or sailor's knot.

So, my double-jointed Venus,
Take this book of verse I send

As a gift from G. Maecenas,
Ever your devoted friend.

Perhaps some Harvard or Harrow Senior will enjoy retranslating this into Latin, hopefully Horatian.

Gc, *hark, hearken, hear. sheen* (conspicuous). *scone* (Du *schoonbrot:* notable bread). *show. scavage; scavenger,* earlier *scavager:* inspector, collector of tolls; then street cleaner. The *n* is intrusive, for smoother flow, as in *messenger,* from *message;* and *passenger,* from Fr *passager. Scavenger's daughter* was an instrument of torture, folkchanged from the name of the Lieutenant of the Tower under Henry VIII, Leonard Skeffington, who devised it; it bent the head so low between the knees that blood flowed from the nose and ears. (Similarly, *Madame Guillotine* was the name given to the slicing instrument the use of which in France was suggested by the doctor and revolutionary Joseph I. Guillotin in 1791; a similar device had earlier been employed in Germany, Italy, and Scotland.)

keu II: bend, curve; hence swollen or hollow. This is another root some scholars divide, for things may bend up or down. Bend a vertical rod, and it may outline a mound, the round of a wave, a bell, a flower, or something hollow; also, reclining. Bend a horizontal rod, and it may form a hole, a cup; but it goes up, hence reaches high, and at the peak, figuratively, are fame, power—the lord. Similarly, twilight may mark the closing in of dark, or the brightening of dawn. The cup you are draining may be half-empty; the one you are serving, half-full. With both light and liquid, you may thus think along two planes—the same item, one root.

Gk, *chasm. codeine:* alkaloid from opium, named for the bell shape of the poppy flower. *codon; coelom.* Suffix *cele:* tumor, as *hydrocele, varicocele;* JWalker lists 10. *coble:* curved boat. *hound:* knob on a masthead (the *d* folk-added from the familiar dog). *cyma, cymba, cymbiform; cymbocephalic. cymatium. kymatology:* of the curving mounds of waves. *Cymbella:* genus of diatoms. *cymbal; chime:* set of bells. *cyphella; cyphonism; cypsela.*

Gk *khaukha:* drinking vessel; *quaich:* two-handled vessel, save in Scotland, where it is usually made of wooden staves and hoops. *kyphosis:* crookback; epithet applied to Richard III of England by his enemies; see *gib.* Gk *khubos,* E *cube, cubicle. cubit:* bend of elbow; then, as a unit of measure, from elbow point to tip of middle finger.

L *cubare:* lie on; *cumbere:* lie down. *couvade, covey. concubine. incubate. incubus. succubus* (more correctly, *succuba*): a female demon that lies beneath a man and by bending him to her purpose saps his strength. *accubation, accumbent, decumbent, incumbent, procumbent, recumbent; succumb. cumulative; accumulate. cumulus. maroon,* from Sp *cimarron,* Gk *khuma:* mountain top, "untamed," was applied to a runaway slave. *Cimarron* is the name of a book by Edna Ferber (1930); it was almost the name of a U.S. territory, is a county in Oklahoma, and a river in New Mexico, the Cimarron region of which is known as Satan's Paradise. The color *maroon,* and *marron:* chestnut, are of unknown origin.

Gibbon, in *The Decline and Fall of the Roman Empire,* chap. 72, tells of Emperor Gordian the Younger: "His manners were less pure, but his character was equally amiable with that of his father. Twenty-two acknowledged concubines, and a library of 62,000 volumes, attested the variety of his inclinations; and from the productions he left behind him, it appears that both the one and the other were designed for use rather than ostentation." He was actually emperor for only 36 days, being killed at Carthage in A.D. 238. He had ruled jointly with his father, Gordian I, who on news of his son's death committed suicide.

They were succeeded by Gordian III, aged thirteen, who six years later was slain by a lieutenant, Philip, who was made emperor by the soldiers' vote. Philip was "an Arab by birth and consequently a robber by profession"; but he was temporarily popular in Rome for the lavish and varied activities of the secular games, which he revived in A.D. 248 to celebrate the founding of the city. (Much earlier the Gordian knot waited in Gordium, capital of Phrygia, where the chariot of the founder, King Gordius, was tied to a pole in a knot the ends of which were hidden, with the prophecy that he who loosed it would be conqueror of Asia. In 333 B.C. Alexander the Great opened it—with his sword. The term *Gordian knot* is now used of a problem solvable only by drastic means.)

Here, too, *cabinet, cadger. huckle; hawker, huckster, hunker:* bent with a pack on the back. *cabook. cage. cajole:* first, chatter like a caged bird; it was earlier *gaioler,* changed by association with *cage. casserole. cavatina. decoy. gaol, jail. gabion, gabionade.*

Gk *khurios:* the Lord; *khuriakon:* the Lord's house. *kermess:* kirk mass; Scot, *kirk. Kyrie eleison!:* Lord, have mercy! *church.* The mineral *churchite* is named after Arthur H. *Church* (d. 1915). *acryology. curiologic. cacuminal.*

Gc, *hip, hop, heap, hoop. hope* springs from *hop;* watch a boy in eager expectation. *hump,* whence *hunchback* (as *lunch* was originally *lump*). A *hunch:* a feeling that good fortune is ahead, may be associated with the belief that rubbing the hump of a hunchback brings good luck. *high, height.* The Gm toast, *Hoch soll er leben!:* May he live on top! *Dreimal hoch!* Three times up!

"Parnassus has its flowers of transient fragrance, as well as its oaks of towering height, and its laurels of eternal verdure."—Johnson, *The Rambler,* 23 Feb. 1751.

co-ax is imitative of the frog, Gk *batrakhos,* as in the chorus of Aristophanes' *The Frogs* (405 B.C.): "Breke-ke-kex, co-ax, co-ax." The play, as performed in 1941 in the Yale University swimming pool, was a spectacle, said one reviewer, "that would make Billy Rose turn an envious shade of batrachian green." Lowell, in *The Biglow Papers* (1867), presents

Old Croakers, deacons of a mire,
That led the deep batrachian choir.

Batrachomyomachy [Battle of the frogs and mice] is a Greek mock epic, a parody of Homer's *Iliad,* also attributed to Homer. Blind Homer is an interesting instance of aptronymics: Gk *homeros* means companion; that is, one that needs a companion, because blind! (Today, the blind use trained dogs.) One of Keats' superb sonnets is *On First Looking Into Chapman's Homer:*

Much have I traveled in the realms of gold
And many goodly states and kingdoms seen;
Round many western islands have I been
Which bards in fealty to Apollo hold.
Oft of one wide expanse had I been told
The deep-browed Homer ruled as his demesne:
Yet never did I breathe its pure serene
Till I heard Chapman speak out loud and bold . . .

Slav *skupshtina* (*kup:* heap; *s:* together; see *ksun*): Yugoslav Parliament. The *s* appears also in *sputnik,* first launched 4 Oct. 1957 (*put:* pilgrimage; *nik:* one who, as in *nudnik* and *beatnik*).

Some suggest that, via the form *kuant,* this root is the source of Gk *Pan,* god of the countryside, who, like the satyr, has the head and body of a man, the horns, ears, and legs of a goat. But behind *Pan* is Skr *Pusan,* Vedic god of nourishment and increase of all things; hence Gk *pas, pan:* all. (For *frying pan* and *panhandler,* see *pet II.*) *OED* gives over 310 words sprung of *pan,* as *panacea; pancreas:* all flesh; *panegyric. pantechnicon:* British for moving van; first, a London bazaar selling all artistic items (Gk *tekhne:* art; see *tekha*). *pandemonium, pantomime*—not counting such words as *diapason; pasigraphy.* There is also the grand *panjandrum,* "with the little round button on top," ending the nonsense poured forth by playwright Samuel Foote (1755) to stump the actor Charles Macklin, who'd boasted he could repeat anything after hearing it once. The *panpipes* are well known, though now seldom heard; other night noises in primitive ears caused *panic,* as did the clamor of "invading Martians" reported one night on early radio.

Several names build upon *Pan. Pandora:* all gifts, was sent to *Prometheus:* forethought, by Zeus, whose wrath he had provoked by teaching man the use of fire; the wily giant refused her, but his brother *Epimetheus:* afterthought, married her, and opened Zeus's wedding gift, *Pandora's box,* whereupon every good thing flew away save hope, glimmering at the bottom. *St. Pantaleone:* all lion, a Roman physician (d. A.D. 305), became the old buffoon *Pantaloon* of the commedia dell'arte; from his costume came *pantaloons,* shortened to *pants,* lengthened (the word) to *pantalettes,* then *panties,* and by both rhyme and reason *scanties;* also *pantywaist, pantyhose; pantaloonery.*

Rabelais in 1533 created *Panurge:* do-all, and *Pantagruel:* all is gruel that comes to the maw; everything serious burlesquely viewed. Rabelais also informed us of *pantagruelion,* "that famous herb, cure for all public ills and private woes," namely, hemp—source of the hangman's rope. (For less permanent distraction, hemp also yields cannabis, marijuana, bhang.) In 1758, Voltaire made the chief figure of his *Candide* the fine philosopher *Pangloss:* explain—or smooth over—all, who shows how every misfortune helps prove that ours is "the best of all possible worlds." The book is a satire, ridiculing the optimism of Leibnitz's *Théodicé* (1710) and of Pope.

From harmony, from heavenly harmony
This universal frame began:
From harmony to harmony
Through all the compass of the notes it ran,
The diapason closing full in man.
—Dryden, *St. Cecilia's Day*

keuero: north wind. L *caurus:* northwest wind. *shower, scour. scurry* is a blend of *scour* and *hurry. hurry, hurry-scurry, flurry, hurl, hurly-burly,* are imitative. *hurricane,* from West Indian (Taino) *hurakan,* was changed to match *hurry.*

When shall we three meet again,
In thunder, lightning, or in rain?
When the hurly-burly's done,
When the battle's lost and won.
—The witches at the opening of *Macbeth*

keup: curve, hollow; lump, bag, etc. An extension of *keu II. coop, cop, cowl, cup. cupel, cupola. cow:* to bend before, *cower. ko(w)tow,* with various other spellings, is Chinese *k'o:* knock, *t'ou:* head: a bowing that puts forehead to ground.

Gk *gyros. gyrate, gyre,* Fr, *girandole. autogyro, circumgyrate; heliogyre.* L *botellus, botulus:* sausage. *botulism.* See *gue 6.* L *guttur:* throat; see *gutta. gut. cud. quid* (for chewing). Gc, *chitterlings. cod:* small bag (see *gue 2*). *peasecod.*

peaseporridge. pease (Gk *pison*) was the English word; heard as a plural, it was folkchanged to *pea. pee* is baby talk, first letter of *piss;* Fr *pipi.*

In *Twelfth Night* Malvolio describes Viola disguised as a youth: "Not yet old enough for a man, nor young enough for a boy, as a squash is before 'tis a peasecod." A *squash* was an unripe, flat *peapod,* now known as a *snowpea,* a delicacy in a Chinese restaurant. In *A Midsummer Night's Dream* one of Titania's fairies is *Peaseblossom,* whom Bottom greets: "I pray you, commend me to Mistress Squash, your mother, and to Master Peasecod, your father."

Apparently from a toast at a 1905 Harvard alumni dinner, Dr. John Collins Bossity of Holy Cross set the "proper Bostonians" in a jingle:

Then here's to good old Boston,
The home of the bean and the cod,
Where the Lowells talk only to Cabots,
And the Cabots speak only to God.

When, despite the Cabot family petition, a judge permitted the new citizens, the Kabotschniks, to change their name to Cabot, several parodies of this jingle appeared; the best remembered merely changed the last line: "And the Cabots speak Yiddish, by God!"

?khalk: chalk. Gk *kalix:* pebble. L *calx, calcis:* chalk, limestone. *calx, calcareous, calcine, calcite; calcium* (see *el 20*). *calculate;* pebbles were used in counting and in games; the illiterate farmer dropped a pebble into a bag as each sheep went through the gate to pasture, and tossed one out as each came back to the fold. *chalk.* Fr, *chausée;* first, made with limestone. *rez-de-chaussée:* ground floor.

kista: basket. Gk *khiste. kistophoros,* borne in a procession; *cistophore,* pictured on an old coin. *cisium. cist. cistern. chest.* W, *cistvaen.* Scot, *kist.*

kla: spread out. *laden. ladle. lathe,* for smoothing out; possibly *lath. last:* obsolete unit of weight, a load. *alastrim. ballast. larboard,* earlier *ladebord:* the loading side; the *r* borrowed from *starboard:* the "steer" side. *load* was originally OE *lad:* journey, way; the meaning changed because of *lade, laden.* a doublet of *load* is *lode;* whence *lodestar, lodestone.* The verb *lead. leitmotif. livelihood* was earlier *livelode.* John Lydgate said that Chaucer was "the lodestar of our language." In Dryden's version of *The Tempest* (i, 1) the Captain cries: "You dogs, is this a time to sleep? Larbord! heave together, lads."

"There is an awful warmth about my heart like a load of immortality"—Keats, letter of 22 Sept. 1818.

kleg: cry out. Imitative. Gk, *klaxon.* L, nasalized, *clang. clack, click. clinkum-clankum; crinkum-crankum. clinchpoop:* an old term for a boor. Gc, *laugh, laughter, laughing jackass.*

"Laughter is nothing else but sudden glory"—Thomas Hobbes, *Leviathan* (1651).

klei: slant, up or down; hence bed, or ladder. Gk *khline:* bed. *clinic.* In the 17th c., a *clinic* was a person (perhaps seeking to avoid persecution) who postponed baptism until his deathbed. *OED* lists 13 and details 11 relevant words beginning *clin(o). aclinic; anticlinal. clinamen. client,* who leans upon someone. *clinochore* and other minerals; *clinobasic, clinohedral,* and other crystals. *clinoid, clinometer, inclinometer.* Gk *kleitoris:* mound, hillock. *clitellum, clition; clitoris; clivus. enclitic, proclitic. heteroclite; isoclinic, microcline, monocline, monoclinic, periclinic; diclinous; triclinium; matroclinous, patroclinous.*

Gk *climax:* ladder. *climactic, climacteric; climax, anticlimax.* From the sloping surface of the terrestrial globe, *clime, climate, acclimat(iz)e.*

L, *declension, decline, declivity; acclivity; proclivity. recline; OED* defines

10 associated words. *inclination, inclined;* from their favorable tone came also *clement, clemency,* then *inclement.* Gc, *hlaedder, ladder; lean, lid.*

"A man ought to read just as inclination leads him"—Johnson, in Boswell's *Life of Samuel Johnson,* 14 July 1763. "Talk to him of Jacob's ladder, and he would ask the number of the steps"—Douglas W. Jerrold, *A Matter-of-Fact Man* (1859).

kleng: turn. Gc, *lank. link,* as in *cuff* and *golf links. flank. flinch, unflinching.*

"Facts are facts and flinch not"—Browning, *The Ring and the Book,* ii.

klep: steal. *klepht; klephtism. kleptic. kleptomania. clepsydra:* the water "steals" away imperceptibly.

"Current democracy seems little more than kleptocracy." Is there honor among thieves?

kleu I: hear, hearken, and their consequences. See *ous.* Skr, *sloka:* first, fame. *s(h)ri; s(h)ruti.* Gk *khleiein:* proclaim, make famous. *Clio:* proclaimer, Muse of History. A number of Greek names end in *kles:* famed of or for. *Sophocles:* famed for wisdom. *Androcles:* famed of men, who took a thorn from a lion's paw and later was spared by the lion in the arena; a story retold in a play by Bernard Shaw. *Damocles:* famed among the people; especially notable, the *sword of Damocles,* which the tyrant Dionysius, at a banquet, hung by a single hair over Damocles' seat, to show under what dangers rulers reigned. *Hercules,* Gk *Heracles:* glory of Hera—an ironical name, as he was son of Zeus and Alcmene, and Zeus's wife Hera was a jealous wife. The name *Hera* means protectress (a *hero* is a protector). *Eteocles:* of true fame; king of Thebes, son of Oedipus and his mother-and-wife, Jocasta.

Clianthus: genus of peas. Gk *khleo:* I glorify; *khledon:* omen. *cledonism:* omission or avoidance of inauspicious words, as when a skyscraper lists no 13th floor; substituting a pleasant word is *euphemism;* see *esu.*

Gc, *list, listen; leer; loud. umlaut, ablaut, anlaut, inlaut, auslaut.* The name *Slav* meant glory; its offshoots include *Slovak, Slovene, Slavonian, Czechoslovakia.* In A.D. 955 Holy Roman Emperor Otto the Great conquered the Slavs; hence E *slave, slavery.* Fr, *esclavage:* literally, slavery; used in 18th c. English of a necklace of several bands of gold, resembling a slave's fetters but implying submission to a husband or lover—as recently a woman's anklet. Various Germanic names spring from the sense "famous in battle": *Ludovic, Ludwig, Lewis;* Fr, *Louis, Louise, Aloysius.*

louis d'or is a gold coin first minted by Louis XIII of France in 1640, found among doubloons and guineas on Stevenson's Treasure Island. Louis' son, "the Sun King," gave his name to a style of furniture, *Louis Quatorze (XIV).* Of this king's several mistresses, one, Françoise Louise de la Baume Le Blanc, Duchesse de *La Vallière,* had her title passed on to a piece of jewelry, the neck-pendant *lavaliere*—now also used of a small, pendant microphone. Another, Marie Angélique de Scorraille de Roussilles, Duchesse de *Fontanges,* went higher but did not last so long. Her title was inherited by a headdress, as described by Addison in 1711 in *The Spectator:* the *fontanges* "rose an ell above the head; they were pointed like steeples, and had loose pieces of crape, which were fringed, and hung down their backs." (An *ell,* modern reader, is 45 inches.) The word *fontange* faded with the fashion; but one mistress of Louis Quinze (XV, another furniture style!) still names a headdress: Jeanne Antoinette Poisson Lenormand d'Etoiles, Marquise de—*Pompadour.*

The name *Lothario,* also from this root, now signifies a seducer, from "the gay Lothario" in Nicholas Rowe's play *The Fair Penitent* (1703); Rowe's 1709 edition of Shakespeare's works was the first that divided the plays into acts and scenes. *Lothario* is also the man urged by a husband to test his wife's virtue, in "The Fatal Curiosity" episode of *Don Quixote* and in several 17th c. English dramas; he is also a character in Goethe's *Wilhelm Meister.* Also rooted here is *Luther* (1453-1546), who started the Reformation in Germany. Read Rosalind Murray's *The Good Pagan's Failure* (1948).

"Listening does not mean simply maintaining a polite silence while you are rehearsing in your mind the speech you are going to make the next time you can grab a conversational opening. Nor does listening mean waiting alertly for the flaws in the other fellow's arguments so that later you can mow him down. Listening means trying to see the problem the way the speaker sees it—which means not sympathy, which is *feeling for* him, but empathy, which is *experiencing* with him"—S. I. Hayakawa, *The Use and Misuse of Language* (1962).

kleu II: wash out; cleanse. Gk, *clysma; clyster; cataclysm.* L, *cloaca. klystron:* oscillator, tube, named after a *clyster pipe.* The strongest *clyster* ("glister": purgative) in literature is in the interlude *The Four P's,* by John Heywood (ca. 1522). The *P's* are: a Palmer, whose palm branch is a sign that he has been to the Holy Land, and whose fee permits stay-at-homes to kiss his holy relics, such as "the great toe of the trinity" and "the buttock-bone of Pentecost," and thus save their souls; a Pardoner, who sells, as from the pope, forgiveness of all sins—past, present, and to come; a Pedlar, who sells everything else; a Pothecary, who sells the quack remedies of the day, to save men's bodies. The Pedlar modestly remarks:

> All ye three can lie as well
> As can the falsest devil in hell

and offers to be judge in a contest as to who can tell the biggest lie. When the Pardoner tells of a woman released from hell because the Devil could not endure her complaining tongue, the Palmer interrupts; he has seen 500,000 women in his travels, but

> I never saw, nor knew, in my conscience,
> Any one woman out of patience—

and at once they all concede the prize to him. But before that the Pothecary told of a constipated woman to whom he administered a glister, then "thrust a tampion in her tewel" (a plug in her anus), so that when the explosion came, the tampion flew 10 miles and knocked down a castle's walls, which filled the moat, so that

> . . . who list to walk thereto
> May wade it over and wet no shoe.

As Heywood says, "a bombard of a clyster!"

kleu III: shut; hook, bar; peg, key. Gk *khleis, khleidos:* key; *khleistos:* closed. *clathrate; cleithral. cleidomancy; cleidomastoid. cleistogamy, cleistogenous. ophicleide:* "keyed" serpent. L *claudere, clausum:* to close; *clavis:* key; *clavus:* nail. *clava, clavicle, clavis. kevel. clavelization, clavate; clavicorn* (beetle); *claviform.* In music: *clavicembalo, clavecin, clavichord, clavier; clef; chiave. Claviceps:* peg-headed, genus of fungi. *clause:* close of a rhetorical period. *close, closet, close-stool. clove, cloy. claustral. claustration; claustrophobia. cloister; recluse. conclave:* first, room in which the Catholic cardinals were locked together until, with white smoke rising toward heaven, one of them emerged as pope. *enclave; autoclave; laticlave; subclavian. enclosure. enclosion. foreclose. exclude. sluice* (*aqua exclusa:* water shut out, separated from the stream). *conclude, include,* *occlude, preclude, seclude, seclusion.* Fr, *cloisonné.* Gc, *lot:* first, to hook to, catch. *allot, lotto. lottery.* "How like a lottery these weddings are!"—Ben Jonson, *A Tale of a Tub* (1633).

As movie mogul Goldwyn is said to have said, "Include me out."

klou: jump, dance; run. Probably Gc *gallop, gauntlet* (earlier, *gantlope*); *interloper; landloper; langlauf. lapwing. leap, lope, loup; orlop, wallop. elope,* whence the childish "We're too young dear, we cantelope." The *cantaloup*—with its several spellings—was first grown in the West at the papal castle *Cantaloupo:* sing and dance, in Ancona, Italy.

kn, ken, kneu: squeeze, compressed; hence hard, tight, narrow. Probably Gk *kastenes,* E *chestnut,* and—from the shape, or the sound when uncut chestnuts are roasted—Sp, *castanets.*

L *nux, nuxem:* nut; *nux vomica. newel; nowel. nucellus; nuclein, nucleolus; nucleus* and *nuclear* reactions. *enucleate. Nuculus:* genus of hard-shelled bivalves. Fr, *noisette; nougat; noyau. neck:* narrow part of a bottle or a body. "Don't stick your neck out"—as though inviting a noose or a knife. *necklace. neckerchief:* head scarf for the neck; compare *handkerchief;* see *caput.*

neck (the verb), *necker,* and *necking,* in the sense of fondling, are not in the 1933 *OED,* although *OED*'s 1976 supplement cites quotations as far back as 1825; by 1970 Germaine Greer could say, in *The Female Eunuch:* "The best behaved teenager necks." *Necker's cube:* a transparent cube that can be viewed as if looking down at the top or up from the bottom, was devised by the Swiss Louis A. Necker in 1832. A similarly reversible perspective is Schröder's staircase; such ocular alternatives animate the work of the artist M. C. Escher.

A *neckverse*—usually the first verse of the Fifty-first Psalm: "Touch not mine anointed, and do my prophets no harm"—was one that saved one's neck. Anyone brought before the king's court in the Middle Ages could plead privilege of clergy and win transfer to the ecclesiastical court by proving he could read, reading and writing then being virtually nonexistent outside the Church. The bishop's representative, always present at the law court, would pronounce *Legit:* He reads; the man might then be branded, but he would not be hanged. A satirical song of the period ran:

If a monk had been taken
For stealing of bacon,
For burglary, murder, or rape,
If he could rehearse
(Well prompt) his neckverse
He never would fail to escape.

legit is now used as an abbreviation for *legitimate,* as the *legitimate theatre* versus the *burlesque* or the *amateur.*

kneiguh: push, press together; lean on. L *nitor, nixus:* make an effort. *nisus. renitent. conictare:* bring together; used of the eyelids. *nictitate. connive:* wink at. Fielding, in *The Modern Husband* (1732), records the resigned male attitude:

Husbands most faults, not public made, connive at;
The trip's a trifle—when the frailty's private.

knid. Gc, *nit. nit-picking.*

ko. Source of various pointing-out words. *he, him, his, her, it. here, hither, hence. hodiernal* (L *hoc die:* on this day). *haecceity. langue d'oc* (*hoc:* yes), whence the Provençal language; opposed to *langue d'oil* (*oui:* yes), which became modern French. *cis* and rarely *citra:* prefixes meaning on this side, as *cisalpine, cispontine;*

OED lists 13 such words; *cismontane, citramontane* (vs. *tramontane, ultramontane*).

cy-pres (Fr *si-pres:* so close as you can; a boon to lawyers). *sic. encore. et cetera:* and the rest; abbreviated *etc.* General semantics maintains that every sentence ends with an implied *etc.* Possibly Gc *hind, behind; hinder, hinterland.*

kob: fit; eventuate pleasantly. Gc, *hap, happen,* and the humorous *happenstance,* from *circumstance. happy, mayhap; mishap.*

Happy the man, whose wish and care
A few paternal acres bound,
Content to breathe his native air
On his own ground;
Whose herds with milk, whose fields with bread,
Whose flocks supply him with attire;
Whose trees in summer yield him shade,
In winter, fire.
—Pope, *Solitude* (1700), at the age of twelve

kogkhos: kernel, grain; notch. *coccus; gonococcus; streptococcus. Chiococca:* genus of madder. *coccid. cochineal:* first, (dye from) woodlouse, from Sp *cochina:* sow, Fr *cochon:* pig; partly imitative. L *coccum:* excrescence on plant. *cocoon. monocoque. scotch; hopscotch:* marks on the ground to hop over.

Lowell, in *My Study Windows* (1870), remarks: "The mind can weave itself warmly in the cocoon of its own thoughts."

kokhlos: spiral shell. Gk *khokhlias:* spiral-shelled snail. *cochlea, cochleate; cochleare:* first, for extracting snail from shell. *cockle, cockleshell.* Nasalized, *conch, conchology. conguis.* Sp, *coquina;* Fr, *caracole.* Read *The Chambered Nautilus,* by Oliver Wendell Holmes.

kokila. Imitative. Skr *kokila:* cuckoo. *koel.* See *auei. coccyx,* shaped like a cuckoo's beak. *coccygeal. cuckoo; cuckold;* see *cucu.* The appellation *cuckold* was very frequent from the 14th into the 18th c.; *OED* lists 14 forms of the word. Dryden asks, in *Absalom and Achitophel* (1681):

Can dry bones live, or skeletons produce
The vital warmth of cuckoldizing juice?

Hearne in 1710 remarked on "a wife who takes care to have him cuckolded every day."

Also imitative is *cock,* with its *cock-a-doodle-doo; cockerel. cocker* (*spaniel*), trained to hunt woodcock (see *ane; auei*). *cockade. cockalorum:* man who crows; *cocky.* The *cockatrice* was folkchanged from L *calcatrix:* tracker, on your trail, from *calx, calcis:* heel; it was a monster hatched from a cock's egg, and its glance was lethal. L *calcatrix* was a translation of Gk *ikhneumon,* E *ichneumon:* a weasel (mongoose) that hunts and digs up crocodile eggs.

Fr, *coquelicot:* poppy, color of the cock's comb. *cockroach* is folkchanged from Sp *cucaracha,* also imitative, meaning first cuckoo, then woodlouse, the bird's food. *cock-a-leekie:* cream chicken soup with leeks.

kolem: reed, stem, pipe. Gk *khalamos. calamary, calamus, calamint. calamite. caramel* (*l.r* shift), from sugar cane. L, *culm. ha(u)lm. calumet:* a long-stemmed American Indian pipe of peace; better to smoke it than to "bury the hatchet" —which the next week might be buried in your skull.

ONorse *marr:* sea, *halmr:* reed; marram grass. *chalumeau, shawm* . . . "With trumpets also, and shawms: O show yourselves joyful before the Lord!"—*The Book of Common Prayer* (1548).

Calamus is a section of 45 poems added in the 1860 edition of Walt Whitman's *Leaves of Grass;* it celebrates the spiritual love of man for man, of which the *calamus* (sweet flag) is a threefold symbol; its leaves represent mortality; its clinging fascicles, friendship; its perennial roots, immortal life, source of the transient blooms.

L *lapsus calami:* slip of the (reed) pen; *lapsus linguae:* slip of the tongue; *lapsus memoriae:* forgetfulness.

kollei: glue. *collage; collagen. Collembole:* order of insects with *collophore:* sucker-like organ. *collenchyma. colletic. Colletotrichum:* genus of fungi. *collidine. colloid. collodion. protocol* (Gk *protos:* first [see *per*]): originally, a sheet glued in front of a book to indicate its nature and contents; in France it developed its present sense of official ordering—abruptly waved aside when at the banquet Macbeth sees Banquo's ghost: "Stand not upon the order of your going."

kom: beside, facing; hence friendly or fighting; with, together or against. Gk *khoinos:* in common; *c(o)enobite. OED* lists 4 and details 20 relevant words, as *coenobium, coenosarc, coenospecies. coenurus:* many-headed, single-tailed bladder worm; cause of staggers in sheep. *koine; epicene:* with characteristics of both sexes, as in Jonson's comedy *Epicoene; or, The Silent Woman* (1609). Rabelais had told a similar story, which Molière dramatized in *Doctor in Spite of Himself* (1666); Fielding made a version, *The Mock Doctor* (1733); Anatole France turned it into a one-act farce, *The Man Who Married a Dumb Wife* (1912).

L *com:* with. As an English prefix, this has three forms. It remains *com* before *b, m,* and *p,* as *combatant, combustion, combine; commandment, commencement, commingle; compel, competent, composition.* It matches a following *l* or *r,* as *collect, collision; correct, correspondent. corespondent,* used only since 1857, is spelled with one *r* to distinguish its special meaning. Before all other consonants *com* changed to *con,* as *conception, condominium, confer, congenital, conjugal, connect, conquer, consolidate, contact, convention. com* is a particularly prolific prefix, running for over 250 columns in *OED;* thus *combat, combination, comfit* (*confectionery*), *commerce. common* (with OL *moenus:* function, or L *munis:* obliging—from the latter also *immune:* exempt from obligation); *commonsensical, commune, community.* Objectors to *communism*—and other political patterns—should ponder Pope's statement in *Essay on Man* (1732):

For forms of government let fools contest,
Whate'er is best administered is best.

L *con:* against, as in *pro and con,* is a prefix for fewer words, as *contrite, convict, convertible.* More usual in this sense is *contra,* as *contraband, contraceptive, contrapuntal, contrary.* See the discussion of *c.o.n.* in the Introduction. *constable, count* (the title), *county. country:* facing the town. The English convicts that were transported to Australia produced that country's first play, in Sydney, on 16 Jan. 1796. Written by the notorious pickpocket George Barrington, its Prologue neatly declares:

From distant climes o'er widespread seas we come,
Though not with much éclat or beat of drum;
True patriots all, for be it understood
We left our country for our country's good.

country dance may be a folkchange from Fr *contredanse,* as in a *square dance,* with the partners or couples facing one another and with a "caller" to signal changes; often danced in a country barn, it is sometimes called a *barn dance.*

Also *counter, encounter, counteract.* Sp, *conquian.* OE *ge-:* with, appears as *e* in *enough* (Gm *genug*); it is *i* or *y* in *handicraft, handiwork, iwis, y-clept,* and some two dozen other words beginning with *y* (detailed in *OED*).

> The law doth punish man or woman
> That steals the goose from off the common,
> But lets the greater felon loose
> That steals the common from the goose.
> —Anonymous folksong, 1764

konemo: shinbone. Gk *khneue:* leg (knee to ankle). *cnemial; gastrocnemius* (bulges like a belly). Gc, *ham. to ham,* and *ham actor* or *ham radio operator,* are folk-changed from *amateur,* with allusion to the many that have vainly tried to capture the spirit of *Hamlet.*

hamshackle: first, to shackle an animal's head to its foreleg in order to keep it still. *hamstrung.* The first syllable of *hamburger,* short for *hamburger steak,* from the German city *Hamburg,* has been "misunderstood" and varied to *beefburger, cheeseburger, wimpyburger,* etc.

konk: waver; hang. L *cunctari, cunctatum:* delay. Quintus Fabius Maximus Verrucosus was surnamed *Cunctator* for the tactics he used against Carthage; see *ia.* Gc, *hang. hangdog. hangfire, hangout, hangover, hang-up.* Note that things are *hung;* persons are *hanged. hank:*

> A fool there was and he made his prayer
> (Even as you and I!)
> To a rag and a bone and a hank of hair
> (We called her the woman who did not care)
> But the fool, he called her his lady fair
> (Even as you and I.)
> —Kipling, *The Vampire*

hanker, hangar: first, a horseshoeing shed, where the horse was suspended. *hinge.*

hanky-panky is a coined term, like *hokey-pokey,* both probably modeled on *hocus-pocus,* which was itself probably an anticatholic combobulation of L *Hoc est corpus (meum):* "This is my body," as though the Eucharist transformation were a juggler's trick; but note *honky-tonk, knick-knack,* and *knock,* which are imitative (see *gen*). *kickshaw:* a trifle, is an English corruption of Fr *quelque chose:* a something; Shallow, in *2 Henry IV,* orders for Falstaff's meal "some pigeons, a couple of short-legged hens, a joint of mutton, and any pretty little tiny kickshaws."

On signing the Declaration of Independence, 4 July 1776, Benjamin Franklin declared: "We must all hang together, or we shall hang separately."

?konops: gnat, mosquito. Gk *khonopeion:* couch with mosquito curtain. *canopy.* Fr, *canapé:* first, a preliminary nibble, on the couch (the ancients ate while reclining). *Conopophagidae:* genus of birds (gnat-eaters).

?kophin: basket. Gk *khophinos. coffer, coffret; coffin.* In England, until the 16th c., there were no coffins, only winding-sheets. "I am told he makes a very handsome corpse, and becomes his coffin prodigiously"—Goldsmith, *The Good-Natured Man* (1768).

kormo: pain. Gm, *harm,* etc.

> For his Aunt Jobiska said, "No harm
> Can come to his toes if his nose is warm."
> —Edward Lear, *The Pobble . . .* (1870)

koro: army, host; war. LL *arberga:* army camp. Via Fr, *auberge.* Gc *harjaz,* OE *here:* army. *harbor, harbinger:* first, army shelters. *harness.* OFr, *herald.* Four terms from English history: *heriot:* feudal payment to a lord upon a tenant's death (i.e., for loss of a soldier); *heretoga:* army leader (from Gm, *Herzog:* duke); *hereship:* raid; and *arrière-ban,* folkchanged from *hari-ban* (by contact with Fr *arrière:* in back): a lord's summons to his vassals to assemble for war.

Also various Teutonic names. *Harold:* army ruler; earlier, *Hari-wold;* the last syllable is first in *Walter,* of the same meaning. *Herman:* man of war. *Oliver:* elfin host. The famous Oliver was one of Charlemagne's twelve peers, bosom friend of *Roland:* glory of the land. The French form was folkchanged to *Olivier:* olive tree, and is the name of the 20th c. English actor Sir Laurence Olivier.

kosel: nut tree. *hazel.* Also called *filbert:* nut of St. Philibert (d. A.D. 684), whose feast day, 24 Aug., is its ripening time. The genus name of hazels is *Corylus.* Its supple green rods were used for whipping; hence, "to anoint with oil of hazel" meant to give a good drubbing. *OED* gives the word well over two columns, not counting *witch hazel,* the forked branches of which are used in divining. *Hazel* is the only nut popularly used as a girl's name.

kost: bone; rib. L *costa:* rib; side. *coast, coastal. costal, intercostal; costate. costrel. accost.* Fr, *cotelette:* little rib; E *cutlet,* changed by influence of *cut. costard:* ribbed apple; whence *costermonger; coster.* W. S. Gilbert, in *The Pirates of Penzance,* muses on human nature:

When the coster's finished jumping on his mother
He loves to lie a-basking in the sun.
O, take one consideration with another,
A policeman's lot is not a happy one.

costard was sometimes used for the head, as when Edgar in *King Lear* declares: "I'se try whether your costard or my ballow [cudgel] be the harder."

krapo: roof. Gc *hrofom;* E *roof.*

There's no roof has not a star above it.
—Emerson, *Musketaquid* (1847)

kred I: belief. *trust* (originally religious): to attribute magic power to. Skr, *s(h)raddha:* offering at a shrine, to an ancestor.

L and E, *credo. creed, credence, credentials; credible, credit, creditor. accredited; discredit. credulity, credulous, incredulous,* etc.

Via Fr, *miscreant:* originally, misbeliever. The 18th c. *incroyable:* "Wert thou not," Carlyle asks in *Sartor Resartus* (1833), "at one period of life, a Buck, or Blood, or Macaroni, or Incroyable, or Dandy, or by whatsoever name such phenomenon is distinguished?" See *haifst; ueid.* Gc, *grant.*

"I hold that the characteristic of the present age is a craving credulity." These words of Carlyle in 1864 apply to our own time; the breakdown of ethical standards has led the unsophisticated to a quest for something to base conduct on, while the tremendous achievements of science have led the unlearned to expect that anything is possible. For example, UFOs (*U*nidentified *F*lying *O*bjects), commonly called *flying saucers,* are considered to bear observers from other planets, perhaps from other stars, perhaps from other galaxies. *incredible.*

Etsi incredibilest credere: And to believe what is most unbelievable.—Terence, *Heauton timoroumenos* [The Self-tormentor] (163 B.C.). *Credo quia absurdum:* I believe because it is absurd.—Tertullian, ca. A.D. 200. "I can believe anything, provided it is incredible"—Oscar Wilde, *The Picture of Dorian Gray* (1891).

kred II: framework. Gc *roost;* whence *rooster* (coined in the U.S.). See *ane.* "A rooster is monarch of his own dunghill."

(k)rek: weave. Gk *khrokhos, khrokhudos:* woolen nap; *crocodilite.* For *crochet,* see *ger III.* Gc, *(night)rail:* woven dress. From the weaving motion, *reel; fisherman's reel, highland reel,* etc.

krep: body. L *corpus. corporal, corporeal, corporation, incorporate. corps, corpse. corpulent; corpus, corpuscle.* The noncommissioned officer *corporal* is from Fr *caporal* (see *caput; kuer*). Ir, *leprechaun:* tiny body. Gc, *midriff.*

kreu: bloody; raw flesh; cruel; cold, freezing. Gk *khreas:* flesh. *creatine, creodont; creophagous. creosote. pancreas.* Gk *khruos:* frost. *crymodynia, cryogen; cryolite, cryometer. crystal, crystallize, crystallographer, crystallomancy,* etc. L *crusta:* first, hardened by freezing. *crust, crustacea. Caucasian:* from the cold region. L *cruor:* blood; *crudus:* raw; whence *crudelis:* hard, pitiless, E *cruel. crude; recrudescence; cruentation.* Fr, *croustade, crouton, écru. custard* was earlier *crustad,* folkchanged by the sound of *mustard;* see *kel VIII.*

John Donne, in *The Bait,* gave a new turn after a first line used before him by Christopher Marlowe, and challenged by Sir Walter Ralegh:

Come live with me, and be my love,
And we will some new pleasures prove
Of golden sands, and crystal brooks,
With silken lines, and silver hooks.

kreup: to become encrusted. Probably an extension of *kreu. scab.* L *ruga:* wrinkle. *rugate, rugose. corrugated.* LL *ruga* was used of a road with houses; whence Fr *rue,* E *ruelle,* Sp *arroyo.*

Via It, *ruffian.* Via Norse, *dandruff* (first syllable of unknown origin), Gc, *gruff, ruffle;* whence *ruff:* large, stiff collar of the 17th c. The *ruffle* of drums is imitative.

kreut. Gc, *reed.*

krup: conceal. Gk *khrupte. crypt* and its doublets *grot, grotto. grotesque.* Prefix *crypto,* as in *cryptogram, cryptonym; cryptorchid:* undescended testicle; and some 50 more such words in *OED. krypton* (see *el 36*). *undercroft. apochryphal.* See *kel VI.* Via SCr *krupa:* groats, came E *graepel:* soft hail.

krut. Two old, stringed musical instruments: the Fr *rote* and the Celt *crowd.*

ksei: rule, ruler. Skr, *kshatriya:* man of the military caste. OPers *khshayathya,* sensibly shortened to *shahzadah, shah; padishah, pasha. Nakshatra, satrap. Ahasuerus* in the Bible, *Xerxes* in less holy history. *chess; check. checkers,* from the checkered pattern of the board; hence, a *checkered career,* mixed black and white. Likewise *exchequer,* and a bank *check, cheque. Czech,* with the same pronunciation, is the native name of what used to be called Bohemia, whence E *bohemian.* (Shakespeare, in *The Winter's Tale,* followed his source, Robert Greene's popular story *Pandosto* [1588; reprinted in 1592, 1595, 1607], in having a ship "[touch] upon the deserts of Bohemia," which, as Shakespeare's rival playwright Ben Jonson was quick to point out, has forests but no desert and emphatically no seacoast.) For *Czechoslovakia,* see *kleu I.* The mineral *scacchite* was named for *Archelangelo Szacchi* (d. 1894).

scacchic: relating to chess. *checkmate* is from *shah mat,* which some trace to Arabic: the king is dead; others more plausibly derive it from Persian: the king is at a loss. Via Sp, E *matador:* he that kills the bull.

ksero: dry. Gk *xeros.* The medical terms *xeransis, xerasia, xeroderma,* etc. Several genera, as *Xeranthemum:* thistle; *Xerophyllum:* turkey-beard; *Phylloxera:* plant lice. The machine for dry reproduction, *Xerox.*

L, probably *sear; sere, serene. Non numero horas nisi serenas:* I count only the hours that are serene—inscription on many a sundial. Also Fr *serein:* fine rain from a clear sky. *serenade;* its meaning influenced by L *sera:* late, evening.

Learn the sweet magic of a cheerful face;
Not always smiling, but at least serene.
—Oliver Wendell Holmes, *The Morning Visit* (1836)

elixir, from Greek via Arabic (*el, al:* the), was originally assumed to be a powder; it was the medieval alchemists' "philosopher's stone," which could transform base metals into gold, cure all human ills, and indefinitely prolong life. Fortunately, it was never found.

Since Macbeth's recognition of his "sear" (see quotation under *saus*), "the yellow leaf" has been used to suggest age.

ksun: together, with. Prefixes from Greek: (1) *sym. OED* lists 26, as *sympalmograph, sympsychology,* then details more in 32 columns, as *symbolism:* thrown together; *symphony:* sounded together; *symposium:* first, drinking together. *sympathy, symptomatic.* (2) *syn. OED* lists 44, as *synthermal, syntoxic,* then details more in 51 columns, as *synagogue; synchronize* (in the film industry abbreviated as *sync*). *syncopation, syncope, synergetic, synonym. synteresis:* innate knowledge of right and wrong.

Russian prefix *so, s:* together, as in *sputnik;* see *keu II.* Polish prefix *se, sejm:* assembly; see *em.* In Latin, however, *se* means away from, without, as in *select, separate. sobriety* is being without drink, not inebriated. Thus also the *s* in *solve* and *dissolve* (*se-luere:* loosen); and *soluble* and *solution,* which are synonyms of *dissoluble* and *dissolution.*

?kuberna: pilot; steer, control. Gk *khubernan,* L *gubernare, gubernatum. gubernatorial. govern, government,* etc., through 13 *OED* columns. *cybernetics,* used in Fr, *cybernétique,* in 1834 by A. M. Ampère, was newly applied in English by Norbert Wiener in 1948. *The Listener* of 1 Nov. 1962 spoke of the rapidly expanding field: "In education, too, cybernetics begins to intrude, as electronic teaching machines make good the lack of human teachers." The American college honor fraternity, *Phi Beta Kappa,* founded at William and Mary College on 5 Dec. 1776, takes its name from the first letters, ΦBK, of *Philosophia Biou Kubernetes:* The love of wisdom is the pilot of life. Would it were widely so!

kue: and, ever. Used as an enclitic, i.e., attached to the main word, as L *que; Senatus Populusque Romanus:* The Senate and the Roman People; *S P Q R* on the standards. *ubiquity. sesqui:* prefix meaning "and a half," as in *sesquicentennial. sesquipedalian:* (words) a foot and a half long.

"The Corporation of the Goosequill—of the Press—of the fourth estate," says Thackeray in *Pendennis,* 30, "she never sleeps. Her officers march along with armies, and her envoys walk into statesmen's cabinets. They are ubiquitous."

kuei I: honor, respect (which may imply fear); consider, pay, atone. Gk *poiein:* esteem, pay, atone. *Pentheus:* god's vengeance; see *men I. Poinae:* Greek goddesses of vengeance, as in Sartre's play *The Flies* (1943), which was based on the *Orestes* of Aeschylus (458 B.C.), in which the goddess Athene established trial by jury, the *Areopagus,* the beginning of the Western system of justice. (Orestes had avenged his father's murder, but to do so had slain his mother; the citizens were unable to decide, but the goddess tempered justice with mercy, freeing Orestes from the tormenting Furies.) *Areopagus* means "the hill of Ares," Greek god of war, Roman Mars. The star *Antares* is "opposite" the planet Mars. See *pag; ue.*

The link between *respect* and *fear* shows through the roots. *Tisiphone:* avenger of murder, is one of the Furies. Gk *timè:* honor, worth; hence *timocracy. Timothy:* honor to god. L *timere:* to fear; *timidus:* afraid. *timorous; timid. Timeo Danaos* has been widely applied; see *keu I.*

From this root also Gk *poine,* L *poena:* blood money, punishment. *pain. penal, penalty, penitentiary, penology. punishment; impunity. subpoena. pine, repine;* not related to *penitent* and *repent* (see *pen*). Note that the word *atone* means simply "at one," in regained harmony.

kuei II: form, make. Gk *poiein:* make. A poet is a maker. *poem, poesy, poetaster, poetry. payyetan:* poet, and *piyyut:* poem, are Hebrew, borrowed from Greek. *epopee. mythopoe(t)ic. onomatopoetic. prosopopoeia. pharmacopoeia. posy,* shortened from *poesy,* was first a verse engraved on, or accompanying, a gift; the gift was so frequently a bunch of flowers that the meaning shifted to the blooms.

Butler, in *Hudibras* (1664), pictured a factotum versifier:

Beside all this, he served his master
In quality of poetaster,
And rhymes appropriate could make
To every month in the Almanack.

Alice, in *Through the Looking Glass,* expresses a common attitude: "'I can repeat poetry as well as other folk, if it comes to that.' 'Oh, it needn't come to that!' Alice said hastily." Keats, in *Sleep and Poetry,* sets down more seriously

the great end
Of poetry, that it should be a friend
To soothe the cares, and lift the thoughts, of man.

While there is poetry, there is hope.

kuei III: restfulness; space of time. L *quies, quietem. quiet; quietus; disquiet; inquietude. quiescent; acquiesce; acquit. quittance. quite; requite. requiem. Requiescat in pace:* May (s)he rest in peace; abbreviated *R.I.P. tranquil.* Fr, *coy.*

Gc, *while; while away* the time; *whilom, whilst, awhile. week.* Joyce did not find the week "restful"; in *Finnegans Wake* he lists "all moanday, tearsday, wailsday, thumpsday, frightday, shatterday"—sparing the shunday to shine! More pleasantly, in the same work, he observes: "Quiet takes back her folded fields."

Hamlet, in his best-known soliloquy, ponders:

To be, or not to be, that is the question . . .
For who would bear the whips and scorns of time,
The oppressor's wrong, the proud man's contumely,
The pangs of disprized love, the law's delay,
The insolence of office, and the spurns
That patient merit of the unworthy takes,
When he himself might his quietus make
With a bare bodkin?

How little these burdens have changed since Shakespeare's day!

kueis. Imitative. Gc, *whine, whisper. whistle. whirr, whish. whisk,* the sound of a brush on cloth; *whiskbroom.* From its brushlike growth, *whiskers. Whist!*—whispered quickly as a signal for silence, less noisy than *Shh!* or *Shush!*—also used as verb or noun. Shakespeare, in *The Tempest,* i, 2:

Curtsied when you have, and kissed
The wild waves whist.

Later, Robert Bridges, in *Shorter Poems* (1890):

The huge unclouded sun,
Surprising the world's whist,
Is all uprisen thereon.

Cotton, in *The Complete Gamester* (1680), tells us that the game "is called whist from the silence that is to be observed in the play." By 1742 Horace Walpole could write: "Whist has spread an universal opium over the whole nation." One of its progeny, *bridge,* first played in Constantinople ca. 1810, now internationally popular, with world-wide contests, probably got its name from Russ *birich:* caller of official proclamations. Whew!

kueit: white, shining. See also *kel V.* Gc, *white; wheat,* from the seeds and flour. *edelweiss. whiting* (fish). *Whitsunday,* from the white robes worn for baptism. *Wheatstone,* short for *Wheatstone's bridge:* for measuring electrical resistance, was devised by Sir Charles *Wheatstone* in 1843.

The bird *wheatear* is folkchanged from *wheaters:* white arse. Folkchange is constantly at work. Less dialectal (and less euphemistic) are such conversions as *pentis* to *penthouse* (see *spend II*), and *crevisse* to *crayfish* (see *gerbh*).

kuel: turn, revolve. Gc, *felly, fallow:* soil turned but not sown. *wheel.* Possibly *clown,* from his somersaulting stunts. By *l.r* shift, some of the words listed under *ker I* have been attributed to this root.

kuelp: vault; bosom, womb. Gk *kholpos:* womb, vagina. The medical terms *colpenchyme, colpeurynter, colpitis, colpocele,* etc. *gulf.* Gc, *whelm:* cover as with a vault. *overwhelm.* Perhaps influential on the words *helm, helmet;* see *kel VI.*

kuenth: suffer. Gk *penthos:* grief. *nepenthe.* Gk, *pathos,* etc. See *guadh.* The *Odyssey* mentions *nepenthes* as a drug to banish grief; English poets have dropped the *s.* Thus Spenser, in *The Faerie Queene,* iv:

In her other hand a cup she hild
The which was with nepenthe to the brim upfild.

Poe, in *The Raven,* seeks for it vainly; see the quotation under *guadh.*

kuep: boil, move violently; hence used of strong emotions. L *cupere, cupido:* desire. *Cupid* is the god not of love, as is commonly considered, but of desire. *cupidity. concupiscence, covet, covetousness.* Also L *vaporem:* vapor; *evaporate.* When all the steam has boiled out of a thing it is *vapid. acapnia* (*a* negative): lack of carbon dioxide.

In Shakespeare there are 59 references to *Cupid.* Thus, in *As You Like It,* the disguised Rosalind, teasing Orlando, says: "Break an hour's promise in love! He that will divide a minute into a thousand parts, and break but a part of the thousandth part of a minute in the affairs of love, it may be said of him that Cupid hath clapped him o' the shoulder, but I'll warrant him heart-whole."

kuer: form, make. Skr, *abkari; carcoon. karma; Visrakarma. prakriti, Prakrit. Sanskrit* (*sam:* together; see *sem*). *samkara. sircar.*

Gk *pelor* (variant *telor*): monster. *peloria. teras, teratos:* marvel, monster. *teratical, teratoid, teratology, teratscopy* (11 such words in *OED*). An 1868 study of minerals informs us that "teratolite is an impure lithomarge, like pholerite." Bailey's word book of 1727 states more comprehensibly: "[teratology] is when bold writers, fond of the sublime, intermix something great and prodigious in everything they write, whether there be foundation for it in reason or not, and this is what is called bombast." Johnson, in his *Dictionary* of 1755, omitting the prodigious monsters, cribs from Bailey: "Teratology: bombast, affectation of false sublimity." Love of the marvelous is *teratism.*

?kuere: ask, seek; hence gain, win. L *quaerere, questum;* L and E *quaestor. quest,* *question; query. acquire, inquire, require. conquest;* Sp, *conquistador. inquest, request. acquisition. disquisition, inquisition, requisition; perquisite. exquisite:* sought out.

conquer, conqueror. William of Normandy, called the Conqueror (in Saxon chronicles rightfully called William the Bastard), won England at the Battle of Hastings, 14 Oct. 1066, but he owed much to Halley's Comet, the appearance of which, accepted as an omen of disaster, broke King Harold's morale. Harold, who wore no helmet, was killed when an arrow pierced his eye. The comet, traced since 12 B.C. and last seen in 1910, is scheduled to reappear in 1986. *comet* is from Gk *aster cometes:* long-haired star. Halley's Comet is shown on the famous Bayeux tapestry (231 feet long, 19½ inches wide) commissioned by William's half-brother Odo, Bishop of Bayeux in Normandy, where it may still be seen in the museum; its 70 woven scenes depict the Norman Conquest. As a matter of fact, William's victory was less a conquest than an assertion of his rights. According to regal and legal custom, Edward the Confessor had named his heir: William of Normandy; on Edward's death, the witenagemot (assembly of bishops and nobles) was persuaded to name the Saxon Harold; William sailed over to maintain his honor.

After the assassination of Julius Caesar in Shakespeare's play:

O mighty Caesar! Dost thou lie so low?
Are all thy conquests, glories, triumphs, spoils,
Shrunk to this little measure?

Man's greatest conquest still awaits, within.

The Catholic Congregation of the Holy Office was established by Pope Innocent III (Lotario dei Conti de Segni) ca. 1210, for the suppression of heresy. Its strong arm, the Inquisition, was set as a tribunal by Pope Gregory IX (Ugelino, Count of Segni) in 1229, spread over Europe, and was severe, although the questioned ones were passed from the clergy to lay officers for torture and the flames. The Inquisition was generally administered by the Dominicans (L *Dominicanes,* broken in popular scorn into *Domini Canes:* Hounds of the Lord). Queen Isabella obtained the Spanish Inquisition from Pope Sixtus IV (Francesco della Rovere) in 1480; it was first headed by Tomás de Torquemada, and was used mainly to spy out "insincere" converts among Jews and Arabs. Jews were banished from Spain in 1492, a little too early for refuge in America.

The French Inquisition was abolished in 1772; the Spanish, not until 1838. Meanwhile, under Pope Pius IV (Giovan Angelo de' Medici), the attention of the Congregation of the Holy Office turned to heretical–including obscene–literature. Typographic printing was spreading books of many sorts. The first *Index Librorum Prohibitorum* was issued in 1564; it was followed in 1571 by the *Index Expurgatorius,* a list of books a Catholic might read if specified passages were expunged or properly altered. Both lists were discontinued by order of the pope on 6 June 1966.

"Upon a time when Burbage played Richard III there was a citizen grew so far in liking with him that before she went from the play she appointed him to come that night to her by the name of Richard III. Shakespeare, overhearing their conclusion, went before, was entertained, and at his game when Burbage came. The message being brought that Richard III was at the door, Shakespeare caused return to be made that William the Conqueror was before Richard III"–John Manningham, *Diary* (1602). William Shakespeare died in 1616; his friend and partner at the Globe Theatre (1598 until it burned down in 1613; see *kerd*),

Richard Burbage, died in 1619. I picture them teasing each other—"Good morrow, Conqueror!" "Happy Hours, Richard!"—chuckling over the memory, long after they'd forgotten the woman's name.

kuerp: twist, move about, revolve. Gk *karpos:* wrist; not to be confused with *karpos:* fruit (see *ker III*). *carpal, carpus.* Prefix *carpo,* as *carpocerite, carpopedal. metacarpal.* Norse, *varve.* Gc (partly imitative), *warble, whir, whirl, whorl. wharf* was first a place where people moved about.

kues. Imitative of the sound of a squeezed bladder. Gk *khustis:* bladder, pouch. *cyst, cystoid, cystectomy, cystecstasy; OED* gives 50 associated words. *cholecyst.* L *queri:* complain; *querimonia:* complaint. *querimonious, querulous. quarrel:* earlier, often, a just quarrel; hence a reason for. Bacon observes: "Wives are young men's mistresses, companions for middle age, and old men's nurses. So as a man may have a quarrel to marry when he will." (Many a marriage is marred by the current sense of quarrel.) Gc, *wheeze.*

kuet: shake, crush, break. A short form of *skut.* Gk *passein:* sprinkle. *paste, impaste. pastel; pastiche.* It, *pasticcio; pasta, pastina.* Fr, *paté, pastry, pasty, pastisserie; patty.* L *quatere, quassum:* shake; *quassare:* shake violently; LL *quassicare:* break. *quash, squash; scotch, scutch. cassation. concussion; concutient; discuss, percussion, succussion. rescue* (short from *re-ex-quassare*): shake off. Sp, *casco; cask, casque. cascara (sagrada):* sacred bark; broken off trees. Fr *casser:* break, annul. *cashier* (: dismiss, discharge); also the ending of *fracas* and *fricassee.*

Macbeth (iii, 1) protests:

We have scotched the snake, not killed it:
She'll close and be herself, whilst our poor malice
Remains in danger of her former tooth . . .
Duncan is in his grave;
After life's fitful fever he sleeps well.

kuetuer: four. Gk, *tetrad. OED* lists 89 words beginning *tetra,* as *tetracoral, tetragamy; tetraselenodont* (*Selene:* the moon): having four crescentic ridges, as a molar tooth. It details 83 words, as *tetrameter, tetrarch. tetracty:* the Pythagorean name of the sum of the first four numbers (1 + 2 + 3 + 4 = 10) regarded as the source of all things. *tetragonism:* the squaring of the circle. *tetrakisdodecahedron:* a solid bounded by 48 triangular planes—e.g. some crystals.

The Tetragrammaton: four-letter word, is the Hebrew word usually transliterated *JHVH,* representing the unspoken name of God. George Wither, in *The Lord's Prayer* (1665), pointed out: "Our English tongue as well as the Hebrew hath a Tetragrammaton, whereby God may be named; to wit, Good." Abraham Tucker, in *The Light of Nature Pursued* (1768), extended the range: "The Quaternion is the holy Tetragrammaton, the same awful name variously pronounced among the sons of men: whether Jeva, Isis, Jove, Theos, Zeus, or Deus, or Tien, Alla, Dios, Idio, Dieu, or Lord; for all these are Tetragrammata."

There are two Greek forms for *four: tettara* and *tessara* (*tessera*). *OED* lists 6 words for the second, as *tessaraglot:* of four languages; *tesseratomic:* of division into four parts. The 12 words *OED* details developed from *tessera* (plural, *tesserae*): first, a quadrilateral tablet, in ancient times broken and divided between host and guest and kept as a sign of recognition and friendliness; thence, a distinguishing token, then a password. From the cubical shape, it was also used of dice; Gibbon, in *The Decline and Fall of the Roman Empire* (chap. 31, p. 3), speaks of the *tesserian* art of dice-playing. The diminutive of *tessera* is *tessella,* used of lozenges, and especially of mosaic chips, at first four-sided, then of various shapes to fit a design; hence *tessellate, tessellation.* There is also Gk *tetartos:* a fourth; *OED* lists 13 such words in relation to crystallography: *tetartohedral, tetartosymmetrical,* etc.

In a few words *tetra* is shortened to *tra.* In the U.S. a *trapezium* (*peza,* It variant of L *pedem:* foot) is a four-sided plane with no sides parallel; a *trapezoid* is such a plane with two sides parallel; in Britain the meanings are reversed. The horizontal bar hanging from two ropes is the (flying) *trapeze;* in the circus, with "the daring young man" (though women, and recently children, fly from one trapeze to the grip of a man on another). A *trapezohedron* is a solid whose sides are *trapezoids* or *trapezia.* Note that *trapezium* and *trapezoid* also name wrist bones near the thumb.

L, *quadrant, quadratic, quadrilateral.* A *quadrangle* is especially a small rectangular park surrounded by buildings, and on college campuses is commonly referred to as *the quad. quatrain, quartet; quartan; quarto. quarter:* a coin, as one-fourth of a dollar; a region, as the *Latin Quarter.* Prefix *quadri,* as *quadrilateral, quadrivalent, quadripara, quadriplegia.* Also *quadru,* as *quadruped, quadruplets. quadrantids* are meteors in the 2 and 3 Jan. shower, the radiant point of which is in the constellation *Quadrans Muralis. OED* has 24 columns beginning with *quad,* as *quadrate, quadraphonic, quadroon, quadrennial, quadriceps.* It has 38 columns beginning *quar,* 13 of which are associated with meanings and combinations of *quarter.*

A *square* has four equal sides. A *squadron,* or *squad,* is a square of soldiers. A *quarrel* was a square-headed bolt for the crossbow; a *quarrelet,* a little square, as in Herrick's *Hesperides* (1648):

Some asked how pearls did grow, and where?
Then spoke I to my girl,
To part her lips, and showed them there
The quarrelets of pearl.

A *quire* was originally a set of four sheets. A *quarantine* (*quadraginta:* four ten times) was first imposed in 1377 at Ragusa, on ships from Egypt and the East. Fr, *cahier:* four sheets; *carillon:* four bells; *quadrille:* a dance for four couples, a card game for four players.

Gc, *cater-cornered, catty-cornered.* Probably *cater-cousin,* sweetly altered to *kissing-cousin. four, fourth, fourteen, forty.*

When man and woman unto forty come,
The man goes to belly, the woman goes to bum.

fardel: fourth of a deal. *farthing. firkin;* first, one-fourth of a barrel. *tankard* (L *tant quartum:* as much as a fourth). A *quart* is a fourth of a gallon. *quarry:* where stones are cut into square blocks.

Some cry up Haydn, some Mozart,
Just as the whim breaks. For my part,
I do not give a farthing candle
For either of them, or for Handel.
—Charles Lamb, letter to Mrs. William
Hazlitt, 24 May 1830

Boethius, in the 6th c., divided the seven liberal arts into the *trivium* (dealing with words): grammar, logic, rhetoric; and the *quadrivium* (dealing with numbers): arithmetic, geometry, astronomy, music. *-vium,* L *via:* way, the seven ways to wisdom. In the 5th c. Martianus Capella, in *The Wedding of Philology and*

Mercury, popular throughout the Middle Ages, had pictured the seven liberal arts as women, each different in complements, clothing, and coiffure. See *men I.*

> So live, that when thy summons comes to join
> The innumerable caravan, which moves
> To that mysterious realm, where each shall take
> His chamber in the silent halls of death,
> Thou go not, like the quarry-slave at night,
> Scourged to his dungeon, but, sustained and soothed
> By an unfaltering trust, approach thy grave
> Like one who wraps the drapery of his couch
> About him, and lies down to pleasant dreams.
> —last sentence of *Thanatopsis,* written by W. C. Bryant when he was seventeen

kuknos: swan. Possibly imitative; see *suen.* Fr, *cygne. cygnet. Cygnus:* a constellation. In Shakespeare's *King John,* v, 7, the King's heir, Prince Henry, says:

> 'Tis strange that death should sing.
> I am the cygnet to this pale faint swan . . .

kuno: dog. Gk *khuon, khunos. khunankhe:* dog strangle; *quinsy. quinsyberry;* see *bhel I. cynarctomachy. cynegetic:* of hunting with dogs. *cynanthropy. cyniatrics.* Three genera: *Cynanchum:* of milkweed; *Cynias:* of dogfish; *Cynoscion:* of weakfish. Several plant genera: *Cynodon:* dog's tooth; *Cynoglossum:* dog's tongue; *Cynocrambe:* dog cabbage; *Cynorrhodon:* dogrose; *Cynara:* artichoke. *cynoid.*

Cynosure: literally, dog's tail; the constellation Ursa Minor, the Lesser Bear, which has the polestar, pointing to the North Pole, at the tip of its tail. Hence, a guiding star; a center of attraction. Milton, in *L'Allegro,* speaks of a place

> Where perhaps some beauty lies,
> The cynosure of neighboring eyes.

OED gives over a dozen words beginning *cyno,* as *cynocephalous.* The word *cynic* may be from *Cynoserges,* a gymnasium where Antisthenes taught Diogenes and others. Diogenes lived in a tub; when Alexander the Great asked what he could do for him, Diogenes replied: "Stand from between me and the sun." But even in those days (the 4th c. B.C.) the Greeks associated the overascetic cynics with the idea of dogs. See *sner I.* Again Milton, in *Comus* (1634):

> O foolishness of men . . .
> To fetch their precepts from the cynic tub
> Praising the lean and sallow Abstinence!

George Meredith, in *The Egoist* (1879): "Cynics are only happy in making the world as barren to others as they have made it for themselves." *OED:* "cynic: one who shows a disposition to disbelieve in the sincerity or goodness of human motives, and is wont to express this by sneers and sarcasms." (Note that *cynicism* has the same sound as *Sinicism:* the practice, or an instance, of Chinese principles or manners.)

The Tasmanian tiger, last seen in 1934, but still being sought, is a marsupial, also called *thylacine;* the species is *Thylacinus cynocephalus:* dog-headed with a pouch.

L *canis, canem:* dog. *Canis, Canidae:* family and genus of the dog, wolf, fox, jackal. The dog stars: *Procyon, Canis Major, Canis Minor, Sirius; Canicula* (which means puppy). *canine, canicular.* Fr *chien; chenille; canaille. kennel.*

The *Canary Islands* were named for the wild dogs there; the bird, a favorite for domestic cages, is from these islands; the color, bright yellow, comes from the bird. (The reverse happened with *cardinal;* see *kerd.*) Incidentally, in the wild state the canary is not yellow but green. *canary* is also (1) a lively dance, from the islands, as in *All's Well That Ends Well,* ii, 1, and *Love's Labor's Lost,* iii, 1 (usually in the plural); (2) a verb, as used by W. Tennant in *Anster Fair* (1812):

The saffron-elbow'd Morning up the slope
Of heaven canaries in her jewelled shoes.

(3) a light, sweet wine, as in *2 Henry IV,* ii, 4, and *Twelfth Night,* i, 3; and (4) a Quicklyism for quandary in *The Merry Wives of Windsor,* ii, 2: "You have brought her into such a canaries as 'tis wonderful: the best Courtier of them all could never have brought her to such a Canarie."

canary grass yields the seed used as food for the caged bird. In the 18th c., *canarybird* was slang for a special type of jailbird: "a rogue or whore" hung in a cage outside the prison, as at Newgate, for public scorn.

Du, *keeshond. Kees,* short for *Cornelius.* Gc, *hound,* the *d* added from an old word meaning to seize, the dog being the seizer. Gm, *Dachshund.* "The dog is man's best friend. Yes, some of my best friends turned out to be sons of bitches." The origin of *bitch* is unknown. *Cave canem:* Beware of the dog (see *keu I*).

kuo. Interrogative, indefinite, and relative pronouns, and words combined therefrom. Skr, *katha.* Pers *chiz:* what thing; hence (the big) *cheese.* Other uses of *cheese* came later. The cheese made from milk—of cows, mares, nanny goats, etc. —was known to the ancients. It *mozzarella* was first used in India, of buffalo milk; see *mut. cheese* is from L *caseus,* whence also *casein. cheesecloth* is loosely woven; the cheese is put in, the liquid squeezed out. The idea that the moon is made of green cheese may use *green* in the sense of unripe, not thoroughly dried, hence pallid, as on a misty night; but *OED* says the notion is applied to a person who will believe any absurdity. *OED* defines *cheeseparing* as referring to a "miserly economist," a skinflint; but Shakespeare uses it to mean thin as a cheese rind when he has Falstaff (*2 Henry IV,* iii, 2) say of Justice Shallow: "I do remember him at Clement's Inn, like a man made after supper of a cheese-paring. 'A was the very genius of famine; yet lecherous as a monkey, and the whores called him mandrake. . . . You might have thrust him and all his apparel into an eelskin." (For *mandrake,* see *manu.*)

The origin of *Cheese it, the cops!* is unknown; Eric Partridge declares it is "obviously" a perversion of *Cease it!*—but why not of the surprised exclamation *Jesus!*? Partridge also mentions *cheese and kisses* as Cockney rhyming slang for *the missus,* and *cheese-eater* as an informer, "obviously" a rat. *cheesecake,* meaning a display (usually in a picture) of attractive feminine parts, was coined by a New York reporter who took photographs of celebrities arriving on transatlantic liners (when they plied the ocean blue), posing the ladies so as to reveal lengths of leg—by analogy with restaurants, such as the noted Lindsay's on Broadway, which displayed in the window their choicest proffering, a cheesecake. The photographer's request to his subject, *Say cheese,* draws its virtue from the way the utterance draws the lips into a smile.

Eugene Field saw especial virtue in a dish:

But I, when I undress me
Each night, upon my knees,
Will ask the Lord to bless me
With apple pie and cheese.

L *qui:* who, *quid:* what, *quantum:* how much, *quot:* how many, *qualis:* what kind, *ubi:* where, *ibi:* there, *unde:* whence, *uter:* either. See *ne.* E, *qua, quality, qualify, quantity, quantum; quibble; quid, quiddity, quidnunc; quillet, quip. quorum:* of whom . . . (thus many). *aliquant, aliquot, aliunde, alibi* (see *al II; kue*). *ibid(em); ubiety, ubiquitous. quota, quotation, quote, quotidian, quotient, quodlibet. posology* (how big a dose). Sp, *conquian* (play with whom?), whence also *cooncan. hidalgo:* son of someone: a propertied but second-rank noble.

Gc, *who, whose, whom; which.* The six questions reporters are taught to ask come from this root; *what, who, when, where, how, why?* As Kipling put it,

I keep six honest serving-men
(They taught me all I knew):
Their names are What and Why and When
And How and Where and Who.

whodunit: the term coined by illiterate mystery-gapers. *then, thence, whence, hence, hither, thither, whither; either, neither; neuter, neutrality.*

Via Fr, *askance* (*as-quam-si*). *quasi* (OL *quam-si:* as if). *OED* does not list the innumerable words beginning with *quasi,* saying instead that it is used parenthetically, or to introduce an etymological explanation (as in the quotation just below). *quasi* can be prefixed to almost any word, as in the jesting suggestion of the "longest" English word, *quasi-antidisestablishmentarianistically. OED* does give 20 quotations, however, one of which is from *Love's Labor's Lost,* iv, 2:

Jaquenetta: God give you good morrow, Master Person.
Holofernes: Master person, quasi pers one. And if one should be pierced, which is the one?

(*Person* was then pronounced—and 10 lines later is spelled—*parson.*) *as if* (Gm *als ob*) has been advanced, first by Hans Vaihinger in 1911, as the fundamental and essential qualification of our view of "reality." What each of us calls the world is his or her personal *quasi universe.*

Out on the far edges of visible space, astronomers have detected *quasi-stellar objects,* abbreviated *QSO;* sometimes called *quasi-stellar radio sources,* shortened by astronomer Hong-yee Chiu to *quasars.*

When Rufus Choate wrote on 9 Aug. 1856 of "the glittering and sounding generalities . . . which make up the Declaration of Independence," Emerson exclaimed: "Glittering generalities! They are blazing ubiquities."

kurmi: (from a) worm. *kermes,* whence *carmine* and *crimson.* Gc, *worm. OED* devotes 12 columns to *worm* and over 6 columns to its compounds, from *wormatic* to *wormy. worm-eater.* J. Beaumont, in *Psyche* (1648), makes a mock title:

Vain son of dust, pull down thy foolish crest,
And in this glass thy feeble Wormship see.

Shakespeare makes frequent use of the worm—in Sonnet 71, and 44 times in the plays—as man's ultimate destiny. The disguised Rosalind in *As You Like It,* iv, 1, laughs at the lovelorn Orlando: "Men have died from time to time, and worms have eaten them, but not for love." The disguised Viola turns the figure in *Twelfth Night,* ii, 4, picturing her own forced restraint to the unsuspecting Duke:

She never told her love,
But let concealment, like a worm i' the bud,
Feed on her damask cheek . . .

Hamlet ruminated (iv, 3) on the skull of Yorick: "A man may fish with the worm that hath eat of a king, and eat of the fish that hath fed of that worm." And Romeo, believing her dead, looks on the unconscious Juliet in the tomb:

Beauty's ensign yet
Is crimson in thy lips and in thy cheeks . . .
With worms that are thy chambermaids. Oh, here
Will I set up my everlasting rest,
And shake the yoke of inauspicious stars
From this world-wearied flesh.

kus: kiss. Imitative. English has grown limited. The olden *osculate* takes longer to pronounce than to perform, although *OED* lists 14 words from its stem, L *osculus,* diminutive of *os:* mouth–including *osculum pacis:* the kiss of peace. The hearty *buss,* earlier *bass,* has inexplicably gone out of favor (save as a teen-agers' game, *blunderbus:* to kiss the wrong party; *omnibus:* to kiss all the girls in the room, etc.). The word echoed along the years from the Roman Catullus (60 B.C.), *Da me basia mille:* Give me a thousand kisses [and then begin again]. One echo is Ben Jonson's *Song to Celia,* which begins:

Kiss me sweet. First give a hundred . . .
Add a thousand, and so more
Till you equal with the store
All the grass that Romney yields,
Or the sands in Chelsea's fields,
Or the drops in silver Thames,
Or the stars that gild his streams.

Herrick, in *Hesperides* (1648), makes this distinction:

Kissing and bussing differ both in this,
We buss our wantons, but our wives we kiss.

Tennyson (1847) praised a man who "nor burnt the grange, nor bussed the milking-maid." Browning (1879) viewed a more sentimental moment: "So blubbered we, and bussed, and went to bed."

The early E *bebass* was defined as "to kiss all over." A *smack,* also imitative, is a slang substitute, but more often than an oscular conjunction it means a quick junction of hand and cheek. Also *kissable. kissing-kin,* or *kissing-cousin;* see *kuetuer.* Quaintly, Bulwer Lytton wrote in his best novel, *Pelham* (1828): "This Hebe, Mr. Gordon greeted with a loving kiss, which the kissee resented."

kiss-off is slang for an abrupt dismissal. A *Judas kiss,* by which Judas revealed Jesus to the executioners, now means a fond greeting as a prelude to dismissal or or other injury. The *kiss of death* has recently been countered by the *kiss of life:* lip-to-lip attempt at resuscitation. Jonathan Swift defined bachelor's fare as "bread and cheese, and kisses." Oscar Wilde, in *The Ballad of Reading Gaol* (1898), was more solemn:

And each man kills the thing he loves,
By each let this be heard . . .
The coward does it with a kiss,
The brave man with a sword!

In *As You Like It* the disguised Rosalind gives advice to her avowed lover, Orlando: "Very good orators, when they are out, they will spit; and for lovers lacking–God warn us!–matter, the cleanliest shift is to kiss."

lab: lick, lap up. Imitative. L *lambentem:* licking. *lambent.* OFr *Lampons!:* Let's lap it up!, cry of medieval students on the way to a tavern; transferred to what they said or wrote when their tongues were loosed by drink; hence, E *lampoon.* (*In vino veritas:* Truth is in the wine.) Gm *Löffel:* spoon. Gc *lap* (verb; for the human *lap* see *leb*).

labh, rabh: take, seize. Gk *lambanein. laphuron:* seized, prey. *astrolabe:* star-taking. *analeptic* (*ana:* away). *catalepsy, epilepsy, narcolepsy. nympholepsy* (see *sneudh*). *prolepsis. syllable:* (letters) taken together. *monosyllabic, dodecasyllable,* etc. *lemma, analemma. dilemma,* with two horns to impale the reasoner.

L *rabere, rapere, raptum; rapidum:* seizing, carrying away. (By some, these are assigned to the root *rep II.*) *rabid, rabies. rage, enraged. rap, rape, rapine; ravish; ravishing; enravish. rap(ta)torial. Raptores:* order of birds of prey; seizers. *rap:* a slight blow (*tap, tip,* and *tit for tat* are imitative). *rave, ravenous.* The bird *raven* is partly imitative of its sound, OE *hraefn* (see *ker IV*). *ravin, ravine:* plunder. *rapacious, rapacity. harpy. rapt, rapture, enrapt, enraptured. rapid, rapidity. correption. erepsin,* coined by J. F. Cohnheim in 1884 by analogy with *pepsin. obreption, subreption; obreptitious, surreptitious. usurp. assart:* to take away trees, make forest land arable; also land thus cleared.

Fielding, in *Jonathan Wild* (1743), iii, makes a neat distinction: "He in a few minutes ravished the fair creature, or would have ravished her, if she had not, by a timely compliance, prevented him."

ladh: hidden; forgotten. Gk, *Lethe:* river of Hades; drinking of it brought forgetfulness; thus the dead put aside life's concerns. *lethargy.*

The Greeks linked remembering and truth; *Alethia:* truth (*a* negative) was a handmaiden of Apollo, god of wisdom. *alethiology* is the branch of logic that deals with truth. Gk, *Alastor:* unforgetting, was one of the names of Zeus. The poem *Alastor, or the Spirit of Solitude* (1816) was Shelley's first important work.

Gk *lanthanein,* L *latere:* lie hidden. *latent. delitescent.* The oxide *lanthana* was so named in 1839 because hidden in erbia; thence *lanthanum* (see *el 57*). *lethal:* deadly, its form influenced by *Lethe,* was L *letalis,* from *letum:* death; see *ol.*

?laed: wound. L *laedere, lesum. lesion. collide, collision; elide, elision.*

laiuo: leftward. L *laevum. l(a)evorotatory. levulose;* opposed to *dextrose.*

laks: salmon. *lax,* early English, was lost after the 17th c., but was revived in the late 19th via Scandinavian or Yiddish; Gm *Lachs.* Also *lox,* usually with bagel; see *bheug II. laspring,* folkchanged from *laxpink:* young salmon. *lox,* an explosive rocket propellant, is from the initial letters of *l*iquid *ox*ygen, used since 1923; it is also a verb.

laku: pool of water. L *lacus, lacuna:* pond. *lake. lagoon. lacunose, lacustrine. lacuna:* a gap.

Wordsworth, in *The Prelude,* iv, noted a clouded sky:

That uncertain heaven, received
Into the bosom of the steady lake.

lal. Imitative. Gk, *Lalage; Eulalie. echolalia, glossolalia. paralalia; mogilalia* (Gk *mogis:* with pain). L, *lallation. lament, lamentation,* etc. *Larus:* genus of gulls.

Gc, *loll; lull. lullaby,* its ending from babytalk, *by, by,* putting the tot to sleep.

Bye, baby bunting. Lollard, especially Wycliffe's "prayer mumblers." *lollop, lolly, lollipop: lollapalooza.*

lolpoop, 17th into 19th c.: one sluggish in the stern. A person forgetting or neglecting the words may sing a tune *la la la.*

Horace, in the Twenty-second Ode, averred:

Still shall I love Lalage,
Sweetly laughing, sweetly prattling.

Coleridge, in *Names,* was less—and more—specific:

Choose thou whatever fits the line;
Call me Sappho, call me Chloris,
Call me Lalage or Doris;
Only, only call me thine.

Poe, a lover of sound, was won by the other name:

My soul was a stagnant tide
Till the fair and gentle Eulalie became my blushing bride—
Till the yellow-haired young Eulalie became my smiling bride.

Nicholas Breton, in *Lullaby* (1592), had his heart elsewhere:

Sing lullaby and lap it warm,
Poor soul that thinks no creature harm.

It is not only infants that one may wish to have sleeping. Thomas Randolph, in his play *The Jealous Lovers* (1632), wrote "A Charm," which King Charles II is said to have sung to one of his mistresses, having set a rendezvous with a new one:

Quiet sleep, or I will make
Erinnys whip thee with a snake,
And cruel Rhadamanthus take
Thy body to the boiling lake
Where fire and brimstone never slake.
Thy heart shall burn, thy head shall ache,
And every joint about thee quake.

Quiet sleep, or thou shalt see
The horrid hags of Tartary,
Whose tresses ugly serpents be;
And Cerberus shall bark at thee;
And all the Furies, that are three—
The worst is called Tisiphone—
Shall lash thee to eternity.
And therefore sleep thou peacefully.

Presumably the king was thereby freed to attend to his other concerns.

?**laos**: of the people. Gk *laos. lay.* A *lay analyst* is one without a professional degree. *laity, laic,* opposed to *clergy, clerical.* See *kel VIII. liturgy.* OE *laewed. lewd:* of the people, hence, ignorant; hence, delighting in coarse pleasure; so the meanings changed.

Names, as *Laertes:* gatherer of the people; *Laocoon:* guardian of . . . ; *Menelaus:* resisting . . . ; *Nicholas:* victorious among the people. Gk *Nike:* goddess of victory; the famous statue *Nike Apteros:* Wingless Victory, was kept thus in Athens so that she could not fly away! *St. Nicholas,* of course, is Santa Claus.

The abbot hath donn'd his mitre and ring,
His rich dalmatic and maniple fine;
And the choristers sing, as the lay-brothers bring
To the board a magnificent turkey and chine.
—R. H. Barham, *The Ingoldsby Legend* (1840)

lap: shine. *lamp.* OFr, *lantern.* preserving the Etruscan diminutive suffix *na,* which is also on E *person.* Gk *Persephone,* goddess of the underworld, is via Etruscan *persona:* mask; first, as worn by the god conducting the dead to Hades. Hence also *parson,* doublet of *person; parsonage; personage, personality, personification, personnel,* etc. *impersonate.*

eclampsis. Nasalized, Gk *lampuris:* glowworm. *Lampyridae:* family of luminous insects. *lampyrine. Lampsilis:* genus of mussels. *lampadedromy:* torch relay race, especially one in honor of Prometheus, who brought fire for man's use. *lampadephore. lampro-,* as *lamprophony, lamprotype.*

Early English lanterns, made of horn, were often folknamed *lanthorns. dark lantern, magic lantern, Chinese lantern* (of paper), and more; and many compounds, as the phosphorescent *lantern fish,* the translucent *lanternshell. lantern jaw.* A *lanternman,* 16th into the 18th c., was a man who emptied privies by *lanternlight;* Nashe, in *Lenten Stuffe* (1599), said: "We will make him tell what manner of lanternman or groom of Hecate's close-stool he is." Such a collector was also dubbed a *goldfinder;* see *kel VI.*

?lapid: stone. L *lapis, lapidem. lapidary. lapilli, lapidify,* same as (from Gk) *petrify. lapidate,* as when a condemned man, or a convicted adulteress, was thrown into a well, which was then filled with stones. *lapis lazuli;* the second word is Arabic, whence also *azure.*

lapidable: deserving to be stoned; oddly defined in a dictionary of 1706, which some later ones copied, as "marriageable, fit for a husband"—probably using the wrong lap. Possibly *leper,* from the stony scales; see *lep I.*

Johnson, in Boswell's *Life of Samuel Johnson* (1775), noted that "in lapidary inscriptions a man is not upon oath," implying the kindly counsel *De mortuis nil nisi bonum:* Of the dead [say] nothing unless good.

las: eager; wanton. L, *lascivus. lascivious. Lares and Penates:* Roman gods of the household; *lar* (plural, *lares*): of the courtyard and structure; *penates:* of the interior and the contents, whence also E *penetrate, impenetrable,* etc.

larva. Lariidae: family of beetles. Gc, *list:* desire. *lust.* Gm *Wanderlust. Die Lustige Witwe:* the merry widow.

Over his keys the musing organist,
Beginning doubtfully and far away,
First lets his fingers wander as they list,
And builds a bridge from Dreamland for his lay.
—Lowell, *The Vision of Sir Launfal* (1848)

lat: moist. Gk *latax:* drop of wine. L *latex, laticem. latex. laticiform.*

lau: booty; gain. Skr, *loot,* but see *leup.* Gk, *apolaustic.* L *lucrum. lucrative, lucre.* OIr, *galore.*

Gc, *guerdon,* via *widarlon:* return gift; blent with L *donum:* gift. (The beginning is a *w.g* alternation, as in ward-guard, warranty-guarantee, etc. Probably a coughlike *khw* was made soft in Gc *w* and crisp in Rom *g.*)

Milton, in *Lycidas* (1637), substitutes *Fury* for *Fate* as he ponders the fortune of man:

Fame is the spur that the clear spirit doth raise
(That last infirmity of noble mind)
To scorn delights, and live laborious days;
But the fair guerdon when we hope to find,
And think to burst out into sudden blaze,
Comes the blind Fury with th' abhorred shears
And slits the thin-spun life.

leb, (s)lab: loose, hanging (as the lip), etc. Gk *lobos;* E *lobe.* L *labi, lapsum:* lapse; *labium, labrum:* lip; *lapsum:* slip, begin to fall; totter under a burden; strive. *labor, laborem:* distress, hardship, work. *laborare, laboratum:* take pains. E *labial, labiate, labium, labellum. labile, labret. lapse, collapse, elapse, prolapse, relapse. supralabial. supralapsarian:* one who believes that God destined some to be damned, and some to be saved, before and regardless of the Fall of man; *sublapsarian:* one who believes that the Fall was predetermined; *infralapsarian:* one who believes that the Fall was permitted by God.

labio-, as *labiodental. lava, lapsus calami,* etc.; see *kolem.* Also *labor, laboratory; belabor; collaborate, elaborate.*

Gc (some partly imitative), *slab; slaver, slobber, slop, slup, slur. sleep:* slacken, as the mouth often does in snoring slumber. *slip, slide, slim. slum, slumgullion, slummock, slump. label. lap, lapel, lappet. lip; OED* gives 5 columns to *lip,* whence also *liplabor, lipless, lip-read, lipstick.* Perhaps *labarum. limp, lump, lumpfish.* From *lump, lunch* (as *hump, hunch*).

slum has recently been euphemized into *ghetto* by those interested in displacing blame. A slum is created by its inhabitants; a ghetto is imposed by those outside. *ghetto* is perhaps from It *borghetto:* small town (see *bheregh*); some suggest it is from Venetian *getto:* foundry, as in Venice, where a Jewish ghetto was established in 1516; though opened by Napoleon in 1797, it still stands, the *Campo del Ghetto Nuovo,* with 10 Jewish families, five synagogues, and a museum of Jewish art.

Perhaps from this root, nasalized, partly imitative, come *slench, sling, slinge, slink; sloven, slur, slurry, slush. slut:* (1) slovenly woman; (2) bitch, as opposed to (male) dog. See *leip I.*

He that in blank verse a sloven can be
Must slur every flight of divine poesy.
—W. H. Ireland, *Scribbleomania* (1815)

Here rests his head upon the lap of earth
A youth to fortune and to fame unknown;
Fair Science frowned not on his humble birth,
And Melancholy marked him for her own.
—Thomas Gray, *Elegy Written in a Country Churchyard* (1751), long the most popular English poem

Oh Sleep! It is a blessed thing,
Beloved from pole to pole.
To Mary Queen the praise be given!
She sent the gentle sleep from heaven
That slid into my soul.
[a felicitous phrase, *that slid into my soul*]
—Coleridge, *The Ancient Mariner* (1798)

leg I: gather, set in order; consider, choose; then read, speak. Gk, *logos, logion. horologe, horology. lexicon.*

In the lexicon of youth which Fate reserves
For a bright manhood, there is no such word
As—fail.
—Bulwer Lytton, *Richelieu,* ii, 2, first performed on 7 Mar. 1839 with William Macready in the title role

Also frequently misquoted, by omitting the qualifying first line, is this statement from the same play:

Beneath the rule of men entirely great
The pen is mightier than the sword.

analects, dialect. alexia, dyslexia. eclectic. prolegomenon. logic, etc. Dunlop's *Encyclopedia of Facts* (1969) lists 362 words ending *(o)logy* (meaning mainly the study of), including *analogy, biology, geology, psychology, sociology, bacteriology, embryology, dermatology, phrenology,* and my *apology* for not giving the rest.

Note *nosology* (Gk *nosos:* disease), and *nostology* (Gk *nostos:* return): the study of senility, "second childhood"; hence also *nostalgia; nostomania. nostalgia de la boue* (Fr *boue:* mud): craving for a life without refinement, with crude ways and coarse pleasures. More recently, in fiction and in life, this had been exceeded by the *mystique de la merde,* taking sustenance from Freud's dictum that "embryologically the anus corresponds to the primitive mouth," with free and frequent use of the once taboo four-letter words. As Tom Lehrer puts it in *Tomfoolery* (1980): "disgusting, in theatrical terms, realistic." See *mer I.*

Gk *to auto:* the same; *tautology. eulogy. logistics. analog(ue); apologue, catalog(ue), decalogue, dialogue. logodaedaly:* skill with words (the ending after *Daedalus,* who made the labyrinth in Crete to hold the Minotaur; see *del II*).

Also *logarithm. paralogical, curiologic. logogriph. logotype:* one or more words cast as a single piece of type; shortened to *logo:* a trademark or other such symbol. *prologue* ("What's past is prologue; let's get on with life's play"); *epilogue. dialectic* (implying logical speech).

logo-, as *logogram, logomachy, logomania, logophobia. logrolling:* exchanging political favors, is suggested as coming from *logos:* word, but is unquestionably influenced by the lumber industry, which sends its *logs,* separately or bound in great rafts, down streams, and the *loggers* have to collaborate to prevent or break up *logjams.* The loggers developed a game, *birling* (imitative, as *birr, whir, whirl*), in which two stand at opposite ends of a log, rolling it in the water under their feet to see how long they can stay on. Of course, as soon as one falls off, the log dips, and the other is also doused in the stream, which should make politicians ponder; but *logrolling* implies working together.

acrilogy. syllogism: a pattern of considering facts together. *Heptalogia* (*a* negative): seven against sense; title of Swinburne's parodies, including a neat one of his own poetry. On the basis of its use in the Bible, John 1:1–5, *Logos* has been identified by devout Christians as the second member of the Trinity, *Logos* in the Greek Septuagint being translated as *Word:* "In the beginning was the Word, and the Word was with God, and the Word was God. He was in the beginning with God; all things were made with him, and without him was not anything made that was made. In him was life, and the life was the light of man. The light shines in darkness, and the darkness has not overcome it." Creation began when

God spoke the words *Fiat lux:* let there be light! And there was light. (The dispute as to what language God spoke has not been settled.)

(1) In the physical sense, L *ligneus:* of wood gathered for fire, or set in order for building. *lignalose. lignify, lignite. lignivorous. lignum vitae. pyroligneous.* (2) With mental application, L *lex talionis* (*talio:* like): an eye for an eye; *retaliation. elect. election; neglect. coil* is shortened from L *colligere, collectum:* to gather together; whence also *cull, collect; select, selection. lectern. legend:* what should be read (L *legendum*). *legion:* chosen; *levied. lecture; lesson. lexigraphy, lexicography; legible, illegible, privilege, sacrilege, sortilege.*

"I have never heard any of your lectures, but from what I can learn I should say that for people who like the kind of lectures you deliver, they are just the kind of lectures such people like."—Letter of recommendation for himself, humorously attributed to Abraham Lincoln by Artemus Ward, 1863.

Also *intellect, intelligent, unintelligible,* etc. *college, colleague. legate, legation, delegate; relegate. legacy. legislature. legitimate, illegitimate. OED* lists 46 related words beginning *leg.* Triplets via L, Fr, Gc: *legal, loyal, leal.* Similarly, *regal, royal,* obsolete E *real,* but Sp *real,* as in *Camino Real:* King's Road, play by Tennessee Williams (1953); see *reg I. allege* ("I deny the allegation and defy the allegator"). *alligator* is a folkchange from Sp *el legarto (de Indias):* the lizard of the Indies (L *ille:* that; Arab *al:* the; L *lacertus:* lizard). *Land o' the Leal* is an olden term for heaven.

Gc, *leech:* early doctor whose medicament was less potent than his healing words, his holy or magic incantation.

The legs on which our body stands have been related by some to *locust:* the jumper; but this origin has no firm leg on which to stand.

leg II: loosening, drooping, dribbling. Gk, *lagomorph:* with drooping ears. *lago-*, as *lagopous, lagophthalmus. acatalectic. catalectic. lagnos:* of loose morals. *algolagnia* combines sadism and masochism: *sadistic,* from Comte Donation Alphonse François (called Marquis) de *Sade* (1740–1814); *masochistic,* from Leopold von Sacher-*Masoch* (1836–1895). The recent (1959) *ALGOL* is an acrostic of *algo*-rithmic *l*anguage: number language for the computer; it has already developed a "dialect," called *DIALGOL.* Arab *Algol:* the Ghoul, is a variable star in the northern constellation Perseus.

L, *lax, laxative, relax. laches. lacmus, delay. relay:* first, of fresh hounds eager (driveling) for the hunt. Nasalized, *languid, languish, languor. lash. lush:* loose, thence *profuse,* was frequent after Shakespeare's use of it in *The Tempest,* ii, 1: "How lush and lusty the grass looks! How green!" Perhaps also *luscious,* influenced by *delicious;* it is *licious* in a 15th c. manuscript.

The word *lush* for a liquorphile (may I say?), whose lips are loosed by liquor —imbibition shakes off inhibition (as the Porter in *Macbeth* was aware), drink drowns discretion, the tipsy trumpet the truth, and all that—was aided by the notorious "City of Lushington," a convivial club on Russell Street, London, for some 150 years (until 1895). It had a Lord Mayor, who lectured each new member on the evils of overdrinking, and four aldermen, elected to represent its four wards: Juniper (Gin), Poverty, Lunacy, and Suicide—a sort of Hogarthian "Drunkard's Progress"; and it was often said of a drunkard: "He's been voting for the Alderman." The *Comic Almanack* of 1846 called medical students "sons of gin and chaff."

Gc, *lack, leach, leak, leash. release, relish. Lackland,* a surname of King John, from whom at Runnymede on 15 June 1215 the barons of England exacted the Magna Carta. Although *John,* under various national guises—*Johannes, Jon, Juan,*

Ivan, Ian, etc.–is the most frequent first name of men in the Western world, no other English king has been called John. See *bhurig.* Conversely, the English people are denominated *John Bull,* after a 1712 satire by John Arbuthnot in which Nicholas Frog represents the Dutch and Lewis Baboon the French; the character *John Bull* caught the fancy of the English. For a time *Brother Jonathan* was used for *the United States,* some say from George Washington's way of addressing his friend Jonathan Trumbull, governor of Connecticut. *A Dictionary of Americanisms* (1951) reports no evidence for this, but does record that when the British retreated from Bunker Hill in 1776, they dressed hay scarecrows as sentries, leaving each with a sign: "Welcome, Brother Jonathan." By 1813, however, as first recorded in the *Troy Post* on 7 Sept. of that year, *United States* had been extended to *Uncle Sam.* His "adventures" were printed in 1816, and by the time of the War between the States, *Uncle Sam* was common nationwide. His costume was taken from cartoons by Seba Smith (d. 1868), who wrote successful satires as Major Jack Downing and who initiated the homespun political commentary continued especially by James Russell Lowell as Hosea Biglow, David Ross Locke as Petroleum V(esuvius) Nasby, Charles Farrar Browne as Artemus Ward, Finley Peter Dunne as Mr. Dooley, and William Rogers as Will Rogers. Abraham Lincoln read the latest Nasby letter to his cabinet before reading them the Emancipation Proclamation.

The New Century Handbook of English Literature (1967) has 44 entries beginning *John,* and lists 51 literary characters with the forename *John.* See *bhurig.* Even so, it overlooks Chesterton's triumphant *Lepanto,* which ends:

> Cervantes in his galley sets the sword back in the sheath,
> (Don John of Austria rides homeward with a wreath.)
> And he smiles, but not as Sultans smile, and settles back the blade . . .
> (But Don John of Austria rides home from the Crusade.)

The Battle of Lepanto, 7 Oct. 1571, brought a heavy naval defeat to the Turks, but lost its effectiveness because of continuing rivalry between the Spaniards and the Venetians. It was financed by the very devout Pope St. Pius V, who in 1570 had anathematized Queen Elizabeth of England; he was the last pope to be denominated a saint.

John is via Gk and L from the Hebr *Yohanan:* the Lord is gracious. Hypocoristic for *John* is *Jack,* although via Fr *Jacques* (pronounced *Zhack,* but by the Elizabethans, *Jakes*) and E *James* (LL *Jacomus,* a variant of *Jacobus*) it may also be traced to Hebr, *Jacob:* he that takes by the heel (wrestles with the Angel; hence also called *Israel:* he that strives with God; and from Jacob's twelve sons came the twelve tribes of Israel. Note that like all spirits since, the angel had to disappear before cockcrow.)

Jack is a widely used term, as Fr *Jacques:* a peasant ("every man Jack of them"), and in various compounds, as *jackanapes* (?*Jack o'Naples:* a rascal, a mountebank); also the tool *jack,* etc. The game *jacks* is short for *jackstones,* earlier *chackstones* (chuck or toss stones). *Jacqueline* is a feminine diminutive of *Jacques.* Every Jack shall have his Jill. John Barleycorn is the personification of (malt) liquor.

lack-Latin was, from the 15th into the 18th c., a term for an ignorant priest. *lackadaisical* was coined by Laurence Sterne, who in *A Sentimental Journey* (1768), pictures himself "sitting in my black coat, and in my lackadaysical manner counting the throbs" (of my pulse). *Alackaday!*

legh: lie, lay, See *phol.* Gk *lokhos:* ambush, lie in wait; hence *lokhein:* childbirth.

lochia. Aristolochia: literally, best for birth, genus of birthwort. *Gelechiidae, Gelechia:* family and genus of moths that "lie in the earth"; see *ge.* L, *less. litter* (to lie on). *wagon-lit.*

Gc, *lie, lay, layer, allay, belay, relay, underlay. beleaguer. laager. stalag,* short for Gm *Stammlager:* base camp, lying-ground. *lager:* beer laid aside for up to six months, for fermentation. *anlage, forlage. lagan,* in Davy Jones's locker (see *ie*). *lair. low. rely* (earlier *relie*), its ending like that of many verbs, as *apply, supply.*

Norse, *law;* the law is "laid down"; a statute "stands up" (see *sta*). *lawless, unlawful,* etc. *Danelaw. by(e)law* (OE *bye:* village). *outlaw. fellow* came via Norse *felag:* the laying down of money (*fe:* cattle, used for barter); hence, companion. *coverlet* came via OFr, *couvre-lit:* bedcover. (Note that *let* is usually a diminutive suffix; JWalker lists 109 such, as *brooklet, cutlet, driblet, fillet, islet, jokelet, pellet, pullet.*)

Byron added this note to a stanza in *Don Juan,* i: "I doubt if *Laureate* and *Iscariot* be good rhymes, but must say, as Ben Jonson did to Sylvester, who challenged him to rhyme with

> I, John Sylvester,
> Lay with your sister.

Jonson answered: "I, Ben Jonson, lay with your wife." When Sylvester exclaimed: "That is not rhyme!" Ben Jonson retorted: "No, but it is true." "Reason is the life of the law"—Sir Edward Coke (d. 1634). "All's love, yet all's law"—Browning, *Saul* (1845).

leguh: slight, light, hence rising. (For *light:* brightness, see *leuk.*) L *levis:* lightweight; *levare:* lighten; lift up, relieve; *levitas, levitatem:* lightness. E *levee;* when the king, or the water, rises. *levator:* lifting muscle. *leaven, lever, levigate; levy; levity. levitate* was formed by analogy with its opposite, *gravitate. Levana* was the Roman goddess of childbirth, lifting the neonate to its mother's arms. *Levant:* region of the rising sun. *carnival:* rising from meat at Shrovetide (see *ker III; sek IX*).

Also *alevin. alleviate; relieve; relevant. elevate, elevator. cantilever. lungs;* earlier, *lights* (from their light weight), still applied to the lungs of animals used for food. Fr, *legerdemain:* sl(e)ight of hand. *champlevé; relevé. pontlevis. bas-relief.* It, *relievo, alto-relievo, basso-relievo, cavo-relievo, mezzo-relievo.* Ir, *leprechaun,* the light sprite with always one shilling in his purse.

Gc, *light(weight); lightsome. OED* has 42 words relating to this *light,* among them *lightfoot,* like Spenser's *lightfoot nymphs* in *The Shepheardes Calender* (1579), June, that "chace the lingring night"; *lighter:* a ship for unloading vessels too heavy to dock; *light-fingered:* dexterous at pilfering; *light-hearted, light-headed; lightly. light-o'-love;* also *light-skirts;* Bishop Hall, in his *Satires* (1597), speaks of the biblical *Song of Songs:*

> Solomon . . .
> Singing his love, the holy spouse of Christ,
> Like as she were some light-skirts of the East.

Shakespeare, in *Much Ado About Nothing,* v, 4, calls: "Let's have a dance . . . that we may lighten our own hearts, and our wives' heels." Stevenson makes a good point in *The Wrong Box* (1889): "Nothing like a little judicious levity!"

lei I: smooth; slimy, slippery. Skr, *pralaya:* in Hindu Philosophy, end of the world; the world slips away. Gk *litos;* plain, smooth. *litotes:* praise by denial: "not so bad!" *alinein:* besmear, anoint; L *linere:* daub, smear. *liniment; illinition. lair:* mud. *loam, lime,* as in *birdlime:* the sticky ooze of the holly bark, spread on branches to catch small birds. *lime-fingered:* given to pilfering; e.g. a *kleptomaniac,* for whom things just stick to the fingers. Bishop Hall in 1624 berated "careless, slothful, false, lime-fingered servants." They persist.

Gk *leios:* smooth. Prefix *leio,* as *leiodere, leiophyllous, leiotrichous.* Huxley mentions the grouping of men by type of hair: *leiotrichi:* smooth; *cymotrichi:* wavy; *ulotrichi:* woolly (see *dhrigh; uel III*). Gk *limne:* muddy place, marsh, pond. *limno-,* as *limnograph, limnology, limnophilous.* Hence L *limus:* slime; *limax:* snail. "The snail leaves a silvery trace, yet it is slime."

Various plants and animals that frequent lakes or muddy places, as *Limicolae:* literally, mud-dwellers (birds); *Limnanthaceae:* marsh-flower family; *limonium:* sea lavender; *Limnetis:* genus of crustaceans; *Limax:* genus of slugs; *Limnaea:* genus of snails; *Limnobium:* genus of frogbit plant; *Limosella:* genus of figwort (mudweed). *limaceous, limacine. limicoline.*

delete first meant to smear out the impression on wax tablets. *lientery:* slimy flow. L *oblivisci:* slip away, out of the mind. *oblivion, oblivious; obliviscible,* a too-forgotten word. Fr, *oubliette:* dungeon entered only by ceiling trap door; place to have one lie forgotten.

Gc, *slack, slick, slide, slight, slime. slowworm. slippery, slip* (also the undergarment a woman can slip off); and *slipper.* See *sleubh. slipslop,* the *slop* a variant from *cowslip,* originally cows' droppings, very slippery when fresh. *sloppy.* Note Fr *salop(e), salopard(e),* the *e* feminine, for a slut; *saloperie:* filthiness, botched work. The *sl* sound is perhaps partly imitative, as in *slippery, slime, slide.*

slipslop: blunder in the use of words, (*OED*) "esp. the ludicrous misuse of one word for another," is from Mrs. Slipslop, the amorous attendant of Lady Booby in Fielding's *Joseph Andrews* (1742), which was begun as a burlesque of Richardson's *Pamela* (Andrews). *OED* illustrates with a man who, in 1826, "among other slipslops," instead of *pasticcios* said *pistachios.* For synonyms of *slipslop,* see *melo.*

oxlip. primrose; see *per VI a.* In England the primrose was from earliest days a source of great delight and the subject of many references in literature, such as "the primrose-breath of May." There is even a flower called *primrose peerless* (the two-flowered narcissus). The primrose is used in heraldry, and even in cookery, as a 1430 recipe tells us: "Take other half-pound of Flowre of rys, iii pound of almandys, half an unce of hony and safroune, and take the Flowre of the prymrose, and grynd hem, and temper hem up with mylke of the almaundys . . ." Wordsworth in 1798 pictured the unimaginative, unresponsive Peter Bell:

> A primrose by the river's brim
> A yellow primrose was to him
> And it was nothing more.

primrose was earlier *prime rose,* first flower of spring, as stated in *The Two Noble Kinsmen* (1612):

> Primrose, firstborn child of Ver,
> Merry Springtime's harbinger.

And in *Hamlet,* Ophelia, responding to her brother's counsel, uses the flower to symbolize the beauty of temptation's lure:

> But, good my brother,
> Do not, as some ungracious pastors do,
> Show me the steep and thorny way to Heaven
> Whilst, like a puffed and reckless libertine,

Himself the primrose path of dalliance treads
And recks not his own rede.

The *primrose path* has been taken so often that it is listed in Eric Partridge's *Dictionary of Clichés* (1940, 1963)—with little effect upon those that tread it.

John of Salisbury (d. 1180) wrote in Latin, beautifully translated by Helen Waddell: "The brevity of our life, the dullness of our senses, the torpor of our indifference, the futility of our occupation, suffer us to know but little; and that little is soon shaken and then torn from the mind by that traitor to learning, that hostile and faithless stepmother to memory, oblivion."

lei II: to get; paid service, also church service, "paid to the gods." See *ken II*. Gk *latreia*. The suffix *latry*, as *idolatry, bibliolatry;* JWalker lists 23 such words. *latrine* is a shortening of L *lavatrina:* lavatory. L *latrocinium:* hiring of a mercenary, came naturally to apply to a robber; hence E *larceny*.

Gk *doulos:* slave, whence *dulocracy. dulosis:* slavery (as among some ants). *dulia:* veneration paid to saints and angels; *hyperdulia* is for the Virgin Mary; *latria* is reserved for the Lord.

leib: pour. L *libare, libatum:* pour out. *libation*. Probably *litus, litoris:* seashore, where the waters pour in. *littoral. Lithuania:* shoreland. It *libeccio:* the south wind, which brings rain from the Mediterranean.

leid I: slacken, yield, leave behind. L *lassus:* weary. *alas. lassitude*—as the nonagenarian viewed the pretty maiden:

A lass! Alas! A lassitude
Seeps through my weary veins tonight . . .

L *lenis:* soft. *lenient, lenitude, lenity* (see *lento*); LL *liticus:* of a serf. *liege*. Gc, *late, latter; latest, last. let, inlet, outlet; leat. let* has come to mean its own opposite: (1) yield, hence allow; (2) sluggish, hence delaying, hindering, as in the legal phrase *without let or hindrance,* or a *let ball* in tennis (often miscalled a *net ball,* which goes into the net; a let ball touches the net but goes over and into the proper court).

leid II: play. L *ludere, lusum. ludicrous. ludo. allude,* etc. *collusion, delusion, illusion. prelude, interlude, postlude, prolusion.*

What stately vision mocks my waking sense?
Hence, dear delusion, sweet enchantment, hence!
—James and Horace Smith, *Rejected Addresses,* 3

When Sheridan's Drury Lane Theatre burned down, he stood watching, drinking wine, and explained: "A man may surely be allowed to take a glass of wine by his own fireside." When the theatre was rebuilt, the committee advertised for an opening-night address. None was deemed suitable, and Byron was invited to write one. The Smith brothers took the opportunity to write *Rejected Addresses,* parodies of current writers, including Wordsworth, Coleridge, Byron, Southey, and Scott. Published in 1812, it ran through 15 editions in two years.

leig I: body, form, shape. OE *lik; lick, lych, lichgate,* through which the corpse is borne into the graveyard. *barley* (OE *bere*) is actually *be*re-*li*ke, the longer term replacing the simple one. A *barn* was first a *barley-house. frolic* (Du *oro:* gay): joylike. Similarly, OE *gelic:* alike; *likeness, likewise; unlikely,* etc. *ilk,* now only in the phrase *of that ilk. like* by intension came to mean fitting, suitable, hence pleasing; thus *to like, likeable, likely.* The suffix *like,* as in *childlike* is still live, as *neutronlike, Nixon-like. each, such, which,* are shortened, respectively, from OE *a gelic:* ever alike; Gothic *swaleiks:* so formed; OE *hwilich:* of what form. From the 16th into the 19th c., *gleek* meant holding three like cards; hence, any three of a kind, as (1714) "Paris with his gleek of wagtails on Mt. Ida" starting the Trojan War.

The very common adverbial suffix *ly,* as in *quickly, uproariously,* is from OE *lik:* like; see *dheigh N 1.*

"Music!" she said drowsily, and such is the force of habit that "I don't," she added, "know anything about music, really. But I know what I like"—Max Beerbohm, *Zuleika Dobson,* 16.

leig II: bind. L *ligare, ligatum. ligament, ligate, ligature, alligation; colligate. oblige, obligation, obligatory. alloy* (bound together); *ally. rally, rely. league,* as *League of Nations*—More effective years to its successor!

lictor. lien. coreligionist; religiosity. etc. *religion:* binding one to God; though Cicero declared it was derived from the root *leg:* thought through again. Fr *lier. liable; liaison.* Shakespeare, in *Richard II,* v, 1:

> I am sworn brother, sweet,
> To grim Necessity, and he and I
> Will keep a league till death.

leigh: lick. Gk *leikhein:* lick up. *electuary. lichen:* licker; *OED* lists 24 related words. *lecher:* literally, licker. Note the Fr anticlerical *prêcheur, lécheur:* preacher, lecher. L *lingere, linctum. linctus. cunnilingus;* see *gn.* A diminutive variant of L *lingua:* tongue, is *ligula:* spoon, strap. *OED* lists 4 such words, as *ligule;* also 5 botanical terms, as *liguliflorate.* Picturing the tongue as the licking organ changed OL *dingua* to *lingua,* whence *lingual, linguistics,* and other words relating to one's mother tongue. See *dinghu.* Via Fr *langue:* tongue, came *language; languet.* Gc *lick, lickerish:* lecherous. *OED* gives over four columns to *lick,* and more than three to its compounds, including *lickpenny, lickpot* (: the first finger), *lickspittle.*

> 'Tis an ill cook that cannot lick his own fingers.
> —*Romeo and Juliet,* iv, 2

leiku: leave, run off, flow away. Gk *ekhleipsis:* leaving out. *eclipse. ecliptic:* annual "path" of the sun, along which eclipses occur. *elleipsis:* falling short. *ellipse, ellipsis, elliptical.*

L *linquere, liqui. liquate, liquefy, liquid, liquor; liquefacient, liquescent; liquidate. deliquescent. delinquent. in flagrante delicto.* See *bhel I. relic, relict, relinquish. Liquidambar:* genus of gum trees. *prolixus:* poured forth. *prolix. lixiviate.*

Gc, *lend, loan. eleven, twelve:* one left, two left, after counting the ten fingers.

leip I: anoint (with grease); adhere; hence remain, continue, live. Gk *aleiphein:* anoint; *lipos:* fat. *aliphetic. aliptes:* anointer, masseur in ancient wrestling school. *liparocele, liparoid, lipase, lipic, lipid, lipoid, lipolysis, lipoma, lipomatosis. OED* lists 9 words beginning *lipo,* as *lipocardiac, lipogenesis, lipoprotein. Liparis:* genus of plants, the twayblade. L *adipum* (Umbrian change of *l* to *d*): animal fat; LL *adiposum. adipose, adipocere.*

Gc, *life, lively; live. liver,* long believed to be the source of blood, hence of life. For *stiff upper lip,* see *leb.*

Emerson, in his essay "Experience" (1842), states "I know a witty physician who . . . used to affirm that if there was a disease in the liver, the man became a Calvinist, and if that organ was sound, he became a Unitarian." The witty doctor's range of patients included only WASPs: *w*hite *A*nglo-*S*axon *P*rotestant*s*—although he did not know this appellation, which is a recent acronym of envious belittling.

Henry James, in *The Madonna of the Future* (1879), cynically sums up our existence: "Cats and monkeys, monkeys and cats—all human life is there."

leip II: leave, leave out; lack, be wanting. Gk *leipein,* in English compounds softened to *lip-*. This developed a number of technical terms. *lipothymia:* wanting spirit; hence swooning. Robert Boyle (of Boyle's law), in a letter of 9 Mar. 1666, suggested that women might be "freed from lipothymias by being pinched, or having cold water thrown in their faces." *lipomorph,* or *lipotype:* a form not native to a region, as cats are lipomorphs of Australia; snakes, of Ireland. See *sneg. lipoxenous, lipoxeny:* of a parasite that after a time leaves its host. *liph(a)emia. lipostomous:* lacking a mouth.

Of letters, *lipogram, lipogrammatic, lipography* (see also *haplography,* under *plek*). Triphiodorus, in the 4th c. A.D., wrote a lipogrammatic *Odyssey,* the 24 books of which, in order, omitted one of the 24 letters of the Greek alphabet, alpha to omega. In the 15th c. a Persian poetaster took some verses to the great poet Jami, saying with pride: "I've omitted the letter alif." After reading the work Jami soberly said: "It would be better if you also omitted the other letters." In the 17th c. Lope de Vega, apostolic prothonotary and founder of the Spanish national drama, wrote five novels, each omitting one of the five vowels. Addison, in *The Spectator,* no. 62 (1711), listed as types of false wit "anagrams, chronograms, lipograms, and acrostics." They persist. Today, on the lawn of an English country church, stands a sign:

CH . . CH
What's missing?
[U R thus invited to attend.]

The following quatrain uses every letter of the English alphabet except the most common, *e:*

A jovial swain should not complain
Of any buxom fair
Who mocks his pain but thinks it gain
To quiz his awkward air.

leis: track, footprint, furrow. L *lira. delirious:* out of the furrow. *lirella.* OE *leornian:* follow the track. *lore. learn, learning, unlearned.* Gc, (the shoemaker's) *last,* measured by the footprint. From tracking an animal, *to last* came to mean to go on, to endure. (For *last* and *latest,* superlatives of *late,* see *leid I.*)

A little learning is a dangerous thing;
Drink deep, or taste not the Pierian spring;
There shallow draughts intoxicate the brain,
And drinking largely sobers us again.
—Pope, *Essay on Criticism*

All that is, at all,
Lasts ever, past recall,
Earth changes, but thy soul and God stand sure.
—Browning, *Rabbi Ben Ezra*

leit: detest. Gc, *loath, loth, loathe, loathsome.* Fr *laid:* ugly. Gm *Leid:* sorrow.

King James I of Britain, in *A Counterblast to Tobacco* (1604), called smoking "a custom loathsome to the eye, hateful to the nose, harmful to the brain, dangerous to the lungs, and in the black stinking fume thereof, nearest resembling the horrible Stygian smoke of the pit that is bottomless." The word *tobacco* comes from Caribbean Indian (Taino) *tabaco,* aided by the West Indian island *Tobago,* shaped like the Indian pipe of peace. *tobacconist. tabatière:* snuffbox. The practice of sniffing snuff is largely out of fashion, although snuff is still available. The word *snuff* is imitative, as are *sniff, sniffle, snivel, snuffle.* Thackeray in 1846 speaks of "a dreamy, hazy, lazy, tobaccofied life." Incidentally, King James's blast was no more effectual than the current U.S. Surgeon General's warning.

leith: go forth; way, course. Gc *lead. load:* first, journey, hence things taken along. *lode. lodestar* (leads the voyager). *lodestone. livelihood* is folkchanged from *livelode:* way of life. *leitmotif* is a hybrid; it begins German and ends French, and is used in English.

> He that forbears
> To suit and serve his need
> Deserves his load.
> —George Herbert, *The Collar* (1633)

leizd: border, strip. Gc, *list:* both an enclosed ground for a tournament, usually in the plural; and a strip on which one makes a list or catalog.

lek I: jump, leap. Gk *lagdon:* a leap and kick; hence, some suggest E *leg;* but see the root *leg I. Lacertilia:* order of reptiles, lizard, chameleon, etc. *polatouche:* flying squirrel. Sp (Arab *al:* the) *alligator.*

lek II: tear. L *lacerare, laceratum:* tear; *lacinare, lacinatum:* tear to pieces. *lacerate. lacinia, lacinula; laciniate, laciniation. OED* defines 10 related words. *lacinious* may be used figuratively, meaning with many windings (cut in); hence *prolix,* as in Urquhart's *Ekskubaluron* (1652): "the sweet labyrinth and mellifluent anfractuosities of a lacinious delectation."

lem: break, cripple. Gc, *lame.* The slang *lam, lambaste,* first meant to lame. *lumber, lumbering:* walking clumsily, was probably influenced by *lumber,* which first, from the main occupation of the *Lombards* in Italy, meant pawnshop, then the junk stored there; then, in the U.S., sawed timber, in the rough. The Lombards derived their name from the *Longobardi:* Long Beards, who invaded Italy in A.D. 568.

lendh I: loin. L *lumbus,* diminutive *lumbulus. umbles* (Fr *lumbles;* the *l* misunderstood as the article *l',* for *le:* the), folkchanged into *humble-pie,* the innards being usually left for the dogs; see *ghdhem.* Also *numbles.*

Gc, *loin.* The idea that *sirloin* was knighted by a king enchanted by the food is folk etymology; the form was *sur:* on, the upper cut of the loin; see *upo.*

lendh II: heath, open ground. Gc, *land. Lambert:* illustrious with land; *Lancelot:* rich with land; *Orlando,* It form of *Roland:* glory of the land. *Landgrave, landloper, landmark, landscape; hinterland.* Fr, *lawn.* Today *lawn* implies human care, as contrasted with *lea:* natural meadow land; see *leuk.*

> To me Art's subject is the human clay,
> And landscape but a background to a torso;
> All Cézanne's apples I would give away
> For one small Goya or a Daumier.
> —W. H. Auden, *Letter to Lord Byron,* iii

lento: gentle; flexible. L *lentus, relent;* see *leid I.* It, *lento, rallentando.* Gc, *lithe. linden:* tree with pliant bast. *Linda,* also short for *Rosalinda:* the gentle dew. *Ethelinda:* gently noble (or noble serpent); Gc *lind, lint:* the lithe animal, i.e. the snake. The serpent, sloughing its skin, thus seemingly renewing itself, was venerated by many primitive peoples; it appears on the caduceus, symbol of the healer, borne by the god Hermes and adopted in 1902 by the medical branch of the U.S. Army.

?**leo**: lion. Homer's *lis* may be borrowed from Hebr *layish:* lion. Gk *leon,* L *leo, leonem. leopard:* the spotted lion; the *pard* perhaps also borrowed from Hebr *barodh:* spotted. *leopardite. leonine. lioncel. lionize.*

Rum, *leu:* coin with lion on it; Bulg, *lev,* same meaning. *pantaloons* is from *St. Pantaleone:* all lion (see *Pan,* under *keu II*). *chameleon:* ground lion. *Leonides:* sons of the lion, clusters of shooting stars from the direction of the constellation *Leo,* fifth sign of the zodiac; see *guei.*

The king of animals was attractive for names. *Leo, Leon. Leonard:* lion-strong. *Leonore:* golden lion; *Leonora, Lenore, Eleanor, Ella.* (*Leopold,* however, means bold for the people; Gc *leuti:* people.) *Leander:* lion-man. The famous Leander swam the Hellespont nightly, from Abydos to Sestos, to visit his beloved Hero; when he drowned in a storm, she plunged after him. Byron was drawn to the swim. Of Don Juan he remarked:

> He could, perhaps, have passed the Hellespont,
> As once (a feat on which ourselves we prided)
> Leander, Mr. Elkenhead, and I did.

Byron swam the Hellespont on 3 May 1810, and in the poem *To Leander,* he pondered:

> But since he crossed the rapid tide,
> According to the doubtful story,
> To woo—and Lord knows what beside,
> And swam for love, as I for glory;
> 'Twere hard to say who fared the best:
> Sad mortals! Thus the gods still plague you!
> He lost his labor, I my jest;
> For he was drowned, and I've the ague.

Leonurus: lion's tail, genus of mothwort. *Leontodon,* a Greek form from Fr, *dandelion:* lion's tooth, from the shape of the leaf. *codling apple* has been connected with *coddle:* to boil lightly, as coddled eggs; but is, rather, folkchanged from Fr *coeur de lion,* perhaps named after the popular English king Richard *Coeur de Lion:* the Lionheart, about whom legends grew while on his return from the Third Crusade he was held in Austria for ransom, 1192–1194.

lep I: peel, cut off; hence scaly; also thin, delicate. Gk *leipein. leper. lepido-,* as in *Lepidoptera:* the order of butterflies and moths, of which there are some 100,000 species (the largest order next to that of the beetles). See *bheid; kel VI.* See also *spider,* under *spend II.* Butterflies are mainly diurnal; moths, mainly nocturnal. The butterfly, alighted, holds its wings spread; the moth closes its wings; see *pal.* The common English butterfly is the color of butter; whence its name. The word *moth* is related to *maggot,* a diminutive of *Mag,* as also in *magpie; Mag* is a shortening of *Margaret;* see *elaia.* The monarch butterfly is the only one that, like many birds, undertakes an annual two-way migration. A young, enthusiastic *lepidopterist* was quite disappointed when he began to read a volume entitled *What Every Young Mother should Know.*

Also *lepto-,* as in *leptodactyl, leptothrix. laparectomy, laparotomy. lepton:* small coin. *Lepidium:* genus of pepperworts. *Lepas:* genus of geese, the barnacle. Stones were early used for chipping or cutting; hence *lapidary.* A similar association developed in L *saxum:* stone, *secare:* cut, and *rupes:* rock, *rumpere, ruptum:* break; whence *rupture.*

How like a moth the simple maid
Still plays about the flame!
—John Gay, *The Beggar's Opera* (1728), i, 4

(So many dead moths lay around oil lamps that "the moth and the flame" became a symbol for overpowering but ruinous attraction.)

lep II: flat, palm of the hand. Gc, *glove*. Du, *luff: loof, aloof. laveer:* to beat to windward.

letro. Gc, leather.

Worth makes the man, and want of it the fellow;
The rest is all but leather or prunella.
—Pope, *An Essay on Man,* iii

leu I: loosen, unbind. Gk *luein. lysin, -lysis,* as *analysis, catalysis, dialysis,* etc. *-lyte,* as *tachylyte. -lytic,* as *hydrolytic. -lyze,* as *analyze, paralyze.* L *solvere, solutum* (*so* from *se:* apart). *soluble, solute, solution, solve, solvent. absolve* and its doublet, *assoil; dissolve, resolve, resolution, absolution. absolute, dissolute, resolute; indissoluble. lues.*

Gc, *loose, lose, loss, lost. lorn, forlorn. forlorn hope* is from Du *verloren hoop:* lost troops; sent on a desperate charge. *leasing:* loose tongue! *loess:* loose soil. *losel:* loose person.

less. The suffix *less,* as *godless, shapeless, hopeless.* In one paragraph of an 1876 letter to Alexander Ellis, the editor of *OED* expressed the impossibility of including all the words ending *less,* but used 23 of them: "The subject is endless and exhaustless. . . . Yours truly, if breathlessly. J. A. H. M[urray]." JWalker lists only 353 words ending *less,* but the suffix is live, and can be added almost at will, even if aimless.

Oh, the little more, and how much it is!
And the little less, and what worlds away!
—Browning, *By the Fireside*

leu II: to dirty. L *lutum:* mud, *lute:* dried clay. *pollution,* a growing world-problem.

lutetia: an oxide of lutetium; see *el 71. Lutetia:* the muddy, swampy place, was a town of the Gallic tribe the Parisii, on an island in the Seine; it grew to be the city of Paris.

"Good Americans, when they die, go to Paris"—Oliver Wendell Holmes, *The Autocrat of the Breakfast-Table.* "There's no good girl's lip out of Paris"—Swinburne, translating Villon.

Paris vaut bien une messe: Paris is well worth a Mass; remark attributed to Henry IV, on the occasion of his acceptance of Catholicism to become king of France (1593); he was crowned at Chartres Cathedral in 1594. By the Edict of Nantes (1598), noble judges (*seigneurs haut justiciers*) were allowed to follow the reformed religion; it was permitted in a few cities, but forbidden within 20 miles of Paris.

leu III. Imitative of singing, of sounds of exaltation or praise. L *laus, laudem:* praise. *laud, laudable, laudatory. lozenge* was applied to a laudatory coat-of-arms or other device, then to the rhomboid shape in which this was framed, then to other things of that shape. *allow* (OFr *alouer*) is a fusion of this root (L *allaudare*) and L *allocare, allocatum:* to place; *allocate* is a doublet of *allow.* Similarly, *collocate* is a doublet of *couch,* via French; whence *accouchement* and the midwife, *accoucheuse.*

Also, from L *locare, locatum,* and *locus* come *local, locality, location, disloca-*

tion, locomotive, etc. *locus. locumtenens:* place-holding; especially, a substitute physician. From the imitative root, also Gc, *lied; Volkslied:* folksong; *Nibelungenlied.* For the *Nibelungs,* see *nebh. liederkranz:* a strong cheese; literally, a garland of songs.

leubh: desire; love; hence trust. L *lubet, libet:* desires (the verb is defective in form, though pervasive in feeling). *libido:* according to Freud, man's basic emotion and driving force. *libidinous. quodlibet:* literally, what you please.

Gc, *love, lovely, lovable,* etc. *lief,* as in "I'd as lief." *livelong* was earlier *lieflong. belief,* etc. *leave:* permission, as *leave of absence;* Du, *furlough. leman,* usually a woman. *The Oxford Dictionary of Quotations* has over 900 entries for *love,* and almost 400 for other forms, as *lover, loving, loveliness.* Love is not only pervasive but inspiring; discount Shakespeare's linking of the lover and the lunatic.

"Love is enough, though the world be a-waning"—William Morris.

Perhaps it was wise to dissemble your love,
But—why did you kick me downstairs?
—Isaac Bickerstaff, ca. 1800

(This Isaac Bickerstaff was an Irish playwright. Swift had used the name *Bickerstaff* to sign a 1708 pamphlet, *Almanac,* in which he prophesied the death of a popular, self-proclaimed prophet, the cobbler John Partridge, whose protest [after the specified day] that he was still alive, and Swift's rejoinder, were so widely popular that Steele signed his *Tatler* essays [1709–1711] as *Bickerstaff*—which means, of course, quarrel-stick.)

leud: bend, stoop; small. Possibly Gk *limos:* hunger. *bulimia:* hungry as an ox. Gc, *little, lout.* Du, *loiter.*

This wimpled, whining, purblind, wayward boy,
This senior-junior, giant-dwarf, Dan Cupid;
Regent of love-rhymes, lord of folded arms,
The anointed sovereign of sighs and groans,
Liege of all loiterers and malcontents.
—*Love's Labor's Lost,* iii, 1

leudh: grow, rise. Originally this was applied to the population, as still in Gm *Leute:* people; also *Latt:* a Latvian. In Greece and Rome, the root was applied to citizens, as opposed to slaves; hence free people (Gk *eleutheros:* free). *eleutheromania.* In botany, *eleutheropetalous, eleutherophyllous.*

L *liber:* free. *liberal;* today somewhat loosely used. *liberation, liberty. libertarian,* etc. *libertine; liege.* The *liberal arts,* as opposed to the servile and the mechanical, were those deemed by the ancients worthy of a free man. In the Middle Ages, the seven liberal arts were divided into the *trivium* and the *quadrivium;* see *kuetuer.* For *library,* see *leup.*

livery was food, then uniforms, supplied free to one's servants. *deliverance, delivery.* While *deliberate* was influenced by *liberate,* it is from L *de-libra:* scales; see *lithra.*

Eternal spirit of the chainless mind!
Brightest in dungeons, Liberty! Thou art,
For there thy habitation is the heart.
—Byron, *Sonnet on Chillon* (1816)

The Swiss François de Bonnivard was imprisoned in Chillon for his political opinions—a practice not unknown in the world today. In a Dublin speech on 10

July 1790, John P. Curran said: "The condition on which God hath given liberty of man is eternal vigilance." Thomas Jefferson, we are told, put the idea more succinctly: "Eternal vigilance is the price of liberty."

leug: bend, fasten, turn; struggle. Gk *lugos:* pliant twig. *lock,* as of hair; *forelock.* Opportunity, being an old man all bald behind, must be grasped by the forelock. *luck,* may it turn your way! *Lygodium:* genus of ferns. L *luctari:* to struggle. *ineluctable:* not to be struggled out of. *reluctance.* L *luxus:* excess; first used of plants. *luxuriant. luxate, eluxate.* Fr, *luxe, de luxe. luxuriate, luxury,* etc. See *leuk.* L *lugere, lucti:* struggle hard, hence grieve. *lugubrious.*

Du, *leek. garlic:* spear leek, from the shape of the leaves. The leek is the symbol of Wales; Shakespeare thus uses it in *Henry V.* Gc, *lock, locket* (Fr *lucarne*). *padlock:* pad, burglar, perhaps imitative of trudging feet, influenced by *pad:* road; whence *footpad:* highwayman on foot.

Falstaff, in *The Merry Wives,* v, 1, exclaims: "This is the third time; I hope good luck lies in odd numbers." A little later, in Windsor Park, the disguised folk surround him, singing:

> Fie on sinful fantasy!
> Fie on lust and luxury! . . .
> Pinch him, and burn him, and turn him about
> Till candles and starlight and moonlight be out.

They suit the action to the words, and Falstaff discovers that "luck" may turn things even; and he learns, as others do (Shakespeare avoids the "cured-endured" cliché), "What cannot be eschewed must be embraced."

leugh: speak falsely. Gc, *lie, lying; belie. warlock:* literally truth-liar, which meetly describes a magician; see *uero.* Shakespeare recognized the complications, using two sorts of *lie* in Sonnet 138:

> Therefore I lie with her, and she with me,
> And in our faults by lies we flattered be.

leuk: shining. Skr, *loka:* open space, the universe. *lokaloka:* mountains at the end of the visible world, holding off the perpetual darkness. *lokapala:* a guardian of the eight cardinal points.

Gk, *leuko,* prefix; *OED* lists 29 such words, as *leucoscope, leucospermous;* and details 20, as *leucocyte, leucorrh(o)ea. leukemia* was earlier *leuchaemia. lussa:* rabies, from the glittering eyes; *lutta:* wormlike cartilage in the tongue of the dog (E *lytta,* supposed cause of rabies, and *alyssum,* supposed cure).

lychnic, lychnidiate, lychnoscope. lychnis: the flaming herb. Before there were street lights, *link;* carried at night by a *linkboy. lynx,* also from the glittering eyes; *lyncean. ounce:* leopard, from Fr *lonce,* the *l* being misunderstood as an article, and dropped.

L *lucere, luxi:* shine; *lucidus:* full of light; OL *lucmen;* L *lumen, luminem:* light; *lustrare, lustratum:* light up, brighten; *luna,* the shining moon. Numerous words shine forth from these stems. *noctiluca:* marine creatures that glow by night (see *nekut*). *Luzula:* genus of wood rushes that sparkle with the morning dew. *lucerne,* with glittering grains. *lucifugous,* like the owl, which hunts at night, and the "twilight-loving" bat; inviting the opposite, *lucipetous,* like the cock, which summons—and the lark, which sings to—the rising sun.

luciferase is an enzyme that, usually with oxygen as a catalyst, enables *luciferin* to produce *bioluminescence:* light from a living organism. This phenomenon is widespread; some forty orders of animals (including the firefly) and some species of squid, shrimp, and fishes are *bioluminescent.* In certain fishes, e.g., the knight-fish, bacteria in an eyelid pouch are the source of the light, an odd symbiosis. Hence *Photoblepharon:* genus of flashlight fish; Gk *blepharon:* eyelid. From *blepharon* came also *anableps:* fish with protrusive eyes, and *ablepsia* (earlier *ablepsy; a* negative): blindness.

Lucina, Roman goddess of childbirth, brings the babe to light. *Lucius. Lucian, Lucia, Lucy, Lucille. Lucifer:* bearer of light (like the Greek Prometheus, who taught man the use of fire—both punished by the gods. In Church Latin, Lucifer was identified with Satan; the name was utilized for a match. And in the 1840s an early type of lighter—sulfuric acid in a glass bubble wrapped in inflammable material; squeezed to produce an instant flame—was called a *promethean.* For *promethium,* see *el 61.*)

Fr, *allumette. limbers:* first, holes to let light through; then applied to water pump-holes on a ship. Also *lucent, lucid, pellucid, elucidate, relucent, translucent. luster, lustrine, lustrum, lustration.* The original meaning of *illustration* lingers in *illustrious:* full of luster. *lucubration, elucubration. luculent. lucule,* on the sun. *lumen;* also shortened to *limn. luminary, luminous; illumination. luna, lunar, lunate.* The *luna moth* is named for the yellow crescents on its wings. *lunatic:* moonstruck (see *me IV*). *lunation, lunette. demilune. LEM: l*unar *e*xcursion *m*odule. *sublunary;* Christopher Marlowe, said Michael Drayton in 1628,

Had in him those brave sublunary things
That the first poets had.

L *lucus a non lucendo:* a grove, from its not being bright, is often cited as an illustration of absurd etymology; actually *lucus* was first the cleared, bright ground before a temple. *luxury, luxuriant,* etc., may have been influenced by L *lux:* light, but see *leug. Fiat lux:* Let there be light! And creation began.

Gc, *light, enlightenment, lightening, lighthouse; lightning, levin. Loki,* Norse god of fire, married *Glut:* glow; their two daughters were *Eisa:* embers, and *Einmyria:* ashes.

low and *leye* were Old English words for *flame. lea:* clear land, meadow. "The lowing herd winds slowly o'er the lea." Frequent also in names, as *Shipley* (sheep); *Cowley; Morley* (moor). In Flemish, *lea* is *loo,* as in *Waterloo,* where Napoleon was sunk; whence perhaps the slang *loo:* watercloset, W.C. The latter, however, may be from the 18th c. cry as the chamber pot was emptied out the window: "Gardyloo!" mistranslating Fr *Gare l'eau:* Watch out for the water! See *gal.* For *light-weight,* see *leguh.*

"Anything for a quiet life, as the man said when he took the sitivation at the lighthouse"—Sam Weller, in Dickens' *The Pickwick Papers.* The introduction of Sam into this series at once made Dickens most popular. Such comparisons as the one above, pertinent yet pert, are called *Wellerisms.* "I'm thirsty myself," as the lady said when the baby fell into the fishpond.

I saw Eternity the other night,
Like a great ring of pure and endless light.
    All calm, as it was bright;
And round beneath it Time, in hours, days, years,
    Driv'n by the spheres
Like a vast shadow mov'd; in which the world
    And all her train were hurl'd.
    —Henry Vaughan (d. 1695)

leup: strip off; bark. Skr, *loot;* but see *lau.* Gk *lepein:* strip the rind. See *lep I.* L *liber, libri:* inner bark; hence, the writing thereon; hence, book. *library,* etc.

ex libris: from the books of; used on a bookplate. *libella.* Fr, *libel:* first, a little book. It, *libretto. lobby* and its doublet *lodge:* first, a roof of bark, a bower. *lodgment, logistics.* Fr, *loge;* It, *loggia.* Gc, *leaf, lift, loft, aloft, leaflet.*

> My library
> Was dukedom large enough.
> —*The Tempest*

lino: flax; linen. Gk *linon,* L *linum.* L *linea:* line. *linen, linin, lint. Linum:* genus of flax. *linnet, lintie;* the bird feeds on flaxseed. *linoleum,* coined by the inventor F. Walton in 1863. *linseed* (oil; lintseed). *linoleic (acid). leno. crinoline:* first made with woof of hair (L *crinis*) and warp of linen. Fr, *lingerie. gridelin* (flax-gray; Fr *gris de lin*). (The fabric *lawn* is from *Laon,* an early French center of linen-making.) *line, lineage; lineaments. linotype* (line o' type). *align,* earlier *aline; alignment. allineation; delineate. collimate,* originally an error in reading L *collineatum. interline; linear; collinear; curvilinear, rectilinear.*

"Love is like linen; often changed, the sweeter"—Phineas Fletcher, *Sicelides* (1614).

lithra: scales. Gk, *litra:* a coin. L *lithra, libra:* scales. *librare, libratum:* weigh. *Libra:* constellation, seventh sign of the zodiac (see *guei*). *libra:* pound (see *leudh*). *librate; deliberate:* weigh in the mind. *deliberately. equilibrium.* It, *lira;* Fr, *livre:* pound. *liter, litre,* etc. *libella, level.*

The basic Roman weight was *libra:* a pound; hence the English abbreviation *lb.* In medieval Europe the basic coinage system counted the *denarius,* 12 of which made a *solidus,* 20 of which made a *pound.* Hence, until the change to the metric system in the 1970s, the English symbols £ *s d* stood for *pounds, shillings, pence.* (For the drug *LSD,* see *gn.*)

> Where both deliberate, the love is slight;
> Whoever loved that loved not at first sight?
> —Marlowe, *Hero and Leander*

lou: wash. Gk *luein,* L *luere:* wash away, release. L *diluvium:* flood. From Greek the suffix *lysis,* as *analysis, catalysis, hydrolysis, paralysis, pyrolysis;* JWalker lists a dozen such; the verbs *analyze,* etc. *pyrolusite:* glass soap.

L, *lather, lave. ablution, lotion. lavabo, lavatory, latrine, lavish. alluvial. absolute, absolution; absolve:* wash away sin. *assoil. dissolve, dissolution; dissolute. solve, solution, solvent. resolute, resolution, resolve. diluent, dilute, diluvial; antediluvian,* when Noah he built himself an ark. *Après nous le déluge,* said Mme de Pompadour to Louis Quinze.

L *lovimentum. lomentum. alluvion, alluvium, collution, colluvies; elution, elutriation, eluvies, eluvium, pediluvium;* see *or, ped.*

OFr *lavandier:* launderer. *launder, laundry. lavender,* used fresh to perfume baths, and dried to freshen laundry. Gc, *lather, loose, lose, loss; forlorn. lye.* The novelist George Gissing, penniless, pictured writers' struggles in *New Grub Street* (1891); when he used the British Museum for his morning wash, a sign was posted in the Men's Room: "For casual ablutions only."

> And still she slept an azure-lidded sleep,
> In blanched linen, smooth and lavender'd.
> —Keats, *The Eve of St. Agnes*

lus: *louse,* once quite familiar. *delouse.* See *guhdher.* John Skelton, in the abusive *Tunnyng of Elynor Rummynge* (1529), calls her

Droupy and drowsy,
Scurvy and lousy,
Her face all bowsy.

Since, in beggars' and thieves' cant, *bowsy* (from *bowse*) was also pronounced *boozy,* it is the source of the frequent *booze.*

L *pediculus:* louse: literally, with little feet (see *ped*). *pediculosis.* Ben Jonson, in *Every Man in His Humour* (1598), gives a summons to revelry: "Helter Skelter, Hang sorrow, care'll kill a cat: uptails all, and a louse for the hangman."

M

ma I: good; timely, early. *manes:* the good ones, Roman euphemism for the gods of the underworld. *immanity.* L *maturus:* seasonable. *mature, immature, premature. Matuta,* Roman goddess of dawn. *matins, matutinal.* Sp, *mañana, madroña. maduro;* seldom smoked today. Fr, *matinée,* now in the afternoon. *maturity* is not a matter of chronology.

ma II. Imitative of a baby's cry, or noise when suckling. See *amma,* with which this root is intertwined. Gk *meter:* mother; *metropolis:* mother city. *metralgia; metritis. metronymic. parametrium. Demeter,* Greek goddess of crops: Mother Earth.

In Tatar, *mama* was used to mean earth; whence *mammont:* a monster that was thought to burrow in the earth; a giant, extinct elephant. Mistaking the *n* for *u,* Fr *mammouth,* whence E *mammoth*—and in 1977 an actual baby mammoth was found near the River Dima in Siberia, preserved for 39,000 years in the permafrost of Mother Earth.

L *mater. alma mater:* kindly, or nourishing, mother; one's college, where the new student *matriculates.* Pope, in *The Dunciad,* expressed his opinion of college class reunions: "And Alma Mater all dissolved in port." *pia mater; dura mater; materia medica.* L *mater* was applied to the trunk of a tree, which nourishes branches and fruit; hence *matter, materialism,* etc. *materialistic; matter-of-fact.* Port, *Madeira:* island rich in timber. Fr, *madrier. maternal, maternity, matrimony. matrix. matriarch, matron, matricide.* See *pa; peter.*

Recent microresearch, led by P. A. M. Dirac, has explored *antimatter:* identical particles with opposite electrical charge or spin, as electron and positron, which upon colliding annihilate each other, releasing energy in the form of gamma rays.

Matricaria: genus of camomile; supposedly of medicinal value. *Maia,* Roman goddess of fertility; whence *May. maieutic. mama, mamma, mammy,* and all the breast-feeding *mammals. mammary. Mammillaria:* genus of cacti, with "nipples." Gc, *mother. mother of pearl. grandmother,* etc. Fr *commère:* godmother; "with the mother," presents the babe at baptism. Scot, *cummer.*

"These pieces of moral prose," Logan Pearsall Smith introduces his collected essays, *All Trivia* (1933), "have been written, dear Reader, by a large Carnivorous Mammal, belonging to that suborder of the animal kingdom which includes the Orang-outang, the tusked Gorilla, the Baboon with his bright blue and red bottom, and the gentle Chimpanzee." Swinburne says, in *Atalanta in Calydon* (1865):

When the hounds of spring are on winter's traces
The mother of months in meadow or plain
Fills the shadows and windy places
With lisp of leaves and ripple of rain.

"Dead!" exclaimed the unhappy heroine of Mrs. Henry Ward's *East Lynne* (1874), "and never called me Mother."

mad: moist; pleasant of taste or sound. Skr *maina;* E *myna bird,* which can be taught words. Gc, *meat,* which first meant all chewed (saliva-moistened) food, as in the opposition "meat and drink." Thus, in *Romeo and Juliet,* iii, 1: "Thy head is as full of quarrels as an egg is of meat." Gc *ge-mate:* meat together; *mate.* Thus *comrade:* room together (see *kam*), and *companion:* bread together (see *pa*). Fr, *matelote; matross. mast:* fodder.

mag: knead; mix. Early houses were made of mixed earth; hence *make. make* developed many meanings, which take 37 columns in *OED,* with 96 numbered divisions and many subdivisions; *make away with, make out,* etc. Also 9 columns of compounds, as *make-believe, making-up, makeless* (*matchless*), *makepeace, makeshift.*

"If you call a tail a leg, how many legs has a dog? Five? No, calling a tail a leg don't *make* it a leg"—Abraham Lincoln.

Gk, *magma. mazocacothesis, mazolysis.* L *massa:* that which adheres like dough; *mass. macerate.* Gc, *mason. match, matchmaker;* on a lower level, *mackerel:* pimp, who makes other matchings. *mingle; mongrel:* mixed breed. *among.*

Thomas Fuller, in *The Cause and Cure of a Wounded Conscience* (1647), states succinctly: "Man can neither make him to whom he speaks, hear what he says, or believe what he hears." Kingsley, in *The Water Babies* (1862), declares: "We will make believe that there are fairies in the world." In a climactic moment of *Peter Pan* (1904), Barrie depends upon the audience to manifest such belief.

maker is used of a poet; *the Maker,* of the Lord.

I sing of a maiden
  That is makeless;
King of all kings
  To her son she ches.
   —15th c. carol

magh: might, power. See *me III.* OPers, *mage; magi,* the Magi that visited Jesus neonate; singular, *magus. magic, archimage.*

Gk *makhane:* invention. *machine, machinist. machination. mechanism, mechanistic. mechanical;* the rude "mechanicals" in *A Midsummer Night's Dream.* Gc, *may, dismay; might, main. Amazon:* female warrior; folk etymology derives this from Gk *a-mazon:* no breast, from the legend that the warrior women cut off the right breast to improve their archery. The suffix *machy:* battle, as *alectromachy, iconomachy, logomachy, naumachy, psychomachy, sciamachy, gigantomachy, tauromachy, theomachy.* The mock-Homeric epic *Batrachomyomachia* [Battle of the frogs and the mice].

The name *Matilda:* mighty in battle, well illustrates how a word may shift its meaning. Shortened to *Maud,* it was, says *OED,* "applied typically to a woman of the lower classes." It developed the pet names *mawkin* and *malkin,* usually used of a slattern or a wanton; from the 13th c. through the 18th, these were also applied to a demon or witch; *Macbeth* begins: "I come, Gray-Malkin!" (the witch's cry to her familiar spirit). By *l.r* shift came *merkin,* shifting from the lewd woman to her pubic hair. Alexander Smith, in *The History of the Most Noted Highwaymen* (1714), relates: "This put a strange whim into his mind, which was, to get the hairy circle of her merkin. . . . This he dry'd well, and combed out, and then returned to the Cardinal, telling him, he had brought St. Peter's beard." Finally, the pox having left so many prostitutes bald below, *merkin* came to mean "a wig for a woman's privy parts." The Australians still sing of "Waltzing Matilda."

Hilaire Belloc, in his *Cautionary Tales* (1907), tells of a different lass:

Matilda told such Dreadful lies
It made one Gasp and Stretch one's eyes;
Her Aunt, who from her Earliest Youth
Had kept a Strict Regard for Truth,
Attempted to believe Matilda:
The effort very nearly killed her.

There was a man in our town, and he was wondrous wise,
He jumped into a bramble bush, and scratched out both his eyes;
And when he saw his eyes were out, with all his might and main,
He jumped into another bush, and scratched them in again.
—Old nursery rhyme

maghos: virgin, of either sex. *maid, maiden, maidenhead, maidenhood. may, mayweed.* Thus also a ship's *maiden voyage,* etc. While some suggest a separate root (see *mari*), it seems likely, from Greek, Cornish, Lithuanian, and other sources, that *marriage* first meant union with a virgin, a maid who has reached *marry-age;* hence also *marital, marry. maritage,* through the 18th c., meant (1) a dowry; (2) the right of a feudal lord (in England, the king) to a sum paid upon the marriage of a vassal.

Virgin, virginity, are from L *virgo, virginis,* possibly from the root *uei:* bend, applied to a young shoot. The constellation *Virgo* is the sixth sign of the zodiac; see *guei.* Some 60 million light-years away, it contains a cluster of some 1,000 galaxies speeding away from us at 1,000 kilometers a second.

The Greek marriage procession chanted *Humen! Humen!*—the god protector of virgins—from which came E *hymen;* see *siu.* Times have changed since the bloody sheet was displayed in the morning, a sign of the broken hymen; and in the morning the happy husband gave the bride the morning gift. Thence, a *morganatic marriage* (Gm *Morgen:* morning; see *mer I*), in which the bride, of inferior rank, could lay no claim to her noble husband's title and estate, but must abide content with the morning gift. See *gn; guel II; per VI c.*

"The perpetual admonition of nature to us is: 'The world is new, untried. . . . I give you the universe a virgin today'"—Emerson, *Literary Ethics* (1828).

virginity gave rise to *Virginia,* named after the virgin queen of England, Elizabeth I. (Note that two women, Elizabeth and Victoria, ruled the land in its greatest years.) Thence *Virginia cowslip, Virginia creeper, Virginia reel,* etc. The *virginal,* an early harpsichord, may be so called because it was played by young girls; or because it was held on the lap, where it is the privilege of a young girl to be held.

"When you're a married man, Samivel, you'll understand a good many things as you don't understand now; but vether it's worth while going through so much to learn so little, as the charity-boy said ven he got to the end of the alphabet, is a matter of taste"—Mr. Weller, in Dickens' *The Pickwick Papers.*

Ickle ockle, blue bockle,
Fishes in the sea;
If you want a pretty maid
Please choose me.

mai I: cut, bite. Ir, *moiley, muley:* hornless; also applied to a meek person. *Malcolm:* originally, bald servant of St. Columba (d. A.D. 597), Irish missionary to the Picts, whose servants shaved their heads—as did the tonsured priests. The American Indians conveniently shaved all their head hair save the long lock for scalping —as do the male followers of "Hare Krishna" today. (*Columba,* from the Latin for *dove,* is also the name of a southern constellation; see *kel III.*)

Gc, *mite:* first, a tiny, biting insect; then, anything small. Thus Fr *mitraille, mitrailleuse,* from the rapid discharge of many small missiles. *maim, mangle; mayhem. emmet, ant.*

mai II: stain, defile. Gk *miastor:* polluter. *miasma; miasmatology. Miastor:* genus of flies. *amianthus:* a type of asbestos (*a* negative) which fire cannot defile. Gc, *mole* (on skin). J. Green, in *A Discourse on the Skin* (1835), stated: "A small mole upon the cheek is sometimes held rather as a heightener of female beauty." If she were unfortunate enough to lack such an adornment, a belle might apply a little black patch, star, heart, or what her fancy chose, long available in cosmetic salons. I have not yet seen this vogue back in fashion, but I have seen a British belle with each of her five fingernails—the two hands matching—painted a different color.

mak: long, large; thin, Gk *makhros:* large. *macron. macro-,* as *macrocosm,* opposed to *microcosm;* see *sme. macrobiotic, macrocephalic. macrology:* long talk with little meaning. A *macromolecule* is a very large molecule, especially a polymer, the linking of up to millions of monomers (: individual molecular units, atoms). *OED* (1933) lists 24 words beginning *macro,* and details 42; the 1976 supplement lists 6 more, and details 29, as *macroglobulin* (having a molecular weight of 1,000,000 or more). The *Encyclopaedia Britannica,* 15th ed., has a 10-volume *Micropaedia* of short entries, and a 19-volume *Macropaedia* of lengthy articles. In many terms, as in *macronucleus* and *micronucleus, macro* is contrasted with *micro;* see *sme.*

Macedonian: literally, tall one. From Macedonia's being deemed a land of mixed races, via French comes *macedoine:* mixture of vegetables or fruit, often jellied. Gk *mekhos:* length; *meco-,* as *mecography, mecodont, mecocephalic; mekometer; param(o)ecium. Mecoptera:* order of longwinged insects, classified between the *Hymenoptera:* membrane-winged, and the *Trichoptera:* hairy-winged.

L *macer:* thin. *emaciated.* Fr, *maigre, meager. malinger,* influenced by Fr *malade,* E *malady. amphimacer:* a metrical foot, which Coleridge in 1807 defined and illustrated:

First and last being long, middle short, amphimacer
Strikes his thundering hoofs like a proud high-bred racer.

maken: poppy. Gk *mekoneion:* poppy juice. *meconium:* fetal excrement at human birth. *meconism. meconophagite,* as De Quincey in *Confessions of an English Opium-Eater* (1822).

L *papaver* led to E *poppy;* Gk *opion:* poppy juice, led to E *opium.* Gm *Mohn* is poppy seed. For *morphine* and *heroin,* derivatives of opium, see *merbh.*

man: hand. L *manus. manual. mandate, mandatory* (L *dare, datum:* give). *mandamus:* "We order delivery into one's hand." *command, commander;* Du, *commodore.* The *Ten Commandments* were put into Moses' hand. *commend, commendation:* "We've got to hand it to you!" *recommend. countermand. demand, remand; emancipation:* taking out of one's hand. It, *mandritto:* right-hand fencing slash. *mancinism:* lefthandedness.

Fr *man(o)euvre, maneuver;* hence *manure,* which first meant to work by hand, to till, to spread. *legerdemain:* light of hand. *manacle; manicure.* For *manifold,* see *menegh. maniple, manipulate. manage;* first, of handling horses. *manager,* etc. Fr, *ménage; menagerie:* first, management or handling of domestic animals, though some trace these two words to L *manere, mansum:* abide (whence also *mansion;* see *men IV*).

Also *manifest, manifesto* (Martin Luther's, 1517; Karl Marx's, 1847). *amanuensis. bimanual. manner. manubrium:* like a handle. *manufacture:* making by hand; *manufactory,* shortened (the "hand" left out) to *factory,* where the work is increasingly done by machine (computers, robots). *manumission. mansuetude:* gentleness, as accustomed to the hand; thus also *mastiff,* trained to the hand, the ending influenced by Fr *mestif:* mongrel. In 18th c. ecclesiastical and learned use (from L *tergere:* wipe) was *manutergium:* a towel.

masturbation (and the learned *manustupration*) are from L *manu stuprare:* to defile with the hand, the ending altered by association with L *turbare, turbatum:* to agitate. *onanism,* sometimes misued to mean masturbation, is more precisely *coitus interruptus:* incomplete coition. Thus, when Judah's son Er died (Bible, Genesis 38), Judah, according to the levirate duty, bade his son Onan to marry the widow Tamar; but "when he went in unto his brother's wife he spilled the semen on the ground."

manichord (: clavichord) is a folkchange from *monochord,* by association with *manus:* hand. Urquhart, in his translation of Rabelais, played upon this when he spoke of Gargantua, in his cradle, *monochordizing* with his fingers—which *OED* misdefines. Some suggest that the vulgar *frig,* for masturbation, may be from OE *frigan:* love (Norse *Frigg,* goddess of love, whence *Friday*); it seems more probably a transfer from L *fricare:* rub; E *friction.*

Also *manus, manuscript:* literally, written by hand. Fr *main:* hand. *maintain. mainpernor:* one that gave *mainprize* (: taking into one's hand); early legal terms meaning to accept a released accused person, guaranteeing his return for trial—before the institution of bail, now often "jumped." (*bail* comes via L *baiulus:* carrier; OFr *baillier:* take charge of. One that *bails out* a boat is a water-carrier.) *maundy* (see *or; ped*).

Gc *munt:* mound, piled by hand for protection; its form influenced by *mount.* Hence *Edmund:* protector; *Osmund:* God guards (*Oscar:* spear of God); *Raymond:* reason protects; *Sigismund:* victory guards; also shortened to *Sig.* Possibly *mundane;* L *mundus* was first used of women's adornment applied by hand, then (like Gk *cosmos* from *cosmetics*) was extended to the ordered universe. Hence *extramundane, ultramundane.* Fr, *monde, demimonde.*

I do not much dislike the matter, but
The manner, of his speech.
—*Antony and Cleopatra,* ii, 2

mano: damp. L, *emanate.* Gc, *moor.* See *mori.*

manu: man. See also *nert.* Skr, *Manu:* one of the 14 progenitors of mankind in

Hindu mythology, probably "the thinker"; see *men I.* From the 16th c. into the 19th, woman was also called *maness. man, men, manhood, mankind. manhandle, manhole, manward, man-eating,* etc. *unmanly. mantrap,* literally set for trespassers, used into the 19th c. Used figuratively by Johnson (Boswell's *Life of Samuel Johnson,* 20 Mar. 1776): "He should have warned us of our danger, before we entered his garden of flowery eloquence, by advertising *Spring-guns and man-traps set here.*" Goldsmith in *She Stoops to Conquer* (1773), mentions a Mrs. Mantrap. Frank Harris in 1923 mischievously pointed out that a virgin is a natural mantrap: L *vir:* man; *gin:* snare, trap (*OED* definition [4]).

Numerous words have *man* as the last element, as *clergyman, gentleman, hangman, henchman, sportsman, workman, yeoman;* JWalker gives 159 relevant words. A *leman* is from OE *loef:* dear; see *leubh. Superman* is a translation of Nietzsche's *Übermensch,* and Bernard Shaw's hope for human redemption, but some regions of the world seem, rather, to be suffering from *supermania.*

For *Northman,* see *ner.* Gc, *Alemanni:* alien men. *Marcomanni:* border men. *Herman:* war man. *fugelman.* Gm *Mensch. minx.* Norse, *ombudsman:* literally, man to see about orders. Russ *moujik, muzhik.* Du, *manikin;* see quotation from Byron, under *sphieu. mannequin. Manneken-Pis:* famous fountain in Brussels, of a boy with the water flowing from his penis.

Manacus: genus of manakins (birds). *mandrill* (*drill:* West African for monkey). *mandriarch; mandrite, archimandrite.*

The *mandragora,* Gk *mandragoras,* also called *mandrake* (*drake* was an early English word for *dragon*), was for centuries a subject of superstition. Its forked roots resemble the human body; but it would destroy anyone uprooting it; a dog was tied to the stem, then called to run, and the mandrake shriek on coming forth would make mad any hearer. Another effect was pictured by John Donne in 1610: "Hannibal, to entrap and surprise his enemies, mingled their wine with mandrake, whose operation is between sleep and poison." A narcotic, it was also supposed to be both an aphrodisiac and a fertilizing agent; Leah (Genesis 30), when her son brought some, invited Jacob to sleep with her, and bore him another son. *OED* states that it is still so used in Palestine. (For *manticore,* see *mer II.*) In Shakespeare's plays, Cleopatra (i, 5) bids her maid

> Give me to drink mandragora
> That I might sleep out this great gap of time
> My Antony is away.

Juliet (iv, 3) in the tomb fears

> Shrieks like mandragora torn out of the earth,
> That living mortals, hearing them, run mad.

And Iago thinks, of Othello (iii, 3), to whom he has fed the notion of his wife's unfaithfulness,

> Not poppy, nor mandragora,
> Nor all the drowsy syrups of the world
> Shall ever medicine you to that sweet sleep
> Which thou owed'st yesterday.

Many other writers, including Chapman, Webster, Thackeray, and Carlyle, have referred to the plant's sleep-inducing power.

In the 15th c. the word was euphemistically folkchanged to *mandglorye,* as though from Fr *main de gloire:* hand of glory. In 1830 John Galt, in *Lawnie Todd,* used the word figuratively: "Earnest employment is the best mandragora for an aching heart."

"Man is the measure of all things"–Protagoras (410 B.C.). "What a piece of work is man!"–*Hamlet* (1602). "Man is Nature's sole mistake"–Lady Psyche, in Gilbert's *Princess Ida* (1884).

?map: signal cloth; sheet. L *mappa,* which Quintilian calls of Carthaginian origin, but which may be from the Hebrew stem *n.w.p.:* move to and fro, as a banner. (Primitive men made no maps.) L *mappa mundi,* OFr *mappemonde. map. mop. moppet:* first, a rag doll. *nappe; napkin, napery. an apron* is a folkchange, misplacing the *n* in *a napron.*

"Map me no maps, Sir; my head is a map, a map of the whole world"–Fielding, *Rape upon Rape* (1730), i, 5.

?margar: pearl. Skr *manjan:* pearl; *manju:* beautiful. Gk *margaron:* pearl. *Margaret:* name of a woman, a daisy, an apple, a pear. *Marguerite. Mag, magpie;* hence *mag:* chatterbox. Also *Margot, Margie, Madge. Fata Morgana, Morgan le Fay* (fairy); sister of King Arthur; to her were attributed magic powers. She was supposed, especially in Sicily, to create the mirage. See *elaia; speik.*

Meg. Long Meg (of Westminster), a notorious virago of the 16th c., was often mentioned by writers, and *Meg* became a general term for a loose woman; hence *Meg's delight. Roaring Meg* was the 15th c. gun at Edinburgh Castle. (A woman's name–as *Big Bertha*–has more than once been applied to a formidable weapon; our most frequent word for a firearm, *gun,* is from *Gunhilda.* As a document of 1330 puts it, "una magna balista de cornu vocatur Domina Gunilda.")

margarin. margaric (acid). margaritiferous, as the oyster. The word *oleomargarine* was first recorded in French, by the chemist Pierre E. M. Berthelot in 1854, of a product made first in 1838; patented in the U.S. in 1873, it was named for (1) the pearl-like bubbles (U.S. Patent no. 146,012 calls them "teats") formed in the process, and (2) the erroneous belief that all oils contain margaric acid. A previous butter substitute was called *butterine.* In England in Aug. 1887, Earl Wemyss foretold: "On Friday next the great fight, Butterine vs Margarine, will come off in the Lords." In Jan. 1888 Parliament chose the second name; at once *The Lancet* (14 Jan. 1888) declared: "The word 'margarine' is, from a scientific point of view, inappropriate." In the 1890s the word was used to mean bogus, as in *margarine liberalism,* which is still rife. As late as 1949 *The Butter and Cheese Review* reported: "Oleo manufacturers do everything to dupe the consumer into thinking their product is butter." Now taken for granted, it is usually called *margarine.* In *OED* the *g* is given as hard, but the American Society of Butterine Manufacturers voted that it should be sounded as *j,* which *OED*'s 1976 supplement states is now common.

mari: nubile girl. *marriable,* more commonly *marriageable.* See *maghos.* L *maritus:* one with a bride. As Byron sees it, in *Don Juan,* iii, 1,

Romances paint at full length people's wooings,
But only give a bust of marriages:
For no one cares for matrimonial cooings,
There's nothing wrong in a connubial kiss:
Think you if Laura had been Petrarch's wife,
He would have written sonnets all his life?

Most of Shakespeare's comedies end with a marriage; *As You Like It* and *A Midsummer Night's Dream,* with multiple matings. In one that does not–*All's Well That Ends Well*–when Bertram, wed against his will by order of the Duke, leaves his wife directly after the ceremony, he protests (ii, 3):

He wears his honors in a box unseen
That hugs his kicky-wicky here at home,

Spending his manly marrow in her arms
Which should sustain the bound and high curvet
Of Mars's fiery steed.

As he departs for the war, his attendant Parolles mutters:

'Tis hard:
A young man married is a man that's marred–

required, espousedly, to keep his "i" from other females.

Note that *marry* is also an exclamation, from the 16th c. into the 19th, a minced oath, *By Mary!* The Nurse says to Juliet, in Shakespeare's play (ii, 5), "Marry, come up." To appease the Virgin one might say *By Mary Gypsy*, which might be shortened to *By Gyp.*

In the Second Folio of Shakespeare, *kicky-wicky* became *kicksy-wicksy;* it has had other forms, and other applications. Thus, in Nashe's *Lenten Stuffe* (1599), it refers to wordplay: "The lousy riddle . . . with eight score more galliard cross-points and kickshi-winshes, of giddy earwig brains." In Victorian England, *kicksies* was slang for trousers; "to turn out a man's kicksies" was to pick his pockets.

Mary, the most common feminine name, after *Virgin Mary*, Hebr *Miryam*, has had many forms, and has passed into other words. *Maria, Marie, Marilyn, Marian(ne); Marion,* whence *marionette* (double diminutive). *Mariolatry. Marihuana* (*marijuana*), a supposed aphrodisiac, is from *Maria Juana, Mary Jane. marigold. rosemary* is folkchanged from *ros marinus:* ocean dew. *mariposite* is a mineral, from *Mariposa* County, Calif. The *mariposa lily* is from Sp *mariposa* (*Mary*, and *posar:* to alight): butterfly. It reminds one of Browning's attraction:

I must learn Spanish, one of these days,
Only for that slow sweet name's sake.

Marinism, however, names the extravagant style of the poet Giovanni Batista *Marini* (1569–1625).

Congreve, in *The Old Bachelor* (1693), v, 10, compares "courtship to marriage, as a very witty Prologue to a very dull play."

marko: horse. Gc, *mare:* female of an equine animal (possibly linked, as *mother*, with the root *ma II;* mare's milk was used by various peoples). Hence various expressions. Used for "the blues," it grew to *nightmare;* see *mer II.* A priest's *mare* was his concubine. *to travel on Shank's mare* was to go on one's own legs; see *skeng. to ride the wild mare:* to be put on a wooden horse, for a whipping. *to ride the two-* (sometimes *three-*) *legged mare:* to be hanged on the gallows. The *flying mare* is a throw in wrestling. A *mare's nest* is something fantastical that doesn't exist, implying a foolish credulity, or a complicated mess. Among several marish sayings, the most persistent is "Money makes the mare go."

marshal was first a groom. When Henry VIII of England saw Anne of Cleves, says Smollet in his *History of England* (1759), "the King found her so different from her picture, that he swore they had brought him a Flanders mare." In its first act of the kind, Parliament in a few months annulled the marriage. Walt Whitman, in *Song of Myself*, was otherwise responsive: "The look of the gray mare shames silliness out of me."

The Press is too much with us, small and great;
We are undone of chatter and *on dit,*
Report, retort, rejoinder, repartee,
Mole-hill and mare's nest, fiction up to date.
–Austin Dobson, *A Pleasant Invective against Printing*

(molded after Wordsworth's sonnet "The world is too much with us; late and soon . . .").

?mas: male. L *mas,* diminutive *masculus. male, masculine, emasculate.*

mat: tool, weapon; beat. L *mateola:* digging tool, club. *malleus:* hammer. *mace, mattock. mall. pall-mall:* ball-mallet. *maul, mallet, malleable. malleus, malleolus.* In 1483 Jakob Sprenger, Dominican inquisitor of Cologne, published *Malleus Maleficorum* (Gm *Hexenhammer:* The hammer of witches), the major text in the uncovering and punishing of "witchcraft." See *netr; sap.* Probably *massacre. marc* (trodden), *march* (beat time), *démarche. mashie* in golf, *massé* in billiards, *stramazon* in fencing. Sp, *machete.*

math: worm. Gc, *moth. mawkish. maggot, maggoty,* influenced by *Mag:* little Margaret; see *margar.*

mavors. L *Mavors,* early name of *Mars,* Roman god of war, whose "son" founded Rome in 753 B.C. This was year 1 of the Roman calendar, *a.u.c.: ab urbe condita:* from the founding of the city. Various lunar calculations (religious and agricultural) became mixed, and a date was usually identified as "during the consulate of —." *A* was also called "the salvation letter," because in criminal trials the judges wrote *A* (*absolvo*) for "not guilty."

The planet *Mars* was named for its blood-red color, from the iron oxide (earthly rust) on its surface. Its two moons are *Phobos* (: dread), ten miles in diameter, and *Deimos* (: terror), five miles; these are the names of the horses that drew the god Mars' war chariot. (The diameter of the Earth's moon is 2160 miles.)

The *Martians* are frequent in scientifiction. The month of *March* "comes in like a lion and goes out like a lamb." Hence also *Marcia, Marcus, Mark,* and *Martin.* For *Mark my words,* see *merk.*

mazdos: pole. *mast* (of a ship). *Malos,* a southern constellation. IE *d* is often changed in Latin to *l,* under Sabine influence. Thus *odere,* E *odor; olere,* E *olfactory;* see *od.* Thus *Ulysses* for *Odysseus.* James Joyce's *Ulysses* is contrapuntal to Homer's *Odyssey.*

Odysseus's parentage explains his sly nature. He is the grandson of Autolycus, the jolly knave of the cony-catching crew whom Shakespeare introduces in act iv of *The Winter's Tale,* and whose appearance singing "When daffodills begin to peer" shifts the play's mood toward spring. Peddler and "snapper-up of unconsidered trifles," Autolycus describes himself in the play as "littered under Mercury"; in Greek mythology he is the son of Hermes (Roman Mercury), patron of merchants and thieves. Autolycus's daughter Anticlea, wife of Laertes, king of Ithaca, was the mother of Odysseus. However, Sisyphus, king of Corinth, the only man that ever outwitted Autolycus, slipped into the Ithacan bed, and in post-Homeric legend he is the father of Odysseus. Thus in Odysseus's background are the two most famous tricksters of ancient days: his father Sisyphus of Corinth, "the most cunning of mankind," and the son of the god of tricksters, his maternal grandfather, Autolycus. See *odi.*

me I. Forms of the personal pronoun. It, *madonna:* my lady. *Mona* (Lisa) is a corruption of *monna, madonna.* Fr, *madame, mademoiselle. mademoiselle* is also the name of a salt-water fish, the silver perch.

Via Ir, *machree; mavourneen:* my darling. Gc, *me, mine, my, myself.* For *I,* see *eg.*

Kathleen Mavourneen! The grey dawn is breaking,
The horn of the hunter is heard on the hill . . .
Oh! why art thou silent, thou voice of my heart?
–Julia Crawford, 1835

me II: to cut grass. Gc, *mead, meadow, math:* what is mowed; figuratively, *aftermath. mow.* If Napoleon had prevailed, we'd be starting the harvest in *Messidor* (L *metere, messum:* reap; Gk *doron:* gift): June 19 to July 18, the tenth month of his short-lived calendar, set in 1792, canceled in 1805; see *kel II.*

me III, megh: great. See *magh; mak.* Skr *maha. maharajah* (feminine, *maharanee*). *Mahabharata:* one of the two great Hindu epics. *Bharata:* literally, storied, is Aryan India. The other epic is the *Ramayana* (*yana:* vehicle; *Rama,* name of three incarnations—the sixth, seventh, and eighth—of the god Vishnu). *Mahayana. mahatma. mahout. Maratha. mahseer:* great-headed fish. By playful euphemism, *mehta:* sweeper (feminine, *matranee*). Possibly *maya:* great art, magic, illusion.

Gk *megas:* great, *megistos:* greatest. Prefix *mega,* as *megaphone, megavolt. megalo-,* as *megalocardia, megalomania; megalopolis* (more or less replaced by the hybrid *megacity,* as *skyscraper* seems to be giving way to *highriser*). *OED* lists 14 words beginning *mega* and details 59 more; it lists 19 others beginning *megalo,* including *megalops:* the large-eyed crab. In its 1976 supplement it lists 16 more *mega* words and details another 15.

Also *acromelagy. almagest* (Arab *al:* the): literally, the greatest work, on astrology. Hermes *Trismegistus:* thrice greatest; legendary priest of Egypt who taught the use of the olive, hieroglyphics, and *geometry* (: land measurement, required annually after the receding of the Nile flood). *omega:* great *O,* last letter of the Greek alphabet; there is also an *omicron:* little *o;* see *mei I* and *sme.* "I am alpha and omega, the beginning and the end"—Bible, Revelation 1:8.

L *magnus, maior, maximus:* great, greater, greatest. *magnanimous, magnate. magistrate,* and, from L *magister, master, mister, mistress.* A *masterpiece* was first a piece presented by an apprentice craftsman, to earn the right to work by himself, as a master in his guild.

magnificent, magnify, magnitude; magnum. magniloquent. bonum magnum: literally, great good; a large potato, also a plum. *magnum opus:* one's chief work. *Magna Carta. magnesium* is named for *Magnesia,* a region in Thessaly rich in minerals; hence also *milk of magnesia; manganese* (see *el 25*); and *magnet* (with over 20 associated words in *OED*).

majesty; major; majority, contrasted with *minority* and *plurality,* which means more than any others but less than half. *majuscule,* opposite of *minuscule;* see *mei I. magisterial, magistral; mayor. palmistry:* mastery of the hand. *mistral.* Names, as *Max, Maximilian, Maxime, Maxine. maxim, maximum; OED* defines 14 relevant words. In the 12th c., Albertus Magnus used *maxim* to describe a basic proposition "not intuitively certain like an axiom," but "practically indisputable." The *maxim machine gun* is named for inventor Hiram S. *Maxim,* 1884; named for his brother, Hudson, is the smokeless gunpowder *maximite,* and for his son Hiram P. the *maxim silencer.* From mining engineer *Max* Braun, in 1872, came *maxite.*

Maia, goddess of growth, which becomes noticeable in her month, *May. Maianthemum:* genus of plants. It, *maestro, magnifico, majordomo.* Gc, *much, more, most. almost.* Scot, *mickel.* "A mickle for a nickel."

The earnest Milton, in *Of Education:* "I call therefore a complete and generous education that which fits a man to perform most justly, skilfully and magnanimously all the offices both public and private of peace and war."

The cynical Bertrand Russell, in *The Conquest of Happiness:* "The megalomaniac differs from the narcissist by the fact that he wishes to be powerful rather than charming, and seeks to be feared rather than loved. To this type belong many lunatics and most of the great men of history."

Ben Jonson, in his fifth song of *Celebration of Charis,* linked three goddesses:

She is Venus when she smiles,
But she's Juno when she walks
And Minerva when she talks

—thus crediting her with loveliness, majesty, and wisdom.

me IV: measure; the setting of time. Skr *masr,* Gk *mene:* the moon, a widespread measure of time. *menses, menstruate; menarche, menopause. meniscus; menology. catamenia; amenorrhea; dismenorrhea; menorrhagia. emmenagogue, emmenic, emmenology. Menaspis:* genus of moonshield sharks, now extinct. *Menispermum:* genus of moonseeds.

L *mensus:* month. *mensal. bimestrial; semester, trimester.* L *metiri, mensum. measure, admeasure, immeasurable.*

—Where Alph, the sacred river, ran
Through caverns measureless to man.
—Coleridge, *Kubla Khan*

metric, centimeter, etc. *diameter:* measure across; *perimeter:* measure around. *metrology. metronome. geometry* (*ge:* earth). *trigonometry* (*tri, trigon:* three, triangle). *isometric.* For *mensuration,* see below.

Gc, *meal:* time to eat. *piecemeal:* a measure of one at a time; thus also *inchmeal* (*The Tempest,* ii, 2), "tear her limb-meal" (*Cymbeline,* ii, 4), and "when worlds of wanwood leafmeal lie" (Gerard Manley Hopkins [d. 1889], *Spring and Fall*).

moon, Monday, month, moonlit; honeymoon (period of sweetness). *moonstruck,* coined by Milton, akin to *lunatic;* see *leuk. moonshine* has long been used of something unsubstantial, unreal; how it came to this is suggested by Rosaline's words in *Love's Labor's Lost:*

Beg another matter,
Thou now request'st but moonshine in the water.

De Quincey, in the opening of his *Confessions of an English Opium-Eater* (1822), protesting Coleridge's excuse of his own habit while condemning De Quincey's, said of his great contemporary: "Coleridge's entire statement upon that subject is perfect moonshine." *eggs in moonshine* was a delicious 18th c. dish (Mrs. Glass, *Cookery* [1767]): eggs hard-boiled, in a "sky" of blanc mange and a "half-moon" of clear jelly. And of course, since the 18th c., *moonshine* has been illicit liquor, first applied to brandy smuggled by moonlight on the Kentish coast of England. In 1901 *Munsey's Magazine* stated: "Georgia and Arkansas have the greatest number of moonshine stills." The more recent *moonlighting* means taking a second job in the evening.

measurable and *measurement* are twinned with *mensurable* and *mensuration* —the former, part Greek; the latter, all Latin. Here also are *commensurate, dimension, immense.*

Various Greek and Latin forms are used as prefixes in modern mensuration tables. For example:

Prefix	*Amount*	*Symbol*		*Prefix*	*Amount*	*Symbol*
deca	10^1	*da*	$10^0 = 1$	*deci*	10^{-1}	*d*
hecto	10^2	*h*		*centi*	10^{-2}	*c*
kilo	10^3	*k*		*milli*	10^{-3}	*m*
mega	10^6	*M*		*micro*	10^{-6}	*u*
giga	10^9	*G*		*nano*	10^{-9}	*n*

Prefix	*Amount*	*Symbol*		*Prefix*	*Amount*	*Symbol*
tera	10^{12}	*T*	*pico* was earlier	*pico*	10^{-12}	*p*
peta	10^{15}	*P*	*micromicro*	*femto*	10^{-15}	*f*
exa	10^{18}	*E*		*atto*	10^{-18}	*a*

10^6=1 followed by 6 zeros, etc. 10^{-3}=0.001, etc.

Other forms for large figures are *googol* = 10^{100}; *googolplex* = $10^{10^{100}}$ (suggested by his young son to mathematician Edward Kasner [d. 1955]). A *centillion* is 10^{600}. A *parsec* is 1.9 × 10^{10} miles. A *light-year* is the distance light travels in a year, 6 × 10^{12} miles. Perhaps our smallest measure is the *atomic mass unit* (*amu*), estimated as 1.6604 × 10^{-24} grams. *Absolute zero,* as which all molecular movement would stop, is –273.16°C; –459.69°F.

There are more microseconds in a minute (60 million) than there will be minutes (52.6 million) in the 20th c. The telephone is linked in microseconds. See *med; medhi.*

> The moon is nothing
> But a circumambulating aphrodisiac
> Divinely subsidized to provoke the world
> Into a rising birthrate.
> —Christopher Fry, *The Lady's Not for Burning* (1948)

med: measure, take measure; hence ponder, judge, prescribe. An extension of *me IV,* this root formed many Latin words: *modicus, modulus, modus; meditari, meditatum; medicina;* etc. Thence *moderate, immoderate,* etc. *modest, immodest. modal; mode* and its doublet *mood* (in grammar; form modified by *mood:* state of mind, see *moro*). *model; mo(u)ld:* pattern.

modern (measured as of our day; influenced by *diurnal,* etc.). *modicum; modify; modulate, module. accommodate, commode, commodious, commodity. meditation,* etc. Meditation is the last of the stations on the eightfold Way to Nirvana; it is of little worth until the other seven are achieved; see *okto. premeditated.*

medical, medication, medicine, medicinal, etc. *remedy.* Fr, *modiste, moulage, turmoil,* folkchanged from L *trimodia:* vessel containing three measures, applied to a mill hopper, which shook as the grain flowed through. W, *metheglin:* literally, honey juice, deemed medicinal; see *medhu.* Gc, *mete, must; meet:* fit. *helpmeet,* a misreading of the Bible, Genesis 2:18: "It is not good that the man should be alone: I will make him an help meet for him"; modified to *helpmate.*

medhi: middle, between; an extension of *med.* Gk *mesos. OED* says that compounds with *meso-* are "almost innumerable"; it lists 92 "examples," as *mesohepaticon,* then in separate items details 104 "especially important" words, as *mesoblast, mesothesis, mesotonic.* Note also that *meso-* often fits as the median between two poles. Thus *dolicocephalic, mesocephalic,* and *brachicephalic,* measuring head sizes; *paleolithic, mesolithic,* and *neolithic,* marking divisions of the stone age; *microstylous, mesostylous,* and *macrostylous; hypogastrium, mesogastrium,* and *epigrastrium.*

Between two extremes is the *mean* (L *medianus:* middle; Fr *moyen*); hence also *median.* Both are defined as "average," but for exactness the three terms should be distinguished. *average* may be from Arab *awariyah:* first, merchandise damaged by sea water; then, equitable division of that loss among all concerned; but see *op I.* In statistics, strictly: (1) The *mean* is the number obtained by adding the lowest and the highest, then dividing by two. (2) The *median* has the same number of figures before it as after: the midmost of a series. (3) The *average,* also called the *mathematical mean,* is obtained by adding all the figures, then dividing by the number of figures. Thus, in the series 9, 12, 14, 19, 22, 24, 24, 27, 29, the mean is 19, the median is 22, and the average is 20. Since all these are dictionaried as "average," any of the three can be chosen according to one's bias; and since, when there are many numbers to be counted, the three "averages" may be far apart, one can understand the scorn in the statement: "The three degrees of the lie: lies, damn lies, and statistics." Also used in statistics is (4) the *mode:* the figure that occurs most frequently; in the above case, 24. As *Punch* remarked in 1846: "You pays your money, and you takes your choice." But Shakespeare knew (*Taming of the Shrew,* i, 1): "There's small choice in rotten apples." Southey in 1808 fervently cried: "Away with the battology of statistics!" (The first element of *battology:* useless repetition, and of *battologize,* is imitative, although "the Father of history," Herodotus, 5th c. B.C., tells of a stammerer named *Battos.*)

Mesopotamia: tract between two rivers. For over two centuries, from before Sir Walter Scott to after Bernard Shaw, *Mesopotamia*—"that sweet word Mesopotamia"—has been used to symbolize something incomprehensible but somehow soothing. Shaw: "There are people who will swallow as inspired revelation any sort of stuff that, so to speak, has the word Mesopotamia in it." The actor David Garrick (d. 1779) said he could pronounce *Mesopotamia* so as to move an audience to tears.

Also *mesial, mesityl. OED*'s 1976 supplement, noting the pronunciation "now usually" *meeso*, earlier *mayso,* lists 29 additional words beginning *meso,* as *mesoconch, mesotarsal,* and details 30 more, as *mesotherm. mesotron* (1938) was changed the next year to *meson:* a subatomic particle intermediate in mass between a proton and an electron.

Gk *meta:* originally, between, beside, mainly because of Aristotle's discussion of *meta*physics next to (after) physics, came also to mean beyond, higher, as in *metachemistry. metabolism* covers the processes of *anabolism,* which builds food into protoplasm, and *catabolism,* which breaks protoplasm into simpler usable substances. *metagalactic:* beyond the Milky Way, our galaxy. *metamorphosis, metaphor, metastasis, metathesis,* and some 260 more. At one point, *OED* gives up: "In the names of isomeric benzene di- derivatives, meta- denotes those compounds in which the two radicals that replace hydrogen in the benzene-ring are regarded as attached to alternate carbon atoms. As the number of these is unlimited, no list is given." Quotations mention a few, as *metanitrometachlorophenol.*

The sage A. K. Coomaraswamy stated that our civilization must move toward *metanoia* or *paranoia. metanoia:* spiritual transformation; see *para,* under *per I.*

L *medius. medium.* The *media,* blamed for many things, are of incalculable influence in our civilization. *medial, mediate,* etc. *immediate, intermediary, intermediate, mediocre, mediocrity. Mediterranean:* (sea in the) middle of the earth. *meridian:* pertaining to midday. *A.M.* and *P.M.*: *ante* and *post meridian:* before and after noon. *mediastinum. monial, mullion. mittens:* half-gloves. *mizzen* (mast). It, *mezzanine, mezzotint, intermezzo.* Fr, *midinette. milieu; moiety; moyen age; Middle Ages; medieval. mesne.* The *Golden Mean* was Aristotle's quest. See *kel VI* (gold); *ne.*

Gc, *mid, amid, middle* and its compounds, as *middling, middleman. middlebrow, middle-class;* both *midway* between low and high. *Middletown* is an imaginary average American town, used to suggest the attitudes and manners of the country middle class. Also *midnight, midstream, midsummer, midway, midwife* (Gm *mid:* with), *mid-Victorian,* etc.

midshipman; humorously, *midshipmite.* The midshipman, ranking between a naval cadet and the lowest commissioned officer, was a frequent butt. Thus *midshipman's butter:* the avocado; *midshipman's half-pay:* nothing a day and find yourself (provide your own board); *midshipman's nuts* ("from soup to nuts"): crumbled crackers as dessert. His status is called *midshipmanship*—as Cowper exclaimed in 1789, "There's a word for you!" See *pigge,* under *ane.*) There is also a fish called the *midshipman,* named for the pattern of luminous spots along its belly like the buttons on the coat.

Midgard (OGm *middenerd*): the Earth; in Norse mythology, midway between heaven and hell, and between *Niflheim:* home of ice, and *Muspellsheim:* home of fire. Midgard (which we inhabit) was formed of the body of the giant Ymir, killed by the gods; his sweat and blood became the oceans; his bones, the mountains; his hairs, the vegetation. His skull, the vault of the sky, is upheld by the four dwarfs, Nordi, Sudri, Austri, and Westri, at the four corners that give names to the four cardinal directions. From Midgard the rainbow bridge, Bifrost, starting at the ash tree Yggdrasill, which shelters the world, leads to Asgard, the abode of the gods. This contains twelve realms, including Valhalla (Norse *valr:* slain; *höll:* royal hall), home of heroes slain in battle and escorted there by one of the twelve Valkyries (*valr:* slain; *kyrja:* chooser), "virgins of slaughter." Alone of the gods, Thor, the thunderer (from whom *Thursday*), because of his heavy tread, may not cross the Bifrost bridge. Yggdrasil is also the horse of Yggr, another name for Odin.

"In the midst of life we are in death"—*The Book of Common Prayer.* Dante begins his *Divine Comedy:* "In the middle of the road of our life"; he was thirty-five, half the expectation of three score and ten. Pope, in *An Essay on Man,* advises:

Know then thyself, presume not God to scan,
The proper study of mankind is man.
Placed on this isthmus of a middle state,
A being darkly wise, and rudely great:
With too much knowledge for the sceptic side,
With too much weakness for the stoic's pride,
He hangs between . . .
Alike in ignorance, his reason such,
Whether he thinks too little, or too much . . .
Sole judge of truth, in endless error hurled,
The glory, jest, and riddle of the world.

medhu: honey, perhaps from its supposed healing qualities; see *med.* Gk *methu:* honey wine. *methyl,* coined in 1835, backformed from *methylene:* wine wood. *amethyst* (*a* negative): supposedly a protection against drunkenness. Gc, *mead.* W, *metheglin. mead* is a mix of honey, water, spices, and bitter herbs; *metheglin* is honey with water, spices, and sweet herbs. *hydromel* is made with honey, water, ginger, cloves, rosemary, ale, and yeast.

Weave a circle round him thrice,
And close your eyes with holy dread,
For he on honey-dew hath fed,
And drunk the milk of Paradise.
—Coleridge, *Kubla Khan*

mei I: little; lessen. Gk *meion:* less. *meiosis. mecogyrous. meionite. m(e)iophylly, m(e)iotherm. Miocene; Miolithic. Ameiurus:* genus of "small-tailed" catfish.

L *nimis:* too much, excessive, is an example of *meiosis,* being literally "not little." *Ne quid nimis:* nothing too much, is the Roman expression of the Golden Mean. Gk *meden agan,* a maxim of Solon, 600 B.C., was inscribed on the Temple of Apollo at Delphi (along with another famous maxim, of Thales, 7th c. B.C., *Gnothi seauton:* Know thyself, repeated by many, including Pope; see quotation under *medhi*). *nimiety.* Gk *mikros:* small; for *micro-*, see *sme.*

L *minus; minuere, minutum. minuend, minuet; minute* (tiny). *minutes* of a meeting or of the day; see *stebh. minor, minus; minimal. minuscule* vs. *majuscule* (see below, and under *me III*). Possibly *mime:* reality made small; *pantomime; mimesis, mimetic, mimic, mimicry. miminypiminy. mimo-*, as *mimology, mimophyre, mimotype. Mimosa, Mimosa pudica* (the sensitive plant); Longfellow, in *Evangeline* (1847), notes:

> At the tramp of a horse's hoof on the turf of the prairies,
> Far in advance are closed the leaves of the shrinking mimosa.

minion and its doublet *mignon,* whence the flower *mignonette,* although some trace these to Fr *minet:* pussy, which may be imitative ("Minny, minny, minny"). In speaking, *minion* may mislead a Jew, as Principal Kelly found one day when, in Elizabethan mood, he said to his monitor Abie Cohen: "Boy, fetch me a minion!" He was surprised at the arrivals; *minyon* is the quorum, 10 males over the age of thirteen, required for Jewish religious services.

A *miniature,* though associated with smallness from the many little pictures on medieval manuscripts, is from *minium,* a coloring; thus also *vermilion* (L *vermis:* worm; whence the dye), *carmine* (Arab *qirmiz:* worm), and *crimson.* For *carminative,* see *kan.* Recently, perhaps from the joint influence of *miniature* and *minimum, mini* has been used as a separate word, and as a prefix in such words as *minicab, miniskirt; mini* has in turn led to *midi-* and *maxi-*, the three thus marking sizes of feminine garments. *minify* is the opposite of *magnify. meatus* is a small body-passage.

Note that *minuscule,* although pronounced with a short *i,* is spelled as from *minus.* Small letters are still indicated in proofreaders' marks as *lc* (*lower case*), from the early days of printing, when each letter was set in place by hand, one line o' type at a time; for then the minuscule letters were arranged in a case *below* the majuscule (capital) letters, for which the proofreader today writes *cap.*

Also *comminute:* pulverize. *mince; diminish, diminution.* It, *diminuendo.* Fr, *menu:* detailed list of separate items for diners not wishing the full table d'hôte. *miniver* (Fr, *vair:* fur; for Cinderella's "glass" slippers, see *ua I*).

minister was first a minor officer, a provider, as the verb *to minister* (to one's needs) still shows; *ministering* to his congregation, a pastor "feeds" his flock. (Antonyms of *minister* are *magister, magistrate.*) Hence *ministry* and its doublets: (1) *mystery:* first, medieval trade, its practice kept within the guild; also, early drama; (2) Fr, *metier:* trade, business. "God will forgive me," said the dying poet Heine, "*c'est son metier*": That's his job. *minstrel.* It, *ministrone.* Port, *muscovado:* lesser-quality granulated sugar. Russ *menshevik:* minority (antonym, *bolshevik*).

From *minus,* the prefix *mis* came into English with two meanings: (1) wrong; (2) bad. Thus (1) *mistake, mistrial, mistranslate. misbehave* smacks of both meanings; (2) *misalliance, misfortune, mischief.* (*bonchief* has dropped out of the language.) Some attribute this prefix to the root *mei II.*

Also *amiss, miss.* The prefix *mis* is given six columns in *OED,* which then details 121 relevant words, as *miscreant:* first, unbeliever (hence, naturally, a scroundrel); *misanthrope, misdemeanor, mistrust. OED*'s 1976 supplement, with numerous additions to the old words, gives 31 new ones, as *misallocation; misdial* (on the telephone); *miscode; mishellene,* as opposed to *philhellene. misregistration* is used of faulty color television, and of computer signals (high, low, or skew). *mismate* is in *OED*'s 1976 supplement; the 1933 *OED* has *mismated,* quoting J. G. Holland, who in 1858 declared: "A mismated match is much worse than unmated life."

Not counted among the above *OED* words are those beginning *mis(o),* from Gk *misos:* hate. Of these, *OED* lists 28, as *misocapnist:* hater of tobacco smoke (smoking); *misoxeny,* the feeling of a *xenophobe:* hater of strangers. It then details 8 such words, as *misanthropy, misogynist. misology* is hatred of reason or discussion (literally, of words). *misoneism* is hatred of new things, but is also used of hatred of the unknown, "best exemplified in children and savages."

Microtinae and *Microtus:* subfamily and genus of rodents, including the lemmings, hordes of which were fabled to drop from the sky, but which actually do rush to drown in the sea.

mei II, expanded as **meig, mein, meit:** change, move away; exchange, arrange for services (hence applied to public office). Gk, *amoeba* (*a* negative): changes but remains one. *am(o)ebean:* alternately answering, as *amoebean verses.* The *Saturday Review* (London), 25 May 1861, spoke of an "amoebean exchange of witticism between the Bench and the Bar." In March, "Spring and Winter sing an amoebean song." *amoebiform:* like the Old Man of the Sea, protean. (The prophetic sea god who could change his shape at will, *Proteus,* is from Gk *protos:* first; see *per I. Proteus* is also a genus of bacteria.) L, *meatus;* and via *commeatus,* Fr, *congé, congee.*

L *mutare, mutatum:* change. *mutation. commute, commutations and permutations. permeate. irremeable. transmute; mutable, immutable. mutual. mew, mews, mo(u)lt.* The verb *mew* was used of birds *moulting:* changing feathers. Then the plural form *mews* (now treated as a singular) was used of the buildings where the royal hunting hawks were kept; then of the royal and noble stables on such grounds. Many short lanes and London streets today are thus called *mews.*

Also, *common:* used together. *The Common:* ground owned by the community, usually a central square of grass, in early days used for grazing. *The Commons:* British Lower House of Parliament, representatives of the "common people." *communicate, excommunicate. communism,* coined in 1840 by Goodwyn Barmby, who in 1841 founded the London Communist Propaganda Society. Karl Marx wrote his *Communist Manifesto* in 1847; in 1849 he came to London to study in the Museum Library, publishing the first volume of *Das Kapital* in 1867.

Hence, too, *community* and *commune. municipal, municipality:* first, a Roman town with its own regulations (*munia capere:* to hold [its own] services). *munificent. remuneration. immune; immunity, immunology.* Also *migrate, emigrate, immigration; transmigration. remuda,* on the western ranch. Gc *gamaidans:* badly changed; wounded. *mad, maim, mayhem; mean. bemean,* virtually supplanted by *demean;* see *men II.*

> If you can talk with crowds and keep your virtue,
> Or walk with kings, nor lose the common touch . . .
> If you can fill the unforgiving minute
> With sixty seconds worth of distance run,
> Yours is the earth, and everything that's in it,
> And—which is more—you'll be a man, my son.
> —Kipling, *If*

"Adieu to common feeling, common prudence, and common sense!"–Rev. Sydney Smith (d. 1845). "Common sense is most uncommon sense."

mei III: fix; fortify. L *murus:* wall; *munire, munitum:* fortify. *murage; mural, mure, immure; intramural, extramural. muniment. premunition,* rarely used, and not to be confused with and used for *premonition* (L *monire:* warn); thus also *premunitory* and *premonitory* (see *men I*). *ammunition,* a shift in Fr, when *la munition* became *l'ammunition. meres* (and bounds). *muromontite* is from L *Muromontania,* Gm *Mauersberg,* in Saxony, where the mineral was found.

But love, first learned in a lady's eyes,
Lives not alone immured in the brain,
But, with the motion of all elements,
Courses as swift as thought in every power . . .
–*Love's Labor's Lost,* iv, 3

mei IV: bind. Skr, *Mitra,* Vedic god. *Mithras,* Persian god of light, from the idea of a bond, a covenant with the Lord, such as Jehovah with Noah after the Flood (Genesis 9:8–17), its sign the rainbow; and with Moses after his forty days on the mount (Exodus 34), its seal the Ten Commandments.

Mithridates, name of rulers, especially *Mithridates VI Eupator,* "the Great," king of Pontus, the most formidable opponent of Rome, who "immunized" himself against poison by taking gradually increased doses. Defeated by Pompey, he died in 63 B.C.–by his own hand. Hence *mithridate,* a supposed panantidote, and half a dozen more words in *OED.* Also used figuratively, as when Southey in 1812 spoke of pernicious ideas, and of those "whom a sound understanding and a mind well-stored have fortified, as with mithridate, against such poison." See also *sta.*

Gk *mitos:* thread. *mitre; mitome, mitosis, mitochondrion. dimity:* of two threads. *samite:* of six threads. See *seks.*

Mithras, God of the Morning, our trumpets waken the Wall!
'Rome is above the Nations, but Thou art over all!'
–Kipling

mei V: gentle, mild. L, *mitigate.* Russ, *mir:* peace, settlement. Pol, *Casimir:* proclaimer of peace. Gc, *mild; Miles, Milo.*

meigh: urinate; squeeze; crush. L, *micturate, micturition.* Gc, *mist, mizzle; mixen. mistletoe,* its glutinous berries supplying birdlime; the *missel thrush* feeds on it and helps propagate it. Washington Irving, in *The Sketch Book* (1820), explains the human use: "The mistletoe is still hung up in farmhouses and kitchens at Christmas; and the young men have the privilege of kissing the girls under it, plucking each time a berry from the bush. When the berries are all plucked the privilege ceases." The plucking has lapsed, but the hanging and kissing continue. The mistletoe is a parasite on the appletree, the elm, willow, thorn, poplar, and more. Shakespeare, in *Titus Andronicus,* ii, 3, calls it baleful; but mistletoe on the oak was held in veneration by the Druids, and was deemed so beneficial in the ills of old age that it was called *Lignum Sancta Crucis:* wood of the holy cross. The mistletoe was the one thing to which Balder was vulnerable, because it was overlooked when his mother Frigga (queen of the Norse gods) pledged "all things" to do her son no harm. Loki, god of evil, persuaded the blind god Hokur to strike Balder with a mistletoe twig, which killed him; see *tre.* (Frigga is usually considered the goddess of married love; Freya, the goddess of love, the northern Venus. Actually, Frigga is of the Aesir family of Scandinavian myth; Freya, of the Vanir family; the two lines of belief merged, and the two goddesses are sometimes fused, and sometimes confused.)

Also *mash* and *mush,* by some attributed to the root *meik;* both are sometimes used figuratively; slang, *mushy.* From the slang sense of "to have a crush on someone," in the 1880s rose the use of *mash* to mean to attempt to rouse the opposite sex. C. G. Leland in 1882 said of the gypsies: "These black-eyed beauties by mashing men for many generations, with shafts shot sideways and most wantonly, at last sealed their souls into the corner of their eyes." Hence a *masher,* defined in *OED* as one "who poses as a 'lady-killer'."

meik: mix. Gk *mixis:* mixing; intercourse. *amphimixis, pseudomixis, apomixis:* the three types of reproduction. *apomist.* L *miscere, mixtum. miscible. immiscible,* like oil and water. *mix, mixture; admix, commix, immix, intermix. panmiscia. promiscuous. miscellaneous; miscegenation.*

Sp, *mestizo;* Fr, *métis; mélange. meddle, medley. maslin. pell-mell* (OFr *meslemesle*). *mustang,* its form influenced by Sp *mostrenco:* straying.

meino: have in mind; complain. Gc, *moan, bemoan. mean, meaning, meaningful, meaningless. OED* devotes 66 columns to the verb *mean* and the noun *meaning.* Plato (d. 348 B.C.), in *The Republic,* points out that "many a man, when he thinks he is reasoning, is actually disputing, because he has not established the meaning of what he is discussing." Bertrand Russell, in *Human Knowledge: Its Scope and Limits* (1948), goes so far as to state that "outside logic and pure mathematics, there are no words of which the meaning is precise." Proving Russell's point is Oliver Wendell Holmes Sr.'s protest: "Just because I say I like sea bathing, that doesn't mean I want to be pickled in brine."

There is precision, if not vision, in the mind of Mr. Grewgious (Dickens, *The Mystery of Edwin Drood*), who states: "If I do not clearly express what I mean, it is either for the reason that, having no conversational powers, I cannot express what I mean, or that having no meaning, I do not mean what I fail to express." Many of us, less analytically—even unwittingly—suffer Mr. Grewgious's plight.

> This world's no blot for us,
> Nor blank; it means intensely, and means good:
> To find its meaning is my meat and drink.
> —Browning, *Fra Lippo Lippi,* which is rich in meaning

mel I, (s)mel: melt, soften; soft, soft substance. This root is intertwined with *mel V.* Perhaps Gk *blennos:* slime; a prefix in English, as in *blennorrhea. blenny:* slimefish. *malakhos:* soft. *maltha. malax. Malaxis:* genus of orchids. *malacology:* study of molluscs; see below. *Malacostraca:* subclass of soft-shelled crustacea. *osteomalacia. malaco-,* as *malacoderm:* soft-skinned; *malaciazooid:* soft-bodied. *amalgam* (Arab *al:* the; the word borrowed, Syrian from Greek, then returned). *Amalthea,* nurse of Zeus: literally, gentle with the god. *ambly-:* dull, blunt, as *amblygon, amblygonite, amblyopia.*

L *mollis:* soft. *mellow; moil, mollify; emollient.* Fr, *mouillé. mullein:* soft-leaved. *Mollusca:* phylum of soft invertebrates, one of which is a *mollusc. Mollugo:* genus of chickweeds. L *blandis:* smooth-tongued. *bland. blandishment;* these may be partly imitative, as is the scornful *bla-bla-bla.*

Gc, *melt; smelt* (the fish). Fr, *enamel. mild. Mildred:* mild power. *mildew,* influenced by *melit:* honey. *mollycoddle,* influenced by *Molly,* pet name for *Mary,* whence also slang *moll.*

Also *mutton.* As the jester Wamba points out to the swineherd in chapter

1 of Scott's *Ivanhoe* (1820), animals, cared for by the serf Saxons, were tended by their Saxon names; when served to the Norman overlords, they were devoured by their French names: *bull–beef* (Fr *boeuf*); *hog, swine–pork* (Fr *porc*); *sheep –mutton* (Fr *mouton*). The origin of most of these words is lost in the mists of prehistory. *bull* is from the IE root *bhel:* to swell (from the prominent phallus). From Fr *mouton* came E *mutton,* and *moutonnée:* shaped like a sheep's back, said of the rocks or foam-crested waves; according to Victor Hugo, "the fleece of the sinister sheep of the sea."

In the earliest modern farce, *Pierre Patelin* (1464; still popular in a lively translation by Moritz Jagendorf), a draper comes to court accusing his shepherd of stealing sheep, but finds that the lawyer is a man who has brazenly cheated him out of a bale of cloth; the draper's angry outcries keep the judge protesting *Revenons à ces moutons!:* Let's come back to these sheep! Repeated by Rabelais as *Retournons à nos moutons!,* the cry has become a catchphrase meaning "Don't change the subject!"

Byron, in *Don Juan,* v, smiles condescendingly

When amatory poets sing their loves
In liquid lines mellifluously bland,
And pair their rhymes as Venus yokes her doves. . . .

mel II: abundance, strength. L *multum:* much. *multum in parvo:* much in little; used of things, as a well-arranged, modern kitchen; or of persons small in bulk but great in comprehensiveness, as the schoolmaster in Goldsmith's *The Deserted Village:*

And still they gazed, and still the wonder grew
That one small head could carry all he knew.

OED states that in the 19th c. the prefix *multi* "came into frequent general use." It lists 102 such words, as *multilingual, multimillionaire;* and details 98, as *multifarious, multipara, multiplex, multiply, multiplicity, multitude.* In 1821 Southey wrote *A Vision of Judgement,* with high praise of King George III; in 1822 Byron mocked this in *The Vision of Judgment,* saying, among other things:

Thus spoke the Demon, later called multifaced
By multiscribbling Southey.

It, *molto,* as *molto allegro.* Possibly *mulct.* L *melior:* better. *ameliorate. meliorism,* for the optimist who believes that "the best of all possible worlds" is still to come.

mel III: dark colored; black. Gk *melas, melanos. melanism, melanin, melanite.* There are 66 associated words in *OED. melano-,* as *melanoma, melanotic. melancholy:* black bile, one of the four humours (see *ugu*). *psilomelane. melampod:* literally, black foot, the plant hellebore, once used as a cathartic. A book of parables in 1643 listed "briony, wormwood, wolfbane, rue, and melampod, the emblems of sedition, malice, fear, ambition, and jealousy."

Melanchthon (see *peisk*). *Melanesian. Melanchroi:* pale, black-haired Caucasians, one of Huxley's divisions of mankind. *Melanthium:* literally, black flower; genus of herbs. *Melampyrum:* black wheat; genus of herb also known as cowwheat. *Corimelaena:* genus including the negro bug. L *mulleus:* reddish-purple shoe of Roman magistrate; E *mule. mullet, surmullet.* Possibly Du *malen:* paint; E *maulstick.* See *kel II; niger.*

Hence loathed Melancholy,
Of Cerberus and blackest Midnight born,

In Stygian cave forlorn,
Mongst horrid shapes, and shrieks, and sights unholy.
—Milton, *L'Allegro* (1631)

Hail, thou goddess sage and holy,
Hail, divinest Melancholy!
Whose saintly visage is too bright
To hit the sense of human sight,
And therefore to our weaker view
O'erlaid with black, staid Wisdom's hue.
—Milton, *Il Penseroso* (1631)

mel IV: limb; then musical section; hence song. Gk *melos. melodeon, melodious, melody,* etc. *melisma. dulcimer. melodrama,* originally with music. *Melpomene:* songstress; Muse of tragedy, which in ancient Greece was sung.

A damsel with a dulcimer
In a vision once I saw;
It was an Abyssinian maid
And on her dulcimer she played.
[*Read it all.*]
—Coleridge, *Kubla Khan*

mel V: grind, grindstone; things ground. Intertwined with *mel I.* L *molaris:* grindstone. *molar* (tooth; the grinder). *mole* (hard lump). *immolate:* first, sprinkle a sacrifice with meal. *multure. emolument:* first, miller's fee. *mill, miller. meal; mealie. miliolite; milium; millet. Melica:* genus of grasses. *ormolu:* ground gold. Gk *mulè:* millstone. *mylo-,* as *mylodont, mylonite, myloglossus. amidin* and *amyloid* (*a* negative).

Russ, *blini, blintz.* Du, *maelstrom.* Fr, *moulin.* Gc, *malm, mold, molder; malt. mull,* now used figuratively: "Let me mull things over."

These were men of pith and thew,
Whom the city never called;
Scarce could read or hold a quill,
Built the barn, the forge, the mill.
—Edmund Blunden, *Forefathers*

melg: wipe off; squeeze out, milk (see *glact*). *milch, milk.* For *Liebfraumilch,* see *per VI c. emulgent, emulsify, emulsion. promulgate. Caprimulgidae, Caprimulgus:* family and genus of birds, the goatsuckers. The Romans told someone who made an impossible proposal, *Mulgere hircos:* Go milk a billy goat!—which Johnson (Boswell's *Life of Samuel Johnson,* 21 July 1763) scornfully applied to skeptics: "Truth sir, is a cow, which will yield such people no more milk, and so they are gone to milk the bull."

melit: honey, sweetness. See also *keneko.* Gk, *Melissa:* the honeybee; also a girl's name. *Meliposa:* genus of honeybees (*ponos:* toil; the busy bee). *hydromel; oenomel. mulse. caramel. melicaris:* like a honeycomb. *Melianthaceae, Melianthus:* family and genus, the honey flower. *melilot:* clover (loved by bees). L *melimelum:* honey apple; *Malus:* genus of apple trees, of which there are over a hundred varieties (see *abel*). *malic (acid), melinite. camomile:* earth apple. *marmalade. melon. Hamamelidaceae, Hamamelis:* family and genus of plants, the medlar.

The *medlar* was an apple, eaten when partly decayed, pulpy and soft, now gone from the market. Drawing a figure from the fruit, Peter Pindar, in *The*

Rights of Kings (1791), said: "The heart should be a medlar, not a crab." Shakespeare uses *medlar* four times: in *Measure for Measure,* iv, 3; *Timon of Athens,* iv, 3; *As You Like It,* iii, 2; and, emphasizing the slang sense: the *pudenda* (from the shape when it splits), especially in the third successive speech of Mercutio with bawdy allusions, in *Romeo and Juliet,* ii,1:

Now will he sit under a medlar tree
And wish his mistress were that kind of fruit
As maids call medlars when they laugh alone.
O Romeo, that she were, O that she were
An open etcetera, and thou a poperin pear!

melli-, as *melliferous, mellifluent. molasses. mildew* is a blend of this root and *mel I:* it was thought to drop down like dew.

Playwright Thomas Heywood, in his study *Hierarchy of the Blessed Angels* (1635), carried on Shakespeare's sonnet-puns on his name:

Mellifluous Shake-speare, whose enchanting Quill
Commanded Mirth or Passion, was but *Will.*

melo: bad. L *malus. malady, malaise, malaria, malefic, malice. petit mal, grand mal. dismal* (L *dies mali:* bad days). *OED* states that *mal* is frequently used to form nonce words, and lists 22, as *malcreated, malhygiene, maladjusted* (now more frequent). It then details more in 14 columns, including *malfeasance, maltreat, maladroit, malapert.* Some may be matched with their opposite: *malediction, benediction; malefactor, benefactor; malevolent, benevolent; malison, benison; malign, benign; malignant, benignant. malism.* Gc, *small:* of little value, first applied to animals.

There are Latin and French phrases. *mala fide(s). mala praxis;* whence *malpractice. mal de flanc. mal de mere. mal à propos;* whence Mrs. *Malaprop* in Sheridan's *The Rivals* (1775), and *malapropism.* Among the lady's verbal aberrations are "Illiterate him, I say, quite from your memory. . . . If I reprehend any thing in this world, it is the use of my oracular tongue, and a nice derangement of epitaphs." See *per VI g.* Earlier (and to some extent still), such blunders were called *Quicklyisms,* from Dame *Quickly,* servant to Doctor Caius in *The Merry Wives of Windsor* (1620), who was ready to help all three of Anne Page's suitors, but speciously (especially) Master Fenton. See also *kuon.* The device of mismouthing the language is attractive to authors, and may be amusing to listeners or readers. For Mrs. Slipslop in Fielding's *Joseph Andrews* (1742), see *lei I.* Winifred Jenkins, Humphry's sweetheart and the maid of Miss Tabitha Bramble in Tobias Smollett's epistolatory novel *Humphry Clinker* (1770), both misspells and misuses words. She thinks that the "mail sex" will agree that "yellow fitts my fizzogmony." She writes: "Dear Molly: You that live in the country have no deception of our doings at Bath. . . . The sarvants at Bath are devils in garnet."

A more recent label for such pseudo slips is *Goldwynism,* from the supposed blunders of movie magnate Samuel *Goldwyn* (fostered by his press agents): "In two words, im possible. . . . I read part of it all the way through. . . . Whoever goes to a psychoanalyst ought to have his head examined. . . . I'll give you a definite maybe." *OED*'s 1972 supplement gives 24 lines to quotations on *Goldwynism,* the first being from the 8 May 1937 *Saturday Evening Post:* "'It sounds like Sam Goldwyn,' Chaplin said; 'we'll pin it on Sam', and he repeated it until it became a world-famous Goldwynism."

mems: flesh. Gk *menigx:* membrane. *meningitis, meningocele, meninx, myringa.* L *membrum:* thigh, fleshy part. *member, dismember; membrane.* For *remember,* see *smer.*

"We are all members one of another"—Paul to the Ephesians, 4:25.

men I: have one's mind roused; hence both to love and to be mad (linked also by Shakespeare: "The lunatic, the lover . . . of imagination all compact"); also to think, remember; show, warn, foretell, and other extensions.

Skr, *mantra:* prayer, counsel, Vedic hymns. *mantra* came to be used of a sacred passage or term for prayer or incantation, supposedly embodying the god invoked, and often repeated lengthily for its potent appeal. Greatest of these is the term *OM,* actually a triphone *a u m,* a compression into one sound of three-times-three "substances" that comprise the universe: the three worlds, earth, atmosphere, and heaven; the three (main) Hindu gods, Brahma, Vishnu, Shiva; and the three sacred Vedic scriptures, Tig Veda, Yajur Veda, Sama Veda. Some add, more personally, another triad, the god Vishnu (the sun), his wife Sri (good fortune), and oneself, praying. *OM* is discussed in various Upanishads, among which the Mandukya is wholly devoted to its powers. Representations of the lingam often bear the Sanskrit sign for *OM,* and the sound is repeated and repeated in pious prayer.

manas: mind. *Ahriman:* hostile spirit. *Ormuzd,* shortened from *Ahuramazda:* wise lord (*ahura:* lord). Via the Orient and Portuguese, *mandarin;* the fruit *mandarine,* from the golden robe of the Chinese official.

Gk *mantis:* seer. *mantic; praying mantis. matos:* automatic. *menthenein:* learn; *mathema:* thing learned; science. E *mathesis:* mental discipline. Metaphysical speculation is derided by Pope in *The Dunciad* (1742), iv:

> Mad mathesis alone was unconfined,
> Too mad for mere material chains to bind.

The suffix *math* was first applied to learning in general; hence *opsimath:* late learner (Gk *opse:* late); *polymath:* learned in many fields; *chrestomathy* (Gk *khrestos:* useful). Later, the term *mathematical* became limited to the precise sciences: arithmetic, geometry, astronomy, optics. (In the quadrivium of medieval studies, music took the place of optics; see *kuetuer.*) In the 16th c., on the analogy of the word *physics, mathematics* with an *s* became the normal form, requiring a singular verb.

Gk *maenad:* orgiastic worshiper or priestess of Dionysus, as the Roman bacchante was of Bacchus. Dryden, in *Alexander's Feast,* tells us:

> Bacchus, ever fair and young,
> Drinking joys did first ordain;
> Bacchus' blessings are a treasure,
> Drinking is the soldier's pleasure,
> Rich the treasure,
> Sweet the pleasure,
> Sweet is pleasure after pain.

From *Bacchus* came *bay,* another name for *laurel,* the leaves of which were made into a wreath, or crown (the *bays* or the *laurels*), for the winners at the *Bacchic* games. Hence also *bayberry;* see *bhel I.* Apollo was the overall god of the Greek games; when he pursued Daphne, upon her prayer the modest nymph was changed into a laurel, which was thereafter used to crown the winners at the contests. Hence also *daphnean:* shy.

The core event of the orgiastic Dionysia or Bacchanalia was the tearing-to-pieces of animals with the bare hands, then devouring them. This, and the Orphic ritual, and the Yasna liturgy of haoma of the Zoroastrians with bread, water, and wine, to ensure immortality, foreran the Eucharist of the Christians (see *ueguh*), which also, until chastened by Paul, tended to degenerate into licentious revelry. The Temple of Dionysus, built in Athens near the theatre for the dramatic contests of the Greater Dionysia, bore a mural of the story of Pentheus (the name means God's vengeance; see *kuei II*). As a young king of Thebes, Pentheus forbade the rites and worship of Dionysus. The god intoxicated the king, then sent him to spy on the women's mysteries, then roused the king's mother, Agave, and her two sisters, in their orgiastic fury, to see and seize a lion and tear it apart. Bearing the severed head of the beast back to the city, the sobering Agave realized that she held her son's head in her hands. (The Dionysia were sometimes called *Omophagia:* eating of raw flesh.)

Euripides presents this story in his play *Bacchae;* in the 405 B.C. postmortem production by the playwright's son, the trilogy containing *Bacchae* won first prize. The play was very popular in the ancient world. In 53 B.C. it was being performed before the kings of Armenia and Parthia when Parthian horseman returned with the head of Crassus (who with Pompey and Caesar had formed the first Roman triumvirate); the actor playing Agave used the head of Crassus in the play, thus informing the kings of their victory.

Bacchae is still considered one of the world's greatest dramas. Robert Graves indicates its eternal significance: "This tearing apart of the young man by the Bacchantes may seem far removed from modern life, but the archives of morbid pathology are filled with such stories. . . . An English or American woman in a nervous breakdown of sexual origin will often instinctively reproduce in faithful and disgusting detail much of the ancient Dionysian ritual. I have witnessed it myself in helpless terror." Euripides wrote 2300 years before Freud. For further discussion of *Bacchae,* see my *Guide to Great Plays* (1956, 1984).

Hence also *manic. mania, maniac,* also used as suffixes indicating excessive attraction, or compulsion, as *kleptomania, monomania, dypsomaniac.* (The opposite failing is a *phobia,* excessive revulsion, as *hydrophobia, Germanophobe.*) The suffix *mancy,* however, developed from the meaning to show, to foretell, as *chiromancy, necromancy.* Under *aeromancy,* my *Dictionary of Early English* (1955) defines 117 words ending *mancy. cotoptromancy* is divination by means of a mirror, which many women have found distressing. Cotgrave's 1611 *Dictionary* defines *anthropomantie* as divination by the raising of dead men; the Roman emperor Heliogabalus is said to have practiced it. (*Heliogabalus* took his imperial name from the sun god, *Helios,* in whose sacrificial temple he had served as a youth.) *OED* in 1933 defines *anthropomancy:* pretended divination by the entrails of men; "pretended" seems an ill-chosen word; the practitioners may have believed in it. The topic is capped by *moromancy:* foolish divination, a 17th c. term that covers them all.

There are 264 recorded *phobia*s, not so many *mania*s—some of which, indeed, do not refer to excessive desire or drive. Thus, *strychnomania* (Gk *strukhnos:* strychnine) is deadly nightshade poisoning. *decalcomania,* for a time an "excessive attraction," has lapsed to a merely descriptive term: the practice of transferring a colored design from paper onto glass, metal, or the skin—in the last case, a pseudo tattoo (*de:* down; *calcare:* press; *calx, calcem:* heel). *Tulipomania* was a truly excessive drive that swept from Holland to England in the late 17th c., with a single bulb selling for hundreds of pounds sterling. Addison, in *The Tatler,* no. 218 (1710), spoke of "a person of good taste . . . had not his head been touched with the tulipomania." The tulip first came into England ca. 1575, from

Persia via Turkey and Holland; Pers *durband* gave English both *turban* and *tulip,* the plant named (*l.r* shift) for the shape of the flower.

Three stages of mania have been noted: *hypomania,* a less intense form; the "normal," or median, *mania;* and the more intense *hypermania.* Some politicians and demagogues suffer from a professional type, *mania concionabunda:* a constant itch to be addressing a public.

Gk *Mnemosyne,* patroness of memory. Hence *mnemonic, mnesic, mnestic.* With *a* negative, *amnesia; amnesty. anamnesis, paramnesia. Mnemosyne,* a Titoness, was by Jupiter the mother of the nine Muses; note that the Muses, the arts, are daughters of memory. Northern mythology lends similar emphasis: the chief Norse god, Odin, bears a raven on each shoulder; one, Hugin, is Thought; the other, Munin, is Memory. Also *music.*

There's music in the sighing of a reed;
There's music in the gushing of a rill;
There's music in all things, if men had ears:
Their earth is but an echo of the spheres.
—Byron

With *a* negative (*ab:* from), *amusia. amuse, amusement,* etc. (*a, ad:* to, with). *museum. mosaic* is from LL *musaicum:* related to the Muses, who were often represented in mosaic design. Wilfrid Blair in 1914 neatly entitled his book of English parodies *Sa Muse s'amuse.* A pleasant number for a dinner at home is "more than the Graces but fewer than the Muses." See *gar.* The nine Muses are *Calliope:* epic poetry; *Clio:* history; *Erato:* love poetry; *Euterpe:* lyric poetry and music; *Melpomene:* tragedy; *Poly(hy)mnia:* singing, rhetoric, mime; *Terpsichore:* dancing and choral singing; *Thalia:* comedy and pastoral poetry; *Urania:* astronomy.

muse: to ponder, came via LL *musum:* sniff about, like a dog; whence also *muzzle. musette, cornemuse. Eumenides:* the kindly spirits, euphemistic term for the Furies; see *fur.*

L *mens, mentem. mental; mention.* For *sentimental,* see *sent.* The brilliant folk that named their exclusive society for high IQs *Mensa* seem to have overlooked that the root of *mens* is *ment,* as in *mentality,* the group's fundamental concern. *mensa* deals not with mind but with matter; L *mensa* means table. (Even the epicure Epicurus, as Frederick W. Hackwood points out in his refreshing book *Good Cheer* (1911), "was less addicted to mensal than to mental converse.") A *mensa* is a flat slab atop the Roman Catholic altar. In early divorces, one was legally removed *a mensa et thoro:* from board and bed. The brightest star in the southern constellation, *Mensa:* the Table, has a magnitude of 5.3, making it just visible to the naked eye. A final assumption: Perhaps, as the Knights of the Round Table roamed the world to wreak righteousness, so the siblings of Mensa probe the world to seek truth. Enough of *mensa,* though, from one who was at school before the "intelligence quotient" became a basis for *mensuration.*

dementia praecox. demented, ament. non compos mentis; whence *nincompoop.* "Hurry Harry" March, in Cooper's *The Deerslayer* (1841), remembers what the officers call "compass meant us" and explains: "*compass* for the point and *meant us* for the intention. Poor Hetty is what I call on the verge of ignorance, and sometimes she stumbles on one side of the line and sometimes on t'other."

L *meminisse:* remember; *monere, monitum:* show, warn. *momento. memento mori:* skull at the feast, or other reminder of our human end. *comment. reminiscent. admonish; monition, monitor, monitory, premonition. Juno Moneta:* sister and wife of Jupiter: the warning goddess, so called by the Romans, with three monitory tales: (1) she advised them to sacrifice a pregnant sow to Cybele, to avert an earthquake; (2) she told them, when they feared for finances in the war against Pyrrhus, that money would never fail those whose cause was just; and (3) the geese that were crated for sacrifice in her temple at the city wall cackled and thus alerted the Romans to the intended surprise attack by the Gauls, 390 B.C. Roman coins were first minted in the Temple of Juno Moneta; hence *mint, money, monetary.* Port, *moidore:* money of gold; Fr, *porte-monnaie.*

Also *monster,* deemed a premonition; *monstrosity, monstrous. monstrance:* showing of the sacred host; also called *ostensorium* (see *ten*). *monument:* public showing. *muster:* showing up for inspection. *summon. Minerva:* goddess of wisdom, who shows how. *mentor.* It, *lentamente, portamento, tardamente, tostamente.*

Gc *minne:* love. *minnesinger. minion:* first, darling; Fr *mignon.* Du, *minikin. mind.* Perhaps *mean:* to signify; and *man:* the being that thinks he thinks. *Zamenis:* genus of snakes, aroused. *Trichomanes:* genus of ferns.

"Mind and matter," said the lady in the wig, "glide swift into the vortex of immensity. Howls the sublime, and softly sleeps the calm ideal, in the whispering chambers of imagination"—Dickens, *Martin Chuzzlewit.*

Space is supposed from what it separates,
Mind is marked by what it conjoins.

men II: stand out, project; threaten. L *minax, minacem. minatory. menace. commination. amenable; adminicle:* standing toward; hence, supporting. *eminent. imminent, prominent. promontory. demeanor.* The verb *demean* has so long been misused to mean belittle that the dictionaries now grant it this meaning, for which it has largely replaced *bemean;* see *mei II.* L *mentum:* chin; hence *mental.* For *mental* referring to the mind, see *men I. mons pubis:* pubic mound of the man; *mons veneris:* Venus mound of the woman. *mound, mount, mountain. amount, paramount; tantamount* (see *kat*). *remount, surmount.* E *mountebank,* It *monte-in-banco:* stand on a bench, as did medieval quacks and buffoons, and early American "soap-box" politicians. *moniliform. mane. monte,* from the pile of cards after the first deal. Fr, *mont-de-piété:* pawnshop!

Ariosto, in *Orlando Furioso* (1516), had a hyperbolic boaster, *Rodomonte:* one who can roll away a mountain; whence *rodomontade. marmot* is partly imitative; likewise *marmoset,* a blend of OFr *marmotter:* mutter, and LL *mus montanus:* mountain mouse. "The mountain will labor, and bring forth a laughable mouse"; so spoke Horace, figuratively, in *Ars Poetica* (18 B.C.). *montage, montane, cismontane, tramontane, ultramontane. piedmontite:* a silicate, from *Piedmont:* mountain foot. *monticule. verumontanum,* inside the male. For *Vermont* and the Green Mountain Boys, see *ters.*

men III: alone, small. Gk *manos:* rare; *monos:* sole. For *ministry,* see *mei I. monometer. monazite; monad. monachal; monastery, monk.* L *monachus* was first a religious solitary or hermit, but was soon applied to *cenobites* (Gk *koinos:* common, *bios:* life), who, though living together, lived apart from other church folk and the laity. The *monk* that is a *monkey* probably came directly from the name *Monekè,* son of Martin the ape in the very popular tale *Reynard the Fox* (1498); but note Turk *maimum:* ape. The Turkish word may have come from Arab *maymum:* that which brings good fortune, a euphemism, since in Arab nations a monkey (as in some places the black cat) is a sign of bad luck. One with a drug habit has "a monkey on his back." Via Italian, the word was also shaped by *monna, ma donna;* also shortened in *Mona Lisa.*

The monkey he got drunk,
He sat on the elephant's trunk,
The elephant sneezed, and fell on his knees,
And what became of the monk, the monk,
And what became of the monk?
–*The Animal Fair,* anonymous

Monongahela is a West Virginia river that at Pittsburgh joins the Allegheny to form the Ohio; all three river names are American Indian in origin.

There are numerous *monk* combinations. *monk's gun,* the 16th c. wheel lock, was named after the monk Schwarz, supposed inventor of it–and of gunpowder, which had been known for centuries in China. *monk's peason:* lice; also *monkey-pease; peason* is the old plural of *pea;* the word implies that the monks, as well as the monkeys, ate them, as one pops a fresh pea into the mouth. *monkery,* for *monastery,* was mainly an anti-Catholic word. Sheridan, in *The Rivals* (1775), uses *monkerony* ironically for *macaroni;* see *haifst.* The originals of "the three wise monkeys" are figures at Nikko, Japan: *Mizaru:* see no evil; *Mikazaru:* hear no evil; *Mazaru:* speak no evil.

Also *monism,* contrasted with *dualism* and *pluralism.* The prefix *mon(o),* as *monarchy, monogamous, monologue, monosyllable;* many more, but to list them would be *monotonous. OED* gives 48 columns to the prefix, from *mon(o)aesthetic* and *monoblastic* to *monoxylous* and *monozoic. malmsey* was first pressed near LL *Malmasia,* earlier *Monemvasia,* small island off Laconia in Greece; the name means with one approach; it could be reached by land only across a dam. Gc, *minnow.*

men IV: remain, dwell. L *manere, mansum. manor, manse, mansion. remain, remnant. meinie; menial:* first, belonging to the household. Fr, *ménage, menagerie* (but see *man*). *messuage,* probably a scribe's error for *mesnage. immanent, permanent. meno-,* as *Menobranchus, Menopoma:* genera of amphibians. For *menopause,* see *me IV.*

manor. to the manor born is a frequent misquotation of Hamlet's remark (i, 4):

But to my mind–though I am native here,
And to the manner born–it is a custom
[*a salvo of trumpets and guns,*
each time the King drinks a pledge]
More honored in the breach than in the observance.

mend: fault. L *menda:* fault; *mendax, mendacem:* false. *mendicant* (full of faults). *maund, maunder. amend; emendation:* turned away from error; E *mend* dropped the initial vowel.

Frederick Temple, Archbishop of Canterbury (1896–1902), said of the clergy: "ecclesiastic beggars. Their mendicity is equalled by their mendacity."

menegh: plenteous. Gc *many, manifold. OED* devotes 5 columns to *many.*

Prithee, pretty maiden, will you marry me?
(Hey but I'm hopeful, willow, willow, waly!)
I may say, at once, I'm a man of propertee–
Hey willow waly O!
Money I despise it;
Many people prize it;
Hey willow waly O!
–W. S. Gilbert, *Patience* (1881)

menth: chew, and what one chews with. Gk *mastax:* jaws. *masticate. malar. masseter. mastic, maxilla. almaciga:* a tree, from Greek via Arabic. By upward extension, *m(o)ustache, mustachio.*

L *mandere:* chew. *mandible, mandibular. manducate* and *manducation* are formal terms, used especially for the receiving of the Eucharist. *mange.* Fr *manger:* eat. *salle à manger. blancmange. manger:* trough for horses' food; where the infant Jesus was cradled. *dog in the manger* has other implications. Gc, *mund; mouth.*

> Sister, my sister, O fleet sweet swallow,
> Thy way is long to the sun and the south;
> But I, fulfilled of my heart's desire,
> Shedding my song upon height, upon hollow,
> From tawny body and sweet small mouth,
> Fill the heart of the night with fire.
> —Swinburne, *Itylus* (1864)

mer I: gleam, sparkle. L *marmor:* marble. *marmolite. marmoreal.* L *merus:* clear, pure; "this exclusively," complete. E *mere.* Thus *merobibe* (from the Latin of Plautus) is a nonce word for a drinker of pure wine, undiluted. Thus also Othello's herald (ii, 2) announces "the mere perdition of the Turkish fleet," and Hamlet calls the world

> an unweeded garden
> That grows to seed; things rank and gross in nature
> Possess it merely.

The word has lapsed in meaning to "only this," as *mere trash,* nothing more or better.

A number of English terms begin *mere. Mere Irish* is not meant in disparagement, but indicates full Irish blood. Such use of *mere* is frequent in Shakespeare: "mere necessity" (*Love's Labor's Lost*), "mere ambition" (*Henry VIII*)," "This is mere falsehood" (*The Winter's Tale*)—where today we might say *sheer.* By extension, *mere* might mean famous, as in *Beowulf* and in runic inscriptions.

In the 15th c., directly from the French, *mere* was used to mean mother. *mere* also meant lake, as in It *mare* and E *maritime,* extended to the sea. Thus E *meresauce:* brine for pickling; *mereswine:* dolphin or porpoise. Possibly *merganser:* waterfowl (L *anser:* goose; E *anserine;* Gm *Gans*), though this has been ascribed to the root *mezg I:* to dip. And possibly via L *murus:* wall, *mere* came to mean boundary. A *meresman* was a surveyor; a *merestone,* a landmark.

Note also the words from the root *(s)mer:* to do for pay. L *meretricem:* prostitute, E *meretricious;* the earlier *meretricate:* to play the whore; and the nonce word *meretriculate:* to deceive like a harlot, used by George Chapman in *May Day* (1611): "I have not been matriculated at the University, to be meretriculated by him." To go further would be mere pedantry.

But we may mention the *merd(e)* words, which came via L *merda,* Fr *merde:* dung. In its 1933 supplement, *OED* lists *merd* as obsolete, but in its 1976 supplement it gives later examples of its use by e. e. cummings; T. S. Eliot; D. H. Lawrence: "A great Merde! to all latter-day Joan-of-Arcism." *OED* gives 6 forms from *merd,* as *merdaille:* the filthy masses (*canaille:* a pack of dogs; see *kuon*); *merdiferous,* as is the dung beetle. The term has a place in French literature. The oriflamme of the avant-garde theatre, Alfred Jarry's *Ubu Roi* (1896), evoked an uproar with its opening word, an obvious offspin: *Merdre!*—as it were, "Shittle!" And Jean Cocteau, in *Orphée* (1926), has the jealous horse, with the gift of speech, tell Orpheus that *Madame Eurydicée reviendra des enfers:* Madame Eurydice will return from the underworld; but the first letters betray the horse's own feelings. Finally, to describe certain insects or to calumniate disliked fellow humans, there are three English words with the one meaning: *merdivorous, cacophagous, coprophagous.* Swinburne added a fourth, calling Emerson *autocoprophagous:* one's mind feeding on its own excretions.

Currently, critic Robert E. Fitch, D.D., speaks of the *mystique de la merde,* the preoccupation of writers with "mud, blood, money, sex, and merde." Freud fortified this emphasis with his dictum that "embryologically the anus corresponds to the primitive mouth" and with his linking of feces, *merde,* with the penis, with gold and money. Onstage the sound of the flushing toilet has become routine. "During my own lifetime," says the English critic Alan Pryce-Jones, "I seem to have heard very little, in the palace of art, except the roar of the flush carrying away the latest detritus." In music and painting, as well as the novel and the drama, sex (secretion) and excretion seem to be linked not only in the body but too often in the mind.

Gc *Morgen. morn, morning. morganatic* (see *maghos*). *morrow.*

Tomorrow and tomorrow and tomorrow
Creeps in this petty pace from day to day
To the last syllable of recorded time,
And all our yesterdays have lighted fools
The way to dusty death. . . .
—Macbeth, upon his Lady's dying (v, 5)

Tomorrow!—Why, tomorrow I may be
Myself with yesterday's sev'n thousand years.
—FitzGerald, *Rubáiyát of Omar Khayyám*

There is a possibility that this root, in the extended sense of catching the eye, hence look, is the source of Fr *morgue,* which first meant a haughty look. This was extended to a place where prisoners were held for examination; then to the place were the dead were examined for identification. The *mortuary* in Paris, called *La Morgue,* gave us *morgue,* which is also used figuratively of the place where records are kept. Thus "from the morgue of the dictionary [Théophile Gautier] dragged forgotten beauties"—Edgar Saltus, *Tales Before Supper* (1887). For such *trouvailles,* browse in my *Dictionary of Early English* (1955).

mer II: rub away, damage, destroy. Skr, *amrita* (*a* negative): drink of immortality; thus also Gk *ambrosia* (*mbrotos:* mortal): food of the gods. (For the drink of the Greek gods, *nectar,* see *nek.*) Possibly this origin of *ambrosia* is folk etymology; some think the word first meant fragrant, as does *ambergris:* gray amber, used for the best perfumes; *amber* is Arabic in origin.

The fabulous monster *manticore,* also *mantiger,* still found in heraldry, is a misreading by Aristotle of OPers *martikhoras:* man-eater. *marasmus. amaranth* (*a* negative), the ending refashioned after Gk *anthos:* flower. *amaranthine:* of indestructible beauty; supposedly of an everlasting flower, but, as Cowper pointed out in *The Task* (1785), ii,

The only amaranthine flower on earth
Is Virtue.

L *mortarium. mortar,* in various senses, as for pounding with a pestle. L *mordere, morsum:* bite; *morbus:* illness; *mors, mortis, mortem:* death. *mordant, mordent; mordacious; morsel;* Fr, *morceau. premorse; remorse.* There is a French religious treatise, translated in 1340 as *The Ayenbite of Inwyt* (i.e., *Remorse of Conscience*). *morbid, morbific, moribund; cholera morbus. mortal, mortify; mortuary, post mortem. rigor mortis. murder. immortality. mortgage; mortmain; amortize.* Sp, *almuerzo:* bite, breakfast. It, *smorzando,* in music. The *mortician*—coined after, and following, the *physician*—is euphemistic for the more literal *under-taker.*

Also *murrain;* Sp, *murrina.* Gc, *mar. mightmare,* commonly associated with *mare,* the female horse, rather than the goblin that rides the dreamer; Fr, *cauchemar.* Gc, *smart:* first, a quick pain, as from a slap; then, quickness of pace or of wit; see *smerd.*

The nightmare Life-in-Death was she,
That thicks man's blood with cold.
—Coleridge, *The Ancient Mariner*

merbh: shine; appear, take shape; shapely. Gk *morphe.* Thus the shapely goddess, *Aphrodite Morpho. Morpho:* genus of butterflies. The god of dreams, *Morpheus,* is more often summoned than the god of sleep, *Somnus* (see *suep I*); one may rest "in the arms of Morpheus."

When opium was recognized as dangerous, a more pleasant name was found for its extract: *morphine,* suggesting pleasant dreams. When morphine in its turn was discouraged, a further extract, *diamorphine,* was developed; but who wants to die o' morphine! Again the peddling euphemists found a welcoming name, *heroin:* try me, and feel like a hero!

The suffix *morph,* for nouns: *morphic, morphous,* for adjectives. JWalker lists 3 words ending *morph,* 18 ending *morphic,* and 13 ending *morphous:* e.g., *allomorph, isomorph; metamorphic, pantomorphic; amorphous, isomorphous. paramorphism, heteromorphy. metamorphosis. morphology.*

Having in mind Busby's words in Shakespeare's *Richard II,* ii, 2—

Like perspectives which rightly gazed upon,
Show nothing but confusion—eyed awry,
Distinguish form—

James Murray coined the word *anamorphose,* the only word in *OED* fortified with a quotation from the dictionary's editor. (Compiling a dictionary, who can resist the temptation to slip in at least one word of one's own?)

L *forma. Formosa,* now Taiwan, named by the Portuguese for its beauty. *form, formal, formula, formulate. conform, deform, inform, information, formation, perform, reform, transform; uniform,* and other forms of these words, as *reformer,* etc. JWalker has 211 words ending *form,* as *vermiform.*

Note that It *formaggio* and, by metathesis, Fr *fromage:* cheese, are both from L *forma,* having been applied first to cheese made in a form or mould.

"Hold fast the form of sound words"—Bible, 2 Timothy 1:13. "Lord, reform Thy world, beginning with me"—Chinese prayer, quoted by F. D. Roosevelt.

?merc: exchange, barter. Probably from the Etruscan, as was *Mercury,* the god of traders and thieves, and messenger of the gods, usually shown with winged heels. From him, the slippery element *mercury,* the only metal that is liquid at ordinary temperatures; see *el 80. Mercury* is also the smallest planet in the solar system and the one nearest the sun. *mercurial. Mercurialis:* genus of plants.

L *merx, mercem:* reward; thanks. In early Christianity this was interpreted as the reward of heaven despite one's sins; hence *mercy,* which also meant thanks. Fr *merci. gramercy:* much thanks. *Gramercy* (the park in New York City), however, is a folkchange from Du *krumme see:* crooked sea; the East River (and marsh) once came that far into Manhattan. The name *Mercedes* is short for Sp *Maria de las Mercedes:* Mary of mercies.

Also *mercantile, merchandise, merchant; market, mart; mercenary. mercerized. mercer;* whence *Mercer Street* in London and New York. *commerce. amerce* (Fr, at one's mercy). "May a miss amerce a mister if he whisk her for a kiss?"

merk: to mark a border; guardian of a border. L *margo, marginem. marge, margent, margin.* Fr, *marquis.* A place for a marquis, the *s* taken as plural, became *marquee. marchioness;* It *marchese.* Gm, *margrave* (*Graf:* count). *march:* boundary. *mark:* first, marking off estate lines. *demarcation. countermark, remark, remarkable.* Fr, *marque, marquetry.* W, *Cymric* (OE *com:* with, *meare:* boundary); whence, *Cambrian.*

And there is nothing left remarkable
Under the visiting moon.
—*Antony and Cleopatra* (her words when he dies)

meu I, meud, (s)meug: damp, flowing; slippery, slimy, Gk *mukos:* mucus. *muketos:* fungi, including the edible mushrooms. *mycelium, mycorrhiza. Phycomyces:* genus of fungi. *myco-,* as *mycoprotein, mycoderma, mycodextrin.* Many are confirmed *mycophagists.* Also *mysophilia:* drawn toward excreta, as is the dung beetle. *mysophobia:* fear of contamination. *myxo-,* as *myxobroma, myxoma, myxomatosis, myxomycetes. Myxine:* genus of slime fish. *Actinomyces:* genus of parasitic bacteria; *actinomycosis. Myxomycetes:* the slime molds. *Myzostoma:* genus of parasites. *mycosis. mycology. Streptomycin,* named by S. Waksmand in 1944.

Gk *murios:* flowing; uncountable. *myriad. myriapod:* the thousand-legger. Gk *muxa:* lamp wick; Fr *mèche, match.* L *emungere, emunctum:* blow the nose. *emunctory; mycteric.* L and E *mucus. mucid, mucin, mucous, mucosity; mucilage. moist. mushroom* was OFr *moisseron,* its form influenced by *mousse:* moss, whence also *muscoid, muscology.*

Also *smuggle:* slip through. *smug.* Fr, *mouchoir. musty,* influenced by *moisty. must:* new wine. *mustard,* the seeds first mixed with grape juice. Norse, *meek. mo(u)ld, mo(u)lder.* Gc, *mud, muddle. mother:* dregs, form influenced by *mother:* female parent (?from the afterbirth). *midden* (*mog:* muck; *dynge:* dung heap). "Any cock can crow on its own midden." *muck, muggy. smock* (slips on). *moist, moisture; mire, quagmire* (for *quake,* see *guebh*). *moss.* "A rolling stone gathers no moss."

One misty moisty morning,
When cloudy was the weather,
I chanced to meet an old man
Clad all in leather.

So begins an 18-stanza broadside ballad, popular from the 1680s, *The Wiltshire Wedding* "between Daniel Do-Well and Doll the Dairy-Maid. With the consent of her old Father Leather-coat and her dear and tender Mother Plodwell." The air for the ballad was used in *The Beggar's Opera* (1728), John Gay's delightful satire of the evils in a system he loved—converted by Bertolt Brecht into *The Threepenny Opera* (1928), a savage satire of a system he would have liked to see destroyed.

meu II: push; move around. L *movere, momentum. move, movement, remove. motion, motive.* Fr, *motif;* Gm, *leitmotiv. commotion, emotion; locomotion,* etc. *moment, momentum.* E *psychological moment* is a valuable term, but is actually a mistranslation of Gm *Das psychologische Moment,* which referred to the moving force, the motive. *momentary, momentous; momentaneous,* since the 18th c. largely replaced by *instantaneous.*

Also *motor, mobile, immobile; automobile, locomobile, pushmobile, snowmobile. promote, remote. mutiny,* Fr, *émeute. motel,* blend of *motor* and *hotel.* It, *mosso. mob,* shortened from L *mobile vulgus:* the fickle crowd. *Motacillidae, Motacilla:* family and genus of birds, the wagtail.

"The automobile has changed our dress, manners, social customs, vacation habits, the shape of our cities, consumer purchasing patterns, common tastes and positions in intercourse"—John Ketas, *The Insolent Chariots.*

mezg I: dip, dive. L *mergere, mersum. merge, merger; emerge, emergency; emersion, immersion; submerge. Merginae, Mergus:* subfamily and genus of *mergansers:* diving geese (Gc *anser:* goose, whence *anserine*).

mezg II: knit. Gc, mesh.

?miles: soldier. L *Miles Gloriosus:* the boastful soldier; title of a play by Plautus (ca. 205 B.C.), and a typical figure in comedy down the ages. *military, militia, militancy. militate:* first, serve as a soldier; then, serve as an argument, usually against.

Special organization for military purposes seems to have been unknown to the early Indo-Europeans; the whole tribe was ready to do battle. Also then unknown was deep-digging; *mine* and *mineral* are probably Celtic words; the Romans went to Britain for tin.

?mimo. Perhaps imitative of rapid repetition. Gk *mimos. mime, mimic, mimesis, mimetic. pantomime. mimeograph. Mimosaceae, Mimosa:* family and genus of plants; see *mei I. Mimulus:* genus, the monkey flower, named for its masklike corolla. *Mimus:* genus, the mockingbird; *mock* is also imitative. See also *mok.*

Out of the cradle endlessly rocking,
Out of the mockingbird's throat, a musical shuttle . . .
As a flock, twittering, rising, or overhead passing . . .
I, chanter of pains and joys, uniter of here and hereafter,
Taking all hints to use them, but swiftly leaping beyond them,
A reminiscence sing.
—Walt Whitman, *Leaves of Grass*

mlub: lead. Perhaps imitative of the thump of lead into water. Gk *molubdus. molybdenum* (see *el 42*). *molybdomancy:* divination by the movement of molten lead. L *plumbum:* lead (see *el 82*); the Latin explains the symbol for the element, *Pb. plumb; plummet,* as with the plumb line. *plumber,* etc. *Plumbaginaceae, Plumbago:* family and genus, the leadwort. *plump* is imitative, sound of a sudden fall; likewise *plunk* and *kerplunk. plunge,* first used of fishing-nets with sinkers of lead. *aplomb.*

mo: strain, tire; heavy mass. Gk *molos:* a load. *mole:* a breakwater. *molar.* L *molestus. molest. demolish, demolition. molecule:* a little mass; first used in its current sense by A. Avogadro in 1811.

"The study of mathematics is apt to commence in disappointment. . . . We are told that by its aid the stars are weighed and the billions of molecules in a drop of water are counted. Yet, like the ghost of Hamlet's father, this great science eludes the efforts of our mental weapons to grasp it"—A. N. Whitehead, *An Introduction to Mathematics* (1911).

mod: assemble. Gc, *moot:* gathering of freemen. *gemot, folkmoot, hallmoot, witenagemot*—all historical. *meet:* come together; etc. Possibly Norse *mal:* agreement, whence *blackmail.*

modhro: *madder,* the plant; from its root, the dye and the color.

mok. Imitative of scornful laughter (see *mimo*). *mock, mockery; mock-heroic,* etc.

The *mockingbird* imitates other songsters. *mock turtle* is usually calf's head; see the comment on Tenniel's illustration, under *ar I.*

It is a modest creed, and yet
Pleasant, if one considers it,
To own that death itself must be,
Like all the rest, a mockery.
—Shelley, *The Sensitive Plant*

mom, mum. Imitative of indistinct speech. Gk *muein:* close lips or eyes. *myopia. mystery:* the thing whispered to the initiate, as especially at the Eleusinian mysteries, in honor of Ceres, which were solemnly observed at Eleusis, near Athens—with a procession from the city to the site—for 1800 years. They were abolished by Theodosius the Great (d. A.D. 395), after whose rule the Roman Empire was split into East and West, capitals Constantinople and Rome.

L *mutus. mute. obmutescent.* LL *muttum,* E *mot;* Fr *bonmot. motet. motto. motmot:* a tropical bird, the name imitative of its cry.

Various dictionaries, from Bailey's in 1721 to the 1890 *Century,* define *momblishness* as muttering talk. This is a spurious word, a misreading of a 1532 printing of Chaucher's *ne momblysnesse,* which should have been, from Fr, *ne m'oubliemies:* forget-me-nots! Momblishness is still to be heard.

momo. Baby talk, expressing astonishment or pleasure. *mum:* act in a dumb show; *mummer, mummery. mum* is also short for *chrysanthemum;* see *andh.*

mori: large body of water (not the ocean, unknown to the early Indo-Europeans). L *mare:* sea. *mare, marine, maritime, mariner, submarine. ultramarine.* Fr, *marinade, marinated.*

Gc, *mere, mermaid. maar:* crater lake. *maremma, marish, morass, moor. marram grass. cormorant:* sea raven. *ormer:* sea ear. *meerschaum:* sea foam. *meerkat:* sea cat. *Merlin* (Celt *Moridunon:* sea dune). Ir, *Muriel:* sea bright. Fr, from Port, *bêche-de-mer:* sea worm. *Pomeranian,* from a province in Prussia, by the Baltic Sea. *rosemary* is a folkchange from *ros marinus:* sea dew. See *spend II.*

mormor. Imitative of rustling, grumbling. L and E *murmur.* Possibly Fr, *marmite:* covered pot, from the sound of the boiling; and Ir *mavourneen,* from the bustle and hum of a party.

moro: foolish. *Moron* is the name of the Fool in Molière's *La Princesse d'Elide* (1664). In 1910 The American Association for the Study of the Feeble-Minded adopted *moron* to designate an adult of the mental age eight to twelve. The 1933 *OED* defines *moron* as a species of salamander. Indeed, Oliver Goldsmith, in *A History of the Earth and Animated Nature* (1774), states: "With respect to the salamander, the whole tribe, from the moron to the gekko, are said to be venomous to the last degree." The 1933 *OED* was printed from earlier fascicules; the supplement of the same year gives the new definition and (in one of its rare admissions of humor) quotes the horrendous jingle from the July 1929 *Eugenics Review:*

See the happy moron.
He doesn't give a damn.
I wish I were a moron.
My god! perhaps I am!

oxymoron: nonsense with a point. *sophomore:* half-wise, half-foolish. *morosophistry.* Urquhart, in his translation of Rabelais (1693), uses *morosoph* for a foolish pretender to wisdom. *morosophist* was used into the 19th c.; K. H. Digby, in *Halcyon Hours* (1870), speaks of "morosophists who love to boast." *morology* means either foolish talk or the study of folly.

Desiderius Erasmus, who wrote *Praise of Folly* in 1509 at the suggestion of his host, Sir Thomas More, punned on that name, giving the work the title *Encomium Moriae.* (More's own *Utopia,* written six years later, also has a punning title; fusing the Greek prefixes *eu* and *ou,* it means "the beautiful place that is no place.")

Two other senses of *moro* may be mentioned. (1) Children used to dance "all around the mulberry bush"—genus *Morus;* earlier *morberry* (*l.r* shift). Hence also *murrey* and *sycamore.* (Some suggest that *syc* is from Hebr *shigmah,* which also means mulberry; but it is probably from Gk *suk:* fig; the figlike variety, *Ficus sycamorus,* is the sycamore of the Bible.) As she was going to bed on her fatal night, Desdemona, in foreboding, sang the tender song:

> The poor soul sat sighing by a sycamore tree,
> Sing all a green willow.
> —*Othello,* iv

The mulberry family, *Moraceae,* has over 900 species; it includes the fig and the breadfruit; it is a source of rubber, hemp, hops for beer, food for silkworms, wood for shoe lasts, berries to eat, and play for children, who—even as I in later years—dance all around the mulberry bush. *morat* was a Saxon drink made of honey and mulberry juice.

(2) Some scholars place under the root *men I* (as though it were related to *mental*) Gc *mood:* state of spirit, and the L *mores* group: E *moral, morality, mores, morose,* etc. *O tempora! O mores!* cried Cicero in his attack upon Cataline, a troubled cry that echoes down the ages to our own troubling times.

The *Immorality Bible,* by omitting a *t,* promised immorality everlasting to all the faithful, for which overoptimistic assurance King James I fined the printer £300. Richard Carew, in 1607, declared that preachers made their sermons "one part allegorical, another anagogical and a third tropological, whereas they should have made one part morological, another mythological and a third pseudological." Any more on this head might be tautological.

morui: ant. Gk *murmax. myrmeco-,* as *myrmecology, myrmecophagous.* There are seven genera from this stem, as Myrmeleon: antlion. L and E *Formica:* a genus of ants; also the laminated plastic. From the stem *formic* come six genera, including the ant-thrush and a beetle. The Greek ant-eating *myrmecophagous* creatures are matched by the *formicivorous* ones in Latin. Also *formicide, formicarium, chloroform, formaldehyde, iodoform. OED* has 16 words beginning *formic.* An *Entomology* of 1816 speaks of ants "enjoying the full sun, which seems the acme of formic felicity." *formication:* sensation of ants crawling on the skin.

David Livingstone, in Zambesia in 1865, could not sleep "because of the attacks by the fighting battalions of a small species of formica." When no word came to the Western world of Livingstone, Gordon Bennett, owner of the *New York Herald,* bade the explorer Henry M. Stanley, a special correspondent of the paper, "Find Livingstone!" Stanley waited to cover the official opening of the Suez Canal; then, on 10 Nov. 1871, seeing a white man in Ujiji, he addressed him in words known to every schoolboy: "Dr. Livingstone, I presume?" Together they went on to Lake Tanganyika, confirming that it is not one of the sources of the Nile.

Every schoolboy knows was Macaulay's overoptimistic expression, as in the statement in the Jan. 1840 *Edinburgh Review:* "Every schoolboy knows who imprisoned Montezuma, and who strangled Atahualpa."

The protean Zeus changed himself into a swarm of ants for his fornication with the nymph Klytoris. See *guher; klei.* Other humans to whom the god made love were (1) Danaë, as a shower of gold. (2) Leda, as a swan. Leda, wife of Tyndareus, was bathing in the Eurotes; Zeus persuaded Aphrodite to transform herself into an eagle, from which the swan fled, seeking refuge in the arms of Leda. Leda, who was already pregnant, brought forth two eggs. From one came Pollux and Helen (of Troy); from the other, the children of Tyndareus, Castor and Clytemnestra. (3) Europa, as a bull; from her, the name of the continent. (4) Antiope, as a satyr. (5) Alcmene, in the shape of her husband, Amphitryon. This event has been celebrated in many comedies, from the *Amphitruo* of Plautus (186 B.C.) to Giraudoux' *Amphitryon 38* (1936), in the American version of which Lynn Fontanne played the lovely, much-loved lady, and Alfred Lunt in the opening scene, as Jupiter, perched on a cloud with Mercury, looking down on the mortal world below. (6) Io, whom Zeus changed into a heifer to escape his jealous wife Hera, who nonetheless sent a gadfly to harass her husband's inamorata. (7) When Zeus was drawn to Semele, Hera planted in her mind the desire to see the god in all his glory; his lightning blazed Semele to ashes.

Among the goddesses with whom Zeus mated were (a) Metis, goddess of wisdom. Because of a prophecy that his offspring would be greater than he, Zeus devoured Metis in the first month of her pregnancy; in due time, there sprang from his head, fully armed, Athene, goddess of wisdom and patroness of the Athenians. (b) Leto, who bore him Phoebus Apollo and Artemis, he the god of sun and science, she the patroness of hunting and of virgins. (c) Hera, sister and chief wife of Zeus, and queen of heaven. They had three children: (i) Hebe (conceived after Hera ate lettuce), goddess of youth (whence the *ephebic oath* upon reaching adulthood) and cupbearer to the gods until Zeus seized upon the excuse that she had fallen into an indecent posture while serving nectar and supplanted her with Ganymede (whence E *catamite*). (ii) Ares, god of war, and (iii) Eileithya, goddess of childbirth. (d) Demeter; their daughter was Persephone. (e) Themis (daughter of Coelus and Terra, Heaven and Earth), who married Zeus unwillingly and became the mother of the three Fates (euphemistically called *Parcae:* Sparers, because they spare no one): Clotho, Lachesis, and Atropos (see *bha I*). Themis also bore Zeus the three Horae: Eunomia, Dikè, and Irenè (*Irenè:* Peace, whence E *eirenarch, (e)irenic, eirenicon*), who presided over the seasons, spring, summer, and winter—fall was not counted along the Mediterranean. Statues of Themis show her with a sword in one hand and a pair of scales in the other. (f) Maia, daughter of Atlas and Pleione; she bore Hermes (Roman Mercury).

It is not known whether the stars were named before the gods. Some scholars maintain that myths were fashioned to explain the shape of the constellations. Three constellations are linked in the story of Maia and her six sisters. The sisters form the seven Pleiades, a star cluster traveling together in the constellation Taurus (second sign of the zodiac; see *guei*), set there by Zeus to protect them from the lustful hunter Orion. Six of the seven are clearly visible to the naked eye; the seventh, Merope, hides in shame, being the only sister that married a mortal. (Other ancient literatures have other myths to explain the dimness of the seventh sister.) The Great Pyramid, outside Cairo, was so built that in 2170 B.C., on the first day of spring, the Pleiades were in line with its southern passageway. Telescopically, as the ancients could not perceive, there are actually several hundred stars in the cluster. The word *pleiad* is still used for a distinguished human group of seven; see *nebh.*

Pleiades means daughters of Pleione. The five other sisters of the dozen borne to Atlas and Pleione form the star cluster the Hyades, also in Taurus. They are a lugubrious cluster; the poet Virgil called them "the rainy Hyades." Nearby is the most impressive of all constellations, Orion, still on his vain chase of the starry virgins. Orion's "belt and sword" are mentioned frequently in ancient and modern literature; they formed the shoulder insignia of the 27th Division of the U.S. Army in World War II and have done so since, helped by the fact that the division commander was General O'Ryan. Orion contains the great star Betelgeuse, and is so large that the middle "star" of the sword is actually a nebular galaxy. When the pansexual, presumptuous Orion sought to ravish Artemis, Zeus had him killed by a scorpion; and the constellation Scorpio (eighth sign of the zodiac; see *guei*) tails him in the sky. The star Antares in Scorpio is the largest that has been measured; its diameter is 450 times that of the sun.

There are 16 words in *OED* relating to *formica:* ant. Gc, *pismire;* see *piss.*

Albert Camus, in *The Fall* (1956), allows man one respite Zeus did not need: "A single sentence will suffice for modern man: he fornicated and read the papers."

mozzo. Gc, *marrow, marrowbone, marrowfat; marrowy. marrow* and its combinations take five columns in *OED.* Definition (2b) reads: "viewed as the seat of animal vitality." Thus, in Shakespeare's poem, Venus tells Adonis: "My flesh is soft and plump, my marrow burning." Dryden also: "At the Spring's approach their marrow burns." *marrowfat balls* make a favorite dumpling for soup.

mregh-m(n)o: brain. Gk *brekhmos:* front of the head above the face. Gc, *brain.* Note that *to brain* means not to equip with brains, but to dash them out, to debrain. Thus Shakespeare, in *1 Henry IV:* "If I were now by this rascal, I could brain him with his lady's fan." The form *brained,* however, may mean equipped with brains, brainy. Again Shakespeare, though disparagingly, in *The Tempest:* "If th'other two be brained like us, the State totters." The human brain has some 2.5×10^{14} intercommunication links, which could be put to good use.

mu: fly. Imitative. Gk *muia,* L *musca. midge, mosquito. Musca:* genus, the fly. *Myiarchinae, Myiarchus:* subfamily and genus, flycatcher, with 100 species. The northern royal flycatcher has "a particularly beautiful erectile crest"; it is red, rimmed and spotted black, and is like a miniature peacock's tail.

Stegomyia: genus, the mosquito. *muscarine. myiasis. musket,* also called *Brown Bess;* see *gun. The Three Musketeers,* by Alexandre Dumas père. (The Arabic word for *handgun* is from the word for *hornet.*) *moppet* is the diminutive of *mop:* child, fool, but is influenced by *poppet, puppet;* see *pa.*

mus: mouse. Skr *musksh:* little mouse, testicle. *musk,* from the gland of the musk deer, near the testicles. From the smell, *muscatel, muscadine, muscardine, moschatel. mugget* is a name of various musk-scented plants, as, more familiarly, the maidenhair and the lily of the valley. *nutmeg.*

Gk *mus,* L *mus, muris:* mouse; diminutive *musculus:* muscle, from its mouse-like movement in the arm. *muscular. murine. mussel;* the *muscle* that opens and closes it is the edible portion of this bivalve. *Mus:* genus of rodents. *Mustelidae:* family, the skunk and weasel, known to the ancients as mice-catchers. *Mya:* genus of bivalves. *Myosotis:* genus of forget-me-nots, the mouse-ear. *Myosurus:* genus, the mousetail. *myalgia; amyous, epimysium, perimysium. myosin, mysticete.*

Gc, *mouse. mousetrap. The Mousetrap,* named by Hamlet (Shakespeare's) when King Claudius asks what play they are watching; also, the mystery drama by Agatha Christie, which opened in London in 1952 and has been running ever since. *mousefish,* the "whale guide." *dormouse,* probably with Fr *dormir:* sleep; early plural *dormouses,* now *dormice.* Also used figuratively, as by Shakespeare in *Twelfth Night,* iii, 2, when Fabian tells the timid Sir Andrew Aguecheek that Viola "did show favor to the youth . . . to awake your dormouse valour, to put fire in your heart and brimstone in your liver." Lewis Carroll, in *Alice in Wonderland,* 7, makes much of the dormouse at the Tea Party, keeping it awake long enough to tell of the three sisters learning to draw "everything that begins with an M, such as mousetraps, and moon, and memory, and muchness." This may have given a hint to the surrealists, whose prescription for "spontaneous writing" includes the instruction: "If thought intervenes, start over at once, with an M."

OED lists 36 scientific terms beginning *myo:* muscle; it details 22 more, from *myocardium* to *myotomy,* plus 3 referring to mice: *myoidal; myomorph,* the division of rodents that includes rats, mice, and dormice; and *myomancy,* divination by the movements of mice, indulged in by some behaviorists.

In Dublin's fair city, where the girls are so pretty,
I first set my eyes on sweet Molly Malone,
As she wheeled the wheelbarrow through streets broad and narrow,
Crying Cockles and mussels! Alive, alive O!

mut: maim. L, *mutilate.* Sp, *mochila:* saddle cover, with holes cut in it to make it fit. It, *mozzarella:* of little lumps; in India, this cheese is made from buffalo milk (and this variety can be obtained at Harrods, in London).

?muth. The origin of Gk *muthos:* myth, is lost in the mists of prehistory. *OED* defines 36 such words, from *myth* to *mythus,* and lists 11 beginning *mytho.*

Thackeray answers himself in *Pendennis* (1850): "What is conscience? What is public or private faith? Mythuses alike, enveloped in enormous tradition." One man's faith is another man's myth. What used to be called the muckraker school still labors to demythologize our heroes. Washington, it seems, never cut down that cherry tree. The widowed Queen Victoria, it is now hinted, secretly married her Scottish gillie (groom) and bore his child. Was Napoleon poisoned? A well-promulgated lie may leap from myth to accepted history. See *bhurig.*

nabh, ombh: navel. Skr *nabhih.* Gk and E *omphalos:* boss of a shield. Applied to the round stone in the Temple of Apollo at Delphi, marking the supposed center of the earth, it came to have the general sense of *center, navel. omphalism:* government from a center. *omphalitis. omphalo-,* as *omphalodium. omphalopsychite:* navel-gazer, to induce reverie or meditation. *omphalomancy:* predicting how many more children a mother will have, by counting the number of knots in the umbilical cord of the first-born.

L and E *umbilicus. umbiliform; umbo.* Fr, *nombril.* Gc, *nave:* hub of wheel. *navel* (on the human body): the place where the umbilical cord, bearing the motherly nourishment, enters the embryo; it closes at birth. (This indicates the answer to one of the riddles the Queen of Sheba posed and Solomon answered: What is it that has ten openings; when one is open nine are closed; when the one closes, the nine open?)

The *navel orange* is named for the (similar) depression where it breaks from the stem. These, and the *nave* of a church, may be from the idea of central location, although the nave of a church is by some attributed to the image of the church as a ship; see *nau II.*

The wounded sergeant in *Macbeth,* i, 2, reporting his commander Macbeth's victory over the rebel Macdonwald, states that he

unseamed him from the nave to the chaps
And fixed his head upon our battlements.

OED, with a question mark, defines *nave* as navel (used thus only this once); but *chaps* means jaws, thus creating a strange upward sword slice.

auger was shortened from *nafu-gar:* nave-spear; then was folkchanged as *a nauger* became *an auger.*

nana. Baby word for woman not the mother. See *me II.* Gk *nanna:* aunt; little old woman. The "little" takes over in scientific terms; *nanism; nano-,* as *nanometer. nanoplankton; nanosecond:* 10^{-9}; see *me IV.*

LL *nonne:* nun. Gc, *nana, nanny. nanny goat. Nan,* a girl's name, is a folkchange of *Mine Ann* to *My Nan.* The same with *Nancy; Ansy* was a pet form of *Agnes;* see *iag I.*

nas: nose. Pkr *nakka* (*naska*). *nark:* informer. L *nares:* nostrils. *nasal; orinasal; nasion, nasitis, nasute. nasturtium:* nose-twister. *naso-,* as *nasofrontal; nasology.* Fr, *pince-nez.* Gc, *nose, nostril* (*thyrl:* hole; whence *thrill:* pierce, and *drill* [a hole, or a troop]; see *ter II*). *nosegay. naze; ness, nozzle; nuzzle.* For *schnozzle,* see *sna.* Hence the Roman love-poet Publius Ovidius *Naso,* author of *Ars Amatoria,* 3 B.C., often inspiring, or referred to in, English works. Thus in *Love's Labor's Lost,* iv, 2, Holofernes praises the "golden cadences of poesy . . . Ovidius Naso was the man. And why, indeed, Naso, but for the smelling out the odoriferous flowers of fancy?" W. S. Gilbert emphasizes the amorous aspect in *Iolanthe,* as the Fairy Queen sings of her secret love of a mortal, Private Willis, sentry outside Parliament:

Oh, amorous dove! Type of Ovidius Naso,
This heart of mine Is soft as thine,
Although I dare not say so.

The origin of the word *puzzle* being obscure, *OED* suggests that it may have come from *pose* (: put a question), as *nuzzle* came from *nose. OED* lists 8 related words, as *puzzle-headed,* 18th c. *puzzleation;* 19th c. *puzzlement.* Ruskin, in *Hortus Inclusus,* exclaimed: "The puzzlement I have had to force that sentence into grammar!" *puzzlement* has won recent vogue from its use by the growing monarch in *The King and I* (1951), the musical (with book) by Oscar Hammerstein II from Margaret Landon's story *Anna and the King of Siam.* As the fictional detective Ellery Queen blandly observed, a puzzle troubles you only when you don't have the answer.

The Miller, who tells a saucy story in *The Canterbury Tales,* is described by Chaucer in the *Prologue* with this detail:

Upon the coping of his nose he had
A wart, and thereon stood a tuft of hairs
Red as the bristles in an old sow's ears.

nau I: fatigued. Scand, *narwhal,* from the pallid color. Yiddish, Russ *nudnyi:* tiresome; *nudnik.* Gc, *need.* "A friend in need is a friend indeed."

nau II: boat, voyage, etc. Gk *naus:* ship; *nautes:* sailor. *Nausicaä:* burner of ships, but hospitable to the ship-wrecked Odysseus; see *odi. nautical; nautilus,* with sail-like membrane. *nau-*, as *naufragous. nauseous:* first, seasick; thence, *noise. Echeneis:* ship-detaining, genus of fish, the remora (sucker fish), supposedly capable of holding back a ship.

Argonaut. aquanaut, aeronaut, astronaut, cosmonaut. L *navis,* E *naval. nave,* in a church, supposedly from the frequent figure of the church as a ship, but see *nabh. navicert, navicular; navigate, circumnavigate; navy. nacelle* (LL *navicella:* little ship). *nef* (ship-shaped). A *naumachy* is a mock sea battle, as onstage or in ancient Rome.

ndher: below. L *inferior, inferius:* lower; *infernus:* under; *inferus:* below; *infra:* beneath. *inferior; infernal; inferno. infra-*, as *infralapsarian, infratemporal. infra-red.* is at the opposite end of visible light waves from ultraviolet. *OED* lists 68 such compounds, mainly anatomical; its 1976 supplement adds 15. *infra dig* is separately discussed, as a colloquial form of L *infra dignitatem:* beneath one's dignity, "unbecoming one's position." *infra* is still a live prefix; see *en. fracas* is from *infra* and It *cassare:* break.

Gc, *under* also is a live prefix, as in *underestimate, undergraduate, underdone, undercover man, undertaker, underwriter;* it takes up 117 columns in *OED.* Avoid *misunderstanding;* note the difference when *under* is not a prefix, but follows the word, as *understand* and *stand under;* similarly, *underbrush, undergo.*

> Oh, their Rafael of the dear Madonnas,
> Oh, their Dante of the dread Inferno,
> Wrote one song–and in my brain I sing it,
> Drew one angel–borne, see, on my bosom!
> –Browning, *One Word More*

ne: negation; perhaps at first little more than a grunt with a headshake; many a person's first impulse when asked to do something is to say No!

Several prefixes are still fruitful. In Sanskrit the grunt became *a,* as in *ahinsa:* nonviolence, practiced by Gandhi; see *etman. amrita* (*mrta:* death): drink of the gods, conveying immortality, like the Greeks' ambrosia. The prefix *a* is also Greek; thus *asymmetry, astigmatic.* Gk *an:* not, and *ana* (which came also to mean back, up, or again); for these two prefixes in English, *OED* lists well over 200 words, as *anabaptist, anaphrodisiac; anadromous:* going back up a river to spawn. *an(a)esthetic, anarchy, anagram, anatomy, anachronism. OED*'s 1972 supplement adds a number of new definitions, and 36 new words, as *anaphase, anaphylaxis, anarthria, anastate.* An *analysand* is a patient undergoing psychoanalysis.

anathema: first, devoted to divine use; then, devoted to evil. In this sense it was a Christian curse; see *an. anacampserote* (erotic again): an herb that is supposed to restore departed love.

The next three prefixes have formed, and continue to form, countless words. (1) L *in:* not. (There is a different, but also fruitful, prefix, Gc *in,* meaning inside, within, into.) Thus "man's *inhumanity* to man"; *infidel, insubordinate.* This prefix changes. Before *l, m,* and *r,* it drops the *n* and repeats these letters, as *illegal, illegitimate; immediate, immunity, irreparable, irreproachable.* Before *p, in* becomes *im,* as *imperfect, impatient.* And the *n* is dropped before *gn,* as *ignorance, ignoble, ignominy.* (2) L *non. nonconformist. nondescript, nonentity; non compos mentis,* whence probably *nincompoop.* (3) Gc *un,* as *ungodly, unimpeachable, unkempt, unlikely, uninformed. Love's Labor's Lost* speaks of Constable Dull's "undressed, unpolished, uneducated, unpruned, untrained, or rather, unlettered, or ratherest, unconfirmed fashion." Defoe, in *Moll Flanders* (1722), comments: "If they will have women worth having, they may find them as uncomeatable as ever." Milton, in *Paradise Lost,* uses three such words to fill a pentameter line; "unshaken, unseduced, unterrified . . . immutable, immortal, infinite." Such words are unnumbered and innumerable, but unlikely to be misunderstood.

nefarious. nescience, which should be distinguished from *ignorance.* Ignorance consists in not knowing what one can and should know; nescience, in not knowing things beyond one's powers. Hence Browning, in *The Inn Album:* "Ignorance is not innocence but sin." Similarly, the head of the British Secret Service in India emphasizes to Kipling's Kim: "There is no sin so great as ignorance. Remember this." See *gn.*

From L *uter:* one of two, came E *either* and its negative *neither.* More directly, from *ne-uter,* came *neuter,* applied first to castrates and in grammar. Thus, grammatically, for the one English adjectival form *good,* Latin requires *bonus* (masculine), *bona* (feminine), *bonum* (neuter); in German these forms are *guter, gute, gutes.* By natural extension *neuter* was applied to one that takes neither side in an argument or conflict; hence *neutral, neutrality, neutralize. OED* lists 4 such words, as *neutrophile,* and details 14. More recently, scientists have discerned within the atom the positively charged positron, the negatively charged electron, and the uncharged *neutron,* with its diminutive *neutrino.* Also *neutretto;* in radio reception, *neutrodyne;* in celestial physics, *neutrosphere. OED*'s 1976 supplement adds 10 *neutron* combinations, from *neutron activation* to *neutron therapy.*

nisi. null, as in *null and void. nullify. annul* is from L *ad nullus:* (bring) to naught. See *oinos. nihil, nihilism. nil:* in scoring games, Americans say zero; the English say nil. The slang term *goose-egg:* zero (from the shape), has become the technical term in tennis, *love,* meaning zero, which is from Fr *L'oeuf:* the egg. For the slang expression *to goose,* see *ane.*

OED has 13 words beginning *nihil*—not to mention a word coined in a letter of 1741 by William Shenstone, from words in a rule of the *Eton Latin Grammar* which every schoolboy knew: "I loved him for nothing so much as his floccinaucinihilipilification of money" (: estimating as worthless). This word was repeated in 1826 by Southey; Scott altered it slightly (three times), as in his *Journal* entry of 18 Mar. 1829: *floccipaucinihilipilification.* A shorter term with the same meaning is *floccipend;* see *vilipend,* below.

annihilate. nihil nimis: nothing too much, the Golden Mean; the opposite of *nimiety.* Coleridge, in *Table Talk* (1834), said: "There is a nimiety—a toomuchness—in all Germans." The Golden Mean is sharpened by Occam's razor (William of Occam, Doctor Invincibilis [?1300-?1349], pupil, then rival, of Duns Scotus, whose name gave English the word *dunce*). The "razor" cuts off excess: "Entities must not be unnecessarily multiplied." In other words, avoid abstractions.

vilipend: to speak with contempt. Occurring only once in Latin, in a play by Plautus, *vilipendere* was probably a copyist's error, a misreading of *nili pendere:* to value at nothing. But, linked with vile, vilipend has thrived; *OED* gives eight derivatives. Thackeray, in *Vanity Fair* (1848), speaks of "menacing the youth with maledictions . . . and vilipending the poor innocent girl as the basest and most artful of vixens."

nemo: nobody; used as a name—e.g., the law-writer in Dickens' *Bleak House,* and Captain Nemo in Jules Verne's *20,000 Leagues Under the Sea* (1870), which anticipated the submarine, and described the periscope so accurately that the man who made one was refused a patent.

neglect, negligence; for casual moments, Fr, *negligee. deny, denigrate; negate, negative. abnegate. renegate;* by folkchange, *runagate;* also *renegade, renegado; reneg(u)e.*

negotiate tells us something of the early Roman citizen's days; it is from *ne-otius:* lack of leisure: an interruption of his usual freedom from business occupations.

Gc, *neither; never; naught; naughty:* of no worth. *nought; no, none, nor, not, nothing. nice* first meant foolish, from L *ne-scire:* not to know. *nestitherapy:* a cure by fasting. *nay, nix, willy-nilly:* will ye, nill ye. *hobnob* first meant have or not have. *never* is also used in compounds, as *never-say-die; never-to-be-forgotten, -gainsaid, -touched,* etc.

necessary is from L *ne* and *cedere, cessum:* yield; see *sed.* Kipling, at the Royal Academy dinner of 1904, queried: "If a tinker in Bedford jail, if a pamphleteering shopkeeper pilloried in London, if a muzzy Scot, if a despised German Jew, or a condemned French thief, or an English admiralty official with a taste for letters, can be miraculously afflicted with the magic of the necessary word, why not any man at any time? Our world, which is concerned only in the perpetuation of the record, sanctions that hope just as kindly and just as cruelly as Nature sanctions love." In case you haven't recognized them, the persons alluded to are, in order: Bunyan, jailed from 1660 to 1672; Defoe, pilloried in 1702; Burns, Heine, Villon, and Pepys. Words, like love, can be used or abused. Of course, Kipling omitted the greatest instance: "If a butcher's son from a hick town . . . [Stratford-upon-Avon]." *hick* (a country shortening of *Richard,* as *Hob* for *Robert, Hodge* for *Roger*) is labeled obsolete in the 1933 *OED,* but restored to current use in *OED*'s 1976 supplement. Thus *The Observer* of 1 May 1927 complains that it is "much easier to write a good play about hicks, boobs, hayseeds, highbrows and sentimentalists than about decent English people." See *aiu; ant; nek.*

nonesuch, as "Chess champion Bobby Fisher is a scacchic nonesuch." *nonsense;* see *sent.*

Why should a dog, a horse, a rat, have life,
And thou no breath at all? Thou'lt come no more,
Never, never, never, never, never!
Pray you, undo this button.
—King Lear, at the death of Cordelia

Shaw, in *Major Barbara,* proves his claim that he stands on Shakespeare's shoulders; the lady exclaims "Never!" seven times.

nebh: mist, cloud; moist. Gk *nephos, nephele. nepho-,* as *nephoscope.* In Aristophanes' comedy *The Birds,* 414 B.C., *Nephelococcugia:* Cloud-Cuckooland, is the home the birds build between earth and heaven, cutting off man's incense and offerings to the gods; the chorus of the birds is one of the greatest Greek lyrics, with its recurring echoing call *tiotiotiotiotinx.*

nephelite: a mineral that turns cloudy then treated with acid; earlier (1800) called *nepheline,* its ending was changed to conform with the names of other minerals. *nephelo-,* as *nephelometer.* L and E *nebula; nebulous, nebulosity.*

Sir William Crookes in 1898 declared: "Still awaiting discovery by the fortunate spectroscopist are the unknown celestial elements aurorium and nebulium." The statement was unfortunate; aurorium remains unknown; nebulium exists only as a green line in the spectrum of gaseous nebulae. The only known element recognized in the nebulae is hydrogen.

nimbrose, nimbus, nimbostratus. imbricate. The *Nibelungs* are "children of the mist."

Neptune, Roman god of the sea. *neptunian:* formed by water action (as opposed to volcanic or plutonic action: water, fire, earth); thus, the white cliffs of

Dover. *Neptune's cup* names a large sponge. *neptunium* (*el 93*) follows uranium (*el 92*), as *Neptune*, the eighth planet, is next after Uranus. For *Pluto* (the ninth planet) and *plutonium* (*el 94*), see *pleu*. Gk *Ouranos:* god of the sky, rain god; see *aue*. *Urania* is the Muse of Astronomy. *Uranus*, seventh planet from the sun, was discovered accidentally in 1781 by Sir William Herschel, who sought to call it *Georgium Sidis:* Star of George, in honor of King George III of England—but all the planets except our own are named after gods. In 1795 Martin H. Klaproth discovered the element that, after the most recently discovered planet, he called *uranium* (*el 92*). In the same year he confirmed the element *menachanite* (*el 22*), which was found near the Cornish town of *Menachen;* Klaproth renamed it *titanium*, the Titans being children of Uranus and his wife Ge, goddess of earth (whence *geography*, etc.; see *ge*). *titanium* is the ninth most abundant element in the earth's crust, and exists in even higher concentration on the moon.

The gigantic Titans have come widely into English—directly in *titanic, titanic acid, titanite*, etc. On its maiden voyage from Southampton to New York, just before midnight on 14 Apr. 1912, the White Star liner, the *Titanic*, struck an iceberg and sank; of the 2,224 persons on board, 1,513 drowned. *Titan*, the largest satellite (sixth out) of Saturn, is the only moon known to have an atmosphere (of methane); its size is exceeded among moons only by Jupiter's Ganymede and, largest of all, Earth's moon. The *Titan rocket*, used by the U.S. to launch space craft, weighs a mere 1,818,500 pounds, but it attains a lift-off thrust of 3,160,000 pounds.

An order of extinct reptiles is called *Titanosuchus;* an order of extinct mammals, *Titanotheres*. *Titanomachy:* the ten-year war of the Titans against their offspring, the gods of Olympus, who finally thrust the Titans into Tartarus.

The first generation of Titans comprised six sons and six daughters: Oceanus, Koios, Krios, Hyperion, Iapetus, Cronus; Thea, Rhea, Themis, Mnemosyne, Phoebe, Thetis. From *Oceanus* we have *ocean, oceanography*, etc. *Hyperion* (Hamlet compares his father to his uncle: "Hyperion to a satyr") means he that looks from above; the first five letters give us all our *hyper* words. The opposite of *hyper* is *hypo:* below; see *uper* and *upo*. But Hyperion was the father of *Helios*, the sun; whence *helium* (see *el 2*). *OED* lists 19 and details 30 words beginning *helio*, as *heliotrope, heliocentric, heliostat*. Its 1976 supplement lists 6 more, and details 6 others, as *heliolithic, helion*.

Helios was the father of *Circe*, the temptress; whence *circean*. An asteroid discovered in 1855 is named *Circe*. And Circe, in turn, with Bacchus, was parent of *Comus:* merrymaking, as in Milton's masque of that name. The *Puritan Review* of 1876 declared: "In Charles II, Comus seems to have seated himself upon the throne of England."

The Titan *Cronus* overthrew his father, Uranus, and castrated him with a pruning hook, akin to the scythe of Father Time; and Cronus's rule was the world's Golden Age. The myth of Cronus is confused; he was probably a pre-Hellenic god of time; from his name we have a number of words (in which the *h* was added during the Renaissance), as *chronaxy, chronic, chronicle, chronological, chronometer. chronogram* (e.g., *M*y *D*ay *C*losed *I*s *I*n *I*mmortality: MDCIII: 1603, the date of the death of the great Elizabeth of England). *crony. anachronism, metachronism, parachronism, prochronism*. The Romans identified Cronus with Saturn, god of agriculture; the *Saturnalia* were harvest festivals, usually marked by more revelry than the American Thanksgiving. From the supposed (astrological) gloomy influence of the planet Saturn came *saturnine*. In alchemy, Saturn is the symbol of lead; hence *saturnism:* lead poisoning.

Out of the seed dripping from the castrated organ of Uranus sprang the three

Erinyes: the Furies (see *fur*), and the Gigantes, the *Hecatonchires:* the hundred-handed. From the foam and seed of the organ as it was tossed into the sea sprang *Aphrodite Anadyomene* (*Aphrodite:* daughter of the foam, from Gk *aphros:* foam; *Anadyomene:* she that emerges). This folk etymology was started by Hesiod in the 8th c. B.C.; *Aphrodite* is altered from the Akkadian goddess *As(h)tarte, Ishtar.*

Eriny is from the ranging root *er:* to rouse, rise up, set in motion. Hence *the Orient;* but also *Eris,* goddess of discord, who tossed to the goddesses the apple that started the Trojan War; see *abel.* From *Eris* came E *erethism, eristic.* Her counterpart is the eternally young *Eros,* son of Aphrodite; from him the many *erotica.* Aphrodite was the mother of Aeneas, who fled from the burning Troy; from *Aphrodite, aphrodisiacs* and the foamlike minerals *aphrite* and *aphrizite;* despite her, *anaphrodisiacs.*

Aphrodite rising from the sea has been a favorite subject for painters; Apelles' painting of her (4th c. B.C.) was one of the three he signed. When a cobbler criticized a sandal strap in his painting, Apelles changed it; when the cobbler went on to criticize the leg, Apelles said (the story came down in Latin): *Ne sutor ultra crepidam:* Cobbler, stick to your last!–hence E *ultracrepidarian:* of a person discussing matters out of his range. This word was first used in 1819, by Hazlitt; but Coleridge acknowledged, in a letter of 1800: "I was a well-meaning *sutor* who had ultracrepidated with more zeal than wisdom."

Cronus's children by his sister Rhea were Zeus, Hestia, Demeter, Hera, Poseidon, and Hades; by Philyra, daughter of Oceanus, he fathered the centaur Chiron, master of medicine.

Iapetus was the father of Atlas (Atlantos), whom Perseus, with the head of Medusa (turning all that look upon it to stone), changed to Mount Atlas, beside the Atlantic Ocean. Atlas was condemned to bear the earth on his head and hands. Hercules, who relieved him for a day, was pictured with the earth on his shoulders on the signboard of London's first Globe Playhouse; Shakespeare alludes to this in *Hamlet,* ii, 2. Hercules is also thus shown in the statue at 530 Fifth Avenue, Radio City, New York.

Atlas literally means bearer; *atlantes* are figures of men as columns supporting an entablature; such figures of women are *Atlantides:* daughters of Atlas. From their mother, Pleione, the Atlantides were also called the *Pleiades;* see *morui.* From the seven Pleiades in the sky, *pleiad* has been used of a group of seven distinguished persons, mainly of poets. The earliest such group consisted of the poets Lycophron, Theocritus, Aratus, Nicander, Apollonius, Philicus, and Homer the Younger, who flourished at the time of Ptolemy II of Egypt (d. 246 B.C.), a patron of the arts. Ptolemy II was also the patron of Euclid and Callimachus; he built a library that housed 200,000 books; he arranged for the first translation of the Old Testament, into Greek; see *dekm.* History, however, by antiphrasis, ironically labels Ptolemy II *Philadelphus:* brother-lover, because he killed two of his brothers–a practice not uncommon among royal families in the Near East and also seen in *Hamlet.* The best-known pleiad is that of 16th c. French poets, chief of whom were Pierre de Ronsard (d. 1585), "father of French lyric poetry," and Joachim du Bellay, "prince of the sonnet," whose *Defence and Illustration of the French Language* (1549) did much to establish the use and usage of French.

The "lost continent" *Atlantis,* mentioned by Plato, Pliny, and other ancient writers, supposedly sank after an earthquake. The geographer Gerhard Kremer (using the Latin translation of his name, *Mercator,* E *mercer*) used the word *atlas* for a volume of maps; see *tol.* And Andreas Vesalius (who made a pilgrimage to the Holy Land in 1564, as a condition of not being burned for dissecting the human body, but who died the same year) used the word *atlas* to name the first vertebra, which supports the head. Hence also *atlantean, atlantite, transatlantic.*

For the stream of words out of *Rhea,* see *sreu.* For *Themis,* see *dhe. Mnemosyne* gives us *mnemonic* and the wide variety of words discussed under *men I.* The struggle between the Titans and the Olympians is also known as the *gigantomachy* (Gk *gigas, gigantos*), whence also *giant, gigantic, giga-,* as in *gigavolts,* where the prefix means 10^9; see *me IV.* Gk *Ouranos* is related to Hindi *varsha,* the rainy season, and *Varuna,* god of the sky. Hence also Gk *oureo, ourein:* to sprinkle; whence *urinate,* etc. Thus the *uretic* advice and warning to a country youngster:

> Stand next to a tree when you make it,
> Perhaps you can aim at some ants;
> No matter how much you may shake it
> The last drop will fall in your pants.

ned: twist, tie, knot. L *nodus. node, nodule, nodus; noose. crunode:* crossknot. *internode.* Fr, *dénouement:* the unraveling of the plot. L *nectere, nexum. net, network; interstices* (see *sta*). *nexus; annex. connection. ouch:* brooch; *a nouch* became *an ouch. lanyard;* OFr *nasle* became *lasne* from the influence of OFr *laz:* noose; then the ending was folkchanged to match *yard:* spar on a ship's mast.

nei: shine, glow; be excited. Hence, both brave, as in *Neil* and *Neilson,* and afraid, as in *nidderling.* Pers *nila. anil,* source of *indigo:* Indian dye. *aniline. nilgai:* blue cow (see *gultur*). *nilak:* lilac. *nidderling* was a corruption of *niddering,* itself an error for the earlier *nithing* (made by William of Malmesbury in 1596); *niddering* was revived by Scott in *Ivanhoe* (1819).

L *nitere, nitidum. neat. net,* in business; *clear,* as opposed to *gross* (see *guertso*). *natty; nitid. nitor. niton:* name given by Ramsay in 1912 to radium emanation because it glows in the dark; now called *radon,* the ending to match that of the other inert gases, argon and neon; see *el 86.*

"Virtue gives a Nitor, Lustre, Splendour, Beauty, and Glory to the Soul"—Theophilus Gale, *The Court of the Gentiles* (1669).

nek: damage, destroy. This is a stonger form of *ne;* see also *nekut.* Gk *nekros:* corpse. *necropolis. necrosis. necro-,* as *necrobiosis, necromancy. necrophagous,* as insects and ghouls; a corpse has often been referred to as food for worms; see *kurmi. necropsy,* short for *necroscopy,* supplanted by the less accurate *autopsy* (: to see with one's own eyes), a post-mortem examination. L *noxa:* harm, *noxius:* harmful. *noxal, noxious, obnoxious.* Via Fr, *nuisance.*

Fr, *noyade:* drowning. In the Loire River at Nantes, in 1793, French Revolutionists drowned between three and five thousand troops of the Vendée; it was the largest noyade since the legendary St. Ursula and her 11,000 virgins in the 4th c.

Necator: genus of hookworm. Gk *nektar* (Skr *taras:* overcoming). *nectar,* the drink of the gods, conveying immortality (for their food, *ambrosia,* see *dhes; mer II*). *nectareous, nectary. nectarine.* L *nocere, noxum:* harm. *nocent, innocent. nocive.*

Coleridge said that "work without hope draws nectar in a sieve."

nekut: night, naturally associated with dark, danger, death. See *nek.* Gk *nux, nukhtos. nyc-,* as *nyctalopia, nictitropism. nyctophobia.* A number of plants and animals, as *Calonycton:* genus of morning-glory. *Nyctanthes:* genus of night flower. *Nyctea:* genus, the snowy owl. *Nyctereutes:* genus, the raccoon dog. *Nycteris:* genus of bats. *Nycticorax:* genus of night heron.

Possibly Gk *akhtis* (omitting the negative *n*): ray of light, daybreak. *actinic. actino-*, as *actinograph, actinology, actinomycin, actinomycosis, actinotherapy. actinium* (see *el 89*). Also, *actinide series. diactinic. tetract. Actinia:* genus, the sea anemone. *Actinomyces:* genus of bacteria. *Actinozoa:* class of marine animals.

L *nox, noctem. nocturn, nocturnal.* Fr, *nocturne.* It, *notturno. equinox. noctambulist* (for *somnabulist,* see *suep*). *nocti-*, as *noctilucent, noctipotent.* "The noctidial day, the lunar periodic month, and the solar year are natural and universal"—Holder, *On Time* (1694). *noctivagant. noctule:* the great bat. *noctuolent:* smelling strongest at night, as some geraniums and jasmines. *Noctuidae, Noctua:* family and genus of night-flying moths. *Noctilio:* genus of bats; whence *noctilionine. Noctiluca:* genus of "night-shining," phosphorescent marine flagellates.

Gc, *night. OED* lists 33 compounds beginning *night,* and separately defines 79 more associated words, as *nightingale* (the middle *n* is a folk addition), which in the breeding season sings by night. *nightmare. nightsoil:* excrementitious matter removed by night from outhouses, cesspools, etc.; it used to be sold as manure. *night-mugging* is no new practice; Shakespeare, in *Richard III* (1594), stated: "There is no man secure / But the Queen's kindred, and night-walking heralds." Milton in 1641 spoke more directly of the danger "to stand to the courtesy of a night-walking cudgeller."

The deadly *nightshade* is euphemistically called *belladonna;* it is also used figuratively, as by O. Winslow in *The Inner Life* (1850): "Satan has ever sought to engraft the deadly nightshade of error upon the life-giving Rose of Sharon." *belladonna* is Italian, meaning beautiful lady; the juice of the plant was used to enlarge the pupil of the eye; but in her discussion of *Flora* (1851) E. Hamilton says: "It was employed by Leucota, a famous poisoner of Italy, to destroy the beautiful women" of whom less beautiful but more powerful ladies were jealous. Its active principle is *atropine;* see *trep.*

Sir Harry Lauder used to sing: "It's a braw brecht moonlecht necht the necht."

Think, in this battered Caravanserai
Whose portals are alternate Night and Day,
How Sultan after Sultan with his pomp
Abode his destin'd hour, and went his way.
—*Rubáiyát of Omar Khayyám,* FitzGerald's 4th ed.

nem: divide, take; allot. Hence custom, law. Gk *nomes:* divided, as allotted land, at first for pasture; hence *nomad:* wanderer with flocks. *Nome:* province in ancient Egypt and modern Greece; city in Alaska, center of the 1898 gold rush; the California gold rush was in 1848. Gk *nomeus:* herdsman; used in English for the man-of-war fish. Gk *nomos:* measure, law. *noma; nomarch:* ruler of a nome. *nomistic. nomo-*, as *nomography, nomothetic. antinomy. -nomy;* JWalker lists 22, as *agronomy, astronomy, economy, gastronomy, taxonomy; autonomy, heteronomy. Deuteronomy. bionomial. metronome.*

The "divine" allotting of justice, ruthless but fair, is *nemesis:* we must accept what we deserve. "It is the wine we tread that we must drink." *anomy:* lawlessness (*a* negative); hence, especially in biological words, observing no regular order, as *anomobranchiate:* with irregular gills; *anomophyllous:* with leaves irregularly placed. *withernam:* taking in reprisal, the medieval eye for an eye.

The division of things led to counting; hence *number.* From classical Greek and Latin poetry, based on quantity, *number* began to be used by the English to mean metrical verse. In *Love's Labor's Lost,* iv, 3, the lovelorn Longaville decides: "These numbers will I tear, and write in prose." Edmund Waller's use of the heroic couplet, in 1625, won great popularity, and followers for over two centuries. As

Dryden wrote, "Our numbers were in their nonage until Waller came." Pope, in his *Epistle to Dr. Arbuthnot* (1735), boasted:

As yet a child, not yet a fool to fame,
I lisped in numbers, for the numbers came.
[See quotation under *kob.*]

In America, Longfellow began one of his best-known poems with the words

Tell me not, in mournful numbers,
Life is but an empty dream. . . .

Thus also, from the Renaissance, *numerous,* which Johnson defined as "harmonious, of parts rightly numbered." Puttentham, in *English Poesie* (1589), states that "[prose is] nothing numerous, nor contrived into measures."

From Latin also we have *numeral, numerical, enumerate, innumerable. numerology. supernumerary,* in the theatre shortened to *super.* L *nummus:* coin. *numismatics, nummary, nummula; nummulite.* Gc, *nim; nimble:* quick to take.

Jack be nimble, Jack be quick,
Jack jump over the candlestick.

Corporal *Nym,* a character in Shakespeare's *Henry V*, was hanged for taking plunder in France; see *taka.*

numb: taken, as by excessive cold; *benumbed.* The *b* was inserted here, and in *nimble* and *number*—L *numerus*—for smoother sounding; likewise in *ramble*—OE *romen,* whence also *roam*—and in *grumble*—IE *ghrem:* to thunder, Fr *grommeler,* OE *grimm,* whence *grim, grimace.* Russ, *pogrom.*

nepot: nephew; grandson. L *nepos, nepotem. nepotism:* first, of Popes favoring their progeny; "the only ones that did not call a priest Father were his own children; they called him Uncle."

ner: below; to the left; hence (facing the sunrise) north. (This allocation occurs also in Arabic and Hebrew.) Skr *Naraka:* the lower regions, hell. Gc, *north, northern,* etc. *Nordic. Norn. Norman, Norse, Norway, Norwegian.* See *ni.*

"Your Roman-Saxon-Danish-Norman English," says Defoe in *The True-Born Englishman,* which begins:

Whenever God erects a house of prayer,
The Devil always builds a chapel there;
And 'twill be found, upon examination,
The latter has the largest congregation.

nert: man. See also *manu.* Skr *nari:* belonging to man, hence woman. *Ardhanari:* the god Shiva as an hermaphrodite. *sundari:* beautiful male strength.

Gk *aner, andros,* also *anthropos* (*ops:* eye, face): man. *andron. androcracy,* some women's view of the present world, despite Barrie's *What Every Woman Knows,* that she is the guiding force behind the male. *monandrous, polyandrous. polyandry:* having several husbands; contrasted with *polygyny:* "the custom, practice, or condition of having a plurality of wives"; both are included in *polygamy. androgyne, gynander, gynandry;* see *guen.*

Alexander: protector of men. *alexin:* blood component, protector against bacteria. *Andrew:* manly. *Leander:* lion-man. Fr, *André.* Hung, *Sandor.* Scot, *Sandy,* short for *Alexander,* but often the nickname of a light-haired lad. *dandy, jack-a-dandy:* first, pet names for *Andrew;* see *haifst.*

alexanders: the meadow parsnip, its flowers "the color of royalty," after

Alexander the Great. *alexandrine:* the metrical six-foot line, the hexameter, first used in a 14th c. poem about Alexander the Great; then, rhymed, the regular form for classical French dramatic poetry; the English preferred the shorter, pentameter, line, and unrhymed (blank) verse. The mineral *andrewsite* is named after Thomas *Andrew* (d. 1858); the mineral *alexandrite,* after *Alexander II* of Russia. *andropogon:* beard grass. *Andromache:* literally, her man a conqueror. *Andromeda:* mindful of her man; also the name of a constellation and of a genus of the heath family. *Andrias:* image of a man; genus of fossil salamanders. *Androsace:* man's cure; genus of primrose.

Also *andrecium; androgen; androsterone. cynanthropy. anthropology. anthropomorphic,* like a bearded god, like animals in fables (e.g., the fox and the "sour grapes"). *OED* defines 75 words beginning *anthrop. lycanthrope; misanthrope; philanthropy; therianthropic. anthropocentric. anthropoid. Eoanthropus; Pithecanthropus* (*erectus:* down from the trees). *anthropophagus,* as Othello explains:

It was my hint to speak, such was the process;
And of the Cannibals that each other eat,
The Anthropophagi; and men whose heads
Do grow beneath their shoulders. This to hear
Would Desdemona seriously incline.

philanthropos: the plant-cleavers, amusingly named; their seeds cling to garments as one brushes by. *philander:* a marsupial, the wallaby, after the first European to describe one, *Philander* de Bruyn (1737). *Philander* is a frequent name in fiction, after Ariosto's *Orlando Furioso* (1506). A ballad of 1682 laments:

Philander, ah Philander! still the bleeding Phyllis cried;
She wept a while, and she forced a smile, then closed her eyes and died.

Hence the sense of *philander* weakened from loving to playing at love; *philanderer:* "professor of the fine art of flirtation." The noun names a man, but "the fine art" belongs at least equally to the ladies; the word *flirt* is imitative of a quick movement, as with a fan. Thus the Earl of Dorset complained in 1665 *To All You Ladies* who

Perhaps permit some happier man
To kiss your hand or flirt your fan.

Usually she flirted it herself, half-hiding, half-revealing, her mocking or inscrutable smile.

Balthasar's song in *Much Ado About Nothing* bids the ladies reconcile themselves:

Sigh no more ladies, sigh no more,
Men were deceivers ever . . .
Then sigh not so, but let them go,
And be you blithe and bonny,
Converting all your sounds of woe
Into Hey nonny nonny.

nes: provide for a journey; return. Skr, *Nasatya:* in Hindu mythology, either of the twin Aswins, sons of the sun, who precede the dawn; they have curative powers. Gk *nostos:* return home; *algos:* pain; E *nostalgia.*

Gc, *harness* (*heri:* army): first, provisions for an army; then, attachment so that one can be directed toward providing.

netr: twist, spin; thread. Gk *nema, nematos:* thread. *nematoid,* etc. *Nematoda:* class of worms. Gk *neuron:* nerve. *neurology; neuron; neurosis, neurotic. nerve, nervous,* etc. *enervate. aponeurosis.* See *sne,* with which this root intertwines.

L, *Natrix:* genus of snakes. *nere, netum:* spin, weave. *needle.* For *net,* see *ned.* Gc, *a nadder,* folkchanged to *an adder. sinew. snood.*

In *Macbeth,* iv, 1, the witches stir their cauldron as they prepare illusions for Macbeth, who is coming to consult them:

Eye of newt, and toe of frog,
Wool of bat, and tongue of dog,
Adder's fork, and blind-worm's sting,
Lizard's leg and howlet's wing,
For a charm of powerful trouble,
Like a hell-broth boil and bubble.

neu I: message, messenger; announcing. L *nuntius:* messenger, probably shortened from *novi ventius:* newly come; see *neuos. announce, annunciation; denounce. enunciate, pronounce, renounce, renunciation,* etc. It, *nuncio, internuncio; pronunciamento.* The *Annunciation,* in Christian doctrine, refers to "the intimation of the incarnation, made by the angel Gabriel to the virgin Mary," which, said Ruskin in *Modern Painters* (1851), has been the most frequent subject of religious painters. It is also the subject of plays—e.g., Paul Claudel's *The Tidings Brought to Mary* (1912). It is observed on Lady Day, 25 Mar. *OED* gives 9 words relevant to *annunciation.*

neu II: nod. L, *nutant, nutation. numen,* the divine spirit whose nod is a command. *numinous, innuendo.*

I do not know which to prefer,
The beauty of inflections
Or the beauty of innuendos,
The blackbird whistling
Or just after.
—Wallace Stevens, 1923

neud: possess, enjoy, use. Gc, *neat:* cattle. Fr, *matelote:* first, one that shares cattle; corrupted in Du, *matross.*

Huguenot: sharer; its form influenced by *Hughes* Besançon, 16th c. Genevan reformer, and/or by the gate *Roi Hughon,* where the Protestants gathered at Tours. See *oito.*

?neuh: near. Gc, *nigh, near, nearest, next. neighbor* is the *nigh boor* (: farmer; thus *Boer.*)

neun, eneuen: nine. Gk *ennea, ennead:* applied first to a collection of the works of Plotinus (d. A.D. 270) in six parts, each containing nine books. *enneatic:* coming once in nine times, as is said of a high wave. *ennea-,* as *enneagynous, enneandrous. enneacontahedron:* polyhedron, especially a crystal, with ninety facets.

L *nova:* ninth. *novem:* nine; originally *noven,* changed to match *septem* and *decem;* thus *September, December, November:* the seventh, tenth, and ninth months, when the year began with March. L *noven* was related to *novus:* new, from early calculation in sets of four (fingers, not counting the thumb) IE *oktu* meant two fours; the next number began a new set; see *neuos.*

The Middle Ages held in high respect the Nine Worthies, the "best that ever were." In the preface to his *Morte d'Arthur* (1485, but written earlier in prison), Sir Thomas Malory lists them:

Three paynims: Hector of Troy, Alexander the Great, Julius Caesar
Three Jews: Duke Joshua, David King of Jerusalem, Judas Maccabeus
Three Christian men: Arthur, Charlemagne, Godfrey of Bouillon
[Godfrey led the First Crusade, took Jerusalem in 1099, refused the title of King, governed as "Advocate of the Holy Sepulcher."]

When Armado, in *Love's Labor's Lost,* wants to put on an entertainment for the Princess, Holofernes suggests, and at once begins to plan, "The Nine Worthies." Two of those he names–Hercules and Pompey–are not on Malory's list.

nones: in the Roman month, ninth day before the ides. The calends was the first day of the new moon and of the month, at which time it was announced when the ides, day of the full moon, would occur; thence the nones. See *kel II.* In Christian times, prayers were said at dawn, then every three hours; the third hour, *tierce;* the sixth, *midday;* the ninth, *none.* Later the hours were shifted; hence *none, noon. novena. nuncheon* (OE *schenche:* pouring out) meant a noon drink, respite for the workers in the field; until the 17th c. it was usually plural, the serfs understandably being thirsty. Also found is the spelling *noontion.* When more time was allowed, the workers might have a lump (broken from a large loaf) of bread; *lump* and *nuncheon* were blended as *luncheon. lump* and *lunch,* as *hump* and *hunch.*

For *nonage:* second childhood, immaturity, see *ne; nonage* used also to mean the ninth part of the movables of a dead person, which went to the clergy of that person's parish. *nonagenarian. nonary. nonagon,* like *pentagon,* etc. *nonuple. nonane:* ninth in the methane series. *nonagesimal:* 90° above the horizon. *nonillion:* in the U.S. and France, 10^{30}; in Great Britain and Germany, 10^{54}.

Gc, *nine, nineteen, ninety;* see *dekm.* As the largest one-figure integer, *nine* is sometimes used for emphasis, as in the vogue expression *on cloud nine;* or as Hotspur puts it, in *1 Henry IV,* iii, 1:

In the way of bargain, mark ye me,
I'll cavil on the ninth part of a hair.

neuos, nu: new, now. Skr, *naya paisa:* new coinage. Gk *neos. neon* (see *el 10*). *neo-*, as *neologism, neomycin, neonate, neophyte, neoplasm, neoteric;* see below. *Neolithic; Neozoic. misoneism,* as with conservatives. See quotations under *smeit. Neophron:* new spirit, a man changed to a vulture in *Metamorphoses,* by Antoninus Liberalis (ca. A.D. 150). An ornithologist who knew his *Antonini* (including two Roman emperors, Titus A. and Marcus Aurelius A.) gave the name *Neophron* to a genus of vultures. *Neotoma:* genus, the wood rat. *Neotragus:* genus, the royal antelope. *Neotropical:* belonging to the hot regions of the "New World."

L *novus. nova:* short for *stella nova:* a new star that bursts upon the sight. *novel, novelty; novice. innovation. renovate* (punned upon in Walter Winchell's word for persons going for a quick divorce to Reno, Nevada: *Renovation:* renewal of marital readiness). *novercal:* a new–i.e., step–mother. Fr, *nouveau riche.*

L *nunc:* now. *quidnunc:* first, an exclamation, What now?! *nuncio, nuntius;* see *neu I. Nunc Dimittis:* first words of the song of Simeon (Vulgate Bible, Luke 2:29), that "sweetest of canticles"; hence, permission to leave. *nunc dimittis* was the Roman formula for manumission of a slave.

Gc, *now, nowadays. new, newlywed. Neustria* (? *New Austria*): latest land taken by the Franks. *Newton:* new town. *newtonite* is from *Newton* County, Arkansas. *Newtonian:* relating to Sir Isaac *Newton* (d. 1727), man of the third famous apple; the first to tell of his deriving therefrom the law of gravity was Voltaire. See *abel.*

news: new tidings from all over the world; reenforced by the fact that its letters begin the four cardinal points of the compass: *N*orth, *E*ast, *W*est, *S*outh. (What do these words have in common: *thorn, seat, stew, shout?* Each is an anagram of a cardinal point of the compass.) *newsworthy.* Many words have been formed with *new,* as *newcomer, newfangled, new-laid* (see below). *Newfoundland* (dog; fish: the cod).

Newgate, site of a notorious prison in London, razed in the 19th c., gave rise to several terms. *Newgate bird:* prisoner, especially one exposed to public scorn in a cage outside the jail. "Must we all march?" asks Falstaff, in *1 Henry IV,* iii, 3, and Bardolph answers: "Yea, two and two, Newgate fashion." "That extraordinary record of human vice and suffering," the *Newgate Calendar,* account of prisoners, was begun in 1773. *Newgate frill:* full beard, from ears around chin, many prisoners being unable to pay the barber. *Newgatory* is a pun on *nugatory.*

"What's the new news at the new court?" Thus Shakespeare launches his exposition in *As You Like It.* "No news but the old news"—which he then provides for the audience.

For *neo-, OED* lists 31 words, from *neoarctic* to *neotype;* and details 38, as *neocomian. neossin* (Gk *neossos:* new-hatched bird): the mucus secreted by the salivary glands of a genus of swift, from which bird's-nest soup is made. The word *new* takes up 7 columns in *OED,* and is followed by over 18 columns of combinations, as *new-bear:* a cow that has just calved; *new year; New Yorker.*

Among several old sayings on the theme of news, one effort at comforting a waiting soul is "No news is good news," which a cynic might interpret as "All news is bad."

ni: down; below. Skr *ni. Upanishad:* literally, sitting down near; a Hindu treatise for initiates; see *sed I.* OE *neathen. neath, beneath, underneath;* the *nether* regions. Coleridge, in *The Ancient Mariner,* tells of

The hornèd moon, with one bright star
Within the nether tip.
[*Is this possible?*]

L *nidus* blent with the root *sei I:* sit, to give us *nest,* wherein the female bird sits and sets. *nidamental, nide, nidify, nidology, nidulent, nidus. An eyas:* nestling hawk, is folkchanged from *a nias.* Shakespeare, in *Hamlet,* calls the child actors then in vogue (rivals of his company) "an eyrie of children, little eyases." Probably *niche.* Gc, *nest, nestling.* The diminutive ending, *ling,* mistaken for the present participial *ing,* hatched the verb *nestle.*

niminy-piminy, imitative of an affected, overdone mincing style, may be related to *nimeity* (see *ne*). It first appeared in print in *The Monthly Review* (1801), as "a niminy-piminy lisp." Usually the *m* doubles back upon itself, making the word *miminy;* this expression has been used by Leigh Hunt, Thackeray, and Robert Louis Stevenson. W. S. Gilbert, in *Patience*, has one of the rival poets sing:

Conceive me, if you can,
A Japanese young man,
Francesca da Rimini, miminy piminy,
Je-ne-sais-quoi young man.

L *nihil, nil* (again see *ne*), gave rise to various expressions. See *guhisl.*

?niger: black. L *niger, nigrum;* Sp, *negro. negroid. Negrillo, Negrito, Negro.* It, *niello:* black enamel. *necromancy* (see *nek*) was changed in LL to *nigromantia:* the black art. *negrophile, negrophobe. nigger. nigrescence. nigrify; nigritude, negritude. nigrosine:* black dye. *denigrate.* It, *nero-antico. Nero,* Roman emperor, A.D. 54–68, black in name and nature. *OED* defines 32 related words beginning *negr,* 35 beginning *nigr.*

Nogella, genus of fennel. The Greek word for fennel is *marathon.* When the Persians invaded Greece in 490 B.C., the courier Pheidippides ran to Sparta—150 miles in two days—for aid. The Spartans hemmed and hawed; and at the fennel field of Marathon the Athenians, under Miltiades, decisively defeated ten times their number of Persians under Darius. Pheidippides—as in Browning's poem, 1879 (Plutarch's suggestion that it was another courier has been ignored by history)—ran from Marathon to Athens with news of the victory, cried it out exultantly, and fell dead. In his memory, the Marathon race, of 26 miles, 385 yards, was added to the Olympic Games. See *bher I; mel III.*

?nitron: sodium carbonate. Gk, *nitron,* possibly from Hebrew. *niter. nitrate:* salt of nitric acid. *nitrite:* salt of nitrous acid. *nitrogen* (see *el 7*). *nitroglycerine. nitroso;* also as a prefix in chemistry, indicating the NO radical. Some forms are probably from Arabic, via Spanish, as *natrolite, natron. natrium* is the earlier name of sodium; hence its symbol, *Na* (see *el 11*).

nogu: naked. Gk *gumnos. gymnasium,* where the Greek youth exercised in the nude. Abbreviated today, as when the sophomore phoned her startled parents that she "weighed 112 pounds, stripped for gym." *gymnast. gymnosophist. OED* gives 67 associated words, mainly botanical, beginning *gymno,* as *gymnogram, gymnosperm. gymkhana* is a blend of *gym* and Hindi *gendkhana:* ball house, racquet court.

L *nudus. nude, nudist,* etc. *denude. nudicaul, nudibranchiate;* but scientists have preferred the Greek prefix. *nudification.* Gc, *naked.*

nudiustertian, however, means the day before yesterday. The *yes* in *yesterday* is altered from L *hesternus,* Gm *Gestern.* See *ghdhies,* which first meant the next day, either before or behind; in some languages, as Gothic and Tocharian, it formed the word for *tomorrow.* Byron, in *Don Juan,* pictures

A group that's quite unique,
Half-naked, loving, natural, and Greek.

Blake, in *Proverbs of Hell,* is more sober, though a bit anticlimactic:

The pride of the peacock is the glory of God,
The lust of the goat is the bounty of God.
The wrath of the lion is the wisdom of God.
The nakedness of woman is the work of God.

not: buttock; back. Gk *notos. notochord. Camponotos:* genus of "backbending" ants. *Gymnonoti:* genus including the electric eel, "naked backs" (without a dorsal fin).

L and E *nates* (plural). *Natica:* genus of marine snails. Via OFr from L *natis, an aitchbone* is folkchanged from *a nachebone.*

?nous: mind, intellect. Thought is something our Indo-European forefathers apparently did not think about; the root for it seems not to occur before the Greeks. "The Greeks had a word for it." To Plato (d. 348 B.C.), *nous* meant the home of the basic idea, the prototype of earthly phenomena, which are merely its manifestations; thus the idea "tree" is before and behind all rooted trees. The word *nous* (now pronounced *noose*) was frequent in the 19th c.; then sounded to rhyme with *house,* it had the colloquial meaning, common sense. "I am glad," said a gentleman in *The Graphic* of 8 Nov. 1884, "my people had the nous to show you to a room where there was a fire." *nous box:* the head. Hence *noetic, noesis.*

noumenon was coined by Kant (d. 1804) to contrast with *phenomenon. paranoia. metanoia:* fundamental change of mind, of moral attitude; see *medhi.*

?o: announcement; foreboding. L *omen, ominem. omen, ominous, abomination. abominable;* up to the 18th c. this was spelled *abhominable,* as though from L *hominem:* man, thus meaning away from man, beastly; the spelling was corrected, but the change in meaning proved permanent. In *Love's Labor's Lost* Holofernes declares: "I abhor such fanatical phantasimes, such insociable and point-device companions, such rackers of orthography. . . . This is abhominable —which he would call abbominable. It insinuateth me of insanie." In the First Folio of Shakespeare, the word *abhominable* occurs 18 times, and always with the *h.*

The greatest *mantra,* or word of power, in Buddhism and Hinduism is *OM,* an announcement of the worshiper's assent to the divine will, the beginning of his ascent on the eightfold Way to godhead (see *okto*). *OM* is actually a triliteral utterance, having the sound of a protracted *aum,* symbolizing earth, sky, and heaven. It is repeated almost endlessly, in prayer, or inwardly as an adjunct to meditation. P. Holroyde, in *Indian Music* (1972), says that it "rings out like the tolling of a cathedral bell."

E *oss:* augur, augury, noun and verb, used from the 4th c. into the 17th, now dialectal, has been assigned to Gk *ossa:* prophecy, but no intermediate terms have been found.

od: smell. Gk *osmein. osmatic, aosmic, anosmia, hyperosmia, hyposmia, parosmia. osmium* (see *el 76*). *osmo-,* as *osmometer. osmonosology, osmology.* The *Universal Reveiw* of Mar. 1889, reacting against the new naturalism, mainly from France, declared: "Literature is much more than osmology, and the world contains something beyond and above its social sewers."

Osmorhiza: genus, the sweet cicelies (Gk *rhiza:* root). Three genera of the rue family—*Agathosma:* good smell, *Barosma:* heavy smell, *Diaosma:* heavenly odor. "You must wear your rue with a difference"—Ophelia, in *Hamlet. Hedeoma:* sweet-smelling; genus, the mock pennyroyal. *euosmite:* pleasant-smelling; fossil resin. But also *Coprosma:* filthy smell, genus of the madder family. *Onosmodium:* ass smell; genus, the false gromwells. Also *osphresus, osphradium. ozone. ozocerite.*

L and E *odor.* Due perhaps to the Sabines, or to association with L *oleum:* oil, the *d* shifted to *l* in L *olere:* smell. *olfactory, redolent. olid; odoriferous, malodorous, deodorant.* Note *odorous;* according to the *Heritage Dictionary,* "usually but not necessarily unpleasant," but in *OED* "more usually sweet-smelling"—with a seasonable instance from 1834:

> Sweetest of younger sisters, odorous-tressed,
> Whose lips are worshipped by the breezes:
> Spring!

odi: hate, disgust. This may have been an offshoot of the preceding root, indicating the feeling roused by a fetid smell. (*fetid,* L *fetere, fetidum,* probably sprang from *fimus:* dung. Via Persian came *asafoetida, asa:* gum.) L and E *odium. odious.* L *in odio,* via French, gave English *annoy,* etc. *noisome.* Fr, *ennui.*

Odysseus, known for his tricky ways, may be of this root. Note, however, in the *Odyssey,* that when the Cyclops Polyphemus asks the captured Odysseus his name, he replies *Odys:* No Man. James Joyce, in conversation, used this as a figure to explain his pouring everything into his book *Ulysses:* "If an artist holds back anything, it is inevitably the god in him, the Zeus, that is sloughed, and No man indeed that remains." The trickiness of Odysseus is illustrated in the fact that when Odysseus blinds Polyphemus and escapes, the other Cyclopes take "No Man" to mean that this was divine action, that Odysseus is beyond their recapture and revenge. See *oku.*

oino: one. (For the negative, see *ne.*) Skr *eka:* one; used by D. I. Mendeléev in 1872 to name a predicted element one below the element in the same group to which *eka* is prefixed, as *ekaboron, ekalead.* "On Friday came news from America that ekaceasium had been discovered" (22 Oct. 1931).

Gk *oinos:* the *one* (ace) on dice; *ace* is from *as,* the smallest Greek coin. Hence also *ambsace:* both aces; in a toss of two dice the lowest possible score; hence, bad luck. L *unus:* one. *unanimous; unify, unit, unite, unity. unicorn. universe. university;* from the British pronunciation, *varsity. uni-,* as *unilateral, uniparous, univalent. OED* lists 68 words beginning *uni,* as *unisexed; unisex* has recently been favored by hairdressers. *OED* then details 52 columns of relevant words, as *uniformed, unique, United States. unison:* of one pitch; Laurence Sterne, in *Tristram Shandy,* vii: "The nymphs joined in unison, and their swains an octave below them."

L, *uncia,* with its doublets *ounce* and *inch. union:* first, a large pearl; also probably *onion* (peel it, and all that's left are tears). *semuncia. coadunation. quincunx:* five in a unitary order; a frequent formation of trees in an orchard. *triune, trinity. Unitarian. Unio:* genus of mussels. *Uniole:* genus, spike grass.

We eat the onion, which may make us cry, but we avoid the Sardonian herb that would make us laugh. (Gk *Sardo:* Sardinia; L *Sardonius risus:* Sardinian laughter; hence E *sardonic.*)

Gc, *a, an* (OE *ane*); *one, once. alone* is all one, by oneself. *lone, lonely, lonesome. anon:* in one (moment); *anon* is also an abbreviation of *anonymous* (see *onomen*). *only.* To atone sets one "at one." *none:* not one (see *ne*). *any.*

Do you know the difference between *leave alone* and *let alone*? The pretty real-estate agent made the distinction when asked by an impertinent customer, "Are you to be let with the apartment?" Not wishing to lose the sale, she neatly replied: "No, I am to be let alone." *to leave one alone* means that others must go away; *to let one alone* means that others must not disturb.

The pretty agent was anticipated by the poet Francis Quarles, who in 1635 wrote (in *Emblems,* book ii, emblem 10) of a house to be let for life (house of the soul?), whose

bills make known
She must be dearly let, or let alone.

One obituary of my late friend Eric Partridge remarked that he was "probably the last lone lexicographer." This neat alliteration overlooks a clear distinction, that between a general dictionary and a specialized one. The publishers of a general wordbook today, in addition to a full-time staff, may, like *Heritage,* have a "Usage Panel," or, like *OED,* a cohort of "word-gatherers." The specialized dictionary–e.g., one of slang words, Eric Partridge's main field (he also compiled clichés and catch phrases)–is still likely to be the work of a single happy drudge. But the occasional bias or whimsicality that marks the one-man work, from Johnson to (shall I say?) Shipley, may still find rare outlet in the cooperatively compiled volumes. Thus *OED*'s Burchfield, as a former pupil of his, Peter Hillman, points out, "was slightly miffed a few years ago when Kingsley Amis remarked that another Oxford Dictionary contained an inordinate number of words connected with drink." And behold, Hillman continues, in *OED*'s third supplement, under *pissed,* meaning drunken, one quotation is from Kingsley Amis, and one from Kingsley's novelist son, Martin. Is this coincidence, or does it smack of a Cheshire-cat grin?

Gm, *einkorn. Turnverein. Zollverein.* Albert *Einstein* (: one stone, which he left not unturned). Scot, *Angus.*

Why should I feel lonely: Is not our planet in the Milky Way?
–Thoreau, *Walden*

Alone. . . . The word is life endured and known.
It is the stillness where our spirits walk
And all but inmost faith is overthrown.
–Siegfried Sassoon, *Alone* (1918)

oito: a going, as to fulfill a pledge; hence, *oath.* See *ei.* Gk *oidos.* Via Celt, *oath.* Gc, *Huguenot:* comrade in oath; see *neud.* What in the U.S. is called a notary public is in England called a commissioner for oaths.

(o)iua: fruit, berry, grape. L and E *uva. uvea, uvula. yew. Iva:* genus, the marsh elder. *Uvularia:* genus, the bellwort. *pyruvic* (*acid*): fire grape. Gc, *acorn:* fruit of the field; related to *acre;* see *ag;* form influenced by *corn.* Some acorns are edible by humans; see *hule.*

okto: eight. In Sanskrit, four twice; counting not the thumb but the fingers. Gk *okto, okta;* L *octo, octavus;* the shift from *o* to *a* by analogy with *hepta:* 7, *ennea:* 9, *dekta:* 10 (*pente:* 5, and *hex:* 6, also use *a* in compounds). *octachord, octad, octagon,* etc. *octan, octane, octant, octaploid; octosyllabic. octave, octet. utas,* perhaps from *ut:* eighth note of the musical scale. *October,* when March was the year's first month. *octopus. octoroon. octillion:* in the U.S. and France, 10^{27}; in Great Britain and Germany, 10^{48}. *OED* has some 75 words beginning *oct. octogenarian. Octavius:* eighth-born. Gc, *eight, eighteen, eightieth.*

"Most of all I envy the octogenarian poet who joined three words–Go, lovely Rose–so happily together, that he left his name to float down through Time on the wings of a phrase and a flower"–Logan Pearsall Smith, "Afterthoughts" (1931). Edmund Waller in 1664 wrote the poem that begins "Go, lovely rose," at the age of eighty-five. When Smith wrote of his envy, he was sixty-six.

The Buddhist eightfold Way, to attain Nirvana, leads through rightness of belief, resolve, speech, action, livelihood, effort, thought, and meditation; see *med.* The term *eightfold* has recently been applied in chemistry to the most frequent interaction of elementary particles.

oku: relating to vision. Skr *aksi:* eye. Various Latin words. *atrox:* black-looking; E *atrocious, atrocity. atrabilious:* black bile, a translation of Gk *melane chole* (see *mel III*). *celox:* fast-looking; *celerity;* see *kel VII. ferox:* wild-looking; *ferocious, ferocity;* see *ghuer. velox:* lively-looking; *velocity;* see *ueg II.*

Gk *ops:* eye, face. *ophthalmos:* eyeball and socket. *myope, nyctalopia. -opsis,* as *coreopsis. -opsia, -opsy,* as *achromatopsia; autopsy. opsin; rhodopsin. Rhodope* Mountains, east of Greece, rosy-looking at dawn. *Europe:* broad-looking, but perhaps this is folk etymology of a Semitic word meaning land of the setting sun. *synopsis. Thanatopsis* (see *dheu I*). *optical, optician, optometrist,* etc. *catoptric,* of reflection; *dioptric,* of refraction; *catadioptric. catoptromancy:* divination with a mirror. *orthoptic; scioptic. metope:* beyond the eyes, the forehead. *metoptic, metopomancy. panopticon.*

As a prefix, *ops* comes from two other Greek forms: (1) *ops:* late, as in *opsigamy, opsimath;* (2) *opson:* dainties, rich fare, as in *opsomaniac:* one with a constant sweet tooth. *opsony* was used of something (as smoked or pickled fish) eaten to give a relish to bread; hence *opsophagist:* one that relishes relish; see *past.*

Ethiop: burnt face. *Ethiopia.* Romeo exclaims of Juliet (i,5):

> O: she doth teach the torches to burn bright.
> It seems she hangs upon the cheek of night
> Like a rich jewel in an Ethiop's ear;
> Beauty too rich for use, for earth too dear.

And in *Love's Labor's Lost,* iv, 3, Dumain, in a love letter, addresses his lady:

> Thou for whom Jove would swear
> Juno but an Ethiop were;
> And deny himself for Jove,
> Turning mortal for thy love.

Shakespeare also uses *Ethiop(e)* in *As You Like It* (iv, 3), *Midsummer Night's Dream* (iv, 2), *Much Ado About Nothing* (v, 4), *Pericles* (ii, 2), *Two Gentlemen of Verona* (ii, 6), and uses *Ethiopian* in *The Merry Wives* (ii, 3) and *A Winter's Tale* (iv, 4).

Cecrops: tail-face, legendary founder of Athens. *Pelops:* furry-eyed, the son of Tantalus, settled Peloponnesia, whose chief cities were Corinth and Sparta, the rival of Athens. Pelops founded the Olympic Games in 776 B.C. Sparta defeated Athens in the 27-year Peloponnesian War, which ended in 404 B.C. *Cyclops:* circle-eyed; just one, in the middle of the forehead; chief of the Cyclopes was Polyphemus; see *odi.*

Also *epopt:* beholder; especially an initiate at the holy mysteries or in secret societies. *stenopaic. diopsite. phlogopite:* fiery-looking; mica. *pyrope:* fire-eye; a garnet. *Oxopidae:* family of hunting spiders. *ophthalmia; ophthalmologist, ophthalmoscope; exophthalmos, lagophthalmus. OED* lists 31 words beginning *ophthalm(o),* and details 17. Gk *opma, omma:* eye, in such English compounds as *ommatidium, ommatophore. Ommastrephes:* eye-turning; genus of cephalopods.

L *oculus:* eye; the ending is not a diminutive, but a suffix denoting action. E *oculus;* also in names, as *oculus Christi:* wild sage; *oculus lucidus:* honeysuckle; *oculus mundi:* an opal. *ocularium:* eyehole in a helmet. *ocular, oculist. ocularist:* maker of artificial eyes. *oculiform. monocular, monocle; binoculars. inoculate. oculo-,* as *oculomotor, oculozygomatic.*

The diminutive of L *oculus* is *ocellus,* and is used in English, usually in the plural, *ocelli. ocellar, ocellation. ocelli-,* as *ocellicyst, ocelliferous.* Fr, *ocelle,* usually figurative in meaning: apple of my eye; darling. *oeillade; oeil-de-boeuf.* Via Fr *aveugle:* blind, from L *ab oculis,* came E *inveigle. ullage:* what's needed to fill a cask to the "eye," i.e., to the bunghole. *antelope,* from Gk *antelops:* flower-eye, a fabulous monster. *antler,* from LL *anteoculare:* (horn) in front of the eye.

The Germanic forms *auga, oga, eiga, oog,* and more, were taboo-changes, to avert the Evil Eye, which was much feared around the world. It has been suggested that the bridal veil, the shaving of a bride's head, certain rites at childbirth, and the mezuzah (a small case containing a roll of parchment inscribed with Deuteronomy 6:4–9 and 11:13–21, traditionally affixed at the side of the entrance door of the Jewish home) are among devices originally intended to avert the Evil Eye.

Gc, *ogle:* to give one the eye; to eye amorously. *The Tatler,* no. 145 (1705), speaks of "a certain sect of professed enemies to the repose of the fair sex, called oglers." *eye.* The *daisy* is the *day's eye. eyelet,* and many other compounds, from *eyeable* and *eyeball* to *eyewink* and *eyewitness.* Scand *vindauga:* wind-eye; E *window.* (The Latin for a wall-opening or window is *fenestra;* whence 13 words in *OED.* Most noted is the *defenestration* in Prague, where, on 21 May 1618, insurgents broke up a government meeting and threw three officials out the window, thus starting the Thirty Years' War.) Perhaps via Gm, from Fr *binocle,* came *pinochle.* The ancient Hebrews swore by their testes (see *tre*); the ancient Greeks swore by their eyes.

"The eye is the window of the soul." "Open the window; light and God stream in."

Thackeray, among his verse satires, has one on *The Sorrows of Werther,* Goethe's juvenile novel of an upright young man in love with a married woman; its end is well known:

So he sighed and pined and ogled,
And his passion boiled and bubbled,
Till he blew his silly brains out
And no more was by it troubled.
Charlotte, having seen his body
Borne before her on a shutter,
Like a well-conducted person
Went on cutting bread and butter.

ol I: destroy. Possibly expanded in L *letalis,* which later added an *h* from *Lethe,* river of oblivion in Hades; whence *lethal.* See *ladh.*

ol II: all. OIr *ule.* The rare L *allers:* learned, degenerated in the scornful E *know-it-all. OED* gives almost 9 columns to the word *all.* It says *all* is a "possible prefix to any adjective of quality," and lists 40, as *all-beauteous, all-content, all-important. all-star, all-wondrous. allodium. allspice.* There were few combinations with the present participle before 1600, but "in modern times their number is unlimited"; *OED* lists 90, as *all-confounding, all-embracing, all-space-filling, all-working.* In the sense of wholly, *all-thing* was used (as still the negative is, in *nothing loath*). Shakespeare had Lady Macbeth (iii, 1) declare of the absence of Banquo:

It had been a gap at our great feast,
And all-thing unbecoming.

With one *l,* there are various combinations. *almighty; also; although. albeit* is a condensation of *although it may be. alone;* sometimes emphatically, *all alone.* Note the difference between *altogether* and *all together; already* and *all ready.*

The frequently written *alright* is not a valid word; yet *all right* may indicate any of three things: (1) one item is completely in order; (2) every one of a number of items is correct; (3) a person approves, or agrees, as to do something. By analogy with the two pairs already in use, for (1) and (3) *alright* may come to be altogether acceptable. See *op I* for *omnis.*

Then let us pray that come it may,
  And come it will for a' that,
That common sense may take the place
  Of common cant and a' that.
  For a' that, and a' that,
  Who cackles trash, and a' that,
  Or be he lord or be he low,
  The man's an ass for a' that.
   —Charles W. Shirley Brooks,
    parody of Robert Burns

oma, am: raw, unripe; bitter; also dark. Gk *Mauros:* dark folks. *Maurus. Mauretania. Moor, Morisco; Moro, Moresque.* From *Moorish,* the E *morris:* a very popular dance, with lively costumes and steps, 15th to 18th c. *morris pike:* a spear. *omophagous,* etc. *margosa, amargoso. marasca, maraschino. maurodaphne:* dark laurel wine. *morel:* the nightshade. *morello.* Also *amaurosis:* darkening of vision. *amarine, amarantite.*

There is a punning L saw: *amare bene est, si non amari:* to love is well, if not to be loved—or "if not bitter." An early English word was *amarous:* bitter, as perhaps after being vainly amorous. Also obsolete are *amaricate:* to embitter; *amarulent, amaritude.*

ombhr: rain. Gk *ombros. ombrology, ombrometer.* L *imber, imbris. imbue. imbrex, imbricem:* hollow tile to lead off rain; on churches this developed into the mischievous *gargoyle* (imitative base *garg;* whence also *gargle* and *gurgle*). *imbricate.* See *andho.*

          Parting day
Dies like the dolphin, whom each pang imbues
With a new colour as it gasps away,
The last still loveliest, till—'tis gone and all is gray.
   —Byron, *Childe Harold's Pilgrimage,* iv

om(s): shoulder. Gk *omos. omodynia. omoplate. omophore:* in Hindu, Manich(a)-ean, and Greek mythology, that which bears the world on its shoulders. *omophorion:* a feminine, later ecclesiastical, garment covering the shoulders. *exomis:* garment that leaves the shoulder(s) bare. *omoplatoscopy. omostegite.*

L *humerus:* shoulder. E *humerus:* bone of upper arm; because it causes a tingling sensation when struck at the elbow, it is punningly called the *funny bone. acromion. Iniomi:* order of fishes. Swedish *os,* plural *osar,* also *osar* singular: ridge, shoulder of ground. H. Miller, in 1854: "There is a wonderful group of . . . osars in the immediate neighborhood of Inverness."

oner: dream. Gk *oneiros. oneirocritic:* interpreter of dreams; for one in action, see *caput. oneiromancy. oneiropompist:* sender of dreams. There are 17 relevant entries in *OED.* For *onerous,* see *enos.* Morpheus is the dream-god, of shapes; the god of sleep is Somnus; see *merbh.*

onogh: nail, claw, hoof. Gk *onux, onukhos. onyx. sardonyx:* onyx of Sardis, ancient capital of Lydia. Hence also *sardonic; herba sardonica,* a poisonous plant that distorts the mouth that takes it. *onycha, onychite, onychoid, onychomancy,* *onychophorous. onychia, paronychia:* beside the nail, a whitlow. *Paronychia:* genus, the whitlowwort, supposedly cures a whitlow. (*whitlow* is from the earlier *whitflawe, whick:* a flaw in a sensitive part; *whick,* quick, as "stung to the quick." *OED* gives 19 columns to *quick* and its compounds, as *quicklime, quicksand, quicksilver.*) *onchyophagist,* an infrequent term for a frequent fellow: one that bites one's nails.

L *unguis. ungual, unguiculate, unguiform, ungulate. Ungulata:* hoofed mammals. *notoungulate.* Gc, *nail; finger-* or *toenail.*

> Care to our coffin adds a nail, no doubt,
> And every grin so merry draws one out.
> —Peter Pindar (John Wolcot),
> *Expostulary Odes* (1782), xv

onomen: name. (While this is deemed by some a separate root, other scholars trace L *nomen, cognomen:* that by which we are known, to the root *gn[o].* To the prolific root *gn,* then, belong all the words mentioned here.) Gk *onoma, onomatos. onomancy, onomastic, onomasticon. antonomasia, paranomasia. onomatopoetic:* made into a name. *allonym; anonymous. synonym, antonym; homonym; cryptonym; eponym. euonymous; heteronymous. metonymy. metronymic. patronymic. paronymous, polyonymous. pseudonym* (Fr, *nọm de guerre, nom de plume*). *toponym. Euonymus:* of good name (a euphemism); genus, the spindle-tree; Pliny called its blossoming a presage of pestilence. *Jerome* (Gk *Hieronymos:* holy name).

L *nomen, nominem. nom, nomen, nomenclature. nominal, nominalism, nominate, nominative. OED* has 10 words beginning *nomen,* and 23 beginning *nomin. nominy,* from the ecclesiastic blessing *in nomine patris:* in the name of the Father, etc., was applied to a rhyming formula, then to rhyming verses to newlyweds, then to rigmarole; it is a good word, but has been little used since the 19th c.

Also *noun, pronoun. renown. monomial, binomial, trinomial; denominator. agnomen, cognomen, praenomen. ignominious, misnomer. nuncupative.* Gc, *name, nameless, namely. a nickname* is folkchanged from *an eke* (extra) *name. by-name, pen name, surname. Christian (christen) name. namesake.*

paronomasia is a sesquipedalian word for a pun; literally, a word beside. A *paronymous* word, a *paronym,* also is a "word beside," another word of the same stem, as *cordial, cordiality. aptronym* is a word coined, I believe, by F.P.A. (columnist Franklin Pierce Adams) to mean an appropriate name, as Mr. Glass, the glazier; Dr. Payne, the dentist.

Most Latin, many English, and all Chinese names are trinomial. In China, the first name is the family name (in English, the last); the second is the generation name, given to all siblings and first-cousins; the third is the personal name.

There are at least ten English words that have two distinct antonyms: *fair—foul, dark; fast—loose, slow; go—come, stop; hard—soft, easy; light—heavy, dark; lose—win, find; old—young, new; quick—dead, slow; right—left, wrong; take—give, bring.*

John Forster, in *Debates on the Grand Remonstrance* (1860), castigates those "postponing Luke to lucre, and setting more store by a handful of marks than by all the doctrines of their namesake saint." (The namesake here, of course, is St. Mark. Thirty "marks" of silver made a *Judas handful. Judas hole:* a peephole, especially for a guard in prison to watch unobserved; wider use today is found for one-way glass. *Judas tree,* on which Judas supposedly hanged himself; its flowers blossom before its leaves appear.) In Catholic France, a first name is still chosen from the register of saints.

Macaulay in 1827 said of Niccolo Machiavelli (1468–1527): "Out of his surname they have coined an epithet [Machiavellian] for a knave, and out of his Christian name a synonym for the Devil [Old Nick]."

eponyms: words from names, may be from fiction or mythology, as *volcanic, jovial, philanderer;* or from actual places or persons. The latter may refer directly to the source, as *Shakespearean, Italianate;* or be applied to actions, attitudes, characteristics, or discoveries, as *sardonic, boycott, guillotine,* and, in science, *diesel, ampere, ohm, mho, volt.*

Surnames in English, as in most West European languages, come mainly from five sources:

1. Sire, ancestor, tribe, as *Johnson* (*Jones,* the commonest name in Wales); *Macintosh, McKinley; O'Reilly, Pavlova* (daughter of *Paul*).
2. Occupation, as *Smith* (commonest name in England), *Murphy* (commonest name in Ireland: sea warrior), *Baker, Clark* (British sounding of *clerk*)
3. Place of residence, as *Berlin(er), Atwell, Cowley* (*lea:* meadow).
4. Personal peculiarities, probably at first nicknames, as *Longfellow, Truman, Kennedy* (: ugly head), *Gray.*
5. Natural objects, as *Berry, Fox, Stone, Shaw, Burns.*

William L'Isle of Wilburgham (d. 1637) had a thought that is still pertinent: "The Saxons did not, as men do nowadays, for a glory of a short continuance, name the places of their conquest after themselves, or some of their great masters; but even according to nature's self." Many place-names are established in memoriam; fewer, like New York's LaGuardia Airport (1939), are given while the persons honored are still in active service (in this case, the mayor of New York City). Note the frequency with which place-names change—e.g., in Russia: *St. Petersburg,* founded in 1703 by Peter the Great as "a window into Europe," was changed to *Petrograd* in 1914; to *Leningrad* in 1924. Street names change even more frequently.

Nature is but a name for an effect
Whose cause is God.
—Cowper, *The Task* (1784)

I am become a name,
For always roaming with a hungry heart
Much have I seen and known, cities of men
And manners, climates, councils, governments . . .
I am a part of all that I have met.
—Tennyson, *Ulysses*

op I: work; originally religious service, then agriculture, then—the gods being kind!—abundance. L *opus, operis:* work; *ops, opis:* abundance. *opus, opuscule;* also *opusculum* ("pretty and pleasing opuscula"). "In this opuscule," said John Morley, "he points out that modern society is passing through a great crisis." That was in 1877. *opera* (L plural of *opus*).

"In how many lives does Love really play a dominant part? The average taxpayer is no more capable of a 'grand passion' than of a grand opera"—Israel Zangwill, "Romeo and Juliet." Zangwill is best known for his description of the United States, *The Melting Pot* (1908).

operate, operation; cooperate; modern *co-ops. opulence.* L *copia* (*co-opis*): abundance; *copious, cornucopia:* horn of plenty. From the sense of abundance came the idea of many times the same thing; hence *copy, copyright; copyist,* etc.

photocopy; now often supplanted by the trade name *Xerox,* both noun and verb (Gk *xeros:* dry). *operose.* Possibly *estovers.*

average may also be from this root; an early term for feudal service, work due the overlord, its form was influenced by OFr *aver:* property, from L *habere:* to have and to hold. *statistical average* (for which see *medhi*) was originally a duty charged on shipped goods (which included "service charge"), then the equal division among investors of any loss by damage to ship and cargo.

L *opi ficium; officium:* performance of (church) service. *office, officer, official, officiate, officious; officinal.* LL *manuoperare:* work with the hand; via Fr *manoeuvre* came *maneuver; manure:* originally, worked (spread) by hand. *hors d'oeuvre:* out of the main action.

L (*opnis*) *omnis:* all (the whole job). *omnibus* (L dative plural of *omnis:* for everyone) has been shortened to *bus. omniana. omnigatherum,* more often *omniumgatherum,* the second element being mock Latin. *omnibenevolent, omnipotent, omnipresent, omniscient:* attributes of the divine. *omni-,* as *omnivorous,* and 85 other *omni-* words in *OED.* For separate use, *omnis* has been superseded by *all;* see *ol II.*

L *optimus,* end of the progression from the simple (good) *bonus* (see *deu*), to the comparative (better) *melior* (see *mel II*), to the superlative (best) *optimus. optimates,* in ancient Greece. *optimum. optimism,* coined by the Jesuits in 1737, felt in every age, although pessimists seem to outnumber their counterparts (L *malus:* bad, *peior:* worse, *pessimus:* worst). Note that in English, too, the simple forms of *good* and *bad* are from different roots than the comparative and superlative forms; they were felt directly, before comparisons pressed in—and comparisons, Mrs. Malaprop is said to have said, are odorous. This remark was first made in 1471, by John Fortescue, in *De Laudibus Legum Angliae;* echoed by Lydgate, Shakespeare (Dogberry, who knew more words than meanings, in *Much Ado About Nothing,* iii, 5), and Swift, it was slyly restored to its original terms in Donne's eighth *Elegy:* "She, and comparisons, are odious." What Mrs. Malaprop said, in Sheridan's *The Rivals,* is: "No caparisons, Miss, if you please. Caparisons don't become a young woman." See *melo.*

Gc, *oft, often.* Though used regularly up to 1875, *oftentimes* is now deemed archaic or literary.

The Rev. Sydney Smith (d. 1845) said of William Whewell: "Science is his forte; omniscience, his foible."

op II: choose. L *opere, optum. opt,* as *I opt out! optative; option. adopt. opine,* now mainly humorous; *opinion, opinionated.* Edmund Burke, in a letter of 1780, spoke of "the coquetry of public opinion, which has her caprices, and must have her way." A man has "a right to his own opinion" only if he has the basic facts behind it and the intelligence to grasp their relevance and significance.

> To hit someone is to adopt his point of view.
> —Paul Valéry

?opak: dark. L *opacus. opacity, opaque.*
or, os: (godly) utterance. *oracle, oracular, orison.*

> Nymph, in thy orisons
> Be all my sins remembered.
> —Hamlet, to Ophelia

oratory: speech; also, place of prayer. *oration, peroration. inexorable;* a word once spoken goeth not back into the mouth, though an aggrieved person might try to make one "eat one's words." *adore.* Dance lovers used to praise *Isadora* Duncan and her *Isadorables.*

Given by some as a separate root, *os,* as L *os, oris:* mouth, entrance, *oral, orle. orifice; orotund. oscillate, oscitancy. ostiary. usher:* doorkeeper. *ostiole. coram* (*co, orem,* by analogy with *clam:* secretly, *palam:* openly): in the face of, fronting the mouth. *Auriga:* charioteer, guiding horses by the mouth; also, a northern constellation. De Quincey, in *The Mail Coach* (1849), describes a driver with "all the skill in aurigation of Apollo himself"; Apollo, you remember, drives the chariot of the sun. His son Phaeton, having begged permission to drive it once, could not manage the steeds; before Zeus struck him with a thunderbolt, the erratic sun had parched the earth of Lydia and blackened the skin of the Ethiopians. Thomas Watson, in *Practical Divinity* (1692), declared: "Sin is the Phaeton that sets the world on fire." Someone with a sense of humor gave the name *phaeton* to a light, open, four-wheeled carriage.

L and E *osculum:* little mouth, as pursed for kissing. Hence *oscular, osculant, osculation. osculum pacis:* the kiss of peace, a rite of the eucharistic service in the primitive Church, survives in the exchanged kissing of cheeks among Europeans. Gk *eirene:* peace, gives us the name *Irene,* sometimes, especially in England, with the final *e* sounded. The word may be related to Gk *eirein:* speak; but *hold your peace* means keep quiet. *kiss the book:* swear solemnly, on the Bible. *kiss (or bite) the dust:* die. More recently, *kiss of life:* an attempt at resuscitation. *kiss the hare's foot:* to be too late, from the speed of the hunted hare. To remind one to be on time, and now for general good luck, one may still keep a rabbit's foot. According to an old saw, kisses are keys. See *kus.*

On Maundy Thursday, which was then the Passover feast, the day before Good Friday of the Crucifixion, Jesus spoke: "A new commandment [*Mandatum novum; Maundy;* see *man*] I give to you, that you love one another" (Bible, John 13:34). This is memorialized in the *pediluvium:* the ceremonial annual washing by the pope of the feet of twelve poor men, symbolizing Jesus' washing the feet of his twelve disciples; see *ped.* The English ceremony at Westminster Abbey is described as "an abbreviated survival of the Pedilavium," but in practice it seems more like a continuation of the pagan Roman practice of distributing baskets of food to the poor after a banquet. The white linen sashes symbolize the cloth with which Jesus wiped the disciples' feet; but at least since the 12th c. the Lord High Almoner (distributor of the royal alms) has given material sustenance rather than spiritual ablution. Queen Mary Tudor in 1556 gave her fur-lined purple gown to the poorest selected old woman. In 1979 Queen Elizabeth II, being fifty-three years of age, gave two purses apiece to 53 men and 53 women, one "for the redemption of Mary's gown" and one for alms, plus a penny apiece in specially minted "maundy money." Thus we are kept mindful of one of the great gifts of Jesus, expressed in his *pediluvium:* humility.

Benjamin Franklin, in *Poor Richard's Almanac* for 1735, exclaimed: "Here comes the orator, with his flood of words, and his drop of reason." This condition has been more morbidly described as "diarrhea of words and constipation of ideas."

In *The Merchant of Venice,* i, 1, Gratiano says there are men

> With purpose to be dressed in an opinion
> Of wisdom, gravity, profound conceit;
> As who shall say: I am Sir Oracle,
> And when I ope my mouth let no dog bark!

O my Antonio, I do know of those
That therefore only are reputed wise
For saying nothing.
Antonio: I'll grow a talker for this gear.
Gratiano: Thanks, i' faith, for silence is only commendable
In a neat's tongue dried, and a maid not vendible.

orbh: deprived—as of parents, of freedom; hence, forced labor. Gk *orphanos,* E *orphan.* Slav, Czech, *robot.* The word *robot* came into English in Samuel Butler's *Erewhon*—turn around *nowhere*—(1872), but was more recently popularized by the production of Karel Čapek's play *R.U.R.* (*Rossum's Universal Robots*) (1922), and by the appearance of robots in scientifiction and life.

orghi: testicle. Gk *orkhis* (genitive *orkhios,* incorrectly *orkhidis*). *orchid,* from the shape of the root. *orchido-,* as *orchidaceous, orchidology. orchidotomy,* shortened to *orchotomy:* cutting into a testicle; *orchidectomy:* removal of testicle(s); loosely, all three words are used to mean castration; see *kastr. orchitis, orchiocele; OED* lists 6 and details 10 relevant *orchi-* terms. See *tre.*

ors: buttock, tail. Gk *oura:* tail. *uro-,* as *uropygial, uropteran.* Note that *uro-* may also refer to *urine,* as *uroscopy;* see *nebh.* Many compounds. *Anthurium:* flower tail; genus, the arium. *anuran:* tailless; frogs and toads. *Urocoptis* (Gk *khoptein:* cut): genus of snails. *Uropeltidae* (Gk *pelte:* small shield): genus of snakes with shieldlike tail end. *coenurus* (Gk *coen:* common): a type of larva. *dasyure* (Gk *dasus:* shaggy): a marsupial mammal. *squirrel* (Gk *skia:* shade; see *skai*). *silure:* literally, sheath tail, "the sly siluris"; fish without scales. *arse* was commonly pronounced, and is now commonly spelled, *ass.* For *jackass,* see *ane; asinus.*

colure (Gk *kholos:* cut, curtailed): great circle of the celestial sphere, the lower part always below the horizon. *cynosure;* see *kuon:* dog. *Cynosure* is the constellation also known as *Ursa Minor:* the Lesser Bear, and the Little Dipper; its star Polaris, at the tip of the tail, is the North Star, the mariner's guide by night. Thus *cynosure* came to mean a center of attraction. (*Ursa Major:* the Great Bear, points to Polaris; see *septm.* For *ursa,* see *rkthos.*)

Towers, and battlements, it sees,
Bosom'd high in tufted trees,
Where perhaps some beauty lies,
The cynosure of neighboring eyes.
—Milton, *L'Allegro*

os: the ash tree. Known from early times, the ash has tough, flexible wood and is used for instruments; and boys can put its winged seeds on the nose. *Beowulf,* Wycliffe, Spenser: "The warlike beech, the ash for nothing ill"; Shakespeare, Dryden, Wordsworth, Scott: "the tough ash-spear so stout and true"; and Tennyson are among the many that mention the ash. It is the only wood that will burn when green.

ost, oss: bone. Gk *osteon. osteopath. OED* lists 57 words beginning *osteo,* as *osteomyelitis,* and details 21, as *osteoblast, osteomalacia, osteometry. endostium, endostosis, exostosis, synostosis; periosteum, teleost. ostreon:* oyster; *ostrakon:* shell, potsherd. *ostracod. ostracon,* used in ancient Athens for voting; hence *ostracize. ostracite.* John Donne, *To the Countess of Bedford,* observes:

Virtue in courtiers' hearts
Suffers an ostracism and departs.

ostraceous, ostraco-, as *ostracoderm, ostracology.* Gk *osphus:* hip bone. *osphyalgia, osphyarthristis.* Gk *astragalos:* ankle ball. *astragal, astragalus.*

L *os, ossis:* bone. *OED* defines 29 relevant words, as *os, ossein, osseus, ossicle; ossify; ossifrage* and its doublet *osprey:* bone-breaker. *ossements:* bare bones. *ossuary:* receptacle for bones of the dead; hence, with grave humor, a *boneyard:* cemetery. Via OFr, *oyster.*

"There is nothing in Christianity or Buddhism that quite matches the sympathetic unselfishness of an oyster"—Saki, *Chronicles of Clovis* (1911). This unselfishness is illustrated in the march of the oysters after the Walrus and the Carpenter in Carroll's *Through the Looking Glass:*

"The time has come", the Walrus said,
"To talk of many things:
Of shoes—and ships—and sealing wax—
Of cabbages—and kings—"

Thus the Walrus devoured the eager and succulent bivalves. (*Cabbages and Kings* is the title of O. Henry's first book. The four lines are also used by Ellery Queen to force the murderer's confession in *The Adventure of the Mad Tea Party.*)

?oti: idleness. *otiose, negotiate* (*neg-otium est:* there is no leisure); see *ne.*

oui: sheep. L *ovis. ovine. oviform* means either sheeplike or egg-shaped; for the latter, see *auei. Ovibovinae, Ovibos:* subfamily and genus, the musk ox. *Ovidae:* family of sheep and goats; fellow travelers, to be sorted out on doomsday. Gc, *ewe.*

My flocks feed not, my ewes breed not, my rams speed not,
All is amiss.
Love is dying, Faith's defying, Heart's denying,
Causer of this.
—Richard Barnfield, *A Shepherd's Complaint* (1598), written at about the time of Shakespeare's sonnets. Two of Barnfield's poems in this volume—"If music and sweet poetry agree" and "As it fell upon a day"—were long thought to be by Shakespeare.

ous, au: ear. Gk *ous, otos. otitis. oto-,* as *otolith, otoscope. otic, entotic, epiotic, parotic. parotid* (gland), *parotoid. diota:* two-eared vessel. *Microtinae. Microtus:* subfamily and genus of "tiny-eared" rodents, including the lemming. *Myosotis:* genus, the forget-me-not; "mouse-eared," from the shape of the leaf. *Aotus:* earless; genus of monkeys. *Haliotis:* ear of the sea; genus of univalve crustaceans, the abalones. *Otididae, Otis:* family and genus of bustards (long-eared). *Plecotus:* genus of long-eared bats. *Otiorhynchidae:* literally, snout and ear; family of weevils.

Gk *lagos:* drooping ear; the hare. *Lagomorpha:* order of rodents, the rabbits and hares. *lagophthalmus. Lagopus:* harefooted; genus, the ptarmigan. *Lagurus:* genus, hare's-tail grass.

L *auris:* ear. *audible, aural, auricle, auricular, auriform; ormer:* sea ear, a mollusk. L *auscultare, auscultatum:* give ear, listen. *auscultation.* The *au* was mistaken for a form of the prefix *ad,* and *ex* was substituted; thence OFr *escouter,* Fr *écouter,* E *scout:* someone sent out to listen and observe. For *scout:* to reject with scorn, see *skeud.*

Fr, *orillion. Oyez:* Hear ye! (for official proclamations, usually called three times, like three cheers). Gc, *ear. OED* gives 6 columns to *ear;* then adds 8 combinations, as *earache. earmark,* first on sheep, to indicate owner. *earwig.*

Polonius, in *Hamlet,* bids his son:

Give every man thine ear, but few thy voice,
Take each man's censure, but reserve thy judgment.

Shakespeare's pompous bore here gives sound advice; it is not his fault that his words have become clichés.

ozd: point, angle, triangle; hence, odd number. Gc, *odd, oddity,* and *the odds* (usually against). *odd-fellow.*

Falstaff, in *The Merry Wives of Windsor,* v, 1, hopefully avers: "There is divinity in odd numbers, either in nativity, chance, or death."

P

pa. Baby talk, usually of the father, which comes after *ma,* of the breast. Hence the protector and, after the weaning, the feeder. See *peter. papa, pappa, pappy, pop.* L *pappa:* food; but *pappus:* grandfather, usually more attentive than the father; in ancient times, he was by the tent to play with the babe while the father was out hunting. (The ancient Roman playwright Plautus doubly marks the "generation gap" by having a grandfather say to his grandson: "You and I should be allies; we have a common enemy.") Hence *pamper.*

This seems to be a widespread root, not only Indo-European. Chinese, *papa.* American Indian (Algonquian), *papoose.* Pers (which is Indo-European) *pad, bad, ban; wan:* protector. *bezoar; durwan; lokapala; padisha; pasha; pashalik; satrap.* SCr, *ban, banat.* Gk and L *pappus.* E *pope, papist.*

pap, a nipple, usually in the plural; some call this a separate root, meaning to swell. *papilla, papilloma, papula; poppet, popsy-wopsy.* Fr *poupée;* E *pup, puppy, puppet. pupa, pupil.* A *pupil*—from the diminutive of L *pupus:* young man (feminine, *pupa*)—was first, legally, a boy up to the age of fourteen, a girl up to the age of twelve. (Romeo's Juliet was fourteen.) *pupa* also means a stage in the development of an insect, between larva and imago. The *pupil* of the eye is named for the tiny image it may show. *pupillary. Papaveraceae, Papaver:* family and genus, the poppy; the flower bells forth. *papaverine:* of opium, derived from the poppy.

Of 34 words in *OED* beginning *papi,* 17, as *papilla,* are related to *pap:* nipple; 4, as *papilionaceous,* to butterfly (see *pal*); and 12, as *papism,* to *pope* and *popery. Paphian,* adjective and noun, is from *Paphos,* a city of Cyprus sacred to Aphrodite; thence applied to a prostitute or to sexual orgies. Byron, in *Hints from Horace* (1811), describes a woman thus: "In turn she'll seem a Paphian or a prude." See *Cyprus,* under *ped.*

Also *pap:* soft food, often used figuratively. *poppy. poppycock:* actually, soft shit (see *caca*). L *pascere, pastum:* feed; *panis:* bread. *pan et circenses* (see *guher*). *pannage. pascual. pasture. repast* first meant feeding again. *pastern:* first, tether for animals at pasture; hence, *pester. pastor,* a shepherd who tends his human flock.

pantry; pantler (the *l* by association with OE *boteler:* butler). *panetela,* shaped like a (long, thin, like the French) breadloaf, as the Fr *pain. panada. pannier:*

breadbasket. *pastille. impanate; panification. pannage, appanage. companion,* with whom one breaks bread. *company; accompany.*

Gk *pastè:* barley mush. It, *pasta; antipasto,* before the main repast. *pasticcio. pastry, pasty, patty.* Fr, *paté, patisserie. pastiche, paste; pastel. impaste. pasteurize* is from the inventor of the process, Louis *Pasteur* d. 1895). *Pasteurella:* genus of bacteria.

LL, *foray;* Fr, *forage.* Possibly *Pasquino:* name of a schoolmaster who lived near the statue (and square) in Rome that in 1510 was given his name; disinterred in 1501, the statue was actually the mutilated figure of Menelaus, outside Troy, with the body of Patroclus; citizens used it to post satirical verses and lampoons; whence *pasquil, pasquinade.*

"*Father* is rather vulgar, my dear. The word papa, besides, gives a pretty form to the lips. Papa, potatoes, poultry, prunes and prism, are all good words for the lips, especially prunes and prism"—Mrs. General in Dickens' *Little Dorrit,* ii, 5. Milton, in *Lycidas,* attacked the pastors that,

for their bellies' sake,
Creep and intrude, and climb into the fold . . .
Blind mouths! that scarce themselves know how to hold
A sheep-hook, or have learned aught else the least
That to the faithful herdman's art belongs!

Johnson objected to "blind mouths," but note its compressed felicity: they that should guide, cannot see; they that should provide, devour.

paen, pe(n): almost. To the primitives, any damage short of death was "almost"; hence this root was extended to mean suffer, endure, be patient. (1) In the *almost* range, *peninsula. penumbra. penult(imate); antepenult.* (2) In the *suffering* range, L *pati, passum:* suffer. *passion,* as in the passion of Christ. *passive. compassion. compatible:* enduring together. *patience, patient. penance* and its doublet *penitence. repent. pain.* Gc, *fiend.*

Isaac Watts (d. 1748) warned: "There's no repentance in the grave."

pag, pak: fix, fasten, bind; first physically, then figuratively. Gk *pekhtos:* fixed, coagulated. *pectin, pectolite, peganite, pegmatite. pachnolite. paxilla. Peganum:* genus of bean capers. *colopexy, hysteropexy. pagurian. Paguridae:* family, the hermit crab, with "fixed tail." *hapax legomenon:* put together once, unique. *Areopagus:* firm, rocky; the hill of Ares (Roman Mars), site of the first Athenian court of justice (see *kuei I*). *parapegm.*

L *pagus:* fixed (staked) boundary. *pagan, paynim; peasant, paysage. pageant.* In *peasant* and *pageant,* the final *t* is an extra ending-sound. LL *pagina:* prop for vines; scaffold; leaf; hence "leaf" of a book, a *page.*

Wine and viniculture were ancient delights. From *pagina* came *propaginem,* shortened to E *prop:* to support; also to prune, trim. Hence *propagate:* first, to fasten vine slips on the trellis, to produce more; then what has grown to the whirl and world of propaganda. *propaganda* is the Latin gerundive form: "what should be propagated," and was first used figuratively in *Congregatio de Propaganda Fidei,* established in 1622 by Pope Gregory XV.

The stalk of a bunch of grapes was L *racemus,* whence *raceme,* and, via French, *raisin.* Fr *raisin* means grape, and strangely, a raisin is a plum—or rather a plum is a raisin. When Jack Horner, while "eating a Christmas pie," stuck in his thumb and pulled out a plum, presumably it was a plum. But later, raisins were substituted in the "plum pudding," and dictionaries now give as one meaning of *plum:* "a raisin used in a pudding or pie." A *plum* in the sense of something especially choice, rises from the ironic story behind the nursery rhyme; that Jack (John)

Horner, one of the couriers of King Henry VIII, bringing back a package ("pie") containing the deeds of 22 confiscated monasteries, "put in a thumb" (put one deed into his own pocket), and complacently remarked: "What a good boy am I!" According to an anonymous mock sermon of 1666, "He that discovered the new star in Cassiopeia . . . deserves not half so much to be remembered, as he that first married mince meat and raisins." Gk *proumnon,* L *prunum,* possibly from Asia Minor, gave English first *plum,* then (*l.r* shift) *prune.*

LL *pagella:* a little page, a small measure; E *pail.* It, *appalto.* L *palus:* stake. *pale, palisade. beyond the pale:* outside the bounds of serious, or respectable, consideration; as later, in U.S. towns, "on the wrong side of the tracks." *Palisades* is the name given to the long line of cliffs along the Hudson River across from New York City, long topped by a wide meadow, then an amusement park; now thick with high-rise residences.

Also *peel:* a square tower; a baker's shovel. *pallet, palette. pole; impale.* LL *tripalium:* torture, with three stakes; hence *travail. travel:* a difficult or dangerous journey, as were all early trips. L *pax, pacis:* a supposedly settling and binding agreement, peace. *Pax vobiscum:* Peace be with you (see *dek*). *pace . . . :* with friendly intent, hoping the named person doesn't mind. *pacific, pacify; pay. pacifist, peace. appease. pact; compact, impact; impinge. dispatch; despatch,* an error in Johnson's *Dictionary,* is now accepted. It, *palafitte.* Gc, *fang. infang thief, outfang thief:* in old English law, thief taken within or outside a lord's jurisdiction. *fay:* join together. *vang:* guy rope to fasten sail.

"When peace has been broken anywhere, the peace of all countries everywhere is in danger"—President Franklin D. Roosevelt, 3 Sept. 1939.

pal, pol: touch, quiver; shake, as with anger. Gk *pallein. catapult* (*cata-:* against). *psallein:* twitch. *Pselaphidae:* family of twitching beetles. But also, from twitching the harp, *psalm, psalmody; psalter. psalterium:* third stomach of a ruminant, folded, like the leaves of a book.

Gk *pelemizein:* to make tremble; *polemikhos:* warlike. *polemarch:* commander of ancient Greek army. *polemic. Ptolemy:* Warlike. Ptolemy I Soter (Savior) was a general under Alexander the Great, upon whose death in Babylon, 323 B.C., Ptolemy took over Libya and Egypt. Founding the great library and museum of Alexandria, he made that city the most important in the world. Sixteen Ptolemys formed the 31st dynasty of Egypt, which ended in 30 B.C. Several Ptolemys married their sisters named Cleopatra (Gk *khleis:* key; key to the fatherland). The famous Cleopatra (the seventh) married in succession two of her brothers, Ptolemy XII and Ptolemy XIII; she killed the second to reign jointly with her son by Julius Caesar, Caesarion, whom Octavius (later Emperor Augustus) killed in 31 B.C. She killed herself—with an asp, as Shakespeare preserved the legend—rather than be exhibited in Octavius's triumph at Rome. Her grandson, from her child by Marc Antony, Ptolemy of Mauretania, the last of the dynasty, was killed in A.D. 40 by Caligula. The name of the family survived; Claudius Ptolemy, ca. A.D. 14, wrote the 13 books of the *Almagest;* and his Ptolemaic system of astronomy, wherein sun, planets, and the stars revolve around the earth, was generally accepted until the late 16th c. Nicolaus Copernicus, in 1507, began to develop the idea that the earth rotates daily, and that the planets revolve around the sun; political and religious complications delayed publication, and a copy of Copernicus's book was brought to him on his deathbed in 1543.

Peleus: shake spear; father of Achilles. L *palpare, palpatum:* touch lightly. *palp.* "A hit, a very palpable hit!"—*Hamlet,* v. *palpus. palpate. palpitation. palpebral,* from the quivering eyelid. L *papilionem:* butterfly. *Papilionaceous. papilotte.*

Papilio: genus of butterflies. *papillon:* spaniel, from the shape of its ears. *mariposa lily* is from Sp *mariposa:* butterfly, a folkchanged blend of piety and beauty –*Maria,* blessed mother of Jesus, and *pausa:* a moment of meditative rest. See *kel IV; lep I.*

Also *pavilion,* from the shape of the tent. *pallesthesia:* sensitivity to vibration. *asypalmograph.* Gc, *feel, flutter.*

"'Tis the still hours of thinking, feeling, loving"–Wordsworth, *On . . . the Coast of Cumberland.*

pan: fabric. Gk *penos:* web. E *panicle.* L *pannus:* piece of cloth. *pawn,* from the pledging of garments at the pawnship. The *pawn* in chess is via OFr *peon:* footsoldier, from L *pedem* (see *ped*). *pane* and *panel,* first used of cloth.

In the nunnery where Piers (of *The Vision of Piers Plowman,* by William Langland, 1360) was cook, there was a Sister *Parnell* (*panel* was the name for a "priest's wench," who kept him warm in winter and "[had] a child in cherry time"). This use came from *Pernel, Peronele,* nicknames of St. *Petronella,* feminine diminutive of *Petrus,* St. Peter–and *peter* was slang for the instrument with which he plied her (later, in rhyming slang, called *dick*). From the 15th c. through the 17th, a married woman overgenerous of her body might be referred to as *Dame Parnell.* A *panel* was thence a harlot. According to a ballad of the period,

> Panels march by two and three,
> Crying "Sweetheart, come with me."

And a *panel joint* was a brothel. But it joined the other sense in prostitution trickery: a *panel joint* was also a room wherein, while the victim was held tight in simulated ecstasy, deft fingers from the adjoining room slid open a panel in the wall and picked the pockets of the man's clothes, lying on a chair set conveniently by. An *impaneled* jury had little mercy if such cheats were caught.

?pare: become visible. L *parere:* appear. *apparent, apparition; apparitor. disappear, reappear. transparent* (when fainter, *translucent;* when nothing shows through, *opaque*).

"Every man has a lurking wish to appear considerable in his native place"–Samuel Johnson, letter to Sir Joshua Reynolds, 17 July 1771.

past: firm. Gc, *fast,* in all senses. *fasten; fastness. steadfast. avast.* With religious application, holding firm on holy days, came *fast,* to go without eating; then more generally, every morning, to *break fast* (*breakfast*). A similar development came with L *jejunus:* fasting. This gave English *jejune;* but also, via LL *disjejunare, disjunare* (further shortened in Fr *diner*), E *dine, dinner, dinette.* See *peku.*

Gk *ariston* (*a* negative): ending a fast–with a feast, as is still usual–gave English *aristology,* the art of dining; see *ar I.* From Gk *sit(i)on:* food made of grain, "the staff of life," came *sit(i)ology, sit(i)omania, sit(i)ophobia.* Gk *opson:* a relish, which adds zest to eating. Gk *opsonin* came to mean victuals, then money for food; modern science has recaptured the earliest sense in E *opsonin:* a constituent of the blood serum that makes the phagocytes (: cell-devourers) relish eating the invading bacteria. (*victuals* is via LL *victualia,* from L *vivus:* alive; whence also Gc, *quick;* see *guei.*)

Also *sitosterol:* any of five steroid alcohols, of the same formula, $C_{22}H_{49}OH$ (see below). A *steroid* is a fat-soluble organic compound, such as the sex hormones. *stereo:* firm, solid; three-dimensional, as in *stereochemistry, stereogram. OED* lists 29 words, and details 7 columns more, beginning *stereo. stereotypy* means (1) the making of printing plates (2) the morbid persistence of a fixed idea.

steric and *steroid* are used of isomers (see *iso*), substances that, like sitosterol, have the same chemical formula, but different arrangements of the atoms within the molecule, and thus different functions in the body. *OED*'s 45 or so words range from the old-fashioned *stereoscope,* which when looked through seemed to give pictures the solidity of three dimensions, to new instruments for *stereophonic* sound and new findings in *stereoisomer* research (with, no doubt, more to come).

Lexicographer Samuel Johnson, "a harmless drudge," as he called his kind, once remarked: "A man is in general more pleased when he has a good dinner on his table, than when his wife talks Greek." Francis Bacon earlier observed that hope is a good breakfast, but a bad supper.

From early Greek and Roman times through the Renaissance, dinner was sumptuous beyond our fancy. When the Holy Roman Emperor Charles II was entertained by Charles V of France, in Jan. 1378, the menu included "roast capons and partridges, civet of hare, meat and fish aspics, lark pasties and rissoles of beef marrow, black pudding and sausages, lampreys with savory rice, entremet of swan, peacock, bitterns and heron 'borne on High', pasties of venison and small birds, fresh- and salt-water fish with a gravy of shad 'the colour of peach blossom', white leeks with plovers, duck with roast chitterlings, stuffed pigs, eels reversed, frizzled beans–fruit wafers, pears, comfits, medlars, peeled nuts, spiced wine." This is perhaps matched by the longest word in Indo-European literature, the main course at the banquet that closes Aristophanes' comedy *Women in Parliament,* a blend that runs through 182 letters. Only science can exceed this; in biochemsitry, *tryptophen synthetase A protein,* spelled in full, would take 1913 letters. Fortunately, the scientists can resort to symbols. (By the way, the granddaughter of Charles V ["the Wise"] is the Catherine who by the Treaty of Troyes [1420] was given in marriage to Henry V of England, and who provided Shakespeare with some comic passages in his play.)

ped: foot. Skr, *pie, naya paisa. pug:* animal footprint. Pers, *pajamas. charpoy:* four-footed table. *seerpaw:* Eastern cap-a-pie, head to foot (see *caput*). *teapoy:* three-footed table, the beginning folkchanged from its use for afternoon tea. *babouche,* via Arabic, which lacks the letter *p.*

Gk *pous, podos:* foot. *polypod, polyp; pseudopod. podium; monopodium, sympodium.* It, *appoggiatura.* Fr, *appui.* Via OFr *puier,* E *pew. antipodes:* feet against feet through the earth. *apus* (*a* negative): the swift,which flies with feet unseen and is rarely seen standing; also *Apus,* the constellation. *podiatry, podology.*

Oedipus was properly translated by Shelley, in his title to Sophocles' play *Oedipus Rex:* Swellfoot the Tyrant. Because of the prophecy that the babe would grow to kill its father and marry its mother, it was hung by its feet and left to die. Cut down by a shepherd, with his feet swollen, Oedipus lived, as shown in the play, to fulfill the prophecy. Made aware, then self-blinded, he moved to a serene death, as shown in the play *Oedipus at Colonus.* (When Sophocles' son charged him with incompetence, the nonagenarian's only defense was to recite to the judges the play's just-written choral lyric in praise of Athens [of which Colonus was a suburb], and the case was dismissed. Produced posthumously in 406 B.C. by Sophocles' grandson, *Oedipus at Colonus* won first prize in the annual dramatic contest of the Greater Dionysia.)

Also *podophyllin. OED* lists 43 relevant words beginning *pod(o),* as *podal(ic);* it details 18, as *podagra* (Gk *agra:* catching, a trap); gout, with 8 related words. *podura:* foot-tail, insect with a terminal forked organ, for leaping. Urquhart, in his translation of Rabelais, uses *pody cody* as an oath, taboo-changed from *body of God.* Note that L *podex, podicem,* E *podex,* means fundament; the verb, *podicate:* to slide along on one's posteriors, as perhaps an unfortunate beginner at ice-skating.

phalerope: wading bird (Gk *phalos:* shining, from the white spot on its head). *trapezium;* transformed into the flying *trapeze* (see *kuetuer*). *octopus. platypus* (see *plat*). The story of *oppidan* is circuitous. First applied to places within walking distance of Rome, it came to be used of the opposition of country and town, then of the contrast between town and gown (university folk within the town, in England, walked to class gowned); finally, of the nonresident student and the colleger, living in the college house (in the U.S., dormitory). Gladstone, in the Jan. 1878 *Nineteenth Century,* spoke of the opposition "between the rural peasant and the oppidan artisan."

Gk *pedan:* leap; push with a steering oar; E *pilot. Pedetes:* genus, the leaping hare. *Polypedates:* the frog, which brought Mark Twain his first success, the tale "The Celebrated Jumping Frog of Calaveras County" (1845). *Lycopodium:* wolf's foot; genus, the club moss. *Podocarpus:* genus, the yew (see *oiua*). *Podophyllum:* genus, the barberry. *Podophthalmia:* order of crustaceans. Russ, *podzol:* ashes underfoot.

JWalker gives 30 words ending *pod,* as *cephalopod, tripod. tripos.* In the early days of Cambridge University, a proctor with a sense of humor set a student on a three-legged stool, called him Mr. Tripos, and called on him to discuss a sheet of Latin verse, in which the student found (whether there or not) an abundance of "indelicate" allusions. When through, Mr. Tripos turned the sheet over and read what all were awaiting, the list of class honors. The word *tripos* was used of this list, then of the honors examination—first, in mathematics. *isopod. apod:* footless.

L *pes, pedem:* foot. *pedal. velocipede:* swift foot. *pedestal. pedestrian,* formerly opposed to *equestrian* (see *eku*). *Pediluvium:* footbath (see *or*). *ped-,* as *pedical, pedicure, pediform. pedesis:* in physics, the Brownian movement of microscopic particles, demonstrated by Robert Brown (d. 1858), who also discovered gymnospermism. *diapedesis.* The *pedlar, peddler,* who *peddles,* was earlier *pedder,* he who goes about on foot to sell his goods; a *hawker* went with cart and horse to *hawk:* cry his wares. Either could have been entangled with the *pie powder* court in early rural England; Fr *pied poudreux:* dusty foot, was used of the court at country markets and fairs, where vagabonds and suspected pickpockets and filchers were summarily tried.

OED has over 22 columns of *ped* words. *pedage* was the old fee for the privilege of using the highway—in France, still called *péage,* though now for cars. The *Scientific American* of 29 June 1889 noted that "the trial court held that bicycling is a form of pedestrianating." *pedalian, sesquipedalian,* used of "foot-and-a-half-long" words. *peduncle. OED* also devotes 14 columns to the word *foot,* plus 11 columns for its compounds. *footback* was a 16th and 17th c. supposedly humorous contrast to *horseback;* compounds run thence from *football* to *footstool, footway, footy. footy* came to mean paltry, of little consequence. W. Dodd, in *The Beauties of Shakespeare* (1752), speaks of many a critic that "foisted in some footy emendation of his own"—such as Theobald's long-acclaimed change of Dame Quickly's report of the dying Falstaff: "His nose was as sharp as a pen, and a table of greene fields," to "'a babbled of green fields." The Penguin *Shakespeare* (1969) suggests that this was probably the hostess's misinterpretation of Falstaff's reciting "green pastures" in the Twenty-third Psalm; she had already put the dying man in "Arthur's bosom" instead of Abraham's. Dame Quickly was noted for her misuse of the language; see *melo.* Other "emendations" are discussed in the Variorum edition of *Henry V.*

L *pediculus:* little foot; louse. *pediculous* (see *lus*). Fr, *calibre, caliber:* first, a shoemaker's last; Gk *kalapous:* wooden foot (*kalon:* firewood, from *kalein:* burn), whence *caliper. vamp:* front of the foot; cut from Fr *avampie* (*avant:* front; *pied* [pronounced *peeay*] ; foot). Sp, *peon.* Fr, *pioneer:* first, foot soldier. *pawn:* footman, as in chess. *pedigree:* crane's foot; present meaning from the shape used to fashion the family tree.

biped, quadruped, milliped (thousand-legger). *tripedal, trivet. breviped, palmiped. parallelopiped,* which spared Samuel Johnson a dusting, by his not using it. He called the woman sweeping the street in front of him a *parallelogram;* startled, she stopped, and he walked cleanly by; had he said "Thou art a parallelo pipe 'ed," she'd have bedusted him. *pedeleon:* lion's foot, was the old name for the plant black hellebore. *pedimane:* hand-foot, of the lemur and the opossum, from the grasping and clasping ability of their hind feet. For *petomane,* see *perd.* For *pawn* at the "hockshop," see *pan.*

Piedmont: at the mountain's foot. *impede; impeach. impediment, impedimenta. repudiate. expedient; expedite. ped-yos; pejoration; impair; pessimism;* see *op I.* Note that *pedagogue, pediatrician,* etc., are, via Latin, from Gk *pais, paidos:* child.

L *peccare* (*?ped-cos:* stumble, "put one's foot in it"): sin. *peccant, impeccable.* Sp, *peccadillo. impedicare,* from L *pedica:* fetter, gives English *impeach;* from this the slang *peach:* to inform on. The fruit *peach* is short for *persicum malum:* Persian fruit; see *abel.*

In 1843, when Sir Charles Napier captured Sindh in India, he supposedly sent back a one-word punning dispatch, the first word of the penitent in the confessional, *Peccavi:* I have sinned. This story was first printed in *Punch,* vi (1844). Twelve years later, James Andrew Broun Dalhousie, tenth earl and first marquis of Dalhousie, and governor general of India, conquered Oudh, a kingdom in the new state of Uttar Pradesh, and *Punch,* xxx, printed:

"Peccavi–I've Sinde" wrote Lord Ellen so proud.
More briefly Dalhousie wrote "Vovi–I've Oude."

(L *Vovi:* I vowed.) In those days, the nearest they had to an atom bomb was an atomizer.

petiole: little foot, leaf stalk; *petiolule,* still littler. *Peziza:* genus of stalkless fungi. *Cypripedium:* genus of orchids; *Cypris* was one of Aphrodite's names. Homer called her *Cyprian;* she was a special object of devotion on *Cyprus,* near which she rose from the sea; see *pa.* L *talus, tarsus:* ankle; *taliped:* club-footed. *Tarsipes:* genus of marsupials.

Gc, *foot, footfall; foot-loose* (and fancy-free). *footprint. fetch, fetlock; fetter.* By a roundabout journey, from *foot*–hence the bottom, a border of cloth, a piece by which weavers marked off the end of a day's work–came *fit,* a division or canto of a poem (as in Lewis Carroll's *The Hunting of the Snark* [1876]); also *fit,* to be or make suitable.

Lives of great men all remind us
We can make our lives sublime,
And, departing, leave behind us
Footprints on the sands of time.
–Longfellow, *A Psalm of Life* (1839)

peg: breast, chest. ?Skr *pakash:* wing. *punkah.* L *pectus, pectorem:* breast. *pectoral. parapet:* breastworks. *parare:* protect, ward off, as in *parasol* (L *sol:* sun); see *per V.* It, *petto.* Fr, *poitrel.* A 15th c. weapon, the *petronel* was held against the chest when fired (first syllable folkchanged by mistaken association with *petra:* rock). *expectorate.*

pei, pi: swell; be fat. Gk *pion. propionic (acid).* Gk *pimele:* fat; E *pimelosis* (Join Weight Watchers!). L *pix, picem:* tar. *pay:* fill seams with tar. *piceous, picoline; pitch, pitchblende.* L *pinus:* pine tree, from the resin. *pinaster, pineal; piñon; pinnace,* first made of pine. L *pituita:* gum and other tree ooze. *pip, pituitary.* Gc *faitidaz;* E *fat, fattened,* etc.

peig, peik: hostile. Gc, *fey, feud, fickle; foe.* Some list here MD *fokken,* and claim this as the source of E *fuck,* but no relation has been traced; the more probable source is *firk,* a good OE word of wide and varied use. Possibly from this root, *firk* came to mean to press hard, strike, shake up and down; move about quickly, "be jiggish"; then, have sexual intercourse. According to Cotgrave's glossary (1611): "firkerie, an odd pranke, or jerke, in whoorisme." Note also J. Fletcher, *Rule a Wife and Have a Wife* (1624), iii, 4: "These five years she has firked a pretty living"; Edmund Gayton, *Pleasant Notes upon Don Quixote* (1654): "Your soberest jades are firkers in corners." Then, by a variant of Gresham's law, the "bad" meaning drove out the others, and the word survived on the vulgar tongue as *fuck.* This origin of *fuck* is detailed in my article in *Maledicta,* i (1977), abbreviated in my book *In Praise of English* (1977). The same "law" is at present transforming the meaning of *gay;* first meaning impetuous, *gay* survives in *nosegay,* which has an invigorating fragrance.

Beautiful as sweet!
And young as beautiful! and soft as young!
And gay as soft! And innocent as gay!
—Edward Young, *Night Thoughts* (1742), iii

peik, peig: adorn by carving and/or coloring. (Much of the ancient marble statuary that has weathered white was originally colored.) Gk *pikros:* sharp. *picrate, picro-,* as *picrolite, picrotoxin; OED* lists 20 such words. L *pingere, pictum. pict,* meaning depict, is described by *OED* as rare. *pictorial, pictograph, picture, picturesque,* etc. *OED* has over 7 columns of words beginning *pict. pigment.* Sp, *pim(i)ento. pint:* first, a painted mark to indicate the quantity. *pinta, pintado. pinto:* a spotted ("painted") horse. *pintano:* a banded fish. *Rembrandt pinxit;* R. painted this. Via Fr *peint, paint, painting. OED* has 8 columns of *paint* words, ending with *paintrix, paintry, painture, painty.*

Pict: ancient northern British tribe; in A.D. 843 merged with the Scots under Kenneth MacAlpine; they painted themselves, as savages have done in America and still do in Africa. (Some say *Pict* is a folkchange from a native name meaning fighter.) *Scot,* with its variants *Scotch, Scottish,* etc., may have been an Irish term of scorn (*Scuit,* pronounced *shite*); its ultimate origin is unknown. *scotch:* to scratch, make a mark, has been traced no further than *ex:* out, with Fr *coche:* notch; hence also the game *hopscotch,* wherein players must hop over the lines to land in the allowed places. "We have scotched the snake, not killed it"—*Macbeth,* iv, 1.

Poikile was a noted portico in Athens, with various paintings; hence, from Gk *poikilo,* L *poecilo:* various, variegated, used as a prefix in English, *poikilitic, poikilocyte, poikilothermic; poeciloblast, poecilopod. poecilonymic:* with a variety of names, as many gods.

This picture that thou here see put,
It was for gentle Shakespeare cut . . .
Reader, look
Not on his picture, but his book.
—Ben Jonson

peisk: fish. L *piscis. Pisces:* constellation, twelfth sign of the zodiac (see *guei*). *piscary, piscatology, piscatory. piscina:* basin for ceremonial ablutions. *piscine. pisci-*, as *pisciculture, piscivorous. OED* has 28 related words beginning *pisc. piscinity* is rife in the vicinity of British streams.

L *crassum piscem:* fat fish, via OFr *craspeis,* was folkchanged to E *grampus,* by association with *grand. porpoise* was "porkfish."

Partly in the mood of the time to translate native names into Greek or Latin—as G. *Schwarzert:* black earth, became *Melanchthon,* etc.—and partly in the hope of averting Catholic attack, Johannes Fischer in 1546 translated the Bible under the name *Piscator;* whence his descendant Erwin *Piscator,* 20th c. creator of the epic theatre.

Gc, *fish. codfish* (*cod:* bag, pouch, as in *peasecod* and *codpiece*). *swordfish, weakfish,* etc. *fishmonger. fish pond.*

"I love any discourse of rivers, and fish and fishing"—Izaak Walton, *The Compleat Angler* (1653). The *Oxford Dictionary of Quotations* includes 67 on *fish* and its compounds.

pek I: attractive, pleasant; glad. Gc, *fain; fair; fawn.*

pek II: to comb, pluck out hair, hence fight; a woolly animal, sheep used for barter, hence money. Gk *(p)ktenos:* comb. *ctenidium; ctenoid* (*c* silent). *Ctenophora:* phylum of free-swimming invertebrates; best known, says *OED,* are the *Beroe* and the *Cydippe. cteno-*, as *ctenobranch, ctenodont.* L and E *pecten. pectinate, pectineous; pectoral* (hairy male chest). *pashm. paxwax. Pecora:* division of hairy, hoofed mammals.

When cattle came to be considered private property, thus could be bartered, via Gc came *fee, fief, feu,* and the *feudal* system. The *d* in *feud* was added by association with LL *alodis:* freehold land. *feodary, feoffee, enfeoff, infeudation,* are all now historical. More directly from the Latin (without the Germanic change of *p* to *f*) came *pecuniary, impecunious,* and, of course, *peculation*—often following injudicious speculation. The first meaning of *peculiar* was "one's own," which is still preserved in such use as "The kangaroo is peculiar to Australia"; the meaning "odd" did not develop until the 17th c., when Edward Topsell noted that the serpent's tongue is peculiar, in that, like the Devil's foot, it is cloven.

Via Fr, *peignoir,* worn when combing. Gc, *fellow. fight,* perhaps from the sheep's resistance to fleecing; in earlier times the wool was torn off.

> She is the sovereign queen of all delights;
> For her the lawyer pleads, the soldier fights.
> —Richard Barnfield, *Encomium of Lady Pecunia* (1598)

peku: cook; ripen (cooked by the sun). See *past.* Skr, *pukka:* ripe, good. Gk *peptein:* cook, ripen, digest. *peptic, eupeptic; dyspepsia. pepsin, peptide, peptone.* Gk *pepon,* L *pepo, peponem:* sun-ripened. *pepo. pumpkin. melon* is short for Gk *melopepon:* sun-ripened fruit; see *abel.* Gk *drupepes:* ripened on the tree; e.g., olives. *drupe.* L *coquere, coctum:* cook, ripen, mature. *cook.* L *culina:* cooking-place. *culinary. concoct:* "cook something up." *concoction. decoct. precocious:* early ripe. Also *apricot,* which came roundabout back from Arabic with the *a* from *al:* the; until the 19th c., usually spelled *apricock,* which Victorian prudery washed away. Fr, *biscuit:* twice cooked, like Gm *Zwieback.* It, *ricotta. terra cotta.* OFr *coiture:* burning; E *quittor.* Gc, *kiln; kitchen. crumpet:* thin-cooked.

> We may live without poetry, music and art,
> We may live without conscience, and live without heart;

We may live without friends, we may live without books,
But civilized man cannot live without cooks.
—Owen Meredith, *Lucile* (1860)

pel I: dust, powder; flour. Gk *poltos;* L *puls, pultes. poultice. pulse:* seeds, as peas and beans. *porridge.* "Pease porridge hot . . ." Gk *palunein:* sprinkle flour, as on sacrificial flesh before the fire. *palynology.* L *pulvis:* dust, powder. *pulverize.* L and E *palea:* chaff. *paillasse; pallet.* L and E *pollen. polenta. Paspalum:* genus, millet. Sp *pulchero.*

pel II: sell. OInd, *fanam:* small coin, via Arabic, which has no *p.* Gk *polein. bibliopole* (see *bibli*). *monopoly.*

pel III: basin. L and E *pelvis. pelvic.* Many modern dances, as an indignant elderly gentleman once remarked, involve (or allow) considerable pelvic pressure. *pelvi-,* as *pelviferous, pelvimyon;* there are 11 such words in *OED.* Also *pelyco-,* as *pelycography; pelycosaurian:* a reptile; fortunately extinct.

pel IV: first, come near; then push, drive, beat. Gk *Apollo* (*a* negative): driver-off of evil. *plesiosaurus* (Gk *plesios:* near; *sauros:* lizard), another extinct one. L *pellere, pulsum:* drive. *compel, compulsory, compulsion. dispel, expel; impel, impulsion, propel, repel, repulse,* etc. "Obey that impulse!"

L *pila* (diminutive *pilotta*): ball; related to *pilus:* hair (see *pel VI*); early balls were of skin stuffed with hair. *pelt, pellet, interpellation.* Sp, *pelota. appeal; repeal. polish; polite* (polished). *pulse, pulsate. pursy. push.* Fr, *pousette. pousse-café:* liqueur, to "drive the coffee down."

Gc, *felt:* beaten wool, etc. *filter* (made of felt). Via Du, *anvil.* For *police, politics,* etc., see *pele.*

"In 1940 Oxford abolished compulsory Greek. And look what happened to the British Empire!"—Peter A. Carmichael, *Reasoning* (1978); a superb example of the fallacy "Post hoc ergo propter hoc."

pel V, ple: full; hence much and many. Gk *polus:* much, *plethos:* many, *ple(i)on:* more, *pleistos:* most. *hoi polloi:* the many; *the hoi polloi* has one article too many. *plethora, plethorical; plethysmograph. pleonasm. pleonaste,* from the many faces of the crystal. *OED* defines *pleiomorphy* and lists 11 words in botany or anatomy that begin *pleio.* It defines 3 words beginning *pleisto;* 41 related words beginning *plen:* full, complete, as *plenitude.* For *pleo-,* it lists 9 words and details 11; it gives 4 related words beginning *pler,* as *pleroma,* and 4 words beginning *plio.* Among these are *pleiomastia, pleiotropism, Pleistocene, pleistoseist* (*seismic:* of an earthquake); *pleomorphism, pleopod; Pliocene, pliohippus.*

OED lists 145 words beginning *poly,* and details 42 columns more, from *polyacanthus* through *polygamy, polytheism, polyvalent,* to *polyzoonite. OED*'s Supplement III in 13 columns lists 117 more, mainly scientific; then details 45 columns of compounds, from *polyacid . . . polytropic . . . polywater . . .* to *polyzoism. polysemia* is used of a word with multiple meanings, as *cell, fine.* Some cooking oils today are advertised as *polyunsaturated.*

L *plere, pletum:* fill; *plenum:* full; *plus,* many; *plures:* more; *plurimus:* most. *E pluribus unum:* out of many, one; motto of the U.S. *plerome. complete, deplete, replete. comply, supply* (for *apply, reply,* see *plek*). *complement. compliment:* first, to fulfill, then appreciation for it. *implement, supplement; accomplish. expletive. maniple:* a handful; *manipulate.* Also *plenary, plenilune, pleniloquence; plenipotentiary, plenteous; plenty; plenum; replenish, replum. pluperfect. plural. plus, nonplus, surplus.* For *plutocracy,* see *plou.* Fr, *terreplein, plein-air.*

Some English words are used always in the plural, as *breeches* (*overalls, trousers, pants, jeans, knickerbockers; pajamas, bloomers, drawers, smallclothes,* etc.—all in plural form because of the human bifurcation), *dregs, riches, scissors, thanks, tongs.* Such words are technically *plurale tantum* (*tantum:* only; more than one, *pluralia tantum*). Contrariwise, some words rarely if ever use a plural form, as *compassion, courage, fun, heat, thunder.* There is also, of course, the collective noun: one form that may, according to its use, call for a singular or a plural verb, as *army, Congress, family, fleet, orchestra.*

L *palus:* marsh. *paludial, paludine. paludism,* now almost wiped out. *Paludicella:* genus of polyzoans. *Paludicola:* order of marsh birds.

L and E *plebs:* the many. *plebe, plebeian; plebiscite. OED* defines 23 terms relating to *plebs.*

Gc, *fill, full, fulfil(l). fulsome.* Compounds, as *full-blown; full dress:* formal evening or court clothes. The suffix *ful,* as in *suspenseful. spoonfuls,* as distinct from separate *spoons full,* indicating how much rather than how many. JWalker lists 179 words ending *ful,* as *bountiful, gleeful, hateful.* See *dheigh N 2 h.*

Come fill the cup, and in the fire of Spring
The winter-garment of Repentance fling;
The Bird of Time has but a little way
To flutter—and the Bird is on the wing.
—FitzGerald, *Rubáiyát of Omar Khayyám*

pel VI: skin, hide. See *pilo.* Gk *pelte:* shield, made first of hide on wood. *peltast:* shield-bearer, in ancient Greece. *pelta, peltate.*

erysipelas: red skin. *epiploon:* fold ("skin") of the peritoneum; Galen's derivation of this from Gk *epiplein:* swim against, because it "swims over the intestines," is folk etymology.

Peltandra: genus, the arrow arum. *Peltigera:* genus of lichens. *Uropeltidae:* tail shield, family of burrowing snakes. L *pellis:* hide. *pell, pellicle. pelage:* any mammal coat except bare skin. *peltry* and the backformation *pelt. pellagra. pillion. pilch.* LL *superpellicum;* E *surplice.* Fr, *pelisse. peel.* L *pallium:* cloak. *pall. palliate:* first, cloaked, covered over. *paletot.* Fr, *paillasse. tarpaulin.*

Gall, *plaid:* first, sheepskin blanket. Du, *veldschoen:* untanned hide shoes. Gc, *fell. film.* To the recent use of film in making pictures, the *OED*'s 1972 supplement devotes almost three columns. See *pel IV.*

"O tiger's heart wrapped in a woman's hide!"—*3 Henry VI* (1590). "For there is an upstart crow, beautified with our feathers, that with his tiger's heart wrapped in a player's hide, supposes he is as well able to bumbast out a blank verse as the best of you; and being an absolute *Johannes fac totum,* is in his own conceit the only Shake-scene in a country"—Robert Greene, *A Groatsworth of Wit . . .* (1592), the first known allusion to Shakespeare.

pel VII: pale, dull-colored; gray, dusky. Gk *pelargos* (*argos:* white): stork. *pelargonium,* from the capsules of the plant; *pelargonic acid* is extracted from its leaves. Note, however, that the *Argonauts* were the 50 heroes on the *Argo,* Jason's ship seeking the Golden Fleece; the ship may have been named for its white sails, or for *Argos* (fertile plain), an important region of ancient Greece. And an *argosy,* early *ragusye,* draws its name from *Ragusa,* an important ancient port on the Adriatic, now known as *Dubrovnik* (*dubrava:* woods). *Argo Navis:* the ship Argo, was the name of a southern constellation, which stronger telescopes divided into four: Carina, Puppis, Pyxis, and Vela.

Pellaea: genus, the cliff brake. *peristeronic* (*l.r* shift): pertaining to the dusky dove. *Pleiad* (plural, *Pleiades*): child of the dove; any of the daughters of *Pleione* and Atlas; see *nebh. poliomyelitis;* inflammation of the gray matter of the spinal chord; abbreviated *polio.*

L *pallere. pale, pallor. appall.* L *pallium. pall:* cloth over a coffin; as a verb, often used figuratively (see below). *palomino.* Via OFr, *favel:* chestnut-colored horse. *to curry favel:* to smooth the horse, came to be used figuratively; then, via folkchange, was transformed into *to curry favor.* Gc, *fallow, falcon, gerfalcon.* W, *llwyd:* Lloyd.

The French have a neat expression: *Tout passe, tout casse, tout lasse,* which may be translated (changing rhyme to alliteration): All things pass, all things perish, all things pall.

pela, plak, plat: spread out; flat, broad, smooth. Gk *pelagos:* flat spread of the inland sea. *plagal. archipelago* (see *arkh*). *pelagic.* The *Pelagian* Islands are in the Mediterranean Sea. *Pelagianism,* however, is the belief of *Pelagius,* a British monk (from over the sea) who denied the doctrine of original sin; his belief was declared heresy in A.D. 416, but many today refuse to accept mankind's guilt for Adam's fall.

Gk *plagios:* spread out; hence a net, as in fishing, and in ancient hand-to-hand combat, especially of captives in the circus arena (recently introduced to capture violent emotionally disturbed persons). *plagio-* as *plagioclase, plagiotropism.* From snaring in a net, *plagiarism* came, first in Greek, to mean snaring, stealing, material property (a slave or a child); then, literary property. This did not seem important until words had monetary value and copyright protection; but it was long scorned. Milton defined a *plagiary* (now the *plagiarist*) as one that borrows without improving. Donne was more emphatic:

> For if one eat my meat, let it be known
> The meat was mine, the excrement is his own.

placental animals, which in pregnancy have a *placenta,* expelled in the afterbirth, are roughly divided from the marsupials of the world by Weber's line (1904): there are about 175 species of marsupials in the South Sea islands and Australia; one species, the opossum, inhabits North America. Such animals have a *marsupium:* pouch; their young are prematurely delivered and attached to nipples in the pouch. The word *marsupium* is from Gk *marsupion,* diminutive of *marsipon:* pouch, probably from Av *marsu:* belly. (Avestan is the earliest language of the Indo- division of Indo-European; the Zend-Avesta are the sacred Zoroastrian writings.)

placoid; plate; platelet, as in the blood. *plateau, platen, plateresque; platform; playa. platyhelminth:* flatworm. *platyrrhine:* flat-nosed. *platysma. Platypus:* flatfoot; an egg-laying mammal. *platypygous; platyscopic. platometry:* art of measuring breadth of a distant or inaccessible object or space. *OED* gives 34 columns to words beginning *plat,* including a list of 48 and a detailed discussion of 5 ending *platy.*

Formed by analogy with *latitude, platitude* appeared in French in 1694, but was apparently not printed in English until 1812. Rossetti, in *Dante and His Circle* (1850), speaks of repartee "with all the profound platitude of medieval wit." A hundred years later, Christopher Fry, in his scintillating play *The Lady's Not for Burning,* asks: "Where in this small-talking world can I find a longitude with no platitude?"

Also *plaice:* a flatfish. Fr, *place;* It, *piazza, plaza.* L nasalized *planta:* sole of the foot; hence *plant:* press the seed in with the foot. *planter, plantation. plantigrade:* walking on the whole sole, as do bears and men. *implant, supplant, transplant.*

Aristocles (d. 347 B.C.; see *ar I*) is known to posterity as *Plato,* from his broad shoulders. *Platonic love:* close friendship between persons of the same sex, close attachment without physical conjunction—sometimes misinterpreted as homosexual, "Socratic," attraction. Cervantes' Don Quixote says: "My love and hers have always been purely Platonic." An English letter of 1645 reports: "The court affords little news at present, but there is a love, called Platonic love, which much sways there of late. It consists of contemplation and ideas of the mind, not in any carnal fruition." A century later, however, Richardson, in the first English novel, *Pamela* (1741), asseverates: "I am convinced, and always was, that Platonic love is Platonic nonsense." W. S. Gilbert in *Patience,* poking fun at the 19th c. exquisites, including Oscar Wilde (whom producer D'Oyly Carte shrewdly sent on an American lecture tour just before the play opened in New York, and who began his visit, at Ellis Island, by declaring, "I have nothing to declare but my genius"), offers a recipe for a dandy, which includes:

> Then a sentimental passion of a vegetable fashion must excite your languid spleen,
> An attachment à la Plato for a bashful young potato, or a not too-French French bean.

The *Platonic bodies,* or solids, are the five regular polyhedra: the tetrahedron, with four faces (the three-sided pyramid); the hexahedron, a cube, with six; the octahedron, with eight; the icosahedron, with twelve; and the dodecahedron, with twenty.

The *Platonic year* is the long-credited time it takes for all the heavenly bodies to complete their movements and return to their original relative positions—some believing that then all history will repeat itself. This "year" was sometimes equated with the period of the revolution of the equinoxes, or some 23,800 of our solar years. But it was estimated in 1585, by Tycho Brache, as 25,816 of our years; in 1651, by Giovanni Riccioli, as 25,920; and in 1659, by Giovanni Cassini, as 24,800.

Plato having defined man as a two-legged animal without feathers, Diogenes brought a plucked cock to the Academy and announced: "Here is Plato's man"—whereupon "with broad flat nails" was added to the definition. *OED* has 15 other words from *Plato,* as when Swift, in *The Tatler,* no. 32 (1709), declared: "I am fallen desperately in love with a professed Platonne, the most unaccountable creature of her sex."

Plato founded the Academy in 387 B.C.; it grew into the world's first university, functioning until closed by the Roman emperor Justinian in A.D. 529. (Justinian's reign included three other emphatic actions. He established the Justinian Code, which is the basis of modern law. He built the cathedral of Hagia [St.] Sophia, which still stands, in Constantinople, now Istanbul. And the violence of modern football spectators was far outshadowed by the Nika riot of A.D. 532. *Nika!:* Win! was the Greek cry that urged on the chariot racers; but the Blues and the Greens, rival factions, gathered in the Hippodrome in a battle that grew into an insurrection; mercenaries were summoned, and 30,000 citizens were slain. Political overtones were kept out of the ancient Olympic Games, but obtruded in the modern Olympics, in Berlin in 1936 and in Moscow in 1980.) Recently *Plato* won the final distinction of being made an entry in a crossword puzzle aid-book: "the only five-letter philosopher ending with *o.*"

Gk *planasthai:* spread, wander. *planet,* as opposed to a fixed star (see *sta*). *airplane, planetary; aplanatic.* Gk *plassein. plasma, plasminogen; -plasm,* as *metaplasm, neoplasm, protoplasm. -plasia,* as *dysplasia, hypoplasia. -plast,* as *chloroplast, mesoplast, protoplast. plaster; plastic. -plasty,* as *anaplasty. plaster of Paris* was first made with gypsum from Paris.

L nasalized, *planus. plan,* spread out; *planar, plain, plane, plank, planchet.*

plano-, as *planometer, planoconcave, planoconvex.* Sp, *llano;* Fr, *esplanade.* It, *piano:* smooth, soft; hence the *pianoforte,* the instrument, shortened to *piano.*

Also *palm:* flat of the hand, and, from the shape of the leaves, *palm tree. palmate, palmitic, palmatifid. palmyra,* folkchanged by false association with the city of *Palmyra,* Syria. *palmiped; palama:* webbing on the feet of aquatic birds. *palmistry:* mastery of the palm; divination by the lines in the hand; chiromancy. A *palmer* was a man who bore a palm branch as a sign that he had been to the Holy Land; for a tale of a palmer, see *The Four P's,* under *kleu II. OED* lists 52 combinations of *palm,* as *palm-color* (as early as the Phoenicians). *palma Christi,* from its handlike leaves and healing effect, like the laying on of hands. There are 8 compounds of *palmati:* relating to leaf, as *palmatilobate.*

Cross my palm with silver: the demand of the gypsy fortune-teller. *to grease one's palm:* to bribe, figuratively making it easy to handle, or hand over, what is desired. *to palm off:* to deceive by giving something of less worth than is expected, as when "the hand is quicker than the eye." *to bear or carry off the palm:* to win, from the palm branch as an emblem of triumph. *Palm Sunday,* "the gateway to Holy Week," memorializes the entrance of Jesus into Jerusalem before the Crucifixion. Branches of palm are blessed and given to Catholics on this day (most in the U.S. come from the Florida Everglades). Kept by the pious, especially in Spain and Italy, the palm branches are burned the next year on Ash Wednesday, the first day of Lént, and used to mark the forehead. At the Ash Wednesday ceremony the priest, tracing the sign of the Cross, bids the recipients "Remember, man: dust thou art, and to dust thou wilt return." *Lent,* from OE *lencten,* as the days perceptibly lengthen in spring, sets a forty-day period of penance and partial fasting in memory of the forty-day fast of Jesus; it ends on Easter Sunday —named after *Eastre,* Teutonic goddess of the dawn of the year, the swing of the sun toward its zenith, the rebirth of the Sun and Son of Righteousness. Hence, President Carter and others that claim to be "born again."

L *placare, placatum:* smooth, calm. *placate, complacent. implacable. placebo. placid, plea, please, pleasant, pleasure.*

> The children in Holland take pleasure in making
> What the children in England take pleasure in breaking.
> —Dutch nursery rhyme

Gael *clandaim:* I plant. *clan:* spread of the family. OFr, *flan.* Sp, *platina:* little silver; *platinum* (see *el 78*). Gc, *feldspar; field, outfield.* Du, *veld. flense. floor; floe. flounder:* the flatfish. *flake; fluke. flag,* as in *flagstone. flaw. flat. flatter:* smooth, caress. ("However flat your words may be, a woman would have them flatter.") *flatfish. flatiron* (see *sa*). *flatware,* etc. Russ *polynya. Polish, Poland, Polak, polka.*

pele: high place, especially one that is fortified. Related (by *l.r* shift and Grimm's law) to *beregh.* Skr *pur:* city. *gopura:* first, a cow city, a suburb where sacred cattle were bred; now, a gate tower. *Saharunpore,* home of the garrulous but friendly old lady in Kipling's *Kim. Singapore, Rampur,* and many more; *jodhpurs;* see Frequent World Forms and Transformations.

Gk *polis:* city. *Minneapolis,* first part American Indian. *Sardanapolis. Nablus,* in Israel, was earlier *Neapolis:* new city. The adjective *Neapolitan* is left from *Neapolis,* now *Naples,* Italy; *OED* lists 7 combinations of *Neapolitan,* including *Neapolitan favor,* euphemism for *syphilis. Constantinople* has the Greek ending; its current name, *Istanbul,* has the Sanskrit. Here also *police, policy, politics,* and the rest of it. *polity. acropolis. megalopolis; metropolis, necropolis. cosmopolitan. isopolity.*

policlinic (a translation of Gm *Poliklinik*): first, treatment and instruction at the patient's house in the city, as opposed to the hospital; then confused with and largely supplanted by *polyclinic:* treatment of outpatients for various diseases. *propolis:* literally, suburb; like cattle in India, bees in Greece were bred in the suburbs; hence *propolis:* beeglue (mainly from poplar or chestnut buds), which held together the bee city, the combs to the hive. From this root may also come *polite, politesse, polish* (from the city's "polished" ways as opposed to rustic "rudeness"); hence also *interpolate:* first, a fuller's term, to smooth between.

tetrapolis: a political union of four towns or cities, as the tetrapolis of "the mighty hunter" Nimrod, great-grandson of Noah; last of the four was Babel. At the Diet of Augsburg (1530), presided over by Charles V, the last German emperor to be crowned by the pope, the Tetrapolitan Confession of the cities of Strassburg (Strasbourg), Memmingen, Constance, and Lindau was presented by Melanchthon; the confession tried to reconcile the rising Protestant faith with the Catholic. The Diet forbade all innovations; Charles gave the German cities one year to return to the faith of their fathers; Luther approved the taking up of arms against Charles. Victories varied until 1555, when the princes and free cities won freedom of worship. Charles abdicated in 1556 and lived in a monastery until his death in 1558.

His talk was like a stream, which runs
With rapid change from rocks to roses:
It slipped from politics to puns,
It passed from Mahomet to Moses;
Beginning with the laws that keep
The planets in their radiant courses,
And ending with some precept deep
For dressing eels, or shoeing horses.
—Winthrop M. Praed, *The Vicar* (1838)

pen: swamp. Gc, *fen.*

Rocks, caves, lakes, fens, bogs, dens, and shades of death.
—Milton, *Paradise Lost,* ii (see quotation from Alexander Pope, under *guhren*)

pend, (s)pen(d): stretch, spin; hang, weigh, hence consider; weigh out money, hence pay. L *pendere, pensum. pendant, pendent, pending. pendulous, pendulum; pensile. appendix. penthouse,* folkchanged from *pentis. pensive. dispensary. spend,* short for *expend; expensive. impend. perpend.* (malice) *prepense. propensity. recompense; stipend. suspend; suspense. vilipend* (but see *ne*). Sp, *peseta, peso.* Gc, *pane, panel* (see *pan*). *pawn. gonfalon. fane, vane; weathervane.*

L, *pound; ponder:* weigh in the mind. *ponderous, imponderable; preponderant.* OFr *painter:* stretched rope, to hold a boat. *pansy* (Fr *pensée:* "that's for thoughts"). *poise, avoirdupois.* Possibly *spontaneous* (L *sponte:* of one's own "stretch").

Also *filipendulous:* hanging by a thread, like the sword of Damocles; hence *Damoclean* (see *kleu I*). *Filipendula:* genus of the rose family.

Russ, *pood.* Gc, *spin, spindle; span, spangle, spanner.* OE *spinthra, spithra:* the spinner; E *spider.* The eight-legged spider, with its spinnerets, is not an *insect* ("cut in" body, with six legs) but an *arachnid,* from *Arachne,* who dared challenge the goddess Athene to a weaving contest, and was turned into a spider. Some scholars state that Shakespeare nodded when he spoke of *Ariachne;* on the contrary, he fused the names of the two greatest mythical thread-bearers—

Arachne, and *Ariadne,* who gave Theseus the ball of thread by which, unrolling it as he went into the Labyrinth, after killing the Minotaur he could retrace his steps. The arguments of those that presume to correct Shakespeare are often threadbare. Some consider Arachne and Ariadne to be aspects of Aphrodite, the eternal rival of Athene: passionate lover vs. wise virgin.

Little Miss Muffet sat on a tuffet,
    Eating her curds and whey.
Along came a spider and sat down beside her,
    And frightened Miss Muffet away.
    —Mother Goose

(*curd; curdled:* coagulated milk, was earlier *crudde,* whence *crude* and the vulgar *crud.* In Afghanistan, where they ferment the milk of mares, you can see the *Kurds,* and watch the way they weigh their whey.)

penkue: five. Skr, *Panchanana;* five-faced, an epithet of the god Shiva. *Panchatantra:* the five books of Bidpai's animal fables (see *ten*). *panchayat:* Hindu village council, five making a quorum. *Punjab:* region of five rivers, affluents of the Hindus River. *punch:* drink of five ingredients. The *Punch* of *Punch and Judy*—which first came from Italy to England in 1666, at Charing Cross, London, as "a mystery play of Pontius (?"Punch") Pilate and Judas"—is short for *Punchinello,* a stock figure in the old puppet show, from Neapolitan *policenella:* young turkey-cock (the man so-called for his beaklike nose), diminutive of L *pullus:* pullet (see *pou*). *pachisi.*

Gk, *pentad. pentamerous. pentagon, pentahedron,* etc. *Pentecost:* five, ten times: the 50th day after the Resurrection, also called Whitsunday, from the white garments of those being baptized. Note that Sunday is counted at both ends; similarly, a week in France is *huit jours:* eight days, and a fortnight (fourteen nights) is *quinze jours:* fifteen days.

L *quintus. quinate, quincunx. quintessence,* etc.; see *el. quintal:* 100 kilograms, however, came, via French, from Arab *qintar:* 100 Arabic pounds. *Quentin:* fifth son. It, *cinquecento.* Fr, *cinquain, cinq(ue).*

Gc, *pempe, finfi;* Gm *fünf;* OE *fif. five, fifth, fifteen, fifty. finger,* one of five; *fist.* Du, *foist.* Norse, *femto-,* as *femtometer;* see mensuration tables under *me IV.*

Frequent in early English, appearing on inn signs, were the *five all's:* the king, who rules all; the lawyer, who pleads for all; the soldier, who fights for all; the farmer (occasionally, later, John Bull), who pays for all; and the parson, who prays for all.

pent: go, go along, come upon. Iran, *path, pathway.* Gk *patein, peripatetic* (*peri:* around), applied first to Aristotle, who taught while walking about the Lyceum in Athens; then to his teachings. Johnson, in *The Rambler,* no. 85 (1751), referred to "the old peripatetic principle that Nature abhors a vacuum." There are 15 associated words in *OED.* "There are many paths to the top of the mountain, but the view is always the same"—Chinese saw.

L *pons, pontem:* bridge. *pons, pontoon, pontonier. pontifex; pontifex maximus:* chief bridge-maker, across the Tiber; Roman head priest; this may be a folkchange from an Etruscan word. *pontiff; pontificate. cispontine, transpontine.* Several special terms come directly from the Latin. *pons asinorum:* the bridge of asses, is the fifth proposition of the First Book of Euclid's geometry: "If two sides of a triangle are equal, the opposite (base) angles are equal." Euclid's diagram is like a bridge, and many schoolboys could not "get across it"; the expression may be applied to anything difficult for a dullard. *pons Varolii* (from Costanzo *Varoli,* a 16th c. Italian anatomist), also called *pons cerebelli:* the band of nerve fibers connecting the underfaces of the two branches of the human cerebellum. Hence E *pontal. pont tournis:* an early type of drawbridge. *pont volant:* flying bridge, used to storm a walled town in medieval sieges. *pontage* (12th through 19th c.): toll paid for crossing a bridge; we've dropped the word but kept the payment. *pont* was also the early form of *punt:* a float, also a flat-bottomed boat, propelled by a pole pushed at the river bed, as in *punting* on English streams.

Gc, *find, found, foundling.* ODu, *footpad. pad,* to go along, is partly imitative of the sound of trudging feet; hence probably also *paddle, piddle, puddle,* and *poodle:* splashing dog. Russ *sputnik* (*s:* with; *put:* go along; the first word of *sputnik zamli:* one who goes along with the earth): first Russian satellite to go into space, 4 Oct. 1957.

"Her ways are ways of pleasantness, and all her paths are peace"—Bible, Proverbs, 3:17.

per: through, ahead, etc. This root has two main aspects, as the one ahead can either help or hinder those that come after. And if you are through, you may have done all you need: *perfection,* or all you can, but not enough: *perdition.* The root has been divided into a number of subroots, but they all seem to be logical extensions of the one basic idea. Producing fertile prefix forms, *per* has brought new words into the language at various times—e.g., as nomads became residents, and as cities, commerce, and civilizations grew. The main prefixes are given here; the structured subdivisions appear at the end of the discussion.

(1) Skr *pra:* before. *Prajapati:* fore-begetter, Vedic creator of the world. *Prakriti:* prototype of female energy. *prana:* before breath; life principle in Vedic thought. *Prakrit:* language "shaped before," the common speech of India, as opposed to *Sanskrit. Pralaya:* before vanishing; the end of the world.

(2) Skr and Gk *para:* alongside. *paradise:* a garden "walled around." *parallel. paragon* is a "stone" (Gk *akone:* whetstone) alongside, used as a touchstone. The verb *paragonize* has been used in two senses: (1) to put into rivalry; (2) to put up, or serve, as a model of excellence.

A *paragram* is a pun that uses letters "alongside." Three sorts of paragram may be distinguished: (1) an exchange of initial letters, also called a *Spooner(ism),* as when *Bob Rank* may slip to *Rob Bank;* (2) a substitution of initial letters, as when Emperor Tiberius Nero's enemies referred to him as *Biberius Mero:* guzzler of neat wine; (3) use of letters with shifting emphasis and sense, as when, upon Boswell's suggestion that Johnson didn't like puns because he couldn't make them, the pundit at once retorted: "If I were punishèd for every pun I shed, no puny shed would hold my punnish head." See *pun,* under *peug.*

paralanguage: beside speech, consists in facial expressions, body movement, gestures of arms and hands. College speech departments may offer a course in gestures appropriate to various moods. Books of folk gestures are available; there is a beautiful (also illustrated) book by A. K. Coomaraswamy, giving the meanings of the hand gestures of the East Indian dance. Folk gestures may have different meanings in different lands; in Malta and Sicily, e.g., an up-and-down headshake means No, while in northern Europe and the U.S. it means Yes. Widely known is Churchill's V for Victory; hold the left palm facing yourself, and in southern Europe the gesture is obscene. Other gestures are more widespread. *Queen Anne's lace* names the delicate flower of the wild carrot, but *Queen Anne's fan* names thumb to nose with outspread wagging fingers, a gesture used in ancient times, by the irrepressible Rabelais, and by impudent children in many lands today.

(3) Gk *peri:* around, as *perimeter.*

(4) Gk and L *pro:* before, for, in behalf of; as *progress, profile. pro* may also be used to mean in place of, as in the Latin phrase, used in English, *quid pro quo:* literally, which for what, a fair exchange. Thus *procaine* (hydrochloride) is *pro:* in place of *(co)caine.*

(5) Gk and L *preter:* beyond, as *preterit, preternatural.*

(6) L *prae:* before, as *praecognitum, praemunire;* more frequently *pre,* as *predict, predestination. Praemonitus, praemunitus:* Forewarned, forearmed.—Roman proverb. William Emerson begins *The Doctrine of Fluxions* (1743) with the warning: "It would be but lost labour for any person unacquainted with these praecognita, to spend any Time in reading this Book."

(7) L *per:* through, as *pervade, persistence.*

(8) Gc *fore* (*p.f* change, Grimm's law): before, as *forebear, forecast.*

(9) Gc *ver;* OE *for.* This evolved to a negative end, coming to mean thorough exhaustion, ruin, or reversal, as *forbear, forbid, forgo.*

Only a representative listing of English words from this prolific root is given below. The following subdivisions, which may employ any of the preceding prefix forms, may also overlap.

(I) Moving about, next to, across, around, through. That which is "made through," completed, thorough, is *perfect* (L *facere, factum:* make; *perficere, perfectum*), *perfectible, perfection.* But also (turn completely) *pervert, perversion, perversity.* Through circumstances we cannot foresee, things come upon us *peradventure, perchance, perhaps.* Skr *palanquin* (*l.r* shift), which bends around the body; *parasang.* Gk, *peripheral. peripatetic* (see *pent*). *paradox, parameter, parasite. palfrey. comparative; compare, comparison. hysteron proteron:* "cart before the horse." *reciprocal. prodigal:* driving or pouring forth; "wasting one's talents," which is a learned pun, as *talent* means both ability and money.

Gk *poros:* passage, whence *pore,* as in the skin; *porous.* After the intinerant peddler, the more permanent *emporium.* L, *perambulate; perambulator,* shortened to *pram. peregrine, pelerine, pilgrim, peregrination. paragraph,* one written next to the other. L *frons, frontem,* Gc *farno:* feather, wing, enabling birds to go; *frond. fern,* from the feathery appearance. Gc, *fare, wayfarer; farther, further. firth, fjord, forward, forth, forthwith. fere, transfer, ferry. impervious:* no way through. *forthright. from, froward, front, frontal, frontier.* Gm *Fahrt:* journey; *Hanneles Himmelfahrt:* Little Hannah's journey to heaven, a play by Gerhart Hauptmann (1893). *Turnverein:* coming together of gymnasts. Let us persist no further.

"Let patience have her perfect work"—Bible, James 1:4. (No human work is perfect. To avert the gods' jealousy, beautiful babies were besmudged by superstitious mothers. The proud architect of the Taj Mahal built it with 20,000 workmen, 1632–43, so that three raindrops could fall through. Shah Jahan, who had commissioned it as a memorial to his wife, *Mumtaz Mahal:* chosen crown of the palace, arranged that the architect would never build another. *Taj,* which used to mean tiara, now names a typical Muslim conical hat.) *paramour.*

Just when we're safest, there's a sunset touch,
A fancy from a flower-bell, someone's death,
A chorus-ending from Euripides,
And that's enough for fifty hopes and fears—
The grand Perhaps.
—Browning, *Bishop Blougram's Apology*

(II) Carrying, crossing, arriving; hence, a place to stop. L, *port, portable, portage, passport, porter; portfolio. porch, portal. portico.* Via Fr, *parterre, portiere. portcullis; portulaca. apartment, compartment, compartmentalize; department. importance, importunate, importune; opportune, opportunity,* etc. *comport; deport, deportment. purport, rapport, report, support, transport, transportation. perdurable; permanent. disport* first meant carrying aside; then, just as *divert:* turn aside, changed in sense to *diversion:* entertainment (Fr, *divertissement*), *disport* was applied to dallying and to the activities now meant by its aphetic form, *sport.* Thus, in Beaumont's *Knight of the Burning Pestle* (1607), Ralph as May lord, summoning in the merry month of May, declares:

> The lords and ladies now abroad, for their disport and play
> Do kiss sometimes upon the grass, and sometimes in the hay.

dally first meant to play amorously; then, to spend time idly or frivolously; to dawdle. *dawdle* is a blend of *daw:* sluggard, and *daddle. diddle, doddle, doodle* are all partly imitative. *sport* came into use as early as 1440; it, too, might mean sexual play, as when Iago in *Othello,* ii, 1, trying to win Roderigo to his purposes, says: "When the blood is made dull by the act of sport, there should be—again to inflame it, and give satiety a fresh appetite—loveliness in favour, sympathy in years, manners . . ."

(III) Venturing, testing the way, taking a chance; hence, valuing; then, buying and selling. Gk *peira:* venture. *peirates. pirate, piracy. empire.* L, *peril, perilous; imperil.* Also (in the sense of trying out) *practice, practical, practitioner; impractical. apraxis. pragmatism.* Via Fr, *barter.* L *pretium:* value. *precious, prize. appraise; praise. appreciate; depreciation. a priori* (vs. *a posteriori*); *preposterous:* full of before-after. *experiment,* etc., *experience, expert. price; purchase.* Gk *pernemi:* sell; hence *porne:* one that sells oneself (see *sta*); *pornography.* L, *Imprimatur:* It may be printed; official permission, as of the Catholic Church. *interpreter:* one between; first, a negotiator.

opportune, opportunity. fortune, which may be good or bad; *fortunate,* good only; *misfortune. fortuitous, fortuity. forsooth.* Gc, *fear, fearful, fearless, fearsome.*

(IV) Come ahead of, look ahead; be ready, quick. L *praestus:* quick. *presto, prestissimo. prestidigitation:* "the hand is quicker than the eye"; but the eye can distinguish tenths of a second; motion pictures seem continuous because the individual pictures ("frames") flow at a faster rate—not less than 16 per second. *prestige:* first, a magic illusion; still often based on illusion.

The language of the English law courts from 1066 to 1362 was Norman French. An abbreviation of LL *prest,* OFr *pret:* ready, indicates how seldom an accused man was acquitted. If the man pleaded "Not guilty," the prosecutor replied: "Guilty (Culpable). Ready to proceed," which the court clerk abbreviated *cul pret—culprit.* Case closed! (In some lands, such days seem not long gone by.)

Via L, *prior, predicate, predict;* via Fr, *preach. preliminary* (*limen:* threshold). *praemonitus praemunitus:* forewarned, forearmed. *preamble. predestination, premature. present, presently:* first, at the present moment, at once; then, because of human nature, in a little while—though there has been a vogue revival of the earlier sense: "He is presently occupied." *pretext:* literally, woven before, as a net, to entrap. *represent, representative.*

Via Gc, *first, before, fore, former, foremost, foretell. Procyon,* a double star in the constellation *Canis Minor:* lesser dog, literally means before the dog (see *kuon*)—i.e., before Sirius, the Dog Star, in the constellation Canis Major. Sirius is the brightest star in the sky, not quite nine light-years from Earth.

Lying face up, to the fore, one is *prone;* face down, *supine* (*sub:* under). *prose* (shortened from L *provertere, proversus:* forward turn) is straight-forward writing, to the end of the line, whereas verse turns back at a metrically measured point, to start a new line.

(V) Coming beyond or before, one may dally, or prepare for others, help or harm. *parapet:* a low protective wall. It *petto:* breast. *rampart. pro* (vs. *con*): in behalf of. L *prodesse* (for *esse,* see *es*): to be helpful to; E *prowess. proud, pride. proud flesh:* literally, coming beyond the skin, around a healing wound. L *prope:* near; *proprior:* nearer; *proximum:* nearest. *proper. approach, appropriate, approximate, proximate. prude, prudish, prudery; prosper, prosperous, prosperity. proximity.* L *pr(a)evenire, pr(a)eventum:* come before. *prevent* (see *gua*).

L *(pre)parare, paratum:* make ready. *prepare. pare. parry. preparedness.* Fr, *parure. apparatus. apparel. parcel. parcener; coparcener* (splitting the inheritance). L *pars, partem. part, partial, impart, impartial; participate, partake; partner. particular, partition, party. depart.* The marriage promise "till death us depart" was, says John Henry Blunt in *The Annotated Book of Common Prayer* (1866), "altered to 'do part' in 1661, at the request of the Puritans, who knew as little of the history of their native language as they did of their national church."

bipartite. particle. Gk, *protagonist; paraphernalia:* first, a married woman's personal property, before her dowry. *impair, repair.* (*despair* is L *de:* from, *sperare, speratum:* hope; hence also *desperate.*) *repartee. parse. portion, proportion, disproportionate.* L *par:* equal. *par, parity, pair, peer* (a man is tried by a jury of his peers). *an umpire* is a folkchange from *a non pair:* odd man out, acting as referee. The same idea occurred with L *testis* (see *tre*). *pari-mutuel. compare.* Fr, *nonpareil. prime:* get something ready to work, as a pump, engine, or early gun.

Note, however, that *proscribe* is opposed to *prescribe. prohibit.* When Stanley in Africa said "Dr. Livingstone, I presume," he meant other than when one says "Don't presume!" (with the noun *presumption*); thus even the one form may have a friendly or a hostile aspect. *protract; procrastinate* (L *crastinus:* tomorrow). There was also *Procrustes* (Gk *prokronein:* draw forward, lengthen), a giant living near Eleusis, where the Athenians went to celebrate the "mysteries." He had a sharp sense of the fitness of things; if a guest did not fit his bed, he stretched the deficient form, or lopped off the excess. A rigid rule or requirement may be referred to as a *Procrustean bed.* Hence *separate, sever, several.*

proctor, as at a college, is short for *procurator* (L *procurare, procuratum:* care for), also shortened to *curator,* as at a museum. *proctal,* however, means anal (Gk *proktos*); whence *proctologist.*

Gc, *for, welfare. further:* to advance one's interests. *furnish, furniture, veneer. frame* (from OE *fremian:* to be helpful; but also to arrange to victimize).

Via Fr, *parasol:* ready for (protection from) the sun. Fr *parapluie:* ready for the rain; but English took *umbrella,* via Italian, from L *umbra:* shade (see *andho*). *parachute:* ready for a fall. From *parachute* came *paratroops; paradoctor,* dropped from a plane in military emergencies or to reach remote countryside. A *paramedic,* however, is more usually a nonphysician working "alongside" a medical man.

(VI) Coming before, one is first. This sense developed in several directions.

(a) First, earliest; in front, beyond, ahead. Gk, *prototype. Prot(er)ozoic. proto-,* as *proton, protoplasm; protein:* first for body growth. *procerity:* tallness. *protocol:* originally, first draft of a treaty; now, who goes first, etc. *protolanguage:* a hypothetical ancestor, as Indo-European. *proso-:* forward, as *prosodemic, prosopopoeia. propaedia:* introductory volume to the 15th edition of the *Encyclopaedia Britannica. prosody:* first, words sung with music. *Proteus:* first god. *Prothalamion:* song before a wedding; coined by Spenser from *Epithalamion:*

upon the wedding; titles of two poems he wrote, in 1595 and 1596. *prow* (opposed to *stern*).

L *pre-:* before, as *preface, premeditated.* L *preter:* beyond, as *preternatural, preterpluperfect.* L *pres; prior, prius; primus:* simple, comparative, and superlative degrees. *prior, priority. primo, imprimis. primum mobile:* first source of motion; in the Middle Ages, added to Ptolemaic astronomy, as an outer sphere. *prime, primeval, primitive.*

> This is the forest primeval,
> The murmuring pines and the hemlocks
> Stand like druids of old . . .
> —Longfellow, *Evangeline*

primordial. primus. prima facie. premier, première. Primulaceae, Primula: family and genus, the primrose, first flower of spring (see *lei I*). *primavera:* earliest green. Fr *printemps:* springtime. Gc, *before:* to the fore. *fore and aft. forenoon. foreboding, forecast, foreclose, foreskin.*

(b) First, as ancestor. L *parere, partum:* give birth; *parens, parentum. parent, parentage, parental; parturient, parturition, postpartum. primapara. primogeniture* (see *gn*). *puerperal* (*puer:* male child; hence *puerile;* see *pou*). *-parous,* as *viviparous;* also, the shorter *viper;* see *auei; guei.*

pauper: bearing little. *forefathers.* (*forbear* is cited under *per VIII,* although it is so often misused that dictionaries list it as a "variant" of *forebear.* Shakespeare knew better. In *2 Henry VI,* iii, 3, he said: "Forbear to judge, for we are sinners all"—recalling the biblical injunction about the first stone. Thus also *forego:* go before, and *forgo:* go without).

(c) First, as most recent, youngest; nearest. L, *pristine. primary* (school); *primer* (short *i;* see *do*). Gc, *heifer, farrow.*

Gm *Jungfrau:* virgin, especially the Virgin Mary. The *Jungfrau* is also a peak in the Swiss Alps; when named, unmounted. *euphroe* (from Du *joncfrouwe:* virgin; not related to the prefix *eu,* for which see *esu*) is a naughty nautical use of the "virgin." No one knows where *virgin* comes from; see *maghos. Virgo* shines in the sky as a constellation, sixth sign of the zodiac; see *guei.* The Virgin also appears, in curious guise, in L *Lac Virginis* and Gm *Liebfraumilch;* see *melg.* The former first named a cosmetic; each now names a variety of wine; both mean, literally, milk of the Virgin. *Blackwood's Magazine* viii (1820), in an aptronymic jingle suggesting port as drink for sailors, sherry (Fr *cheri:* sweetheart) for lovers, and ale for physicians, includes:

> The parsons should grow misty
> On good Lac Virginis or Lachrima Christi.

Note may be taken here of the *virago,* which does come from L *vir:* man. In the Bible, Genesis 2:23: "She shall be called woman, because she was taken out of the man." In Hebrew, *ishshah:* woman; *ish:* man. But in Vulgate Latin, *Haec vocebitur virago, quoniam de viro sumpta est.* Thus *virago* first meant, in English, a manly woman, then a bold, then a stormy one. In this mood, some (by male folk etymology) have explained woman as woe to man. This derivation slips into Latin as well; the name *Eva,* of Adam's mate and temptress, is an anagram of L *vae:* woe, well known in the old saying still too often true: *Vae victis:* Woe to the vanquished (see *uai*). Women may counter these male thrusts by pointing to the spirit of love personified in Mary, mother of Jesus, for *Eva* is also an anagram of *Ave:* Hail, as in the eloquent song of prayer *Ave Maria.* Thus the first woman looks forward to the Savior. *Ave atque vale:* Hail and fare well.

(d) First (born before), as eldest. Gk *prestus. presbyopia. Presbyterian. Prester John.* Fr, *prêtre:* priest, naturally called *Father. OED* has 26 words beginning *presby.*

(e) First, as standing forth, outstanding. *probity. probate, probe, prove, proof.* In the expressions "The proof of the pudding is the eating thereof" and "The exception proves the rule," we retain the early meaning: test. *probable; approve. improve* (*in:* into, as an intensive); *improbable, improbity* (*in,* negative). *disapprove, reprobate, reprove.*

Of *prime* quality. A *prime number* is a number that has no factors but itself and 1. The first few primes are 1, 2 (the only even prime), 3, 5, 7, 11, 13, 17, 23, 29; they become more distantly spread, but reach into infinity. They recently reached into the media. The London *Times,* on 22 Sept. 1980, pictured the dismay of Vice-Admiral B. R. Inman, director of the U.S. National Security Agency, upon the suggestion of an unbreakable secret code: multiply two prime numbers of over fifty digits each (computer supplied); take their product as the code base, and no cryptographer, however supplied with computers and brains, can possibly break the code. This, said Director Inman, may "seriously damage the ability of this government to protect national security information." A curious turn of thought! The product of two prime numbers, if again divisible only by itself, 1, and the two primes, is called a *prime product;* thus $7 \times 23 = 161$.

Christian Goldbach, in a 1742 letter to the Swiss mathematician Leonhard Euler, announced what is known as *Goldbach's conjecture,* which has never been disproved: that every even number greater than 2 is the sum of two primes. A. de Polignac in 1849 declared that every positive even number is a difference of two primes (in infinitely many ways). And it has been proved (by Borodkin) that every "sufficiently large" odd number is the sum of three primes—"sufficiently large" being over $3^{3^{15}}$, which, Solomon W. Colomb informs me, is slightly less than $10^{10,000,000}$. Largest known prime: $2^{132049} - 1$; ca. 40,000 digits.

Twin primes are prime numbers separated by one even number, as 5 . . . 7; 51 . . . 53; 191 . . . 193; 227 . . . 229. For perfect numbers, see *dhe I.*

(f) First, as chief. *paramount.* From L *princeps* (*capere, captum:* take), *principal, principality; principle. princess, prince.* "The Prince of Darkness is a gentleman." Baudelaire warned that "the cleverest ruse of the Devil is to persuade us he doesn't exist." Shakespeare, in *Love's Labor's Lost,* iii, calls Dan Cupid "Dread prince of plackets, king of codpieces." A *placket* is a slit in the top of a skirt, used (*OED* says *sensu obscoenu*) as slang for *vagina.* See *bheudh; burd; tel. brothel* first meant a prostitute; it took its present meaning from It *bordello,* Fr *bordel,* both used also in English. *bordel* first meant hovel.

primacy. primate. premium, premier. prime-time, as in broadcasting. *prime minister. primum mobile,* Aristotle's name for what Bernard Shaw called the Life Force, and what countless persons have spoken of as God. *imperator, emperor; empress. imperial, imperious. prior, prothonotary. Parcae.* Gm, *Frau, Fräulein. Führer.*

(g) First, ahead of the rest, hence alone. L *proprius:* held apart, one's own. *proper, improper, property, proprietor, impropriety.* Fr *mal à propos;* whence Mrs. *Malaprop* in Sheridan's *The Rivals* (1775), who mangled the language with such expressions as "He is the very pineapple of politeness. . . . She's as headstrong as an allegory on the banks of the Nile." *malapropisms* found a defender a century later, in Lewis Carroll's *Through the Looking Glass* (1872): "When I use a word," Humpty-Dumpty said in a rather scornful tone, "it means just what I want it to mean—neither more nor less. The question is, which is to be master—that's all." See *melo.*

appropriate, misappropriate. L *privus:* alone, by oneself; hence *lone, lonely, lonesome.* (Note that *alone* is a compression of *all one;* similarly, *atonement* is the state of being *at one.*) *privacy, private, privation. privilege:* first, a law regarding an individual. *deprive, privity, privy* (council). A *privateer*—the ending borrowed from *volunteer*—was a person, or a privately owned ship, authorized by royal "letters of marque," in 1651 and later, to capture the ships of England's enemies—Dutch, French, or Spanish.

Shakespeare, in *Twelfth Night,* iii, 4, said: "Go off, I discard you: let me enjoy my private." *OED* has 16 columns of relevant words, from *privacy* to *privy seal. privy* also means hidden; *privy to:* in the secret; it is also used to mean latrine. In Elsinor Castle (supposedly Hamlet's) in Denmark, I was shown "the King's secret": a small chamber, with a hole in the floor, beneath which flowed the castle moat; and I recognized that *privy* had been translated into Danish, then retranslated into English as "secret."

Today's "liberated" woman, if she read Chaucer, might approve the thought in his prologue to *The Miller's Tale:*

A housbonde shal not be inquisityf
Of Goddes pryvetee, nor of his wyf.
So he may find Goddes foyson plenty there,
Of the remenant nedeth not enquere.

As Dryden said of Chaucer himself, "Here is God's plenty!"

(VII) Things drawing near may embrace or strike each other. *approach, propinquity. proximate, approximately; peroneal; pregnant* (see *gn*). Fr, *rapprochement;* but also *reproach. press, pressure; compress, depression, express, oppress, repress, suppress. reprimand, print, imprint, reprint.*

Coming together, creatures may form some sort of symbiotic relationship, as that of a *parasite* (*para:* alongside; *sitos:* food, whence also *sit(i)ology*). Hence also *parasitology. parasite:* a plant or animal that lives in or on another, and draws its sustenance from its host. Often, as in the case of the louse and the mistletoe, it does little or no harm; but *parasitism* has several subdivisions. (1) *brood parasitism:* of birds that lay and leave their eggs in other birds' nests, as the cowbird and the cuckoo; from the latter comes E *cuckold,* noun and verb. (2) *parasitoidism:* of the parasite that kills its host. Some ants, wasps, flies, and bees lay eggs in or on the host, and, upon hatching, the larvae devour the host. The thread-waisted wasp paralyzes the host, then seals it in a mud cell for the larva to consume. (3) *lipoxeny* (see *leip II*): of a parasite that after a time leaves the host, as certain fungi. (4) *hyperparasitism:* of a parasite on a parasite, as a protozoon in the digestive tract of a flea living on a dog. (5) *symbiosis:* living together; that pattern of coexistence in which each member of a pair draws aid or sustenance from the other, in mutual companionship. A most special symbiotic couple is the jellyfish and the sea slug in the Bay of Naples, described by Lewis Thomas in *The Medusa and the Snail* (1979).

'Tis pleasure, sure, to see one's name in print;
A book's a book, although there's nothing in't.
—Byron, *English Bards and Scotch Reviewers* (1809)

(VIII) Gc *ver* (pronounced *fair*), OE *for:* completion, thence exhaustion, ruin; reversal. *forfend, forgather, forgo, forsake, forswear; forspent. forbidden* (Gm *verboten*). *forgive* is an Old English translation of L *pardonare:* pardon. *forlorn;* but *forlorn hope* is folkchanged from Du *verloren hoop:* lost troop. *forget;* but note that *forgetive* is a blend of *forge* and *(inven)tive. forbear* (see *per VI b*).

The prefix *per* may also be used in the negative sense, as in *perjury* (L *ius, iuris:* oath, law) and *perdition* (L *perdere, perditum:* lose, from *per,* and *dare:* give). Also the ethnophaulistic "perfidious Albion" (L *fides:* faith; *albus:* white; the color from the usual approach to England via France, upon which one beholds first the white chalk cliffs of Dover, as the Alps are named for their snow-white peaks). An *ethnophaulism,* if you need ask, is a racial slur.

per N. These prefixes can run on endlessly. Let us conclude with statistics.

(1) *pra:* before. Having moved along the Indo- branch, this form came into Europe mainly after the Europeans went into India; the only word from *pra* in *OED* is *prakrit.* From Gk *prason:* leek, *prasios:* leek-green, *OED* lists 5 words and details 5, as *prase.* For *praseodymium,* see *el 59.* The sweet candy, *praline,* now mainly from New Orleans, is named after Marshall Duplessis *Praslin,* whose chef confected it ca. 1670.

(2) *para:* alongside, beside; beyond; hence also amiss, wrong. *OED* lists 87 words from anatomy and 44 from chemistry, and details in 65 columns over 400 more, as *paraclete, paradiastole, parallelopiped, paraplegia. parallax* (see *al II*). *paramorph. paranymph:* bridesmaid or best man; in ancient Greece, one that went with the groom to fetch the bride, symbolizing the primitive carrying-off of the female. There is still a similar practice in India, as the bride is escorted to the home of the husband. On the country roads of India, the man walks before the bride and her bridesmaids, brandishing a sword.

(3) *peri:* around, about. *OED* lists 128 words beginning *peri,* and details 41 columns more. Thus *period* is *peri-odos:* a going around, cycle of days, etc. *period* is listed with 7 columns of derivatives. *perish* is *per-ire:* to go completely; *peril* is from L *periculum,* from *ex-per-ire:* to try out, hence run a risk. Lancelot Gobbo, in *The Merchant of Venice,* ii, 2, reads his own palm, seeing amours with 15 wives, 11 widows, and 9 maids; but, while he will escape drowning thrice, he will "be in peril of [his] life with the edge of a featherbed." Perish the thought. Note that *peri* also means fairy; see *peri,* under *gn.*

(4) *pro:* before, in behalf of. This prefix, like *anti,* is in continuous use. One can be pro- or anti-Nixon; thus with most anyone and anything you choose. For *pro:* before in time, *OED* lists 37 words, as *proethnic:* said of a primitive people before its division into separate ethnic groups; in this sense, *pre* is more frequent; see (6) below. For *pro:* before in space, *OED* lists 25 words, as *procerebrum:* the forebrain, and details 360 columns, from *proaeresis* (Milton, 1644, *proairesis*): deliberate first choice, to *proxy,* shortened from *procuracy.*

(5) *preter:* beside, beyond, above. *OED* lists 35 words, and details 34 more, as *preternatural, preternuptial, preterea.*

(6) *prae, pre:* before. *OED* gives *prae* 6 columns, but this spelling has generally been replaced by *pre,* for which, says *OED,* "casual combinations can be formed at will, and are unlimited in number." It lists 274 words, then in 264 columns details others, as *precinct:* girded in front; *precognition; pretend, pre-Shakespearean.*

(7) *per:* through, thorough; sometimes, as we have seen, through to a bad end. *OED* gives 175 columns of *per* words, which to some extent blend with *peri.* It explains the special use of *per* in chemistry, indicating the largest combination of one element with another; thus *peroxide* means with the greatest proportion of oxygen—the smallest proportion being *protoxide.* Thus also *perbromic acid,* HBO_4.

(8) *fore:* before, in front. *OED* lists 212 words, and details others in 52 columns, as *forecastle, forefathers, foremost; foresight,* opposed to the easier *hindsight.*

(9) *for:* usually implying negative, or something wrong. Many such words are obsolete, as *forsay:* renounce; *forfare:* perish; *forlapped:* dead drunk. *OED* lists 84 *for* words, and details 18 columns more, as *forbid:* speak against; *forget:* lose hold (now only mental).

A number of Latin expressions beginning *per* or *pro* are still used in English legal, formal, or learned reference. These include: *per accidens:* by chance, without intent, not intrinsic; opposed to *per se:* in and of itself, intrinsically. *per angusta ad augusta:* through travail to triumph. *per ardua ad astra:* through struggle to the stars; motto of Britain's Royal Air Force.

per diem: by the day. *per mensem:* by the month. *per annum:* by the year. *per cent(um):* of each hundred. *per contra:* on the other hand. *per curiam:* by the court. *per capita:* by heads, apiece; vs. *per stirpes:* by families or groups, each branch then subdividing its share among its members. *per extensum:* lengthily. *per minima:* through the minutest particles or details. *per quod:* whereby. *per favore* (It): as a favor; Please! *per veritatem vis:* power through truth; motto of Washington University.

pro aris et focis (altars and hearths): for faith and home. *pro bono publico:* for the general good. *pro confessio:* according to the confession. *pro Deo et Patria:* for God and country; motto of American University. *pro fas aut nefas:* by fair means or foul, by hook or by crook. *pro forma:* to observe the formalities. *pro hac vice:* for this turn (occasion) only. *pro nunc:* for now. *pro rata:* in proportion to one's share. *pro re nata:* for the matter born; equipped for the contingency. *pro scientia et religione:* for science and religion; motto of Denver University. *pro tanto:* to such an extent. *pro tempora:* for the time being.

perd: fart. No less than three imitative roots are assigned to this word; the act was once as unrestrained as among (at least the pre-Communist) Chinese the uninhibited belch, a sign to a host that one has enjoyed one's dinner. From the root *peis,* via Gc, come *feist, fizgig, fizzle.* From the root *pezd,* perhaps *pediculosis,* of the foul-smelling insect; but see *lus.* Via Fr *perdrix, partridge,* from the whir of its sudden flight. *petard,* from the loud noise; as in *Hamlet,* iii, "the enginer Hoist with his own petar." Fr, *pet;* Gc, *fart.*

Even the "divine" Sarah Bernhardt paled during the 1899 vogue of Joseph Pujol, the "petomane" whose musical expulsions of anal wind captivated society; as the famous diseuse Yvette Guilbert reported, "The laughter and hysterical screams could be heard a hundred yards from the Moulin Rouge." Pujol's biography was translated into English in 1976, and eight producers vied for the motion-picture rights. His "art," however, is old; in A.D. 430 St. Augustine wrote, in *The City of God,* xiv, 24: "There are those that can break wind backward so artfully you would think they sang." Juan Luis Vives, tutor to Henry VIII's daughter Mary, in his commentary on that work, mentions a German at the court of Maximilian (ca. 1500) "that could rehearse any song whatsoever with his tail." *razz,* shortened from *raspberry,* is Cockney rhyming slang, the full rhyming expression—the Cockney usually does not give the rhyme—being *raspberry tart.* Eric Partridge, in *Shakespeare's Bawdy* (1947, 1968), tells us that this is the sound in Hamlet's mind when he taunts Polonius: "Bzz, bzz" (sounded *bts,* as *czar* was earlier and is sometimes still spelled, and sounded, *tsar*).

Oddly, what in English is called a *Spooner* and *Spoonerism,* in French is *contrepet,* the instance, and *contrepeterie,* the practice: transferring initial letters or syllables so as to make other, and often risqué, sense. Thus Rabelais turned *femme folle à la messe* to *femme molle à la fesse:* foolish woman at the mass; woman with the flaccid ass. *à Beaumonte le vicomte* became *à beau con le vit monte.*

The most notable *fart* in English literature is that in Chaucer's *The Miller's Tale.* In her husband's absence, Nicholas is lying with fair Alison, when a clerk, Absalon, comes and begs for a kiss. Alison, in the dark night, comes to the window—and squats. Absalon, leaving, reflects that a woman has no beard; he comes vengefully back with a red-hot poker and begs for one more kiss:

This Nicholas had risen for to pisse . . .
And up the window he did hastily
And out his ers he putteth prively
Over the buttock, to the haunche-bone.
And therewith spoke this clerk, this Absalon:
"Spek, swete brid, I noot not wher thou art."
This Nicholas anon let flee a fart
As great as it had been a thunder-dent,
That with the stroke he was almost y-blent;
And he was ready with his iron hote,
And Nicholas amid the ars he smote.

The victim's anguished cry betrayed the adulterous lovers. More expulsive anecdotes are recorded under *wind* in my *Scholar's Glossary of Sex* (1968), published under the name Roy Goliard. And among the many images of love, perhaps none is more eccentric and borborygmous than the Cavalier quatrain:

Love is the fart
Of every heart;
It pains a man when 'tis kept close,
And others doth offend when 'tis let loose.

—done by Suckling, who also invented the game of cribbage, but worthy of Donne, who in 1635 seized upon *The Flea:*

Mark but this flea, and mark in this
How little that which thou denyst me is:
It sucked me first, and now sucks thee,
And in this flea our two bloods mingled be;
Thou knowst that this cannot be said
A sin, nor shame, nor loss of maidenhead.

(He pictures her "purpling" her nail by killing it, and ends:)

Just so much honor, when thou yieldst to me,
Will waste, as this flea's death took life from thee.

History does not record whether this poem by the royal chaplain and Dean of St. Paul's achieved its purpose.

perk: pray, entreat. L *peccari:* beg. *preces:* prayers. *pray.* "To plow is to pray; to plant is to prophesy."

deprecate; imprecation. precarious: depending upon prayer. L *postulare, postulatum:* request. *postulate, expostulation. prithee. procacity:* first, of a suitor. Fr, *priedieu.*

In act ii of Suckling's *Aglaura,* produced at court in the Christmas season of 1637, Orsames sings a song to the Platonic ladies Semantha and Orithie—platonic love being an affectation of the time (see *pela*)—a song that advises a victim of the Platonic snub:

Why so pale and wan, fond lover,
  Prithee, why so pale?

Will, when looking well can't move her,
Looking ill prevail?
Prithee, why so pale? . . .

Quit, quit for shame, this will not move;
This cannot take her.
If of herself she cannot love,
Nothing can make her.
The Devil take her!

Charles L. Squier, in *Sir John Suckling* (1978), calls attention to the "frequent" pun in *fond:* loving, and foolish; and to "the sexual pun in take."

?pers: mask. L *persona:* theatre mask. *person, personality,* etc. *parson:* person of the church; *person* was pronounced *parson. parsonage. Persephone:* wife of Hades; goddess of the underworld, who wore a mask when meeting the dead.

pes: tail. Gk *peos;* L and E *penis. pencil; penicillin, penicillium.* The sexual allusion is clear in the drinking toast, "Here's lead in your pencil!"

pet I: rush, leap, fly; also fall. "Whatever goes up must come down." Skr *patram:* feather. *talipot:* palm leaf. Gk *pteron:* feather, wing; *ptenos:* feathered. *ptenoglossate, ptenopleural. stearoptene:* flying, volatile. *OED* lists 32 words beginning *pter(o),* as *pterograph, pterotheca,* and details 24, as *pterodactyl, pteridology, pterigoid.* It lists 8 more beginning *pterid(o).* For *pteryg(o):* wing, fin, it lists 19 words, details 4. *Pterygote* includes all winged insects. *pterigium:* in 1684, "the nymphae of a woman's secret parts"; in 1884, "an ocular tumor."

The suffix *pterous,* as *apterous, lepidopterous;* JWalker lists 15. *peripteral. helicopter:* helix-winged. *apteryx. archeoptery. acanthopterygian.* Gk *ptilon:* soft feathers, down. *coleoptile.*

Gk *piptein* (reduplicated): fall. *ptomaine,* from Gk *ptoma:* fallen body, corpse, via It *ptomaina,* coined by Professor Selmi of Bologna in 1876. *ptosis. asymptote:* not falling together. *aptote, diptote, triptote. perepeteia. proptosis. symptom.* Gk *potamos:* flowing water. *hippopotamus:* river horse. *Mesopotamia:* between rivers; see *medhi.*

L *petere:* go forward, seek. *centripetal* (opposed to *centrifugal*). *petition. petulant. appetency, appetite. appetizer. compete, competition.* A *competitor* was first a fellow-seeker, cooperating; in *Antony and Cleopatra,* v, 1:

. . . thou my brother, my competitor,
In top of all design, my mate in empire,
Friend and companion in the front of war.

But as with *prevent* (see *gua*), human nature intervened, to make competitors rivals.

Also *impetuous, impetus; perpetual, perpetuate; repeat, repetition.* OL *petna,* L *penna, pinna:* feather, wing. *pen; penknife,* for sharpening quill pens. *penmanship. penna, pennate, pennant, pennon. pinnacle. pinnate. OED* lists 5 words beginning *pinnati,* and details 3 more, as *pinnatiped;* it also lists 3 beginning *pinnato* (botanical all). *pinnule.*

propitious: first, rushing forward, well-disposed; said of the gods. Probably also L *peior, pessimum:* fallen far. *pejorative, pejorism, pessimism.* Schopenhauer in 1819 used Gm *Pessimismus,* which was Englished by Coleridge; some trace these terms to *ped:* at the foot, bottom.

Gc, *fit, fern, feather.*

"The optimist proclaims that we live in the best of all possible worlds, and the pessimist fears this is true"—James Branch Cabell, *The Silver Stallion* (1926), iv.

There are three lessons I would write,
Three words as with a burning pen,
In tracings of eternal light
Upon the hearts of men.
—Schiller, *Hope, Faith, and Love*

pet II: open out, spread. Gk and E *petalon:* petal. *pan, patella, paten:* round dish for bread at the Eucharist; thence (L *patina:* dish) *patina:* film on old bronze, etc. L *(s)patere:* to be open. *space, spacious;* probably *spatula* and *spade:* spread out. *patent* (long *a*). The copyright *patent* (short *a*) was originally *letters patent* (L *litterae patentes*): open letters from the king granting a title or monopoly right. Now, while legally "protected," patents in the Record Office may be seen by anyone, and some inventors (especially of drugs or complex objects) prefer to keep their products unpatented and secret. *patera, patio. patulous.* Sp, *paella,* cooked in a pan.

L *pandere, passum:* to spread out, open, expand, extend. *pandiculation. pandy. penny,* from its spread in a circle; it once was a large coin. *pace* (Fr, *pas*), *pass, passage, passenger* (Fr *passager*); *passer-by; passport. passim. compass, surpass, trespass. expand, expanse; repand. mile* is from L *mille passus:* a thousand paces; the Roman mile was 1618 English yards, 142 yards short of our mile. An old advertisement said: "I'd walk a mile for a Camel," but a miss is as good as a mile.

peter: father. Gk *peter,* L and E *pater. paternal.* The Roman *Jupiter* is a blend of Gk *Zeus-peter:* king of the gods and polyparent. *patriarch, patrician. expatriate, repatriate. impetrate. perpetrate:* first, to behave like a father, through and through. *allopatric, sympatric. eupatrid:* of a fine father; noble. *repair* (to a place) first meant to go home. *OED* gives 67 relevant words beginning *patr,* as *patriot, patriotism. unpatriotic.* A *patrix* is a die used to form a matrix.

Patrick is from *patrician. pattern. patter,* first meaning rapid talk, was imitative of the priest's mechanical muttering of the Lord's Prayer: *Pater noster:* Our Father (which art in heaven); then of the showman's glib "spiel"; then of the sound of raindrops. *pitter-patter. patronymic. patronomatology:* study of the origin of personal names; a word listed in dictionaries, but apparently never used. *patrology. petrology* is from Gk *petros:* stone, rock; whence also *petrify.* For the pun on which the Catholic Church was erected, see *caput.* Also *saltpeter. parsley* is via L from Gk *petroselinon:* rock celery. *petroleum:* oil from the rocks; *petro* and all its combinations. "Step on the gas!" refers, of course, not to any gas but to *gasoline,* which is made chiefly from crude petroleum.

patruity; relationship of a father's brother, a *paternal* uncle. *patrimony* may be the end result of *matrimony. patron, patronage;* Du *patroon. parricide.* It, *padre, padrone.* Fr, *père.* Gc, *father, fatherland, unfatherly.* See *da; ma II; pa; per N; tara.*

Guy de Maupassant, in *My Uncle Sosthenes* (1883), stated that "patriotism is the egg from which wars are hatched." Samuel Johnson, from his disappointing experience with Lord Chesterfield, in his *Dictionary* defined *patron* as "commonly a wretch who supports with insolence and is paid with flattery."

?peti. Imitative. Baby talk for little things; it grew to other uses. *petty officer:* enlisted man in the navy. *petty bourgeois. petty cash. petty* (or *petit*) *larceny. petit mal; petit point. petits fours.* The feminine *petite. petticoat;* sometimes used disrespectfully of the wearer, as perhaps by Byron in the quotation below.

pettitoes: pig's feet, for food; originally *giblets,* from Fr *petite oie:* little goose (*oie* being from L *avis:* bird; see *auei*). *pettifogger;* the second element may imply one who "fogs things up," or is possibly from the famous *Fugger* family of merchants, financiers, and philanthropists of the 14th through the 16th c. It, *piccolo*. Sp *pequeno*, Port diminutive *pequenino*, E *pickaninny*. *a ninny* is a shift from *an innocent* (simpleton), its form influenced by It *ninno:* child.

Queen Elizabeth I stated: "I thank God I am endued with such qualities that if I were turned out of the Realm in my petticoat I were able to live in any place in Christome." This is not what led Lord Byron to remark (*Don Juan*, c): "I for one venerate a petticoat."

peu I: to feel shame; repel. Perhaps imitative, as in the exclamation *Pyeu!* L *pudere:* to be ashamed. *pudency, pudic. impudent. repudiate.* L *pudendum*, usually in the plural, *pudenda:* things to be ashamed of, from the curiously clinging notion that one should be ashamed of the genital organs, a belief fostered by Adam and Eve's fig leaf and continued through the Christian centuries, a belief affecting statuary and painting as well as spoken and written words.

peu II: cleanse. An extension of the preceding root. L *purus; purgere, purgatum:* make pure. *pure, purify; Puritan. purge; Purgatory. spurge*, used as a *purgative. purblind*, earlier *pure-blind; pure* used to mean free from other matter, unadulterated, completely what it should be.

compurgation, depurate. Fr, *purée. expurgate.* Bowdler is the most notorious expurgator, giving us E *bowdlerize* (see *esu*); but he is far from the first. Lord Roscommon, in his *Essay on Translated Verse* (1684), declared:

Immodest words admit of no defence,
For want of decency is want of sense.

Thackeray, as editor, rejected a poem by Elizabeth Barrett Browning because it contained the word *harlot.* Contrariwise, Charles Lamb wrote to Southey: "—the scene for the most part laid in a brothel. O tempora, O mores! but as friend Coleridge said when talking bawdy to Miss ——, 'to the pure all things are pure'." See *kens*.

peue: cut, strike, dig into; then (physical transferred to mental), think over, consider, etc. Gk *paiein:* beat; *anapaistos:* stricken back. E *anap(a)est:* the metrical foot, ⏑⏑–, which reverses the earlier dactyl, –⏑⏑. L *putare, putatum:* prune; consider. *putamen. putative. amputate. compute, count, account. deputation, deputy. dispute, disputation; impute; reputation*, etc. L *puteus:* a well. *pit, puteal.* L *pavire:* beat. *pave, pavement.* A *macadamized* pavement has in the one word elements of four languages: *mac:* Celtic; *adam:* Hebrew; *ize:* Greek; *d:* Germanic.

It, *pozzolano:* volcanic ashes used in cement, first at the town of *Pozzuoli* (near Naples), ancient *Puteoli:* little springs, where the water wells. L *pavere:* to be struck with fear. *pavid, impavid.*

In Köhln, a town of monks and bones,
And pavements fang'd with murderous stones,
And rags, and hags, and hideous wenches,
I counted two and seventy stenches,
All well defined, and several stinks!
Ye nymphs that reign o'er sewers and sinks,
The River Rhine, it is well known,
Doth wash your city of Cologne;
But tell me, Nymphs, what power divine
Shall henceforth wash the river Rhine?
—Coleridge, *Cologne*

p(e)ug: fist; strike, prick, pierce. Gk *pugme:* fist; also a measure of length, elbow to knuckle of closed fist; hence *pygmy, pygm(a)ean.* L *pugnare:* fight, first with fists. *pugilist; pugnacious. impugn, inexpugnable; oppugn; repugnant.* Via Fr, *poniard.* Possibly *prick,* played upon by Shakespeare in *Romeo and Juliet,* ii, 4: "The bawdy hand of the dial is now upon the prick of noon"; and in Sonnet 20, a rebuttal to those claiming he was homosexual.

L nasalized *pungere, punctum:* punctual. *pivot, poignant; point,* made by pricking. *appoint, appointment, reappoint. disappoint* first meant to remove from office. *pointillism. pun,* probably from It *puntiglio:* a fine point. *punctilious.* An earlier English form was *pundigrion,* from which *pun* evolved (in like manner, *mob,* etc.) "in good King Charles's Golden Days" (title of a 1939 play by Bernard Shaw), when, said *The Gentleman's Magazine,* 1791, "punning was the language of the Pulpit as well as of the Court." Swift, who in 1716 wrote *A Modest Defense of Punning,* less modestly called Thomas Sheridan "the greatest punner of this town next myself." Thomas (grandfather of playwright Richard Brinsley) Sheridan, in his 1719 *Ars Punica* gave 34 rules for the art. Rule 32, "Never speak well of another punster," became the general practice. Coleridge is said in his conversation to have been afflicted with "punorhea." *OED* lists 8 and details 5 words beginning *rhea:* flow, stream, (electric) current; JWalker gives 9 words ending *rhoea;* but both missed *punorhea. OED* has *punnet,* and in its 1982 supplement it quotes Henry James's remark in the *Atlantic Monthly,* 1866: "Blunt and I made atrocious puns. I believe, indeed, that Miss Blunt herself made one little *punkin,* as I called it." And as every jolly Catholic knows, the Roman Catholic Church was founded on a pun (Matthew 16:18). The *New York Times* of 28 Mar. 1983 mentions a book of *punjabs* by Alan Rubin, *Gopher Broke,* which consists of drawings with "punning punch lines." The title is illustrated with a pocket gopher, the pockets empty—which follows the pattern Lewis Carroll gives to Alice: "We called him tortoise because he taught us." To addicts of *punnology,* including the present author, may be applied the term *pungent!* See *paragram,* under *per 2.* Fr *pointe* took on meaning in the same way, evolving from a physical point to a mental quip.

punch: strike with the fist, or perforate with a tool, a *punch.* Hence also *pounce:* first, to prick, or the hole made by pricking; then, the pricking claws of a bird of prey; hence, *to pounce upon.* Also *puncheon:* a perforating instrument; a large cask, a perforated vessel, for pouring.

Also *punctuate, punctuation, punctule, puncture. pungent. compunction, expunge. counterpane, counterpoint.* It, *spontoon:* a 17th and 18th c. officer's weapon combining a spear and a battle-ax. *trapunto.* Gc, *bung. fight. fist, fisticuffs* (*cuff* [verb and noun]: strike; a blow). *Faust(us),* whose tale of selling his soul to the Devil for knowledge and power has been told by Marlowe and by Goethe; "I'll burn my books."

peuor: fire; color of flames. Gk *pur. pyre,* for burning corpses or the condemned. *pyralic, pyrene, pyretic. apyretic; pyresis:* fever. *Pyrex.* (iron) *pyrites:* fool's gold. *OED* has 29 columns of relevant words beginning *pyr(o),* as *pyromancy, pyromaniac, pyrotechnics.* The *Encyclopaedia Britannica* has a chart of the characteristics of eight *pyroxenes. pyruvic (acid),* CH_3COCOH, coined from *pur,* and L *uva:* grape. *empyrean.*

From Gk *purros:* fiery red, come another dozen words, as *pyrrhous, pyrrhite, pyrrhotite, pyrrole.* L *birro:* red. It, *sbirro:* policeman, from the red uniform. *burro:* donkey, from the color. *Borachio* in *Much Ado About Nothing* (Sp *borracho:* drunken), from the red complexion of the drunkard. *Pyrrha,* who lights a fire in a man's heart, is the name Horace gives his beloved in his odes, of which there have been more than ninety English translations. Emperor Augustus called Horace "a most immaculate libertine."

Note other sources of the same form in English. The *pyrrhic dance* was an ancient Greek dance in armor miming fighting movement; part of the training of Spartan youth, it was named for its supposed creator, *Purrixos.* The *pyrrhic foot,* in verse, two short syllables, ⏑⏑, is named for the two quick steps of this military dance. *pyrrhic victory* comes from the routing of the Romans by *Pyrrhus,* king of Epirus, in the battle of Heraclea, 279 B.C., with such slaughter of his own men that Pyrrhus exclaimed: "One more such victory, and we are lost." And *Pyrrhonism* names the philosophy of *Pyrrhon* of Elis (d. 272 B.C.), founder of the Greek school of Skepticism. Wise men, he said, suspend judgment as to the certainty of our knowledge, and are content to accept things as they appear. This idea was widely influential in 17th c. Europe, and has many followers today.

You have the Pyrrhic dance as yet;
Where is the Pyrrhic phalanx gone?
Of two such lessons, why forget
The nobler and the manlier one?
You have the letters Cadmus gave—
Think ye he meant them for a slave?
—Byron, *Don Juan,* c, 3

Cadmus, according to Greek legend, gave man the alphabet.

phol: to make slide; hence, to trick, deceive. L *fallere, falsum. fail, failure, fail-safe. fallible, infallible. fallacious, fallacy. false, falsify. fault; default. Fallit me:* It fails me; I do not know.

Note that the past tense of the irregular verb *fall, fell,* becomes the present of a regular verb, and thus several other verbs, usually with a wider or stronger meaning:

fall, fell: to drop down	*fell, felled:* to make drop down
lie, lay: to go down	*lay, laid:* to make go down
find, found: to come upon	*found, founded:* to make come into being
bind, bound: to confine	*bound, bounded:* to mark the confines of

Whoever thinks a faultless piece to see
Thinks what ne'er was, nor is, nor e'er will be.
—Pope, *Essay on Criticism*

Pope added:

To err is human, to forgive, divine.

(Any suggestions for the improvement of this work, sent in care of the publisher, will be gratefully received.)

?phulax: watcher, guard. Gk *phulaktron:* guard; *phulaktrion:* watchman's post; later, amulet. E, *phylacterian, phylactery, phylactic. phylaxis. anaphylaxis:* unusual susceptibility, especially to protein, coined by Charles Richet, French physiologist, in 1893. *calciphylaxis. Phylactrocarp:* literally, fruit case. In wider use is the word *prophylactic.* Isaac Watts, in his *Logick* (1725), observed: "Medicine is justly distributed into prophylactick, or the art of preserving health; and therapeutick, or the art of restoring health."

phylacteries are small leather boxes containing four texts of Scriptures—Exodus 13:1–10, 11–16; Deuteronomy 6:4–9, 11:13–21—written in Hebrew on vellum, one worn on the left arm, near the heart, and one on the forehead, by pious Jews during the weekday morning prayer, not on the Sabbath. The Hebrew word for these is *tephillin,* possibly related to Hebr *naphal:* he prostrated himself. They are set as "a reminder of the obligation to keep the law." Scott refers to them in *Kenilworth.*

The *mezuzah* (Hebr: doorpost), in a case at the right of the entrance to the home of a pious Jew (or to every room), is a tiny scroll with Deuteronomy 6:4–9 and 11:13–21 printed on one side and the divine name *Shaddi* on the other. There should be a space or transparency. so that *Shaddi* is seen. The Deuteronomy passage begins *Shema:* Hear . . . (O Israel, the Lord is our God, the Lord is One). When entering or leaving, the pious Jew touches the mezuzah with his finger, puts the finger to his lips, and repeats Psalm 121:8: "The Lord will keep your going out and your coming in from this time forth and for evermore." Israel Zangwill, in *The Children of the Ghetto* (1892), says: "They don't kiss the Mezuzah often in that house—the impious crew."

Later the word *phylactery* came into more general use to mean an amulet, a charm. Thus Benjamin H. Malkin in his 1809 translation of *Gil Blas:* "Good books . . . a never-failing phylactery against the blue devils" (*contre l'ennui*).

A reminder: "to thoughtful observers the whole world is a phylactery. . . . Happy are they who make their phylacteries speak in their lives"—Sir Thomas Browne, *Christian Morals* (1682).

p(i)lo: hair (see *pel VI*). *pilar;* the *pile* of a carpet; *pilose; depilatory. pileum; pileus:* hairy cap of a fungus. *pelage:* coat of a mammal, hair or fur. *horripilation:* hair standing on end.

peel, to strip off, first meant to deprive of hair, as Delilah betrayed Samson. In the 16th c. a *pilpate* was a tonsured priest; in the 17th, he was a *pilledow* (pronounced *daw*)—both were terms of scorn. Into the 19th c., used by Burns and Carlyle, *pilgarlic* was a belittling term for a *baldpate.* Sir Edmund Gosse in *Critical Kit-Kats* (1893), uses the adjective figuratively: "It is a pilgarlicky mind that is satisfied with saying 'I like you, Dr. Fell;/ The reason why I cannot tell.'" Martial, in A.D. 85, in his Epigram 32, blazed this trail: "I do not like you, Hylas; I cannot tell you why" (and on it ran). Threatened with expulsion from Oxford in 1683, Thomas Brown was told by Dean John Fell that he'd be pardoned if he could paraphrase impromptu Martial's Epigram 32. At once he responded:

I do not love thee, Dr. Fell,
The reason why I cannot tell,
But this I know, and know full well,
I do not love thee, Dr. Fell.

Coleridge, Carlyle, and Agatha Christie (in *Murder Is Easy* [1938]) are among those that have quoted this jingle; but whether they use *like* or *love,* they always use the negative. I cannot tell why Edmund Gosse untied the *not.*

Early balls were made of animal hair packed into hide; hence L *pila:* ball. E *pill:* first, a little sphere of medicine; its diminutive, *pilule. piles:* ball-like hemorrhoids. *pelt:* first, to strike with a ball. *complot* was first a winding into a ball; then, figuratively, a bunching together to plan activity; later shortened to *plot.* By a similar transference, *platoon:* a large ball, came to mean a gathered group of soldiers. OFr, *pellet;* Sp, *pelota. pelon:* hairless; but *pellon:* fur riding coat. Fr, *poilu:* a hairy (tough) soldier.

In tragic life, God wot,
No villain need be! Passions spin the plot:
We are betrayed by what is false within.
—George Meredith, *Modern Love* (1862)

From sloughing the i came *plush* and *pluck*. Originally *pluck* meant to cut or tear off the hair or wool, as sheep in early days were plucked, not shorn. Then, the feathers plucked off fowl; then, the heart, liver, and lights of game, plucked by the huntsmen and given as reward to the dogs; plucked also by farmers for food. Because it was considered to be the seat of courage, *pluck* came in 19th c. sportswriters' cant to be used of someone courageous ("heartful," from Fr *coeur:* heart), meaning courageous persistence in spite of difficulty, the main sense of the noun *pluck* today. The persistence of folk physiology is apparent in the fact that writers in search of variety have gone right back to the viscera to say "That guy's got guts" or more affectedly to speak of intestinal fortitude. See *pleus.*

With art, we do not pluck; we gaze.

Gk *berron:* shaggy. *burl. burlesque:* first, flocks of wool; then, figuratively, trifles, nonsense. L *burra:* "hairy," coarse linen, used as table cover; hence *bureau, bureaucracy, bureaucrat,* etc.

From the meaning shreds, *pillage* was applied to the spoils of war; whence OE *piller:* thief. And from the 15th into the 19th c., *caterpillar* (: hairy little cat) was also applied to a plunderer, often with a contrast, as by Scott: "We have become the caterpillars of the island, instead of its pillars." *caterpillar tread,* of tractor and army tank, is named for the manner of its movement.

cat (L *cattus,* feminine *catta*) may be African in origin; the cat was worshiped in Egypt; see *kam.* Dick Whittington's cat, sent as his contribution to a merchant ship bound for Africa, brought him a fortune; as the churchbells had foretold, he was thrice Lord Mayor of London. The real Richard Whittington (d. 1423) became the subject of several legends. Skeptics have suggested that the animal *cat* came as a folk fable, fashioned from Whittington's work as an *acatour* (OE: provider of provisions; the provider for the royal household became an *achatour;* whence E *cater, caterer*). But Whittington was not a caterer; he was a mercer; he made loans to Kings Henry IV and Henry V; he left funds for homes for the aged, and for the rebuilding of Newgate Prison (see *kuon*); and his property, still held by the Mercers Society, is today worth millions of pounds.

In 1760 the anonymous *Life and Adventures of a Cat* became very popular; its opening, "Tom the Cat is born of poor but honest parents," is the source of the name *tomcat* for the male—and of Bertrand Russell's remark that the cleverest dog cannot tell you that he is born of poor but honest parents.

There are a number of words based on *cat,* as *catboat, cat brier.* Old, deceitful marketing practices are caught in the phrases that if you "buy a pig in a poke" you may open it and "let the cat out of the bag." The diminutive of *cat* is *kitten,* also *kitling* and the pet name *Kitty. to kittle* is to give birth. By metathesis *kittle* became *tickle,* which has a sexual connotation. *OED* lists 7 *cat* phrases and 42 combinations, then details over a dozen more, as *cat and dog* (raining *cats and dogs*), *catcall, caterwaul. cat-o'-nine-tails:* a short-handled whip with nine leather thongs (the fierce ones tipped with lead); see *ane. catsup*—so spelled by Swift, also *catchup,* but now more usually *ketchup*—is our form of a Chinese word first meaning fish brine.

Humorously, perhaps, from the caterwauling squeak of a poorly played fiddle, came *catgut;* but the intestines used for strings were never from the cat; they were from sheep, horses, and donkeys. *catlap,* a drinker's contemptuous term for a weak drink, may have been suggested by Shakespeare's remark, in *The Tempest,* ii, 1: "They'll take suggestion as a cat laps milk." Of plants, *catkin, cattail, catmint;* in the U.S., *catnip.* Washington Irving, in *Salmagundi* (1824), spoke of "the healing qualities of hoarhound, catnip, and pennyroyal." A *catnap* may also help. The finest *cat's-eyes* come from Ceylon (now Sri Lanka) and Malabar.

Arabic for Ceylon was *Serendib;* see *bher I.* Try not to be a *cat's-paw,* to pluck the monkey's roasted nuts from the fire.

pip. Imitative. *peep.* "Not a peep out of you!" *pipe. pigeon.* Gael, *pibroch.* Gc, *fife.*

?pippa: *pepper.* Skr *pippala:* the bo tree (see *bheudh*). *peepul:* sacred tree. *pepper* (*l.r* shift). *salt-and-pepper:* (1) cloth woven of dark and light threads; (2) human hair beginning to turn gray. See *sal I.* From *pepper* came *pep:* vigor, as though stimulated by peppery food. *OED* lists 39 words, and details 24 more, as *peppercorn, peppermint.* Probably *pimpernel,* although this may be a French shift from L *bipinnella, bipennis:* two-winged, from the shape of the leaf. *The Scarlet Pimpernel* (1905) is the title of a once very popular novel by the Baroness Orczy, and the *nom de guerre* of the novel's hero, a seeming fop, Sir Percy Blakeney, who was actually an astute and active rescuer of aristocrats condemned in the French Revolution.

The *Pippa* (short for *Philippa,* feminine of *Philip;* see *bhili*) in Browning's poem *Pippa Passes* is an innocent girl who, as she walks, sings songs that change the lives of persons that hear them; her best-known song is:

The year's at the Spring,
And day's at the morn;
Morning's at seven;
The hillside's dew-pearled.
The lark's on the wing;
The snail's on the thorn;
God's in his heaven
—All's right with the world.

piss. Imitative; also in Fr, *pisser; pissoir.* This outdoor public urinal is also called a *vespasian,* after the Roman emperor *Vespasian,* who sold the accumulated liquid to launderers for their bleaching. When Titus, Vespasian's son, objected, the father held some of the gold toward him and made the since then famous remark: "Money doesn't smell." Christopher Morley, on a tour of London pubs that had survived the German blitz, came upon "the loveliest of all London's vespasians, opposite the door of the Anchor"—across the Thames from St. Paul's.

pissabed: farmer's term for the dandelion; see *leo.* Flaubert, in an 1887 letter to playwright Ernest Feydeau, said of the pyramids: "Jackals piss at their feet, and the bourgeois climb them."

Pope, egoist though he was, kept the *i* out of the title of his epigram "To a Lady Who P–st at the Tragedy of Cato," which indicates how politics may affect theatregoers:

While maudlin Whigs deplored their Cato's fate,
Still with dry eyes the Tory Celia sate;
But while her pride forbids her tears to flow
The gushing waters find a vent below.

One must hope that she was equipped with a *bourdalou:* a portable urinal, such as French ladies wore beneath their gowns while listening to the long but stern and moving sermons of Louis *Bourdaloue,* court preacher to "the Sun King," Louis XIV. In those days there were no benches in the cathedral; worshipers stood. Nor did women wear anything underneath their petticoats until the mid-19th c.; drawers were first donned, less for sanitary than for provocative reason, in the French demimonde.

?pius: devout. L *pius. pious. pietism. piety. pity. piteous, pitiful, pitiless. pittance. impiety, impious, expiate, inexpiable.* L *piare, piatum. appease. piacular.* It,

Pietà: representation of the mournful Mary holding the body of Jesus. Fr, *mont-de-piété:* pawnshop.

plab. Imitative. Gc, *flap. flabby,* earlier *flappy.* Also *flip, flippant; fillip. flop. flabbergasted:* a blend of *flabby* and *aghast.* "I have had ample sufficiency; any more would be flippity-flop" (a jocose Midwestern way, at least in my father's time, of refusing another portion of food).

plak: strike. Gk *plektron; plessein. plectrum; plessor. plexor. apoplexy;* the Romans translated Gk *apoplexia* as *sideratio:* struck by the stars, which in their courses "affect human lives." *paraplegia. plague. Plegadis:* genus of birds, the ibis, with striking beak. *Symplegades:* the Clashing Rocks, cliffs at the entrance to the Hellespont, which in Greek mythology crushed whatever was caught between them. *Aplectrum* (*a* negative): genus of orchis, the puttyroot, without spurs.

L nasalized *plangere, planctum:* to strike one's breast, as in mourning. *plain, plaint, plaintiff, plaintive. plangent. complain, complainant, complaint.* Things struck off may move away; hence *plankton* (see *ie*). Gc, *flaw:* a sudden blow of wind. *fling.*

"When complaints are freely heard, deeply considered, and speedily reformed, then is the utmost bound of civil liberty attained that wise men look for"—Milton, *Areopagitica* (1644), which also contains the words: "Give me the liberty to know, to utter, and to argue freely, according to conscience, above all liberties."

?plaud: beat the hands. Perhaps an offshoot of the preceding. *plaudits, applaud. applause. plosion, explode, explosion, implosion. plausible:* first, worthy of applause; hence acceptable.

pleik: to tear. Gc, *flay. fleck. flitch.* Probably *flesh. the Dunmow flitch:* a side of bacon given, in Essex, England, to any couple that on the first anniversary of marriage can swear that they have lived in perfect harmony and fidelity; initiated in 1244 by Robert Fitz-Walter of *Dunmow* Manor, the custom continues.

plek: bend, fold; braid, twist, weave. This root has two main offshoots, changing from *p* to *f* to *b,* following Grimm's law for labials.

(I) The *p* forms. From Greek, a number of rhetorical terms. *ploce:* a weaving of repetitions through a passage. *symploce:* a combination of *anaphora:* repetition at the beginning of successive units, and *epistrophe:* repetition at the end. *anadiplosis:* folding back; the beginning of a unit repeats the preceding end; Puttenham, in *The Art of Poesie* (1589), gives an example: "Comfort it is to have a wife, Wife chaste and wise." And John Wesley in 1791 instructs: "The word repeated is pronounced the second time louder and stronger than the first."

simple, simplify, simplicity. simpleton. See *dhe II; sem I. O Sancta Simplicitas!* exclaimed Jan Huss on seeing an old peasant bring a faggot for the fire by which Huss was being burned at the stake, 1415. Gathering indignation started the Hussite War, 1419–34, which kept Bohemia free from Catholic domination until 1620.

A *diploma* was first a twofold (once-folded) sheet. A *diplomat* carried an official diploma of authority. Thus, via Fr, *diplomacy; OED* has 14 words related to this art. The prefix *diplo* occurs in many scientific terms; *OED* lists 31, as *diplocardiac:* having the two parts of the heart separate (as in birds and mammals), and details 11, as *diploidion:* an ancient Greek woman's garment. *diplopia:* double vision.

aplotomy (*a* negative): simple incision. *aplome:* a simple mineral, as andradite. The negative is actually Gk *ἁ, ha:* single, simple, as in *haploid; OED* gives 12 words beginning *haplo,* as *haplocardiac, haplomorphic. haplography* is the omission of one or more letters in writing (see *lipogram,* under *leip II*); its opposite, the repetition of letters, is *dittography.*

haplology, sounding only once what should have been sounded twice, has contributed to language change, as in *calamitous* (L *calamitatosus*), *fastidious* (*fastitidium*), *pacifist* (*pacificist*), *surgery* (*chirurgerie*), *viper* (*vivipara*), *England* (*Angleland*); also *formicide, homily, idolatry, palmistry, tragicomedy,* and more. Some doublings remain; thus *repetitive* did not become *repetive;* nor did *philology* become *philogy.* The opposite of *haplology* (which also retains the doubling) is *epenthesis:* insertion of an extra sound; this also changed a number of words, as *beloved, blackamoor.* Both *peasant* and *tyrant* have an added final *t.*

Fourfold versions of one text, presented together, are called *tetrapla;* thus Origen, in the 3d c., set together four Greek translations of the Old Testament. Also *hexapla, octapla,* etc. The secular book most often published in this fashion is the *Rubáiyát* [Quatrains] of the astronomer-astrologer Gheyas Od-Din Abu Ol-Fath Umar Ebn Ebrahim Ol-Khayyám (*khayyám:* tent-maker; probably his father's profession) (d. 1122), more briefly, *Omar Khayyám.* The *Rubáiyát* has appeared in two pentaplas (both with English, French, and German): one adding Arabic and Persian (1334, 1955); the other adding Italian and Danish (1898). It has also appeared in a tetrapla containing four variant editions of Edward FitzGerald's translation—which offers the reader more quatrains than the original.

Symplocarpus: fruit folded together; a genus of plants, the skunk cabbage. *Symplocos:* genus, the sweetleaf.

L *plectere, plexus:* fold, weave. *plexus. solar plexus:* network of nerves behind the belly, "sun" of the abdominal nervous system. *complexion:* originally the temperament, determined by the intermingling of the four humours—hot, cold, dry, moist—in the human body; then, as betrayed by the coloring of the face.

complex. Oedipus complex: incorrectly named, the "complex" is explained as the jealously close attachment of a son to the mother who has nursed and reared him; Oedipus was separated from his parents at birth; when grown, he unwittingly married the stranger who had borne but not bred him. *perplex, duplex, triplex, multiplex. OED* has 10 relevant words beginning *plex,* and 21 beginning *pli.*

plat, pleach, pleat, plait; pliable, pliant. plight, as in *sorry plight* (the *gh* from blending with *plight:* pledge, exercise, from OE *plegan,* whence also *play*). *ply, apply, application.* Fr, *appliqué. comply, compliant, reply,* from the blank sheet folded in, for response, in early letters. *deploy. imply,* and its doublet, *employ. two-ply,* etc. *plywood. display, splay, splayfoot.*

complicate, duplicate, explication, implicate; replica, replicate, supplicate. suppliant. supple, supplement; complement, compliment. explicit. exploit. L *Explicitus est:* It is unrolled; words at the end of a scroll, as *Finis* at the close of a book. (Often, as with the Jewish Torah in the synagogue, the scroll is on two rods, so that it rolls onto one as it rolls off the other—the two rods being held apart to leave a section for reading—and thus is always protected.) *complicity, accomplice; duplicity. triple, quadruple, quintuplets,* etc. *decuple, centuple, multiple, multiplication. Plectognathi:* twisted jaws; order of fish.

(II) The *f* forms. L *flectere, flexum:* bend. *flex* (your muscles). *flexible, inflexible. flexor, flexion, flexuous. flexure, circumflex* (ˆ). *inflection, reflect, retroflex.*

flask: first, a bottle plaited around, as now for Chianti wine. *flagon.* It, *fiasco:* first, a spoiled flask, used for cheap liquor. *flax,* its fibers woven. Possibly *floss.* Fr, *fauteuil,* Gm, *faldstool:* a folding stool. From the Germanic base, *fol,* came E *fold, unfold, manifold, refold, twofold, threefold,* etc.

(III) The *b* forms. Sp, *dubloon, doblon;* Port *dobra:* gold coins. Fr, *doublure:*

doubled, with a lining. *double, double entendre* (Fr *double entente*): twofold meaning. Gm, *Doppelgänger:* one's double; also Englished as *doubleganger.*

Thoreau, in *Walden* (1853), perhaps remembering Occam's razor as he ponders beside Walden Pond, gives this good advice: "Simplify, simplify." But Oscar Wilde, in *The Importance of Being Earnest* (1895), demurs: "Truth is never pure, and rarely simple."

pleu: flow. From ever-flowing came *Pluto,* lord of the underworld and all the treasures of the earth; his name is enhanced as *Ploutodores:* enhancer of wealth. *Pluto,* smallest and farthest planet, comes after *Neptune,* eighth planet, and Roman god of the waters. Just after Pluto was discovered, the chemical element therefore named *plutonium* was isolated; it comes in the series of elements right after *neptunium* (see *el 93; el 94; nebh*). Jupiter *Pluvius* was Roman king of the gods (and heaven) as rain-bringer and wielder of the lightning bolt. Hence *pluvial, pluvious. plover,* the rain bird. *plutonic* is used of igneous rock, water, etc., deep underground. *Pluto,* code name for the pipes supplying petrol from Britain to the Allies in France during 1944, is an acrostic of *P*ipe *l*ine *u*nder *t*he *o*cean.

By metathesis came *pulmonary* and the *pulmo-* compounds: relating to the lungs. When tossed into water after a fowl is plucked, the heart, liver, etc., sink; the lungs float; hence they are called *the lights. OED* lists 17 and details 16 *pulmo-* words, including *Pulmonata:* order of mollusks, and *Pulmonaria:* order of arachnids.

Germanic shift to *f* (*flug*) led to E *flow. fly,* action and creature; *flying* is flowing in air. *flight; fleet,* adjective and noun; for *flea,* see *plou. float, flotilla; flotsam* (see *ie*). *flit; fluster. flutter.* Combined with the idea of *feather* (see *pet I; pleus*), which helps a bird to fly, came *fledge. fledgling; flèche; fletcher:* maker of arrows; remaining as a name. By metathesis again (*flug* to *fugl*) came *fowl; Vogel,* the *v* sounded *f,* is German for *bird.*

In Gaelic came the form *linn:* a stream, or a ravine where a stream flows; hence *Brooklyn. Lincoln:* colony by the stream. *Dublin* was once a muddy stretch (see *dher*) along the River Liffy, which, in *Finnegans Wake,* as two washerwomen talk across its endless and widening flow, James Joyce extends to the "Misses Liffy" that divides the U.S. *metheglin* is spiced mead, which among the Gaelic warriors flowed freely; see *medhu.*

"However far a bird may fly, it takes its tail along"—warning to those that hope to change their nature in a new environment.

pleus: pluck. OL *plusma,* L *pluma:* feather. *plumage, plumate, plume, plumose; plumule.* Gc, *fleece.* From shearing a sheep came the sense of fleecing a person, seen also in the slang *to skin* someone: to strip of money or property. For *pluck,* see *pilo.*

plor: search out; exclaim, cry out. Partly imitative. *deplore, deplorable. explore, exploration.*

plou: flea. Probably Gk *psulla. psylla:* plant louse. *psillid. Psyllidae:* family of plant lice.

L, *Pulex. puceron. puce:* flea color. In French, *puce* means flea; whence the ironic query (instead of an answer) to a person seeking absurdly minute details: *Comment peut-on voir si une puce est pucelle?* (which loses much in translation): How can one tell whether a flea's a virgin? *La Pucelle* is used of Joan of Arc. For *pucelle,* diminutive of *pullus:* young animal, see *pou; ane.*

fleabane; fleabite. flea market, especially large in Paris. *flea circus,* a 19th and 20th c. sideshow. The flea can jump 30 times its own height, can draw 80 times its own weight. See quotation under *perd.*

A fly and a flea in a flue
Were imprisoned; so what could they do?
"Let us fly", said the flea;
"Let us flee," said the fly;
So they flew through a flaw in the flue.

(There are two more long vowels; *flay* and *flow* must be aggrieved at their omission.)

?plumbum: lead. Gk *molubdos. molybdenum* (see *el 42*). L *plumbum. plumb. plumber; plumbago. plummet, plunge. aplomb. plumb line.* The Latin and Greek forms may have come from Iberian; lead was mined in Spain as early as 2000 B.C. The Romans had standard sizes of lead pipes for their aqueducts, and also used lead in making counterfeit silver coins. Their word *plumbum* gives English the abbreviation *Pb* for the chemical element lead; see *el 82. OED* lists 8 words beginning *plumbo,* and details 27 relevant words beginning *plumb,* as *plumbisolvent, plumbless* (depths).

In the Bible, Amos 7:7–8, we read: "Behold, the Lord stood upon a wall built with a plumb line, with a plumb line in His hand. And the Lord said to me: 'Amos, what seest thou?' And I said, 'A plumb line.' Then the Lord said 'Behold, I am setting a plumb line in the midst of my people Israel; I will never again pass by them.'"

Generations later, in *A Truthful Song,* Rudyard Kipling observed:

How very little, since things were made,
Things have altered in the building trade!
Your glazing is new, and your plumbing's strange,
But otherwise I observe no change;
And in less than a month, if you do as I bid,
I'll learn you to build me a Pyramid!

pneu: breathe. This is a nasalized form of *pleu,* imitative of a strong exhalation. From Greek came *pneuma:* the vital spirit, *pneumatic, pneumonia, pneumodynamics,* and other *pneumo-* compounds; and medical terms such as *apnea, dyspnea, eupnea:* healthy breathing, *hypernea.* From this root, via OE *fneasan,* came the (again imitative) *sneeze.*

po(i): drink. Gk *symposium:* first, a coming together to drink. L *potare, potum. potion, potable. potatory, potation. poison;* "Name your poison." Russ, *pirog.* Gc, *beer, beverage; bib, bibulous; imbibe, imbibition.*

potato is from American Indian (Taino) *batata.* The sweet variety of the tuber was brought to Europe from South America; the white potato came from Sir Walter Ralegh's Virginia; the first planter in England tried to eat the flowers. By the end of the 17th c. the "Irish potato" was Ireland's major crop; its blight in 1845–46 led to the migration of many Irish to the United States. The brothers A. W. and J. C. Hare, in *Guesses at Truth* (1827), remind us that "every Irishman, the saying goes, has a potato in his head." We are told that there are 240 ways of preparing potatoes.

When first introduced into England the potato was, like some other "roots," thought to be of aphrodisiac virtue; hence its inclusion in Sir John Falstaff's lascivious cry (*The Merry Wives,* v, 3): "Let the sky rain potatoes, let it thunder to the tune of Greensleeves, hail kissing-comfits, and snow eringoes." (My Lady Greensleeves is the unfaithful wife in the popular ballad. Kissing-comfits are breath-sweeteners. *eryngo:* a sweetmeat made from the candied root of the sea holly, also deemed an aphrodisiac.) One can understand why Mrs. Page explains, of the women's plot against the obese and libidinous Falstaff:

Against such lewdsters and their lechery
Those that betray them do no treachery.

Deus sit propitius isti potatori is the last line of a medieval Goliardic song; the stanza may be Englished thus:

My uttermost desire is in a tavern to die,
So that in my final hour I shall not be dry;
And may the angel choir sing a liquid chant:
"God, keep the wine aflowing for this bon vivant!"

poieo: make. Gk, via L and Fr, *onomatopoetic. poem. poet:* maker. See *kuei II. poetaster:* a taster, who never drank deep of the fount of inspiration. *poetize; poetry.* John Aubrey (d. 1697), in *Brief Lives,* records that when George Withers was suspected of treason, John Denham begged King Charles not to hang him, for as long as Withers lived, Denham would not be the worst poet in England. The king acquiesced.

pol: thumb. L *pollex, pollicem. pollex, pollical.* The thumb, opposed to the four fingers, permits monkeys and men to grasp. *pollice trunco:* with thumb cut off, to avoid military service; hence *poltroon.* This derivation, put forward by the French scholar Claude de Surmaise in the 17th c., is probably folk etymology, but it passed into falconry; a *poltroon* is a trained bird of prey with the talons of its hind toes clipped, so that it will bring its catch back to the hunter untorn. *OED* suggests that *poltroon:* coward, is from It *poltro:* lazy good-for-nothing, from an assumed *poltro:* couch. It seems more likely that it is from It *poltrone:* colt, which is timid, always shying away; see *pou.*

timid is from L *timere:* to fear. For the protest in the *Aeneid, Timeo Danaos et dona ferentes,* see *keu I.*

?popul: people. L *S P Q R: Senatus Populusque Romanus:* the Senate and the Roman people; letters on the standard of the Republic. *people; populace; popular, populous, population; depopulate, repopulate; unpopular. public, publican; republican,* etc. *publication, publicist, publicity; publish.* Sp, *pueblo.*

"Publish and be damned!"—the Duke of Wellington.

porko I: young pig. *pork; porcine. porpoise:* pigfish. It *porcellana;* relating to a sow; hence the *cowrie:* Venus shell, from its resemblance to a sow's vulva; from the hard shell, applied by Marco Polo to Chinese ware, via Fr, came *porcelain.* Du, *aardvark:* earth pig, a burrowing animal; muzzled hogs have long been used in Spain to root up truffles. Gc, *farrow.*

porko II. Gc, *furrow.* Tennyson, in *The Princess* (1847), vii:

Now sleeps the crimson petal, now the white;
Nor waves the cypress in the palace walk,
Nor winks the gold fin in the porphyry font:
The firefly wakens: waken thou with me . . .
Now slides the silent meteor on, and leaves
A silent furrow, like thy thoughts in me.

Coleridge, in *The Ancient Mariner* half a century earlier, was more literal:

The fair breeze blew, the white foam flew,
    The furrow followed free;
We were the first that ever burst
    Into that silent sea.

porpur: purple. Possibly from a Semitic source. *purple;* in heraldry *purpure. purpureal, purpurine.* Gk *porphura:* shellfish, of the genus *Murex;* the royal purple dye is from the fish. *Porphyra:* genus of purple algae. *porphyrio:* the purple coot, or water hen. *porphyre:* a small serpent; "most beautiful and well-coloured," wrote Robert Greene, 1684, "but being toothless hurteth none but himself." *porphin, porphyroid, porphyrine, porphyrate. porphyrite; porphyry. OED* has 28 words and 5 combinations beginning *porphyr;* and 6 columns for *purple* and its derivatives, as *purply, purple fish.* R. W. Brown, in *Composition of Scientific Words* (1954), under *purple,* adds 7 names of plants or animals.

One born while one's father was emperor in Byzantium (later Constantinople, now Istanbul) was *porphyrogenite:* born in the porphyry-lined room of the Imperial Palace (whence the "imperial purple"), a term first applied to the patron of arts and letters Emperor Constantine VII (905–959), who was poisoned by his son and successor, Romanus II. The learned Anna Comnena (1083–1148) was *porphyrogenita;* after an unsuccessful conspiracy against her brother, Emperor John II, she retired to a convent, where she wrote the historical *Alexiad.* The two terms were later applied to children of reigning monarchs elsewhere.

Queen Gertrude, in *Hamlet,* iv, 7, telling of Ophelia's drowning, relates:

. . . fantastic garlands did she make
Of crowflowers, nettles, daisies, and long purples,
That liberal shepherds give a grosser name,
But our cold maids do dead men's fingers call them.

Among the "grosser" names is *wanton widow,* from which Queen Gertrude well might flinch; but her words are an excellent example of emblematic speech (see *guel II*), the items representing the situation:

crowflowers	*nettles*	*daisies*	*long purples*
fayre mayde	stung to the quick	virgin bloom	cold hand of death

Porphyrian may mean "relating to the Neo-Platonic *Porphyrius"* (233–306), the opponent of Christianity who developed the *Porphyrian tree,* tracing mankind from primal substance; in the skeleton herewith, the attributes of man are listed first in each opposed pair:

Substance	
Corporeal	Incorporeal
Body	
Animate	Inanimate
Living	
Sensible	Insensible
Animal	
Rational	Irrational
Man	

This pattern has been replaced by the more precise taxonomic grouping mentioned in Notes on Usage. Roman Emperor Constantine I in 325 ruled that the Arians were Porphyrians, heretics all. Abraham Cowley in 1656 held high

That right Porphyrian tree which did true logic show;
Each leaf did learned notions give,
And the apples were demonstrative.

Thomas Hood, in a parody of *The Raven,* called *Ravings,* "by E. A Poe–t," included:

I sighed, for my feelings were gushing
Round Mnemosyne's porphyry throne,

Like lava liquescent lay gushing,
And rose to the porphyry throne—
To the filigree footstool were gushing
That stands on the steps of the throne.

poti: lord; power. Skr *patih:* master. *padishah. shah. pasha. Prajapati:* Lord of creation. Gk, *Poseidon:* master of earth; god of earthquakes and the sea. *despot:* first, master of the house; see *dem.* L *potere* (*pot-esse;* see *es*), *posse:* be able. *potent, potentate, ignipotent, impotent, prepotent, omnipotent, plenipotential. ventripotent,* as a glutton. *potential. power, powerful; possible, possibly; possession.* Fr, *puissant. posse comitatus:* power of the county, legal phrase empowering a sheriff to appoint deputies, especially in the American "Wild West," to corral frontier "bad men" (cattle rustlers and horse thieves); the group thus appointed was called a *posse.*

Carlyle, in his *French Revolution* (1837), i, 1, declared: "France was long a despotism tempered by epigrams." Churchill, in a speech of 12 Nov. 1936, stated that the English government "go on in strange paradox, decided only to be undecided, resolved to be irresolute, adamant for drift, solid for fluidity, all-powerful for impotence."

"Books, we are told, propose to *instruct* or to *amuse.* Indeed! . . . not pleasure, but power. All that is literature seeks to communicate power; all that is not literature, to communicate knowledge"—De Quincey, *Letters to a Young Man.*

pou: little. Hindi, *rajput:* literally, king's son. Gk *pais, paidos:* child. *pedagogue:* leader of a child; first, a slave that escorted a boy to school (see *ag*). *pederast* (Gk *eran:* lust, related to *Eros:* god of desire). *pediatrician; pedant* (for *pedantocracy,* see *deph*). *orthopedics. encyclop(a)edia.* (Note that L *pes, pedis:* foot, formed many English words; see *ped.*) Via It *paggio, page:* a young gentleman serving a nobleman or lady, in early training toward knighthood.

Ho, pretty page with the dimpled chin
That never has known the barber's shear,
All your wish is woman to win,
This is the way that boys begin.
Wait till you come to Forty Year.
—Thackeray, *The Age of Wisdom*

Several additional forms in Latin are:

(1) *parvus:* small, little. *OED* lists 6 words beginning *parvi,* as *parvipotent,* and details 4, as *parvitude. parvoline:* a foul-smelling, oily liquid from decaying mackerel and horse flesh, so named, said G. Williams, who coined the word in 1855, because of its "small volatility." It was the first ptomaine analyzed. *parvis:* clear ground in front of a church; shortened from *paradise:* an enclosed garden, the original name of the forecourt of St. Peter's in Rome. The parvis of Notre Dame de Paris was recently excavated, revealing the remains of a still-earlier cathedral.

(2) *puer:* boy, *puerile; puerperal. pubescent:* developing pubic hair, beginning to mature (physically). Thus also *puberty, pubes, pubic, puberulent.*

(3) *putus:* boy. It, *putti:* little Cupids in paintings or statuary.

(4) *pupa:* girl, doll. *pupa, pupil, puppet; puppy.* Fr, *pucelle;* see *plou.*

(5) *paucus:* few, little. *paucity.* It, *poco.*

(6) *parum:* too little. *paraffin:* of little affinity with other substances; L *finis:* border, end.

(7) *pauper:* of small means, *poor. pauper, poverty, impoverish.*

(8) *paulus:* small. *Paul:* the little one. *Pauline, Paulinus. pusillus:* very small. *pusillanimous. paulopost future:* a tense in Greek grammar, picked up by English writers to mean in the very near future (but sometimes with the implication that it's a dream future, really never); used, e.g., by Shelley, Southey, and Thoreau; Stevenson spoke of a *paulopast.* Lowell, in *A Fable for Critics* (1848), said:

Here comes Dana, abstractedly loitering along,
Involved in a paulo-post-future of song,
Who'll be going to write what'll never be written.
Till the Muse, ere he think of it, gives him the mitten.

(9) *pullus:* young animal. *polecate, poulard, pullet, poult, poulterer, poultry. pony. poltroon:* one that is as timid as a young animal; but see *pol.* From *pullus,* via It diminutive *pulcina:* chick hen, came the further diminutive *Punchinello,* shortened to *Punch,* the little fellow that trounces Judy in the puppet show, but gets his comeuppance at the end.

Gc, *few, filly, foal, fowl.* Possibly *catchpole:* officer that arrested debtors, called *chicken-catcher* in scorn; but this may be a folkchange from the earlier *catchpoll:* head-catcher.

"Poverty has strange bedfellows"—Bulwer-Lytton, *The Caxtons* (1850)

prai: beloved, hence precious; hence also at peace with, allowed to do as one pleases; thus applied to a free member of the community, as opposed to a slave. Skr *priya:* dear, precious. *sapphire.* LL *exfridare:* remove from peace; Fr *effrayer,* E (*a* negative) *affray. afraid.* Then, the *a* dropped, *fray, fright, frighten.* Gc *fridu,* Gm *Friede:* peace.

free, freedom. freemason is folkchanged from Fr *frère maçon. friend* first meant a loving one.

frith—by metathesis also *firth*—first meant peace, then freedom from molestation; hence enclosed ground, as pasture land or a game preserve. Hence also, historically, *frithburger:* freeman; *frith-guild:* a guild of protectors of the peace. *frithstool, fridstool:* a stone stool at the altar of a church, or beside the figure of a saint, which afforded inviolable sanctuary; also called *freedstool.*

The word *free* takes up 10 columns in *OED,* and 14 more are given to its combinations, as *freeborn, Free Church, free-handed, freelance, free press, freethinker, free will* (vs. determinism, predestination). *freehold,* used of property, especially in England, means owned without restriction, not leased; it is also used figuratively, as by Samuel Rutherford in a letter of 9 Sept. 1637: "The whole army of the redeemed sit rent-free in heaven. . . . We are all freeholders." (In 1661, Rutherford's book *Rex Lex* [1644] was burned by the hangman.)

A *belfry* was originally a movable (free) tower to place against the wall of a besieged city; for the first syllable, see *bheregh.* The *r.l* shift came by association with *bell,* as the tower came to be used for a church chime detached from the church building, as the Campanile on Plaza San Marco, Venice. The name *Campanile,* from the metal the bell was made of, found in *Campania,* Italy, is derived from L *campus:* field; whence also *camp, campus, campaign, champignon, champagne, champion, campanulate. encamp; decamp.* From LL *excampare:* leave the field of battle, came *scamper,* then *scamp. champerty* (Fr *champart:* part of a field); first, division of the produce of a field; now, an (illegal) bargain to share winnings in a lawsuit.

Freda: peaceful lass; *Frederick:* peaceful ruler; *Humphrey:* peace through power; *Geoffrey:* peace in the land; *Siegfried:* peace by conquest; *Godfrey:* peace of God. Norse, *Freya* or *Frija;* and *Frigg* (sometimes deemed the one wife of Odin, sometimes considered two, with him leaving the one for the other):

goddess of love; hence *Friday,* translating L *Venus dies.* Also Norse was *Tuesday:* from *Tui,* god of war (the Roman war god *Mars* gave French *mardi,* as in *Mardi gras;* also the month *March;* see *dei* and *ker III*); *Wednesday:* from *Woden, Odin,* chief Norse god; and *Thursday:* from *Thor,* whence also *thunder. Saturday* was named after the Roman god *Saturn.* For *Sunday,* see *sauel. Monday* is the moon's day (see *me IV*). Du, *freebooter;* by folkchange *filibuster.*

"I only ask to be free. The butterflies are free. Mankind will surely not deny to Harold Skimpole what it concedes to the butterflies"—Dickens, *Bleak House. Butterflies Are Free* (1969) is the title of a moving play by Leonard Gershe about a blind man.

Seneca observed that "the comfort of having a friend may be taken away, but not that of having had one."

"Anacharsis, coming to Athens, knocked at Solon's door, and told him that he, being a stranger, was come to be his guest, and contract a friendship with him; and Solon replying 'It is better to make friends at home', Anacharsis replied, 'Then you that are at home make friendship with me'"—Plutarch, *Parallel Lives, Solon,* ca. A.D. 100.

?pres: press. L *premere, pressum. press, compress, depress, impress, oppress, repress, suppress. pressure.* The impression of the printing press; hence *the press:* newspapers, included in *the media.* Hence also *print,* via Fr, from L *imprimere. reprimand. pregnant:* weighty, cogent, may be from this root, but is more probably a figurative use of *pregnant:* heavy with child; see *gn.*

For you know dear, I may without vanity hint—
Though an angle should write, still 'tis *devils* must print.
—Thomas Moore, *The Fudges in England* (1835)

"Despotism can no more exist in a nation until the liberty of the press be destroyed, than the night can happen before the sun is set"—C. C. Colton, *Lacon* (1830).

"The liberty of thinking and of publishing whatever one likes . . . is the fountainhead of many evils"—Pope Leo XIII, *Immortale Dei* (1885). "Why should freedom of speech and freedom of the press be allowed? Why should a government that is doing what it believes to be right allow itself to be criticized? It would not allow opposition by lethal weapons. Ideas are much more fatal things than guns"—Nikolai Lenin, speech in Moscow, 1920. "Free press: two hundred men imposing their prejudices on two hundred million"—L. L. Levinson, *The Left-Handed Dictionary* (1963).

preu: hop. Gc *frogga. frog.* Du *vro:* jump with joy. *frolic.*

How dreary—to be—Somebody!
How public—like a frog—
To tell one's name—the livelong June—
To an admiring Bog!
—Emily Dickinson, #288

preus: burning, freezing (the sensations are alike; extremes meet). L *prurire, pruritum:* burn, itch. *pruritus; pruriency, prurient; prurigo.* It *pruina:* hoar frost. *pruinose.* Gc, *frost, freeze.* Perhaps *friz* and *frizzle,* partly imitative of the sound of frying.

?prika: mark with dots; prick. Gc, *prick,* in all its senses. *pricket, prickle, prickly pear,* etc. The slang word *prig:* to pilfer, was first used of horse thieves, who galloped away.

Spenser begins the First Canto of *The Faerie Queene:* "A gentle knight was pricking on the plain": applying the spurs. A different application is made in Beaumont's *The Knight of the Burning Pestle* (1611), by the bumbling old Merrithought, who'd like to live on laughter, and is always breaking into song:

With hey, trixy, trilery, whicksin,
The world it runs on wheels;
When the young man's prick's in
Up goes the maiden's heels.

prokto: anus. Gk *proktos;* E *proctology, proctoscope. proctor* is shortened from *procurator;* see *cura. OED* lists 30 words, mainly medical and surgical, beginning *proct,* as *proctectomy. proctuchous,* opposed to the *aprocta,* which are creatures lacking an anus; no vertebrate is normally *aproctous. proctalgia,* sometimes used figuratively of those that pain us in the anus.

(p)ster: sneeze. Imitative. *sternutation. sternutator. stertorous, ptarmic. ptarmica:* the sneezewort; whence, possibly, *arnica.*

pu: decay, rot. Partly imitative of the sound of disgust. Gk *puon. empyema, pyaemia. pyo-,* as *pyoid, pyorrhea;* some dozen medical or technical terms, as *pyoneumothorax. pyroxanthin. Pyrhium:* genus of fungi.

L *pus, puris. pus, pustule, purulent, suppurate. puter, putrem; putere:* stink. *putid;* in a note to *Davidus* (1635), Cowley speaks of "the putid officiousness of some grammarians"; hence *putidity. putrid; putrefy, putrefaction, putrescent; putrescine.* Fr, *punaise.* It, *olla-podrida;* Fr, *potpourri. Putorius:* the polecat (skunk) family. Gc, *fulmar:* foul gull, from the odor. *foumart:* foul marten, the skunk; *skunk* is from an Algonquian Indian word. *putois:* brush for decorating pottery, first made of skunk's hair. The *polecat weed* is skunk cabbage. *putanism:* harlotry, condemned as foul. It *putta,* Fr *putain:* whore.

In the 16th and 17th c., *polecat* was used, in scorn, of a prostitute. In *The Merry Wives,* iv, 4, Ford beats Falstaff, disguised as the fat old fortune-teller Mother Prat, crying: "I'll prat her! Out of my door, you witch, you hag, you bagge, you polecat, you ronyon! Out, out! I'll conjure you, I'll fortunetell you!" Falstaff runs off, glad he's not again in the basket of dirty laundry, to be dumped once more into the Thames.

Gc, *filthy; defile. foul, foul-mouthed. fog:* coarse grass, left unmowed; *foggage, fuzzy.*

puk: bushy, haired. Gc, *fox,* from its tail. *vixen.* See *ulp,* of which this may be a taboo-change.

For Love is of the valley, come thou down
And find him, by the happy threshold, he,
Or hand in hand with Plenty in the maize,
Or red with spirted purple of the vats,
Or foxlike in the vine . . .
—Tennyson, *The Princess*

This breathes a memory of the Song of Solomon 2:15:

Take us the foxes, the little foxes,
that spoil the vines.

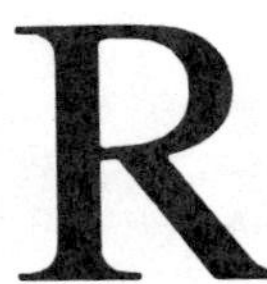

rad I, red: gnaw, scrape, scratch; thence filth (as a dog might scratch ground after excretion). L *radere, rasum. abrade, abrasion. rascal, rapscallion* (earlier, *rascallion*). *raze;* also *rase* and *race. race:* a scratch, was a common word from the 16th into the 19th c., used especially of a mark made on timber with a racing knife. *ramentum:* a fragment scraped off, a mote. Sir Gilbert Blaine, an early 19th c. physician, considered "the salivary glands one of the outlets for the ramenta of the bones." Hence *ramentaceous:* covered with scratches or, in the case of the stems of some plants, tiny scales.

erase, rasure, erasure. razor, razorback, razorbill, razor clam. razee: a 19th c. warship with the upper deck(s) cut away, for speedier action; in 1815 the British warships *Indefatigable, Majestic,* and *Saturn* were cut down to razees. O. W. Holmes, in *Elsie Venner* (1860), used the word figuratively: "The hulks and the razees of enslaved or half-enslaved intelligences."

rail: marsh bird. *Rasores:* order of birds that scratch for food; *rasorial,* opposed to *raptorial. Raptores:* order of birds that seize their prey. *radula:* scraper. *rash:* (skin) eruption. For *rash:* reckless, see *kret. tabula rasa:* wax tablet or slate scraped clean; a fresh, untrammeled mind.

L *rodere, rostum:* gnaw. *rodent; corrode, corrosive; erosion. rostrum:* prow of a ship, from its resemblance to a scraping beak. On the speaker's platform in the Roman forum were placed the prows of the ships captured from the Antiates in A.U.C. 415; hence the transferred meaning of *rostrum.* (*A.U.C.: ab urbe condita:* from the founding of the city [in 753 B.C.]; thus, the Roman calendar's 415 is our 338 B.C.)

The second *r* in *rostrum* helped form an instrumental suffix—that which, or he who. The suffix is manifest in English in three forms: (1) via Fr, *eur* (JWalker lists 30 words with this ending, as *amateur, chauffeur, entrepreneur*); (2) *or* (JWalker lists 600 relevant words, as *ambassador, anchor, bachelor, corridor*); and (3) *er* (JWalker lists some 3300 relevant words, as *idler, informer, wrongdoer*). *stabber* means either that which or one who stabs; see *dheigh N 13.*

"Every man of education would rather be called a rascal, than accused of deficiency in the graces"—Johnson, in Boswell's *Life of Samuel Johnson,* May 1776.

rad II. L *radius:* rod, etc. *ray. X-ray;* when found, the nature of the ray was unknown (like the *X* in algebra). *rayon. radiant, radiation, radiator. irradiate. radio,* and its multiplex offshoots, as *radiobiology, radiotherapy, radioactive. radius:* a bone of the forearm, was first used by Aulus Cornelius Celsus, a 1st c. Roman. Perhaps also *radicle:* root, and *radix.* A *radical* is one that seeks to get at the roots of things, usually to root them out. See *uerad.*

Samuel Butler (d. 1902), in his *Notebooks,* published in 1912, remarked: "The healthy stomach is nothing if not conservative. Few radicals have good digestion."

rap: tuber. L *rapa:* turnip. *rape. rampion,* with edible root. Via It *cavolo rapa,* Fr *chou-rave, kohlrabi:* cabbage with turniplike stem. *ravioli:* diminutive of It *rava;* then applied to a pasta with various fillings.

?re, red: backward, over again. Used in English in thousands of words, as *regain, remarriage; readjust, redeem* (L *emere:* buy), *redeliver, redintegrate, revision, revolve; regard* and its doublet *reward.* (Note that *redrumped* means with a red rump, as certain parrots, finches, thrushes, orioles.) Also several hundred words beginning *retro,* as *retroactive, retromingency, retroversion. retrovert* is applied physically; *introvert* and *extrovert,* usually metaphysically, first so used by Carl Jung in 1918. William McDougall in 1926 averred: "The characteristic neurosis of the extrovert is hysteria, while that of the introvert is neurasthenia or psychasthenia."

There are actually two uses of *re-* and two uses of the form *re:*

1. *back,* as in *recede, recline, reduce* (cut back; literally, lead back).
2. "Go back and do it over": *again,* as in *reiterate, repeat, reenter.*
3. *re,* from L *res:* thing. See *rei II.*
4. *re:* a note in music (*do, re, mi*), from L *?resonare:* resound. Shakespeare, in *Romeo and Juliet,* iv, 5, has the Nurse's servant Peter (played by the company comic, Will Kemp) jestingly threaten the musicians: "I'll re you, I'll fa you, do you note me?"—to which the first musician retorts: "If you re us and fa us, you note *us.*"

re- is given 5 columns in the 1933 *OED,* but *OED*'s 1982 supplement lists 156 words with 5 columns of quotations, and follows these with over 1200 relevant words, from *reable* (a verb) . . . *reelected* . . . *retranslate* . . . to *rezero, rezone.*

OED states that the number of English forms with *re* can be "practically infinite." Other scholars trace *re, retro,* to *uret,* which came by metathesis from *uert;* see *uer II 5. rear* is short for *arrear,* which via Fr *arrière* is from LL *ad retro:* backward.

Note also the *re* (*do, re, mi*) naming the second tone of the diatonic scale (from *?resonare, ?responsum*); and, directly from Latin, the *re* (also *in re,* from L *res, rem, re:* thing) that means in the matter of. See *rei II.*

Keep you to the rear of your affection,
Out of the shot and danger of desire . . .
Be wary, then; best safety lies in fear.
Youth to itself rebels, though none else near.
—Laertes to his sister, Ophelia, *Hamlet,* i, 3

rebh: to cover, roof. Gc, *rib; the ribs,* "roof" of the chest. Slang *rib:* to tease, from poking or tickling at the ribs. *spareribs* (see *sper I*). *rep:* ribbed silk fabric. *reef.* Probably *orb:* cover, surface of a globe; whence *orbicular, orbit, periorbita. OED* defines 22 related *orbi-* words; it also lists 8 and details 5 beginning *orbito,* mainly anatomical terms.

O my aged Uncle Arly!
Sitting on a heap of barley
Thro' the silent hours of night,—
Close beside a leafy thicket:—
On his nose there was a cricket,—
In his hat a railway-ticket;—
(But his shoes were far too tight.)

Long ago, in youth, he squandered
All his goods away, and wandered
To the Tiniskoop hills afar.
There, on golden sunsets blazing
Every evening found him gazing,—
Singing—"Orb, you're quite amazing!
How I wonder what you are!"
—Edward Lear, *Nonsense Songs* (1870)

(This is one of Lear's "autobiographical" pieces. Uncle Arly is clearly *UNc LEAR ly,* the nonsensical author. *tin* was English slang for money, as in the imaginary *Tiniskoop, tin's coop.* The stanza form is borrowed from *The Lady of Shalott,* by Tennyson, to whom Lear sent a copy of this; as also to Ruskin, who had said Lear's *Book of Nonsense* was his favorite reading. If I suggest your trying Lear's recipe for crumbobblious cutlets, you may well be leary.)

reg I: stretch out, reach for; movement in a straight line; army formation; director of such movement; hence leader, ruler. Skr, *raj, rajah; maharajah* (feminine, *ranee, maharanee*): great ruler; *rye,* as in *Romany rye:* gypsy leader. Gk *orekhtos:* stretched out. *orectic:* desiring, hungry. *anorexia* (literally, not to reach for): loss of appetite.

Many forms from L *regere, regens, rexi, rectum:* guide, direct, control; *regnare, regnatum:* have royal power, rule. *rectangle, rectilinear, rectify, recto. rector, rectory; rectitude. regimen, regiment, regime.* Via Fr, *realm, régie. rectum:* straight part of large intestine (in animals), leading to the anus. *regulate. rule, ruler* (for making straight lines, and to govern). Via Fr, *règle;* diminutive *reglet.*

regal, regale, regalia (in kingly style). Fr *roi. royal, viceroy. rex;* the feminine form, *regina,* is the official title of the Queen of England, where postboxes, wagons, etc., bear the initials *ER:* Elizabeth Regina. *regent, regnant; regicide.* Via Fr, *rennet:* little queen, a variety of apple. *region:* direction, boundary, of land ruled.

interregnum; reign. In *sovereign* the *g* is intrusive, by folk association with *reign*ing monarch; the word was earlier *sovran* (as in Milton's *Comus* and *Paradise Lost*), from L *super:* above; see *uper.*

Rotten Row: the name of 3 lanes in London—in Battersea Park, Hampstead Heath, and Hyde Park—is a cockney corruption of Fr *route du roi:* King's Way. There are also in London 7 separate streets named *Kingsway,* and 3 named *King's Way,* with over 250 more beginning *King.* Also Sp *Camino Real:* King's Way; title of a play by Tennessee Williams (1953). Thus Sp *real:* coin with king's head; Port *rei, reis, milreis.* Hence also *riyal:* monetary unit of Saudi Arabia worth 20 gursh; of Yemen, worth 40 bugshas. The capital of Saudi Arabia is *Riyadh:* Royal City.

Compounds of L *regere* include *dirigere, directum:* set straight, guide. *direct, direction, directory;* via Fr, *directoire; dress, dresser; dressage.* L *pergere:* stretch out; via It, *pergola.* The imperative *dirige* is the first word in the Roman Catholic Office of the Dead (Psalm 5:8: "Guide me, O Lord, in Thy Righteousness"); thence E *dirge.*

dirigible. The first dirigibles were large balloons made rigid from within, like the *zeppelin,* named after Count *Zeppelin,* the designer (who, incidentally, fought with the Union Army in the American Civil War). Then nonrigid, limp balloons were tried; the first model, the *A limp,* was unsuccessful; the second model, the *B limp,* became the *blimp.*

Other compounds gave English *arrect, correct, corrective; erect, erection, erectile.* Via Fr (*l.r* shift), *alert.* It, *Risorgimento. insurrection.* Via Sp, *surge, insurgent, resurgent; resurrection.*

L *rogare, rogantis, rogatum:* to stretch out one's hands for; in later, more polite periods, to request, ask. *rogation, abrogate, arrogate, arrogant. derogatory; prerogative.* L *prorogare:* extend, protract. *prorogation, prorogue. rogue:* first, asker, beggar. *subrogate, surrogate, supere(r)rogatory. ergo* (*e-rego:* literally, from the direction; therefore), which Shakespeare's gravedigger in *Hamlet* turned into *argal,* used since to indicate clumsy reasoning. LL *corrogata:* asked to do together; via Fr, *corvée:* unpaid labor, especially that exacted of French peasants (up to 1726) to maintain the roads.

Gc, *rack, rake, rail* (fence), *railroad;* all straight-lined. *rake:* a dissolute man, is an abbreviation of *rakehell,* from OE *rakel:* rash; such a fellow, said Nicholas Udall in 1542, as one would find were one to rake hell; he'd be raking the coals for hellfire.

Nasalized, *rank* (*and file*). A *rank* smell was influenced by *rancid* (Fr *rance*). *reck, reckon:* plan it straight. *reckless. right, right-angled; upright,* both physically and morally. *forthright. downright,* now a term of emphasis.

rule, and as a *ruler,* naturally *rich,* which first meant kingly, powerful. *riches* was first singular, from Fr *richesse.* Hence also *Richard.* The German *Reich. Reichtag.* (Gm *Tag:* day, is from meeting on an appointed day. *diet:* assembly, is similarly from L *dies:* day.) *Rigsdag. rix-dollar.* The last element in *bishopric,* and in *Alaric, Aubrey, Frederic(k), Heinrich, Henry* (: ruler of the home). *Reginald, Roderick;* Gc *Reginhart,* Gm *Reinhart. Reynard:* name given the trickster fox in the medieval beast epic. The epic, based on folktales and Aesop's fables, and translated from Flemish by Caxton in 1481, includes *Bruin* the bear, *Chanticleer* the cock, *Tybert* the cat (*tabby*), and more. In the 18th and 19th c. an *old maid* was said to be in her *tabbyhood.* The *tabby* cat (an old maid's companion) is named for its stripes, from *at-attabiyah,* a suburb of Baghdad (named after Prince *Attab*) where a watered silk of this pattern was made.

"Remember, it is as easy to marry a rich woman as a poor woman"—Thackeray, *Pendennis,* 28. First catch your hare.

"A man in the right relies easily on his rectitude, and therefore goes about unarmed. His very strength is his weakness. A man in the wrong knows that he must look to his weapons; his very weakness is his strength. Therefore it is that in this world the man that is in the wrong almost invariably conquers the man that is in the right, and invariably despises him"—Anthony Trollope, *Barchester Towers* (1857).

reg II: dye, preservative. Skr *laksha* (*l.r* shift). *Lakshmi,* Hindu goddess of beauty. *lac:* an insect of the subfamily *lacciferinae;* also the dark red dye that the female lac secretes. *lacquer; shellac.* From the teeming insects, *lac* (also *lakh*) came to be used of a large sum; a lac equals 100,000 rupees, a rupee being (in 1982) about 12 cents. *raga,* a figurative use of color applied to sound (an idea developed in 19th c. France, as in Rimbaud's sonnet *Vowels* and Baudelaire's sonnet "Color and sound and fragrance correspond"). Gk *rhegos:* cover, dye. *regolith.* (*lithos:* stone, as in *lithography, monolith. lithosphere,* with atmosphere and hydrosphere, constitutes man's surroundings. For *lithium,* see *el 3.*)

reg III: moist, wet. L *rigare. irrigation.* Gc *regen. rain, rainbow, rain* and its compounds, as *rainfall, rainy,* take up over 8 columns in *OED.* See *bheug II.*

rei I: scratch, tear, cut; flow through. See also *ergh.* L, *rima, rimose. riparian:* torn by the stream; probably also *river:* the tearer; *rive. rivulet.* Sp, *ria, rio.* Fr, *rivage, rivière. riverside. rival:* one sharing a stream; hence, first, a neighbor, an aid, as in *Hamlet:* "If you do meet Horatio and Marcellus, the rivals of my watch . . . ," but alas, thence, a competitor. *rivalry. arrival, arrive, derive.* Gc, *Rhine:* flowing stream; *Rhenish. rife, rift. ripe; reap. rove. row on row. regatta:* first, a row of gondolas lined up for a race. For *row a boat,* see *ere.*

In the Bible Hosea, though he has faith in ultimate redemption by the Lord, prophesies punishment for Israel's current sins, "for they have sown the wind, and they shall reap the whirlwind."

rei II: thing. L *res publica. republic,* etc. *in re:* in the matter of. *reify. realism. reism;*

not in *OED,* where *real* takes up 4 columns. *reality, unreal; really, realize,* etc. *rebus,* the ablative plural of *res,* in the phrase *non verbis sed rebus:* not by words but by things, besides meaning "Don't talk; act; show me!" came to be used of the practice, or game, of indicating words by objects; thus a picture of an eye and a tin container would signify "I can."

Reification: treating an abstraction or imaginary creation as though it were an actual thing, may cause considerable confusion of mind and inadvisable action. The Loch Ness monster and flying saucers are among the comparatively harmless reifications.

He will watch from dawn to doom
The lake-reflected sun illume
The yellow bees in the ivy-bloom,
Nor heed, nor see, what things they be,
But from these create he can
Forms more real than living man,
Nurslings of immortality!
—Shelley, *Prometheus Unbound,* i

reidh: ride. *palfrey* (Gk *para-:* beside; *l.r.* shift): a horse to ride side saddle. *raddle:* wooden horse. *curry, currycomb* (LL *corredere:* make ready to ride. For *curry favor,* see *pel VII. curry,* the powder and the sauce, is from Tamil *kari.*)

Gc, *raid, ride, road. array.* In 1725 the French took E *riding coat* into their language; a century later it returned as E *redingote.* The word *raid* lapsed from use in the 16th c.; it was revived by Scott in *The Lay of the Last Minstrel* (1805); but the action of *raiding,* in one part of the world or another, has been uninterrupted. *riding:* any of the three government districts of Yorkshire, is a folkchange from OE *thriding:* a third part, as *North Thriding* was compressed to *North Riding.*

The road was a ribbon of moonlight over the purple moor,
And the highwayman came riding—
Riding—riding—
The highwayman came riding, up to the old inn door.
—Alfred Noyes, *The Highwayman*

reig I: bind. LL *ex-corrigia:* bound together; thongs. *scourge.* Gc, *rig:* to bind sails to mast; hence, to manipulate a ship's rigging; later used of a fraudulent practice, as in *thimblerig* or a shellgame ("Under which of the three is the pea?"). Recent signs in New York banks and stores have warned customers against sidewalk *riggers* and their tricks, now usually the shifting of three playing cards ("Which one is the picture?").

Perhaps from *ship's rigging,* the verb *rig* came to be used to mean climb up and down, then—first in slang—to jump up and down, to behave wantonly, "to perform the act of supersaliency." John Fletcher, in *The Wild Goose Chase* (1619), protested

That this Bilbo-Lord shall reap the maidenhead
That was my due; that he shall rig and top her.

Shakespeare looks upon Cleopatra (ii, 3):

Age cannot wither her, nor custom stale
Her infinite variety . . . for vilest things
Become themselves in her, that the holy priests
Bless her when she is riggish.

James Joyce, in *Ulysses,* twists from God: "They believe in rod, the scourge almighty, creator of hell upon earth and in Jacky Tar."

reig II: stretch out. An extension of *reg I.* L *rigere:* stiffen, as from cold. *rigid; rigescent. rigor* (*mortis*). Gk *hrigos:* cold. *frigid, frigidity, frigorific; refrigerator,* in speech often abbreviated *fridge. rhigoline:* a local anesthetic, which "freezes"; a petroleum naphtha, first used in 1866. Fr, *sang-froid:* in or with cold blood. Gc, *reach.*

> Ah, but a man's reach should exceed his grasp,
> Or what's a heaven for?
> —Browning, *Andrea del Sarto*

rendh: tear off, tear up. Gc, *rend, rent, rind.*

rep I: creep. L *reptum. repent* (accent on the first syllable). *reptile. reptant, reptilian; OED* has 14 associated words.

Alexander Pope reminds us of the form attributed to the serpent in the Garden of Eden:

> Eve's tempter thus the Rabbins have exprest,
> A Cherub's face, a reptile all the rest.

rep II: snatch. See *labh.* L *rapere, raptum. rape, ravish;* note the contrasted meanings of *ravishing. rapt, enrapt. Raptores:* order of birds that seize their prey; *raptatorial, raptorial* (see *rad I*). *rapacious, ravin. erepsin. subreption* and *subreptitious* remain as ecclesiastical or legal terms; for more general use they have been smoothed to *surreption* and *surreptitious.*

Lucretia, wife of Lucius Tarquinius Collatinus, in 509 B.C. was raped by Tarquinius Sextus; she told of her ravishing, then killed herself. Under Lucius Junius Brutus, the Romans ended the Tarquin rule and founded the Republic. Shakespeare tells the story in *The Rape of Lucrece,* and in *Macbeth* speaks of "Tarquin's ravishing strides."

rep III: beam. Norse, *raft.* Gc, *rafter.*

"A monarchy is a merchantman which sails well, but will sometimes strike on a rock and go to the bottom; a republic is a raft which will never sink, but then your feet are always in the water"—Fisher Ames, speech in the House of Representatives, 1795.

ret: pole. *rod.* The Bible (Proverbs 13:24) says: "He that spareth his rod hateth his son"; the common saw is from Butler's *Hudibras,* ii, 844;

> Love is a boy, by poets styl'd;
> Then spare the rod, and spoil the child.

A *rod* is also a measure, 5½ yards. *dowsing* or *divining rod. rood,* especially *The Rood:* the cross of Jesus; now archaic, though it lingered somewhat longer in the oath *By the rood*—used by Shakespeare (Hamlet to his mother in the closet scene), Scott, and Tennyson. A *rood* is also a small piece of land, a quarter acre.

> I often wish that I had clear
> For life six hundred pounds a year;
> A handsome house to lodge a friend,
> A river at my garden's end,
> A terrace walk, and half a rood
> Of land, set out to plant a wood.
> —Swift, *Imitation of Horace,* ii, 6

reth: round, roll. L *rota:* wheel. *rotate, rota, rotary, rotation. rote. rotulus* (diminutive), *rotella. rotiform. rotogravure. role, rowel. control* (LL *contrarotulare:* keep a second roll, register, as a check). *Rotary International,* organized in Chicago on 23 Feb. 1905 for service to the community, had expanded by 1980 to 18,900 local Rotary clubs in 154 countries. It is named for its symbol, a cogwheel, which turns to transmit motion.

L *rotundus. rotunda. rotundity. round, orotund* (blended with *os, oris:* mouth). *roll, enroll.* It, *rondo.* Sp, *rodeo.* Fr *rouler. roulette. barouche* (L *birota*), originally a two-wheeled carriage. *rondeau, rondel, roundelay:* poems that turn upon themselves, or have a recurring refrain. *refrain* is via OFr *refraindre,* from LL *refrangere:* break back. Nathaniel P. Willis modestly remarked in *Melanie* (1835):

> When another sang the strain,
> I mingled in the old refrain.

refrain from is from *re:* back, and *frenum:* bridle.

reu. Imitative of the sound of wind or animal cries. *Rudra,* Vedic god of storms. L *rugir:* bellow. *raucous, riot; roar, rough. rut:* an animal's sexual rousing. L *rumor* first meant to howl. *murmur. rumor.* ONorse, *rout:* clamor.

In his *Jabberwocky,* Charles Dodgson explained "uffish thought" as "a state of mind when the voice is gruffish, the manner roughish, and the temper huffish. . . ." Other words from *Jabberwocky–burble, galumphing, frabjous, chortle–* were helped to popularity by Kipling's use of them in his *Stalky and Co.* (1899). *chortle* is a fusion of *chuckle* and *snort.* The *ish* words are partly imitative. JWalker gives 288 relevant words ending *ish,* as *childish, coquettish, fiendish, roguish, sheepish, snobbish.*

> Rumor is a pipe
> Blown by surmises, jealousies, conjectures,
> And of so easy and so plain a stop
> That the blunt monster with uncounted heads,
> The still-discordant wavering multitude,
> Can play upon it.
> –Shakespeare, *2 Henry IV*

r(e)udh: ruddy. See *keiro.* Gk *eruthros:* red. *erythema. erythro-,* as *erythroblast, erythrocite, erythromycin. erysipelas,* referred to by Chaucer in *The Parson's Tale* and by others, also called *St. Anthony's Fire;* in Spenser's *The Faerie Queene, St. Fraunces' Fire* is probably the same; see *sak.* L *rubeus:* red. *rubella, rubeola, rubefacient, rubeosis, rubescent, erubescence. rubor. rubric:* heading, marginal note or direction, first written or printed in red. *rubricate.* Probably *Rubus:* genus of the rose family. *rutilant.* Via Fr, *rouge, roux, russet. rissole, rubicund. rubidium,* from the red lines in its spectrum (see *el 37*). *rubiginous, rubigo, ruby.*

L *robus:* red. *robustus:* oak; hence hard, strong. *robust. corroborate:* make firm. *rudd; ruddy; rust.* Probably *robot:* slave, hard worker (Czech; Gm *Arbeit:* work) made popular by Karel Čapek's play *R.U.R.* (Rossum's Universal Robots), produced in New York in 1923; see *orbh.* Also, via Gk *orphanos,* came E *orphan.* The stem in Armenian, OSlavic (*rabota*), Gothic, etc., also meant slavery, hard work; OE *earfodh:* hardship, trouble–the fate of many poor orphans. Also *roble, roborant, roburite.*

A slang variant of *robustious* is *rambunctious;* also *rumbustious,* as ruddy after drinking rum. See *kel VI; urod.*

reu(g): belch. Partly imitative. L, *eruct, eructation.* Gc, *reek.*

reuos: clear space, open field. L *rural; rustic, rusticate, rusticity.* OFr *rustre:* boor; first, country fellow. Du, *Boer. neighbor:* near farmer; see *bheu.* From *rustre,* E *roister. Ralph Roister Doister,* the first English comedy, was probably first performed ca. 1553 by the boys of Westminster School; its author, Nicholas Udall, was headmaster there.

rummage: first, arrange in a ship's hold. Gc, *ream. rhumb.* Via Sp, *rumba. room.* Gm *Lebensraum.* For a while, *Ruritania* was a popular term for an idyllic land of romance, from the country of Ruritania in Anthony Hope Hawkins' novel *The Prisoner of Zenda* (1894).

reup, reub: snatch, break. *rip, reave, bereave.* A prisoner of war, or a victim, was usually stripped; persons being beheaded often left what they were wearing to the executioner on his promise of a quick, clean stroke; from a garment as booty came *robe.* What is left of the spoils is *rubble.* Hence also *rob, robber; rover. usurp:* to snatch the use of. *abrupt, corrupt, disrupt, erupt, interruption, irruption. bankrupt* is from the broken (or confiscated) bench of the unsuccessful Italian moneylender.

roture. rout: to break the enemy ranks; also a broken-up group. *route* (L *rupta via*): a way broken through. *routier. routine:* following a beaten path. *rupestrian:* consisting of broken rock. *rupture, rutter. rubato* is "stolen time" in music.

In a speech of 1771, Edmund Burke said: "the greater the power, the greater the abuse." Gibbon, in *The Decline and Fall of the Roman Empire,* (1776), 21, pictured the plague of all democracies: "Corruption, the most infallible symptom of constitutional liberty." In a letter of 1904 the First Baron Acton set the idea in an (often misquoted) epigram: "Power tends to corrupt, and absolute power corrupts absolutely." He was blaming an abstraction, "power," for an urge in human nature; it would seem sounder to say that the possession of power gives a corrupt person opportunity to exercise his will. (Volcanic eruptions—not to mention the sun—show how short-lived, despite Napoleon and Hitler, is the range of human power.)

?ridè: laugh. L *ridere, risum. arride. riant, ridicule, ridiculous; risible. risorius:* cheek muscle; *risus, deride, derision.*

"Ridicule is the best test of truth"—Earl of Chesterton, letter to his son, 6 Feb. 1752.

rkthos: a bear. Gk *arktos. arctic, arctician; antarctic. arctogeal:* the northern earth. *Arcturus:* the bear guardian, the brightest star in the constellation *Boötes* (Plowman), at the tail of *Ursa Major* (Great Bear), in the northern sky. L *ursus. ursine, urson. Ursula. Orson,* spelling influenced by It *orso:* bear; the derivation from *horson:* whore-son, is folk etymology. Celt, *Arthur.*

There grew pied wind-flowers and violets,
Daisies, those pearled Arcturi of the earth,
The constellated flower that never sets.
—Shelley, *The Question*

?rud: rough. L *rudimentum:* rough beginning; fashioned after *elementum. rude, rudiments. erudite* (*e:* out, removing the rough); *erudition.*

The Rev. R. H. Barham (d. 1845) wrote (the Latin is an inscription on St. Paul's Cathedral, London, designed by Wren):

I've always considered Sir Christopher Wren,
As an architect, one of the greatest of men;
And talking of epitaphs, much I admire his:

"Circumspice, si monumentum requiris",
Which an erudite verger translated for me:
"If you ask for his monument, Sir-come-spy-see!"

Circumspice: Look around. The motto of the College of the City of New York is *Respice, Adspice, Prospice:* Look back, look around, look ahead. Wren helped rebuild London after the Great Fire of 1666; he built 52 churches there; St. Paul's, 1675-1716. It is still a "monument." E. Clerihew Bentley built the architect into one of his clerihew verses:

Sir Christopher Wren
Said: "I'm going to dine with some men.
If anybody calls
Say I'm designing St. Paul's."

sa: satisfy. Via L *satis:* enough, came *sate, satiate, satiety; satisfy; saturate; assets. satyr:* never sated, is of unknown origin. See *aig; sap. sad* first meant sated, hence heavy; as still in *sadiron,* a solid flatiron heated on the stove, as contrasted with a hollow iron to be filled with hot water or steam. From its figurative use—first meaning full of food, then a mixture, a medley—came the literary term *satire.* Similarly, the literal sense of *farce* was stuffing; thus the chronicler Jean Froissart in 1370 wrote of his patron:

The good Enguerrand de Courci
Often farced my fist for me
With a bag of gold louis.

The theatrical *farce* was first "stuffed" between the acts of a serious drama, to quiet the bored or restless audience.

satisfaction. Wordplayfully, "The leader of the opposition sat his faction on the left." When voting in Parliament, the Yeas (the ruling party) stand to the right of the Speaker; the Nays (disagreeing) stand to the left. This is one reason why *the Left,* and *leftist,* have come to designate the minority, the dissident, and by extension the extremist, the revolutionary. A second reason is that the opposite of *right* is both *left* and *wrong;* and the majority, the "right-minded," so label those that disagree with them. Those that are not "right" are wrong, and should be left.

"Satire is a kind of glass, wherein beholders do generally discover everybody's face but their own"—Swift, *Battle of the Books* (1697), preface.

sab: juice. *sap;* but see *sap.* It, *zabaglione.*

sag: to sense, seek; hence take, know. Gk, *exegesis. hegemony. hegumen:* head of monastery of Eastern Orthodox Church. L, *sagacious, sagacity; presage.* Gc, *sake,* *forsake; seek, sought.* Former legal terms of tenure: *soc, socage, soke, soken.* ONorse, *ransack.*

Eli, Eli, lama sabacthani!: My God, my God, why hast thou forsaken me?—last cry of the man Jesus on the Cross, before he resumed his godhead.

"Forsaking all others, keep only unto her, as long as ye both shall live"—*The Book of Common Prayer,* defied by the divorce rate.

sai: suffering. This root gives us words for the physical and the mental aspects: *sore* and *sorry.* Note that, by way of slang, *sore* can move from the physical to the emotional realm.

sak: to make holy. L *sacer:* dedicated (perhaps for sacrifice), holy. *sacrament, sacred, sacerdotal; sacrifice, sacrilege* (L *legere:* gather, steal; see *leg I*), whence *sacrilegious,* often misspelled as though from *religion,* which is from *re-ligatum:* bound back (see *leig II*). *sacrum:* bone used in sacrifices; *sacroiliac* (L *ilium:* groin). *sacristan* and its doublet, *sexton. consecrate;* also *desecrate, obsecrate; execration.*

His death, which happened in his berth,
At forty-odd befell;
They went and told the sexton, and
The sexton tolled the bell.
—Thomas Hood, *Faithless Sally Brown* (1826)

From the nasalized form we have *sacrosanct, sanctum;* via Fr, *sanctity, sanctimony, sanction,* and the lengthy list of *saints.* Via Du, *Santa Claus* (Saint Nicholas). A *sanctuary* is an *asylum* (Gk *a* negative; *sulon:* the right to take): a place from which no one may be rightfully taken.

corposant: holy body, is the name given by sailors to the light sometimes seen on mastheads during electric storms; it is also called *St. Elmo's fire,* from the patron saint of sailors. *St. Anthony's,* also *St. Fraunces', Fire:* erysipelas; see *reudh.*

A number of saints are involved in words, of which the following are some of the most familiar. *St. Andrew's Cross,* X-shaped. *Cross of St. Anthony,* T-shaped. *Great St. Bernard:* breed of dog developed by monks at the hospice of St. Bernard, at a pass in the Alps between Switzerland and Italy; the dog is often portrayed with a cask at the neck, as for the rescue of snowbound travelers in distress. *St. Germaine pear:* with especially juicy pulp. *St. Gobain glass:* plate glass made at St. Gobain, France. *St. Jeffry's Day:* "neither before Christmas nor after," it falls on 31 Feb.; *on St. Jeffry's Day* is a pietistic way of saying *never. St. Johnston's riband* or *tippet:* the hangman's noose; used, e.g., by Scott in *Old Mortality* (1816). *St. Leger:* horserace for three-year-olds, run annually at Doncaster, Yorkshire, England. *St. Louis group:* deposits of limestone near St. Louis and along the upper Mississippi, sometimes 250 feet thick (the crystalline variety of limestone being marble). *St. Lubbock's Day:* heavily humorous name for the English bank holidays, four a year, established by Sir John Lubbock's Act of 1871. *St. Omer's,* also *St. Homer's, St. Thomas's, worsted:* cloth manufactured at St. Omer, France. *St. Vitus,* also *St. John's, St. Guy's, dance:* chorea, a dancing mania of the Middle Ages. "They that are taken with it," said Robert Burton in *The Anatomy of Melancholy* (1621), "can do nothing but dance till they be dead, or cured." Also used figuratively, as by Southey in 1804 of Coleridge: "His mind is in a perpetual St. Vitus dance—eternal activity without action." See *reudh.* (Chorea has lapsed, today, to involuntary muscular movements of the arms and face.)

The word *saint,* as earlier in Latin and French, has been attached to various words, especially ecclesiastical ones, as *St. Cross, St. Faith, St. Thrift, St. Trinity.* Chaucer, in *The Knight's Tale* (1386), refers to *St. Charity,* as does Shakespeare, in *Hamlet,* iv, 5, when the mad Ophelia sings:

By Gis and by Saint Charity
Alack! and fie for shame!
Young men will do't, if they come to't,
By cock, they are to blame.
Quoth she, before you tumbled me,
You promised me to wed.

(*Gis* and *cock* are minced forms of *Jesus* and *God,* though the latter, in this context, has a sexual overtone.) The *London Gazette* in 1710 described a summer parade as a procession "in honor of St. Sudario" (: sweating).

St. Distaff's Day is the day after "the twelve days of Christmas"—Twelfth Night being the Feast of Epiphany—when, after the seasonal festivities, women resumed spinning and other feminine chores. As Herrick commented in *Hesperides* (1648):

Give St. Distaff all the right,
Then bid Christmas sport good night.

The *distaff* side of the family was the feminine branch (in early England, contrasted with the spear side). OE *dis:* bunch of flax; unspun flax, wool, etc., was put on the rod or staff of the spinning wheel, to be turned into thread by the spinster woman. (If she did not marry, she remained a spinster.)

In *The Tatler,* Steele gave Bickerstaff a sister, Jenny Distaff, whose marriage to Tranquillus is pleasantly detailed. See *leubh.*

"Yea, though I walk through the valley of the shadow of death, I fear no evil, for Thou art with me; Thy rod and Thy staff they comfort me"—Bible, Psalm 23.

"Accidents will occur in the best-regulated families; and in families not regulated by that pervading influence which sanctifies while it enhances the—a—I would say, in short, by the influence of Woman, in the lofty character of Wife, they may be expected with confidence, and must be borne with philosophy"—Mr. Micawber, in Dickens' *David Copperfield.*

sakkara: gravel, pebble; sugar. *saccharin(e). saccharify, saccharimeter,* etc. *Saccharomyces:* genus of sugar fungi; yeast. *saccharose.* Via Arab, *sugar* and its doublet, *jaggery:* dark brown sugar. *sucrate, sucrose. seersucker:* literally, milk and sugar; a thin, cotton fabric. *crocodile:* pebble worm; named for its hard, knotty back.

Bacon, in Essay 40, comments: "It is the wisdom of the crocodiles, that shed tears when they would devour." Antony's description of the creature, in *Antony and Cleopatra,* ii, 7, is less informative.

sal I: salt. Gk *hals:* the salt sea. *halogen:* salt-producing, as bromine, chlorine, fluorine, iodine. Sodium and chlorine, each poisonous, combine (NaCl) to give us common table salt. *halophyte, halomancy. OED* defines 11 *halo-* words. In Brittany are *halobiontes:* sheep that feed on the grass of the salt marshes; the lamb comes to the cook already salted.

L, *sal, saline; saltpeter:* rock salt. It, *salami, salmi, salmagundi.* Fr, *salad. sauce. sausage. salary* was the allowance of salt, or money for salt, to preserve soldiers' food while an army was on the march. *Attic salt* is the refined or poignant wit of Athens, capital of Attica, sometimes contrasted with *Italian vinegar,* more biting and insolent comment. The negative compounds *insulse* and *insulsity* were used to mean stupid and stupidity. Milton, in his tract on *Divorce* (1642), sought to justify "the councells of God and Fate from the insulsity of mortal tongues."

(Note that in compounds the vowels are often changed; thus also *sapid, insipid.*) Berkeley, in 1732: "In our times a dull man is said to be insipid or insulse." *OED* calls *insulse* and *insulsity* "now rare."

In the 16th and 17th c., *salty* was used to mean what today is called *peppy:* full of pep, pepper; see *pippa;* then *salt* came to be applied to sexual desire. Thus also *salacious:* full of salt; *saucy* (L *salire:* to leap; to be lustful). Othello (iii, 3) speaks of illicit lovers

. . . as prime as goats, as hot as monkeys,
As salt as wolves in pride . . .

lusty also implies good health (L *salus, salvus*); hence *Salute!:* Good health to you! *salutary, salutation; salubrious.* A *salvo* is a loud salute, as with guns; or a saving clause in a contract (Read the fine print!); or a mental reservation. *save, salve, salvation, savior.* From the Portuguese for *savior* came the country *El Salvador. salvage.* The plant *sage,* which is supposed to have healing powers; see *sap.*

A forest is a salubrious place. LL *salvaticus:* of the wood, via French, gave English *savage.* Earlier came L *silvaticus,* and from it *silvan, sylvan; Sylvia.* Still earlier was Gk *xylon:* wood, whence *xylophone* and technical terms such as *xylograph,* with 5 derivative words; *OED* lists 16 words and details 10 beginning *xylo.* See *hule.*

sir-reverence (cut from "saving"—sparing—"your reverence") is a 16th–18th c. euphemism for feces—begging pardon, as it were, for the mention. Shakespeare, in *A Comedy of Errors,* iii, 2, speaks of "such a one, as a man may not speak of, without he say sirreverence." Richard Head, in *The English Rogue* (1665), gives us a glimpse of what London's unpaved streets were like, when he tells of a man "sirreverencing in a paper, and running to the window with it." Among many other instances, from Jonson to Dryden, I mention only Smollett's sarcastic comment in *Humphry Clinker* (1771): "as a plate of marmalade would improve a pan of sirreverence."

Gc, *salt, saltcellar, saltine.* Via Gc *sulza,* Dan *sylt:* salt marsh, E *silt. souse.* To take something *cum grano salis:* with a grain of salt, is to try to make it acceptable to the taste; such an item must therefore be taken with doubt and caution. Salt was used to purify and preserve; hence it became a symbol of these; a pinch of salt was put in "holy water," and "the devil's feast" was a meal without salt—*pace* those now medically advised not to take salt. Kipling remarked that a kiss without a moustache is like an egg without salt. It seems strange that the endless and subtle variety of tastes upon the palate is compounded of but four basic savors: salt, sweet, sour, and bitter.

"Let your speech be always with grace, seasoned with salt"—Epistle of Paul to the Colossians 4:6: "Ye are the salt of the earth; but if the salt have lost its savour, wherewith shall it be salted?"—Matthew 5:13.

sal II: willow. L, *sallow, salicin,* obtained from the bark. *sargasso* (*l.r* shift), from the shape of the leaf. When Lady Suffolk received a fragile package from Spain, Alexander Pope, at his Twickenham estate (his home from 1719 until his death, in 1744), planted the twigs her package had been wrapped in, and thus grew the first weeping willow in England.

?sang: blood. L *sanguine, sanguinary.* Fr, *sang-froid.* Sp, *sangría,* from the color.

Senlac! sanguelac,
The lake of Blood!
—Tennyson, *Harold,* iii

sano: healthy. *sane, sanity; sanitation; insanity, sanitarium.* Fr, *sainfoin:* healthy hay. Juvenal, in *Satires,* x: *Orandum est ut sit mens sana in corpore sano:* One should pray for a sound mind in a sound body.

sap: juice; taste. Thus the delicious sap annually tapped from the maple tree. For food of good taste came *sapid, savor, savory, sage;* contrariwise, *insipid.* For persons of good taste—hence discerning, wise—came *sapient, savant, sage, sapor,* and the slang *savvy,* perhaps via Fr *Savez-vous?:* Do you know? Via *irony* (with a plethora of juice, hence foolish) come the slang *sap, sappy, saphead* (thus Gk, *hydrocephalous:* fluid in the head, which enlarges the skull but compresses the brain). *Homo sapiens,* as we optimistically label our species.

A *sapling* is the juicy child of a tree. There are 60 words in JWalker ending *ling:* small or insignificant, as *darling, fledgling, foundling, gosling, priestling, suckling.* "The witling sat whittling under the willow." A *codling* is (1) a small codfish; (2) a tapering variety of apple; from its shape the suggestion has been made that it is derived from Norman Fr *querdelyon:* lion's heart; but the hearts of lions were rarely seen in northern France. From EE *inkle, inkling* may be imitative, as of a bell that faintly tinkles in the mind.

A *changeling* was an ugly, malformed, or otherwise obnoxious infant, obviously left by the fairies that had carried off the genuine and well-endowed child born to the parents. In *A Midsummer Night's Dream* the cause of the quarrel between Oberon, king of the Fairies, and his queen, Titania, is "a little changeling boy"—the superb natural one the fairies had carried off. From the empty-headed justice of the peace, *Shallow,* in Shakespeare's *2 Henry IV,* came *shallowling.* In 1646 *The British Bellman* commented: "Whores, when they have drawn in silly shallowlings, will ever find some trick to retain them."

savory, the aromatic mint, from L *satureia,* provides a good example of polyglot variation. The English word was folkchanged to match *savor* and *flavor.* Fr *sarriette* added a diminutive. Also folkchanged was It *santoreggia:* a flavor fit for a saintly queen. Sp *ajedra,* coming via Arabic dishes, kept the first letter of the Arabic article *al:* the. (Another odd international variation springs from L *episcopus;* E *bishop* and Fr *évêque,* from this one source, have not one letter in common.)

The Latin expression *Verbum sapienti satis est:* A word to the wise is enough, is often shortened, for English use, to *Verbum sap*—although Byron, in *Don Juan* (i, 53), preferred *Verbum sat.* Also from Latin, *suction, succulent;* see *seu I.* In *OED, saponaceous, saponify,* and 11 other *sapo-* words. *soap* was first a dye (vegetable juice) with which German warriors made their flowing hair a frightening red. (In the far East, the common people still regard a red-headed woman as a witch.) A *soap bubble* is perhaps the only separate molecule visible to the naked eye; it is, we are told, 1/600,000 of an inch thick. A *soapbox* speaker is one that uses this sort of makeshift platform, like the earlier stump speaker on the village green. A *soap opera* is a sentimental (emotionally mushy, "soapy") afternoon (now also evening) program on the air, often sponsored by soap or detergent manufacturers.

Related along the Germanic line, partly imitative, are *sip, sieve* (flows through), *sift, seep, sop, soap, soak, sup, supper; suck, suckle, honeysuckle. sieve* has developed various meanings: (1) It is a symbol of vain folly; to carry water in a sieve was one of the exploits of Simple Simon. (2) It is used of a person that cannot keep a secret, as in *All's Well That Ends Well,* i, 3, 108. (3) It is also a vessel for witches to sail in; Scott, in *Letters on Demonology* (1830), mentions "another frolic they had, when, like the weird sisters in Macbeth, i, 3, they embarked in sieves." (4) The expression *sieve and shears* is used in divination; also, especially, *to turn the riddle*—a riddle being a coarse-meshed sieve riddled with holes—

to identify a thief. (5) The sieve of Eratosthenes provided an early way of sifting out the prime numbers: Strike out every second number after 2, every third number after 3, every fifth number after 5, and every seventh number after 7, and what's left are the prime numbers. See *per VI e.* (Eratosthenes was a Greek astronomer of Cyrene in the 3d c. B.C.; he became head of the great library in Alexandria; he established a series of historical dates beginning with the fall of Troy, and he calculated the circumference of the earth.)

> Nor bring, to see me cease to live,
> Some doctor full of phrase and fame,
> To shake his sapient head, and give
> The ill he cannot cure a name.
> —Matthew Arnold, *A Wish*

"Soap and education are not so sudden as a massacre, but they are more deadly in the long run"—Mark Twain, *Sketches Old and New* (1900).

sauel, suen: sun. Gk (*sauel-yo*) *helios. Helios,* the sun god. *helium* (see *el 2*). *heliacal; aphelion, perihelion, anthelion, parhelion. helio-,* as *heliocentric, heliochrome; OED* lists 15 relevant words beginning *helio,* and details 36 more, as *heliotrope:* flower that turns to follow the sun. Thus also from L *sol:* sun, *girasole* and *turnsole.* Hence also *solar, solanine, solarium. insolate. parasol;* see *per V.* Gc, *sun, Sunday, sunny* (see *prai*). *south, southern. sunny side up:* direction given to a chef when ordering a fried egg (with the yellow circle atop).

"Sunday is not like another day. On Sunday, people may walk, but not throw stones at birds"—Samuel Johnson

saus: dry; perhaps a consequence of the sun's action. Gk *austeros. austere. austerity* (from dryness, roughness, to harshness to severe self-discipline). Gk *auein:* to dry, kindle. L *urere, ustum:* burn. Hence *auster:* the south wind, the south. *Australia* means the southern land; originally the supposed continent and all the islands of the Great Southern Ocean. Describing the various applications of *aust-, OED* details 12 words. The *Austral* signs are the six signs of the zodiac from Libra to Pisces. (*Austria,* however, is folkchanged from Gm *Oesterreich:* Eastern kingdom.) *austromancy* is divination using the direction of the winds, the south wind being most favorable in England.

OFr, *sorrel:* dry brown color. Gc, *sear, sere.*

> I have lived long enough; my way of life
> Is fall'n into the sear, the yellow leaf.
> —*Macbeth,* v, 3

se I: to sow, and that which is sown, the seed. *season* first meant sowing time. *insert,* as seeds are sown. Affixed came *semen,* the male seed; *seminary* first meant a seed plot; then, a nursery. *disseminate. insemination.* Cleopatra, in Shakespeare's play, i, 4, calls her eunuch, Mardian, *unseminar'd.*

secular: first, the seed of men; then, generation (in Fr, *siècle:* century); then, men of the world as distinct from the celibate men of the church. The Inquisition, with its arrangements to punish for violations of Church ordainments, or "to destroy the body to save the soul," was known as the *secular arm* of the Church; thus the clergy, preaching about a God of love, did not engage in torture. See *Dominicans,* under *dem.* Franklin, in 1737, said: "Truth . . . scorns the aid of the secular arm."

colza is "kohl seed"; *kohl:* cabbage, as in *coleslaw.*

"All knowledge and wonder (which is the seed of knowledge) is an impression of pleasure in itself"—Francis Bacon, *Advancement of Learning* (1605).

se II: long; late. *serotinous:* late-blooming. Via Fr, *soiree.* OE *sith* is archaic, but, combined in *sithenes,* survives as *since.*

Adriana, unsuspecting of the confusion of the twin brothers and therefore suspicious of her husband, in *The Comedy of Errors,* ii, 1, laments:

> Since that my beauty cannot please his eye,
> I'll weep what's left away, and weeping die.

sed: put down. This root developed in three directions: (I) to put down the buttocks—stop, sit, dwell; (II) to put down the foot—walk, go; and (III) to put down the fists or weapons—yield.

(I) sit, dwell. Skr, *Upanishad:* sitting beside; treatise on Hindu philosophy, explaining the Vedas; see *ni.* Gk *hedra:* seat, chair. *cathedral: see* of a bishop. *ex cathedra:* the pope speaking from his *seat* of Catholic authority. *synezesis:* sitting together, combining. Gk *edaphos:* floor, soil. *edaphic:* of the ground, on which primitive man squatted. *edaphology. -hedron:* sides, as surface to sit on; *dihedral, icosahedron,* etc. *exedra:* portico, with bench for disputation. *Sanhedrin:* Jewish official council, usually 72 men sitting together. *ephedra:* sitting on; name of the plant (also known as *horsetail*) from which the powder *ephedrine* was extracted. Gk (*pi-sed*) *piezein:* sit on, press. *piezoelectricity, piezometer, sympiezometer.*

L *cathedra:* chair. Fr, *chaise, chaise-longue.* L *sedere, sedens, sessum:* sit, abide, dwell, hold court. *seat, sedate, sedative, sedentary; sedan chair;* a religious *see. sessile, session, sediment; sewer:* servant. *sit. siege:* sit down before; *besiege. hostage* (LL *obsides: h* added because of influence of *hostile*): one held sitting, for ransom, etc. Possibly *sitology:* study of food, from L *sitos:* meal; sit down to eat.

Also *sedulous, assiduous. assess, assizes. insidious, insessorial. obsession. possession:* to dwell with. *sit; set:* to cause to sit. *setter:* dog trained to sit, awaiting command. *settle, settlement. soot,* which settles down. *nest,* where a bird sits. *nestling. nide, nidulation, nidify. eyas* (*a nyas* became *an eyas*): a young falcon taken from its nest to be trained to hunt. *preside, president. dissident. resident, residue. subside, subsidy. supersede. soil:* earth; L *solium:* seat. *cosset:* first, to sit with; then, to pet, as Mary's little lamb. Fr, *séance, bienséance.* L, *Alsatian,* Fr, *Alsace:* dwelling on the other side (of the Rhine). Gc, *saddle. sitz bath. ersatz.*

(II) walk, go. Gk *hodos:* way. *hodograph, odograph, odometer. episode; exodus. method, period, synod. stomodeum:* on the way to being a mouth, in an embryo. *-ode,* as *anode, cathode, electrode.* L *accedere, accessum:* approach, also assent (thus blending with *sed III*). *access, accession. ancestor, antecedent. exceed, excess. intercede, precede, precession; precedent, predecessor. procedure, proceed, process, procession, access, recede, recess. abscess:* going away. *secede. succeed,* in both senses, from the nouns *success* and *succession.* Thus contestants *succeeding* the first one may not *succeed; successive* attempts may be *unsuccessful. retrocede. recession* (an economics term preferred to *panic*). *cesspool;* shortened from *recess pool.*

(III) yield. *cease, surcease. cede, cession, accede; concede, concession, decease. necessary:* "unyielding"; see *ne.*

"Government, even in its best state, is a necessary evil"—Thomas Paine, *Common Sense,* 10 Jan. 1776.

> If it were done when 'tis done, then 'twere well
> It were done quickly; if the assassination
> Could trammel up the consequence, and catch
> With his surcease success; that but this blow

Might be the be-all and the end-all here,
But here, upon this bank and shoal of time,
We'd jump the life to come.
—*Macbeth,* i, 7

segh: seize, hold; have, pause. Several variants developed in Greek. *skhedios:* holding briefly; on the spur of the moment. *sketch;* Fr, *esquisse. skhole:* leisure, which in ancient Greece was largely devoted to discussion; hence *school, scholar, scholastic, scholium,* etc. *ekhein:* hold, *epi:* on; a "hold on time" forms an *epoch. apocha* was a legal receipt, acknowledgment that one holds something (as money). A *cleruch* was a Greek citizen entitled to hold, and settle on, conquered land. The *daduchus* held the torch at the Eleusinian mysteries. *eunuch* is discussed below. From having a state of mind came E *hectic:* first, habitual. Milton spoke of "that hectic disposition to evil, the source of all vice." In this sense the more common term now is *hectic flush,* which is perhaps misused when one says that things are *hectic* (feverish?). *cachexy* is a bad thing held (see *caca*). *pleonexia. entelechy:* actuality, term coined by Aristotle from the idea of "having the whole"; *enteles:* the whole.

Gk *skhema:* form. *scheme, schematic. ischium* (L *os innominata:* the bone not to be named): the bone that holds the body when sitting. *ischuria:* a holding back; retention of urine; *ischuretic. ischemia:* holding back of the blood; local anemia (Gk *haima:* blood, whence also *h(a)emoglobin, hemophilia, hemorrhage, hemorrhoids,* etc.).

eunuch (Gk *eune:* bed) was first one that guarded the Oriental harem; perhaps first emasculated in the 9th c. B.C. by King Ninus for his wife Semiramis. There are two sorts of *eunuch:* the *spado* has only his testicles removed (hence *spaded*); the *castrato* has all his external sex organs severed. Young boys in the papal choirs were made eunuchs so that their high-pitched voices would not change. When such a choir visited London, it was hissed out of the country. In 1761 Charles Churchill wrote:

Never shall a truly British age
Bear a vile race of eunuchs on the stage.

The practice continued, however. A note in French, written by Rossini in 1863 and presently housed in a glass case in La Scala, Milan's famous opera house, states: "Twelve singers of three sexes, men, women, and castrati, will suffice." The practice continues for other reasons as well. In Denmark, from 1929 to 1959, some 900 men, mainly sex offenders, were eunuchized. This was also the fate of some 400 rapists and child-molesters in Los Angeles in the twenty years before 1975; after an American Civil Liberties Union protest in that year, however, doctors, fearing malpractice suits, refused to eunuchize the convicts.

holding, in the sense of capture, led to Gm *Sieg:* victory; hence the names *Siegfried* and *Sig(is)mund,* sometimes shortened to *Sig.* The German toast, before and after Hitler, is *Sieg heil!*

And let a scholar all earth's volumes carry,
He will be but a walking dictionary.
—George Chapman, *Tears of Peace* (1616)

"Public schools are the nurseries of all vice and immorality"—Henry Fielding, *Joseph Andrews* (1742), ii, 5.

But from the first 'twas Peter's drift
To be a kind of moral eunuch;
He touched the hem of Nature's shift,

Felt faint—and never dared to lift
The closest, all-concealing tunic.
—Shelley, *Peter Bell the Third* (1819), iv

sei: leave, leave off; delay; settle down. L *sinere, situm:* set down. *site, situation, situs; desinence, desition.* L *silere, silens, silitum. silence.* The prolific *ponere:* put down, place, is short for *po-sinere* (see *ap*).

God makes such nights, all white and still,
Fur'z you can look or listen;
Moonshine and snow on field and hill,
All silence and all glisten.
—J. R. Lowell, *The Biglow Papers,*
2d ser., introduction

seiku: flow. L *siccatus:* flowed out, dry. *siccative; desiccated; exsiccate. hortus siccus:* dry garden. Via Fr, *sec* (used of wine, as opposed to *sweet*). It, *secchio. secco:* painting on dry plaster. *sack* (earlier *seck*): a strong wine. Gm *Seidel:* mug.

"If sack and sugar be a fault, God help the wicked!"—*1 Henry IV,* ii, 4. And read the encomium of sherris-sack in *2 Henry IV,* iv, 3, which ends: "Skill in the weapon is nothing without sack, for that sets it a-work; and learning, a mere hoard of gold kept by a devil till sack commences it and sets it in act and use." "If I had a thousand sons," Falstaff adds to his panegyric, "the first humane principle I should teach them should be to forswear thin potations, and to addict themselves to sack."

sek: cut. See *tem.* Early man found and fashioned tools. To shells and to stones sharp or chipped sharp he added hilts or handles, the better to scrape, scratch, dig, cut apart. Then the basic roots for these tools, for the operations performed, for the things made with them, took on wider meaning. Thus, *to scratch or incise letters* (on stone, wood, wax, clay, papyrus) produced *scribes* and *scribblers*—and current *scrabblers.* To cut, as diamond-shapers and butchers are aware, demands the knowledge and skill to separate wisely. Here we approach the wide avenues of science, and here this root spreads into eight more forms (discussed here), plus two that dropped the *s* (*see kel VIII; ker III*).

(I) *sek:* cut, L *secare, secantem, sectum. secant; secateur:* pruning shears; *sect, section, sector. bisect, dissect. trisect,* etc. *sicarian:* killer with a knife. *intersect, intersection, transect, venesection, vivisection.*

An insect is "cut in"; in the 16th and 17th c., insects were called *cutwaists.* William Harrison, in *The Description of England* (1577), says of L *insecta:* "The cut-wasted (for so I English the word) are the hornets, wasps, bees, and the like." Go to the ant, thou skeptic, and be wise to the shape there. It is estimated that insects comprise 80 percent of all animal life. Over a million species have been registered and described; entomologists tell us that as many more are crawling, hopping, or flying around us unrecognized, and that thousands are newly registered every year.

bug, possibly Welsh in origin, first meant hobgoblin; this sense survives in such words as *bugaboo, bugbear, bogy.* The *boogeyman* was in the mind of James Whitcomb Riley when he wrote, in *Little Orfant Annie* (1980): "The gobble-uns'll git you ef you don't watch out." (For *goblin,* Gk *khobalos,* see *el 27.*) With cognates in Scandinavian, *bug* is a vague word for various disliked grubs, larvae, and insects, as *potato bug, bedbug* (which, says *OED,* emits an offensive odor when touched). The word has also been applied to disliked humans, as an arsonist, a *fire bug,* and scornfully to a person in a superior position, a *big bug.* Benjamin

Franklin, in a letter of 26 Sept. 1772 to Georgiana Shipley, is apparently the first to have noted the neat juxtaposition (suggesting an epitaph for her late pet squirrel):

Here Skugg Lies snug As a bug In a rug.

Note that the *bugger* who commits *buggery:* sodomy, draws his name from *Bulgar* (the Bulgarian heretics of the 16th c. having been thus calumniated). The word *bugger,* however, in all innocence and even affection, has come to mean fellow, chap, youngster: "He's a cute little bugger."

L *resecare,* used of the danger of ships' being cut asunder by rocks, emerged in E *risk.* L *saxum:* stone, chipped off the rock. *saxatile, saxicoline, saxifrage. sex,* which (as Adam knew) cuts female from male, has (strangely?) not been traced further back than the Latin. Aldous Huxley states in *Along the Road* (1925): "Since Mozart's day composers have learned the art of making music throatily and palpitatingly sexual." African drumbeaters knew it long before. Lawrence Durrell, in *Tunc,* closed the subject: "No more about sex; it's too boring."

(The German musical prodigy Mozart was entangled in the vogue of classicalizing names. He was baptized Johannes Crysostomus Wolfgangus Theophilus; the last of these, a Greek name, was made more familiar as Latin *Amadeus,* which is *Gottlieb* in German, but which in his usual signature Mozart made French: Wolfgang Amadé Mozart. *Amadeus,* a play by Peter Shaffer, at the London National Theatre [Olivier] in 1980, in New York in 1981, plays upon the jealousy of the Italian Salieri, court composer to Joseph II of Austria, and the suspicion that he poisoned the German Mozart, who died in 1791, at the age of thirty-five).

The word *aprosexia* is not connected with *sex;* via Gk *a,* negative, *prosexein:* turn (the attention), it is applied to an abnormal inability to concentrate. Fixing persistently on one idea is *hyperprosexia;* turning constantly to side issues is *paraprosexia.* Man's major drives are for security and power; sex is a side issue, to keep him going.

L *signum. sign; signal, signature; signet, signify, significant. consign, countersign, design, designate; ensign; insignia. resignation. sigil, sigillate* (L *sigillum,* diminutive of *signum*). A *sennet* is a trumpet call signaling an entrance or an exit. A *tocsin* (LL *toccare:* touch) is an alarm bell.

Via OFr, from L *absecare,* came *an otch,* which has been folkchanged to *a notch.*

E *scarlet* is roundabout from Arabic, which had borrowed L *sigillatum* to apply to a shorn cloth, which might be blue, green, or brown as well as the brilliant red that survived in the word because it was "the king's color." John Locke, in *Human Understanding* (1690), made a surprising comparison: "His friend demanding what scarlet was, the blind man answered: It was like the sound of a trumpet." The relationship between sight and sound was stressed by the 19th c. French poets (see *reg II*) and by Francis Thompson in his magnificent *Ode to the Setting Sun* (1893):

High was thine Eastern pomp inaugural,
But thou dost set in statelier pageantry,
Lauded with tumults of a firmament;
Thy visible music-blasts make deaf the sky,
Thy cymbals clash to fire the Occident,
Thou dost thy dying so triumphally:
I *see* the crimson blaring of thy shawms!

Gc, *saw, seesaw. sedge:* sharp-edged stalks; mind your fingers! *skin,* sliced off the animal. *sickle, scythe.* "Time the mower whets his scythe." OE *sax:* knife; *Saxon:* knife man. The Saxon Hengist and his brother Horsa, invited to Britain in 446 by King Vortigern to help him fight the Picts, cried *nemet oure saxes!* as the signal for their men to massacre their hosts. Hence also *Saxony, Essex, Middlesex, Sussex, Wessex.*

(II) *skei, sqei:* cut, split; divide, part, drop off. Gk *skhizein. schism, schismatic. schist, schedule* (pronounced *shedule* in Britain, *skedule* in the U.S.): first, a splinter of wood or a scrap of papyrus, to make a note on. *schizo-,* as *schizocarp, schizoid, schizophrenia. schizomysete:* bacteria that multiply by splitting, as "fission fungi." *OED* lists 27 *schizo* words, as *schizogenic; schizognathous:* with cleft palate; and it details 30 words beginning *schism* or *schist.*

L *scutum:* shield; first, cut-and-joined boards covered with hide. *scutum. ancile.* Fr *écu:* coin with shield design, first, of Louis IX of France. It, *scudo;* Fr, *escudo. escutcheon. esquire:* first, a knight's shield-bearer; *squire. shear; shiver; skewer.* L *scindere, scidi, scissum:* divide, cut, tear. *abscess, abscind, abscissa. scission, scissile, scissors, scissortail. exscind, prescind, rescind.*

L *caedere, cecidi, caesus:* cut, cut to pieces. See *skhai* below. From this came *suicide, fratricide* (hence, "the mark of Cain"), etc. *caesarian* comes from the legend that Julius Caesar was delivered *a caeso matris utere:* from his mother's cut womb. In ancient times, this operation was performed only when a woman had died, in an attempt to save the unborn child; Julius Caesar's mother was alive when he wrote the *Gallic Wars.* The family name *Caesar* was probably Etruscan. *Julius* is shortened from *Jovilis:* descendant of Jove. Julius Caesar was born in Quintilis, the fifth month when March was first; in his honor the month was renamed *July,* whereafter his adopted son and heir, Emperor Augustus, took the next month, with as many days, *August.*

When Emperor Tiberius Caesar was offered a month of 31 days, he refused it, saying: "There are only twelve months; what will you do when there are thirteen Caesars?" History provided only twelve Caesars, but the names of the other months remained unchanged. From the first emperor also came the adjective *august,* and from *Caesar* came *kaiser, czar* (*tsar*). *Caesaria:* city of Caesar, became Sp *Xeres:* Jerez, which gave early English *sherris;* this, taken as a plural, is now *sherry.* Other English words that were formed because the final *s* sound was taken as a plural are *pea* ("Pease porridge hot . . ."), *cherry, gentry, marquee, shay; shimmy* (Shake your chemise!).

Julius Caesar began his bid for power when in 49 B.C. he crossed the River Rubicon, the river between Gaul and Italy that no general was supposed, unbidden, to cross; one's *Rubicon* may be used to mean one's moment of critical decision. Caesar exclaimed *Alea jacta est:* The die is cast. From *alea,* E *aleatory.* (Note that *Cherubicon* is the hymn sung during the Great Entrance of the choir of the Eastern Orthodox Church, symbolizing the worship of the cherubim before God. *cherub* and *cherubic* are from Hebrew.)

L, *caesura. cement* (chipped bits). *cestus:* ancient knuckle-dusters. *circumcision. chisel. concise; decide, indecision; excise, excision; incise, incision.* Fr, *précis. precise; succise. sallet.* L *scire, sciens, scientum:* divide, discriminate, hence know. *science, scientific, pseudoscience, scientology,* etc. *scilicet. sciolist. scire facias. adscititious. conscience, conscientious. conscious.* Shakespearean characters express opposed ideas about conscience. Richard III (v, 3) cries "Conscience is but a word that cowards use"; he goes fiercely into battle—and dies. Hamlet (iii, 10), pondering "the dread of something after death," observes: "Thus conscience doth make cowards of us all." Julius Caesar (ii, 2) remarks:

Cowards die many times before their deaths;
The valiant never taste of death but once.

Also *prescient.* For the distinction between *nescience* and *ignorance,* see *ne. nice* and *nicety* were originally, via OFr, contractions of *nescient. omniscient* (see *op I*). *plebiscite:* division of the people, in voting.

Gc, *shin* (divides the leg). OFr, *chine.* Gc, *Wiener schnitzel:* Vienna cutlet. *shed. watershed;* in the U.S. "the Great Divide": water to the west flows to the Pacific; to the east, to the Atlantic. *sheath:* first, sticks fitted together. *ship* (hewn wood). *shiver,* as *Shiver my timbers! skipper* (Du *schipper*). *ski* (in Scandinavia pronounced *she*). *shite, shit,* dropped from the animal; earlier *skate, skite,* as in *blatherskite. blather:* to talk nonsense loquaciously, as with verbal diarrhea. *skate:* shitter, originally a Scotch term of contempt, is now softened in the colloquial "He's a good skate." The Scotch song *Maggie Lauder,* by F. Sempill, 1650, a favorite with the American Army in the Revolution, contains the line: "Jog on your gait, ye blatherskate." Variants are *bletherumskite* and *blatherskite.* An informative Paston family letter written in 1449, relates: "I cam abord the Admirall, and bade them stryke [pull down their flag] in the Kyngys name, and they bade me skyte in the Kyngys name." (Note that *sk,* as still in Scandinavian tongues, was long sounded *sh* in English.)

(III) *(s)kel:* cut, sharp. L, *scalp, scalpel, scalper, scauper. sculptor, sculpture, sculpturesque,* and the more recent *sculpt. colter, cult; cutlass. cultivate:* dig the ground. *cultrate. culture* and all that. The wide field of *agriculture.* OFr, *caul.* Gc, *shale, shell. skill* (in cutting, dividing). *shoal;* via Du, *school* of fish (cut apart). *shelf* (cut wood). *scale:* first, the dish ("shell") of the balance for weighing. The *scales* of a fish resemble cut-off chips. Norse, *skoal:* first, a drinking cup made from a skull; *skull,* from its separation from the torso.

(IV) *skep:* hack, scrape, dig. Gk *khoptein:* strike off. *comma:* first, a clause marked off; then, the punctuation mark (,). *apocopate, apocope. pericope;* four syllables, not to be confused with the trisyllabic *periscope. syncope.* A *capon* is a castrated cock (barnyard variety). Via Fr, *hatchet, hash, hatch:* to engrave. *Coptis:* genus of plant, the crowfoot, named for its divided leaves. Russ, *kopeck;* first, a coin bearing the image of the czar with a lance.

Scylla: the tearing one; monster guarding one side of the Strait of Messina. *Charybdis,* the whirlpool on the other side, is of unknown origin. *between Scylla and Charybdis* is used of the danger of running into one evil while seeking to avoid another. *The Man in the Moon* (1609), speaks, alliteratively if not quite accurately, of "the very sink of sensuality and pool of putrefaction; a Scylla to citizens and Charybdis to countrymen."

Gk *skuphos:* cup; first made of hollowed wood. *scyph-,* prefix in plant and animal names, as *scyphiform, scyphomedusa; OED* lists 14. *scyphus:* a deep cup. *scyphogeny. scyphomancy:* divination using a cup, as with tea leaves. *OED* lists 6 words beginning *scyphi,* as *scyphiferous;* and 9 beginning *scypho,* as *scyphostoma:* cup-mouthed. Gk *scaphos:* dug out, thence boat-shaped, as *scaphocephalic. scapula:* first, shovel; then, shoulder blade, from its shape plus its use in digging.

L, *scabrous:* scratched, rough. LL, *scabble; chap.* OE, *nuthatch.* Sp, *quebracho:* ax-breaker. Gc, *hack. shape, landscape. scab; scabies. scoop. shabby; shaft.* The suffix *ship,* as in *workmanship,* was applied first to cutting with stone; then was gradually widened to apply to skill, quality, or office, as in *championship, deanship;* see *dheigh N 33. shipshape. shave, shaver, shavings.* Via Swiss, *sapsago.*

(V) *(s)ker:* cut, cut off, drop. Gk *scato-:* excrement, excrementitious, as *scatology, scatomancy; OED* lists 7 associated terms. *skatole. scoria, scorify.*

stercoriaceous. L *scrobis:* ditch, pit. *scrobiculate:* pitted. *scrofula,* listed with 12 relevant words in *OED.* From dropping the *s* came L *corium:* cut-off hide, leather. E *corium, currier. cuirass,* first made of leather. For *carnal, carnation, chair,* etc., see *ker III.* L (*kert-sna:* cut food) *cena, cenacle.* Gc, *scrap, scrape, scarp. sharp, scrub, shrub.* Gm, *dreck.*

(VI) *skeri:* cut, scrape, separate, sift. Gk *khrinein.* L *cernere, cretum* (earlier *certum*): separate, discriminate, judge. *certain, certainty, uncertain. certificate, certify; certiorari; certitude. crisis, criterion* (from Gk *khrinein, khrisis:* decision; *khrites:* judge); *critic, critikin, uncritical, hypercritical. hypocrisy. hematocrit. apocrine. diacritical. oneirocritic:* interpreter of dreams, e.g., the Greek oracles, whose stone "sleeping beds" for petititoners may still be seen outside the ruins of their temples; and Joseph and Daniel in the Bible. *concern, decern, decree; discern, discriminate, incriminating, recrimination. criminal, crime* (see *ker IV*). *eccrinology; endocrene, exocrene; recrement. crayon:* of sifted earth, was borrowed from French by John Evelyn, who wrote in his *Diary:* "The prospect was so tempting that I designed it with my crayon" (1644). *cribriform:* sievelike. With L *se-:* apart, came *secern, secret, secrete, secretion.* Via Sp, *garble,* and possibly *garbage:* things sifted out.

L *scribere, scriptum:* scratch; then write. *scribe, circumscribe, ascribe, conscription, describe, inscription; manuscript,* abbreviated *ms.* (*Ms* has recently grown into use as a written form of address for a female of any age, either Miss or Mrs.) *postscript,* in letters often abbreviated *P.S.;* the one following this would be *P.P.S. prescribe, prescription, proscribe, subscribe, superscription, transcribe, transcription,* etc. *scribble, scrabble, script. Scripture, scriptorium. scrivener:* Chaucer blandly remarked that any error in his writings should be ascribed to ("aret it to") Adam *Scrivener*—"a votary of the desk," as Lamb described him, "a notched and cropt scrivener—one that sucks his substance as certain sick people are said to do, through a quill."

Gc, *shrivel. riddle,* as with bullets; for the puzzling *riddle,* see *ar I. shrift, shrive. Shrovetide:* the three days before Ash Wednesday, the first day of Lent; on them, confessions are heard and penance is prescribed. *Lent* is from OE *lengten:* spring, when the days clearly lengthen; it is the period of 40 weekdays before Easter, a period of restraint (originally observed by fasting from dawn to dusk, as the Muslims still do in the month of Ramadan), its duration being suggested by the 40-day fasts of Moses, Elijah, and Jesus.

> A man must serve his time to every trade
> Save censure—critics all are ready made.
> Take hackneyed jokes in Miller, got by rote,
> With just enough of learning to misquote;
> A mind well skilled to find or forge a fault;
> A turn for punning, call it Attic salt . . .
> Fear not to lie, 'twill seem a sharper hit;
> Shrink not from blasphemy, 'twill pass for wit;
> Care not for feeling—pass your proper jest—
> And stand a critic, hated yet caressed.
> —Byron, *English Bards and Scotch Reviewers*

(VII) *skhed:* cut. L, *shingle:* a cut piece for roofing. Gc, *shatter.*

(VIII) *ske(r)u:* cut, dig, poke, push. *scrotum:* a bag "pushed" from the belly at the crotch; its form influenced by L *scrantum:* a quiver, a container. Via OFr *escroc:* shred, came E *scroll,* a folkchange influenced by *roll,* because the cut section, written on, was rolled up for keeping. Hence also *escrow,* now a legal term.

screed: first, a strip cut off; used to write a list on, as of grievances. Russ *krai:* edge, led to the name *Ukrainian:* bordering land.

L *scrutinium:* investigation of (*scruta:* bits cut or torn off), E *scrutiny. shred. shroud:* cut garment, later limited to burial cloth; the plural, *shrouds,* is still used for cut ropes for masts and sails, etc.

shrew: small mammal with long, pointed nose overhanging the upper lip and used for digging. In 180 of the 290 species of shrew, a curious behavior pattern is expressed; when disturbed, they form a daisy chain, a young one taking an older one's tail in its mouth, the mother leading. In the 13th c. the term *shrew* was applied to an ugly person, but soon became limited to a scolding, malignant woman. The shrew's saliva is toxic; never kiss a shrew! *shrewd,* from the noun, has softened in meaning, but still bears a disagreeable overtone. *Beshrew me!:* Curse me!, takes force from the common speech of the human shrew.

"Bid fair peace be to my sable shroud"—Milton, *Lycidas.*

(IX) *(s)kreu:* divide, cut, bite, scrape, pluck. Gk *khoris:* bedbug, biting insect. *corum. Coreopsis:* genus of plants with buglike seeds. *coriander:* plant that smells like the bedbug, an odor once widely familiar. *coriaceous.*

Gk *carpos:* fruit, cut or plucked off. The spirit of the spring breeze, Zephyr, won the love of the nymph *Chloris,* from whom, in nature's mythological fashion, we get E *chlorophyll,* the greening essence (*chloris* means green). The fruit of that union was a son, *Carpos,* which by the same mythological process became the Greek word for fruit. Hence *carpel, onocarpic, amphicarpic,* etc. *scarce:* picked out. *carpology.*

excerpt. L *carnis:* flesh, cut off. *carnage, carnal, carnassial. carnation* first meant flesh color; hence also *carnelian. carnival* (but see *ker III; leguh*). *carnivorous, caruncle.* Via OFr, *carrion, charnel.* "This my hand will rather/The multitudinous seas incarnadine"—*Macbeth,* ii, 2, 59. *incarnate;* deliberately distorted in "He's the very devil incardinate"—*Twelfth Night,* v, 1, 182. *incarnation, reincarnation.*

L, *cortex:* bark, cut off. *decorticate. excoriate, quarry:* first, parts of a deer cut off and tossed as a reward to the expectant hounds. LL, *scorbutic* (Russ *skrobota:* scratch); *scurf, scurvy.* L *scrupus:* sharp stone. *scrupulous:* literally, full of sharp little stones, hence to be handled with care. *scruple.* L *curtus:* cut short. *curt, curtal, curtail, curtate. kirtle.*

Gc, *harvest:* cutting and plucking time. *harrow. shear, shears, share.* "Turn your swords into plowshares." *share and share alike:* divided parts. *scabbard; scar. shard. short. shirt;* "cutty sark"—Burns, *Tam o'Shanter* (see *ker II*). *skirt. skirmish:* first, the cut-hide covering of a shield; then, close combat with sword and dagger. Also *screen, scrim, scrimmage. scrod:* young codfish (weighing less than three pounds), especially one split to cook.

This was the most unkindest cut of all.
—Julius Caesar of his friend Brutus's
blow (iii, 2, 183)

Flo was fond of Ebenezer—
"Eb," for short, she called her beau.
Talk of tides of love, great Caesar!
You should see them—Eb and Flo.
—Thomas Augustin Daly, *The Tides of Love* (1909)

seks, sueks: six. Gk *hex. hexad, hexagon. OED* lists 47 and details 41 relevant words, from *hexachord* to *hexyl.* Gk *hexamiton:* woven with six threads; via OFr, *samite:* heavy silk cloth—a word used in a line Tennyson employs four times (*The Coming of Arthur,* 284; *The Passing of Arthur,* 199, 312, 321) to describe the "Lady of the Lake," who has given to and takes from King Arthur the sword Excalibur; her arm above the water is "clothed in white samite, mystic, wonderful." (The bewitching *hex* is from Gm *Hexe:* witch. See *kagh.*)

L *sex, sextus. sexagenarian; sextant;* etc. *OED* lists 38 and details 53 relevant words beginning *sex-, sexi-,* or *sext-.* (For the *sex* of living things, see *sek I. sexton* and its doublet, *sacristan* are roundabout from L *sacer;* see *sak.*) *bissextile;* originally, leap year doubled the sixth day before the March calends. *senary.* It, *sestina.* The *sestet,* following the octet, completes the fourteen lines of a sonnet. Fr, *semester* (L *sex-mens-tris:* originally, a period of six months); study hours, as well as working hours, have a way of growing shorter. Sp, *siesta* (L *sexta hora:* sixth hour after sunrise; noon).

sistine: referring to one of the Popes *Sixtus;* the last was Pope Sixtus V (d. 1590). Especially, in reference to Pope Sixtus IV, who in 1473 began the building of the Sistine Chapel in the Vatican palace. The chapel is noted for the murals and ceiling painted by Michelangelo, although the *Encyclopaedia Britannica,* in its 1885 edition, commented that it "lost its chief attraction when Raphael's Sistine Madonna was sold by the monks." It is in the Sistine Chapel that the College of Cardinals meets to select a new pope.

Gc, *six, sixth, sixty; sixpence. sixteenmo,* short for *sextodecimo:* sheet so folded as to make 16 printed pages.

As Noel Coward saw his kind,

> Mad dogs and Englishmen go out in the midday sun;
> The Japanese don't care to, The Chinese wouldn't dare to;
> Hindus and Argentines sleep firmly from twelve to one,
> But Englishmen detest a siesta.

seku I: follow. L *sequi, secutum. sect, sectarian. sequacious; sequel, sequela; sequence; consecutive, consequence, inconsequential. non sequitur:* it does not follow; an error in logic. *sequestered. subsequent; ensue. execute:* follow out. *exequatur* (L *exsequatur:* he may follow his task): official recognition of a consul by the government to which he is accredited. *persecute; prosecute.* Sp, *seguidilla;* follow your partner. Fr, *sue, suit, suitor. pursuant, pursue, pursuit; pursuivant. suite.* Fr, *suivez. intrinsic* (Fr *intrinsèque*); *extrinsic.*

exequies, obsequies; obsequious; at first applied to one that follows submissively, *obsequious* followed the noun *obsequies* to refer to the rites following death. Shakespeare thus uses the word, in Sonnet 31; in *Hamlet,* i, 2; and in *Richard III,* i, 2, where Anne, come with the corpse to

> obsequiously lament
> The untimely fall of virtuous Lancaster,

is interrupted by the murderer, Gloucester, soon to be King Richard III, who at once proceeds to woo her, and wins her hand. Shakespeare's Tudor picture of Richard as a villain has been challenged by recent historians; see *gib.* Back in 1649 G. Daniel exclaimed: "How byassed all human actions are!"

L *secundus. secundines:* afterbirth, following the neonate. *OED* details 11 words beginning *secund. second* is the one following *one;* we say *third, fourth, fifth,* etc., but not *twoth.* Fr, *seconde:* parry in fencing; It, *secondo:* second player or singer in a duet.

L *signum:* mark to be followed. *sign, signpost, significant, signify. assign, consign. design, designate, resign. insignia.* L *socius:* follower, fellow worker. *sociable, social. socialism;* coined, in French, ca. 1830, by Pierre Leroux; applied to the teachings of Saint-Simon and Robert Owen. *society, sociology,* etc. *associate, consociate, disassociate* (shortened to *dissociate*).

Life's but a walking shadow,
. . . .
It is a tale
Told by an idiot, full of sound and fury,
Signifying nothing.
–*Macbeth*, v, 5

Along the cool sequestered vale of life
They kept the noiseless tenor of their way.
–Gray, *Elegy in a Country Churchyard* (1751)

Among the astute observations of Samuel Johnson is his opinion of medical men (objects of scorn or mockery from before Molière to after Bernard Shaw): "It is incident to physicians, I am afraid, beyond all other men, to mistake subsequence for consequence." This is the error in logic called *post hoc ergo propter hoc:* after this, therefore because of this.

seku II: remark, with the early implication of divine vision. Gk, *thespian,* from *Thespis,* legendary founder of Greek drama; hence, divinely spoken; see *dhes.* Norse, *skald, scold. saga.* Gc, *see, seem, seemly. sight. say, saying, saw:* old saying.

the justice,
In fair round belly with good capon lined,
With eyes severe, and beard of formal cut,
Full of wise saws and modern instances . . .
–"Seven Ages of Man," in *As You Like It,* ii, 7

Good to the heels the well-worn slipper feels
When the tired player shuffles off the buskin;
A page of Hood may do a fellow good
After a scolding from Carlyle or Ruskin.
–Oliver Wendell Homes, *How Not to Settle It*

sel I: abode. L *solum:* foundation, bottom. *sole* of the foot. *solum.* Fr, *entresol; salon, saloon.*

sel II: good spirit, happy. Gk, *exhilarating; hilarious.* L, *solace, consolation, console. desolate* (but see *sue*). Gc *selig:* blessed; used today when referring to the dead. In English, degenerated to *seely,* then *silly:* first, unlearned, rustic, innocent; then, feeble-minded; happy; idle. Coleridge, in *The Ancient Mariner* (1798), speaks of "the silly buckets on the deck"—for rain water, but there had been no rain. *sillabub* (earlier *sillibub*): literally, happy belly; cream with sugar in wine.

sillyism (better, *sillygism,* after *syllogism*): an (un)intentionally amusing nonsensical remark. *the silly season* was an early newspaper term for August and September, when (in the good old days before the wireless, world wars, and world-wide terrorism) there was little news, and the papers resorted to trivial items, and even hoaxes, as space-fillers. Although published a little early in the year (*New York Sun,* 13 Apr. 1844), Edgar Allan Poe's account of "Mr. Monck Mason's Flying Machine," which in 75 hours crossed the Atlantic from North Wales to South Carolina, qualifies as a silly season "balloon hoax."

"It's over, and can't be helped, and that's one consolation, as they always says in Turkey ven they cuts the wrong man's head off"—Sam Weller, in Dickens' *The Pickwick Papers* (a good example of a Wellerism).

sel III: take. Gk *Hellen:* seizer; legendary ancestor of the *Hellenes,* the Greeks, whence *Hellenism,* etc. Probably L *consulere senatum:* to take the senators together; *consultare, consultatum:* to take advice. *consul, consult, consultation, counsel,* etc; but see *kel II.* Gc, *sell:* let one take. *sale. handsel:* to seal the bargain.

sel IV: leap; gush out; quake. Gk, *halteres:* organs taking the place of hind legs in some insects, helping them jump; the singular form, *halter,* is also called *balancer. Altica:* genus of jumping beetles. L *salire, saltus. salient, saltation, saltatory; sally. saltigrade,* e.g., the kangaroo, which walks by leaps and bounds. It, *saltimbanco.* Fr, *somersault. saltant, saltus. assail, assault. desultory. subsultory.* Possibly *exile. exult:* jump for joy. *insult:* literally, leap upon. *result.* Fr, *sauté. tressilate* (*tres:* very, *saillir:* leap). Probably the fish that leaps upstream, the *salmon.* (The salmon and the eel return to their native waters to spawn, recognizing the natal stream by its smell.) For *salty* and *salacious,* see *sal.*

It, *saltarello:* lively dance. *saltire:* arranged like St. Andrew's Cross (X), from the shape of the old stirrup cord used when mounting a house; thus *in* or *per saltire,* used in heraldry. Shoes are often laced *saltirewise.*

Salian, of the *Salii:* priests of the god Mars, from their leaping dances in the mimic warlike ritual. *Salii* was latter applied to a tribe of Franks near the cascading river *Sala;* thence, the *Salic law,* by which title to the crown could not pass along the female line, established in 1322 when Charles IV of France succeeded his brother Philip, excluding Edward III of England, whose claim came through his mother. In *Henry V,* i, 2, the Salic law is so explained as to justify Henry's invasion of France; but is attributed—as in Shakespeare's source, Holinshed's *Chronicles*—to a King Pharamond, who died in 426.

selk: drag, draw along. Gk, *hulk, hulking.* L, *sulcate; sulcus,* as where a furrow's been drawn. Possibly *sulky:* carriage; and *seal,* which draws itself closely along the ground.

selp: fat. Gc, *salve. quack,* short for *quacksalver.* See *cal.*

sem I: one, same, as one, together. Skr, *samath:* tomb of a holy man. *samathi:* intense personal meditation, like that attained through yoga. *samsara:* oneness of the soul through generations. *samskara:* bringing oneself together; purification rites.

A number of prefixes have developed from Gk *ha, ȧ. acolyte:* with the teacher, on the Way. *adelpho-:* from the same womb; *adelphi:* brother; *adelphous; mono-* and *bio-adelphous. Philadelphia* (see *bhili*). *amnion:* gathering together. *amoeba:* moving as one. *hama-:* together. *hamacratic:* governing together. *hamadryad:* nymph who lives together with her tree; born with it, she dies when it does. *haplo-:* single, once. *hapax legomenon:* a word or thing occurring only once. *haplodont. OED* lists 8 and details 4 words beginning *haplo. haplography:* writing one letter, syllable, or word where two belong; the reverse is *dittography. haplology* (opposite of *dittology*): making one sound instead of two, sometimes a cause of language change, as when *pacificist* became *pacifist;* see *plek.* Gk *hen:* unit. *henad. hendiadys:* making units—i.e., two nouns joined by *and* taking the place of a noun and an adjective; a 1586 example says of a horse: "on iron and bit he champed." *henopoetic:* of a number of things viewed as one. *henotheism:*

having one's own (or tribal) god. *henotic:* unifying. *hendeca:* one and ten; *hendecasyllabic; OED* lists 9 and details 4 related words.

Gk *sun:* together. E *syn* changes to *syl* before *l;* to *sym* before *b* and *p.*

syl. OED details 13 words, as *syllable:* able to take (letters) together; *syllabus;* the varieties of *syllogism:* two premises, together leading inevitably to a logical conclusion.

sym. OED lists 26 words and details others in 30 columns, as *symbiosis, symbol, sympathetic, symptom.* For *symbiotic,* see *black,* under *kel VI.*

syn. OED lists 45 words and details others in 40 columns, as *synagogue:* led together; *synchronize, syncopated, syndicate.*

OED also lists 14 words related to *syphilis:* loving together; see *bhili.*

Gk *homos:* same; *homoios:* similar; *heteros:* other one; hence different. *Homoousian, Homoiousian, Heteroousian;* see *es. homeopathy:* inducing symptoms similar to the disease; opposed to *allopathy* (*allos:* other). *OED* lists 12 and details 16 words beginning *hom(o)eo;* it lists 66 and details 55 relevant words beginning *homo,* as *homonym, homophone, homologous. homogenized:* made the same throughout. It lists 63 words and details 80 beginning *hetero; heterogeneous* vs. *homogeneous. OED* calls the word *heteroclite* "very common in the 17th and 18th centuries." *homily:* sermon to a gathering. *Homer:* one going with, a companion; the great Greek epic poet was blind. *hyphen:* linking together. Also *homalo:* equal, flat, as *homalographic.*

L *sem-per:* the same throughout, hence everlasting; double perpetuity in E *sempiternal; OED* lists 7 related words. *sempervive:* everliving; the house leek. *sengreen:* evergreen.

A few Latin phrases current in English are *semper eadem:* always the same; motto of Queen Elizabeth I of England. *semper fidelis:* always faithful; motto of the U.S. Marines. *semper paratus:* always ready; motto of the Boy Scouts; also the motto of the U.S. Coast Guard. A member of the Guard's Women's Brigade is known as a *spar*—a clever coinage because (1) a spar supports a ship's rigging, and (2) the letters of *spar* may be formed from *s*emper *par*atus or from the first letters of the motto and the first letters of its translation: *s*emper *par*atus, *a*lways *r*eady.

assembly; Fr, *ensemble. semblance, resemblance, resemble; dissemble.* L *simul:* at the same time. *simultaneous,* fashioned after *instantaneous;* see *sta.* L *similis:* of the same appearance, like. *similar, similacrum; similitude, simulate. simile;* Falstaff (*1 Henry IV,* i, 2) says to Prince Hal: "Thou hast the most unsavory similes."

assimilate, dissimilar, dissimulation; verisimilitude. Compounded with Gk *plous,* L *plex:* fold, came *haploid; simple, simplex, simplify;* see *plek. Simple Simon* is familiar from the nursery rhyme. Among other English Simons is *Simon Pure,* a Quaker in Susannah Centlivre's play *A Bold Stroke for a Wife* (1717); impersonated by Colonel Feignwell, he proves his identity; hence the phrase *the real Simon Pure:* genuine. (Susannah's husband was cook to Queen Anne.) *Simon Legree* (from the brutish slave-dealer in *Uncle Tom's Cabin* (1852) may be used generally of a cruel taskmaster. *Simon Magus,* revered as a magician, then baptized, tried to buy from the apostle Peter the power of bestowing "the Holy Spirit" (Acts 8:18–24); from him came *simony* and 15 related words (see *OED*). For *Simon,* called *Peter,* on whom the Catholic Church rests, see *caput.* The name *Simon* is Hebr *Shim^c^on,* E *Simeon:* literally, hearing (*Shema Israel:* Hear, O Israel [Deuteronomy 6:4]); but is also Gk *Simon:* literally, snub-nosed.

It, *semplice,* in music. L *singulus:* one by itself. *single, single out. OED* gives over 8 columns to the various uses of *single,* and 6 more to its compounds, as *singlet, single-handed; singleton,* in card games. *singular:* odd, one of a kind; but not plural. *singularity* has recently been used by astronomers to name the mass point at which light turns in upon itself; see *kel VI.* Ponder the fact that *alms* has no singular.

Norse, *seem; seemly:* going together, fitting. Gc, *same, some.* Also the suffix *some* (pronounced *sum*): likeness, tendency toward, as *adventuresome, handsome, quarrelsome, toothsome;* JWalker lists 59 such words. (*chromosome*—first and last *o* long—was coined in 1888 by the anatomist Wilhelm von Waldeyer-Hartz, from Gk *chroma:* color and *soma:* body; see *teue.*) *some* is also the first element in a number of words, as *somebody, sometimes, somewhat, somewhere.*

You, for example, clever to a fault,
The rough and ready man that write apace,
Read somewhat seldomer, think perhaps even less.
—Browning, *Bishop Blougram's Apology*

From Slavic, *skupshtina:* Yugoslavia's Parliament; *sobranje:* Bulgaria's Assembly. *Soviet:* together. *Samoyed* (*sam,* and L *edere:* eat, self-eater, cannibal): Russian name for the Nenets, a Siberian tribe. *samovar:* self-cooker.

Nothing in the world is single;
All things, by a law divine,
In one another's being mingle.
Why not I, with thine?
—Shelley, *Love's Philosophy*

sem II. Gc, *summer.*

Sumer is icumen in,
Lhude sing cuckoo!
Ewe bleateth after lamb,
Loweth after calve cu;
Bullock starteth, bucke farteth,
Merry sing, cuckoo!
—First recorded in 1250 by a monk of Reading Abbey, where it is sung annually

How swift the summer goes,
Forget-me-not, pink, rose,
The young grass when I started,
And now the hay is carted,
And now my song is ended,
And all the summer spended . . .
Only the winds that blew,
The rain that makes things new,
The earth that hides things old,
And blessings manifold.
—John Masefield, *The Everlasting Mercy*

There is also the triply punning Guy Wetmore Carryl, who, at the end of his telling of the tale *Little Red Riding Hood,* twists the seasonal trope into an unreasonable toper:

If a swallow cannot make a summer
It can bring on a summary fall.

semi: half. See *sem I.* Four English prefixes have developed here, with overlapping meanings.

(1) L *semi. OED* list 38 words beginning *semi,* the earliest being *semicircular,* used in 1432. It adds that nonce compounds of *semi* came into frequent use in the 19th c., and illustrates "but a small proportion" in over 10 columns, as *semi-cannibalic. semicipher* is used in scorn of an insignificant person. *OED* then details 21 columns of more common *semi* words, as *semifinals, semicolon. semi-bousy:* half-drunk. Also both *semidemi* and *demisemi.*

Some words begin *sesqui* (L *semis-que:* and a half). *OED* lists 42, then details 16, as *sesquicentennial; sesquipedalian,* from Horace's *sesquipedalia verba:* words a foot and a half long ("noddle-puzzling sesquipedalian words"). The first element of the Roman coins *sesterce* and *sestertium* is contracted from *sesqui.* And *sandblind* is a folkchange from *sem, semi-, blind.*

(2) L *demi,* says *OED,* "may be prefixed to almost any substantive, often to adjectives, sometimes to verbs." *OED* lists 53 such words, and details 60, as *demilune, demimondaine.* The *Demiurge* is said by some to be the active center of the world, carrying out the will of the wholly contemplative Supreme Being; by others, the author of evil, opponent of the Supreme Being. A *demijohn,* which usually held from five to eight gallons, is in all likelihood from *Dame Jeanne,* an otherwise unremembered burly French lady.

(3) Gk, *hemi. OED* lists 68 and details others in 9 columns, as *hemipteron; hemiplegia* (*plege:* stroke); *hemisphere, hemistich* (*ch* sounded *k*). This *hemi* should not be confused with the distinct *h(a)em.*

(4) *h(a)em,* from Gk *haima, haimat-:* blood. *OED* details 17 *h(a)ema* words, as *haemagogue, haematine, haemapophysis.* It lists 36 *h(a)emato* or *h(a)emo* words, as *haematotic, haemochrome, haemoscope;* and details 22, as *hemocyanin, hemophilia, hemophobia, hemorrhage. hemorrhoid:* a tumor of the veins around the anus, is usually plural; but to the ancients (Pliny) it was a serpent whose bite caused unstanchable bleeding. *hemoglobin* spreads into 6 other words. *hematite:* a blood-red iron ore.

Browning, in *Bishop Blougram's Apology,* speaks of

demireps
That love and save their souls in new French books.

Shakespeare's Richard II (ii, 1) speaks of England:

This other Eden, demi-paradise,
This fortress built by Nature for herself
Against infection and the hand of war,
This happy breed of men, this little world,
This precious stone set in the silver sea . . .

sen: old. L *senex:* old man; *senectutus:* old age; *senilis, senior, senatus.* E *senescent, senectitude; senile. senior, seniority; senate, senatorial,* etc. Fr, *monsieur:* my sire; *seigneur, signor, monseigneur, monsignor. sir, sire.* Port, *senhor, senhora, senhorita.* Sp, *señor, señora, señorita.* It, *signor, signore, signorina. senicide;* H. H. Johnson, in *The Fortnightly Review* (1889), declared that "the ancient Sardi of Sardinia considered it a sacred duty for the young to kill their old relatives."

sengu. Gc, *sink, sank.* Scand, *sag.*

senguh. Gc, *sing, sang, song, sung. songster;* originally feminine, like *spinster;*

songstress has a second feminine ending superimposed. See *suen.* Gm, *Meistersinger:* master of the art of song. *Minnesinger* (*Minne:* love; *Minnelied:* love song).

There was a jolly miller once,
  Lived on the river Dee;
He worked and sang from morn till night;
  No lark more blithe than he,
And this the burden of his song
  Forever us'd to be:
I care for nobody, not I,
  If no one cares for me.
   —Isaac Bickerstaffe, *Love in a Village* (1763)

For a day and a night Love sang to us, played with us,
  Folded us round from the dark and the light,
And our hearts were fulfilled with the music he made with us,
Made with our hands and our lips while he stayed with us,
  Stayed in mid passage his pinions from flight
      For a day and a night.
   —Swinburne, *At Parting*

seni: separate, by oneself. L *sine:* without. *sincere* (probably from L and E *caries:* decay): without decay; but some suggest it means without wax (Gk *keros,* L *cera*), which was used to restore cracked statues. *sinecure:* first, benefice without "cure of souls" (care of parishioners); thus, an easy post.

In phrases: *sine die:* adjourned without a set date for reconvening. *sine prole:* without offspring (see *al I*). *sine qua non:* without which not, indispensable; *sinequanonical.* In prudish Victorian days, *sinequanons* was one of the odd euphemisms (sometimes with humorous intent) for *breeches.*

Gc, *sunder, asunder; sundry.*

Fr, *sans:* without; the form influenced by Fr *absence* (L *ab-esse;* see *es*). *sans serif* in printed type. *OED* lists 12 phrases from French; best-known are *sans cérémonie; sans gêne:* free and easy, tomboyish. (*Madame Sans-Gêne* (1893) is a play by Victorien Sardou about a madcap washerwoman become Maréchale [wife of the Marshal] Lefèvre; she protects the reputation of Emperor Napoleon's wife and briefly intrigues the emperor; a one-act version by the present author was enacted on television by Sarah Churchill.) *sanspareil:* unequaled; *sans peur et sans reproche:* fearless and faultless (applied first to the Chevalier de Bayard, who died in battle in 1524); *sans souci:* carefree.

The historical *sans-culotte* is represented by 7 English words in *OED;* meaning, literally, without knee breeches, it was a term of scorn used by the nobles to refer to the French Revolutionists, the common men, who wore long trousers, pantaloons. *pantaloons,* shortened to *pants,* is itself shortened from *Pantaleone;* see *keu II. culotte* is a diminutive of Fr *cul:* backside; the nobles wore tight knee breeches with fancy buckles, and long hose. (Camille Desmoulins, whose fiery speech brought on the storming of the Bastille on 14 July [French Independence Day] 1789, thus beginning the French Revolution, was, like many revolutionary leaders, killed by his successors; on Robespierre's orders he and Danton were executed on 5 Apr. 1794. At his trial Desmoulins [b. 1760] said: "I am as old as the good sansculotte Jesus, an age fatal to Revolutionists." Danton's cry to the people on 2 Sept. 1792, rousing them to revolt, was *De l'audace, encore de l'audace, et toujours de l'audace!*)

In the U.S., in somewhat looser shape, knee breeches are called *knickerbockers,* from the costume of Diedrich *Knickerbocker* (: marble baker), the supposed Dutch author of Washington Irving's *History of New York* (1809). *Father Knickerbocker,* thus garbed, is often used to personify New York City. *knee breeches,* also *britches,* worn by golf players and clasped four inches below the knees, are called *plus fours.*

Ah, make the most of what we yet may spend,
Before we too into the dust descend,
Dust into dust, and under dust, to lie,
Sans Wine, sans Song, sans Singer, and–sans End!
–FitzGerald, *Rubáiyát of Omar Khayyám*

Last scene of all,
That ends this strange eventful history,
Is second childishness and mere oblivion,
Sans teeth, sans eyes, sans taste, sans everything.
–"Seven Ages of Man," in *As You Like It,* ii, 7

senk: burn. Gc, *singe.*

sent: to notice, take a direction. L *sentire, sensum:* to sense. *sensation, sense, sensitive, sensible, sentient, sentience; sentence, sentiment. sensorium; sensory, sensual, sensuality; sensuous, sensorimotor. senseless, nonsense.* Jane Austen's first novel, *Sense and Sensibility* (written 1797–98, published 1811), brought her immediate recognition. Its picture of two contrasted sisters and their thwarted lives has been much admired, and is still sometimes read.

assent, consensus; consent; dissension, dissent; insensate, insensitive; presentiment; resent, etc. "Resentment is a union of sorrow with malignity; a combination of a passion which all endeavor to avoid with a passion all concur to detest" –Samuel Johnson.

present is from *pre-esse:* to be before (see *es*). *scent* (noticed); *sentinel, sentry.* Gc, *send, godsend.* Scot, *withershins:* the wrong direction. (*with:* back, against, as in *withdraw, withhold, withstand;* originally meaning close together, *with* may imply joined in cooperation or joined in conflict; see *uid.*)

"Nonsense and faith, (strange as the conjunction may seem) are the two supreme symbolic assertions of the truth that to draw out the soul of things with a syllogism is as impossible as to draw out Leviathan with a hook. The well-meaning person who, by merely studying the logical side of things, has decided that 'faith is nonsense', does not know how truly he speaks; later it may come back to him in the form that nonsense is faith"–G. K. Chesterton, *A Defence of Nonsense* (1901).

sep: bury; venerate the dead. L, *sepulcher; sepulture.*

septem: seven. Gk *hepta.* An English prefix, as in *heptachord, heptad, heptagon, hebdomad, hebdomadary.* (Donne, in a 1631 sermon, spoke scornfully of the *hebdomadary righteous:* those that deem good behavior on Sunday sufficient for the week.) L *septem. septan, septangular, septennial, septuple. September,* seventh month when March was first. A *Septembrist* was one of the revolutionists that massacred royalists in Paris in Sept. 1792. The term was also applied to the Portuguese, who in Sept. 1836 brought about the restoration of the country's 1822 constitution. *Black September* is the group of Arab terrorists (an outgrowth of al-Fatah, headed by Abd al-Rahman abd al-rauf Arafat al-Qud al Husseinie before he took command of the PLO, *P*alestine *L*iberation *O*rganization) which has sought to avenge the unexpected defeat of Syrian and guerrilla forces in what it calls "Black September," 1970; the group pledged to attack not only in Israel but all over the world, its most spectacular strike to date being the killing of 11 Israeli athletes at the 1972 Olympic Games in Munich.

OED lists 45 and details 18 relevant words beginning *hept(a),* as *heptamerous; Heptateuch:* the first seven books of the Old Testament. It also details 8 beginning *hebdo,* as *hebdomically:* according to the mystical number seven. It lists 7 and details 37 relevant words beginning *sept,* as *septemfluous:* flowing in seven branches, as does the Nile; *septenary.*

Gc, *seven, seventh, seventeen, seventy,* etc.

> Seven cities* warr'd for Homer, being dead,
> Who living, had no roof to shroud his head.
> —Thomas Heywood, *Hierarchie of the Blessed Angels* (1635)

Note that *septum* comes from L *sepire, septum:* to divide; hence, a hedge, also a membrane. And *septic(a)emia* comes from Gk *septikhos:* putrefying (plus *haima:* blood); whence also *septic, septicine, septicity, aseptic, antiseptic.*

Septentrion(es) is a name for the seven brightest stars (visible to the naked eye) of the constellation Ursa Major, the Great Bear, a circumpolar group in the northern sky which never sets. To the Hindus, these stars represent the seven *Rashis,* the great sages. In Greek legend, Callisto was a nymph serving Artemis; she bore Zeus a son, *Arcus* (ancestor of the *Arcadians*), and angry Artemis changed her into a bear. When Arcus was about to slay the bear, Zeus changed Callisto into the Great Bear constellation, and set her son Arcus into the near sky as *Arcturus:* guardian of the bear (in the constellation *Arctophylas,* with the same meaning). The star Arcturus speaks the prologue in Plautus's play *Rudens* [The Rope], 194 B.C., perhaps the masterpiece of Roman comedy.

Other names are used for *Septentrion.* It may be called the *Plow,* interpreting *Septem-triones:* seven plow oxen. It may also be called the *Wagon;* when Arcturus is called *Boötes:* the Wagoner. The early word for *wagon* was *wain,* and the constellation was also called *churl's* (peasant's) *wain.* This was later folkchanged to *Charles's Wain* (by association with King *Charlemagne*) because of its nearness to Arcturus, which was similarly folk-understood as *Arturus,* for King *Arthur,* who is linked in legend with Charlemagne. Homer, in the *Odyssey,* v, mentions "the Great Bear, by others called the Wain." In Shakespeare's *1 Henry IV,* ii, 1, the hour of night is judged by the fact that "Charles' Wain is over the new chimney." The group of seven is more commonly known today as the *Big Dipper.*

"The sluggard is wiser in his own conceit than seven men that can render a reason"—Bible, Proverbs 26:16.

> As I was going to St. Ives
> I met a man with seven wives,
> Each wife had seven sacks,
> Each sack had seven cats,
> Each cat had seven kits;
> Kits, cats, sacks, and wives,
> How many were going to St. Ives?
> —Nursery riddle, 1730

ser I: arrange, interlace, join together, compose. L, *series, sertularian; assert, desert* (*de:* away); *dissertation; exert, insert; serried.* L *sortem:* fortune, the way events

*Argos, Athens, Chios, Colophon, Rhodes, Salamis, Smyrna.

are arranged. *sort, assorted; consort; resort. sorcerer; sortilege. sermon* (*sermo religiosus:* composed for church), *sermonet(te), sermonize.*

ser II: press together; protect, serve. Gk *heros:* protector. *conserve, deserve, observe, preserve, reserve.* Fr, *reservoir.* Probably *servant, serve, service, servile, servitude. sear:* catchlock on gun. Via LL, *seraglio,* influenced by Turk *serai:* palace. Also, via Pers, *serai, caravanserai.* It, *sirvente* (*cavaliere;* see *horse,* under *ane*). Fr, *concierge; sergeant.* Gc, *serf.*

> All service ranks the same with God—
> With God, whose puppets, best and worst,
> Are we; there is no last nor first.
> —Browning, *Pippa Passes,* iv

ser III: flow, whirl, boil, Skr, *apsaras:* water nymph in the Hindu heaven. *samsara:* flowing through; the cycle of birth, suffering, death, and rebirth in the Buddhist "wheel of life," from which the devout seek to escape, to attain *Nirvana* (*nirva:* extinguished, *nir:* out, and *vati* [see *aue*]).

Gk *orrhos:* watery fluid; in English pathological terms, as *orrhocyst, orrhoid, orrhous.* Also *hormone;* used by Hippocrates, 5th c. B.C., to mean a vital principle; given its modern sense by E. H. Starling in 1903. L *serum:* watery fluid, whey. *sérac; serum.* Gc, *strudel,* from the boiling stir.

serk: repair, mend. L *sarcire, sartum; sartor. sartorial. Saruna:* genus of bacteria. Carlyle, in *Sartor Resartus* [The Tailor Repatched]: *The Life and Opinions of Herr Teufelsdröckh* (1833–34), reaches the conclusion that all symbols, all human institutions, like clothes, are temporary. This work contains three especially notable chapters: "The Everlasting No," "The Center of Indifference," and "The Everlasting Yea." (*Teufelsdröckh* means Devil's dung.)

serp: creep. Gk *herpein. herpes; herpetology.* L *serpere. serpent. serpentine; serpigo. Serpula:* genus of marine worms. *Serpens:* a northern constellation near the constellation *Serpentinus.* Also the constellation *Ophiuchus:* holding a serpent; Gk *ophis* (diminutive *ophidion*): snake; whence E *ophidian, ophiology, ophite. OED* lists 13 and details 24 relevant words beginning *ophi.* Milton, in *Paradise Lost,* ii, pictures the archrebel of heaven:

> Incenst with indignation Satan stood
> Unterrified, and like a Comet burn'd
> That fires the length of Ophiuchus huge
> In th' arctick sky, and from his horrid hair
> Shakes Pestilence and Warr.

seu I: sap, juice; humid; dripping; absorbing liquid. Gk *huetos:* rain. *hyetograph, hyetometer; OED* lists 8 *hyeto* words. *isohyet.* (*hueto* is cognate with *hudro;* see *aus.*) L *sugere, suctum. suck, suckle, honeysuckle. sugent; sugillate:* to apply a leech or a sucking cup. *sumen:* sow's udder. Gael, *sowens. supper:* first, bread sopped in broth for a light evening meal. OFr *souper:* soup, from an imitative group: *sip, sob, sop, soup, sup;* see also *sap.*

seu II: boil; miry. Gc, *seethe, sod, sodden* (*sod* is also a shortening of *sodomite;* see *gn*); *suds.* Obsolete E *suddle:* to wallow in mire; figuratively, to do sloppy work; hence *sutler:* bad cook; first, one that peddled provisions to soldiers.

seu III: to give birth. Gc, *son.* Robert Burton remarked, in *The Anatomy of Melancholy* (1621), that "when the son swore, Diogenes struck the father."

seug. Gc, *sick, sicken, sickly; sickness.* Some have linked these words with *seu I:* suck, it having been a Teutonic belief that disease was caused by the sucking of a demon. This notion persists in the stories of the blood-sucking vampire, in India,

China, Malayasia, and Indonesia, but mainly in Slavic lands. *The Standard Dictionary of Folklore* (1950), states that in 18th c. Hungary "the uproar about vampires was as great as that during the witch hunts of colonial New England." The excitement persists in the popularity of the many books, films, and plays about Count Dracula and his gory breed. (*Dracula* is coined from a diminutive of L *drago:* dragon; see *manu*.) The first story, written in 1897 by Bram Stoker, is set in Transylvania, in the Hungarian mountains; a medieval King *Drag* of Romania, called "the Impaler," is thought by some to be the source of the Dracula legend. *Draconian:* severe, cruel, is drawn from the frequent mention of the death penalty in the first code of laws in Athens, drawn up by *Draco* ca. 621 B.C.

?silva: forest. See *sal.* L, *Sylvanus,* Roman god of forests and fields. *Silas,* a shortening of *Silvanus,* is an appropriate name for a countryman. *silvan, sylvan. Sylvia:* a girl's given name; also, a genus of warblers, the thrush; see *trozdos.* OFr, *savage.* See also *aqua.*

Who is Sylvia? what is she,
That all our swains commend her?
—*The Two Gentlemen of Verona,* iv, 2

s(i)u: bind; sew. Skr, *sutra:* thread, string; figuratively, string of aphorisms or ideas. *Kamasutra:* book of love counsel. Gk *humen:* membrane, especially that occluding the virginal vagina, the *hymen. hymeneal. hymenoptera* (plural): membrane-winged, as ants, bees, wasps. Gk *humnos:* song for brides; also for virgins dedicated to a god or goddess, as nuns "married to Jesus." *hymn, hymnody,* etc. L *suere, sutum. suture, subulate, subuliform. accoutre.* Fr, *couture. haute couture, couturier.* Gc, *seam, sew.*

Cassius, in *Julius Caesar* (i, 2):

Caesar said to me, 'Dar'st thou, Cassius, now
Leap in with me into this angry flood,
And swim to yonder point?' Upon the word,
Accoutred as I was I plunged in . . .
Caesar cried, 'Help me, Cassius, or I sink!'
I, as Aeneas, our great ancestor,
Did from the flames of Troy upon his shoulder
The old Anchises bear, so from the waves of Tiber
Did I the tired Caesar.

skai: gleam, dim light; shadow. Skr *chitra:* variegated, speckled. *chit, chitty. chintz. cheeta. chital:* spotted deer.

Gk *skia:* shadow. *squirrel* (*skia,* and *oura:* tail). *skiagram. skiascope.* Around 1896 *skiagraphy* was used interchangeably with *radiography.* The *Skiapodes* were a mythical people of Libya whose feet were so large they used them as sunshades. L and E *scintilla, scintillate.* By metathesis, *stencil, tinsel.*

My love is of a birth as rare
As 'tis of object strange and high;
It was begotten by despair
Upon impossibility.
Magnanimous Despair alone
Could show me so divine a thing
Where feeble Hope could ne'er have flown
But vainly flapt its tinsel wing.
—Andrew Marvell (d. 1678), *The Definition of Love* [of God].

(s)kamb: bend, change; exchange, barter. LL *cambiare. cambist.* Sp, *cambio.* Scot, *excambion.* Ir, *gombeen.* Fr, *change, exchange. Plus ça change, plus c'est la même chose:* The more a thing changes, the more it is the same. (The distance between the two wheels of the ancient chariot equals the gauge of the modern railroad.) *cambium:* where bark changes to wood.

Gc, *change, changeable, unchanging,* etc. By another route—the changing course of a stream, hence curve of field—this root is related to *camp, campus, campaign,* etc.; see *prai.* It *Cambio non è furto:* Exchange is not robbery, was first used in English by John Heywood, in 1546; Smollett, in *Humphry Clinker* (1771), added a word that improved it, and in *Roderick Random* (1784) again applied it: "Casting an eye upon my hat and wig, he took them off, and clapping his own on my head, declared that a fair exchange was no robbery."

skand: climb; but also stumble. Gk *scandalon:* stumbling block. *scandal,* and its doublet, *slander. scandalum magnatum,* since the reign of Richard II (deposed by Parliament in 1399, in favor of Henry IV, as in Shakespeare's *Richard II*): malicious report against a person of high rank or position; in the 18th and 19th c. often abbreviated as *scanmag* and used of any scandalous gossip. Thomas Hook, in *Sayings* (1826), wrote: "I can give you a daily abstract of fashionable scanmag."

L *scandere:* climb. *scan, scandent, scansion, scansorial. scantling. ascend, condescend, descendant, transcendant. ascension.* Ascension Day, the fortieth day after Easter, is celebrated as marking the ascent of Christ to heaven. L *scalae:* steps. Fr *echelon, escalade, escalator. scale:* climb the heights; also, up and down on the scales, physical and musical.

The pigeon *scanderoon* is from *Iskanderun* (a town in Syria named after Alexander the Great) where, by these carrier pigeons, the English factor received regular news from Aleppo, especially of the safe arrival of ships.

(s)kel: curving, crooked. Gk *skhelos:* leg. *isoceles. triskelion. scalene; scolex; scoliosis. scolion (melos):* crooked song, was invented by Terpander, "the father of Greek music," in the 7th c. B.C.; its verses were begun by a guest at a banquet; he then handed a branch to another guest, who had to continue as cleverly as he could, then passed the branch on. The closest thing to this in modern times seems to have been the game of making limericks at convivial Victorian parties. If you have quick-witted guests, try it some time; it's fun.

Gk *kholon:* limb, member; bends at elbow or knee. A *colon* was a member of a sentence, then the mark (:) that sets it apart; thence, *semicolon* (;). *cylinder. calender:* machine with rollers. Scand, *scowl; skulk.* Fr, *scelerat.* Gc, *shoulder.*

skelo: dry up, wither; be hard. Gk *skhellein:* dry up; *skhleros:* hard. *OED* defines 52 relevant words beginning *scler(o),* as *sclerotic, scleroderma, sclerometer. scleragogy:* hard bodily discipline. *sclerosis, arteriosclerosis.* Gk *skheleton,* E *skeleton,* though this is probably folk etymology: the word is in all likelihood (as Klein points out) borrowed from Syrian, from Akkad *shalamtu,* referring to the whole corpse; it is then related to Hebr *Shalom,* usually translated Peace, but originally Wholeness.

(s)keng. A nasalized variation of *skel:* that which bends. Gc, *shank. on shank's mare:* walking.

skern. Gc, *scorn.*

sketh: injure. Gc, *scathe, scathing; scatheless.* Gm *Schade:* shame. *Schadenfreude:* delight in the discomfiture of another person.

(s)keu: cover, conceal. See *kem I.* Gk *khutos:* a hollow, receptacle. Suffix *cyte:* cell, as *cystocyte, leucocyte, phagocyte.* For prefix *cyto, OED* lists 12 words and details 4, as *cytoblast. cytode* was suggested by Haeckel in 1866, to name the lowest form of life, a protoplasm without a nucleus.

Gk *skutos:* shield; first, covered with hide. *scutage:* shield money, paid in lieu of military service, as by some knights of old, and some drafted men in the American Civil War. *scutum.* Via Fr, *scutcheon; escutcheon. scuttle:* first, a leathern vessel; whence *scullery. skillet.* It, *scudo:* coin with design of a shield. *Scutellaria:* genus of plants, the skullcap. *zucchetto:* small skullcap, worn by a dignitary of the Roman Catholic Church; when worn by an orthodox Jew it is called a *yarmulke.* (No biblical injunction orders the wearing; the name *yarmulke* may be from Turk *yagmurluk:* rain cover, *yagmur:* rain.)

Via Fr, *esquire:* first, one that carried a knight's shield; *squire; equerry.* L *custodia:* guard, protection. *custos; custodian; custody.* "Confine her; set a guard! *Sed quis custodiet ipses custodes?* but who will watch the watchers themselves? Your wife is cunning, and begins with them"—Juvenal, *Satires,* 6. Hence the Oriental "bed guard," the *eunuch,* ensuring at least no swelling evidence.

L *cutus:* animal skin. *cutaneous, subcutaneous; cuticle, cutis.* L *culus:* rump. *culet, culot, culottes:* breeches covering the rump; for *sans-culottes,* see *seni.* Fr, *bascule; recoil. cul-de-sac:* dead end. L *cunnus:* sheath, *cunt;* see *gn. obscure;* via It, *chiaroscuro.*

Gc, *scum, scumble; skim. meerschaum:* literally, sea foam. *shame;* cover your nakedness, as Eve after the apple. *hide:* (1) conceal; (2) skin. *hoard, house, huddle, hut. heaven,* also *sky;* both cover the earth. Hence *skyscraper*—Gm *Wolkenkratzer:* cloud-scraper—often now, more literally, highriser. *hose,* which cover the legs; also *shoe. swathe, swaddle, swaddling clothes.* Norse, *skillet.* Russ, *kishke:* sheath, gut.

A volume could be written on the charges of "obscurity" laid by his contemporaries against the poet Browning. Of his book-length *Sordello* it was said that the only lines one could understand were the first and the last, and that these were both lies.

[First] Who will, may hear Sordello's story told.
[Last] Who would, has heard Sordello's story told.

Of the many jibes and parodies, one will have to suffice. In 1883 Browning wrote:

Wanting is what?
Summer redundant,
Blueness abundant,
Where is the blot?

And almost at once (21 Apr. 1883) *Punch* printed:

Browning is—what?
Riddle redundant,
Baldness abundant;
Sense,—who can spot?

George Eliot, however, stood firmly for Browning, declaring that "[in his] best poems he makes us feel that what we took for obscurity in him was superficiality in ourselves." Current opinion finds the poet not obscure but profound.

skeub: push, thrust. Scand, *scoff.* Gc, *scuff; scuffle* and its doublet, *shuffle. shove, shovel. scoop. scupper,* originally *scupper-hole.* Perhaps *scow:* boat propelled from the shore. Perhaps *scop,* whose songs were often verbal thrusts at the enemy; the word fell out of use between 888 and 1848, when Bulwer-Lytton, in *Harold,* wrote: "I have heard scops and harpers sing."

(s)keud: push; make a hole in something; throw. Norse, *scot:* money tossed down; tax. A Roman lawyer's palindrome is *Si nummi immunis:* Pay my fee, and you go scot free." Gc, *scoot, skeet, skit, skitter, skittish;* all partly imitative. *sheet:* first the rope of a sail; thence the cloth. *shoot. shut:* push a bar across; *shutter. shuttle, shuttlecock. wainscot. scout:* to fleer at; for *boy scout,* see *ous. scud. shoat:* just weaned; a pusher. *scuttle:* hole in a ship's deck, smaller than a hatchway, for quick communication or climbing out. *scuttlebutt:* first, *scuttled butt:* a barrel of fresh water on deck, with a hole, for a quick drink; hence (slang) gossip whispered there. Hence also *scuttle:* to cut holes in the hull to sink a ship. *scuttle about:* rush to and fro, is from the earlier *scuddle,* a frequentative of *scud.*

(s)keup: tuft. Gc, *sheaf. shop:* first, a shed. *scruff,* from the tuft of hair at the back of the neck. Via Du, *hops,* which grows in tufts. *scut:* tuft of a tail, as a rabbit's.

(s)khai: strike, cut; fall, fell. See *sek II.* L *caedere, caesum. caesarian;* see *sek II. chisel.* The suffix *cide:* JWalker has 31 related words, as *patricide, regicide.* Until 1650 *suicide* was referred to as self-homicide. In 1671 Milton's nephew Edward Phillips, in *New World of Words,* objected that *suicide* might mean killing a sow (Gc *sus:* sow; see *sue*). Note that *stillicide* refers to drops falling, as from eaves onto a neighbor's land; see *stei.*

skot: dark. Gk, *scotoma. OED* has 7 relevant words beginning *scoto.* Gc, *shade* and its doublet, *shed. shadow.* See *skai.*

The shades of night were falling fast
As through an Alpine village passed
A youth who bore, 'mid snow and ice,
A banner with the strange device,
Excelsior!
—H. W. Longfellow

(s)krei: cry out. Imitative; see *ker IV.* A number of birds: *cormorant, crow, raven, rook, shrike. croak. scream, screak; screech* and its doublet, *shriek; squeak, squeal;* all imitative.

L *crimen* first meant a cry of distress; the response added the meanings charge, judgment, then crime. *OED* has 23 relevant words beginning *crim.* Also *incriminate, discrimination; recriminate.*

Poe's *The Raven* is a brilliant tour de force, which, he explained, he built around "the saddest word in the language": "Quoth the Raven, Nevermore."

(s)kualo: large fish. L and E *squalus:* shark. *squaloid. squalene,* from shark-liver oil. *Squalodon:* shark-tooth; genus of fossil whales. Possibly *squalid:* first, foul with slime; *squalor,* etc.

squama: fish scales. *squamose; desquamate, esquamate. OED* details 20 associated words, and lists 12 compounds with *squamo* and *squamoso.* Gc, *walrus* (*hross:* horse). *narw(h)al; roqual. whale.*

The Walrus and the Carpenter
Were walking hand in hand;
They wept like anything to see
Such quantities of sand:
'If this were only cleared away,'
They said, 'it would be grand.'
—Lewis Carroll, *Through the Looking Glass*

skut: shake. See *kuet.* Gc, *shudder.*

(s)lagu: seize, take. Gk nasalized, *lambanein; eilemmai, leptos. lemma:* an assumption. *dilemma. analeptic, cataleptic, epilepsy. nympholepsy, nympholept;* see *sneubh. astrolabe:* star-taker. *prolepsis, syllepsis. syllable:* a taking together of letters. *monosyllable,* etc. *syllabification; OED* lists 17 associated words. Gc, *latch* (*on to*).

Edward Coke (d. 1634), first Lord Justice of England, who established common law, was so impressed with the power of words, and the vital need for precision, that he declared: "Syllables govern the world."

slak: strike; and from knowing when and how to strike, clever. Gc, *slay, slaughter, onslaught, overslaugh. sledge* (*hammer*). *slag,* which is stricken off. Via ONorse, *sleight* (of hand); *sly.*

(s)leidh: slip. Gc, *slide, slid. sled, sledge, sleigh, sleigh ride.* For *slime,* on which one may slip, see *lei I.*

slenk: coil, wind; hurl. Gc, *sling; slink. slingshot,* as aimed by country boys at birds, and David at Goliath. *slang* (Norw *slengja kjaeften:* sling the jaw). *slanging match:* railing, the 16th c. flyting. *slanguage.*

Hamlet (ii, 2), being emotionally mixed, mixes his metaphors:

Whether 'tis nobler in the mind to suffer
The slings and arrows of outrageous fortune,
Or to take arms against a sea of troubles
And by opposing end them.

(s)leu: relax, and associated ideas. *slouch, slow. sloth* (earlier *slowth*). *slowworm* is folkchanged from *slimeworm;* see *lei I. slumber* (OE *slumen:* doze). *slosh, sludge, slush, sleet. slug, slugged, slur. logy.* "Go to the ant, thou sluggard; consider her ways; and be wise"—Proverbs 6:6.

All nature seems at work. Slugs leave their lair—
The bees are stirring—birds are on the wing—
And Winter, slumbering in the open air,
Wears on his smiling face a dream of Spring!
And I the while, the sole unbusy thing,
Nor honey make, nor pair, nor build, nor sing.
—Coleridge, *Work Without Hope*

(s)leubh: notion of sliding. L *lubricus:* sliding, physically, then morally. *OED* details 18 words, mainly physical. *lubricant, lubricate; lubricous, lubricity, lewd. lewdness.* Gc, *slip, slipover; slipper,* which slips on. *slipslop,* etc; see *lei I. cowslip, oxlip. slop; slope. sloop* (slides along).

(s)li: bluish. L *lividus. livid.* OSlav *sliva:* plum, from the color. *slivovitz.* Gc, *sloe.*

smarakt. Gk *smaragdos:* via Fr, *emerald,* probably Semitic in origin. The name *Esmeralda.* The emerald is a variety of beryl; it was worked in Egypt as early as 1650 B.C. at what were later called Cleopatra's Mines, east of Aswan. It was supposed to drive away evil spirits, to preserve chastity, but also to assist in childbirth. In early England, its color in a gown was deemed a deliberate allure, as of My Lady Greensleeves in the old ballad. Since 1946 it has been made synthetically.

Has anybody here seen Kelly,
Kelly of the Emerald Isle?

(s)me: smear, fling, speck. Gk *mikros:* small. *micrify; microbe; micron. omicron;* see *mei I.* The prefix *micro,* as *microscope, microphone; micromicro;* see table of measurements, under *me IV.* L *mica;* first, crumb; then fused or confused with L *micare:* glisten; hence E *mica, micaceous, micelle.* For *small,* see *melo.*

Comparing the number of words beginning *micro* with those beginning *macro* (see *mak*) and *mega* (see *me III*) makes it plain that men have deemed it more important, or have devised better instruments, to examine little things than large ones. The 1933 *OED* lists 56 words beginning *micro* and details 135 more, from *microbat* to *microzyme.* The 1976 supplement lists some 140 words and details 22 columns more. These range from *microanalyze* to *microwelding,* and include *microdot, microfiche,* and words relating to the use of computers, and tiny crystals, *chips.* The 1976 supplement adds that the form is now freely prefixed, as in *micropanorama,* or as in the figurative "looking for tiny needles in micro-haystacks." *micrurgy:* research on cells, etc., under the microscope. There are also *microminiaturization,* as in transitors, and the *submicroscopic* world.

Why has not man a microscopic eye?
For this plain reason, man is not a fly.
–Pope, *Essay on Man*

smegh: taste. Imitative. Gc, *smack* (the lips). *smack* (with the hand) also is imitative.

(s)mei I: smile. L *mirus:* to be smiled at. *admirable; admire. Miranda:* to be admired; heroine of *The Tempest. Mirabel. marvel; miracle; mirage; mirador, mirific. mirror.* L *mirabile dictu* (Virgil, *Georgics,* ii): wonderful to relate. *comity:* smiling together. Gc, *smile, smirk.*

Steven Runciman, in *Byzantine Civilization* (1933, 1956), tells us that Emperor Constantine the Great sent his mother Helena (the former concubine of Emperor Constantius I, who incidentally died, A.D. 306, at British York, Eboracum) "to Jerusalem, and there, with miraculous aid seldom nowadays vouchsafed to archaeologists, she found the very site of Calvary and unearthed the True Cross itself and the crosses of the thieves and the Lance and the Sponge and the Crown of Thorns and all the attendant relics of the Passion. The discovery thrilled Christendom."

smei II: cut, pound. *smith, smithy. blacksmith, goldsmith, locksmith,* etc., and the legion of *Smiths.*

Under the spreading chestnut tree
The village smithy stands;
The smith, a mighty man is he,
With large and sinewy hands,
And the muscles of his brawny arms
Are strong as iron bands.
–Longfellow, *The Village Blacksmith* (1842)

(s)meit: throw; send. The first sense seems to have been to throw, as cow dung at a wall, to dry for fuel. I have seen freight cars at a siding in India with their south sides completely covered with spats of drying dung. Hence *smite; smectic, smectite; smegma.* From the meaning *spot* (on the wall; where the dung strikes) came *macula, maculation, mackle; immaculate.*

L *mittere, missum:* send. *mass, mess, message, missal, missile, mission, missive; mittimus. admit; commissariat; commit, committee, commission; demit, dismiss; entremit, emit, intermission, intermittent; intromission; manumission. omit; permission, permit; pretermit; remiss; remit, remittance* (man); *submit, transmit. premise, premiss; promise, compromise, surmise.*

There is sound counsel for many occasions in the warning, in *The Book of Common Prayer* (1548), to avoid "the two extremes, of too much stiffness in refusing, and of too much easiness in admitting, any variation." Pope, in his *Essay on Criticism,* put it more concisely:

Be not the first by whom the new are tried,
Nor yet the last to lay the old aside.

"A wise physician is a John the Baptist, who recognizes that his only mission is to prepare the way for one greater than himself–Nature"–Arthur S. Hardy.

?(s)meld: melt, soften: grind. Gk, *meldometer.* Via OFr, *enamel.* L *mollis:* soft. *mollify.* Gc, *smalt, smelt; malt, meal.* Probably a variation of roots *mel I* and *mel V.*

(s)mer. This root seems to have taken three paths. (1) Its basic meaning seems to have been to keep in mind, be concerned about. (2) From this: what one deserves, a share, portion, part. (3) Thence, a part of the body, especially a limb; the thigh.

Skr, *smriti:* that which is remembered; tradition (in Hindu religion).

Gk *meros:* part. *OED* lists 10 words beginning *mero:* part, and details 13, as *meroblastic, merosymmetry;* it lists 7 beginning *mero:* relating to the thigh, detailing only *meros.* Two English suffixes, *mere* and *merous,* as in *metamere, paramere; dimerous, pentamerous,* sometimes written *2-merous,* etc., *heteromerous, polymerous.* Also *isomer, monomer, dimer,* etc. *merism, merismatic, meristem.*

The *Moirai* (singular, *Moira*) are the three Fates, allotters of one's portion in life. Clotho holds the distaff; Lachesis manipulates the thread; Atropos cuts it. The Romans called them the *Fates,* from *fatum:* that which is spoken; also the *Parcae,* from *parcere:* to spare, show mercy, in euphemistic hope of a generous portion. (Their Latin names are *Nona, Decuma, Morta.* From *Nona, nones,* the ninth day before the ides of each month; on it, no marriages were allowed. *Nonacris* was the mountain from which the River Styx flowed to Hades. *Decuma:* a tithe, was the tenth part of a man's possessions, which he must give to the gods. And *Morta* marks the end of all mortals.) There is still wide belief in the Moirai in Greece.

Gk, *martyr:* one kept in mind as evidence of a miracle, etc. L *merere, meritum:* deserve. *merit, meritorious. emeritus:* first, of retired military men; then, of professors. *demerit. meretricious.* A 17th c. dictionary word was *meretricate:* to play the whore. See *mer I.*

L *memor:* mindful. *memory, remember, remembrance. memento* (*mori*); *memorize, memorabilia. memorial.* Fr, *memoir(s). memorandum,* sometimes shortened to *memo. commemorate.* L *membrum:* limb. *member, dismember. membrane,* etc. *meninx. meningitis, myringa, myringitis.*

L *mora:* carefulness; *morari, moratum:* to take one's time; delay. LL and E *moratorium. moratory. demur. remora:* large fish, once believed to cling to and delay ships. Gc, *mourn:* to keep in (sorrowful) memory. Norse, *Mimir:* giant that guards the well of Wisdom; Wisdom is the daughter of Memory. In Greek mythology, Memory (Mnemosyne) is mother of the Muses. Truth (Wisdom's sister) also lies at the bottom of a well. From the bottom of a well, one can see the stars by day.

"Memory, the warder of the brain"–*Macbeth.* "It's a poor memory that only works backward"–Lewis Carroll, *Through the Looking Glass.*

smerd: pain. *smart.* See *mer II.*

smeru: grease. Gk *muron:* sweet juice, unguent. *Myristica, Myroxyton:* genera of tropical trees. *myrobalan:* dried fruit of tropical trees. *Amyris:* genus of the rue family. L and E *medulla:* influenced by L *medius,* from its middle position as bone marrow; see *mozzo. medulla oblongata.* Gc, *smear.* Sw, *smörgasbord:* goose-fat table.

(s)meugh. Gc, *smoke. smog:* blend of *smoke* and *fog,* as over misplaced cities. There are only guesses as to where *fog* comes from.

(s)na. This is another root that developed in three directions from its basic sense of liquid flow, or flowing, floating, in liquid.

(I) swim. Gk *nekhein. nekton:* creatures that swim (see *ie*). *nectocalyx. nectopod:* the foot as a swimming organ. Numerous plant and animal names, as *Naius, Nama:* plants; *Nectria:* fungi; *Eunectes:* good swimmers, the anaconda snakes; *Necturus:* aquatic salamanders; *Pleuronectidae:* family of flatfish.

Gk *naias, naiados. naiad,* river nymph; *nereid:* sea nymph. Gk *nesos:* island; floats on the water (*Austronesia, Melanesia, Micronesia. Polynesia*). *Peloponnesus. cheronese:* almost an island; a peninsula.

L *natare. naiant,* in heraldry. *natant, natation, natatorium. supernatant.*

On desperate seas long wont to roam
Thy hyacinth hair, thy classic face,
Thy Naiad airs have brought me home
To the glory that was Greece
And the grandeur that was Rome.
—Poe, *To Helen*

(II) drip. Partly imitative, of dripping mucus and sniffling nose. Gc, *sniff, sniffle, snivel, snot. snap, snatch.* Churchill commented on the Munich Agreement, 5 Oct. 1938: "The German dictator, instead of snatching the victuals from the table, has been content to have them served to him, course by course."

snoop. snub: turn up the nose. *snuff, snuffle, schnauzer. snout. schnozzle.* For his time, the comedian Jimmy Durante made known the term *schnozzola;* but the most outstanding historical and literary possessor of an outstanding proboscis is Savinien Cyrano de Bergerac (1619–1655), who wrote *Voyages* (to the sun and to the moon) and was made the hero of Edmond Rostand's romantic drama *Cyrano* (1897).

Laurence Sterne picked up at a bookstall Bruscambille's *Pensées facetieuses,* with a prologue on noses; and in Book IV of Sterne's *Tristram Shandy* (1760–67), Slawkenbergius's tale is of a man whose nose is so enormous that many refuse to believe it is natural; bets and quarrels ensue, between the nosarians and the antinosarians. This recounting, with its sly sexual symbolism, led to a short story, *The Nose* (1836), by Gogol. Bruscambille was the *nom de plume* of Deslauriers (so popular that others appropriated his pen name), one of a cluster of 16th and 17th c. French satirists whose works were forbidden on pain of death, but who maintained a flow of underground political and religious satires and farces.

Some of the metaphysical poets, following Donne's observation that "love based on beauty, soon as beauty dies," wrote in mock praise of ugliness; witness Sir John Suckling's *The Deformed Mistress* (1638):

Her nose I'd have a foot long, not above,
With pimples embroder'd, for those I love,
And at the end a comely pearl of snot,
Considering whether it should fall or not.

See *nas.*

(III) More pleasantly, what flows into the mouth; to suckle, drink. OInd *snauti:* she gives milk. Gk *nekhtar,* possibly Semitic in origin, from wine used at sacrifices. *nectar,* drink of the gods; *OED* defines 22 words beginning *nectar,* as *nectarine, nectary. snack.*

L *nutrio, nutritum. nutrix:* wet nurse. *nourish, nurse, nurture, nutrient, nutriment, nutrition, nutritious.*

As Berowne looks on life in *Love's Labor's Lost,* iv, 3,

From women's eyes this doctrine I derive:
They sparkle still the right Promethean fire;
They are the books, the arts, the Academe,
That show, contain, and nourish all the world.

(s)ne: spin, sew; thence thread, bowstring, cord; sinew, nerve. Gk *nema:* thread. *chromonema, protonema; treponeme. nemato-,* as *nematocyst,* with stinging thread; *nematode; nematophore. Nematomorpha:* hairlike worms. Gk *neuron:* nerve. *neuralgia, neurasthenia; neuron, neurosis, neurotoxin. aponeurosis; perineurium. OED* lists 54 *neur(o)* words, as *neuradynamia* (*a* negative): nervous debility; and details 55, as *neurologist, neur(h)ypnology; neurilemma,* now usually *epineurism. Neuroptera:* order of insects with four transparent membranous wings. *OED*'s 1976 supplement lists 81 new words, as *neurolinguist, neuropsychosis;* and details 33, from *neuroanatomy* to *neurovirulence. neuroleptic, neurotransmitter;* and new applications of *neuron* and *neurotic.*

L *nervus,* by metathesis from Gk *neuron. nerve, nervous; enervate, unnerved.* Gc, *needle; sinew, snood.* See *netr.*

In the biblical warning (Matthew 19:24), "It is easier for a camel to go through the eye of a needle, than for a rich man to enter into the kingdom of God," the needle's eye may seem an exaggerated figure. Actually, in ancient Near Eastern walled towns, the postern gate, from its narrowness and pointed top, was called "the needle's eye," and a camel could go through it—by kneeling. Shakespeare seems to have been aware of this. In *Richard II* (v 5), the king, in the castle dungeon and expecting to be killed, has thoughts of the next world. He tries to summon words to express them—"Come, little ones"—then laments: "It is as hard to come as for a camel to thread the postern of a small needle's eye." (The appeal "Come, little ones"— Vulgate *parvulos*—brings to mind "for of such is the kingdom of heaven.")

There is, of course, the proverbial needle in a haystack. And *Gammer Gurton's Needle,* the first English comedy on a native theme, probably by William Stevenson of Cambridge (1566)—*Ralph Roister Doister* (1553), by Nicholas Udall of Westminster School, follows the classical pattern—is a farcical hunt for the old woman's needle, which is suddenly found when her man Hodge sits down.

sneg: creep. Gc, *snail. snake. sneak; sneakers* (for athletes and muggers). *snark,* coined by Lewis Carroll in 1896, is a portmanteau word, blending *snake* and *shark.* But beware, lest the snark be a boojum. "What I tell you three times is true"—*The Hunting of the Snark,* first fit.

Boswell records, in his *Life of Samuel Johnson,* 13 Apr. 1778: "Johnson said that he could repeat a complete chapter of *The Natural History of Iceland* from the Danish of Horrebow; the whole of it was exactly thus: Chap Lxxii Concerning Snakes: There are no snakes to be met with throughout the whole island." Johnson could just as well have memorized Chapter Xlii of the 1758 translation, which reads: "There are no owls of any kind in the whole island." By altering one letter in the name of the place, the sons of St. Patrick have claimed the snakes as a logomorph (see *leip*) of Ireland.

(s)neiguh: snow. L *nix, nivis. nivosity; nival.* Fr, *névé:* especially, perpetual snow where a glacier is forming. Gc, *snow. OED* gives 8 columns to the word *snow* and its compounds, as *snowbound, snow-capped;* lists 9 animals and 12 birds beginning *snow;* then details 28 relevant words, as *snowball, snowfall, snowplow; snowmanship.*

Emerson hailed "the frolic architecture of the snow." George Ellis, in 1810, summed up *The Twelve Months:*

Snowy, Flowy, Blowy,
Showery, Flowery, Bowery,
Hoppy, Croppy, Droppy,
Breezy, Sneezy, Freezy.

sneit: cut. Gc, *Wiener schnitzel:* little cut (of veal), Vienna style. Gm *Schneider:* tailor. *snick, snickersnack. snickersnee,* earlier *snick and snee,* the first part folk-changed by influence of the second, from *stick and snee:* stab and cut. Also *snath:* scythe. *specktioneer:* head harpooner on a whaling ship; see *sphei I.*

Ko-Ko, the Lord High Executioner in Gilbert's *The Mikado,* when asked to describe the (imaginary) execution, exults:

Oh never shall I Forget the cry
Or the shriek that shriekèd he,
As I gnashed my teeth When from the sheath
I drew my snickersnee!

The slaying of the jabberwock, in Lewis Carroll's *Through the Looking Glass,* is equally triumphant:

One, two! one, two! And through and through
The vorpal blade went snickersnack!
He left it dead And with its head
He went galumphing back.

(s)ner I. Imitative. Gc, *snarl, sneer, snore, snort. chortle* is a blending, by Lewis Carroll, of *chuckle* and *snort.* Yiddish, *schnorrer.* The *Norns:* literally, the whisperers, were the three Norse Fates: *Urdur:* past, *Verdandi:* present, *Skuld:* future. They dwelt at the roots of the sacred tree Yggdrasill, watering it from the fountain *Norna* to keep it in good growth.

The *sneer* is a major weapon of the cynical and the conceited. Pooh-Bah, Lord High Everything Else (except Executioner) in *The Mikado,* declares: "I can trace my ancestry back to a protoplasmal primordial atomic globule. Consequently, my family pride is something in-conceivable. I can't help it. I was born sneering." And as the Rev. William Paley, in *Moral Philosophy* (1785), v, helplessly asked: "Who can refute a sneer?"

(s)ner II: twist. Skr, *nautch.* Gk *narke:* cramp, torpor. *narcosis; narcolepsy. narcotic;* first used in French, in 1314. *OED* defines 16 words beginning *narco.* Pliny, and Plutarch (1st c. A.D.) explain that the *narcissus* was named for its narcotic effects. Its best-known variety is *narcissus poeticus.* Sappho speaks of "laughing narcissus that loves the rain." Shelley calls it, of flowers, "the fairest among them all."

OED's 1976 supplement adds the word *narcissism,* from the mythological *Narcissus,* who fell in love with his reflection in a pool and was changed into the flower, frequent at the waterside. Psychiatry has used the term since Havelock Ellis's *Alienist* (1898). The 1976 supplement also adds *narc, nark,* slang for *narcotics agent,* and *narco* (for either agent or addict); and lists 4 new compounds of *narco,* as *narcosynthesis,* plus 2 columns of further new relevant material.

Gc, *snare, ensnare. narrow:* first, twisted tight.

O infinite virtue! Cam'st thou smiling from
The world's great snare uncaught?
–*Antony and Cleopatra,* iv, 8

But for the unquiet heart and brain
A use in measured language lies,
The sad mechanic exercise
Like dull narcotics, numbing pain.
–Tennyson, *In Memoriam,* v

(s)neubh: marry. Gk *numphe:* bride. *nymph* (see *or*). *nymphae:* the labia minora. *nymphet,* a diminutive, had a voguish revival with the popularity of Vladimir Nabokov's *Lolita* (1955), in which Humbert Humbert was what the *Encyclopaedia Britannica* calls "possessed by overpowering desire for very young girls."

nymphomania: excessive lustfulness in a woman, should be distinguished from *nympholepsy:* the ecstasy that overcomes a man "when he catches a glimpse of a nymph," generalized as a yearning for the unattainable. See *slagu. OED* lists 26 associated *nymph* words. *Nymphaea:* genus of aquatic plants, the yellow lily. *Nymphaeaceae:* the water-lily family.

Some dictionaries define *houri* (Pers *huri:* with beautiful black eyes) as "a nymph of the Mohammedan paradise"; 72 houris are promised each believer; as with all nymphs, their virginity is perpetually renewed. See *aue; gn.*

L *nubere, nuptum:* marry; *nubilis:* of marriageable age. *nubile, nuptials; connubial* (*bliss*). *nubere* first meant to cover, veil, as a bride still does; originally, some say, this was done to ward off the evil eye. From this sense, the veiled, overcast sky: *nubecula, nubia, nubiform, nubilate, nubilous. nuance.*

solo: whole, firm; sound, correct. Gk *holos:* whole. *OED* lists 37 *holo* words, as *holozoic,* and details 16, as *holograph:* wholly written in one's own hand. *holocaust* first meant sacrifice (burning) of a complete victim, not just the heart or entrails (the rest being kept to nourish the priests); now, a complete, disastrous conflagration.

catholic (Gk *kata:* throughout): universal, as *of catholic taste:* appreciative of the best of every sort. *solicitous:* wholly concerned. *solicitation.* Via Fr, *insouciant:* not concerned. *solemn:* first, of a wholly religious rite, wholly holy. Possibly *salubrious, save,* etc., but see *sal.* L *solidus:* firm. *solid, solidarity; consolidate,* etc. *solidus:* old Roman coin; *soldo:* Italian coin; *sol:* old French coin, modern *sou.* L *solidatus:* one given coins (pay), via Fr *soldour* became E *soldier. Soldanella:* genus, mountain bindweed, with leaves shaped like a coin. *Solidago:* genus of goldenrod, once believed to heal, make whole. *solideme,* in linguistics. *soliped:* whole-footed, with uncloven hoof; *solidungulate,* in zoology.

Note that *holor* was an early English *l.r* shift from *whorer:* fornicator; thus the Wife of Bath explains her sex's fallibility, in Chaucer's prologue to her *Tale:*

And if that she be fair, then, verry knave,
Thou sayst that every holour wol her have;
She may no while in chastitie abide
That is assailed up-on ech a syde.

so(s), se: various verbal and nominative forms. Gk *hoi,* as in *hoi polloi:* the many. (*polloi* is plural of *polus:* much, many, as in the many English words beginning *poly;* see *pel V.*) L and E *sic:* thus. *si:* if; *nisi:* if not. *quasi:* as if; for its many uses in English, see *kuo.* Gc, *so, such. yes, yea. she.*

Run, run, Orlando, carve on every tree
The fair, the chaste, the unexpressive she.
—*As You Like It*, iii, 2

speik, (s)pik: a pointed instrument; from the pointed beak, some birds. Sp, *picaro. pick,* as in *pickax, toothpick. picket, pike.* Via Fr, *piquant, pique, piqué, piquet.* Possibly the *r* slipped in for the consequence, *prick.* L *pica:* magpie; *picus:* woodpecker. Skr, *pikas:* Indian cuckoo. E *pie, magpie; pecker, woodpecker.* (1) From the black-and-white *magpie,* E *pied, parti-colored:* first, in the 14th c., of the "pyed freres," friars wearing black-and-white habits; then, more generally, as in *pied* court fools, and Browning's *Pied Piper of Hamelin. piebald.* of a horse (*bald* first meant white; see *bhel I*). (2) From the magpie's gathering miscellaneous items in its nest—e.g., a jeweled ring from a bureau top near an open window—came (a) L *pica:* legal index, as of ecclesiastical rules; E *pica:* type size (though some suggest these, too, are from the black and white on the page); (b) *to pie,* as in *pieing type:* mixing letters up after printing, before sorting (in the old days) to put them back in the proper boxes; (c) the *pie* we enjoy eating, with its mixed ingredients, as mince and other meat pies. Eric Partridge suggests that the magpie may have been the first pie-crusted bird, earlier than the "four and twenty blackbirds baked in a pie." For *apple-pie order,* see *caput.*

The *mag* in *magpie* is a nickname for *Margaret,* as likewise *Jenny* wren, *Nanny* goat, etc. Skr *manjani:* flower bud. Gk *margaron:* pearl; E *Margaret, Margarita,* etc.; *margaric, margarine* (see *elaia; margar*).

(s)peis: breathe. Partly imitative. L *spirare, spiratum. spirit, spiritual,* etc. *spiracle. aspire, aspiration. conspiracy. expire, inspiration:* breath of the gods. *respiration. suspire. sprightly. perspire,* and its synonym *transpire,* now mainly used figuratively. Fr, *esprit* (*de corps*). From OFr *souspirail:* breathing-hole, came E *cesspit,* folkchanged to *cesspool.*

Through the unheeding many he did move,
A splendor among shadows, a bright blot
Upon the gloomy scene, a Spirit that strove
For truth, and like the Preacher found it not.
—Shelley's sonnet "Lift not the painted veil
which those who live Call life . . ."

spek: see, regard. Gk *skheptomai* (by metathesis): watch. *skheptos:* watcher. *skeptic. scope.* English suffixes: *scope,* as in *horoscope, kaleidoscope, microscope, periscope, telescope* (JWalker lists 56); *scopy,* as in *spectroscopy, urinoscopy* (JWalker lists 19). *episcopal;* whence *bishop,* etc. *haruspex:* inspector of the entrails, for divining; from the first element, E *hernia:* protruding gut (see *gher V*). *scopophobia:* hatred of being kept under watch. *scopophilia:* voyeurism (a sexual turn of man's first aid to knowledge, curiosity); thus denigrated by Freud, to whom *Webster's Third New International Dictionary* supinely and absurdly kowtows by adding to its definition of *scopophilia:* "often sublimated (as in a desire for learning)." Thus, sincere students are unwitting voyeurs!

L *specere, spectum. spectacle, spectator, spectrum, speculate. species* and its doublet, *spice. special, especial; specious. specify. specimen. aspect, circumspect, expect, expectancy, expectation, inspect, introspection; perspective, perspicacity, perspicuous; prospect, prospectus; respect, irrespective, retrospection. spectacles; specter. suspect, suspicion;* Fr, *soupçon. auspices, auspicious; conspectus, conspicuous. despise, despicable, despite, spite, respite. frontispiece;* ending folkchanged from *frontispice.* Via Fr, *espionage.* Gc, *spy. spiegeleisen* (Gm *Spiegel:* mirror): a variety of cast iron.

When Hamlet, distraught after the Ghost's revelations, visits his beloved Ophelia, seeking sympathy and strengthening, she behaves like a frightened child; this is perhaps the most important *unshown* scene in all of drama. Hamlet is thereby thrown back on his own resources, with no loved one to hear, comfort, and sustain him. The uncomprehending Ophelia reports the visit to her father:

O! what a noble mind is here o'erthrown;
The courtier's, soldier's, scholar's eye, tongue, sword;
Th' expectancy and rose of the fair state,
The glass of fashion, and the mould of form,
The observed of all observers, quite, quite down!

spel: recite, tell. Gc, *spell;* you must recite the proper formula to cast a spell. Hence *spellbinder.* Also *spell out, spelling,* and the too frequent *misspelling.*

OE *spel:* news. *gospel:* news of God, as in the four gospels of the New Testament. *evangel* (Gk *eu:* good; *aggelos,* pronounced *angelos*): messenger of God, as with *The Tidings Brought to Mary,* a play by Paul Claudel (1912). *evangelical. gossip* is from *God-sib:* relation in God; the talkative godmother. See *ghau.*

?spelugx: cavern. *spelean. speleology; speluncar, spelunker.*

spend I: to pour a ritual libation; hence, to solemnize a promise. Gk *spondee:* two long syllables, the meter used in ritual verses. L *spondere, sponsum. sponsion, sponsor. respond, respondent, responsible, irresponsible. correspondent, corespondent,* etc. *despond, despondency.* Via Fr, *espouse, spouse.*

In Bunyan's *Pilgrim's Progress,* "The name of the slough was Despond."

(s)pend II: stretch, spin, work. An expansion of the root *sphei I.* Gk *ponein:* to toil. *geoponics:* tilling the soil; see *ge.* L *pendere, pensum,* frequentative *pensare:* weigh; then weigh in the mind. *painter,* stretching from boat to shore. *pendant, pendent, dependent, independent. penthouse,* folkchanged from *pentis.* Fr, *poise, avoirdupois. antependium; append, appendix; appendicitis. compendium; depend, expend, spend. stipend, compensate, recompense, dispense, dispensation; indispensable. impend. penchant, pendulum; pensive. perpend, perpendicular. (malice) prepense. propend; suspend, suspenders. pension, suspense. vilipend* (see *ne*).

spontaneous combustion, as of oil-soaked rags; sometimes alleged of humans after excessive consumption of alcohol; Dickens, in the preface to *Bleak House* (1853), says: "It was shown upon the evidence that she had died the death to which this name of spontaneous combustion has been given." *spontaneous generation.* Cowper, in his *Notes to Pindar's Odes* (1656), speaks of "the generation of serpents, which is spontaneous sometimes." In his 1857 *Botany,* Arthur Henfrey states: "The idea of spontaneous generation of organic bodies is now exploded." The 1933 *OED* declares that the possibility "has been a subject of debate in more recent times." It still occurs in speculations as to how life first came upon the earth.

Via Fr *pensée:* weighed in the mind, a thought, came E *pansy.* The mad Ophelia says: "There's rosemary, that's for remembrance; pray, love, remember; and there is pansies, that's for thoughts."

Gc, *span, spanner;* possibly *spangle.* Gc *spinnan;* E *spin, spindle, spinster.* Gc *spinthra,* E *spinner.* Gc *spithra,* E *spider.* The spider is not an insect; insects have six legs, spiders have eight. Spiders are *arachneans, arachnids,* from the fabled *Arachne;* see *pend.* They are numerous–30,000 species have been described–but they are far fewer than the beetles; see *bheid.* Of the harvestman spider, better known as *daddy-longlegs,* there are 3,400 species; the legs may be 20 times the body length; the male has a protrusible penis; the female, a retractible ovipositor, which lays the eggs in the soil.

> Little Miss Muffet Sat on a tuffet
> Eating her curds and whey;
> Along came a spider And sat down beside her,
> And frightened Miss Muffet away.
> —A reassuring nursery rhyme

sper I: pole; spit, for cooking. Gc, *spar,* on a ship; *spear, spire. spareribs* was first *spearribs,* as on a spit; for *rib,* see *rebh.* The name of the greatest English playwright, *Shakespeare,* was spelled in 13 ways; he had a grandfather named *Shakeshaft.*

sper II: coil, twist. Gk *speira. Spirnea:* genus of plants of the rose family, with twisting pods, the flowers of which yield acetosalicilic acid; when this was synthetically produced, by H. Dreser in 1899, he named it *aspirin* (*a* negative): not from the flower.

spiral, spire (coiled); *spireme. spirivalve; spirochete.* The plant genera *Spirodela, Spartina, Spartium. sparteine.* Sp, *spartene, esparto.*

sper III. Gc, *sparrow; sparhawk* is short for *sparrow hawk.* OFr *esparvin,* E *spavin,* from the resemblance of the motion of a *spavined* horse to that of a hopping sparrow. See *spingo.*

sp(h)ei I: broad, spread out; broad strip; move; cut out, draw out, stretch; prosper. Gk *spadè,* via Latin, gave English *spathe* (diminutive, *spatula*); also applied to broad shoulders; via French it gave English *epaulet, épaulière.* Applied also to flattened metal, as the broadsword; hence Fr *épée;* It, *spadassin:* swordsman; *espadon:* two-handed sword. To *spay* is to draw out the ovaries of an animal; a *spado* is a castrated man. A *spade* is a flat shovel; the diminutive *spadille* is the ace of spades. *spadix:* first, the broken spread of a pine-tree branch. *spathic.*

A flat, broad, wooden chip became E *spoon.* From its figurative use to describe a fond lover, as though he hoped to spoon-feed the maiden, came the verb *to spoon.* A *Spooner* (the instance) or *Spoonerism* (the practice): the involuntary or humorous shifting of initial sounds, is from the Rev. William A. *Spooner,* warden of New College, Oxford (d. 1930): "It is kisstomary to cuss the bride"—although Ronald Knox, Catholic chaplain at Oxford in Spooner's time, in *Literary Distractions* (1958), protestingly calls him "a man known to fame, but unjustly, for I believe he never in his life perpetrated a Spoonerism." This statement is accepted by G. Grigson, who in his *Faber Book of Nonsense Verse* reaches out to a few "select [prose] Spoonerisms"—as "Which of us has not felt in his heart a half-warmed fish?"—but calls them "manufactured in Oxford and fathered upon William Archibald Spooner," and adds a note that the earlier writings of the Oxford don Charles Dodgson (Lewis Carroll) had given Oxonians a taste for nonsense.

> A little nonsense now and then
> Is relished by the best of men.

The students *may* have spun a mighty mischievous hoax; but it is usually futile to fly in the face of a folk tale.

Being spread out requires space; hence *spacious, spatial;* also *span:* to spread across space; *inspan, outspan.* For *expand,* etc., see *pet II. fathom* first meant the outstretched arms. *spick-and-span; nail and span new,* and *span-new* are from the early *span:* a chip of wood cut off; *spick* is a form of spike. But from *spei* in the sense of swell came *spick and speck:* fat meat (as blubber; whence also the first element of *specktioneer;* see *sneit*). A *spang* is a strip of land.

Things stretched out may become narrow, lean; hence *spare.* This developed the further sense of *sparing:* being frugal; also "Spare the rod and spoil the child"; see *ret.* What helps the body stretch out, the vertebra, is a *spondyl;* hence *spondylitis, spondylus. OED* lists 4 words beginning *spondylo.* Possibly, from stiffening one's spine and stretching one's resources, came the slang *spondulix:* money. J. H. Bloomfield, not knowing in what sense his words would come true, said in *A Cuban Expedition* (1896): "As long as the Cubans can raise the spondulix, they'll get plenty of people to fit out expeditions."

From the meaning "a chip of wood" came Gk *sphen:* wedge; E *sphene:* mineral with wedge-shaped crystals. *OED* lists 19 words beginning *sphen(o)* and details 4, as *sphenoid, sphenotic.*

Things that spread may prosper; hence L *sperare, speratum:* hope. Thus *prosper, prosperity,* etc. Fr, *esperance. Esperanto,* with only partial success as a world-wide language. Hence *desperate, despair.* Gc *spuon:* prosper. *speed:* first, success, as in the farewell wish *Good speed* or *God speed you.* A *good speed penny* may still be put into a new purse, for good luck. *OED* gives over 11 columns to *speed* and its combinations, as *speed limit, speedometer, speedy.* A *speedyman* used to carry "from Oxford to Westminster intimations of vacancies at New College."

"Nothing puzzles me more than time and space; and yet nothing troubles me less, as I never think about them"—Lamb, letter to Southey, 9 Aug. 1815.

sp(h)ei II: a point. L and E *spica. spicate. spike. spicule, spiculum. aspic:* variety of lavender; also *spike lavender; spikenard* (the *nard* is from Skr *naladam:* reed, sap, via LL *spica nardi—l.r* shift). *spinney.* L *porcus,* OFr *porc espin:* spiny hog; E *porcupine.*

Gc, *spit:* pointed bar. *spitz,* with tapered muzzle. *spile, spill:* to bespatter; also, a strip of paper used to light something. *spire, acrospire, spoke.* For *spoken word,* see *sphereg.* Possibly *conspicuous,* but see *spek.*

In *Hamlet,* i, v, the Ghost says he is forbidden to tell a tale that would make

> each particular hair to stand on end
> Like quills upon the fretful porpentine.

sp(h)el I: to take as booty; split; flay. L *spolium. spoil, spoils* of war; *spoliation. spoilsport. despoliation.* Gc, *spall; spool. spelt:* grain; to be split open. *split, spilth. spill:* first, to shed blood. The slang phrase *to spill the beans* first meant to make a mess of; then, to divulge (accidentally or on purpose) something of importance; it was first used in this second sense in the U.S., and in England by Dorothy Sayers in *The Unpleasantness at the Bellona Club* (1928).

sp(h)el II: shine. L *splendere. splendid, splendor; resplendent.*

sp(h)er I: spread; sow, sprout. Gk *speirein:* scatter. *diaspora. sporadic.* Via Fr, *spore. OED* lists 20 and details 19 relevant *spor(o)* words. *sperm, spermatozoon. angiosperm:* the division of flowering plants, the dominant vegetation on earth, made up of some 250,000 species, with a life span from a few weeks to several thousand years. Gk *angeoin:* of seeds in an ovary; diminutive of *angos:* vessel. *spermaceti* (*ceti:* of the whale). *asparagus,* of which we eat the sprouts; sometimes folk-changed to *sparrowgrass.* Thus "Rabelais the Younger" wrote in 1819:

> Some score hundred sparrowgrass,
> As it's now call'd by every ass.

Gc, *spread, sprit, bowsprit. spirt, spurt; sprout. sprawl.* Via It, *spritz.* Possibly *spheroid, spherical. sphere:* an even spread in all directions, the way in which some say the universe is expanding, like a balloon.

When the twin gondoliers ruled Barataria, in Gilbert's *The Gondoliers,* a result of their egalitarian beliefs was that

Ambassadors cropped up like hay,
Prime Ministers and such as they
Grew like asparagus in May.

sp(h)er II: kick; stir with foot, heel. Gc, *spur, spurn, sprain, spoor. spar* first meant to fight with spurs, as did the game cock; sometimes, extra (steel) spurs were fastened on. See also *sphereg. to win one's spurs,* now generalized, first meant to earn knighthood, the right to ride (spur) a horse to war. *on the spur of the moment:* produced by opportunity.

George Chapman, in *The Revenge of Bussy D'Ambois* (1613), vi, 1, spoke of "Danger, the spur of all great minds."

(s)p(h)er(e)g: jerk, shatter; scatter; cry out. Partly imitative. L *spargere, sparsum; adspergere:* sprinkle. *asperse, asperges:* sprinkling of holy water before High Mass. *aspersion:* first, a physical showering; then, a damaging imputation on one's name or reputation. *spray:* a sprinkling of water; also, a small branch, easily swaying. *sprig, sprag. sparse:* widely scattered; hence few. *disperse, interspersed. Spergula:* genus, the spurry; named for its scattering seeds.

Gc, *spark, sparkle. spar:* mineral with good cleavage; i.e., one that breaks into crystals, as *feldspar. spat* first meant a spattering raindrop, such as led a man venturing onto the unpaved streets to wear *spatterdashes* (soon shortened to the once-fashionable *spats*). *spat* and *spatter* are imitative (as are also *spit* and its past tense, *spat*).

spring, in all senses. Spring is "the time of beginning," when plants spring up; fall is the time when leaves and fruit (seeds) fall down. *springlet. sprinkle. spry. freckles* are scattered on the skin.

Also *speak, speech, bespeak. spokesman. OED* devotes 12 columns to *speak,* including *speak for, on, to, out, up,* etc., and details 13 words, as *speak-easy* (so the police won't hear), *speaking trumpet* (so the deaf will). A *speakhouse* or *speakroom* is the place in a convent or monastery where visitors are received.

The early past tense of *speak* was *spake; spoke* was fashioned after *break, broke* (earlier *brake*). For the *spoke* of a wheel, see *sphei II.* When Queen Elizabeth I was asked whether she believed in Christ's presence in the Sacrament of the Mass, she responded:

'Twas God the Word that spake it,
He took the bread and brake it,
And what the Word did make it,
That I believe, and take it.

(s)p(h)ieu. Imitative. Gk *ptuein:* spit. *hemophysis. ptyalin,* found in the saliva. *ptyalism. OED* has 7 relevant words beginning *pty.* L *spuere, sputum.* E *sputum; conspue. puke.* Port, *cuspidor.* Gc, *spit, spittoon, spittle, spue, spew. spout, sputter, splutter.*

"Because thou art lukewarm, and neither cold nor hot, I will spue thee out of my mouth"–Bible, Revelation 3:16.

Edward FitzGerald, remembered for his translations of *The Rubáiyát of Omar Khayyám,* forgettably wrote: "Mrs. Browning's death is rather a relief to me, I must say: no more *Aurora Leighs,* thank God!" When Browning saw this, in 1889, his righteous indignation produced lines that end:

Kicking you seems the common lot of curs—
While more appropriate greeting lends you grace:
Surely to spit there glorifies your face—
Spitting from lips once sanctified by hers.

Byron evinced a similar feeling toward a greater poet in a private letter to his friend and publisher John Murray, 12 Oct. 1820: "No more Keats, I entreat . . . there is no bearing the driveling idiotism of the Mankin."

(s)pingo. Imitative. Gc, *finch. spink,* another name for the *chaffinch.* (*chaff:* husk of grain, to be stripped from the edible kernel; hence, worthless stuff. See *geph.*)

As soon
Seek roses in December—ice in June;
Hope constancy in wind, or corn in chaff;
Believe a woman—or an epitaph,
Or any other thing that's false, before
You trust in critics.
—Byron, *English Bards and Scotch Reviewers*

(s)pleid: split, cleave. Gk, *splice. splint, splinter, split.* Gc, *flinders, flint.*

(s)poim: foam. L, *spume. pumex. pumice; pounce:* powder. Gc *feim, foam.* The nightingale, in Keats' *Ode,* sang:

Perhaps the selfsame song that found a path
Through the sad heart of Ruth when, sick for home,
She stood in tears amid the alien corn;
The same that oft-times hath
Charm'd magic casements, opening on the foam
Of perilous seas, in faery lands forlorn.

?(s)pong: sponge. Gk *spoggos* (double gamma is sounded *ng*). *sponge. spunk:* touchwood, tinder, ready to spark; hence also the figurative application to a *spunky* person. Also *punk,* used to light firecrackers, etc. Perhaps from the fact that punk smoulders, but does not flame, came the slang *punk:* one that tries to seem important, but is insignificant.

L, *fungus; fungoid,* etc. The fungus, often parasitic, is without chlorophyll, hence not green; it includes yeasts, molds, smuts, and mushrooms; over 250,000 species have been named and described, from *abgliophragma* to *zythiostoma;* and some 700 new ones are added every year. The most popular fungus is the edible mushroom; the nonedible ones, some intoxicant, some poisonous, are from their shape often called *toadstools,* though seldom, save with Alice in Wonderland, do toads thus employ them—although Spenser, in *The Shepheardes Calender* (1579), December, records:

The grislie Todestoole growne there mought I se
And loathed paddocks lording on the same.
[*paddock* is the diminutive of OE *pad,* a toad.]

The word *mushroom* is associated with OFr *moisseron,* its form influenced by Fr *mousse:* moss. *mushroom* is also used figuratively of rapid growth, as of a city sprung "over night" near a new gold field; and, recently, of the mushroom-shaped cloud from an exploded atom bomb, "a supermundane mushroom of boiling dust up to 20,000 feet."

John Donne (d. 1631), in a sermon on eternity, said: "Methusalem, with all his hundreds of years, was but a mushroom of a night's growth to this day . . .

that hath no *pridie,* nor *postridie;* yesterday doth not enter it in, nor tomorrow shall not drive it out."

srebh: suck in. Partly imitative. L *sorbere. sorb, sorption, sorbefacient. absorb, absorbent,* etc. Also used figuratively. *adsorption, reabsorb, resorb.* Via It, *sorbet;* its variant *sherbet* is Semitic, as is *syrup,* still imitative. Gc (*l.r* shift) *slurp. sip.*

Dickens is scornful in *The Old Curiosity Shop,* 57: "Did you ever taste beer?" "I had a sip of it once," said the small servant. "Here's a state of things!" cried Mr. Swiveller. . . . "She *never* tasted it—it can't be tasted in a sip."

srep: seize; cut off, trim; hook, sickle. Gk *harpe:* sickle. *harpy. harpoon* was influenced by this root. L *sarpere:* cut off, prune. *sarment(um):* originally, a cutting from a tree or vine; now applied to a creeping stalk that "emits roots as it runs along," as does the strawberry. *sarmentose; OED* details 6 associated words, including *sarmentous:* twiggy.

sreu: bubble; flow. Gk *rhein:* flow; *rheuma:* stream. *rheum, rheumatic, rheumatism,* etc. *rheumatism* was first "a defluxion of rheum"; *rheum* was watery matter, as that secreted by the mucous membranes or glands, as drops from the eyes or nose; connected with the theory of bodily humors as the cause of disease. Hence also the suffix *rrhea;* JWalker lists 9 such, as *diarrhea, pyorrhea; gonorrhea* (see *gn*).

The prefix *rheo: OED* lists 8 such words, and details 5, as *rheoscope. rheostat* was coined by Sir Charles Wheatstone (d. 1875). *rhyolite:* rock (lava) flow. *hemorrhoids. catarrh:* a flowing down. *Catarrhina:* primates (gorilla, orangoutan, and chimpanzee) with downward nostrils.

Callirhoe: beautifully flowing; a sea nymph. Gc, *stream, streamer. maelstrom. strudel* (Gm *Strudel:* whirlpool, eddy), from the boiling.

Gk *rhuthmos:* flow of verse. *rhythm; OED* defines 15 associated words. For *rhyme, OED* defines 13. *rhyme* was spelled *rime* until the Renaissance, when it was linked with Greek spelling, as in *rhythm;* the old form persists, as in Coleridge's *The Rime of the Ancient Mariner.* (*rime:* hoarfrost, is from OE *hrima.*)

"I was never so berhymed since Pythagoras' time, that I was an Irish rat!" exclaims Rosalind in *As You Like It,* iii, 2, when she finds trees embellished with Orlando's verses to her—which Touchstone bawdily mimics, "for a taste":

If a hart do lack a hind,
Let him seek out Rosalind.
If a cat will after kind,
So be sure will Rosalind . . .
He that sweetest rose will find
Must find love's prick and Rosalind.

It was folklorily said that in Ireland, rats were killed by rhyming, to which notion Shakespeare's is not the only literary reference:

Songs no longer move;
No rat is rhymed to death, nor maid to love . . .

laments Pope, in his *Satires of Donne* (1735).

Some rhyme a neebor's name to lash,
Some rhyme (vain thought) for needfu' cash;
Some rhyme to court the country clash,
An' raise a din;
For me, an aim I never fash;
I rhyme for fun.
—Burns, *Epistle to James Smith*

(s)rig: the notion of coldness. L *frigus, frigoris. frigid, frigorific,* etc. *refrigeration; fridge. rigid; rigescent, rigorous. rhigolene:* petroleum product used as an early local anesthetic, "freezing" the body part. Fr, *sang-froid:* cold blood. J. P. Andrews, in 1790, spoke of "the sang-froid of a chessplayer."

sta: stand, stay; hence, a standing-place; a thing that stands; something unmoving, firm, solid, hard; and other offshoots. L *sto, stare:* stand; *stans, stantem:* standing; *status:* stood. *Stet* is the imperative Let it stand. Archimedes, the "Eureka!" man, 3d c. B.C., declared: "Give me a place to stand (*pou sto*) and I will move the earth." *non obstante.*

stand, standing (*rank:* where one stands). *stanch:* to make stand, to stop. *staunch:* standing against opposition. *stanchion. stank:* standing water; early form of *tank.* The military *tank* was manufactured secretly, and shipped in boxes falsely labeled "tank"; the name stuck.

Only a selection of the many words derived from this root is presented here. *OED* gives 44 columns to *stand* and its phrases, plus 11 columns for compounds, from *standage* and *standard* to *standstillism* and *stand-up.* There are a further 21 columns for *state* and its compounds; 12 columns for *station;* and 17 columns for *stay.* For *stay:* a support, see *stak.*

From OInd *sthana* came *thana,* a police station in India. *Hindustan* is where the Hindus stay; thus also *Pakistan, Afghanistan, Baluchistan.*

stance, circumstance, circumstantial; substance, substantive, substantial; substitute. constant; Constance. Constantine, the Roman emperor (306–377), and his new city in the East, *Constantinople* (see *pele*). *extant; distant:* standing apart. *stanza. instant:* standing at the moment; *instantaneous. instance. understanding; misunderstand.*

standard is from OFr *estandard:* extended, but some of its meanings come from association with *stand. state, estate, status; static; statistics:* how things stand. *stator, stay.* Things that stand too long grow *stale. staddle, stadholder. staid, staith.*

Via Gc *stelt:* to cause to stand, came *still, stilts, stilted. stilling; stillion. gestalt.* OL *stlocus. local, location; locus. locum tenens:* deputy; especially a doctor taking another's place; Fr, *lieutenant.*

stat as a technical affix gives us *statoblast, statoscope, rheostat, gyrostat, areostat.* A *thermostat* keeps the temperature *stable*—hence also the verb *stabilize,* and the *stable* where horses stand in a *stall.* To *stall* a person is to keep him standing. *forestall, install, installation, installment. stalwart:* standing worthily. *pedestal.* A horse kept in a stall is a *stallion;* hence also *steed* (OE *steda*). Gc *stod:* stud. Thus, too, *establish, establishment; stead, homestead, instead; steady, steadfast.* During an *armistice* the armies stand still.

statue, statuary, and *statute* all stand. *statuesque; stature. static, station, stationary. stationery* was sold by a *stationer,* who kept a *standing* (permanent) shop, as opposed to a temporary stand or stall in the market. Hence also *grandstand.*

From reduplicated or affixed forms, with vowel change, came *destine:* to set how things are to stand; *destiny; destination. destitute:* standing alone, apart. *instauration, institution, restitution; substitute. constant, constitution*—yours and your country's. *constituents. superstitious, interstice.* Samuel Johnson's *Dictionary* defines *network* as "anything reticulated or decussated, at equal distances, with interstices between the intersections"—a heavy-handedly humorous instance of what logicians call *ignotum per ignotius:* (explaining) the unknown by the more unknown. (Some protest that a lexicographer should indulge his sense of humor after working hours.) See *er; ned.*

obstinate. As Laurence Sterne points out in *Tristram Shandy,* "'Tis known by the name of perseverance in a good cause–and of obstinacy in a bad one." An *obstacle* is a little something that stands in the way. L *obstare,* whence also, via Fr, *oust* and *ouster.* From L *constare:* to stand together (for sale), came *cost;* we may still say, "Those will stand you five dollars." A prostitute was one who stood forth to exhibit or proclaim her wares.

A number of words end with the *st* of this root. *arrest* (LL *arrestare; ad:* to; *re:* back; *stare:* stand); *assist, consist, contrast* (stand opposite); *desist; exist, existentialism. insist, persist, post, presto!, resist, subsist, subsistence. celestial* probably adds the root *skai:* gleaming, thus standing bright, up there in the sky. *star* ("like a diamond in the sky"): one of the standing, "fixed" bodies in the sky, as opposed to the "shooting stars," the comets, and also to the planets (Gk *planetes:* wanderers; see *pele III*). Through the atmosphere, the stars twinkle; Beatrice, in *Much Ado About Nothing,* ii, 1, says: "There was a star danced, and under that I was born."

store, storage, restore: stand on its own feet again. L *restaurare* first meant to hold back, make stand, as by fastening to a stake; then it was used figuratively. Over the first restaurant, in Paris, 1765, Boulanger (his name means baker) set a sign in Latin: "Come all whose stomachs call, and I shall restore you." L *restaurabo:* I shall restore, has as its present participle *restaurantem;* hence, *restaurant.* (The word has also been folk-explained as *rest-au-errant:* stopping place for the wanderer.) *to rest* means, literally, to stay back, hence to remain; the rest is clear. *restive:* holding back, though perhaps eager to go.

A *post* is a standing pole. *post* as in *postbox, post office,* was originally a relay station, a stage of a journey, with fresh horses and riders posted, standing ready at each stage to speed the delivery of messages or materials. Hence *stagecoach; posthaste.* The English theatrical *stage* was first erected in the courtyard, with balcony, of an inn at the *post-stage;* this gave its shape to the early unroofed theatre in England. *stadium.* In navigation came the word *steer:* to keep standing in the proper direction; *starboard:* steering side; *stern:* where the rudder was; also *stow:* setting the cargo to stay.

The summer solstice occurs when the sun (L *sol:* sun; whence *solar, solarium*) seems to stand still before the turn from the longest day and shortest night for the half-year journey to the winter solstice. This second stand and turn, lifting primitive man from his fear of everlasting dark to the glad return of brightness, is the season of the greatest festivals of joy. The happiest holidays, in many faiths, come at the time when primitive man rejoiced that the sun had won its fight, and was lengthening its hold upon the hours. Thus even the Christ Mass. In A.D. 386 Pope Siricius decreed that Jesus' birthday be celebrated on Dec. 25. Speculation sets it, historically, "between May and August"; but St. John Chrysostum (Gk *khrusostos:* golden-mouthed) explained: "The worshipers of Mithra [Persian god of light] call December 25 the birthday of the sun; but is not our Lord the sun of righteousness?" Thus the primitive joy received the Catholic sanction.

Mithra is also the Supreme Being in More's *Utopia.* Incidentally, "the son of the sun," Mithridates VI, the Great, king of Pontus, gave English the word *mithridatism:* induced immunity to poison, by his taking gradually increased doses. See *mei IV.* The word has been used figuratively, as by Lowell in 1866: "Our constitutions adapt themselves to the slow poison of the world until we become mithridatized at last." In his *Essay on Man,* Alexander Pope pictures this process more vividly:

Vice is a monster of so frightful mien
As to be hated, needs but to be seen;
Yet seen too oft, familiar with her face,
We first endure, then pity, then embrace.

Greek forms from the root *sta* include *Anastasius; apostle, apostate; apostasy. ecstasy:* standing out of oneself. *diastalsis; diastasis; peristaltic; anastasis, catastasis; hypostasis, epistasis. epistemology; metastasis. prostate:* standing in front (of the bladder). *system:* that by which things stand together. Also compounds with *histo:* tissue, which enables things to stand, as *histology, histolysis, anhistous, histamine. OED* lists 21 and details 8 *histo-* words; in its 1976 supplement there are 11 more.

stylite: from St. Simeon *Stylites,* who for 30 years stood on a pillar, winning many converts. *stele, epistyle, hypostyle. obstetrix:* she that stands by; *obstetrician.* (*midwife* is from Gm *mid:* with.)

Also *stalk,* the standing part of a plant. *stem. stamen:* pollen-bearing organ of a plant. *stamen* was also the warp in the ancient upright loom; this was applied to the thread spun by the Fates at one's birth, the strength and length of which determined the span of one's life. Hence *stamina:* the degree of "vital impulse" in one. (L *stamina,* plural of *stamen,* is now used in English as a singular.) *stamineal.*

stool, usually standing on three legs; *faldstool* (folding). *steel,* which stands firm (see *stak*). *sterling;* OFr *ester* with diminutive ending; also *stater:* a coin held in the Treasury as a standard.

Sweet is a legacy, and passing sweet
The unexpected death of some old lady,
Or gentleman of seventy years complete,
Who's made "us youth" wait too too long already,
For an estate, or cash, or country seat,
Still breaking, but with stamina so steady
That all the Israelites are fit to mob its
Next owner for their double-damned post-obits.
—Byron, *Don Juan,* i

Byron's letters make facetious mention of his mother-in-law, Lady Noel, whose death meant a large inheritance for him. The "Israelites" are the money-lenders who advance sums on such expectations, "us youth" is a self-mocking allusion to Falstaff's remark at the Gadshill robbery (*1 Henry IV,* ii, 2): "They hate us youth. . . . What, ye knaves, young men must live!"

Absence of occupation is not rest;
A mind quite vacant is a mind distressed.
—William Cowper, *Retirement*

stag: drip, seep; pool. Skr *tagada,* Gujarati *tankh:* pool, reservoir. The Portuguese blended this with the Latin form (below); whence also Fr *estang;* OE *stank:* standing water; E *tank* (see *sta*). Gk *stazein:* drip, ooze; *stagon:* drop. *stacte, stactometer. epistaxis:* nosebleed. Gk *stalkhos:* dripping. In many caves, where mineral-rich water drips, *stalactites* hang down like icicles from the rock above, and *stalagmites* form upward like cones, on the cavern floor. Sometimes they meet and fuse; they form many shapes, and may be colored, according to the nature of the mineral; in various parts of the world, they are tourist spectacles. L *stagnum:* pond. *stagnant, stagnate. stagnicolous:* growing by the pond.

stai: stone. See also *stei.* Gm *Stein;* hence the name *Stein* and its many combinations, as *Goldstein, Goldstone, Silberstein, Silverstone, Steinberg, Steinman.* The London telephone directory for 1980 has 31 names beginning *Steen,* 112 *Steins,* and some 250 names in combinations from *Steinaker* to *Steinweg,* including the *Steinway* piano.

They're a curious family, Stein;
There's Gert, and there's Ep, and there's Ein.
Gert writes like a monkey,
Ep's sculpture is junky,
And only ten understand Ein.

This incomprehension, and the new complexities Einstein probed, led J. C. Squire to add a couplet reversing Pope's epitaph on Sir Isaac Newton:

Nature, and Nature's laws, lay hid in night;
God said *Let Newton be!* and all was Light.

It did not last: The Devil, howling *Ho!*
Let Einstein be! restored the status quo.

Scales in England measure weight by the *stone:* 14 pounds. Racehorses everywhere have their weight measured by the stone, their height by the hand (a *hand* being four inches). In some lands criminals and adulteresses were once *stoned,* as by putting them in a well or pit, then filling it with stones; such executions have occurred recently in Iran. Jesus, as reported in John 8:7, was more restrained: "He that is without sin among you, let him first cast a stone."

"Stonewall" Thomas Jackson was a Confederate general in the American Civil War.

Via Du, *steinbok.* Sw, *tungsten:* heavy stone (see *el 74*). JWalker lists 36 relevant words ending *stone,* as *brimstone, milestone, millstone* (figuratively, around one's neck), *tombstone, whetstone. felstone:* rock stone; *rock* (whence, via Fr, *rococo*) seems to be Celtic in origin.

Choosing each stone, and poising every weight,
Trying the measures of the breadth and height,
Here pulling down, and there erecting new,
Founding a firm state on proportions true,
—Andrew Marvell, *The First Anniversary of . . . Oliver Cromwell*

stak: stand firm, support. An emphatic form of *sta. stay:* support. Hence, literally, a woman's *stays:* corset; plural because they were made in two pieces, laced together; often strengthened with strips of whalebone. Also used figuratively, and probably punningly, as by Byron in *Don Juan,* xv:

But Virtue's self, with all her tightest laces,
Has not the natural stays of strict old age.

Hence *stayless; stay-binding, stay-tape,* etc. Russ *Stalin;* E *steel.*

"Stay me with flagons, comfort me with apples: for I am sick of love"—Song of Solomon.

stam: stem, hold back. Imitative. Gc, *stammer. stem the tide* (as Canute showed his flattering warriors he could not). Gm *stumm:* dumb. *stum, stumble.*

"Wisely and slow; they stumble that run fast."
—*Romeo and Juliet,* ii, 3.

And he that strives to touch the stars
Oft stumbles at a straw.
—Spenser, *The Shepheardes Calender* (1579), July

stebh: first, a stem; then, to encircle, fasten around, hold, press, pound, step on. Gk *stephein:* to tie around, as a wreath. *stemma, stem.* In Latin, *stemma* was used of a scroll on which one's "family tree" was spread; in Old English, *stemm* was a tree trunk.

Stephen; see *bhereu. stephane:* diadem, halo, as in Greek statuary. *OED* has 6 related words beginning *stephan;* as *stephanome:* for measuring halos and other such forms in a foggy or rainy sky. *stephanite,* however, was named in 1845 for Archduke *Stephan* of Austria.

Gk *staphule:* a bunch of grapes for pressing; *staphyline. Staphylococcus* (*coccos:* berry) was coined in 1882 by Alexander Ogston. *OED* defines 8 associated words, as *staphylinid:* a rove beetle.

Sp *estampar. stampede.* Gc, *staff, distaff* (see *sak*). *stamp, step, stoop. stump.* Gm *Stamm:* stem, base; *Lager:* bed, camp. *Stammlager* was shortened to *stalag,* used for prisoners of war.

"Step by step each mile goes by; minute by minute, each life."

(s)teg. cover. hide. Skr *sthagati:* he hides. *thug:* first, a sneak thief. Pers *taj:* dervish's cap. Gk, *stegein:* cover; *steganos:* covered. *stegodon, stegosaur; OED* lists 10 words beginning *stego. steganography:* secret writing. L *tegere, tectum* (verb); *tegumentum* (noun): cover. *tetrix,* (plural, *tetrices*). *tegula, tegular; tegument, integument. detect, detective. obtected. protection. toga, togated; togs.* Fr, *tile, tuille.* Via OIr, *shanty;* some used to speak of the "shanty Irish." Gc, *deck:* the "cover" of a ship; to cover with ornaments; *bedeck. thatch.*

Seasons of mists and mellow fruitfulness,
Close bosom-friend of the maturing sun;
Conspiring with him how to load and bless
With fruit the vines that round the thatch-eaves run.
—Keats, *To Autumn*

steg(h): a stick; to shove, to stick. Gk *stokhos:* a pointed stake, used for target practice. *stochastic:* first, to aim at a mark; hence, guessing. Norse *staka:* to push, as with a stick. *stagger. stake.* Gc, *stack, stag, staggard. stockade. attach, attaché; attack. detach.* Nasalized, *sting.* See *steibh; steig.*

stei: solid fat; to thicken (drop by drop); compress, stiffen; hard. Gk, *stearoptene,* which is volatile (see *per I*). *steatite, steatocele. OED* states that *ster(o)* is used in "many chemical compounds"; it lists 3 and details 11; e.g., *stearin* comprises the three glycerides (combinations of stearic acid and glycerine): *monostearin, distearin,* and *tristearin.* For *steato, OED* lists 8, and details 10, as of the "steatogynous functions of the sweat glands." Women who are *steatopygous* are prized in some countries, as among the African bushmen; Darwin, in *The Descent of Man* (1871), was surprised that "with many Hottentot women the posterior part of the body projects in a wonderful manner." See *cal.*

L *stilla:* trickle, drop. *stillatim* (in prescriptions): a drop at a time. *stillatitious; stilliform.* Stevenson, in *An Apology for Idlers,* bowing to the advantages of schooling, avers: "I still remember that emphyteusis is not a disease, nor stillicide a crime." *Emphyteusis:* in ancient, and early English, law, a perpetual right, as of use of or of crossing land belonging to another. *stillicide:* the dripping of water, as from eaves, especially onto another person's property; a cause of many quarrels and lawsuits. Thomas Hardy, in *Wessex Poems* (1898), hearkens to

. . . the muted measured note
Of . . . a lone cave's stillicide.

eavesdropping today has a more inquisitive significance. Hence also a *still,* where liquor is made by dripping. *OED* defines 22 relevant *still* words. Also *instill, distill, distillation. distillery,* especially when illegal, is shortened to *still,* as in *moonshine still, wildcat still.* During and since Prohibition there has been a bond between liquor and politics (and crime). As a character in Jesse Stuart's *Men of the Mountains* states, "I'll send him a carload of cracked corn to fill up his moonshine still if he'll line up the votes just right!"

Gc, *stiff.* possibly *stifle. stop:* first, to stop up with tow, as the space between boat planks. *stopple, estop, estoppel.* From Gm *Stein,* E *stone,* come many proper names; see *stai* (another source of the word *stone,* an important tool of early man; hence *the Stone Age*). *OED* gives 14 columns to the word *stone* and its combinations, then details 12 more, as *stone-blind, stone's throw, stonewort. stonify* has been supplanted by *petrify;* see *peter.* Also *astonish, astound,* as though stricken to stone, stone-struck. *grindstone, hailstone, keystone, soapstone,* etc. *holystone* is a soft sandstone, humorously named from sailors kneeling while using it to scrub the deck. *touchstone,* originally a hard stone (as basalt, used to test gold by comparing the scratches it makes with those made by other metals and alloys), came to be used more generally; by Shakespeare as the name of the philosophical jester in *As You Like It.* The word *touch* is probably imitative, of a tapping sound, from L *toccare;* whence also, via Fr, *touché,* and possibly *tocsin,* etc. (see *steu*).

"Let's stop somebody from doing something"–A. P. Herbert. "Speak, Cousin, or if you cannot, stop his mouth with a kiss"–*Much Ado About Nothing,* ii, 1.

steibh, steip: press, stick; stick together, agree. L *stipes:* tree trunk. *stipare, stipatum:* compress. *stipate, stipe.* Via Fr, *costive. constipation; obstipation.* Via Sp, *steeve,* on a ship; *stevedore.* Gc, *stiff, stipple; stipule; stipend:* fixed pay. *stipulate;* in ancient Rome, breaking a twig or straw sealed a bargain. See *stegh; steig.*

steig: stick, prick; pointed, sharp; focus. Gk *stizein:* tattoo. *stylus. style:* first a pointed instrument for writing; then, the manner of writing (both physical and figurative). *stylish, stylist,* etc. The *y* instead of *i* comes from confusion with Gk *stulon:* gnomon, the Gk upsilon regularly changing to E *y.* It, *stiletto. stigma; astigmatism* (*a* negative). L, *instigate.*

Nasalized, *stinguere. distinct, distinguish; extinguish, extinct.* Note: *undistinguished,* but *indistinguishable.*

tiger, from its fangs and claws. Via OFr *estiquette,* E *ticket:* first, a little note, such as was stuck on a board at a law court, announcing legal seizure of an inheritance, etc. *etiquette,* in its present sense, was borrowed from French later; Lord Chesterfield seemed aware of his innovation when, referring to the pope, he underlined the word in a letter to his son on 19 Mar. 1750: "Without hesitation kiss his slipper, or whatever the *etiquette* of the court requires."

Gc, *stick, stickleback. steak,* which was first cooked on a spit. *stitch. thistle.* For *snickersnack,* see *sneit.* See also *stegh; steibh.*

steigh: step; go up. Gk *steikho:* climb; applied to the movement of verse. (In English the combining form *stich* is pronounced *stick.*) *stichic, stichous; stichomythia. distich, hemistich, tristich, tristichous.*

acrostic: successive letters down the beginning of the lines of a poem spell a name or other word(s), as the first letters of James Branch Cabell's *Sonnet for Maya* spell "This is nonsense." The acrostic may spread even farther: In *Testament of Love* (1386), by Thomas Usk, the first letters of the 32 chapters spell "Margarete of virtu have merci on thin Usk." *telecrostic:* similarly down (rarely up) at the ends of the lines. A *cross-acrostic* works as in Edgar Allan Poe's *A Valentine,* which he presents as a riddle. Here are the last 4 of its 20 lines:

Its letters, although naturally lying,
Like the knight Pinto (Mundez Ferdinando)–
Still form a synonym for truth, Cease trying!
You will not read the riddle though you do the best you *can* do.

Take the 17th letter of line 17 ("Its letters . . ."); the 18th of line 18, and so on. So far, so *good.* Get the whole poem, do the same from the first letter of line 1, and you have the name of the valentine's recipient, Frances Sargent Osgood–a clever stunt rather than a poem.

paracrostic: verse that in its first line begins words with the letters that start the remaining lines. The prophetic verses of the Sibylline oracles, said Cicero, were paracrostics. *orthostichous.* Via OIt *catastico:* a step-by-step record, E *cadaster.*

stoichiometry: measurement of the atomic weight of the elements, going up regularly; coined in 1792 by Jeremias B. Richter.

Gc, *stickle, stile. sty,* rising on the eye. From OE *stigrap:* step rope, *stirrup.*

Jog on, jog on, the footpath way,
And merrily hent the stile-a;
A merry heart goes all the day,
Your sad tires in a mile-a.
–*The Winter's Tale*

stel: put, put on; solid, firm. This is an expansion of the root *sta.* Gk *stellein:* put in order; send. *apostle, epistle. epistolary. apostate* is from Gk *apo:* away, and the root *sta:* stand. *systole, diastole; systaltic, diastaltic; peristalsis.* Gk *stolè:* equipment; E *stole:* robe, garment.

L *stolo:* branch. *stolon.* L *stolidus:* firm. *stolid; stolidity. stultify.* Via It, *pedestal.* Gc, *stall, stalwart, stalk. stout.* Gm, *gestalt.*

"The men of culture are the true apostles of equality"–Matthew Arnold, *Culture and Anarchy.*

sten: narrow. Gk *stenos. Steneosaurus;* the *e* crept in by linkage with *Teleosaurus. stenocephaly. stenography. OED* lists 22 *steno* words, and details 16, as *stenochrome, stenosis.*

(s)tene: thunder. Imitative. *stentorian. Stentor* was a warrior in the Trojan War (*Iliad,* v) with a voice "as of fifty men shouting." *OED* gives 10 associated words, as *stentorophone.* L *tonare. detonate. astonish, astound, stun. tornado;* see *ker I.* The Scandinavian god of thunder is *Thor,* whence *Thursday. tonite; tonitruous.* L *tinnitare,* frequentative of *tinnire:* ring. *tinnitus:* ringing in the ears. *tintamarre. tintinnabulation,* doubled for echoic emphasis; see *jing.*

Keeping time, time, time,
In a sort of Runic rhyme,
To the tintinnabulation that so musically wells
From the bells, bells, bells, bells,
Bells, bells, bells–
From the jingling and the tinkling of the bells.
–Poe, *The Bells*

ster I, stel, (s)tern: spread, extend, stretch; be rigid, stiff, thorny. Gk *stratos:* spread, applied to an army. *stratagem, strategy. stratocracy.* Gk and E *stroma. stramineous.* Gk *sternon:* breastbone. *sternum; episternum.* L *sternere, stratum:* spread out. *stratum,* plural *strata; substratum. street. consternation. prostrate, prostration.* L *struere, structum:* pile up. *structure, construct, constructivism. destruction, destroy. instruct, instrument,* etc. *obstruct; substructure.* L *constringere, constrictum:* constrain, constrict. L *endo:* within; *industry, industrious.* OL *stlocus. locus, locomotive,* etc. *local. OED* defines 21 words related to *local, location;* 14 relevant words beginning *loco;* 18 beginning *locu;* and 4 Latin phrases used in English, as *locus classicus.* L (by metathesis) *latus:* wide. *lateral, bilateral, latitude, latitudinarian. dilate.* Possibly L and E *lamina, lamination. laminitis:* inflammation of the sensitive plates (*laminae*) of a horse's hoof. *lamella.* Fr, *estrade. omelet* is from a French interpretation of *la lemele:* thin spread, with the diminutive ending *ette.*

Gaulish, *strath.* Gc, *stern, strain, strand, stretch, strew. thorn.* Via Sw, *turbot:* spiny flatfish. "Wherever a man lives, there will be a thornbush near his door"—J. B. Cabell.

straw, from strewing it for mattresses. The *strawberry* may be named for its little strawlike runners, but see *bhel I.* The word has had two special applications: (1) *strawberry leaves,* referring to a duke, from the eight leaves that adorn the ducal coronet; (2) *strawberry mark,* a reddish birthmark, often used in the old melodrama to identify a character, and parodied in the J. M. Morton farce *Box and Cox* (1847), which was burlesqued, with music by Arthur Sullivan, as *Cox and Box,* by F. C. Burnand, which ends:

> "Have you a strawberry mark on your left arm?
> No?! Then you are my long-lost brother."

> Bring hither the Pink, and purple Columbine,
> With Gilliflowers:
> Bring Coronation, and Sops-in-wine,
> Worn of paramours,
> Strew me the ground with daffadowndillies,
> And Cowslips, and Kingcaps, and loved Lilies;
> The pretty Paunce
> And the Chevisaunce
> Shall match with the fair flower Delice.
> —Spenser, *The Shepheardes Calender* (1579), April

(s)ter II: stiff, solid. Gk *stereos. stere. OED* lists 29 *stereo* words, as *stereognostic,* and details 35, as *stereochrome, stereoscope, stereotype. cholesterol. steric, sterigma. sterile, sterilize.* L *stirps* (plural, *stirpes*): family stem, line of descent. *stirpiculture. extirpate.* L *torpere. torpedo:* first used of the fish that can stun with an electric shock. *torpid, torpor.*

Gc, *stare. starch. stark* (naked). *start* (of surprise); *startle.* possibly *upstart. start:* to begin, has not been traced. *start,* a 17th c. Dutch term of contempt for the English, is from *staart:* tail, as though the English had recently come down from the trees. For the contemporary English opinion of the Dutch, see *teuta.*

redstart and other birds; *starling,* possibly *stork. ostrich* (*avis struthio*), *throstle, thrush;* see *trozdos.* Possibly *throat. stride, strive, struggle, strut. stiff* (as in rigor mortis). Into the 18th c. *starve* meant to die slowly, of cold, hunger, or disease. ("Let not poor Nellie starve"; Charles II's dying concern for his favorite mistress, Nell Gwyn, was heeded by his brother and successor James II, who paid her debts, granted her £1500 annual pension, and had her buried in St. Martin's-in-the-Field, at the corner of what is now Trafalgar Square in London. Admiral Horatio Nelson, who died in 1805 while winning the battle of Trafalgar, was not so successful with his mistress, Amy Lyon, whom he knew when she was Lady Emma Hamilton. On the brink of the battle he wrote a document "bequeathing" her to the nation; part of the story is told in Terence Rattigan's play *A Bequest to the Nation* [1970]. Despite Nelson's concern, nine years later Emma was in debtors' prison in London; she died, as the *Encyclopaedia Britannica* puts it, "in impecunious exile.") See *ueid.*

Confucius (d. 479 B.C.), in his *Analects,* declared: "He with whom neither slander that gradually soaks into the mind, nor accusations that startle like a wound in the flesh, are successful, may indeed be called intelligent."

ster III: star. (This may be a blend with the root *sta,* the stars as standing, fixed bodies.) Pers *Sitareh.* E *Esther.* Gk and E *aster.* Gk *astron. asteria. asterisk. asterism,* an early word for *constellation. asteroid, astral, astrophobia. diaster. disaster:* the stars turned away. *Astronaut, astronomy. Astraea,* goddess of justice, set in the sky as the constellation *Virgo,* sixth sign of the zodiac; see *guei.*

The *Encyclopaedia Britannica* calls *astrology* "for 2,000 years a dominant influence on religion, philosophy and science in Europe." In other lands it is much older. The "science" was applied to agriculture and human lives in Chaldea and Egypt before 3000 B.C.; the signs of the zodiac (see *guei*) go back at least to King Sargon I of Babylon (2637–2582 B.C.). Astrology was as widespread in the Middle Ages as it is today, and more respected. When Charles V of France came to the throne in 1364, he founded and equipped a College of Astrology at the University of Paris, to which he brought Doctor of Astrology Thomas of Pisano, from the University of Bologna, at the then princely salary of 100 francs a month. Doctor John Dee was Astrologer Royal to Queen Mary Tudor of England, and instructed Queen Elizabeth I.

There is reason to believe that Shakespeare was less gullible. In *King Lear,* i, 2, when Gloucester says, "These late eclipses in the sun and moon portend no good to us," his villainous bastard Edmund replies: "This is the excellent foppery of the world, that, when we are sick in fortune—often the surfeit of our own behaviour—we make guilty of our own disasters the sun, the moon, and the stars; as if we were villains by necessity, fools by heavenly compulsion, knaves, thieves and treachers by spherical predominance; drunkards, liars and adulterers by an enforced obedience of planetary influence . . . —an admirable evasion of whoremaster man, to lay his goatish disposition to the charge of a star! . . . 'Sfoot! I should have been that I am had the maidenliest star in the firmament twinkled on my bastardizing." And Cassius, in *Julius Caesar,* less loquaciously but with equal emphasis exclaims:

> The fault, dear Brutus, is not in our stars,
> But in ourselves, that we are underlings.

James M. Barrie in 1917 took *Dear Brutus* as the title for his play that develops this theme.

With *l.r* shift came L and E *Stella. stellar. stellate, constellation. Estelle.* Gc, *star, starlet. starlight. OED* lists 11 words beginning *astro,* and details 37, including *astrologaster:* a foolish, lying astrologer. Its 1972 supplement has a column of new material for old entries, and lists 16 and details 13 new relevant words. *astrolabe:* early navigators' instrument.

astrophel: a flower named by Spenser in his elegy on the death of his friend Sir Philip Sidney, who, dying at the siege of Zutphen, 22 Sept. 1586, passed a cup of water to another wounded man, saying: "Thy necessity is greater than mine." Spenser wrote:

> That herb, of some, starlight is called by name . . .
> From this day forth do call it astrophel.

Spenser no doubt had in mind Philip Sidney's sonnet series *Astrophel and Stella* (1580–84), which recorded, contemporaries said, Sidney's love for the first earl of Essex's daughter, Penelope Devereux, who in 1580 was married against her will to Lord Rich. Divorced by him, she married not Sidney but Lord Mountjoy, Earl of Devonshire, her earlier lover. Philip Sidney's sonnet series is wholly star-spun. Stella is loved by Astrophel (*astrophil:* star-lover), a transformed abbreviation of the poet's name, *Phil sid, sid* being from *sidus, sideris:* star (see *sueid I*).

ster IV: rob. Gk (*l.r.* shift), *stalk:* follow secretly. *steal, stealth.* In *As You Like It,* after Touchstone has explained the seven stages of a quarrel, the old Duke observes: "He uses his folly like a stalking-horse, and under the presentation of that he shoots his wit." Americans are perhaps familiar with the Indians' literal use of the stalking-horse, under its belly shooting their arrows at unsuspecting buffaloes or other prey.

The emperor, Jones, in Eugene O'Neill's play (1920), declares: "For de little stealin' dey gets you in jail soon or late. For de big stealin' dey makes you emperor and puts you in de Hall o' Fame when you croaks."

(s)teu: knock, beat, thrust, push; project, projection; piece knocked off. Gk *tupos:* to strike; later, to make a mold. *type, typical, typify, typography, typewriter; antitype, archetype. daguerreotype;* first element, from the name of the inventor, Louis *Daguerre* (1839). *logotype,* often shortened to *logo. OED* lists 23 words beginning *typ(o),* and details 21. Thus (used by Oliver Wendell Holmes in 1882), *typomania:* craze for seeing oneself in print. *typtology:* the study of spirit rapping, as on tables at a seance. *typolite:* a stone bearing a fossil impression, as of a leaf.

Nasalized, *tympan, timpano. tympanum:* eardrum. Via Fr, *timbre.* Also *tambour* and its diminutive, *tambourine.* A *timbrel* was like a tambourine, jingled and tapped by May Day merrymakers.

Fr *timbre:* postage stamp, came by a lengthy route. The word was used of a struck bell, then of the hemispherical table bell; then of the same-shaped skull cap, used in heraldry as a crest over a coat-of-arms; thence the crest stamped on official documents; thence, *stamp*—and *postage stamp.* Into English, in the 17th and 18th c., came words relating to stamp collecting—*timbrology, timbrophile, timbromaniac*—which were supplanted by *philately,* etc. See *ker I; tol.*

Probably from this root came *tip:* a projection; also *tip:* to push over, as the *tip cart, dump cart* (first, for dung; now frequent in agriculture and industry). Here, too, are *tumble; tumbler:* first a glass with a rounded bottom, so that it had to be emptied before it was set down; *tumbrel:* refuse disposal cart; used during the French Revolution to carry prisoners to the guillotine, as vividly described in Dickens' *Tale of Two Cities* (1859).

OED lists 14 anatomical terms beginning *tympan(o).* It details 19 with more general application. Thus *tympany* is (1) a drum, (2) a stretched membrane, and (3) a figurative term for *pregnancy,* as when Richard Tarlton, in *News Out of Purgatory* (1590), remarks that "the maid fell sick, and her disease was thought to be a tympany with two heels." Donne goes a stage farther, speaking of "this tympany, or false conception, by which spiritual power is blown up and swelled with temporal—a temptation still, to spiritual leaders with ascendancy over mobs." One thinks of 20th c. religious leaders, cultists, or such as the Ayatollahs of Iran. *tympany* is also (4) bombast, an inflated quasi-literary style.

tympanism is defined by Thomas Blount, in *Glossographia* (1661), as "a kind of torturing used by the Jews, by beating one to death with cudgels and drumsticks, *Hebrews* 11, 35; *Maccabees* 6, 19." The second reference is to *2 Maccabees* 6:18–30, wherein the Jews are not torturing but tortured, and the pious old Eliazar, refusing even to pretend to eat pork, lest his act serve as a bad example to the youth, is flogged to death. Flogging has been an almost universal form of punishment. It is vividly pictured as used on American slaves, as at the death of Tom, in Harriet Beecher Stowe's *Uncle Tom's Cabin* (1852); it was long usual in the British navy, and was not wholly forbidden by the English law of 1948. Corporal punishment (its milder name) is still employed in many parts of the world; its abolition in American schools remains the subject of controversy. When Samuel Johnson heard that a certain schoolmaster did not use the rod, he said: "What is spared at one end is spoiled at the other."

Folkplay on *tympany* produced *Tin Pan Alley:* a passage from 45th to 46th Street west of Broadway, in New York's theatre district; the name was then applied to the district and the (usually fortissimo) music produced or played there.

Tyndareus: the pounder, was the husband of Leda, who, seduced by Jove in the form of a swan, gave birth to Helen of Troy; but there was a division of seed in the egg, which hatched the twins Castor and Pollux. When Castor, son of Tyndareus, was killed, Pollux, son of Zeus, and therefore immortal, asked to share his brother's fate; Zeus permitted them to alternate in Hades, then set them as a constellation in the sky, where they continue to shine as Gk *Dioscuri:* sons of the god; L *Gemini:* twins, third sign of the zodiac (see *guei*). From them, the exclamation *By Jiminy!*

L *stupere:* knock hard. *stupefy, stupendous; stupor, stupid. styptic.* L *studere:* push on; *studium:* application, zeal. *study, studious; student; studio.* L *tudes:* hammer; via Fr, *toil. tundere, tusum. tund, tussal, tussicular. tussis:* pounding in the chest. *contuse, contusion. Tussilago:* genus, the coltsfoot, formerly used to relieve a cough. *obtund, obtuse; retund, retuse.* LL *pertusiare. pierce. tuck* of a drum, partly imitative; *tucket;* Fr, *tocsin;* It, *toccata, toccatella, toccatina.*

Gc, *stake, stockade; stoke, stoker. stook* of corn. *chock. stoss, stutter, stoop, stub; stipple, steep, steeple.* A *steeplechase* was first a cross-country race to a distant but visible church steeple, the horses leaping obstacles in the way. Du *linstock* (*lont:* match); *maulstick* (*malen:* paint). From OE *astiepen:* deprive; *stepchild,* etc.

Friedrich von Schiller, in *The Maid of Orleans* (1801), declared: "Against stupidity the gods themselves struggle in vain."

(s)teue: compact; to condense, to stop up. Related to *stei.* Skr, *stupa, stupe, tope.* A *toper* was first one that clapped hands to seal a bargain, then drank on it; then found other occasions to drink. (*swap* first meant to strike each other's hands to confirm an agreement.) Gk *stuppe,* L *stuppa;* tow; used to plug crevices. *stiffle; stop, stopple; estop; stuff.*

stoman: an opening, receptacle; hence mouth, stomach. Gk and E *stoma:* first, mouth. Gk *stomakhos:* gullet, orifice of an organ; later extended to the digestive organ, E *stomach.* The four stomachs of the ruminants are the *rumen, reticulum* (or honeycomb), *omasum* (or manyplus), and the true stomach, the *abomasum.* The London *Daily Chronicle* of 26 July 1901 pointed out that "the oyster and his fellow-molluscs, like man himself, possess that test of biological greatness, a true stomach."

stomatology. With *caca:* dung, came *stomacace:* scurvy of the gums. *astomous* (*a* negative): with no mouth. *anastomosis. ancyclostomiasis* (Gk *agkhulos:* crooked): hookworm. *OED* gives 6 columns to the word *stomach* and its compounds, as *stomacher, stomach pump, stomach-warmer, stomach ache;* 6 more columns detail related words. *OED* also lists 11 and details 14 *stomat(o)* words, as *stomatic,* referring to the mouth. *stomatod(a)eum* was formed in 1887, to "correct" the irregularly fashioned *stomod(a)eum,* coined in 1876. *Stomatopoda:* order of crustaceans. *Stomoisia:* genus, the bladderwort.

stomach is often used figuratively; the noun, for courage, pride, anger, or ill-will; the verb, mainly negative, in the sense of to put up with, as *I can't stomach that.*

The astute Henry V, in Shakespeare's play, addressing his men before battle with the outnumbering French, knew that no one would step forward to accept his offer:

> He which hath no stomach to this fight,
> Let him depart; his passport shall be made,
> And crowns for convoy put into his purse:
> We would not die in that man's company
> That fears his fellowship to die with us.

strebh: turn, twist, whirl. Gk *strephein:* turn; *strophos:* twisted cord or band. *strophe* was first used of the Greek dramatic chorus, turning from right to left; *antistrophe,* of its counterturn; then the terms were applied to the verses sung by the chorus while thus moving. *anastrophe. apostrophe. catastrophe,* which has been humorously misapplied; it is not hard to grasp the Page's meaning when, in *2 Henry IV,* ii, 1, he shouts at Falstaff resisting arrest:

> Away, you scullion! you rampallion! you fustilarian!
> I'll tickle your catastrophe.

epistrophe. monostrophe. boustropedon: turning like an ox in plowing; used of early writing or carving, in which the lines go alternately from right to left, then from left to right.

Streptomycin, from "twisted fungus." *Streptococcus:* bacterium that gathers in twisting chains. *OED* lists 14 biological *strept(o)* terms, as *streptobacterial, streptocolysin,* and details 3. *strophanthin. Ommastrephes:* genus of cephalopods. *Strophanthus:* genus of tropical plants; source of African arrow poison, also of the glucoside strophanthin, used for heart ailments. *Strepsiptera:* order of insects; the wingless females and larvae are parasitic of bees and wasps; *strepsipterous. Streptothrix:* bacteria with interlaced filaments.

Gk *strabos:* whirling, crooked. *strabismus. strabismometer, strabotomy; OED* defines 7 *strab(o)* words. *strobic, strobile, stroboscope; OED* defines 11 *strobo* words. *strap* and its doublet, *strop. diastrophism. strophulus.* Perhaps *strip* and *stripe,* though these have not been traced. The *Mobius strip* was devised by August *Mobius* in 1827: take a strip of paper, say an inch wide, a foot or so long; twist it once and glue the ends together; draw a line along the middle of the strip, and you will find that it has but one side.

In an essay of 1831, E. Caird mentions "a view which supposes man to be afflicted with a kind of intellectual strabismus, so that he can never see with one of his mental eyes without shutting the other."

streig, streng: squeeze (hence powerful); stroke, scrape; furrow, groove. L *striga:* furrow. *stria, striate, striga, strigil, strigose. strain; strict; stricture; strait. constrain, constrict; distrain, distress; obstriction; restrain, restrict.* Possibly Fr, *prestige. tricot.* Nasalized, *string; stringent, stringency. strand; strangle, strangulated. strong, strength.* It, *stringendo, stretto. Strongyle:* order of parasitic worms; *strongylosis.* Gc, *stress, strike, strickle.*

It matters not how strait the gate,
How charged with punishment the scroll,
I am the master of my fate,
I am the captain of my soul.
—William Ernest Henley, *Invictus* (1874)

stre(p): make noise. Imitative. Gk *ptarmikhos. Ptarmica:* the sneezewort; also folk-changed to *arnica.* Gk *ptarnusthai;* L *sternutare, sternutatum,* frequentative of *sternuere:* to sneeze. *sternutation, sternutative. stertere:* stertorous. L *strepere:* make a noise, roar. *strepitous; obstreperous.* It, *sterpitoso.*

(s)trid, strig: squeak, buzz; grind, rasp. Imitative. Gk, *trismus:* lockjaw. *strident; stridulation.* From *stridence,* through *stridor,* to *stridulousness, OED* defines 15 relevant words. *Strix:* genus of owl; see *ul.*

Amphitrite (wife of Poseidon, who rules the waves; *amphi:* both) can be heard on the beaches both sides of the sea; she was one of the fifty Nereids, daughters of Nereus and Doris; Doris was daughter of Oceanus (they were all at sea). Poseidon saw Amphitrite dancing on the island of Naxos; when she shrank from him, he sent a dolphin to persuade her to accept him; when the dolphin succeeded, Poseidon set him as a constellation in the northern sky. See *guelbh.*

suad: sweet, pleasant. Gk *hedone:* pleasure. *OED* lists *hedonic, hedonism,* and 6 more *hedo* words. *Hedychium:* sweet snow; genus of plants. *algedonic:* mixing pain and pleasure. *Aedes* (*a* negative): genus of mosquito.

L *suadere, suasum:* try to persuade. *suasion, suave, suavity. assuage, assuasive; dissuade, persuade, persuasion.* It, *soave.* Gc, *sweet, sweeten. sweetbread; sweetheart. sweet* and its compounds take up 24 columns in *OED.*

In 1876 Walter Pater protested: "I wish they wouldn't call me a hedonist; it produces such a bad effect on the minds of people who don't know Greek." None the less, two years later Edward Dowden persisted: "This devotion to beauty, to beauty alone . . . was a kind of hedonist asceticism."

suard: Gk *sardonios. sardonic,* from the plant *Sardonia* (also called *apium risus:* laugh-bringing apium), in the belief that this plant from the island *Sardinia* twisted the face into a scornful laugh.

sue, se: personal relations, one's own; his, hers, its; hence, a group as a unit. Skr *stridhana:* her own; a woman's property. *swadeshi:* of one's own region; applied, as in India, to a boycott of foreign (i.e., British) goods. *swami:* one's own master.

Gk *ethos:* group, group practice, custom. *ethos, ethics, cacoethes* (see *caca*). *ethnic, ethnology. OED* gives 30 related words, from *ethnagogue* to *ethnopsychology.*

hetaira (*hetaera*): one's own woman, companion. Respectable women in most of ancient Greece were largely confined to the home and to domestic chores, so that, said Xenophon, 4th c. B.C., of growing girls, "they might see, hear, and inquire as little as possible." Hence the men often sought the company of *hetaerai,* who were frequently Ionians of intelligence and education, "making them" (says *The Oxford Companion to Classical Literature*) "more agreeable companions than the cloistered Athenian women." The most famous *hetaera* was Aspasia of Miletus, the lifelong companion of the Athenian statesman Pericles (d. 429 B.C.). Landor wrote a series of imaginary letters between Pericles and Aspasia (1836), as well as an imaginary conversation between Pericles and Sophocles.

Gk *idios* (*sued-ios*): one's own. *idiom, idiot, idiosyncrasy. OED* lists 27 and details 24 *idio* words, as *idiomorphous, idionomy, idiopsychological,* as opposed to *heteropsychological.*

L *sed, se:* self. Latin phrases used in English: *per se. felo-de-se,* which first meant accidental death while committing a felony, then was used of suicide. To commit a felony was virtually a form of suicide; until the mid 19th c. in England, felonies were punishable by death. *OED* gives 45 columns to *self* and its compounds, as *self-abuse, self-consistent, self-sufficiency, self-willed. se:* by oneself, came to mean apart, without; in this sense it is an English prefix to innumerable words, as *secret, secrete; secure* (whence *sure*); *seduce:* lead astray; *segregate:* part from the herd; *separate, sever; several:* existing apart; *sex:* cut apart, as Eve from Adam; see *sek.* "Of their own kind" were the Sabines, who occupied two of the seven hills that became Rome; the "rape of the Sabine women" while their men were at the Roman games, 753 B.C., gave Romulus and his fellows their next generation. Some 700 years later, the wealthy Maecenas gave the poet Horace a villa in the Sabine hills, where Horace often relaxed, on his "Sabine farm."

L *sodalis:* for oneself; a companion. *sodality.* L *solus:* by oneself, alone. *sol. solfidian* (but see *sel II*). *sullen.* L *suus* (genitive *sui*): of oneself; *suicide. sui generis:* of its own kind, unique. Gm *Ding an sich,* Kant's term (1781) for an essence beyond human experience, prime substance, "the thing in itself."

L *suescere, suetum:* to accustom oneself. *custom, accustom. assuetude, consuetudinary. desuetude. mansuetude:* accustoming to the hand; whence *mastiff:* a dog thus trained.

Gc *sik* became the Danish suffix *sk.* Thus *bask:* to bathe oneself in sunshine, or in the sun of someone's favor. *busk:* prepare oneself; whence *bustle:* busy oneself. Gc, *self, sib, sibling, gossip. swain:* for oneself; first, an attendant. OIr, *Sinn Fein:* We Ourselves, a society founded ca. 1905.

Kipling pictures *The Prodigal Son* rejoicing:

Here come I to my own again–
Fed, forgiven, and known again–
Claimed by bone of my bone again
And sib to flesh of my flesh.

"After an existence of nearly twenty years of innocuous desuetude, these laws are brought forth." President Grover Cleveland said he used these words, in his message to Congress, 1 Mar. 1886, to "please the Western taxpayers, who are fond of such things."

suei I: hiss, whistle. Imitative. L *sibilare, sibilatum. sibilancy, sibilant, sibilate; siffle.* It *zufolo.* Possibly *sibyl,* from the snake sacred to Apollo, at whose temples, especially at Delphi, prophetesses–the sibyls–uttered their predictions. The Cumaean sibyl offered twelve books of prophecies to Tarquinius Superbus, last king of Rome. When told that her price was considered excessive, she destroyed three of the books and offered the remainder at the same price. Finally, Tarquinius bought the last three books at the price she had asked for all twelve. When his son Tarquinius Sextus was rash enough to rape the wife of Lucius Tarquinius Collatinus, Lucretia, she killed herself, and the roused Romans, led by Lucius Junius Brutus, drove out the Tarquin family and established the Republic. When the Tarquins tried to recapture Rome, they were foiled by the valor of Horatio at the Tiber bridge, as told in Macaulay's poem. In *Julius Caesar,* Cassius, trying to persuade Brutus to remove another "tyrant," refers to his glorious ancestor; and Shakespeare's *Rape of Lucrece* is one of the many retellings of her story–vividly pictured in the play *Le Viol de Lucrèce,* by André Obey (1931), which in the same year was made into an opera by Benjamin Britten.

Also *persiflate:* to banter lightly. *persiflage.* Lord Chesterfield, in a letter of

1757, was the first to use this word in English: "Upon these delicate occasions you must practice the ministerial shrugs and persiflage." Hannah More in 1779 presented the feminine attitude toward "the cold compound of irony, irreligion, selfishness, and sneer, which make up what the French . . . so well express by the word persiflage." Carlyle, in *Heroes and Hero-Worship* (1840), said of Voltaire: "They felt that, if persiflage be the great thing, there never was such a persifleur."

Dies irae, dies ille,
Solvet saeculum in favilla,
Teste David cum Sibylla.
—Day of wrath and doom impending,
David's word with Sibyl's blending,
The century in ashes ending.
—Thomas of Celano, ca. 1250

suei II: turn, swing rapidly. Gc, *swap, sway, sweep, swift.* Also *swift,* the bird, which darts across the sky; and *swiftlet,* a small Oriental species whose nest, held together by its saliva, is the base of bird's-nest soup.

swipe, sideswipe; switch. Possibly *swim,* but see *suem.*

sueid I: shine. L *sidus, sideris:* star. sidereal. *consider:* originally, consult the stars. *consideration.* L *desiderare, desideratum.* Also E *desideratum. desiderate:* hope for from the stars; shortened to *desire. undesirable. OED* has 15 words beginning *desir,* plus 12 beginning *desider.*

"She doted upon . . . captains and rulers clothed most gorgeously, horsemen riding upon horses, all of them desirable young men." The "she" referred to, "who bestowed her harlotries upon them," was not Catherine the Great of Russia but Oholibah (Bible, Ezekiel 23:1–7); making the point clear and the punishment understandable, "the word of God came . . . Oholibah is Jerusalem"—which was consequently captured and destroyed in 587 B.C.

sueid II: sweat. Gk (*suidros*) *hidros. hidrosis.* L *sudor. sudation. sudoriferous, sudorific, sudatorium* (compressed to *sudorium*). *exude; transude.* Via Fr, *suint. sandiver* is a folkchange from *suin de verre:* glass sweat. Possibly Scand, *sauna.* Gc, *sweat, sweater, sweatshirt.*

"In the sweat of thy face shalt thou eat bread, till thou return unto the ground, for dust thou art and unto dust shalt thou return"—Bible, Genesis 3:19.

"I have nothing to offer but blood, toil, tears, and sweat"—Churchill, House of Commons, 13 May 1940.

(s)uekuos: juice. Gk *opos:* vegetable juice; *opion:* poppy juice. *opiate, opium, opiumism.* The *opium poppy* is *Papaver* (: poppy) *somniferous* (: sleep-bringer); whence also *papaveraceous, papaverine;* see *pa.*

OED lists 24 varieties of poppy—*black, prickly, yellow*—and 25 combinations, from *poppy bed* to *poppy water;* and it details *poppy head, poppy seed, poppywort.* For *poppycock* (called "U.S. slang"), see *pa.*

Iago, when he has roused Othello to suspicion of his faithful wife (iii, 3), gloats:

not poppy, nor mandragora,
Nor all the drowsy syrups of the world,
Shall ever medicine you to that sweet sleep
Which thou owedst yesterday.

suel: burn; brightness without flame. *Svarga:* Hindu heaven; *Surya:* sun god. Gk *Selene:* moon goddess; Keats, in 1818, tells of her love for Endymion. *selenium;*

see *el 34. OED* defines 33 *selen* words relating to the moon or the element. *Selachii:* order of phosphorescent fish. Gc, *sweal, swelter, sweltry; sultry.*

James Howell, in *Epistolae Ho-Elianae* (1645), averred that "the sphear of the moon is peopled with Selenites or Lunary men." The belief was reiterated as late as 1864, but–although many have seen the man in the moon; indeed, he comes on stage in the Pyramis and Thisbe performance in *A Midsummer Night's Dream* –Selenites have not been popular in scientifiction. Since humans have landed on the moon, talk of a native population has died out.

suem: move in water; swim. *swim, swam, swum. swimmeret. swimmingly. sound:* water one can swim across; a channel, as Long Island *Sound. to sound:* to plumb or probe the depths. *soundless:* rarely used for *unfathomable.* Fr, *sonde:* sounding line; hence *radiosonde, rocketsonde.* For the audible *sound,* and supersonic activity, see *suen.*

Mother, may I go out to swim?
Yes, my darling daughter.
Hang your clothes on a hickory limb,
But don't go near the water.
–Nursery rhyme, its variations discussed in Walter de la Mare's *The Scarecrow* (1945)

suen: sound. L *sonus, sonare, sonatum. sonant, sone, sonnet, sonneteer, sonorescent, sonority, sonorous.* It, *sonata, sonatina. sound, resound. assonance, consonance; dissonance. consonant. unison.* For *sing, sang, song,* and *sung,* see *senguh. sonar:* the first letters of *so*und *na*vigation *r*anging. Recently, aviation crossed the *sonic barrier:* as a plane approaches the speed of 738 miles per hour, it moves, with the *sonic boom* (explosive sound), into *supersonic* speed.

Gc, *swan* (see *kuknos*). Socrates, facing death (as reported in Plato's *Phaedo*), demanded: "Will you not allow that I have as much of the spirit of prophecy in me as the swan? For they, when they perceive that they must die, having sung all their life long, do then sing more lustily than ever, rejoicing in the thought that they are going to the god they serve." Chaucer (*The Parlement of Foules*) and Shakespeare (*The Phoenix and the Turtle; The Merchant of Venice,* iii, 2; and *Othello,* v, 2) are among those that speak of the *swan song:* a burst of glorious song at dying. In folklore, the swan is considered dumb until its dying.

Varieties of the graceful bird are called *mute swan, trumpeter swan, whistling swan,* or *whooper;* the last term seems most appropriate, for, despite the fable, the most frequent sound the bird utters resembles a croak. One aspect of the bird is caught in the prologue to Chaucer's *Canterbury Tales:* "A fat swan loved he best of any roast." *OED* gives 4 columns to the word *swan* and special combinations, as *swan quill:* swan's feather used as a pen; then defines 21 relevant words. *swan-upping,* changed to *swan-hopping:* nicking the beak to mark ownership–now obsolete. Most of the swans in England belong to the Crown.

From the bird's actual and fabled beauty (as of the "ugly duckling" that grew to be a swan) the name has been applied to master poets–*the Mantuan swan:* Virgil; *the Swan of Avon:* Shakespeare.

The American dialectal exclamation, as in "*Wal, I swan,* I must be gettin' on," may be compressed from *I'se warrant:* I'll be bound; or may be a mincing folk-change from *I'm sworn.*

sueng: swing. Gc, *sway, swag, swagger, swing; swinge:* to make swing. *swingletree:* (1) bar to hang hemp over, for beating; (2) pivoted crossbar on a vehicle, to which, on a carriage, cart, or plow, traces are fastened so as to give the horse freedom of movement. In the second sense, *swingletree* is sometimes folk-changed to *singletree;* also called *whiffletree, whippletree.*

swank. A *swanker* was first a person of swaggering, ostentatious behavior. In the 18th and 19th c. it was a challenge to drain a pint of beer in three draughts, the first of which was called *Neckum;* the second, *Sinkum;* and the third, proudly, *Swankum*—shortened to *swank.*

suep I: sleep. Gk *Hupnos:* god of sleep; hence, *hypnosis. OED* lists 29 words beginning *hypn(o),* and details 14. The term *neurohypnotism* was coined by James Braid in 1842; for a time the practice was also known by his name, as when Quain's *Dictionary of Medicine* (1882) warned that "the too ready adoption of hypnotism or Braidism may do harm rather than good." The practice came to be used with mentally disturbed patients; hence *hypnoanalysis,* which Freud tried before he turned to *psychoanalysis,* which induces talk while the patient remains conscious.

L *Somnus,* Roman god of sleep (for *Morpheus,* god of dreams, see *merbh*). L and E *sopor. soporific. OED* details 15 relevant words beginning *sopi* or *sopo,* as *sopient, soporiferous.* It lists 17 words beginning *somn,* as *somnambulism;* 9 others beginning *somni,* 8 of these relating to *somniloquy:* talking in one's sleep; then details 20, as *somnivolent.* Lowell, in a letter of 1890, says that some consider the nightingale a *somnifuge.*

somnolent, insomnia. Insomnia has troubled many in all times, and *somnifers:* methods of inducing sleep, have varied down the ages. Ancient, marble dreaming-beds, guides to the oracles, may still be seen at Delphi and at Ephesus. Medieval recipes included the witch doctor's mixture of frog spittle, dew gathered from the leaves of the mandragora, and peacock's urine, stirred together with the knucklebone of a stillborn seventh son. These, in our more enlightened times, have been replaced by sleeping pills and sedatives of varying degrees of effectiveness and addictive lure. Sometimes, as young parents and errant husbands know, it is not one's own sleep that is the desideratum. In desperate cases, one may resort to television or a Mickey Finn; or to soft music or a lullaby. An ironic lullaby that was popular in the 17th c. is given under *lal.*

suep II: toss, cast, scatter. Partly imitative. L, *dissipate.* Gc, *swab.*

(s)uer I: watch out for; guard, protect; cover. Skr *varna:* to cover, hence color. Gk *horan:* watch; *ephoros:* overseer, guard. *ephor,* as in Sparta. *pylorus:* literally, gatekeeper. *propylaeum; pylon, propylon. tetrapylon:* with four gates. *Arcturus* (Gk *arkhtos:* bear): bear guard; brightest star in the constellation Boötes, keeping watch over the Great Bear. Possibly *Ouranus,* god of the sky, which covers Earth; but see *aue.* Gk *orama:* view. *cosmorama, diorama, panorama.*

L, *cover, covert, coverture, uncover. aperire, apertum* (*a* negative): to open. *aperient:* that which opens the bowels. Fr, *apéritif, aperitive:* that which opens the taste-buds. *aperture, overt, overture. operculum; OED* details 8 related words. *pert, malapert. apricate:* lie open to the sun. L *vereor, vereri:* watch with religious regard. *revere, reverence.* Even in ancient Rome, modesty induced euphemism; *veretrum* was used of "the private parts"; whence E *Veretillum:* genus of sea pens, from their phallic shape; also *verecund:* modest, bashful. Similarly, Gk *ais, aidos:* reverence, bashfulness, gave that language *aidoia:* the privy parts, and came into English in *edea, edeitis, edeology, edeoscopy.* For L, *pudenda:* the shameful parts, see *peu I.*

L *servus:* first, guardian of the herd. *servile, servitude; serf; serve, servant, serviceable,* etc. Fr, *sergeant. conserve, deserve. one's just deserts. dessert*—the main service removed; usually the table is cleared before dessert, or the final course is served in another room. *disservice. observe, observance, observation, observatory. preserve.* "Self-preservation is the first law of nature."

ward and *guard* are doublets; words via French tend to begin *g(u);* via Germanic languages, *w.* Hence *warden, warder, warrant, warranty, ware, wary, aware, beware. weir. Edward* (*ead:* wealth). *award, reward, unrewarded. wardrobe. steward:* first, warder of the sty. *warren, warn.* Thus also *guardian, disregarded, rear guard, guarantee, guaranty; garrison* (OE *warison*), *garret, garment, garnish, garage*—all with the basic notion of covering or protecting.

Canterbury was OE *Cantwarabyrig* (see *bhereg*): guards of Kent town. From the pace of the pilgrims to Canterbury Cathedral, as in Chaucer's *Tales,* came *canter. louver:* medieval watchtower on a wall or roof, is a fusion of the French article *le:* the, and the noun *l'ouvert:* the open place. Gm *Wehrmacht; Landwehr.*

"The virtue which requires to be ever guarded is scarcely worth the sentinel" —Oliver Goldsmith, *The Vicar of Wakefield* (1766). Goldsmith is perhaps the only writer to have achieved a masterpiece—though minor—in each of the four major literary forms: poetry, *The Deserted Village;* essay, *Citizen of the World* ("Chinese Letters"); novel, *The Vicar of Wakefield;* drama, *She Stoops to Conquer.*

(s)uer II, sur: sound; talk. See also *uer VI.* Imitative of whisper, buzz. *swear, answer. swarm* (of buzzing bees). *swirl.* Gk *rhema:* word; *rhetor:* orator. *rhetor, rhetoric,* etc. Coleridge, in *Table Talk* (1830): "The object of rhetoric is persuasion—of logic, conviction—of grammar, significancy. A fourth term is wanting, the rhematic, or logic of sentences." Byron, in *Don Juan:*

His speech was a fine example, on the whole,
Of rhetoric, which the learn'd call rigmarole.

Gk *eiron:* a sayer, who speaks but utters not his thoughts. *irony. susurration. syrinx:* first, a shepherd's pipe. From the hollow pipe, *syringe; syringotomy. Syringa:* genus, the mock orange, from its hollow stem. *Sorex:* genus, the shrew, from its sound; *soricine.* Possibly *Hermes,* messenger of the gods, himself the god of eloquence and science, who was pictured as a youth with *caduceus* (: rod), *petasus* (: brimmed hat), and *talaria* (: winged sandals); identified with the Roman god Mercury; see *el 80.* Hence *hermeneutics:* art of interpretation; when related to Scripture, *hermeneutics* is distinguished from *exegesis:* exposition. *hermaphrodite.*

Irony is a blow delivered as a caress, an insult presented as a compliment.

L *verbum:* word. *verb. verbalize; veracious,* used of a man of his word. *veracity. verbatim; verbose. verbocination.* For *reverberate,* see *uer II. adverb; proverb. Verbum sap* (see *sap*). Via Fr *verbier:* chatter, E *verbiage. very* first meant a true word, actual—*the very thing;* it takes almost 8 columns in *OED. veriment, verisimilitude, verism,* etc. Probably *verve,* first used by Dryden in the dedication of his *Aeneid* (1697): "If he be above Virgil and is resolved to follow his own verve (as the French call it), the proverb will fall heavily upon him: Who teaches himself has a fool for his master."

OED lists 6 and details 4 words related to *veratine,* a liniment (used by Mrs. Carlyle in 1865) made from a poisonous alkaloid; it makes one sneeze, and its name comes from the folk belief that sneezing shows a remark is true.

L *surdus* (from the buzzing in the ears?): hard of hearing, muted. *absurd:* at first, out of tune. Voltaire observed that "as long as people believe in absurdities, they will commit atrocities." It, *sordamento, sordellina, sordine, sordino.* In mathematics, Euclid (*Geometry,* x) used Gk *alogos:* reasonless, to apply to irrational numbers; this was translated into Arabic as *açamm:* deaf, then back into Latin and so to English as *surd.* See the quotation under *deik.*

Gc, *word. OED* devotes 13 columns to *word,* with almost 4 more for other forms, as *wordmonger, wordless.* Byron, in *Lara,* ii, deems it a pity

to mar
The mirthful meeting with a wordy war.

Quantities of words have been noted. The London *Times,* 1 Oct. 1979, achieved (intentional) bathos when it gave the final figure here: "The Lord's Prayer, 56 words; the Ten Commandments, 197; the American Declaration of Independence, about 500; the European Economic Community directive on import of caramel, 26,911." Despite official logorrhea and gobbledegook, English can be concise in relation to other languages, as shown by the count of syllables in various translations of the Latin Vulgate Gospel According to Mark:

Average in

Teutonic languages, 32,650	Romance languages, 40,200
Slavic languages, 36,500	Indo-Iranian languages, 43,100
in French, 36,500	in English, 29,000

"There is nothing so absurd but some philosopher has said it"–Cicero, *Of Divination.* "In the beginning was the word"–and it will mark the ending.

(s)uer III, (s)qet(p): cut, pluck. *sword. sharp. harrow; harvest. acarpous* (*a* negative). For words from Gk *karpos:* fruit, see *ker III. carport* and *car pool* relate to automobiles; see *kers I.*

London, thou art the flower of cities all! . . .
Fair be their wives, right lovesome, white and small . . .
Thy famous Mayor, by princely governance,
With sword of justice thee ruleth prudently.
–William Dunbar, *London* (1501)

suesor: sister. L *soror. sororal.* L *sobrinus* (*sororinus*): mother's sister's child; cousin. *cozen:* first, to call oneself a cousin, to claim kinship for advantage; to sponge, deceive. *OED* calls this derivation uncertain; some suggest It *cozzonare,* from L *coctionem:* horse-trader, hence a cheat. But *cousin,* in Elizabethan days and to some extent even now, is used loosely; *cousin, Coz,* may indicate a tie merely of affection. *cozen;* thence *cozenage.*

cousin-german; german is a folkchange from *gen-men:* of the same germ (see *gn*); of ideas closely related, the form now is *germane;* thus also *human, humane; urban, urbane*–the first being physical; the second, of the spirit.

Gc, *sister, sisterhood. sorority.* Thus *brotherhood, fraternity; motherhood, maternity; fatherhood, paternity*–the Germanic form with *hood* is closer to the hearth and heart; the form via Latin and French is more formal, legalistic, or smacking of the hospital and the college secret society.

Besides giving over 4 columns to *sister, OED* has 13 related entries.

Cousins indeed, and by their uncle cozen'd
Of comfort, kingdom, kindred, freedom, life!
–*Richard III,* iv, 3

sui, sei: leave off, settle down. Gk *siope:* silence. *aposiopesis:* in rhetoric, breaking off midsentence, not completing an idea;. in word formation, a breaking off after a syllable, as *cab(riolet), photo(graph). prosiopesis:* leaving off the first element, as *(tele)phone, (omni)bus.* Sometimes both the regular and the changed form are used, as *history, story; example, sample; disport, sport; acute, cute.*

Pope, in *Peri Bathos: The Art of Sinking in Poetry* (1727), mockingly spoke of the rhetorical "apotheopesis, an excellent figure for the ignorant, as 'What shall I say?' when one has nothing to say."

suombh: spongy. Gc, *sump, swamp.*

Chesterton, surveying *The Victorian Age in Literature,* 2, observed that "Hardy went down to botanize in the swamp."

suord: dirty, black. L, *sordes, sordid.* Gc, *swart, swarthy.* The frequent name *Schwartz* and its compounds, as *Schwartzkopf:* blackhead.

sus: pig, snout. Also *plowshare,* which works the ground like a hog rooting; from this sense came E *socket.* Gk *hus:* hog; with the feminine ending *aina, hyena; hyocine. Hyoscyamus:* genus, the henbane, poisonous to swine. Possibly *hystrix:* hairy swine; porcupine, spiny pork (note Fr *porc,* E *pork*).

L *sus. Sus:* genus of swine. *OED* gives 3 columns to *swine,* then details 13 words beginning *swine.* The diminutive of *sus, suculus,* from the wallowing, led to *sully, soil, soilure; sullage* (in the 17th and 18th c. often *sulliage*). *suilline.* Gc, *sow, swine.*

In Browning's *Soliloquy of a Spanish Cloister,* an unnamed monk eructs his hatred of Brother Lawrence. The poem begins "Gr–r–r–There go, my heart's abhorrence," and ends "Gr–r–r–you swine!" Within, mocking Lawrence's request for help in translating, the monk asks: "What's the Greek name for swine's snout?" The monk was thinking of Brother Lawrence; Browning was perhaps thinking of the Bible, Proverbs 11:22, which states: "Like a gold ring in a swine's snout is a beautiful woman without discretion."

In Matthew there are two references to *swine.* The injunction "Neither cast ye your pearls before swine" (7:6) is generally applied to unappreciative persons. Then Jesus, among assorted reported miracles, transplants the demons plaguing two men into the Gadarene swine, which "rushed violently down the steep bank into the sea, and perished in the waters" (8:32).

swine is now used to represent greediness or uncleanness; in the farmyard the usual terms are *hog* (feminine, *sow*) and *pig;* the wild variety is a *boar. OED* gives 3 columns to *swine,* listing 49 combinations; then it details 15, as *swinery; swine's-feather:* a pointed stake used against cavalry in the 17th and 18th c.; *swinestone.* Since one pig in every litter was devoted to St. Anthony, patron saint of swineherds, and when grown was given to the church, the littlest pig (naturally) came to be called an *anthony.*

Possibly *syphilis:* swine-lover; but see *bhili. k(e)elson:* timber parallel to a ship's keel to strengthen the flooring–*swine, cat, dog, horse,* have been used to designate *timber.* And figuratively, Walt Whitman, in *Song of Myself* (1855), states: "A kelson of creation is love."

T

t, th: base of demonstratives. Gc, *der, die, das.* E, *the, there, then; that, those, this, these; they, their, them. thence, thither; thus.* Via L, *tales* (plural of *talis:* such a one): call to serve on a jury; hence *talesman. tandem:* at length; applied in pedantic humor to horses hitched one behind the other (Indian style). *tantamount. tauto:* the same, as in *tautochrome, tautology,* etc. The ending of *ibidem,* also shortened to *idem;* see *ei.*

A query applicable to life today was put forward in a lecture by Artemus Ward (Charles Farrar Browne [d. 1867]): "Why is this thus? What is the reason of this thusness?"

ta, ti: melting. Gk *tektos:* melted. *eutectic, eutexia.* L, *tabes, tabescent, tabefaction, tabitude. tiglic (acid). laurustine:* laurellike shrub with purgative force. Gc, *thaw; dew.*

> O! that this too too solid flesh would melt,
> Thaw, and resolve itself into a dew!
> —Hamlet's first soliloquy (i, 2)

tag I: touch. L *tangere, tactum. tact, tactile, tactometer. tangent,* first used in mathematics in 1583. *tangible, intangible. taste; tax,* which touches everyone, and often taxes one's patience. Hence *taximeter,* which measures the amount (see *tag II*). *attain, attaint. contact, contagion, contagious.* From L *contagsminatum:* threatened, *contaminate. contiguity, contiguous. intact, integrate, integrity.* The game of *tag.*

In the Bible, John 20:17, Jesus upon his resurrection says to Mary Magdalene: *Noli me tangere:* Touch me not, and the phrase is used of pictures of the scene, as by Raphael and Holbein. The expression is also used in four other senses: (1) of an eroding ulcer of the face; also figuratively, of a person or thing that thus pains one; (2) of a kind of balsam that forcefully expels its ripe seeds when touched; (3) of a person to be let alone, or who wears a forbidding aspect. Landor, in his examination of Shakespeare, 1846, speaks of a *noli-me-tangeretarian.* (4) as a general warning or prohibition. A variation of this was the flag of the American Revolution, with its rattlesnake and the words "Don't tread on me."

Integer vitae scelerisque purus: With life untainted and free from guilt.—Horace, *Odes,* 23.

tag II: arrange, order. Gk (*tag-ti*) and E *taxis:* arrangement. *tactics, tactician.* Perhaps *taxi, taxicab,* and *taximeter* belong here instead of with the preceding root. *taxodont. taxonomy;* established for plants by Carolus Linnaeus (d. 1778); from 1865 to 1900 a vain effort was made to change this word and its compounds to the more strictly etymological *taxinomy. taxite, ataxia. eutaxy,* as rare as it is pleasing. *hypotaxis, paratasis.* And *syntax.*

tak: be silent. L *tacere, tacitus. Tacè* (Latin imperative): Be still!, long used in English classrooms. *tacet,* in music. *tacit, taciturn, taciturnity.* A misnomer for the Roman Cornelius *Tacitus* (A.D. 53–118), who was both author and orator.

?taka. E, *take, tackle. OED* gives 40 columns to *take* and its compounds. *wapentake* (ONorse *vapn:* weapon, probably taken and brandished as an affirmative vote).

In Old English, *tacan* superseded *niman,* of the same meaning, which survives in *nimble*—and in Shakespeare's name for Falstaff's follower, *Nym* (: taker), in *The Merry Wives of Windsor* and *Henry V;* in the latter play, we hear that he is hanged for looting churches. *nimble-fingered.*

?tara. Imitative. L (Ennius, 3d c. B.C., *Annals,* 2) *Ut tuba terribili sonitu taratantara dixit:* And the trumpet in terrible tones called taratantara. The call has sounded down the ages. Thus Gilbert, in *The Pirates of Penzance* (1879), has the police protest that "a policeman's lot is not a happy one":

When the foeman bares his steel
Tarantara, tarantara!
We uncomfortable feel,
Tarantara.

The sound became linked with the spread of *diddle* (*daddle, doodle, diddle-daddle, fiddle-faddle, twaddle, twiddle, tweedle*—mainly imitative nonsense terms). The form *diddle* was first used of moving back and forth, as in a dancing step; then of sounding a tune without singing the words. It was then used as a repetitive jingle, in nursery rhymes. The best-known of all nursery rhymes begins

Heigh diddle diddle
The cat and the fiddle.

Charles Lamb's favorite, which he'd begin to recite in company when bored, was

Diddle diddle dumpling, my son John
Went to bed with his breeches on . . .

Thomas Preston's play *Cambises* (1597), "a most lamentable tragedy mixed ful of pleasant mirth," mentions a new dance called *hey-diddle-diddle.* Among the street cries of old London was heard the lure, *Diddle diddle diddle dumplings, piping hot!*

In 1803 James Kenny wrote a farce, *Raising the Wind,* the chief character of which, Jeremy *Diddler,* was a sponging liar and cheat; its popularity led to E *diddle:* to tell a fib. An obvious "whopper" of a fib was a *tar(r)adiddle.* H. S. Leigh, in *Only Seven,* a parody of Wordsworth, wrote:

I wondered hugely what she meant
And said: "I'm bad at riddles,
But I know where little girls are sent
For telling tarradiddles."

W. S. Gilbert uses this in *Iolanthe.* When Strephon is trying to explain to his sweetheart, Phyllis, that the "young lady" he has been seen kissing in the park is actually his mother (ever-youthful because she is a fairy), the jealous peers break into his account with repeated incredulous mocking:

Taradiddle, taradiddle, tol lol lay.

In 18th c. London there was a feud between the rival musicians Handel and Bononcini, partly personal, partly a struggle for German or Italian influence on English music. For the opera *Muzio Scevola,* Bononcini composed the second act; Handel, the third; the public preferred Handel. In 1716 John Byram mocked the musical moil:

Some say Buononcini can't hold a candle
To the virtuoso Handel;
Others insist Handel's a ninny
Compared to the genius Buononcini.
Strange how such a fuss can be
Twixt Tweedledum and Tweedledee.

(*tweedle* may be imitative of the high squeal of a fiddle.) Carlyle and Thackeray used Byram's new names. Lewis Carroll adopted them for the two fat little men in *Through the Looking Glass*—described, and pictured by Tenniel, as *enantiomorphs:* mirror images of each other. Tweedledee recites "The Walrus and the Carpenter"; see *ost.*

A *paradiddle* is a rapid roll, as on a snare drum, beating alternately with left and right drumsticks, a turn toward the early sense of *diddle,* with a tentative touch of trumpeting *tara.* For a minstrel show of 1892, Henry J. Sayers wrote the popular song "Ta-ra-ra boom-de-ay."

taur: bull. Gc, *steer.* L and E *Taurus,* a constellation, second sign of the zodiac (see *guei*); it includes the Pleiades and the Hyades. Sp, *toreador, torero, toro. taurine, tauriform.* LL *buti:* falcon, and *taurus* become E *bittern;* the bird's cry was likened by Pliny (d. A.D. 79) to the call of an ox. *OED* lists 3 and details 7 words beginning *tauro. tauromachy:* bullfighting, as still in Spanish lands. *Minotaur:* offspring of Pasiphaë, who mated with a sacred bull that her husband Minos, legendary king of Crete, kept in the Labyrinth devised by Daedalus; see *del II.* The Minotaur fed regularly on seven youths and seven maidens exacted as tribute from Athens until one of them, Theseus, slew the monster. Theseus retraced his way out of the Labyrinth with the help of a thread given him by Ariadne, daughter of Minos. Among others, Chaucer tells Ariadne's story, in *The Legend of Good Women;* Elizabeth Barrett Browning, in *Paraphrase on Nonnus;* see *pend.*

tekh(s): weaving; building (first, with wood). Gk *techne:* skill, craft. *technical, technique; technology. pantechnicon, polytechnic. tectonic. architect:* master builder (*arch* as in *monarch*). *architectonic. tectology. Tectona:* genus, the verbena tree, used in carpentry. *technetium;* see *el 43.*

L *texere, tectum:* weave, construct, compose. *text, textile; texture.* Via Fr, *tissue. toil:* a net ("in his toils"). *toilette, toilet.* For *toil:* work hard, see *steu. thixle:* ax. *context, contextual; pretext.* L *tela:* web, warp. *telary. subtle* was first the thread that goes under (*sub*) the warp; then came to be used figuratively. *tessitura,* in music. *test. Taxidead:* genus, the badger. Du, *dachshund:* builder-dog, from its digging.

Milton, in *Of Education,* speaks of "Ornate rhetorick taught out of the rule of Plato . . . to which poetry would be made subsequent, or indeed rather precedent, as being less subtle and fine, but more simple, sensuous, and passionate." And Browning, in *Red Cotton Night-Cap Country,* looks toward

> That far land we dream about,
> Where every man is his own architect.

tekhu(s): to speed. Gk *toxon:* bow, arrow; *toxikhon:* arrow poison. *toxic, toxin, intoxication. antitoxin. autotoxin; autointoxication. toxophil,* a biochemical term meaning to have affinity for a toxin; but *toxophilite:* amateur of archery; thus *Toxophilus,* title of a 1545 book by Roger Ascham, secretary to Queen Elizabeth. Thackeray in 1845 spoke of contests "for which we toxophilites muster strong"—as amateurs of the bow still muster. *toxicology:* study of poisons.

The use of the word *toxikhon* in the sense of poison came from dropping the second word of the Greek phrase *toxikhon pharmakhon. pharmakhon* moved along a range of meanings, from enchantment, spell, to poison; then drug, ointment, medicine. Hence E *pharmacy, pharmaceutical,* and the whole *pharmacopoeia* (for *poeia,* see *kuei II*). For the poison, *OED* lists 7 *tox,* 10 *toxi,* and 5 *toxo* words. It details 24 words, a few related to archery; the *toxarch* was captain of the archers guarding Athens.

Toxifer: suborder of mollusks with barbed teeth like arrowheads.

Taxus: genus, the yew, favorite wood for bows; see *oiua. Taxodium:* literally, like the yew; genus, the bald cypress.

> O! many a shaft, at random sent,
> Finds mark the archer little meant!
> And many a word, at random spoken,
> May soothe or wound a heart that's broken.
> —Scott, *Lord of the Isles,* 5

tel, tal: ground, floor; board; slope. L *tellus, telluris:* earth. *tellurian, telluric. tellurion. tellurium* (see *el 52*). *talus:* ground slope; in medieval days, a surface supposedly indicating underground gold. Possibly *tilt,* from the sloping posture of jousting horsemen. Possibly reduplicated L *titulus:* first, sign on a board, label; thence *title, titular; entitle* and its doublet, *intitule. tilde; tittle. titer, titrate.* The first element of *tittle-tattle* was drawn from the second, as in several such pairings; the second is imitative of the repeated *ta.ta.ta* (ODu *tateln:* stammer).

The Clown in *The Winter's Tale,* iv, 4, protests: "Is there no manners left among maids? Will they wear their plackets where they should bear their faces? Is there not milking time, when you are going to bed, or kiln hole, to whistle off these secrets, but you must be tittletattling before all our guests?" Sometimes the expression is applied to a person. Thus Addison (appropriately in *The Tatler,* no. 157 [1710]) speaks of "your Castanets or impertinent Tittle-Tattles, who have no other variety in their discourse but that of talking slower or faster."

tem: cut. Gk *temnein. tomos:* a cut piece. *tome* (one section of a scroll, etc.). *acrotomous; apotome; dichotomy; epitome. entomology;* insects seem cut in; see *sek I. tomium. trichotomy. autotomy:* casting off a damaged member, as a lizard its tail, a spider its leg, a crab its claw. *tmesis:* cut between, a verbal device used to lend emphasis, as in *absodamnlutely. esteem, estimate:* first, cutting ore to evaluate it; thence also the short form, *aim.*

L *tondere, tonsum:* haircutting. *tonsorial* (parlor); *tonsure. tonsurate* is the state of the ecclesiastically shorn, though earlier came Delilah's shaving of Samson, leading to the tumbling of the pillars of the Philistine temple. The American Indian shaved all but the crown of the head, leaving long locks for the scalping (which removed some of the topskin as well), as a trophy, or to collect a bounty. *Omnibus notum tonsoribus:* Every barber knows; this remark by Horace (*Satires,* vii) was valid until the advent of the daily newspaper, the tonsorial parlors being the male hotbed of gossip, which barbers eagerly absorbed and freely dispensed. Horace's words are therefore truer than Macaulay's throwaway remark "as every schoolboy knows," for the schoolboy listens to little, too too little.

The barber's chair, "that fits all buttocks," was an Elizabethan term for a strumpet. Shakespeare uses it literally, with interesting elaboration, in *All's Well That Ends Well,* ii, 2; but Motteux, in his translation of Rabelais' *Pantagruel,* makes the figurative use clear, dividing strumpets into "bonarobas, barber's chairs, and hedge-whores," roughly as one today might specify kept women, call girls, and streetwalkers.

Temenos: cleared and holy ground around a temple, for sacrifice, divine service, or divination; see *temp.* (The grass plot beside London's Westminster Abbey bears a sign: "This is holy ground." A church in London's Kensington bears an amusing but probably effective sign: "No Parking. Violators will be prayed for.") *Artamus:* cut artistically; genus of songsters. *Tomistoma:* cutting mouth; genus of crocodiles.

atom (*a* negative): that which cannot be cut; now we know better. As early as the 5th c. B.C. came the idea (of Leucippus, spread by "the laughing philosopher"

Democritus) that the universe is composed of atoms. Times change and ideas change with them; in 1871 R. H. Hutton queried: "Why do scientific men attach less and less [credit] to the atom theory of matter?" *diatom.* An *atom* was also the smallest medieval measure of time, 15/94 of a second.

47 atoms = 1 ounce
8 ounces = 1 ostent
1 1/2 ostents = 1 moment
2 2/3 moments = 1 part
1 1/2 parts = 1 minute
2 minutes = 1 point
5 points = 1 hour

There are thus 22,560 atoms in an hour.

OED has 26 relevant entries beginning *atom,* to which its 1972 supplement adds about 5 columns of new uses and combinations, as *atom-smasher.* JWalker lists 9 words ending *tom* and 54 ending *tomy,* as *craniotomy, lithotomy. anatomize* is an intensive of *atomize.* The *atomizer* was in every home medicine cabinet early in this century. *anatomy;* hearing this, and thinking the first sound was the article *an,* produced *atomy,* which was used to mean (1) a skeleton, cut to the bone; (2) a person puny in size, like Tom Thumb, or in personality.

In *Romeo and Juliet,* i, 4, Mercutio pictures Queen Mab:

She is the fairies' midwife, and she comes
In shape no bigger than an agate stone . . .
Drawn with a team of little atomies
Athwart men's noses as they lie asleep—

Then, for 20 more lines, he tells the kinds of dream Mab brings to various persons.

teme: dark, obscure. Skr *tamas:* darkness. *tamala-pattram:* dark leaf. *malabathrum:* ointment from the malabar leaf, yielding a perfume prized in antiquity. *tamas:* ignorance, in Hinduism. Via Port, *tombac:* dark-red alloy.

L and E *tenebrae. tenebrous; OED* lists 13 *tenebr* words. *tenebrio:* a night prowler. In the dark, one may be frightened or (and) rash; hence *timid,* etc., but also *temerarious; temerous, temerity; OED* lists 11 such words. *temulant:* clouded with drink; hence, preferably, *abstemious.*

temp: stretch, extend. This root, an extension of the root *ten,* has stretched in several directions.

(1) Physically. Pers *taftah. taffeta:* the warp is stretched on the loom; a *temple* is a device for keeping it taut. Gk *tapes:* first, a hanging, as a rug or carpet. *tapestry* (earlier *tapissery*), the intrusive *t* for smoother flowing. In poems by Milton and Dryden, *tapestry* is pronounced in two syllables. Hence also *tape,* now widely used. *red tape. tapetum. tapis:* carpet; *on the tapis:* under consideration.

(2) Religiously. A stretch of land set aside by the augurs, to observe the stars; in the Near East, there are still a number of open-air observatories. Hence L *templum:* temple. *template. contemplate,* and the *contemplative* life. Familiarity breeds *contemplation.* The *Knights Templars* were established in 1119, the name from their headquarters; King Baldwin II of Jerusalem accorded them space in his palace grounds on the site of the Temple of Solomon.

(3) Physiologically. Where the human skin is stretched thinnest is the *temple.* Hence *temporal:* relating to the temple, and 13 *tempero* words in *OED.*

(4) Ethically. To stretch one's will power is to *tempt.* Hence also *attempt, temptation.* Fr, *attentat.* A *tentacle* is a feeler, used to test; *OED* gives 16 relevant words. Thus *tentative,* as putting one's toes in the water.

(5) Chronologically. L *tempus, temporis:* span of time. *temporal, temporary.*

tempo and *tempus,* in music. *contemporaneous; contemporary. contretemps. extemporaneous, extempore.* L *tempestas:* the times, the weather; E *tempest, tempestuous. Tempus fugit,* which Austin Dobson revises:

Time goes, you say? Ah no!
Alas, Time stays, *we* go.

There is a tendency for words that stretch along a polarity to move toward one end; thus *humor, humorous,* are usually good. Everyone has a *temperature;* but if "the baby has temperature," it is bad. Similarly *temper.* Here also *temperance, tempera, temperament; attemper, distemper.* From *temper* (as the wind to the shorn lamb) came *tamper.* In grammar, the *tense* indicates the time.

Note Hamlet's advice to the Players (iii, 2): "Use all gently: for in the very torrent, tempest and—as I may say—whirlwind of passion, you must acquire and beget a temperance, that may give it smoothness."

ten, ton: stretch, strain, swell, extend; hence things that are thin, and things that stretch, as strings on a musical instrument; hence pitch. *tone.* Skr *tantra:* thread; hence, guiding doctrine. *Pachatantra:* the five books of Bidpai's Fables. (*Bidpai,* probably of the 5th c. A.D., is from Skr *vidyapati:* chief pundit. *pancha:* five, as in E *punch,* of 5 ingredients; see *penkue.*) *tatty.* Pers, *sitar.*

Gk *tanoein, tenein:* stretch; *ektasis:* thing stretched out; *tonos:* string, and from a stretched-string instrument, pitch. *taenia, tone, tonality, tonic. intone, detonate.* Fr, *ton:* style; *haut ton:* high style. *atonic, oxytone, pretone. tenor:* holder; dominates the song. *tenoroon; tenorino; countertenor. baritone:* between tenor and bass. *barytone* (heavy), *monotonous, syntony; tritone.*

atelectasis; bronchiectasis; ectasis, entasis. entatic: that which swells, was formerly used to mean aphrodisiac. *epitasis. peritoneum. protasis. telangiectasis,* which in some cases is a birthmark. *tenesmus. tetanus;* Gk *tetanos:* muscular spasm; *OED* details 14 related words, and lists 5 beginning *tetano,* as *tetanocannabine:* tension and spasm from cannabis; see *kann.*

L *tendere, tensum, tentum:* stretch, make tense, draw out; *tenere, tenui:* hold fast; *tenuis:* drawn out, thin; *tenuare, tenuatum:* make thin, lessen, enfeeble. *tenable, tenacious, tenancy, tenant, tenement. tenor.*

Far from the madding crowd's ignoble strife,
. . . .
They kept the noiseless tenor of their way.
—Gray, *Elegy Written in a Country Churchyard*

tenue, tenure. In music, *tenuto, sostenente, sostenuto. tennis* (Fr *Tenez!:* Hold!, the cry of the server). *tendon. tenography, tenotomy; OED* lists 8 *teno* words and 5 beginning *tenonto,* as *tenontophyme. tenuity; OED* gives 6 *tenui* words, as *tenuipede:* thin-footed. *tenuous, attenuated. extenuating. retinaculum; tenaculum.*

abstain: "It is easier to abstain than to restrain." *attain, contain, content, contents, continue, detain, detention; entertain; lieutenant, locum tenens. maintain:* hold by hand. *obtain, pertain; pertinent, pertinacious; retain; rein(s); retinue; sustain, sustenance. tend, tendency, tender; tense, tension;* Fr, *détente. tent:* stretched hide or canvas. *tentative. tentorium,* from the shape. *tentigo. tenter:* frame for stretching cloth; hence, also figuratively, *on tenterhooks.*

attend, contend, contention. distend; extend, extensive, extent; intend, intendant, intense, intensive. intention. ostensible. ostensorium: monstrance (see *men I*). *ostentation:* stretched "like a peacock's tail." *portend, portent. pretend, pretense; subtend; superintendent.* Via OFr *estandard, standard,* though some of its meanings are derived from association with *stand;* see *sta.*

Gc, *dunnage. thin. thing:* subject of consideration. The current sense of *thing* came roundabout from Scand *thing, ting:* assembly, a set meeting, where any thing might be discussed. This early sense remains in *Folket(h)ing:* Denmark's Parliament; *Stort(h)ing:* Norway's Parliament; *Tynwald:* the Isle of Man's Assembly; *husting(s):* court called by the king; also in such English place-names as *Tinwald, Dingwall.* From this also came such facetious terms as *dingus, thingamy, thingamabob, thingamajig.* (Some etymologists attribute the words in this paragraph to a root *tenk,* as an extension of this root.) For the imitative root *ten:* thunder, see *stene.* See also *temp.*

"One of the principal features of my entertainment is that it contains so many things that don't have anything to do with it"—Artemus Ward (C. F. Browne), "Lecture on the Mormons" (1863).

A thing of beauty is a joy forever;
Its loveliness increases; it will never
Pass into nothingness . . .
[Read it all.]
—Keats, *Endymion*

And take courage from the words of Leigh Hunt in *A Rustic Walk:*

Learn the right
Of coining words in the quick mint of joy.

Juvenal, in his *Satires,* iii, describes the ambitious, omnivolent Greek: "Scholar, orator, geometrician, painter, physical training instructor, diviner, rope-dancer, physician, magician, the hungry little Greek can do everything; order him to Heaven—and he'll go there." *The Greeks Had a Word for It:* title of a play (1929) by Zoë Akins, whose first name is Greek, meaning life; see Byron, under *guei.* Browning, in his *Soliloquy of a Spanish Cloister,* asks: "What's the Greek name for Swine's Snout?" See *sus.* Casca's words in *Julius Caesar,* i, 2, "It's Greek to me," are widely used as an admission of ignorance.

Ben Jonson, in *A Fit of Rhyme Against Rhyme,* wrote:

Greek was free from rhyme's infection,
Happy Greek, by this protection,
Was not spoiled . . .

Graikai: Greek, probably from Illyrian, a lost Indo-European language, was first the name of a tribe of Epirus.

Thoreau, in his (vain) *Plea for Captain John Brown,* in his typically unworldly way, said: "He would have left a Greek accent slanting the wrong way, and righted up a falling man." Brown, a violent abolitionist, was hanged for treason after his attack on the U.S. arsenal at Harpers Ferry, Virginia, in 1859, but in 1861 the Union soldiers were singing:

John Brown's body lies amouldering in the grave,
But his soul is marching on.

"Harlequin without his mask is known to present a very sober countenance, and was himself, the story goes, the melancholy patient whom the doctor advised to go and see Harlequin"—Thackeray, *The English Humorists, Swift* (1851). Jack Point sings the same point in Gilbert's *Yeomen of the Guard:*

Oh a private buffoon is a light-hearted loon,
If you listen to popular rumor . . .
Though your wife ran away with a soldier that day,

And took with her your trifle of money,
Bless your heart, they don't mind—they're exceedingly kind,
They don't blame you—as long as you're funny!

And, as Browning wryly remarks, in *Any Wife to Any Husband:* "It all comes to the same thing at the end."

teng: soak, dip into a liquid. L *tingere, tinctum:* moisten; dye. *tinge, tint,* earlier *tinct. tinctorial, tincture, intinction. aquatint, monotint.* Fr *teint. taint, untainted.* Sp, *tent:* a "tinted" red sweet wine. *distain,* shortened to *stain*—as *disport* was shortened to *sport.* Gc, *dunk. Dunker:* a German-American Baptist dipped three times when baptized.

tenq: firm, thickened; thick mass. Gc, *tight.* Dan and E *tang:* seaweed; see also quotation under *dinghu. tangle, entangle, disentangle.*

O what a tangled web we weave
When first we practice to deceive!
—Scott, *Marmion,* vi

tep: to be warm. L *tepere, tepidum. tepidarium;* between the *frigidarium* and the *calidarium* in the ancient Roman bath. Note L *calidus,* Fr *chaud;* in English-speaking lands, the letter *C* on a water tap means cold; in French, hot.

The gem *topaz,* which glows at night, and *tapas:* Hindu asceticism, are linked with warmth. The topaz is ninth of the twelve jewels in the walls of the "holy city of Jerusalem coming down out of heaven from God," as shown by the angel to John in Revelation 21:2.

t(e)r I (sometimes extended as *trem, trep, tres*): tremble. Gk *treron:* timid. *Treron:* genus, the pigeon. *tromometer:* measures faint earth tremors. L, *terrible, terrific, terrify, terror. deter, deterrent. tremor; tremble; tremendous; tremulous.* It, *tremolant, tremolo. Tremandra:* genus of plants with quivering anthers. *Tremella:* genus of quivering fungi. *tremelline, tremellose. trepid, trepidation, intrepidity.*

t(e)r II, tor: rub, as to remove husk, hence thresh; plow, turn, hence drill, bore, gnaw, press, crush, etc. Gk *tribein:* rub. *tribade. diatribe. tripsis. Tribonema:* genus of algae. *tripsin,* the enzyme, was so named by German phsyiologist W. F. Kühne in 1874 because it was obtained by rubbing the pancreas with glycerine—its ending as in *pepsin.*

Gk *teredon:* boring worm. *trite, trituration. teredo. Termitidae, Termes:* family and genus, the woodworm. *termite;* actually not a worm but a white ant. *toreutic:* of chased metal work, in relief. Gk *trema:* bore. *monotreme. trematode. tryma. helicotrema:* spiral bore; hole in the cochlea of the ear. *trauma. Cutiterebra:* genus, the botfly, skin-borer. *trone:* first, the hole wherein the tongue of a balance (rubs as it) moves.

trogon: gnawing bird. *tragos:* gnawing goat; whence *tragedy* (: goat song); see *aig. troglodyte. trepan. Tripsacum:* genus of grass with smooth spikes. *Triticum:* genus, cereal grass, for threshing. *Trypetidae, Trypeta:* family and genus of boring flies. *Xylotrya:* woodborer; genus of marine bivalves.

Gk *teres, teretis:* rounded or smoothed by rubbing. *terete, terebra, teredo. lithotrity:* crushing stones within the bladder, for natural evacuation, to avoid an operation. *teres major* and *teres minor,* smooth muscles.

L *terere, tritum:* plow, rub, grind, wear away, pierce. *atresia* (*a* negative): occlusion of a body passage. *trite:* figuratively, worn from much use. *attrite, attrition. attritus. contrite, contrition. detriment, detrition, detritus. Septentrion:* literally, seven plow oxen (*triones*); the seven stars of the constellation the Great Bear, near the North Pole; see *septm. septentrional:* northern. L *tornare:* first, turn in a lathe; bore. *turn, return; attorn, attorney, attornment. tour. contour, detour, tournament, tourney. tourniquet. turnip* (earlier *nepe*), from the root. *turnpike. turnsole.* L *tribulum:* sledge for threshing. *tribulation.*

Gc, *thresh, threshold. thrash. thread.* The "Old Lady of *Threadneedle* Street" is the Bank of England, so called from its location. Celt *trugant:* idle rogue. *truant. drill* (a hole). For *throw, thrust,* see the extension of this root, *treud.*

t(e)r III, tar: pass across, cut, break off or through; bore through, reach a goal. Skr *ava:* down; *taruti:* passes over; E *avatar. Dhanvantari:* Vedic physician of the gods. Pers *sarai:* inn, caravanserai. Gk, *nectar, nectarine;* see *sna.* L, *term, terminal, termination, terminus. co(n)terminous;* the form with *n* is more usual. *OED* defines 9 relevant words. Thomas Love Peacock, in *Crochet Castle* (1831), 9, speaks of "the neighboring lords, his conterminal bandits." *determine, determination; exterminate; interminable; terminology. terse.*

As a prefix, *trans:* across, beyond, begins many words, as *transatlantic, transfer, transgress, translate; OED* gives 96 columns of *trans* words, few of them transitory. From L *trans* came Fr *très:* beyond, then very; it is used in English as a direction in music, and appears in *trespass, tressilate, trestle. transom. truculent.* Nasalized, *trench, trenchant; truncate, trunk* (limbs and branches off). *detruncate. obtruncate* ("Off with his head!"). *trinket:* first, a small knife. *trance.*

Gc *thirl;* by metathesis, *thrill. drill. nostril. through, thorough. thrum. trumeau. tram, tramway. Sic transit gloria mundi:* Thus goes the glory of the world. —Thomas à Kempis (d. 1471), *Imitation of Christ.*

ter(e)q, torq: turn, twist. *torque, torques, torsade, torsel, torsion. tort, tortious. torticollis:* wryneck. *tortuous. torture. torturous. contort, contortions; distort, distortion; extort, retort.* L *tricae:* twisted ways, perplexities. *extricate, intricate, inextricable.* Via It, *intrigue. nasturtium* (taste a leaf and your nose will twitch). *tortoise* is from LL *tartuca:* the infernal animal, from *Tartarus;* folkchanged from its twisted legs. It suffered a sea change, by sailors, into *turtle,* and thus is linked with the *turtle dove,* though that *turtle* is imitative of the bird's cooing. OFr *torte:* twisted bread, became E *tart,* which as an "open pie" became slang for *prostitute.*

Tortricidae, Tortrix: family and genus of moths. *Tortulaceae:* family of mosses. A *torch* was first a twist of rags or hay. *torcular, torchon.* L *tornus:* turner's wheel. *tornoria:* a larva. *torment:* first, an instrument for twisting, to hurl a missile or make a victim howl. *tormentil:* plant supposed to relieve toothache. Sp, *tornado:* twister; blended with L *tonare:* thunder (see *ker I*). *tormina:* bowel-twisting. *torquated:* wearing a chain of twisted metal. *truss; trousse; trousseau. retroussé.* Norse, *thwart, athwart.* Gc, *queer.*

Stephen Vincent Benét, in *Western Star* (1943), i, spoke of

That queer sense of relief and shame
Which comes to those who make sensible decisions.

terp: delight, please. Gk, *Terpsichore:* delight in dancing; Muse of the dance. The Greek chorus danced; for *chorus,* see *gher IV. Euterpe:* well-pleasing; Muse of music and lyric song.

ters: dry. L *torrere,* present participle *torrens, torrentis; tostum:* dry up, roast, scorch; by metonymy (describing streams), boiling, rushing, roaring. It might seem strange that *torrent,* meaning swift water, should come from a root meaning dry; but from early times speed was associated with "scorching"—as even today, in games, an especially swift pitch may be called "a scorcher." *torrential. OED* lists 17 compounds beginning *torrent. torrentine:* of fish in mountain streams. Also British *torsk,* Norse *cusk,* U.S. *cod.*

L *tersa, terra:* dry earth, as in *terra firma, terra cotta. terrain, territory; extraterritorial, terrestrial, extraterrene, extraterrestrial. inter,* earlier *interr,* as still in *interring. interment.* It, *terrazzo;* Fr, *terrace. terrane, terrene, terrine. tureen:* first, earthenware. *terrigenous, terricolous. parterre. subterranean. Mediterranean:* middle of the earth. *terramara:* dry earth deposit. *Terramycin,* from an earth mold. *terraqueous. terreplein. torrid, torrefaction; torrefy.*

Gk *tarsos:* flat board for drying figs; then used of the flat sole of the foot; then, by extension, of the ankle (perhaps with a thought of *torq:* to twist); E *tarsus. trass:* spread of volcanic earth, perhaps shortened from *terrace.* OFr *fumeterre:* earth smoke; E *fumitory;* once used against scurvy. *traulism:* stammering, supposedly caused by a dry mouth.

Both *terrevert* and *verditer* mean earth-green. *verdigris:* green of Greece, blent with Fr *gris:* gray. *Vermont* is the "Green Mountain State"; see *men II.* The Green Mountain Boys were formed in 1770 to protect the "New Hampshire grants" from New York claimants; under Ethan Allen they were valiant in the American Revolution. Vermont, in 1791, was the first state admitted to the Union after the original thirteen. Also from this root are words for the green of spring: *vert, verdant, verdure. verjuice; verd antique. vireo; virescent; virid, viridescent.* The *verderer* was in charge of the green growth of the royal fields and forests of Old England. Sp *verdugo:* young green shoot, which bends without breaking, came via French to English as *farthingale:* hoopskirt.

The French have a neat term, *vert galant* (spring in an old man's heart), for an elderly man still in quest of woman: "homme entreprenant auprès des femmes, malgré un certain age"—applied especially to the first Bourbon king of France, Henry IV, assassinated in 1610, called "the Great," as in some respects he apparently was.

Note that L *tersta, testa:* earthen pot, came into French as *tête:* first slang, then the standard term, for *head.* The circumflex accent in French often indicates an *s* dropped from the Latin, but retained in English, as *conquête, conquest; tempête, tempest; bête, beast, bestial; crête, crest.*

Gc, *toast,* Gm *Durst:* thirst.

"One realm we have never conquered—the pure present. One great mystery of time is terra incognita to us—the instant. . . . The quick of all time is the instant" —D. H. Lawrence, preface to *New Poems* (1918).

t(e)u: consider, regard. L *tueri, tutum. tutelage, tutelary, tuition. intuition, intuitive.* What is regarded is guarded, hence *tutus:* safe. A *tutor* was first a guardian. *OED* lists 15 relevant *tutor* words, including *tutorial, tutrix; tutress,* shortened from *tutoress.* Perhaps from this source is *tutsan:* of plants with supposed healing qualities, though from some early spellings it seems to be derived from Fr *toute-saine:* all-healing. Perhaps also Gc, *thew:* a general custom; more common in the plural, and used by Shakespeare (*2 Henry IV,* iii, 2) to mean bodily power. Thus also Scott, in *Rob Roy,* 3: "My fellow-traveller, to judge by his thews and sinews, was a man who might have set danger at defiance." This meaning became the usual one, as, figuratively, in J. C. Muir's *Pagan or Christian* (1860): "Real wealth lies in the sinewy force of moral thewness."

From the 13th c. into the 17th, *thew* was used to mean instruct; hence the noun *thew* for an instrument of punishment for women who did not heed their husbands; some say the instrument was the collistrigium, an iron collar, wearing which the woman was carted through the town (men were set at the town center, in a pillory); others identify the thew with the cucking stool, on which the woman was ducked in the town pond.

Logan Pearsall Smith, in *All Trivia* (1933), remembers "that Stonehenge circle of elderly disapproving faces–Faces of the Uncles, Schoolmasters and the Tutors who frowned on my youth."

t(e)u(e): swell; lumped; compress. This took various forms in Greek and Latin.

Greek

(1) *turos:* cheese. *boustouros, bouturon:* cow cheese; E *butter. tyrocidine:* an antibiotic. *tyrosine:* an amino acid formed by putrefaction of cheese. *tyrotoxicon; tyromancy. tyrothricin:* literally, hairy cheese; a mixture of antibiotics from soil bacteria, including the *Tyrotrix* family. Note also the unrelated L *tiro:* recruit, beginner; whence E *tyro, tirocinium. tyronic:* amateurish.

(2) *tule:* swelling, stuffing for a bolster, etc. *tylarus:* pad on the undersurface of the toe of some birds, as the chicken. *tyloma:* callus. *Tylopoda:* camel, from its padded feet. *Typhaceae, Typha:* family and genus, the cattail, once used for stuffing pillows.

(3) *soma:* body. *soma, somatic, somatogenic, somatology. somite, psychosomatic. acrosome, autosome, mitosome, trophosome,* etc. *somatovisceral, somatocyst,* etc. *Somateria:* genus, the eider duck, its body wool called *eiderdown.* A *somatist* is one who seeks the causes of mental disorders in bodily conditions. Note that in these words *som(e)* is pronounced with a long *o*; for the suffix *some* pronounced *sum,* see *dheigh N 37.*

(4) *sos, sotos:* whole, sound, safe. *Soter:* Zeus as "savior." *soterial. soteriology:* study of salvation; specifically, of Jesus as redeemer. *creosote:* literally, flesh-saver; coined by Baron Karl von Reichenbach in 1832 (Gk *khreos:* flesh; whence also *creophagous:* flesh-eating).

(5) *soros:* heap. *sorus, sorosus. soredium:* thallus bud in lichens: *OED* lists 5 derivatives. *sorites:* series of syllogisms, which, said Addison (*Spectator,* no. 239 [1711]), is "commonly called a Pile of Faggots."

(6) *tumbos:* tomb, entomb. LL *cata-tumba, catacumba,* perhaps influenced by L *cumbere:* lie down. E *catacomb(s); catacumbal.*

Latin

(7) *tumere:* swell. *tumefacient, tumefy, tumescent, tumid. tumor. contumacy:* swollen with pride. *contumelious, contumely. detumescence; intumesce, intumescent.*

(8) *tumulare:* cover with a mound. L and E *tumulus. tumular. tumultus:* swollen with people; crowd, confusion, noise. *tumult, tumultuous,* etc.

(9) *tuber:* swelling. L and E *tuber; tuberous, tuberose. tubercular, tuberculin, tubercle, tuberculosis. protuberance. tubercles* in the lungs were first noted in 1689, by Richard Morton, in London. *Tuberaceae, Tuberculariaceae:* families of fungi. *Tuber, Tuberularia:* genera of fungi. *tuberaceous.* (*tube,* however, is from L *tubus:* pipe; whence also *tuba, tubule, tubulous; intubate.*)

LL *tufer,* by metathesis *trufe.* E *truffle;* whence *trifle. trifle* is also the modest appellation of a delicious dessert, described by Oliver Wendell Holmes in *Elsie Venner* (1891), 7, as "That most wonderful object of domestic art called trifle . . . with its charming confusion of cream and cake and almonds and jam and jelly and wine and cinnamon and froth."

(10) *totus:* swollen to capacity; full; all. *total, totality; totipalmate.* Fr, *tout, surtout.* It, *tutti,* in music; *tutti-frutti,* in gastronomy. *teetotum.* See *teuta.*

The swelling fruit the *tomato* came via Sp from Nahuatl Indian *tomatl,* the end changed to match the other New World gift to Europe, the *potato.* See *abel.*

Tartuffe: puffed up with pride, is the hypocrite in Molière's play of that name (1664), which was at once damned by the clergy. The Queen Mother demanded that it never be shown again, and it was not—until she died, when it became an instant and lasting success. Lord Morley (d. 1923) declared of "the Sun King": "The best title of Louis XIV to the recollection of posterity is the protection he extended to Molière."

Gc, *thumb:* swelled finger; *thigh:* swelling of the leg. *tholepin. thousand* (*thus-hundr*): a "swollen" hundred. If one spells out our numbers, one reaches a thousand before coming to an instance of the letter *a;* and after the thousands, one must wait for a quadrillion before meeting another; then, for a parsec.

The tumult and the shouting dies;
The Captains and the Kings depart:
Still stands Thine ancient sacrifice,
An humble and a contrite heart.
—Kipling, *Recessional* (1897)

teuta: the tribe; hence, everyone worthy of consideration. L *totus, totum* (see *teue 10*). *factotum:* do-all, jack-of-all-trades. *teetotal, teetotaler; t* sound doubled for emphasis. *totum.* Fr *toton;* then *T-totum, teetotum:* a top spun by the fingers, the body a cube, with a letter on each side; *OED* calls it "a favorite Victorian toy." It was popular in England from the 16th c.; on the Continent, from medieval times. Defoe in 1720 had "a very fine ivory T-totum." The sheep-shopkeeper in *Through the Looking Glass* asks Alice: "Are you a child, or a teetotum?" It was also used figuratively, of a whirligig "teetotum brain" or, as in W. S. Gilbert's *Utopia Limited,* "She'll waltz away like a teetotum."

As a game, each player puts down an equal sum as a stake; children perhaps use marbles. In turn, the players spin; when the teetotum stops and falls, the letter on top tells what that player should do:

Latin	*French*	*German*	*English*	*Meaning*
D depone	*D da*	*S stell ein*	*P*	Put down (new stake)
A aufer	*A accipe*	*H halb*	*H*	Take half (of stakes)
N nihil	*R rien*	*N nichts*	*N*	Nothing (next player spins)
T totum	*T tout*	*G ganz*	*T*	Take all

This cube-bodied top, called a *dreidl* (Hebr): top, or *trendel* (Gm): top, also forms part of the traditional play on the Jewish festive days of *Hanukkah* (: dedication). In 168 B.C. Antiochus IV Epiphanus ordained the worship of Zeus in the Temple of Jerusalem; in 165 the Jews, led by the Hasmodean Maccabees, especially Judah, retook and rededicated the temple. According to the Talmud story, the one-day supply of consecrated oil burned miraculously for eight days, until the fresh supply arrived; hence the eight-branched *menorah* (: candelabrum). Except for chess, games among pious Jews were played mainly on festive days; but a top is essentially a child's toy, and children should not gamble. So the rabbis, with properly paternal solicitude, noted that the gaming letters on the top—*N, G, H, S*—were also the initial letters of the words meaning "Great Miracle Happened There"; and also, in numerology, had the same value, 385, as the letters in *Messiah*—a providential sign! So even today, in Jewish families, the *dreidl*—perhaps filled with chocolate chips, jelly beans, or other tiny goodies—is spun in memory of the Maccabee triumphs.

From the root *teuta* came also the name of the tribe *Teuton;* Gm *Deutsch;* Du, *Plattdeutsch.* During the 16th and 17th c., when the Dutch and the English were rivals in discovery and colonization, the Dutch bore a broom on their ships' masthead as a sign that they "swept the seas," and the English used *Dutch* in many ethnophaulic combinations. Among the most frequent are *Dutch treat* (you pay your own way); *Dutch uncle; Dutch luck:* undeserved good fortune; *double Dutch; in Dutch.* There are many more, as *Dutch anchor:* something important left behind. *Dutch auction:* announcing a high figure, then gradually lowering it until someone bids. *Dutch bargain,* made over liquor. *Dutch courage,* induced by liquor. *Dutch feast:* when the host gets drunk before the guests do (very impolite!). *Dutch comfort:* "Thank God it was no worse!" *Dutch defense:* surrender. *Dutch gold:* alloy of copper and gold; cheap imitation of gold leaf. *Dutch nightingale:* a frog. *Dutch praise:* commendation that's really a condemnation; damning with faint praise. *Dutch reckoning:* lump sum, higher than if itemized. *Dutch wife* (for a hot climate): a pillow between the legs. To bring the most shame upon oneself, the saying, "If that's not so, I'm a Dutchman!" For the reciprocal Dutch opinion of the English, see *ster II.*

tit, tik. Imitative. A baby word for something small. *tit, teat; titbit, tidbit. tomtit; tit for tat.* L *titillare, titillatum. titillate. tickle;* by metathesis, *kittle; kit, kitling; kitten, kitty.* Gm *Zitze:* teat; *Kitze:* kid: *Katze:* cat; *kitzel:* tickle. See *ane.* To *kid* someone is to treat him as a credulous child.

Good luck, she is never a lady,
But the cursedest quean alive.
Tricksy, wincing, and jady,
Kittle to lead or drive.
Greet her—she's hailing a stranger!
Meet her—she's busking to leave!
Let her alone for a shrew to the bone,
And the hussy comes plucking your sleeve.
—Kipling, *Kim*

There is early sexual implication in the *kit-tick* sounds. Langland, in *Piers Plowman* (1362), speaks of a woman "tickle of her tail." The word *tickle-tail* has been used in three senses: (1) a wanton woman; (2) a schoolmaster, or the rod he employs; also *tickle-toby* (*toby:* buttocks); (3) the children's game of "threading the needle"—which phrase is also a figure for the sexual act, as in the tale of the judge who, by moving the needle he holds and has challenged a complainant to thread, shows how she might have avoided what she claims was rape.

tickle-tackle: tricky maneuvering. *tick-tack* came via Fr *tric-trac.* There is also the game of *tick-tack-toe,* three in a row (crosses or circles). Randle Cotgrave, in his 1611 *Dictionarie of the French and English Tongues,* defines *amourettes* as "wanton love toys, ticking, ticklings, dalliances." *kitty,* as also *pussy,* is slang for *vagina.* In *Measure for Measure,* i, 2, Lucio expresses fear that Claudio might foolishly lose his life "for a game of tick-tack" (a kind of backgammon scored by putting a peg in a hole).

to, tu: pointing-out words. L *tant:* so much. *tantamount. tandem:* at length; the second element, in L and E *idem, ibidem* (see *i*). L *talis:* such. *tales, talesman.* Gc, *the;* Du *de,* as in *de-affodil,* the *asphodel,* E *daffodil, daffadowndilly,* etc.; *de-kooi:* the cage; E *decoy.* The middle of *nevertheless. this, these, that, those; they, their, them.* L *tuum.* via Fr, *tutoyer. thou, thee, thy, thine. then, than. there, thither, thence. though, although.*

Gk *tauto,* contracted from *to auto:* the same. *OED* lists 18 *taut(o)* words, as *tautozonal,* and details 12. Coleridge in 1825 coined *tautogorical,* to be used of symbols, which express "the same subject but with a difference," as opposed to metaphors and similitudes, which express "a different subject but with a resemblance."

Samuel Pepys, in his diary entry for Christmas 1665, remarked: "Strange to say what delight we married people have to see these poor fools decoyed into our condition."

toc. Imitative of the sound of knocking. LL *toccare, toccatum:* touch. It, *toccata, toccatella. tuck, tucket, tocsin* (OProv *tocar senh:* touch the bell; LL *signum:* sign, signal). *touchy. touchstone.* Fr, *touché.* See *stei.*

tol, tel, tal, (t)la: lift, support; weigh, weight; and from weighted gold and silver, money, pay. Skr, *tola:* Indian unit of weight. Via Port, *tael:* Eastern unit of weight; former Chinese unit of money, by weight.

Gk *tlenai, talanton:* weight; L *talentum,* E *talent:* first a coin, then a valuable quality. Gk *telos:* payment, charge. *toll.* From Gk *phil:* love, *a* negative, and *telos:* no further charge, M. Herpin, an avid stamp collector, in 1864 suggested the word *philately.* See *steu; ker I.*

Emphatically reduplicated, Gk *Tantalos:* the Sufferer, *Tantalus,* son of Zeus, who for variously reported sins was condemned to stand up to his neck in water, which receded whenever he bent to drink, under fruit trees the branches of which swayed from his reach. Hence *tantalize. tantalum* (see *el 73*).

Atlas, Atlantic: bearer (of the Earth). *atlas* was first used of a book of maps by Mercator (1585), from the figure of Atlas supporting the world (the frontispiece to such books); his maps from 1568 use what we call the *Mercator projection. Atlas,* a Titan, was transformed by Perseus (with the head of the Gorgon Medusa, which turned all who looked upon it into stone) into *Mount Atlas.* (This may be Greek folk etymology, from a Berber name for the mountain.) Hence, *Atlantic Ocean. Atlantes* (male), *Atlantides* ("daughters of Atlas"): figures used as pillars. From this root also *telamon* (plural, *telamones*): males supporting pillars; the female figures are called *caryatid(e)s,* from the handmaids at the Temple of Diana at *Karyai;* see *nebh.*

Atalanta, daughter of King Schoeneus of Boeotia and Clymene of Arcadia, was pledged to marry the man who outran her; if one tried and failed, he would die. She lost to Melanion (some legends say Hippomenes), who in succession tossed aside three golden apples given him by Aphrodite, which Atalanta could not forbear stopping to pick up. She was so speedy that she was first to pierce the wild boar that was ravaging Calydon. In *The Earthly Paradise* (1868), by William Morris, the first tale is "Atalanta's Race." Swinburne's *Atalanta in Calydon* (1865) brought him fame. The name *Atalanta*—from Gk *a:* the same, and *talanton:* weight, value—means of the same value (as a man). According to some legends, Atalanta was one aspect of Artemis.

Mary Manley set her popular, slanderous romance *Atalanta* (1709) on a Mediterranean island; the name was probably suggested by Francis Bacon's *New Atlantis* (1616). From Manley's book, for some time a scandalous story was called an *atalantis.* Here also "the lost *Atlantis,*" a continent somewhere under the Atlantic Ocean.

L *tolerare, toleratum:* bear, support, endure. *tolerate; intolerant.* L *ferre, tuli, (t)latum:* raise, carry, bear. *ablation, ablative, allative. collate; collation. correlate. delate; dilatory, elation. extol. legislate,* etc. *illation; oblate. prelate. prolate. relate, relation, relationship; relative, relativity. sublate, sublation; superlative.* L *transferre, translatum:* carry across. *transfer, transference; OED* gives 15 associated words. *tralatitious. translate, translation.* It *tradutorre, traditore:* translator, traitor. *acceptilation:* bearing acceptance, that is, forgiveness, of a debt or of a sin. L *talio:* repay. *lex talionis:* an eye for an eye. *talion. retaliate,* Gc, *thole* (archaic; used by Burns and Barrie).

Our gay musical *fiddle* is probably from LL *vitulare:* to be joyful, from a cry of joy, and *tulo:* raise. *Vitula* was the Roman goddess of jubilation and triumph. Hence, via Italian and French, E *viola, violin,* etc. Used mainly for dancing, the word *fiddle* came to be associated with triviality, then with nonsense, as in *fiddling around.* Hence also *fiddle-faddle;* sometimes shortened to *fidfad; fiddle-de-dee; fiddlesticks! OED* lists 12 and details 14 *fiddle* words.

When I consider how my light is spent
Ere half my days, in this dark world and wide,
And that one talent which is death to hide
Lodged with me useless . . .
They also serve who only stand and wait.
—Milton, *On His Blindness* (1652)

"My old friend Mrs. Carter could make a pudding as well as translate Epictetus"—Johnson, in Boswell's *Life of Samuel Johnson* (1791).

tolku: talk. L *(t)loqui, locutum. locution. loquacious; loquitur. allocution; circumlocution; collocution, colloquy. elocution, eloquent; grandiloquent, magniloquent. soliloquy. obloquy. ventriloquism:* belly-talk.

"Light griefs are loquacious, but the great are dumb"—Seneca, *Hippolytus,* ii. Lucius Seneca, tutor to Nero (A.D. 49) and at first his counselor; finally ordered by Nero (A.D. 69) to take his own life (he did so); author of philosophic essays and nine tragedies. His *Thyestes* was the prototype of the Elizabethan "blood and thunder" melodrama of revenge.

tong: to seem (to one); to think it so. *methinks* is defined as "it seems to me." The Romans had assurance: "What I think is so, is so"; L *tongere:* to know. OE *thyncan:* to seem, had a causative form, *thencan:* to make seem; hence, to think. *think, thank, thought.* Gm *denken:* think; *danken:* thank; *Gedanken:* thought. OE *thanc* developed a series of meanings: thought, thoughtfulness; favorable thought; thankfulness, thanks. To think is to thank. Methinks man has daily cause for thanksgiving.

You have two ends: one for sitting, one for thinking. Heads you win, tails you lose.

"I never could find any man who could think for two minutes together"—Rev. Sydney Smith, *Sketches of Moral Philosophy* (ca. 1810).

"God, I thank thee that I am not like other men"—Prayer of the Pharisee, Bible, Luke 18:11. The passage continues with the tax collector, who "beat his breast, saying, 'God, be merciful to me a sinner.' I tell you this man went down to his house justified rather than the other; for every one who exalts himself shall be humbled, but he who humbles himself will be exalted."

top: arrive, reach a place. Gk *topos:* place. *atopic:* out of place, *atopy; ectopia. Ectopistes:* genus of wandering pigeons. *topiary,* from Gk *topia,* diminutive plural of *topos:* place. For the prefix *top(o), OED* lists 8 words, from *topolatry:* excessive reverence for a place, to *topotypically;* and it details 13, from *topograph* to *topophone:* an instrument, patented in 1880, for checking distance and direction of sounds in a fog at sea, so that the pilot may not be totally at sea. *topography; toponym.*

The sense of *topic:* subject, is drawn from Aristotle's study of rhetoric, ca. 335 B.C., *ta topikha:* concerning commonplaces; hence *topical.*

Utopia, the title of a book by Sir (Saint) Thomas More (1516 in Latin, 1551 in English), was formed in wordplay, which most discussions of it fail to point out. It fuses two Greek prefixes, *ou:* not, and *eu:* good; thus, the good place that is no place. *Eutopia* is mentioned in the 1516 preface; and Sidney, in his *Apologie for Poetry* (1580), mentions "Sir Thomas More's Eutopia." The early and widespread popularity of More's book is shown by Rabelais' reference to *Utopians* in 1546. Jeremy Bentham, in his *Plan of Parliamentary Reform* (1817), mentions a *Cacotopia:* the worst of all possible places. The Latin printing of *Utopia,* at Louvain, was supervised by More's friend Erasmus—whose satire *Praise of Folly* (1509), written when he was in England, also has a punning title, *Encomium Moriae:* of More, his host, and of Folly (E *moron*). For *encomium,* see *ued.*

"An acre in Middlesex is better than a principality in Utopia"—Macaulay, *Lord Bacon* (1837).

tragh: draw, pull, carry. L *trahere, tractum. trace, traces. tract, tractable, intractable; tractate; tractile, traction, track, trail, train; trait. tram,* as in *tramway;* but also *tram silk,* the woof in weaving good material. *trawl. treat, treatise, treaty.*

"Being so long in the lower form [at Harrow] I gained an immense advantage over the cleverer boys. I got into my bones the essential structure of the ordinary British sentence—which is a noble thing. Naturally, I am biassed in favor of boys learning English; and then I would let the clever ones learn Latin as an honor, and Greek as a treat"—Winston Spencer Churchill, *My Early Life* (1930).

Via Fr, *tret* (as in *tare and tret:* from the 15th c. into the 19th, an allowance; *tare* for the wrapping or container; *tret* for waste in carriage, transport, etc.); *tret* was an allowance of 4 pounds in every 104 (1/26). *abstract, attract, contract, detract, distract, extract, protract, retract, subtract;* also the noun forms, as *abstraction. attractive. attrahent, contrahent; subtrahend. entreat. strass:* silk pulled apart in making a skein. It, *trattoria* (*trattare:* draw, treat). Afrikaans, *trek.* Du, *trigger, triggerfish* (from its dorsal spine). *trigger-happy.* Russ, *droshky.* Gc, *drag, dragnet; dredge. draggle, bedraggled, drail, dray. drawl, drogue.*

Hamlet, when his mother asks him to sit by her to watch the play, turns to Ophelia, saying, "No, good Mother, here's metal more attractive."

Longfellow, in *Elegiac Verse,* gives sound advice:

If you would hit the mark, you must aim a little above it;
Every arrow that flies feels the attraction of earth.

James Thomson, in *The Seasons* (*Winter*), pictures

The redbreast . . .
Against the window beats, then brisk alights
On the warm hearth, then hopping o'er the floor
Eyes all the smiling family askance,
And pecks, and starts, and wonders where he is—
Till, more familiar grown, the table-crumbs
Attract his slender feet.

tre, tri: three. Skr *teapoy* (earlier *tripoy*): three-legged (see *pod*); folkchanged from its use at afternoon tea. *Trimurti:* three-formed, the Hindu trinity: Brahma the Creator, Vishnu the Preserver, S(h)iva the Destroyer; sometimes represented as one body with three heads. *Tripura:* triple city. *Trisirias:* fever as a three-headed demon marking the three symptoms: heat, cold, and sweating. Pers *sitar:* three-stringed instrument—today usually with 7 main strings and 13 under, resonating. *sitar* is also the Turkish word for *star.*

Gk, *trias, trireme, trierarch. triclinium:* couch on three sides of Greek and Roman banquet table (see *klei*). *triskelion. trichotomy:* early division of man into body, mind, and spirit (soul); Freud preferred *id, ego,* and *superego. tricerion:* three-branched candlestick of the Eastern Orthodox Church. *tridactyl:* three-fingered. *triglyph:* carving, as on an arch, with three grooves. *tribrach, trilogy, trio, triolet. triplet, tristich, tercet.* It, *terzo. triad.*

The *triad* is the most common of all divisions; most things, as Aristotle pointed out, have a beginning, a middle (body), and an end. Several hundred of "the triads of the Island of Britain" have come to us from 9th c. Wales. They list, with a mixture of chauvinism and xenophobia, "three notable qualities of the four nations: in a Welshman, genius, generosity and mirth; in an Englishman, coolness, boldness and industry; in an Irishman, flattery, cunning and ostentation; in a Frenchman, gallantry, courtesy and inconstancy." More objective, and still valid, is the triad of "the three dignities of poetry: the union of the true and the wonderful, the union of the beautiful and the wise, the union of nature and art."

The notorious Chinese San Ho Hui Society, founded in 1725 "to oust the Manchu dynasty," and perhaps still a tong, claimed to be a union of heaven, earth, and man. Triads still function in Chinese activities.

Also *tierce. terce:* prayer at the third hour after sunrise. *tercel:* male hawk; according to folk belief, only a third of these birds are male. *triplex, triploid, triplicity. triangle. trigon:* ancient three-sided lyre or harp; also known as *trigonon. tripod, trivet.* For *tripos,* see *ped. trine, triune, trinity. tritium* (see *el*).

Gk and L *tri* overlap. *trey.* It, *trio, trecento. trammel:* first, three-spotted; then, a mesh. *triumvir.* The first *triumvirate* was that of Pompey, Caesar, and Crassus (*Dives:* the rich), at Rome in 60 B.C. L *tertius:* third. *tern. ternal; tertian, tertiary. sesterce* (*semi-terce*): coin worth two asses and half of a third. *trimester. triarii:* Roman soldiers of the third rank. *tribe:* first, the third division of the Roman people; hence, *tribunal, tribune:* chosen to represent the tribe. *tribute; tributary; attribute, contribute, distribute, retribution. triceps:* three-headed; muscle of the upper arm. *trivium,* followed by the *quadrivium* (see *kuetuer*). *trivial:* (gossip) where three roads meet. *travail:* originally an instrument of torture, with three stakes. *trident.*

"If I were asked to what the singular prosperity and growing strength of the American people ought mainly to be attributed, I should reply: to the superiority of their women"—Alexis de Tocqueville, *Democracy in America* (1840), ii, 3.

L *terstis, testis:* a third (person) standing by (see *sta*); hence, a witness (cf. *umpire*). *testis, testicle,* explained in dictionaries as "witness or evidence of virility," is actually the obverse: the virility is evidence, or pledge, of one's honest word. As the 13th c. Jewish commentator Rashi explained: "When one swears, one takes a sacred object in his hand. The circumcision was the first precept of the Lord to Abraham, and had also come to him through great pain; hence it was particularly precious to him, and so he ordered his servant to put his hand upon it while taking the oath." Rashi came near the explanation, but balled it up. Actually, the swearer put his hands upon the organs of male affirmation, swearing by his manhood, implying, "If I prove false, you may cut off my balls." With the growth of modesty and civil law, Christians instead began to swear on the Bible, or on holy relics such as the crown of thorns (of which there were three in Paris in the 13th c.), or one of Jesus' baby teeth, or—claimed by several churches—the snip of his circumcision.

Hence, *testament.* The Old and the New Testament of the Bible were, respectively, a "covenant with the Lord" and his "last will and testament." *testify, testator, testimonial, testimony; intestate. attest, contest, detest, obtest; protest, Protestant, protestation.* Note that *test,* however, is from L *testa:* first, shell or shard; then a clay, brick, earthen pot. The clay pot was used in assaying metals; hence *test;* also *testaceous.* Via Late Latin slang came Fr *tête:* head; see *ters.* Also from the slang, E *testy.* A *teston;* with Henry VIII, known as a *tester:* a shilling coin with a head on it. L, *teste John Doe:* witness John Doe. *testamur:* we attest, as on an English university certificate or diploma.

Many mathematical and other scientific terms arise from the *three* fold. *trivalent, trinomial; tricrotic, tricuspid. trocar. trisect. trigonometry. trihedron, trisoctrahedron* (3 X 8 faces). *triplicate. triatomic. triazial, triazine, triazole. trillion. trimerous:* with three equal divisions. *triethyl, triphenyl, triphenylmethane. trissaccharide. tritanopia. tridymite. trilobite:* three-lobed arthropod (extinct). *Tribulus:* genus, the three-pointed bean caper. *Trithrinax, Thrinax:* genera of palms with three-pointed leaves. *Tribolium:* genus of beetles. *Triceratops:* three-horned dinosaur (long gone). *Trillium:* genus of plants with three petaled flowers. *Triteleia:* genus of lily with trimerous flowers. *trifoliate. Trias:* the threefold era before the Jurassic. *Tertiary:* of the era before the Mesozoic, which was formerly called the Secondary Age of the Earth. *OED* lists 176 such special *tri* words, and details other relevant words in 74 more columns.

As *thrid* became *third,* so *three* and *ten* became *thirteen.* There are two stories behind the notion that thirteen at table brings bad luck (one will die within the year). Norse mythology tells us that twelve gods were feasting in Valhalla; Loki, the god of strife, joined them uninvited; the god Balder died (see *meigh*). Jesus sat with his twelve disciples at the Paschal feast, the Last Supper; Jesus died. Judas, we are told, hanged himself on an elder tree, and in the tree alphabet, the elder is thirteenth.

three and its compounds, especially *three* self-fortified, 3 X 3 = 9, are holy symbols. Holy is the combination of human body, mind, and soul (*3*) with the elements of substance—earth, air, fire, water (*4*)—and the divine compounded essence (*9*), which combined (multiplied) equal *108.* There are 108 beads on the Eastern rosary, which the pious Buddhist clicks off as he circles a stupa 108 times. A. K. Coomaraswamy speaks of "the 108 auspicious symbols that may ornament the Buddha's foot." A man who attains his 108th year is triply blessed.

"Ko Wan Tze thought thrice before acting. Twice would have been enough"—Confucius, *Analects,* ca. 500 B.C.

Sp, *tresillo:* card game with three players. As Columbus was nearing land, he saw three "islands"; drawing closer, he realized that they were three mountains on one body of land; with the Spanish word for *trinity,* he named the island *Trinidad.*

Russ, *troika:* carriage drawn by three horses abreast. Gc, *three, thrice, thirty. riding:* one of the three administrative districts of Yorkshire, England; by folk-change, North *Thirding* became North *Riding. threescore and ten:* the "allotted" span of human life, now often extended. As Ecclesiastes 4:12 reminds us: "A cord with three strands is not quickly broken." Via Gc, *drill:* heavy cloth, from L *trilis:* triple-twilled, three-threaded; whence also *trellis. twill* came via OE *twilic* from L *bilix:* two-threaded. From *twill* came Scot *tweal;* misread in 1829 by James Lock, a London dealer, as cloth from the region of the River Tweed, *tweal* became E *tweed.* The river, which marks part of the English-Scottish border, has gone into folklore, though it is outranked by a rival stream:

Says Tweed to Till—
"What gars ye rin sae still?"
Says Till to Tweed—
"Though ye rin wi' speed
And I rin slaw,
For ae man that ye droon
I droon twa."

"All good things come in threes"–an optimistic saw, perhaps from the good fairy's usual grant of three wishes.

treb: build, beam; dwelling. L *trabs, trabis:* beam. *trabea:* state robe in ancient Rome, adorned with "beams" (horizontal stripes). *trabeated, trabeation, trabecula. trave.* Via It, *architrave:* basic beam. By metathesis, L *taberna:* tent, booth, hut. *tabernacle, tavern. contubernal:* companion of the tent.

Gc *throp, thorp:* gathering place, hence hamlet. *thorpe,* still used in placenames, as *Allthorpe, Allerthorpe* (Celt *Aelfweard's thorpe*); *Mablethorpe* (Gc *Malbert's*); *Oglethorpe* (Norse *Otkell's*).

Also *troop,* Fr *troupe;* hence also Fr *de trop:* too many. It, *troppo,* in music.

John Henry (later Cardinal) Newman, a close friend of R. H. Froude at Oxford and after, wrote in a letter of 1835: "Dear Froude is pretty well, but is languishing for want of his Oxford contubernians."

trep: turn; find. Gk *trepein:* to turn; *tropos:* a turning. *trope, tropism. tropic. Tropic of Cancer* (north), *Tropic of Capricorn* (south): lines where the sun attains an altitude of 90° and turns back; between them stretches the torrid zone; see *ios. entropy:* the measure of heat that can be turned into energy, has been given new use: "The basic probability concept, entropy, and its quantum, the bit, are now part of the metalanguage of linguistics"–*Language* xl (1964): 210. *Atropos:* the unturnable; relentless Greek Fate who cuts the thread of life. *Atropa:* genus, the deadly nightshade. *atropine:* the active principle of the drug obtained from the deadly nightshade; sometimes called *tropine.* The deadly nightshade is also called *belladonna:* beautiful lady; it was used in medieval Italy as a cosmetic; see *nekut.* The *belladonna lily* is named for "the charmingly blended red and white of its perianth, resembling the complexion of a beautiful woman." Hence *apotropaion:* a good-luck charm used to turn away evil; e.g., a rabbit's foot, or the *apotropaic* expression *D V* (*Deo volente:* God willing).

tropology. troposphere. turpitude: turning from proper paths. *Heliotropium:* genus of flowers that turn to follow the sun; thus also, via It, *turnsole.* Turning in response to light is *phototropism;* to heat, *thermotropism;* to the earth's gravity, *geotropism. chromatotrope; allotropy. isotropy. aeolotropy,* from *Aeolus:* the rapid one, god of the winds, from whom also the *Aeolians* and the *aeolian harp.*

A *trophy* was first a memorial for having turned back an enemy. A *trope* was first the turning back of classical verse, unlike prose, which runs straight on; then, the figurative use of a word, turning from its literal application; hence, a figure of speech. From such association with poetry and song came the sense of a "finder" of good words and lines, as Fr, *trouvère, troubadour;* then, good "finds," from Fr *trouvaille:* (treasure) trove. Thus also *contrive, retrieve.* A blend of *apt* and *contrivance* gave us *contraption. OED* has 8 columns of relevant *trop* words; thus Urquhart, in *Ekskubalauron* (1652), says he could have enlarged his discourse "tropologetically, by metonymical, ironical, metaphorical and synecdochial instruments of elocution."

Gk *tropis:* keel, on which a boat turns, is used in E *tropis:* the "keel" of some sponges, and in *tropidosternal:* of a division of birds with a keeled breastbone. *Oxytropis:* literally, sharp-keeled; genus of the pea family. *Monotropa:* genus, the Indian pipe. *Tropaeolum:* a genus of South American climbing plant whose leaves, like a shield, and flowers, like a helmet, give it the appearance of an ancient trophy. *Notropis:* back-turner; genus, the minnow.

He was in logic a great critic,
Profoundly skilled in analytic,
He could distinguish, and divide

A hair 'twixt south and south-west side . . .
For rhetoric, he could not ope
His mouth, but out there flew a trope;
He knew what's what, and that's as high
As metaphysic wit can fly.
—Samuel Butler, *Hudibras* (1663), i

treud: push, press; threaten, oppress. Akin to *ter II.* L *trudere, trusum. abstruse. detrude, extrude, intrude, obtrude, protrude, retrude,* and their noun forms, *intrusion,* etc. Gc, *threat, threatening. throe; throw, thrust.*

As some great Tyrian trader, from the sea,
Descried at sunrise an emerging prow . . .
And saw the merry Grecian coaster come,
Crated with amber grapes, and Chian wine,
Green bursting figs, and tunnies steeped in brine,
And knew the intruders on his ancient home,
The young light-hearted Masters of the waves . . .
—Matthew Arnold, *Scholar-Gipsy* (1853)

trozdos: the thrush. Partly imitative. Gk *struthion. ostrich. Struthio:* genus, the ostrich; *struthioid, struthious.* In 17th c. England the ostrich (there unseen) was called *struthiocamel.*

L *turdus:* thrush. LL *exturdire,* Fr *étourdi,* E *sturdy:* first, like a thrush drunk on grapes; hence, reckless; hence the more favorable current sense. Gc, *throstle; thrush.* Michael Drayton, in *Idea; The Shepherd's Garland* (1593), 3, to the poet:

Crave the tuneful nightingale to help you with her lay,
The ousel and the throstlecock, chief music of our May.

Browning, in his *Home Thoughts from Abroad:*

That's the wise thrush; he sings each song twice over,
Lest you should think he never could recapture
That first fine careless rapture!

And hear Shakespeare's song in *The Winter's Tale,* iv, 2.

tuegh: press; sudden pain, felt or inflicted. Gc, *tweak, twitch.* Nasalized, *twinge.* OE *thwong. thong.*

At last he rose, and twitch'd his mantle blue;
Tomorrow to fresh woods, and pastures new.
—Milton, *Lycidas*

tueis: shake, move to and fro; break into flame. scorch. Gk (*tueisein*). *seiein:* shake; *seismos:* earthquake. *seismic, seismograph. seismology,* etc. Occasionally used figuratively, as in *seismic with laughter. siriasis:* sunstroke, as under *Sirius,* the Dog Star, brightest in the heavens. The dog days, when Sirius rises, have from ancient times been deemed the hottest and most unwholesome; they are also the days when dogs are most likely to run mad.

sistrum: a rattle; first used in Egyptian worship of Isis. Gc, *whittle,* as the knife moves back and forth. *thwaite:* cleared land, from to and fro of ax and scythe. Du, *doit:* a small coin "hewn off"; now used especially in negative figurative expressions, as *not a doit.*

Trinculo, in *The Tempest,* ii, 2, coming upon the prostrate Caliban, pictures him as a prize exhibit for "holiday fools. . . .When they will not give a doit to relieve a lame beggar, they will lay out ten to see a dead Indian."

tuer I: whirl, confusion. Gk *turbe,* L *turbo, turbinis:* violent motion, spinning. *turbid, turbo; turbine, turbojet. turbit:* a pigeon, ever turning. *turbinate. turbulent. disturb, perturb. imperturbable. Turbo:* genus of snails shaped like a top. *Turbellaria:* class of flatworms whose cilia stir the water. By metathesis, OFr *turber, truber. trouble, troublesome,* etc. *trowel:* "That was laid on with a trowel!"*—As You Like It,* i, 2; repeated by Congreve, Benjamin Disraeli, etc.

tuer II: grasp, seize; hold; hard. Gk *siren:* she that seizes when victims are drawn by her alluring song, has degenerated to the warning shriek of the alarm siren. Gc, *quartz.* This is from early *zwerg:* dwarf, applied to the hard stone; similarly, *nickel* (dwarf, spiteful sprite) was named because its copperlike ore yielded no copper; and cobalt (*kobold:* demon of the mine) took its name from the miners' belief that it diminished the silver ore found with it.

"What song the Syrens sang, or what name Achilles assumed when he hid himself among women, though puzzling questions, are not beyond all conjecture" —Sir Thomas Browne, *Hydriotaphia: Urne Buriall* (1658), 5.

Of Browne's book, *The New Century Handbook of English Literature* (1967) states: "Succeeding generations of critics have continued to commend it as an example of nearly flawless English prose"; but I have yet to find any of the conjectures as to "what song the Syrens sang." The only human who heard the song and survived was Odysseus, who had his ear-plugged crew tie him to a mast so that he would not seek to swim to the sweet and fatal siren.

tuerk: cut. Gk *sarkh:* flesh. *sarco-,* as *sarcology; sarcocarp:* the fleshy part of fruit. *sarcode:* animal protoplasm. *OED* lists 16 *sarco* words and details 34 relevant words beginning *sarc. sarcinoid. sarcophagous:* flesh-eating. *sarcophagal:* term of scorn used by vegetarians of flesh-eaters. "I am a vegetarian," remarked Dr. Kim Alier, "—at second hand; I eat the steer that eats the grass."

The *sarcophagus,* a limestone coffin used by the ancient Greeks, was supposed to consume the body buried therein. Other technical terms include *anasarca:* dropsy throughout the flesh; *coenosarc, endosarc; sarcenchyme. syssarcosis:* flesh (muscle) that holds bones together.

sarcasm first implied biting the lips; *sarcastic.* Carlyle, in *Sartor Resartus,* ii, observes: "Sarcasm, I now see to be, in general, the language of the devil."

U

ua I: change, bend, turn apart. Hindi *varanda,* perhaps from Portuguese; E *veranda.*

L *varus:* bent, knock-kneed, is the basis of a number of English words for infirmities or disease. *varus:* clubfoot. (L *varix, varicem*), *varicose (vein).* (L *varius:* changeable, spotty), E *varix. varicella:* chickenpox; *variola:* smallpox. Hence also *vary, variance, variety, various; variorum* (edition). *variegated. divaricate. prevaricate:* first, to walk crookedly; then, figuratively, to talk crookedly.

vair: parti-colored, used of fur; represented in heraldry by alternating azure and argent. *miniver;* see *mei I.* In the Middle Ages, *vair* was used to trim robes and slippers. Thus Cinderella's OFr *vair* slippers (all stories then came by word of mouth) were heard as Fr *verre* (same sound, but meaning glass), and the little "cinder girl" left behind one glass slipper—as indeed only a fairy godmother could provide.

ua II: harm, swelling. Gc, *wen. wound.* William Congreve confessed himself dazzled at first sight of Lesbia:

> But soon as e'er the beauteous idiot spoke,
> Forth from her coral lips such folly broke,
> Like balm the trickling nonsense heal'd my wound,
> And what her eyes enthral'd, her tongue unbound.

uab: cry, wail. L, *vapulate* (literally, to cry in pain): to be flogged. Pedagogue Samuel Parr wrote in a letter of 1783 of "blunders for which a boy ought to vapulate." *vapulation* was routine in the British Navy until the 19th c.; Lowell wrote in 1886 that he was not "arguing in favour of a return to those vapulatory methods." See *cat,* under *pilo.* Gc, *weep.*

uad: pledge. L *vas, vadis.* Legal terms, as *vadiation, vadium, vadimonium (vadimony);* E *vas,* especially *praedial.*

wage, wages, wager. wed, wedding, wedlock. "Age and wedlock tame man and beast"—an early English saw; Eugene O'Neill, in *Welded* (1924), bitterly refers to *bedlock.* With the shift of *g* and *w* (as also in *warden, guardian,* etc. [see *suer I*]), *gage, engagement. mortgage:* death pledge. *dégagé.*

uadh: move ahead (in water, to wade); go. L *vadere:* go. *vadum:* shallow place; ford. *vade mecum:* go with me; a memorandum book or the like. *Quo vadis?:* Whither goest thou?—Bible, John, 16:5; also the title of the novel by Henryk Sienkiewicz, who won the Nobel Prize for literature in 1905. *vadose:* of water not far underground. *invade, evade, pervade,* and their noun forms, *invasion,* etc. Via Sp, *vamo(o)se:* literally, Let's go! Via Gc, *wade, waddle* (like a duck).

"Depart,—be off, excede,—evade,—erump!"—Oliver Wendell Holmes, *The Autocrat of the Breakfast-Table* (1858), 11.

uag I, uaq: bend, curve; wander indecisively. L *vagari, vagatum:* ramble. *vagabond. vagary; vagrant. vague. vagus:* longest cranial nerve, from the neck to the abdomen. *divagation. extravagant. solivagant* (often delightful). *vacillate. convex:* curve together.

Gc, *wankle:* unsteady, fickle; whence *wench, wince, winch, wink;* the slang term *wonky;* and, nasalized, *wangtooth:* curved, i.e., the molar. *lapwing* was earlier *lappewinke:* flickering about.

uag II: sheath, pod. L and E, *vagina.* As L *gladius:* sword, became slang for *penis,* it was natural for the receptacle of the penis to be given the name for the sheath; slang in Latin, *vagina* became the technical term in English. *OED* details 9 combinations of *vagina* and lists 8 words beginning *vagini,* 8 beginning *vagino,* as *vaginipennous:* with wings in a sheath; *vaginolabial; vaginofixation.* See *kal.*

Via Sp, from the shape of the pod and with diminutive ending, E *vanilla. invagination. evaginate,* as one might turn gloves inside out.

Lady Holland, Sydney Smith's daughter, published his life and papers in 1855, among these his remark: "Ah, you flavour everything, you are the vanilla of society."

uagh, (s)uagh: sound. Gk *ekhe:* sound, resound; *ekho. echo. catechesis:* teaching by word of mouth. *catechism. catechize; catechumen.* L *vagire, vagitus:* cry. E *vagitus:* cry of the emerging human neonate. Gc *sough,* partly imitative.

The nymph *Echo* loved Narcissus, who repulsed her; Aphrodite then made him fall in love with his own image, seen in a pond. Freud coined the word *narcissism;* but more pleasantly the youth became the beautiful pondside flower that Sappho called "laughing narcissus that loves the rain." But Pan desired Echo; fleeing him, she faded into a voice that can but repeat the last sound it has heard. *echo poems* repeat, often with a humorous change, the last sounds of lines. Byron approximates an echo line in *The Bride of Abydos* (1813):

> Hark! To the hurried question of Despair:
> "Where is my child?"—an echo answers: Where?

Much earlier and more deftly, a Cambridge pamphlet, *Hygisticos* (1643), presented the struggle of a Glutton with his Conscience (which ends with hope of a cure):

> *Glutton:* My belly do I deify.
> *Conscience:* Fie! . . .
> *Glutton:* My joy's a feast, my wish is wine.
> *Conscience:* Swine!
> . . . .
> *Glutton:* If all be true that thou dost tell,
> They that fare sparingly fare well.
> *Conscience:* Farewell.

Macbeth (act v) makes a plea that is urgent in many a land today:

> If thou couldst, doctor, cast
> The water of my land, find her disease,
> And purge it to a sound and pristine health,
> I would applaud thee to the very echo,
> That should applaud again.

uai. Exclamation of distress. L *Vae victis:* Woe to the vanquished. According to Plutarch's *Lives,* this expression was first used by the Gaul Brennus, in 390 B.C., when the conquered Romans complained that he was tampering with the scales that weighed their tribute. It has since been used by many, including Plautus, Livy, Erasmus, and Bernard Shaw (*Caesar and Cleopatra* [1897], ii).

ONorse, *wail.* Gc, *woe, wellaway.* "Woe is me"; apparently first used in the Bible, Isaiah 6:5.

uak: cow. L *vacca. vaccinus:* of a cow. Dr. Edward Jenner, of Gloucestershire, noticing that dairymaids who'd had *vaccinia:* cowpox, did not get the then-endemic smallpox, in 1796 inoculated eight-year-old James Phipps, thus achieving *vaccine* and *vaccination*—for which Parliament granted him £30,000. Hence the spread of *vaccinotherapy.* When smallpox was not fatal, it left the victim badly pockmarked, yet thereafter immune; hence, many English families hired servants who had already had the disease, to minimize the danger of contagion for their children. In many countries today, children are vaccinated prior to their first day of school.

Sp, *vaquero:* cowboy; folkchanged in the American West to *buckayro, buckaroo. OED* has three columns of *vacc* words, including *vaccicide,* and *vaccimulgence:* the milking of cows.

ual: power, strength. L *valere, valentem, validus. Ave atque vale:* Hail and fare well. *valence, monovalent, bivalent,* etc. *valerian:* a plant, and the drug from its root (from *Valeria,* a province in Pannonia [now part of Hungary and Yugoslavia] conquered by Augustus in 9 B.C.). *valiant; valid, invalid. value; invaluable:* so worthwhile its value cannot be measured. *validity.* L *valetudo:* state of health. Like other words covering a polarity, it moved, even in Roman times, to one end (as "a temperature" usually means a high one for a human); hence *valetudinarian; OED* defines 7 associated words.

avail; convalescence. countervail. devaluate. equivalent, invalidate. prevalent; prevail. revalescent, revaluate, revaluation. Gc, *wield. springal(d):* powerful youth. *herald:* first, an army officer (Gc *heri:* army, whence also *harry;* see *koro*).

A number of names: L, *Valeria. Valentine.* St. Valentine's Day (14 Feb., celebrated from medieval times as the day birds begin to mate) used to involve various ways of choosing one's *valentine:* sweetheart, for the year. The day is still celebrated with gifts and sentimental or comic *valentines:* cards of greeting and good wishes. Gc, *Arnold:* eagle strength. *Gerald:* powerful with the spear; *Geraldine. Harold:* army leader; also *Walter. Oswald:* divine power. *Reginald, Reynold:* powerful judge. *Magna est veritas et praevalebit:* Great is truth, and shall prevail, said Thomas Brooks in 1662. A cynic has suggested the translation "Great is truth, and will prevail a bit."

ual(s): palisade; curve, turn. This root turned in two directions, partly from military use. Stakes were used to make ramparts; channels or trenches were dug beside them (as sometimes today, for horse jumping). Hence L *vallus:* stake, palisade; *vallere, vallatus:* to fortify with a rampart; entrench. *vallation, circumvallate, contravallation.* From the spaces between the stakes, *interval.* Gc, *wall.* And curving down from a hillside came *vale, valley* (Some assign the *valley* words to a root *ualu.*)

vaudeville rose from *Vau de Vire:* Valley of the Vire, in Normandy, which in the 15th c. was famous for its songs. Via OFr *à val:* to the valley, came *vail,* and *avale:* to lower.

"Every valley shall be exalted, and every mountain and hill shall be made low" —Bible, Isaiah 40:4.

For love is of the valley, come thou down
And find him, by the happy threshold, he,
Or hand in hand with Plenty in the maize,
Or red with spirted purple of the vats,
Or foxlike in the vine . . .
—Tennyson, *The Princess,* 1

uat: inspire. L *vates:* prophet. *vates, vatic, vaticination.* (The pope's palace, the *Vatican,* is named for *Vatican Hill* in Rome, from an Etruscan word.) Gc *wood:* mad, was used into the 19th c.; *OED* gives over 2 columns to *wood:* mad, furious. For the *wood* from trees, see *uidhu.* Also Anglo-Saxon *Wodin,* whence *Wednesday;* Scand *Odin.* Possibly *Edda:* collection of early Icelandic writings, as of Snorri Sturluson (d. 1241).

ud: up, out, away. Gk *husteron* (comparative): higher, latter, later. *hysteron proteron:* that which should come later comes before, as "My dame that bred me up and bare me in her womb"—often referred to as "the cart before the horse." *hysterology:* inversion. *hysteranthos:* of plants the leaves of which come after the flowers. *hysterogenic:* of later origin or formation (opposite of *protogenic*). *hysteresis:* slackening of magnetic force.

hubristic: away from proper behavior—violent, insolent, overproud. *OED* calls this word "irregular for hybristic," which it does not list, even though both *hubris* and *hybris* are in *OED*'s 1933 supplement, there described as "university slang" unless applied to Greek tragedy; the Greek form is *hubris.* Also *hybrid:* away from its kind; first, the offspring of a tame sow and a wild boar. *OED* lists 10 associated words, only one of which—*hybridous*—is in Johnson's *Dictionary* (1755).

Hystrix: literally, with hair up; genus of (1) porcupine, (2) bottle-brush grass, both named for their spikes. Gc, *out, about, but.* Du *Uitlander,* E *outlander; outlandish. utter:* speak out. *uttermost;* also shortened to *utmost. outlaw, outline,* etc. *OED* gives the word *out* 10 columns; then lists several hundred combinations that have been used, as *outbargain, outbrawl, outqueen;* then details in 100 columns additional *out* words, as *outbabble, outfit, outrage, outright, outside*—at the end of which the reader's patience may well be *outworn.*

From Gc *gar:* all, and *aus:* out, came *carouse:* to drink all out. Many old drinking cups were made in such a shape (e.g., that of a lion couchant with a hole in its base) that they could not be set down until emptied.

udero: womb, belly. Gk *hustera. hysteria;* the cause was believed to lie in the womb. *hysterics, hysteritis; hysterology, hysterodynia; hysterectomy. OED* lists 11 relevant words beginning *hyster(o)* and details 23 more.

L and E *venter,* possibly via a taboo change. *vesica:* bladder, blister. *vesicant, vesicotomy, vesicular, vesicatory, vesicle. ventral, ventriloquism* (: belly talk). *OED* lists 7 *ventri* combinations and details 21, as *ventripotent:* gluttonous, big-bellied, like the fellow next door, like the man in Rabelais who trundles his belly before him on a wheelbarrow.

Several words, like *ventose, ventosity,* combine the ideas of stomach and wind; for *wind,* see the next root, *ue.* E *venter* has had several meanings: (1) women (*first venter, second venter,* etc.) with offspring from the same man; (2) any one of the four stomachs of a ruminant (for their specific names, see *stoman*); (3) the thick, fleshy part of a muscle; (4) any one of the three main cavities in man containing viscera—namely, abdomen, chest, and head; (5) in lower forms of animal life, what corresponds to the belly in mammals.

ue, aue, uen: blow; vapor, wind. Skr, *mahatma* (*maha:* great; *atma:* vapor, spirit). *Nirvana:* blowing out; in Hindu belief, the end of man's series of lives, when by virtue he has attained absorption into the universal essence. *Vayu,* Hindu god of wind.

Probably Gk *aer:* air. *aerial; aeroplane* (simplified to *airplane*). *aeration, aerobatics, aerodynamics; aeroembolism; aeromancy; aerosol; aerostat; aerothermodynamic;* 6 columns of relevant words in *OED,* including, probably, *(aerie) eyrie:* nest of a bird, especially the eagle, perched high on a mountain peak. *Aëllo:* literally, storm swift; a Harpy. *anaerobic:* of the *anaerobe,* a microorganism that lives without free oxygen; *anaerobiosis.*

Gk *aetmos:* vapor. *atmosphere,* first used by John Wilkins, in 1638, of the moon, which has no atmosphere. *atmolysis; atmidometer.* L *ventus:* wind. *vent, ventiduct, ventail, ventilation. ventosity* (see *udero*). L *vannus. van:* wing; a fan for winnowing. *fan.* (*fan* is also short for *fanatic:* first, one inspired by a god, from L *fanum:* temple; see *dhes.* Similarly, *wood:* mad; see *uat.*)

Gc *weather, weatherbeaten. withered. wind, windmill, winnow, wing. wheedle:* first, wagging the tail. *winze:* vent or airshaft in a mine. *window* (Norse *windauga:* wind's eye). "Open the window, light and God stream in."

"Though all the winds of doctrine were let loose to play upon the earth, so Truth be in the field, we do injuriously by licensing and prohibiting to doubt her strength. Let her and Falsehood grapple; who ever knew Truth put to the worse, in a free and open encounter?"—Milton, *Areopagitica; or Speech for the Liberty of Unlicensed Printing* (1644). *Areopagitica* is derived from *Areopagus:* the Hill of Mars (Greek Ares), where sat the Athenian supreme court, and whence Paul (Bible, Acts 17) addressed the Athenians.

uebh(s): weave, move back and forth; objects woven or the like, as a honeycomb. Pers, *baft:* woven cotton cloth. Gk *huphe:* web. *hypha:* threadlike part of fungus.

Perhaps from this root, from the to-and-fro of a wedding march and chant, Gk (*huph-nos*), *humnos,* E *hymn;* hence *hymen,* etc. See *siu.* L *vepsa,* by metathesis, *vespa:* wasp, which weaves its hive. *vespiary:* wasp's nest (the ending as in *aviary*). *Vespidae:* family of wasps; *vespine.*

Gc *web. webster:* female weaver, survives as a name, as on a dictionary. *weave, weft, woof, wafer, waffle. wave. waver; wobble. goffer:* to plait. *gopher,* from its web of burrows. *wax; beeswax,* woven by the bees.

"Instead of dirt and poison we have rather chosen to fill our hives with honey and wax; thus furnishing mankind with the two noblest of things, which are sweetness and light"–Swift, *Battle of the Books* (1697), preface. Matthew Arnold, in *Culture and Anarchy* (1869), added: "The pursuit of perfection, then, is the pursuit of sweetness and light."

ued: sing. Gk *aoid. odeum. odeon,* now usually the name of a concert hall. L *ode, oda:* lyric song. *ode, epode, monody. melody, melodious;* 14 such words in *OED. hymnody, psalmody, palinode. parody; prosody; rhapsody. threnody. comedy; tragedy;* see *ter II.* Comedy was first a song for a *khomos:* celebration, revel; whence also *encomium:* praise at a celebration, as for a conquering hero. *encomiast.* Three olden musical instruments: *melodeon, melodion* (*mel:* sweet; see *melit*); *terpodion* (*terp:* delight, as in *Terpsichore;* see the root *terp.*).

uedh: thrust, strike. Gk *osmos:* thrusting. *osmose,* backformed from *osmosis; osmotic. endosmosis* (*exosmosis*): the interpenetrating fluid passes inward (outward) through the porous partition. Used figuratively, as in *Nation,* 18 Oct. 1900: "the subtile interchange–a sort of moral osmosis–between the higher conquering race and the lower conquered one."

ueg I: weave. L *velum:* sail, cloth. *veil, unveil; reveal, revelation.* Fr, *voile, velum, velar, velic. vexillum:* military standard; *vexillary:* standard-bearer. *velamen:* membrane; *velarium:* awning over Roman auditorium. Possibly *wife,* the veiled one.

Veronica's veil: the cloth with which Veronica wiped the face of Jesus on his way to Calvary, on which his face is miraculously represented; it is preserved in St. Peter's Basilica, in Rome. Reflecting an aptness frequent in early and legendary names, *Veronica* is from LL *vera iconica:* true image; see *ueik II; uero.*

ueg II. Ideas of vigor, liveliness, watchfulness. Skr *vajra:* thunderbolt. L *vegere, vegetatum:* enliven; *vegetator:* enlivener, exciter. *vegetable, vegetation, vegetarian. vegetate.* L *velox, velocem:* fast. *velocity; velocipede. velites:* lightly armed, swift Roman infantry. *vigil, vigilant, vigilante.* The *Chicago Times* as late as 1950 (23 May) felt called on to protest: "We have not adopted lynch law as a proper antidote; for we know that vigilanteism threatens all our civilization." *vigor, vigorous.* "Eternal vigilance is the price of liberty."

Fr, *vedette, reveille, surveillance.* Gc, *wake, awaken; wait, watch. waft* was backformed from *wafter,* a 17th c. term for a convoy vessel. From Gm *Biwak,* via Fr, *bivouac.*

On Fame's eternal camping-ground
Their silent tents are spread,
And glory guards, with solemn round,
The bivouac of the dead.
–Theodore O'Hara, 1849

uegh: move to and fro; transport. Gk *ochlos,* partly imitative, from the noisy stir of a crowd. *ochlocracy:* mob rule. *ochlophobia. ochlesis:* malaise from overcrowding. *OED* defines 8 *ochl(o)* words.

L *vehere, vectum. vehicle. inveigh:* to move against; *invective; advection, convect, convection. evection; vector. vex:* agitate (first physically, now emotionally); and the frequent *vexation.*

Gc, *way, away, always. Norway:* the north way. *wag, waggle.* The first syllable of *walleyed* is folkchanged from *wag. wagon,* and its doublet, *wain.* Moving to balance on a scale gave English *weigh, weight, weighty; wee.* The ocean *wave; waver.* Via Fr *voguer:* to wave, came *vogue,* the flow of fashion.

voyage; Fr, *Bon voyage! convoy, envoy, convey, conveyance.* Possibly *via:* by way of. *viaduct, viatic. viaticum;* see *dheigh N 36. deviate, devious, undeviating, impervious; obviate, obvious, previous; trivium* and *quadrivium; trivia, trivial.* It, *La Traviata:* the woman led astray; opera by Giuseppe Verdi, 1853. Possibly *vein,* which transports the blood; *venation, venose, venule, venesection.*

wiggle; for *wriggle,* see *uer II 6. polliwog* means wiggling head; *tadpole* means toad head (*poll:* head, as counted at the polls, or for a poll tax). Also from *wiggling, earwig* (keep it out of your hair!).

Multiplication is vexation,
Division is as bad;
The Rule of Three doth puzzle me,
And Practice drives me mad.
—Unknown scholar, 1570

ueguh: make a vow. Possibly partly imitative. Gk *eukhe:* vow, prayer. *Euchite:* since the 4th c., a monk devoted to perpetual prayer. *euchology:* prayerbook. Not related to *Eucharist;* see *gher I.* Apparently not related to the card game *euchre* (earlier *yuker*), of unknown origin, which was reportedly first played in America. The *Pall Mall Gazette* of 3 Feb. 1889 says it "was probably acclimatized on the Mississippi by the Canadian voyageurs, being a form of the French game of triomphe." Mark Twain, in *Roughing It* (1872), said: "At night, by the camp fire, we played euchre and seven up, to strengthen the mind." And in Bret Harte's lively verses *The Heathen Chinee,* it was the game played by Ah Sin with extra cards up his sleeve.

L *vovere, votum. votary, votive; devote, devotion, devout. vow, avow.* Possibly *woo.*

"Devotion! Daughter of astronomy!"—Edward Young, *The Complaint; or, Night-Thoughts on Life, Death and Immortality* (1742), ix, chief work of "the graveyard school."

uei (which may add *g, k, m, n, t*): flexible twig used for binding; hence curve, bend, give way, yield, change. Gk *iris, iridis;* terms applied to the curve of the rainbow; from the color, the *iris* of the eye, and the flower; also, *Iridaceae:* family, the iris. *iridescent. iritis. iridium* (see *el 77*). Hence *iridoline; iridosmine,* usually found with platinum. Gk *inos:* fiber; *inosite* (also called *inositol*).

L *viere, visum:* bend; *vis, vitis:* vine, tendril; from the shape (that of a screw), E *vise. viticulture. Vittaria:* genus, the ribbon fern. *vitta, vittate,* in plants. *vimen:* slender shoot; *viminal. vetch; Vicia:* genus, the vetch. *vinculum:* the plant periwinkle, folkchanged from *vincapervinca:* the winding plant.

The ultimate source of *vine, wine, vinegar,* and the whole family of *vineyard* and other *vinous* products is lost in antiquity. There are Fr *vin,* Russ *vino,* L *vinum,* Gk *oinos;* but also the non-Indo-European Hebr *yayin,* Ugaritic *yn,* Ethiopian *wayn.* There are hundreds of varieties of grape wine; and Moritz Jagendorf, in his comprehensive *Folk Wines* (1963), describes wines from over a hundred other sources—fruits, flowers, vegetables, herbs, etc. There are also hundreds of quotations about wine, of which three may here suffice. Tennyson, in *The Miller's Daughter,* enjoys pleasant

after-dinner talk
Across the walnuts and the wine.

The Bible, Proverbs 23:31–32, issues a warning: "Look not thou upon the wine when it is red. . . . At the last, it biteth like a serpent, and stingeth like an adder." And FitzGerald, in his translation of *The Rubáiyát,* passes on Omar Khayyám's enthusiasm:

In divine
High piping Pehlevi, with Wine! Wine! Wine!
Red wine! the nightingale cries to the Rose,
That yellow cheek of hers t' incarnadine.

L *vices:* yield, change, replace. *vicar. vicariously, vicissitude. vice,* as in *viceroy, vice-president,* etc. Fr, *viscount. vice versa.* The *Vikings,* who on their piratic forays appeared suddenly around the bends (bays and inlets) of the European coast.

Gc, *witch* or *wych:* with pliant branches, as the *wych elm* and the *witch hazel. wattle, wicker, wicket, withy. weak:* pliant, yielding. *wicked* first meant yielding to the Tempter. *week:* the recurrent turn of time. *wire,* first bent around a slave's ankle; now thus worn sometimes as a symbol of amorous bondage. Scot *wissel:* change; used financially in Gm *Wechsel:* money exchange. Via French, possibly *garland,* a circle of flowers, as the Hawaiian lei.

In the Spring a livelier iris changes on the burnished dove;
In the Spring a young man's fancy lightly turns to thoughts of love.
–Tennyson, *Locksley Hall,* I

ueid: look at, see; object of vision. "Seeing is believing"; hence, know. Among some peoples, as the Celts, easily seen, white.

Skr, *Veda:* knowledge, as in the sacred books of the Hindus, *Atharva-Veda, Rig-Veda, Sama-Veda. Vedanta. Gaekwar:* literally, watcher of the sacred cow; title of the Maratha rulers of Baroda, India. *vidya:* knowledge; *avidya:* limited knowledge.

Gk *eidos:* form. *eidetic; eidolon; idol, idolatry, idolum. idyl:* little picture. *idea:* form in the mind, as with the philosophical idealist, who follows Plato. *ideally, idealism, ideological. OED* lists 9 relevant *ide(o)* words, and details others in 10 columns. As suffixes, meaning shaped like, resembling. JWalker lists 17 relevant words ending *ode,* as *nematode,* and 204 ending *oid,* as *anthropoid, celluloid, planetoid. kaleidoscope:* view of beautiful forms. Gk *Haides* (*a* negative): Hades, the unseen. Gk *histor:* having seen, hence knowing. *historical, historiographer,* etc. *history;* also shortened to *story. polyhistor.*

L (*videre, visum*), *Vide* (imperative): See ___; instruction to a reader, abbreviated *v. videlicet;* L *videre licet:* it is permitted (easy) to see; abbreviated *viz. visor,* also *visard, vizor. visual* and its compounds, as *audiovisual, visuopsychic, visuosensory. visa;* looked at and checked. *vision; vista, invisible. advise, advice; evidence, evident; envy, invidious. improvident; improvise, improvisation; prevision; provide, providence, provision, proviso. prudent, prudence, jurisprudence. revise, revision; supervise, supervision; survey. visit:* see often; *visitant, visitation,* etc. Via Fr, *view, interview, preview, review, revue.*

Nature fits all her children with something to do;
He who would write and can't write can surely review.
–J. R. Lowell, *A Fable for Critics* (1848)

Fr, *idée fixe; vis-à-vis. visage, envisage. clairvoyance; voyeur; belvedere. bevue. blunder:* to see poorly.

Via Celt, *penguin:* literally, white head. *vendace:* whitefish; also *gwyniad. Guinevere:* white-cheeked. *Gwendolin(e):* also shortened to *Gwen. druid;* Caesar mentions the Druids (*dru-vid:* oak-knowing), with their holy oak tree and their use of its mistletoe. *winter:* the white season. *Vienna;* L *Vindo-bona:* the pleasant white place; settled by the Celts.

Ir *colcannon* (*cole:* cabbage): mixture of cabbage and white potatoes. Irish comedian Isaac Sparks founded the *Colcannon Club* in London in 1774, in gusty opposition to the more "exquisite" Macaroni Club, (founded in 1764), which, said Horace Walpole in a letter of 1764, "is composed of all the travelled young men who wear long curls and spying glasses." (A spying glass was a monocle dangled on a ribbon; see *haifst; kred I.*) A little later, in *Convention Hall* (1812), Peter Pindar asked a rhetorical question:

And will it not be deemed a daring thing
To ogle through a spying-glass the King?

Gc forms include a number of words now archaic or historical. *wist:* to know. *iwis; God wot! wite:* accuse. OE *aetwitan:* to see and blame, survives as *twit. witenagemot:* gathering of the wise men, an early Anglo-Saxon assembly. More-current words include *wit,* which first meant the faculty of understanding. Insofar as wit is applied to an unexpected resemblance, said Dryden, it must both surprise and delight, as "My mistress' bosom is as white as snow–and as cold." *witling. witticism* (the ending as in *criticism*). *witness,* who in the U.S. takes the *witness stand;* in Britain, speaks from the *witness box. unwitting; witless. wise, wisdom. to wit.* Again from Dryden (*The Hind and the Panther* [1687], iii): "Much malice mingled with a little wit."

Possibly *wistful* (blent with *wishful*). With *w.g* shift (as *ward, guard,* etc.), *guide, guise, disguise. guy rope.*

In these days of wife-"swapping" and multiple cohabitation, there is room for revival of the old word *wittol:* an aware and complaisant cuckold. Byron uses the word in *Don Juan,* i; Scott, in *Kenilworth,* 36. Shakespeare, in *The Merry Wives,* ii, 2 (where the disguised Ford, suspicious of his wife, urges Falstaff to make advances to her), uses *wittol, wittolly, cuckoldly,* and–six times–*cuckold.* The *sign of cuckoldry* was an outcropping of horns, invisible only to the afflicted husband; see *cucu.* The *badge of wittolry* was asses' ears. The most prominent wittol in history was Sir William Hamilton, British ambassador to Naples, who after 1793 lived with his wife Emma and Admiral Horatio Nelson until Nelson's death at Trafalgar in 1805. In 1801 Emma had a daughter, Horatia, whom Nelson acknowledged; Emma's life makes raunchy reading. See *ster II.*

wiseacre is folkchanged from *wise sayer. wizard:* a male witch, though earlier *witch* referred to either sex; see *ueik III. wizard* is now mainly used figuratively, in semihumorous exaggeration; the slang *wiz* is partly blent with *whiz,* imitative of speed. Here also the suffix *wise:* in the shape of, resembling, as *likewise, otherwise, counterclockwise;* JWalker lists 18 such combinations. *-wise* has recently been overworked as a vogue suffix, e.g., in "speaking *economicswise.*" This generous attachment, however, is no newfangled obnoxiety; Joshuah Sylvester, in his translation of Du Bartas in 1599, wrote (see *uel III 2*):

And also mingled (linsey-woolsie-wise)
Their gold-ground Tissue with too mean supplies.

Cowper neatly remarked: "Knowledge is proud that he has learned so much,

Wisdom is humble that he knows no more." FitzGerald, in his translation of *The Rubáiyát of Omar Khayyám:*

With them the seed of wisdom did I sow,
And with mine own hand wrought to make it grow;
And this was all the harvest that I reaped:
I came like water, and like wind I go.

All things bright and beautiful,
All creatures great and small,
All things wise and wonderful,
The Lord God made them all.
–Cecil F. Alexander, 1848

u(e)idh: separate. L *vidua:* bereft; used rarely of an unmarried woman. In Spain, the term used in formally addressing a woman whose husband has died is *Vidua. vidual, viduate. widow.* L *dividere, divisum. divide, divisive, division. dividend:* "that which should be divided." *device, devise. point-device:* properly sorted, perfectly arranged. *indivisible. individual.* Via Port, *viuva:* rockfish. *widow-bird (whidah),* from its long, black tail feathers.

Thus he grew up, in logic point-device,
Perfect in grammar, and in rhetoric nice.
–Longfellow, describing Einhard, in
Tales of a Wayside Inn (1872)

John Stark addressed his soldiers before the battle of Bennington, 16 Aug. 1777: "My men, yonder are the Hessians. They were bought for seven pounds and ten pence a man. Are you worth more? Prove it. Tonight the American flag floats from yonder hill, or Molly Stark sleeps a widow!" Need I add that the British forces, under Gentleman Johnny Burgoyne, were defeated?

ueik I: settle; neighborhood. Skr *vaisya:* settler, herdsman. The four major Indian castes were *Sutra:* menials, unskilled laborers; *Vaisya:* farmers, later also merchants; *Kshatriya:* military men, governors; *Brahmin:* first, priests.

Gk *oikhos:* house. *oecus:* main room in an ancient house. *oikist, oecist:* housebuilder in a new place; founder of a colony. Gk *paroikhos:* dwelling beside. *parish, parochial. Perioeci:* Spartans who were not householders and who therefore lacked political rights. *androecium:* the male "house" (division) of a plant. *autoecious, monoecious, paroecious.* Most males are happy that mankind is *dioecious;* women too.

Gk *oikhein:* inhabit; manage. *economics,* and all the concerns of *economy. OED* lists *oecumenical* and *oecology,* but its 1972 supplement gives "the now more usual form," *ecumenical, ecology.* And *ecology* has spawned *ecophene, ecosphere, ecotone, ecotype, ecotypical. ecospecies:* interfertile groups within a species.

L *vicus:* hamlet. L and E *villa:* country house. *vicinage, vicinity. village.* Via Fr, *ville.* This appears in scores of names, as *Deauville.* There is an odd *Sottesville:* literally, town of the silly women, in Normandy; population in 1980 ca. 27,000. Fr *hôtel de ville:* town hall. *villain:* first, farmer; hence, lacking city civility; hence, scoundrel. *villein* retains the sense of peasant. *villainy.* It, *villanella:* rustic dance; Fr, *villanelle:* poem; Sp, *villancico:* song.

OE *wick:* usually a dependent village, survives in *bailiwick,* administered by a bailiff; also in place names, as *Berwick, Chiswick, Warwick.*

In Gilbert's *The Pirates of Penzance* (1880), the daughters of the General, captured by the pirates (who are all noblemen "gone wrong," but now reforming), recognize their happy fate:

We shall quickly be parsonified,
Conjugally matrimonified
By a doctor of divinity
Who resides in the vicinity.

ueik II: likeness. Gk *eikhon:* image. *icon, iconic; iconoclast; iconolatry. iconostasis:* place in the Greek Orthodox Church where an icon stands. *Veronica* (see *ueg I; uero*). Gk *aikhos:* unseemly. *aecidium:* fruit of a parasitic fungus.

The Semites respect the command to make no graven image of the Lord; Muslim mosques are adorned with admirable Arabic calligraphy.

ueik III: divination. L *victima:* beast for sacrifice; usually the entrails are the source of prophecy. *victim.* Gc *wicca:* wizard; *wicce:* witch. See *ueid. bewitch. wile* and its doublet, *guile. beguile.*

The wiles and guiles that women work,
Dissembled with an outward show,
The tricks and toys that in them lurk
The cock that treads them shall not know.
—Shakespeare(?), *The Passionate Pilgrim* (1599)

ueip, ueib: tremble; move back and forth; wrap around. L *vibrare, vibratum. vibration, vibrate.* It, *vibrato. vibrant. vibraculum.*

Gc, *whip,* from its swing. *whippet:* restless dog. *whippoorwill* is imitative of the bird's call. Possibly Gm *Weib,* E *wife:* the veiled one, from the flutter of the veil in the wind; see *ueg I. hussy* is shortened from *housewife. waif:* something flapping about; hence, a lost article blown by the wind, then a stray child. Also *waive, waiver.* Possibly *weave, wave,* and *waver* (see *uebh*). *wipe,* as with a *wisp:* a bunch of straw used as a wiper. *will-o'-the-wisp:* literally, William with a bunch of straw. *wimple. gimlet.* Fr, *guimpe, gimp, guipure.*

Whenas in silks my Julia goes,
Then, then (methinks) how sweetly flows
The liquefaction of her clothes.
Next, when I cast my eyes and see
That brave vibration each way free,
O how that glittering taketh me!
—Robert Herrick, Vicar of Dean Prior, *Hesperides* (1648)

ueis: slime, rot; strong smell, poison. Hindi, *bish, bikh:* aconite poison. L and E *virus. virulent, viscid, viscosity, viscous. Viscum:* genus, the mistletoe, from the ooze of its *viscin:* birdlime.

Gc, *ooze. wizen:* rot, shrivel; more frequent in the participial form, *wizened. weichselwood.* Perhaps some animals that smell, especially at rutting time; *weasel, wisent, bison.*

Coleridge, in his *Notes and Lectures upon Shakespeare* (1834), speaks of "the corrosive virus which inoculates pride with a venom not its own."

uek(s): speak. Gk (*uepos*) Gk and E *epos, epopee; epic. Calliope:* of the beautiful voice; see *cal.* L *vox, vocis; vocare, vocatum. voice, vox. Vox populi, vox dei:* The voice of the people is the voice of God. Persons that quote this are usually unaware of Alcuin's A.D. 800 letter to Charlemagne: "Those should not be heeded who keep saying the voice of the people is the voice of God, for the riotousness of the crowd is always very close to madness."

viva voce. televox. vocal. semivocal, univocal. equivocal; Fr, *equivoque. irrevocable. vocation, avocation. vocable, vocabulary; vocative. evocative; vociferate, vociferous. vouch, avouch. vowel.* (Between them, *b* and *t* can contain the five vowels, long and short: *bat, bet, bit, bot, but; bait, beat, bite, boat, boot, bout,* and *bought.* Are there any other such consonants? *facetiously* contains all the vowels in forward order; *duoliteral,* in reverse.) *avowal, disavow.* Fr, *avoué. advowee; advowson. advocate, convocate, equivocate; invocate; convoke, evoke, invoke, provoke, revoke,* and their noun forms, *convocation,* etc. *convicium* (in law): reviling.

Gc *ne-uaihts. naught. not. nothing.*

Revelation 1:10: "I was in the Spirit on the Lord's day, and I heard behind me a great voice as of a trumpet." Shelley was in a different spirit when he wrote *Lines . . . Near Naples:* "The city's voice itself is soft, like Solitude."

When Falstaff said, in *1 Henry IV,* i, 2, "'Tis my vocation, Hal; 'tis no sin for a man to labour in his vocation," he was speaking of robbery.

uel I: see. *litmus* (paper) changes to let us see: red with acids, blue with alkalis.

uel II: wish for, will; enjoy. L *velle:* desire; *voluntas:* of one's own will; *voluptas:* delight. *velleity. volition; voluntary. involuntary; volunteer. benevolent; malevolent. nolens volens,* reversed in *willy-nilly (will-ye, nill-ye). voluptuary, voluptuous.*

"From the poetry of Lord Byron they drew a system of ethics compounded of misanthropy and voluptuousness—a system in which the two great commandments were to hate your neighbor and to love your neighbor's wife"—Macaulay, *On Moore's Life of Lord Byron* (1831).

Gc, *well, weal, wealth; commonweal. wallop,* also *gallop:* first, delight in running. *gallant. gala, galanty show; gallivant. gallimaufry:* first, delight in eating. *William:* will to protect.

Joyce, in *Ulysses* (Scylla and Charybdis) (1922), declared: "A man of genius makes no mistakes. His errors are volitional and are the portals of discovery."

uel III: seize, tear, wound; twitch; pluck; hence wool, first torn off by hand; apparently so in Tudor times, for Marlowe's "Come live with me and be my love," among various "delights," promises the maiden

A gown made of the finest wool
Which from our pretty lambs we pull.

(1) Gk, *helot:* an original inhabitant of Laconia, seized by the Spartans; hence, a serf. L *vellere, velsum:* tear; *vulnus, vulneris:* a wound. *vulnerable. invulnerable,* as several legendary heroes—but always with a fatal flaw: for the Greek Achilles, the heel his mother held when she dipped him in the immunizing Styx; for the German Siegfried, a fallen leaf on his shoulder when he bathed in the immunizing blood of the dragon Fafnir, which he had slain; for the Norse god Balder, the mistletoe (see *meigh*). Also *avulsion, convulsion; divulsion, divulsive; evulsion; revulsion. vellicate; vellication:* twitch. *vulsellum:* forceps for tearing. *vulture:* the tearing bird.

Know ye the land where the cypress and myrtle
Are emblems of deeds that are done in their clime?
Where the rage of the vulture, the love of the turtle
Now melt into sorrow, now madden to crime?
—Byron, *The Bride of Abydos*

Gk *lukhos,* L *lupus:* wolf, the tearing animal. *lupine, lycanthropy. lyceum:*

gymnasium where Aristotle taught, so named because adjacent to the Temple of Apollo *Lukheios:* the wolf-slayer.

Gc, *wolf, wolverine. wolfram:* wolf-soot, named in scorn as lessening the extraction of the more valued tin. *wer(e)wolf:* man-wolf. *Adolph:* noble wolf; *Bardolph:* bright wolf; *Randal (Randwulf):* shielding wolf; *Ralph (Radwulf):* counsel wolf. (For a wolf council, see Kipling's *Jungle Book.* Gm *Rat:* council; hence *Rathaus:* city hall; *Ratskeller:* first, tavern in city hall cellar. *Mit Rat und Tat:* By word and deed.) Norse *vair* (*l.r* shift): the slain in battle. *Valhalla:* hall for the mighty slain; *Valkyrie:* chooser of the slain, bearing them to Valhalla; see *medhi.*

(2) Gk *lenos* (*ulenos*), L *lana:* wool. *lanate, lanose, laniferous, lanigerous. flannel. lanolin.* Via Fr, *delaine.* L and E *lanugo:* the down on us at birth. *lanuginous.* L *vellus:* fleece. *velours, velure, velvet. svelte,* as though pulled slender. L and E *villus:* shaggy hair, tuft. *villiform, villocity, villous.*

Gc *wulla. wool, woolen. linsey-woolsey:* first part from *Lindsey,* a sheep-growing village in Suffolk, England; second part partly reduplicative. Being a mixture of coarse wool woven on a cotton warp, *linsey-woolsey* came to be used figuratively of a coarse or confused medley. Thus Shakespeare in *All's Well That Ends Well,* iv, 1. *The Examiner,* no. 532 (1832), condemned "a perking, prurient, linsey-woolsey species of composition" (see *ueid*). *wool-gathering. woolly.*

Bory de St. Vincent (d. 1846) classified mankind by the hair: *leiotrichous:* straight; *cymotrichous:* wavy; and *ulotrichous:* woolly (see *lu 1*).

> And if such as came for wool, sir, went home shorn,
> Where is the wrong I did them?
> —Browning, *Mr. Sludge, the Medium*

uelk: wet. Gc, OE *welk, wilk. wilt. welkin:* cloudy sky. Pistol, in the Boar's Head Tavern with his cronies (*2 Henry IV,* ii, 4), mingle-mangles Marlowe's *Tamburlane:*

> These be good humours, indeed! Shall pack horses,
> And hollow pampered jades of Asia,
> Which cannot go but thirty mile a day,
> Compare with Caesars, and with Cannibals,
> And Trojan Greeks? Nay, rather damn them with
> King Cerberus, and let the welkin roar.

When the welkin is reached, in poetry, it usually rings, resounds, or roars.

uelt: open field; wildwood. Gc, *weald. waldgrave:* count of the forest (Gm *Graf:* count). *weld:* wild plant. *wold. vole:* field mouse. *wilder:* to lose one's way; *bewilder. wild.* Du, *wildebeest. wilderness* is the place of the wild beast (*der* from OE *deor:* animal, whence *deer;* see *dheu I*). Gm, *waldhorn. Tynwald:* legislature of the Isle of Man; assembly in the field (*thing, ting:* assembly, as in *hustings;* see *kel VI*).

uelu: turn, curve; roll; hence enfold, envelop (as Cleopatra in the carpet, to meet Caesar). Gk *alytarch:* chief of police at the ancient Olympic Games, from his round stick. Gk and E *helix. helical, helicopter* (*pteron:* wing): spiral-winged. *Helicon,* tortuous mountain in Boeotia, sacred to the Muses. Gk *eilein:* twist. *Helen* ("the bright one"): literally, a torch made of twisted reeds. The *Hellespont* (so called because *Helle,* daughter of the king of Thebes, drowned there) was the "bridge" (*pontem*) between Europe and Asia, at its narrowest point three-quarters of a mile wide. (Xerxes crossed it in 480 B.C. to invade Greece. Alexander the Great crossed it in the opposite direction in 334 B.C. to conquer the Near East. Troy stood at its southern Asian tip.)

Gk *elutron:* sheath. *elytron; hemielytron:* of insects, the front wings hardened to covers. *ileus:* colic, severely twisting. *inulin. Inula:* genus of the thistle family. *Helenium:* genus, the sneezeweed. *Helonias:* genus of bog herbs. *helminth:* parasitic worm. *anthelmintic; helminthiasis; helminthology; nemahelminth; platyhelminth.*

Gk *loma:* fringe. L *lorum:* thong. *lore:* space between eyes and beak. *lorica, loricate. lorimer:* maker of bits for horses; now mainly a proper name. *Cycloloma:* genus of the goosefoot plant; the wing of the calyx encloses it. *Isoloma:* genus of the gesneria family, with equal fringe. *Tricholoma:* genus, the agarics, hairy-fringed.

L *volvere, volutum:* turn. *volute. volutoid. volt:* turn, in horse management. It, *volti.* Fr, *volte-face. voussoir:* stone in arch. *voluble; volume; voluminous.* For *vale, valley,* see *uals. vault:* arch; *vault:* jump over; *vaulting. volar:* of the palm of the hand, cupped, as to hold water. *valve:* first, leaf of a folding door. *bivalve. valvulae; valvate. volva:* cuplike base of fungi. *volvulus:* twisted intestine. *vulva. Volvox:* genus of flagellates. *valgus:* bowlegged. *circumvolution, convolution, convolve; devolve; devolution; evolve, evolution,* etc. *involve; involute. involucre* (for *filthy lucre,* see *lau*). *involvement. intervolve; obvolute. revolve, revolver; revolt, revolution,* etc.

Gc, *well:* bubble up (Gm *Welle*: wave); from the past tense *welled* came *weld. wale, weal:* mark of blow on flesh. *wallow, welter.* Probably *willow,* from its flexible twigs. *OED* gives 4 columns to *willow,* including 51 compounds, as *willow grouse; willow beauty:* an insect.

From time immemorial the willow has been used as a symbol of sorrow and loss. An old English ditty is sung pathetically and prophetically by Desdemona in Shakespeare's *Othello* (1605), iv, 3: "Sing all a green willow must be my garland." W. S. Gilbert puts it to comically pathetic use in *The Mikado* (1885), ii, when Ko-Ko sings:

On a tree by a river a little tom-tit
Sang willow, titwillow, titwillow . . .

The more practical Benjamin Franklin, in *Poor Richard's Almanack* (1754), pointed out: "Willows are weak, but they bind the faggot."

walk; waltz (Fr, *valse*). *whelk:* spiral-shelled mollusk. *wallet;* one might still refer to paper money in one's pocket as one's roll.

Macbeth (i, 7), pondering the pathway to the throne, tells himself

I have no spur
To prick the sides of my intent, but only
Vaulting ambition, which o'erleaps itself,
And falls on the other.

uem: expectorate; vomit. Gk *emein. emetic. OED* defines 8 associated words. Used figuratively, as by Dickens in *The Uncommercial Traveler* (1860): "sneaking Calais, prone behind its bar, invites emetically to despair."

L *vomere, vomitum. vomitive; vomit. vomit grass,* to which dogs turn for its emetic power. *OED* defines 15 associated words. *vomito:* virulent yellow fever. *vomitory:* (1) a pill or potion to induce vomiting; (2) more usually in the Latin form *vomitorium,* and always found in the plural, *vomitoria,* what Gibbon makes clear in *The Decline and Fall of the Roman Empire* (1776): "Sixty-four vomitories (for by that name the doors were very aptly distinguished) poured forth the immense multitude"–as at stadia after football games today. See *ar I.*

Marlowe, in *Dr. Faustus* (produced ca. 1588), illustrates the contemporary belief in astrology in Faustus's anguished regret at having sold his soul to the Devil:

You stars that reigned at my nativity,
Whose influence hath allotted death and hell,
Now draw up Faustus like a foggy mist
Into the entrails of yon labouring cloud,
That when you vomit forth into the air
My limbs may issue from your smoky mouth,
So that my soul may but ascend to heaven.

uen: to desire; strive after. This root sprouted words along two paths of primitive man's needs: hunting and sex (in earliest times, perhaps not far apart).

(1) Hunting, with early man, was of course not a pastime, but a necessity, to obtain food. Skr *vanija. banian:* Hindu trader in skins, etc; hence *banyan tree,* under which traders traditionally gathered. Possibly also *bandar,* as in Kipling's *Jungle Books,* and *wanderoo:* monkey of the forest. L *venari, venatum:* hunt; *venator:* hunter. *venatic, venery, venison.* Slav, *vaivode, voivode:* hunter; then army leader. Gc, *gain, regain. rowen.*

(2) L *Venus, Veneris,* goddess of desire and beauty (Greek Aphrodite), to whom Paris awarded the golden apple that doomed Troy; her girdle was an infallible warranty of love. *Venice* originally meant city of the beloved. *Venice treacle:* a supposed panantidote for poisons, a mithridate; see *sta. Venetian glass* was supposed to break into shivers if poison was poured in; today it is highly prized, and its manufacture is still a tourist attraction.

As the word *potion* led to *poison,* so L *venenum:* love potion, led to *venom*—possibly from the frequent results of drinking one; possibly from the observation that hell hath no fury like a woman scorned, when it doesn't work. Hence *venomous, venin, envenom. Venus* is the second planet from the sun; its supposed inhabitants would etymologically be *Venerians;* but science-fiction writers prefer to call them *Venusians.* The goddess has also given her name to various plants and animals, as *Venus's bath, Venus's flower basket, Venus's-flytrap, Venus's hair, Venus's looking-glass; OED* lists 33 names. *mound of Venus* has one meaning in palmistry, another in anatomy.

Slav, *Wend, Wanda. Vanir,* Norse god of fertility. *Vanadis,* a name of Freya, Norse goddess of love; whence *vanadium* (see *el 23*); *vanadinite, vanadous,* etc.

C'est Vénus tout entière à sa proie attachée.—Racine, *Phèdre* (1677).

uendh: turn, wind; wanderer. Gc, *wend,* and the *Wends.* The past tense of *wend* was *went,* which has been preserved as the past tense of *go. wind* (long *i*), also *wynd:* alley. *wand:* flexible rod. *wander; wanderlust. windlestraw:* dry stalk of grass. Du, *wentletrap:* winding stairs; seasnail with a spiral shell. *Vandal* (earlier *Wandal*): wanderer. The *Penny Cyclopedia* (1842) said the Teutonic Vandals "are often confounded with the Wends." The Vandals reached Spain; hence *Andalusia* (LL *Vandalicia*); first found there was aluminum silicate, thence called *andalusite.* The Vandals under Genseric sacked Rome in 455; they held Carthage for 94 years.

Time and again fiction has triumphed over fact. Aristophanes' picture helped destroy Socrates. Shakespeare's Richard III defies historians. So it was with the Vandal; Dryden in 1694 presented the common notion that

Goths and Vandals, a rude Northern race,
Did all the matchless monuments deface.

Thus, in *OED, vandalic, vandalistic, vandalism, vandalize:* "recklessly or ruthlessly destructive of anything beautiful or venerable." Against this stands the *Encyclopaedia Britannica* (1888 ed.): "There does not seem to be, in the story of the capture of Rome by the Vandals, any justification for the charge of wilful and objectless destruction of public buildings." Time and neglect wrought ruin; the Vandals are blamed.

uer I: high, raised; a swelling. Gk *aerein:* raise. *aorta:* literally, that which is hung. *endaorta. arsis* (see below). *artery, arterial; arteriosclerosis,* etc. Related to Gk *aera:* air, as in *aeroplane,* etc.; see *ue. meteor* when in the air; *meteorite* when it reaches earth (the ending *ite,* in mineralogy, signifies stone).

L and E *verrusa* (also *verruga*): wart. *verrusous. serious:* elevated. Gm, *wart. warble:* wartlike growth on horses or cattle, from the larva of what is therefore called the *warble fly.* The trilling *warble* is partly related to *whirl,* partly imitative.

The word *arsis* turned *arsy-varsy.* In early prosody, it was associated with the rising hand or foot in beating time, hence an unaccented syllable; in Late Latin it became linked with the rising voice, hence the accented syllable. Its converse, *thesis,* correspondingly means the accented syllable, and vice versa.

uer II: turn, spin, twist, wind; rub (as turning a twig in tinder to beget a flame); hence also twig, rod. This root developed a number of extensions as the basic meaning spread.

(1) *uerb(h), uerp:* turn, sew together. Skr, *rupa:* form (spun into being). Gk *rhabdos:* rod. *rhabdomancy:* divination with a rod; especially for water, minerals, etc. *OED* lists 13 words beginning *rhabdo* and details 11 relevant words. *rhapsody. Rhapis:* genus, the fan palm. Nasalized, *rhombus. Rhamnus:* genus, the buckthorn. *Raphiolepis:* genus, the hawthorn.

Gk *rhopalos:* club. From its shape, gradually thickening, E *rhopalic:* of successive words, each a letter or a syllable longer than the one before; and *rhopalic verses,* each a foot longer, as Herrick's *Wishes for His Supposed Mistress* (each stanza repeating the pattern):

Whoe'er she be,
That not impossible she
That shall command my heart and me . . .

L *verbera:* rods, whips. *verberation, reverberate. verbena, vervain;* holy rods, from the sacred laurel, were used to strike a bargain or conclude a treaty. Gc, *warp.*

(2) *uerg.* L *vergere:* turn, bend. *virga:* young shoot; hence *virgin.* (Similarly, Gk *talea:* rod, came to mean nubile maiden.) The constellation *Virgo,* sixth sign of the zodiac; see *guei. Virginia:* colony of the virgin queen, etc. *virgate, virgulate. virgule:* comma (little curved rod). *verge:* first, rod as a sign of office, as carried by a *verger;* then, *within the verge:* within the limits of authority; hence *verge* as border, edge. *converge, diverge.* Gc (nasalized), *wrench, wrinkle.* See also *uerg,* discussed below as a separate root.

(3) *uergh:* twist. Gc, *worry;* this was first physical, meaning to strangle, to seize by the throat, as might a dog or a wolf. Nasalized, *wrangle, wring. wrong:* twisted. (Similarly, *tort:* legal term for a wrong, came via L *tortum:* twisted; whence also *torture:* first, twisting the arm behind the back; also *tortuous* and *torturous.*)

"Live long enough, and you'll eventually be wrong about everything"–Russell Baker, *New York Times Magazine,* 27 Feb. 1983.

(4) *uerm.* L *vermis:* worm (which *does* turn). *vermiculated. vermeil, vermilion:* dye and color from the cochineal "worm." *vermicelli. vermiform (appendix). OED* has over 14 columns of associated words, from *Vermes:* worm division of

the animal kingdom, to *vermouth:* wormwood. *vermin;* its variant, *varmint,* is a cowboy's term of contempt for a meek greenhorn. Gc, *worm.*

(5) *uert:* turn, spin. See *tereq.* L *vertere, versum.* L and E *vertex. vortex* (plural *vortices*). *vortiginous. vorticism:* the whirlabout artistic school that preferred vortices to cubes. It has been suggested that by metathesis, *uert* becoming *uret,* the prefixes *re* and *retro* were formed; see *re.*

verse, verset, versicle, versify, version. well-versed. versatile. "Anyone may be an honourable man, and yet write verse badly"—Molière, *Le Misanthrope* (1666), iv. *versicolor. verso. vice versa. versus,* abbreviated *vs. vertical,* contrasted with *horizontal,* from Gk *horizein:* to divide; *horos:* boundary, limit; whence also *horizon.* "Both man and woman bear pain and sorrow (and, for aught I know, pleasure) best in a horizontal position"—Laurence Sterne.

Here also, *prose* (via Fr) from L *proversus:* turn ahead, which does not turn with the meter, as does verse, but turns at the end of the line. *prosaic.* (*prosody* is of different origin, *pro* and Gk *oide:* song, as in tragedy, etc.) Arthur Clutton-Brock explains why it is hard to quote good prose. Read "The Defects of English Prose," in his *More Essays on Books* (1921).

Also *vertigo. vertebra, vertebrate, invertebrate; Vertebrata:* animals with a spinal column, which permits the head to turn. *vervel. diverticulum. dextrorse, extrorse, introrse, retrorse; sinistrorse:* counterclockwise. *quaquaversal:* turning every which way, as some geological strata, and flighty minds. *tergiversation:* turning one's back. Possibly *dorsal, dorsum; doss house, dossal, dosser, dossier. adverse, adversary, adversity.*

Sweet are the uses of adversity,
Which like the toad, ugly and venomous,
Wears yet a precious jewel in his head;
And this our life, exempt from public haunt,
Finds tongues in trees, books in the running brooks,
Sermons in stones, and good in everything.
—*As You Like It,* ii, 1

Byron, in *Don Juan,* xii, 50, mentions one "sweet use": "Adversity is the first path to truth."

Also *advertise:* turn attention to. *animadvert. anniversary. averse, aversion. avert. conversant; conversation, converse, convert; controversy. divers, diverse; diversion. divert;* Fr, *divertissement* (see *per II*). *divorce; divorcé, divorcee. evert; extrovert, introvert. inadvertent. inverse, invert. malversation. obverse, obvert. perverse, perversion, pervert.* "Not versions but perversions": St. Jerome thus dismissed translations of the Bible before his own, the Latin Vulgate (for "the vulgar," the common man), A.D. 382–405. *vertilago. retroversion; reverse, reversion, revert.*

Is there no bright reversion in the sky
For those who greatly think, or bravely die?
—Pope, *Elegy to . . . an Unfortunate Lady*

subversive, subvert. transverse, traverse. universal, universe, university. OED has 16 columns of relevant words beginning *vers,* over 13 columns of *vert* words, and 3 columns of words beginning *vort.* The Roman god of the changing year was *Vertumnus;* his festival, on August 13, was celebrated when fruit was turning ripe. *suzerain* came via Fr *souvrain:* literally, turned upward; thence also *sovereign:* the one above, its ending changed to match *reign;* see *upo.*

Russ, *verst.* Gc, *worth, worthless, worthwhile, worthy.* For the *Nine Worthies,* see *neun. wurst, liverwurst.* The suffix *ward,* as *inward, outward, toward, upward;* also with nouns, as in *heavenward, homeward, seaward, southward, wayward. unstraightforward.* JWalker lists 28 such *ward* words, and 8 *wards,* as *backwards.*

weird: first, the way fate turns, as in the expression *to dree one's weird:* to endure one's fate–used by Langland, Gower, and Chaucer; then mainly in Scotland, until Sir Walter Scott, in *The Heart of Midlothian* (1818), brought it back to general use in English. The "Weird sisters" as in Macbeth, were the three Norns, who spun human destiny; folkchange brought the meaning of weird to *uncanny.*

(6) *ureik:* turn back and forth; brush. Gk *erikha:* heath, underscrub; used for brushes. *Ericaceae, Erica:* family and genus, heath. *Hypericaceae, Hypericum:* family and genus, St.-John's-wort, literally (*hypo*) under heath. Perhaps OFr *guietre:* instep, E *gaiter.* Via It, *brusque:* first, a butcher's broom, and its doublet, *brisk. briar.*

> There grows a bonny brier bush in our kail yard.
> –James Hogg, *Jacobite Relics* (1819)

Gc, *wry; wriggle; wrist,* which permits the hand to turn.

(7) *ureip:* spin, rub. This root generates heat, which may be turned sexward; hence Gc *riban:* to be wanton; E *ribald, ribaldry. euripus:* first, the narrow strait separating the largest Greek island, Euboea, from Magnesia in Thessaly, noted for its fierce, whirling currents; hence, any strait of violent currents (which rub the shore). Also used figuratively, as in the *Pall Mall Gazette,* 16 Feb. 1884: "Although all nations are nowadays more or less unquiet, Paris seems to be in a very euripus of change."Aristotle said that the air in the upper parts of houses *ueripizes:* whirls about.

(8) *ureit:* twist, twine around. *wreath, wreathe. wrath, wroth; writhe.*

(9) *uremb.* Probably *rump,* which moves back and forth, especially as young women walk. Possibly *rumple, rimple; ramp, rampant* (in heraldry, on the hind legs); *romp.*

(10) *urizd.* Gc, *wrest, wrestle.*

> Weave the warp, and weave the woof,
> The winding-sheet of Edward's race.
> Give ample room, and verge enough
> The characters of hell to trace.
> –Gray, *The Bard* (1757); based on the tradition that when Edward I conquered Wales, he ordered the execution of all Welsh bards. The poem closes with a "prophecy" of the glories of the poets under the House of Tudor.

uer III: find. Gk *heuriskein:* heuristic. *Eureka!:* I have found it!, Archimedes' cry as he ran naked from the bath, having hit upon the principle of buoyancy, which enabled him to tell whether the gold crown of his king, Hieron II of Syracuse, contained any baser metal. By the aptronymic pattern of legend, *Archimedes* means chief watcher; see *arkh.*

uer IV: watch for, watch out for; guard; perceive. Gk *Arcturus:* bear guard; see *ger V; rkthos. ephor. panorama.* L, *revere; reverence* (see *sirreverence,* under *sal I*). Gc, *ward, warden, warder, guard, guardian; rear guard. rearward, wardrobe. Edward:* guard of wealth. *steward, award, reward. wary, aware, beware.*

Shakespeare has the Chorus open act ii of *Henry V* with the announcement of England's invasion of France:

Now all the youth of England are on fire,
And silken dalliance in the wardrobe lies;
Now thrive the armourers . . .

Thoreau, in *Walden* (1854), admonishes: "Beware of all enterprises that require new clothes."

uer V: cover. L *operire. operculum. aperire:* uncover, open. *aperient, aperitive; aperture.* Via Fr, *overt, overture. pert, malapert.* OFr, *garment, garnish, garniture. garret; garrison* and its doublet, *warison.* Gc, *warn; warren. warrant(y), guarantee. weir.*

Go, soul, the body's guest,
Upon a thankless arrant:
Fear not to touch the best,
The truth shall be thy warrant.
—Sir Walter Ralegh, *The Lie*

uer VI: speak. Skr *vratam:* vow. Gk *eirein,* E *irony. rhematic. rhetor, rhetorical. rhetorical question:* one that insinuates its answer into the listener's mind, e.g., the questions posed by Brutus in Shakespeare's play (iii, 2) after the assassination of Caesar: "Who is here so base that would be a bondman? . . ."

L *verbum* (see *sap*). *verb, adverb. proverb. verbose.* Gc *word, word lore. OED* gives 13 columns to *word* and such combinations as *word of honor, word-of-mouth; the last word* (a feminine prerogative); *a word and a blow; word-for-word*—then details 16 *words*, from *wordage* to *wordy.* Also, *What's the good word?* See the Bible, John 1:1.

Disraeli called Gladstone (four times prime minister) "a sophistical rhetorician, inebriated with the exuberance of his own verbosity." (Insults were polished in Queen Victoria's days.) Wycherley, in *The Plain Dealer* (1676), caustically observed: "Fair words butter no cabbage"—though the more frequent vegetable was served by Scott in *The Legend of Montrose*, 3: "There is a southern proverb, fine words butter no parsnips." Emerson, in *The Poet* (1844), neatly observed: "Each word was at first a stroke of genius."

uer VII: water. See *aue.* Gk, *urea, ureta, urethra, uretic, uric (acid, oxide). diuretic. enuresis. OED* details *dysuria, ischuria,* and lists 9 *-uria* words, as *albuminuria, glucosuria.* L, *urinary, urine. OED* lists 43 relevant *ur* words; 9 *urino* words, as *urinoscopist;* and 15 words beginning *uro,* as *urogenital, urology, uropoietic;* but note also *uro-:* tail, as *uropygial;* thus also *cynosure* and *squirrel. aurochs* is the wet ox.

u(e)rad: branch, root. See *rad II.* Gk *rhiza:* root. *rhizome. rhizophagous. OED* lists 24 and details 11 words beginning *rhiz(o). coleorhiza; mycorrhiza. licorice, liquorice* (Gk *glukurrhiza:* sweet root; folkchanged to approach L *liquor*). L *radix, radicem:* root. *race:* mainly ginger root. *radish, radix; radicle. deracinate.* A *radical* is one that wants to get at the roots of evils, to eradicate them. In a broadcast of 25 Oct. 1929, Franklin Delano Roosevelt (the only U.S. president to serve three terms) declared, with little more wit than wisdom: "A radical is a man with both feet planted firmly in the air."

L and E *ramus:* branch. *ramage, ramiform; ramifications; ramify. ramose, ramulose; rampion.* Gc, *root. rutabaga. mangel-wurzel. wort; bitterwort, lustwort, sneezewort, spearwort;* JWalker lists 20 such words.

square root needs no explanation. The *cube root* of *125* is *5.* The *fourth root* of *81* is *3*. A *digital root* is determined by adding the digits of a number, adding again until only one digit remains; it has no practical use that I know of, save in some forms of numerology. The digital root of a man born 8/19/1893 is *3*. And *3* is the luckiest number. Next is 7. The two limits, *1* and *9*, are unlucky; the others are varyingly neutral. Figure out your luck.

(u)er(e)dh: grow properly. Skr, *vriddhi:* vowel increase, in Indian grammar. Gk *orthos:* straight, right. *orthodox* (see *dek*). *orthoepy; orthography. orthopedics. orthotropian:* tendency of plants to grow vertically. *orthoptera:* straight-winged; order of insects including the grasshopper and the cockroach. *OED* lists 19 words and details 11 columns of words beginning *orth(o). orthostichous* (see *steig*). *orthocephalic:* a skull the breadth of which is 3/4 to 4/5 of its length; between *brachycephalic* (short) and *dolichocephalic* (long). From L *arduus:* high, *arduous.* For *hetero,* see *sem I.*

Sir Daniel Wilson, in *Archaeology . . . of Scotland* (1851), observed: "I have met with brachycephalic Scots." *Nil mortalibus ardui est:* No height too arduous for mortal men.—Horace, *Odes,* 37.

uerg: work; do. Gk *(u)ergon. erg, ergon. ergograph. ergosphere* is the energy-producing layer (not yet confirmed) of the black hole; see *kel VI. energy; energumen; ergasia. exergue. allergy. alurgite:* wrought by the sea. *anergy* (*a* negative). *adrenergic, cholinergic.*

surgeon (earlier *chirurgeon*): literally, hand worker; see *gher IV. surgery. demiurge. dramaturgy. liturgy. zymurgy. thaumaturge:* worker of wonders; *theurgy:* divine work, magic. *George:* earth worker; *georgic. synergetic, synergist. synergism:* (1) working together, e.g., drugs; (2) the doctrine that human will and divine grace must work together for salvation. *telergy,* the force behind telekinesis and telepathy. (*telepathy* was coined in 1882 by Frederic W. H. Myers.)

Gk *organon:* tool. *organ; organicism; organism. organon. orgasm. orgy. Panurge:* ready to do anything; companion of *Pantagruel:* ready to gobble anything. "All is grist that comes to the mill," according to Rabelais.

Gc, *work. clockwork, earthwork, handiwork, overwork;* JWalker lists 16 such words. *irksome. bulwark* (*bole:* tree trunk). *boulevard:* first, the work of fortifying. *breastworks, fireworks. wright,* as in *cartwright, playwright, wheelwright. wrought.*

The boy responds to the doctor, Celeberrimus, in Abraham Tucker's 1768 *The Light of Nature Pursued* (chapter on vision): "I can easily understand how any tract of land or water can become an organism. I remember, when I was a stripling, the vast Pacific Ocean, commonly, yea vulgarly, not to say newspaperically, nor yet teatabellically, called, appellated, and as the saying is, annominated the South Sea, was made an engine, I mean organism, to pick people's pockets, and ruin half the nation." (When George I in 1718 became governor of the South Sea Company, which was organized to trade, mainly in slaves, with Spanish America, interest soared, ministers took bribes—and in 1720 the South Sea Bubble burst.)

This noble ensample to his sheep he yaf,
That first he wroghte, and afterward he taughte.
—Chaucer, *The Canterbury Tales,* prologue of *The Parson's Tale*

And constancy lives in realms above,
And life is thorny, and youth is vain;
And to be wroth with one we love
Doth work like madness in the brain.
—Coleridge, *Christabel,* ii

uero: true; pledge, promise; hence fidelity; kindness. L *verus. aver. veracious, veracity, verity; verify; verism.* E *verisimilitude,* Fr *vraisemblance. veridical; verdict* (see *deik*). *Veronica* (see *ueg I*). *voir dire:* oath of a witness to speak the truth. *veratrine:* chemical that causes sneezing, which was long taken as a sign that what one says is true. *very,* as in *the very one:* truly, has lapsed into a general intensive. *Varangians:* Northmen who "pledged faith" and founded a Russian dynasty; they had been rovers and pirates; later (Anglo-Saxons and Danes) they became the faithful bodyguards of the Byzantine emperors.

heortology: study of festivals (the first syllable meaning kindness). *severe* (*se:* apart): absence of kindness; *severity. asseverate. persevere:* first, to be very strict. Gc, *warlock;* see *leugh.*

Of the countless remarks about truth, let three men's words suffice. Lowell, in *The Present Crisis,* pictures

Truth forever on the scaffold, Wrong forever on the throne,

but implies its relativity:

New occasions teach new duties; Time makes ancient good uncouth;
They must upward still, and onward, who would keep abreast of truth.

T. H. Huxley, in *Science and Culture,* indicates its course: "It is the customary fate of new truths to begin as heresies and to end as superstitions." Its basic value is urged by Robert Bridges, in his *Hymn of Nature:*

Gird on thy sword, O man, thy strength endue,
In fair desire thine earth-born joy renew.
Live thou thy life beneath the making sun
Till Beauty, Truth, and Love in thee are one.

uers: sweep, stir up confusion; strife. L *averruncate* (*a* negative); *verriculate; verricule.* Fr *guerre:* war; Sp and E, *guerrilla.* Gc, *war, worse, worst.* "War doesn't prove who is right, only who is left."

The isles of Greece, the isles of Greece!
Where burning Sappho loved and sung,
Where grew the arts of war and peace,
Where Delos rose, and Phoebus sprung!
Eternal summer gilds them yet,
But all, except their sun, is set.
—Byron, *Don Juan,* iii

ues I: linger, dwell; parts of the verb *to be.* Skr *bustee:* village slum. Gk *Hestia,* goddess of the hearth; Roman *Vesta,* with the *vestal virgins.* Gk *astu:* city; hence *astute,* as contrasted with the ways of the countryman come to town, a *cony* (in the country, the city fellow is a *greenhorn*). *asteism:* polite and ingenious mockery, as sought by the *New Yorker*–Noel Coward would-be sophisticates, typified in the legend of Alexander Woollcott as presented in George S. Kaufman and Moss Hart's play *The Man Who Came to Dinner* (1934)—who calls his nurse "Miss Bedpan," and would greet an actress "Miss Cast."

Norse *vesa* (imperative *ves*): be; E *wassail:* Be hale! Gc, *was, were.*

ues II: clothe. L *vestis:* garment. *vest, vestment, vesture; vestry:* where the clergy don their priestly garb. *investiture. devest, divest; invest, investment; reinvest. revest. revet. transvestite. travesty,* as "a travesty of justice." Gc, *wear.*

ue(s)n: sell. L *vendere, venditum. venalis:* for sale. *venal:* with soul for sale. *vend, vendor, vendible; vendition; vendue.*

uesper: evening. (The first element, *ue:* down, is drawn from the setting sun.) Gk *Hesper(os),* L *Vesper:* evening star. *hesperian. Hesperides:* daughters of the west; in Greek mythology, the three nymphs that guarded the golden apples in a garden at the western extreme of the known world.

vespers. vespertine: at the farthest end of daylight from *matutine, matutinal,* from *Matuta,* Roman goddess of dawn; the *t* in *vespertine* follows the pattern of the dawn word; see *ma I. Vespertilionidae, Vespertilio:* family and genus of bats, twilight fliers. Via OIt *vispistrello* came E *pipistril,* a tiny bat. *OED* has 13 *vesper* entries.

Gc, *west, western, westerly.* The *Visigoths* were the western Goths.

Up lads! For Vesper comes; to waiting eyes
Upon Olympus Vesper lifts his ray.
—Catullus, *Carmen,* lxii

ue(s)r: Spring. L *ver. vernal, vernant, vernation.* Via Sp, *verano:* the dry season in Latin America. *primaveral.* On the Mexican *primavera tree* the flowers appear early, like a yellow cloud, before the leaves; also known as *white mahogany,* the wood is a favorite in cabinet-making. Four genera of plants begin with this spring root: *Aruncus, Eranthemum, Eranthis; Eryngium,* one of which is an *eryngo.*

uet: year; hence both yearling and one of many years. Gk *etos:* year. *etesian:* annual wind currents, as on the Aegean. *trieteric:* once every three years, like some ancient festivals. L *vetus, veterem:* old. *veteran, inveterate. veterinarian; veterinary:* first, of old animals; abbreviated *vet.*

L *vitulus:* yearling. *veal, vellum. vitulary, vituline. vitellus:* literally, little calf; yolk of the egg. Hence *vitellarium, vitelligenous. vitellin:* protein in yolk. Gc, *wether, bellwether.*

The *Spectator* of 25 Mar. 1882 spoke of "the gregariousness and bellwetherishness of the English people, who must all do the same thing at once." Not only the English . . .

ugu, ud: moist; sprinkle. Gk *hugros:* damp. *hygrometer, hygroscope. hygrophobia:* a revulsion from liquids, especially wine or water, should be distinguished from the disease *hydrophobia;* see *aue. OED* lists 10 and details 13 *hygr(o)* words. *hygroma:* wet tumor.

L (*ugu-mr, umere*), *humere:* be wet. (The *h* in these words is a folk addition, from *humus:* earth, source of fresh water.) *humectant, humid, humidity; humour* (see below). L *udus:* wet. *udograph, udometer.* L *uliginis:* moisture. *uliginous, uliginose. Ulex:* genus, the furze. From Gc *uhso, ox, aurochs* (see *uer VII*). *wake:* trail of a ship; originally (ONorse) water seen through a hole in the ice; also used figuratively, of an after effect: *in its wake.*

In ancient and medieval thought, one's temperament was determined by the admixture of the four bodily *humours* (: moistures)—*blood:* sanguine; *phlegm:* phlegmatic; Gk, *choler,* L, *bile:* choleric, bilious; and *melancholy* (*black bile*): melancholic, atrabilious. Hence a man who could overcome the dominance of his humour (said Johann Lavater in his *Aphorisms on Man* [1788], 609—which William Blake admired and annotated) was to be venerated: "the sanguine who has checked volatility and rage for pleasure; the choleric who has subdued passion and pride; the phlegmatic emerged from indolence; and the melancholy who has dismissed avarice, suspicion, and asperity."

Like other words that cover a range, a polarity—e.g., *temper, temperature*—*humor* has moved toward one end; while we may speak of a person as being in a bad humor, the word usually implies good; hence *humorous, humorist.* Thus, too, *curiosity:* "*a* curiosity" is an oddity, like a two-headed rooster or three-dimensional chess; but curiosity, while it "killed a cat," makes man persevere, climb Mount Everest, seek the Loch Ness monster, split the atom. First the curiosity, then perhaps the use.

J. Hayward in 1632 spoke of "a noble and solid curiosity of knowing things in their beginnings"—which, I make bold to say, impelled the preparation of this book. But Horatio Smith, 200 years later, wrote: "curiosity—looking over other people's affairs, and overlooking our own." *OED* gives 18 major meanings of *curious,* and adds this note: "The only senses now really current are 5, 16, and (in some applications) 9." The original sense of both noun and adjective implied taking great care; see *cura.*

The *temper* words—*temperature,* measured first by the pulse count; *temperance, temperate, temporal, temporary, temporize,* etc.—all hinge upon a balance or *tempering:* mixing ("God tempers the wind to the shorn lamb"; not from the Bible, but in Laurence Sterne's *A Sentimental Journey* [1768]), and all spring from L *tempus, temporis:* time (see *temp*). We are told that *tempus fugit:* time flies. Take your time—while you have it.

Sterne also said, in *Tristram Shandy:* "As we jog on, either laugh with me, or at me, or in short do anything—only keep your temper." So be it as you read on.

In all thy humours, whether grave or mellow,
Thou'rt such a touchy, testy, pleasant fellow,
Hast so much wit, and mirth, and spleen about thee,
There is no living with thee, or without thee.
—Addison, *The Spectator,* no. 68 (1711)

ui(d): split in half. This root itself split. Thus it means apart, hence separate, individual; but also "in two," two parts together; which, again, may be joined in friendship and cooperation, or facing in opposition. Thus *with* may mean either working together, or working against, as in *withstand* (see below). *guerdon:* first, a return gift (see *do*).

In the sense of individual: Skr, *vihara:* place apart, for Buddha; hence, temple, monastery. *vimana:* temple tower. Gk (*uidios*), *idios. idiot, idiotic, idiocy. idiolect. idiom, idiomatic. idiosyncrasy* (Gk *khrasis:* mixture).

In the sense of two parts asunder—Skr *visarga:* breath at the end of a word. *pachisi* (*vimsati:* 20; *pancha:* 5; see *penkue*): the highest throw is 25. From Gk *eikhosi,* L *viginti:* two tens, *icosahedron. vicenary, vicennial, vigesimal.* Port, *vintem:* coin worth 20 reis.

In the sense of split, hence faulty—L and E *vitiligo:* blemish. With moral application, L *vitium. vice, vicious, vitiate; vitiosity. vituperation* (see *per V*).

Gc, *wide, width. with* in the sense of together has replaced (Gm *mit*) OE *mid,* which remains in *midwife, amid, amidst, middle.* Never meddle in the middle of a muddle. *with* in the sense of against is mainly obsolete; it remains in *withhold, withstand; widdershins (withershins):* direction against the apparent movement of the sun (see *sent*). *withers:* the "resisting" part of a horse, the back between the shoulder blades. *OED* gives 17 columns to the development of the word *with;* it lists 31 obsolete compounds, as *withdrive:* repel; and it details 19 more compounds, most of them obsolete, as *withgang:* success; *witherwin:* an adversary, especially God's adversary, the Devil. Lest we blame the Devil too often, Hannah More, in *Moses* (1782), shrewdly points out:

Did not God
Sometimes withhold in mercy what we ask,
We should be ruined at our own request.

uidhu: tree. L *Gallus:* a Gaul, man of the forest. *Gallia* was the name of France in ancient times, when it was mainly wildwood; Julius Caesar's history of his wars begins *Gallia est omnis divisa in partes tres:* all Gaul is divided into three parts. *gallicism,* etc. *gallium* (see *el 31*). *galosh* is from *solea Gallica:* Gallic sandal. LL *gallicula* (folkchanged from *caligula*): military boot. From his constantly wearing *caligulae,* Roman Emperor Gaius Caesar became known as *Caligula.* Succeeding his uncle Tiberius in A.D. 37, he ruled moderately for a year, then became ill, probably insane, and reveled in torture and bloodshed until his assassination in A.D. 41. He made his horse a consul. His best-known remark was the exclamation, "Would that the Roman people had but one neck!"

Welsh *gwydd:* wildwood. *Gael:* man of the wildwood. *Goidelic:* of the Gaelic language. Gm, *wood.*

"Raise the stone, there shalt thou find me; cleave the wood and there am I"—*Sayings of Our Lord* (1897), Logion v, 23.

?uio: violet. Gk *ion:* violet. *ioeides:* violetlike. *iodine,* from the color of its vapor (see *el 52*). *iodide; iodism,* etc. *iolite. iodine* and *chloroform* fused to make *iodoform. Violaceae, Viola:* family and genus, the violet. From the flower's often being hidden beneath the leaves comes the figurative use *shrinking violet,* likely to be a *wallflower:* a lass who waits by the wall for an invitation while the other girls are dancing around the ballroom—unless mothers sic their sons because of the social or financial standing of the girl's parents. (*sic* here is a form of *Seek!* used to loose a dog upon its prey: *Seek him!*)

> Blue! gentle cousin of the forest-green,
> Married to green in all the sweetest flowers,
> Forget-me-not, the bluebell, and that Queen
> Of secrecy, the violet.
> —Keats, *Sonnet, Blue* (1818)

uiro: man, and the vital force in man. L *vis, vim* (plural, *vires*): force; *violare, violatum:* treat with force. *vim. violate, violation, violence, inviolate.* L *vir:* man. *virile, virilescence, virility. virtual, virtuosity. virtuous, virtu.* For over a thousand years, until Queen Victoria died, *virtue* in a man meant courage, honor; in an unmarried woman, virginity ("She maintained her virtue"); in a married woman, fidelity. Now, except for the merely mechanical phrase *in virtue of,* the word seems almost archaic. Quite obsolete is the verb *evirtuate:* to exercise one's manly qualities toward a worthy goal. *virago:* a woman usurping the role of a man. *Triumvirate* (see *tre*); *duumvir, decemvir,* etc. *evirate:* deprive of manhood; *eviration.*

Quirinus, Sabine god of war, whom the conquering Romans fused with Mars, although later he was associated with Romulus. The *Quirinal,* the Sabine home, was the one of the seven hills of Rome that became the seat of government. *Quirites:* all the Roman men; originally the men of the Sabine town Cures, which Rome absorbed. *Cures* is from *co(m):* together, and *vires:* men; thence *curia, curial.* E *cry* is shortened from L *quiritare:* cry out, originally, an appeal to the Roman people for help or justice. *decry, decrial; descry.*

Gc *wer(e)wolf.* Via Fr, *loup-garou:* man into wolf (see *ulkuo*). *wergeld:* man-money, payment, usually for homicide, amount determined by the rank of the victim, in lieu of other penalty. Also the *world,* wherein man functions (Gc *wer:* man, and *aldh,* as in *elders*).

> The world is too much with us; late and soon,
> Getting and spending, we lay waste our powers:
> Little we see in Nature that is ours;

We have given our hearts away, a sordid boon!
—Wordsworth, *Sonnet*

How many would, with Swinburne (*Dolores*),

change in a trice
The lilies and languors of virtue
For the raptures and roses of vice!

ul: howl. Imitative. L *ululare, ululatum. ululate, ululation.* Gc, *owl, owlet, owlish. howl.* Via Fr, *howlet.* In some dialects, as of northern New York farmers, *hoot owl* becomes *hoodle. hoot* is also imitative; thence *hue (and cry).*

In the 16th c. grew the legend of Till *Ulenspiegel* (: Owlglass), a peasant trickster who outwitted the narrow, condescending townsmen and the complacent clergy; his stories in English translation, 1560, were widely popular. Ben Jonson pictured

A Howleglass
On his father's ass;
With owl on fist
And glass on wrist—

and in *The Poetaster,* iii, 1, exclaimed:

What, do you laugh,
Howleglass! You perstemptuous varlet!

In 1867 Charles de Coster wrote *The Legend of Ulenspiegel,* imbuing Till with the spirit of freedom in the struggle of the Protestant Netherlands against Catholic Spain; the work has been called "the Bible of Flanders"; it is divided into six books, each with a song of Till; it ends with his beloved Nele at the grave of Till, who then—with an upheaval of the earth and a dispersal of the dust of death—rises and exclaims: "'Can any bury Ulenspiegel the spirit and Nele the heart of Mother Flanders?' He went forth with her, singing his sixth song; but no man knoweth where he sang the last song of all." In 1894 Richard Strauss revived Till in a symphonic poem.

In the 16th and 17th c., when, to encourage home manufacture of garments, England forbade the exporting of sheep and wool, the smugglers by night, from their birdcalls to signal the Channel boats, were called *owlers;* their practice, *owling.* See *strid.*

ulkuo: the flesh-tearing animal, the wolf. In many parts of the world, some things are *taboo.* The best-known taboo stories are of Adam and Eve, Pandora's box, Cupid and Psyche, Orpheus and Eurydice; Bluebeard; but mention of sacred things has been widely taboo. Even today, pious Jews will not speak the name of their Lord. Among primitive peoples, the animal associated with the tribe—as the American Indian totem—was often held unmentionable; and the early names for *wolf* in Greek, Latin, and German seem fashioned to preserve taboo. The practice is world-old, but we have borrowed the term from more modern primitives; it is Tongan *tabu: ta:* mark; *bu:* especially. The main island of this Polynesian group is named *Tongatabu.*

Gk *lukhos:* wolf. *lycanthrope.* Fr, *loup-garou.* Gm, *werewolf.* Several genera of plants: *Lycopersion:* potato ("destroy wolf"); *Lycopodium:* club moss ("wolf's foot"); thus, too, *Lycopus:* horehound; *Lycopsis:* bugloss ("wolf sight").

L *lupus:* wolf. *lupine, lupulus, lupus.* Sp, *lobo, robalo* (from *lobarro, l.r* shift):

wolf fish. *Lupercalia,* the ancient festival on Feb. 15, begun at the *Lupercal,* grotto at the foot of the Palatine hill in Rome, celebrating Pan as *Lupercus;* a dog was sacrificed. After the assassination of Caesar, Mark Antony opens his speech to his "Friends, Romans, Countrymen" (Shakespeare's play, iii, 2) by reminding them:

> You all did see that on the Lupercal
> I thrice presented him a kingly crown,
> Which he did thrice refuse . . .

lyceum: gymnasium where Aristotle taught, its name from the neighboring Temple to Apollo *Lukheios:* wolf-slayer (see *uel III*). Fr, *lycée.* From Fr *loup* (feminine, *louve*), came the wolf field the *Louvre,* where the palace of the French kings was built, now one of the world's greatest museums. From its popularity at the palace came *louvre,* an 18th c. dance. S. Jenkyns, in *The Art of Dancing* (1729), makes grace preeminent,

> Whether her steps the minuet's mazes trace,
> Or the slow louvre's more majestic pace.

Norse, *Ralph.* See *uel III,* with which this root overlaps. African *aardwolf;* Du *aard:* earth. *wolframite. wolfram.* See also *ulp.*

The wolf is frequent in folk references: the wolf in sheep's clothing; the shepherd boy that cried "Wolf! Wolf" when there was no wolf, thus went unheeded when the wolf attacked his flock; the tale of Little Red Riding Hood; the saying that when the wolf (rapaciousness, hunger) comes in at the door, love flies out the window.

The American Indian comes into the story of the wolf. The Wolf tribe in New York was called in scorn by other Algonquians *tuksit:* round foot, implying that they easily fell down in surrender. In their region thus came the names *Tuxedo* and *Tuxedo Lake,* which were acquired by the Griswold family in payment of a debt. There the family established the exclusive *Tuxedo Club;* and there in the late 1880s Griswold Lorillard first appeared in a dinner jacket without tails, a *tuxedo.* By a twist of slang, one may now refer to a man in a tuxedo as a "wolf."

ulp: fox. See note on *taboo,* under *ulkuo.* Gk *alopex. alopecia:* first, fox mange. *Alopecurus:* genus, the foxtail. L *vulpes.* The genus *Vulpes:* the red fox. *vulpicide:* the triumphant English fox hunter. *vulpine. vulpinism:* cunning as a fox.

Vulpecula: the Little Fox, sometimes called *Vulpecula cum Ansere:* Little Fox with the Goose, is a northern constellation between *Sagitta:* the Arrow, and *Cygnus:* the Swan. (There is also a southern constellation *Sagittarius:* the Archer, pictured as a centaur with drawn bow, ninth sign of the zodiac; see *guei. OED* defines 13 relevant words beginning *sagit.*) Cygnus contains the Northern Cross; it lies in a most impressive section of the Milky Way, like a swan with outspread wings and trailing legs. Its head star, Deneb, has an intrinsic brightness some 1,000 times that of Earth's sun; its star Number 61, though comparatively faint, was the first star to have its distance from Earth measured scientifically.

Gc, *fox* (feminine, *vixen*); see *puk.* From the reputation of the fox came the early cartoon character *Foxy* Grandpa and the more generally used adjective *foxy.* And, of course, there is the tale of the fox and the "sour grapes"—these words now a general expression for seeming to disregard what one cannot attain. *foxed:* of discolored books. *foxglove. foxhole:* a soldier's quick trench. *fox trot:* a once popular dance.

> Suspicion all our lives shall be stuck full of eyes,
> For treason is but trusted like the fox,

Who, ne'er so tame, so cherish'd, and locked up,
Will have a wild trick of his ancestors.
—*1 Henry IV,* v, 2

"Catch us the foxes, the little foxes, that spoil the vines, for our vineyards are in blossom." What concern made King Solomon tuck this appeal into his love song?

upo: near, down, under; up from under, hence over. The comparative degree of *upo* was *uper:* over, above, beyond. The two forms overlap; they may be only partially distinguished, and will be summed up together in paragraph (III) below.

(I) *upo* forms. Skr *upa:* near. *upala:* precious stone; *opal, opalescent. Upanishad:* to sit down beside; a Sanskrit treatise. L *sub:* under. *submarine, subterfuge. supine:* down on the back; face down is *prone.* It, *sotto:* low; *sotto voce. soutane:* first, an undergarment. L *surgere:* come up from under; *resurgere. resurrectum. surge, assurgent; insurgent, insurrection; resurge, resurgent, resurrection.* A *resurrectionist,* in 18th and 19th c. England, was a man that dug up corpses to sell to doctors for anatomical research. Via Fr, *resource, source, resourceful; sortie. souse:* the swoop of a hawk to its prey. *soubrette. so(u)briquet:* first, to chuck under the chin.

Gc, *up, uproar. open. above, aboveboard. eaves, eavesdrop* (see *stei*). Also (morally "under" or "going beyond") *evil.* From standing under, hence serving, came *valet, varlet, vassal.*

(II) *uper* forms. Gk *hyper,* L *super:* above. The slang *super!,* which grew to the reduplicating *superduper!* Dickens contributed *extra super,* the tailor's description of his cloth for Nicholas Nickleby. In 1979 a book was published called *Superlearning,* with a chapter on *supermemory,* and sections on *superperformance* and *superrapport,* presumably to create a *superman* able to pay the new *supertaxes.* Also *super,* short for *supernumerary* in the theatre, sometimes shortened to *supe*—which might also mean *superintendent. superb. sovereign* (see *uer II 5*). *insuperable. superiority.* A *superiority complex,* we are told, may be a mask over feelings of inferiority. *supernal,* as opposed to *infernal;* also *external, internal* (see *ndher*). *supreme.*

In the 1964 Disney motion picture *Mary Poppins,* Julie Andrews sang the happy word *supercalifragilisticexpialidocious*—how soon these gems fade from the memory! In search of its roots, fancy with me, fancy-free: *cal,* root of wholesome beauty (see *cal*). *fragile:* delicate, expensive. *istic:* adjectival ending, as in *spiritualistic. expi:* expiate, cleansed of all sins; expedition. *ali:* aliment, well-nourished, as in "Alimentary, my dear Watson!"—another Sherlock Holmes success—and "That's up my alley." *do-re-mi:* a merry note; also *dough:* bread, the staff of life, and *dough:* money, the staff of power. Ending on a strong sound (like *precocious*) plus a suffix meaning *full of* (all the good things suggested before). A magic, happy, wholesome word indeed! *OED*'s Burchfield says he will include the word in the dictionary's Supplement IV. I wonder what he will do about its etymology.

Science has *supercool, supernova, superheterodyne,* etc., but largely dismisses the *supernatural.*

sirloin is the upper (*sur*) part of a loin of beef, folkchanged from the notion that a king was so pleased that he knighted the cut—a sword slap attributed to Henry VIII, James I, and Charles II. Two sirloins, uncut, are thence a baron of beef. (Incidentally, 21 related words beginning *baron* are defined in *OED*).

L *supra:* beyond. Via It, *soprano.* Fr *soubresaut, sombresaut,* gave English *somersault,* folkvaried as *summersault.* Gm *über;* Nietzsche's *Übermensch* was translated by G. B. Shaw as Superman, although the German word was used as early as 1527. L *summa:* highest. The Romans, adding a column of figures, put the total at the top, not, as we usually do, at the bottom; hence, the *sum* at the *summit.* A *summary* sums it up. *summation, consummate.*

(III) Compounds from prefixes of I and II.

(a) *hyper:* overmuch, excessive. *OED* lists 75 words, then details more in 12 columns—e.g., *hyperbole,* in speech; *hyperbola,* in mathematics; *hyperborean:* of the extreme north; *hypercritical; hypersensitive; hyperdynamic. hypermnesia:* unusual power of memory. England has *hypermarkets. Hyperion* the Titan, son of Uranus (god of heaven) and Gea (goddess of earth), means, literally, he that looks from above. Identified with Apollo, he was a paragon of manly beauty; Hamlet compares his father to his uncle: "Hyperion to a satyr." *supersonic,* faster than the speed of sound; *hypersonic:* five or more times the speed of sound. (The speed of sound is roughly 1,087 feet per second; crossing the "sound barrier" produces a sharp report called a *sonic boom.*)

(b) *hypo:* beneath, under, underhand. *OED* lists 133 words, and details others in 20 columns, as *hypothetical; hypochondriac:* beneath the breastbone cartilage, therefore the belly, once thought to be the seat of the affliction.

Guy Wetmore Carryl in 1898 begins his comic retelling of the fable of the fox persuading the raven to sing (and thus drop the coveted cheese):

Without the slightest basis
For hypochondriasis . . .

(The suffix *iasis,* indicating disease—of which JWalker gives 14 instances, as *satyriasis; trypanosomiasis,* more familiarly known as sleeping sickness—is always pronounced with the accent on the long *a,* except for *elephantiasis,* which presses a long *i.*)

hypotenuse. hypocrisy. hypotiposis: vivid description, bringing the object "under one's eyes." *hypocorism:* a pet name. In chemistry, *-ic* is strongest, as *sulfuric acid; -ous* (*sulfurous acid*) is weaker; *hyposulfurous* is next under in the series.

(c) *hypsi, hypso:* high, lofty. *OED* lists 10 words for the first, 9 for the second. It details 3 words beginning *hypsi,* as *hypsistarian:* of the 4th c. sect that worshiped God as the "Most High"; and 5 beginning *hypso,* as *hypsometry:* measurement of altitudes.

(d) *over:* above, across, exceedingly. *OED* lists over 200 words, then details more in 146 columns, as *overboard, overnight, overalls; overeat, overflow; overlook, overrule, overturn.* It would *overtax* one's patience to *oversee* them all.

(e) *sub:* under. These compounds are more complicated. There are a number of Latin phrases used in English; among the more frequent are: *sub hasta:* under a spear, i.e., by auction. *sub Jove frigido:* under a chilly sky. *sub judice:* under court consideration. *sub plumbo:* under lead, i.e., the pope's seal. *sub rosa:* under the rose, in secret (see *urod*). *sub sigilla:* under the seal (of confession), confidentially. *sub silentio:* met with silence, ignored.

The prefix *sub* is assimilated before *c,* as in *success; f,* as in *suffering; g,* as in *suggestion; m,* as in *summon; p,* as in *suppose; r,* as in *surrogate.* Its form *subs* becomes *sus,* as in *susceptible, suspend, sustain.* It is still live, and may be prefixed to many words, though it is mainly used for scientific compounds, as *subgenus, subclass.* (Note that *subway* in the U.S. is for trains; in England, for pedestrians beneath dangerous crossroads; the trains in England run on the Underground; in Paris, on the Metro[politan].) For *suffix,* see *dheigh N.*

OED lists over 200 *sub* words, then details others in 163 columns, as *subject, subjunctive, sublimation, submissive, subordinate, suborn, subscribe, subsistence, substantial, suburbanite.* In mathematics, *sub* reverses the ratio. Thus *decuple:* 10:1, *subdecuple:* 1:10; *triple:* 3:1, *subtriple:* 1:3; *subnovitripartient:* 1:9 3/8, or 8:75.

(f) *subter:* beneath. *OED* lists 19 words and details 20, as *subterfuge; subternatural,* as opposed to *natural, supernatural, preternatural.*

(g) *super:* above, beyond. *OED* lists almost 200 words, as *supersalient:* the way horses and elephants mate; *supertelluric.* It then details others in 78 columns, as *supererogatory, superfluity, superhuman, superlative, supercilious, superstitious. supermarket.* A small *grocery* (which once meant wholesale, by the *gross*) may puff up its name to *superette;* this word, which has no stem, is only a prefix conjoined with a (contradictory) suffix.

(h) *supra:* above. When used alone, as in a footnote, *supra* means mentioned before. *OED* lists 102 words, as *supralineal, suprarational,* and details others in 4 columns, as *suprarenal; supraliminal,* as opposed to *subliminal* and the rare *liminal; supraspinal; supraspinatus:* muscle that raises the arm.

(i) *sur,* via French, is a variant of *super. OED* lists 24 words and details more in 26 columns, as *surcharge, surcingle, surcoat, surname, surrealism. surrender; surreptitious; survey, survivor.* Macbeth (i, 7) ponders:

If the assassination
Could trammel up the consequence, and catch
With his surcease, success . . .

Anything more might seem *superfluous.*

ureg: push, drive away. L *urgere,* present participle *urgens, urgentem. urge, urgency, urgent.* OFr *urakjo:* pushed away; *garçon* (feminine, *garce;* diminutive, *garcette*), nautical term for a piece of rope, whence E *gasket;* also used for flogging. For a similar figurative application, see E *euphroe,* from Gm *Jungfrau. gossoon* is an occasional English variant of Fr *garçon.*

Gc, *wrack, wreak, wreck, wreckage. wretch. rack* (of driven clouds).

There is an optimistic thought for today in Addison's *Cato,* v, 1, produced at Drury Lane, London, in 1713:

But thou shalt flourish in immortal youth,
Unhurt amid the wars of elements,
The wrecks of matter, and the crash of worlds.

?urod: rose. Primitive man probably took little time to pluck flowers; there seems to be no general Indo-European term for *rose.* But it is unquestionably Western man's most cherished bloom, and around the world no other flower has been so tenderly cultivated, refashioned in many forms of variant and radiant beauty. (A "flower show" in China once consisted of "one perfect rose.") From the 16th c. through the 18th, the *rosemary*—combining the favorite flower and the favorite name, recalling the Virgin Mary—was also called the *anthus,* as the flower *par excellence.* Actually, *rosemary* is folkchanged from *ros marinus:* sea dew. *rose* and its forms, *rosebuds,* and *roses* are the subject of 259 entries in the *Oxford Dictionary of Quotations.*

In the Middle Ages a rose was an emblem of secrecy. When a host had a rose above his table, it meant that the talk was private. Roses were carved or painted on ceilings of council chambers and confessionals; hence *sub rosa:* under the rose, confidential.

OIran *urda,* Pers *gul* (*l.r* shift): rose, with *ab:* water, named the sweet drink, *julep. bedeguar:* wind rose, a mosslike gall on a rose bush, induced by the insect *cynips rosae.*

Gk *rhodon:* rose. *rhododendron* (*dendron:* tree). *Rhodora. rhodium* (see *el 45*). Minerals, as *rhodochrosite, rhodolite, rhodonite. rhodopsin:* purple-red pigment in the eye; responds to red light. *cynorrhodon:* the dogrose.

L *rosa.* Many surnames, as *Rose, Rosenberg, Rosenkrantz,* came into being as a result of early 19th c. regulations, in Germany and elsewhere, requiring the use of a surname.

rosary. OED gives 10 columns to *rose,* listing such combinations as *rose cup, rose briar, rose aphis, rose cockatoo;* then almost 13 columns to detailing words, from *roseac . . . roseate . . . roseola:* rash, as in German measles, . . . *rosette, rosewood, rosewort . . .* to *rosicler. rose noble:* a 15th.–16th c. gold coin. *rose ryal:* coin issued by James I. *rosa solis* was earlier *ros solis:* the plant sundew, and a liqueur flavored with its juice.

The *Rosicrucians* (: Rosy Cross, translation of the name of the group's founder, Christian *Rosenkreuz*) were members of a secret society supposedly founded in 1414; they must have guarded their secrets well, for the name first came into print in 1614; they claimed special powers, as for the transmutation of metals, implementation of the elements, prolongation of life.

Go, lovely rose!
Tell her, that wastes her time and me,
That now she knows,
When I resemble her to thee,
How sweet and fair she seems to be.
Then die! that she
The common fate of all things rare
May read in thee;
How small a part of time they share
That are so wondrous sweet and fair!
—Edmund Waller, 1645

?x. This letter, first taking its shape in Greek, has developed various uses.

(1) In mathematics, it is the Roman numeral for ten. In arithmetic, placed between two numbers, it is a directive to multiply. In algebra, it is used to label the first unknown quantity, to be found.

(2) In religion, as a cross, it stands for Christ, or Christian. Informally, *Xmas* is Christmas. *XP*—in Greek the first two letters of the name *Christos*—is also used (on medallions, in architecture, etc.) as a symbol of Christ.

(3) At the end of a letter, usually multiplied, *X* is the sign of a kiss. Sometimes the sender adds, on the back of the envelope, the letters *S W A K:* sealed with a kiss. Most persons outgrow this practice. See *kus.*

(4) Miscellaneous uses. On a map or diagram, *X* "marks the spot" to which attention is directed. More recently, *X* marks a motion picture deemed "unsuitable for minors." The *X-ray* was so called because its nature was unknown; X-rays were at first called *Roentgen rays* after their discovery by Wilhelm K. *Roentgen,* who was awarded the 1901 Nobel Prize in Physics therefor.

?xenos: strange, stranger. *xenophile, xenophobe* (see *bhili*). *euxenite:* literally, good to strangers; a mineral with infrequent, "strange" elements. *pyroxene:* strange to fire, coined in 1796 by Abbé René J. Haüy, who believed the mineral does not occur in igneous rocks. *xenotine:* strange honor; a mineral erroneously named in 1832 by F.-S. Beudant, who explained that he was naming it "empty honor" (Gk *kenos*) because Berzelius wrongly thought it contained a new metal.

OED lists 22 words beginning *xen(o)* and details 13, as *xenagogue:* leader of strangers, a guide—now routine for tourists, often with a "spiel" learned by rote, and not well informed. *xenelasy:* Spartan regulation banning strangers; many lands today restrict immigration and forbid noncitizens to work, buy property, etc. *xenon:* rare, unreactive element (see *el 54*). Also *xenia; xenogamy; xenogenous. xenodochy:* hospitality, or a hospice, for pilgrims. See *ghostis.*

?yack. Imitative. *yack;* reduplicated as *yackety-yack.*

yap. Imitative. *yap, yawp. yell, yelp* (see *ghel*). *gulp.* Via OFr *japper,* E *jape:* (1) joke, trick; (2) to have carnal intercourse. A character in *Hickscorner* (1510) complains: "He japed my wife and made me cuckold." George Gascoigne, in *The Delectable History of . . . Don Bartholomew of Bath* (1592), bluntly advises: "In thy journey, jape not overmuch." Because of this meaning, around 1600 the word dropped from general use; until revived in sense (1), by Scott, Lamb, and others. Hence also *japery:* playing pranks.

Z

?zip. Imitative of the sound of swift movement. *zip. zipper. zippy:* full of pep. The *Zip Code* of the U.S. Post Office is an acrostic, but it sounds as though someone thought that *zip* was a good word, suggesting speedy service, and then hunted for words the three letters might initiate; *Z*one *I*mprovement *P*rogram is what was found, but it's hard to see how improvement of the "zones" is involved.

When Marco Polo recorded his travels, the name he used for Japan was *Zipango.*

Zoilism deserves final mention: the attitude of a captious or malignant critic, from *Zoilus* of Amphipolis in the 4th c. B.C., called "the scourge of Homer." *OED* gives 18 quotations of the use of his name, from one in 1565 to Coleridge's in 1834: "How then comes it that not only single Zoili, but whole nations have combined in unhesitating condemnation of our great dramatist?" To paraphrase that great dramatist, Be thy work as radiant as a diamond, as fresh as a new-budded rose, it shall not escape the zoilist. "Let not," wrote Sir Thomas Browne, "let not zoilism nor detraction blunt well-intended labours."

Finis Coronat Opus

Sancho Panza said he could recognize, at the beginning of the alphabet book, the sign of the Cross. At the end, had he traveled that far, he might have found a benediction, a well-wishing word. All departures, indeed, involve a minor ritual.

We of the English-speaking world usually wish one another *good-bye,* which of course is a contraction of *God be with ye.* In the Near East, Semitic tongues, with the same intention but more specifically, extend a wish for peace: Hebrew *Shalom,* Arabic *Salaam.*

East is East and West is West, and neighborly may they meet. On many Western lips is an informal parting wish: *So long.* And *So long,* first on the lips of British soldiers, by way of Malay *Salang,* came from that Arabic wish for peace, *Salaam.* The Roman said *Vale:* Be you well. Everywhere, from men of good will, comes the same world-embracing wish: Readers, neighbors, friends, may ye, may we, fare well.

Index of English Words

and word forms, and of foreign phrases used in English, each followed by the root(s) under which it appears. Roots are given alphabetically in the body of the book.

A

a: *oino*
aardvark: *er, porko I*
aardwolf: *ert*
ab-: *ap*
abaft: *ap*
abandon: *bha*
abase: *beu*
abate: *bat, dheigh*
abatement: *bat*
abbess: *dheigh N 13*
abbreviate: *braghu*
abcee: *do*
abdicate: *deik*
abduct: *api, deuk*
abecedarian: *do, ker II*
abeecee: *do*
aberration: *eres*
abet: *bheid*
abgliophragma: *spong*
abhor: *ghers*
abide: *bheidh*
abiogenesis: *ap, gn*
abject: *ie*
abjure: *ieuos*
abkari: *kuer*
ablation: *tol*
ablative: *tol*
ablaut: *kleu I*
able: *gebh*
ablepsia: *leuk*
ablution: *lou*
abnegate: *ne*
abnormal: *dheigh N 5, gn*
abolish: *al I, ap, dheigh N 20*
abomasum: *stoman*
abominable: *o*
aborigines: *ap*
abortion: *ap, ergh*
abound: *aue*
about: *ud*
above: *upo I*
aboveboard: *upo I*
Abra: *do*
abracadabra: *do*
abrade: *rad I*
abrasion: *rad I*
abridge: *braghu*
abrogate: *reg I*
abrupt: *reup*
abscess: *sed II, sek II*
abscind: *sek II*
abscissa: *sek II*
abscond: *dhe I*
absey: *do*
absolute: *leu I, lou*
absolute zero: *me IV*
absolution: *leu I, lou*
absolve: *leu I, lou*
absorb: *srebh*
absorbent: *srebh*
abstain: *ten*
abstemious: *teme*
abstract: *tragh*
abstraction: *tragh*
abstruse: *treud*
absurd: *suer II*

abundant: *aue*
abut: *bhaut*
abyss: *guadh*
acantha: *ak*
acanthion: *ak*
acanthopterygian: *pet I*
acanthus: *ak*
acapnia: *kuep*
a cappella: *caput*
acarpous: *ker III*
acatalectic: *kat, leg II*
acaulescent: *kaul*
acauline: *kaul*
accede: *sed III*
accelerate: *kel VII*
accent: *kan*
accentor: *kan*
acceptance: *kap*
acceptilation: *tol*
access: *sed II*
accession: *sed II*
accete: *sed III*
accident: *kad I*
accidie: *kad II*
acclaim: *kel II*
acclamation: *kel II*
acclimate: *klei*
acclimatize: *klei*
acclivity: *klei*
accolade: *ker I*
accommodate: *med*
accompany: *pa*
accomplice: *plek I*
accomplish: *pel V*
accord: *kerd*
accordant: *kerd*
accordion: *kerd*
accost: *kost*
accouchement: *leu III*
accoucheuse: *leu III*
account: *peue*
accoutre: *siu*
accredited: *kred I*
accrue: *ker VI*
accubation: *keu II*
accumbent: *cub, keu II*
accumulate: *keu II*
accurate: *cura*
accusative: *kau III*
accuse: *kau III*
accustom: *seu*
ace: *oino*
acharnement: *ker III*
Acheron: *kau II*
achieve: *caput*
Achilles: *uel III*
achromatic: *gher I*
achromatopsia: *oku*
acid: *ak*
acidity: *ak*
acidophil(e): *bhili*
acidophilus: *bhili*
acidulous: *ak*
acknowledge: *gn*
aclastic: *kal*
aclinic: *klei*
acme: *ak*
acmite: *ak*
acne: *ak*
acolyte: *kel VII, sem I*
aconite: *gerbh, ken I*
acorn: *ag, oiua*
acoustics: *keu I*
acquaint: *gn*
acquaintance: *gn*
acquiesce: *kuei III*
acquire: *kuere*
acquisition: *kuere*
acquit: *kuei III*
acrasia: *kere*
acratia: *kar*
acre: *ag*
acreage: *ag*
acrid: *ak*
acrilogy: *leg I*
acrimonious: *dheigh N 2 d*
acrimony: *ak*
acrobat: *ak, gua*
acrocarpous: *ker III*
acrodont: *denk*
acromelagy: *me III*
acromion: *oms*
acronym: *ak*
acrophobia: *ak*
acropolis: *ak, pele*
acrosome: *teue 3*
acrospire: *sphei II*
acrostic: *leip II, steigh*
acrotomous: *tem*
act: *ag*
Actinia: *nekut*
actinic: *nekut*
actinide: *nekut*
actinium: *el 89, nekut*

actinograph: *nekut*
actinology: *el 89, nekut*
Actinomyces: *nekut*
actinomycin: *nekut*
actinomycosis: *meu I, nekut*
actinon: *el 86*
actinotherapy: *nekut*
Actinozoa: *nekut*
acumen: *ak*
acupuncture: *ak*
acute: *ak*
acyrology: *dheigh N 30, keu II*
adage: *eg III*
adagio: *ie*
adamant: *dam*
adapt: *ap*
add: *do*
addendum: *do*
adder: *netr*
addition: *do*
adduce: *deuk*
Adelaide: *dei*
Adelia: *dei*
Adeline: *dei*
adelite: *dei*
Adella: *dei*
adelocodonic: *dei*
adelomorphous: *dei*
adelopod: *dei*
adelpholite: *guelbh*
adelphous: *guelbh, sem I*
adenoid: *engu*
adenoma: *engu*
adept: *ap*
adhere: *ghais*
adhesion: *ghais*
adhibit: *ghebh*
adieu: *dei*
adipocere: *leip I, keneko*
adipose: *leip I, dheigh N 2 g*
adjacent: *ie*
adjective: *ie*
adjoin: *ieug*
adjourn: *dei*
adjudicate: *dheigh N 10, ieuos*
adjunct: *ieug*
adjuration: *ieuos*
adjure: *ieuos*
adjust: *ad, ieuos*
admeasure: *me IV*
adminicle: *men II*
admirable: *smei I*
admire: *smei I*
admission: *dheigh N 19*
admit: *smeit*
admix: *meik*
admonish: *dheigh N 20, men I*
ado: *ad*
adolescent: *al I*
Adolph: *dei, uel III, ulkuo*
adopt: *op II*
adorn: *ar I*
adrenergic: *uerg*
adscititious: *sek II*
adsorption: *srebh*
adult: *al I*
adulterate: *al II*
adulterer: *al II*
adultery: *al II*
adumbrate: *andho*
advance: *ant*
advantage: *ant*
advective: *uegh*
advent: *gua*
adventitious: *gua*
adventure: *gua*
adverb: *uer VI*
adverbial: *dheigh N 5*
adversary: *uer II 5*
adverse: *uer II 5*
adversity: *uer II 5*
advertise: *dheigh N 25, uer II 5*
advice: *ueid*
advise: *ueid*
advocate: *ueks*
advowee: *ueks*
advowson: *ueks*
adytum: *do*
adz: *aguesi*
aecidium: *ueik II*
Aedes: *suad*
aegis: *aig*
Aëllo: *ue*
aeration: *ue*
aerial: *ue*
aerobatics: *ue*
aerobic: *guei*
aerodynamics: *ue*
aerodyne: *deu*
aeroembolism: *ue*
aeromancy: *men I, ue*
aeronaut: *nau II*
aeroplane: *ue, uer I*
aerosol: *ue*

aerostat: *sta, ue*
aerostic: *ak*
aerothermodynamic: *ue*
aerugo: *aios*
aesthetics: *aus*
aestival: *aidh*
aestivate: *aidh, ghei*
affable: *bha I*
affair: *dhe I*
affect: *dhe I*
affectation: *dhe I*
affected: *dhe I*
affection: *dhe I*
afferent: *bher I*
affetuoso: *dhe I*
affiance: *bheidh*
affidavit: *bheidh*
affiliate: *dhe II, dhel*
affinity: *fin*
affirm: *dhar*
affirmative: *dhar*
affix: *dheigh*
afflatus: *beu*
afflict: *bhlag*
affluent: *ben*
afforest: *dhur*
affray: *prai*
affront: *frons*
afraid: *prai*
aft: *ap*
after: *ap*
Agathosma: *od*
age: *aiu*
ageless: *aiu*
agendum: *ag*
agent: *ag*
ageratum: *ger IV*
agglomeration: *gel II*
agglutinate: *gel II*
aggrandize: *grand*
aggravate: *guer*
aggregate: *ger I*
aggression: *ghredh*
aggrieved: *guer*
agile: *ag*
agist: *ie*
agitate: *ag*
Aglaia: *gel I*
agnail: *angh*
agnate: *gn*
Agnes: *iag I*
agnomen: *onomen*
agnostic: *gn, ne*
agomphious: *gembh*
agony: *ag*
agora: *ger III*
agoraphobia: *ger III*
agraffe: *ger III*
agrarian: *ag*
agree: *gar*
agreeable: *gar*
agrestrial: *ag*
agriculture: *ag, sek III, ker I*
agriology: *ag*
agro: *ag*
agronomy: *nem*
ah: *jing*
Ahasuerus: *ksei*
ahem: *hum*
ahi: *anghui*
ahinsa: *ne*
Ahriman: *men I*
ahura: *ane*
Ahuramazda: *ane, men I*
ai: *jing*
Aileen: *dheu I*
aileron: *aks*
aim: *aios, tem*
aimless: *aios, leu I*
air: *ag, el*
airplane: *pela, ue*
aisle: *aks*
aitchbone: *not*
akimbo: *bheug II*
alackaday: *leg II*
alar: *aks*
Alaric: *reg I*
alas: *leid I*
alastor: *ladh*
alate: *aks*
alb: *albh*
albedo: *albh*
albeit: *ol II*
Albert: *bhel I*
albino: *albh*
Albion: *per VIII*
albite: *albh*
album: *albh*
albumen: *albh*
albuminuria: *uer VII*
alcazar: *kastr*
alchemy: *au I, kers II*
Alcmene: *morui*
alderman: *al I, dheigh N 27*

ale: *alu, per VI c*
aleatory: *al III, dheigh N 35, sek II*
Alecto: *dheu I*
alectryomachy: *magh*
Alemanni: *manu*
alert: *reg I*
alethiology: *el 57, ladh*
alevin: *leguh*
Alexander: *caput, nert, uelu*
alexander: *nert*
alexandrine: *nert*
alexandrite: *nert*
alexia: *leg I*
algebraically: *dheigh N 1, leig I*
algedonic: *suad*
-algia: *glokh*
ALGOL: *leg II*
algolagnia: *leg II*
alias: *al II*
alibi: *al II, kuo*
Alice: *dei*
alien: *al II*
alienation: *lino*
aliform: *aks*
align: *lino*
alignment: *lino*
alike: *leig I*
aliment: *al I*
alimentary: *al I*
Aline: *dei*
aliped: *aks*
aliphatic: *leip I*
aliptes: *leip I*
aliquant: *kuo*
aliquot: *kuo*
aliunde: *kuo*
alkali: *el 19*
all: *ol II*
Allah: *dekm*
allative: *tol*
allay: *legh*
allegation: *leg I*
allege: *leg I*
allegory: *al II, ger I*
allergy: *uerg*
alleviate: *leguh*
alley: *al III, ei I*
alligation: *leig II*
alligator: *al II*
alliteration: *deph*
allocate: *leu III*
allocution: *tolku*
allogen: *al II*
allograph: *al II*
allomorph: *merbh*
allonym: *onomen*
allonymous: *al II*
allopathy: *al II, guadh, sem I*
allopatric: *peter*
allot: *kleu III*
allotropy: *al II*
allow: *leu III*
alloy: *leig II*
allspice: *ol II*
allude: *leid II*
alluvial: *lou*
ally: *leig II*
almaciga: *menth*
almagest: *me III*
alma mater: *al I, amma, ma II*
almighty: *ol II*
almost: *me III, ol II*
alms: *amma*
alone: *oino, ol II, per VI g*
along: *ant, del III*
aloof: *lep II*
alopecia: *ulp*
Alopecurus: *ulp*
Aloysius: *kleu I*
alpenhorn: *ker II*
alpenstock: *steu*
alphabet: *do*
alphos: *albh*
Alps: *per VIII*
already: *ol II*
alright: *ol II*
Alsace: *sed I*
Alsatian: *sed I*
also: *ol II*
altar: *ger I*
alter: *al II*
altercation: *al II*
alternate: *al II*
althea: *al I*
although: *ol II*
Altica: *sel IV*
altimeter: *al I*
altitude: *al I*
alto: *al I*
altogether: *ol II*
alto-relievo: leguh
altruism: *al II*
alumette: *leuk*
aluminium: *el 13*

aluminum: *el 13*
alumnus: *al I*
alurgite: *uerg*
always: *uegh*
alyssum: *leuk*
alytarch: *uelu*
A.M.: *dei, per VI a*
am: *es*
amah: *amma*
Amalthea: *mel I*
amanuensis: *man*
amaranth: *mer II*
amaranthine: *mer II*
amarantite: *oma*
amargoso: *oma*
amaricate: *oma*
amarine: *oma*
amaritude: *oma*
amarous: *oma*
amarulent: *oma*
amateur: *rad I*
amatory: *amma*
amaurosis: *oma*
amazement: *dheigh N 28*
Amazon: *magh*
ambage: *ag*
ambassador: *ag, rad I*
amber: *gher III*
ambergris: *gher III, mer II*
ambidextrous: *ambhi*
ambient: *ambhi, ei I*
ambiguous: *ag*
ambit: *ambhi, ei I*
ambition: *ambhi, ei I*
amble: *al III, ambhi, ei I*
amblygon: *mel I*
amblygonite: *mel I*
amblyopia: *mel I*
ambrosia: *dhes, mer II*
ambsace: *ambhi, oino*
ambulance: *ambhi*
ambulate: *al III*
ameliorate: *mel II*
Amen: *bhes I*
amenable: *men II*
amend: *mend*
amenorrhea: *me IV*
ament: *men I*
amerce: *mere*
Americana: *an*
americum: *el 95*
amethyst: *med*
amiable: *amma*
amiant(h)us: *mai II*
amicable: *amma*
amice: *ie*
amid: *medhi, uid*
amidin: *mel V*
amidst: *uid*
amine: *bhes I*
aminophenal: *bhes I*
aminopterin: *bhes I*
Amish: *bhes I*
amity: *amma*
ammocoete: *bhes I*
ammodyte: *bhes I*
Ammon: *bhes I*
ammonia: *bhes I, el 7*
ammophilous: *bhes I*
ammotherapy: *bhes I*
ammunition: *mei III*
amnesia: *men I*
amnesty: *men I*
amnion: *sem I*
amoeba: *mei II, sem I*
amoebean: *mei II*
amoebiform: *mei II*
among: *mag*
amorous: *amma*
amorphous: *merbh*
amortize: *mer II*
amount: *men II*
amour: *amma*
ampere: *onomen*
amphibious: *ambhi, guei*
amphibole: *guel II*
amphibology: *guel II*
amphibrach: *braghu*
amphicarpic: *ker III, sek IX*
amphimacer: *mak*
amphimixis: *meik*
amphisbaena: *gua*
Amphitryon: *morui*
amphora: *ambhi, bher I*
amphoteric: *ambhi*
ample: *ambhi*
amplexicaul: *kaul*
ampoule: *bher I*
ampule: *ambhi*
ampulla: *ambhi*
amputate: *ambhi, peue*
amrita: *mer II, ne*
amu: *me IV*
amuse: *men I*

amusement: *men I*
amyloid: *mel V*
amyous: *mus*
Amyris: *smeru*
an: *oino*
ana: *an*
anabaptist: *an, guebh*
anabasis: *gua*
anableps: *leuk*
anacampserote: *nebh*
anacampsis: *kam*
anacamptic: *an*
anachronism: *nebh*
anachronistic: *nebh*
anaclastic: *an, kal*
anacoluthon: *kel VII*
anadiplosis: *plek I*
anaerbiosis: *ue*
anaerobe: *ue*
anaerobic: *ue*
an(a)esthetic: *aus*
anaglyph: *gleubh*
anagoge: *ag*
anagram: *gerbh, leip II*
analects: *leg I*
analemma: *labh*
analeptic: *labh, slagu*
analgesia: *ne*
analogous: *dheigh N 2 f, leg I*
analog(ue): *leg I*
analogy: *leg*
analphabeti: *an*
analysand: *ne*
analysis: *an, leu I, lou, ne*
analyze: *leu I, lou*
anamnesia: *ne*
anamnesis: *men I*
anamorphose: *merbh*
anapest: *peue*
anaphase: *ne*
anaphora: *bher I, plek I*
anaphrodisiac: *fur, nebh*
anaphylaxis: *ne, phulax*
anaplasty: *pela*
anarchy: *an, arkh, ne*
anarthia: *ne*
anarthrous: *ar I*
anasarca: *tuerk*
anastasis: *sta*
anastate: *ne*
anastrophe: *strebh*
anathema: *an, dhe I*
anatomy: *tem*
anatropous: *an*
ancestor: *ant, sed II*
anchor: *ank, rad I*
anchorite: *ghe*
ancient: *ant*
ancile: *sek II*
ancillary: *ker I*
and: *ant*
Andalusia: *uendh*
andalusite: *uendh*
André: *nert*
andrecium: *nert*
Andrew: *nert*
andrewsite: *nert*
Andrias: *nert*
Androcles: *kleu I*
androcracy: *nert*
androecium: *ueik I*
androgen: *nert*
androgenous: *an, gn*
androgyne: *guen, nert*
android: *andh*
Andromache: *nert*
Andromeda: *nert*
andron: *nert*
andropetalous: *andh*
androphagous: *bhag*
andropogon: *nert*
Androsace: *nert*
androsterone: *nert*
anecdote: *do*
anemo-: *ane*
anemone: *ane*
anemophilous: *bhili*
anergy: *uerg*
anfractuous: *bhreg*
anger: *angh*
angina: *angh*
angle: *ank*
Angle-land: *ank*
angler: *ank*
Anglophile: *ank*
Anglo-Saxon: *ank*
angst: *angh*
anguiliform: *anghui*
anguine: *anghui*
anguish: *angh*
angular: *ank*
Angus: *oino*
anhelation: *ane*
anhistous: *sta*

anhydrous: *aue*
anil: *nei*
aniline: *nei*
animadvert: *ane, uer II 5*
animal: *ane*
animate: *ane*
animation: *ane*
animosity: *ane, dheigh N 2 d*
animus: *ane*
anion: *ei I*
ankle: *ank*
ankylosis: *ank*
anlage: *legh*
anlaut: *kleu I*
annals: *at*
anneal: *aidh*
annex: *ned*
anniversary: *at, eir, uer II 5*
annotate: *gn*
announce: *neu I*
annoy: *odi*
annual: *at*
annuity: *at*
annul: *ne*
annular: *ano*
annulet: *ano*
annunciation: *neu I*
anode: *sed II*
anodyne: *an, ed, ne*
anoint: *enguo*
anomobranchiate: *nem*
anomophyllous: *nem*
anomy: *nem*
anon: *oino*
anonymous: *onomen*
anorexia: *reg I*
Anselm: *kel VI*
anserine: *ghans, mezg I*
answer: *ant, suer II*
antagonist: *ag, ant*
antagonize: *ag*
antarctic: *rkthos*
Antares: *kuei I*
ante: *ant*
ante-bellum: *dau, duo*
antecedent: *ant, sed II*
antechamber: *kam*
antediluvian: *dheigh N 7, lou*
antelope: *oku*
antemeridian: *ant, dei*
ante-Nixon: *ant*
antependium: *spend II*
antepenult: *al II, paen*
anterior: *ant*
anth-: *andh*
anthelion: *sauel*
anthelmintic: *uelu*
anthem: *bha I*
anther: *andh*
anthesis: *andh*
anthony: *sus*
anthos: *urod*
-anthous: *andh*
anthracite: *dheigh N 22, ken I*
anthraconite: *ken I*
anthrax: *ken I*
anthropocentric: *kent, nert*
anthropoid: *nert, ueid*
anthropology: *nert*
anthropomancy: *men I*
anthropomantie: *men I*
anthropomorphic: *nert*
anthropophagus: *dheigh N 2 f, nert*
Anthurium: *ors*
anthypophora: *ant*
anti-: *ant*
antiae: *ant*
anti-American: *dheigh N 7*
antibiotic: *ant*
antic: *ant*
Antichrist: *ant*
anticipate: *ant, kap*
anticlimax: *klei*
anticlinal: *klei*
anticyclone: *ker I*
antidote: *do*
antigen: *gn*
antilogy: *ant, dheigh N 30*
antimatter: *ma II*
antimony: *el 51, nem*
anti-Nixon: *ant, per N 4*
antinomy: *el 51*
antinosarians: *sna II*
Antiope: *morui*
antipasto: *ant, pa*
antipathy: *ant, guadh*
antiphlogistic: *bhel I*
antiphon: *bha I*
antipodes: *ped*
antique: *ant*
antiseptic: *septm*
antistrophe: *strebh*
antithesis: *dhe I*
antitoxin: *tekhus*

antitype: *steu*
antler: *oku*
antonomasia: *onomen*
antonym: *onomen*
anuran: *ors*
anus: *ano, kel IV*
anvil: *pel IV*
anxiety: *angh*
anxious: *angh*
any: *oino*
aorta: *uer I*
Aotus: *ous*
apartment: *per II*
apathy: *guadh*
Apelles: *nebh*
aperient: *suer I, uer V*
aperitif: *suer I*
aperitive: *suer I, uer V*
aperture: *suer I, uer V*
apex: *ap*
aph(a)eresis: *ie*
aphasia: *bha I*
aphelion: *sauel*
aphesis: *ie*
aphetic: *ie*
aphrite: *nebh*
aphrizite: *nebh*
aphrodisiac: *fur, nebh*
Aphrodite: *fur, nebh*
aphyllous: *beu*
apiculture: *ker I*
aplanatic: *pela*
Aplectrum: *plak*
aplomb: *mlub*
aplome: *plek I*
aplotomy: *plek I*
apnea: *pneu*
apocalypse: *ap, kel VI*
apocha: *segh*
apocopate: *sek IV*
apocope: *sek IV*
apocrine: *ker III, sek VI*
Apocrypha: *ap*
apocryphal: *krup*
apodeictic: *ap, deik*
apodosis: *do*
apolaustic: *lau*
Apollo: *or, pel IV*
apologue: *leg I*
apology: *leg I*
apomict: *meik*
apomixis: *meik*
aponeurosis: *netr, sne*
apophasis: *bha I*
apophthegm: *dhe I, duo*
apoplexy: *ap*
aposiopesis: *sui*
apostasy: *sta*
apostate: *stel*
apostle: *sta, stel*
apostrophe: *strebh*
apothecary: *ap, dhe I*
apothem: *dhe I*
apotheosis: *dhes*
apotome: *tem*
apotropaic: *trep*
apotropaion: *trep*
apozem: *ies*
appall: *pel VII*
appalto: *pag*
appanage: *pa*
apparatus: *per V*
apparel: *per V*
apparent: *pare*
apparition: *pare*
apparitor: *pare*
appeal: *pel IV*
appear: *pare*
appease: *pag*
append: *spend II*
appendage: *pend*
appendicitis: *dheigh N 23, spend II*
appendix: *kel IV, pend, spend II*
apperception: *kap*
appetency: *pet I*
appetite: *pet I*
appetizer: *pet I*
applaud: *plaud*
applause: *plaud*
apple: *abel*
apple-pie order: *caput*
application: *plek I*
appliqué: *plek I*
apply: *plek I*
appoggiatura: *ped*
apposite: *ap*
apposition: *ap*
appraise: *per III*
appreciate: *dheigh N 10, per III*
approach: *per V, per VII*
appropriate: *per V, per VI g*
approve: *bheu, per VI e*
approximately: *per VII*
appui: *ped*

apricate: *suer I*
apricot: *peku*
April: *ap, me II*
a priori: *per III*
aprocta: *prokto*
aproctous: *prokto*
apron: *map*
aprosexia: *sek I*
apsaras: *ser III*
apt: *ap*
apterous: *pet I*
apteryx: *pet I*
aptitude: *ap*
aptote: *pet I*
aptronym: *onomen*
aptronymic: *es*
apus: *ped*
Apus: *ped*
apyretic: *peuor*
aqua: *akua*
aquacade: *akua*
aquamarine: *akua*
aquanaut: *nau II*
aquarelle: *akua*
aquarium: *akua, dheigh N 35*
Aquarius: *akua, guei*
aquatic: *akua*
aquatint: *akua, teng*
aqua vitae: *guei*
aqueduct: *akua, deuk*
aqueous: *akua, dheigh N 2*
aquiline: *akua*
arable: *are*
Arachne: *pend*
arachnid: *spend II*
arachnidan: *dheigh N 7*
arc: *arq*
arcade: *arq*
Arcadia: *cal, es*
arcane: *areq*
Arcas: *septm*
arch: *arkh, arq*
archaeology: *arkh*
archaic: *arkh*
archaism: *dheigh N 21*
archangel: *arkh*
archbishop: *arkh*
archdeacon: *ken II*
archegonium: *arkh, gn*
archeoptery: *pet I*
archetype: *arkh, steu*
archeus: *arkh*
archfiend: *arkh*
archimage: *arkh, magh*
Archimedean: *arkh*
archipelago: *arkh, pela*
architect: *arkh, tekhs*
architectonic: *tekhs*
architrave: *treb*
archives: *arkh*
archliar: *arch*
arciform: *arq*
arctic: *rkthos*
arctician: *rkthos*
Arcturus: *rkthos, septm, suer I, uer IV*
arcuate: *arq*
Ardhanari: *nert*
arditi: *kar*
arduous: *ueredh*
are: *es*
Areopagus: *kuei I, pag*
Ares: *kuei I*
argent: *arg, el 47*
argentiferous: *arg*
Argentina: *arg*
argentine: *arg*
argil: *arg*
argon: *el 13*
argonaut: *arg, nau II, pel VII*
argosy: *pel VII*
argue: *arg*
argument: *arg*
argyrol: *arg*
Ariadne: *pend, taur*
Aries: *guei*
arista: *ar I*
Aristocles: *ar I*
aristocracy: *ar I, da II, dheigh N 11, kar*
Aristolochia: *legh*
aristology: *ar I, past*
Aristotelian: *ar I*
Aristotle: *ar I*
arithmetic: *ar I, men I*
arithmogram: *ar I*
ark: *areq*
arm: *ar I*
armada: *ar I*
armadillo: *ar I*
armature: *ar I*
armiger: *ger VI*
armistice: *dheigh N 18, sta*
armoire: *ar I*
armomancy: *ar I*
arms: *ar I*

arnica: *pster, strep*
Arnold: *ual*
arquebus: *keg*
arrange: *ker I*
arrant: *ei*
arrear: *re*
arrect: *reg I*
arrest: *sta*
arride: *ridè*
arrière-ban: *koro*
arrival: *rei I*
arrive: *ergh, rei I*
arrogant: *reg I*
arrogate: *reg I*
arrow: *arq*
arroyo: *kreup*
arse: *ors*
arsenic: *el 33, el 40, gel I*
art: *ar I*
Artamus: *tem*
arterial: *uer I*
arteriosclerosis: *skelo, uer I*
artery: *uer I*
artful: *ar I*
arthro-: *ar I*
Arthur: *rkthos*
Arthur, King: *septm*
article: *ar I*
articulate: *ar I*
artifice: *ar I, dhe I*
artillery: *ar I*
artisan: *ar I*
artist: *ar I*
artless: *ar I*
Aruncus: *uesr*
Aryan: *ari*
asafoetida: *odi*
ascend: *skand*
ascension: *skand*
ascertain: *ker III, sek VI*
ascorbic acid: *ker III*
ascribe: *ker III, sek VI*
ascription: *ker III, sek VI*
aseptic: *septm*
Asgard: *medhi*
ash: *os*
Ashtoreth: *dekm*
Ash Wednesday: *ker III, sek VI*
as if: *kuo*
ask: *anghui*
asoins: *eku*
asparagus: *spher I*
aspartame: *ker I*
aspect: *spek*
aspen: *apsa*
asperges: *sphereg*
asperse: *sphereg*
aspersion: *sphereg*
aspic: *sphei II*
aspiration: *speis*
aspire: *speis*
aspirin: *sper II*
assail: *sel IV*
assart: *labh*
assault: *sel IV*
assay: *ag*
assembly: *sem I*
assent: *sent*
assert: *ser I*
assess: *sed I*
assets: *sa*
asseverate: *uero*
assiduous: *sed I*
assign: *sek I, seku I*
assimilate: *sem I*
assist: *sta*
assizes: *sed I*
associate: *ad, seku I*
assoil: *leu I, lou*
assorted: *ser I*
assuage: *suad*
assuasive: *suad*
assuetude: *seu*
assume: *em*
assure: *cura*
assurgent: *upo I*
Assyriologue: *leg I*
Astarte: *dekm*
astatine: *el 85*
asteism: *ues I*
aster: *ster III*
asteria: *ster III*
asterisk: *ster III*
asterism: *ster III*
asteroid: *ster III*
asthenic: *bheu*
asthma: *ane*
astigmatism: *steig*
astomous: *stoman*
astonish: *stei, stene*
astound: *stei, stene*
Astraea: *ster III*
astragal: *ost*
astragalus: *ost*

astral: *ster III*
astrolabe: *labh, slagu, ster III*
astrologaster: *ster III*
astrology: *ster III*
astronaut: *nau II, ster III*
astronomy: *men I, nem, ster III*
astrophel: *ster III*
astrophobia: *bhegu, ster III*
astute: *ues I*
asura: *ane*
Aswin: *nes*
asymptote: *pet I*
at: *ad*
Atalanta: *tol*
ataman: *caput*
ataractic: *dher*
ataraxia: *dher*
atavism: *atos*
ataxia: *tag II*
atelectasis: *ten*
atheism: *dheigh N 21*
atheist: *dhes, ne*
Athelstan: *dei*
Athena: *guel II, morui*
athletic: *bheu*
athwart: *tereq*
athymia: *dheu I*
atlantean: *nebh*
atlantes: *nebh, tol*
Atlantic: *nebh, tol*
atlantides: *nebh, tol*
Atlantis: *nebh*
Atlas: *nebh*
atlas: *nebh, tol*
atlasite: *nebh*
atma: *etman*
atman: *etman*
atmidometer: *ue*
atmolysis: *ue*
atmosphere: *reg II, ue*
atom: *el, ne, tem*
atomizer: *tem*
atomy: *tem*
atone: *kuei I, oino*
atonement: *per VI g*
atonic: *ten*
atopic: *top*
atopy: *top*
atrabilious: *atr, oku*
atresia: *ter II*
atrium: *atr*
atrocious: *atr, dheigh N 2 d, oku*
atrocity: *atr, em, oku*
Atropa: *trep*
atropine: *trep*
atropos: *trep*
attach: *stegh*
attack: *stegh*
attain: *tag I, ten*
attaint: *tag I*
attemper: *temp 5*
attempt: *temp 4*
attend: *ten*
attentat: *temp 4*
attenuated: *ten*
attest: *tre*
Attic salt: *sal I*
atto-: *me IV*
attorn: *ter II*
attorney: *ter II*
attornment: *ter II*
attract: *tragh*
attractive: *tragh*
attrahent: *tragh*
attribute: *tre*
attrite: *ter II*
attrition: *ter II*
attritus: *ter II*
Atwell: *onomen*
auantic: *saus*
aubade: *albh*
auberge: *koro*
Aubrey: *reg I*
auburn: *albh*
A.U.C.: *mavors, rad I*
auction: *aug*
aucupate: *kap*
audacious: *au IV, dheigh N 2 b*
audacity: *em, dheigh N 36*
audible: *aus, ous*
audience: *aus*
audio: *aus*
audio frequency: *aus*
audiometer: *aus*
audiophile: *aus*
audio-visual: *aus, ueid*
audit: *aus*
audition: *aus*
auditorium: *aus*
auger: *nabh*
aught: *aiu*
augment: *aug*
augur: *aug*
augury: *aug*

August: *me IV, sek II*
august: *aug, sek II*
aumildar: *dhar*
aunt: *amma*
aural: *aus, ous*
aureate: *aues*
aureole: *aues*
Aureomycin: *aues*
auricle: *aus, ous*
auricular: *ous*
auriform: *aus, ous*
Auriga: *or*
aurigation: *or*
aurochs: *uer VII, ug, ugu*
aurora: *aues*
aurorium: *nebh*
aurum: *aues*
auscultation: *aus, ous*
auslaut: *kleu I*
auspices: *auei, spek*
auspicious: *spek*
austere: *saus*
Australia: *aues, aus II*
Austri: *medhi*
Austria: *aues, aus II*
Austronesia: *sna I*
autantonym: *gleubh*
author: *aug*
authority: *aug*
authorize: *aug*
autobiography: *guei*
autochthonous: *ghdhem*
autoclave: *kleu III*
autocracy: *da II, kar*
autoecious: *ueik I*
autogenous: *gn*
autograph: *bergh*
autogyro: *gue, keup*
autointoxication: *tekhus*
autolatry: *dheigh N 36*
automatic: *men I*
automobile: *meu II*
automysophobia: *bhegu*
autonomy: *nem*
autopsy: *nek, oku*
autosome: *teue 3*
autotelic: *ker I*
autotoxin: *tekhus*
autumn: *se I*
auxesis: *aug*
auxiliary: *aug*
avail: *ual*
avale: *uals*
avaricious: *au IV*
avast: *kel VII, past*
avatar: *au I, dheigh N 13, ter III*
avenge: *deik*
avenue: *gua*
aver: *uero*
average: *medhi, op I*
averruncate: *uers*
averse: *uer II 5*
aversion: *uer II 5*
avert: *uer II 5*
Avestan: *ger IV*
aviary: *auei*
aviation: *auei*
aviculture: *auei*
avid: *au IV*
avidya: *ueid*
avocation: *ueks*
avoid: *bha II, eu*
avoirdupois: *ghebh, pend, spend II*
avouch: *ueks*
avoué: *ueks*
avow: *ueguh*
avowal: *ueks*
avulsion: *uel III*
avuncular: *au III, dheigh N 9*
awaken: *ueg II*
award: *suer I, uer IV*
aware: *suer I, uer IV*
away: *uegh*
awe: *agh*
awhile: *kuei III*
awkward: *ap*
ax: *aguesi*
axial: *aks*
axil: *aks*
axilla: *aks*
axillary: *aks*
axiology: *ag*
axiom: *ag*
axis: *aks*
axle: *aks*
axon: *aks*
ay: *aiu, i*
ayah: *ters*
aye: *aiu*
azalea: *ar II*
azoic: *guei*
azote: *guei*
azygous: *dheigh N 2 f, ieug*

B

baa: *jing*
Baal: *dekm*
Baalist: *dekm*
babble: *baba*
babe: *baba*
baboon: *baba*
babouche: *ped*
baby: *baba*
baccalaureate: *bacca*
Bacchanalia: *men I*
bacchanalia: *bacca*
bacchante: *bacca, men I*
Bacchus: *men I*
bacciferous: *bacca*
bacciform: *bacca*
baccivorous: *bacca, bhag*
bachelor: *bacca, rad I*
bacillus: *bak*
bacon: *bhe*
Bacon, Francis: *tol*
bacteria: *bak*
bactericidal: *bak*
bacteriology: *bak, leg I*
bad: *bheidh*
baft: *uebh*
bagel: *bheug II*
bagnio: *bhe*
baguette: *bak*
baignoire: bha
bail: *man*
bairn: *bher I*
bait: *bheid*
bake: *bhe*
Baker: *onomen*
baksheesh: *bhag*
balalaika: *baba*
balance: *duo*
balcony: *bhelk*
bald: *bhel I*
Baldur: *uel III*
bale: *ben*
baleful: *dheigh N 2 h*
balk: *bhelk*
ball: *beu, guel II*
ballad: *guel II*
ballast: *kla*
ballerina: *guel II*
ballet: *guel II*
ballista: *guel II*
ballistics: *guel II*
ballock: *beu*
balloon: *beu*
ballot: *beu*
baloney: *el 84*
ban: *bha I, pa*
banal: *bha I*
banat: *pa*
band: *bha II, bhendh*
bandage: *bhendh*
bandar: *uen*
bandit: *bha I*
bandoleer: *bha II*
baneberry: *bhel I*
bang: *bheg*
banian: *uen*
banish: *bha I*
bank: *bheg*
bankrupt: *bheg, reup*
banner: *bha I*
Bannockburn: *bhereu*
banns: *bha I*
banquet: *bheg*
banshee: *guen*
banyan: *uen*
baphia: *guebh*
baptisia: *guebh*
baptism: *guebh*
Baptist: *guebh*
baptize: *guebh*
bar: *bhoros*
barbaria: *guer*
barbarian: *baba*
barbarous: *baba*
barber: *bhar*
barberry: *bhel I*
barbula: *bhar*
bard: *gar*
Bardolph: *uel III, ulkuo*
bargain: *bhergh*
baritone: *guer, ten*
barium: *el 38, el 56, guer*
bark: *bhago*
barley: *bhares, leig I*
barm: *bhereu*
barmy: *bhereu*
barn: *bhares, leig I*
barometer: *guer*
baron: *upo II*
Barosma: *od*
barouche: *duo, reth*
barrier: *bhoros*

barrister: *bhoros*
barrow: *bher I, bher II*
barrulet: *bhoros*
barytes: *el 56, guer*
barythemia: *dheu I, guer*
barytone: *ten*
bascule: *skeu*
base: *gua*
baseball: *gua*
basic: *gua*
basifuge: *bheug I*
basis: *gua*
bask: *sue*
bas-relief: *leguh*
bass: *bhar*
basso-relievo: *leguh*
baste: *bhaut*
bat: *bhlag, dheigh*
batadar: *dhar*
batberry: *bhel I*
bated: *dheigh*
bath: *bhe*
bathe: *bhe*
bathetic: *guadh*
bathorse: *guadh*
bathos: *guadh*
bathybius: *guadh, guei*
bathymetry: *dheigh N 36*
bathysphere: *guadh*
batman: *bhares, guadh*
Batrachomyomachia: *magh*
Batrachomyomachy: *keu II*
batten: *bhad*
batter: *bat, dheigh*
battery: *bat, dheigh*
battle: *bat, dheigh*
battledore: *bat, dheigh*
battlement: *bat*
battologize: *medhi*
battology: *glokh, medhi*
battue: *dheigh*
bavardage: *bhel II*
bawd: *beu*
bawl: *bhel II*
bayadere: *guel II*
bayberry: *bhel I*
bays: *bacca, men I*
be: *bheu*
beadle: *bheudh*
beagle: *garg*
beak: *bheid*
beam: *bheu*
bear: *bher I*
bearberry: *bhel I*
beard: *bhar*
beast: *ters*
beat: *bhaut*
beatific: *deu, dhe I*
beatification: *deu, dhe I*
beatify: *deu, dhe I, dheigh N 15*
beatitude: *deu*
beatnik: *keu II*
Beatrice: *deu*
beau: *deu*
Beau Brummel: *bhe*
Beaufort (scale): *deu*
beau geste: *deu*
beauteous: *dheigh N 2 h*
beautiful: *dheigh N 2 h*
beautifullest: *dheigh N 13*
beauty: *deu*
beaver: *bhel I*
bebass: *ambhi, kus*
becack: *ambhi*
bêche-de-mer: *mori*
become: *gua*
becoming: *ambhi*
bed: *bhedh*
bedbug: *sek I, sek IX*
bedeck: *ambhi, steg*
bedeguar: *urod*
bedlock: *uad*
bedraggle: *ambhi*
bedraggled: *tragh*
bee: *bhei*
beech: *bhago*
beef: *ane, mel I*
beefburger: *konemo*
Beefeater: *ieu*
Beelzebub: *dekm*
been: *bheu*
beer: *per VI c, poi*
beeswax: *uebh*
beetle: *bat, bhau, bheid*
beetle-browed: *bat*
before: *per IV, per VI a*
befriend: *ambhi*
beguile: *ambhi, ueik III*
behalf: *kel VIII*
behavior: *ambhi, ghebh*
beheading: *caput*
behest: *kei I*
behight: *kei I*
behind: *ko*

behold: *kel VII*
behoof: *kap*
behoove: *kap*
belabor: *leb*
belay: *legh*
belch: *bhel II*
beleaguer: *legh*
belfry: *bheregh, prai*
belie: *leugh*
belief: *leubh*
bell: *bhel II*
belladonna: *deu, nekut, trep*
belle: *deu*
Bellerophon: *guhen*
belles-lettres: *deph*
bellicose: *dau, dheigh N 2 g, duo*
belligerent: *dau, duo, ger VI*
Bellona: *duo*
bellow: *bhel II*
bellows: *beu*
bellwether: *uet*
belly: *beu*
bellyful: *dheigh N 2 h*
belong: *del III*
beloved: *ambhi*
belvedere: *deu, ueid*
bema: *qua*
bemean: *ambhi, mei II*
bemoan: *meino*
ben: *bend*
bench: *bheg*
bend: *bhendh*
beneath: *ni*
benedict: *deu*
benediction: *deu, deik, melo*
benefactor: *deu, dhe I, melo*
benefice: *deu, dhe I*
beneficence: *deu, dhe I*
beneficial: *deu, dhe I*
beneficiary: *deu*
benefit: *deu, dhe I*
benevolent: *deu, melo, uel II*
benighted: *ambhi*
benign: *deu, gn, melo*
benignant: *gn, melo*
benison: *deu, melo*
benthos: *guadh, ie*
benumbed: *nem*
Benzedrine: *deu*
benzene: *deu*
benzocaine: *deu*
benzoin: *deu*
benzoline: *deu*
benzoyle: *hule*
bequeath: *guet*
bequest: *ambhi, guet*
berceuse: *bher I*
bereave: *ambhi, reup*
bereavement: *dheigh N 28*
berkelium: *el 97*
Berlin(er): *onomen*
berm: *bherem*
Bernard: *kar*
berry: *bhel I, bheregh*
Berry: *onomen*
berserk: *bhel I*
Bertha: *bhel I*
Bertha, Big: *margar*
beryllium: *el 4*
beshrew: *ambhi, sek VIII*
besiege: *sed I*
bespeak: *sphereg*
best: *bhad*
betoken: *deik*
béton: *gue, keup*
betray: *do*
betrothal: *deru*
better: *bhad*
Betula: *gue*
betula: *keup*
beverage: *poi*
bevue: *ueid*
bewail: *ambhi*
beware: *ambhi, suer I, uer IV*
bewilder: *uelt*
bezoar: *pa*
Bharata: *me III*
Biathanatos: *dheu I*
bib: *poi*
Bible: *bibli*
bibliography: *bibli*
bibliolatry: *dheigh N 36, lei II*
bibliomancy: *bibli*
bibliophile: *bhili*
bibliopole: *bibli, pel II*
bibulous: *poi*
bicameral: *kam*
bicorn: *ker II*
bid: *bheudh*
biddy: *bhe*
bide: *bheidh*
biennial: *at*
bier: *bher I*
bifarious: *bha I*

Bifrost: *bedhi*
bifurcate: *bhurig, duo*
big: *beu*
bigamy: *geme*
bigeminal: *iem*
bight: *bheng III*
bilberry: *bhel I*
bile: *gel I, ugu*
bilge: *beu*
bilingual: *dinghu*
bilious: *ugu*
bill: *beu, bheid*
billet: *beu*
billet-doux: *alku*
billow: *beu*
Bilqis: *gn*
bimanual: *man*
bimestrial: *me IV*
binary: *duo*
bind: *bhendh*
binnacle: *ghebh*
binoculars: *oku*
binomial: *nem, onomen*
bio-: *guei*
bioadelphous: *sem I*
biographer: *gerbh*
biography: *guei*
biology: *leg*
bioluminescence: *leuk*
biomedical: *guei*
biontic: *es*
bipartite: *per V*
biped: *duo, ped*
birch: *bhel I*
birdlime: *lei I*
Birds, The: nebh
Birmingham: *kei II*
birth: *bher I*
biscuit: *bhe, duo, peku*
bisect: *sek I*
bishop: *sap, spek*
bismuth: *el 83*
bison: *ueis*
bissextile: *seks*
bit: *bheid, duo*
bite: *bheid*
biting: *dheigh N 13*
bitter: *bheid, sal I*
bitterwort: *uerad*
bitumen: *gue*
bivalent: *ual*
bivalve: *uelu*
bivouac: *ambh, ueg II*
black: *bhel I, kel VI*
blackball: *bhes I*
blackberry: *bhel I*
blackguard: *kel VI*
black hole: *kel VI*
blackjack: *kel VI*
blackmail: *kel VI, mod*
black market: *kel VI*
black mass: *kel VI*
bladder: *beu*
blade: *beu*
blain: *beu*
blame: *bha I*
blanch: *bhel I*
blancmange: *bhel I, menth*
bland: *mel I*
blandishment: *mel I*
blank: *bhel I*
blanket: *bhel I*
blare: *bhel II*
blasé: *beu*
blasphemy: *bha I*
blast: *beu*
blather: *beu*
blatherskite: *sek II*
blaze: *bhel I*
blazer: *bhel I*
bleach: *bhel I*
bleak: *bhel I*
bleat: *bhel II*
bleeding: *beu*
blend: *bhel I*
blennorrhea: *mel I*
blenny: *mel I*
Blephilia: *kel VI*
blimp: *kel IV, reg I*
Blimp, Colonel: *kel IV*
blind: *bhel I*
blini: *mel V*
blink: *bhel I*
blintz: *mel V*
blister: *beu*
blitzkrieg: *guer*
bloat: *beu*
blob: *beu*
blockhead: *bhelk, caput*
blood: *beu, ugu*
bloom: *beu*
blossom: *beu*
blot: *beu*
blow: *beu*

blue: *bhel I, kel VI*
blue devils: *kel VI*
blue gown: *kel VI*
blue laws: *kel VI*
blues, the: *kel VI*
blue stocking: *kel VI*
bluff: *buff*
blunderbus: *kus*
blush: *bhel I*
bo: *bheudh*
board: *bher II*
boast: *beu*
boat: *bheid*
boatswain: *bheid*
bob: *ane*
bode: *bheudh*
bodega: *dhe I*
Bodhisattva: *bheudh, es*
Boer: *bheu, reuos*
bogy: *jing, sek I*
boil: *beu*
bold: *beu*
bolder: *dheigh N 13*
bole: *beu*
bolero: *beu*
boll: *beu*
bolometer: *guel II*
Bolshevik: *bel*
bolson: *burs*
bolster: *bel*
bomb: *bomb*
bombasine: *bomb*
bombast: *bomb*
bombazine: *bomb*
bombic: *bomb*
bombous: *bomb*
bombus: *bomb*
bombycinous: *bomb*
bombykol: *bomb*
bombylious: *bomb*
bombyx: *bomb*
bonafide: *bheidh, deu*
bona fides: *bheidh*
bonanza: *deu*
bonbon: *deu*
bond: *bhendh*
bondage: *bheu*
bonehead: *caput*
bonhomie: *deu, ghdhem*
bonito: *deu*
bonne: *deu*
bonne bouche: deu
bonny: *deu*
bonum magnum: me III
bonus: *deu*
bon voyage: *uegh*
boo: *jing*
booby: *baba*
book: *bhago, leup*
boom: *bheu*
boon: *bha I, deu*
boor: *bheu, reuos*
boot: *bhad*
bootblack: *bhad*
Boötes: *septm*
booth: *bheu*
bootlegger: *bhad*
bootless: *bhad*
bootlick: *bhad*
bootstraps: *bhad*
booze: *lus*
Borachio: *peuor*
bordello: *bher II*
border: *bher II*
bore: *bher II*
boredom: *dhe I*
boron: *el 5*
borough: *bheregh*
borrow: *bheregh*
bosom: *beu*
both: *ambh*
bother: *guou*
bottle: *guou*
bottom: *bhudh*
botulism: *gue, keup*
bough: *bhagus*
bouillabaisse: *beu*
bouillon: *beu*
boulder: *beu*
boulevard: *beu, uerg*
bountiful: *pel V*
bounty: *deu*
Bourbon: *bhereu*
bourgeois: *bheregh*
bourne: *bhereu*
bourse: *burs*
boustrophedon: *bheug II, guou, strebh*
bout: *bheng II*
boutique: *dhe I*
bovine: *ane, guou*
bow: *bhagus, bheng II*
bowdlerism: *kleu I*
bowdlerize: *esu, kens, peu II*
bowel: *gue, keup*

bower: *bheu*
bowery: *bheu*
bowl: *beu*
bowlegs: *bheug II*
bowwow: *jing*
boyau: gue, keup
boycott: *onomen*
brace: *braghu*
bracelet: *braghu*
brach: *bhrag*
brachinate: *braghu*
brachistochrone: *braghu*
brachycephalic: *braghu, caput, ueredh*
brachylogy: *braghu, dheigh N 30*
brad: *bhar*
Brahman: *ueik I*
braid: *bhel I*
Braidism: *suep I*
braille: *do*
brain: *mregh-mno*
brained: *mregh-mno*
brainy: *mregh-mno*
braise: *bhereu*
brake: *bhreg, sphereg*
bramberry: *bhel I*
bramble: *bherem*
branchia: *garg*
branchiform: *garg*
brand: *bhereu*
brandish: *bhereu*
brandy: *bhereu*
bras: *braghu*
brash: *bhreg*
brass: *el 29, el 30*
brassiere: *braghu*
brave: *baba*
bravo: *baba*
bravura: *baba*
brawn: *bhereu*
brazier: *bhereu*
breach: *bhreg*
bread: *bher I*
break: *bhreg, sphereg*
breakage: *dheigh N 4*
breakfast: *ieium, past*
bream: *bhel I, bherem*
breast: *bhreus*
breastworks: *uerg*
breath: *bhereu*
breathing: *bhereu*
breathlessly: *leu I*
breed: *bhereu*
breeze: *bhereu*
bregma: *mregh-mno*
breve: *braghu*
brevet: *braghu*
breviary: *braghu*
breviped: *ped*
brevity: *braghu*
brew: *bher I, bhereu*
brewery: *bhel I*
Brewster: *bhereu*
Briareus: *guer*
brick: *bhreg*
bridegroom: *ghdhem*
bridge: *bhar, bhru*
Bridget: *bhe*
Bridgit: *bhe*
bridle: *bhel I*
brief: *braghu*
brier: *uer II 6*
brigade: *guer*
brigadier: *guer*
brigand: *guer*
brigantine: *guer*
brim: *bherem*
brimstone: *bhereu, stai*
bring: *bher I*
brisk: *uer II 6*
brisket: *bhreus*
broach: *bhreg*
broadcast: *ger VI*
brocade: *bhreg*
broccoli: *bhreg*
brochure: *bhreg*
broil: *bhereu*
broke: *bhreg, sphereg*
broken: *bhreg*
broker: *bhreg*
bromatology: *el 35*
bromine: *el 35*
bronchia: *garg*
bronchiectasis: *ten*
bronchitis: *dheigh N 23, garg*
bronchospasm: *dheigh N 34*
bronchus: *garg*
Bronx cheer: *bhel I*
brooch: *bhreg*
brood: *bhereu*
Brooklyn: *pleu*
broom: *bherem*
broth: *bhereu*
brothel: *bher II, per VI f*
brother: *bhrater*

brotherhood: *suesor*
brow: *akua, bhru*
brown: *bhel I*
browse: *bhreus*
bruin: *bhel I*
bruise: *bhreg*
brummagem: *kei II*
brunette: *bhel I*
brush: *bherem*
brusque: *uer II 6*
brute: *guer*
bubble: *beu*
bubo: *beu*
buccal: *beu*
buccinator: *kan*
bucellas: *guou*
bucentaur: *guou*
Bucephalus: *caput, guou*
buceros: *guou*
Buchloë: *guou*
buck: *bhugo*
buckaroo: *uak*
bucket: *beu*
buckle: *beu*
buckwheat: *bhago*
bucolic: *ker I*
Buddha: *bheudh*
buff: *buff*
buffalo: *buff*
buffer: *buff*
buffet: *buff*
buffo: *buff*
buffoon: *buff*
bug: *sek I*
bugaboo: *jing, sek I*
bugbear: *sek I*
bugger: *hum, sek I*
buggery: *hum, sek I*
bugle: *guou*
bugloss: *glokh*
build: *bheu*
bulba: *beu*
bulbiform: *dheigh N 14*
bulimia: *guou, leud*
bulk: *beu*
bulkhead: *bhelk*
bull: *ane, beu, mel I*
bullet: *beu*
bulletin: *beu*
bullion: *beu*
bullock: *ane, beu*
bully: *beu*
bulwark: *uerg*
bumblebee: *kem IV*
bumpkin: *bheu*
bunco: *bheg*
bund: *bhendh*
bundle: *bhendh*
bung: *peug*
Bunsen burner: *el 37*
buoy: *bha II*
burbot: *bhereu*
burden: *bher I, burd*
burdock: *dheu II*
bureau: *peuor*
bureaucracy: *peuor*
bureaucrat: *peuor*
burg: *bheregh*
-burg: *bheregh*
burgher: *bheregh*
burglar: *bheregh*
burglaree: *geme*
burgomaster: *bheregh*
burial: *bheregh*
burl: *peuor*
burlesque: *peuor*
burly: *bher I*
burn: *bhereu*
burnish: *bher III*
Burns: *onomen*
burr: *bhar*
burrito: *peuor*
burro: *peuor*
bursa: *burs*
bursar: *dheigh N 13*
bursiform: *burs*
bursitis: *burs*
burst: *bhreg*
bury: *bheregh*
bushel: *bhaut*
business: *dheigh N 29*
busk: *sue*
buss: *kus*
bust: *eus*
bustard: *auei*
bustee: *ues I*
bustle: *sue*
but: *ambhi, ud*
butcher: *bhugo*
butler: *guou*
butt: *bhaut, guou*
butter: *guou, teue 1*
butterflies: *prai*
butterfly: *guou, lep I*

butterine: *margar*
buttery: *guou*
buttock(s): *bhaut*
button: *bhaut*
buttress: *bhaut*
butyl: *guou*
butyraceous: *guou*
butyric: *guou*
buxom: *bheug II*
buzz: *hum, jing*
by: *ambhi*
by(e)law: *bheu, legh*
by-name: *onomen*
byre: *bheu*
bzz, bzz: *perd*

C

cab: *kapr*
cabaret: *kam*
cabas: *kap*
cabbage: *kap*
cabinet: *kagh, keu II*
cable: *kap*
cabook: *keu II*
caboose: *bhendh, kel VI*
cabrilla: *kapr*
cabriolet: *kapr*
cacaphony: *caca*
cacca: *caca*
cachalot: *kap*
cache: *ag*
cachepot: *ag*
cachet: *ag*
cachexy: *caca, segh*
cackle: *ane, coc, jing*
cacochroia: *gher I*
cacodyl: *caca*
cacoëpy: *caca*
cacoëthes: *caca, seu IV*
cacogenesis: *gn*
cacography: *caca*
cacomistle: *caca*
caconym: *caca*
cacuminal: *gue, keu II*
cadaster: *steigh*
cadaver: *kad I*
cade: *ke*
cadelle: *kat*
cadence: *kad I*
cadenza: *kad I*
cadet: *caput*
cadge: *kagh*
cadger: *keu II*
Cadmus: *el 48*
caducity: *kad I*
caducous: *kad I*
c(a)ecum: *kaiko, kel IV*
caeoma: *kau I*
Caesarian: *sek II, skhai*
c(a)esium: *el 55*
c(a)esius: *kait*
caesura: *sek II, skhai*
cage: *kagh, keu II*
cahier: *kuetuer*
caisson: *kap*
caitiff: *kap*
caja: *kap*
cajeta: *kap*
cajole: *kagh, keu II*
calamary: *kolem*
calamint: *kolem*
calamite: *kolem*
calamitous: *plek I*
calamity: *kal, kel VIII*
calamus: *kolem*
calash: *ker I*
calcareous: *khalk*
calcine: *el 20, khalk*
calciphylaxis: *phulax*
calcite: *khalk*
calcium: *el 20, el 38, khalk*
calculate: *khalk*
Calcutta: *gher I*
calefacient: *dhe I, kel I*
calendar: *kel II*
calender: *skel*
calends: *kel II, neun*
Calendula: *kel II*
calenture: *kel I*
calf: *ane*
caliber: *kau I*
californium: *el 98*
Caligula: *uidhu*
caliper: *ped*
calisthenics: *cal*
call: *gal*
calla (lily): *cal*
Callicarpa: *cal*
callicebus: *cal*
calligraphy: *cal*
Calliope: *ueks*

calliope: *cal*
Callipyge: *cal*
callipygian: *cal*
Callirrhoë: *cal, sreu*
Callisto: *cal*
Callitriche: *cal*
callowness: *dheigh N 29*
Calluna: *cal*
calm: *kau I*
calomel: *cal*
Calonyction: *cal, nekut*
calophantic: *cal*
calophyllum: *cal*
calorescence: *kel I*
caloric: *kel I*
calorie: *guher, kel I*
calorifacient: *kel I*
calorific: *kel I*
calorimeter: *kel I*
calotte: *kel VIII*
caltrop: *dra*
calumet: *kolem*
calumny: *kel IX*
Calvary: *keleuo*
Calvatia: *keleuo*
Calvin: *keleuo*
calvities: *keleuo*
calx: *khalk*
calybite: *kel VI*
Calypso: *kel VI*
calyptra: *kel VI*
calyptrogen: *kel VI*
cam: *gembh*
camara: *kam*
camaraderie: *kam*
camarilla: *kam*
cambist: *skamb*
cambium: *skamb*
Cambrian: *merk*
Camelina: *ghdhem*
camellia: *ghdhem*
camera: *kam*
Camino Real: *reg I*
camisado: *kem I*
camise: *kem I*
camisole: *kem I*
camp: *kam, prai*
campaign: *kam, prai, skamb*
campanile: *prai*
campanulate: *prai*
Campephagidae: *kam*
Campephilus: *kam*
Campodea: *kam*
Camponotos: *not*
Camponotus: *kam*
campus: *kam, prai, skamb*
can: *gn, kamm*
cañada: *kann*
canaille: *kuon*
canal: *kann*
canapé: *konops*
canary: *ane, kuon*
canarybird: *kuon*
Canary Islands: *kuon*
canasta: *kann*
cancer: *kar*
Cancer: *guei, kar*
Cancer, Tropic of: *trep*
cancroid: *dar*
candelabrum: *kand*
candent: *kand*
candid: *dheigh N 13, kand*
candidate: *kand*
Candide: *kand*
candle: *kand*
cane: *kann*
canescent: *kand*
canicular: *kuon*
Canidae: *kuon*
canine: *kuon*
canions: *kann*
Canis: *kuon*
canister: *kann*
canities: *kand*
canker: *kar*
canna: *kann*
cannabis: *kann*
cannel: *kann*
cannelloni: *kann*
cannon: *kann*
cannula: *kann*
canon: *kann*
canopy: *konops*
canorous: *kan*
cant: *kan*
cantabile: *kan*
cantaloupe: *klou*
cantankerous: *kanth*
cantata: *kan*
cantatrice: *kan*
canteen: *kanth*
canter: *kan, suer I*
Canterbury: *bheregh, kan, suer I*
canthus: *kanth*

cantilever: *leguh*
cantle: *kanth*
cantlet: *kanth*
canto: *kan*
canton: *kanth*
cantor: *kan*
canvas: *kann*
canvass: *kann*
canyon: *kann*
canzone: *kan*
cap: *caput*
capable: *kap*
capacious: *kap*
capacity: *em, kap*
cap-a-pie: *caput*
caparison: *caput*
cape: *caput*
Capella: *kapr*
caper: *kapr*
capercailzie: *kapr*
capias: *kap*
capillary: *caput*
capistrate: *kap*
capital: *caput*
capitalism: *caput*
capo: *caput, ghers*
capon: *sek IV*
capote: *ghers*
cappricio: *ghers*
Caprella: *kapr*
Capreolus: *kapr*
Capri: *kapr*
capric: *kapr*
capriccio: *kapr*
caprice: *caput, ghers, kapr*
capricious: *caput, kapr*
Capricorn: *guei, kapr, ker II*
Capricorn, Tropic of: *trep*
caprification: *kapr*
Caprifoliaceae: *kapr*
Caprimulgidae: *kapr, melg*
caprine: *kapr*
caproic: *kapr*
capsa: *kap*
Capsella: *kap*
Capsicum: *kap*
capsize: *caput*
capstan: *caput, kap*
capsule: *kap*
captain: *caput*
captation: *kap*
caption: *kap*
captious: *kap*
captivate: *kap*
captive: *kap*
captivity: *kap*
captor: *kap*
capture: *kap*
capuche: *caput*
capuchin: *caput*
caput mortuum: *caput*
car: *kers I*
caracole: *kokhlos*
caramel: *kolem, melit*
carat: *ker II*
caravanserai: *ser II, ter III*
carbon: *el 6, ker V*
carbonaceous: *ker V*
carbonado: *ker V*
Carbonari: *ker V*
carborundum: *ker V*
carboxyl: *ker V*
carbuncle: *ker V*
carcinogen: *gn, kar*
carcinoma: *kar*
carcoon: *kuer*
cardia: *kerd*
cardiac: *kerd*
cardialgia: *dheigh N 6, kerd*
cardinal: *kerd*
cardiology: *kerd*
Cardiospermum: *kerd*
carditis: *kerd*
cardoncillo: *kars*
cardoon: *kars*
Carduus: *kars*
care: *cura, gal*
careen: *kar, kers I*
careering: *kers I*
careful: *cura*
careless: *dheigh N 26*
carelessness: *cura*
caress: *ka*
Carex: *kars*
carfax: *bhurig*
cargo: *kers I*
caricature: *kers I*
caries: *ker VII, seni*
carillon: *kuetuer*
carina: *kar*
cariole: *kers I*
carious: *ker VII*
cark: *kers I*
Carl: *ger V*

Carline: *ger V*
carline: *kars*
Carmelites: *dem*
Carmen: *kan*
carmen: *kan*
carminative: *kars*
carmine: *kurmi*
carnage: *ker III, sek IX*
carnal: *ker III, sek IX*
carnassial: *sek IX*
carnation: *ker III, sek IX*
carnelian: *ker II, sek IX*
carnival: *ker III, leguh*
carnivorous: *bhag, ker III, sek V, sek IX*
caroche: *kers I*
Caroline: *ger V*
carouse: *ud*
carp: *ger I, ker III*
carpal: *kuerp*
carpel: *ker III, sep IX*
carpenter: *kers I*
carpet: *ker III*
carpinus: *ker III*
carpogonium: *ker III*
carpology: *sek IX*
car pool: *suer III*
carpopedal: *kuerp*
carpophagous: *bhag, ker III*
carpophore: *ker III*
carpophyll: *ker III*
carport: *suer III*
Carpos: *sek IX*
carpus: *kuerp*
carriage: *kers I*
carrion: *ker III, sek IX*
carroccio: *kers I*
carrot: *ker II*
carry: *kers I*
cart: *ger I, kers I*
cartilage: *kert*
cartilaginous: *kert*
cartwright: *uerg*
caruncle: *ker III, sek IX*
carve: *gerbh*
caryatides: *tol*
cascade: *kad I*
cascara: *kuet*
casco: *kuet*
case: *kad I, kap*
casein: *kuo*
casement: *kap*
cash: *kap*
cashier: *kuet*
Casimer: *mei V*
cask: *kap, kuet*
casket: *kap*
casque: *kuet*
cassation: *kuet*
casserole: *keu II*
Cassida: kadh
Cassis: kadh
cassone: *kap*
cast: *ger VI*
castaway: *ger VI*
caste: *kastr*
castellan: *kastr*
castellated: *kastr*
castigate: *ag, kastr*
cast iron: *el 26*
castle: *kastr*
castoff: *ger VI*
Castor: *morui*
castramentation: *kastr*
castrate: *kastr*
castrato: *segh*
casual: *kad I*
casualty: *kad I*
cat: *ane, kam, kat, pilo*
catabasis: *gua*
catabolism: *guel II, kat*
catacaustic: *kau I*
catachrisis: *kat*
cataclasm: *kat*
cataclysm: *kat, kleu II*
catacomb(s): *kat, teue 6*
catacumbal: *teue 6*
catadioptric: *oku*
cataglottism: *kat*
catalectic: *kat, leg II*
catalepsy: *labh*
cataleptic: *slagu*
catalog(ue): *leg I*
catalysis: *leu I, lou*
catamaran: *kat*
catamenia: *me IV*
catamidiate: *kat*
catamite: *ga, jing, kat, morui*
catamount: *kam, kat*
catamountain: *ane*
cat and dog: *pilo*
catapult: *pal*
cataract: *kat*
catarrh: *kat, sreu*
Catarrhina: *kat, sreu*

catastasis: *sta*
catastrophe: *kat, strebh*
catatonic: *ten*
catawampus: *kat*
catcall: *pilo*
catch: *kap*
catchpole: *pou 9*
catchpoll: *kap, pou 9*
catechesis: *uagh*
catechism: *uagh*
catechize: *uagh*
catechumen: *uagh*
categorize: *ger III*
category: *ger III*
cater: *ane*
cater-cornered: *kuetuer*
cater-cousin: *kuetuer*
caterer: *pilo*
caterpillar: *kam, pilo*
caterwaul: *kam, pilo*
catgut: *pilo*
cathedral: *kat, sed I*
catheter: *ie, kat*
cathode: *sed II*
catholic: *kat, solo*
catholicon: *kat*
cathouse: *ane*
cation: *ei I*
catkin: *pilo*
cat-lap: *pilo*
catmint: *pilo*
catmium: *el 48*
cat nap: *ane*
catnip: *ane, pilo*
catocathartic: *kat*
catogenic: *kat*
cat-o'-nine-tails: *ane, pilo*
catoptric: *oku*
catoptromancy: *men I, oku*
cats and dogs: *pilo*
cat's cradle: *ane*
cat's-eye: *ane, pilo*
catsup: *pilo*
cattail: *pilo*
cattle: *caput*
catty-cornered: *kuetuer*
Caucasian: *kreu*
cauchemar: *mer II*
caudal: *kel VIII, kau III*
caudate: *kel VIII*
caudle: *kel I*
caul: *kel VIII, sek III*
ca(u)ldron: *kel I*
Caulerpa: *kaul*
caulescent: *kaul*
cauliflower: *kaul*
cauline: *kaul*
caulis: *kaul*
Caurus: *keuero*
causal: *kau III*
causate: *kau III*
cause: *kau III*
causerie: *kau III*
causeway: *khalk*
caustic: *kau I*
cautel: *keu I*
cautelous: *keu I*
cauterize: *kau I*
caution: *keu I*
cavalcade: *ane*
cavalier: *ane*
cavalry: *ane*
cavatina: *keu II*
caveat: *keu I*
caveat emptor: *em*
cavicorn: *ker II*
cavil: *kel IX*
cavo-relievo: *leguh*
caw: *jing*
cay: *kagh*
cease: *sed III*
Cecil: *kaiko*
cecity: *kaiko*
Cecrops: *oku*
cedar: *kedr*
cede: *sed III*
ceil: *kait*
ceiling: *kait*
celandine: *ghel I*
celebration: *kel VII*
celebrity: *kel VII*
celerity: *kel VII, oku*
celery: *peter*
celesta: *kait*
celestial: *kait, sta*
celibate: *kailo*
Céline: *kait*
cell: *kel VI*
cellar: *kel VI*
cellophane: *bha II*
cellular: *dheigh N 9, kel VI*
celluloid: *es*
cellulose: *dheigh N 2 g*
cement: *sek II*

cemetery: *kei II*
cenacle: *ker III, sek V*
cenobite: *ei I, guei, kom*
cenosite: *ken III*
cenotaph: *dhembh*
cenozoic: *guei*
Cenozoic: *guei, ken III*
censor: *kens*
censorious: *kens*
censorship: *kens*
census: *kens*
cent: *dekm*
centaur: *dekm*
centenary: *dekm*
centennial: *dekm*
center: *kent*
centi-: *me IV*
centillion: *me IV*
centimeter: *me IV*
cento: *kent*
centralization: *kent*
centrifugal: *bheug I, kent, pet I*
centripetal: *bheug I, kent, pet I*
centrobaric: *guer, kent*
centrosome: *kent*
Centunculus: *kent*
centuple: *plek I*
cephalic: *caput*
Cephalonia: *caput*
cephalopod: *ped*
ceramics: *ker V*
cerastes: *ker II*
cerastium: *ker II*
Ceratodus: *ker II*
ceratoid: *ker II*
ceraunite: *ker VII*
ceraunograph: *ker VII*
ceraunoscope: *ker VII*
cere: *keneko*
cereal: *ker VI*
cerebellum: *ker II*
cerebrose: *ker II*
cerebrum: *ker II*
cerecloth: *el 58, keneko*
cerement: *keneko*
ceremonious: *dheigh N 2 d*
ceremony: *keneko*
Ceres: *el 58, ker VI*
Cereus: *keneko*
Cerinthe: *keneko*
Cerion: *keneko*
cerite: *el 57, el 58*
cerium: *el 57, el 58, ker VI*
cernuous: *ker III*
cerography: *el 58*
ceromancy: *el 58*
ceroplasty: *el 58*
cerotic: *el 58*
certain: *ker III, sek VI*
certainty: *sek VI*
certificate: *ker III, sek VI*
certify: *ker III, sek VI*
certiorari: *sek VI*
certitude: *ker III, sek VI*
cerulean: *kait*
cerumen: *keneko*
ceruse: *keneko*
cerussite: *keneko*
cervelat: *ker II*
cervical: *ker II*
cervine: *ker II*
cesium: *el 37, el 55*
cession: *sed III*
cesspool: *sed II, speis*
cestrum: *kent*
cestus: *kent, sek II*
chafe: *dhe I, kel I*
chafer: *geph*
chaff: *geph, kel I*
chaffer: *geph*
chaffinch: *spingo*
chafing dish: *kel I*
chair: *ker III, sek V*
chaise: *sed I*
chaise longue: *sed I*
chalk: *khalk*
challenge: *kel IX*
chalumeau: *kolem*
Chamaecyparis: *ghdhem*
Chamaedaphne: *ghdhem*
Chamaelirium: *ghdhem*
chamber: *kam*
chamberlain: *kam*
chameleon: *ghdhem*
chamfer: *kanth*
chamois: *kem II*
chamomila: *ghdhem*
c(h)amomile: *abel, ghdhem*
champagne: *kam, prai*
champaign: *kam, prai*
champerty: *prai*
champignon: *kam, prai*
champion: *kam, prai*
championship: *sek IV*

champlevé: *leguh*
chance: *kad I*
chancellor: *kad I*
chancre: *kar*
chancy: *kad I*
change: *skamb*
changeable: *skam*
changeling: *sap*
channel: *kann*
chanson: *kan*
chant: *kan*
chantage: *kan*
chantecler: *ane, kan*
chanticleer: *kel II*
chaogenesis: *gn*
chaos: *cal, ghi*
chap: *sek IV*
chapel: *caput*
chaperon: *caput*
chaplain: *caput*
chapman: *abel*
chapter: *caput*
charabanc: *kers I*
character: *gher I*
characterization: *gher I*
charactery: *gher I*
charade: *char*
chard: *kars*
chargé d'affaires: *kers I*
charisma: *gher II*
charismatic: *gher II*
charitable: *dheigh N 3*
charity: *amma, dheigh N 36, ka*
charivari: *ker II*
charlatan: *char*
Charlemagne: *ger V, septm*
Charles: *ger V*
Charles's Wain: *ger V, septm*
charlie: *bhar*
charm: *gal, kan*
charnel: *ker III, sek IX*
Charon: *gher II, kau II*
charpoy: *ped*
chary: *gal*
Charybdis: *sek IV*
chase: *kap*
chasm: *ghi, keu II*
chassis: *kap*
chaste: *kastr*
chasten: *kastr*
chastity: *dheigh N 36, kastr*
chastize: *kastr*
chateau: *kastr*
chatelain: *kastr*
chatoyant: *kam*
chattel: *caput*
chatter: *jing*
chaudmellé: *kel I*
chaudpisse: *kel I*
chaudron: *kel I*
chauffeur: *kel I, rad I*
chaussée: *khalk*
cheat: *kad I*
check: *ksei*
checkers: *ksei*
checkmate: *dheigh N 10, ksei*
cheer: *ker II*
cheerfulness: *ker II*
cheese: *kuo*
cheeseburger: *bheregh, konemo*
cheesecloth: *kuo*
cheeseparing: *kuo*
cheetah: *kait, skai*
cheiranthus: *gher IV*
Chem: *au I*
chemise: *kem I*
chemistry: *au I, gheu, kers II*
chemotherapy: *au I*
chenille: *kuon*
chenopod: *ghans*
cheque: *ksei*
cherish: *ka*
chernozem: *kers II*
cheronese: *sna I*
cherry: *sek II*
chersonese: *ghers*
cherub: *sek II*
cherubic: *sek II*
Cherubicon: *sek II*
chervil: *gher II*
chess: *kap, ksei*
chest: *kista*
chevalier: *ane*
cheverel: *kapr*
chevron: *kapr*
chevrotain: *kapr*
chew: *gieu*
chiaroscuro: *kel II, skeu*
chiave: *kleu III*
chick: *ane, auei*
chickabiddy: *bhe*
chicory: *kerd*
chief: *caput*
chieftain: *caput*

chiliad: *gheslo*
chill: *gel I*
chime: *keu II*
chimney: *kam, kau I*
chin: *genu*
chine: *sek II*
chintz: *kait, skai*
Chiococca: *kogkhos*
chiromachy: *gher IV*
chiromancy: *gher IV, men I*
Chiron: *dekm, gher IV*
chironomy: *gher IV*
chiropodist: *gher IV*
chiropractor: *gher IV*
chirotonize: *gher IV*
chirurgeon: *gher IV, uerg*
chisel: *sek II, skhai*
chit: *kait, skai*
chital: *kait, skai*
chitterlings: *geu, gue, keup*
chitty: *skai*
chloretone: *gel I*
chloride: *gel I*
chlorine: *gel I, el 17*
Chloris: *sek IX*
chloroacetophenone: *gel I*
chloroform: *dheigh N 14, morui*
chloroma: *gel I*
Chloromycetin: *gel I*
chlorophyll: *beu, gel I, sek IX*
chloroplast: *pela*
chlorosis: *gel I*
chlorotile: *gel I*
choana: *gheu*
chobdar: *dhar*
choir: *gher IV*
chokeberry: *bhel I*
chokidar: *dhar*
choler: *gel I, ugu*
cholera: *gel I*
cholera morbus: *mer II*
choleric: *gel I, ugu*
cholesterol: *gel I, ster II*
cholic: *gel I*
cholinergic: *uerg*
chomage: *kau I*
chondrodite: *ghren*
chondroid: *ghren*
chondroma: *ghren*
chonolith: *gheu*
choragus: *ag, gher IV*
choral: *aulo*
chorale: *gher IV*
chorea: *sak*
choriamb: *gher IV*
choric: *gher IV*
chorion: *ghe*

choristate: *ghe*
chorister: *gher IV*
choristophyllous: *ghe*
chorizontes: *ghe*
chortle: *reu*
chorus: *gher IV*
chou: *kaul*
chowder: *kel I*
chrestomathy: *men I*
chrismatory: *gher I*
Christ: *gher I*
Christian: *gher I*
Christian name: *onomen*
Christmas: *gher I*
Christopher: *gher I*
chromatic: *gher I*
chromatophore: *gher I*
chromatoscope: *gher I*
chrome: *gher I*
chromium: *el 24, gher I*
chromolithograph: *gher I*
chromonema: *sne*
chromophyll: *gher I*
chromosome: *dheigh N 37, gher I*
chronaxy: *ag, gher IV, nebh*
chronic: *gher IV, nebh*
chronicle: *nebh*
chronogram: *gher IV, leip II, nebh*
chronograph: *gher IV*
chronological: *dheigh N 5, nebh*
chronometer: *gher IV, nebh*
chronoscope: *gher IV, nebh*
Chrysemys: *uem*
chthonian: *ghdhem*
chthonic: *ghdhem*
chthonography: *ghdhem*
chub: *geu*
chubby: *geu*
chukar: *kau II*
chukker: *ker I*
church: *keu II*
chute: *kad I*
chyle: *gheu*
chylify: *gheu*
chyluria: *gheu*
chyme: *gheu*

chymify: *gheu*
chymotrypsin: *ter II*
chytra: *gheu*
Cicindelidae: *kand*
cierge: *keneko*
cilia: *kel VI*
cimarron: *keu II*
cimelia: *kei II*
cimeliarch: *kei II*
cinch: *kenk I*
cinct: *kenk I*
cincture: *kenk I*
cinema: *kei I*
cinematography: *dheigh N 16*
Cineraria: *ken I*
cinerarium: *ken I*
cinerary: *ken I*
cingulum: *kenk I*
cinquain: *penkue*
cinq(ue): *penkue*
cinquecento: *penkue*
cinter: *kenk I*
circa: *ker I*
circadian: *dei*
Circaëtus: *ker IV*
Circe: *nebh*
circean: *nebh*
circle: *ker I*
circuit: *ei I*
circuitous: *ker I*
circular: *ker I*
circularize: *ker I*
circum-: *ker I*
circumbendibus: *ker I*
circumcision: *ker I, sek II*
circumference: *ker I*
circumflex: *plek II*
circumgirate: *gue, keup*
circuminsession: *ker I*
circumjacent: *ie*
circumlocution: *ker I, tolku*
circumnavigate: *ker I, nau II*
circumscribe: *ker III, sek VI*
circumspect: *spek*
circumstance: *ker I, sta*
circumstantial: *ker I, sta*
circumvallate: *uals*
circumvene: *gua*
circumvolution: *uelu*
circus: *ker I*
cirque: *ker I*
ciruela: *keneko*
cisalpine: *ko*
cisium: *kista*
cismontane: *men II*
cispontine: *ko, pent*
cist: *kista*
cistern: *kista*
cistophore: *kista*
cistvaen: *kista*
citadel: *kei II*
citation: *kei I*
cite: *kei I*
citizen: *kei I*
citracaucasian: *ko*
citramontane: *ko*
citrate: *kedr*
citric: *kedr*
citron: *kedr*
citronella: *kedr*
citrul: *kedr*
Citrullus: *kedr*
citrus: *kedr*
city: *kei II*
civic: *kei II*
civil: *kei II*
civility: *kei II*
civilization: *kei II*
clack: *gal, kleg*
cladceran: *ker II*
cladocean: *kal*
claim: *kel II*
clairvoyance: *kel II, ueid*
clam: *gel I, kel VI*
clamant: *kel II*
clamber: *gel I*
clammy: *gel I*
clamor: *kel II*
clamp: *gel I*
clan: *pela*
clandestine: *kel VI*
clang: *kleg*
clank: *kleg*
clap: *coc*
Clara: *kel II*
clarabella: *deu*
Clarence: *kel II*
claret: *kel II*
Claribel: *kel II*
clarify: *dhe I, kel II*
clarinet: *kel II*
clarion: *kel II*
clarity: *dheigh N 36, kel II*
Clark: *onomen*

clasp: *gel I*
class: *kel II*
classical: *kel II*
classify: *kel II*
clastic: *kal*
clathrate: *kleu III*
clatter: *gal*
claustral: *kleu III*
claustration: *kleu III*
claustrophobia: *kleu III*
clava: *kleu III*
clavate: *kleu III*
clavecin: *kleu III*
clavelization: *kleu III*
clavicembalo: *kleu III*
Claviceps: *kleu III*
clavichord: *kleu III*
clavicle: *kleu III*
clavicorn: *ker II, kleu III*
clavier: *kleu III*
claviform: *kleu III*
clavis: *kleu III*
clay: *gel I*
claymore: *kal, kel VIII*
clean: *gel I*
cleanse: *gel I*
Cleanthus: *kleu I*
clear: *kel II*
cleat: *gel I*
cleave: *gel I, gleubh*
cledonism: *kleu I*
clef: *kleu III*
cleft: *gleubh*
cleidomancy: *kleu III*
cleidomastoid: *kleu III*
cleistogamy: *kleu III*
cleistogenous: *kleu III*
cleithral: *kleu III*
clematis: *kal*
clemency: *klei*
clement: *klei*
clench: *gel I*
clepsydra: *aue, klep*
clergy: *kal, kel VIII*
clerical: *kal, kel VIII*
clerihew: *el 9*
cleruch: *segh*
clever: *gel I*
clew: *gel I*
click: *kleg*
client: *klei*
cliff: *gel I, gleubh*
climacteric: *klei*
climactic: *klei*
climate: *klei*
climax: *klei*
climb: *gel I*
clime: *klei*
clinamen: *klei*
clinch: *gel I*
clinchpoop: *kleg*
cling: *gel I*
clinic: *klei*
clink: *kleg*
clinkum-clankum: *kleg*
clinobasic: *klei*
clinochore: *klei*
clinohedric: *klei*
clinoid: *klei*
clinometer: *klei*
Clio: *kleu I*
clip: *gel I*
clitellum: *klei*
clition: *klei*
clitoridectomy: *dheigh*
clitoris: *klei*
clivus: *klei*
cloaca: *kleu II*
clockwork: *uerg*
clod: *gel I*
cloisonné: *kleu III*
cloister: *kleu III*
clone: *kel VII*
clonus: *kel VII*
close: *kleu III*
close-stool: *kleu III*
closet: *kleu III*
clot: *gel I*
cloth: *gel I*
cloud: *gel I*
cloudberry: *bhel I*
cloudlet: *legh*
clout: *gel I*
clove: *gleubh, kleu III*
cloven: *gleubh*
clover: *gel I*
clown: *gel I, kuel*
cloy: *kleu III*
club: *gel I*
clue: *gel I*
clump: *gel I*
clutch: *gel I*
clutter: *gel I*
clysma: *kleu II*

clyster: *kleu II*
Clytemnestra: *men I*
cnemial: *konemo*
coaction: *ag*
coadunation: *oino*
coagulate: *ag*
coast: *kost*
coastal: *kost*
coaxial: *aks*
cobalt: *el 27, gen, geu, tuer II*
coble: *keu II*
cobweb: *geu*
coccid: *kogkhos*
coccus: *kogkhos*
coccygeal: *kokila*
coccyx: *kokila*
cochineal: *kogkhos*
cochlea: *kokhlos*
cochleare: *kokhlos*
cochleate: *kokhlos*
cock: *ane, auei, kokila*
cockaleekie: *ane*
cockatoo: *ane*
cockatrice: *ane, dheigh N 18, kokila*
cockboat: *kau III*
cocker: *kokila*
cockerel: *ane, kokila*
cockle: *kokhlos*
cockney: *auei*
cockroach: *ane, kokila*
cocksure: *ane, auei*
cocoon: *kogkhos*
cocotte: *auei*
Cocytus: *kau II*
cod: *geu, gue, keup*
coddle: *gue, leo*
code: *ane, kau III*
codeine: *keu II*
codex: *ane, kau III*
codfish: *geu, keup, peisk*
codicil: *kau III*
codify: *dheigh N 15, kau III*
codling: *kerd, leo, sap*
codon: *keu II*
codpiece: *burd, geu, gue, keup, peisk*
coelom: *keu II*
coenobite: *men III*
coenobium: *kom*
coenosarc: *kom, tuerk*
coenurus: *ors*
coercion: *areq*
coetaneous: *aiu*
Coeur de Lion: *leo*
coeval: *aiu*
coexistence: *dheigh N 8*
coffer: *kophin*
coffin: *kophin*
coffret: *kophin*
cogency: *ag*
cogitate: *ag*
cognate: *gn*
cognition: *gn*
cognizant: *gn*
cognomen: *onomen*
cogwheel: *geu*
cohabit: *ghebh*
cohere: *ghais*
coherent: *ghais*
coil: *leg I*
coincide: *kad I*
coincidence: *kad I*
coition: *ei I*
coitus: *ei I*
col: *ker I*
colander: *kagh*
colcannon: *kaul, ueid*
cold: *kaul*
colder: *dheigh N 13*
coleopteron: *kel VI*
coleoptile: *pet I*
coleorhiza: *kel VI, uerad*
coleslaw: *kaul*
coleus: *kel VI*
coli, Escherichia: *kel IV*
colitis: *ker I*
collaborate: *leb*
collage: *kollei*
collagen: *kollei*
collapse: *leb*
collar: *ker I*
collate: *tol*
collation: *tol*
colleague: *leg I, leig II*
collect: *leg I, kom*
college: *leg I*
Collembola: *kollei*
colliculus: *gue, kel IV*
collide: *laed*
collidine: *kollei*
colligate: *leig II*
collimate: *lino*
colline: *gue, kel IV*
collinear: *lino*
collision: *kom, laed*

collistrigium: *teu*
collocate: *leu III*
collocution: *tolku*
collodion: *kollei*
colloid: *kollei*
collophore: *kollei*
colloquy: *tolku*
collusion: *leid II*
colobium: *kal*
coloboma: *kal*
cologne: *ker I*
colon: *kel IV, ker I, skel*
Colonel: *kel IV*
colonel: *gue, kel IV*
colonial: *ker I*
colonic: *kel IV*
colonnade: *gue, kel IV*
colopexy: *pag*
colophon: *kel IV*
colophony: *kel IV*
color: *kel VI*
colpenchyma: *kuelp*
colpenrynter: *kuelp*
colpitis: *kuelp*
colpolcele: *kuelp*
colter: *sek III*
Columba: *kel III, mai I*
columbarium: *kel III*
Columbella: *kel III*
Columbia: *kel III*
Columbine: *kel III*
columbine: *kel III*
Columbus: *kel III*
column: *gue, kel IV*
columnar: *kel IV*
colure: *ors*
colza: *kaul*
coma: *kei II*
comatose: *dheigh N 2 g*
comb: *gembh*
combat: *bat, dheigh*
combatant: *kom*
combe: *gue*
combine: *duo, kom*
combustible: *eus*
combustion: *eus, kom*
come: *gua*
comedy: *aus, ued*
comestible: *ed*
comet: *kuere*
comfit: *dhe I*
comfort: *bheregh*
comity: *smei I*
comma: *kel IV, sek, sek IV*
command: *man*
commander: *man*
commandment: *kom, man*
commence: *ei I*
commencement: *ei I, kom, man*
commend: *man*
commendation: *man*
commensurate: *me IV*
commerce: *merc*
commercial: *dheigh N 5*
commination: *men II*
commingle: *kom*
commissariat: *smeit*
commission: *dheigh N 19, smeit*
commit: *smeit*
commitment: *dheigh N 28*
committee: *smeit*
commix: *meik*
commode: *med*
commodious: *med*
commodity: *med*
commodore: *man*
common: *mei II*
Commons: *mei II*
commonweal: *uel III*
commotion: *meu II*
commune: *mei II*
communicate: *mei II*
communion: *dheigh N 19*
Communist: *mei II*
community: *mei II*
commutations: *mei II*
commute: *mei II*
compact: *pag*
companion: *mad, pa*
company: *pa*
comparative: *per I*
compare: *per I, per V*
comparison: *per I*
compartment: *per I, per II*
compartmentalize: *per I, per V*
compass: *pet I*
compassion: *paen*
compatible: *paen*
compel: *kom, pel IV*
compendious: *pend*
compendium: *pend, spend II*
compensate: *pend, spend II*
compensation: *pend*
compete: *pet I*

competent: *kom*
competition: *kom, pet I*
competitor: *pet I*
complacent: *pela*
complainant: *plek I*
complaint: *plek I*
complement: *pel V, plek I*
complete: *pel V*
complex: *plek I*
complexion: *plek I*
complicate: *plek I*
complicity: *plek I*
compliment: *pel V, plek I*
complot: *pilo*
comply: *pel V, plek I*
comport: *per II*
composite: *ap*
composition: *ap, kom*
compound: *ap*
compress: *per VII, pres*
comprise: *dheigh N 25*
compromise: *dheigh N 25, smeit*
compulsion: *pel IV*
compulsory: *pel IV*
compunction: *peug*
compurgation: *peu II*
compute: *peue*
comrade: *kam, mad*
Comus: *nebh*
con: *gn*
conarium: *ke*
conation: *ken II*
conceal: *kel VI*
concede: *sed III*
conceit: *kap*
conceive: *gn, kap*
concentrate: *kent*
conception: *gn, kap, kom*
concern: *ker III, sek VI*
concert: *kan, ker III*
concession: *sed III*
conch: *kokhlos*
conchology: *kokhlos*
concierge: *ser II*
conciliate: *kel II*
concise: *sek II*
conclave: *kleu III*
conclude: *kleu III*
concoct: *peku*
concoction: *peku*
concomitant: *ei I*
concord: *kerd*
concourse: *kers I*
concrescence: *ker VI*
concrete: *ker VI*
concubine: *cub, gue, keu II*
concupiscence: *kuep*
concur: *kers I*
concussion: *kuet*
concutient: *kuet*
condemn: *da II*
condemnation: *dheigh N 19*
condense: *dens*
condescend: *skand*
condign: *dek*
condiment: *dhe I*
condition: *deik*
condolence: *del II*
condominium: *kom*
condone: *do*
condottiere: *deuk*
conducive: *deuk, dheigh N 24*
conduct: *deuk*
conductor: *deuk*
conduit: *deuk*
cone: *ke*
coney: *gn*
Coney Island: *gn*
confabulation: *bha I*
confection: *dhe I*
confederation: *bheidh*
confer: *kom*
conference: *bher I*
confession: *bha I*
confidant: *bheidh*
confide: *bheidh*
confident: *bheidh*
configuration: *dheigh*
confinement: *fin*
confirm: *dhar*
confiteor: *bha I*
conflagration: *bhel I*
conflict: *bhlag*
confluence: *beu*
conform: *merbh*
confound: *gheu*
confrere: *bhrater*
confront: *frons*
confuse: *gheu*
confute: *bhaut, gheu*
congé: *mei II*
congee: *mei II*
congener: *gn*
congenial: *gn*

congenital: *gn, kom*
congeries: *ger VI, ges*
congested: *ger VI*
congestion: *ges*
congius: *kokhlos*
conglomerate: *gel I*
congratulations: *gar*
congregation: *ger I*
congress: *ghredh*
conidium: *ken I*
coniology: *ken I*
conionycetes: *ken I*
coniospermous: *ken I*
conjecture: *ie*
conjoin: *ieug*
conjugal: *dheigh N 5, ieug, kom*
conjugation: *ieug*
conjunction: *ieug*
conjunctivitis: *ieug*
conjure: *ieuos*
connate: *gn*
connect: *kom*
connection: *ned*
conning tower: *gn*
connive: *kneiguh*
connoisseur: *gn*
connotation: *gn*
connubial: *sneubh*
Conopaphagidae: *konops*
conquer: *kom, kuere*
conqueror: *kuere*
conquest: *kuere*
conquian: *kom, kuo*
conquistador: *kuere*
conscience: *sek II*
conscientious: *sek II*
conscious: *sek II*
conscribe: *sek VI*
conscript: *ker III*
conscription: *sek VI*
consecrate: *sak*
consecutive: *seku*
consensus: *sent*
consent: *sent*
consequence: *seku I*
conserve: *ser II, suer I*
consider: *sueid I*
consideration: *sueid I*
consign: *sek I, seku I*
consilient: *sel IV*
consist: *sta*
consociate: *seku I*
consolation: *sel II, seu IV*
console: *sel II*
consolidate: *kom*
consonant: *kom*
consort: *ser I*
conspectus: *spek*
conspicuous: *spek, sphei II*
conspiracy: *speis*
conspue: *sphieu*
constable: *ei I, kom*
constant: *sta*
Constantinople: *pele*
constellation: *ster III*
consternation: *ster I, ster II*
constipated: *steibh*
constituents: *sta*
constitute: *sta*
constitution: *sta*
constrain: *ster I, streig*
constrict: *ster I, streig*
construct: *ster I*
constructivism: *ster I*
consuetudinary: *sue*
consul: *sel III*
consult: *kel II, sel III*
consultation: *sel III*
consume: *em*
consummate: *upo II*
consumption: *em*
contact: *kom, tag I*
contagion: *tag I*
contagious: *tag I*
contain: *ten*
contaminate: *tag I*
contemplate: *temp 2*
contemplation: *temp 2*
contemplative: *temp 2*
contemporaneous: *temp 5*
contemporary: *temp 5*
contend: *ten*
content: *ten*
contention: *ten*
contents: *ten*
co(n)terminous: *ter III*
contest: *tre*
context: *tekhs*
contextual: *tekhs*
contiguity: *tag I*
contiguous: *tag I*
continue: *ten*
contline: *kanth*
contort: *tereq*

contortions: *tereq*
contour: *ter II*
contraband: *bha I, kom*
contraceptive: *kom*
contract: *tragh*
contradictory: *dheigh N 35*
contrahent: *tragh*
contraption: *trep*
contrapuntal: *kom*
contrary: *kom*
contrast: *sta*
contravallation: *uals*
contravene: *gua*
contretemps: *temp 5*
contribute: *tre*
contrite: *kom, ter II*
contrition: *ter II*
contrive: *trep*
controversy: *uer II 5*
contubernium: *treb*
contumacy: *teue 7*
contumelious: *teue 7*
contumely: *teue 7*
contusion: *steu*
convalescence: *ual*
convection: *uegh*
convene: *gua*
convenient: *gua*
convent: *gua*
convention: *gua, kom*
converge: *uer II 2*
conversant: *uer II 5*
conversation: *uer II 5*
converse: *uer II 5*
conversion: *uer II 5*
convert: *uer II 5*
convertible: *kom*
convex: *uag I, uegh*
convey: *uegh*
conveyance: *uegh*
convicium: *ueks*
convict: *kom*
convocate: *ueks*
convocation: *ueks*
convoke: *ueks*
convolution: *uelu*
convolve: *uelu*
convoy: *uegh*
convulsion: *uel III*
coo: *jing*
cook: *peku*
cool: *gel I*
coomb: *gue*
cooncan: *kuo*
coop: *gue, keup*
cooperate: *op I*
co-ops: *op I*
coordinate: *ar I*
cop: *el 29, kap, keup*
coparcener: *per V*
cope: *kal*
copepod: *kap*
Copernican: *pal*
copious: *op I*
copper: *el 29, kap*
coppice: *kal*
coprolite: *caca*
coprolith: *keku*
coprology: *caca, keku*
coproperty: *keku*
coprophagous: *bhag, caca, keku*
coprophilous: *caca*
Coprosma: *keku, od*
copse: *kal*
Coptis: *sek IV*
copula: *ap*
copulate: *ap*
copy: *op I*
copyist: *op I*
copyright: *op I*
coquelicot: *kokila*
coquette: *auei*
coquina: *kokhlos*
Cora: *ker VI*
coracine: *ker IV*
coracle: *sek*
coracoid: *ker IV*
coralberry: *bhel I*
coram: *or*
coranto: *kers I*
corbeau: *ker IV*
corbel: *ker IV*
corbine: *ker IV*
cordate: *kerd*
cordial: *kerd*
cordiform: *kerd*
core: *kerd*
coreligionist: *leig II*
corema: *ker III*
Coreopsis: *sek IX*
coreopsis: *ker III*
coreopsy: *oku*
corespondent: *kom, spend I*
coriaceous: *ker III, sek IX*

coriander: *sek IX*
Corinna: *ker VI*
corium: *ker III, sek V*
corm: *ker III*
cormorant: *ker IV, mori*
cornea: *ker II*
Corneille: *ker IV*
cornel: *ker II*
cornelian: *ker II*
Cornelius: *ker II*
cornemuse: *men I*
corner: *ker II*
cornet: *ker II*
cornice: *ker I*
corniculate: *ker II*
cornucopia: *ker II, op I*
corona: *ker II*
corporal: *caput, krep*
corporation: *krep*
corporeal: *krep*
corposant: *sak*
corps: *krep*
corpse: *krep*
corpulent: *krep*
corpus: *krep*
corpuscle: *krep*
corral: *kers I*
correct: *kom, reg I*
corrective: *reg I*
correlate: *tol*
correption: *labh*
correspond: *spend I*
correspondent: *kom*
corridor: *kers I, rad I*
corrode: *rad I*
corrosive: *rad I*
corrupt: *reup*
corsair: *kers I*
cortex: *ker III, sek IX*
corum: *sek IX*
corvée: *reg I*
corvine: *ker IV*
Corvus: *ker IV*
Corydalis: *ker II*
corymb: *ker II*
Coryneum: *ker II*
coryphaeus: *ker II*
cosmetics: *cal, kens*
cosmetology: *kens*
cosmic: *kens*
cosmo-: *kens*
cosmogony: *gn, kens*
cosmology: *kens*
cosmonaut: *cal, nau II*
cosmopolitan: *cal, kens, pele*
cosmorama: *cal, suer I*
cosmos: *cal, kens*
cosset: *sed*
cost: *sta*
costal: *kost*
costard: *kost*
costate: *kost*
costermonger: *kost*
costive: *steibh*
costrel: *kost*
cot: *geu*
cote: *geu*
cottage: *geu*
couch: *leu III*
couch grass: *guei*
coulée: *kagh*
coulisse: *kagh*
couloir: *kagh*
co(u)lter: *kel VIII*
council: *kel II*
counsel: *kel II, sel III*
count: *ei I, kom, peue*
countenance: *dheigh N 8*
counter: *kom*
counteract: *kom*
countermand: *man*
countermark: *merk*
counterpane: *peug*
counterpoint: *peug*
countersign: *sek I*
countertenor: *ten*
countervail: *ual*
country: *kom*
county: *ei I, kom*
coup: *kal*
coupe: *kal*
couple: *ap*
coupon: *kal*
courage: *kerd*
courageous: *dheigh N 2, kerd*
courante: *kers I*
courier: *kers I*
course: *kers I*
court: *gher IV*
courteous: *dheigh N 2 a, gher IV*
courtesan: *gher IV*
courtesy: *gher IV*
court holy water: *gher IV*
courtier: *gher IV*

courtly love: *ane*
courtship: *dheigh N 33*
courtyard: *gher IV*
cousin: *suesor*
coutel: *kel VIII*
couth: *gn*
couture: *siu*
couturier: *siu*
couvade: *cub, gue, keu II*
cove: *gue*
coven: *gua*
covenant: *gua*
Covent Garden: *bhe, gua*
cover: *suer I*
coverlet: *legh*
covert: *suer I*
coverture: *suer I*
covet: *kuep*
covetous: *kuep*
covey: *cub, keu II*
cow: *grou, keup*
coward: *kel VIII*
cowardice: *kel VIII*
cowberry: *bhel I*
cowcatcher: *guhen*
cower: *geu, keup*
cowl: *caput, keup*
Cowley: *leuk*
cowslip: *grou, lei I, sleubh*
coxa: *kenk III*
coxaglia: *kenk III*
coxcomb: *ane, auei*
coxitis: *kenk III*
coxswain: *ane, kau III*
cozen: *suesor*
cozenage: *suesor*
crab: *gerbh, kar*
crab apple: *kar*
crabbed: *kar*
crabby: *kar*
crack: *ker IV*
cradle: *ger I*
craftsman: *dheigh N 27*
craftsmanship: *dheigh N 33, sek IV*
crake: *ger II, ker IV*
cram: *ger I, ger III*
Crambe: *ker I*
crambo: *ker I*
cramp: *ger I*
cranberry: *bhel I, ger II*
crane: *ger II*
craniometry: *dheigh N 36*
craniotomy: *tel*
cranium: *ker II*
crank: *ger I*
crass: *kert*
crate: *kert*
crater: *kere*
crateriform: *kere*
craven: *ker IV*
crawl: *gerbh, kar*
crayfish: *gerbh, kar, kueit*
crayon: *ker III, sek VI*
creak: *ker IV*
cream: *gher I*
create: *ker VI*
creation: *ker VI*
creationism: *ker VI*
creative: *kreu*
creature: *ker VI*
crèche: *ger I*
credence: *kred I*
credentials: *kred I*
credible: *kred I*
credit: *kred I*
creditor: *kred I*
credo: *kred I*
credulity: *kred I*
credulous: *kred I*
creed: *kred I*
creek: *ger I*
creel: *kert*
creep: *ger I*
cremation: *ker V*
crematory: *ker V*
cremocarp: *ker III*
creodont: *kreu*
creole: *ker VI*
creophagous: *kreu*
creosote: *kreu, teue 4*
crepe: *ker I*
crepitate: *ker IV*
crescendo: *ker VI*
crescent: *ker VI*
cress: *gras*
crest: *ker I, ters*
crestate: *ker I*
cretaceous: *ker III*
Crete: *ker VI*
crevasse: *ker IV*
crevice: *ker IV*
crew: *ker VI*
crib: *ger I*
cribriform: *ker III, sek VI*

cricket: *ker IV*
cricoid: *ker I*
crim. con.: *ker IV*
crime: *ker III, ker IV, sek VI, skrei*
criminal: *ker III, ker IV, sek VI*
crimp: *ger I*
crimson: *kurmi*
cringe: *ger I*
crinite: *ker I*
crinkle: *ger I*
crinkum-crankum: *kleg*
crinoline: *ker I, lino*
criocephalous: *ker II*
criocerate: *ker II*
crioceratite: *ker II*
criosphinx: *ker II*
crious: *ker II*
cripple: *ger I*
crisis: *ker III, sek VI*
crisp: *ker I*
crispate: *ker I*
crissum: *ker I*
criterion: *ker III, sek VI*
crith: *ghers*
critic: *ker III, sek VI*
criticism: *ker III*
criticize: *sek VI*
critikin: *sek VI*
croak: *ger II, ker IV*
crochet: *ger I*
crocidolite: *krek*
crock: *ger I*
crocodile: *ker I, sakkara*
croft: *ger I*
cromlech: *ker I*
crone: *ker III*
Cronus: *nebh*
crony: *nebh*
crook: *ger I*
crooked: *ger I*
crop: *ger I*
cross: *cruc, ger I*
crossbow: *bheug II*
crouch: *ger III*
croup: *ger III*
croupier: *ger III*
croustade: *kreu*
crouton: *kreu*
crow: *ger II, ker IV*
crowbar: *ker IV*
crowberry: *bhel I*
crowd: *krut*
crown: *ker I*
crozier: *ger I*
crucial: *cruc, ger I*
crucible: *ger I*
crucifer: *ger I*
crucifix: *cruc, ger I*
cruciform: *ger I*
crucify: *cruc, ger I*
crud: *pend*
crude: *pend*
crudity: *dheigh N 36*
cruel: *kreu*
cruise: *cruc*
cruiser: *cruc*
cruller: *ger I*
crumb: *ger I*
crumble: *ger I*
crumpet: *ger I, peku*
crumple: *ger III*
crunode: *ned*
crupper: *ger I*
crusade: *cruc*
crust: *kreu*
crustacea: *kreu*
crustaceous: *dheigh N 2 a*
crutch: *ger I*
crux: *cruc, ger I*
cry: *gal, ker IV, uiro*
crymodyma: *kreu*
cryogen: *kreu*
cryolite: *kreu*
cryometer: *kreu*
crypt: *kru*
cryptogamous: *geme*
cryptogram: *krup*
cryptonym: *krup, onomen*
cryptorchid: *krup*
crysanthemum: *andh*
crystal: *kreu*
crystallize: *kreu*
crystallographer: *kreu*
crystallomancy: *kreu*
ctenidium: *pek II*
ctenobranch: *pek II*
ctenodont: *pek II*
ctenoid: *pek II*
Ctenophora: *pek II*
cubbyhole: *geu*
cube: *keu II*
cubicle: *cub, gue, keu II*
cubit: *cub, gue, keu II*
cubitus: *cub*

cuckold: *cucu, kokila, per VII*
cuckoldize: *cucu*
cuckoo: *cucu, kokila*
cuckoo-buds: *cucu*
cuckoo clock: *cucu*
cuckoopint: *cucu*
cuculiform: *cucu*
cucullaris: *caput*
cucullated: *caput*
cud: *gue, keup*
cudgel: *geu*
cue: *kau III*
cuirass: *sek V*
cuisses: *kenk III*
cul-de-sac: *skeu*
culinary: *peku*
cull: *leg I*
cullis: *kagh*
culm: *kolem*
culminate: *gue*
culmination: *kel IV*
culot: *skeu*
culottes: *skeu*
culpable: *kal*
culport: *kal*
culprit: *per IV*
cult: *ker I, sek III*
cultivate: *ker I, sek III*
cultrate: *kel VIII, sek III*
culture: *ker I, sek III*
culver: *kel III*
cumbersome: *dheigh N 37*
cummer: *ma II*
cummerbund: *bhendh, kam*
cumulative: *keu II*
cumulus: *keu II*
cunctation: *konk*
cunnilingus: *gn, leigh, skeu*
cunning: *gn*
cunny: *gn*
cunt: *gn, geu, skeu*
cup: *gue, keup*
cupboard: *bher II*
cupel: *gue, keup*
cupful: *dheigh N 2 h, pel V*
Cupid: *fur, kuep*
cupidity: *fur, kuep*
cupola: *gue, keup*
cupule: *gue*
curate: *cura*
curative: *cura*
curator: *per V*
curb: *ker I*
curd: *pend*
curdled: *pend*
cure: *cura*
curettage: *cura*
curette: *cura*
curia: *uiro*
curial: *uiro*
curiologic: *keu II, leg I*
curiosity: *cura, ugu*
curious: *cura*
curium: *el 96*
curl: *ger I*
curmudgeon: *ger II*
current: *kers I*
curricular: *kers I*
curriculum: *kers I*
currier: *sek V*
curry: *pel VII, reidh*
currycomb: *reidh*
curse: *kers I*
cursive: *kers I*
cursory: *kers I*
curt: *ker III, sek IX*
curtail: *ker III, sek IX*
curtal: *ker III, sek IX*
curtate: *sek IX*
curtsy: *gher IV*
curule: *kers I*
curvature: *ker I*
curve: *ker I*
curvet: *ker I*
curvilinear: *lino*
cushion: *kenk III*
cusk: *ters*
cuspidor: *sphieu*
custard: *kreu*
custodian: *dheigh N 6, skeu*
custody: *skeu*
custom: *sue*
custos: *skeu*
cut: *kel VIII*
cutaneous: *skeu*
cute: *ak*
cutic: *skeu*
cuticle: *skeu*
cutlass: *kel VIII, sek III*
cutler: *kel VIII*
cutlery: *kel VIII*
cutlet: *kel VIII, kost, legh, skeu*
cuttlefish: *gue, keup*
cybernetics: *kuberna*

cyclamate: *ker I*
cyclamen: *ker I*
cyclas: *ker I*
cycle: *ker I*
cycl(o)-: *ker I*
Cyclobothra: *ker I*
Cycloconium: *ker I*
Cycloloma: *ker I, uelu*
cyclone: *ker I*
cyclonic: *ker I*
Cyclonium: *ker I*
cyclopedia: *ker I*
Cyclops: *ker I, oku*
cyclorama: *ker I*
cyclosis: *ker I*
cyclostomatous: *stoman*
cygnet: *kuknos*
Cygnus: *kuknos*
cylinder: *skel*
cyma: *keu II*
cymatium: *keu II*
cymba: *keu II*
cymbal: *keu II*
cymbella: *keu II*
cymbiform: *keu II*
cymborephalic: *keu II*
cymotrichous: *uel III*
Cymric: *merk*
cynanche: *bhel I*
Cynanchum: *kuon*
cynanthropy: *kuon, nert*
cynaraceous: *kuon*
cynarctomachy: *kuon*
cynegetic: *kuon*
Cynias: *kuon*
cyniatrics: *kuon*
cynic: *kuon*
cynicism: *kuon*
cynocephalus: *kuon*
cynocrambe: *kuon*
cynodon: *kuon*
cynoglossum: *glokh, kuon*
cynoid: *kuon*
cynorrhodon: *kuon*
Cynoscion: *kuon*
cynosure: *kuon, ors, uer VII*
cyphella: *keu II*
cyphonism: *keu II*
cy-pres: *ko*
cypripedium: *ped*
cypsela: *keu II*
cyst: *kues*
cystecstasy: *kues*
cystectomy: *kues*
cystocyte: *skeu*
cystoid: *kues*
cytoblast: *skeu*
cytrode: *skeu*
czar: *sek II*

D

dachshund: *kuon, tekhs*
dactyl: *do, peue*
dactylioglyph: *do, gleubh*
dactyliomancy: *do*
dactylodeiktous: *do*
dactylograph: *do*
dactyloid: *do*
dactylology: *do*
dad: *tara*
da-da: *da I, tara*
dadaism: *tara*
daddle: *per II*
daddy: *da I, tara*
dado: *do*
daduchus: *segh*
daedal: *leg I*
daedalian: *del II*
Daedalus: *taur*
daffadowndilly: *to*
daffodil: *to*
daft: *dhabh*
daguerreotype: *steu*
daily: *dei*
daimon: *da II, dei, esu*
dainty: *dek*
dairy: *dheigh*
dais: *deik, guel II*
daisy: *agher, oku*
dale: *dhel II*
Dama: *eku*
damage: *da II*
dame: *dem*
damn: *da II*
damnable: *da II*
damnation: *da II, dheigh N 35*
Damoclean: *pend*
Damocles: *kleu I*
damp: *dhem*
dampen: *dhem*
damper: *dhem*

damsel: *dem*
Danaë: *morui*
dance: *gher IV*
dandelion: *den, kerd, leo*
dandruff: *kreup*
dandy: *haifst, nert*
Danelaw: *legh*
danger: *dem*
dank: *dhem*
daphnean: *men I*
dapple: *abel*
dare: *dhers*
Darius: *dhar*
dark: *dher*
darling: *sap*
darn: *der*
dastard: *dhe II*
dasyure: *ors*
date: *do*
dative: *do*
datum: *do*
daub: *albh*
daughter: *dhugter*
daunt: *dam*
dauphin: *guelbh*
davy: *el 9*
dawdle: *per II*
dawn: *agher*
day: *agher, dei*
daze: *dhe II*
dazzle: *dhe II*
deacon: *ken II*
dead: *dheu II, dheu IV*
deaf: *dheu I, dheu II*
deafen: *dheu I, dheu II*
deal: *da II*
dean: *dekm*
deanship: *sek IV*
dearth: *dheu II, dheu IV*
death: *dheu II, dheu IV*
debacle: *bak*
debar: *bhoros*
debate: *bat, dheigh*
debenture: *ghebh*
debilitate: *bel*
debility: *bel*
debit: *ghebh*
debon(n)aire: *deu*
debouch: *beu*
debruise: *bhreg*
debt: *ghebh*
debtor: *ghebh*
debut: *bhaut*
deca-: *me IV*
decadence: *kad I, kru*
decagon: *dekm*
decagram: *dekm*
decalcomania: *men I*
decalescent: *kel I*
decalogue: *leg I*
decamp: *kam, prai*
decant: *kanth*
decapitation: *caput*
decay: *kad I*
decease: *sed III*
deceit: *kap*
deceive: *kap*
decelerate: *kel VII*
December: *dekm, me IV*
decemvir: *dekm, uiro*
decenary: *dekm*
decennial: *dekm*
decern: *sek VI*
deci-: *me IV*
decide: *sek II*
deciduous: *kad I*
decimate: *dekm, dheigh N 10*
decision: *sek*
deck: *steg*
deckle: *steg*
declaim: *kel II*
declare: *kel II*
decline: *klei*
declivity: *klei*
decoct: *peku*
decolleté: *ker I*
decorticate: *sek IX*
decoy: *kagh, keu II, to*
decrease: *ker VI*
decree: *ker III, sek VI*
decrement: *ker VI*
decrepit: *ker IV*
decrepitate: *ker IV*
decrial: *uiro*
decry: *ker IV, uiro*
decumbent: *cub, keu II*
decuple: *plek I, upo III e*
decurrent: *kers I*
dedication: *deik*
deduce: *deuk*
deduct: *deuk*
deed: *dhe I*
deem: *dhe I*
deep: *dhel II, dheub*

deer: *dheu I, dheu II*
deface: *dhe I*
defaced: *dhe I*
defamatory: *bha I*
default: *phol*
defeat: *dhe I*
defecate: *dhe I*
defect: *dhe I*
defector: *dhe I*
defend: *guhen*
defenestration: *oku*
defense: *guhen*
defer: *bher I*
defiance: *gheidh*
deficient: *dhe I*
deficit: *dhe I*
defile: *guhisl*
define: *fin*
definition: *fin*
definitive: *fin*
deflate: *beu*
deflect: *plek*
deflower: *beu*
defoliation: *beu*
deforestation: *dhur*
deform: *merbh*
defray: *bhreg, prai*
defunct: *bheng III*
defy: *bheidh*
dégagé: uad
degenerate: *gn*
degrade: *ghredh*
degree: *ghredh*
deha: *dheigh*
dehiscence: *ghi*
dehydrate: *aue*
deicer: *dei*
deicide: *dei*
deictic: *deik*
deific: *dhe I*
deify: *dei*
deign: *dek*
Deimos: *duei, mavors*
deism: *dei*
deity: *dei*
dejection: *ie*
delaine: *uel III*
delate: *tol*
delay: *leg II*
delegate: *leg I*
delete: *lei I*
deliberate: *lithra*
deliberately: *lithra*
delice: *dheigh N 18*
delicious: *dheigh N 2 c, dheigh N 18*
delimit: *elei*
delineate: *lino*
delinquent: *leiku*
delirious: *leis*
delirium: *dheigh N 35*
delitescent: *ladh*
deliverance: *leudh*
delivery: *leudh*
dell: *dhel*
Della: *dei*
delouse: *lus*
Delphi: *guelbh*
delphinestrian: *guelbh*
Delphinidae: *guelbh*
delphinium: *guelbh*
deluge: *lou*
delusion: *leid II, dheigh N 19*
de luxe: *leug*
delve: *dhel II*
demagogic: *dheigh N 17*
demagogue: *ag, da II*
demarcation: *merk*
démarche: mat
deme: *da II*
demean: *ambhi, mei II, men II*
demeanor: *men II*
demented: *men I*
dementia praecox: *men I*
demerit: *smer*
demijohn: *semi*
demilune: *semi*
demimondaine: *cal*
demimonde: *cal, man, semi*
demisemi: *semi*
demit: *smeit*
demiurge: *da II, semi, uerg*
democracy: *da II, kar*
Democratic: *da II*
demoiselle: *dem*
demolish: *mo*
demon: *da II, dei, esu*
demoniacal: *da II, dei*
demonocracy: *dheigh N 11*
demonstration: *men I*
demur: *smer*
demythologize: *muth*
dendral: *deru*
dendrite: *deru*
dendro-: *deru*

dendrochronology: *deru*
dendroid: *deru*
dendrology: *deru*
denigrate: *ne*
Denis: *dei*
denominator: *onomen*
denotation: *gn*
dénouement: *ned*
denounce: *neu I*
dense: *dens*
density: *dens*
dent: *denk*
dental: *denk*
dentifrice: *bhreg, denk*
dentist: *denk*
deny: *ne*
deodand: *dei*
deodar: *deru*
deodorant: *od*
department: *per II*
depend: *pend*
depending: *pend*
dephlogisticated: *bhel I*
depict: *peik*
depilatory: *pilo*
deplete: *pel V*
deplorable: *plor*
deplore: *plor*
deploy: *plek I*
deplume: *pleus*
depopulate: *da II, popul*
deport: *per II*
deportment: *per II*
depose: *ap*
deposit: *ap*
deprecate: *perk*
depreciation: *per III*
depress: *pres*
depression: *per VII*
depth: *dhel II, dheub*
depurate: *peu II*
deputation: *peue*
deputy: *peue*
deracinate: *uerad*
derange: *ker I*
deride: *ridè*
derision: *ridè*
derive: *ergh, rei I*
derma: *der*
Dermaptera: *der*
dermatitis: *der*
dermatology: *der, leg I*
derogatory: *reg I*
descant: *kan*
descend: *skand*
descendant: *skand*
describe: *ker III, sek VI*
description: *sek VI*
descry: *ker IV, uiro*
desert: *ser I*
deserve: *ser II, suer I*
desiccated: *seiku*
desiderate: *sueid I*
desideratum: *sueid I*
design: *sek I, seku I*
designate: *sek I, seku I*
desinence: *sei*
desire: *sueid I*
desist: *sta*
desition: *sei*
desk: *deik, guel II*
desolate: *sel II*
desolation: *sue*
despair: *per V, sphei*
despatch: *pag*
desperate: *per V, sphei*
despise: *spek*
despite: *spek*
despoliation: *sphel I*
despond: *spend I*
despondency: *spend I*
despot: *dem*
desquamate: *skualo*
dessert: *suer I*
destination: *sta*
destine: *sta*
destiny: *sta*
destitute: *sta*
destrier: *deks*
destroy: *ster I*
destruction: *ster I*
desuetude: *sue*
desultory: *sel IV*
detach: *stegh*
detain: *ten*
detect: *steg*
detective: *steg*
détente: *ten*
detention: *ten*
deter: *ter I*
deteriorate: *de*
determination: *ter III*
determine: *ter III*
deterrent: *ter I*

detest: *tre*
detonate: *stene, ten*
detour: *ter II*
detract: *tragh*
detriment: *ter II*
detrition: *ter II*
detritus: *ter II*
de trop: *treb*
detrude: *treud*
detruncate: *ter III*
detumescence: *teue 7*
deuce: *duo*
deuterium: *el 1, iso*
Deuteronomy: *nem*
devaluate: *ual*
devanagari: *dei*
devastate: *eu*
devest: *ues II*
deviate: *uegh*
device: *ueidh*
devil: *guel II*
devilfish: *guel II*
devilish: *guel II*
devil's advocate: *guel II*
devil's bit: *guel II*
devious: *uegh*
devise: *ueidh*
devoid: *eu*
devoir: *ghebh*
devolution: *uelu*
devolve: *uelu*
devote: *ueguh*
devotion: *ueguh*
devour: *garg*
devout: *ueguh*
dew: *dheu I, ta*
Dewali: *dei*
Dexedrine: *dek I*
dexiocardia: *kerd*
dexter: *dek I*
dexterity: *dek I*
dext(e)rous: *dek I*
dextroamphetamine: *dek I*
dextrorotation: *dek I*
dextrorse: *dek I, es*
dextrose: *dek I, uer II 5*
Dhanwantari: *ter III*
dharma: *dhar*
dharmasala: *dhar*
dharmashastra: *dhar*
dharna: *dhar*
diabetes: *gua*
diablerie: *guel II*
diabolic: *guel II*
diacaustic: *kau I*
diaconate: *ken II*
diacritical: *sek VI*
diactinic: *nekut*
di(a)eresis: *ie*
diagnosis: *gn*
diagonal: *ghenu*
diagram: *gerbh*
dial: *dei*
dialect: *leg I*
dialectic: *leg I*
diallage: *al II*
dialogue: *leg I*
dialysis: *leu I*
diameter: *me IV*
diamond: *dam*
Diana: *dei, deiu*
dianthus: *andh*
diapason: *keu II*
diapetesis: *ped*
diaphanous: *bha II*
diaphragm: *bhareku*
diarrhea: *sreu*
diary: *dei*
diaspora: *spher I*
diastalsis: *sta*
diastaltic: *stel*
diastasis: *sta*
diastole: *stel*
diastrophism: *strebh*
diathesis: *dhe I*
diathrosis: *ar I*
diatom: *tem*
diatribe: *ter II*
Dicentra: *kent*
dichlorodiphenyltrichloromethane: *duo*
dichotomy: *duo, tem*
dichromatic: *duo, gher I*
diclinous: *klei*
dicorticate: *ker III*
dictate: *deik*
dictator: *deik*
diction: *deik*
dictum: *deik*
diddle: *per II*
didymium: *duo*
didymous: *duo*
didynamous: *duo*
die: *dheu II, dheu IV, do*
diesel: *onomen*

Dies irae: dei
diesis: *ie*
dies non: dei
diet: *ai I, dei, reg I*
different: *bher I*
difficult: *dhe I*
diffidence: *bheidh*
diffident: *bheidh*
diffraction: *bhreg*
diffuse: *ghes*
dig: *dheigh*
digest: *ger VI, ges*
digestion: *ges*
digit: *deik*
digital: *deik*
digitalis: *deik*
dignify: *dek*
dignity: *dek*
digression: *ghredh*
dihedral: *sed I*
Dikè: *morui*
dike: *dheigh*
dilatory: *tol*
dildo: *burd*
dilemma: *labh, slagu*
diligent: *leg I*
diluent: *lou*
dilute: *lou*
diluvial: *lou*
dime: *dekm*
dimension: *me IV*
dimer: *smer*
dimerous: *smer*
diminutive: *dheigh N 24*
dimity: *mei IV*
dimple: *dhel II, dheub*
dine: *ieiun, past*
dinette: *past*
Ding an sich: sue
dingus: *ten*
dinner: *ieiun, past*
dinosaur: *duei*
dinothere: *duei*
diocesan: *dheigh N 7*
dioecious: *ueik I*
Diomedes: *dei*
Dion: *dei*
Dionae: *dei*
Dione: *dei*
dionise: *dei*
Dionysia: *dei, men I*
Dionysiac: *dei*
Dionysius: *dei*
Dionysus: *dei*
diopsite: *oku*
dioptric: *oku*
diorama: *suer I*
Dioscuri: *dei, ker VI*
Diosma: *dei, od*
diota: *ous*
dip: *dhel II*
diphtheria: *deph*
diphthong: *duo*
diplocardiac: *kerd, plek I*
diploidion: *plek I*
diploma: *duo, plek I*
diplomacy: *duo, plek I*
diplomat: *duo, plek I*
diplopia: *plek I*
dipsomaniac: *men I*
dipsopathy: *guadh*
diptote: *pet I*
diptych: *bheag II*
dire: *duei*
direct: *reg I*
direction: *reg I*
directoire: *reg I*
directory: *reg I*
dirge: *reg I*
dirigible: *reg I*
diriment: *em*
disadvantage: *dheigh N 4*
disagreeable: *gar*
disappear: *pare*
disarm: *ar I*
disarrange: *ker I*
disassociate: *seku I*
disavow: *ueks*
disbar: *bhoros*
disburse: *burs*
disc: *deik, guel II*
discern: *ker III, sek VI*
discerp: *ker III*
discerptible: *ker III*
disciple: *dek, kap*
discipline: *dek, kap*
discobolus: *guel II*
discomfiture: *dhe I*
discord: *kerd*
discourse: *kers I*
discredit: *kred I*
discrepancy: *ker IV*
discriminate: *sek VI*
discursive: *kers I*

discus: *deik, guel II*
discuss: *kuet*
disdain: *dek*
disdainful: *dheigh N 2 h*
disease: *ie*
disembogue: *beu*
diseme: *dheie*
disenchanting: *kan*
disentangle: *tenq*
disfigure: *dheigh*
disgrace: *gar*
disgruntled: *gru*
disguise: *ueid*
dish: *deik, guel II*
dishabille: *ghebh*
disingenuous: *gn*
disinherit: *ghe*
disjoin: *ieug*
disjunctive: *ieug*
disk: *deik, guel II*
dismal: *dei, melo*
dismay: *magh*
dismember: *mems, smer*
dismiss: *smeit*
disparate: *per V*
dispatch: *pag*
dispel: *pel IV*
dispensary: *pend*
dispensation: *spend II*
dispense: *pend, spend II*
disperse: *sphereg*
display: *plek I*
disport: *per I, per II*
dispose: *ap*
disproportionate: *per V*
disprosium: *ei I*
disprove: *bheu*
disputation: *peue*
dispute: *peue*
disquiet: *kuei III*
disquisition: *kuere*
disregarded: *suer I*
disrupt: *reup*
dissect: *sek I*
dissemble: *sem I*
disseminate: *se I, sei*
dissension: *sent*
dissent: *sent*
dissertation: *ser I*
disservice: *dheigh N 18, suer I*
dissident: *sed I*
dissilient: *sel IV*
dissimilar: *sem I*
dissimulation: *sem I*
dissipate: *suep II*
dissociate: *seku I*
dissoluble: *ksun*
dissolute: *leu I, lou*
dissolution: *lou, ksun*
dissolve: *ksun, leu I, lou*
dissuade: *suad*
distaff: *sak, stebh*
distain: *teng*
distant: *sta*
distearin: *stei*
distemper: *temp 5*
distend: *ten*
distil(l): *stei*
distillation: *stai, stei*
distillery: *stei*
distinct: *steig*
distinguish: *steig*
distort: *tereq*
distortion: *tereq*
distract: *tragh*
distrain: *streig*
distress: *streig*
distribute: *tre*
district: *streigh*
disturbance: *dheigh N 8*
ditch: *dheigh*
ditto: *deik*
dittography: *plek I*
ditty: *deik*
diuretic: *aue, uer VII*
diurnal: *dei*
diuturnal: *dei*
diuturnity: *dei*
diva: *dei*
divagation: *uag I*
divaricate: *ua I*
dive: *dheub*
diverge: *uer II 2*
divers: *uer II 5*
diverse: *uer II 5*
diversion: *uer II 5*
diverticulum: *uer II 5*
divertissement: *uer II 5*
divest: *ues II*
divide: *ueidh*
dividend: *ueidh*
divination: *dei*
divine: *dei*
divining rod: *dei*

divinity: *dei*
division: *ueidh*
divisive: *ueidh*
divorce: *uer II 5*
divorcé: *uer II 5*
divorcee: *uer II 5*
divulsion: *uel III*
divulsive: *uel III*
dizdar: *dhar, dheigh*
dizzy: *dheu I*
do: *dhe I*
doblon: *plek III*
dobra: *plek III*
docent: *dek*
docile: *dek*
dock: *deuk, dheu I, dheu II*
docoglossa: *glokh*
doctor: *dek*
doctrinaire: *dek*
doctrine: *dek*
document: *dek*
doddle: *per II*
dodecahedron: *dekm, duo*
dodecosyllabic: *labh*
dog: *ane*
dogberry: *bhel I*
dog days: *tueis*
doge: *deuk*
dogma: *dek*
dogmatic: *dek*
dog-whipper: *ane*
doit: *tueis*
dolce far niente: dhe I
doldrums: *dheu I*
dole: *da II, del I, del II*
doleful: *del II*
dolerite: *del I*
dolichocephalic: *ueredh*
doll: *do*
dolorous: *del II*
dolphin: *guelbh*
dolt: *dheu I, dheu II*
-dom: *dhe I*
domain: *dem*
dome: *dem*
domestic: *dem*
domicile: *dem*
dominate: *dam, dem*
domineer: *dem*
dominical: *dem*
Dominicans: *dem*
dominie: *dem*
dominion: *dem*
domino: *dem*
don: *dem*
donation: *do*
donative: *do*
donjon: *dem*
donkey: *dheu I*
donor: *do*
doodle: *per II*
doodler: *coc*
doom: *dhe I*
dope: *dhel II*
Doppelgänger: *plek III*
dopper: *dhel II*
dor: *dhren*
doron: *do*
Dorothea: *dei, do*
Dorothy: *dei*
dorsal: *uer II 5*
dorsum: *uer II 5*
dose: *do*
dossal: *uer II 5*
doss house: *uer II 5*
dossier: *uer II 5*
dot: *do*
double: *duo, plek III*
double entendre: *plek III*
doublet: *duo*
doublure: *plek III*
doubt: *bheu, duo*
douche: *lead*
dough: *dheigh*
doughty: *dheugh*
dour: *deru*
dove: *dheu I*
dowager: *do*
dowel: *dheubh*
down: *dheu I, dheu II*
downcast: *ger VI*
downright: *reg I*
downward: *dheu I*
downy: *do*
dowry: *do*
doxology: *dek*
doxy: *dek*
doyen: *dekm*
doze: *dheu II*
dozen: *duo*
drab: *der, dher*
drabbing: *der*
drabble: *dher*
dracaena: *derk*

Draconian: *derk, seug*
Draconic: *derk*
Dracula: *seug*
draff: *dher*
draft: *dheragh*
Drag: *seug*
drag: *dheragh, tragh*
draggle: *tragh*
dragnet: *tragh*
dragon: *derk*
dragonet: *derk*
dragoon: *derk*
drail: *tragh*
drama: *dere*
dramatize: *dere*
dramaturgy: *uerg*
drape: *der*
drastic: *dere*
draught: *dheragh*
draughts: *dheragh*
draw: *dheragh*
drawl: *tragh*
dray: *dheragh, tragh*
dreaminess: *dheigh N 29*
dreary: *dhreu*
dredge: *dheragh, tragh*
dregs: *dher*
dress: *reg I*
dressage: *reg I*
dresser: *reg I*
driblet: *legh*
drift: *dhreibh*
drill: *ter III, tre*
drink: *dheragh*
drip: *dhreu*
drive: *dhreibh*
drivel: *dher*
drizzle: *dhreu*
drogue: *tragh*
dromedary: *dru*
drone: *dhren*
droop: *dhreu*
drop: *dhreu*
dropsy: *aue*
droshky: *dheragh*
dross: *dher*
drove: *dhreibh*
drown: *dheragh*
drowse: *dhreu*
druid: *ueid, deru*
drunken: *dheragh*
drupe: *deru, peku*
Drury Lane: *bhe*
dryad: *deru*
duad: *duo*
dual: *duo*
dualism: *men III*
dub: *duo, dheubh*
dubious: *bheu, duo*
dubitation: *bheu*
Dublin: *dher, pleu*
dubloon: *duo, plek III*
ducal: *deuk*
ducat: *deuk*
duchess: *deuk*
duchy: *deuk*
duck: *ane*
ducking stool: *ane*
duckling: *ane, sap*
duct: *deuk*
ductile: *deuk*
due: *ghebh*
duel: *duo*
duenna: *dem*
duet: *duo*
duftedar: *dhar*
dug: *dhel I*
duke: *deuk*
dulcet: *dlku*
dulciana: *dlku*
dulcify: *dlku*
dulcimer: *dlku, mel IV*
Dulcinea: *dlku*
dulia: *lei II*
dull: *dheu I, dheu II*
dullard: *dheu II*
dulocracy: *lei II*
dulosis: *lei II*
dumb: *dheu II*
dump: *dhel II, dheub*
dun: *dheu I, dheu II*
dunce: *ne*
dune: *dheu I*
dungeon: *dem*
duniwassal: *ghdhem*
dunk: *teng*
Dunker: *teng*
dunnage: *ten*
duodecimal: *duo*
duodenum: *kel IV*
duplex: *duo, plek I, plex*
duplicate: *duo, plek I, plex*
duplicity: *dheigh N 2 c, duo, plek I, plex*
durable: *deru*

dura mater: *ma II*
duramen: *deru*
durance: *deru*
duration: *deru*
duress: *deru*
during: *deru*
durwan: *pa*
dusk: *dheu I, dheu II*
dust: *dheu I*
dutiable: *ghebh*
dutiful: *ghebh*
duty: *ghebh*
duumvir: *uiro*
dwindle: *dheu II*
dwine: *dheu II*
Dyaus: *dei*
Dyauspitar: *dei*
dynamic: *deu*
dynamite: *deu*
dynamo: *deu*
dynamometer: *deu*
dynasty: *deu*
dyne: *deu*
dyscrasia: *kere*
dysentery: *en*
dyslexia: *leg I*
dysmenorrhea: *me IV*
dyspepsia: *peku*
dysplasia: *pela*
dyspnea: *pneu*
dysprosium: *el 66*
dysuria: *uer VII*

E

each: *leig I*
eager: *ak, akua*
eagle: *akua*
ear: *ak, ous*
early: *aier*
earnest: *er III, ergh*
earth: *el, er*
earthenware: *er*
Earthian: *ert*
Earthman: *ert*
earthwork: *uerg*
earwig: *uegh*
ease: *ie*
east: *aues, aus III*
Easter: *aues, aus III*
eastern: *aues*
easy: *ie*
eat: *ed*
eau de vie: akua
eaves: *upo I*
eavesdrop: *upo I*
eavesdropping: *stei*
ebb: *ap*
ebriate: *ebrius*
ebriety: *ebrius*
ebullient: *beu*
ecaudate: *eghs*
ecbolic: *guel II*
eccentric: *kent*
ecchymosis: *gheu*
Ecclesiastes: *kel II*
ecclesiastic: *kel II*
ecclesiastical: *eghs*
ecclesiology: *kel II*
eccrinology: *ker III, sek VI*
ecdysiast: *do*
ecdysis: *do, eghs*
echelon: *skand*
Echeneis: *nau II*
echino: *anghui*
echinodorus: *anghui*
echinops: *anghui*
echinus: *anghui*
Echo: *uagh*
echo: *uagh*
echolalia: *lal*
éclair: *kel II*
eclampsis: *lap*
eclectic: *leg I*
eclipse: *eghs, leiku*
ecliptic: *eghs, leiku*
ecology: *ueik I*
ecomiast: *ued*
ecomium: *ued*
economics: *ueik I*
economy: *ueik I*
ecophene: *ueik I*
ecospecies: *ueik I*
ecosphere: *ueik I*
ecosystem: *ueik I*
ecotone: *ueik I*
ecotype: *ueik I*
ecstasy: *sta*
ectasis: *ten*
ectoblast: *eghs*
ectoderm: *der*
ectogenous: *eghs*

ectomorphic: *eghs*
ectopia: *top*
Ectopistes: *top*
ectoplasm: *dheigh N 31, eghs*
écu: *sek II*
ecumenical: *ueik I*
eczema: *ies*
edaphic: *sed I*
edaphology: *sed I*
Edda: *uat*
eddy: *et, eti*
edea: *suer I*
edentate: *denk*
Edgar: *ghaiso*
edge: *ak*
edible: *ed*
edict: *deik*
edifice: *aidh, dhe I*
edify: *aidh, dhe I*
edition: *do*
Edmund: *man*
education: *deuk*
educe: *deuk*
Edward: *suer I, uer IV*
effable: *eghs*
efface: *dhe I, eghs*
effect: *dhe I*
effective: *dhe I*
effeminate: *dhe II, dhel I*
efferent: *bher I*
effervesce: *bher I*
effete: *dhe II, dhel I*
efficacious: *dhe I*
efficient: *dhe I*
effigy: *dheigh*
efflorescence: *beu*
efflorescent: *eghs*
effluvium: *beu, bhleu*
effort: *bheregh*
effrontery: *frons*
effulgent: *bhel I*
effusive: *eghs, gheu*
effutiation: *eghs*
eftsoons: *ap*
egest: *ger VI*
egg: *ak, auei*
ego: *eg I*
egocentric: *kent*
egoism: *eg I*
egotism: *eg I*
egregious: *ger I, ger III*
egress: *ghredh*
eiderdown: *dheu II*
eidetic: *ueid*
eidolon: *ueid*
eight: *okto*
eighteen: *okto*
eightieth: *okto*
Eileen: *dheu I*
einkorn: *oino*
Einmyria: *leuk*
Einstein: *oino*
einsteinium: *el 99*
Eire: *eis*
eirenarch: *morui*
eirenic: *morui*
(e)irenicon: *morui, or*
Eisa: *leuk*
eisteddfod: *bheu, sed*
either: *kuo, ne*
ejaculate: *ie*
ejaculatory: *dheigh N 35*
eject: *ie*
ekaboron: *oino*
ekacaesium: *oino*
ekalead: *oino*
eke: *aug*
elaborate: *leb*
elapse: *leb*
elation: *tol*
elbow: *bhagus, elei*
elder: *al I*
elders: *uiro*
eldest: *al I*
El Dorado: *aues*
Eleanor: *leo*
Eleazer: *dekm*
elect: *leg I*
election: *leg I*
electricity: *dheigh N 2 c, gher III*
electrocardiogram: *gher III, kerd*
electrocution: *gher III*
electrode: *sed II*
electromagnetic: *gher III*
electron: *el, gher III*
electronic: *gher III*
electuary: *leigh*
eleemosynary: *amma*
elegant: *leg I*
element: *el*
Eleocharis: *gher II*
elephantiasis: *upo III b*
eleutheromania: *leudh*
eleutheropetalous: *leudh*

eleutherophyllous: *leudh*
elevate: *leguh*
elevator: *leguh*
eleven: *oino*
elide: *laed*
Elijah: *dekm*
eliminate: *elei*
Elisha: *dekm*
elision: *laed*
ell: *elei*
Ella: *leo*
ellagic: *gel I*
ellipse: *en, leiku*
ellipsis: *leiku*
elliptical: *leiku*
elocution: *tolku*
elongate: *del I*
elope: *klou*
eloquent: *tolku*
El Salvador: *sal I*
else: *al II*
elucidate: *leuk*
elucubration: *leuk*
elude: *leid II*
eluxate: *leug*
elytron: *uelu*
emaciated: *mak*
emacity: *em*
emanate: *dheigh N 10, mano*
emancipation: *kap, man*
emasculate: *mas*
embassy: *ag*
embellish: *deu*
embers: *eus*
emblem: *guel II*
embolden: *beu*
embolism: *guel II*
embonpoint: *deu*
embracer: *bher I*
embroider: *bhar*
embroil: *bher I*
embryo: *guer*
embryology: *guer, leg I*
eme: *kei II*
emend: *mend*
emerald: *smarakt*
emerge: *mezg I*
emergency: *mezg I*
emeritus: *smer*
emersion: *mezg I*
emetic: *uem*
émeute: meu II
emigrate: *mei II*
Emil: *im*
Emilia: *im*
eminent: *men II*
emit: *smeit*
emmenagogue: *me IV*
emmenic: *me IV*
emmenology: *me IV*
emolument: *mel V*
emotion: *meu II*
empathy: *guadh*
emperor: *per VI f*
emphatic: *en*
emphyteusis: *stei*
empire: *per III*
employ: *plek I*
employee: *plek I*
emporium: *dheigh N 35, per I*
empress: *per VI f*
empressement: *pres*
emption: *em*
empyema: *pu*
empyrean: *peuor*
emulate: *im*
emulgent: *melg*
emulous: *im*
emulsify: *melg*
emulsion: *melg*
emunctory: *meu I*
Emys: *uem*
enable: *en*
enamel: *mel I, smeld*
enamored: *amma, en*
enarthrosis: *ar I*
enc(a)enia: *ken III*
encamp: *kam*
encase: *kap*
encaustic: *kau I*
enceinte: *kenk I*
enchanting: *kan*
enchase: *kap*
enchondroma: *ghren*
enchorial: *ghe*
enchymatous: *gheu*
enclave: *kleu III*
enclitic: *klei*
enclosion: *kleu III*
enclosure: *kleu III*
encore: *ad, eir, ko*
encroach: *ger I*
encyclical: *ker I*
encyclop(a)edia: *ker I*

end: *ant, anti*
endaorta: *uer I*
endeavor: *ghebh*
endemic: *da II*
endless: *leu I*
endoblast: *en*
endocardium: *kerd*
endocarp: *ker III*
endocrene: *sek VI*
endocrine: *en, ker III, sek VI*
endoderm: *der*
endogamy: *en, geme*
endomorph: *en*
endon: *en*
endosark: *tuerk*
endosmosis: *uedh*
endothelium: *dhe II, dhel I*
endow: *do*
endure: *deru*
endysis: *do*
enema: *ie*
enemy: *amma*
energamen: *uerg*
energy: *uerg*
enervate: *netr, sne*
enfeoff: *pek II*
enfilade: *guhisl*
enforce: *bheregh*
engaged: *en*
engagement: *uad*
engender: *en gn*
engine: *gn*
engineer: *gn*
England: *ank, plek I*
English: *ank*
engrained: *ger V*
engrave: *ghrebh I*
engross: *gher I*
engrossing: *gher I, guretso*
enhance: *al I*
enigma: *ai II*
enjoin: *ieug*
enjoy: *ga*
enjoyable: *ga*
enlightenment: *leuk*
enmity: *amma*
enneacontahedron: *neun*
ennead: *neun*
enneagynous: *neun*
enneandrous: *neun*
enneatic: *neun*
enormous: *gen*
enough: *enek*
enraged: *labh*
enrapt: *labh*
enraptured: *labh*
ensconce: *kam*
ensemble: *sem I*
ensign: *sek I*
ensnare: *sner II*
ensue: *seku I*
ensure: *cura*
entangle: *tenq*
entasis: *ten*
entelechy: *ker I, segh*
entelodont: *ker I*
enter: *en*
enteritis: *en*
enterokinase: *en*
enterospasm: *dheigh N 34*
enterprise: *en*
entertain: *en, ten*
enthusiasm: *dhes*
enthusiastic(al): *dheigh N 17*
enthusiastically: *dheigh N 1*
enthymeme: *dheu I, dheu II*
entire: *tag I*
entitle: *tel*
entity: *es*
entomb: *teue 6*
entomology: *en, tem*
entomophagous: *bhag*
entotic: *ous*
entrails: *en*
entrance: *en*
entreat: *tragh*
entremets: *smeit*
entrepreneur: *rad I*
entresol: *sel I*
entropy: *trep*
entrorse: *uer II 5*
enumerate: *nem*
enunciate: *neu I*
enuresis: *aue, uer VII*
envious: *dheigh N 2 d*
envisage: *ueid*
envoy: *uegh*
envy: *ueid*
enzyme: *ieug*
eoan: *aues*
Eoanthropus: *nert*
eoanthropus: *aues*
Eocene: *ken II*
eocene: *aues*

eohippus: *aues, eku*
eolithic: *aues*
eon: *aiu*
eosin: *aues*
epact: *ag*
epaulet: *sphei I*
épaulière: *sphei I*
épée: *sphei I*
ependyma: *do*
epenthesis: *dhe I, plek I*
ephebic: *ga, iegua*
ephedrin: *sed I*
ephemera: *amer*
ephemeral: *amer, dheigh N 5*
ephemerid: *amer*
ephemeris: *amer*
ephemeron: *amer*
ephetae: *ie*
ephor: *suer I, uer IV*
epic: *ueks*
epic(al): *dheigh N 17*
epicardium: *kerd*
epicarp: *ker III*
epicedium: *kad II*
epicene: *kom*
epichorial: *ghe*
Epicrates: *kar*
epicrises: *ker III*
epicritic: *ker III*
epidemic: *da II*
epidermis: *der*
epididymus: *duo*
epigastrium: *medhi*
epigene: *gn*
epigenesis: *gn*
epigenous: *gn*
epiglottis: *glock*
epigone: *gn*
epigonium: *gn*
epigraph: *gerbh*
epigram: *gerbh*
epigynous: *guen*
epilepsy: *labh, slagu*
epilogue: *leg I*
Epimetheus: *el 61, keu II*
epimysium: *mus*
epiotic: *ous*
epiphany: *bha II*
epiphyte: *bheu*
epiploon: *pel VI*
episcopal: *spek*
episode: *aud, en, sed II*
epistasis: *sta*
epistaxis: *stag*
epistemology: *sta*
episternum: *ster I*
epistle: *stel*
epistolary: *stel*
epistrophe: *plek, strebh*
epistyle: *sta*
epitaph: *dhembh*
epitasis: *ten*
epithalamion: *per VI a*
epithelium: *dhe II, dhel I*
epitome: *tem*
epizeuxis: *ieug*
e pluribus unum: pel V
epoch: *segh*
epode: *aud, ued*
eponym: *onomen*
epopee: *kuei, ueks*
epopt: *oku*
epos: *ueks*
epsilon: *bhili*
equable: *ane*
equality: *ane*
equanimity: *ane*
equation: *ane*
equator: *ios*
equerry: *skeu*
equestrian: *eku*
equilibrium: *lithra*
equimultiple: *mel II*
equine: *eku*
equinox: *aiu, ios*
equiponderate: *spend II*
equisetum: *eku*
equitation: *eku*
equivalent: *ual*
equivocal: *ueks*
equivocate: *ueks*
equivoque: *ueks*
equus: *eku*
era: *aios*
eradicate: *uerad*
Eranthemum: *uest*
Eranthis: *uest*
erase: *rad I*
erasure: *rad I*
Eratosthenes: *sap*
erbium: *el 68*
ere: *aier*
erect: *reg I*
erectile: *reg I*

erection: *reg I*
eremite: *er*
erepsin: *labh, rep II*
erethism: *nebh*
erg: *uerg*
ergasia: *uerg*
ergo: *reg I*
ergograph: *uerg*
ergon: *uerg*
Erica: *uer II 6*
Ericaceae: *uer II 6*
Erin: *eis*
Erinyes: *dheu I, nebh*
Eriocaulon: *kaul*
Eris: *nebh*
eristic: *nebh*
Eros: *fur, nebh*
erosion: *rad I*
erotica: *fur, nebh*
eroticism: *fur*
erotomania: *fur*
err: *ei I, eres, sta*
errand: *ei I*
errant: *ei I, ergh*
erratic: *eres*
erratum: *eres*
erroneous: *eres*
error: *eres*
ersatz: *sed I*
Erse: *eis*
erstwhile: *aier*
eruct: *reug*
eructation: *reug*
erudite: *rud*
erudition: *rud*
erupt: *reup*
Eryngium: *uest*
eryngo: *poi, uest*
erysipelas: *pel VI, reudh*
erythema: *reudh*
erythroblast: *reudh*
erythrochroic: *gher I*
erythrocite: *reudh*
erythrogenesis: *gn*
Erythromycin: *reudh*
escalade: *skand*
escalator: *skand*
escape: *caput*
escarbuncle: *ker V*
escarole: *ed*
eschatology: *eghs*
escheat: *kad I*
esclavage: *kleu I*
escritoire: *ker III*
escrow: *sek VIII*
escudo: *sek II*
esculent: *ed*
escutcheon: *sek II*
esoteric: *en*
ESP: *guadh*
espadon: *sphei I*
esparto: *sper II*
especial: *spek*
esperance: *sphei I*
Esperanto: *sphei I*
espionage: *spek*
esplanade: *pela*
espouse: *spend I*
esprit: *speis*
esquamate: *skualo*
esquire: *sek II, skeu*
esquisse: *segh*
essay: *ag*
essence: *es*
essential: *el, es*
Essex: *sek I*
establish: *sta*
establishment: *sta*
estate: *sta*
esteem: *aios, tem*
Estelle: *ster III*
estimable: *tem*
estimate: *aios, tem*
estival: *aidh*
estivate: *aidh*
estop: *stei, steue*
estopple: *stei*
estovers: *op I*
estrade: *ster I*
estrogen: *eis*
estrone: *eis*
estrus: *eis*
estuary: *aidh*
et cetera: *eti*
etch: *ed*
Eteocles: *kleu I*
eternal: *aiu*
eternity: *aiu*
etesian: *uet*
Ethelinda: *lento*
ether: *aidh*
ethics: *sue*
Ethiop: *oku*
Ethiopia: *oku*

ethnic: *sue*
ethnology: *sue*
ethnophaulism: *per VIII*
et hoc genus omne: eti
ethos: *sue*
etiology: *ai I*
etiquette: *steig*
etymology: *es*
etymon: *es*
eucalyptus: *esu, kel VI*
Eucharist: *esu, gher I, gher II, men I*
euchite: *ueguh*
euchology: *ueguh*
eudaemonic: *da II*
eudemon: *esu*
eudemonism: *esu*
eudiometer: *dei*
Eudora: *do*
eugenics: *gn*
euglena: *gel I*
Eulalia: *lal*
eulogy: *esu; leg I*
Eumenides: *dheu I, fur, men I, nebh*
Eunectes: *sna I*
eunuch: *segh*
Euonymous: *onomen*
euonymous: *onomen*
euosmite: *od*
eupatrid: *peter*
eupeptic: *peku*
euphemism *bha I, esu, kleu I*
euphemistic: *bha I*
euphemy: *esu*
euphony: *esu*
Euphorbiaceae: *esu*
euphoria: *bher I, esu*
euphotic: *bha II, eu*
Euphrasia: *guhren*
euphrasy: *guhren*
euphroe: *ieu, per VI c*
Euphrosyne: *guhren*
Euphues: *esu*
euphuism: *bheu, esu*
eupnea: *pneu*
eureka: *uer III*
euripus: *uer II 7*
Europa: *morui*
Europe: *el 63, oku*
europium: *el 63*
eurus: *eus*
eutaxy: *tag III*
eutectic: *ta*
Euterpe: *terp*
eutexia: *ta*
euthanasia: *dheu I*
euxenite: *xenos*
euzeolite: *esu*
evacuate: *eu*
evade: *uadh*
evaginate: *uag II*
Evan: *ieu*
evanescent: *eu*
evangel: *spel*
evangelical: *spel*
evaporate: *kuep*
evasive: *dheigh N 24*
Eve: *per VI c*
evening: *ap*
event: *gua*
eventide: *da II*
eventuate: *gua*
ever: *aiu*
Everard: *kar*
evert: *uer II 5*
every: *aiu*
everything: *aiu*
evidence: *ueid*
evident: *ueid*
evil: *upo I*
evirate: *uiro*
eviration: *uiro*
evirtuate: *uiro*
evitable: *eu*
evite: *bha II*
evocative: *ueks*
evoe: *euoi*
evoke: *ueks*
evolution: *uelu*
evolutionism: *ker VI*
evolve: *uelu*
evulsion: *uel III*
evzone: *ios*
ewe: *oui*
ewer: *akua*
exa-: *me IV*
exacerate: *eghs*
exacerbate: *eghs*
exact: *ag*
exaction: *ag*
exaggerate: *ges*
exalt: *al I*
examine: *ag*
example: *em*
excambion: *skamb*

ex cathedra: kat, sed I
exceed: *sed II*
excel: *gue, kel IV*
excellent: *kel IV*
excelsior: *gue, kel IV*
except: *kap*
excerpt: *ker III*
excess: *sed II*
exchange: *skamb*
exchequer: *ksei*
excind: *sek II*
excipient: *kap*
excise: *eghs, kens, sek II*
excision: *sek II*
excissate: *seiku*
excite: *kei I*
exclaim: *kel II*
exclude: *kleu III*
exclusive: *dheigh N 24*
excommunicate: *mei II*
excoriate: *sek IX*
excrement: *ker III, sek V*
excrementitious: *sek V*
excrete: *ker III*
excruciating: *cruc*
exculpate: *kal*
excurrent: *kers I*
excursion: *kers I*
excursus: *kers I*
excuse: *kau III*
execration: *sak*
execute: *seku I*
executive: *dheigh N 24*
exedra: *sed I*
exegesis: *sag*
exemplary: *em*
exemplify: *em*
exempt: *em*
exemption: *em*
exequator: *seku I*
exequier: *seku I*
exercise: *areq*
exergue: *uerg*
exert: *ser I*
exeunt: *ei I*
exfoliate: *beu*
exhalation: *ane*
exhale: *ane*
exhaust: *au II*
exhaustless: *eghs, leu I*
exheredate: *ghe*
exhibition: *ghebh*
exhilarating: *sel II*
exhortation: *gher II*
exhume: *ghdhem*
exigent: *ag*
exiguous: *ag*
exile: *al III, sel IV*
exist: *es, sta*
existentialism: *eghs, es*
exit: *ei I*
ex libris: leup
exocrene: *sek VI*
exocrine: *ker III*
exodus: *eghs, sed II*
exogamy: *geme*
exomis: *oms*
exonerate: *enos*
exophthalmos: *oku*
exorcise: *arek*
exorcism: *arek*
exordium: *ar I*
exosmosis: *uedh*
exoteric: *eghs, en*
exotic: *eghs*
expand: *eghs, pet II*
expanse: *pet II*
expatriot: *peter*
expect: *spek*
expectancy: *spek*
expectation: *spek*
expectorate: *peg*
expedient: *ped*
expedite: *ped*
expel: *pel IV*
expend: *pend, spend II*
expensive: *dheigh N 24, pend*
experience: *per III*
experiment: *per III*
expert: *per III*
expiate: *pius*
expire: *speis*
explication: *plek I*
explicative: *dheigh N 24*
explicit: *plek I*
explode: *plaud*
exploit: *plek I*
exploration: *plor*
explore: *plor*
explosion: *plaud*
expose: *ap, eghs*
expostulation: *perk*
expound: *ap*
express: *per VII, pres*
expunge: *peug*
expurgate: *peu II*

exquisite: *kuere*
extant: *sta*
extemporaneous: *temp 5*
extempore: *temp 5*
extenuating: *ten*
exterior: *eghs*
exterminate: *eghs, ter III*
external: *eghs*
extinct: *steig*
extinguish: *steig*
extirpate: *ster I, ster III*
extol: *tol*
extort: *tereq*
extract: *tragh*
extraction: *eghs*
extragalactic: *eghs*
extramatrimonial: *eghs*
extramundane: *man*
extramural: *mei III*
extraneous: *eghs, gn*
extraordinary: *eghs*
extrapolate: *eghs*
extrasensory: *eghs*
extraterrene: *ters*
extraterrestrial: *ters*
extravagance: *uag I*
extravagant: *eghs*
extreme: *eghs*
extricate: *tereq*
extrinsic: *seku I*
extrovert: *re, uer II 5*
extrude: *treud*
exuberant: *eudh*
exult: *in II, sel IV*
exultation: *eghs*
ex voto: eghs
exzodiacal: *eghs*
eyas: *ni, sed I*
eye: *akue, oku*
eyeable: *oku*
eyeball: *oku*
eyelet: *oku*
eyewink: *oku*
eyewitness: *oku*
eyrie: *ue*

F

Fabian: *ia*
fable: *bha I, dhabh*
fabric: *dhabh*
fabricate: *dhabh*
fabulous: *bha I*
façade: *dhe I*
face: *dhe I*
facet: *dhe I*
facetious: *dhe I*
facient: *dhe I*
facile: *dhe I*
facility: *dhe I*
facinorous: *dhe I*
facsimile: *dhe I*
fact: *dhe I*
faction: *dhe I*
factional: *dhe I*
factionary: *dhe I*
factionate: *dhe I*
factioneer: *dhe I*
factitious: *dhe I*
factor: *dhe I*
factory: *dhe I, dheigh N 35, man*
factotum: *dhe I, teuta*
factual: *dhe I*
faculty: *dhe I*
fade: *burd*
fading: *burd*
fail: *fall, phol*
fail-safe: *fall, phol*
failure: *fall, phol*
fain: *pek I*
fainéant: *dheigh*
faint: *dheigh*
fair: *dhes, onomen, pek I*
fairy: *bha I*
faith: *bheidh*
faithful: *bheidh*
faithless: *dheigh N 26*
falcon: *pel VII*
faldstool: *plek II, sta*
fall: *fall, phol*
fallacious: *fall, phol*
fallacy: *fall, phol*
fallible: *phol*
fallow: *ker I, kuel*
false: *fall, phol*
falsify: *phol*
falter: *fall, phol*
fame: *bha I*
famine: *fall*
famished: *fall*
famous: *bha I*
fan: *ue*
fanam: *pel II*
fanatic: *dhes, ue*

fanciful: *bha II*
fancy: *bha II*
fane: *dhes, pend*
fang: *pag*
fantastic: *bha II*
fantastic(al): *dheigh N 17*
fantasy: *bha II*
fantoccini: *bha II*
far: *per I*
farce: *bhareku, sa*
farcical: *dheigh N 5*
fardel: *da II, kuetuer*
fare: *per I*
farina: *bhares*
farinaceous: *bhares*
farkleberry: *bhel I*
farm: *dhar*
farmer: *dhar*
farouche: dhur
farrago: *bhares*
farrow: *per VI c, porko I*
fart: *perd*
farther: *per I*
farthing: *kuetuer*
farthingale: *ters*
fasces: *bhasko*
fascinate: *beu, bhasko*
fascinator: *bhasko*
fascism: *bhasko*
Fascist: *bhasko*
fashion: *dhe I*
fast: *onomen, past*
fasten: *past*
faster: *dheigh N 13*
fastidious: *bhar, plek I*
fastness: *past*
fat: *pi*
fatal: *bha I*
fata morgana: *elaia*
fate: *bha I*
Fates: *bha I, morui, smer*
father: *peter*
fatherland: *peter*
fathom: *sphei I*
fattened: *pi*
faubourg: *dhur*
faucet: *phol*
fault: *fall, phol*
faultless: *phol*
fauna: *beu*
Faunus: *beu*
Faust: *peug*
fauteuil: *plek II*
favel: *pel VII*
favor: *ghoue*
favorite: *ghoue*
fawn: *dhe II, pek I*
fay: *pag*
fealty: *bheidh*
feasance: *dhe I*
feasible: *dhe I*
feast: *dhes*
feat: *dhe I*
feather: *pet I*
feature: *dhe I*
febrifuge: *bheug I*
February: *me IV*
feces: *dhe I*
feckless: *dhe I*
fecund: *dhe II, dhel I*
fecundity: *dhe II, dhel I*
federal: *bheidh*
Federal(ist): *da II*
Fedora: *do*
fedora: *do*
fee: *bha I, pek II*
feeble: *bhel II*
feel: *pal*
feign: *dheigh*
feint: *dheigh*
feldspar: *pela, sphereg*
felicitations: *dhe II, dhel I*
felicity: *dhe II, dheigh N 2 c, dhel I*
fell: *fall, pel VI, phol*
Fell, Dr.: *pilo*
fellatio: *dhel I*
fellow: *legh, pek II*
felly: *kuel*
felo-de-se: sue
felonious: *fur*
felstone: *stai*
felt: *pel IV*
female: *dhe II, dhel I*
feminine: *dhe II, dhel I*
femto-: *penkue*
femto: *me IV, penkue*
femtometer: *penkue*
fen: *pen*
fence: *guhen*
fend: *guhen*
fender: *guhen*
fennel: *dhel I, niger*
fens: *guhen*
fenugreek: *dhel I*

feodary: *pek II*
feofee: *pek II*
feral: *dhes, ghuer*
fere: *per I*
ferial: *dhes*
ferment: *bhereu*
fermium: *el 100*
fern: *pet I*
ferocious: *dheigh N 2 d, ghuer, oku*
ferocity: *em, ghuer, oku*
ferrule: *uei I*
ferry: *per I*
fertile: *bher II*
fertilize: *dheigh N 25*
fervent: *bhereu*
fest: *dhes*
-fest: *dhes*
festival: *dhes*
festive: *dhes*
festoon: *dhes*
fetal: *dhel I*
fetch: *ped*
feticide: *dhel I*
fetid: *odi*
fetish: *dhe I*
fetlock: *ped*
fetter: *ped*
fetus: *dhel I*
feu: *pek II*
feud: *peig, pek II*
feverish: *dheigh N 20*
few: *pou 9*
fey: *peig*
fiancée: *bheidh*
fiasco: *plek II*
fiat: *dhe I*
Fiat lux: leuk
fibula: *dheigh*
-fic: *dhe I*
ficelle: *guhisl*
fichu: *dheigh*
fickle: *peig*
fictile: *dheigh*
fiction: *dhe I, dheigh*
fictitious: *dhe I*
fiddle: *tol*
fiddle-de-dee: *tol*
fiddle-faddle: *tol*
fiddlesticks: *tol*
fideicide: *bheidh*
Fidei Defensor: bheidh
fideism: *bheidh*
fidelious: *bheidh*
fidelity: *bheidh*
fidfad: *tol*
Fidius: *bheidh*
fiduciary: *bheidh*
fief: *pek II*
field: *pela*
fiend: *paen*
fierce: *ghuer*
fiesta: *dhes*
fife: *pip*
fifteen: *penkue*
fifth: *penkue*
fifty: *penkue*
fight: *pek II, peug*
figment: *dheigh*
figure: *dheigh*
Filago: *guhisl*
filament: *guhisl*
Filaria: *guhisl*
filbert: *bhel I, kosel*
file: *guhisl*
filet: *guhisl*
filial: *dhel*
filibuster: *prai*
filigree: *ger V, guhisl*
Filipendula: *pend*
filipendulous: *pend*
fill: *pel V*
fillet: *legh*
fillip: *plab*
filly: *pou 9*
film: *pel VI*
filter: *pel IV*
filthy: *pu*
final: *fin*
finality: *dheigh N 36*
finalize: *fin*
finance: *fin*
finch: *spingo*
find: *pent*
fine: *fin*
finery: *fin*
fines herbes: fin
finesse: *fin*
finger: *penkue*
finical: *fin*
finicking: *fin*
finicky: *fin*
finis: *fin*
finish: *fin*
finite: *fin*

finochio: *dhel I*
fire: *el, peuor*
fireworks: *peuor, uerg*
firk: *bhreg, peig*
firkin: *kuetuer*
firm: *dhar*
firmament: *dhar*
first: *per IV*
firth: *per I*
fish: *peisk*
fission: *bheid*
fissure: *bheid*
fist: *penkue, peug*
fisticuffs: *peug*
fit: *ped, pet I*
Fitz: *dhel I*
five: *penkue*
fix: *dheigh*
fixation: *dheigh*
fixture: *dheigh*
fjord: *per I*
flabbergasted: *plab*
flabby: *plab*
flagellation: *bhleg*
flageolet: *beu*
flagitious: *bhlag*
flagon: *plek II*
flagrant: *bhel I*
flagstone: *pela*
flail: *bhlag*
flair: *bhrag*
flake: *pela*
flambeau: *bhel I*
flamboyant: *bhel I, dheigh N 8*
flame: *bhel I*
flamingo: *bhel I*
flammable: *bhel I*
flan: *pela*
flank: *kleng*
flannel: *uel III*
flap: *coc, plab*
flapdoodle: *coc*
flapdragon: *esu*
flare: *beu*
flask: *plek II*
flat: *pela*
flatfish: *pela*
flatiron: *pela*
flatter: *pela*
flatulent: *beu*
flatus: *beu*
flatware: *pela*
flautist: *beu*
flavescent: *bhel I*
flavoprotein: *bhel I*
flavor: *beu*
flaw: *pela*
flax: *plek II*
flay: *pleik*
flea: *plou*
fleabane: *plou*
fleabite: *plou*
flea market: *plou*
flèche: *pleu*
fleck: *pleik*
fledge: *pleu*
fledgling: *pleu, sap*
flee: *bheug I, pleu*
fleece: *pleus*
fleet: *pleu*
flense: *pela*
flesh: *pleik*
fletcher: *pleu*
flex: *plek II*
flexible: *plek II*
flexion: *plek II*
flexor: *plek II*
flexuous: *plek II*
flexure: *plek II*
Flies, The: fur
flight: *pleu*
flighty: *dheigh N 36*
flinch: *kleng*
flip: *plab*
flippant: *plab*
flippity-flop: *plab*
flirt: *nert*
flit: *pleu*
flitch: *pleik*
float: *pleu*
floccinaucinihilipilification: *ne*
floccipend: *ne*
floe: *pela*
flog: *bhlag*
floor: *pela*
flop: *plab*
Flora: *beu*
flora: *beu*
florid: *beu*
florine: *el 9*
florist: *beu*
floss: *plek II*
flotilla: *pleu*
flotsam: *ie, pleu*

flounder: *pela*
flour: *beu*
flourish: *beu*
flout: *beu*
flow: *beu, pleu*
flower: *beu*
flue: *pleu*
fluent: *beu*
flugelhorn: *ker II*
fluid: *beu*
fluke: *pela*
fluoride: *beu*
fluorine: *beu, el 9, guhdhei*
flurry: *keuero*
flush: *beu*
fluster: *pleu*
flute: *beu*
flutter: *pal, pleu*
flux: *beu*
fly: *pleu*
flyflapper: *coc*
flyswatter: *coc*
foal: *pou 9*
fob: *haifst*
foe: *peig*
fog: *pu*
foggage: *pu*
foible: *bhel II*
foil: *beu*
foist: *penkue*
fold: *plek II*
foliage: *beu*
folio: *beu*
Folket(h)ing: *ten*
folkmoot: *mod*
follicle: *beu*
folly: *beu*
fontange: *kleu I*
fool: *beu, bhel I*
foolhardy: *beu*
foot: *akua, ped*
footback: *ped*
football: *ped*
footfall: *ped*
footle: *bhaut*
foot-loose: *ped*
footpad: *leug, pent*
footprint: *ped*
footstool: *ped*
footway: *ped*
footy: *ped*
fop: *haifst*
forage: *pa*
foralite: *bher II*
foramen: *bher II*
foray: *pa*
forbear: *bher I, per VI b, per VIII*
forbid: *bheudh, per N 9*
forbidden: *per VIII*
forceful: *dheigh N 2 h*
forceps: *kap*
ford: *per I*
fore: *per IV*
forearmed: *per VI a*
forebear(s): *bher I, per VI b*
forecast: *ger VI, per VI a*
forecastle: *per N 8*
foreclose: *dhur, per VI a*
forefathers: *per VI b, per N 8*
forego: *per VI b*
foreign: *dhur*
forelock: *leug*
foremost: *per IV, per N 8*
forenoon: *per VI a*
forensic: *bhoros, dhur*
foresight: *per N 8*
foreskin: *gn, per VI a*
forest: *dhur*
forestall: *sta*
forestry: *dheigh N 36*
foretell: *per IV*
forewarned: *per VI a*
forfare: *per N 9*
forfeit: *dhur*
forfend: *guhen, per VIII*
forficate: *bher II*
forgather: *ghedh, per VIII*
forge: *dhabh*
forgery: *dhabh*
forget: *per N 9*
forgetive: *per VIII*
forgive: *ghebh*
forgo: *per VI b, per VIII*
fork: *bhurig*
forlapped: *per N 9*
forlorn: *leu I, lou, per VIII*
form: *merbh*
formal: *merbh*
formaldehyde: *morui*
formation: *merbh*
former: *per IV*
formic: *morui*
formica: *morui*
formicary: *morui*

formication: *morui*
formicide: *morui*
formicivorous: *morui*
Formosa: *merbh*
formula: *merbh*
formulate: *merbh*
fornicate: *guher*
fornication: *guher*
forsake: *per VIII, sag*
forsay: *per N 9*
forspent: *per VIII*
forswear: *per VIII*
fort: *bheregh*
forte: *bheregh*
forth: *per I*
forthright: *per I, reg I*
forthwith: *per I*
fortify: *bheregh*
fortissimo: *bheregh*
fortitude: *bheregh*
fortuitous: *bher I, per III*
fortuity: *per III*
fortunate: *per III*
fortune: *bher I, per III*
forty: *kuetuer*
forum: *bhoros, dhur*
fosse: *bhedh*
foujdar: *dhar*
foul-mouthed: *pu*
found: *pent*
foundation: *bhudh*
founder: *bhudh*
foundling: *pent, sap*
foundry: *gheu*
fount: *dhen*
fountain: *dhen*
four: *kuetuer*
fourchée: *bhurig*
fourchette: *bhurig*
four humours: *ugu*
fourteen: *kuetuer*
fourth: *kuetuer*
fowl: *pleu, pou 9*
fox: *puk, ulp*
Fox: *onomen*
foxed: *ulp*
foxglove: *ulp*
foxhole: *ulp*
fox trot: *ulp*
foxy: *ulp*
fra: *bhrater*
fracas: *bhreg, kuet, ndher*
fraction: *bhreg*
fractious: *bhreg*
fracture: *bhreg*
fragile: *bhreg*
fragment: *bhreg*
frail: *bhreg*
frailty: *bhreg, dheigh N 36*
frame: *per V*
francium: *el 87*
Franciscans: *dem*
Francophile: *bhili*
frangible: *bhreg*
franion: *bhreg, kad II*
frankfurter: *bheregh*
frantic: *guhren*
fraternal: *bhrater*
fraternity: *bhrater, seusor*
fratricide: *bhrater, sek II*
Frau: *per VI f*
fraught: *eik*
Fräulein: *per VI f*
fray: *bhreg, prai*
Freda: *prai*
Frederick: *prai, reg I*
free: *prai*
freebooter: *prai*
freeborn: *prai*
Free Church: *prai*
freedom: *prai*
free-handed: *prai*
freehold: *prai*
freelance: *prai*
freemason: *prai*
free press: *prai*
free thinker: *prai*
free will: *prai*
freeze: *preus*
freight: *eik*
frenetic: *guhren*
frenulum: *ghren*
frenum: *dhar, ghren*
frenzy: *guhren*
freshly: *dheigh N 1*
fret: *ed*
Freya: *prai*
friable: *bhreg*
friar: *bhrater*
fricassee: *bhreg, kuet*
fricative: *bhreg*
Friday: *prai*
fridge: *srig*
friend: *prai*

friendship: *dheigh N 33, sek IV*
frig: *bhreg*
frigacious: *bheug I*
Frigg: *prai*
fright: *prai*
frighten: *prai*
frigid: *reig II, srig*
frigidity: *reig II*
frigorific: *reig II, srig*
frith: *prai*
frithstool: *prai*
frizz: *preus*
frizzle: *preus*
frog: *preu*
frolic: *leig I, preu*
frolicsome: *dheigh N 37*
from: *per I*
frond: *per I*
front: *frons, per I*
frontage: *frons*
frontal: *per I*
frontier: *frons, per I*
frontispice: *frons, nebh*
frontispiece: *frons, spek*
frontward: *frons*
frost: *preus*
froward: *per I*
fructify: *bhrud*
frugal: *bhrud*
fruit: *bhrud*
fruition: *bhrud*
fruity: *dheigh N 36*
frumentaceous: *bhrud*
frumenty: *bhrud*
fry: *bhereu*
fub: *haifst*
fucivorous: *bhag*
fuck: *bhreg, peig*
fugacity: *bheug I*
fuge: *bheug I*
fugelman: *manu*
fugitive: *bheug I*
fugue: *bheug I*
Führer: *per VI f*
fulcrum: *bhelk*
fulfil(l): *pel V*
fulgent: *bhel I*
fuliginous: *dheu I*
full: *pel V*
full-blown: *pel V*
full dress: *pel V*
fulmar: *pu*
fulminate: *bhel I*
fulsome: *pel V*
fume: *dheu I*
fumigate: *ag, dheu I*
fumitory: *ters*
funambulist: *al III, dhun*
Funaria: *dhun*
function: *bheug III*
fund: *bhudh*
fundament: *bhudh*
fundamental: *bhudh*
fungivorous: *bhag*
fungoid: *spong*
fungus: *spong*
funicle: *dhun*
funicular: *dhun*
funipendulous: *dhun*
funipotent: *dhun*
funis: *dhun*
funnel: *gheu*
furcate: *bhurig*
furfur: *ghren*
Furies: *dheu I*
furious: *dheu I*
furlough: *leubh*
furnace: *guher*
furnish: *per V*
furniture: *per V*
furrow: *porko II*
further: *per I*
furtive: *dheu I*
fury: *dheu I*
fuse: *gheu*
fustigate: *ag*
futile: *gheu*
future: *bheu*
fuzzy: *pu*
-fy: *dhe I*
fylfot: *es*

G

gabble: *baba, gen*
gabfest: *dhes*
gabion: *kagh, keu II*
gabionade: *kagh, keu II*
gable: *caput*
Gabriel: *dekm*
gad: *ghedh*
gadolinite: *el 39, el 64*

gadolinium: *el 64*
Gaekwar: *guou, ueid*
Gael: *uidhu*
gage: *uad*
gain: *uen*
gala: *uel II*
galactagogue: *glact*
Galactia: *glact*
galactometer: *glact*
galactonic: *glact*
galactopoietic: *glact*
galactorrhea: *glact*
galactose: *glact*
galactrophagous: *bhag*
galanty show: *uel II*
Galatea: *glact*
galax: *glact*
galaxia: *glact*
galaxy: *glact*
gale: *ghel I*
galimatias: *gal*
gall: *gel I*
gallant: *uel II*
gallantry: *dheigh N 36*
Gallia: *uidhu*
Gallicism: *uidhu*
gallimaufry: *uel II*
gallinaceous: *gal*
gallium: *el 31, gal, uidhu*
gallivant: *uel II*
gallnut: *gel I*
gallop: *klou, uel II*
galore: *lau*
galosh: *uidhu*
galways: *bhar*
gam: *kam*
gamb: *kam*
gambado: *kam*
gambit: *kam*
gambler: *dheigh N 13*
gamete: *geme*
gametophore: *geme*
gamic: *geme*
gammadion: *es*
gammon: *kam*
gamogenesis: *geme*
gamophyllous: *geme*
gander: *ghans*
Gandhiji: *guen*
ganglion: *gel I*
gannet: *ghans*
gantlet: *klou*
Ganymede: *ga, jing, morui*
gaol: *kagh, keu II*
gap: *ghi*
gape: *ghi*
garage: *suer I*
garb: *ghrebh II*
garbage: *ghrebh II, sek VI*
garble: *ghrebh II, ker III, sek VI*
garboard: *ghedh*
garçon: ureg
garden: *gher IV*
gardenia: *gher IV*
gardyloo: *gal, leuk*
garfish: *ghaiso*
Gargantua: *garg*
gargantuan: *dheigh N 7, garg*
gargle: *garg, ombhr*
gargoyle: *garg, ombhr*
garland: *uei*
garlic: *ghaiso, leug*
garment: *suer I, uer V*
garnet: *ger V*
garnish: *suer I, uer V*
garniture: *uer V*
garret: *uer V*
garrison: *suer I, uer V*
garrulous: *gal*
garter: *ken III*
garuda: *guel III*
gas: *ghi*
gasket: *ureg*
gastric: *gras*
gastrin: *gras*
gastr(o)-: *gras*
gastrocnemius: *gras, konemo*
gastrology: *gras*
gastromancy: *gras*
gastronomy: *gras*
gather: *ghedh*
gaud: *ga, jing*
gaudeamus: ga
gaudy: *jing*
Gaul: *uidhu*
gaur: *guou*
gauze: *bha II*
gavel: *ghebh*
gawk: *ghoue*
gay: *es, peig*
gayel: *guou*
Gea: *fur, uesper*
gee: *esu*
gelatine: *gel I*

geld: *ghel II*
gelding: *ghel II*
Gelechiidae: *legh*
gelid: *gel I*
gem: *gembh*
gemel: *iem*
gemellus: *iem*
gemination: *iem*
Gemini: *guei, iem*
gemmate: *gembh*
gemote: *mod*
gemsbok: *kem II*
gendarme: *gn*
gender: *gn*
gene: *gn*
genealogy: *dheigh N 30, gn*
general: *gn*
generalissimo: *gn*
generate: *gn*
generation: *gn*
generator: *gn*
generatrix: *gn*
generous: *gn*
genes: *gn*
genesis: *gn*
genetics: *gn*
genial: *ghenu, gn*
genie: *gn*
genitals: *gn*
genitive: *gn*
genitor: *gn*
genius: *gn*
genocide: *gn*
genre: *gn*
gens: *gn*
genteel: *gn*
gentile: *gn*
gentle: *gn*
gentleman: *gn*
gentry: *gn, sek II*
genuflect: *ghenu*
genuine: *ghenu*
genus: *gn*
geocentric: *ge*
geode: *ge*
geodesy: *da II*
Geoffrey: *prai*
geogony: *gn*
geography: *ge, gerbh, nebh*
geoid: *ge*
geology: *ge, leg I, nebh*
geometry: *ge, me IV, men I*
geoponics: *spend II*
George: *ge, uerg*
georgic: *uerg*
Georgics: *ge*
geotropism: *trep*
Gerald: *ghaiso, ual*
Geraldine: *ual*
geranium: *ger I*
Gerard: *ghaiso, kar*
gerbe: *ghrebh II*
gerent: *ger VI*
gerfalcon: *pel VII*
geriatrics: *eis, ger IV*
germ: *gn*
german: *gn, suesor*
German: *gal*
germander: *deru, ghdhem*
germane: *gn, suesor*
germanite: *gal*
germanium: *el 32, gal*
Germanophobe: *gal, men I*
Germantown: *gal*
germinal: *gn*
germinate: *gn*
gerocomical: *ger IV*
gerocomy: *ger IV*
gerontarchical: *ger IV*
gerontic: *ger IV*
gerontocracy: *ger IV*
gerontocratic: *ger IV*
gerontogeous: *ger IV*
gerontology: *ger IV*
gerontomorphic: *ger IV*
gerontophil: *ger IV*
Gertrude: *ghaiso*
gerund: *ger VI*
gerundive: *ges*
Gervais: *ghaiso*
gest: *ger VI, ges*
Gestalt: *sta, stel*
gestation: *ger VI, ges*
gesticulate: *ger VI, ges*
gesture: *ger VI, ges*
geyser: *gheu*
ghat: *gher I*
ghetto: *leb*
giant: *gigas, nebh*
giantism: *gigas*
gibbosity: *gib*
gibbous: *gib*
giblet: *bheid*
giddy: *ghau*

Gifola: *guhisl*
gift: *ghebh*
giga-: *me IV*
gigantic: *gigas, nebh*
gigantomachy: *gigas, magh, nebh*
Gigas: *gigas*
gigavolts: *nebh*
gilbert: *bhel I*
Gilbertian: *bhel I*
gilbertite: *bhel I*
gild: *gel I*
gill: *ghi*
gillyflower: *beu*
gilt: *gel I, ghel II*
gimbal: *iem*
gimlet: *ueip*
gimp: *ueip*
ginger: *ker III*
gingerly: *gn*
gingivitis: *gieu*
girandole: *gue, keup*
girasole: *gue, sauel*
gird: *gher IV*
girdle: *gher IV*
girt: *gher IV*
girth: *gher IV*
gist: *ie*
give: *ghebh*
gizzard: *ieku-rt*
glacial: *gel I*
glacier: *gel I*
glacis: *gel I*
glad: *gel I*
gladiate: *kal*
gladiator: *kal*
gladiolus: *kal*
gladius: *kal*
glair: *gel I*
glaive: *kal*
glamour: *gerbh*
glance: *gel I*
glare: *gel I*
glass: *gel I*
glaucoma: *gel I*
glaucous: *gel I*
glaze: *gel I*
gleam: *gel I*
glebe: *gel II*
glee: *gel I*
gleeful: *pel V*
gleek: *leig I*
Gleet: *leuk*
glib: *gel I*
glide: *gel I*
glimpse: *gel I*
glint: *gel I*
glissade: *gel I*
glisten: *gel I*
glister: *gel I*
gloaming: *gel I*
gloat: *gel I*
globe: *gel II*
globule: *gel II*
glomery: *gerbh*
Gloria: *glor*
glorify: *glor*
gloriole: *glor*
glorious: *glor*
glory: *glor*
gloss: *gel I, glokh*
glossary: *glokh*
glossolalia: *glokh, lal*
glottis: *glokh*
glove: *lep II*
glow: *gel I*
glower: *gel I*
glucose: *dlku, glact*
glucosuria: *uer VII*
glue: *gel II*
glume: *gleubh*
glut: *garg*
gluten: *gel II*
glutinous: *gel II*
glutton: *garg*
glycerin: *dlku*
glyph: *gleubh*
glyptic: *gleubh*
gnar: *ghenu*
gnarl: *ghenu*
gnash: *ghenu*
gnat: *ghenu*
gnathic: *ghenu*
gnathonic: *ghenu*
gnaw: *ghenu*
gnome: *gn*
gnomon: *gn*
gnosis: *gn*
gnostic: *gn*
go: *onomen*
goat: *ghaido*
goatee: *bhar*
gobble: *baba, gen, jing*
goblin: *gen*
God: *per VI f*

god: *ghau*
godchild: *ghau*
godfather: *ghau*
Godfrey: *ghau, prai*
godhead: *ghau*
godless: *leu I*
godmother: *ghau, ma II*
godparent: *ghau*
godsend: *ghau*
goffer: *uebh*
Goidelic: *uidhu*
goiter: *gue, gutta*
gold: *andh, el 79, gel I*
gold bricks: *kel VI*
gold digger: *kel VI*
golden: *kel VI*
golden mean: *medhi, mei I*
golden rule: *kel VI*
goldfinder: *kel VI, lap*
gold rush: *nem*
goldsmith: *kel VI*
Goldwynism: *melo*
Golgotha: *keleuo*
goliard: *garg, gher II*
goliardic: *dheigh N 17*
gombeen: *skamb*
gomphosis: *gembh*
gonad: *gn*
gonfalon: *guhen, pend*
goniometer: *ghenu*
gono-: *gn*
gonococcus: *kogkhos*
gonorrhea: *gn, sreu*
gonosphere: *gn*
gonyaulax: *ghenu*
gonys: *ghenu*
good: *ghedh*
good-by(e): *ghau, kailo*
goodness: *ghedh*
googol: *me IV*
googolplex: *me IV*
goose: *ane, ghans*
gooseberry: *bhel I*
goose-egg: *ane*
goosestep: *ane*
gopher: *uebh*
gopura: *guou, pele*
goral: *guou*
Gordian knot: *keu II*
gorge: *garg*
gormandize: *garg*
gorse: *ghers*
gosh: *esu*
goshawk: *ghans*
gosling: *ane, ghans, sap*
gospel: *spel*
gospodin: *ghostis*
gossamer: *ane*
gossip: *ghau, spel, sue*
gouache: *akua, akw*
gourmand: *garg*
gourmet: *garg*
gout: *gutta*
govern: *kuberna*
government: *kuberna*
grab: *ghrebh II*
grabble: *ghrebh II*
grace: *gar*
graceless: *gar*
gracile: *gar*
gracioso: *gar*
gracious: *gar*
grackle: *ger II, ker IV*
gradatim: *ghredh*
gradation: *ghredh*
grade: *ghredh*
gradient: *ghredh*
gradual: *ghredh*
gradually: *dheigh N 1*
graduation: *ghredh*
graepel: *kru*
graffiti: *gerbh*
graffito: *gerbh*
graft: *gerbh*
grail: *kere*
grain: *ger V, gher I*
gram: *gerbh, gras*
grama: *gras*
Gramercy: *merc*
gramicidine: *gras*
gramineous: *gras*
graminivorous: *bhag, gras*
grammar: *gerbh*
gramophone: *gerbh*
grampus: *peisk*
granary: *ger V*
grand: *grand*
grandam: *grand*
grandee: *grand*
grandeur: *grand*
grandiloquent: *grand, tolku*
grandiose: *grand*
grand mal: melo
grandmother: *grand, ma II*

grandstand: *sta*
grange: *ger V*
granite: *ger V*
granivorous: *bhag*
grant: *kred I*
granulated: *ger V*
granule: *ger V, gher I, ghren*
granulose: *ger V*
grape: *ger III*
graph: *gerbh*
graphite: *el 82, gerbh*
graphology: *gerbh*
graphomania: *caca*
grapple: *ger III*
grasp: *ghrebh II*
grate: *kert*
gratify: *gar*
gratis: *gar*
gratitude: *gar*
gratuity: *gar*
graupel: *kreup*
grave: *gherbh I, guer*
gravel: *gher I*
gravel-blind: *caput*
graveless: *caput*
gravid: *guer*
gravitate: *guer, leguh*
gravity: *guer*
gravy: *ger V*
Gray: *onomen*
gray: *gher III*
graybeard: *gher III*
graylag: *gher III*
grayling: *gher III*
great: *gher I*
Great Bear: *cal*
great-grandchild: *grand*
greave: *ghrebh I*
greedy: *gher II*
green: *gel I, kel VI*
green-eyed: *kel VI*
green gallant: *kel VI*
green gown: *kel VI*
greenhorn: *kel VI*
greenhouse: *kel VI*
Greensleeves: kel VI
Greensleeves, Lady: *poi*
greensward: *kel VI*
greenwood: *kel VI*
gregarious: *ger I*
Gregorian: *per I*
Gregory: *ker III*
grenade: *ger V*
gressorial: *ghredh*
grey: *gher III*
greyhound: *gher III*
grid: *kert*
griddle: *kert*
gridelin: *lino*
gridiron: *kert*
grief: *guer*
grievance: *guer*
grieve: *guer*
griff: *ghreib*
griffe: *ghreib*
griffon: *ghreib*
griffonage: *ghreib*
grill: *kert*
grille: *kert*
grilse: *gher III*
grim: *ghrem, nem*
grimace: *ghrem, nem*
grind: *gher I, ghren*
grindstone: *stei*
grip: *ghrebh II*
gripe: *ghrebh II, ghreib*
grippe: *ghreib*
gripsach: *ghreib*
grisaille: *gher III*
grisette: *gher III*
grist: *gher I, ghren*
gristle: *gher I, ghren*
grits: *gher I*
grizzled: *gher III*
grizzly bear: *gher III*
groan: *jing*
groat: *gher I*
groats: *gher I*
grocer: *duo, gher I*
grocery: *upo*
grog: *gher I, ker I*
groggy: *ker I*
grogram: *gher I*
groom: *ghdhem*
groove: *ghrebh I*
grope: *ghrebh I*
grosbeak: *gher I*
groschen: *gher I, guretso*
grosgrain: *gher I, guretso*
gross: *duo, gher I, guretso*
grosz: *gher I, guretso*
grot: *krup*
grotesque: *krup*
grotto: *krup*

grouch: *gru*
ground: *ghren*
group: *ger I*
grouse: *gru*
grovel: *ger III*
growl: *jing*
grub: *ghrebh I*
grudge: *gru*
gruel: *gher I*
gruesome: *gher I*
gruff: *kreup*
gruffish: *reu*
grumble: *ghrem, nem*
grunt: *gru*
gruntled: *gru*
grutch: *gru*
guarantee: *suer I, uer V*
guaranty: *suer I*
guard: *suer I, uer IV*
guardian: *suer I, uer IV*
guardianship: *dheigh N 33*
Guatama: *guou*
gubernatorial: *kuberna*
guerdon: *lau, uid*
guerrilla: *uers*
guest: *ghostis*
guhr: *ies*
guide: *ueid*
guile: *ambhi, ueik*
guillotine: *keu I, onomen*
guimpe: *ueip*
Guinevere: *ueid*
guipure: *ueip*
guise: *ueid*
gulf: *kuelp*
gull: *gel I*
gullet: *garg*
gulp: *yap*
gun: *guhen, margar*
Gunther: *guhen*
gurges: *garg*
gurgitation: *garg*
gurgle: *garg, ombhr*
gurnard: *gru*
guru: *guer*
guruji: *guen*
gush: *gheu*
gust: *gheu*
gut: *gheu, keup*
guttate: *gutta*
gutter: *gutta*
guttersnipe: *gutta*
guttural: *gue, gutta, keup*
Gwendolin: *ueid*
gwyniad: *ueid*
gymkhana: *nogu*
gymnasium: *gn, nogu*
gymnast: *nogu*
Gymnoconia: *ken I*
gymnogram: *nogu*
gymnosophist: *nogu*
gymnosperm: *nogu*
gymnospermism: *ped*
Gymnoti: *not*
gynander: *guen, nert*
gynantherous: *ner II*
gynarchy: *guen*
gynecologist: *guen*
gynecology: *dheigh N 30*
gynecomasha: *guen*
gynecomastia: *guen*
gynecomorphous: *guen*
gynephobia: *guen*
gynocracy: *guen*
gyps: *gue*
gyrate: *keup*
gyre: *gue*
gyro: *keup*
gyromancy: *gue*
gyroplane: *gue*
gyroscope: *gue*
gyrostat: *sta*

H

habeas corpus: *ghebh*
habile: *ghebh*
habiliments: *ghebh*
habilitate: *ghebh*
habit: *ghebh*
habitat: *ghebh*
habitation: *ghebh*
habitude: *ghebh*
hacienda: *dhe I*
hack: *keg, sek IV*
hackberry: *bhel I*
hackbut: *keg*
hackery: *ker I*
hackle(s): *keg*
hackney: *keg*
hackneyed: *keg*
hackster: *keg*

hackwork: *keg*
Hades: *kau II, ueid*
haecceity: *ko*
haemagogue: *semi*
haemapophysis: *semi*
haematine: *semi*
haemochrome: *semi*
haemoscope: *semi*
hafnium: *el 72*
haft: *kap*
hag: *kagh, kau III*
hagberry: *bhel I, kagh, kau III*
hagfish: *kagh*
haggard: *kagh*
haggis: *kau III*
haggle: *kau III*
hagiocracy: *iag I*
hagiographic: *iag I*
hagioscope: *dheigh N 32, iag I*
hagiosidere: *iag I*
ha-ha: *ha, kagh*
hahnium: *el 105*
hail: *kailo*
hailstone: *kaghlo, stei*
hake: *keg*
hakenkreuz: *keg*
halberd: *kelp*
hale: *kailo*
half: *kel VIII*
halibut: *bhau*
Halicore: *ker VI*
halidome: *dhe I, kailo*
Haliotis: *ous*
halitosis: *ane*
halitus: *ane*
hall: *kel VI*
hallmoot: *mod*
hallucination: *al III*
halobiontic: *sal I*
halogen: *el 35, el 85, gn, sal I*
halomancy: *sal I*
halophyte: *sal I*
halse: *kailo*
halt: *kal, kel VII*
halter: *kelp*
halteres: *sel IV*
halve: *kel VIII*
-ham: *kei II*
ham: *konemo*
hamacratic: *sem I*
hamadryad: *deru, sem I*
hamburger: *bheregh, konemo*
hamesucken: *kei II*
hamlet: *kei II*
hammer: *ak*
hamshackle: *konemo*
hamstrung: *konemo*
handicraft: *kom*
handiwork: *kom, uerg*
handkerchief: *caput*
handsel: *sel III*
handsome: *dheigh N 37*
hang: *konk*
hangar: *konk*
hangdog: *konk*
hangfire: *konk*
hangnail: *angh*
hangover: *konk*
hang-up: *konk*
hank: *konk*
hanker: *konk*
hanky-panky: *konk*
hanuman: *ghenu*
hap: *kob*
hapax legomenon: pag, plek I, sem I
haplocardiac: *plek I*
haplodont: *sem I*
haplography: *plek I, sem I*
haploid: *plek I, sem I*
haplology: *plek I, sem I*
haplomorphic: *plek I*
happen: *kob*
happenstance: *kob*
happy: *kob*
harangue: *ker I, koro*
harbinger: *koro*
harbor: *koro*
hard: *kar, onomen*
harden: *kar*
hardihood: *kar*
hardship: *dheigh N 33, kar*
hardtack: *kar*
hardware: *kar*
hardy: *dheigh N 13, kar*
hare: *kas*
hark: *keu I*
harlotry: *dheigh N 36*
harm: *kormo*
harmonious: *dheigh N 2 d*
harmony: *ar I*
harness: *nes*
Harold: *koro, ual*
harpoon: *srep*
harpy: *labh, srep*

(h)arquebus: *keg*
harrier: *kas*
harrow: *ker III, sek IX, suer III*
harry: *koro, ual*
harsh: *kars*
hart: *ker II*
hartebeest: *ker II*
hartshorn: *el 7, ker II*
harvest: *ker III, sek IX, suer III*
hash: *sek IV*
haste: *haifst*
hasten: *haifst*
hasty pudding: *haifst*
hat: *kadh*
hatch: *sek IV*
hatchel: *keg*
hatchet: *sek IV*
hate: *kad II*
hateful: *pel V*
hatred: *ar I, kad II*
hauberk: *ker I*
haugh: *kel VI*
haughty: *al I*
ha(u)lm: *kolem*
haunt: *kei II*
hausse-col: *ker I*
haustellum: *au III, aus*
haustorium: *au III, aus*
hautboy: *al I*
haute couture: siu
have: *ghebh, kap*
haven: *kap*
havildar: *dhar*
haw: *ha*
hawk: *kap*
hawker: *gue*
hawse: *ker I*
hawser: *al I*
hay: *kagh, kau III*
haycock: *geu*
haystack: *geu*
hazardous: *dheigh N 2 e*
hazel: *kosel*
he: *ko*
head: *caput*
heading: *caput*
headline: *caput*
headland: *caput*
headlong: *caput*
headman: *caput*
headmaster: *caput*
headstrong: *caput*
heady: *caput*
heal: *kailo*
healthy: *kailo*
heap: *keu II*
hear: *keu I*
hearken: *ken I*
heart: *kerd*
hearth: *ker V*
heat: *kai*
heath: *kaito*
heathen: *kaito*
heather: *kaito*
heaume: *kel VI*
heave: *kap*
heaven: *kam, kem I, skeu*
heavenward: *uer II 5*
heavy: *kap*
hebdomad: *septm*
hebdomadary: *septm*
hebdomically: *septm*
Hebe: *ga, iegua*
hebeanthus: *iegua*
hebegynous: *iegua*
hebepetalous: *iegua*
hebephrenia: *ga, iegua*
hebetude: *iegua*
hecatomb: *dekm*
heckle: *keg*
hectare: *dekm*
hectic: *segh*
hecto-: *me IV*
hectoliter: *dekm*
hector: *segh*
Hector: *segh*
Hedeoma: *od*
hedgeberry: *bhel I*
hedonic: *suad*
hedonian: *suad*
hedonist: *suad*
-hedron: *sed I*
Hedychium: *ghei, suad*
heed: *kadh*
heel: *kenk III*
heft: *kap*
hegemony: *sag*
hegira: *kel II*
hegumen: *sag*
heifer: *per VI c*
height: *keu II*
heinous: *kad II*
Heinrich: *kei II, reg I*
heir: *ghe*

Hel: *kel VI*
Helen: *dheu I, uelu*
Helenium: *uelu*
Helga: *kailo*
heliacal: *sauel*
helical: *uelu*
helicogyre: *keup*
Helicon: *uelu*
helicopter: *pet I, uelu*
helicotrema: *ter II*
heliocentric: *kent, nebh, sauel*
heliochrome: *gher I, sauel*
heliolithic: *nebh*
helion: *nebh*
heliophilous: *bhili*
Helios: *nebh, sauel*
heliostat: *nebh*
heliotrope: *nebh, sauel, trep*
helium: *el 2, nebh, sauel*
helix: *uelu*
hell: *kel VI*
Hellenes: *dheu I*
Hellenism: *sel III*
Hellespont: *uelu*
helm: *kelp, kuelp*
helmet: *kel VI, kuelp*
helminth: *uelu*
helminthiasis: *uelu*
helminthology: *uelu*
helmsman: *kelp*
Héloise: *kailo*
Helonias: *uelu*
helot: *uel III*
help: *kelb*
helpless: *kelb*
helpmate: *kelb, med*
helpmeet: *kelb, med*
helve: *kelp*
hem: *kem III, kem IV*
hematite: *semi*
hematocrit: *sek VI*
hematose: *semi*
hemeralopia: *amer*
hemerocallis: *cal*
hemielytron: *uelu*
hemiplegia: *semi*
hemipteron: *semi*
hemisphere: *semi*
hemistich: *semi, steigh*
hemocyanin: *semi*
hemoglobin: *semi*
hemophilia: *segh, semi*
hemophobia: *semi*
hemoptysis: *sphieu*
hemorrhage: *segh, semi*
hemorrhoid: *semi*
hemorrhoids: *segh, sreu*
hempe: *kel VIII*
hen: *ane, kan*
hence: *ko, kuo*
hendecasyllabic: *sem I*
hendiadys: *sem I*
henopoetic: *sem I*
henotheism: *sem I*
henotic: *sem I*
Henry: *kei II, reg I*
heortology: *uero*
hepar: *ieku-rt*
heparin: *ieku-rt*
hepatic: *ieku-rt*
hepatitis: *ieku-rt*
heptachord: *septm*
heptad: *septm*
heptagon: *septm*
Heptalogia: *leg I*
heptamerous: *septm*
her: *ko*
Hera: *kleu I, morui*
Heracles: *kleu I*
herald: *ual*
herbivorous: *bhag, dheigh N 2 f*
Hercules: *kleu I, nebh*
herd: *kerdh*
herdsman: *kerdh*
here: *ko*
heredity: *ghe*
heresiarch: *ie*
heresy: *ie*
heretic: *dek, ie*
heretoga: *koro*
heriot: *koro*
heritage: *ghe*
Herman: *koro, manu*
hermeneutics: *suer II*
Hermes: *suer II*
hermit: *er*
hermitage: *er*
hero: *kleu I*
herpes: *serp*
herpetology: *serp*
herring: *keiro*
herringbone: *keiro*

herring pond: *keiro*
hership: *koro*
Herzog: koro
hesitate: *ghais*
hesperian: *uesper*
Hesperides: *uesper*
Hesper(us): *uesper*
hest: *kei I*
Hestia: *ues I*
hetaera: *sue*
heterochromatic: *dek*
heterochrome: *dek*
heteroclite: *keli, sem I*
heterodoxy: *dek*
heterodyne: *dek*
heterogeneous: *dek, gn, sem I*
heterogenesis: *dek*
heteromerous: *smer*
heteromorphy: *merbh*
heteronymous: *onomen*
Heteroousian: *es, sem I*
heterophyllous: *beu*
heterozygous: *ieug*
hetman: *caput*
heuristic: *uer III*
hew: *kau III*
hex: *kagh, seks*
hexachord: *seks*
hexad: *seks*
hexagon: *seks*
hexapla: *plek I*
hexyl: *seks*
hiatus: *ghi*
hibernate: *ghei*
Hibernian: *eis*
hidalgo: *dhel I, kuo*
hide: *kei II, skeu*
hidrosis: *sueid II*
hiemal: *ghei*
hieratic: *eis*
hieroglyphics: *dheigh N 17, eis, gleubh*
hi-fi: *aus*
high: *gue, keu II*
high cockalorum: *ane*
highriser: *me III, skeu*
hight: *kei I*
hilarious: *sel II*
Hilda: *kal*
hill: *gue, kel IV*
hillbilly: *kel IV*
hillock: *gue, kel IV*
hilt: *kal*
hilum: *guhisl*
him: *ko*
Himalayas: *ghei*
Hinayana: *ei I*
hind: *kei II, kem II, ko*
hinder: *ko*
hindsight: *per N 8*
hinge: *konk*
hinterland: *ko, lendh II*
hip: *keu II*
hippalectryon: *eku*
hippocras: *da II*
Hippocrates: *da II*
Hippocratic: *da II*
Hippocrene: *eku*
Hippodamia: *eku*
hippodrome: *dra, eku*
hippoglossus: *glokh*
hippogriff: *ghreib*
Hippolyta: *eku*
hippophagous: *bhag*
hippopotamus: *eku, pet I*
hirsute: *ghers*
his: *ko*
hispid: *ghers*
hiss: *jing*
histamine: *sta*
histology: *sta*
histolysis: *sta*
historical: *ueid*
historiographer: *ueid*
history: *ueid*
hither: *ko*
h'm: *hum*
hoar: *keiro*
hoard: *kel VI, skeu*
hoarding: *kert*
hoarfrost: *keiro*
hoarse: *kai*
hoax: *gher II*
hobnob: *ne*
hock: *kenk III*
hockey: *keg, kenk III*
Hocktide: *kenk III*
hocus-pocus: *gher II, konk*
hodden: *kel VII*
hodiernal: *ko*
hodograph: *sed II*
hoe: *kau III*
hog: *mel I, sus*
hoi polloi: pel V, sos
hoity-toity: *dheigh N 36*

hokey-pokey: *konk*
hold: *kel VII*
hole: *kel VI*
Holland: *kal, kel VIII*
hollandaise: *kel VIII*
hollow: *kel VI*
hollowness: *dheigh N 29*
holly: *kailo, kel V*
hollyhock: *kailo*
holm: *gue, kel IV*
holmia: *el 67*
holmium: *el 67, kel IV*
holm oak: *kel V*
holocaust: *kau I, solo*
holograph: *al II, gerbh, solo*
holour: *solo*
holozoic: *solo*
holster: *kel VI*
holt: *kal, kel VIII*
holy: *kailo*
holystone: *stei*
homage: *ghdhem*
hombre: *es, ghdhem*
home: *kei II*
homelike: *kei II*
homely: *kei II*
homeopathy: *al II, es, guadh, sem I*
Homer: *keu II, sem I*
homespun: *kei II*
homestead: *sta*
homeward: *uer II 5*
homicide: *es, ghdhem*
homily: *sem I*
hominid: *es, ghdhem*
hominoid: *ghdhem, gn*
hominy: *es*
homo: *es, ghdhem, sem*
homochromous: *gher I*
homoeoteleuton: *es*
homogamous: *es*
homogeneous: *es, ghdhem, gn, sem I*
homogenized: *es, gn, sem I*
homogenous: *gn*
homograph: *es*
Homoiousian: *es, sem I*
homologous: *dheigh N 2 f, leg I*
homolographic: *sem I*
homologue: *sem I*
homologus: *sem I*
homonym: *es, onomen, sem I*
Homoousian: *es, sem I*
homophone: *es, sem I*
Homo sapiens: *sap*
homosexual: *es, ghdhem*
homunculus: *ghdhem*
hone: *ke*
honest: *honos*
honesty: *honos*
honey: *keneko*
honeycomb: *keneko*
honeydew: *keneko*
honeymoon: *keneko, me IV*
honeysuckle: *keneko, seu I*
honi soit: ken III
honky-tonk: *konk*
honor: *honos*
honorable: *honos*
honorarium: *honos*
honorific: *honos*
hood: *kadh*
-hood: *kait*
hoodie: *kadh*
hoodle: *kueit, ul*
hoof: *kaph*
hook: *keg*
hooker: *keg*
hoop: *keu II*
hoosegow: *ieuos*
hoot: *ul*
hop: *keu II*
hope: *eu, keu II*
hope chest: *eu*
hopeful: *eu*
hopeless: *dheigh N 26, eu, leu I*
hopscotch: *kogkhos, peik*
Horae: *eir, morui*
horal: *eir*
horary: *eir*
Hordeum: *ghers*
horehound: *keiro*
horizon: *uer II 5*
horizontal: *uer II 5*
hormone: *ser III*
horn: *ker II*
hornbeam: *ker II*
hornbill: *ker II*
hornblende: *ker II*
hornbook: *ker II*
hornet: *ker II*
horntail: *ker II*
hornworm: *ker II*
hornwort: *ker II*
horny: *ker II*
horologe: *eir, leg I*

hurtleberry: *bhel I*
husband: *bheu, kel VI*
husbandry: *bheu*
husk: *kel VI*
hussar: *dheigh N 13, kers I*
husting(s): *kel VI, ten*
hut: *kel VI, skeu*
hutch: *kel VI*
hutment: *kel VI*
Huxley: *leuk*
Hyades: *morui*
hyalite: *dheigh N 22*
hybrid: *ud*
hybridous: *ud*
hybris: *ud*
hydantoic: *aue*
hydatic: *aue*
hydra: *aue*
hydrangea: *aue*
hydrant: *aue*
hydraulic: *aue, aulo*
hydrocele: *keu II*
hydrocephalic: *aue, caput*
hydrocephalus: *sap*
hydrochoerus: *ghers*
hydrocycle: *aue*
hydroelectric: *aue*
hydroextractor: *aue*
hydrogen: *aue, el 1, gn, iso*
hydrokinetics: *aue*
hydrolitic: *leu I*
hydrolysis: *lou*
hydromel: *medhu, melit*
hydrophic: *duo*
hydrophobia: *aue, bhegu, duo, men I*
hydrophore: *aue*
hydrosphere: *reg II*
hydrotherapy: *dhar*
hydroxide: *aue*
hydroxyl: *hule*
hydruria: *aue*
hydurilic: *aue*
hyena: *sus*
hyeometer: *seu I*
hyetograph: *seu I*
Hygeia: *guei*
hygiene: *guei*
hygroma: *ugu*
hygrometer: *ugu*
hygroscopic: *ugu*
hyla: *hule*
hylic: *hule*
hylobates: *hule*
hylophagous: *hule*
hylotheism: *hule*
hylozoic: *hule*
hylozoist: *hule*
hymen: *maghos, siu, uebh*
hymeneal: *siu*
hymenocallis: *cal*
hymenography: *dheigh N 16*
hymenoptera: *mak, siu*
hymn: *siu, uebh*
hymnody: *aud, siu, ued*
hyoscine: *sus*
Hyoscyamus: *sus*
hyper-: *upo III a*
hyperbaton: *gua*
hyperbola: *guel II, upo III a*
hyperbole: *guel II, upo III a*
hyperborean: *dheigh N 7, upo III a*
hypercritical: *sek VI, sker VI, upo III a*
hyperdynamic: *upo III a*
Hypericaceae: *uer II 6*
Hypericum: *uer II 6*
Hyperion: *nebh, upo III a*
hyperkinesia: *kei I*
hypermania: *men I*
hyperparisitism: *per VII*
hyperpnea: *pneu*
hyperprosexia: *sek I*
hypersensitive: *upo III a*
hypha: *uebh*
hyphen: *sem I*
hypnagogic: *ag*
hypnoanalysis: *suep I*
hypnosis: *suep I*
hypo-: *upo III b*
hypocaust: *kau I*
hypochondria: *ghren*
hypochondriac: *ghren, upo III b*
hypochondriasis: *upo III b*
hypocorism: *upo III b*
hypocoristic: *ker VI*
hypocrisy: *ker III, sek VI, upo III b*
hypocritical: *ker III*
hypogastrium: *medhi*
hypomania: *men I*
hypoplasia: *pela*
hypostasis: *sta*
hypostyle: *sta*
hyposulfurous: *upo III b*
hypotaxis: *tag II*
hypotenuse: *ten, upo III b*

I

image: *im*
imagination: *im*
imago: *im*
imbecile: *bak*
imbibe: *poi*
imbibition: *poi*
imbricate: *nebh, ombhro*
imbrue: *bhereu*
imbue: *ombhro*
imburse: *burs*
imitate: *im*
immaculate: *smeit*
immanity: *ma I*
immaterial: *en*
immature: *ma I*
immeasurable: *me IV*
immediate: *medhi, ne*
immense: *me IV*
immersion: *mezg I*
immigration: *mei II*
imminent: *men II*
immiscible: *meik*
immix: *meik*
immobile: *meu II*
immoderate: *med*
immodest: *med*
immolate: *mel V*
immorality: *moro*
immortal: *ne*
immortality: *mer II*
immovable: *en*
immune: *mei II*
immunity: *mei II, ne*
immunology: *mei II*
immure: *mei III*
immutable: *mei II, ne*
imp: *bheu*
impact: *pag*
impair: *ped, per V*
impale: *pag*
impanate: *pa*
impaneled: *pan*
impart: *per V*
impartial: *dheigh N 5, per V*
impaste: *kuet, pa*
impatient: *ne*
impavid: *peue*
impeach: *ped*
impecunious: *pek II*
impede: *ped*
impediment: *ped*
impedimenta: *ped*
impel: *pel IV*
impend: *spend II*
impending: *pend*
impenetrable: *las*
impenitence: *dheigh N 8*
imperator: *per VI f*
imperceptible: *kap*
imperfect: *dhe I, en, ne*
imperial: *bhar, per VI f*
imperil: *per III*
imperious: *per VI f*
impersonal: *pers*
impersonate: *lap*
impervious: *per I, uegh*
impetrate: *peter*
impetuous: *pet I*
impetus: *pet I*
impiety: *pius*
impinge: *pag*
impious: *pius*
implacable: *pela*
implant: *pela*
implement: *pel V*
implicate: *plek I*
implore: *plor*
implosion: *plaud*
imply: *plek I*
imponderable: *pend, spend II*
importance: *per II*
importunate: *per II*
importune: *per II*
impose: *ap*
impotent: *poti*
impound: *bend*
impoverish: *pou 7*
impractical: *per III*
imprecation: *perk*
impregnable: *gn*
impregnate: *gn*
impress: *per VII, pres*
impression: *pres*
imprimatur: *per III*
imprint: *per VII*
improbable: *per VI e*
improbity: *per VI e*
impromptu: *em*
improper: *per VI g*
impropriety: *per VI g*
improve: *per VI e*
improvisation: *ueid*
improvise: *ueid*
impudent: *peu I*

impugn: *peug*
impulse: *pel IV*
impunity: *kuei I*
impute: *peue*
in: *en*
inadvertent: *uer II 5*
inamorata: *amma*
inaugurate: *aug*
incandescent: *kand*
incantation: *kan*
incarnadine: *ker III, sek IX*
incarnation: *ker III, sek IX*
incendiary: *kand*
incense: *kand*
incentive: *kan*
inception: *kap*
incest: *en*
inch: *oino*
inchmeal: *me IV*
inchoate: *kagh*
incident: *kad I*
incidental: *kad I*
incinerator: *ken I*
incipient: *kap*
incise: *sek II*
incision: *sek II*
incite: *kei I*
inclement: *klei*
inclination: *klei*
inclined: *klei*
inclinometer: *klei*
include: *kleu III*
incomparable: *en*
incomplete: *en*
inconsequential: *seku I*
inconsistent: *dheigh N 8*
incorporate: *krep*
increase: *ker VI*
incredible: *dheigh N 3, kred I*
incredulous: *kred I*
increment: *ker VI*
incriminate: *ker IV*
incriminating: *sek VI*
incroyable: *kred I*
incubate: *keu II*
incubator: *cub*
incubus: *cub, gue, keu II*
incumbency: *cub*
incumbent: *cub, gue, keu II*
incunabula: *kei II*
incur: *kers I*
incurable: *cura*
indecision: *sek II*
indemnify: *da II*
indent: *den*
indenture: *den*
independent: *spend II*
index: *deik*
indication: *deik*
indict: *deik*
indigence: *eg II*
indigene: *gn*
indigenous: *gn*
indigent: *eg II*
indigestion: *ges*
indignant: *dek, gn*
indigo: *el 49*
indissoluble: *leu I*
indistinguishable: *steig*
indite: *deik*
indium: *el 49*
individual: *ueidh*
indivisible: *ueidh*
indoctrinate: *dek*
indolent: *del II*
indomitable: *dom*
induce: *deuk*
induct: *deuk*
induction: *en*
indurate: *deru*
industrious: *ster I*
industry: *ster I*
inebriety: *ebri*
ineffable: *bha I*
ineluctable: *leug*
inept: *ap*
inert: *ar I*
inertia: *ar I*
inestimable: *aios*
inevitable: *bha II, eu, uegh*
inexpiable: *pius*
inexpugnable: *peug*
inextricable: *tereq*
infallible: *phol*
infamous: *bha I*
infangthief: *pag*
infant: *bha I*
infantry: *bha I, dheigh N 36*
infarct: *bhareku*
infect: *dhe I*
infelicity: *dhe II, dhel I*
infer: *bher I*
inferior: *endher, ndher*
infernal: *endher, ndher*

inferno: *endher, ndher*
infest: *dhers*
infeudation: *pek II*
infidel: *bheidh, ne*
infinite: *fin, ne*
infinitesimal: *fin*
infirm: *dhar*
infirmary: *dhar*
in flagrante delicto: bhel I, leiku
inflame: *bhel I*
inflammable: *bhel I*
inflation: *beu*
inflection: *plek II*
inflexible: *plek II*
inflict: *bhlag*
influence: *beu*
influenza: *beu*
inform: *dheigh N 14, merbh*
information: *merbh*
informer: *rad I*
infraction: *bhreg*
infra dig: *en, endher*
infralapsarian: *leb, ndher*
infrangible: *bhreg*
infrared: *en, ndher*
infraspinatus: *en*
infratemporal: *ndher*
infringe: *bhreg*
ingenious: *gn*
ingenuity: *gn*
ingenuous: *gn*
ingest: *ger VI, ges*
ingrate: *gar*
ingratiate: *gar*
ingratitude: *gar*
ingredient: *ghredh*
inguen: *engu*
inguinal: *engu*
inguinocrual: *engu*
inguinoscrotal: *engu*
inhabitant: *ghebh*
inhale: *ane*
inhere: *ghais*
inherent: *ghais*
inherit: *ghe*
inhibition: *ghebh*
inhumanity: *ne*
inhume: *ghdhem*
inimical: *amma*
Iniomi: *oms*
iniquity: *en*
initial: *ei I*
initiation: *ei I, en*
initiative: *ei I*
injection: *ie*
injunction: *ieug*
injury: *ieuos*
injustice: *ieuos*
ink: *kau I*
inkling: *sap*
inlaut: *kleu I*
inlet: *leid I*
inn: *en*
innate: *gn*
inner: *en*
innocent: *aiu, nek*
innumerable: *ne, nem*
inoculate: *oku*
inordinate: *ar I*
inosite: *uei*
inositol: *uei*
inquest: *kuere*
inquietude: *kuei III*
inquire: *kuere*
inquisition: *kuere*
inroad: *reidh*
insanity: *sano*
inscribe: *ker III*
inscription: *sek VI*
insect: *en, sek I*
insectivore: *bhag*
insectivorous: *bhag*
insensate: *sent*
insensitive: *sent*
insert: *se I, ser I*
insessorial: *sed I*
inside: *en*
insidious: *sed I*
insignia: *seku I*
insipid: *sap*
insist: *sta*
insistence: *dheigh N 8*
insolate: *sauel*
insolent: *al I*
insomnia: *suep I*
inspan: *sphei I*
inspect: *spek*
inspection: *en*
inspiration: *speis*
install: *sta*
installation: *sta*
installment: *sta*
instant: *sta*
instantaneous: *sta*

instauration: *sta*
instead: *sta*
instil(l): *stai, stei*
instinct: *steig*
institute: *sta*
institution: *sta*
instruct: *ster I*
instrument: *ster I*
insubordinate: *ne*
insular: *aku, akua*
insulation: *akua*
insulin: *akua*
insulse: *sal I*
insulsity: *sal I*
insult: *al I, sel IV*
insuperable: *upo II*
insupportable: *dheigh N 3*
insure: *cura*
insurgent: *reg I, upo I*
insurrection: *reg I, upo I*
intact: *tag I*
intangible: *tag I*
integer: *tag I*
integrate: *tag I*
integrity: *tag I*
intellect: *leg I*
intellectual: *gn, leg I*
intelligent: *leg I*
intense: *ten*
intensive: *ten*
intention: *ten*
intercalary: *kel II*
intercede: *sed II*
intercept: *kap*
interchange: *en*
intercollegiate: *en*
intercourse: *kers I*
intercrural: *en*
interdiction: *deik*
interfere: *bher II*
interim: *en*
interior: *en*
interject: *ie*
interline: *lino*
interlinear: *dheigh N 9*
interloper: *en, klou*
interlude: *leid II*
intermediary: *medhi*
intermediate: *medhi*
interment: *ters*
intermezzo: *medhi*
interminable: *ter III*
intermission: *smeit*
intermittent: *smeit*
intermix: *meik*
internal: *en*
internecine: *aiu, nek*
internist: *en*
internuncio: *neu I*
interpellation: *pel IV*
interpolate: *pele*
interpreter: *per III*
interregnum: *reg I*
interrupt: *en, reup*
interscription: *ker III*
intersect: *sek I*
intersection: *sek I*
interspersed: *sphereg*
interstice: *sta*
intervene: *en, gua*
interview: *ueid*
intervolve: *uelu*
intestate: *tre*
intestine: *en*
intimate: *dheigh N 10, en*
intinction: *teng*
intitule: *tel*
into: *en*
intolerant: *tol*
intone: *ten*
intoxication: *tekhus*
intractable: *tragh*
intragallactic: *en*
intramural: *en, mei III*
intransigent: *ag*
intravenous: *en*
intrepidity: *ter I*
intricate: *en, tereq*
intrigue: *tereq*
intrinsic: *seku I*
introduce: *deuk, en*
introduction: *deuk*
introit: *ei I*
intromission: *en, smeit*
introrse: *uer II 5*
introspection: *en, spek*
introvert: *en, re, uer II 5*
intrude: *treud*
intrusion: *treud*
intubate: *teue 9*
intumesce: *teue 7*
intumescent: *teue 7*
intussusception: *kap*
Inula: *uelu*

inulin: *uelu*
inure: *op I*
invade: *uadh*
invagination: *uag II*
invalid: *ual*
invalidate: *ual*
invaluable: *ual*
invasion: *uadh*
invective: *uegh*
inveigh: *uegh*
inveigle: *oku*
invent: *gua*
invention: *en*
inverse: *uer II 5*
invert: *uer II 5*
invertebrate: *uer II 5*
invest: *ues II*
investigate: *en*
investiture: *ues II*
investment: *ues II*
inveterate: *uet*
invidious: *ueid*
invincible: *dheigh N 3*
inviolate: *uiro*
invisible: *en, ueid*
invocate: *ueks*
involucre: *uelu*
involuntary: *uel II*
involute: *uelu*
involve: *uelu*
involvement: *uelu*
invulnerable: *uel III*
inward: *uer II 5*
Io: *morui*
iodide: *uio*
iodine: *el 53, uio*
iodism: *uio*
iodoform: *uio, morui*
iolite: *uio*
ion: *ei I*
ipseity: *i*
ipso facto: *i*
irascible: *dheigh N 3, eis*
irate: *eis*
ire: *eis*
Ireland: *eis*
irenarch: *or*
Irene: *or*
irenic: *or*
Iridaceae: *uei*
iridescent: *uei*
iridium: *el 77, uei*
iridoline: *uei*
iridosmine: *uei*
iris: *uei*
Irish: *eis*
iritis: *uei*
irksome: *uerg*
iron: *aios, eis, el 26*
irony: *suer II, uer VI*
irradiate: *rad II*
irremeable: *mei II*
irreparable: *ne*
irrepressible: *en*
irreproachable: *ne*
irresistible: *en*
irrespective: *spek*
irresponsible: *spend I*
irrevocable: *ueks*
irrigation: *reg III*
irruption: *reup*
is: *es*
ischemia: *segh*
ischium: *segh*
ischuria: *uer VII*
ishwara: *eik*
Isidore: *do*
isinglass: *beu*
Islam: *dekm, eis*
island: *akua*
isle: *akua*
islet: *akua, legh*
iso-: *iso*
isobar: *guer*
isochime: *ghei*
isochromatic: *iso*
isochronous: *iso*
isoclinic: *klei*
isohyet: *seu I*
isolate: *akua*
Isolde: *ieg*
Isoloma: *uelu*
isomer: *smer*
isomeric: *iso*
isometric: *me IV*
isomorph: *merbh*
isopolity: *pele*
isosceles: *iso, skel*
isotherm: *iso*
isotope: *el, iso*
issue: *ei I*
isthmus: *ei I*
itaconic: *gerbh*
Italianate: *onomen*

Italian vinegar: *sal I*
Italy: *ker I*
item: *i*
iterate: *ei I*
ithyphallic: *beu*
itinerant: *ei I*
itinerary: *ei I*
Iva: *oino*
iwis: *kom, ueid*
ixora: *eik*

J

jack: *ker I*
jackadandy: *haifst*
jackanapes: *haifst*
jaconet: *gua*
jactation: *ie*
jactitation: *ie*
jaeger: *iag II*
Jagannath: *gua*
jagat: *gua*
Jagendorf: *iag II*
jaggery: *ker I, sakkara*
jagheedar: *bhar*
jail: *kagh, keu II*
jamb: *kam*
jangle: *jing*
janitor: *ei I*
January: *ei I, me IV*
Janus: *dei, ei I*
jape: *yap*
japery: *yap*
jardiniere: *gher IV*
jargon: *garg, gel I*
jasione: *eis*
Jason: *eis*
jatrophe: *eis*
jaundice: *dheigh N 18*
jaunty: *gn*
jealous: *ia*
jealousy: *ia*
jecoral: *ieku-rt*
jejune: *ieiun, past*
jejunum: *ieiun, kel IV*
Jello: *gel I*
jelly: *gel I*
jemador: *dhar*
jeopardy: *iek*
Jerome: *onomen*
Jersey: *akua*
Jerusalem: *dekm, tis*
jess: *ie*
jest: *ger VI*
jet: *ie*
jetsam: *ie, pleu*
jettison: *ie*
jetty: *ie*
jeu: *iek*
jewel: *iek*
jiminy: *morui*
jingle: *jing*
jinx: *iu II*
jiva: *guei*
jobber: *dheigh N 13*
jocose: *dheigh N 2 g, iek*
jocular: *iek*
jodhpurs: *pele*
jog: *jing*
joggle: *jing*
John: *leg II*
John Bull: *leg II*
Johnson: *onomen*
join: *ieug*
joinery: *ieug*
joint: *ieug*
joist: *ie*
joke: *iek*
jokelet: *iek, legh*
jokull: *ieg*
Jones: *onomen*
jongleur: *iek*
jordan: *gher IV*
joss: *dei*
jostle: *ieug*
journal: *dei*
journey: *dei*
joust: *ieug*
Jove: *dei*
jovial: *dei, onomen*
jowl: *geph*
joy: *ga, jing*
joyous: *ga, jing*
jubilant: *iu II*
Jubilate: *iu II*
jubilation: *iu II, jing*
judas: *onomen*
Judas kiss: *kus*
Judas tree: *onomen*
judge: *deik*
judicate: *deik*
judicatory: *deik, ieuos*

judicial: *deik*
judiciary: *deik, ieuos*
judicious: *deik, dheigh N 2 c, ieuos*
juggernaut: *gua*
juggle: *iek*
juggler: *iek*
jugular: *ieug*
juice: *ieug*
ju-ju: *iek*
Jukes: *caca*
julep: *urod*
Jules: *dei*
Julian: *dei, per I*
julienne: *dei*
Julius: *dei, sek II*
July: *aug, me IV, sek II*
junction: *ieug*
juncture: *ieug*
June: *ieu, me IV*
Jungfrau: *per VI c*
junker: *ieu*
Juno: *dei, deiu, ieu*
Juno Moneta: *men I*
junta: *ieug*
junto: *ieug*
Jupiter: *dei*
juramentado: *ieuos*
jurat: *ieuos*
juridical: *deik, ieuos*
jurisdiction: *deik, ieuos*
jurisprudence: *ieuos*
juror: *ieuos*
jury: *deik, ieuos*
just: *ieuos*
justice: *dheigh N 18, ieuos*
justify: *dhe I, ieuos*
jut: *ie*
juvenal: *ieu*
juvenescent: *ieu*
juvenile: *ieu*
juxtaglomerula: *ieug*
juxtapose: *ieug*
juxtaposition: *ieug*
juxtapositive: *ieug*
jynx: *iu II*

K

kailyard: *kaul*
kainite: *ken III*
kaiser: *sek II*
kakistocracy: *caca*
Kakos: *caca*
kale: *kaul*
kaleidophone: *cal*
kaleidoscope: *cal, spek, ueid*
kali: *el 19*
Kali: *gher I*
Kalighat: *gher I*
Kallikak: *caca*
Kama: *ka*
Kamasutra: *ka, siu*
karma: *kuer*
karyokinesis: *kar*
karyolysis: *kar*
karyostenosis: *kar*
katha: *kuo*
Kavi: *keu I*
keel: *gel I, geu*
k(e)elson: *sus*
keeshond: *ker II, kuon*
ken: *gn*
Kenelm: *kel VI*
Kennedy: *onomen*
kennel: *kann, kuon*
kenning: *gn*
Kent: *kanth*
kephalotomy: *caput*
keralin: *kailo*
keratinize: *ker II*
keratose: *ker II*
kerchief: *caput*
kerite: *keneko*
kermes: *kurmi*
kernel: *ger III*
kerosene: *keneko*
kerplunk: *mlub*
kestrel: *ker IV*
ketch: *kap*
ketchup: *pilo*
kevel: *kleu III*
key: *kagh*
keylessness: *dheigh N 29*
kickshaw: *konk*
kid: *tit*
kidnap: *el 29*
kidney: *auei*
kieselguhr: *ies*
kill: *guel I*
killador: *dhar*
kiln: *peku*
kilo-: *me IV*

kilogram: *gheslo*
kilometer: *gheslo*
kin: *gn*
kinchin: *gn*
kind: *gn*
kindergarten: *gher IV, gn*
kindle: *gn*
kindred: *ar I, gn*
kine: *guou*
kinematics: *kei I*
kinematograph: *kei I*
kinesthesia: *kei I*
king: *gn, reg I*
kingdom: *dhe I*
kingly: *leg I*
Kingsway: *reg I*
kinship: *dheigh N 33*
kirk: *keu II*
kirmess: *keu II*
kirtle: *ker III, sek IX*
kishke: *skeu*
kiss: *kus, or*
kissing comfits: *poi*
kissing cousin: *kuetuer, kus*
kiss-off: *kus*
kist: *kista*
kistophoros: *kista*
kit: *tit*
kitchen: *peku*
kith: *gn*
kitling: *tit*
kitten: *ane, kam, tit*
kittle: *kam, pilo, tit*
kitty: *kam, tit*
klaxon: *kleg*
klepht: *klep*
klephtism: *klep*
kleptic: *klep*
kleptocracy: *klep*
kleptomania: *klep, men I*
kloof: *gleubh*
klystron: *kleu II*
Klytoris: *morui*
knapsack: *gen*
knar: *gen*
knave: *gen*
knead: *gen*
Knecht: *gen*
knecker: *kn*
knee: *genu*
kneel: *genu*
knell: *gen*
knickerbockers: *seni*
knife: *gen*
knight: *gen*
knight-errantry: *dheigh N 36*
knighthood: *kait*
Knights Templars: *temp 2*
knit: *gen*
knob: *gen*
knock: *gen, konk*
knoll: *gen*
knot: *gen*
knout: *gen*
know: *gn*
knowledge: *gn*
knuckle: *gen*
knurl: *gen*
kobold: *gen*
koel: *kokila*
kohlrabi: *rap*
koine: *kom*
kolach: *ker I*
kolo: *ker I*
koniscope: *dheigh N 32*
kopeck: *sek IV*
Koran: *kel II*
Krishna: *au I, kers II*
Kriss Kringle: *gn*
krummhorn: *ker II*
krypton: *el 36, krup*
kshatriya: *ksei, ueik I*
kudos: *keu I*
kunkur: *kar*
Kurd: *pend*
Kursaal: cura
kymatology: *keu II*
kyphosis: *keu II*
Kyrie eleison: *keu II*

L

laager: *legh*
labarum: *leb*
labefaction: *dhe I, leb*
label: *leb*
labellum: *leb*
labial: *leb*
labiate: *leb*
labile: *leb*
labiodental: *leb*
labium: *leb*

labor: *leb*
laboratory: *leb*
labret: *leb*
lac: *reg II*
Laccifernae: *reg II*
lacerate: *lek II*
Lacerta: *lek I*
lacertian: *lek I*
Lacertilia: *lek I*
laches: *leg II*
Lachrymae Christi: *dakru*
lachrymal: *dakru*
lachrymator: *dakru*
lachrymogenic: *dakru*
lacinia: *lek II*
laciniate: *lek II*
lacinula: *lek II*
lack: *leg I, leg II*
lackadaisical: *leg II*
Lackland: *leg II*
Lack-Latin: *leg II*
lacmus: *leg II*
lacquer: *reg II*
lacrosse: *ger I*
lactary: *glact*
lactate: *glact*
lactation: *glact*
lacteal: *glact*
lactescent: *glact*
lactic: *glact*
lactiferous: *glact*
lactometer: *glact*
lacuna: *laku*
lacunose: *laku*
lacustrine: *laku*
Lac Virginis: per VI c
ladder: *klei*
laden: *kla*
ladle: *kla*
lady: *dheigh, gn*
Lady Bountiful: *deu*
ladyfinger: *dheigh*
lady-trifles: *dheigh*
Laertes: *laos*
l(a)evorotary: *laino*
lagan: *ie, legh*
lager: *legh*
lagomorph: *leg II*
Lagomorpha: *ous*
lagoon: *laku*
lagophthalmus: *leg II, oku, ous*
lagopous: *leg II*
Lagopus: *ous*
Lagurus: *ous*
laic: *laos*
lair: *legh, lei I*
laity: *laos*
lake: *laku*
laksha: *reg II*
Lakshmi: *reg II*
Lalage: *lal*
la la la: *lal*
lallation: *lal*
lam: *lem*
lamb: *ane*
lambaste: *bhaut*
lambent: *lab*
Lambert: *lendh II*
lame: *lem*
lamella: *ster I*
lament: *lal*
lamentation: *lal*
lamina: *ster I*
lamination: *ster I*
laminitis: *ster I*
lammelicorn: *ker II*
lammergeier: *ghi*
lamp: *lap*
lampadephore: *lap*
lampatedromy: *lap*
lampoon: *lab*
lamprophony: *lap*
lamprotype: *lap*
Lampsilis: *lap*
Lampyrides: *lap*
lampyrine: *lap*
lanate: *uel III*
Lancaster: *kastr*
Lancelot: *lendh II*
lancination: *lek II*
land: *lendh II*
landgrave: *lendh II*
landloper: *klou, lendh II*
landmark: *lendh II*
landscape: *lendh II, sek IV*
Landwehr: *suer I*
langlauf: *klou*
language: *dinghu*
languid: *leg II*
languish: *leg II*
languor: *leg II*
laniferous: *uel III*
lanigerous: *uel III*
lank: *kleng*

lanolin: *uel III*
lanose: *uel III*
lantern: *lap*
lanternfish: *lap*
lantern jaws: *lap*
lanternman: *lap*
lantern shell: *lap*
lanthana: *ladh*
lanthanides: *el 57*
lanthanum: *el 57, ladh*
lanthorn: *lap*
lanuginous: *uel III*
lanugo: *uel III*
lanyard: *ned*
Laocoön: *keu I, laos*
lap: *geu, lab, leb*
laparectomy: *lep I*
laparotomy: *lep I*
lapel: *leb*
lapidable: *lapid*
lapidary: *lapid, lep I*
lapidate: *lapid*
lapidify: *lapid*
lapis lazuli: *lapid*
lapoop: *lal*
lappet: *leb*
lapse: *leb*
lapsus: *kolem, leb*
lapwing: *klou, uag I*
larboard: *kla*
larceny: *ken II, lei II*
Lares: *las*
lariat: *ap*
Lariidae: *las*
larva: *las*
lascivious: *las, sleub*
lash: *leg II*
laspring: *laks*
lassitude: *leid I*
last: *kla, leid I, leis*
latch: *slagu*
late: *leid I*
latent: *el 57, ladh*
lateral: *ster I*
latest: *leid I*
latex: *lat*
lathe: *kla*
lather: *lou*
laticiferous: *lat*
laticlave: *kleu III*
Latin: *ker I*
latitude: *ster I*
latitudinarian: *ster I*
latria: *lei II*
latrine: *lei II, lou, per VI g*
-latry: *lei II*
latter: *leid I*
laud: *leu III*
laudable: *leu III*
laudatory: *leu III*
laugh: *kleg*
laughing jackass: *kleg*
laughter: *kleg*
launder: *lou*
launderer: *lou*
laundry: *lou*
laurustine: *la*
lava: *leb*
lavabo: *lou*
lavaliere: *kleu I*
lavander: *lou*
lavatory: *lou*
lave: *lou*
laveer: *lep II*
lavender: *lou*
lavish: *dheigh N 20, lou*
law: *leg I, legh*
lawful: *leg I*
lawless: *legh*
lawn: *lendh II, lino*
lawrencium: *el 103*
lax: *laks, leg II*
laxative: *leg II*
lay: *laos, legh, phol*
layer: *legh*
lay figure: *elei*
lb.: *leudh*
lea: *lendh II, leuk*
leach: *leg I, leg II*
lead: *el 82, kla, leith, mlub, plumb*
leaf: *leup*
leafmeal: *me IV*
league: *leig II*
leak: *leg I, leg II*
leakage: *dheigh N 4*
leal: *leg I*
lean: *klei*
Leander: *leo, nert*
leap: *klou*
learn: *leis*
leash: *leg II*
leasing: *leu I*
leat: *leid I*
leather: *letro*

leave: *leip, leubh*
leaven: *leguh*
leavings: *leip*
Lebensraum: *reuos*
lecher: *leigh*
lectern: *leg I*
lectual: *gn*
lecture: *leg I*
Leda: *morui*
lee: *kel I*
leech: *leg I*
leek: *leug*
leer: *kleu I*
lees: *legh*
Left: *sa*
left: *leip, sa*
leftist: *sa*
leg: *lek I*
legacy: *leg I*
legal: *leg I*
legate: *leg I*
legation: *leg I*
legend: *leg I*
legerdemain: *leguh, man*
legible: *leg I*
legion: *leg I*
legislate: *tol*
legislation: *tol*
legislature: *leg I*
legit: *kn*
legitimate: *dheigh N 10, leg I*
Leicester: *kastr*
leiodere: *lei I*
leiophyllus: *lei I*
leiotrichi: *lei I*
leiotrichous: *lei I, uel III*
leitmotif: *kla, leith*
L.E.M.: *leuk*
leman: *leubh*
lemma: *labh, slagu*
lend: *leiku*
length: *del III*
lenient: *leid I*
lenitive: *leid I*
lenity: *leid I*
leno: *lino*
Lent: *dei, del III, sek VI*
lentamente: *men I*
lento: *lento*
Leo: *guei, leo*
Leonard: *kar, leo*
Leonides: *leo*
leonine: *leo*
Leonodont: *leo*
Leonora: *leo*
Leonore: *leo*
Leonurus: *leo*
leopard: *leo*
leopardite: *leo*
Leopold: *leo*
leper: *lapid, lep I*
Lepes: *lep I*
Lepidium: *lep I*
lepidoptera: *lep I*
lepidopterous: *pet I*
leprechaun: *krep, leguh*
leptodactyl: *do, lep I*
lepton: *lep I*
leptothrix: *lep I*
lesbian: *es*
lesion: *laed*
-less: *leu I*
less: *leu I*
lesson: *leg I*
let: *leid I*
lethal: *ladh, ol I*
lethargy: *el 57, ladh*
Lethe: *el 57, kau II, ladh*
Lett: *leudh*
letter: *deph*
lettuce: *glact*
leu: *leo*
leucocyte: *leuk, skeu*
leucorrh(o)ea: *leuk*
leucoscope: *leuk*
leucospermous: *leuk*
leukemia: *leuk*
lev: *leo*
levalose: *laino*
Levana: *leguh*
Levant: *leugh*
levant: *leguh*
level: *lithra*
lever: *leguh*
levigate: *ag, leguh*
levin: *leuk*
levitate: *leguh*
levity: *leguh*
levy: *leguh*
lewd: *laos*
lewdness: *sleub*
Lewis: *kleu I*
lexical: *dheigh N 5*
lexicon: *leg I*

lexigraphy: *leg I*
lex talionis: *leg I, tol*
leye: *leuk*
liable: *leig II*
liaison: *leig II*
libation: *leib*
libeccio: *leib*
libel: *leup*
liberal: *leudh*
libertarian: *leudh*
libertine: *leudh*
liberty: *leudh*
libidinous: *leubh*
libido: *leubh*
libra: *leudh*
Libra: *guei*
library: *leup*
librate: *lithra*
libretto: *leup*
lich: *leig I*
lichen: *leigh*
lich gate: *leig I*
lick: *leigh*
lickerish: *leigh*
licorice: *dlku, uerad*
lictor: *leig II*
lid: *klei*
lie: *legh, leugh, phol*
Liebfraumilch: per VI c
lied: *leu III*
liederkranz: *leu III*
lief: *leubh*
liege: *leid I, leudh*
lien: *leig II*
lientery: *lei I*
lieutenant: *sta, ten*
life: *leip I*
Life Force: *per VI f*
lift: *leup*
ligament: *leig II*
ligature: *leig II*
light: *leguh, leuk, onomen*
lighten: *leguh*
lightening: *leuk*
lighter: *leguh*
light-fingered: *leguh*
lightfoot: *leguh*
light-headed: *leguh*
lightly: *leguh*
lightning: *leuk*
light-o'-love: *leguh*
light-skirts: *leguh*
lightsome: *leguh*
light-year: *al II, me IV*
lignaloes: *leg I*
ligneous: *leg I*
lignify: *leg I*
lignite: *leg I*
lignivorous: *bhag II, leg I*
lignum vitae: *leg I*
ligule: *leigh*
like: *leig I*
likeable: *leig I*
likelihood: *kait*
likely: *leig I*
likeness: *leig I*
likewise: *leig I, ueid*
lilac: *nei*
limaceous: *lei I*
limacine: *lei I*
Limax: *lei I*
limb: *elei*
limber: *elei*
limbers: *leuk*
limbmeal: *me IV*
lime-fingered: *lei I*
limen: *elei*
limerick: *elei*
Limicolae: *lei I*
limicoline: *lei I*
limit: *elei*
limitation: *elei*
limn: *leuk*
Limnanthaceae: *lei I*
Limnetis: *lei I*
limnobium: *guei*
limnograph: *lei I*
limnology: *lei I*
Limonium: *lei I*
limophilous: *lei I*
Limosella: *lei I*
limp: *leb*
limulus: *elei*
Lina: *dei*
Lincoln: *pleu*
linctus: *leigh*
Linda: *lento*
linden: *lento*
line: *lino*
lineage: *lino*
lineaments: *lino*
linear: *lino*
linen: *lino*
lingam: *gn*

linger: *del III*
lingerie: *lino*
lingonberry: *bhel I*
lingot: *gheu*
lingua franca: *dinghu*
lingual: *leigh*
linguist: *dinghu*
liniment: *lei I*
linin: *lino*
link: *kleng, leuk*
linn: *pleu*
linnet: *lino*
linoleic: *lino*
linoleum: *lino*
linotype: *lino*
linseed: *lino*
linsey-woolsey: *uel III*
linstock: *steu*
lint: *lino*
lintel: *elei*
Linum: *lino*
lion: *leo*
lioncel: *leo*
Lionel: *leo*
lionize: *leo*
lip: *leb*
Liparis: *leip I*
liparocele: *leip I*
liparoid: *leip I*
lipase: *leip I*
lipic: *leip I*
lipid: *leip I*
lipocardiac: *leip I*
lipogenesis: *leip I*
lipogram: *leip II*
lipogrammatic: *leip II*
lipography: *dheigh N 16, leip II*
lipoid: *leip I*
lipolysis: *leip I*
lipoma: *leip I*
lipomatosis: *leip I*
lipomorph: *leip II*
lipoprotein: *leip I*
lipos: *leip I*
lipostomous: *leip II*
lipothymia: *leip II*
lipotype: *leip II*
lipoxenous: *leip II*
lipoxeny: *leip II*
liquate: *leiku*
liquefacient: *leiku*
liquefy: *leiku*
liquescent: *leiku*
liquid: *leiku*
liquidambar: *leiku*
liquidate: *leiku*
liquor: *leiku*
lira: *lithra*
lirella: *leis*
list: *kleu I, las, leizd*
listen: *kleu I*
liter: *lithra*
literal: *deph*
literary: *deph*
literature: *deph*
literocracy: *deph*
lithe: *lento*
lithium: *el 3*
lithobium: *guei*
lithography: *reg II, el 3*
lithophagous: *bhag II*
lithosphere: *reg II*
lithotrity: *ter II*
Lithuania: *leib*
litigate: *ag*
litmus: *uel I*
litotes: *lei I*
litra: *lithra*
litter: *legh*
littérateur: *deph*
little: *leud*
littoral: *leib*
liturgy: *uerg*
live: *leip I*
livelihood: *kla, leith*
livelong: *leubh*
lively: *leig I, leip I*
liver: *leip I*
liverwurst: *uer II 5*
livery: *leudh*
livid: *sli*
Livingston, Dr.: *morui*
livre: *lithra*
lixiviate: *leiku*
lizard: *lek I*
llano: *pela*
Lloyd: *pel VII*
load: *kla, leith*
loam: *lei I*
loan: *leiku*
loath: *leit*
loathe: *leit*
loathsome: *leit*
lobby: *leup*

lobo: *ulkuo*
lobster: *lek I*
local: *leu III, sta, ster I*
locality: *leu III*
location: *leu III, sta, ster I*
loch: *laku*
lochia: *legh*
lock: *leug*
locket: *leug*
locomobile: *meu II*
locomotion: *meu II*
locomotive: *leu III, ster I*
locumtenens: *leu III, sta, ten*
locus: *leu III, ster I*
locus classicus: ster I
locust: *lek I*
locution: *tolku*
lode: *kla, leith*
lodestar: *kla, leith*
lodestone: *kla, leith*
lodge: *leup*
lodgment: *leup*
loess: *leu I*
loft: *leup*
loganberry: *bhel I*
logarithm: *ar I, leg I*
loge: *leup*
loggia: *leup*
logic: *leg I*
logion: *leg I*
logistics: *leg I, leup*
logo: *leg I, steu*
logo-: *leg I*
logodaedaly: *leg I*
logogram: *leg I*
logogriph: *leg I*
logomachy: *leg I, magh*
logomania: *leg I*
logophobia: *leg I*
Logos: *leg I*
logos: *leg I*
logotype: *leg I, steu*
logrolling: *leg I*
logy: *sleu*
-logy: *leg I*
loin: *lemdh I*
loka: *leuk*
lokaloka: *leuk*
lokapala: *leuk, pa*
Loki: *leuk*
loll: *lal*
lollapalooza: *lal*
Lollard: *lal*
lollipop: *lal*
lollop: *lal*
lolly: *lal*
lombard: *bhar, del III*
Lombards: *lem*
lone: *oino, per VI g*
lonely: *oino, per VI g*
lonesome: *oino, per VI g*
long: *del III*
longevity: *aiu, del III*
Longfellow: *onomen*
longicorn: *kel II*
longitude: *del III*
loo: *leuk*
loof: *lep II*
loom: *lem*
loose: *leu I, lou*
loot: *lau, leup*
lope: *klou*
loquacious: *tolku*
loquitur: *tolku*
lord: *gn*
lore: *uelu*
lorica: *uelu*
loricate: *uelu*
lorimer: *uelu*
lorn: *leu I*
lose: *leu I, lou, onomen*
losel: *leu I*
loss: *leu I, lou*
lost: *leu I*
lot: *kleu III*
loth: *leit*
Lothario: *kleu I*
lotion: *lou*
lottery: *kleu III*
lotto: *kleu III*
loud: *kleu I*
Louis: *kleu I*
loup: *klou*
loup-garou: uiro, ulkuo
louse: *lus*
lout: *leud*
louver: *suer I*
Louvre: *haifst, ulkuo*
louvre: *ulkuo*
lovable: *dheigh N 3, leubh*
love: *leis, leubh*
lovely: *leubh*
low: *kel II, legh, leuk*
lox: *laks*

loyal: *leg I, leg II*
lozenge: *leu III*
LSD: *gn, leu I*
lubricant: *sleubh*
lubricate: *sleubh*
lubricity: *sleubh*
lucent: *leuk*
lucerne: *leuk*
Lucia: *leuk*
Lucian: *leuk*
lucid: *leuk*
Lucifer: *leuk*
luciferase: *leuk*
luciferin: *leuk*
lucifugous: *leuk*
Lucille: *leuk*
Lucina: *leuk*
lucipetous: *leuk*
Lucius: *leuk*
luck: *leug*
lucrative: *lau*
lucre: *lau*
lucubration: *leuk*
lucule: *leuk*
luculent: *leuk*
Lucy: *leuk*
ludicrous: *leid II*
ludo: *leid II*
Ludovic: *kleu I*
Ludwig: *kleu I*
lues: *leu I*
luff: *lep II*
lugubrious: *leug*
lukewarm: *kel I*
lull: *lal*
lullaby: *lal*
lumber: *bhar, del III, lem*
lumberjack: *bhar*
lumber pie: *bhar*
lumen: *leuk*
luminary: *leuk*
luminosity: *dheigh N 2 d*
luminous: *leuk*
lump: *leb*
lumpfish: *leb*
lumpish: *dheigh N 20*
luna: *leuk*
lunar: *leuk*
lunate: *leuk*
lunatic: *leuk*
lunation: *leuk*
lunch: *leb*
luncheon: *neun*
lunette: *leuk*
lungs: *leguh*
Lupercal: *ulkuo*
Lupercalia: *ulkuo*
Lupercus: *ulkuo*
lupine: *uel III, ulkuo*
lupulus: *ulkuo*
lupus: *ulkuo*
luscious: *leg II*
lush: *leg II*
Lushington: *leg II*
lust: *las*
luster: *leuk*
lustration: *leuk*
lustrine: *leuk*
lustrum: *leuk*
lustwort: *uerad*
lute: *leu II*
lutetia: *leu II*
Lutetia: *el 71*
lutetium: *el 71, leu II*
Luther: *kleu I*
luxate: *leug*
luxe: *leug*
luxuriant: *leug, leuk*
luxuriate: *leug*
luxury: *leug, leuk*
Luzula: *leuk*
-ly: *leig I*
lycanthrope: *nert, ulkuo*
lycanthropy: *uel III*
lycée: *ulkuo*
lyceum: *uel III, ulkuo*
lychnic: *leuk*
lychnidiate: *leuk*
Lychnis: *leuk*
Lychnoscope: *leuk*
Lycopersion: *ulkuo*
Lycopodium: *ped, ulkuo*
Lycopsis: *ulkuo*
Lycopus: *ulkuo*
lye: *lou*
Lygodium: *leug*
lying: *leugh*
lyncean: *leuk*
lynx: *leuk*
lyric(al): *dheigh N 17*
lysin: *leu I*
lysis: *leu I*
lytta: *leuk*

M

ma: *tara*
maar: *mori*
macadamized: *peue*
macaroni: *haifst, men III*
macaronic: *haifst*
macaroon: *haifst*
mace: *mat*
macédoine: *mak*
Macedonian: *mak*
macerate: *mag*
machete: *mat*
Machiavellian: *onomen*
machicolate: *kagh*
machination: *magh*
machine: *magh*
machinist: *magh*
machree: *kerd, me I*
-machy: *magh*
mackerel: *mag*
Mackintosh: *onomen*
mackle: *smeit*
macrobiotic: *mak*
macrocephalic: *caput, mak*
macrocosm: *kens, mak*
macroglobulin: *mak*
macrology: *mak*
macromolecule: *mak*
macron: *mak*
Macropaedia: *mak*
macrostylous: *medhi*
macula: *smeit*
maculation: *smeit*
mad: *mei II*
madam: *dem*
madame: *me I*
madder: *modhro*
Madeira: *ma II*
mademoiselle: *dem, me I*
Madge: *margar*
madonna: *dem, me I*
madroña: *ma I*
maduro: *ma I*
maelstrom: *mel V, sreu*
maenad: *men I*
Mag: *lep I, margar, math*
mage: *magh*
maggot: *lep I, math*
maggoty: *math*
Magi: *magh*
magi: *magh*
magic: *magh*
magic(al): *dheigh N 17*
magisterial: *me III*
magistral: *me III*
magistrate: *me III*
magma: *mag*
Magna Carta: *me III*
magna cum laude: *me III*
magnanimous: *ane, me III*
magnate: *dheigh N 10, me III*
magnesia: *el 12*
magnesium: *el 12, el 38, me III*
magnet: *el 12, me III*
magnificent: *dhe I, me III*
magnify: *me III*
magniloquent: *me III, tolku*
magnitude: *me III*
magnum: *me III*
magnum bonum: *deu*
magpie: *elaia, lep I, margar, speik*
Mahabharata: me III
maharajah: *me III, reg I*
maharanee: *me III, reg I*
mahatma: *etman, me III, ne*
Mahayana: *ei I, me III*
mahout: *me III*
mahseer: *ker II, me III*
Maia: *amma, me III*
Maianthemum: *me III*
maid: *maghos*
maiden: *maghos*
maidenhead: *maghos*
maidenhood: *maghos*
maieutic: *amma, ma II*
maim: *mai I, mei II*
main: *magh*
mainprize: *man*
maintain: *man, ten*
majesty: *me III*
major: *me III*
major-domo: *dem*
majority: *me III*
majuscule: *me III, mei I*
malabathrum: *teme*
malachite: *dheigh N 22*
malaciazooid: *mel I*
malacoderm: *der, mel I*
malacology: *mel I*
malacon: *mel I*
Malacostraia: *mel I*
maladjusted: *deu, melo*

maladroit: *melo*
malady: *deu, mak, melo*
mala fides: bheidh, melo
malaise: *deu, melo*
malapert: *melo, suer I, uer V*
Malaprop, Mrs.: *melo, per VI g*
malapropism: *melo*
malar: *menth*
malaria: *melo*
malax: *mel I*
Malaxis: *mel I*
Malcolm: *mai I*
malcreated: *melo*
mal de flanc: melo
mal de mer: melo
male: *mas*
malediction: *deik, deu, melo*
malefactor: *deu, dhe I, melo*
malefic: *deu, dhe I, melo*
maleficence: *deu, dhe I*
maleficiate: *deu*
malentendu: *deu*
malevolent: *deu, melo, uel II*
malfeasance: *deu, dhe I, melo*
malhygiene: *melo*
malic: *abel, melit*
malice: *melo*
malicious: *deu*
malign: *deu, gn*
malignant: *gn, melo*
malinger: *deu, mak*
malism: *deu, melo*
malison: *deu, melo*
mall: *mat*
malleolus: *mat*
mallet: *mat*
malleus: *mat*
Malleus Maleficorum: mat
malm: *mel V*
malmsey: *men III*
malodorous: *deu, od*
malpractice: *deu, melo*
malt: *mel V, smeld*
maltha: *mel I*
maltreat: *deu, melo*
Malus: *mazdos, melit*
malversation: *uer II 5*
mama: *amma, tara*
mame: *ma II*
mamma: *amma, ma II*
mammal: *amma, ma II*
mammalia: *amma*
mammary: *amma, ma II*
mammilla: *amma*
Mammillaria: *ma II*
mammoth: *ma II*
mammy: *ma II*
mamont: *ma II*
man: *men I*
manacle: *man*
Manacus: *manu*
manage: *man*
manager: *man*
manakin: *manu*
mañana: ma I
manas: *men I*
mancinism: *man*
mancipate: *kap*
-mancy: *men I*
mandamus: *man*
mandarin: *men I*
mandate: *man*
mandatory: *man*
mandible: *menth*
mandibular: *menth*
mandragora: *manu*
mandrake: *manu*
mandriarch: *manu*
mandrill: *manu*
mandrite: *manu*
mandritto: *man*
manducate: *menth*
mane: *men II*
manes: *ma I*
maness: *manu*
maneuver: *man, op I*
manganese: *el 25, me III*
mange: *menth*
mangel-wurzel: *uerad*
manger: *menth*
mangle: *mai I*
manhandle: *man*
mania: *men I*
maniac: *men I*
mania concionabunda: *men I*
Maniai: *dheu I*
manichord: *man*
manicure: *cura, man*
manifest: *dhers, man*
manifesto: *man*
manifold: *menegh, plek II*
manikin: *manu, men I*
maniple: *man, pel V*
manipulate: *dheigh N 10, man, pel V*

mannequin: *manu*
manner: *man*
manometer: *men III*
manor: *men IV*
manse: *men IV*
mansion: *men IV, sue*
mansuetude: *man, sue*
mantic: *men I*
manticore: *mer II*
mantis: *men I*
mantra: *men I*
Manu: *manu*
manual: *man*
manubrium: *man*
manufactory: *man*
manufacture: *dhe I, man*
manumission: *man, smeity*
manure: *man, op I*
manus: *man*
manuscript: *ker III, man, sek VI*
many: *menegh*
map: *map*
mar: *mer II*
maraschino: *oma*
marasmus: *mer II*
Maratha: *me III*
marathon: *niger*
marble: *mer I, mer II*
marc: *mat*
March: *mavors, me IV, prai*
march: *mat, merk*
marchioness: *merk*
Marcia: *mavors*
Marcomanni: *men I*
Marcus: *mavors*
Mardi gras: *dei, prai*
mare: *marko, mori*
maremma: *mori*
Margaret: *elaia, lep I, margar, speik*
margaret: *elaia, lep I, margar*
margaric: *margar, speik*
margarin(e): *elaia, margar, speik*
Margarita: *elais, speik*
margaritiferous: *margar*
marge: *merk*
margent: *merk*
margin: *merk*
margosa: *oma*
Margot: *margar*
margrave: *merk*
Marguerite: *map*
marinade: *mori*
marinated: *mori*
marine: *mori*
mariner: *mori*
mariposa: *pal*
marish: *mori*
marital: *maghos*
maritime: *mori*
Mark: *mavors*
mark: *merk*
market: *merc*
Mark Twain: *duo*
marmalade: *abel, melit*
marmite: *mormor*
marmolite: *mer I*
marmoreal: *mer I, mer II*
marmorean: *dheigh N 7*
marmoset: *men II*
marmot: *men II, mus*
maroon: *keu II*
marosca: *oma*
marque: *merk*
marquee: *merk, sek II*
marquetry: *merk*
marquis: *merk*
marram: *mori*
marriage: *maghos*
marron: *keu II*
marrow: *mozgo*
marry: *maghos*
Mars: *mavors*
marshal: *marko*
marsupial: *pela*
marsupium: *pela*
mart: *merc*
martial: *mavors*
Martian: *mavors*
Martin: *mavors*
martin: *mavors*
martite: *mavors*
martlet: *mavors*
martyr: *smer*
martyrdom: *dhe I*
marvel: *smei I*
masculine: *mas*
mash: *meigh*
masher: *meigh*
mashie: *mat*
maslin: *meik*
masochism: *leg II*
masochistic: *leg II*
mason: *mag*
mass: *mag, smeit*

massacre: *mat*
massé: *mat*
mast: *mad, mazdos*
master: *me III*
mastic: *menth*
masticate: *menth*
mastiff: *man, sue*
mastodon: *den*
mastoid: *es*
masturbate: *man*
matador: *ksei*
match: *mag, meu I*
matchless: *mag*
matchmaker: *mag*
mate: *mad*
matelot: *mad, neud*
mater: *ma II*
material: *amma*
materialism: *ma II*
materialistic: *ma II*
materia medica: *ma II*
maternal: *amma, ma II*
maternity: *amma, ma II, suesor*
math: *me II*
mathematical: *men I*
mathematics: *men I*
mathesis: *men I*
Matilda: *kal, magh*
matinee: *ma I*
matins: *ma I*
matranee: *me III*
matriarch: *ma II*
Matricaria: *ma II*
matricide: *ma II*
matriculate: *amma, ma II*
matrimony: *amma*
matrix: *amma*
matroclinous: *amma, klei*
matron: *amma, ma II*
matross: *mad, neud*
matter: *amma, ma II, men I*
mattock: *mat*
mature: *ma I*
maturity: *ma I*
Matuta: *ma I*
matutinal: *ma I, uesper*
Maud: *magh*
maul: *mat*
maulstick: *mel III, steu*
maund: *mend*
maunder: *mend*
maundy: *man*
Maundy Thursday: *or*
Mauretania: *oma*
Maurus: *oma*
mavourneen: *me I, mormor*
mavrodaphne: *oma*
mawkish: *math*
maxi-: *mei I*
maxilla: *menth*
maxim: *me III*
maximite: *me III*
maxim silencer: *me III*
maximum: *me III*
maxite: *me III*
May: *amma, ma II, me III, me IV*
may: *magh, maghos*
maya: *me III*
mayhap: *kob*
mayhem: *mai I, mei II*
mayor: *me III*
mayweed: *maghos*
Mazda: *ane*
mazer: *sme*
mazocacothesis: *caca, mag*
mazolysis: *mag*
McKinley: *onomen*
me: *me I*
mead: *me II, medhu*
meadow: *me II*
meager: *mak*
meal: *me IV, mel V, smeld*
mealic: *mel V*
mean: *medhi, mei II, meino, men I*
meaning: *meino*
meaningful: *meino*
meaningless: *dheigh N 26, meino*
measles: *sme*
measure: *me IV*
measureless: *me IV*
measurement: *me IV*
meat: *mad*
meatus: *mei I*
mechanic: *magh*
mechanism: *magh*
mechanistic: *magh*
mecocephalic: *mak*
mecodont: *mak*
mecography: *mak*
Mecoptera: *mak*
meddle: *meik*
media: *medhi*
medial: *medhi*
median: *medhi*

mediastinum: *medhi*
mediate: *medhi*
medical: *med*
medication: *med*
medicine: *med*
medieval: *aiu*
mediocre: *ak, medhi*
mediocrity: *medhi*
meditation: *med*
Mediterranean: *medhi*
medium: *medhi*
medley: *meik*
medulla: *smeru*
meek: *meu I*
meerkat: *mori*
meerschaum: *mori, skeu*
meet: *med, mod*
Meg: *margar*
mega-: *me IV*
megacity: *me III*
Megaera: *dheu I*
megalocardia: *kerd, me III*
megalomania: *me III*
megalopolis: *me III, pele*
megalops: *me III*
megaphone: *me III*
megathere: *ghuer*
megavolt: *me III*
mehtar: *me III*
meinie: *men IV*
m(e)iogyrous: *mei I*
meionite: *mei I*
m(e)iophyllous: *mei I*
meiosis: *mei I*
Meistersinger: *senguh*
mekometer: *mak*
Melampyrum: *mel III*
melancholic: *ugu*
melancholy: *gel I, mel III, ugu*
Melanchthon: *pele*
Melanesia: *sna I*
Melanesian: *mel III*
mélange: *meik*
melanin: *mel III*
melanism: *mel III*
Melanochroi: *mel III*
melanoma: *mel III*
melanotic: *mel III*
Melanthium: *mel III*
meldometer: *smeld*
Melianthaceae: *melit*
Melianthus: *melit*
Melica: *mel V*
meliceris: *keneko, melit*
melilot: *melit*
melinite: *abel, melit*
meliorism: *mel II*
Melipona: *melit*
melisma: *mel IV*
Melissa: *melit*
melliferous: *melit*
mellifluent: *melit*
mellifluous: *beu*
mellivorous: *bhag*
mellow: *mel I*
melodeon: *mel IV, ued*
melodion: *ued*
melodious: *mel IV, ued*
melodrama: *mel IV*
melody: *aud, mel IV, ued*
melon: *abel, melit, peku*
Melpomene: *mel IV*
melt: *mel I, smeld*
member: *mems, smer*
membrane: *mems, smer*
memento: *men I, smer*
memento mori: *caput*
memoirs: *smer*
memorabilia: *smer*
memorandum: *smer*
memorial: *smer*
memorize: *dheigh N 25, smer*
memory: *smer*
menace: *men II*
ménage: *man, men IV*
menagerie: *man, men IV*
menarche: *me IV*
Menaspis: *me IV*
mend: *mend*
mendacious: *mend*
mendacity: *em, mend*
mendelevium: *el 101*
Mendelian: *geme*
mendicant: *mend*
mendicity: *mend*
Menelaus: *laos*
menial: *men IV*
meningitis: *mems, smer*
meningocele: *mems*
meninx: *mems, smer*
meniscus: *me IV*
Menobranchus: *men IV*
menology: *me IV*
menopause: *me IV*

Menopoma: *men IV*
menorrhagia: *me IV*
Menospermum: *me IV*
Mensa: *men I*
mensal: *me IV*
menses: *me IV*
menshevik: *mei I*
menstruate: *me IV*
mensurable: *me IV*
mensuration: *me IV*
mental: *men I, men II*
mentality: *men I*
mention: *men I*
mentor: *men I*
menu: *mei I*
meow: *jing*
mercantile: *merc*
mercaptan: *kap*
Mercedes: *merc*
mercenary: *merc*
mercer: *merc*
mercerized: *merc*
merchandise: *merc*
merchant: *merc*
mercurial: *merc*
Mercurialis: *merc*
Mercury: *el 80, merc*
mercury: *el 16, el 80, merc*
mercy: *merc*
mere: *mer I, mori*
merely: *mer I*
meres: *mei III*
meretricious: *smer*
merganser: *ghans, mezg I*
merge: *mezg I*
merger: *mezg I*
Merginae: *mezg I*
Mergus: *mezg I*
mericarp: *ker III*
meridian: *dei, medhi*
meringes: *mems*
merism: *smer*
merismatic: *smer*
meristem: *smer*
merit: *smer*
meritorious: *smer*
Merlin: *mori*
mermaid: *mori*
merobile: *smer*
meroblastic: *smer*
meros: *smer*
merosymmetry: *smer*
merriment: *braghu*
merry: *braghu*
merryandrews: *haifst*
mesaticephalic: *medhi*
mesenchyma: *gheu*
mesh: *mezd II*
mesial: *medhi*
Mesidor: *me II*
mesityl: *medhi*
mesne: *medhi*
meso-: *medhi*
mesoblast: *medhi*
mesocarp: *ker III*
mesocephalic: *medhi*
mesoconch: *medhi*
mesoderm: *der, medhi*
mesogastrium: *medhi*
mesohepaticon: *medhi*
mesolithic: *medhi*
mesology: *medhi*
meson: *medhi*
mesonephron: *engu*
mesoplast: *pela*
Mesopotamia: *medhi, pet I*
mesostylous: *medhi*
mesotarsal: *medhi*
mesothelium: *dhel I*
mesotherm: *medhi*
mesothesis: *medhi*
mesothorax: *dhar*
mesotonic: *medhi*
Mesozoic: *guei*
mess: *smeit*
message: *smeit*
messenger: *keu I*
messeter: *menth*
messuage: *men IV*
mestizo: *meik*
metabasis: *gua*
metabolic: *guel II*
metabolism: *guel II, kat, medhi*
metacarp: *ker III*
metacarpal: *kuerp*
metachemistry: *medhi*
metachronism: *nebh*
metagalactic: *medhi*
metagenesis: *gn*
metamere: *smer*
metamorphic: *merbh*
metamorphosis: *medhi, merbh*
metanoia: *medhi*
metaphor: *bher II, medhi*

metaphysics: *medhi*
metaplasm: *medhi*
metastasis: *medhi*
metathesis: *dhe I, medhi*
mete: *med*
metempsychosis: *bhes*
meteor: *uer I*
meteorite: *uer I*
meteorology: *leg I*
metheglin: *pleu, med, medhu*
methinks: *tong*
method: *sed II*
methodism: *dheigh N 21*
methyl: *medhu*
methylene: *hule, medhu*
métier: *mei I*
Metis: *morui*
métis: *meik*
metonymy: *onomen*
metope: *oku*
metopic: *oku*
metopomancy: *oku*
metralgia: *ma II*
metric: *me IV*
metritis: *ma II*
metro: *upo III e*
metrology: *me IV*
metronome: *me IV*
metronymic: *ma II, onomen*
metropolis: *amma, ma II, pele*
metropolitan: *amma, upo III e*
metrorrhagia: *amma*
mew: *ane, jing, mei II*
mewl: *ane*
mews: *mei II*
mezuzah: *phulax*
mezzanine: *medhi*
mezzotint: *medhi*
mho: *gerbh, onomen*
miaoul: *ane*
miasma: *mai II*
miasmatology: *mai II*
Miastor: *mai II*
mica: *sme*
micaceous: *sme*
micelle: *sme*
mickle: *me III*
micrify: *sme*
micro-: *me IV*
microanalyze: *sme*
microbe: *guei, sme*
microcephalous: *caput*
microcline: *klei*
microcosm: *kens*
microdot: *sme*
microfiche: *dheigh, sme*
microhaystacks: *sme*
micromicro: *sme*
microminiaturization: *sme*
micron: *sme*
Micronesia; *sna I*
micropanorama: *sme*
microphone: *sme*
microphyllous: *beu*
microscope: *sme, spek*
microsome: *dheigh N 37*
microstylous: *medhi*
Microtinae: *mei I, ous*
Microtus: *mei I, ous*
microwelding: *sme*
micrurgy: *sme*
micturate: *meigh*
micturition: *meigh*
mid: *medhi*
midden: *meu I*
middle: *medhi, uid*
Middle Ages: *medhi*
middlebrow: *medhi*
middle-class: *medhi*
middleman: *medhi*
Middlesex: *sek I*
middling: *medhi*
Midgard: *medhi*
midge: *mu*
midinette: *medhi*
midnight: *medhi*
midriff: *krep*
midshipman: *medhi*
midshipmite: *medhi*
midstream: *medhi*
midsummer: *medhi*
midway: *medhi*
midwife: *medhi, sta, uid*
might: *magh*
mignon: *mei I, men I*
mignonette: *mei I*
migraine: *ker II*
migrate: *mei II*
mil: *gheslo*
milch: *melg*
mild: *mel I*
mildew: *mel I, melit*
Mildred: *mel I*
mile: *gheslo, pet II*

Miles: *mei V*
milestone: *stai, stei*
milfoil: *gheslo*
milieu: *medhi*
miliolite: *mel V*
militancy: *miles*
military: *miles*
militate: *miles*
militia: *miles*
milium: *mel V*
milk: *melg*
Milky Way: *glact*
mill: *mel V*
millefiori: *gheslo*
millennium: *at, dheigh N 35, gheslo*
miller: *mel V*
millet: *mel V*
milli-: *me IV*
milliard: *gheslo*
million: *dheigh N 19*
millionaire: *gheslo*
milliped: *gheslo, ped*
millstone: *stai*
Milo: *mei V*
milreis: *reg I*
mime: *mei I, mimo*
mimeograph: *mimo*
mimesis: *mei I, mimo*
mimetic: *mei I, mimo*
mimic: *mei I, mimo*
mimicry: *mei I, mimo*
miminypiminy: *mei I*
Mimir: *smer*
mimology: *mei I*
mimophyre: *mei I*
Mimosa: *mimo*
mimosa: *mei I*
Mimosaceae: *mimo*
mimotype: *mei I*
Mimus: *mimo*
Mimusops: *mimo*
minatory: *men II*
mince: *mei I*
mind: *men I*
mine: *me I, miles*
mineral: *miles*
Minerva: *men I*
minestrone: *mei I*
mingle: *mag*
mini: *mei I*
miniature: *mei I*
minicab: *mei I*
minify: *mei I*
minikin: *men I*
minimal: *mei I*
minimum: *mei I*
minion: *ag, mei I, men I*
miniskirt: *mei I*
minister: *mei I*
ministry: *mei I*
miniver: *mei I, ua I*
minnesinger: *men I, senguh*
minnow: *men III*
minor: *mei I*
Minos: *taur*
Minotaur: *taur*
minstrel: *mei I*
mint: *men I*
minuend: *mei I*
minuet: *mei I*
minus: *mei I*
minuscule: *mei I*
minute: *mei I*
minutes: *mei I*
minyan: *ag*
minyon: *mei I*
minx: *manu*
Miocene: *mei I*
Miolithic: *mei I*
mir: *mei V*
Mirabel: *smei I*
mirabile dictu: smei I
miracle: *smei I*
mirador: *smei I*
mirage: *smei I*
Miranda: *smei I*
mire: *meu I*
mirific: *smei I*
mirror: *smei I*
mirth: *braghu*
mirza: *gn*
misadventure: *gua*
misalliance: *mei I*
misallocation: *mei I*
misanthrope: *mei I, nert*
misappropriate: *per VI g*
misbehave: *mei I*
miscegenation: *gen, gn, meik*
miscellaneous: *meik*
mischief: *caput, mei I*
miscible: *meik*
miscode: *mei I*
miscreant: *kred I, mei I*
misdemeanor: *mei I*

miser: *esu, kerd*
miserable: *kerd*
miserabilism: *kerd*
misericord: *kerd*
miserly: *kerd*
misery: *esu, kerd*
misfeasance: *dhe I*
misfortune: *mei I, per III*
mishap: *kob*
mis-hit: *mei I*
mismate: *mei I*
misnomer: *onomen*
misoneism: *neuos*
mispronunciation: *mei I*
misregistration: *mei I*
Miss: *dheigh N 13*
miss: *mei I*
missal: *smeit*
missel: *meigh*
missile: *smeit*
mission: *smeit*
missive: *smeit*
misspelling: *spel*
mist: *meigh*
mistake: *mei I*
mistellene: *mei I*
mister: *me III*
mistletoe: *meigh*
mistral: *me III*
mistranslate: *mei I*
mistress: *dheigh N 13*
mistrial: *mei I*
mistrust: *mei I*
misunderstanding: *mei I, ndher, sta*
misunderstood: *ne*
mite: *mai I*
miter: *mei IV*
Mithras: *mei IV*
mithridate: *mei IV*
Mithridates: *mei IV*
mithridatism: *sta*
mitigate: *mei V*
mitochondria: *mei IV*
mitome: *mei IV*
mitosis: *mei IV*
mitosome: *teue 3*
Mitra: *mei IV*
mitrailleuse: mai I
mittens: *medhi*
mittimus: *smeit*
mix: *meik*
mixen: *meigh*
mixture: *meik*
mizzen: *medhi*
mizzle: *meigh*
mnemonic: *men I, nebh*
Mnemosyne: *men I, nebh*
mnesic: *men I*
mnestic: *men I*
moan: *meino*
mob: *meu II*
mobile: *meu II*
mochila: *mut*
mock: *mimo, mok*
mockery: *mok*
mock-heroic: *mok*
mockingbird: *mimo, mok*
mock turtle: *mok*
modal: *med*
mode: *med, medhi*
model: *med*
moderate: *med*
modern: *med*
modest: *med*
modicum: *med*
modify: *med*
modiste: *med*
modulate: *med*
module: *med*
moidore: *men I*
moiety: *medhi*
moil: *mel I*
Moira: *smer*
Moirai: *smer*
moist: *meu I*
moisture: *meu I*
molar: *mel V, mo*
molasses: *melit*
mold: *med, mel V*
molder: *mel V*
mole: *mai II, mel V, mo*
molecule: *mo*
molest: *mo*
moll: *mel I*
mollify: *mel I, smeld*
Mollugo: *mel I*
Mollusca: *mel I*
mollusk: *mel I*
mollycoddle: *mel I*
molt: *mei II*
molto: *mel II*
molybdenum: *el 42, mlub, plumb*
molybdomancy: *el 42, mlub*
momblishness: *mom*

moment: *meu II*
momentaneous: *meu II*
momentary: *meu II*
momentous: *meu II*
momentum: *meu II*
momma: *tara*
mona: *me I*
monachal: *men III*
monad: *men III*
monandrous: *nert*
monarch: *arkh*
monarchy: *dheigh N 12, men III*
monastery: *men III*
monazite: *men III*
Monday: *me IV, prai*
monde: *cal, man*
monetary: *men I*
money: *men I*
mongrel: *mag*
monial: *medhi*
moniliform: *men II*
monism: *men III*
monition: *men I*
monitor: *men I*
monitory: *men I*
monk: *men III*
monkery: *men III*
monkey: *men III*
monkey on one's back: *cub*
monkeyrony: *men III*
monk's gun: *men III*
monk's peason: *men III*
mon(o)aesthesia: *men III*
monobasic: *gua*
monoblastic: *men III*
monocarpic: *ker III, sek IX*
monochordizing: *man*
monochrome: *gher I*
monocle: *oku*
monocline: *klei*
monoclinic: *klei*
monocogue: *kogkhos*
monocular: *oku*
monodactylous: *do*
monodelphia: *guelbh*
monody: *aud, ued*
monoecious: *ueik I*
monogamous: *men III*
monogamy: *geme*
monoglot: *glokh*
monograph: *gerbh*
monolith: *reg II*
monologue: *men III*
monomania: *men I*
monomer: *mak, smer*
monomial: *onomen*
Monongahela: *men III*
monopoly: *pel II*
monostearin: *stei*
monostrophe: *strebh*
monosyllabic: *labh*
monosyllable: *men III, slagu*
monotheism: *dhes*
monotint: *teng*
monotonous: *men III, ten*
monotreme: *ter II*
Monotropa: *trep*
monovalent: *ual*
monoxylous: *men III*
monozoic: *men III*
monster: *men I*
monstrance: *men I*
monstrosity: *men I*
monstrous: *men I*
montage: *men II*
montane: *men II*
mont-de-piété: men II, pius
monte: *men II*
month: *me IV*
monticule: *men II*
montigenous: *gn*
monument: *men I*
moo: *jing*
mood: *med*
moon: *me IV*
moonlighting: *me IV*
moonlit: *me IV*
moonshine: *me IV*
moon-struck: *me IV*
Moor: *oma*
moor: *mano, mori*
moot: *mod*
mop: *map*
mope: *mom*
moppet: *map, mu*
moral: *moro*
morality: *moro*
morass: *mori*
moratorium: *smer*
moratory: *smer*
morbal: *mer II*
morbid: *mer II*
morbific: *mer II*
morceau: mer II

mordacious: *mer II*
mordant: *mer II*
mordent: *mer II*
more: *me III*
More, Sir Thomas: *moro*
morel: *oma*
morello: *oma*
mores: *moro*
Moresque: *oma*
morganatic: *maghos, mer I*
Morisco: *oma*
morn: *mer I*
morning: *mer I*
Moro: *oma*
Morocco: *oma*
morological: *moro*
moromancy: *men I*
moron: *moro*
morose: *moro*
morosophist: *moro*
morosophistry: *moro*
Morpheus: *merbh, oner*
morphine: *merbh*
Morpho: *merbh*
morphology: *merbh*
Morris: *oma*
morrow: *mer I*
morsel: *mer II*
mortar: *mer II*
mortgage: *mer II, uad*
mortician: *mer II*
mortify: *mer II*
mortmain: *mer II*
mortuary: *mer II*
Morus: *moro*
moschatel: *mus*
Moslem: *dekm*
mosquito: *mu*
mosso: *meu II*
most: *me III*
mot: *mom*
Motacilla: *meu II*
Motacillidae: *meu II*
motel: *meu II*
motet: *mom*
moth: *lep I, math*
mother: *amma, ma II, meu I*
motherhood: *suesor*
motherless: *amma*
mother-of-pearl: *ma II*
motif: *meu II*
motion: *meu II*
motive: *meu II*
motmot: *mom*
motor: *meu II*
motto: *mom*
mouche volant: *guel III*
mouchoir: meu I
mouillé: *mel I*
moujik: *manu*
moulage: *med*
mo(u)ld: *med, meu I*
mo(u)lder: *meu I*
moulin: *mel V*
mound: *cal, man*
mount: *men II*
mountain: *men II*
mountebank: *bhag, men II*
mount of Venus: *uen*
mourn: *smer*
mouse: *mus*
mousetrap: *mus*
mouth: *akua, menth*
moutonnée: *mel I*
move: *meu II*
movement: *meu II*
mow: *me II*
moyenage: *medhi*
mozzarella: *mut*
Mrs.: *dheigh N 13*
Ms: *dheigh N 13*
much: *me III*
mucid: *meu I*
mucilage: *meu I*
mucin: *meu I*
mucivorous: *bhag*
muck: *meu I*
muckraker: *muth*
mucosity: *meu I*
mucous: *meu I*
mucus: *aues, meu I*
mud: *meu I*
muddle: *meu I*
mugget: *mus*
muggy: *meu I*
mugwort: *mu*
mulberry: *moro*
mule: *ane, mel III*
muley: *mai I*
mull: *mel V*
mullein: *mel I*
mullet: *mel III*
mullion: *medhi*
mulse: *melit*

multifarious: *bha I, mel II*
multilingual: *mel II*
multimillionaire: *mel II*
multipara: *mel II*
multiple: *plek I*
multiplex: *mel II, plek I*
multiplication: *plek I*
multiplicity: *mel II*
multitude: *mel II*
multum in parvo: mel II
multure: *mel V*
mum: *mom, momo, tara*
mumble: *mom*
mummer: *momo*
mummery: *momo*
mump: *mom*
munch: *mom*
mundane: *cal, man*
mundanity: *cal*
municipal: *kap, mei II*
municipality: *mei II*
munificent: *dhe I, mei II*
muniment: *mei III*
Munin: *men I*
munitions: *mei III*
murage: *mei III*
mural: *mei III*
murder: *mer II*
mure: *mei III*
Murex: *porpur*
Muriel: *mori*
murine: *mus*
murmur: *mormor*
muromontite: *mei III*
Murphy: *onomen*
murrain: *mer II*
murrey: *moro*
murrina: *mer II*
Mus: *mus*
Musca: *mu*
muscadine: *mus*
muscardine: *mus*
muscarone: *mu*
muscat: *mus*
muscatel: *mus*
muscle: *mus*
muscoid: *meu I*
muscology: *meu I*
muscovado: *mei I*
muscular: *mus*
muse: *men I*
Muses: *men I*
musette: *men I*
museum: *men I*
mush: *meigh*
mushroom: *meu I, spong*
music: *men I*
musk: *mus*
musket: *mu*
musketeer: *mu*
Muslim: *dekm*
Muspellsheim: *medhi*
mussel: *mus*
Mussulman: *dekm*
must: *med, meu I*
mustang: *meik*
mustard: *meu I*
Mustelidae: *mus*
muster: *men I*
musty: *meu I*
mutable: *mei II*
mutation: *mei II*
mute: *mom*
mutilate: *mut*
mutiny: *meu II*
mutter: *mom*
mutton: *mel I*
muttonchops: *bhar*
mutual: *mei II*
muzzle: *men I*
my: *me I*
myalgia: *mus*
mycelium: *meu I*
mycoderma: *meu I*
mycodextrin: *meu I*
mycology: *aues, meu I*
mycophagist: *meu I*
mycophagous: *bhag II*
mycoprotein: *meu I*
mycorrhiza: *meu I, uerad*
mycosis: *meu I*
mycteric: *meu I*
Myiarchus: *mu*
myiasis: *mu*
mylodont: *mel V*
myloglossus: *mel V*
mylonite: *mel V*
myna: *mad*
myocardia: *kerd*
myocardium: *mus*
myoidal: *mus*
myomancy: *mus*
myomorph: *mus*
myope: *oku*

myopia: *mom*
myosin: *mus*
myosotis: *au II, mus, ous*
myotomy: *mus*
Myoxylon: *smeru*
myriad: *meu I*
myriapod: *meu I*
myringa: *mems, smer*
myringitis: *smer*
myriorama: *suer I*
Myristica: *smeru*
myrmecology: *morui*
myrmecophagous: *morui*
myrmeleon: *morui*
myrobalan: *smeru*
myself: *me I*
mysophilia: *meu I*
mysophobia: *meu I*
mystagogue: *mom*
mystery: *mei I, mom*
mystic: *mom*
mysticete: *mus*
myth: *mom, muth*
mythologize: *dheigh N 25*
mythopoe(t)ic: *kuei II*
Myxine: *meu I*
myxobroma: *meu I*
myxoma: *aues, meu I*
myxomatosis: *meu I*
myxomycetes: *meu I*
Myzostoma: *meu I*

N

nacelle: *nau II*
nag: *gen, gher I*
naiad: *sna I*
naiant: *sna I*
nail: *onogh*
nainsook: *nei*
Naius: *sna I*
naive: *gn*
naked: *nogu*
Nakshatra: *ksei*
Nama: *sna I*
name: *onomen*
nameless: *onomen*
namely: *onomen*
namesake: *onomen*
Nan: *nana*
nana: *nana*
Nancy: *nana*
nanism: *nana*
nanny: *nana*
nanny goat: *nana*
nano: *me IV*
nanometer: *nana*
nanoplankton: *nana*
nanosecond: *nana*
nap: *ken I*
napery: *map*
napkin: *map*
nappe: *map*
Naraka: *ner*
narc: *sner II*
narceine: *sner II*
narcissism: *sner II*
Narcissus: *uagh*
narcissus: *sner II, uagh*
narco: *sner II*
narcolepsy: *labh, sner II*
narcosis: *sner II*
narcosynthesis: *sner II*
narcotic: *sner II*
nard: *sphei II*
nark: *nas, sner II*
narrate: *gn*
narrative: *gn*
narrow: *sner II*
narw(h)al: *nau I, skualo*
nasal: *nas*
Nasatya: *nes*
nascent: *dheigh N 8, gn*
nasitis: *nas*
nasofrontal: *nas*
nasology: *nas*
nasturtium: *nas, tereq*
nasute: *nas*
natal: *gn*
natant: *sna I*
natation: *sna I*
natatorium: *sna I*
nates: *not*
Natica: *not*
nation: *gn*
native: *gn*
nativity: *gn*
natrium: *nitro*
Natrix: *netr*
natrolite: *nitro*
natron: *nitro*
natty: *nei*

nature: *gn*
naufragous: *nau II*
naught: *aiu, ne*
naughty: *ne*
naumachy: *magh, nau II*
nauplius: *nau II*
nauseous: *dheigh N 2 a, nau II*
Nausicaä: *kau I, nau II*
nautch: *sner II*
nautical: *nau II*
nautilus: *nau II*
naval: *nau II*
nave: *nabh, nau II*
navel: *nabh*
navicert: *nau II*
navicular: *nau II*
navigate: *ag, nau II*
navy: *nau II*
nay: *ne*
naya paisa: *neuos, ped*
naze: *nas*
Nazi: *ari*
ncytalopia: *oku*
neap: *ken I*
near: *neuh*
neat: *nei, neud*
neath: *ni*
nebula: *nebh*
nebulium: *nebh*
nebulosity: *nebh*
nebulous: *nebh*
Necator: *nek*
necessary: *ne, sed III*
neck: *kn*
neckerchief: *kn*
Necker's cube: *kn*
neckful: *kn*
necklace: *kn*
neckverse: *kn*
necrobiosis: *nek*
necromancy: *men I, nek, niger*
necrophagous: *nek*
necropolis: *nek, pele*
necropsy: *nek*
necrosis: *nek*
nectar: *dhes, nek, sna III, ter III*
nectareous: *nek*
nectarine: *nek, sna III, ter III*
nectary: *nek, sna III*
nectocalyx: *sna I*
nectopod: *sna I*
Nectria: *sna I*
Necturus: *sna I*
nee: *gn*
need: *nau I*
needle: *netr, sne*
nef: *nau II*
nefandous: *dheigh N 2 e*
nefarious: *bha I, ne*
negate: *ne*
negative: *ne*
neglect: *leg I, ne*
negligee: *ne*
negligence: *ne*
negligent: *leg I*
negotiate: *ne, oti*
Negrillo: *niger*
Negrito: *niger*
Negro: *niger*
Negroid: *niger*
Negrophile: *niger*
Negrophobe: *niger*
neighbor: *bheu, neuh, renos*
Neil: *nei*
neither: *kuo, ne*
nekton: *ie, sna I*
Nelson: *nei*
nemahelminth: *uelu*
nematocyst: *sne*
Nematoda: *netr*
nematode: *sne, ueid*
nematoid: *netr*
Nematomorpha: *sne*
nematophore: *sne*
nemesis: *nem*
Nemo: *ne*
neoarctic: *neuos*
neocomian: *neuos*
neodymium: *el 60*
Neolithic: *neuos*
neologism: *neuos*
neomycin: *neuos*
neon: *el 10, neuos*
neonate: *gn, neuos*
Neophron: *guhren, neuos*
neophyte: *bheu, neuos*
neoplasm: *neuos, pela*
neossin: *kei II, neuos*
neossology: *kei II*
neoteric: *neuos*
Neotoma: *neuos*
Neotragus: *neuos*
neotropical: *neuos*
neotype: *neuos*

Neozoic: *guei, neuos*
nepenthe: *guadh*
Nephelai: *nebh*
nephelite: *nebh*
nephelo-: *nebh*
Nephelococcugia: *nebh*
nephelometer: *nebh*
nephew: *nepot*
nephinium: *pleu*
nepho-: *nebh*
nephoscope: *nebh*
nephralgia: *engu*
nephridium: *engu*
nephrite: *engu*
nephritis: *engu*
nepotism: *nepot*
Neptune: *nebh, pleu*
neptunian: *nebh*
neptunium: *el 93, nebh*
nereid: *sna I*
nereis: *dheu I*
Nerita: *dheu I*
Nero: *niger*
nero antico: *niger*
nerve: *netr, sne*
nervous: *netr, sne*
nescience: *ne*
ness: *nas*
-ness: *ghedh*
nessberry: *bhel I*
nest: *ni, sed I*
nestle: *ni*
nestling: *ni, sed I*
net: *ned, nei*
nether: *ni*
network: *ned, sta*
neuralgia: *dheigh N 6, sne*
neurasthenia: *sne*
neurology: *netr*
neuron: *netr, sne*
neuropathy: *guadh*
neurosis: *netr, sne*
neurotic: *netr*
neurotoxin: *sne*
neustria: *neuos*
neuter: *kuo, ne*
neutral: *ne*
neutrality: *kuo, ne*
neutralize: *ne*
neutretto: *ne*
neutrino: *ne*
neutrodyne: *deu, ne*
neutron: *el, ne*
neutronlike: *leig I*
never: *aiu, ne*
nevertheless: *to*
nevus: *gn*
new: *neuos*
new-bear: *neuos*
newcomer: *neuos*
newel: *kn*
newfangled: *neuos, pag*
Newfoundland: *neuos*
Newgate: *neuos*
new-laid: *neuos*
newlywed: *neuos*
news: *neuos*
newsworthy: *neuos*
Newton: *neuos*
Newtonian: *neuos*
newtonite: *neuos*
new year: *neuos*
New Yorker: *neuos*
next: *neuh*
nexus: *ned*
nibble: *ken I*
Nibelungenlied: leu III
Nibelungs: *nebh*
nice: *ne, sek II*
nicety: *sek II*
Nicholas: *laos*
nickel: *el 28, tuer II*
nickname: *aug, onomen*
nictitate: *kneiguh*
nidamental: *ni, sed*
niddering: *nei*
nidderling: *nei*
nide: *ni, sed I*
nidify: *ni, sed I*
nidology: *ni*
nidulant: *ni*
nidulation: *ni, sed I*
nidus: *ni*
niece: *nepot*
niello: *niger*
Niflheim: *medhi*
Nigella: *niger*
niggard: *ken I*
nigger: *niger*
niggle: *ken I*
nigh: *neuh*
night: *nekut*
nightingale: *ghel I, nekut*
nightmare: *mer II, nekut*

night-mugging: *nekut*
nightshade: *nekut*
nightsoil: *nekut*
nighttime: *aiu*
nigrescence: *niger*
nigrify: *niger*
nigritude: *niger*
nigrosene: *niger*
nihil: *guhisl, ne*
nihilism: *guhisl, ne*
Nike: *laos*
nil: *guhisl, ne*
nilgai: *gultur, nei*
nilgau: *gultur*
nim: *nem*
nimble: *nem, taka*
nimbrose: *nebh*
nimbrostratus: *nebh*
nimbus: *nebh*
nimiety: *ne*
niminy-piminy: *ni*
nincompoop: *men I*
nine: *neun*
nineteen: *neun*
ninety: *neun*
Nine Worthies: *neun, uer II 5*
ninny: *peti*
ninth: *neun*
Niobe: *el 41*
niobium: *el 41*
nip: *ken I*
Nirvana: *ser III, ue*
nisi: *ne, sos*
nisus: *kneiguh*
nit: *knid*
niter: *nitron*
niton: *nei*
nitor: *nei*
nit-picking: *knid*
nitrate: *nitron*
nitric: *nitron*
nitrid: *nei*
nitrite: *nitron*
nitrogen: *el 7, nitron*
nitroglycerin: *nitro*
nitroso: *nitro*
nitrous: *nitron*
nival: *sneiguh*
nivosity: *sneiguh*
nix: *ne*
Nixonlike: *leig I*
no: *aiu, ne*
nobelium: *el 102*
nobility: *gen*
noble: *gen*
nocent: *nek*
nocive: *nek*
nock: *kn*
noctambulist: *nekut*
noctidial: *nekut*
Noctilio: *nekut*
Noctiluca: *nekut*
noctilucent: *nekut*
noctipotent: *nekut*
noctivagant: *nekut*
noctivagous: *dheigh N 2 f*
Noctua: *nekut*
Noctuidae: *nekut*
noctule: *nekut*
noctuolent: *nekut*
nocturnal: *nekut*
nocturne: *nekut*
nod: *ken I*
nodi: *ned*
nodule: *ned*
nodus: *ned*
Noël: *gn*
noise: *nau II*
noisette: *kn*
noisome: *odi*
nolens volens: uel II
noli me tangere: tag I
nom: *onomen*
noma: *nem*
nomad: *nem*
nomarch: *nem*
nombril: *nabh*
nom de guerre: onomen
nom de plume: onomen
Nome: *nem*
nome: *nem*
nomen: *onomen*
nomenclature: *kel II, onomen*
nomeus: *nem*
nominal: *onomen*
nominalism: *onomen*
nominate: *onomen*
nominative: *onomen*
nomistic: *nem*
nomograph: *nem*
nomography: *nem*
nomothetic: *nem*
nonage: *aiu, ne, neun*
nonagenarian: *dekm, dheigh N 7, neun*

nonagesimal: *neun*
nonagon: *neun*
nonane: *neun*
nonary: *neun*
nonchalant: *kel I*
non compos mentis: men I
nonconformist: *ne*
nondescript: *ne*
none: *ne, oino*
nonentity: *ne*
nones: *neun*
nonesuch: *ne*
nonillion: *neun*
non obstante: sta
nonpareil: *per V*
nonplus: *pel V*
nonsense: *ne, sent*
non sequitur: seku I
nonuple: *neun*
nook: *kn*
nooky: *kn*
noon: *neun*
noose: *ned*
nor: *ne*
Nordi: *medhi*
Nordic: *ner*
norm: *gn*
normal: *gn*
Norman: *manu, ner*
Normandy: *ueik I*
Norn: *ner, sner I*
Norse: *ner*
north: *ner*
northern: *ner*
Norway: *ner, uegh*
Norwegian: *ner*
nosarians: *sna II*
nose: *nas*
nosegay: *nas, peig*
nosology: *leg I*
nostalgia: *dheigh N 6, leg I, nes*
nostology: *leg I*
nostomania: *leg I*
nostril: *nas, ter III*
not: *ueks*
notable: *gn*
notary: *gn*
notch: *sek I*
note: *gn*
nothing: *ne, ueks*
notice: *gn*
notify: *gn*
notion: *gn*
notochord: *not*
notorious: *dheigh N 2 d, gen*
notoungulate: *onogh*
Notropis: *trep*
notturno: *nekut*
nougat: *kn*
nought: *ne, ueks*
noun: *onomen*
nourish: *sna III*
nouveau riche: neuos
nova: *neuos*
novel: *neuos*
novelty: *neuos*
November: *me IV, neun*
novena: *neun*
novercal: *neuos*
novice: *dheigh N 18, neuos*
now: *neuos*
nowadays: *neuos*
nowel: *kn*
noxal: *nek*
noxious: *nek*
noyade: *nek*
noyau: *kn*
nozzle: *nas*
nuance: *sneubh*
nub: *gen*
nubecula: *sneubh*
nubia: *sneubh*
nubiform: *sneubh*
nubilate: *sneubh*
nubile: *sneubh*
nubilous: *sneubh*
nucellus: *kn*
nucivorous: *bhag*
nuclear: *kn*
nuclein: *kn*
nucleolus: *kn*
nucleotide: *kn*
nucleus: *kn*
Nucula: *kn*
nude: *nogu*
nudibranchiate: *nogu*
nudicaul: *kaul, nogu*
nudifidian: *nogu*
nudist: *nogu*
nudiustertion: *nogu*
nudnick: *keu II, nau I*
nugget: *gheu*
nusiance: *nek*
null: *ne*

nullify: *ne*
numb: *nem*
number: *nem*
numbles: *lendh I*
numen: *neu II*
numeral: *nem*
numerator: *nem*
numerical: *nem*
numerology: *nem*
numerous: *nem*
numinous: *neu II*
numismatics: *nem*
nummary: *nem*
nummular: *nem*
nummulite: *nem*
nun: *nana*
Nunc Dimittis: *neuos*
nuncheon: *neun*
nuncio: *neu I*
nuncupative: *kap, onomen*
nuptials: *sneubh*
nurse: *sna III*
nurture: *sna III*
nut: *kn*
nutant: *neu II*
nutation: *neu II*
nuthatch: *keg, kn, sek IV*
nutmeg: *mus*
nutria: *aue*
nutrient: *sna III*
nutriment: *sna III*
nutrition: *sna III*
nutritious: *sna III*
nutty: *dheigh N 3*
nux vomica: *kn*
nuzzle: *nas*
nyctalopia: *nekut*
Nyctanthes: *nekut*
Nyctea: *nekut*
Nyctereutes: *nekut*
Nycteris: *nekut*
Nycticorax: *nekut*
nyctitropism: *nekut*
nyctophobia: *nekut*
nylghau: *gultur*
Nym: *taka*
nymph: *gn, sneubh*
nymphae: *sneubh*
Nymphaea: *sneubh*
Nymphaeceae: *sneubh*
nymphet: *sneubh*
nympholepsy: *labh, slagu*
nympholept: *slagu*
nymphomania: *sneubh*

O': *au II, au IV*
oak: *aig II*
oakum: *gembh*
oar: *ere*
oast: *aidh*
oath: *oito*
obbligato: *leig II*
obdurate: *deru, dheigh N 10*
obedience: *aus*
obeisance: *aus*
obese: *ed*
obey: *aus*
obfuscate: *dheu I*
obituary: *ei I*
object: *ie*
objection: *ie*
objective: *ie*
objurgate: *ag*
objurgation: *ieuos*
oblate: *tol*
obligation: *leig II*
obligatory: *leig II*
oblige: *leig II*
oblique: *elei*
obliterate: *deph*
oblivion: *lei I*
oblivious: *lei I*
obliviscible: *lei I*
oblong: *del III*
obloquy: *tolku*
obmutescent: *mom*
obnoxious: *nek*
obreption: *labh*
obreptitious: *labh*
obscure: *skeu*
obsecrate: *sak*
obsequies: *seku I*
obsequious: *dheigh N 2 d, seku I*
observance: *suer I*
observation: *suer I*
observatory: *suer I*
observe: *ser II, suer I*
obsession: *sed I*
obsolescent: *al I*
obsolete: *al I*

obstacle: *sta*
obstetrician: *sta*
obstetrics: *sta*
obstetrix: *sta*
obstinate: *sta*
obstipation: *steibh*
obstreperous: *strep*
obstriction: *streig*
obstruct: *ster I*
obtain: *ten*
obtected: *steg*
obtest: *tre*
obtrude: *treud*
obtruncate: *ter III*
obverse: *uer II 5*
obvert: *uer II 5*
obviate: *uegh*
obvious: *uegh*
obvolute: *uelu*
ocarina: *auei*
Occam's razor: *ne*
ocean: *nebh*
Occident: *kad I*
occipital: *caput*
occiput: *caput*
occlude: *kleu III*
occult: *kel VI*
occupation: *kap*
occupy: *kap*
occur: *kers I*
oceanography: *nebh*
ocellar: *oku*
ocellation: *oku*
ocelle: *oku*
ocelli: *oku*
ocellicyst: *oku*
ocelliferous: *oku*
ochlocracy: *da II, dheigh N 11, kar, uegh*
ocitancy: *or*
octachord: *okto*
octad: *okto*
octagon: *okto*
octan: *okto*
octane: *okto*
octangular: *dheigh N 9*
octant: *okto*
octapla: *plek I*
octaploid: *okto*
octave: *okto*
Octavius: *okto*
octet: *okto, seks*
octillion: *okto*
October: *me IV, okto*
octogenarian: *okto*
octopus: *okto*
octoroon: *okto*
octosyllabic: *okto*
ocular: *oku*
ocularist: *oku*
ocularium: *oku*
oculiform: *oku*
oculist: *oku*
oculomotor: *oku*
oculozygomatic: *oku*
oculus: *oku*
od: *esu, hule*
odd: *ozd*
oddity: *ozd*
odds: *ozd*
ode: *aud, ued*
-ode: *sed II*
Odeon: *ued*
odeum: *ued*
Odin: *men I, prai, uat*
odious: *odi*
odium: *odi*
odograph: *sed II*
odometer: *sed II*
odontology: *den*
odor: *mazdos, od*
odoriferous: *od*
odorous: *od*
Odsbodkins: *esu*
odyl: *hule*
Odysseus: *mazdos, odi, oku*
odzooks: *esu*
oecist: *ueik I*
oecus: *ueik I*
Oedipus complex: *plek I*
oeillade: *oku*
oenology: *em*
oenomel: *em, melit*
Oenone: *em*
oenophilist: *em*
Oenothera: *em*
(o)estrus: *eis*
of: *ap*
off: *ap*
offal: *ap*
offend: *guhen*
offensive: *guhen*
offer: *bher I*
office: *dhe I, op I*
officer: *dhe I, op I*

official: *dhe I, op I*
officiate: *op I*
officinal: *op I*
officious: *dhe I, op I*
oft: *op I*
often: *op I*
oftentimes: *op I*
ogle: *oku*
ohm: *gerbh, onomen*
-oid: *es*
oikist: *ueik I*
oil: *elaia*
oily: *elaia*
ointment: *enguo*
Olax: *od*
old: *al I, onomen*
Old Mortality: *sak*
Old Nick: *onomen*
oleaginous: *elaia*
olecranon: *ker II*
oleo: *elaia*
oleograph: *elaia*
oleomargarine: *elaia, margar*
oleophilic: *elaia*
olfactory: *mazdos, od*
Olga: *kailo*
olid: *od*
oligarchy: *arkh, dheigh N 12*
oligoclase: *kal*
olio: *auku*
olive: *elaia*
olive branch: *elaia*
Oliver: *koro*
olive stick: *elaia*
Olivier: *koro*
olla-podrida: *auku, pu*
-ology: *dheigh N 30, leg I*
Olympic Games: *fur*
OM: *men I, o*
omaphagous: *oma*
omasum: *stoman*
ombre: *ghdhem*
ombrology: *ombhro*
ombrometer: *ombhro*
ombudsman: *ambh, bheudh, manu*
omega: *bes I, me III*
omelet: *ster I*
omen: *o*
omicron: *bhes I, me III*
ominous: *o*
omission: *dheigh N 19*
omit: *smeit*
Ommastrephes: *strebh*
ommatidium: *oku*
Ommatostrephes: *oku*
omniana: *op I*
omnibenevolent: *op I*
omnibus: *kus, op I*
omnigatherum: *op I*
omnipotent: *dheigh N 8, op I, poti*
omnipresent: *op I*
omniscient: *op I, sek II*
omnivorous: *bhag, garg, op I*
omodynia: *oms*
omophagous: *bhag*
omophore: *oms*
omophorion: *oms*
omoplate: *oms*
omoplatoscopy: *oms*
omostegite: *oms*
omphalism: *nabh*
omphalodium: *nabh*
omphalomancy: *nabh*
omphalopsychite: *nabh*
omphalos: *nabh*
onanism: *man*
once: *oino*
onchyia: *onogh*
oncology: *enek*
oncometer: *enek*
oncotomy: *enek*
ondine: *aue*
ondograph: *aue*
ondometer: *aue*
ondoyant: *aue*
one: *oino*
oneirocritic: *caput, oner, sek VI*
oneiromancy: *oner*
oneiropompist: *oner*
onerous: *enos*
onion: *oino*
only: *oino*
onocarpic: *sek IX*
onomancy: *onomen*
onomasticon: *onomen*
onomatopoetic: *kuei II, onomen, poieo*
onomestic: *onomen*
Onosmodium: *od*
onslaught: *slak*
onto: *de*
ontogeny: *es, gen, gn*
ontologism: *es*
ontology: *es*
onus: *enos*

onycha: *onogh*
onychite: *onogh*
onychoid: *onogh*
onychomancy: *onogh*
onycophagist: *onogh*
onyx: *onogh*
oocyte: *auei*
oogamy: *auei*
oogenesis: *auei, gn*
oogonium: *auei, gn*
oolite: *auei*
oology: *auei*
oom: *kei II*
ooze: *aue, aeis*
opacity: *opak*
opal: *upo I*
opalescent: *upo I*
opaque: *opak*
open: *upo I*
opera: *op I*
opéra bouffe: *buff*
operate: *op I*
operation: *op I*
operculum: *suer I, uer V*
ophicide: *anghui*
ophidian: *anghui, serp*
ophiolatry: *serp*
ophiology: *anghui*
ophiophagous: *bhag*
ophite: *anghui, serp*
Ophiuchus: *serp*
ophthalmia: *oku*
ophthalmologist: *oku*
ophthalmoscope: *oku*
opine: *op II*
opinion: *op II*
opinionated: *op II*
opisthognathous: *ghenu*
oppidan: *ped*
opportune: *per III*
opportunity: *per III*
oppose: *ap*
opposite: *dheigh N 22*
opposition: *ap*
oppress: *per VII, pres*
opprobrium: *bher I*
oppugn: *peug*
opsigamy: *oku*
opsimath: *men I, oku*
opsin: *oku*
opsomaniac: *oku*
opsonic: *oku*
opsonin: *oku, past*
opsony: *oku*
opsophagist: *oku*
opt: *op II*
optative: *op II*
optical: *oku*
optician: *oku*
optics: *men I*
optimates: *op I*
optimism: *op I*
optimum: *op I*
option: *op II*
optometrist: *oku*
opulence: *op I*
opus: *op I*
opuscule: *op I*
opusculum: *op I*
or: *aier*
oracle: *or*
oracular: *or*
oral: *or*
oration: *or*
oratory: *or*
orb: *cal, rebh*
orbicular: *cal, rebh*
orbit: *cal, rebh*
orchard: *gher IV*
orchestra: *ergh*
orchestration: *ergh*
orchid: *orghi*
orchidaceous: *dheigh N 2 a, orghi*
orchidology: *orghi*
orchidotomy: *orghi*
orchiocele: *orghi*
orchitis: *orghi*
orchotomy: *orghi*
ordeal: *da II*
order: *ar I*
ordinal: *ar I*
ordinary: *ar I*
ore: *aios, el 29*
orectic: *reg I*
O'Reilly: *onomen*
organ: *uerg*
organicism: *uerg*
organism: *uerg*
organon: *uerg*
orgasm: *uerg*
orgeat: *ghers*
orgy: *uerg*
Orient: *aues, nebh*
orient: *ergh*

orifice: *dhe I, or*
oriflamme: *aues*
origin: *ergh*
original: *ergh*
originate: *ergh*
orillion: *ous*
orinasal: *nas*
oriole: *aues*
Orion: *morui*
orisons: *or*
Orlando: *koro, lendh II*
orle: *or*
orlop: *klou*
Ormazd: *ane*
ormer: *mori, ous*
ormolu: *mel V*
Ormuzd: *men I*
ornament: *ar I*
ornate: *ar I*
orogeny: *gn*
orotund: *or, reth*
orphan: *orbh, rudh*
orpiment: *el 16, el 33*
orrhocyst: *ser III*
orrhoid: *ser III*
orrhous: *ser III*
orris: *uei I*
Orson: *rkthos*
orthocephalic: *ueredh*
orthoclase: *kal*
orthodontics: *dek*
orthodox: *ueredh*
orthodoxy: *dek*
orthoepy: *dek, ueredh*
orthognathous: *dek, ghenu*
orthography: *dek, ueredh*
orthopedics: *ueredh*
Orthoptera: *ueredh*
orthopterans: *dek*
orthoptic: *dek, oku*
orthostichous: *steigh, ueredh*
orthotropian: *ueredh*
O'Ryan, Gen.: *morui*
osar: *oms*
Oscar: *ghaiso*
oscillate: *or*
oscines: *kan*
oscitancy: *kei I*
osculant: *or*
oscular: *or*
osculate: *kus*
osculation: *or*
osculum: *or*
osmatic: *od*
osmium: *el 76, od*
osmology: *od*
osmometer: *od*
osmonosology: *od*
Osmorhiza: *od*
osmose: *uedh*
osmosis: *uedh*
osmotic: *uedh*
Osmund: *man*
osphradium: *od*
osphresis: *od*
osphyalgia: *ost*
osphyarthritis: *ost*
osprey: *auei, bhreg, ost*
oss: *ost*
ossein: *ost*
ossements: *ost*
osseus: *ost*
ossicle: *ost*
ossifrage: *bhreg, ost*
ossify: *ost*
ossivorous: *bhag*
ossuary: *ost*
ostensible: *ten*
ostensorium: *ten*
ostentation: *ten*
osteoblast: *ost*
osteomalacia: *mel I, ost*
osteomyelitis: *ost*
osteopath: *ost*
ostiary: *or*
ostiole: *or*
ostler: *ghostis*
ostraceous: *ost*
ostracism: *ost*
ostracite: *ost*
ostracize: *ost*
ostracod: *ost*
ostracoderm: *ost*
ostracology: *ost*
ostracon: *ost*
ostreophagous: *bhag*
ostrich: *auei, ster II, trozdos*
Oswald: *ual*
otalgia: *au II*
otary: *au II*
other: *al II*
otic: *ous*
Otididae: *ous*
Otiorhynchidae: *ous*

otiose: *dheigh N 2 g, oti*
Otis: *ous*
otitis: *ous*
otocranial: *au II*
otolith: *ous*
otorrhea: *au II*
otoscope: *ous*
otter: *aue*
oubliette: *lei I*
ouch: *ned*
ought: *eik*
ounce: *leuk, oino*
Ouranos: *aue, suer I*
oust: *sta*
ouster: *sta*
out: *ud*
outbabble: *ud*
outbargain: *ud*
outbrawl: *ud*
outcast: *ger VI*
outfangthief: *pag*
outfield: *pela*
outfit: *ud*
outfitter: *dheigh N 13*
outlander: *ud*
outlandish: *ud*
outlaw: *legh, ud*
outlet: *leid I*
outline: *ud*
outqueen: *ud*
outrage: *ud*
outright: *ud*
outside: *ud*
outspan: *sphei*
outward: *uer II 5*
outworn: *ud*
oval: *auei*
ovary: *auei*
ovation: *euoi*
oven: *auku*
over: *upo III d*
overalls: *upo III d*
overboard: *upo III d*
overcast: *ger VI*
overeat: *upo III d*
overflow: *upo III d*
overlook: *upo III d*
overnight: *upo III d*
overreacher: *dheigh N 13*
overrule: *upo III d*
oversee: *upo III d*
overslaugh: *slak*
overt: *suer I, uer V*
overtax: *upo III d*
overture: *suer I, uer V*
overturn: *upo III d*
overwhelm: *kuelp*
overwork: *uerg*
Ovibos: *oui*
Ovibovinae: *oui*
Ovidae: *oui*
oviduct: *auei*
oviform: *dheigh N 14, oui*
oviparous: *auei, per VI b*
ovule: *auei*
owe: *eik*
owl: *ul*
owler: *ul*
owlet: *ul*
owling: *ul*
owlish: *ul*
own: *eik*
ox: *ugu*
oxalic: *ak*
Oxopidae: *oku*
ox(s)lip: *lei I, sleubh*
oxygen: *ak, el 8, gn*
oxymoron: *moro*
oxyphil(e): *bhili*
oxytone: *ten*
Oxytropis: *trep*
oyez: *ous*
oyster: *ost*
ozocerite: *od, keneko*
ozone: *el 8, od*

P

pablum: *pa*
pace: *pet II*
pacè: pag
pachisi: *penkue, uid*
pachnolite: *pag*
pachycardian: *bhengh*
pachycephalic: *bhengh*
pachyderm: *bhengh, der*
pachydermatic: *bhengh*
pachyntic: *bhengh*
Pachysandra: *bhengh*
Pachystina: *bhengh*
pacific: *dhe I, dheigh N 17, pag*
pacifist: *pag, plek I*

pacify: *pag*
pact: *pag*
paddle: *pent*
padishah: *ksei, pa, poti*
padlock: *leug*
padre: *peter*
padrone: *peter*
paella: *pet II*
pagan: *pag*
page: *pag, pou*
pageant: *pag*
pagoda: *bhag*
pagurian: *pag*
Paguridae: *pag*
pail: *pag*
paillasse: *pel I, pel VI*
pain: *keui I, paen*
painter: *pend, spend II*
painting: *peik*
paintrix: *peik*
paintry: *peik*
painture: *peik*
painty: *peik*
pair: *per V*
pajamas: *ped*
pal: *bhrater*
palafitte: *pag*
palanquin: *per I*
pale: *pag, pel VII*
Paleolithic: *ker I*
paleology: *ker I*
paleothere: *ghuer*
Paleozoic: *quei*
paletot: *pel VI*
palette: *pag*
palfrey: *per I, reidh*
palimpsest: *bhes I, ker I*
palindrome: *dra, gerbh, ker I*
palingenesis: *gn, ker I*
palinode: *aud, ker I, ued*
palisade: *pag*
pall: *pel VI, pel VII*
Palladian: *gn*
palladium: *el 46, gn*
Pallas: *gn*
Pallas Athene: *gn*
pallesthesia: *pal*
pallet: *pag, pel I*
palliate: *pel VI*
pall-mall: *mat*
pallor: *pel VII*
palm: *pela*
palmer: *pela*
palmiped: *ped*
palmistry: *me III*
palomino: *pel VII*
palp: *pal*
palpable: *pal*
palpate: *pal*
palpebral: *pal*
palpitation: *pal*
Paludicella: *pel V*
Paludicola: *pel V*
paludine: *pel V*
paludism: *pel V*
palynology: *pel I*
pamper: *pa*
pamphelet: *bhili*
pamphlet: *bhili*
Pan: *aig, keu II*
pan: *keu II, pet II*
panacea: *keu II*
panada: *pa*
Panchanana: *penkue*
Panchatana: *penkue*
Panchatantra: *penkue, ten*
panchayat: *penkue*
pancratium: *kar*
pancreas: *keu II*
pandemonium: *da II, dei, dheigh N 35, keu II*
pandicular: *pet II*
Pandora: *keu II*
pandy: *pet II*
pane: *pan, pend*
panegyric: *ger I, keu II*
panel: *pan, pend*
panetela: *pa*
Pangloss: *glokh, keu II, pet I*
panic: *keu II*
panicle: *pan*
panification: *pa*
panjandrum: *keu II*
panmixia: *meik*
pannage: *pa*
pannier: *pa*
panorama: *keu II, suer I, uer V*
panpipes: *keu II*
panpsychism: *bhes*
pansy: *mori, pend, spend II*
Pantagruel: *keu II, uerg*
pantagruelion: *keu II*
pantaloonery: *keu II*
pantaloons: *keu II, leo, seni*

pantechnicon: *keu II, tekhs*
pantheon: *keu II*
panther: *ghuer*
pantler: *pa*
pantomime: *keu II, mimo*
pantry: *pa*
pants: *keu II, seni*
pantyhose: *keu II*
pantywaist: *keu II*
Panurge: *keu II, uerg*
pap: *pa*
papa: *pa*
Papaver: *pa*
Papaveraceae: *pa*
papaveraceous: *dheigh N 2 a*
papaverine: *pa*
paper: *bibli*
Paphian: *pa*
Papilio: *pal*
papilionaceous: *pa, pal*
papilla: *pa*
papilloma: *pa*
papillon: *pal*
papillote: *pal*
papism: *pa*
papist: *pa*
papoose: *pa*
pappa: *pa*
pappus: *pa*
pappy: *pa*
papula: *pa*
par: *per V*
parabasis: *gua*
parable: *guel II*
parabola: *guel II*
parabolic: *guel II*
paraboloid: *guel II*
parachor: *ghe*
parachroma: *gher I*
parachronism: *nebh*
parachronium: *nebh*
parachute: *kad I, per V*
paraclete: *kel II, per N 2*
paracrostic: *steigh*
paradigm: *deik*
paradise: *dheigh, per 2*
paradisiac: *dheigh*
paradoctor: *per V*
paradox: *per I*
paraffin: *pou 6*
paragon: *ak, per 2*
paragram: *per 2*
paragraph: *gerbh, per I*
paralanguage: *per 2*
parallax: *al II, per N 2*
parallel: *al II, per 2*
parallelogram: *gerbh*
parallelopiped: *ped, per N 2*
paralogical: *leg I*
paralogize: *leg I*
paralogy: *leg I*
paralysis: *lou*
paralyze: *leu I*
paramedic: *per V*
paramere: *smer*
parameter: *per I*
parametrium: *ma II*
paramorphism: *merbh*
paramount: *ad, kat, men II, per VI f*
paramour: *amma, per I*
paranomesia: *onomen*
parapegm: *pag*
parapet: *peg, per V*
paraphernalia: *bher I, per V*
paraplegia: *per N 2, plak*
paraprosexia: *sek I*
parapsychology: *dheigh N 30*
parasang: *per I*
parasite: *per I, per VII*
parasitism: *per VII*
parasitoidism: *per VII*
parasitology: *per VII*
parasol: *per V, sauel*
parataxis: *tag II*
paratroops: *per V*
parbleu: esu
parboil: *beu*
Parcae: *morui, per VI f, smer*
parcel: *per V*
parcener: *per V*
pardie: *dei*
pardon: *do, per VIII*
pardoner: *pela*
pare: *per V*
paregoric: *ger I*
parent: *per VI b*
parentage: *dheigh 4 N, per VI b*
parental: *per VI b*
parenthesis: *dhe I, en*
paresis: *ie*
parget: *ie*
parhelion: *sauel*
pari-mutuel: *per V*
Paris: *em, leu II*

parish: *ueik I*
parity: *per V*
parlance: *guel II*
parlando: *guel II*
parley: *guel II*
parleyvoo: *guel II*
parliament: *guel II*
parlor: *guel II*
parochial: *ueik I*
parody: *aud, ued*
paroecious: *ueik I*
parole: *quel I*
paronomasia: *onomen*
Paronychia: *onogh*
paronymous: *onomen*
parotic: *ous*
parotid: *au II, ous*
parotoid: *ous*
paroxysm: *ak*
parricide: *peter, skhai*
parry: *per V*
parse: *per V*
parsec: *al II, me IV*
Parsi: *ane, ger IV, iag I*
parsley: *caput, peter*
parson: *pers*
parsonage: *pers*
part: *per V*
partake: *per V*
parterre: *per II*
parthenogenesis: *gn*
Parthenon: *gn*
parthenophobia: *bhegu*
partial: *per V*
participate: *kap, per V*
particle: *per V*
particular: *dheigh N 9, per V*
partition: *per V*
partner: *per V*
partridge: *perd*
parturient: *per VI b*
parturition: *per VI b*
party: *per V*
parure: *per V*
parvenu: *gua*
parvipotent: *pou 1*
parvis: *dheigh, pou 1*
parvitude: *pou 1*
parvoline: *pou 1*
pas: *pet II*
pascual: *pa*
pasha: *ksei, pa, poti*
pashalik: *pa*
pashm: *pek II*
pasigraphy: *keu II*
Paspalum: *pel I*
pasquil: *pa*
pasquinade: *pa*
Pasquino: *pa*
pass: *pet II*
passage: *pet II*
passenger: *keu I, pet II*
passer-by: *pet II*
passim: pet II
passion: *paen*
passive: *paen*
passport: *pet II*
pasta: *kuet, pa*
paste: *kuet, pa*
pastel: *kuet, pa*
pastern: *pa*
Pasteurella: *pa*
pasteurize: *pa*
pasticcio: *pa*
pastiche: *kuet, pa*
pastille: *pa*
pastina: *kuet*
pastor: *pa*
pastry: *kuet, pa*
pasture: *pa*
pasty: *kuet, pa*
paté: *kuet, pa*
patella: *pet II*
paten: *pet II*
patent: *pet II*
pater: *peter*
patera: *pet II*
paternal: *peter*
path: *pent*
pathetic: *guadh*
pathogen: *guadh*
pathology: *guadh*
pathos: *guadh, kuenth*
pathway: *petn*
patience: *paen*
patient: *paen*
patina: *pet II*
patio: *pet II*
patisserie: *kuet, pa*
patriarch: *peter*
patrician: *peter*
patriclinous: *klei*
patrimony: *peter*
patriot: *peter*

Pelops: *oku*
peloria: *kuer*
pelota: *pel IV, pilo*
pelt: *pel IV, pel VI, pilo*
pelta: *pel VI*
Peltandra: *pel VI*
peltast: *pel VI*
peltate: *pel VI*
Peltigera: *pel VI*
pelto: *peg*
peltry: *pel VI*
pelvic: *pel III*
pelviferous: *pel III*
pelvimyon: *pel III*
pelvis: *pel III*
pelycography: *pel III*
pelycosaurian: *pel III*
pen: *bend, pet I*
penal: *kuei I*
penalty: *kuei I*
penance: *paen*
Penates: *las*
penchant: *pend, spend II*
pencil: *pes*
pendant: *pend, spend II*
pendent: *pend, spend II*
pending: *pend*
pendulous: *pend, spend II*
pendulum: *pend, spend II*
penetrate: *las*
penguin: *ueid*
penicillin: *pes*
penicillium: *pes*
peninsula: *akua, al II, paen, sna I*
penis: *kal, pes*
penitence: *paen*
penitentiary: *kuei I*
penknife: *pet I*
penmanship: *pet I*
penna: *pet I*
pen name: *onomen*
pennant: *pet I*
pennate: *pet I*
pennon: *pet I*
penny: *pet II*
penology: *kuei I*
pensée: spend II
pensila: *pend, spend II*
pension: *pend, spend II*
pensive: *pend, spend II*
pentad: *penkue*
pentagon: *ghenu, penkue*
pentahedron: *penkue*
pentamerous: *penkue, smer*
pentapla: *plek I*
Pentateuch: *dheugh*
pentateuch: *dheugh*
Pentecost: *dekm, penkue*
Pentheus: *kuei I, men I*
penthouse: *kueit, pend, spend II*
penult: *al II, paen*
penultimate: *akua*
penumbra: *al II, andho, paen*
penury: *paen*
peon: *ped*
people: *da II, popul*
pep: *pippa*
pepo: *peku*
pepper: *pippa*
peppercorn: *pippa*
peppermint: *pippa*
pep pill: *dek*
pepsin: *peku*
peptic: *peku*
peptide: *peku*
peptone: *peku*
peradventure: *per I*
perambulate: *al III, per I*
perbromic acid: *per N 7*
perceive: *kap*
percent: *dekm*
perception: *kap*
perceptive: *dheigh N 24*
perchance: *per I*
percolate: *kagh*
percurrent: *kers I*
percussion: *kuet*
perdition: *do, per VIII*
perdu: *do*
perdurable: *deru, per II*
père: peter
peregrination: *ag, per I*
peregrine: *ag, per I*
perepeteia: *pet I*
perfect: *dhe I, per I*
perfectible: *per I*
perfection: *dhe I, per I*
perfidious: *per VIII*
perfidy: *bheidh*
perforate: *bher II*
perform: *merbh*
perfume: *dheu I*
perfunctory: *bheug III*
perhaps: *kob, per I*

peri: *gn*
pericardium: *kerd*
pericarp: *ker III*
perichondrium: *ghreu*
periclase: *kal*
Pericles: *sue*
pericline: *klei*
pericope: *sek*
peridontal: *denk*
perihelion: *sauel*
peril: *per III, per N 3*
perilous: *per III*
perimeter: *bher I, me IV, per 3*
perimysium: *mus*
perinephral: *engu*
perineurium: *sne*
period: *kel IV, per N 3, sed II, sek IV*
Perioeci: *ueik I*
periorbita: *rebh*
peripatetic: *pent, per I*
peripheral: *per I*
periphery: *bher I*
peripteral: *pet I*
periscope: *ne, sek IV, spek*
perish: *ei I, per N 3*
perissad: *kei II*
perissodactyl: *kei II*
peristalsis: *stel*
peristaltic: *sta*
peristeronic: *pel VII*
peritoneum: *pel VI, ten*
peritonitis: *dheigh N 23*
periwinkle: *uei*
perjury: *ieuos, per VIII*
permanent: *per II*
permeate: *mei II*
permission: *smeit*
permit: *smeit*
permutations: *mei II*
pernicious: *nek*
peronial: *per VII*
peroxide: *per N 7*
perpend: *pend, spend II*
perpendicular: *pend, spend II*
perpetrate: *peter*
perpetual: *pet I*
perpetuate: *pet I*
perplex: *plek I*
perquisite: *kuere*
persecute: *seku I*
Persephone: *pers*
persevere: *uero*
persiflage: *suei I*
persiflate: *suei I*
persifleur: suei I
persist: *sta*
persistence: *per 7*
person: *kuo, pers*
personality: *pers*
perspective: *spek*
perspicacious: *spek*
perspicuous: *spek*
perspire: *speis*
persuade: *suad*
persuasion: *suad*
pert: *suer I, uer V*
pertain: *ten*
pertinacious: *ten*
pertinent: *ten*
pervade: *per 7, uadh*
perverse: *uer II 5*
perversion: *per I, uer II 5*
perversity: *per I*
pervert: *per I, uer II 5*
peseta: *pend, spend II*
peso: *pend, spend II*
pessimist: *op I, pet I*
pester: *pa*
peta-: *me IV*
petal: *pet II*
petalon: *pet II*
petar(d): *perd*
Peter: *caput*
petiole: *ped*
petiolule: *ped*
petit: *peti*
petite: *peti*
petition: *pet I*
petits fours: *guher*
petomane: *perd*
petrify: *caput, dhe I, peter*
petro: *peter*
petrochemistry: *caput*
petrodollar: *caput*
petroglyph: *caput, gleubh*
petrolatum: *caput*
petroleum: *caput, elaia, peter*
petrology: *caput, peter*
petronel: *peg*
petrosal: *caput*
petticoat: *peti*
pettifogger: *peti*
pettitoes: *peti*
petty: *peti*

petulant: *pet I*
pew: *ped*
Peziza: *ped*
Phaeton: *or*
phagocyte: *bhag, skeu*
phalangeal: *bhelk*
phalanx: *bhelk*
phalarope: *ped*
phallus: *beu*
phanerogram: *bha II*
phantasm: *bha II*
phantasmagoria: *bha II*
phantom: *bha II*
pharmaceutical: *tekhus*
pharmacopoeia: *kuei II, tekhus*
pharmacy: *tekhus*
pharynx: *bher II*
Ph.D.: *hum*
Phemius: *bha I*
phenomenon: *bha II*
Philadelphia: *bhili, guelbh*
philander: *nert*
philanderer: *nert*
philanthropos: *nert*
philanthropy: *nert*
philately: *ker I, steu, tol*
philharmonic: *bhili*
philhellene: *mei I*
Philip: *bhili, eku*
philodendron: *deru*
philosopher: *bhili*
philosophy: *bhili*
-philous: *bhili*
philter: *bhili*
philtrum: *bhili*
Phlegethon: *bhel I, kau II*
phlegm: *bhel I, ugu*
phlegmatic: *bhel I, ugu*
phlegmon: *bhel I*
phlobaphene: *guebh*
phlogiston: *bhel I*
phlogopite: *bhel I, oku*
phlox: *bhel I*
phobia: *bhegu, men I*
Phobos: *mavors*
phoenix: *guhen*
-phone: *bha I*
phoneme: *bha I*
phonetic: *bha I*
phonograph: *gerbh*
phonography: *dheigh N 16*
phony: *esu*
-phore: *bher I*
phosphorescent: *bha II, el 15*
phosphorous: *bha II, el 15*
phot: *bha II*
photic: *bha II*
Photoblepharon: *leuk*
photocopy: *op I*
photogenic: *bha II*
photograph: *bha II*
photography: *el 15*
photostat: *bha II*
phototropism: *trep*
photuris: *el 15*
phreatic: *bhereu*
phrenic: *guhren*
phrenitis: *guhren*
phrenology: *guhren, leg I*
phronesis: *guhren*
Phronima: *guhren*
phthaline: *guhdher*
phthinode: *guhdhei*
phthinoplasm: *guhdhei*
phthiriatic: *guhdher*
phthirophagous: *guhdher*
phthisic: *guhdhei*
phthisicky: *guhdhei*
phthisiology: *guhdhei*
phthisis: *guhdhei*
phthisozoics: *guhdhei*
phylacterian: *phulax*
phylactery: *phulax*
phylactic: *phulax*
phylactrocarp: *phulax*
phylaxis: *phulax*
phylloclade: *kal*
phyllodium: *beu*
phyllophagous: *bhag*
Phylloxera: *ksero*
phylogeny: *bheu, gen, gn*
phylum: *bheu*
physics: *bheu*
physiognomy: *gn*
physiology: *bheu*
physique: *bheu*
-phyte: *bheu*
pi: *bher I*
piacular: *pius*
pia mater: *ma II*
piano: *pela, bheregh*
pianoforte: *bheregh, pela*
piazza: *pela*
pibroch: *pip*

picaro: *speik*
piccolo: *peti*
pick: *speik*
pickaninny: *peti*
pickax: *speik*
picket: *speik*
pico-: *me IV*
picrate: *peik*
picric: *peik*
picrite: *peik*
picrolite: *peik*
picrotoxin: *peik*
Pict: *peik*
pict: *peik*
pictograph: *peik*
pictorial: *peik*
picture: *peik*
picturesque: *peik*
picturing: *peik*
piddle: *pent*
pie: *ped, speik*
piebald: *speik*
piecemeal: *me IV*
pied: *speik*
Piedmont: *ped*
piedmontite: *men II*
piepoudre: *ped*
pierce: *steu*
pierrot: *caput*
Pietà: *pius*
pietism: *pius*
piety: *pius*
piezoelectricity: *sed I*
piezometer: *sed I*
pigeon: *pip*
pigment: *peik*
pigsty: *dheu II*
pike: *speik*
pilar: *pilo*
pilch: *pel VI*
pile: *pilo*
piles: *pilo*
pileum: *pilo*
pileus: *pilo*
pilgarlic: *pilo*
pilgrim: *ag, per I*
pill: *pilo*
pillage: *pilo*
piller: *pilo*
pillion: *pel VI*
pilose: *pilo*
pilot: *ped*
pilpate: *pilo*
pilule: *pilo*
pim(i)ento: *peik*
pimpernel: *pippa*
pine: *kuei I*
pinnacle: *pet I*
pinnate: *pet I*
pinnule: *pet I*
pinochle: *oku*
pint: *peik*
pinta: *peik*
pintado: *peik*
pintle: *bend*
pinto: *peik*
pinxit: peik
pioneer: *ped*
pious: *dheigh N 2, pius*
pipe: *pip*
pipi: *keup*
pipistrel: *uesper*
Pippa: *pippa*
piquant: *dheigh N 8, speik*
pique: *speik*
piqué: *speik*
piquet: *speik*
piracy: *per III*
pirate: *per III*
pirog: *poi*
piscary: *peisk*
piscatology: *peisk*
Piscator: *peisk*
piscatorial: *peisk*
Pisces: *guei, peisk*
pisciculture: *ker I, peisk*
piscina: *peisk*
piscine: *peisk*
piscinity: *peisk*
piscivorous: *bhag, dheigh N 2 f, peisk*
pismire: *morui, piss*
piss: *piss*
pissabed: *kerd, piss*
pissoir: *piss*
pit: *peue*
pitchfork: *bhurig*
piteous: *dheigh N 2 h, pius*
Pithicanthropus: *nert*
pitiful: *dheigh N 2 h, pius*
pitiless: *pius*
Pittsburgh: *bheregh*
pity: *pius*
pivot: *ker I, peug*
pizzle: *bat*

placate: *pela*
place: *pela*
placebo: *pela*
placenta: *pela*
placental: *pela*
placid: *pela*
placket: *burd, per VI f*
placoid: *pela*
plagal: *pela*
plague: *plak*
plaice: *pela*
plaid: *pel VI*
plain: *pela, plak*
plaint: *plak*
plaintiff: *plak*
plaintive: *plak*
plait: *plek I*
plan: *pela*
planar: *pela*
planchet: *pela*
plane: *pela*
planet: *pela, sta*
planetarium: *dheigh N 35*
planetary: *pela*
planetoid: *ueid*
plangent: *plak*
plank: *pela*
plankton: *ie, plak, sna I*
planoconcave: *pela*
planoconvex: *pela*
planometer: *pela*
plant: *pela*
plantain: *pela*
plantar: *dheigh N 9*
plantation: *pela*
planter: *pela*
plantigrade: *ghredh, pela*
plap: *coc*
plasma: *pela*
plasminogen: *pela*
plaster: *pela*
plastic: *pela*
plat: *plek I*
plate: *pela*
plateau: *pela*
platelet: *pela*
platen: *pela*
plateresque: *pela*
platform: *pela*
platinoid: *el 78*
platinum: *el 78, pela*
platitude: *pela*
Plato: *ar I, pela*
platometry: *pela*
Platonic: *pela*
platoon: *pilo*
platyhelminth: *pela, uelu*
platypus: *ped, pela*
platypygous: *pela*
platyrrhine: *pela*
platyscopic: *pela*
platysma: *pela*
plaudits: *plaud*
plausible: *plaud*
play: *plek I*
playa: *pela*
playwright: *verg*
plaza: *pela*
plea: *pela*
pleach: *plek I*
plead: *pela*
pleasant: *pela*
please: *pela*
pleasure: *pela*
pleat: *plek I*
plebe: *pel V*
plebian: *pel V*
plebiscite: *pel V, sek II*
plebs: *pel V*
Plectognathi: *plek I*
plectrum: *plak*
Plegadis: *plak*
pleiad: *nebh*
Pleiades: *morui, nebh, pel VII*
plein-air: *pel V*
Pleiocene: *ken III*
pleiomastia: *pel V*
pleiomorphy: *pel V*
pleiotropism: *pel V*
Pleistocene: *pel V*
pleistoseist: *pel V*
plenary: *pel V*
pleniloquence: *pel V*
plenilune: *pel V*
plenipotential: *poti*
plenipotentiary: *pel V*
plenitude: *pel V*
plenteous: *pel V*
plenty: *pel V*
plenum: *pel V*
pleomorphism: *pel V*
pleonasm: *pel V*
pleonaste: *pel V*
pleonexia: *segh*

pleopod: *pel V*
pleriosaurus: *pel IV*
pleroma: *pel V*
plerome: *pel V*
plessor: *plak*
plethora: *pel V*
plethorical: *pel V*
plethysymograph: *pel V*
Pleuronectidae: *sna I*
plexor: *plak*
plexus: *plek I*
pliable: *plek I*
pliant: *plek I*
plight: *plek I*
Pliocene: *pel V*
pliohippus: *pel V*
ploce: *plek I*
plosion: *plaud*
plot: *pilo*
plover: *pleu*
plowshares: *sek IX*
pluck: *ker III, pilo*
plum: *pag*
plumage: *pleus*
plumate: *pleus*
plumb: *mlub, plumb*
Plumbaginaceae: *mlub*
Plumbago: *mlub*
plumbago: *el 82, plumb*
plumbate: *el 82*
plumbbob: *el 82*
plumber: *el 82, mlub, plumb*
plumbisolvent: *plumb*
plumbless: *plumb*
plumb line: *el 82, mlub, plumb*
plume: *pleus*
plummet: *mlub, plumb*
plumose: *pleus*
plump: *mlub*
plumule: *pleus*
plunge: *mlub, plumb*
pluperfect: *dhe I, pel V*
plural: *pel V*
pluralism: *men III*
plus: *pel V*
plus fours: *seni*
plush: *pilo*
plutarchy: *pel V*
Pluto: *el 94, pleu*
plutocracy: *pel V, pleu*
plutocrat: *pleu*
plutonium: *el 94, pleu*
pluvial: *pleu*
pluvious: *pleu*
Pluvius, Jupiter: *pleu*
ply: *plek I*
plywood: *plek I*
P.M.: *dei*
pneuma: *pneu*
pneumatic: *pneu*
pneumoconiosis: *ken I*
pneumodynamics: *pneu*
pneumonia: *pneu*
poach: *beu*
pocket: *beu*
poco: *pou 5*
pococurante: *cura*
podagra: *ag, ped*
podex: *ped*
podiatry: *eis, ped*
podicate: *ped*
podium: *ped*
Podocarpus: *ped*
podology: *ped*
Podophthalmia: *ped*
podophylein: *ped*
Podophyllum: *ped*
Podura: *ped*
pody cody: *ped*
podzol: *ped*
poem: *kuei II, poieo*
poephagous: *bhag*
poesy: *kuei II, poieo*
poet: *kuei II, poieo*
poetaster: *kuei II, poieo*
poetess: *dheigh N 13*
poetize: *poieo*
poetry: *dheigh N 36, kuei II, poeio, tre*
pogron: *ghrem, nem*
poignant: *peug*
Poikile: *peik*
poikilitic: *peik*
poikilocyte: *peik*
poikilothermic: *peik*
poilu: *pilo*
Poinae: *kuei I*
point: *peug*
point-device: *ueidh*
pointillism: *peug*
poise: *pend, spend II*
poison: *poi*
poitrel: *peg*
Polack: *pela*
Poland: *pela*

Polaris: *ors*
polarity: *ant, ker I*
pole: *ker I, pag*
polecat: *pou 9, pu*
polemarch: *pal*
polemic: *pal*
polenta: *pel I*
police: *pele*
policlinic: *pele*
policy: *deik, pele*
polio: *pel VII*
poliomyelitis: *dheigh N 23, pel VII*
polish: *pel IV, pele*
polite: *pel IV, pele*
politesse: *pele*
politics: *pele*
polity: *pele*
polka: *pela*
poll: *kap*
pollard: *kap*
polled: *kap*
pollen: *pel I*
pollex: *pol*
pollical: *pol*
pollution: *leu II*
Pollux: *morui*
pollywog: *kap*
polonium: *el 84*
polony: *el 84*
poltroon: *pol, pou 9*
polyacanthus: *pel V*
polyandrous: *nert*
polyandry: *guen, nert*
polydelphia: *guelbh*
Polygala: *glact*
Polygalacea: *glact*
polygamy: *geme, guen, nert, pel V*
polygenism: *gn*
polygeny: *gn*
polyglot: *glokh*
polygon: *ghenu*
polygyny: *guen, nert*
polyhedron: *neun*
polyhistor: *ueid*
polylingual: *dinghu*
polymath: *men I*
polymerous: *smer*
Polynesia: *sna I*
polynomial: *nem*
polyonymous: *onomen*
polyp: *ped*
Polypedates: *ped*
polyphagous: *bhag*
Polyphemus: *bha I*
polyphyllous: *beu*
polypnea: *pneu*
polypod: *ped*
polyptych: *bheug II*
polytechnic: *tekhs*
polytheism: *dhes, pel V*
polyunsaturated: *pel V*
polyvalent: *pel V*
polyzoonite: *pel V*
pomegranate: *ger V*
Pomeranian: *mori*
pompadour: *kleu I*
pomposity: *dheigh N 2 d*
pond: *bend*
ponder: *pend, spend II*
ponderous: *pend, spend II*
poniard: *peug*
pons: *pent*
pontifex: *pent*
pontiff: *dhe I, pent*
pontificate: *dhe I, pent*
pontlevis: *leguh*
pontonier: *pent*
pontoon: *pent*
pony: *pou 9*
pood: *pend*
poodle: *pent*
poor: *pou 7*
pop: *pa*
pope: *pa*
popery: *pa*
poppet: *pa*
poppycock: *caca, pa*
popsy-wopsy: *pa*
populace: *da II*
popular: *popul*
population: *da II, popul*
populous: *popul*
porcelain: *porko I*
porch: *per II*
porcine: *porko I*
porcupine: *porko I, sphei II*
pore: *per I*
pork: *mel I, porko I*
pornocracy: *kar*
pornography: *per III*
porous: *per I*
porphin: *porpur*
Porphyra: *porpur*
porphyrate: *porpur*

porphyre: *porpur*
Porphyrian: *porpur*
porphyrine: *porpur*
porphyrio: *porpur*
porphyrite: *porpur*
porphyrogenite: *porpur*
porphyroid: *porpur*
porphyry: *porpur*
porpoise: *peisk, porko I*
porridge: *pel I*
port: *per II, per VI c*
portable: *per II*
portage: *per II*
portal: *per II*
portamento: *men I*
portcullis: *kagh, per II*
porte-monnaie: men I
portend: *ten*
portent: *ten*
porter: *per II*
portfolio: *beu, per II*
portico: *per II*
portière: *per II*
portion: *per V*
portulaca: *per II*
pose: *ap*
Poseidon: *poti*
poser: *ap*
position: *ap*
positive: *ap*
posology: *kuo*
posse: *es, poti*
possession: *poti, sed I*
possessor: *dheigh N 13*
possible: *es, poti*
possibly: *poti*
post: *ap, sta*
post-: *ap*
post-bellum: *duo*
postbox: *sta*
postdate: *do*
posterior: *ap*
posthaste: *sta*
posthumous: *ghdhem*
postiche: *ap*
postillion: *ap*
postiminy: *em*
postlude: *leid II*
postmeridian: *dei*
post-mortem: *mer II*
post office: *sta*
post partum: *per VI b*
postpone: *ap*
postprandial: *ed*
postscript: *ker III, sek VI*
postulate: *perk*
posture: *ap*
posy: *kuei II*
potable: *poi*
potash: *el 19*
potassium: *el 19*
potation: *poi*
potato: *kap, poi*
potatory: *poi*
potecary: *pela*
potent: *poti*
potentate: *dheigh N 10, poti*
potential: *poti*
potion: *poi*
potpourri: *pu*
pouch: *beu*
poulard: *plou, pou 9*
poult: *plou, pou 9*
poulterer: *plou, pou 9*
poultice: *pel I*
poultry: *plou, pou 9*
pounce: *peug*
pound: *bend, lithra, pend, spend II*
pourparler: guel II
pousse-café: *pel IV*
poussette: *pel IV*
pout: *beu*
poverty: *pou 7*
power: *poti*
powerful: *poti*
pozzolano: *peue*
practical: *per III*
practice: *per III*
practitioner: *per III*
praecognitum: *per 4*
pr(a)edial: *uad*
praenomen: *onomen*
praise: *per III*
Prajapati: *per 1, poti*
Prakrit: *kuer, per 1, per N 1*
Prakriti: *per 1*
prakriti: *kuer*
Pralaya: *per 1*
pralaya: *lei I*
praline: *per N 1*
pram: *per I*
prana: *per 1*
prandial: *ed*
prase: *per N 1*

praseodymium: *el 59*
pray: *perk*
prayers: *perk*
preach: *deik, per IV*
preacher: *dheigh N 13*
preamble: *al III, ei I, per IV*
prebend: *ghebh*
precarious: *perk*
precaution: *keu I*
precede: *sed II*
precedent: *sed II*
precentor: *kan*
precept: *kap*
precession: *sed II*
preciloblast: *peik*
precilonymic: *peik*
precilopod: *peik*
precinct: *kenk I, per N 6*
precious: *per III*
precipice: *caput, dheigh N 18, kap*
precipitate: *caput*
précis: *sek II*
precise: *sek II*
preclude: *kleu III*
precocious: *dheigh N 2 d, peku*
precocity: *em*
precognition: *per N 6*
precumbent: *keu II*
precursor: *kers I*
predecessor: *sed II*
predestination: *per 6, per IV*
predicate: *deik, per IV*
predict: *deik, per 6, per IV*
predominate: *dem*
preempt: *em*
preen: *enguo*
preface: *bha I, per VI a*
prefatory: *bha I*
prefect: *dhe I*
prefer: *bher I*
prefix: *dheigh*
pregnancy: *gn*
pregnant: *gn, per VII, pres*
prejudice: *ieuos*
prelate: *tol*
preliminary: *em, per IV*
prelude: *leid II*
premature: *per IV*
premeditated: *med, per VI a*
premier: *per VI a, per VI f*
première: per VI a
premise: *smeit*
premiss: *smeit*
premium: *em, per VI f*
premonition: *men I*
premorse: *mer II*
premunition: *mei III*
prepare: *per V*
preparedness: *per V*
prepense: *pend, spend II*
preponderance: *dheigh N 8*
preponderant: *pend*
preponderate: *spend II*
preposition: *ap*
preposterous: *ap, per III*
prepotent: *poti*
prerogative: *reg I*
presage: *sag*
presbyopia: *gua, per VI d*
presbyter: *gua*
Presbyterian: *per VI d*
prescient: *sek II*
prescind: *sek II*
prescribe: *ker III, per VI a, sek VI*
prescription: *ker III, per IV, sek VI*
present: *per IV*
presentiment: *sent*
presently: *per IV*
preserve: *ser II, suer I*
pre-Shakespearean: *per N 6*
preside: *sed I*
president: *sed I*
presidential: *dheigh N 5*
press: *per VII, pres*
pressure: *per VII, pres*
Prester John: *per VI d*
prestige: *deik, streig*
prestigious: *deik*
prestidigitator: *deik*
presume: *em*
presumption: *em*
pretend: *per 5, per N 6, ten*
pretense: *ten*
preterea: *per N 5*
preterit: *ei I, per 5*
pretermit: *smeit*
preternatural: *per VI a, per N 5*
preternuptial: *per N 5*
preterpluperfect: *per VI a*
pretext: *per IV, tekhs*
pretone: *ten*
pretzel: *braghu*
prevail: *ual*
prevalent: *ual*

prevaricate: *ua I*
prevent: *gua, per V*
preview: *ueid*
previous: *uegh*
prevision: *ueid*
price: *per III*
prick: *peug, prika, speik*
pricket: *prika*
prickle: *prika*
prickly: *prika*
pride: *per V*
pridian: *dei*
prie-dieu: *dei, perk*
priest: *per VI d*
priestling: *sap*
prig: *prika*
primacy: *per VI f*
prima facie: *dhe I, per VI a*
primapara: *per VI b*
primary: *per VI c*
primate: *dheigh N 10, per VI f*
primavera: *per VI a, uesr*
primaveral: *uesr*
prime: *per V, per VI a, per VI e*
prime minister: *per VI f*
primer: *per VI c*
prime time: *per VI f*
primeval: *aiu, per VI a*
primigenial: *gn*
primitive: *per VI c*
primo: *per VI a*
primogenital: *gn*
primogenitor: *gn*
primogeniture: *gn, per VI b*
primordial: *ar I, per VI a*
primrose: *lei I, per VI a*
primrose path: *lei I*
Primula: *per VI a*
Primulaceae: *per VI a*
primum mobile: per VI f
primus: *per VI a*
prince: *kap, per VI f*
princeling: *sap*
Prince of Darkness: *per VI f*
princess: *dheigh N 13, per VI f*
principal: *kap, per VI f*
principality: *kap, per VI f*
principle: *kap*
print: *per VII, pres*
prior: *per IV, per VI a, per VI f*
priority: *per VI a*
pristine: *per VI c*
prithee: *perk*
privacy: *per VI g*
private: *per VI g*
privation: *per VI g*
privilege: *leg, per VI g*
privity: *per VI g*
privy: *per VI g*
prize: *per III*
pro: *per V*
pro-: *per N 4*
proaeresis: *per N 4*
proalcoholism: *per N 4*
probable: *bheu, per VI e*
probate: *per VI e*
probe: *bheu, per VI e*
probity: *bheu, per VI e*
problem: *guel II*
procacity: *perk*
procaine: *per 4*
procaleusmatic: *kel VII*
procedure: *sed II*
proceed: *sed II*
procerebrum: *per N 4*
procerity: *per VI a*
process: *sed II*
procession: *sed II*
prochronism: *nebh*
proclaim: *kel II*
proclitic: *klei*
proclivity: *klei*
proconsular: *dheigh N 9*
procrastinate: *per V*
procreate: *ker VI*
Procrustean: *per V*
proctal: *per V*
proctalgia: *prokto*
proctectomy: *prokto*
proctology: *per V, prokto*
proctor: *per V, prokto*
proctoscope: *prokto*
proctuchus: *prokto*
procuration: *prokto*
procuratory: *prokto*
procure: *prokto*
procuress: *prokto*
Procyon: *kuon, per IV*
prodigal: *ag, eg III, per I*
prodigious: *eg III*
prodigy: *ag, eg III*
produce: *deuk*
production: *deuk*
proethnic: *per N 4*

profane: *dhes*
profanity: *dhes*
profess: *bha I*
professor: *bha I, dheigh N 13*
proffer: *bher I*
proficient: *dhe I*
profile: *guhisl, per 4*
profit: *dhe I*
pro forma: merbh
profound: *bhudh*
profusion: *gheu*
progenitor: *gn*
progeny: *gn*
proglottid: *glokh*
prognathous: *ghenu*
prognosis: *gn*
program: *gerbh*
progress: *ghredh, per 4*
project: *ie*
projection: *ie*
prolapse: *leb*
prolate: *tol*
prolepsis: *labh, slagu*
proletariat: *al I*
proliferate: *al I*
prolific: *al I*
prologue: *leg I*
prolong: *del III*
prolusion: *leid II*
prolusite: *lou*
Prometheus: *el 61, keu II*
promethium: *el 61*
prominent: *men II*
promiscuous: *meik*
promise: *smeit*
promontory: *men II*
promote: *meu II*
prompt: *em*
prompter: *em*
promulgate: *melg*
prone: *per IV, upo I*
pro-Nixon: *per N 4*
pronoun: *onomen*
pronounce: *neu I*
pronunciamento: *neu I*
proof: *bheu, per VI e*
prop: *pag*
propaganda: *pag*
propagate: *pag*
propel: *pel IV*
propend: *spend II*
propensity: *pend*
proper: *per V, per VI g*
property: *per VI g*
prophet: *bha I*
prophylactic: *phulax*
propinquity: *per VII*
propitious: *pet I*
propolis: *pele*
proponent: *ap*
proportion: *per V*
propose: *ap*
propound: *spend II*
proprietor: *per VI g*
proptosis: *pet I*
propulsion: *pel IV*
propylaeum: *suer I*
propylon: *suer I*
prorogation: *reg I*
prorogue: *reg I*
prosaic: *uer II 5*
proscribe: *ker III, sek VI*
prose: *per IV, uer II 5*
prosecute: *seku I*
prosenchyma: *gheu*
prosodemic: *per VI a*
prosody: *aud, per VI a, ued, uer II*
prosopopeia: *kuei II, per VI a*
prospect: *spek*
prospectus: *spek*
prosper: *per V, sphei I*
prosperity: *per V, sphei I*
prosperous: *per V*
prostate: *sta*
prosthesis: *dhe I*
prosthetics: *dhe I*
prosthodontics: *den*
prostitute: *sta*
prostrate: *ster I*
prostration: *ster I*
protactinium: *el 91*
protagonist: *ag, per V*
protasis: *ten*
protean: *dheigh N 7*
protection: *steg*
protein: *per VI a*
Proterozoic: *tre*
protest: *tre*
Protestant: *tre*
protestation: *tre*
Proteus: *mei II, per VI a*
prothalamion: *per VI a*
prothallus: *dhel I*
prothesis: *dhe I*

prothonotary: *gn, leip II, per VI f*
protocol: *kollei, per VI a*
protogenic: *ud*
protolanguage: *per VI a*
proton: *el, per VI a*
protonema: *sne*
protopathic: *guadh*
protoplasm: *dheigh N 31, pela, per VI a*
protoplast: *pela*
prototype: *per VI a*
protoxide: *per N 7*
protract: *tragh*
protrude: *treud*
protuberance: *teue 9*
proud: *per V*
prove: *bheu, per VI e*
provender: *ghebh*
proverb: *uer VI*
provide: *ueid*
providence: *ueid*
provision: *ueid*
proviso: *ueid*
provocative: *dheigh N 24*
provoke: *ueks*
provost: *ap*
prow: *per VI a*
prowess: *per V*
proximate: *dheigh N 10, per V, per VII*
proximity: *per V*
proxy: *per N 4, prokto*
prude: *per V*
prudence: *ueid*
prudent: *ueid*
prudery: *per V*
prudish: *per V*
pruinose: *preus*
prune: *pag, reth*
pruriency: *preus*
prurient: *preus*
prurigo: *preus*
pruritus: *preus*
P.S.: *sek VI*
psalm: *pal*
psalmody: *aud, pal, ued*
Psalter: *pal*
psalterium: *pal*
psammite: *bhes I*
Pselaphidae: *pal*
psephism: *bhes I*
psephite: *bhes I*
pseudomixis: *meik*
pseudonym: *es, onomen*
pseudopod: *ped*
pseudopodium: *dheigh N 35*
psilanthropy: *bhili*
psilology: *bhili*
psilomelane: *bhes I, mel III*
psilosis: *bhes I*
psilosopher: *bhili*
psilothron: *bhes I*
psora: *bhes I*
psoriasis: *bhes I*
psyche: *bhes*
psychedelic: *dei*
psychiatry: *dheigh N 36*
psychic: *bhes*
psychoanalysis: *bhes, suep I*
psychology: *bhes, leg I*
psychomachy: *magh*
psychopath: *bhes*
psychosomatic: *teue 3*
psychotic: *bhes*
psylla: *plou*
psyllid: *plou*
Psyllidae: *plou*
ptarmic: *pster*
Ptarmica: *pster, strep*
ptarmica: *strep*
ptenoglossate: *pet I*
ptenopleural: *pet I*
pteridology: *pet I*
pterigium: *pet I*
pterigoid: *pet I*
Pteris: *pet I*
pterodactyl: *do, pet I*
pterograph: *pet I*
pteroma: *pet I*
pterotheca: *pet I*
Pterygote: *pet I*
Ptolemaic: *pal*
Ptolemy: *pal*
Ptolemy II: *nebh*
ptomaine: *pet I*
ptosis: *pet I*
ptyalin: *sphieu*
ptyalism: *sphieu*
puberty: *pou 2*
puberulent: *pou 2*
pubes: *pou 2*
pubescent: *pou 2*
pubic: *pou*
public: *da II, popul*
publican: *popul*
publication: *popul*

publicist: *popul*
publicity: *da II, popul*
publish: *popul*
puce: *plou*
pucelle: *plou, pou 4*
Pucelle, La: *plou*
puceron: *plou*
pucker: *beu*
puddle: *pent*
pudency: *peu I*
pudendum: *peu I*
pudic: *peu I*
pueblo: *da II, popul*
puerile: *pou*
puerperal: *per VI b, pou 2*
puff: *buff*
puffin: *buff*
puffy: *buff*
pug: *ped*
pugilist: *peug*
pugnacious: *dheigh N 2 b, peug*
puissant: *poti*
puke: *sphieu*
pukka: *peku*
Pulex: *plou*
pullet: *legh, pou 9*
pulley: *ker I*
Pulmonaria: *pleu*
pulmonary: *pleu*
Pulmonata: *pleu*
pulsate: *pel IV*
pulse: *pel I, pel IV*
pulverize: *pel I*
pumpkin: *peku*
pun: *peug*
punaise: *pu*
Punch: *penkue, pou 9*
punch: *penkue, peug, ten*
puncheon: *peug*
punctilious: *peug*
punctual: *peug*
puncture: *peug*
pundigrion: *peug*
pungent: *peug*
punish: *kuei I*
punitive: *kuei I*
Punjab: *penkue*
punk: *spong*
punkah: *peg*
punner: *peug*
punnet: *peug*
punnology: *peug*
punster: *peug*
punt: *pent*
puny: *gn*
pup: *pa*
pupa: *pa, pou 4*
pupil: *pa, pou 4*
pupillary: *pa*
puppet: *pa, pou 4*
puppy: *pa*
purblind: *peu II*
purchase: *kap, per III*
pure: *peu II*
purée: *peu II*
purfle: *guhisl*
purgative: *peu II*
purgatory: *peu II*
purge: *ag, peu II*
purify: *peu II*
Puritan: *peu II*
purlieu: *al III, ei I*
purple: *porpur*
purport: *per II*
purpure: *porpur*
purpureal: *porpur*
purpurine: *porpur*
purr: *ane, jing*
purse: *burs*
pursuant: *seku I*
pursue: *seku I*
pursuit: *seku I*
pursuivant: *seku I*
pursy: *pel IV*
purulent: *pu*
pus: *pu*
push: *pel IV*
pushmobile: *meu II*
pusillanimous: *ane*
pussy: *ane*
pustule: *pu*
putamen: *peue*
putanism: *pu*
putative: *peue*
puteal: *peue*
Puteoli: *peue*
putid: *pu*
putidity: *pu*
putois: *pu*
Putorious: *pu*
putrefaction: *pu*
putrefy: *pu*
putrescent: *pu*
putrescine: *pu*
putrid: *pu*
putti: *pou 3*

puzzle: *ap*
puzzlement: *ap*
pyaemia: *pu*
pyeu: *peu I*
pygal: *cal*
pygidium: *cal*
pygmean: *peug*
pygmy: *peug*
pyknic: *bheu*
pylon: *suer I*
pylorus: *kel IV, suer I*
pyoid: *pu*
pyoneumothorax: *pu*
pyorrhea: *pu, sreu*
pyoxanthin: *pu*
pyralic: *peuor*
pyre: *peuor*
pyretic: *peuor*
pyrexia: *peuor*
pyrites: *peuor*
pyrogenous: *gn*
pyroligneous: *leg I*
pyrolusite: *lou*
pyrolysis: *lou*
pyromancy: *peuor*
pryomania: *peuor*
pyrope: *oku*
pyrotechnics: *peuor*
pyroxene: *xenos*
pyruvic acid: *oina*
Pythium: *pu*
pythogenesis: *gn*
pyuria: *nebh*

Q

QSO: *kuo*
qua: *kuo*
quack: *guebh, selp*
quacksalver: *guebh*
quad: *kuetuer*
quadrangle: *kuetuer*
quadrant: *kuetuer*
quadrantid: *kuetuer*
quadratic: *kuetuer*
quadrilateral: *kuetuer*
quadrille: *kuetuer*
quadrillion: *kuetuer*
quadripara: *kuetuer*
quadriplegia: *kuetuer*
quadrivalent: *kuetuer*
quadrivium: *kuetuer, uegh*
quadruped: *kuetuer, ped*
quadruple: *plek I, plex*
quadruplets: *kuetuer*
quaestor: *kuere*
quagmire: *guebh, meu I*
quaich: *keu II*
quaint: *gn*
Quaker: *guebh*
Quaker gun: *guebh*
qualify: *kuo*
quality: *kuo*
qualm: *guel I*
quanta: *kuo*
quantity: *kuo*
quantum: *kuo*
quaquaversal: *uer II 5*
quar: *kuetuer*
quarantine: *kuetuer*
quarrel: *kues, kuetuer*
quarry: *kerd, kuetuer, sek IX*
quart: *kuetuer*
quartan: *kuetuer*
quarter: *kuetuer*
quartet: *kuetuer*
quartz: *tuer II*
quasar: *kuo*
quash: *kuet*
quasi: *sos*
quasi-: *kuo*
quatrain: *kuetuer*
quay: *kagh*
quean: *guen*
quebracho: *ker IV, sek IV*
queen: *guen*
Queen Anne's fan: *per I*
Queen Anne's lace: *per I*
Queensberry: *bhel I*
queer: *tereq*
quell: *guel I*
Quentin: *penkue*
querimonious: *kues*
quern: *guer*
querulous: *kues*
query: *kuere*
quest: *kuere*
question: *kuere*
queue: *kau III*
quibble: *kuo*
quick: *el 80, guei, onogh, onomen*
quicklime: *el 20, onogh*
Quicklyism: *kuon, melo*
quicksand: *onogh*

quicksilver: *el 16, el 80, guei, onogh*
quid: *gue, keup, kuo*
quiddity: *kuo*
quiddle: *kuo*
quidnunc: *kuo*
quid pro quo: *per 4*
quiescent: *kuei III*
quiet: *kuei III*
quietus: *kuei III*
quillet: *kuo*
quinate: *penkue*
quincunx: *oino, penkue*
quinquagesima: *penkue*
quinquecostate: *penkue*
quinquefoliate: *penkue*
quinquennial: *penkue*
quinsy: *angh, kuon*
quinsyberry: *bhel I, kuon*
quintal: *penkue*
quintessence: *el, es, penkue*
quintuplets: *plek I*
quip: *kuo*
quire: *kuetuer*
Quirimus: *viro*
Quirinal: *ker IV, viro*
Quirinus: *ker IV*
Quirites: *ker IV, viro*
quitch: *guei*
quite: *kuei III*
quittance: *kuei III*
quittor: *peku*
quiver: *guebh*
qui vive: *guei*
quixotic: *dlku*
quodlibet: *kuo*
quorum: *ag, kuo*
quota: *guet, kuo*
quotation: *kuo*
quote: *kuo*
quoth: *guet*
quotidian: *dei, kuo*
quotient: *kuo*
Quo vadis?: uadh

R

rabble: *baba*
rabid: *labh*
rabies: *labh*
race: *ergh, rad I, uerad*
raceme: *pag*
racialism: *dheigh N 21*
rack: *reg I, ureg*
raddle: *reidh*
radiant: *rad II*
radiation: *rad II*
radiator: *rad III*
radical: *rad II*
radicle: *uerad*
radio: *rad II*
radioactive: *rad II*
radiobiology: *rad II*
radiosonde: *suem*
radiotherapy: *rad II*
radish: *uerad*
radium: *el 84, el 88*
radius: *kel VI, rad II*
radix: *uerad*
radon: *el 86, nei*
radula: *rad I*
raft: *rep III*
rafter: *rep III*
raga: *reg II*
rage: *labh*
raid: *reidh*
rail: *rad I, reg I*
railroad: *reg I*
rain: *reg III*
rainbow: *bheug II, reg III*
raise: *ergh*
raisin: *pag*
raj: *reg I*
rajah: *reg I*
rajput: *pou*
rake: *reg I*
rakehell: *reg I*
rallentando: *lento*
rally: *leig II*
Ralph: *uel III, ulkuo*
Rama: *au IV, me III*
ramage: *uerad*
Ramayana: *au IV, ei I, me III*
ramble: *nem*
rambunctious: *rudh*
ramentaceous: *rad I*
ramentum: *rad I*
ramification: *uerad*
ramiform: *uerad*
ramify: *uerad*
ramose: *uerad*
ramp: *ker I*
rampart: *per V*

rampion: *rap, uerad*
Rampur: *pele*
ramulose: *uerad*
ramus: *uerad*
ranch: *ker I*
Randal: *uel III, ulkuo*
Randolph: *ulkuo*
randy: *ulkuo*
ranee: *reg I*
range: *ker I*
ranivorous: *bhag*
rank: *ker I, reg I*
rankle: *derk*
ransack: *sag*
ransom: *em*
rap: *labh*
rapacious: *labh, rep II*
rapacity: *labh*
rape: *labh, rap, rep II*
Raphael: *dekm*
Raphiolepis: *uer II 1*
rapid: *labh*
rapidity: *labh*
rapine: *labh*
rapport: *per II*
rapprochement: *per VII*
rapscallion: *rad I*
rapt: *labh, rep II*
raptatorial: *rep II*
Raptores: *labh, rad I, rep II*
raptorial: *labh, rep II*
rapture: *labh*
rare: *er, kere*
rarity: *er*
rascal: *rad I*
rase: *rad I*
rash: *kret, rad I*
Rasores: *rad I*
rasorial: *rad I*
raspberry: *bhel I, perd*
rasure: *rad I*
rat: *ane*
rate: *ar I*
rathe: *kret*
rather: *kret*
ratify: *ar I, dheigh N 15*
ratio: *ar I*
ratiocination: *ken II*
Ratskeller: *uel III*
raucous: *reu*
rave: *labh*
raven: *ker IV*
ravenous: *labh*
ravin: *labh, rep II*
ravine: *labh*
ravioli: *rap*
ravish: *labh, rep II*
ravishing: *labh*
raw: *kreu*
ray: *rad II*
Raymond: *man*
rayon: *rad II*
raze: *rad I*
razee: *rad I*
razor: *rad I*
razorback: *rad I*
razorbill: *rad I*
razor clam: *rad I*
razz: *bhel I, perd*
re: *re, rei II*
re-: *re*
reabsorb: *srebh*
reach: *reig II*
reaction: *ag*
read: *ar I*
readjust: *re*
ready: *reidh*
real: *leg I, reg I, rei II*
realism: *rei II*
reality: *rei II*
realize: *rei II*
really: *rei II*
realm: *reg I*
ream: *reuos*
reap: *rei I*
reappear: *pare*
rear: *ergh, re*
rear guard: *suer I, uer IV*
rearward: *uer IV*
reason: *ar I*
reasonable: *ar I*
reave: *reup*
rebarbative: *bhar*
rebate: *bat, dheigh*
rebel: *dau*
rebellion: *dau, duo*
rebuff: *buff*
rebus: *rei II*
rebut: *bhaut*
recado: kap
recalcitrant: *dra*
recalescence: *kel I*
recant: *kan*
recede: *sed II*

receipt: *kap*
receive: *kap*
recension: *kens*
recent: *ken III*
receptacle: *kap*
reception: *kap*
recess: *sed II*
recession: *sed II*
recidivist: *kad I*
recipe: *kap*
reciprocal: *per I*
reciprocate: *kap*
reciprocity: *dheigh N 2 d*
recitation: *kei I*
reck: *reg I*
reckless: *dheigh N 26, reg I*
reckon: *reg I*
reclaim: *kel II*
reclamation: *kel II*
recline: *klei*
recluse: *kleu III*
recognizant: *gn*
recognize: *gn*
recommend: *man*
recompense: *pend*
recondite: *dhe I*
reconnaissance: *gn*
record: *kerd*
recoup: *kal*
recourse: *kers I*
recover: *kap*
recreation: *dheigh N 19, ker VI*
re-creation: *ker VI*
recrement: *sek VI*
recrimination: *ker IV, sek VI*
recruit: *ker VI*
rectangle: *reg I*
rectify: *reg I*
rectilinear: *lino*
rectitude: *reg I*
recto: *reg I*
rector: *reg I*
rectory: *reg I*
rectum: *kel IV, reg I*
recumbent: *keu II*
recuperate: *kap*
recur: *kers I*
recurrent: *dheigh N 8, kers I*
recusant: *kau III*
red: *kel VI, reudh*
redactor: *ag*
red-blooded: *kel VI*
redcap: *kel VI*
rede: *ar I*
redeem: *em, re*
redeliver: *re*
redemption: *em*
red-handed: *kel VI*
red herring: *kel VI*
redingote: *kel VI*
red-letter: *kel VI*
redolent: *od*
redoubt: *deuk*
redrumped: *re*
reduction: *deuk*
reduplicate: *duo, gn*
reed: *kreut*
reef: *rebh*
reek: *reug*
refectory: *dhe I*
refer: *bher I*
refine: *fin*
reflect: *plek II*
reflection: *plek II*
reflex: *plek II*
refold: *plek I*
reforestation: *dhur*
reform: *merbh*
reformation: *dheigh N 19*
reformer: *merbh*
refractory: *bhreg, dheigh N 35*
refrain: *dhar, ghren*
refreshed: *dheigh N 13*
refrigeration: *srig*
refrigerator: *reig II*
refuge: *bheug I*
refugee: *bheug I*
refund: *gheu*
refuse: *gheu*
refutation: *bhaut, gheu*
refute: *bhaut, gheu*
regain: *re, uen*
regal: *leg I, reg I*
regale: *reg I*
regalia: *reg I*
regard: *re, suer I*
regatta: *rei I*
regeneration: *gn*
regent: *reg I*
regicide: *reg I, skhai*
régie: reg I
regime: *reg I*
regiment: *reg I*
regina: *guen, reg I*

Reginald: *reg I, ual*
region: *reg I*
register: *ger VI, ges*
registrar: *dheigh N 13*
registration: *ges*
regle: *reg I*
reglet: *reg I*
regnant: *reg I*
regolith: *reg II*
regress: *ghredh*
regulate: *reg I*
Reich: *reg I*
Reichstag: *reg I*
reify: *rei II*
reign: *reg I*
Reil's island: *akua*
reimburse: *burs*
reincarnation: *sek IX*
reindeer: *dheu I, ker II*
reinforce: *bheregh*
rein(s): *ten*
reinvest: *ues II*
reis: *reg I*
reiteration: *ei I*
reject: *ie*
rejoice: *jing*
rejoin: *ieug*
rejoinder: *ieug*
relapse: *leb*
relate: *tol*
relation: *tol*
relationship: *tol*
relative: *tol*
relativity: *tol*
relay: *leg II*
relegate: *leg I*
relent: *lento*
relevant: *leguh*
relevé: *leguh*
relic: *leiku*
relict: *leiku*
relieve: *leguh*
relievo: *leguh*
religion: *leig II*
religiosity: *leig II*
relinquish: *leiku*
relucent: *leuk*
reluctance: *leug*
rely: *legh, leig II*
remand: *man*
remark: *merk*
remarkable: *merk*
remarriage: *re*
remedy: *med*
remember: *smer*
remiss: *smeit*
remit: *smeit*
remittance: *smeit*
remonstrance: *dheigh N 8*
remonstrate: *men I*
remora: *smer*
remorse: *mer II*
remote: *meu II*
remount: *men II*
remuda: *mei II*
remuneration: *mei II*
renaissance: *gn*
renascence: *gn*
rend: *rendh*
render: *do*
rendition: *do*
renegade: *ne*
renege: *ne*
renitent: *kneiguh*
rennet: *reg I*
renoun: *onomen*
renounce: *neu I*
renovate: *neuos*
Renovation: *neuos*
rent: *do, rendh*
renunciation: *neu I*
rep: *rebh*
repair: *per V, peter*
repand: *pet II*
reparation: *per V*
repartee: *per V*
repast: *pa*
repatriate: *peter*
repeal: *pel IV*
repeat: *pet I*
repel: *pel IV*
repent: *paen, rep I*
repetition: *pet I*
repine: *kuei I*
replenish: *pel V*
replete: *pel V*
replica: *plek I*
replicate: *plek I*
replum: *pel V*
reply: *plek I*
repopulate: *da II, popul*
report: *per II*
repose: *ap*
represent: *per IV*

representative: *per IV*
repress: *pres*
reprimand: *per VII, pres*
reprint: *per VII*
reproach: *per VI e, per VII*
reprobate: *bheu, per VI e*
reprove: *per VI e*
reptant: *rep I*
reptile: *rep I*
reptilivorous: *bhag*
republic: *rei II*
Republican: *da II*
repudiate: *ped, peu I*
repugnant: *peug*
repulse: *pel IV*
reputation: *peue*
request: *kuere, perk*
requiem: *kuei III*
requiescat: *kuei III*
require: *kuere*
requisition: *kuere*
requite: *kuei III*
rescind: *sek II*
rescript: *ker III*
rescue: *kuet*
research: *ker I*
resemblance: *sem I*
resemble: *sem I*
resent: *sent*
reserve: *ser II*
reservoir: *ser II*
resident: *sed I*
residue: *sed I*
resign: *seku I*
resignation: *sek I*
resilient: *sel IV*
resist: *sta*
resolute: *leu I, lou*
resolution: *leu I, lou*
resolve: *leu I, lou*
resorb: *srebh*
resort: *ser I*
resound: *suen*
resource: *upo I*
resourceful: *upo I*
respect: *spek*
respiration: *speis*
respite: *spek*
resplendent: *sphel II*
respond: *spend I*
respondent: *spend I*
responsible: *spend I*
rest: *sta*
restaurant: *sta*
restitution: *sta*
restive: *dheigh N 24, sta*
restlessness: *dheigh N 29*
restore: *sta*
restrain: *streig*
restrict: *streig*
result: *sel IV*
resume: *em*
résumé: *em*
resurge: *upo I*
resurgent: *reg I, upo I*
resurrection: *reg I, upo I*
resurrectionist: *upo I*
resuscitate: *kei I*
retain: *ten*
retaliate: *tol*
retaliation: *leg I*
retch: *ker IV*
retiary: *er*
reticent: *tak II*
reticulate: *er*
reticule: *er*
reticulum: *er, stoman*
retina: *er*
retinaculum: *ten*
retinue: *ten*
retort: *tereq*
retract: *tragh*
retribution: *tre*
retrieve: *trep*
retroactive: *ag, re*
retrocede: *sed II*
retroflect: *plek II*
retroflex: *plek II*
retrograde: *ghredh*
retrogress: *ghredh*
retrorse: *uer II 5*
retrospection: *spek*
retroussé: *tereq*
retroversion: *uer II 5*
retrovert: *re*
retrude: *treud*
return: *ter II*
reunion: *dheigh N 19*
revalescent: *ual*
revalidate: *ual*
revaluation: *ual*
reveal: *ueg I*
reveille: *ueg II*
revel: *dau*

revelation: *ueg I*
revelry: *duo*
revenant: *gua*
revenge: *deik*
revenue: *gua*
reverberate: *uer II 1*
revere: *suer I, uer IV*
reverence: *suer I*
reverse: *uer II 5*
reversion: *uer II 5*
revert: *uer II 5*
revest: *ues II*
revet: *ues II*
review: *ueid*
revise: *ueid*
revision: *ueid*
revoke: *ueks*
revolt: *uelu*
revolution: *uelu*
revolve: *re, uelu*
revolver: *uelu*
revulsion: *uel III*
reward: *re, suer I, uer IV*
rex: reg I
Reynard: *kar, reg I*
Reynold: *ual*
rhabdomancy: *uer II 1*
Rhapis: *uer II 1*
rhapsody: *aud, ued, uer II 1*
rhea: *peug*
rhematic: *suer II, uer VI*
Rhemnus: *uer II 1*
Rhenish: *el 75*
rhenium: *el 75*
rheoscope: *sreu*
rheostat: *sreu, sta*
rhetor: *suer II, uer VI*
rhetoric: *suer II*
rhetorical: *uer VI*
rheum: *sreu*
rheumatic: *sreu*
rheumatism: *sreu*
rhigolene: *reig II, srig*
Rhine: *rei I*
rhizome: *uerad*
rhizophagous: *bhag, uerad*
rhodium: *el 45, urod*
rhodocrosite: *urod*
rhododendron: *deru, urod*
rhodolite: *urod*
rhodonite: *urod*
Rhodope: *oku*
rhodopsin: *oku, urod*
Rhodora: *urod*
rhopalic: *geu, uer II 1*
rhumb: *reuos*
rhyme: *sreu*
rhyolite: *sreu*
rhyparographer: *caca*
rhyparography: *caca*
rhypophagous: *bhag*
rhythm: *sreu*
ria: *rei I*
Rialto: *burs, ergh*
riant: *ridè*
rib: *rebh*
ribald: *uer II 7*
ribaldry: *uer II 7*
riband: *bhendh, ker I*
ribbon: *bhendh, ker I*
riboflavin: *bhel I*
rich: *reg I*
Richard: *kar, reg I*
richer: *dheigh N 13*
ricotta: *peku*
riddle: *ar I, ker III, sek VI*
ride: *reidh*
ridge: *ker I*
ridicule: *ridè*
ridiculous: *ridè*
riding: *reidh, tre*
rifacimento: *dhe I*
rife: *rei I*
rift: *rei I*
rig: *reig I*
rigescent: *reig II, srig*
rigger: *reig I*
rigging: *reig I*
riggish: *reig I*
right: *onomen, reg I, sa*
right-angled: *reg I*
righteous: *dheigh N 2 a*
righteousness: *dheigh N 29*
rigid: *reig II, srig*
rigor: *reig II*
rigor mortis: *mer II*
rigorous: *srig*
Rigsdag: *reg I*
Rig-Veda: *ueid*
rill: *ergh*
rima: *rei I*
rime: *sreu*
rimose: *rei I*
rimple: *ker I*

rind: *rendh*
rinderpest: *ker II*
ring: *ker I, ker IV*
rinse: *ken III*
rio: *rei I*
riot: *reu*
R.I.P.: *kuei III*
rip: *reup*
riparian: *rei I*
ripe: *rei I*
rise: *ergh*
risible: *ridè*
risk: *sek I*
Risorgimento: *reg I*
risorious: *ridè*
rissole: *reudh*
risus: *ridè*
rite: *ar I*
ritual: *ar I*
rivage: *rei I*
rival: *ergh, rei I*
rivalry: *ergh, rei I*
rive: *rei I*
river: *ergh, rei I*
riverside: *rei I*
rivulet: *ergh, rei I*
rix-dollar: *reg I*
Riyadh: *reg I*
riyal: *reg I*
road: *reidh*
roam: *ergh, nem*
roar: *kere, reu*
rob: *reup*
robalo: *uekuo*
robber: *reup*
robe: *reup*
Robert: *bhel I*
roble: *reudh*
roborant: *reudh*
robot: *orbh, reudh*
roburite: *reudh*
rocambole: *beu*
rock: *caput, stai*
rocketsonde: *suem*
rococo: *stai*
rod: *ret*
rodent: *rad I*
rodeo: *reth*
Roderick: *reg I*
rodomontade: *men II*
rogation: *reg I*
Roger: *ghaiso*
roger: *ap*
rogue: *reg I*
roister: *reuos*
Roland: *koro, lendh II*
role: *reth*
roll: *reth*
rondeau: *reth*
rondel: *reth*
rondo: *reth*
rood: *ret*
roof: *krapo*
rook: *ker IV*
rookery: *ker IV*
rookie: *ker IV*
room: *reuos*
roost: *ane, kred II*
rooster: *ane, kred II*
root: *uerad*
rorqual: *skualo*
Rosa: *urod*
Rosalinda: *lento*
rose: *urod*
rosemary: *mori, urod*
rostrum: *rad I*
rota: *reth*
rotary: *reth*
rotate: *reth*
rotation: *reth*
rote: *krut, reth*
rother: *ker II*
rotiform: *reth*
rotogravure: *reth*
Rotten Row: *reg I*
rotunda: *reth*
rotundity: *reth*
roture: *reup*
rouge: *reudh*
rough: *reu*
roughcast: *ger VI*
roughish: *reu*
roulade: *reth*
roulette: *reth*
round: *reth*
roundelay: *reth*
rout: *reu, reup*
route: *reup*
routier: *reup*
routine: *reup*
roux: *reudh*
rove: *rei I*
rover: *reup*
row: *ere, rei I*

rowdy: *reu*
rowel: *reth*
rowen: *uen*
royal: *leg I, reg I*
rubato: *reup*
rubble: *reup*
rubefacient: *reudh*
rubella: *reudh*
rubeola: *reudh*
rebeosis: *reudh*
rubescent: *reudh*
rubicund: *reudh*
rubidium: *el 37, reudh*
rubiginous: *reudh*
rubigo: *reudh*
rubric: *reudh*
ruby: *reudh*
ruck: *ker I*
rucksack: *ker I*
rudd: *reudh*
rudder: *ere*
ruddy: *reudh*
rude: *rud*
Rudens: *septm*
rudiments: *rud*
Rudra: *reu*
rue: *kreup*
ruelle: *kreup*
ruffian: *dheigh N 7*
ruffle: *kreup*
rugate: *kreup*
rugose: *kreup*
rule: *reg I*
ruler: *reg I*
rum: *ker I*
rumba: *reuos*
rumbustious: *reudh*
rumen: *stoman*
rummage: *reuos*
rumor: *reu*
rump: *uer II 9*
rumple: *ker I*
run: *ergh*
runagate: *ne*
rung: *ker I*
runnel: *ergh*
runt: *ker II*
rupa: *uer II 1*
rupestrian: *reup*
rupture: *lep I, reup*
rural: *reuos*
Ruritanian: *reuos*
rusma: *gher I*
russet: *reudh*
Russia: *ere*
rust: *reudh*
rustic: *reuos*
rusticate: *reuos*
rutabaga: *uerad*
ruthenium: *el 44*
rutherfordium: *el 104*
rutilant: *rudh*
rutter: *reup*
rye: *reg I*

S

Sabine: *sue*
sabulous: *bhes I*
saburra: *bhes I*
saccharify: *sak*
saccharimeter: *sakkara*
saccharin(e): *ker I, sakkara*
saccharometer: *ker I*
Saccharomyces: *sakkara*
saccharose: *ker I, sak*
sacerdotal: *dhe I, sak*
sack: *seiku*
sackbut: *bhaut*
sacrament: *sak*
sacred: *sak*
sacrifice: *dhe I, sak*
sacrilege: *leg I, sak*
sacrilegious: *sak*
sacristy: *sak*
sacroiliac: *sak*
sacrology: *tuerk*
sacrosanct: *sak*
sacrum: *sak*
sad: *sa*
saddle: *sed I*
sadiron: *sa*
sadism: *leg II*
sadistic: *leg II*
safe: *solo*
sag: *sengu*
saga: *seku II*
sagacious: *sag*
sagacity: *sag*
sage: *sal I, sap*
Sagittarius: *guei*
Saharunpore: *pele*

sailor: *dheigh N 13, rad I*
sainfoin: *sano*
saint: *sak*
St. Andrew's Cross: *sak*
St. Anthony: *sak*
St. Anthony's Fire: *reudh*
St. Bernard: *sak*
St. Charity: *sak*
St. Elmo's Fire: *sak*
St. Germaine pear: *sak*
St. Gobain glass: *sak*
St. Jeffrey's Day: *sak*
St. Johnston's ribband: *sak*
St. Leger: *sak*
St. Louis group: *sak*
St. Lubbock's Day: *sak*
St. Omer's worsted: *sak*
St. Sudario: *sak*
St. Valentine: *ual*
St. Vitus's dance: *sak*
sake: *sag*
sal: *sal I*
salaam: *dekm, eis*
salacin: *sal II*
salacious: *sal I*
salad: *sal I*
salamander: *gn*
salami: *sal I*
sal ammoniac: *el 16*
salary: *sal I*
sale: *sel III*
Salem: *eis*
Salian: *sel IV*
Salic law: *sel IV*
salient: *sel IV*
saline: *sal I*
salle à manger: cura
sallet: *sek II*
sallow: *sal II*
sally: *sal I, sel IV*
salmagundi: *sal I*
salmi: *sal I*
salmon: *sel IV*
salon: *sel I*
saloon: *sel I*
salt: *sal I*
saltant: *sel IV*
saltarello: *sel IV*
saltation: *sel IV*
saltatory: *sel IV*
saltcellar: *sal I*
saltigrade: *ghredh, sel IV*
saltimbanco: *sel IV*
saltine: *sal I*
saltire: *sel IV*
saltirewise: *sel IV*
saltpeter: *caput, el 53, peter, sal I*
saltus: *sel IV*
salty: *sal I*
salubrious: *sal I, solo*
salutary: *sal I, solo*
salutation: *sal I*
salute: *sal I, solo*
salvage: *dheigh N 4, sal I, solo*
salvation: *sal I*
salve: *sal I, selp*
salvo: *sal I*
samadh: *sem I*
samadhi: *sem I*
samarium: *el 62*
same: *sem I*
samite: *mei IV, seks*
samovar: *sem I*
Samoyed: *sem I*
sample: *em*
samsara: *sem I, ser III*
samskara: *kuer, sem I*
sanctify: *sak*
sanctimonious: *sak*
sanction: *sak*
sanctity: *sak*
sanctuary: *sak*
sanctum: *sak*
sand: *bhes I*
sandal: *kand*
sandalwood: *kand*
sandara: *reg II*
sandarac: *kand*
sandblind: *bhes I, caput, semi*
sanderling: *bhes I*
sanders: *kand*
sandiver: *sueid II*
Sandor: *nert*
sandpiper: *bhes I*
sandwich: *bhes I*
sandworm: *bhes I*
sandwort: *bhes I*
Sandy: *bhes I, nert*
sane: *sano*
sang: *senguh*
sang-froid: *reig II, sang, srig*
sangría: *sang*
sanguinary: *sang*
sanguine: *sang, ugu*

sanguivorous: *bhag*
Sanhedrin: *sed I*
sanitarium: *sano*
sanitary: *sano*
sanitation: *sano*
sank: *sengu*
sans cérémonie: seni
sans-culotte: *seni*
sans gêne: seni
Sanskrit: *kuer*
sans pareil: seni
sans peur: seni
sans serif: *seni*
sans souci: kei I, seni
Santa Claus: *el 28, sak*
santal: *kand*
santalaceous: *kand*
Santa Sophia: *guhren*
sap: *sab, sap*
saphead: *sap*
sapid: *sap*
sapient: *sap*
sapling: *sap*
saponaceous: *sap*
saponify: *sap*
sapor: *sap*
sapphic: *es*
sapphire: *prai*
sappy: *sap*
saprophyte: *bheu*
sapsago: *guher, sek IV*
sarangousty: *ker II*
sarcasm: *tuerk*
sarcastic: *tuerk*
sarcenchyme: *tuerk*
Sarcina: *serk*
sarcinoid: *tuerk*
sarcocarp: *tuerk*
sarcode: *tuerk*
sarcophagal: *tuerk*
sarcophagous: *tuerk*
sarcophagus: *bhag, tuerk*
Sardanopolis: *pele*
sardonic: *oino, onomen, suard*
sardonyx: *onogh*
sargasso: *sal II*
sarmentose: *srep*
sarmentum: *srep*
sartor: *serk*
sartorial: *serk*
sate: *sa*
satem: *dekm*
Sati: *es*
satiate: *sa*
satiety: *sa*
satire: *sa*
satiriasis: *upo III b*
satisfaction: *dhe I, sa*
satisfy: *dhe I, sa*
satrap: *ksei, pa*
sattva: *es*
saturate: *sa*
Saturday: *prai*
Saturn: *nebh, prai*
Saturnalia: *nebh*
saturnine: *nebh*
saturnism: *nebh*
satyr: *aud, caput, keu II, sa*
sauce: *sal I*
saucy: *sal I*
sauna: *sueid II*
sausage: *sal I*
sauté: *sel IV*
savage: *sal I, silva*
savant: *sap*
save: *sal I, solo*
saveloy: *ker II*
savior: *sal I*
savoir-faire: dhe I
savoir-vivre: guei
savor: *sap*
savory: *sap*
savvy: *sap*
saw: *sek I, seku II*
saxatile: *sek I*
saxicolous: *sek I*
saxifrage: *bhreg, sek I*
Saxon: *sek I*
say: *seku II*
saying: *seku II*
sbirro: peuor
scab: *sek IV*
scabbard: *bhergh, sek IX*
scabble: *sek IV*
scabies: *sek IV*
scabrous: *sek IV*
scacchic: *ksei*
scacchite: *ksei*
scaglia: *kel VIII*
scagliola: *kel VIII*
scald: *kel I, kel VIII*
scaldino: kel I
scale: *kel VIII, sek III, skand*
scalene: *skel*

scall: *kel VIII*
scallop: *kel VIII*
scalp: *sek III*
scalpel: *sek III*
scalper: *sek III*
scalping: *tem*
scamp: *kam, prai*
scamper: *kam, prai*
scan: *skand*
scandal: *skand*
scandalize: *dheigh N 25, skand*
scandaroon: *skand*
scandent: *skand*
scandium: *el 21*
scanmag: *skand*
scansion: *skand*
scansorial: *skand*
scant: *kem II*
scanties: *keu II*
scantling: *skand*
scaphocephalic: *sek IV*
scapula: *sek IV*
scar: *ker III, sek IX*
Scaramouche: *ker III*
scarce: *ker III, sek IX*
scarify: *ker III*
scarlet: *sek I*
scarp: *sek V*
scathe: *sketh*
scatheless: *sketh*
scathing: *sketh*
scatology: *sek V*
scauper: *sek III*
scavage: *keu I*
scavenger: *keu I*
scelerat: *skel*
scent: *sent*
Schadenfreude: sketh
schanz: *kam*
schedule: *sek II*
schematic: *segh*
scheme: *segh*
scherzo: *skern*
schism: *sek II*
schismatic: *sek II*
schist: *sek II*
schizo-: *sek II*
schizocarp: *ker III, sek II*
schizogenic: *sek II*
schizognathous: *sek II*
schizoid: *sek II*
schizomycete: *sek II*
schizophrenia: *guhren, sek II*
schnauzer: *sna II*
schnorrer: *sner I*
schnozzle: *sna II*
scholar: *segh*
scholastic: *segh*
scholium: *dheigh N 35, segh*
school: *segh, sek III*
schoolboy: *morui*
Schwartz: *suord*
sciamachy: *magh*
science: *sek II*
scientific: *dhe I, sek II*
scientology: *sek II*
scilicet: *sek II*
scintilla: *skai*
scintillate: *skai*
sciolist: *sek II*
scioptic: *oku*
scire facias: sek II
scissile: *sek II*
scission: *sek II*
scissors: *sek II*
scissortail: *sek II*
scleragogy: *skelo*
scleroderma: *skelo*
sclerometer: *skelo*
sclerotic: *skelo*
scoff: *skeub*
scold: *seku II*
scolex: *skel*
scolion: *skel*
scoliosis: *skel*
sconce: *kam*
scone: *keu I*
scoop: *sek IV, skeub*
scoot: *skeud*
scop: *skeub*
scope: *spek*
scopophilia: *spek*
scopophobia: *spek*
scorbutic: *ker III, sek IX*
scorcher: *ters*
score: *ker III*
scoria: *sek V*
scorify: *sek V*
scorn: *skern*
Scorpio: *guei, morui*
scorpion: *ker III*
Scot: *peik*
scot: *skeud*
scotch: *kogkhos, kuet, peik*

scotoma: *skot*
scour: *cura, keuero*
scourge: *reig I*
scout: *au II, ous, skeud*
scow: *skeub*
scowl: *skel*
Scrabble: *gerbh*
scrabble: *ker III, sek VI*
scrap: *ker III, sek V*
scrape: *ker III, sek V*
scratch: *gerbh, ker III*
scrawl: *gerbh, krak*
screak: *skrei*
scream: *jing, skrei*
screech: *jing, skrei*
screed: *sek VIII*
screen: *sek IX*
scribble: *gerbh, ker III, sek VI*
scribe: *ker III, sek VI*
scrim: *sek IX*
scrimmage: *ker III, sek IX*
scrimp: *ker I*
script: *ker III, sek VI*
scriptorium: *ker III, sek VI*
Scripture: *ker III, sek VI*
scrivener: *ker III, sek VI*
scrobiculate: *sek V*
scrod: *sek IX*
scrofula: *sek V*
scroll: *sek VIII*
scrotum: *sek VIII*
scrub: *bherem, ker III, sek V*
scruff: *skeup*
scrum: *ker III*
scrummage: *ker III*
scruple: *ker III, sek IX*
scrupulous: *sek IX*
scrutiny: *ker III, sek VIII*
scudo: *sek II, skeu*
scuff: *skeub*
scuffle: *skeub*
sculpt: *sek III*
sculptor: *sek III*
sculpture: *sek III*
sculpturesque: *sek III*
scum: *skeu*
scumble: *skeu*
scupper: *skeub*
scurf: *ker III, sek IX*
scurry: *keuero*
scurvy: *ker III, sek IX*
scut: *skeup*
scutage: *skeu*
scutch: *kuet*
Scutellaria: *skeu*
scuttle: *skeud*
scuttlebutt: *skeud*
scutum: *sek II*
Scylla: *sek IV*
scyphiform: *sek IV*
scyphogeny: *sek IV*
scyphomancy: *sek IV*
scyphomedusa: *sek IV*
scyphostoma: *sek IV*
scyphus: *sek IV*
scythe: *sek I*
seal: *sek I, selk*
seam: *siu*
seance: *sed I*
sear: *ksero, saus, ser II*
search: *ker I*
season: *se I*
seat: *sed I*
seaward: *uer II 5*
sec: *seiku*
secant: *sek I*
secateur: *sek I*
secchio: *seiku*
secco: *seiku*
secede: *sed II*
secern: *ker III, sek VI*
seclude: *kleu III*
seclusion: *kleu III*
second: *seku I*
secondarily: *seku I*
seconde: *seku I*
secondo: *seku I*
secret: *ker III, sek VI, sue*
secrete: *ker III, sek VI, sue*
secretion: *sek VI*
sect: *sek I, seku I*
sectarian: *seku I*
section: *sek I*
sector: *sek I*
secundines: *seku I*
secure: *cura, sue*
securiform: *sek I*
sedan chair: *sed I*
sedate: *sed I*
sedation: *dheigh N 19*
sedative: *sed I*
sedentary: *sed I*
sedge: *sek I*
sediment: *sed I*

sedition: *ei I*
seduce: *deuk, sue*
seduction: *deuk*
sedulous: *del I, sed I*
see: *sed I, seku II*
seed: *se I*
seek: *sag*
seel: *kel VI*
seem: *seku II, sem I*
seemly: *seku II, sem I*
seep: *sap*
seerband: *ker II*
seerpaw: *ker II, ped*
seersucker: *ker I, sakkara*
seesaw: *sek I*
seethe: *seu II*
segment: *sek I*
segregate: *sue*
segregation: *ger I, ger III, sue*
seguidilla: *seku I*
Seidel: *seiku*
seigneur: *sen*
seismic: *tueis*
seismograph: *tueis*
seismology: *tueis*
sejm: *em, ksun*
Selachii: *suel*
select: *ksun, leg I*
selection: *leg I*
Selene: *suel*
Selenite: *suel*
selenium: *el 34, suel*
selenotropic: *el 34*
self: *sue*
self-abuse: *sue*
self-consistent: *sue*
self-sufficiency: *sue*
self-willed: *sue*
selig: *sel II*
sell: *sel III*
selvage: *dheigh N 4*
semantics: *dheie*
semaphore: *bher II, dheie*
semasiology: *dheie*
sematic: *dheie*
semblance: *sem I*
semeiotics: *dheie*
Semele: *morui*
sememe: *dheie*
semen: *se I*
semester: *me IV, seks*
semibousy: *semi*
semicannibalic: *semi*
semicipher: *semi*
semicircular: *semi*
semicolon: *semi, skel*
semidemi: *semi*
semifinals: *semi*
seminary: *se I*
semivocal: *ueks*
semper fidelis: sem I
semper paratus: sem I
sempervive: *sem I*
sempiternal: *aiu, sem I*
semplice: *sem I*
sempre: *sem I*
semuncia: *oino*
senary: *seks*
senate: *sen*
senatorial: *sen*
send: *sent*
senectitude: *sen*
senescent: *sen*
sengreen: *sem I*
senhor: *sen*
senhora: *sen*
senhorita: *sen*
senicide: *sen*
senile: *sen*
senior: *sen*
seniority: *sen*
sennet: *sek I*
señor: *sen*
señora: *sen*
señorita: *sen*
sensation: *sent*
sense: *sent*
senseless: *sent*
sensibility: *sent*
sensible: *sent*
sensitive: *sent*
sensorimotor: *sent*
sensorium: *sent*
sensory: *sent*
sensual: *sent*
sensuality: *sent*
sensuous: *sent*
sentence: *sent*
sentience: *sent*
sentient: *sent*
sentiment: *sent*
sentinel: *sent*
sentry: *sent*
separate: *ksun, per V, sue*

septan: *septm*
septangular: *septm*
September: *me IV, septm*
Septembrist: *septm*
septemfluous: *septm*
septenary: *septm*
septennial: *septm*
septentrional: *ter II*
Septentrion(es): *septm, ter II*
septic: *septm*
septic(a)emia: *septm*
septicine: *septm*
septicity: *septm*
Septuagint: *dekm*
septum: *septm*
septuple: *septm*
sepulcher: *sep*
sepulture: *sep*
sequacious: *seku I*
sequel: *seku I*
sequela: *seku I*
sequence: *dheigh N 8, seku I*
sequestered: *dheigh N 13, seku I*
sérac: *ser III*
seraglio: *ser II*
serai: *ser II*
serang: *ker II*
seraphical: *dheigh N 5*
seraskier: *ker II*
sere: *ksero, saus*
serein: *ksero*
serenade: *ksero*
serendipity: *bher I*
serene: *ksero*
serf: *ser II, suer I*
sergeant: *ser II, suer I*
series: *ser I*
serious: *uer I*
sermon: *ser I*
sermonette: *ser I*
sermonize: *ser I*
serotinous: *se II*
Serpens: *serp*
serpent: *serp*
serpentine: *serp*
serpigo: *serp*
Serpula: *serp*
serried: *ser I*
sertularian: *ser I*
serum: *ser III*
serval: *ker III*
servant: *ser II, suer I*
serve: *ser II, suer I*
service: *ser II*
serviceable: *suer I*
servile: *ser II, suer I*
servitude: *ser II, suer I*
sesquicentennial: *kue, semi*
sesquipedalian: *kue, ped, semi*
sessile: *sed I*
session: *sed I*
sesterce: *semi, tre*
sestertium: *semi*
sestet: *seks*
sestina: *seks*
set: *sed I*
setter: *sed I*
settle: *sed I*
settlement: *sed I*
seven: *septm*
seventeen: *septm*
seventh: *septm*
seventy: *septm*
sever: *per V, sue*
several: *per V, sue*
severe: *uero*
severity: *uero*
sew: *siu*
sewer: *akua, sed I*
sex: *sek I, sue*
sexagenarian: *seks*
sextant: *seks*
sexual: *sek I*
shabby: *sek IV*
shade: *skot*
shadow: *skot*
shaft: *sek IV*
shah: *ksei, poti*
shahzadah: *gn, ksei*
Shakespearean: *onomen*
shako: *dek II*
shakta: *kak*
Shakti: *kak*
shale: *sek III*
shallowling: *sap*
shalom: eis, skelo
sham: *skeu*
shame: *skeu*
shank: *skeng*
shanty: *steg*
shape: *sek IV*
shapeless: *leu I*
shard: *ker III, sek IX*
share: *ker III, sek IX*

sharp: *ker III, sek V, suer III*
shatter: *sek VII*
shave: *sek IV*
shaver: *sek IV*
shavings: *sek IV*
Shaw: *onomen*
shawm: *kolem*
shay: *sek II*
she: *sos*
sheaf: *skeup*
shear: *ker III, sek II, sek IX*
shears: *sek I, sek IX*
sheath: *sek II*
shed: *sek II, skot*
sheen: *keu I*
sheep: *ane, mel I*
sheepberry: *bhel I*
sheet: *skeud*
sheeve: *steibh*
shelf: *sek III*
shell: *kel VIII, sek III*
shellac: *kel VIII, reg II*
shelter: *kel VIII*
shepherd: *kerdh*
sherbet: *srebh*
sherry: *per VI c, sek II*
shield: *kel VIII, sek II*
shilling: *kel VIII*
shimmy: *kem I, sek II*
shin: *sek II*
shingle: *sek VII*
shingles: *kenk I*
ship: *sek II, sek IV*
-ship: *dheigh N 33, sek IV*
Shipley: *leuk, onomen*
shipshape: *sek IV*
shirt: *ker III, sek IX*
shit: *sek II*
Shiva: *kei II*
shive: *sek II*
shiver: *geph, sek II*
shoal: *sek III*
shoat: *skeud*
shoe: *skeu*
shoot: *skeud*
shop: *skeup*
shore: *ker III*
short: *ker III, sek IX*
shoulder: *skel*
shove: *skeub*
shovel: *skeub*
shovelful: *pel V*
show: *keu I*
shower: *keuero*
s(h)raddha: *kred I*
shred: *ker III, sek VIII*
shrew: *sek VIII*
shrewd: *sek VIII*
s(h)ri: *kleu I*
shriek: *skrei*
shrift: *ker III, sek VI*
shrike: *skrei*
shrimp: *ker I*
shrink: *ker I*
shrive: *ker III, sek VI*
shrivel: *ker I, sek VI*
shroud: *sek VIII*
Shrovetide: *sek VI*
Shrove Tuesday: *ker III*
shrub: *bherem, ker III, sek V*
s(h)ruti: *kleu I*
shudder: *skut*
shuffle: *skeup*
shut: *skeud*
shutter: *skeud*
shuttle: *skeud*
shuttlecock: *bat*
sib: *sue*
sibilancy: *suei I*
sibilant: *suei I*
sibilate: *suei I*
sibling: *sue*
sibyl: *suei I*
sic: *uio*
sic: ko, sos
sicarian: *sek I*
siccative: *seiku*
sick: *seug*
sicken: *seug*
sickle: *sek I*
sickly: *seug*
sickness: *seug*
sideburns: *bhar*
sidereal: *sueid I*
sideroscope: *dheigh N 32*
sideswipe: *suei II*
Sieg: *segh*
siege: *sed I*
Siegfried: *prai, segh, uel III*
siesta: *seks*
sieve: *ker III, sap*
siffle: *suei I*
sift: *sap*
sight: *seku II*

sigil: *sek I*
sigillate: *sek I*
Sigismund: *man, segh*
sigmoid: *kel IV*
sign: *sek I, seku I*
signal: *sek I*
signature: *sek I*
signet: *sek I*
significant: *sek I, seku I*
signify: *sek I, seku I*
signor: *sen*
signore: *sen*
signorina: *sen*
signpost: *seku I*
Sikh: *kak*
sikhara: *ke*
Silas: *silva*
silence: *sei*
silent: *sui*
"silent *e*": *esu*
silicon: *el 14*
sillabub: *sel II*
silladar: *dhar*
silly: *sel II*
silt: *sal I*
silure: *ors*
silvan: *sal I, silva*
silver: *el 47*
similacrum: *sem I*
similar: *sem I*
simile: *sem I*
similitude: *sem I*
Simon Pure: *sem I*
simony: *sem I*
simple: *plek I, sem I*
Simple Simon: *sem I*
simpleton: *plek I*
simplex: *sem I*
simplicity: *em, plek I*
simplify: *dhe I, plek I, sem I*
simulate: *sem I*
simultaneous: *aiu, sem I*
sin: *es*
Sinai: *ane*
since: *se II*
sincere: *keneko, seni*
sinciput: *caput*
sinecure: *cura, seni, ug*
sine die: seni
sine prole: seni
sine qua non: seni
sinequanonical: *seni*
sinequanous: *seni*
sinew: *netr*
sing: *senguh*
Singapore: *pele*
singe: *senk*
Singh: *kak*
single: *sem I*
single-handed: *sem I*
singlet: *sem I*
singleton: *sem I*
singular: *sem I*
singularity: *sem I*
Sinicism: *kuon*
sinister: *deks*
sinistrorse: *deks, es, uer II 5*
sink: *sengu*
sinner: *es*
Sinn Fein: *sue*
Sinologue: *leg I*
sip: *sap, seu I, srebh*
sir: *sen*
sircar: *ker II, kuer*
sirdar: *dhar, ker II*
sire: *sen*
siren: *tuer II*
siriasis: *tueis*
Sirius: *per IV, tueis*
sirloin: *lendh I, upo II*
sir-reverence: *sal I*
sister: *suesor*
sisterhood: *suesor*
sistrum: *tueis*
sit: *sed I*
sitar: *ten*
site: *sei, sui*
sit(i)ology: *past, per VII, sed I*
sit(i)omania: *past*
sit(i)ophobia: *past*
sitosterole: *past*
situation: *sei, sui*
situs: *sui*
sitz bath: *sed I*
six: *seks*
sixpence: *seks*
sixte: *seks*
sixteenmo: *seks*
sixth: *seks*
sixty: *seks*
skald: *seku II*
skatole: *sek V*
skeet: *skeud*
skeleton: *skelo*

skeptic: *spek*
sketch: *segh*
skewer: *sek II*
ski: *sek II*
skiagram: *skai*
skiagraphy: *skai*
skiapodes: *skai*
skiascope: *skai*
skill: *kel VIII, sek III*
skillet: *skeu*
skim: *skeu*
skin: *sek I*
skipper: *sek II*
skirmish: *ker III, sek IX*
skirt: *ker III, sek IX*
skit: *skeud*
skitter: *skeud*
skittish: *skeud*
skoal: *kel VIII, sek III*
skulduggery: *kel VIII*
skulk: *skel*
skull: *kel VIII, sek III*
skunk: *pu*
Skupshtina: *keu II, sem I*
sky: *skeu*
skyscraper: *me III, skeu*
slab: *leb*
slag: *slak*
slang: *slenk*
slap: *sphereg*
slaughter: *slak*
Slav: *kleu I*
slave: *kleu I*
slaver: *leb*
slavery: *kleu I*
slavish: *dheigh N 20*
slay: *slak*
sled: *sleidh*
sledge: *slak, sleidh*
sleek: *lei I*
sleep: *leb*
sleet: *sleu*
sleigh: *sleidh*
sleighride: *sleidh*
sleight: *slak*
slench: *leb*
slick: *lei I*
slid: *sleidh*
slide: *leb, lei I, sleidh*
slight: *lei I*
slim: *leb*
slime: *lei I*
sling: *leb, slenk*
slinge: *leb*
slingshot: *slenk*
slink: *leb, slenk*
slip: *leb, lei I, sleub*
slipover: *sleub*
slipper: *lei I, sleub*
slippery: *lei I*
slipshod: *sleub*
slipslop: *sleub*
slit: *kel VIII*
slivovitz: *sli*
slob: *leb*
slobber: *leb*
sloe: *sli*
slogan: *gal*
sloka: *kleu I*
sloop: *sleubh*
slop: *lei I, sleubh*
slope: *sleubh*
slosh: *sleu*
slouch: *sleu*
Slovak: *kleu I*
sloven: *leb*
Slovene: *kleu I*
slowworm: *lei I*
sludge: *sleu*
slug: *sleu*
sluggard: *sleu*
slughorn: *gal*
sluice: *kleu III*
slum: *leb*
slumber: *sleu*
slumgullion: *leb*
slummock: *leb*
slump: *leb*
slup: *leb*
slur: *leb, sleu*
slurp: *srebh*
slurry: *leb*
slush: *leb, sleu*
slut: *leb*
sly: *slak*
smack: *kus, smegh*
smaggle: *meu I*
smallpox: *uak*
smalt: *smeld*
smart: *mer II, smerd*
smear: *sme*
smectic: *smeit*
smectite: *smeit*
smegma: *smeit*

smelt: *mel I, smeld*
smile: *smei I*
smirk: *smei I*
smite: *sme, smeit*
Smith: *onomen, smei II*
smith: *smei II*
smithy: *smei II*
smock: *meu I*
smog: *smeugh*
smoke: *smeugh*
smoothy: *dheigh N 1*
smorgasbord: *bher II, ghans, smeru*
smorzando: *mer II*
smrite: *smer*
smug: *meu I*
snack: *sna III*
snail: *sneg*
snake: *sneg*
snap: *sna II*
snare: *sner II*
snark: *sneiguh*
snarl: *ghenu, sner I*
snatch: *sna II*
snath: *sneit*
sneak: *sneg*
sneakers: *sneg*
sneer: *sner I*
sneeze: *jing, pneu*
sneezewort: *uerad*
snick: *sneit*
snickersnack: *sneit*
snickersnee: *sneit*
sniff: *leit, sna II*
sniffle: *jing, sna II*
snivel: *leit, sna II*
snood: *netr, sne*
snoop: *sna II*
snore: *jing*
snorkle: *sner I*
snort: *jing, sner I*
snot: *sna II*
snout: *sna II*
snow: *sneiguh*
snowberry: *bhel I*
snowdrift: *dhreibh*
Snowman, Abominable: *sneiguh*
snowmobile: *meu II*
snub: *sna II*
snuff: *leit, sna II*
snuffle: *leit, sna II*
snug: *ker III*
so: *sos*
soak: *sap*
soap: *sap*
soapberry: *bhel I*
soapbox: *sap*
soap opera: *sap*
soapstone: *stei*
soave: *suad*
sob: *sap*
sober: *ebrius*
Sobranje: *sem I*
sobriety: *ebrius, ksun*
soc: *sag*
socage: *sag*
sociable: *seku I*
social: *seku I*
socialism: *seku I*
society: *seku I*
sociology: *leg I, seku I*
socket: *sus*
Socrates: *da II*
sod: *seu II*
sodality: *sue*
sodden: *seu II*
sodium: *el 11, nitron*
sodomy: *gen, gn*
soil: *sed I, sus*
soilure: *sus*
soiree: *se II*
soke: *sag*
soken: *sag*
sol: *solo*
solace: *sel II*
solanine: *sauel*
solar: *sauel*
solarium: *dheigh N 35, sauel*
solar plexus: *plek I*
Soldanella: *solo*
soldier: *dheigh N 13, solo*
soldo: *solo*
sole: *sel I, sue*
solemn: *solo*
solfatara: *el 16*
solicit: *kei I*
solicitation: *solo*
solicitous: *solo*
solid: *solo*
Solidago: *solo*
solidarity: *solo*
solideme: *solo*
solidungulate: *solo*
solidus: *solo*
soliloquy: *sue, tolku*

soliped: *solo*
solipsism: *sue*
solitary: *sue*
solitude: *sue*
solivagant: *uag I*
solivagous: *dheigh N 2 f*
solo: *sue*
solstice: *sta*
soluble: *leu I*
solum: sel I
solute: *leu I*
solution: *ksun, leu I, lou*
solve: *ksun, leu I, lou*
solvent: *leu I, lou*
soma: *teue 3*
Somateria: *teue 3*
somatic: *teue 3*
somatist: *teue 3*
somatocyst: *teue 3*
somatogenic: *teue 3*
somatology: *teue 3*
somatovisceral: *teue 3*
somber: *andho*
sombrero: *andho*
some: *sem I*
somersault: *sel IV, upo II*
somite: *teue 3*
somnambulism: *suep I*
somnambulist: *al III, ei I*
somnifacient: *dhe I*
somnific: *dheigh N 17*
somniloquy: *suep I*
somnolent: *suep I*
Somnus: *suep I*
son: *seu III*
sonant: *suen*
sonar: *suen*
sonata: *suen*
sonatina: *suen*
sone: *suen*
song: *senguh*
songster: *senguh*
songstress: *senguh*
sonic: *suen*
sonic boom: *upo III a*
sonnet: *suen*
sonneteer: *suen*
sonorescent: *suen*
sonority: *suen*
sonorous: *suen*
soot: *sed I*
sooth: *es, esu*
soothe: *es*
soothsayer: *es*
sop: *sap, seu I*
Sophia: *guhren*
sophism: *guhren*
sophist: *guhren*
sophistry: *guhren*
Sophocles: *ar I, kleu I, sue*
sophomore: *guhren, moro*
Sophronia: *guhren*
Sophronisba: *guhren*
soporific: *suep I*
soprano: *upo II*
sorb: *srebh*
sorbefacient: *srebh*
sorbet: *srebh*
sorcerer: *ser I*
sordamento: suer II
sordellina: suer II
sordes: *suord*
sordid: *suord*
sordine: *suer II*
sordino: *suer II*
sore: *sai*
soredium: *teue 5*
Sorex: *suer II*
soricine: *suer II*
sorites: *teue 5*
sororal: *suesor*
sorority: *suesor*
sorosus: *teue 5*
sorption: *srebh*
sorrel: *saus*
sorrowful: *dheigh N 2 h*
sorry: *sai*
sort: *ser I*
sortie: *upo I*
sortilege: *leg I, ser I*
sorus: *teue 5*
sostenente: ten
sostenuto: *ten*
Soter: *teue 4*
soterial: *teue 4*
soteriology: *teue 4*
sotto: upo I
sotto voce: upo I
sou: *solo*
soubrette: *upo I*
so(u)briquet: *upo I*
soufflé: *beu*
sought: *sag*
sound: *aue, suem, suen*

soundless: *suem*
soup: *sap, seu I*
soupçon: *spek*
sour: *sal I*
source: *upo I*
souse: *sal I, upo I*
soutane: *upo I*
south: *sauel*
Southampton: *kei II*
southern: *sauel*
southward: *uer II 5*
souvenir: *gua*
sovereign: *reg I, uer II 5, upo II*
Soviet: *sem I*
sow: *se I, sus*
sowens: *seu I*
space: *pet II, sphei I*
spacious: *pet II, sphei I*
spadassin: *sphei I*
spade: *pet II, sphei I*
spadille: *sphei I*
spadix: *sphei I*
spado: *segh, sphei I*
spake: *sphereg*
spall: *sphel I*
span: *pend, spend II, sphei I*
spang: *sphei I*
spangle: *pend, spend II*
spanner: *pend, spend II*
spar: *sper I, spher II, sphereg*
spare: *sphei I*
spareribs: *rebh, sper I*
sparhawk: *sper III*
spark: *sphereg*
sparkle: *sphereg*
sparrow: *sper III*
sparrowgrass: *spher I*
sparse: *sphereg*
sparteine: *sper II*
sparterie: *sper II*
Spartina: *sper II*
Spartium: *sper II*
spasm: *sphei I*
spasmatic: *sphei I*
spasmodic: *sphei I*
spat: *sphereg*
spated: *segh*
spathe: *sphei I*
spathic: *sphei I*
spatial: *sphei I*
spats: *sphereg*
spatter: *sphereg*
spatula: *pet II, sphei I*
spavin: *sper III*
spay: *sphei I*
speak: *sphereg*
spear: *sper I*
spearwort: *uerad*
special: *spek*
species: *spek*
specify: *spek*
specimen: *spek*
specious: *spek*
speck: *sphei I*
specktioneer: *sneit, sphei I*
spectacle: *spek*
spectacles: *spek*
spectator: *spek*
specter: *spek*
spectroscopy: *spek*
spectrum: *spek*
speculate: *spek*
speed: *sphei I*
spelean: *spelugx*
speleology: *spelugx*
spell: *spel*
spellbinder: *spel*
spelling: *spel*
spelt: *sphel I*
speluncar: *spelugx*
spelunker: *spelugx*
spend: *pend*
Spergula: *sphereg*
sperm: *spher I*
spermaceti: *spher I*
spermatozoon: *spher I*
spew: *sphieu*
sphalerite: *sphel I*
sphene: *sphei I*
sphenoid: *sphei I*
sphenotic: *sphei I*
sphere: *spher I*
spherical: *spher I*
spheroid: *es, spher I*
spicate: *sphei II*
spice: *spek*
spick: *sphei I*
spicule: *sphei II*
spiculum: *sphei II*
spider: *pend, spend II*
spiegeleisen: *spek*
spike: *sphei II*
spikenard: *sphei II*
spile: *sphei II*

spill: *sphei II, sphel I*
spilth: *sphel I*
spin: *pend, spend II*
spindle: *pend, spend II*
spine: *sphei II*
spinel: *sphei II*
spink: *spingo*
spinneret: *pend*
spinney: *sphei II*
spinster: *sak, spend II*
spiny: *sphei II*
spiracle: *speis*
Spiraea: *sper II*
spiral: *sper II*
spire: *sper I, sper II, sphei II*
spireme: *sper II*
spirit: *speis*
spiritual: *speis*
spirituality: *dheigh N 36*
spirivalve: *sper II*
spirochete: *sper II*
Spirodela: *sper II*
spirt: *spher I*
spit: *sphei II, sphieu*
spite: *spek*
spittle: *sphieu*
spittoon: *sphieu*
spitz: *sphei II*
splay: *plek I*
splayfoot: *plek I*
splendid: *sphel II*
splendor: *sphel II*
splice: *speid*
splint: *spleid*
splinter: *spleid*
split: *sphel I, spleid*
splutter: *sphieu*
spoil: *sphel I*
spoilsport: *sphel I*
spoke: *sphei II, sphereg*
spokesman: *sphereg*
spoliation: *sphel I*
spondee: *spend I*
spondulix: *sphei I*
spondyl: *sphei I*
spondylitis: *sphei I*
spondylus: *sphei I*
sponge: *spong*
sponsion: *spend I*
sponsor: *spend I*
spontaneous: *pend, spend II*
spontoon: *peug*
spool: *sphel I*
spoon: *sphei I*
Spoonerism: *per 2, sphei I*
spoonfuls: *dheigh N 2 h, pel V*
spoor: *spher II*
sporadic(al): *dheigh N 17, spher I*
spore: *spher I*
sporran: *burs*
sport: *per II*
sportsman: *dheigh N 27*
spouse: *spend I*
spout: *sphieu*
sprag: *sphereg*
sprain: *pres, spher II*
sprawl: *spher I*
spray: *sphereg*
spread: *spher I*
sprig: *sphereg*
sprightly: *speis*
spring: *sphereg*
springal(d): *ual*
springbok: *bhugo*
springlet: *sphereg*
sprint: *sphereg*
sprit: *spher I*
spritz: *spher I*
sprout: *spher I*
spry: *sphereg*
spume: *spoim*
spunky: *spong*
spur: *spher II*
spurge: *peu II*
spurn: *spher II*
spurry: *spher I, sphereg*
spurt: *spher I, spher II*
sputnik: *keu II, ksun, pent*
sputter: *sphieu*
sputum: *sphieu*
spy: *spek*
squad: *kuetuer*
squadron: *kuetuer*
squalene: *skualo*
squalid: *skualo*
squall: *skualo*
Squalodon: *skualo*
squaloid: *skualo*
squalor: *skualo*
squalus: *skualo*
squama: *skualo*
squamose: *skualo*
square: *kuetuer*
squash: *kuet*

squawberry: *bhel I*
squeal: *jing, skualo*
squeamish: *suei II*
squib: *suei II*
squire: *sek II*
squirrel: *ors, skai*
stabber: *rad I*
stabilize: *sta*
stable: *sta*
stack: *stegh*
stacte: *stag*
stactometer: *stag*
staddle: *sta*
stadholder: *sta*
stadium: *sphei I, sta*
staff: *stebh*
stag: *stegh*
stage: *sta*
stagecoach: *sta*
staggard: *stegh*
stagger: *stegh*
stagnant: *stag*
stagnate: *stag*
stagnicolous: *stag*
staid: *sta*
stain: *teng*
staith: *sta*
stake: *stegh, steu*
stalactite: *dheigh N 22, stag*
stalag: *legh, stebh*
stalagmite: *stag*
stale: *sta*
Stalin: *stak*
stalk: *sta, stel, ster IV*
stalking-horse: *ster IV*
stall: *sta, stel*
stallion: *sta*
stalwart: *sta*
stamen: *sta*
stamina: *sta*
stamine: *sta*
stamineal: *sta*
stammer: *stam*
stamp: *stebh*
stampede: *stebh*
stance: *sta*
stanch: *sta*
stanchion: *sta*
stand: *sta*
standard: *sta, ten*
standing: *sta*
stanza: *sta*
staphyline: *stebh*
staphylinid: *stebh*
Staphylococcus: *stebh*
staple: *stebh*
star: *sta, ster II*
starboard: *bher II, sta*
starch: *ster II*
stare: *ster II*
stark: *ster II*
starlet: *ster II*
starlight: *ster II*
starling: *ster II*
starosta: *ster II*
start: *ster II*
startle: *ster II*
starve: *ster II*
state: *sta*
stater: *sta*
statesman: *dheigh N 27*
static: *sta*
station: *sta*
stationary: *sta*
stationery: *sta*
statistics: *sta*
statoblast: *sta*
stator: *sta*
statoscope: *sta*
statuary: *sta*
statue: *sta*
statuesque: *sta*
stature: *sta*
status: *sta*
statute: *sta*
staunch: *sta*
stay: *sta, stak*
stead: *sta*
steadfast: *past*
steady: *sta*
steak: *steig*
steal: *ster III*
stealth: *ster III*
stean: *stai*
stearic acid: *cal*
stearin: *stai, stei*
stearoptene: *pet I, stei*
steatite: *stai, stei*
steatocele: *stei*
steatogynous: *stei*
steatolysis: *cal*
steatopygian: *cal*
steatopygous: *stai*
steed: *sta*

steel: *el 26, sla, sta, stak*
steenbok: *stai*
steep: *steu*
steeple: *steu*
steer: *sta, taur*
steganography: *steg*
steganopodous: *dheigh N 2 e*
stegnotic: *steg*
Stegodon: *steg*
stein: *stai*
steinbok: *stai*
stele: *sta, stel*
Stella: *ster III*
stellar: *ster III*
stellate: *ster III*
stem: *sta, stam*
stemma: *stebh*
stencil: *skai*
Steneosaurus: *sten*
stenocephaly: *sten*
stenochrome: *sten*
stenography: *gerbh, sten*
stenopaic: *oku*
stenosis: *sten*
Stentor: *stene*
stentorian: *stene*
stentorophonic: *stene*
step: *stebh*
stepfather: *steu*
stephane: *stebh*
stephanite: *stebh*
stephanome: *stebh*
Stephen: *stebh*
stepson: *steu*
stercoraceous: *sek V*
stere: *ster II*
stereochemistry: *past*
stereochrome: *ster II*
stereognostic: *ster II*
stereogram: *past*
stereoisomer: *past*
stereophonic: *past*
stereoscope: *past, ster II*
stereotypy: *past, ster II*
steric: *ster II*
sterigma: *ster II*
sterile: *ster II*
sterilize: *ster II*
sterling: *sta*
stern: *sta, ster I*
sternum: *ster I*
sternutation: *pster, strep*
sternutative: *strep*
sternutator: *pster*
steroid: *past*
stertorous: *pster, strep*
stet: *sta*
stevedore: *steibh*
stew: *dheu I*
steward: *dheu I, suer I, uer IV*
stichic: *steigh*
stichomythia: *steigh*
stick: *steig, steu*
stickle: *steigh*
stickleback: *steig*
stiff: *stai, stei, steibh*
stifle: *stai, stei, steue*
stigma: *steig*
stile: *steigh*
stiletto: *steig*
still: *sta, stei*
stillatiform: *stei*
stillatim: *stai, stei*
stillatitious: *stei*
stillicide: *stei, skhai*
stilted: *sta*
stilts: *sta, stel*
sting: *stegh*
stint: *steu*
stipate: *steibh*
stipe: *steibh*
stipend: *pend, steibh*
stipes: *steibh*
stipple: *steibh, steu*
stipulate: *steibh*
stipule: *steibh*
stir: *tuer I*
stirpiculture: *ster I*
stirps: *ster I*
stirrup: *steigh*
stitch: *steig*
stochastic: *stegh*
stock: *steu*
stockade: *stegh, steu*
Stockholm: *kel IV*
stoichiometry: *steigh*
stoke: *steu*
stoker: *steu*
stole: *stel*
stolid: *stel*
stolidity: *stel*
stolon: *stel*
stoma: *stoman*
stomacace: *stoman*

stomach: *stoman*
stomach ache: *stoman*
stomacher: *stoman*
stomach pump: *stoman*
stomach-warmer: *stoman*
stomatic: *stoman*
stomatology: *stoman*
Stomatopoda: *stoman*
stomodeum: *sed II, stoman*
Stomoisia: *stoman*
Stone: *onomen*
stone: *stai*
stone-blind: *caput*
stook: *steu*
stool: *sta*
stoop: *stebh, steu*
stop: *stai, stei, steue*
stopple: *stei, steue*
store: *sta*
stork: *ster II*
storm: *tuer I*
Stort(h)ing: *ten*
story: *ueid*
stoss: *steu*
stout: *stel, ster I*
stove: *sta*
stow: *sta*
strabismometer: *strebh*
strabismus: *strebh*
strabotomy: *strebh*
strain: *ster I, streig*
strait: *streig*
stramazon: *mat*
stramineous: *ster I*
strand: *ster I, streig*
strange: *eghs*
stranger: *eghs*
strangle: *streig*
strangulated: *streig*
strap: *strebh*
strass: *tragh*
strata: *ster I*
stratagem: *ag, ster I*
strategy: *ag, ster I*
strath: *ster I*
stratocracy: *ster I*
stratum: *ster I*
straw: *kau III, ster I*
strawberry: *bhel I, ster I*
stream: *sreu*
streamer: *sreu*
street: *ster I*
strength: *streig*
strenuous: *ster I*
strepitoso: strep
strepitous: *strep*
Strepsiptera: *strebh*
Streptocarpus: *strebh*
Streptococcus: *strebh*
Streptomycin: *meu I, strebh*
Streptothrix: *strebh*
stress: *streig*
stretch: *ster I*
stretto: *streig*
strew: *ster I*
stria: *streig*
striate: *streig*
strickle: *streig*
strict: *streig*
strictness: *dheigh N 29*
stricture: *streig*
stride: *ster I*
stridence: *strid*
strident: *strid*
stridor: *strid*
stridulation: *strid*
stridulousness: *strid*
strigil: *streig*
strigose: *streig*
strike: *streig*
string: *streig*
stringency: *streig*
stringendo: streig
stringent: *streig*
stripling: *sap*
strive: *ster I*
Strix: *strid*
strobic: *strebh*
strobile: *strebh*
stroboscope: *strebh*
stroma: *ster I*
strong: *streig*
Strongyle: *streig*
strongylosis: *streig*
strontium: *el 38*
strop: *strebh*
strophanthin: *strebh*
Strophanthus: *strebh*
strophe: *strebh*
strophulus: *strebh*
structure: *ster I*
strudel: *ser III, sreu*
struggle: *ster I*
Struthio: *trozdos*

struthiocamel: *trozdos*
struthioid: *trozdos*
struthious: *trozdos*
strychnomania: *men I*
stud: *sta*
student: *steu*
studio: *steu*
studious: *steu*
study: *steu*
stuff: *steue*
stultify: *stel*
stum: *stam*
stumble: *stam*
stump: *stebh*
stun: *stene*
stunted: *steu*
stupa: *steue*
stupe: *steue*
stupefy: *steu*
stupendous: *dheigh N 2 e, steu*
stupid: *steu*
stupor: *steu*
sturdy: *trozdos*
stutter: *steu*
sty: *dheu I, steigh*
style: *steig*
stylist: *steig*
stylite: *sta*
stylus: *steig*
styptic: *steu*
Styx: *kau II*
suasion: *suad*
suave: *suad*
suavity: *suad*
subahdar: *dhar*
subaltern: *al II*
subclass: *upo III e*
subclavian: *kleu III*
subconscious: *dheigh N 2 d*
subcutaneous: *skeu*
subdecuple: *upo III e*
subdolous: *del I*
subdue: *deuk*
subgenus: *upo III e*
sub hasta: upo III e
subito: *ei I*
subjacent: *ie*
subject: *ie, upo III e*
subjective: *ie*
sub Jove frigido: upo III e
sub judice: upo III e
subjugate: *ieug*
subjunctive: *ieug, upo III e*
sublate: *tol*
sublation: *tol*
sublimation: *elei, upo III e*
sublime: *elei*
subliminal: *elei*
sublunary: *leuk*
submarine: *mori, upo I*
submerge: *mezg I*
submicroscopic: *sme*
submissive: *upo III e*
submit: *smeit*
subnovitripartient: *upo III e*
subordinate: *ar I, upo III e*
suborn: *ar I, upo III e*
sub plumbo: upo III e
subpoena: *kuei I*
subreption: *labh*
subrogate: *reg I*
sub rosa: upo III e
subscribe: *ker III, sek VI, upo III e*
subscription: *sek VI*
subsequent: *seku I*
subside: *sed I*
subsidy: *sed I*
sub sigilla: upo III e
sub silencio: upo III e
subsist: *sta*
subsistence: *sta, upo III e*
substance: *sta*
substantial: *sta, upo III e*
substantive: *sta*
substitute: *sta*
substratum: *ster I*
substructure: *ster I*
subsume: *em*
subtend: *ten*
subterfuge: *bheug I, upo I*
subternatural: *upo III f*
subtle: *tekhs*
subtract: *tragh*
subtrahend: *tragh*
subtriple: *upo III e*
subulate: *siu*
subuliform: *siu*
suburb: *dhur*
suburbanite: *upo III e*
subvention: *gua*
subversive: *uer II 5*
subvert: *uer II 5*
subway: *upo III e*
succeed: *sed II*
succeeding: *sed II*
succentor: *kan*

success: *sed II, upo III e*
succession: *sed II*
successive: *sed II*
succinct: *kenk I*
succise: *sek II*
succivorous: *bhag*
succor: *kers I*
succose: *seu I*
succuba: *cub, que, keu II*
succubus: *cub*
succulent: *sap, seu I*
succumb: *cub, keu II*
succursal: *kers I*
succussion: *kuet*
such: *leig I, sos*
suck: *sap, seu I*
suckle: *sap, seu I*
suckling: *sap*
sucramine: *ker I*
sucrate: *ker I, sakkara*
sucre: *ker I*
sucrose: *ker I, sakkara*
suction: *sap, seu I*
suctorial: *seu I*
sudarium: *dheigh N 35*
sudation: *sueid II*
sudatorium: *dheigh N 35, sueid II*
sudden: *ei I*
sudoriferous: *sueid II*
sudorific: *sueid II*
sudorium: *sueid II*
Sudra: *ueik I*
Sudri: *medhi*
sue: *seku I*
suffer: *bher I*
suffering: *upo III e*
suffice: *dhe I*
sufficient: *dhe I*
suffix: *dheigh N*
suffrage: *bhreg*
suffragette: *bhreg*
sugar: *ker I, sakkara*
sugent: *seu I*
suggest: *ger VI*
suggestion: *ges, upo III e*
sugillate: *seu I*
suicide: *sek II, skhai, sue*
suilline: *sus*
suint: *sueid II*
suit: *seku I*
suite: *seku I*
suitor: *seku I*
suivez: seku I
sulcate: *selk*
sulcus: *selk*
sulfur: *el 16*
sulky: *selk*
sullage: *sus*
sullen: *sue*
sully: *sus*
sulphur: *el 16*
sultry: *suel*
sum: *upo II*
sumen: *seu I*
summary: *upo II*
summation: *upo II*
summer: *sem II*
summersault: *upo II*
summit: *upo II*
summon: *men I, upo III e*
sump: *suombh*
sumptuary: *em*
sumptuous: *em*
sun: *sauel*
Sunday: *prai, sauel*
sunder: *seni*
sundry: *seni*
sung: *senguh*
sunn: *kann*
Sunna: *dheigh*
sunny: *sauel*
sup: *sap, seu I*
super: *nem, upo II*
superabundance: *aue*
superannuated: *at*
superb: *bheu, upo II*
supercilious: *kel VI, upo III g*
supercool: *upo II*
supererogatory: *reg I, upo III g*
superette: *upo III g*
superfetate: *dhel I*
superficial: *dhe I*
superfluity: *upo III g*
superfluous: *beu, bhleu, upo III i*
superheterodyne: *upo II*
superhuman: *upo III g*
superintendent: *ten, upo II*
superior: *bheu*
superiority: *upo II*
superiority complex: *upo II*
superjacent: *ie*
superlative: *ar I, dheigh N 24, tol, upo III g*
superman: *dheigh N 27, upo II*
supermarket: *upo III g*
supernal: *upo II*

supernatant: *sna I*
supernatural: *upo II*
supernova: *upo II*
supernumerary: *nem, upo II*
supersalient: *upo III g*
superscription: *ker III, sek VI*
supersede: *sed I*
supersonic: *suen, upo III a*
superstition: *sta*
superstitious: *sta, upo III g*
supertelluric: *upo III g*
supervene: *gua*
supervise: *ueid*
supervision: *ueid*
supervisor: *dheigh N 13*
supine: *per IV, upo I*
supper: *sap, seu I*
supplant: *pela*
supple: *plek I*
supplement: *pel V, plek I*
suppliant: *plek I*
supplicate: *plek I*
supply: *pel V*
support: *per II*
suppose: *upo III e*
suppress: *pres*
suppurate: *pu*
supralabial: *leb*
supraliminal: *upo III h*
supralineal: *upo III h*
suprarational: *upo III h*
suprarenal: *upo III h*
supraspinal: *upo III h*
supraspinatus: *upo III h*
supreme: *upo II*
surcease: *sed III, upo III i*
surcharge: *upo III i*
surcingle: *kenk I, upo III i*
surcoat: *upo III i*
surd: *suer II*
sure: *cura, sue*
surety: *cura*
surface: *dhe I*
surfeit: *dhe I*
surge: *reg I, upo I*
surgeon: *gher IV, uerg*
surgery: *plek I, uerg*
surmise: *smeit*
surmount: *men II*
surmullet: *mel III*
surname: *onomen, upo III i*
surpass: *pet II*
surplice: *pel VI*
surplus: *pel V*
surrealism: *upo III i*
surrender: *do, upo III i*
surreption: *rep II*
surreptitious: *labh, rep II, upo III i*
surrogate: *reg I, upo III e*
surtout: *teue 10*
surveillance: *ueg II*
survey: *ueid, upo III i*
survivor: *upo III i*
Surya: *suel*
susceptible: *kap, upo III e*
suspect: *spek*
suspend: *pend, spend II, upo III e*
suspenders: *spend II*
suspense: *pend, spend II*
suspenseful: *pel V*
suspicion: *spek*
suspicious: *dheigh N 2 c*
suspire: *speis*
Sussex: *sek I*
sustain: *ten, upo III e*
sustenance: *ten*
susurration: *suer II*
sutler: *seu II*
sutra: *siu*
suttee: *es*
suture: *siu*
suzerain: *uer II 5*
Svarga: *suel*
svelt: *uel III*
swab: *suep II*
swaddle: *skeu*
swaddling: *skeu*
swadeshi: *sue*
swag: *sueng*
swagger: *sueng*
swain: *sue*
swami: *sue*
swamp: *suombh*
swan: *suen*
swank: *sueng*
swap: *steue, suei II*
swarm: *suer II*
swart: *suord*
swarthy: *suord*
swastika: *es, keg*
swathe: *skeu*
sway: *suei II, sueng*
sweal: *suel*
swear: *suer II*

sweat: *sueid II*
sweater: *sueid II*
sweatshirt: *sueid II*
sweep: *suei II*
sweet: *sal I, suad*
sweetbread: *suad*
sweeten: *suad*
sweetheart: *kerd, suad*
swelter: *suel*
sweltry: *suel*
swift: *suei II*
swiftlet: *suei II*
swim: *suei II, suem*
swimmeret: *suem*
swimmingly: *suem*
swine: *mel I, sus*
swineherd: *kerdh*
swing: *sueng*
swinge: *sueng*
swingletree: *sueng*
swipe: *suei II*
swirl: *suer II*
switch: *suei II*
sword: *suer III*
swordfish: *peisk*
sycamore: *moro*
sycophant: *bha II*
syllabification: *slagu*
syllable: *labh, sem I, slagu*
syllabus: *sem I*
syllepsis: *slagu*
syllogism: *dheigh N 21, leg I, sem I*
sylph: *gn*
sylvan: *sal I, silva*
Sylvanus: *silva*
Sylvia: *sal I, silva*
Sylvian fissure: *akua*
sylvite: *akua*
symbiosis: *guei, ksun, per VII, sem I*
symbol: *sem I*
symbolism: *ksun*
symmetry: *dheigh N 36*
sympalmograph: *pal*
sympathetic: *guadh, sem I*
sympathy: *ksun*
sympatric: *peter*
symphony: *bha I, ksun*
symphysis: *bheu*
sympiezometer: *sed I*
Symplegades: *plak*
Symplocarpus: *plek I*
symploce: *plek I*
Symplocos: *plek I*
symposium: *ksun, poi*
symptom: *ksun, pet I, sem I*
symptomatic: *ksun*
synadelphite: *ksun*
syn(a)ersis: *ie*
synagogue: *ag, ksun, sem I*
synarthrosis: *ar I*
sync: *ksun*
syncarp: *ker III*
synchondrosis: *ghren*
synchronize: *ksun, sem I*
synchytrium: *gheu*
syncopated: *sem I*
syncopation: *ksun*
syncope: *ksun, sek IV*
syncretism: *kere*
syndic: *deik*
syndicate: *deik, sem I*
syndication: *deik*
syndrome: *dra, ksun*
syndyasmian: *ksun*
synecdoche: *eghs*
synergetic: *ksun, uerg*
synergism: *uerg*
synergist: *uerg*
synesis: *ie*
synezesis: *sed I*
synod: *sed II*
synonym: *es, ksun, onomen*
synopsis: *oku*
syntax: *tag II*
synteresis: *ksun*
synthesis: *dhe I*
syntony: *ten*
syphilis: *bhili, sem I, sus*
Syringa: *suer II*
syringe: *suer II*
syringotomy: *suer II*
syrinx: *suer II*
syssarcosis: *tuerk*
systaltic: *stel*
system: *sta*
systole: *stel*
syzygy: *ieug*

T

tabatière: leit
tabby: *reg I*

tabefaction: *ta*
tabernacle: *treb*
tabes: *ta*
tabescent: *ta*
tabitude: *ta*
tabula rasa: *rad I*
tace: *tak*
tacet: *tak*
tache: *dek II*
tachyglossus: *glokh*
tachylite: *leu I*
tacit: *tak*
taciturn: *tak*
taciturnity: *tak*
Tacitus: *tak*
tack: *dek II*
tackle: *taka*
taco: *dek II*
tact: *tag I*
tactician: *tag II*
tactics: *tag II*
tactile: *tag I*
tactometer: *tag I*
taenia: *ten*
taffeta: *temp 1*
tag: *dek II, tag I*
tagatose: *glact*
tahsildar: *dhar*
tail: *dek II*
tailor: *dheigh N 13*
taint: *teng*
taj: *per I, steg*
take: *deik, onomen, taka*
tale: *del I*
talent: *tol*
tales: *t, to*
talesman: *t, to*
talion: *tol*
taliped: *ped*
talipot: *pet I*
talisman: *ker I*
talk: *del I*
talose: *glact*
talukdar: *dhar*
talus: *tel*
tamas: *teme*
tambour: *steu*
tambourine: *steu*
tame: *dam*
tamper: *temp 5*
tandem: *de, t, to*
tang: *denk, jing, tenq*
tangent: *tag I*
tangible: *tag I*
tangle: *jing, tenq*
tank: *sta*
tankard: *kuetuer*
tansy: *dhel I*
tantalize: *tol*
tantalum: *el 73*
Tantalus: *el 41, el 73, tol*
tantamount: *t, to*
tantra: *ten*
tap: *labh*
tapas: *tep*
tape: *temp 1*
tapestry: *temp 1*
tapetum: *temp 1*
taphrina: *dhembh*
tapis: *temp 1*
tar: *deru*
tardamente: men I
tarragon: *derk*
Tarsipes: *ped*
tarsus: *ters*
tart: *der, tereq*
Tartuffe: *teue 10*
taste: *tag I*
tattoo: *de*
tatty: *ten*
tauriform: *taur*
taurine: *taur*
tauromachy: *magh, taur*
Taurus: *guei, morui, taur*
taut: *deuk*
tautegorical: *to*
tautochrone: *t, to*
tautology: *dheigh N 30, leg I, t, to*
tautophony: *t, to*
tavern: *treb*
tax: *tag I*
taxi: *kapr, tag II*
taxicab: *tag II*
taxidermy: *der*
taximeter: *tag I, tag II*
taxis: *tag II*
taxite: *tag II*
Taxodium: *tekhus*
taxodont: *tag II*
taxonomy: *tag II*
Taxus: *tekhus*
teach: *deik*
teacher: *rad I*
team: *deuk*

teapoy: *ped, tre*
tear: *dakru, der*
teat: *tit*
technetium: *el 43, tekhs*
technical: *tekhs*
technique: *tekhs*
technology: *tekhs*
tectology: *tekhs*
Tectona: *tekhs*
tectonic: *tekhs*
tectrix: *steg*
teem: *deuk*
teetotal: *teuta*
teetotaler: *teuta*
teetotum: *teue 10, teuta*
tegula: *steg*
tegular: *steg*
tegument: *steg*
teinoscope: *ten*
telaesthesia: *eghs*
telamon: *tol*
talangiectasia: *ten*
telary: *tekhs*
telegnosis: *ker I*
Telegonus: *ker I*
telegony: *gn, ker I*
telegram: *gerbh*
telegraph: *ker I*
telekinesis: *kei I*
Telemachus: *ker I*
telepathy: *guadh, ker I, uerg*
telephone: *bha I, gn, ker I*
telergy: *uerg*
telescope: *dheigh N 32, ker I, spek*
telesterion: *ker I*
television: *arkh, ker I*
televox: *ueks*
telium: *ker I*
tell: *del I*
tellurian: *tel*
telluric: *tel*
tellurion: *tel*
tellurium: *el 34, el 52, tel*
Tellus: *el 52*
telson: *ker I*
temenos: *tem*
temerarious: *teme*
temerity: *teme*
temerous: *teme*
temper: *temp 5, ugu*
tempera: *temp 5*
temperament: *temp 5*
temperance: *temp 5, ugu*
temperature: *temp 5, ugu*
tempest: *temp 5, ters*
tempestuous: *temp 5*
Templars: *temp 2*
template: *temp 2*
temple: *temp 1, temp 3*
tempo: *temp 5*
temporal: *temp 3, temp 5, ugu*
temporary: *temp 5, ugu*
temporize: *ugu*
tempt: *temp 4*
temptation: *temp 4*
tempus: temp 5
tempus fugit: temp 5
temulent: *teme*
ten: *dekm*
tenable: *ten*
tenacious: *dheigh N 2 b, ten*
tenaculum: *ten*
tenancy: *ten*
tenant: *ten*
tend: *ten*
tendency: *ten*
tender: *ten*
tendon: *ten*
tenebrae: *teme*
tenebrous: *teme*
tenement: *ten*
tenesmus: *ten*
tenet: *ghdhu*
tennis: *ane, ten*
tenography: *ten*
tenon: *ten*
tenontophyme: *ten*
tenor: *ten*
tenorino: ten
tenoroon: *ten*
tenotomy: *ten*
tense: *temp 5, ten*
tension: *ten*
tent: *ten, teng*
tentacle: *temp 4*
tentative: *temp 4, ten*
tenter: *ten*
tenterhooks: *ten*
tenth: *dekm*
tentigo: *ten*
tentorium: *ten*
tenue: ten
tenuipede: *ten*
tenuity: *ten*

tenuous: *ten*
tenure: *ten*
tenuto: ten
tepid: *tep*
tepidarium: *tep*
tera-: *me IV*
teratical: *kuer*
teratohedral: *kuetuer*
teratoid: *kuer*
teratology: *kuer*
teratoscopy: *kuer*
teratosymmetrical: *kuetuer*
terbium: *el 65*
tercel: *tre*
tercet: *tre*
terebra: *ter II*
teredo: *ter II*
teres: ter II
terete: *ter II*
tergiversation: *uer II 5*
term: *ter III*
Termes: *ter II*
terminal: *ter III*
termination: *ter III*
terminology: *ter III*
terminus: *ter III*
termite: *ter II*
Termitidae: *ter II*
tern: *tre*
ternal: *tre*
Teron: *ter I*
terpodion: *ued*
Terpsichore: *terp*
terra: *ters*
terrace: *ters*
terra cotta: *peku, ters*
terra firma: *ters*
terrain: *ters*
terra incognita: *ters*
terramara: *ters*
Terramycin: *ters*
terrane: *ters*
terraqueous: *ters*
terrazzo: *ters*
terrene: *ters*
terreplein: *pel V, ters*
terrestrial: *ters*
terrevert: *ters*
terrible: *ter I*
terricolous: *ters*
terrific: *dhe I, ter I*
terrify: *ter I*
terrigenous: *ters*
terrine: *ters*
territory: *ters*
terror: *ter I*
terse: *ter III*
tertian: *tre*
Tertiary: *tre*
tertiary: *tre*
terzo: *tre*
tessaraglot: *kuetuer*
tessella: *kuetuer*
tessellate: *kuetuer*
tessellation: *kuetuer*
tessera: *kuetuer*
tesseratomic: *kuetuer*
tesserian: *kuetuer*
tessitura: *tekhs*
test: *tekhs, tre*
Testament: *tre*
testament: *tre*
testamur: *tre*
testator: *tre*
teste: *tre*
tester: *ane*
testes: *tre*
testicle: *tre*
testify: *tre*
testimonial: *tre*
tetanus: *ten*
tête-à-tête: *caput*
tetra-: *kuetuer*
tetracoral: *kuetuer*
tetract: *nekut*
tetrad: *kuetuer*
tetragamy: *kuetuer*
tetragonism: *kuetuer*
Tetragrammaton: *gerbh, kuetuer*
tetrahedron: *kuetuer*
tetrakisdodecahedron: *kuetuer*
tetrameter: *kuetuer*
tetrapla: *plek I*
tetrapolis: *pele*
tetrapylon: *suer I*
tetrarch: *kuetuer*
tetraselenodont: *kuetuer*
tetter: *der*
Texidea: *tekhs*
text: *tekhs*
textile: *tekhs*
texture: *tekhs*
thalassian: *eku*
thalassic: *eku*

thalassophilous: *eku*
thalattocracy: *eku*
Thalia: *dhal, el 81*
thallic: *dhal*
thallium: *dhal, el 81*
thallophyte: *dhal*
thallous: *dhal*
thallus: *dhal*
than: *t, to*
thanadar: *dhar*
thanatism: *dheu I*
thanatognomic: *dheu I*
Thanatopsis: *dheu I, oku*
thanatotic: *dheu I*
thank: *tong*
Thanksgiving: *tong*
that: *t, to*
thatch: *steg*
thaumaturge: *uerg*
thaw: *ta*
the: *t, to*
thee: *to*
theelin: *dhel I*
their: *t, to*
theism: *dhes*
thelitis: *dhel I*
thelium: *dhel I*
thelyblast: *dhel I*
thelyotokous: *dhel I*
them: *t, to*
theme: *dhe I*
Themis: *dhe I, morui*
then: *kuo, t, to*
thence: *kuo, t, to*
theobromine: *dhes, garg*
theocentric: *dhes*
theocratic: *dhes*
theodicy: *deik, dhes*
Theodore: *do, dei*
theodore: *do*
theomachy: *dhes, magh*
theophany: *bha II, dhes*
theorem: *dhes*
theory: *dhes*
therapeutic: *dhar*
theravada: *aus*
there: *t, to*
thereomorphic: *ghuer*
Thereva: *ghuer*
theriac: *ghuer*
therianthropic: *ghuer, nert*
Theridiidae: *ghuer*
therm: *guher*
thermae: *guher*
thermaesthesia: *guher*
thermal: *guher*
thermion: *guher*
thermocall: *guher*
thermochemistry: *guher*
thermodynamics: *deu, guher*
thermometer: *guher*
thermopaulion: *guher*
thermophile: *guher*
thermopote: *guher*
thermos: *guher*
thermostat: *sta*
thermotropism: *trep*
theroid: *ghuer*
theropod: *ghuer*
these: *t, to*
Theseus: *taur*
thesis: *dhe I*
thespian: *seku II*
Thespis: *seku II*
theurgy: *uerg*
thew(s): *teu*
they: *t, to*
thigh: *teue 10*
thigmotaxis: *dheigh*
thigmotropism: *dheigh*
thimblerig: *reig I*
thin: *ten*
thine: *to*
thing: *ten*
thingamabob: *ten*
thingamajig: *ten*
thingamy: *ten*
think: *tong*
thio acid: *dheu I*
Thiobacillus: *dheu I*
thiocyanic: *dheu I*
thionic: *dheu I*
thiophenal: *dheu I*
third: *tre*
thirst: *ters*
thirteen: *dekm, tre*
thirty: *dekm, tre*
this: *t, to*
thither: *t, to*
thixle: *tekhs*
thixotropy: *dheigh*
thole: *tol*
tholepin: *teue 10*
thong: *tuegh*

Thor: *el 90, es, prai, stene*
thorax: *dhar*
thorium: *el 90*
thorn: *ster I*
thorough: *ter III*
thorp: *treb*
those: *t, to*
thou: *to*
though: *to*
thought: *tong*
thousand: *teue 10*
thrash: *ter II*
thrasonical: *dhers, ghenu*
thread: *ter II*
threat: *treud*
threatening: *treud*
three: *tre*
threefold: *plek II*
three-ply: *plek I*
threescore: *tre*
threnody: *aud, dhren, ued*
thresh: *ter II*
threshold: *ter II*
thrice: *tre*
thrill: *ter III*
Thrinax: *tre*
throat: *ster I*
throe: *treud*
throne: *dhar*
throstle: *stene, trozdos*
throttle: *ster I*
through: *ter III*
throw: *treud*
thrum: *ter III*
thrush: *stene, trozdos*
thrust: *treud*
thug: *steg*
thulium: *el 69*
thumb: *teue 10*
thurible: *dheu II*
thurifer: *dheu I*
Thursday: *medhi, prai*
thus: *t*
thwaite: *tueis*
thwart: *tereq*
thy: *to*
Thyestes: *tolku*
thyme: *dheu I, dheu II*
thymus: *dheu I*
thyroid: *dhur*
ticket: *steig*
ticking: *tit*
tickle: *ane, pilo, tit*
tickle-tackle: *tit*
tickle-tail: *ane, tit*
tickling: *tit*
ticktack: *tit*
tick-tack-toe: *dek II*
ticktock: *dek II*
tidbit: *tit*
tide: *da II*
tidings: *da II*
tie: *deuk*
tierce: *neun, tre*
tiffany: *bha II*
tiger: *steig*
tight: *tenq*
tiglic: *ta*
til: *tel*
tilde: *tel*
tile: *steg*
till: *ant, del I*
tiller: *del II*
tilt: *del II, tel*
timber: *dem*
timbre: *steu*
timbrel: *steu*
time: *da II*
timid: *kuei I, teme*
timocracy: *dheigh N 11, kuei I*
timorous: *kuei I*
Timothy: *kuei I*
timothy grass: *kuei I*
timpano: *steu*
tin: *el 50*
tinctorial: *teng*
tincture: *teng*
ting: *jing*
tinge: *teng*
tinglass: *el 83*
tingle: *jing*
tink: *jing*
tinker: *dheigh N 13, jing*
tinnitus: *stene*
tinsel: *skai*
tint: *teng*
tintamarre: *stene*
tintinnabulation: *jing, stene*
tirocinium: *ken II, teue 1*
Tisiphone: *dheu I, kuei I*
tissue: *tekhs*
tit: *tit*
Titan: *nebh*
Titanic: *nebh*

titanic: *nebh*
titanic acid: *nebh*
titanite: *nebh*
titanium: *el 22, nebh*
Titanomachy: *nebh*
Titanosuchus: *nebh*
Titanotheres: *nebh*
Titan rocket: *nebh*
titbit: *tit*
titer: *tel*
tit for tat: *labh*
titillate: *tit*
titlark: *tit*
title: *tel*
titrate: *tel*
tittle: *tel*
tittle-tattle: *tel*
titular: *tel*
tmesis: *tem*
to: *de*
toadstool: *spong*
toast: *ters*
tobacco: *leit*
tobaccofied: *leit*
tobacconist: *leit*
toccata: *steu*
toccatella: steu
toccatina: steu
tocsin: *sek I, steu*
today: *agher*
toe: *deik*
together: *ghedh*
toil: *steu, tekhs*
toilet: *tekhs*
toilette: *tekhs*
token: *deik*
tola: *tol*
tolerate: *tol*
toll: *tol*
tomato: *teue 10*
tomb: *teue 6*
tombac: *teme*
tombstone: *stai, stei*
tome: *tem*
Tomistoma: *tem*
tomium: *tem*
tomtit: *tit*
ton: *dheu I, ten*
-ton: *dheu III*
tonality: *ten*
tone: *ten*
tongs: *denk*
tongue: *dinghu*
tonic: *ten*
tonite: *stene*
tonitrous: *stene*
tonsillitis: *dheigh N 23*
tonsorial: *tem*
tonsurate: *tem*
tonsure: *tem*
tonypandy: *bhurig*
too: *de*
tooth: *denk*
toothpick: *speik*
toothsome: *dheigh N 37*
topaz: *tep*
tope: *steue*
toper: *steue*
topiary: *iso*
topic: *iso, top*
topical: *iso, top*
topography: *gerbh, top*
topolatry: *top*
toponym: *onomen, top*
topophone: *top*
topsy-turvy: *derbh*
torch: *tereq*
torchon: *tereq*
torcular: *tereq*
toreador: *taur*
torero: taur
toreutic: *ter II*
torment: *tereq*
tormentil: *tereq*
tormentor: *dheigh N 13*
tormina: *tereq*
tornado: *ker I, stene, tereq*
tornaria: *tereq*
toro: *taur*
torpedo: *stene*
torpid: *stene*
torpor: *stene*
torquated: *tereq*
torque: *tereq*
torques: *tereq*
torrefaction: *ters*
torrefy: *ters*
torrent: *ters*
torrential: *ters*
torrentine: *ters*
torrid: *ters*
torsade: *tereq*
torsel: *tereq*
torsion: *tereq*

torsk: *ters*
tort: *tereq, uer II 3*
torticollis: *tereq*
tortile: *tereq*
tortious: *tereq*
tortoise: *tereq*
Tortricidae: *tereq*
Tortrix: *tereq*
Tortulaceae: *tereq*
tortuous: *tereq*
torture: *tereq*
torturous: *tereq*
tostamente: men I
total: *teue 10*
totality: *teue 10*
totipalmate: *teue 10*
touch: *stei*
touché: *stei*
Touchstone: *stei*
touchstone: *stei*
tough: *denk*
tour: *ter II*
tournament: *ter II*
tourney: *ter II*
tourniquet: *ter II*
tout: *teue 10*
tow: *deuk*
toward: *de, uer II 5*
town: *dheu III*
toxarch: *tekhus*
toxic: *tekhus*
toxicology: *tekhus*
Toxifer: *tekhus*
toxin: *tekhus*
toxophil: *tekhus*
toxophilite: *tekhus*
Toxotes: *tekhus*
trabea: *treb*
trabeated: *treb*
trabeation: *treb*
trabecula: *treb*
trace: *tragh*
traces: *tragh*
trachea: *dher*
trachelotomy: *dhregh*
trachoma: *dher*
track: *tragh*
tract: *tragh*
tractable: *tragh*
tractate: *tragh*
tractile: *tragh*
traction: *tragh*
trade: *dra*
tradition: *do*
traduce: *deuk*
traduction: *deuk*
tragedian: *dheigh N 7*
tragedy: *aig, ter II, ued*
tragelaph: *aud*
traghetto: ie
tragically: *dheigh N 1, leig I*
trail: *tragh*
train: *tragh*
trait: *tragh*
traitor: *do*
trajectory: *ie*
tralatitious: *tol*
tram: *ter III, tragh*
trammel: *tre*
tramontane: *men II*
tramp: *dra*
trample: *dra*
trampoline: *dra*
tramway: *ter III*
trance: *ei I, ter III*
transact: *ag*
transatlantic: *nebh, ter III*
transcendent: *skai*
transcribe: *ker III, sek VI*
transducer: *deuk*
transect: *sek I*
transfer: *bher I, ter III, tol*
transference: *tol*
transfix: *dheigh*
transform: *merbh*
transfusion: *gheu*
transgress: *ter III*
transgression: *ghredh*
transient: *ei I*
transit: *ei I*
transition: *ei I*
transitive: *ei I*
transitory: *ter III*
translate: *ter III, tol*
translation: *tol*
translator: *do*
transliterate: *dephi*
translucent: *leuk*
transmigration: *mei II*
transmit: *smeit*
transmute: *mei II*
transom: *ter III*
transparent: *pare*
transpire: *speis*

transplant: *pela*
transpontine: *pent*
transport: *per II*
transportation: *per II*
transverse: *uer II 5*
transvestite: *ues II*
trap: *dra*
trapeze: *kuetuer, ped*
trapezium: *kuetuer, ped*
trapezohedron: *kuetuer*
trapezoid: *kuetuer*
trappings: *der*
traps: *der*
trapunto: *peug*
trass: *ters*
traulism: *ters*
trauma: *ter II*
travail: *pag, tre*
travel: *pag*
traverse: *uer II 5*
travesty: *ues II*
Traviata, La: uegh
trawl: *tragh*
tray: *deru*
treacle: *ghuer*
tread: *dra*
treason: *do*
treat: *tragh*
treatise: *tragh*
treaty: *tragh*
trecento: *tre*
trechometer: *dhregh*
tree: *deru*
trefoil: *beu*
trek: *tragh*
trellis: *tre*
trema: *ter II*
Tremandra: *ter I*
trematode: *ter II*
tremble: *ter I*
Tremella: *ter I*
tremelline: *ter I*
tremellose: *ter I*
tremendous: *dheigh N 22, ter I*
tremolant: *ter I*
tremolo: *ter I*
tremor: *ter I*
tremulous: *ter I*
trench: *ter III*
trenchant: *ter III*
trepan: *fin, ter II*
trephine: *fin*
trepid: *ter I*
trepidation: *ter I*
treponeme: *sne*
très: ter III
tresillo: tre
trespass: *pet II, ter III*
tressilate: *sel IV, ter III*
trestle: *ter III*
tret: *tragh*
trey: *tre*
triad: *tre*
triarii: *tre*
Trias: *tre*
triatomic: *tre*
triaxial: *tre*
triazine: *tre*
triazole: *tre*
tribade: *ter II*
tribe: *tre*
Tribolium: *tre*
tribrach: *braghu, tre*
tribulation: *ter II*
Tribulus: *tre*
tribunal: *tre*
tribune: *tre*
tributary: *tre*
tribute: *tre*
triceps: *tre*
Triceratops: *tre*
tricerion: *keneko, tre*
Tricholoma: *uelu*
Trichomanes: *men I*
Trichoptera: *mak*
trichotomy: *tem, tre*
triclinium: *klei, tre*
tricorn: *ker II*
tricot: *streig*
tricrotic: *tre*
tricuspid: *tre*
tridactyl: *tre*
trident: *den, tre*
tridymite: *tre*
trierarch: *tre*
trieteric: *uet*
trifle: *bhel, bhel I, teue 9*
trifoliate: *tre*
trifurcate: *bhurig*
trig: *deru*
triganon: *tre*
trigeminous: *iem*
trigger: *tragh*
triggerfish: *tragh*

trigger-happy: *tragh*
triglochin: *glokh*
triglot: *tre*
triglyph: *gluebh, tre*
trigon: *tre*
trigonometry: *dheigh N 36, ghenu, me IV, tre*
trihedron: *tre*
trillion: *tre*
Trillium: *tre*
Trilobite: *tre*
trilogy: *tre*
trim: *deru*
trimaran: *kat*
trimerous: *tre*
trimester: *me IV, tre*
Trimurti: *tre*
trine: *tre*
trinity: *oino, tre*
trinket: *ter III*
trinomial: *onomen, tre*
trio: *tre*
triolet: *tre*
trip: *dra*
tripartite: *dheigh N 22*
tripedal: *ped*
triphenylmethane: *tre*
triple: *plek I, upo III e*
triplet: *tre*
triplex: *plek I, tre*
triplicate: *tre*
triplicity: *tre*
triploid: *tre*
tripod: *ped, tre*
tripos: *ped*
Tripsacum: *ter II*
tripsis: *ter II*
triptote: *pet I*
triptych: *bheug II, tre*
Tripura: *tre*
trireme: *ere, tre*
trisagion: *iag I*
trisect: *sek I, tre*
triseme: *dheie*
Trisiras: *tre*
triskelion: *skai, tre*
Trismegistus: *me III*
trismus: *strid*
trisoctahedron: *tre*
trissaccharide: *tre*
tristearin: *stei*
tristich: *steigh, tre*
tristichous: *steigh*
Tristram: *ieg*
tritanopia: *tre*
tritaph: *dhembh*
trite: *ter II*
Triteleia: *tre*
Trithrinax: *tre*
Triticum: *ter II*
tritium: *el 1, iso, tre*
tritone: *ten*
trituration: *ter II*
triumphal: *dheigh N 5*
triumvir: *tre*
triumvirate: *tre, uiro*
triune: *oino, tre*
trivalent: *tre*
trivet: *ped, tre*
trivia: *uegh*
trivial: *tre, uegh*
trivium: *kuetuer, tre, uegh*
trocar: *tre*
trochaic: *dhregh*
trochal: *dhregh*
trochanter: *dhregh*
troche: *dhregh*
trochee: *dhregh*
trochilics: *dhregh*
trochilus: *dhregh*
trochlea: *dhregh*
trochoid: *dhregh*
troglodyte: *aud, ter II*
trogon: *aud, ter II*
troika: *tre*
trone: *ter II*
troop: *treb*
Tropaeolum: *trep*
trope: *trep*
tropedosternal: *trep*
trophosome: *teue 3*
trophy: *trep*
tropic: *trep*
tropine: *trep*
tropis: *trep*
tropism: *trep*
tropologetically: *trep*
tropology: *trep*
troposphere: *trep*
troppo: treb
trot: *dra*
troth: *deru*
troubadour: *trep*
trouble: *tuer I*

tutress: *teu*
tutrix: *teu*
tutsan: *teu*
tutti: *teue 10*
tutti-frutti: *teue 10*
tuum: *to*
tuxedo: *ulkuo*
twain: *duo*
twat: *caput*
twat-scourer: *caput*
twayblade: *duo*
tweak: *tuegh*
tweedle: *tara*
twelve: *duo*
twenty: *dekm, duo*
twice: *duo*
twig: *duo*
twilight: *duo*
twill: *duo, tre*
twin: *duo*
twine: *duo*
twinge: *tuegh*
twist: *duo*
twister: *ker I*
twit: *ueid*
twitch: *tuegh*
two: *duo*
twofold: *plek II*
two-ply: *plek I*
tylarus: *teue 2*
tyloma: *teue 2*
Tylopoda: *teue 2*
tympan: *steu*
tympano: *steu*
tympanum: *steu*
tympany: *steu*
Tyndareus: *steu*
Tynwald: *ten, uelt*
type: *steu*
Typha: *teue 2*
Typhaceae: *teue 2*
typhoid: *dheu I, ker I*
typhoon: *ker I*
typhus: *dheu I, ker I*
typical: *steu*
typify: *steu*
typography: *steu*
typolite: *steu*
typomania: *steu*
typtology: *steu*
tyro: *ken II, teue 1*
tyrocidine: *teue 1*
tyromancy: *teue 1*
tyronic: *teue 1*
tyrosine: *teue 1*
tyrothricin: *teue 1*
tyrotoxicon: *teue 1*
Tyrotrix: *teue 1*

U

uberous: *eudh*
ubiety: *kuo*
ubiquitous: *kuo*
ubiquity: *kue*
udder: *eudh*
udograph: *ugu*
udometer: *ugu*
uffish: *reu*
UFO: *kred I*
Uitlander: ud
ukase: *au I*
Ukrainian: *sek VIII*
Ulenspiegel, Till: *ul*
Ulex: *ugu*
uliginous: *ugu*
ullage: *oku*
ulna: *elei*
Ulotrichi: *uel III*
ulotrichous: *uel III*
ulterior: *al II*
ultimate: *al II, dheigh N 10*
ultima Thule: *el 69*
ultimatum: *al II*
ultimogeniture: *gn*
ultracrepidarian: *nebh*
ultramarine: *mori*
ultramicroscopic: *al II*
ultramontane: *men II*
ultramundane: *man*
ultrasonic: *al II*
ultraviolet: *al II, en, ndher*
ululate: *ul*
ululation: *ul*
Ulysses: *mazdo*
umbel: *andho*
umbilical: *nabh*
umbilicus: *nabh*
umbiliform: *nabh*
umbles: *lendh I*
umbra: *andho*
umbrage: *andho*

umbrella: *andho, per V*
umlaut: *kleu I*
umpire: *per V*
unanimous: *ane, oino*
unavoidable: *bha II, eu*
uncertain: *sek VI*
unchanging: *skamb*
uncia: *oino*
unciform: *ank*
uncinal: *ank*
uncinus: *ank*
uncle: *au II, au IV*
Uncle Remus: *ere*
Uncle Sam: *leg II*
un-come-at-able: *ne*
uncommunicative: *dheigh N 24*
unconfirmed: *ne*
uncouth: *gn*
uncritical: *sker VI*
unction: *enguo*
unctuous: *enguo*
uncus: *ank*
undate: *aue*
under: *endher, ndher*
underbrush: *bherem, ndher*
undercover man: *ndher*
undercroft: *krup*
underdone: *ndher*
underestimate: *ndher*
undergraduate: *ndher*
underground: *endher, upo III e*
underlay: *legh*
underling: *sap*
underneath: *ni*
understand: *ndher, sta*
understanding: *sta*
undertaker: *mer II, ndher*
underwriter: *ndher*
undesirable: *sueid I*
undeviating: *uegh*
undine: *aue, gn*
undiplomatic: *duo*
undistinguished: *steig*
undo: *ant*
undose: *aue*
undressed: *ne*
undulant: *aue*
unearth: *ant*
uneducated: *ne*
unfatherly: *peter*
unflinching: *kleng*
unfold: *plek II*
ungodly: *ne*
ungual: *onogh*
unguent: *enguo*
unguiculate: *onogh*
unguiform: *onogh*
Ungulata: *onogh*
ungulate: *onogh*
unicorn: *ker II, oino*
uniform: *merbh, oino*
unify: *oino*
unilateral: *oino*
unimpeachable: *ne*
unintelligible: *leg I*
Unio: *oino*
Uniole: *oino*
union: *oino*
unionocracy: *kar*
uniparous: *oino*
unique: *oino*
unisexed: *oino*
unison: *oino*
unit: *oino*
Unitarian: *oino*
unite: *oino*
United States: *oino*
unity: *oino*
univalent: *oino*
universal: *uer II 5*
universe: *oino, uer II 5*
university: *oino, uer II 5*
univocal: *ueks*
unjust: *ieuos*
unkempt: *gembh, ne*
unlawful: *legh*
unlearned: *leis*
unlettered: *ne*
unlikely: *leig I, ne*
unlimited: *elei*
unlock: *ant*
unloose: *ant*
unnerved: *sne*
unnumbered: *ne*
unpatriotic: *peter*
unpolished: *ne*
unpopular: *popul*
unpruned: *ne*
unreal: *rei II*
unrewarded: *suer I*
unrivaled: *ergh*
unseduced: *ne*
unseminared: *se I*
unshaken: *ne*

unstraightforward: *uer II 5*
unsuccessful: *sed III*
untainted: *teng*
unterrified: *ne*
until: *anti, dek III*
unto: *anti*
untoward: *do*
untrained: *ne*
untranslatable: *dheigh N 3*
unveil: *ueg I*
unwanted: *eu*
unwitting: *ueid*
up: *upo I*
Upanishad: *ni, sed I, upo I*
upbraid: *bhel I*
upright: *reg I*
uproar: *kere, upo I*
upsilon: *bhili*
upstart: *ster II*
upward: *uer II 5*
urachus: *geu*
uranism: *aue*
uranium: *aue, el 52, el 92, nebh*
Uranus: *el 52, nebh*
urban: *dhur, suesor*
urbane: *dhur, suesor*
urbanity: *dhur*
urchin: *ghers*
urea: *nebh, uer VII*
uredo: *eus*
ureto: *uer VII*
ureter: *nebh*
urethra: *uer VII*
uretic: *nebh, uer VII*
urge: *ureg*
urgency: *ureg*
urgent: *ureg*
uric: *aue, nebh, uer VII*
uridine: *nebh*
urinal: *aue, nebh*
urinalysis: *aue, nebh*
urinary: *uer VII*
urinate: *aue, nebh*
urinator: *aue*
urine: *nebh, uer VII*
urinoscopist: *uer VII*
urinoscopy: *spek*
urinous: *aue*
urning: *ane*
Urocoptis: *ors*
urogenital: *aue, nebh, uer VII*
urology: *uer VII*
Uropeltidae: *ors*
uropoietic: *uer VII*
uropteran: *ors*
uropygial: *ors, uer VII*
uroscopy: *aue*
urosome: *dheigh N 37*
urotoxic: *aue*
ursine: *rkthos*
urson: *rkthos*
Ursula: *rkthos*
urtica: *eus*
urticaria: *eus*
urtication: *eus*
usher: *or*
usquebaugh: *guei*
ustion: *eus*
ustulation: *eus*
usucapion: *kap*
usurer: *dheigh N 13*
usurp: *labh, reup*
utas: *okto*
uterus: *udero*
utmost: *ud*
Utopia: *moro, top*
utter: *al II, ud*
utterly: *ud*
uttermost: *ud*
uvea: *oiua*
uvula: *oiua*

V

vacancy: *eu*
vacant: *eu*
vacate: *eu*
vacation: *eu*
vaccicide: *uak*
vaccimulgence: *uak*
vaccination: *uak*
vaccine: *uak*
vaccinia: *uak*
vaccinotherapy: *uak*
vacillate: *uag I*
vacuity: *eu*
vacuous: *eu*
vacuum: *eu*
vada: *aus*
vade mecum: *uadh*
vadiation: *uad*
vadimonium: *uad*

vadium: *uad*
vadose: *uadh*
vae victis: uai
vagabond: *uag I*
vagary: *uag I*
vagina: *kal, uag II*
vagrant: *uag I*
vague: *uag I*
vail: *uals*
vain: *eu*
vair: *ua I*
Vaisya: *ueik I*
vaivode: *uen*
vajra: *ueg II*
vale: *ual, uals*
valedictory: *deik*
valence: *ual*
valentine: *ual*
Valeria: *ual*
valerian: *ual*
valet: *upo I*
valetudinarian: *ual*
valgus: *uelu*
Valhalla: *kel VI, medhi, uel III*
valiant: *ual*
valid: *ual*
validity: *ual*
Valkyrie: *medhi, uel III*
vallation: *uals*
vallecula: *uals*
valley: *uals*
valse: *uelu*
value: *ual*
valvate: *uelu*
valve: *uelu*
valvulae: *uelu*
vam(o)ose: *uadh*
van: *ue*
vanadinite: *uen*
Vanadis: *uen*
vanadium: *el 23, uen*
vanadous: *uen*
Vandal: *uendh*
vandalism: *dheigh N 21, uendh*
vandalize: *uendh*
vandyke: *bhar*
vane: *pend*
vang: *pag*
vanguard: *anti*
vanilla: *uag II*
Vanir: *uen*
vanish: *eu*
vanity: *eu*
vapid: *kuep*
vapor: *kuep*
vapulate: *uab*
vapulation: *uab*
vapulatory: *uab*
vaquero: *uak*
Varangians: *uero*
variance: *ua I*
varicella: *ua I*
varicocele: *keu II*
varicose: *dheigh N 2 g, ua I*
variegated: *ua I*
variety: *ua I*
variola: *ua I*
variorum: *ua I*
various: *ua I*
varix: *ua I*
varlet: *upo I*
varmint: *uer II 4*
varna: *suer I*
varsha: *aue, nebh*
varsity: *oino*
Varuna: *nebh*
varus: *ua I*
varve: *kuerp*
vary: *ua I*
vas: *uad*
vaseline: *aue*
vassal: *upo I*
vast: *eu*
vates: ken II, uat
vatic: *uat*
Vatican: *uat*
vaticinate: *ken II*
vaticination: *uat*
vaudeville: *uals*
vault: *uelu*
vaulting: *uelu*
vaunt: *eu*
Vayu: *ue*
veal: *ane, uet*
vector: *uegh*
Veda: *ueid*
Vedanta: *ant, ueid*
vedette: *ueg II*
vegetable: *ueg II*
vegetarian: *ueg II*
vegetate: *ueg II*
vegetation: *ueg II*
vehicle: *uegh*
veil: *ueg I*

vein: *uegh*
velamen: *ueg I*
velar: *ueg I*
velarium: *ueg I*
veld: *pela*
velic: *ueg I*
velites: ueg II
velleity: *uel II*
vellicate: *uel III*
vellication: *uel III*
vellum: *uet*
velocipede: *ped, ueg II*
velocity: *dheigh N 2 d, oku, ueg II*
velours: *uel III*
velum: *ueg I*
velure: *uel III*
velvet: *uel III*
venal: *uesn*
venality: *dheigh N 36*
venatic: *uen*
venation: *uegh*
vend: *do, uesn*
vendace: *ueid*
vendible: *uesn*
vendition: *uesn*
vendor: *do, uesn*
vendue: *uesn*
veneer: *per V*
venerable: *dheu I, uen*
venerate: *uen*
veneration: *dheu I*
venereal: *dheu I, uen*
Venerians: *dheu I, uen*
venery: *dheu I, uen*
venesection: *sek I, uegh*
venial: *uen*
Venice: *uen*
venin: *uen*
venison: *uen*
venom: *uen*
venomous: *uen*
vent: *ue*
ventail: *ue*
venter: *udero*
ventiduct: *ue*
ventose: *udero*
ventosity: *udero, ue*
ventral: *udero*
ventriloquism: *tolku, udero*
ventripotent: *poti, udero*
venture: *gua*
venturesome: *dheigh N 37*
venue: *gua*
venule: *uegh*
Venus: *aue, dheu I, uen*
Venusians: *uen*
Venus's girdle: *uen*
Venus's-hair: *uen*
Venus's bath: *uen*
Venus's flower basket: *uen*
Venus's-flytrap: *uen*
Venus's looking-glass: *uen*
veracious: *suer II, uero*
veracity: *em, suer II, uero*
veranda: *ua I*
verano: *uesr*
veratrine: *suer II, uero*
verb: *suer II, uer VI*
verbalize: *suer II*
verbatim: *suer II*
verbena: *uer II 1*
verbiage: *suer II*
verbocination: *suer II*
verbose: *suer II, uer VI*
verbosity: *dheigh N 2 d*
verboten: bhendh
Verbum sap: sap, suer II
verdant: *ters*
verd antique: *ters*
verderer: *ters*
verdict: *deik, uero*
verdigris: *ters*
verditer: *ters*
verdure: *ters*
verecund: *suer I*
Veretillum: *suer I*
verge: *uer II 2*
verger: *uer II 2*
veridical: *deik, uero*
verify: *deik, dhe I, uero*
veriment: *suer II*
verisimilitude: *sem I, suer II, uero*
verism: *uero*
verity: *uero*
verjuice: *ieug, ters*
vermeil: *uer II 4*
Vermes: *uer II 4*
vermicelli: *haifst, uer II 4*
vermiculated: *uer II 4*
vermiform: *kel IV, uer II 4*
vermilion: *uer II 4*
vermin: *uer II 4*
vermivorous: *bhag*
Vermont: *men II, ters*

vermouth: *uer II 4*
vernal: *uesr*
vernant: *uesr*
vernation: *uesr*
Veronica: *uero*
Veronica's veil: *ueg I*
verriculate: *uers*
verricule: *uers*
verruca: *uer I*
verrucous: *uer I*
versatile: *uer II 5*
verse: *per IV, uer II 5*
versed: *uer II 5*
verset: *uer II 5*
versicle: *uer II 5*
versicolor: *uer II 5*
versify: *uer II 5*
version: *uer II 5*
verso: *uer II 5*
verst: *uer II 5*
versus: *uer II 5*
vert: *ters*
vertebra: *uer II 5*
Vertebrata: *uer II 5*
vertebrate: *uer II 5*
vertex: *uer II 5*
vertical: *uer II 5*
vertigo: *uer II 5*
vertilago: *uer II 5*
Vertumnus: *uer II 5*
verumontanum: *men II*
vervain: *uer II 1*
verve: *uer VI*
vervel: *uer II 5*
very: *suer II, uero*
vesica: *udero*
vesicant: *udero*
vesicatory: *udero*
vesicle: *udero*
vesicotomy: *udero*
vesicular: *udero*
Vespasian: *el 7, piss*
vespasian: *el 7, piss*
Vesper: *uesper*
vespers: *uesper*
Vespertilio: *uesper*
Vespertilionidae: *uesper*
vespertine: *uesper*
vespiary: *uebh*
Vespidae: *uebh*
vespine: *uebh*
vest: *ues II*
Vesta: *ues I*
vestal: *ues I*
vestment: *ues II*
vestry: *ues II*
vesture: *ues II*
vetch: *uei*
veteran: *uet*
veterinary: *uet*
vex: *uegh*
vexation: *uegh*
vexillary: *ueg I*
vexillum: *ueg I*
via: *uegh*
viable: *dheigh N 3*
viaduct: *deuk, uegh*
viatic: *uegh*
viaticum: *uegh*
vibraculum: *ueip*
vibrant: *ueip*
vibrate: *ueip*
vibration: *ueip*
vibrato: *ueip*
vicar: *dheigh N 13, uei*
vicariously: *uei*
vice: *sta, uei, uid*
vicenary: *uid*
vicennial: *uid*
vice-president: *uei*
viceroy: *reg I, uei*
vice versa: *uei, uer II 5*
Vicia: *uei*
vicinage: *ueik I*
vicinity: *ueik I*
vicious: *uid*
vicissitude: *uei*
victim: *ueik III*
victuals: *guei, past*
vide: ueid
videlicet: ueid
vidual: *ueidh*
viduate: *ueidh*
vidya: *ueid*
Vienna: *ueid*
view: *ueid*
vigesimal: *uid*
vigil: *ueg II*
vigilant: *ueg II*
vigilante: *ueg II*
vignette: *em*
vigor: *ueg II*
vigorous: *ueg II*
vihara: *uid*

Vikings: *uei*
vilipend: *guhisl, ne, pend, spend II*
villa: *ueik I*
villain: *ueik I*
villainy: *ueik I*
villancico: ueik I
villanella: *ueik I*
villanelle: *ueik I*
ville: *ueik I*
villein: *ueik I*
villiform: *uel III*
villosity: *uel III*
villous: *uel III*
villus: *uel III*
vim: *uiro*
vimana: *uid*
vimen: *uei*
viminal: *uei*
vimineous: *uei*
Vinca: *uei*
vinculum: *uei*
vindicate: *deik*
vindictive: *deik*
vine: *em*
vinegar: *ak, em*
vinegarroon: *em*
vineyard: *em*
viniculture: *em*
vinometer: *em*
vintage: *em*
vintner: *em*
Viola: *uio*
viola: *tol*
Violaceae: *uio*
viola da gamba: *kam*
violate: *uiro*
violation: *uiro*
violence: *uiro*
violet: *uio*
violin: *tol*
viper: *auei, guei, per VI b, plek I*
virago: *per VI c, uiro*
vireo: *ters*
virescent: *ters*
virgate: *uer II 2*
virgin: *maghos, per VI c, uer II 2*
virginal: *maghos*
Virginia: *maghos, uer II 2*
Virgo: *guei, ster III, uer II 2*
virgulate: *uer II 2*
virgule: *uer II 2*
virid: *ters*
viridescent: *ters*
viril: *uiro*
virilescence: *uiro*
virility: *uiro*
virtu: *uiro*
virtual: *uiro*
virtue: *uiro*
virtuosity: *uiro*
virtuous: *uiro*
virulent: *ueis*
virus: *ueis*
visa: *ueid*
visage: *ueid*
visarga: *uid*
vis-à-vis: *ueid*
viscid: *ueis*
viscin: *ueis*
viscosity: *ueis*
viscount: *ei I, uei*
viscous: *ueis*
Viscum: *ueis*
vise: *uei*
Vishvakarma: *kuer*
Visigoths: *uesper*
vision: *ueid*
visit: *ueid*
visitant: *ueid*
visitation: *ueid*
visor: *ueid*
vista: *ueid*
visual: *ueid*
visuopsychic: *ueid*
visuosensory: *ueid*
vital: *guei*
vitality: *guei*
vitals: *guei*
vitaphone: *guei*
vitellarium: *uet*
vitelligenous: *uet*
vitellin: *uet*
vitellus: *uet*
vitiate: *uid*
viticulture: *ker I, uei*
vitiosity: *uid*
Vitrasura: *anghui*
vitta: *uei*
Vittoria: *uei*
vittate: *uei*
vitulary: *uet*
vituline: *uet*
vituperation: *uid*
viuva: *ueidh*

W

waive: *ueip*
waiver: *ueip*
wake: *ueg II, ugu*
waldgrave: *uelt*
waldhorn: *ker II, uelt*
wale: *uelu*
walk: *uelu*
wall: *uals*
wallet: *uelu*
walleyed: *oku*
wallflower: *uio*
wallop: *klou, uel II*
wallow: *uelu*
walrus: *skualo*
Walter: *koro, ual*
waltz: *uelu*
wan: *eu*
wand: *uendh*
wander: *uendh*
wanderlust: *las, uendh*
wanderoo: *uen*
wane: *eu*
wangtooth: *uag I*
wanhope: *eu*
wankle: *uag I*
want: *eu*
wanton: *deuk, eu*
wapentake: *taka*
war: *uers*
warble: *kuerp, uer I*
ward: *uer IV*
warden: *suer I, uer IV*
warder: *suer I, uer IV*
wardrobe: *suer I, uer IV*
ware: *suer I*
warlock: *leugh, uero*
warm: *guher*
warmth: *guher*
warn: *suer I, uer V*
warp: *uer II 1*
warrant: *suer I*
warranty: *suer I, uer V*
warren: *suer I, uer V*
wart: *uer I*
Warwick: *ueik I*
wary: *suer I, uer IV*
was: *ues I*
WASP: *leip I*
wasp: *uebh*
wassail: *ues I*
waste: *eu*
watch: *ueg II*
water: *el*
watercress: *grand*
Waterloo: *leuk*
wattle: *uei*
wave: *uebh, uegh, ueip*
waver: *uebh, ueip*
wax: *uag, uebh*
way: *uegh*
W.C.: *leuk*
weak: *uei*
weakfish: *peisk*
weal: *uel II, uelu*
weald: *uelt*
wealth: *uel II*
wear: *ues II*
weasel: *ueis*
weather: *ue*
weather-beaten: *ue*
weathervane: *pend*
weave: *uebh, ueip*
web: *uebh*
webster: *uebh*
wed: *uad*
wedding: *uad*
wedlock: *uad*
Wednesday: *prai, uat*
wee: *uegh*
week: *kuei I, uei*
weep: *uab*
weft: *uebh*
weichselwood: *ueis*
weigh: *uegh*
weight: *uegh*
weighty: *uegh*
weir: *suer I, uer V*
weird: *uer II 5*
welcome: *gua*
weld: *uelt, uelu*
welfare: *per V*
welkin: *uelk*
well: *uel II, uelu*
wellaway: *uai*
Wellerism: *sel II*
welter: *uelu*
wen: *ua II*
wench: *guen, uag I*
wend: *uendh*
Wends: *uendh*
went: *uendh*
wentletrap: *uendh*
were: *ues I*
wer(e)wolf: *uel III, uiro, ulkuo*

wergeld: *uiro*
Wessex: *sek I*
west: *uesper*
Westchester: *kastr*
westerly: *uesper*
western: *uesper*
Westri: *medhi*
wether: *uet*
whale: *skualo*
wharf: *kuerp*
what: *kuo*
wheat: *kueit*
wheatear: *kueit*
wheatstone: *kueit*
wheedle: *ue*
wheel: *kuel*
wheelwright: *uerg*
wheeze: *kues*
whelk: *uelu*
whelm: *kuelp*
when: *kuo*
whence: *kuo*
where: *kuo*
whet: *kued*
whether: *kuo*
whetstone: *stai, stei*
whew: *kueis*
which: *kuo, leig I*
whidah: *ueidh*
while: *kuei III*
whilom: *kuei III*
whilst: *kuei III*
whine: *jing, kueis*
whinny: *jing*
whip: *ueip*
whippet: *ueip*
whippoorwill: *ueip*
whir: *kuerp*
whirl: *kuerp*
whirlwind: *ker I*
whirr: *kueis*
whish: *kueis*
whisk: *kueis*
whiskers: *bhar, kueis*
whiskey: *akua, guli*
whisper: *jing, kueis*
whist: *bhar, jing, kueis*
whistle: *jing, kueis*
white: *kel VI, kueit*
whither: *kuo*
whiting: *kueit*
whitlow: *onogh*
Whitsunday: *kueit, penkue*
whittle: *tueis*
whiz: *ueid*
who: *kuo*
whodunit: *kuo*
whole: *kailo*
wholesome: *kailo*
whom: *kuo*
whore: *ka, keilo*
whorl: *kuerp*
whortleberry: *bhel I*
whose: *kuo*
why: *kuo*
wicked: *uei*
wicker: *uei*
wicket: *uei*
widdershins: *uid*
wide: *ei I, uid*
widow: *ueidh*
widow-bird: *ueidh*
widowhood: *kait*
width: *uid*
wield: *ual*
Wiener schnitzel: *sek II, sneit*
wife: *ueg I, ueip*
wiggle: *uegh*
wild: *uelt*
wildebeest: *uelt*
wilder: *uelt*
wilderness: *uelt*
wildwood: *uelt*
wile: *ueik III*
William: *kel VI, uel II*
willie-wa: *ker I*
will-o'-the-wisp: *kel VI, ueip*
willow: *sal II, uelu*
willy-nilly: *ne, uel II*
willy-willies: *ker I*
wilt: *uelk*
wimple: *ueip*
wince: *uag I*
winch: *uag I*
wind: *ue, uendh*
windlestraw: *uendh*
windmill: *ue*
window: *oku, ue*
wing: *ue*
wink: *uag I*
winnow: *ue*
winter: *ueid*
winze: *ue*
wipe: *ueip*

wire: *uei*
wisdom: *ueid*
wise: *ueid*
wiseacre: *ueid*
wisent: *ueis*
wisp: *ueip*
wissel: *uei*
wist: *ueid*
wistful: *ueid*
wit: *ueid*
witch: *ueid, ueik III*
witchhazel: *uei*
wite: *ueid*
witenagemot: *mod, ueid*
withdraw: *sent*
withdrive: *uid*
withe: *uei*
withered: *ue*
withernam: *nem*
withers: *uid*
withershins: *sent, uid*
witherwin: *uid*
withgang: *uid*
withhold: *sent*
within: *en*
withstand: *sent, uid*
withy: *uei*
witless: *ueid*
witling: *sap, ueid*
witness: *ueid*
witticism: *ueid*
wittol: *ueid*
wittoldry: *ueid*
wittolly: *ueid*
witty: *dheigh N 36*
wiz: *ueid*
wizard: *ueid, ueik III*
wizen: *ueis*
wizened: *ueis*
wobble: *uebh*
Wodin: *uat*
woe: *uai*
wold: *uelt*
wolf: *uel III, ulko*
wolfberry: *bhel I*
wolfram: *el 74, uel III, ulkuo*
wolframite: *ulkuo*
wolverine: *uel III, ulkuo*
woman: *per VI c*
wonky: *uag I*
wood: *uat, uid*
wooden horse: *ane*
woodpecker: *speik*
woof: *uebh*
wool: *uel III*
woolen: *uel III*
Worcestershire: *kastr*
word: *suer II, uer VI*
wordage: *uer VI*
wordless: *suer II*
wordlore: *uer VI*
wordmonger: *suer II*
wordy: *suer II, uer VI*
work: *uerg*
workmanship: *sek IV*
world: *uiro*
worm: *uer II 4*
worry: *uer II 3*
worse: *uers*
worst: *uers*
wort: *bhes I, uerad*
worth: *uer II 5*
Worthies, the Nine: *neun, uer II 5*
worthless: *uer II 5*
worthwhile: *uer II 5*
worthy: *uer II 5*
wot: *ueid*
wound: *ua II*
wrack: *ureg*
wrangle: *uer II 3*
wrath: *uer II 5, uer II 8*
wreak: *ureg*
wreath: *uer II 5, uer II 8*
wreathe: *uer II 8*
wreck: *ureg*
wreckage: *ureg*
wrench: *uer II 2*
wrest: *uer II 10*
wrestle: *uer II 10*
wretch: *ureg*
wriggle: *uer II 6*
wright: *uerg*
wring: *uer II 3*
wrinkle: *uer II 2*
wrist: *uer II 6*
writhe: *uer II 5, uer II 8*
wrong: *sa, uer II 3*
wrongdoer: *rad I*
wroth: *uer II 8*
wrought: *uerg*
wrought iron: *el 26*
wry: *uer II 6*
wurst: *uer II 5*
wych: *uei*
wynd: *uendh*

x: *x*
xanthic: *eku*
xanthophyll: *eku*
Xanthippe: *eku*
xanthous: *eku*
xenagogue: *ghostis, xenos*
xenelasia: *ghostis*
xenelasy: *xenos*
xenial: *ghostis*
xenodochy: *ghostis*
xenon: *el 54, ghostis, xenos*
xenophile: *bhili, ghostis, xenos*
xenophobe: *ghostis, xenos*
xenotine: *kuei I, xenos*
xeransis: *ksero*
Xeranthemum: *ksero*
xerasia: *ksero*
xeroderma: *ksero*
xerodermy: *der*
xerophthalmia: *ksero*
Xerophyllum: *ksero*
Xerox: *beu, ksero, op I*
Xerxes: *ksei, uela*
XP: *x*
X-ray: *x*
xylem: *hule*
xylocarp: *ker III*
xylograph: *sal I*
xylophagous: *bhag, hule*
xylophone: *sal I*
Xylotrya: *ter II*

Y

yacht: *iag II*
yack: *yack*
yackety-yack: *jing*
yager: *iag II*
Yajna: *iag I*
yakska: *iag I*
yap: *yap*
yard: *gher IV*
yarmulke: *skeu*
yasna: *iag I*
yaw: *iag II*
yawn: *ghi*
yawp: *yap*
y-clept: *kom*
ye: *iu I*
yea: *i*
yean: *aguhno*
yeanling: *aguhno*
year: *eir*
yearn: *gher II*
yeast: *ies*
yell: *ghel I, yap*
yellow: *gel I, kel VI*
yellowbelly: *kel VI*
yellow fever: *kel VI*
yelp: *ghel I, jing, yap*
yeoman: *ieu*
yes: *i, sos*
yesman: *i*
yesterday: *ghdhies, nogu*
yesteryear: *ghdhies*
yestreen: *ghdhies*
yet: *i*
yew: *ei II, oiua*
Yggdrasill: *medhi*
ylem: *hule*
Ymir: *medhi*
yodel: *in II, jing*
yoga: *ieug*
yogi: *ieug*
yoke: *ieug*
yokel: *ieug*
yolk: *gel I*
yoni: *gn*
yore: *eir*
you: *iu I*
young: *ieu*
youngling: *ieu*
youngster: *ieu*
youth: *ieu*
yowl: *iu II, jing*
ytterbium: *el 70*
yttrium: *el 39*
Yuga: *ieug*
yuletide: *da*

Z

zabaglione: *sab*
Zamenis: *men I*
zamindar: *dhar, ghdhem*
Zarathustra: *ger IV*
zeal: *ia*
zealot: *ia*
zealous: *ia*

zemstvo: *ghdhem*
zenana: *guen*
zeolite: *ies*
Zeppelin, Count: *reg I*
zeppelin: *reg I*
zetetic: *ia*
zeugma: *ieug*
Zeus: *dei, el 61, guel II*
zeuxite: *ieug*
zinc: *el 30, den*
zingerone: *ker II*
Zingiber: *ker II*
zingiberene: *ker II*
zip: *zip*
Zip Code: *zip*
zipper: *zip*
zippy: *zip*
zircon: *el 40, gel I*
zirconium: *el 40, gel I*
zodiac: *guei*
zodiacal: *guei*
zoe: *guei*
zoetic: *guei*
Zollverein: *oino*
zonal: *ios*
zonar: *ios*
zone: *ios*
zonule: *ios*
Zonuridae: *ios*
zoo: *guei*
zooblast: *guei*
zoogamy: *guei*
zooid: *guei*
zoolite: *guei*
zoology: *guei*
zoon: *guei*
zoophagous: *bhag*
zoophyte: *bheu*
Zoroaster: *ger IV*
Zoroastrian: *ger IV*
zoster: *ios*
Zostera: *ios*
zucchetto: *skeu*
zufolo: suei I
zwieback: *bhe, duo*
zwitterion: *duo*
zygodactyl: *ieug*
zygoma: *ieug*
zygomatic: *ieug*
zygospore: *ieug*
zygote: *ieug*
zymin(e): *ieug*
zymogen: *ieug*
zymosis: *ieug*
zymurgy: *ieug, uerg*
zythiostoma: *spong*

JOSEPH T. SHIPLEY is author of the highly acclaimed *In Praise of English* (an alternate selection of the Book-of-the-Month Club) as well as twenty-six other books, including *The Quest for Literature, Dictionary of Word Origins,* and *Dictionary of Early English.* In a long and distinguished career he has been president of the New York Drama Critics Circle, was a founder of Yeshiva College, and has taught at the City College of New York. He holds a Ph.D. in comparative literature.